...d

...s

...between two towns along
...s and other main roads this is
...ssarily the shortest.

...utes, are average off-peak driving
...e times should be used as a
...traffic delays, rest breaks or fuel

...y between Glasgow and Norwich
...tes.

Journey times

Distances in miles (one mile equals 1.6093 km)

Atlas contents

Scale 1:200,000 or 3.16 miles to 1 inch

Map pages and distance times	inside front cover
Route planning	*II–XX*
Route planner	*II–VII*
Traffic signs	*VIII–IX*
Channel hopping	*X–XI*
Ferries to Ireland and the Isle of Man	*XII–XIII*
Caravan and camping sites in Britain	*XIV–XVII*
Road safety cameras	*XVIII–XIX*
Map pages	*XX*
Road map symbols	**1**
Road maps	**2–173**
Britain 1:200,000 scale	2–169
Some islands are shown at slightly smaller scales.	
Ireland 1:1,000,000 scale	170–173
Motorways	**174–179**
Restricted junctions	174–177
M25 London Orbital	178
M6 Toll Motorway	179
Street map symbols	**180**

Towns, ports and airports	**181–231**
Town plans	182–228
Major airports	229–231
Channel Tunnel terminals	27
Central London	**232–247**
Central London street map	232–241
Central London index	242–247
District maps	**248–259**
London	248–251
Birmingham	252–253
Glasgow	254–255
Manchester	256–257
Newcastle	258–259
Index to place names	**260–308**
County, administrative area map	260
Place name index	261–308
Map pages and distance times	inside back cover

28th edition June 2013
© AA Media Limited 2013
Original edition printed 1986.

Cartography:
All cartography in this atlas edited, designed and
produced by the Mapping Services Department of AA
Publishing (A05048).

This atlas contains Ordnance Survey data © Crown
copyright and database right 2013 and Royal Mail data
© Royal Mail copyright and database right 2013.

 Land &
Property
Services.
This atlas is based upon Crown
Copyright and is reproduced with
the permission of Land and Property
Services under delegated authority from the Controller of
Her Majesty's Stationery Office, © Crown copyright and
database rights 2013, Licence number 100,363.
Permit No. 130002.

 Ordnance
Survey
Ireland's National Mapping Agency
© Ordnance Survey Ireland/
Government of Ireland. Copyright
Permit No. MP000913.

Publisher's Notes:
Published by AA Publishing (a trading name of AA Media
Limited, whose registered office is Fanum House, Basing
View, Basingstoke, Hampshire RG21 4EA, UK.
Registered number 06112600).

All rights reserved. No part of this publication may be
reproduced, stored in a retrieval system, or transmitted
in any form or by any means – electronic, mechanical,
photocopying, recording or otherwise – unless the
permission of the publisher has been given beforehand.

ISBN: 978 0 7495 7454 3 (leather)
ISBN: 978 0 7495 7453 6 (standard)

A CIP catalogue record for this book is available from The
British Library.

Disclaimer:
The contents of this atlas are believed to be correct
at the time of the latest revision, it will not contain any
subsequent amended, new or temporary information
including diversions and traffic control or enforcement
systems. The publishers cannot be held responsible or
liable for any loss or damage occasioned to any person
acting or refraining from action as a result of any use
or reliance on material in this atlas, nor for any errors,
omissions or changes in such material.
This does not affect your statutory rights.

The publishers would welcome information to correct
any errors or omissions and to keep this atlas up to
date. Please write to the Atlas Editor, AA Publishing,
The Automobile Association, Fanum House, Basing
View, Basingstoke, Hampshire RG21 4EA, UK.
E-mail: *roadatlasfeedback@theaa.com*

Acknowledgements:
AA Publishing would like to thank the following for their
assistance in producing this atlas:
RoadPilot® Information on fixed speed camera
locations provided by and © 2013
RoadPilot® Driving Technology. Crematoria data provided
by the Cremation Society of Great Britain. Cadw, English
Heritage, Forestry Commission, Historic Scotland,
Johnsons, National Trust and National Trust for Scotland,
RSPB, The Wildlife Trust, Scottish Natural Heritage,
Natural England, The Countryside Council for Wales (road
maps).

Road signs are © Crown Copyright 2013. Reproduced
under the terms of the Open Government Licence.

Transport for London (Central London Map),
Nexus (Newcastle district map).

Printer:
Printed in China by Leo Paper Products.

Route planner

REPUBLIC
OF
IRELAND

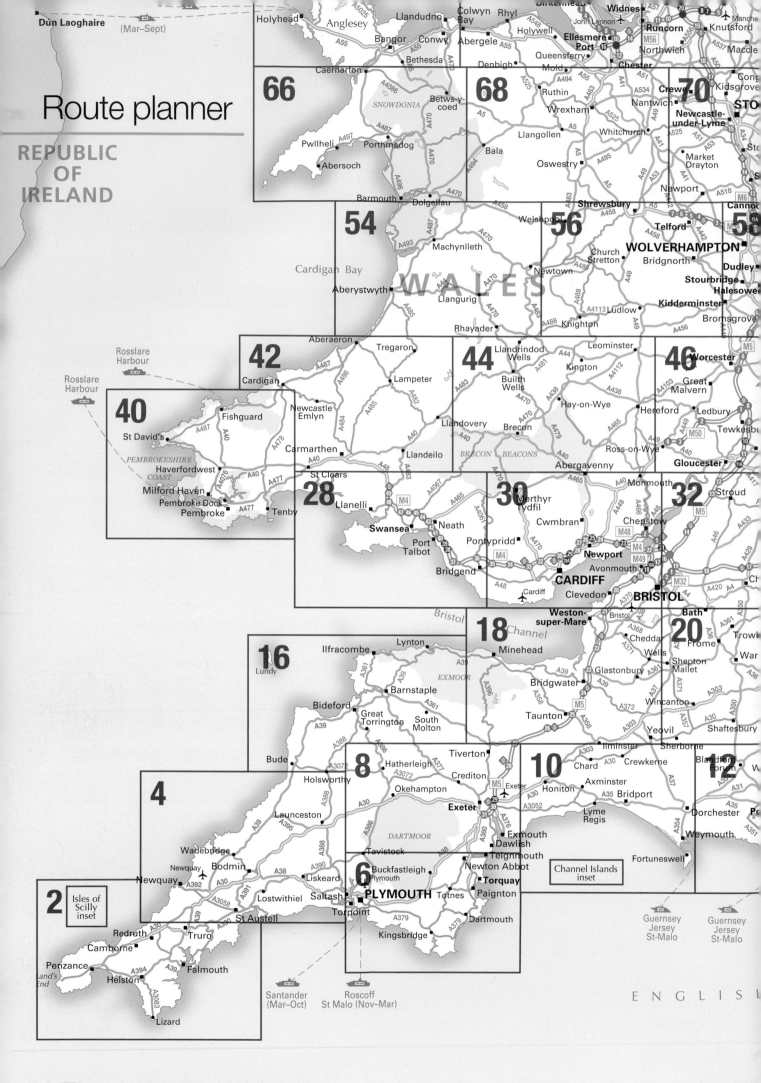

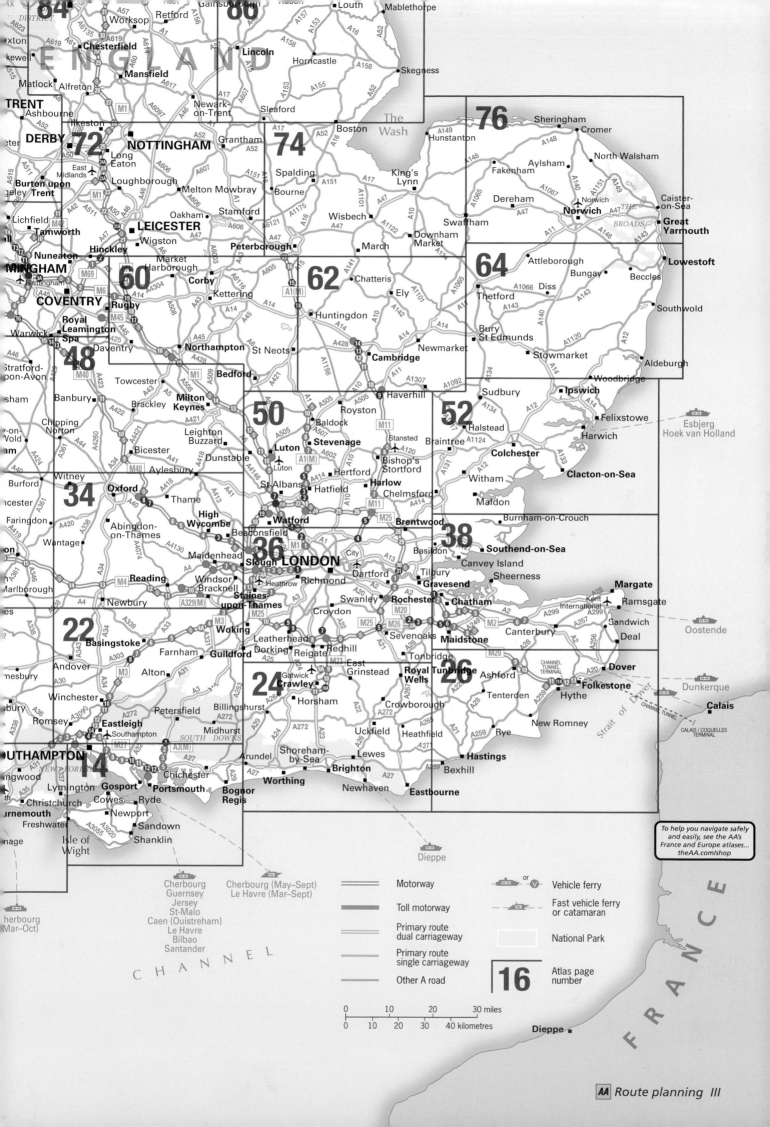

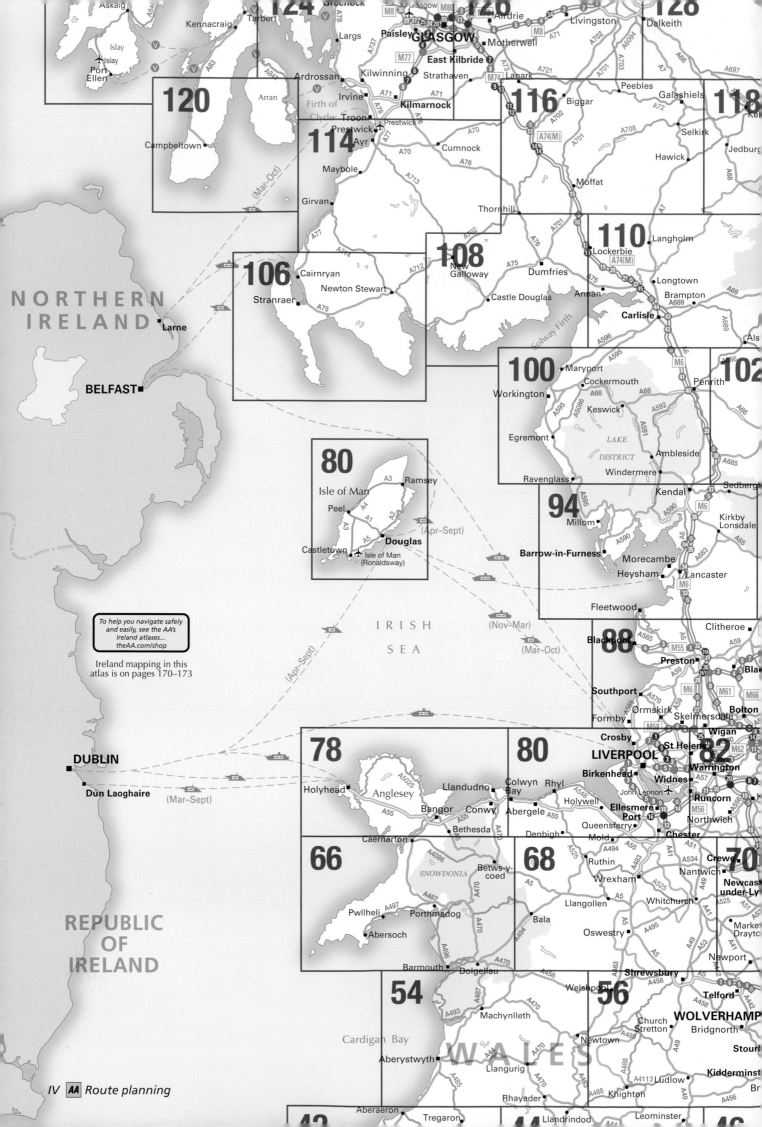

124 **Greenock**

126

128

Askaig
Kennacraig · Tarbert
Port Askaig
Islay
Port Ellen

120
Campbeltown
Arran
Firth of Clyde
(Mar–Oct)

Paisley **GLASGOW** M80 Airdrie Livingston Dalkeith
M8 Motherwell M8
East Kilbride Peebles Galashiels
116 Biggar
118
Selkirk
Hawick Jedburgh
Kel

Ardrossan
Irvine
Kilwinning
Kilmarnock Strathaven Lanark
Troon Cumnock
Prestwick
Ayr
Maybole A70
Girvan A713

114
Moffat
Thornhill

106
Cairnryan
Newton Stewart
Stranraer

108
New Galloway Dumfries
Castle Douglas

110
Lockerbie Langholm
A74(M)
Longtown
Annan Brampton
Carlisle Als

NORTHERN
IRELAND
Larne

BELFAST

100
Maryport
Cockermouth
Workington Keswick
Egremont
LAKE
DISTRICT Ambleside
Ravenglass Windermere

102
Penrith
M6
Kendal Sedbergh
Kirkby Lonsdale

94
Millom
Barrow-in-Furness
Morecambe
Heysham Lancaster
M6
Fleetwood

80
Isle of Man
A3 Ramsey
Peel A4
A1 A2
A3 A5
Castletown A5 **Douglas**
Isle of Man
(Ronaldsway)

To help you navigate safely
and easily, see the AA's
Ireland atlases…
theAA.com/shop

Ireland mapping in this
atlas is on pages 170–173

IRISH

SEA

(Apr–Sept)

(Nov–Mar)

(Mar–Oct)

88
Clitheroe
Blackpool A585 M55 A59
Preston
Bla

DUBLIN
Dún Laoghaire
(Mar–Sept)

(Apr–Sept)

78
Holyhead
Anglesey
A55
Bangor Conwy
Bethesda
A5025
Llandudno
Colwyn Bay Rhyl
Abergele A55
Holywell
Queensferry

80
LIVERPOOL Crosby St Helens
Birkenhead
Widnes John Lennon
Ellesmere Port Runcorn
Northwich
Chester M56

82
Wigan
Warrington

Southport
Ormskirk Skelmersdale
Formby M58 **Bolton**
M6 M61 M66

66
Caernarfon
SNOWDONIA
Betws-y-coed
A487 A470
Pwllheli A497
Porthmadog
Abersoch
Barmouth Dolgellau A470

68
Ruthin
Wrexham
Llangollen
Bala
Oswestry

70
Crewe
Nantwich
Newcastle-under-Ly
Whitchurch
Market Drayton
Newport

REPUBLIC
OF
IRELAND

Cardigan Bay

54
Machynlleth
Newtown
Aberystwyth
Llangurig

WALES

56
Welshpool
Shrewsbury
Church Stretton
Telford
WOLVERHAMP
Bridgnorth
Stourl
Kiddermins

Aberaeron
Tregaron
Rhayader Knighton
Llandrindod Ludlow
Leominster

Br

42 **44** **46**

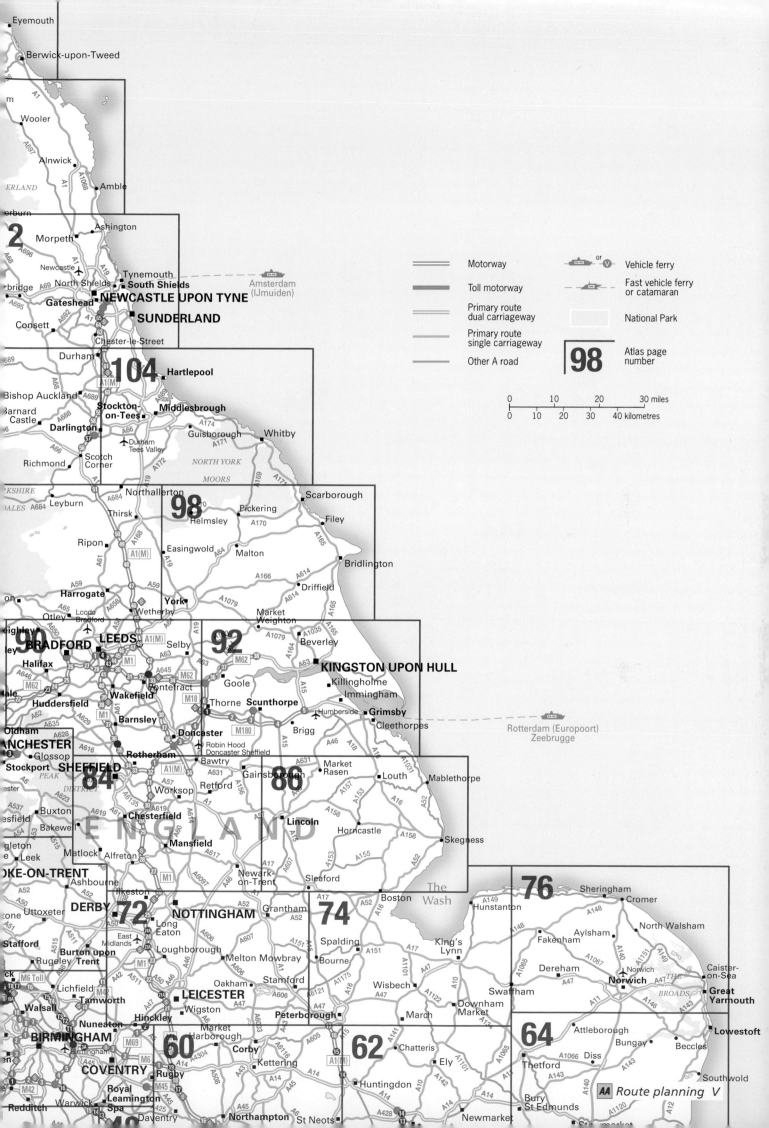

Motorway

Toll motorway

Primary route
dual carriageway

Primary route
single carriageway

Other A road

Vehicle ferry

Fast vehicle ferry
or catamaran

National Park

98 Atlas page
number

0 10 20 30 miles
0 10 20 30 40 kilometres

AA Route planning V

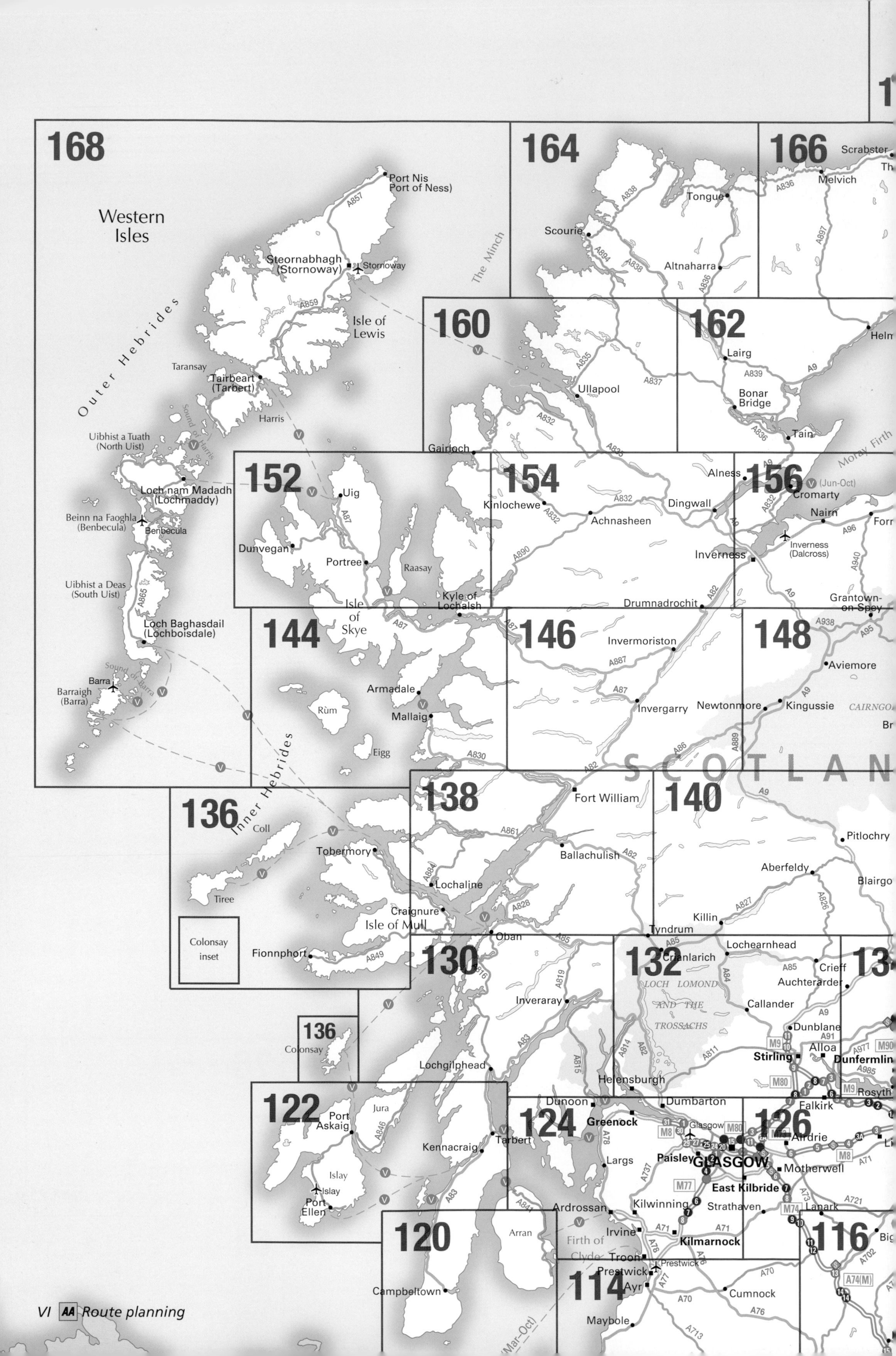

168

Western Isles

Outer Hebrides

Taransay
Tairbeart (Tarbert)
Harris
Uibhist a Tuath (North Uist)
Beinn na Faoghla (Benbecula)
Benbecula
Loch nam Madadh (Lochmaddy)
Uibhist a Deas (South Uist)
A865
Loch Baghasdail (Lochboisdale)
Sound of Barra
Barra
Barraigh (Barra)

Steornabhagh (Stornoway)
Stornoway
A857
A859
Isle of Lewis
Sound of Harris

160
Gairloch
Ullapool
A835
A832

152
Uig
A87
Dunvegan
Portree
Raasay
Isle of Skye
Kyle of Lochalsh

164
Scourie
A894
A838
A838
Tongue
Altnaharra
A836

166
Scrabster
Melvich
A836
A897
Th

162
Lairg
A839
A9
Bonar Bridge
A837
Tain
A836
Hel

154
Kinlochewe
A832
Achnasheen
A890

156
Alness
A832
Dingwall
A9
Cromarty
Nairn
Inverness (Dalcross)
Inverness
A96
For
A940
Moray Firth

144
Isle of Skye
A87
Armadale
Rùm
Mallaig
Eigg
A830

Inner Hebrides

146
A887
Invermoriston
A87
Invergarry
A82

148
Grantown-on-Spey
A938
A95
Aviemore
Newtonmore
Kingussie
CAIRNGO
A9
A889
Br

SCOTLAN

136
Coll
Tobermory
A884
Tiree
Lochaline
Craignure
Isle of Mull
Fionnphort
A849

Colonsay inset

138
A861
Fort William
Ballachulish
A82
A828
Oban
A85

140
A9
Pitlochry
Aberfeldy
Blairgo
A826
Killin
A827
Tyndrum

130
A816
Inveraray
A83
A819
A85

132
Crianlarich
A85
Lochearnhead
Crieff
A84
Auchterarder
LOCH LOMOND AND THE TROSSACHS
Callander
Dunblane
A91
M9
Stirling
Alloa
A977
M90
M80
Dunfermlin
A985
Rosyth

13

136
Colonsay

122
Jura
Port Askaig
A846
Kennacraig
Islay
Islay
Port Ellen

Lochgilphead
Tarbert
A83

124
Dunoon
Greenock
Largs
A78
Dumbarton
A737
Helensburgh
A814
A82
A811
A815

126
Glasgow
M8
M80
Airdrie
Paisley
GLASGOW
M8
Motherwell
A71
M77
East Kilbride
Strathaven
Kilwinning
A73
M74
Lanark
A721
Ardrossan
Kilmarnock
Irvine
A71
Troon
Prestwick
Prestwick
Ayr
A77
A70
Cumnock
A70
A76
Maybole
A713

116
L
Big
A702
A74(M)

120
Arran
Campbeltown
Firth of Clyde

114

1

The Minch

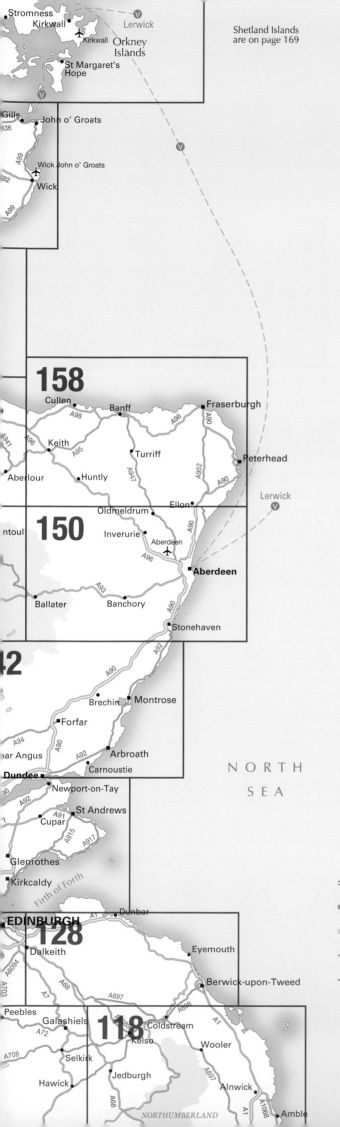

Stromness
Kirkwall
Lerwick
Kirkwall
Orkney
Islands
St Margaret's
Hope
Gills
John o' Groats
Wick John o' Groats
Wick

Shetland Islands
are on page 169

FERRY INFORMATION

Hebrides and west coast Scotland

calmac.co.uk	0800 066 5000
skyeferry.co.uk	01599 522 236
western-ferries.co.uk	01369 704 452

Orkney and Shetland

northlinkferries.co.uk	0845 6000 449
pentlandferries.co.uk	0800 688 8998
orkneyferries.co.uk	01856 872 044
shetland.gov.uk/ferries	01595 743 970

Isle of Man

steam-packet.com	08722 992 992

Ireland

irishferries.com	08717 300 400
poferries.com	08716 642 020
stenaline.co.uk	08447 70 70 70

North Sea (Scandinavia and Benelux)

dfdsseaways.co.uk	08715 229 955
poferries.com	08716 642 020
stenaline.co.uk	08447 70 70 70

Isle of Wight

wightlink.co.uk	0871 376 1000
redfunnel.co.uk	0844 844 9988

Channel Islands

condorferries.co.uk	0845 609 1024

Channel hopping (France and Belgium)

brittany-ferries.co.uk	0871 244 0744
condorferries.co.uk	0845 609 1024
eurotunnel.com	08443 35 35 35
ldlines.co.uk	0844 576 8836
dfdsseaways.co.uk	08715 229 955
poferries.com	08716 642 020
transeuropaferries.com	01843 595 522
myferrylink.com	0844 2482 100

Northern Spain

brittany-ferries.co.uk	0871 244 0744
poferries.com	08716 642 020

158
Cullen
Banff
Fraserburgh
Keith
Turriff
Peterhead
Aberlour
Huntly
Ellon
Oldmeldrum
150
Inverurie
Aberdeen
Lerwick
Aberdeen
Ballater
Banchory
Stonehaven
42
Brechin
Montrose
Forfar
ar Angus
Arbroath
Carnoustie
Dundee
Newport-on-Tay
St Andrews
Cupar
Glenrothes
Kirkcaldy
Firth of Forth

EMERGENCY DIVERSION ROUTES

In an emergency it may be necessary to close a section
of motorway or other main road to traffic, so a
temporary sign may advise drivers to follow a diversion
route. To help drivers navigate the route, black symbols
on yellow patches may be permanently displayed on
existing direction signs, including motorway signs.
Symbols may also be used on separate signs with
yellow backgrounds.

For further information see *www.highways.gov.uk*,
trafficscotland.org and *traffic-wales.com*

NORTH
SEA

EDINBURGH
128
Dalkeith
Dunbar
Eyemouth
Berwick-upon-Tweed
Peebles
Galashiels
118
Coldstream
Kelso
Wooler
Selkirk
Jedburgh
Hawick
Alnwick
Amble
NORTHUMBERLAND

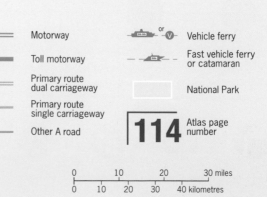

══════ Motorway	Vehicle ferry
══════ Toll motorway	Fast vehicle ferry or catamaran
══════ Primary route dual carriageway	National Park
────── Primary route single carriageway	
────── Other A road	**114** Atlas page number

0   10   20   30 miles
0   10   20   30   40 kilometres

Traffic signs

Signs giving orders

**Signs with red circles are mostly prohibitive.
Plates below signs qualify their message.**

Entry to
20mph zone

End of
20mph zone

Maximum
speed

National speed
limit applies

School crossing
patrol

Stop and
give way

Give way to
traffic on
major road

Manually operated temporary
STOP and GO signs

No entry for
vehicular traffic

No vehicles
except bicycles
being pushed

No cycling

No motor
vehicles

No buses
(over 8
passenger
seats)

No
overtaking

No
towed
caravans

No vehicles
carrying
explosives

No vehicle or
combination of
vehicles over
length shown

No vehicles
over
height shown

No vehicles
over
width shown

Give priority to
vehicles from
opposite
direction

No right turn

No left turn

No
U-turns

No goods vehicles
over maximum
gross weight
shown (in tonnes)
except for loading
and unloading

No vehicles
over maximum
gross weight
shown
(in tonnes)

Parking
restricted to
permit holders

No stopping during
period indicated
except for buses

No stopping during
times shown
except for as long
as necessary to set
down or pick up
passengers

No waiting

No stopping
(Clearway)

**Signs with blue circles but no red border mostly give
positive instruction.**

Ahead only

Turn left ahead
(right if symbol
reversed)

Turn left
(right if symbol
reversed)

Keep left
(right if symbol
reversed)

Vehicles may
pass either
side to reach
same
destination

Mini-roundabout
(roundabout
circulation – give
way to vehicles
from the
immediate right)

Route to be
used by pedal
cycles only

Segregated
pedal cycle
and pedestrian
route

Minimum speed

End of minimum
speed

Buses and
cycles only

Trams only

Pedestrian
crossing
point over
tramway

One-way traffic
(note: compare
circular 'Ahead
only' sign)

With-flow bus and
cycle lane

Contraflow bus lane

With-flow pedal cycle lane

Warning signs

Mostly triangular

Distance to
'STOP' line
ahead

Dual
carriageway
ends

Road narrows on
right (left if
symbol reversed)

Road
narrows on
both sides

Distance to
'Give Way'
line ahead

Crossroads

Junction on
bend ahead

T-junction with
priority over
vehicles from
the right

Staggered
junction

Traffic merging
from left ahead

The priority through route is indicated by the broader line.

Double bend first
to left (symbol
may be reversed)

Bend to right
(or left if symbol
reversed)

Roundabout

Uneven road

Reduce
speed
now
Plate below
some signs

Two-way
traffic crosses
one-way road

Two-way traffic
straight ahead

Opening or
swing bridge
ahead

Low-flying aircraft
or sudden
aircraft noise

Falling or
fallen rocks

Traffic signals
not in use

Traffic signals

Slippery road

Steep hill
downwards

Steep hill
upwards

Gradients may be shown as a ratio i.e. 20% = 1:5

Tunnel ahead

Trams crossing ahead

Level crossing with barrier or gate ahead

Level crossing without barrier or gate ahead

Level crossing without barrier

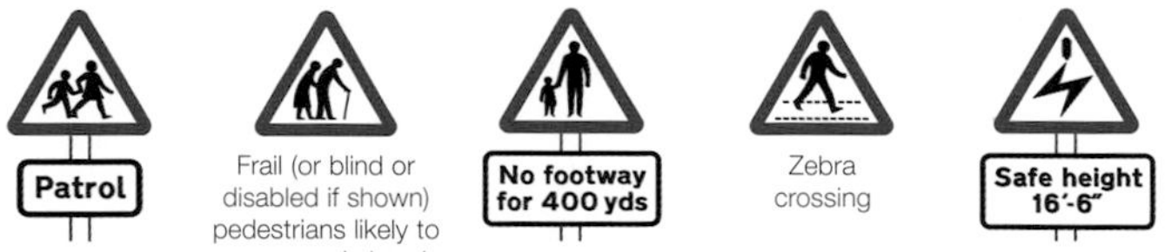

Patrol
No footway for 400 yds
Safe height 16'-6"

School crossing patrol ahead (some signs have amber lights which flash when crossings are in use)

Frail (or blind or disabled if shown) pedestrians likely to cross road ahead

Pedestrians in road ahead

Zebra crossing

Overhead electric cable; plate indicates maximum height of vehicles which can pass safely

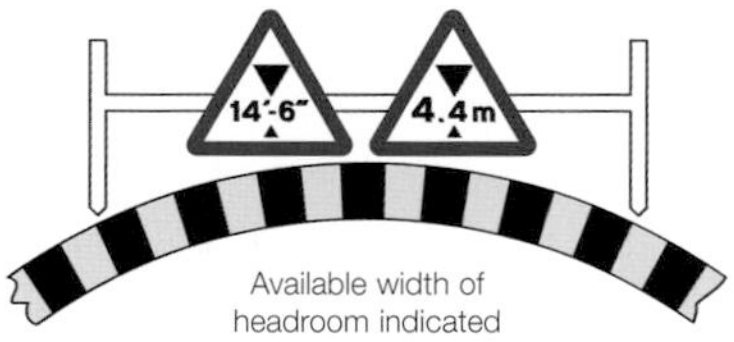

14'-6"
4.4m

Available width of headroom indicated

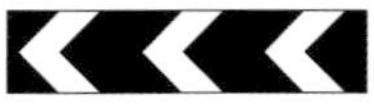

Sharp deviation of route to left (or right if chevrons reversed)

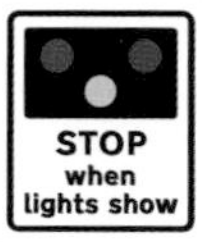

STOP when lights show

Light signals ahead at level crossing, airfield or bridge

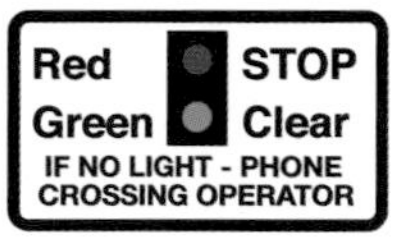

Red STOP
Green Clear
IF NO LIGHT - PHONE CROSSING OPERATOR

Miniature warning lights at level crossings

Cattle

Wild animals

Wild horses or ponies

Accompanied horses or ponies

Cycle route ahead

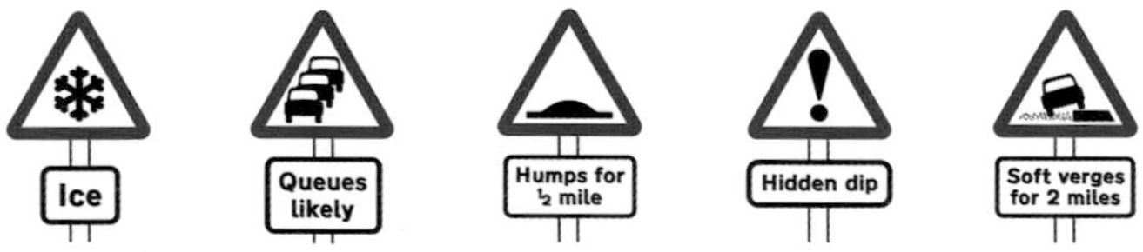

Ice
Queues likely
Humps for ½ mile
Hidden dip
Soft verges for 2 miles

Risk of ice

Traffic queues likely ahead

Distance over which road humps extend

Other danger; plate indicates nature of danger

Soft verges

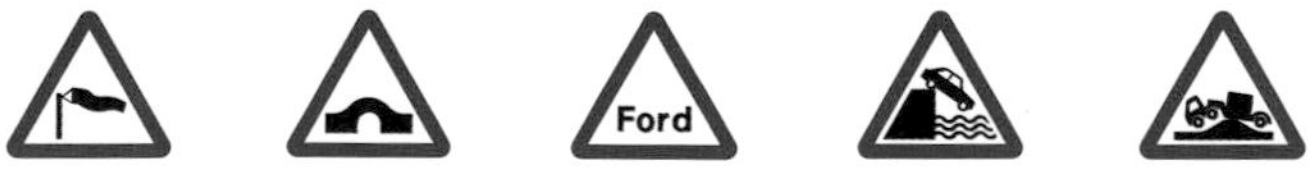

Ford

Side winds

Hump bridge

Worded warning sign

Quayside or river bank

Risk of grounding

Direction signs

Mostly rectangular

Signs on motorways – blue backgrounds

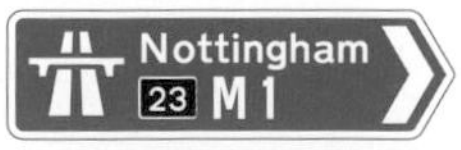

Nottingham
23 M1

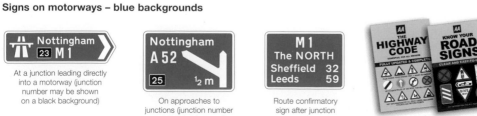

At a junction leading directly into a motorway (junction number may be shown on a black background)

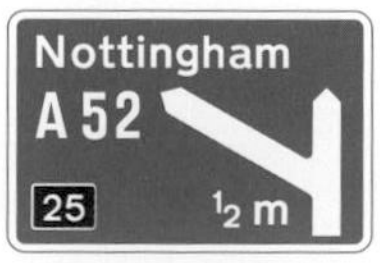

Nottingham
A 52
25
½ m

On approaches to junctions (junction number on black background)

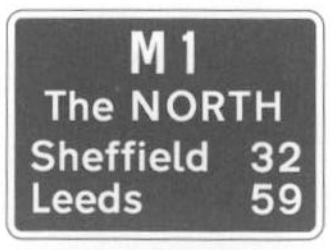

M 1
The NORTH
Sheffield 32
Leeds 59

Route confirmatory sign after junction

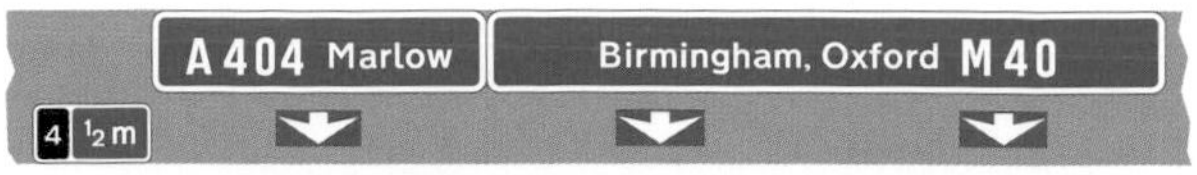

A 404 Marlow
Birmingham, Oxford M 40
4 ½ m

Downward pointing arrows mean 'Get in lane'
The left-hand lane leads to a different destination from the other lanes.

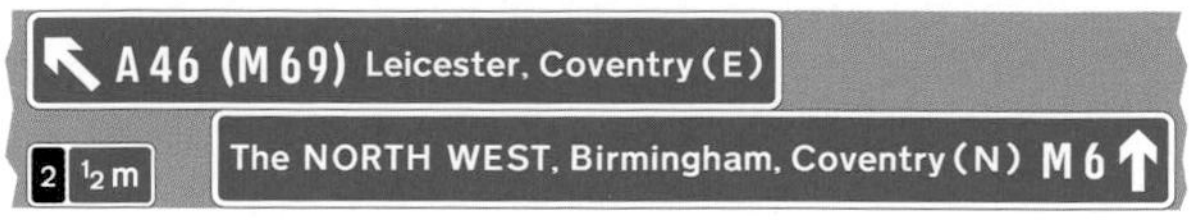

A 46 (M 69) Leicester, Coventry (E)
2 ½ m
The NORTH WEST, Birmingham, Coventry (N) M 6

The panel with the inclined arrow indicates the destinations which can be reached by leaving the motorway at the next junction

Signs on primary routes - green backgrounds

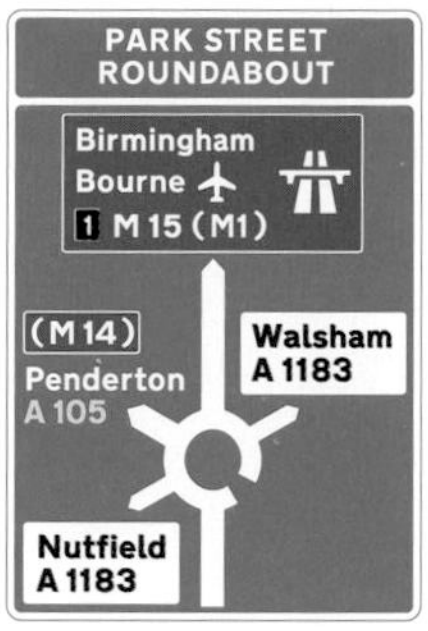

PARK STREET ROUNDABOUT
Birmingham
Bourne
1 M 15 (M1)
(M 14)
Penderton
A 105
Walsham
A 1183
Nutfield
A 1183

On approaches to junctions

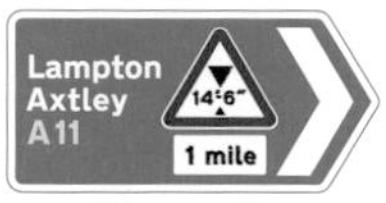

Lampton
Axtley
A 11
14'6"
1 mile

At the junction

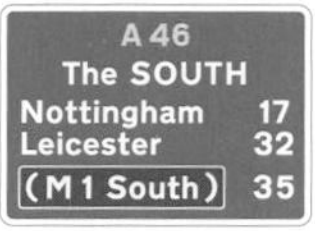

A 46
The SOUTH
Nottingham 17
Leicester 32
(M 1 South) 35

Route confirmatory sign after junction

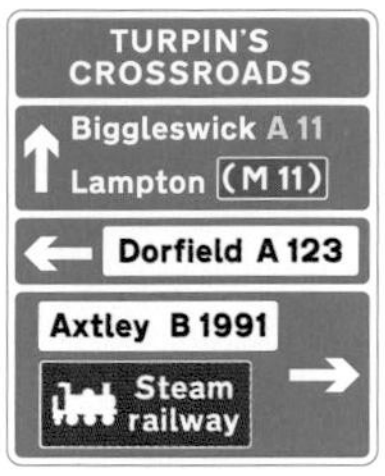

TURPIN'S CROSSROADS
Biggleswick A 11
Lampton (M 11)
Dorfield A 123
Axtley B 1991
Steam railway

On approaches to junctions

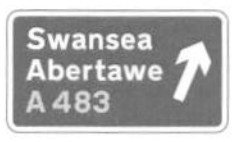

Swansea
Abertawe
A 483

On approach to a junction in Wales (bilingual)

Blue panels indicate that the motorway starts at the junction ahead.
Motorways shown in brackets can also be reached along the route indicated.
White panels indicate local or non-primary routes leading from the junction ahead.
Brown panels show the route to tourist attractions.
The name of the junction may be shown at the top of the sign.
The aircraft symbol indicates the route to an airport.
A symbol may be included to warn of a hazard or restriction along that route.

Signs on non-primary and local routes - black borders

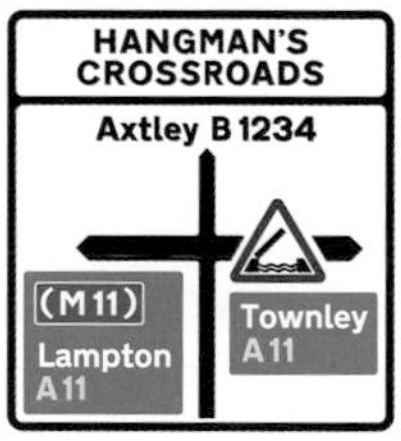

HANGMAN'S CROSSROADS
Axtley B 1234
(M 11)
Lampton
A 11
Townley
A 11

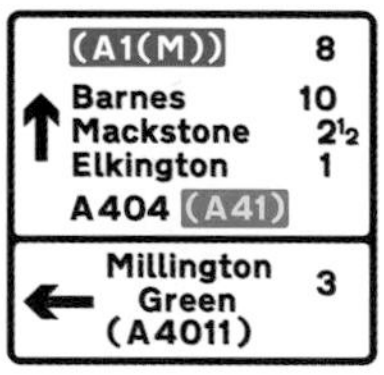

(A1(M)) 8
Barnes 10
Mackstone 2½
Elkington 1
A 404 (A 41)
Millington Green (A4011) 3

On approaches to junctions

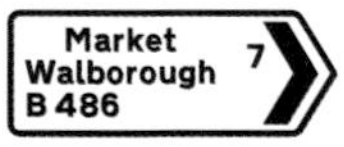

Market
Walborough
B 486
7

At the junction

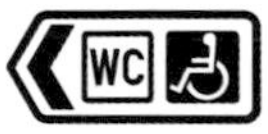

WC

Direction to toilets with access for the disabled

Green panels indicate that the primary route starts at the junction ahead.
Route numbers on a blue background show the direction to a motorway.
Route numbers on a green background show the direction to a primary route.

Emergency diversion routes

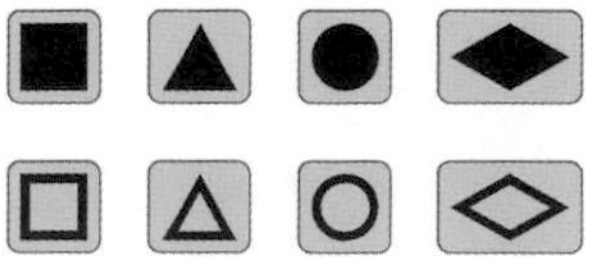

In an emergency it may be necessary to close a section of motorway or other main road to traffic, so a temporary sign may advise drivers to follow a diversion route. To help drivers navigate the route, black symbols on yellow patches may be permanently displayed on existing direction signs, including motorway signs. Symbols may also be used on separate signs with yellow backgrounds.

For further information see highways.gov.uk, trafficscotland.org and traffic-wales.com

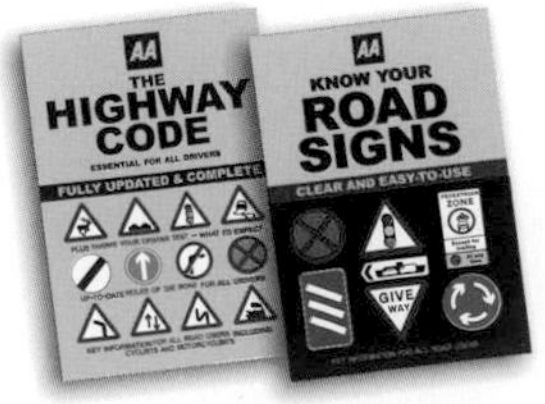

THE HIGHWAY CODE
KNOW YOUR ROAD SIGNS

Note: The signs shown in this road atlas are those most commonly in use and are not all drawn to the same scale. In Scotland and Wales bilingual versions of some signs are used, showing both English and Gaelic or Welsh spellings. Some older designs of signs may still be seen on the roads. A comprehensive explanation of the signing system illustrating the vast majority of road signs can be found in the AA's handbook *Know Your Road Signs*. Where there is a reference to a rule number, this refers to *The Highway Code*, which is detailed in the AA's guide. Both of these publications are on sale at theaa.com/shop and booksellers.

Channel Hopping

For business or pleasure, hopping on a ferry across to France, Belgium or the Channel Islands has never been easier.

The vehicle ferry routes shown on this map give you all the options, together with detailed port plans to help you navigate to and from the ferry terminals. Simply choose your preferred route, not forgetting the fast sailings; then check the colour-coded table for ferry operators, crossing times and contact details.

Bon voyage!

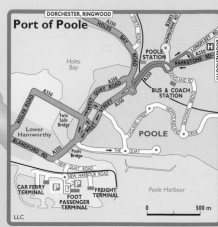

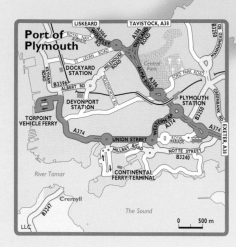

- 🚢 Fast ferry
- 🚢 Conventional ferry

ENGLISH CHANNEL FERRY CROSSINGS AND OPERATORS

From	To	Journey Time	Operator	Telephone	Website
Dover	Calais	1 hr 30 mins	P&O Ferries	0871 664 2020	poferries.com
Dover	Dunkerque	1 hr 30 mins	DFDS Seaways	0871 522 9955	dfdsseaways.co.uk
Dover	Calais	1 hr 30 mins	LD Lines/DFDS	0844 576 8836	ldlines.co.uk
Dover	Calais	1 hr 30 mins	My Ferry Link	0844 2482 100	myferrylink.com
Folkestone	Calais (Coquelles)	35 mins	Eurotunnel	0844 335 3535	eurotunnel.com
Newhaven	Dieppe	4 hrs	LD Lines	0844 576 8836	ldlines.co.uk
Plymouth	Roscoff	6–8 hrs	Brittany Ferries	0871 244 0744	brittany-ferries.co.uk
Plymouth	St-Malo	10 hrs 15 mins (Nov–Mar)	Brittany Ferries	0871 244 0744	brittany-ferries.co.uk
Poole	Cherbourg	4 hrs 15 mins (Mar–Oct)	Brittany Ferries	0871 244 0744	brittany-ferries.co.uk
Poole	Guernsey	3 hrs	Condor	0845 609 1024	condorferries.co.uk
Poole	Jersey	4 hrs 30 mins	Condor	0845 609 1024	condorferries.co.uk
Poole	St-Malo	7–12 hrs (with stop at Channel Is.)	Condor	0845 609 1024	condorferries.co.uk
Portsmouth	Caen (Ouistreham)	6–7 hrs	Brittany Ferries	0871 244 0744	brittany-ferries.co.uk
Portsmouth	Cherbourg	3 hrs (May–Sept)	Brittany Ferries	0871 244 0744	brittany-ferries.co.uk
Portsmouth	Cherbourg	4 hrs 30 mins(day) 8 hrs(o/night)	Brittany Ferries	0871 244 0744	brittany-ferries.co.uk
Portsmouth	Cherbourg	5 hrs (May–Sept, Sunday only)	Condor	0845 609 1024	condorferries.co.uk
Portsmouth	Guernsey	7 hrs	Condor	0845 609 1024	condorferries.co.uk
Portsmouth	Jersey	10 hrs 30 mins	Condor	0845 609 1024	condorferries.co.uk
Portsmouth	Le Havre	5 hrs 30 mins–8 hrs	LD Lines	0844 576 8836	ldlines.co.uk
Portsmouth	Le Havre	4 hrs 30 mins (Mar–Sept)	LD Lines	0844 576 8836	ldlines.co.uk
Portsmouth	St-Malo	9–11 hrs	Brittany Ferries	0871 244 0744	brittany-ferries.co.uk
Ramsgate	Oostende	4 hrs 30 mins	Transeuropa	01843 595 522	transeuropaferries.com
Weymouth	Guernsey	2 hrs 30 mins	Condor	0845 609 1024	condorferries.co.uk
Weymouth	Jersey	4 hrs	Condor	0845 609 1024	condorferries.co.uk
Weymouth	St-Malo	5 hrs 30 mins	Condor	0845 609 1024	condorferries.co.uk

Ferry services listed are provided as a guide only and are liable to change at short notice.

Please check sailings before planning your journey.

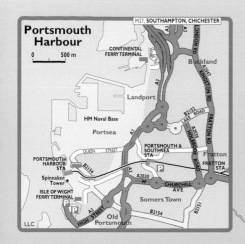

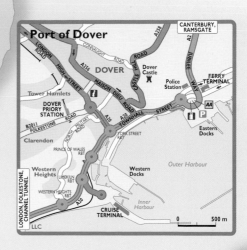

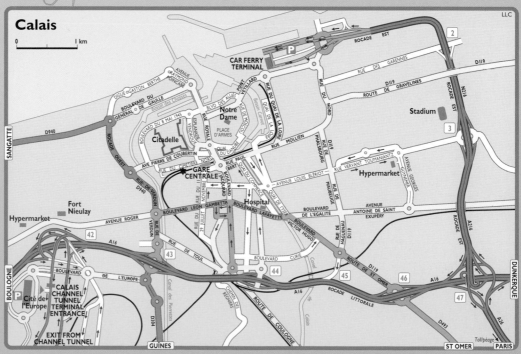

Ferries to Ireland and the Isle of Man

With so many sea crossings to Ireland and the Isle of Man this map will help you make the right choice.

The vehicle ferry routes shown on this map give you all the options, together with detailed port plans to help you navigate to and from the ferry terminals. Simply choose your preferred route, not forgetting the fast sailings; then check the colour-coded table for ferry operators, crossing times and contact details.

Fast ferry   Conventional ferry

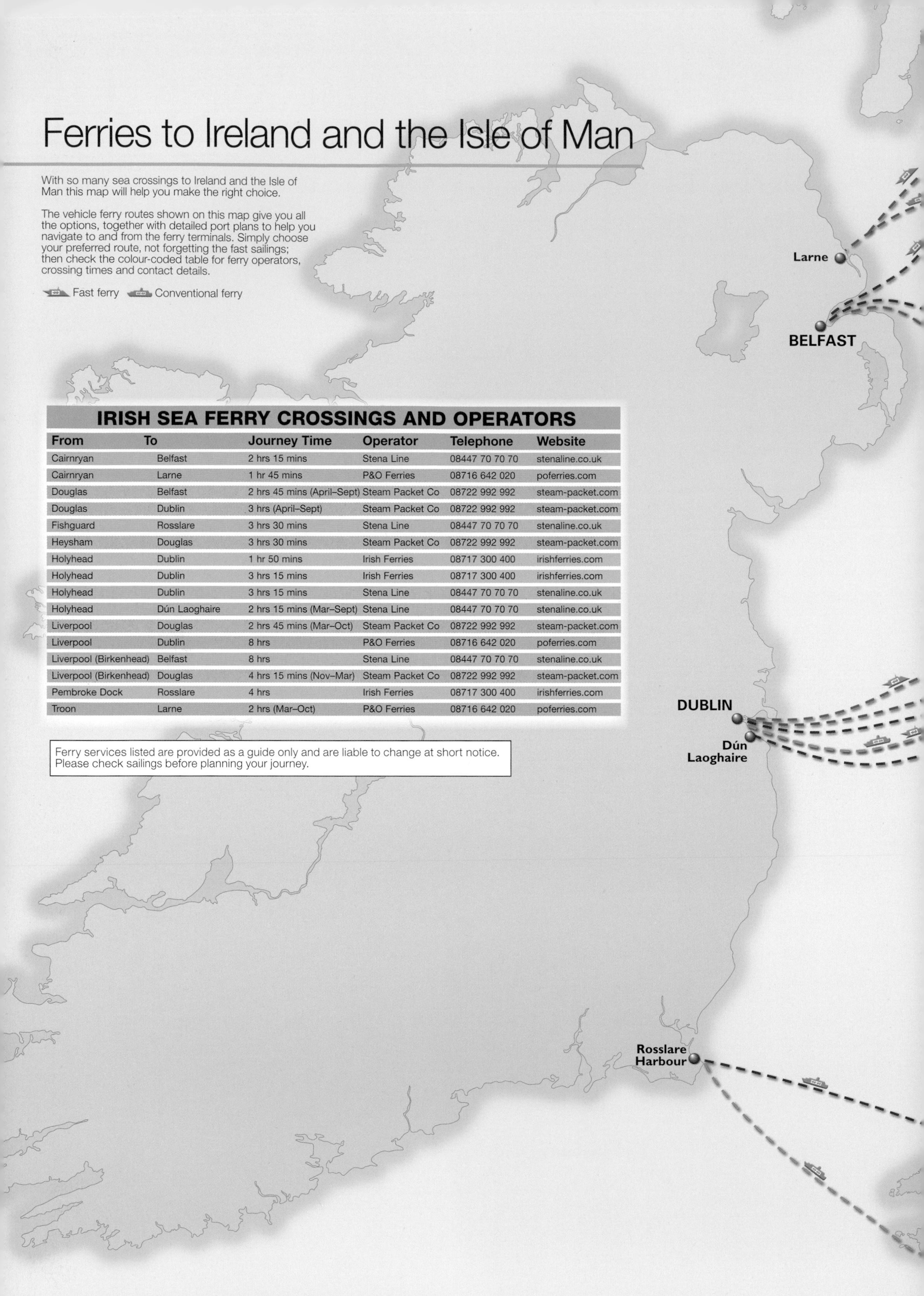

Larne

BELFAST

IRISH SEA FERRY CROSSINGS AND OPERATORS

From	To	Journey Time	Operator	Telephone	Website
Cairnryan	Belfast	2 hrs 15 mins	Stena Line	08447 70 70 70	stenaline.co.uk
Cairnryan	Larne	1 hr 45 mins	P&O Ferries	08716 642 020	poferries.com
Douglas	Belfast	2 hrs 45 mins (April–Sept)	Steam Packet Co	08722 992 992	steam-packet.com
Douglas	Dublin	3 hrs (April–Sept)	Steam Packet Co	08722 992 992	steam-packet.com
Fishguard	Rosslare	3 hrs 30 mins	Stena Line	08447 70 70 70	stenaline.co.uk
Heysham	Douglas	3 hrs 30 mins	Steam Packet Co	08722 992 992	steam-packet.com
Holyhead	Dublin	1 hr 50 mins	Irish Ferries	08717 300 400	irishferries.com
Holyhead	Dublin	3 hrs 15 mins	Irish Ferries	08717 300 400	irishferries.com
Holyhead	Dublin	3 hrs 15 mins	Stena Line	08447 70 70 70	stenaline.co.uk
Holyhead	Dún Laoghaire	2 hrs 15 mins (Mar–Sept)	Stena Line	08447 70 70 70	stenaline.co.uk
Liverpool	Douglas	2 hrs 45 mins (Mar–Oct)	Steam Packet Co	08722 992 992	steam-packet.com
Liverpool	Dublin	8 hrs	P&O Ferries	08716 642 020	poferries.com
Liverpool (Birkenhead)	Belfast	8 hrs	Stena Line	08447 70 70 70	stenaline.co.uk
Liverpool (Birkenhead)	Douglas	4 hrs 15 mins (Nov–Mar)	Steam Packet Co	08722 992 992	steam-packet.com
Pembroke Dock	Rosslare	4 hrs	Irish Ferries	08717 300 400	irishferries.com
Troon	Larne	2 hrs (Mar–Oct)	P&O Ferries	08716 642 020	poferries.com

Ferry services listed are provided as a guide only and are liable to change at short notice. Please check sailings before planning your journey.

DUBLIN

Dún Laoghaire

Rosslare Harbour

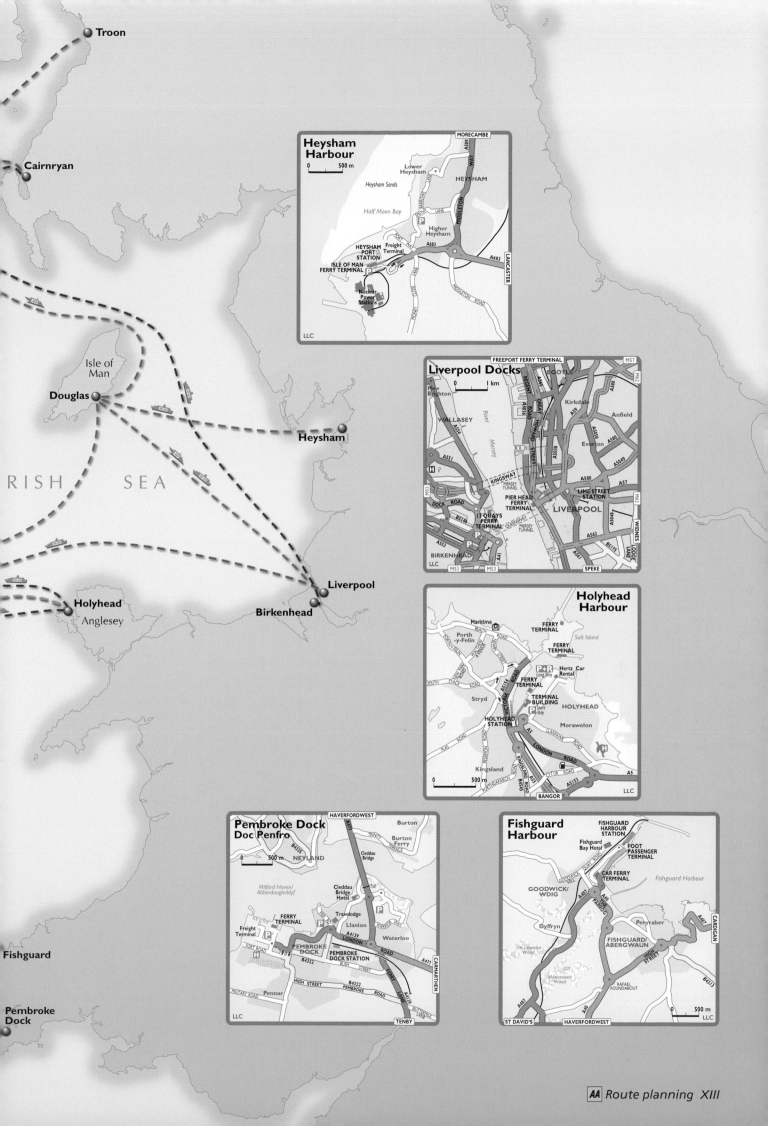

Troon

Cairnryan

Isle of
Man

Douglas

RISH   SEA

Heysham

Liverpool

Holyhead
Anglesey

Birkenhead

Fishguard

**Pembroke
Dock**

Heysham Harbour

0   500 m

MORECAMBE

Lower
Heysham

HEYSHAM

Heysham Sands

Half Moon Bay

Higher Heysham

P

HEYSHAM PORT STATION

Freight Terminal

ISLE OF MAN FERRY TERMINAL

Nuclear Power Stations

A683

A683

MIDDLETON ROAD

LANCASTER

LLC

Liverpool Docks

FREEPORT FERRY TERMINAL

M57

0   1 km

BOOTLE

New Brighton

WALLASEY

Kirkdale

Anfield

River Mersey

Everton

KINGSWAY

PIER HEAD FERRY TERMINAL

LIME STREET STATION

DOCK ROAD

12 QUAYS FERRY TERMINAL

LIVERPOOL

Mersey Tunnel

BIRKENHEAD

LLC   M53   M53   SPEKE   WIDNES

Holyhead Harbour

Maritime

FERRY TERMINAL

Salt Island

Porth-y-Felin

FERRY TERMINAL

P+R Long Stay   Hertz Car Rental

FERRY TERMINAL

Stryd

TERMINAL BUILDING

HOLYHEAD

HOLYHEAD STATION

Morawelon

Kingsland

LONDON ROAD

A5

BANGOR   LLC

0   500 m

Pembroke Dock
Doc Penfro

HAVERFORDWEST

Burton

0   500 m   NEYLAND

Burton Ferry

Cleddau Bridge

Milford Haven/ Abberdaugleddyf

Cleddau Bridge Hotel   Toll

FERRY TERMINAL   Travelodge

P   Llanion

Freight Terminal   P   A4139 LONDON ROAD   Waterloo

PEMBROKE DOCK

PEMBROKE DOCK STATION

CARMARTHEN

Pennar   High Street   PEMBROKE ROAD

MILITARY ROAD

LLC   TENBY

Fishguard Harbour

FISHGUARD HARBOUR STATION

Fishguard Bay Hotel   FOOT PASSENGER TERMINAL

CAR FERRY TERMINAL

GOODWICK/ WDIG   Fishguard Harbour

Dyffryn   Penyraber

FISHGUARD/ ABERGWAUN

Tre-Llewelyn Wood

HIGH STREET

CARDIGAN

RAFAEL ROUNDABOUT

ST DAVID'S   HAVERFORDWEST   A40   0   500 m   LLC

Caravan and camping sites in Britain

These pages list the top 300 AA-inspected Caravan and Camping (C & C) sites in the Pennant rating scheme. Five Pennant Premier sites are shown in **green**, Four Pennant sites are shown in **blue**.

Listings include addresses, telephone numbers and websites together with page and grid references to locate the sites in the atlas. The total number of touring pitches is also included for each site, together with the type of pitch available. The following abbreviations are used: C = Caravan CV = Campervan T = Tent

To find out more about the AA's Pennant rating scheme and other rated caravan and camping sites not included on these pages please visit *theAA.com*

ENGLAND

Alders Caravan Park
Home Farm, Alne, York
YO61 1RY
Tel: 01347 838722   **97 R7**
alderscaravanpark.co.uk
Total Pitches: 87 (C, CV & T)

Andrewshayes Caravan Park
Dalwood, Axminster
EX13 7DY
Tel: 01404 831225   **10 E5**
andrewshayes.co.uk
Total Pitches: 150 (C, CV & T)

Apple Tree Park C & C Site
A38, Claypits, Stonehouse
GL10 3AL
Tel: 01452 742362   **32 E3**
appletreepark.co.uk
Total Pitches: 65 (C, CV & T)

Appuldurcombe Gardens Holiday Park
Appuldurcombe Road, Wroxall,
Isle of Wight
PO38 3EP
Tel: 01983 852597   **14 F10**
appuldurcombegardens.co.uk
Total Pitches: 130 (C, CV & T)

Atlantic Bays Holiday Park
St Merryn, Padstow
PL28 8PY
Tel: 01841 520855   **4 D7**
atlanticbaysholidaypark.co.uk
Total Pitches: 70 (C, CV & T)

Ayr Holiday Park
St Ives, Cornwall
TR26 1EJ
Tel: 01736 795855   **2 E5**
ayrholidaypark.co.uk
Total Pitches: 40 (C, CV & T)

Back of Beyond Touring Park
234 Ringwood Rd, St Leonards,
Dorset
BH24 2SB
Tel: 01202 876968   **13 J4**
backofbeyondtouringpark.co.uk
Total Pitches: 80 (C, CV & T)

Bagwell Farm Touring Park
Knights in the Bottom,
Chickerell, Weymouth
DT3 4EA
Tel: 01305 782575   **11 N8**
bagwellfarm.co.uk
Total Pitches: 320 (C, CV & T)

Bardsea Leisure Park
Priory Road, Ulverston
LA12 9QE
Tel: 01229 584712   **94 F5**
bardsealeisure.co.uk
Total Pitches: 83 (C & CV)

Barn Farm Campsite
Barn Farm, Birchover, Matlock
DE4 2BL
Tel: 01629 650245   **84 B8**
barnfarmcamping.com
Total Pitches: 50 (C, CV & T)

Barnstones C & C Site
Great Bourton, Banbury
OX17 1QU
Tel: 01295 750289   **48 E6**
Total Pitches: 49 (C, CV & T)

Beaconsfield Farm Caravan Park
Battlefield, Shrewsbury
SY4 4AA
Tel: 01939 210370   **69 P11**
beaconsfield-farm.co.uk
Total Pitches: 60 (C & CV)

Bellingham C & C Club Site
Brown Rigg, Bellingham
NE48 2JY
Tel: 01434 220175   **112 B4**
*campingandcaravanningclub.co.uk/
bellingham*
Total Pitches: 64 (C, CV & T)

Bingham Grange Touring & Camping Park
Melplash, Bridport
DT6 3TT
Tel: 01308 488234   **11 K5**
binghamgrange.co.uk
Total Pitches: 150 (C, CV & T)

Bo Peep Farm Caravan Park
Bo Peep Farm, Aynho Road,
Adderbury, Banbury
OX17 3NP
Tel: 01295 810605   **48 E8**
bo-peep.co.uk
Total Pitches: 104 (C, CV & T)

Briarfields Motel & Touring Park
Gloucester Road, Cheltenham
GL51 0SX
Tel: 01242 235324   **46 H10**
briarfields.net
Total Pitches: 72 (C, CV & T)

Broadhembury C & C Park
Steeds Lane, Kingsnorth, Ashford
TN26 1NQ
Tel: 01233 620859   **26 H4**
broadhembury.co.uk
Total Pitches: 110 (C, CV & T)

Brokerswood Country Park
Brokerswood, Westbury
BA13 4EH
Tel: 01373 822238   **20 F4**
brokerswoodcountrypark.co.uk
Total Pitches: 69 (C, CV & T)

Budemeadows Touring Park
Widemouth Bay, Bude
EX23 0NA
Tel: 01288 361646   **16 C11**
budemeadows.com
Total Pitches: 145 (C, CV & T)

Burrowhayes Farm C & C Site & Riding Stables
West Luccombe, Porlock,
Minehead
TA24 8HT
Tel: 01643 862463   **18 B5**
burrowhayes.co.uk
Total Pitches: 120 (C, CV & T)

Burton Constable Holiday Park & Arboretum
Old Lodges, Sproatley, Hull
HU11 4LJ
Tel: 01964 562508   **93 L3**
burtonconstable.co.uk
Total Pitches: 140 (C, CV & T)

Calloose C & C Park
Leedstown, Hayle
TR27 5ET
Tel: 01736 850431   **2 F7**
calloose.co.uk
Total Pitches: 109 (C, CV & T)

Camping Caradon Touring Park
Trelawne, Looe
PL13 2NA
Tel: 01503 272388   **5 L11**
campingcaradon.co.uk
Total Pitches: 75 (C, CV & T)

Capesthorne Hall
Congleton Road, Siddington,
Macclesfield
SK11 9JY
Tel: 01625 861221   **82 H10**
capesthorne.com
Total Pitches: 50 (C & CV)

Carlton Meres Country Park
Rendham Road, Carlton,
Saxmundham
IP17 2QP
Tel: 01728 603344   **65 M8**
carlton-meres.co.uk
Total Pitches: 96 (C & CV)

Carlyon Bay C & C Park
Bethesda, Cypress Avenue,
Carlyon Bay
PL25 3RE
Tel: 01726 812735   **3 R3**
carlyonbay.net
Total Pitches: 180 (C, CV & T)

Carnevas Holiday Park & Farm Cottages
Carnevas Farm, St Merryn
PL28 8PN
Tel: 01841 520230   **4 D7**
carnevasholidaypark.co.uk
Total Pitches: 195 (C, CV & T)

Carnon Downs C & C Park
Carnon Downs, Truro
TR3 6JJ
Tel: 01872 862283   **3 L5**
carnon-downs-caravanpark.co.uk
Total Pitches: 150 (C, CV & T)

Carvynick Country Club
Summercourt, Newquay
TR8 5AF
Tel: 01872 510716   **4 D10**
carvynick.co.uk
Total Pitches: 47 (CV)

Castlerigg Hall C & C Park
Castlerigg Hall, Keswick
CA12 4TE
Tel: 017687 74499   **101 J6**
castlerigg.co.uk
Total Pitches: 48 (C, CV & T)

Cayton Village Caravan Park
Mill Lane, Cayton Bay,
Scarborough
YO11 3NN
Tel: 01723 583171   **99 M4**
caytontouring.co.uk
Total Pitches: 310 (C, CV & T)

Cheddar Bridge Touring Park
Draycott Rd, Cheddar
BS27 3RJ
Tel: 01934 743048   **19 N4**
cheddarbridge.co.uk
Total Pitches: 45 (C, CV & T)

Cheddar Mendip Heights C & C Club Site
Townsend, Priddy, Wells
BA5 3BP
Tel: 01749 870241   **19 P4**
*campingandcaravanningclub.co.uk/
cheddar*
Total Pitches: 90 (C, CV & T)

Chiverton Park
East Hill, Blackwater
TR4 8HS
Tel: 01872 560667   **3 J4**
chivertonpark.co.uk
Total Pitches: 12 (C, CV & T)

Church Farm C & C Park
The Bungalow, Church Farm,
High Street, Sixpenny Handley,
Salisbury
SP5 5ND
Tel: 01725 552563   **21 J11**
churchfarmcandcpark.co.uk
Total Pitches: 35 (C, CV & T)

Chy Carne Holiday Park
Kuggar, Ruan Minor,
Helston
TR12 7LX
Tel: 01326 290200   **3 J10**
chycarne.co.uk
Total Pitches: 30 (C, CV & T)

Claylands Caravan Park
Cabus, Garstang
PR3 1AJ
Tel: 01524 791242   **95 K11**
claylands.com
Total Pitches: 30 (C, CV & T)

Clippesby Hall
Hall Lane, Clippesby,
Great Yarmouth
NR29 3BL
Tel: 01493 367800   **77 N9**
clippesby.com
Total Pitches: 120 (C, CV & T)

Cofton Country Holidays
Starcross, Dawlish
EX6 8RP
Tel: 01626 890111   **9 N8**
coftonholidays.co.uk
Total Pitches: 450 (C, CV & T)

Colchester Holiday Park
Cymbeline Way, Lexden,
Colchester
CO3 4AG
Tel: 01206 545551   **52 G6**
colchestercamping.co.uk
Total Pitches: 168 (C, CV & T)

Constable Burton Hall Caravan Park
Constable Burton, Leyburn
DL8 5LJ
Tel: 01677 450428   **97 J2**
cbcaravanpark.co.uk
Total Pitches: 120 (C & CV)

Coombe Touring Park
Race Plain, Netherhampton,
Salisbury
SP2 8PN
Tel: 01722 328451   **21 L9**
coombecaravanpark.co.uk
Total Pitches: 50 (C, CV & T)

Corfe Castle C & C Club Site
Bucknowle, Wareham
BH20 5PQ
Tel: 01929 480280   **12 F8**
*campingandcaravanningclub.co.uk/
corfecastle*
Total Pitches: 80 (C, CV & T)

Cornish Farm Touring Park
Shoreditch, Taunton
TA3 7BS
Tel: 01823 327746   **18 H10**
cornishfarm.com
Total Pitches: 50 (C, CV & T)

Cosawes Park
Perranarworthal, Truro
TR3 7QS
Tel: 01872 863724   **3 K6**
cosawestouringandcamping.co.uk
Total Pitches: 59 (C, CV & T)

Cote Ghyll C & C Park
Osmotherley,
Northallerton
DL6 3AH
Tel: 01609 883425   **104 E11**
coteghyll.com
Total Pitches: 77 (C, CV & T)

Cotswold View Touring Park
Enstone Road, Charlbury
OX7 3JH
Tel: 01608 810314   **48 C10**
cotswoldview.co.uk
Total Pitches: 125 (C, CV & T)

Cove C & C Park
Ullswater, Watermillock
CA11 0LS
Tel: 017684 86549   **101 M6**
cove-park.co.uk
Total Pitches: 50 (C, CV & T)

Crealy Meadows C & C Park
Sidmouth Road, Clyst St Mary,
Exeter
EX5 1DR
Tel: 01395 234888   **9 P6**
Total Pitches: 120 (C, CV & T)

Crows Nest Caravan Park
Gristhorpe, Filey
YO14 9PS
Tel: 01723 582206   **99 M4**
crowsnestcaravanpark.com
Total Pitches: 49 (C, CV & T)

Dell Touring Park
Beyton Road, Thurston,
Bury St Edmunds
IP31 3RB
Tel: 01359 270121   **64 C9**
thedellcaravanpark.co.uk
Total Pitches: 50 (C, CV & T)

Diamond Farm C & C Park
Islip Road, Bletchingdon
OX5 3DR
Tel: 01869 350909   **48 F11**
diamondpark.co.uk
Total Pitches: 37 (C, CV & T)

Dibles Park
Dibles Road, Warsash,
Southampton
SO31 9SA
Tel: 01489 575232   **14 F5**
diblespark.co.uk
Total Pitches: 14 (C, CV & T)

Dolbeare Park C & C
St Ive Road, Landrake,
Saltash
PL12 5AF
Tel: 01752 851332   **5 P9**
dolbeare.co.uk
Total Pitches: 60 (C, CV & T)

Dornafield
Dornafield Farm, Two Mile Oak,
Newton Abbot
TQ12 6DD
Tel: 01803 812732   **7 L5**
dornafield.com
Total Pitches: 135 (C, CV & T)

East Fleet Farm Touring Park
Chickerell, Weymouth
DT3 4DW
Tel: 01305 785768   **11 N9**
eastfleet.co.uk
Total Pitches: 400 (C, CV & T)

Eden Valley Holiday Park
Lanlivery, Nr Lostwithiel
PL30 5BU
Tel: 01208 872277   **4 H10**
edenvalleyholidaypark.co.uk
Total Pitches: 56 (C, CV & T)

Eskdale C & C Club Site
Boot, Holmrook
CA19 1TH
Tel: 019467 23253   **100 G10**
*campingandcaravanningclub.co.uk/
eskdale*
Total Pitches: 100 (CV & T)

Exe Valley Caravan Site
Mill House, Bridgetown,
Dulverton
TA22 9JR
Tel: 01643 851432   **18 B8**
exevalleycamping.co.uk
Total Pitches: 50 (C, CV & T)

Fallbarrow Park
Rayrigg Road, Windermere
LA23 3DL
Tel: 015395 69835   **101 M11**
slholidays.co.uk
Total Pitches: 32 (C & CV)

Fernwood Caravan Park
Lyneal, Ellesmere
SY12 0QF
Tel: 01948 710221   **69 N8**
fernwoodpark.co.uk
Total Pitches: 60 (C & CV)

Fields End Water Caravan Park & Fishery
Benwick Road, Doddington,
March
PE15 0TY
Tel: 01354 740199   **62 E2**
fieldsendcaravans.co.uk
Total Pitches: 52 (C, CV & T)

Fishpool Farm Caravan Park
Fishpool Road, Delamere,
Northwich
CW8 2HP
Tel: 01606 883970   **82 C11**
fishpoolfarmcaravanpark.co.uk
Total Pitches: 50 (C, CV & T)

Flusco Wood
Flusco, Penrith
CA11 0JB
Tel: 017684 80020   **101 N5**
fluscowood.co.uk
Total Pitches: 46 (C & CV)

Forest Glade Holiday Park
Kentisbeare, Cullompton
EX15 2DT
Tel: 01404 841381   **10 C3**
forest-glade.co.uk
Total Pitches: 80 (C, CV & T)

Forest Park
Northrepps Road, Cromer
NR27 0JR
Tel: 01263 513290   **77 J3**
forest-park.co.uk
Total Pitches: 262 (C, CV & T)

Globe Vale Holiday Park
Radnor, Redruth
TR16 4BH
Tel: 01209 891183   **3 J5**
globevale.co.uk
Total Pitches: 138 (C, CV & T)

Golden Cap Holiday Park
Seatown, Chideock,
Bridport
DT6 6JX
Tel: 01308 422139   **11 J6**
wdlh.co.uk
Total Pitches: 108 (C, CV & T)

Golden Square Touring Caravan Park
Oswaldkirk, Helmsley
YO62 5YQ
Tel: 01439 788269   **98 C5**
goldensquarecaravanpark.co.uk
Total Pitches: 129 (C, CV & T)

Goosewood Caravan Park
Sutton-on-the-Forest, York
YO61 1ET
Tel: 01347 810829   **98 B8**
flowerofmay.com
Total Pitches: 100 (C & CV)

Green Acres Caravan Park
High Knells, Houghton,
Carlisle
CA6 4JW
Tel: 01228 675418 **110 H8**
caravanpark-cumbria.com
Total Pitches: 30 (C, CV & T)

Greenacres Touring Park
Haywards Lane, Chelston,
Wellington
TA21 9PH
Tel: 01823 652844 **18 G10**
greenacres-wellington.co.uk
Total Pitches: 40 (C & CV)

Greenhill Leisure Park
Greenhill Farm, Station Road,
Bletchingdon, Oxford
OX5 3BQ
Tel: 01869 351600 **48 E11**
greenhill-leisure-park.co.uk
Total Pitches: 92 (C, CV & T)

Grouse Hill Caravan Park
Flask Bungalow Farm,
Fylingdales, Robin Hood's Bay
YO22 4QH
Tel: 01947 880543 **105 P10**
grousehill.co.uk
Total Pitches: 175 (C, CV & T)

Gunvenna Caravan Park
St Minver, Wadebridge
PL27 6QN
Tel: 01208 862405 **4 F6**
gunvenna.co.uk
Total Pitches: 75 (C, CV & T)

Gwithian Farm Campsite
Gwithian Farm, Gwithian,
Hayle
TR27 5BX
Tel: 01736 753127 **2 F5**
gwithianfarm.co.uk
Total Pitches: 87 (C, CV & T)

Harbury Fields
Harbury Fields Farm, Harbury,
Nr Leamington Spa
CV33 9JN
Tel: 01926 612457 **48 C2**
harburyfields.co.uk
Total Pitches: 32 (C & CV)

**Hawthorn Farm
Caravan Park**
Station Road, Martin Mill,
Dover
CT15 5LA
Tel: 01304 852658 **27 P2**
keatfarm.co.uk
Total Pitches: 147 (C, CV & T)

Heathfield Farm Camping
Heathfield Road, Freshwater,
Isle of Wight
PO40 9SH
Tel: 01983 407822 **13 P7**
heathfieldcamping.co.uk
Total Pitches: 60 (C, CV & T)

**Heathland Beach
Caravan Park**
London Road, Kessingland
NR33 7PJ
Tel: 01502 740337 **65 Q4**
heathlandbeach.co.uk
Total Pitches: 63 (C, CV & T)

Hele Valley Holiday Park
Hele Bay, Ilfracombe,
North Devon
EX34 9RD
Tel: 01271 862460 **17 J2**
helevalley.co.uk
Total Pitches: 50 (C, CV & T)

Hidden Valley Park
West Down, Braunton,
Ilfracombe
EX34 8NU
Tel: 01271 813837 **17 J3**
hiddenvalleypark.com
Total Pitches: 100 (C, CV & T)

High Moor Farm Park
Skipton Road, Harrogate
HG3 2LT
Tel: 01423 563637 **97 K9**
highmoorfarmpark.co.uk
Total Pitches: 320 (C & CV)

Highfield Farm Touring Park
Long Road, Comberton,
Cambridge
CB23 7DG
Tel: 01223 262308 **62 E9**
highfieldfarmtouringpark.co.uk
Total Pitches: 120 (C, CV & T)

**Highlands End
Holiday Park**
Eype, Bridport, Dorset
DT6 6AR
Tel: 01308 422139 **11 K6**
wdlh.co.uk
Total Pitches: 195 (C, CV & T)

**Hill Cottage Farm
C & C Park**
Sandleheath Road, Alderholt,
Fordingbridge
SP6 3EG
Tel: 01425 650513 **13 K2**
hillcottagefarmcampingand
caravanpark.co.uk
Total Pitches: 75 (C, CV & T)

Hill Farm Caravan Park
Branches Lane, Sherfield English,
Romsey
SO51 6FH
Tel: 01794 340402 **21 Q10**
hillfarmpark.com
Total Pitches: 70 (C, CV & T)

Hill of Oaks & Blakeholme
Windermere
LA12 8NR
Tel: 015395 31578 **94 H3**
hillofoaks.co.uk
Total Pitches: 43 (C & CV)

Hillside Caravan Park
Canvas Farm, Moor Road,
Thirsk
YO7 4BR
Tel: 01845 537349 **97 P3**
hillsidecaravanpark.co.uk
Total Pitches: 35 (C & CV)

Hollins Farm C & C
Far Arnside, Carnforth
LA5 0SL
Tel: 01524 701508 **95 J5**
holgates.co.uk
Total Pitches: 12 (C, CV & T)

Homing Park
Church Lane, Seasalter,
Whitstable
CT5 4BU
Tel: 01227 771777 **39 J9**
homingpark.co.uk
Total Pitches: 43 (C, CV & T)

Honeybridge Park
Honeybridge Lane, Dial Post,
Horsham
RH13 8NX
Tel: 01403 710923 **24 E7**
honeybridgepark.co.uk
Total Pitches: 130 (C, CV & T)

Hurley Riverside Park
Park Office, Hurley,
Nr Maidenhead
SL6 5NE
Tel: 01628 824493 **35 M8**
hurleyriversidepark.co.uk
Total Pitches: 200 (C, CV & T)

Hylton Caravan Park
Eden Street, Silloth
CA7 4AY
Tel: 016973 31707 **109 P10**
stanwix.com
Total Pitches: 90 (C, CV & T)

**Jacobs Mount
Caravan Park**
Jacobs Mount, Stepney Road,
Scarborough
YO12 5NL
Tel: 01723 361178 **99 L3**
jacobsmount.com
Total Pitches: 156 (C, CV & T)

Jasmine Caravan Park
Cross Lane, Snainton,
Scarborough
YO13 9BE
Tel: 01723 859240 **99 J4**
jasminepark.co.uk
Total Pitches: 68 (C, CV & T)

Juliot's Well Holiday Park
Camelford, Cornwall
PL32 9RF
Tel: 01840 213302 **4 H5**
juliotswell.com
Total Pitches: 39 (C, CV & T)

**Kenneggy Cove
Holiday Park**
Higher Kenneggy, Rosudgeon,
Penzance
TR20 9AU
Tel: 01736 763453 **2 F8**
kenneggycove.co.uk
Total Pitches: 45 (C, CV & T)

Kloofs Caravan Park
Sandhurst Lane, Bexhill
TN39 4RG
Tel: 01424 842839 **26 B10**
kloofs.com
Total Pitches: 50 (C, CV & T)

Kneps Farm Holiday Park
River Road, Stanah,
Thornton-Cleveleys, Blackpool
FY5 5LR
Tel: 01253 823632 **88 D2**
knepsfarm.co.uk
Total Pitches: 40 (C & CV)

**Ladycross Plantation
Caravan Park**
Egton, Whitby
YO21 1UA
Tel: 01947 895502 **105 M9**
ladycrossplantation.co.uk
Total Pitches: 130 (C, CV & T)

Lamb Cottage Caravan Park
Dalefords Lane, Whitegate,
Northwich
CW8 2BN
Tel: 01606 882302 **82 D11**
lambcottage.co.uk
Total Pitches: 45 (C & CV)

Langstone Manor C & C Park
Moortown, Tavistock
PL19 9JZ
Tel: 01822 613371 **6 E4**
langstone-manor.co.uk
Total Pitches: 40 (C, CV & T)

Lebberston Touring Park
Filey Road, Lebberston,
Scarborough
YO11 3PE
Tel: 01723 585723 **99 M4**
lebberstontouring.co.uk
Total Pitches: 125 (C & CV)

Lee Valley C & C Park
Meridian Way, Edmonton,
London
N9 0AR
Tel: 020 8803 6900 **37 J2**
visitleevalley.org.uk
Total Pitches: 100 (C, CV & T)

Lee Valley Campsite
Sewardstone Road, Chingford,
London
E4 7RA
Tel: 020 8529 5689 **51 J11**
visitleevalley.org.uk
Total Pitches: 81 (C, CV & T)

Lemonford Caravan Park
Bickington (near Ashburton),
Newton Abbot
TQ12 6JR
Tel: 01626 821242 **7 K4**
lemonford.co.uk
Total Pitches: 82 (C, CV & T)

Lickpenny Caravan Site
Lickpenny Lane, Tansley, Matlock
DE4 5GF
Tel: 01629 583040 **84 D9**
lickpennycaravanpark.co.uk
Total Pitches: 80 (C & CV)

Lime Tree Park
Dukes Drive, Buxton
SK17 9RP
Tel: 01298 22988 **83 N10**
limetreeparkbuxton.co.uk
Total Pitches: 106 (C, CV & T)

Lincoln Farm Park Oxfordshire
High Street, Standlake
OX29 7RH
Tel: 01865 300239 **34 C4**
lincolnfarmpark.co.uk
Total Pitches: 90 (C, CV & T)

Little Cotton Caravan Park
Little Cotton, Dartmouth
TQ6 0LB
Tel: 01803 832558 **7 M8**
littlecotton.co.uk
Total Pitches: 95 (C, CV & T)

Little Lakeland Caravan Park
Wortwell, Harleston
IP20 0EL
Tel: 01986 788646 **65 K4**
littlelakeland.co.uk
Total Pitches: 38 (C, CV & T)

Long Acres Caravan Park
Station Road, Old Leake,
Boston
PE22 9RF
Tel: 01205 871555 **87 L10**
longacres-caravanpark.co.uk
Total Pitches: 40 (C, CV & T)

Long Hazel Park
High Street, Sparkford, Yeovil
BA22 7JH
Tel: 01963 440002 **20 B9**
longhazelpark.co.uk
Total Pitches: 50 (C, CV & T)

Lower Polladras Touring Park
Carleen, Breage, Helston
TR13 9NX
Tel: 01736 762220 **2 G7**
lower-polladras.co.uk
Total Pitches: 39 (C, CV & T)

Lowther Holiday Park
Eamont Bridge, Penrith
CA10 2JB
Tel: 01768 863631 **101 P5**
lowther-holidaypark.co.uk
Total Pitches: 180 (C, CV & T)

Lytton Lawn Touring Park
Lymore Lane, Milford on Sea
SO41 0TX
Tel: 01590 648331 **13 N6**
shorefield.co.uk
Total Pitches: 136 (C, CV & T)

**Manor Wood Country
Caravan Park**
Manor Wood, Coddington,
Chester
CH3 9EN
Tel: 01829 782990 **69 N3**
cheshire-caravan-sites.co.uk
Total Pitches: 45 (C, CV & T)

Maustin Caravan Park
Kearby with Netherby,
Netherby
LS22 4DA
Tel: 0113 288 6234 **97 M11**
maustin.co.uk
Total Pitches: 25 (C, CV & T)

Mayfield Touring Park
Cheltenham Road, Cirencester
GL7 7BH
Tel: 01285 831301 **33 K3**
mayfieldpark.co.uk
Total Pitches: 72 (C, CV & T)

Meadow Lakes
Hewas Water, St Austell
PL26 7JG
Tel: 01726 882540 **3 P4**
meadow-lakes.co.uk
Total Pitches: 190 (C, CV & T)

Meadowbank Holidays
Stour Way, Christchurch
BH23 2PQ
Tel: 01202 483597 **13 K6**
meadowbank-holidays.co.uk
Total Pitches: 41 (C & CV)

Merley Court
Merley, Wimborne Minster
BH21 3AA
Tel: 01590 648331 **12 H5**
shorefield.co.uk
Total Pitches: 160 (C, CV & T)

**Middlewood Farm
Holiday Park**
Middlewood Lane, Fylingthorpe,
Robin Hood's Bay, Whitby
YO22 4UF
Tel: 01947 880414 **105 P10**
middlewoodfarm.com
Total Pitches: 100 (C, CV & T)

Minnows Touring Park
Holbrook Lane,
Sampford Peverell
EX16 7EN
Tel: 01884 821770 **18 D11**
ukparks.co.uk/minnows
Total Pitches: 59 (C, CV & T)

Moon & Sixpence
Newbourn Road, Waldringfield,
Woodbridge
IP12 4PP
Tel: 01473 736650 **53 N2**
moonandsixpence.eu
Total Pitches: 65 (C, CV & T)

Moss Wood Caravan Park
Crimbles Lane, Cockerham
LA2 0ES
Tel: 01524 791041 **95 K11**
mosswood.co.uk
Total Pitches: 25 (C, CV & T)

Naburn Lock Caravan Park
Naburn
YO19 4RU
Tel: 01904 728697 **98 C11**
naburnlock.co.uk
Total Pitches: 100 (C, CV & T)

Newberry Valley Park
Woodlands, Combe Martin
EX34 0AT
Tel: 01271 882334 **17 K2**
newberryvalleypark.co.uk
Total Pitches: 120 (C, CV & T)

Newlands C & C Park
Charmouth, Bridport
DT6 6RB
Tel: 01297 560259 **10 H6**
newlandsholidays.co.uk
Total Pitches: 240 (C, CV & T)

Newperran Holiday Park
Rejerrah, Newquay
TR8 5QJ
Tel: 01872 572407 **3 K3**
newperran.co.uk
Total Pitches: 357 (C, CV & T)

Newton Mill Holiday Park
Newton Road, Bath
BA2 9JF
Tel: 0844 272 9503 **20 D2**
newtonmillpark.co.uk
Total Pitches: 106 (C, CV & T)

**Northam Farm
Caravan & Touring Park**
Brean, Burnham-on-Sea
TA8 2SE
Tel: 01278 751244 **19 K3**
northamfarm.co.uk
Total Pitches: 350 (C, CV & T)

**North Morte Farm
C & C Park**
North Morte Road, Mortehoe,
Woolacombe, N Devon
EX34 7EG
Tel: 01271 870381 **16 H2**
northmortefarm.co.uk
Total Pitches: 180 (C, CV & T)

**Oakdown Country
Holiday Park**
Gatedown Lane,
Sidmouth
EX10 0PT
Tel: 01297 680387 **10 D6**
oakdown.co.uk
Total Pitches: 150 (C, CV & T)

**Oathill Farm
Touring & Camping Site**
Oathill, Crewkerne
TA18 8PZ
Tel: 01460 30234 **11 J3**
oathillfarmleisure.co.uk
Total Pitches: 13 (C, CV & T)

Old Hall Caravan Park
Capernwray, Carnforth
LA6 1AD
Tel: 01524 733276 **95 L6**
oldhallcaravanpark.co.uk
Total Pitches: 38 (C & CV)

Orchard Park
Frampton Lane, Hubbert's Bridge,
Boston
PE20 3QU
Tel: 01205 290328 **74 E2**
orchardpark.co.uk
Total Pitches: 87 (C, CV & T)

Ord House Country Park
East Ord,
Berwick-upon-Tweed
TD15 2NS
Tel: 01289 305288 **129 P9**
ordhouse.co.uk
Total Pitches: 79 (C, CV & T)

Oxon Hall Touring Park
Welshpool Road,
Shrewsbury
SY3 5FB
Tel: 01743 340868 **56 H2**
morris-leisure.co.uk
Total Pitches: 105 (C, CV & T)

Padstow Touring Park
Padstow
PL28 8LE
Tel: 01841 532061 **4 E7**
padstowtouringpark.co.uk
Total Pitches: 150 (C, CV & T)

**Park Cliffe Camping &
Caravan Estate**
Birks Road, Tower Wood,
Windermere
LA23 3PG
Tel: 01539 531344 **94 H2**
parkcliffe.co.uk
Total Pitches: 60 (C, CV & T)

Parkers Farm Holiday Park
Higher Mead Farm, Ashburton,
Devon
TQ13 7LJ
Tel: 01364 654869 **7 K4**
parkersfarmholidays.co.uk
Total Pitches: 100 (C, CV & T)

Parkland C & C Site
Sorley Green Cross,
Kingsbridge
TQ7 4AF
Tel: 01364 654869 **7 J9**
parkersfarmholidays.co.uk
Total Pitches: 100 (C, CV & T)

Pear Tree Holiday Park
Organford Road, Holton Heath,
Organford, Poole
BH16 6LA
Tel: 0844 272 9504 **12 F6**
peartreepark.co.uk
Total Pitches: 154 (C, CV & T)

Penderleath C & C Park
Towednack, St Ives
TR26 3AF
Tel: 01736 798403 **2 D6**
penderleath.co.uk
Total Pitches: 75 (C, CV & T)

Penrose Holiday Park
Goonhavern, Truro
TR4 9QF
Tel: 01872 573185 **3 K3**
penroseholidaypark.com
Total Pitches: 110 (C, CV & T)

Pentire Haven Holiday Park
Stibb Road, Kilkhampton, Bude
EX23 9QY
Tel: 01288 321601 **16 C9**
pentirehaven.co.uk
Total Pitches: 120 (C, CV & T)

Piccadilly Caravan Park
Folly Lane West, Lacock
SN15 2LP
Tel: 01249 730260 **32 H11**
Total Pitches: 41 (C, CV & T)

Pilgrims Way C & C Park
Church Green Road, Fishtoft,
Boston
PE21 0QY
Tel: 01205 366646 **74 G2**
pilgrimsway-caravanandcamping.com
Total Pitches: 22 (C, CV & T)

Polborder House C & C Park
Bucklawren Road, St Martin, Looe
PL13 1NZ
Tel: 01503 240265 **5 M10**
polborderhouse.co.uk
Total Pitches: 31 (C, CV & T)

Polmanter Touring Park
Halsetown, St Ives
TR26 3LX
Tel: 01736 795640 **2 E6**
polmanter.com
Total Pitches: 270 (C, CV & T)

Porlock Caravan Park
Porlock, Minehead
TA24 8ND
Tel: 01643 862269 **18 A5**
porlockcaravanpark.co.uk
Total Pitches: 40 (C, CV & T)

**Portesham Dairy Farm
Campsite**
Portesham, Weymouth
DT3 4HG
Tel: 01305 871297 **11 N7**
porteshamdairyfarm.co.uk
Total Pitches: 90 (C, CV & T)

Porthtowan Tourist Park
Mile Hill, Porthtowan, Truro
TR4 8TY
Tel: 01209 890256 **2 H4**
porthtowantouristpark.co.uk
Total Pitches: 80 (C, CV & T)

**Quantock Orchard
Caravan Park**
Flaxpool, Crowcombe, Taunton
TA4 4AW
Tel: 01984 618618 **18 F7**
quantock-orchard.co.uk
Total Pitches: 69 (C, CV & T)

Ranch Caravan Park
Station Road, Honeybourne,
Evesham
WR11 7PR
Tel: 01386 830744 **47 M6**
ranch.co.uk
Total Pitches: 120 (C & CV)

Ripley Caravan Park
Knaresborough Road, Ripley,
Harrogate
HG3 3AU
Tel: 01423 770050 **97 L8**
ripleycaravanpark.com
Total Pitches: 100 (C, CV & T)

River Dart Country Park
Holne Park, Ashburton
TQ13 7NP
Tel: 01364 652511 **7 J5**
riverdart.co.uk
Total Pitches: 170 (C, CV & T)

Riverside C & C Park
Marsh Lane, North Molton Road,
South Molton
EX36 3HQ
Tel: 01769 579269 **17 N6**
exmoorriverside.co.uk
Total Pitches: 42 (C, CV & T)

Riverside Caravan Park
High Bentham, Lancaster
LA2 7FJ
Tel: 015242 61272 **6 E7**
riversidecaravanpark.co.uk
Total Pitches: 61 (C & CV)

Riverside Caravan Park
Leigham Manor Drive,
Marsh Mills, Plymouth
PL6 8LL
Tel: 01752 344122 **95 P7**
riversidecaravanpark.com
Total Pitches: 259 (C, CV & T)

Riverside Holidays
21 Compass Point, Ensign Way,
Hamble
SO31 4RA
Tel: 023 8045 3220 **14 E5**
riversideholidays.co.uk
Total Pitches: 77 (C, CV & T)

**River Valley
Holiday Park**
London Apprentice,
St Austell
PL26 7AP
Tel: 01726 73533 **3 Q3**
rivervalleyholidaypark.co.uk
Total Pitches: 45 (C, CV & T)

Rosedale C & C Park
Rosedale Abbey, Pickering
YO18 8SA
Tel: 01751 417272 **105 K11**
flowerofmay.com
Total Pitches: 100 (C, CV & T)

**Rose Farm Touring &
Camping Park**
Stepshort, Belton,
Nr Great Yarmouth
NR31 9JS
Tel: 01493 780896 **77 P11**
rosefarmtouringcp.co.uk
Total Pitches: 145 (C, CV & T)

Ross Park
Park Hill Farm, Ipplepen,
Newton Abbot
TQ12 5TT
Tel: 01803 812983 **7 L5**
rossparkcaravanpark.co.uk
Total Pitches: 110 (C, CV & T)

Rudding Holiday Park
Follifoot, Harrogate
HG3 1JH
Tel: 01423 870439 **97 M10**
ruddingholidaypark.co.uk
Total Pitches: 141 (C, CV & T)

Rutland C & C
Park Lane, Greetham,
Oakham
LE15 7FN
Tel: 01572 813520 **73 N8**
rutlandcaravanandcamping.co.uk
Total Pitches: 130 (C, CV & T)

St Helens Caravan Park
Wykeham,
Scarborough
YO13 9QD
Tel: 01723 862771 **99 K4**
sthelenscaravanpark.co.uk
Total Pitches: 250 (C, CV & T)

St Mabyn Holiday Park
Longstone Road, St Mabyn,
Wadebridge
PL30 3BY
Tel: 01208 841677 **4 H7**
stmabynholidaypark.co.uk
Total Pitches: 120 (C, CV & T)

**Seaview International
Holiday Park**
Boswinger, Mevagissey
PL26 6LL
Tel: 01726 843425 **3 P5**
seaviewinternational.com
Total Pitches: 201 (C, CV & T)

Severn Gorge Park
Bridgnorth Road, Tweedale,
Telford
TF7 4JB
Tel: 01952 684789 **57 N3**
severngorgepark.co.uk
Total Pitches: 10 (C & CV)

Shamba Holidays
230 Ringwood Road,
St Leonards, Ringwood
BH24 2SB
Tel: 01202 873302 **13 K4**
shambaholidays.co.uk
Total Pitches: 150 (C, CV & T)

Shrubbery Touring Park
Rousdon, Lyme Regis
DT7 3XW
Tel: 01297 442227 **10 F6**
shrubberypark.co.uk
Total Pitches: 120 (C, CV & T)

Silverbow Park
Perranwell, Goonhavern
TR4 9NX
Tel: 01872 572347 **3 K3**
chycor.co.uk/parks/silverbow
Total Pitches: 100 (C, CV & T)

Silverdale Caravan Park
Middlebarrow Plain,
Cove Road, Silverdale,
Nr Carnforth
LA5 0SH
Tel: 01524 701508 **95 K5**
holgates.co.uk
Total Pitches: 80 (C & CV)

**Skelwith Fold
Caravan Park**
Ambleside, Cumbria
LA22 0HX
Tel: 015394 32277 **101 L10**
skelwith.com
Total Pitches: 150 (C & CV)

**Somers Wood
Caravan Park**
Somers Road, Meriden
CV7 7PL
Tel: 01676 522978 **59 K8**
somerswood.co.uk
Total Pitches: 48 (C & CV)

Southfork Caravan Park
Parrett Works,
Martock
TA12 6AE
Tel: 01935 825661 **19 M11**
southforkcaravans.co.uk
Total Pitches: 27 (C, CV & T)

**South Lytchett Manor
C & C Park**
Dorchester Road, Lytchett
Minster, Poole
BH16 6JB
Tel: 01202 622577 **12 G6**
southlytchettmanor.co.uk
Total Pitches: 150 (C, CV & T)

Springfield Holiday Park
Tedburn St Mary, Exeter
EX6 6EW
Tel: 01647 24242 **9 K6**
springfieldholidaypark.co.uk
Total Pitches: 48 (C, CV & T)

**Stanmore Hall
Touring Park**
Stourbridge Road,
Bridgnorth
WV15 6DT
Tel: 01746 761761 **57 N6**
morris-leisure.co.uk
Total Pitches: 131 (C, CV & T)

Stowford Farm Meadows
Berry Down, Combe Martin
EX34 0PW
Tel: 01271 882476 **17 K3**
stowford.co.uk
Total Pitches: 700 (C, CV & T)

Stroud Hill Park
Fen Road, Pidley
PE28 3DE
Tel: 01487 741333 **62 D5**
stroudhillpark.co.uk
Total Pitches: 60 (C, CV & T)

**Sumners Ponds
Fishery & Campsite**
Chapel Road, Barns Green,
Horsham
RH13 0PR
Tel: 01403 732539 **24 D5**
sumnersponds.co.uk
Total Pitches: 85 (C, CV & T)

**Sun Haven Valley
Holiday Park**
Mawgan Porth, Newquay
TR8 4BQ
Tel: 01637 860373 **4 D8**
sunhavenvalley.com
Total Pitches: 109 (C, CV & T)

Sun Valley Holiday Park
Pentewan Road, St Austell
PL26 6DJ
Tel: 01726 843266 **3 Q4**
sunvalleyholidays.co.uk
Total Pitches: 29 (C, CV & T)

**Swiss Farm
Touring & Camping**
Marlow Road, Henley-on-Thames
RG9 2HY
Tel: 01491 573419 **35 L8**
swissfarmcamping.co.uk
Total Pitches: 140 (C, CV & T)

**Tanner Farm Touring
C & C Park**
Tanner Farm, Goudhurst Road,
Marden
TN12 9ND
Tel: 01622 832399 **26 B3**
tannerfarmpark.co.uk
Total Pitches: 100 (C, CV & T)

**Tattershall Lakes
Country Park**
Sleaford Road, Tattershall
LN4 4LR
Tel: 01526 348800 **86 H9**
tattershall-lakes.com
Total Pitches: 186 (C, CV & T)

Tehidy Holiday Park
Harris Mill, Illogan, Portreath
TR16 4JQ
Tel: 01209 216489 **2 H5**
tehidy.co.uk
Total Pitches: 18 (C, CV & T)

Teversal C & C Club Site
Silverhill Lane, Teversal
NG17 3JJ
Tel: 01623 551838 **84 G8**
campingandcaravanningclub.co.uk/teversal
Total Pitches: 126 (C, CV & T)

The Grange Touring Park
Yarmouth Road,
Ormesby St Margaret,
Great Yarmouth
NR29 3QG
Tel: 01493 730306 **77 Q9**
grangetouring.co.uk
Total Pitches: 70 (C, CV & T)

The Inside Park
Down House Estate,
Blandford Forum
DT11 9AD
Tel: 01258 453719 **12 E4**
theinsidepark.co.uk
Total Pitches: 125 (C, CV & T)

The Laurels Holiday Park
Padstow Road, Whitecross,
Wadebridge
PL27 7JQ
Tel: 01209 313474 **4 F7**
thelaurelsholidaypark.co.uk
Total Pitches: 30 (C, CV & T)

The Old Brick Kilns
Little Barney Lane, Barney,
Fakenham
NR21 0NL
Tel: 01328 878305 **76 E5**
old-brick-kilns.co.uk
Total Pitches: 65 (C, CV & T)

The Old Oaks Touring Park
Wick Farm, Wick,
Glastonbury
BA6 8JS
Tel: 01458 831437 **19 P7**
theoldoaks.co.uk
Total Pitches: 100 (C, CV & T)

**The Orchards Holiday
Caravan Park**
Main Road, Newbridge,
Yarmouth, Isle of Wight
PO41 0TS
Tel: 01983 531331 **14 D9**
orchards-holiday-park.co.uk
Total Pitches: 171 (C, CV & T)

The Quiet Site
Ullswater, Watermillock
CA11 0LS
Tel: 07768 727016 **101 M6**
thequietsite.co.uk
Total Pitches: 100 (C, CV & T)

Tollgate Farm C & C Park
Budnick Hill, Perranporth
TR6 0AD
Tel: 01872 572130 **3 K3**
tollgatefarm.co.uk
Total Pitches: 102 (C, CV & T)

Townsend Touring Park
Townsend Farm, Pembridge,
Leominster
HR6 9HB
Tel: 01544 388527 **45 M3**
townsendfarm.co.uk
Total Pitches: 60 (C, CV & T)

**Treago Farm
Caravan Site**
Crantock, Newquay
TR8 5QS
Tel: 01637 830277 **4 B9**
treagofarm.co.uk
Total Pitches: 90 (C, CV & T)

Trencreek Holiday Park
Hillcrest, Higher Trencreek,
Newquay
TR8 4NS
Tel: 01637 874210 **4 C9**
trencreekholidaypark.co.uk
Total Pitches: 194 (C, CV & T)

Trethem Mill Touring Park
St Just-in-Roseland, Nr St Mawes,
Truro
TR2 5JF
Tel: 01872 580504 **3 M6**
trethem.com
Total Pitches: 84 (C, CV & T)

Trevella Tourist Park
Crantock, Newquay
TR8 5EW
Tel: 01637 830308 **4 C10**
trevella.co.uk
Total Pitches: 313 (C, CV & T)

Troutbeck C & C Club Site
Hutton Moor End, Troutbeck,
Penrith
CA11 0SX
Tel: 017687 79149 **101 L5**
*campingandcaravanningclub.co.uk
/troutbeck*
Total Pitches: 54 (C, CV & T)

Truro C & C Park
Truro
TR4 8QN
Tel: 01872 560274 **3 K4**
trurocaravanandcampingpark.co.uk
Total Pitches: 51 (C, CV & T)

Tudor C & C
Shepherds Patch, Slimbridge,
Gloucester
GL2 7BP
Tel: 01453 890483 **32 D4**
tudorcaravanpark.com
Total Pitches: 75 (C, CV & T)

Two Mills Touring Park
Yarmouth Road,
North Walsham
NR28 9NA
Tel: 01692 405829 **77 K6**
twomills.co.uk
Total Pitches: 81 (C, CV & T)

Ulwell Cottage Caravan Park
Ulwell Cottage, Ulwell,
Swanage
BH19 3DG
Tel: 01929 422823 **12 H8**
ulwellcottagepark.co.uk
Total Pitches: 77 (C, CV & T)

Vale of Pickering Caravan Park
Carr House Farm, Allerston,
Pickering
YO18 7PQ
Tel: 01723 859280 **98 H4**
valeofpickering.co.uk
Total Pitches: 120 (C, CV & T)

Wagtail Country Park
Cliff Lane, Marston, Grantham
NG32 2HU
Tel: 01400 251955 **73 M2**
wagtailcountrypark.co.uk
Total Pitches: 49 (C & CV)

Warcombe Farm C & C Park
Station Road, Mortehoe
EX34 7EJ
Tel: 01271 870690 **16 H2**
warcombefarm.co.uk
Total Pitches: 250 (C, CV & T)

Wareham Forest Tourist Park
North Trigon, Wareham
BH20 7NZ
Tel: 01929 551393 **12 E6**
warehamforest.co.uk
Total Pitches: 200 (C, CV & T)

Watergate Bay Touring Park
Watergate Bay, Tregurrian
TR8 4AD
Tel: 01637 860387 **4 C9**
watergatebaytouringpark.co.uk
Total Pitches: 171 (C, CV & T)

Waterrow Touring Park
Wiveliscombe, Taunton
TA4 2AZ
Tel: 01984 623464 **18 E9**
waterrowpark.co.uk
Total Pitches: 45 (C, CV & T)

Waters Edge Caravan Park
Crooklands, Nr Kendal
LA7 7NN
Tel: 015395 67708 **95 L4**
watersedgecaravanpark.co.uk
Total Pitches: 26 (C, CV & T)

Wayfarers C & C Park
Relubbus Lane, St Hilary,
Penzance
TR20 9EF
Tel: 01736 763326 **2 F7**
wayfarerspark.co.uk
Total Pitches: 39 (C, CV & T)

Wells Holiday Park
Haybridge, Wells
BA5 1AJ
Tel: 01749 676869 **19 P5**
wellsholidaypark.co.uk
Total Pitches: 72 (C, CV & T)

Westwood Caravan Park
Old Felixstowe Road,
Bucklesham, Ipswich
IP10 0BN
Tel: 01473 659637 **53 N3**
westwoodcaravanpark.co.uk
Total Pitches: 100 (C, CV & T)

Whitefield Forest Touring Park
Brading Road, Ryde, Isle of Wight
PO33 1QL
Tel: 01983 617069 **14 H9**
whitefieldforest.co.uk
Total Pitches: 80 (C, CV & T)

Whitemead Caravan Park
East Burton Road, Wool
BH20 6HG
Tel: 01929 462241 **12 D7**
whitemeadcaravanpark.co.uk
Total Pitches: 95 (C, CV & T)

**Whitsand Bay Lodge &
Touring Park**
Millbrook, Torpoint
PL10 1JZ
Tel: 01752 822597 **5 Q11**
whitsandbayholidays.co.uk
Total Pitches: 49 (C, CV & T)

Widdicombe Farm Touring Park
Marldon, Paignton
TQ3 1ST
Tel: 01803 558325 **7 M6**
widdicombefarm.co.uk
Total Pitches: 180 (C, C & T)

Widemouth Fields C & C Park
Park Farm, Poundstock, Bude
EX23 0NA
Tel: 01288 361351 **16 C11**
widemouthbaytouring.co.uk
Total Pitches: 156 (C, CV & T)

Wild Rose Park
Ormside,
Appleby-in-Westmorland
CA16 6EJ
Tel: 017683 51077 **102 C7**
wildrose.co.uk
Total Pitches: 226 (C, CV & T)

Wilksworth Farm Caravan Park
Cranborne Road,
Wimborne Minster
BH21 4HW
Tel: 01202 885467 **12 H4**
wilksworthfarmcaravanpark.co.uk
Total Pitches: 85 (C, CV & T)

Wolds Way C & C
West Farm, West Knapton,
Malton
YO17 8JE
Tel: 01944 728463 **98 H6**
rydalesbest.co.uk
Total Pitches: 70 (C, CV & T)

Wooda Farm Holiday Park
Poughill, Bude
EX23 9HJ
Tel: 01288 352069 **16 C10**
wooda.co.uk
Total Pitches: 200 (C, CV & T)

Woodclose Caravan Park
High Casterton,
Kirkby Lonsdale
LA6 2SE
Tel: 01524 271597 **95 N5**
woodclosepark.com
Total Pitches: 29 (C, CV & T)

Wood Farm C & C Park
Axminster Road,
Charmouth
DT6 6BT
Tel: 01297 560697 **10 H6**
woodfarm.co.uk
Total Pitches: 175 (C, CV & T)

Woodhall Country Park
Stixwold Road, Woodhall Spa
LN10 6UJ
Tel: 01526 353710 **86 G8**
woodhallcountrypark.co.uk
Total Pitches: 80 (C, CV & T)

Woodlands Grove C & C Park
Blackawton, Dartmouth
TQ9 7DQ
Tel: 01803 712598 **7 L8**
woodlands-caravanpark.com
Total Pitches: 350 (C, CV & T)

Woodland Springs Adult Touring Park
Venton, Drewsteignton
EX6 6PG
Tel: 01647 231695 **8 G6**
woodlandsprings.co.uk
Total Pitches: 81 (C, CV & T)

Woodovis Park
Gulworthy, Tavistock
PL19 8NY
Tel: 01822 832968 **6 C4**
woodovis.com
Total Pitches: 50 (C, CV & T)

Woolsbridge Manor Farm Caravan Park
Three Legged Cross,
Wimborne
BH21 6RA
Tel: 01202 826369 **13 K4**
woolsbridgemanorcaravanpark.co.uk
Total Pitches: 60 (C, CV & T)

Yeatheridge Farm Caravan Park
East Worlington,
Crediton
EX17 4TN
Tel: 01884 860330 **9 J2**
yeatheridge.co.uk
Total Pitches: 85 (C, CV & T)

Zeacombe House Caravan Park
Blackerton Cross, East Anstey,
Tiverton
EX16 9JU
Tel: 01398 341279 **17 R7**
zeacombeadultretreat.co.uk
Total Pitches: 50 (C, CV & T)

SCOTLAND

Aird Donald Caravan Park
London Road, Stranraer
DG9 8RN
Tel: 01776 702025 **106 E5**
aird-donald.co.uk
Total Pitches: 100 (C, CV & T)

Beecraigs C & C Site
Beecraigs Country Park,
The Visitor Centre, Linlithgow
EH49 6PL
Tel: 01506 844516 **127 J3**
beecraigs.com
Total Pitches: 36 (C, CV & T)

Blair Castle Caravan Park
Blair Atholl, Pitlochry
PH18 5SR
Tel: 01796 481263 **141 L4**
blaircastlecaravanpark.co.uk
Total Pitches: 241 (C, CV & T)

Brighouse Bay Holiday Park
Brighouse Bay, Borgue,
Kirkcudbright
DG6 4TS
Tel: 01557 870267 **108 D11**
gillespie-leisure.co.uk
Total Pitches: 190 (C, CV & T)

Cairnsmill Holiday Park
Largo Road, St Andrews
KY16 8NN
Tel: 01334 473604 **135 M5**
cairnsmill.co.uk
Total Pitches: 62 (C, CV & T)

Castle Cary Holiday Park
Creetown, Newton Stewart
DG8 7DQ
Tel: 01671 820264 **107 N6**
castlecary-caravans.com
Total Pitches: 50 (C, CV & T)

Craigtoun Meadows Holiday Park
Mount Melville, St Andrews
KY16 8PQ
Tel: 01334 475959 **135 M4**
craigtounmeadows.co.uk
Total Pitches: 57 (C, CV & T)

Drum Mohr Caravan Park
Levenhall, Musselburgh
EH21 8JS
Tel: 0131 665 6867 **128 B5**
drummohr.org
Total Pitches: 120 (C, CV & T)

Faskally Caravan Park
Pitlochry
PH16 5LA
Tel: 01796 472007 **141 M5**
faskally.co.uk
Total Pitches: 300 (C, CV & T)

Gart Caravan Park
The Gart, Callander
FK17 8LE
Tel: 01877 330002 **133 J6**
theholidaypark.co.uk
Total Pitches: 128 (C & CV)

Glenearly Caravan Park
Dalbeattie
DG5 4NE
Tel: 01556 611393 **108 H8**
glenearlycaravanpark.co.uk
Total Pitches: 39 (C, CV & T)

Glen Nevis C & C Park
Glen Nevis, Fort William
PH33 6SX
Tel: 01397 702191 **139 L3**
glen-nevis.co.uk
Total Pitches: 380 (C, CV & T)

Hoddom Castle Caravan Park
Hoddom, Lockerbie
DG11 1AS
Tel: 01576 300251 **110 C6**
hoddomcastle.co.uk
Total Pitches: 200 (C, CV & T)

Huntly Castle Caravan Park
The Meadow, Huntly
AB54 4UJ
Tel: 01466 794999 **158 D9**
huntlycastle.co.uk
Total Pitches: 90 (C, CV & T)

Invercoe C & C Park
Glencoe, Ballachulish
PH49 4HP
Tel: 01855 811210 **139 K6**
invercoe.co.uk
Total Pitches: 60 (C, CV & T)

Linnhe Lochside Holidays
Corpach, Fort William
PH33 7NL
Tel: 01397 772376 **139 K2**
linnhe-lochside-holidays.co.uk
Total Pitches: 85 (C, CV & T)

Linwater Caravan Park
West Clifton,
East Calder
EH53 0HT
Tel: 0131 333 3326 **127 L4**
linwater.co.uk
Total Pitches: 60 (C, CV & T)

Lomond Woods Holiday Park
Old Luss Road, Balloch,
Loch Lomond
G83 8QP
Tel: 01389 755000 **132 D11**
holiday-parks.co.uk
Total Pitches: 100 (C & CV)

Milton of Fonab Caravan Site
Bridge Road, Pitlochry
PH16 5NA
Tel: 01796 472882 **141 M6**
fonab.co.uk
Total Pitches: 154 (C, CV & T)

River Tilt Caravan Park
Blair Atholl, Pitlochry
PH18 5TE
Tel: 01796 481467 **141 L4**
rivertilt.co.uk
Total Pitches: 30 (C, CV & T)

Sands of Luce Holiday Park
Sands of Luce, Sandhead,
Stranraer
DG9 9JN
Tel: 01776 830456 **106 F7**
sandsofluceholidaypark.co.uk
Total Pitches: 100 (C, CV & T)

Seaward Caravan Park
Dhoon Bay, Kirkcudbright
DG6 4TJ
Tel: 01557 870267 **108 E11**
gillespie-leisure.co.uk
Total Pitches: 26 (C, CV & T)

Shieling Holidays
Craignure, Isle of Mull
PA65 6AY
Tel: 01680 812496 **138 C10**
shielingholidays.co.uk
Total Pitches: 90 (C, CV & T)

Skye C & C Club Site
Loch Greshornish, Borve,
Arnisort, Edinbane,
Isle of Skye
IV51 9PS
Tel: 01470 582230 **152 E7**
campingandcaravanningclub.co.uk /skye
Total Pitches: 105 (C, CV & T)

Thurston Manor Leisure Park
Innerwick, Dunbar
EH42 1SA
Tel: 01368 840643 **129 J5**
thurstonmanor.co.uk
Total Pitches: 120 (C, CV & T)

Trossachs Holiday Park
Aberfoyle
FK8 3SA
Tel: 01877 382614 **132 G8**
trossachsholidays.co.uk
Total Pitches: 66 (C, CV & T)

Witches Craig C & C Park
Blairlogie, Stirling
FK9 5PX
Tel: 01786 474947 **133 N8**
witchescraig.co.uk
Total Pitches: 60 (C, CV & T)

WALES

Anchorage Caravan Park
Bronllys, Brecon
LD3 0LD
Tel: 01874 711246 **44 G7**
anchoragecp.co.uk
Total Pitches: 110 (C, CV & T)

Barcdy Touring C & C Park
Talsarnau
LL47 6YG
Tel: 01766 770736 **67 L7**
barcdy.co.uk
Total Pitches: 80 (C, CV & T)

Beach View Caravan Park
Bwlchtocyn,
Abersoch
LL53 7BT
Tel: 01758 712956 **66 E9**
Total Pitches: 47 (C, CV & T)

Bodnant Caravan Park
Nebo Road, Llanrwst,
Conwy Valley
LL26 0SD
Tel: 01492 640248 **67 Q2**
bodnant-caravan-park.co.uk
Total Pitches: 54 (C, CV & T)

Bron Derw Touring Caravan Park
Llanrwst
LL26 0YT
Tel: 01492 640494 **67 P2**
bronderw-wales.co.uk
Total Pitches: 48 (C & CV)

Bron-Y-Wendon Caravan Park
Wern Road, Llanddulas,
Colwyn Bay
LL22 8HG
Tel: 01492 512903 **80 C9**
northwales-holidays.co.uk
Total Pitches: 130 (C & CV)

Bryn Gloch C & C Park
Betws Garmon,
Caernarfon
LL54 7YY
Tel: 01286 650216 **67 J3**
campwales.co.uk
Total Pitches: 160 (C, CV & T)

Caerfai Bay Caravan & Tent Park
Caerfai Bay, St Davids,
Haverfordwest
SA62 6QT
Tel: 01437 720274 **40 E6**
caerfaibay.co.uk
Total Pitches: 106 (C, CV & T)

Cenarth Falls Holiday Park
Cenarth,
Newcastle Emlyn
SA38 9JS
Tel: 01239 710345 **41 Q2**
cenarth-holipark.co.uk
Total Pitches: 30 (C, CV & T)

Deucoch Touring & Camping Park
Sarn Bach, Abersoch
LL53 7LD
Tel: 01758 713293 **66 E9**
deucoch.com
Total Pitches: 70 (C, CV & T)

Dinlle Caravan Park
Dinas Dinlle,
Caernarfon
LL54 5TW
Tel: 01286 830324 **66 G3**
thornleyleisure.co.uk
Total Pitches: 175 (C, CV & T)

Eisteddfa
Eisteddfa Lodge, Pentrefelin,
Criccieth
LL52 0PT
Tel: 01766 522696 **67 J7**
eisteddfapark.co.uk
Total Pitches: 100 (C, CV & T)

Erwlon C & C Park
Brecon Road, Llandovery
SA20 0RD
Tel: 01550 721021 **43 Q8**
erwlon.co.uk
Total Pitches: 75 (C, CV & T)

Fforest Fields C & C Park
Hundred House,
Builth Wells
LD1 5RT
Tel: 01982 570406 **44 G4**
fforestfields.co.uk
Total Pitches: 60 (C, CV & T)

Hendre Mynach Touring C & C Park
Llanaber Road, Barmouth
LL42 1YR
Tel: 01341 280262 **67 L11**
hendremynach.co.uk
Total Pitches: 240 (C, CV & T)

Home Farm Caravan Park
Marian-Glas,
Isle of Anglesey
LL73 8PH
Tel: 01248 410614 **78 H8**
homefarm-anglesey.co.uk
Total Pitches: 102 (C, CV & T)

Islawrffordd Caravan Park
Tal-y-bont, Barmouth
LL43 2AQ
Tel: 01341 247269 **67 K10**
islawrffordd.co.uk
Total Pitches: 105 (C, CV & T)

Llys Derwen C & C Site
Ffordd Bryngwyn, Llanrug,
Caernarfon
LL55 4RD
Tel: 01286 673322 **67 J2**
llysderwen.co.uk
Total Pitches: 20 (C, CV & T)

Pencelli Castle C & C Park
Pencelli, Brecon
LD3 7LX
Tel: 01874 665451 **44 F10**
pencelli-castle.com
Total Pitches: 80 (C, CV & T)

Penisar Mynydd Caravan Park
Caerwys Road, Rhuallt,
St Asaph
LL17 0TY
Tel: 01745 582227 **80 F9**
penisarmynydd.co.uk
Total Pitches: 75 (C, CV & T)

Pen-y-Bont Touring Park
Llangynog Road, Bala
LL23 7PH
Tel: 01678 520549 **68 B8**
penybont-bala.co.uk
Total Pitches: 95 (C, CV & T)

Plas Farm Caravan Park
Betws-yn-Rhos,
Abergele
LL22 8AU
Tel: 01492 680254 **80 B10**
plasfarmcaravanpark.co.uk
Total Pitches: 54 (C, CV & T)

Pont Kemys C & C Park
Chainbridge, Abergavenny
NP7 9DS
Tel: 01873 880688 **31 K3**
pontkemys.com
Total Pitches: 65 (C, CV & T)

Riverside Camping
Seiont Nurseries, Pont Rug,
Caernarfon
LL55 2BB
Tel: 01286 678781 **67 J2**
riversidecamping.co.uk
Total Pitches: 73 (C, CV & T)

River View Touring Park
The Dingle, Llanedi,
Pontarddulais
SA4 0FH
Tel: 01269 844876 **28 G3**
riverviewtouringpark.com
Total Pitches: 60 (C, CV & T)

The Plassey Leisure Park
The Plassey, Eyton,
Wrexham
LL13 0SP
Tel: 01978 780277 **69 L5**
plassey.com
Total Pitches: 90 (C, CV & T)

Trawsdir Touring C & C Park
Llanaber, Barmouth
LL42 1RR
Tel: 01341 280611 **67 K11**
barmouthholidays.co.uk
Total Pitches: 70 (C, CV & T)

Trefalun Park
Devonshire Drive, St Florence,
Tenby
SA70 8RD
Tel: 01646 651514 **41 L10**
trefalunpark.co.uk
Total Pitches: 90 (C, CV & T)

Tyddyn Isaf Caravan Park
Lligwy Bay, Dulas,
Isle of Anglesey
LL70 9PQ
Tel: 01248 410203 **78 H7**
tyddynisaf.co.uk
Total Pitches: 30 (C, CV & T)

Well Park C & C Site
Tenby
SA70 8TL
Tel: 01834 842179 **41 M10**
wellparkcaravans.co.uk
Total Pitches: 100 (C, CV & T)

Ynysymaengwyn Caravan Park
Tywyn
LL36 9RY
Tel: 01654 710684 **54 E4**
ynysy.co.uk
Total Pitches: 80 (C, CV & T)

CHANNEL ISLANDS

Beuvelande Camp Site
Beuvelande, St Martin,
Jersey
JE3 6EZ
Tel: 01534 853575 **11 c1**
campingjersey.com
Total Pitches: 150 (C, CV & T)

Fauxquets Valley Campsite
Castel, Guernsey
GY5 7QL
Tel: 01481 255460 **10 b2**
fauxquets.co.uk
Total Pitches: 120 (CV & T)

Rozel Camping Park
Summerville Farm, St Martin,
Jersey
JE3 6AX
Tel: 01534 855200 **11 c1**
rozelcamping.co.uk
Total Pitches: 100 (C, CV & T)

Road safety cameras

First, the advice you would expect from the AA - we advise drivers to always follow the signed speed limits – breaking the speed limit is illegal and can cost lives.

Both the AA and the Government believe that safety cameras ('speed cameras') should be operated within a transparent system. By providing information relating to road safety and speed hotspots, the AA believes that the driver is better placed to be aware of speed limits and can ensure adherence to them, thus making the roads safer for all users.

Most fixed cameras are installed at accident 'black spots' where four or more fatal or serious road collisions have occurred over the previous three years. It is the policy of both the police and the Department for Transport to make the location of cameras as well known as possible.
By showing camera locations in this atlas the AA is identifying the places where extra care should be taken while driving. Speeding is illegal and dangerous and you MUST keep within the speed limit at all times.

Gatso™   Truvelo™   SPECS™   Traffipax™

There are currently more than 4,000 fixed cameras in Britain and the road mapping in this atlas identifies their on-the-road locations.

 This symbol is used on the mapping to identify **individual** camera locations - with speed limits (mph)

 This symbol is used on the mapping to identify **multiple** cameras on the same stretch of road - with speed limits (mph)

 This symbol is used on the mapping to highlight SPECS™ camera systems which calculate your **average speed** along a stretch of road between two or more sets of cameras - with speed limits (mph)

Mobile cameras are also deployed at other sites where speed is perceived to be a problem and mobile enforcement often takes place at the fixed camera sites shown on the maps in this atlas. Additionally, regular police enforcement can take place   on any road.

Speed Limits	Built up areas*	Single carriageways	Dual carriageways	Motorways
Types of vehicle	MPH (km/h)	MPH (km/h)	MPH (km/h)	MPH (km/h)
 **Cars & motorcycles** (including car derived vans up to 2 tonnes maximum laden weight)	30 (48)	60 (96)	70 (112)	70 (112)
 **Cars towing caravans or trailers** (including car derived vans and motorcycles)	30 (48)	50 (80)	60 (96)	60 (96)
 **Buses, coaches and minibuses** (not exceeding 12 metres (39 feet) in overall length)	30 (48)	50 (80)	60 (96)	70 (112)
 **Goods vehicles** (not exceeding 7.5 tonnes maximum laden weight)	30 (48)	50 (80)	60 (96)	70† (112)
 **Goods vehicles** (exceeding 7.5 tonnes maximum laden weight)	30 (48)	40 (64)	50 (80)	60 (96)

* The 30mph (48km/h) limit usually applies to all traffic on all roads with street lighting unless signs show otherwise.
† 60mph (96km/h) if articulated or towing a trailer.

Read this before you use the atlas

Safety cameras and speed limits

The fixed camera symbols on the mapping show the maximum speed in mph that applies to that particular stretch of road and above which the camera is set to activate. The actual road speed limit however will vary for different vehicle types and you must ensure that you drive within the speed limit for your particular class of vehicle at all times.

The chart above details the speed limits applying to the different classes. Don't forget that mobile enforcement can take account of vehicle class at any designated site.

Camera locations

1 The camera locations were correct at the time of finalising the information to go to press.

2 Camera locations are approximate due to limitations in the scale of the road mapping used in this atlas.

3 In towns and urban areas camera locations are shown only on roads that appear on the road maps in this atlas.

4 Where two or more cameras appear close together, a special symbol is used to indicate multiple cameras on the same stretch of road.

5 Our symbols do not indicate the direction in which cameras point.

6 On the mapping we symbolise more than 4,000 fixed camera locations. Mobile laser device locations, roadwork cameras and 'fixed red light' cameras cannot be shown.

Be alert to accident black spots even before seeing the cameras

The AA brings you a Smart Phone app that provides 'real-time' updates of safety camera locations

The AA Safety Camera app brings the latest safety camera location system to your Smart Phone. It improves road safety by alerting you to the location of fixed and mobile camera sites and accident black spots.

The AA Safety Camera app ensures that you will always have the very latest data of fixed and mobile sites on your Smart Phone without having to connect it to your computer. Updates are made available automatically.

Powered by **RoadPilot**®

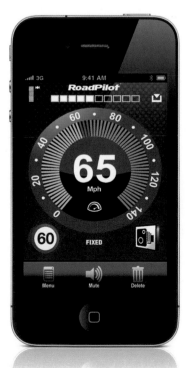

Visual Countdown
To camera location

Your Speed
The speed you are travelling when approaching a camera. Dial turns red as an additional visual alert

Camera Types Located
Includes fixed cameras (Gatso, Specs etc.) and mobile cameras

Speed Limit at Camera

Smart Phone Apps

Map pages

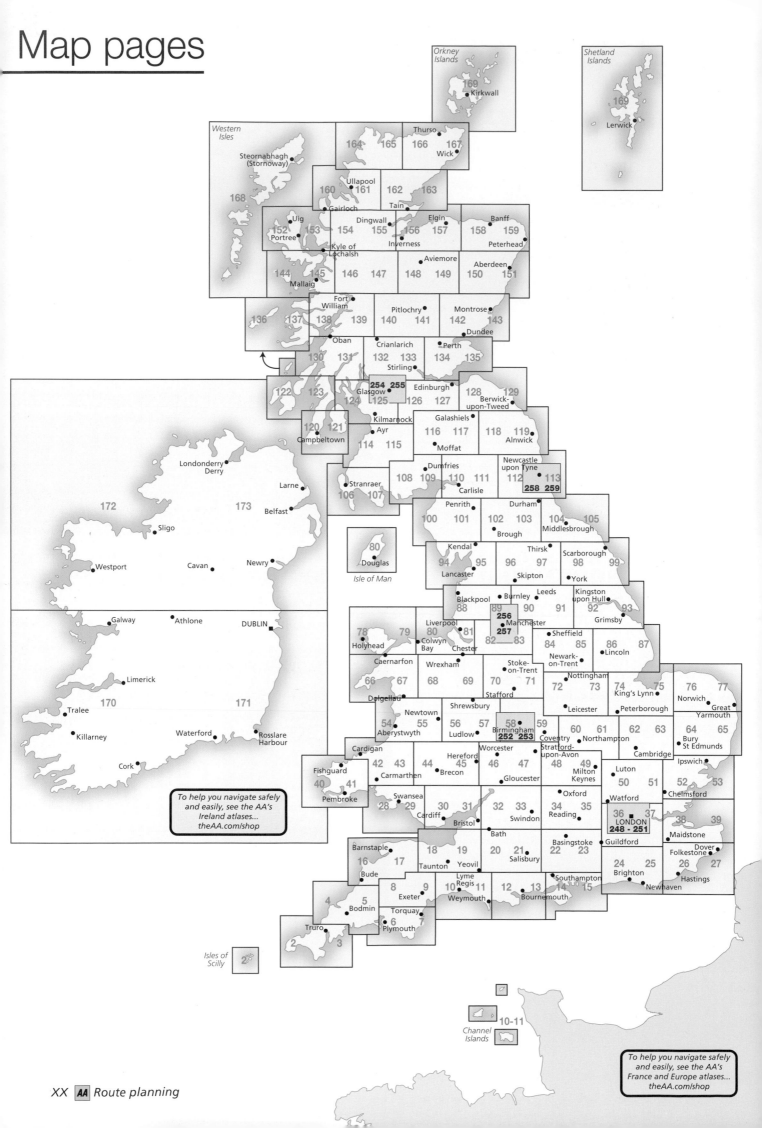

Orkney Islands

Shetland Islands

Western Isles

Steornabhagh (Stornoway)

168

Thurso
164 165 166 167 Wick

160 Ullapool 161 162 163
Gairloch Tain

Uig Dingwall Elgin Banff
152 153 154 155 156 157 158 159
Portree Inverness Peterhead
Kyle of Lochalsh

144 145 146 147 148 149 150 151
Mallaig Aviemore Aberdeen

136 137 138 139 140 141 142 143
Fort William Pitlochry Montrose
Dundee

Oban Crianlarich Perth
130 131 132 133 134 135
Stirling

122 123 254 255 Edinburgh 128 129
124 Glasgow 125 126 127 Berwick-upon-Tweed

120 121 Kilmarnock
Campbeltown Ayr 116 117 118 119
114 115 Galashiels Alnwick
Moffat

Londonderry Derry
Larne
172 173
Belfast

Sligo

Westport Cavan Newry

Galway Athlone DUBLIN

To help you navigate safely and easily, see the AA's Ireland atlases... theAA.com/shop

170 171

Limerick

Tralee
Killarney Waterford Rosslare Harbour
Cork

Dumfries Newcastle upon Tyne
108 109 110 111 112 113
Stranraer Carlisle 258 259
106 107

Penrith Durham
100 101 102 103 104 105
Brough Middlesbrough

Kendal Thirsk Scarborough
94 95 96 97 98 99
Lancaster Skipton York

80 Blackpool Burnley Leeds Kingston upon Hull
Douglas 88 89 90 91 92 93
Isle of Man 256 Grimsby
257 Manchester
82 83 Sheffield
78 79 Liverpool 84 85 86 87
Holyhead 80 81 Newark-on-Trent Lincoln
Colwyn Bay Chester
Caernarfon Stoke-on-Trent
66 67 68 69 70 71 72 73 74 75 76 77
Dolgellau Stafford Nottingham King's Lynn Norwich
Newtown Shrewsbury Leicester Peterborough Great Yarmouth
54 55 56 57 58 59 60 61 62 63 64 65
Aberystwyth Ludlow Birmingham Cambridge Bury St Edmunds
Cardigan 252 253 Coventry Northampton Ipswich
Hereford Worcester Stratford-upon-Avon
42 43 44 45 46 47 48 49 50 51 52 53
Fishguard Brecon Gloucester Milton Keynes Luton Chelmsford
40 41 Carmarthen Oxford
Pembroke Swansea Watford 36 37
28 29 30 31 32 33 34 35 LONDON 38 39
Cardiff Swindon Reading 248 - 251 Maidstone
Bristol Guildford Dover
Bath Basingstoke 24 25 26 27 Folkestone
Barnstaple 20 21 22 23 Brighton Hastings
16 17 18 19 Salisbury Southampton Newhaven
Bude Taunton Yeovil 14 15
Lyme Regis
8 9 10 11 12 13 Bournemouth
4 5 Exeter Weymouth
Bodmin Torquay 6 7
2 Truro Plymouth
3

Isles of Scilly 2

10-11

Channel Islands

To help you navigate safely and easily, see the AA's France and Europe atlases... theAA.com/shop

Road map symbols

Motoring information

M4 Motorway with number	**BATH** Primary route destination	▼ 5 ▼ Distance in miles between symbols	**50** Speed camera site (fixed location) with speed limit in mph
T4 Toll motorway with toll station	**A1123** Other A road single/dual carriageway	or **V** Vehicle ferry	**40** Section of road with two or more fixed speed cameras, with speed limit in mph
11 Motorway junction with and without number	**B2070** B road single/dual carriageway	Fast vehicle ferry or catamaran	**60** **60** Average speed (SPECS™) camera system with speed limit in mph
3 Restricted motorway junctions	Minor road more than 4 metres wide, less than 4 metres wide	- - - - Railway line, in tunnel	**V** Fixed speed camera site with variable speed limit
S Fleet Motorway service area	Roundabout	Railway station and level crossing	**P·R** Park and Ride (at least 6 days per week)
Motorway and junction under construction	Interchange/junction	++++++++ Tourist railway	City, town, village or other built-up area
A3 Primary route single/dual carriageway	Narrow primary/other A/B road with passing places (Scotland)	✈ H Airport, heliport	628 637 ▲ Lecht Summit Height in metres, mountain pass
1 Primary route junction with and without number	Road under construction/ approved	**F** International freight terminal	Sandy beach
3 Restricted primary route junctions	╠═════ Road tunnel	**H** 24-hour Accident & Emergency hospital	National boundary
S Primary route service area	Toll → Road toll, steep gradient (arrows point downhill)	**C** Crematorium	County, administrative boundary

Touring information To avoid disappointment, check opening times before visiting.

Scenic route	❊ Garden	- - - - National trail	Air show venue
i Tourist Information Centre	♣ Arboretum	☼ Viewpoint	Ski slope (natural, artificial)
i Tourist Information Centre (seasonal)	Vineyard	⁖ Hill-fort	National Trust property
V Visitor or heritage centre	Country park	♞ Roman antiquity	National Trust for Scotland property
⚲ Picnic site	Agricultural showground	Prehistoric monument	English Heritage site
Caravan site (AA inspected)	Theme park	✕ 1066 Battle site with year	Historic Scotland site
▲ Camping site (AA inspected)	Farm or animal centre	Steam railway centre	Cadw (Welsh heritage) site
▲ Caravan & camping site (AA inspected)	Zoological or wildlife collection	Cave	★ Other place of interest
Abbey, cathedral or priory	Bird collection	✕ ⌘ Windmill, monument	Boxed symbols indicate attractions within urban areas
Ruined abbey, cathedral or priory	Aquarium	⌐ Golf course (AA listed)	⊙ World Heritage Site (UNESCO)
✗ Castle	RSPB RSPB site	County cricket ground	National Park
Historic house or building	National Nature Reserve (England, Scotland, Wales)	Rugby Union national stadium	National Scenic Area (Scotland)
Museum or art gallery	Local nature reserve	International athletics stadium	Forest Park
Industrial interest	Wildlife Trust reserve	Horse racing, show jumping	Heritage coast
Aqueduct or viaduct	⋯⋯⋯⋯ Forest drive	⚑ Motor-racing circuit	Major shopping centre

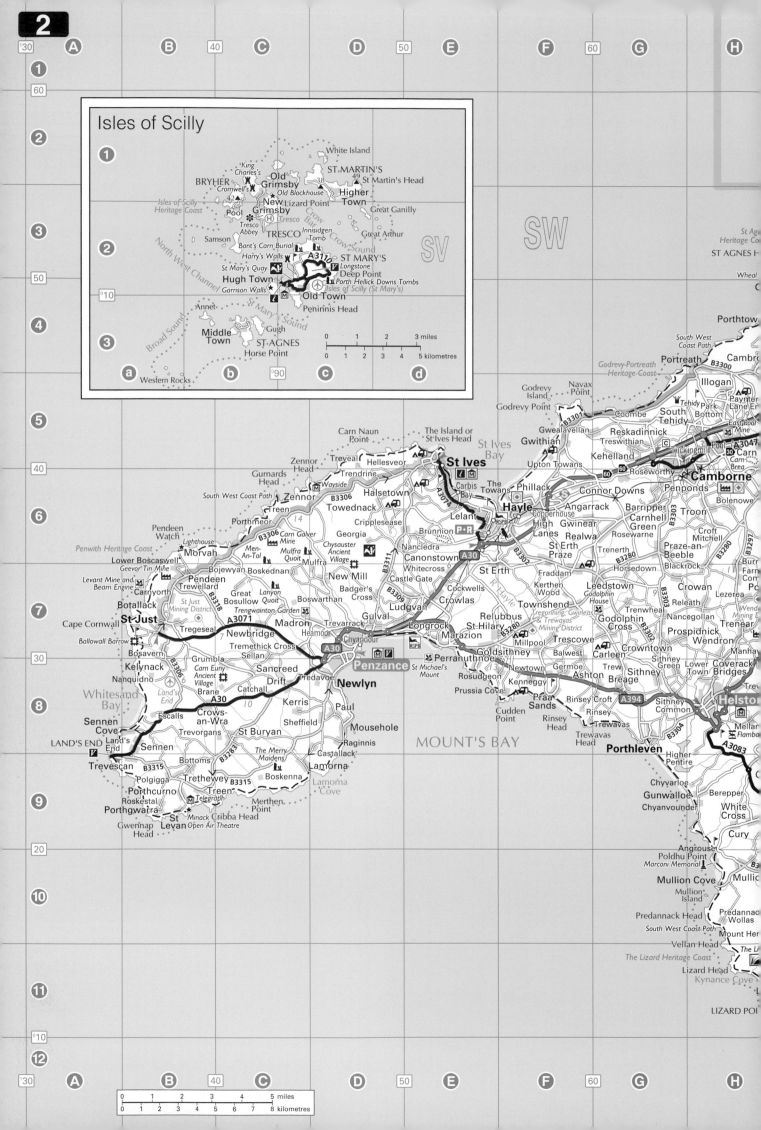

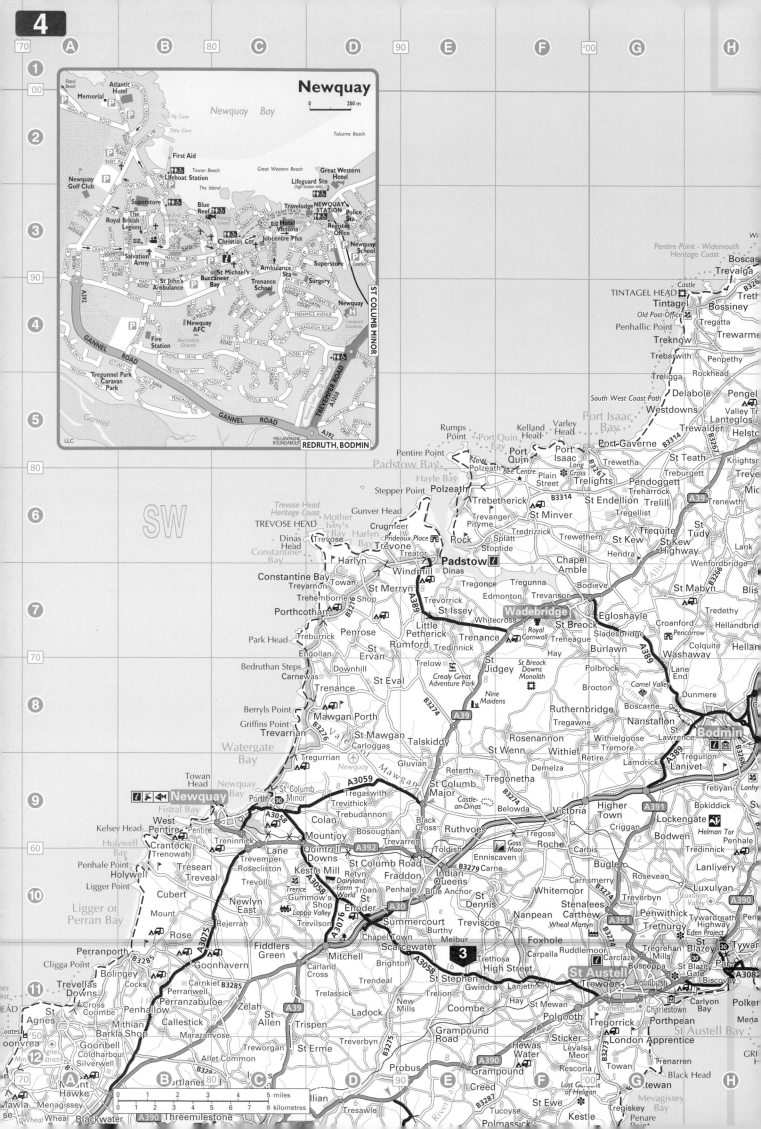

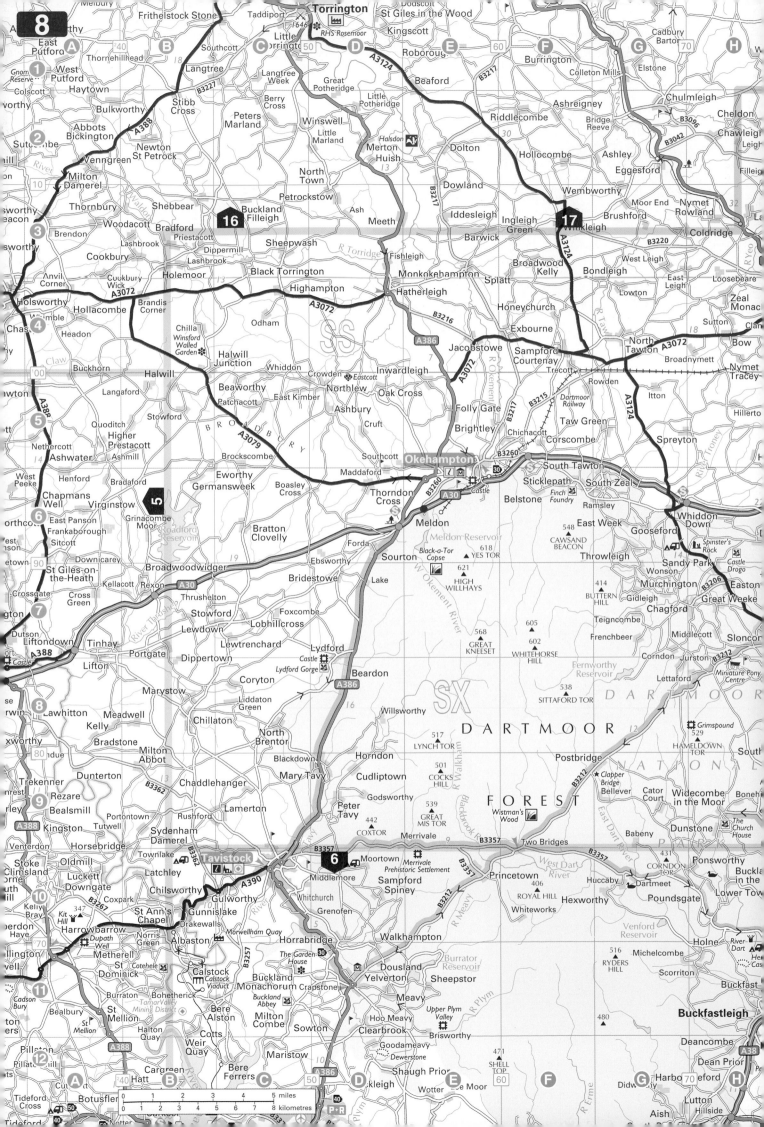

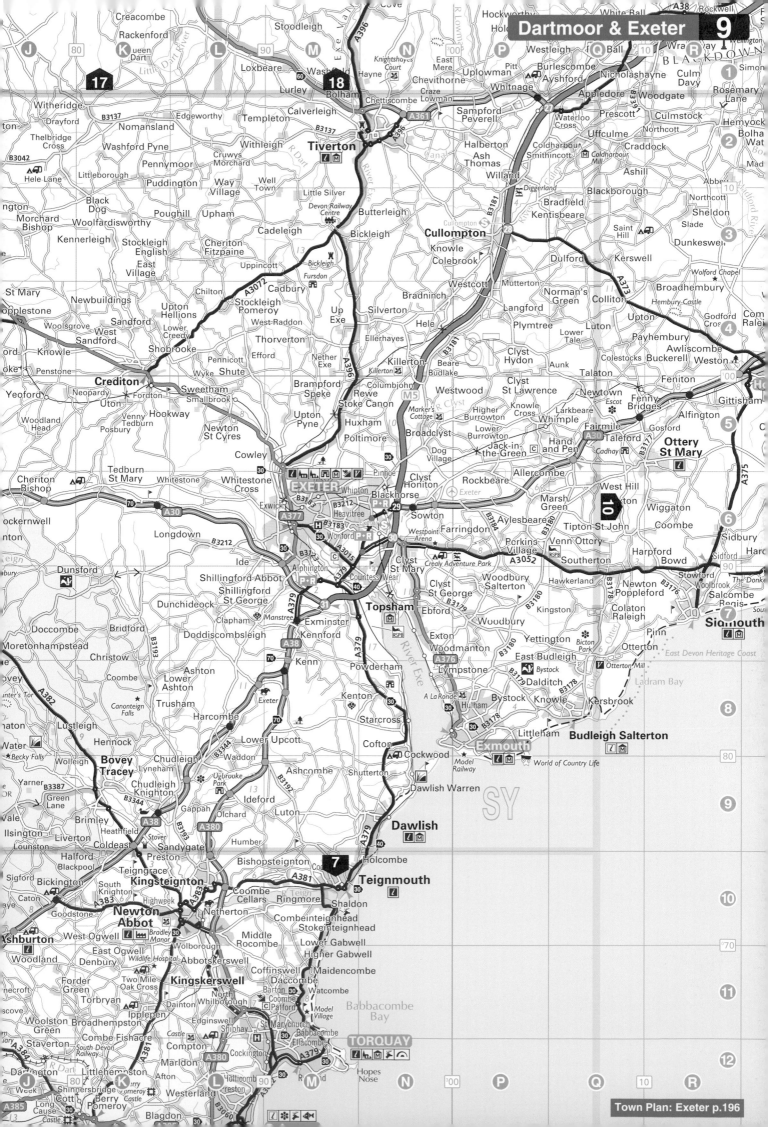

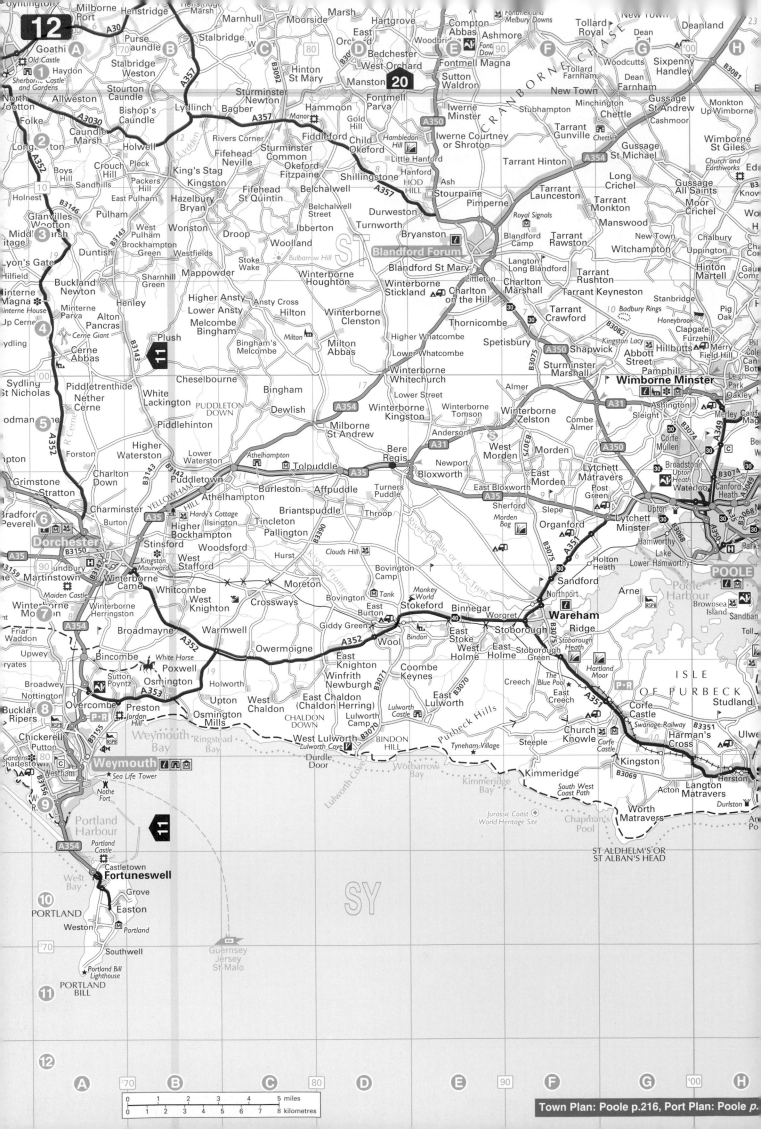

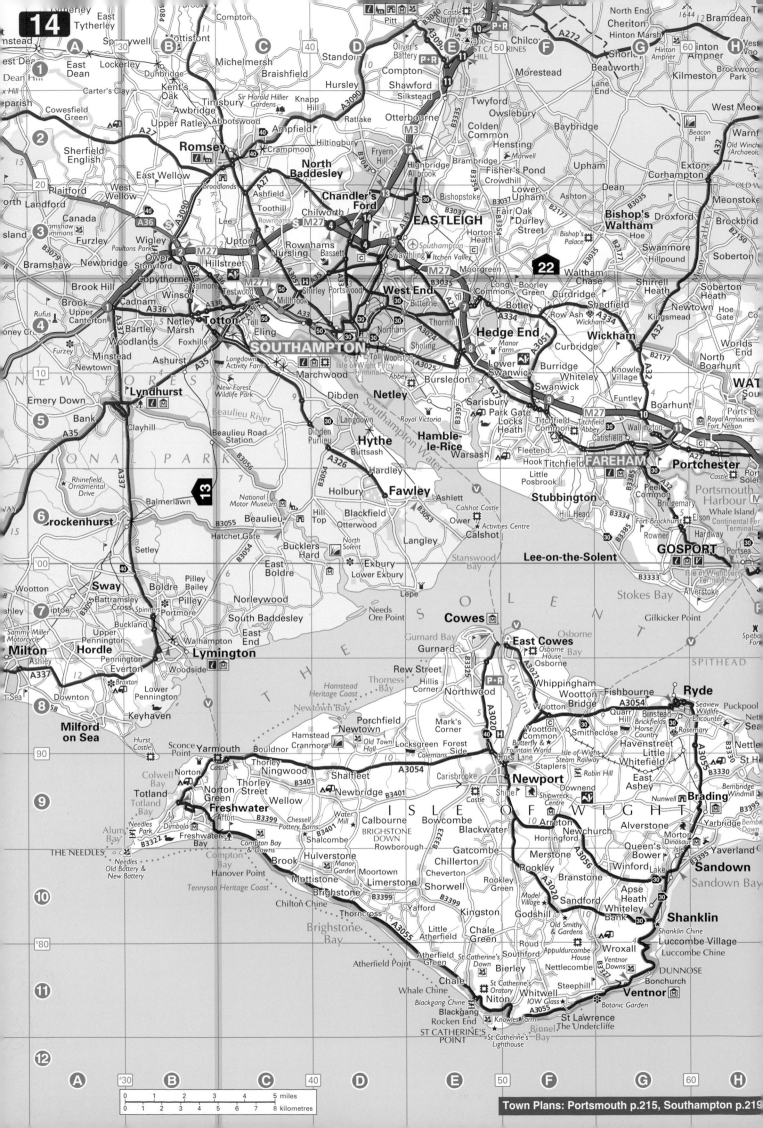

Town Plan: Taunton p.224

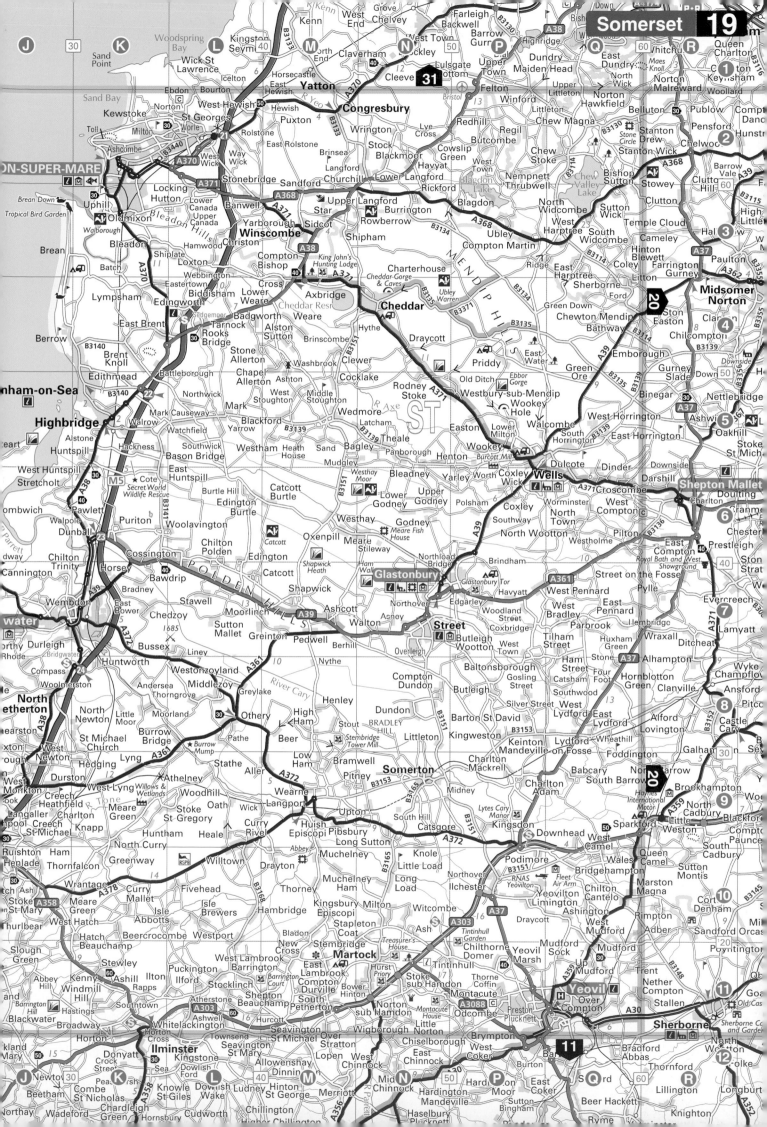

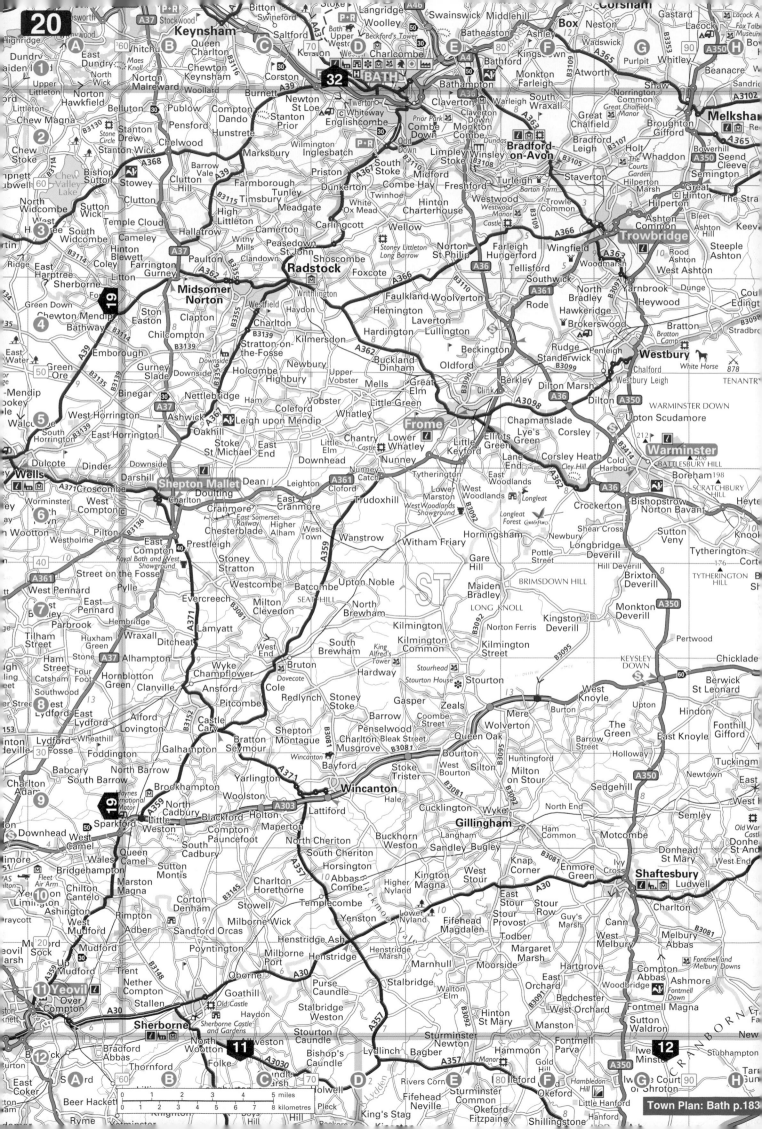

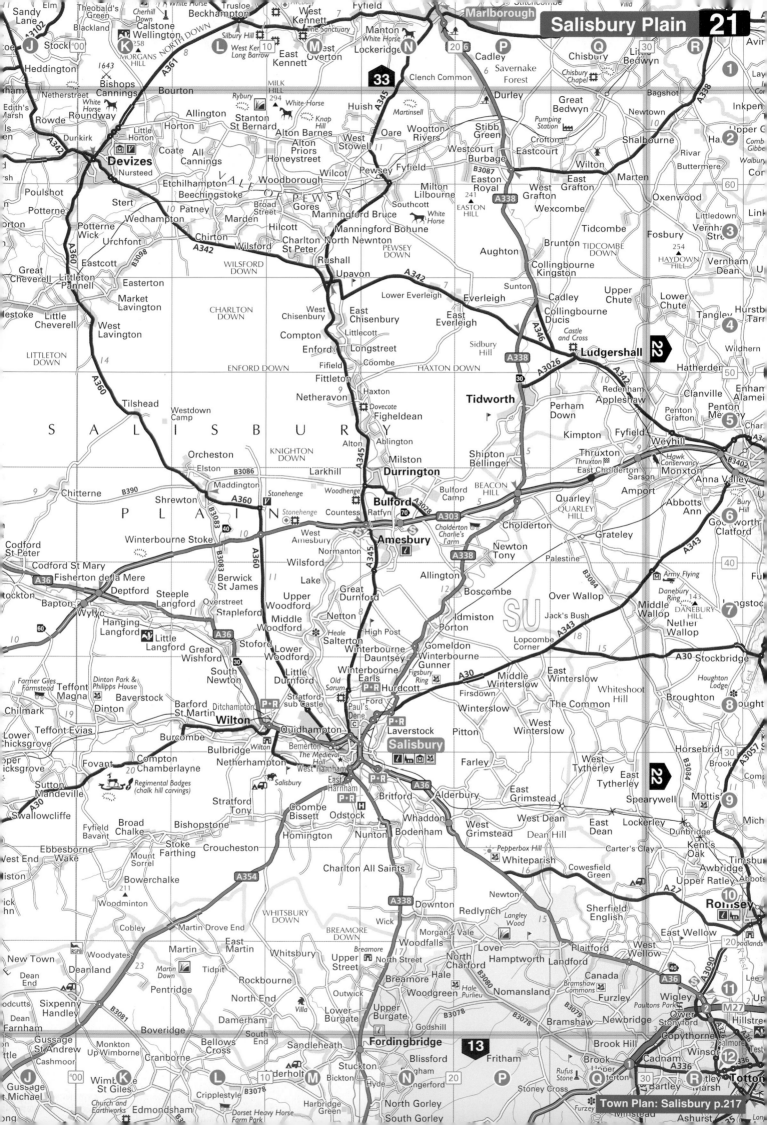

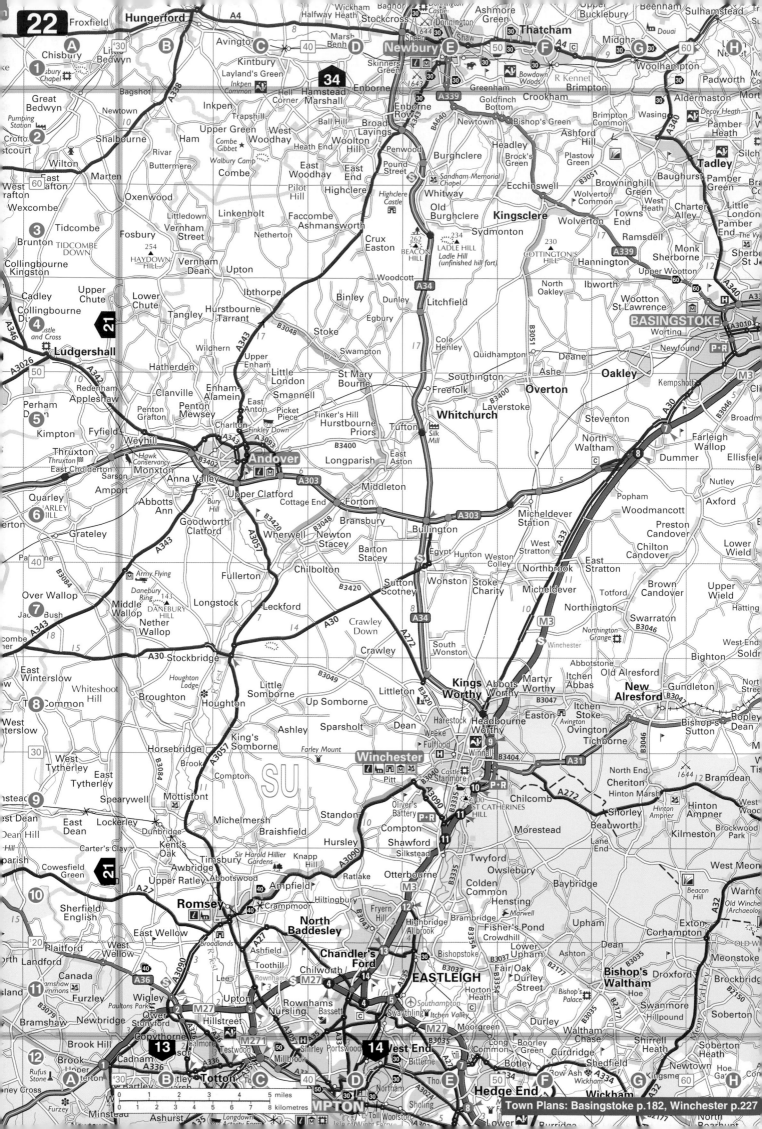

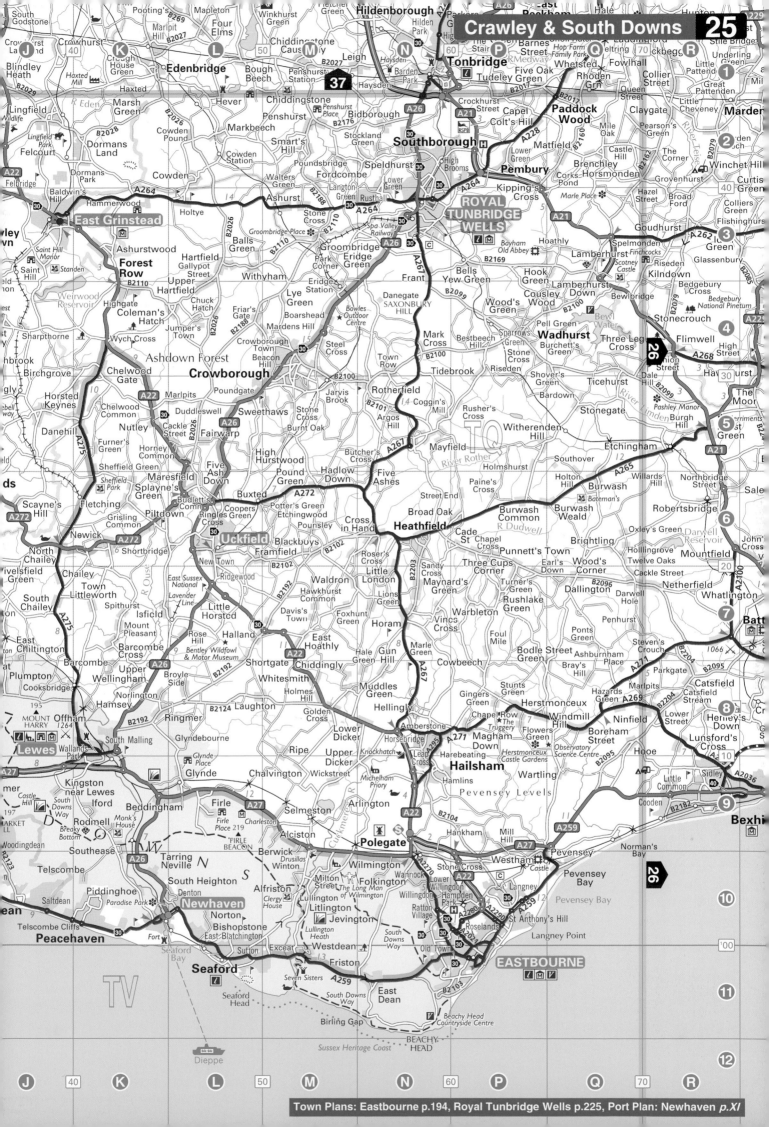

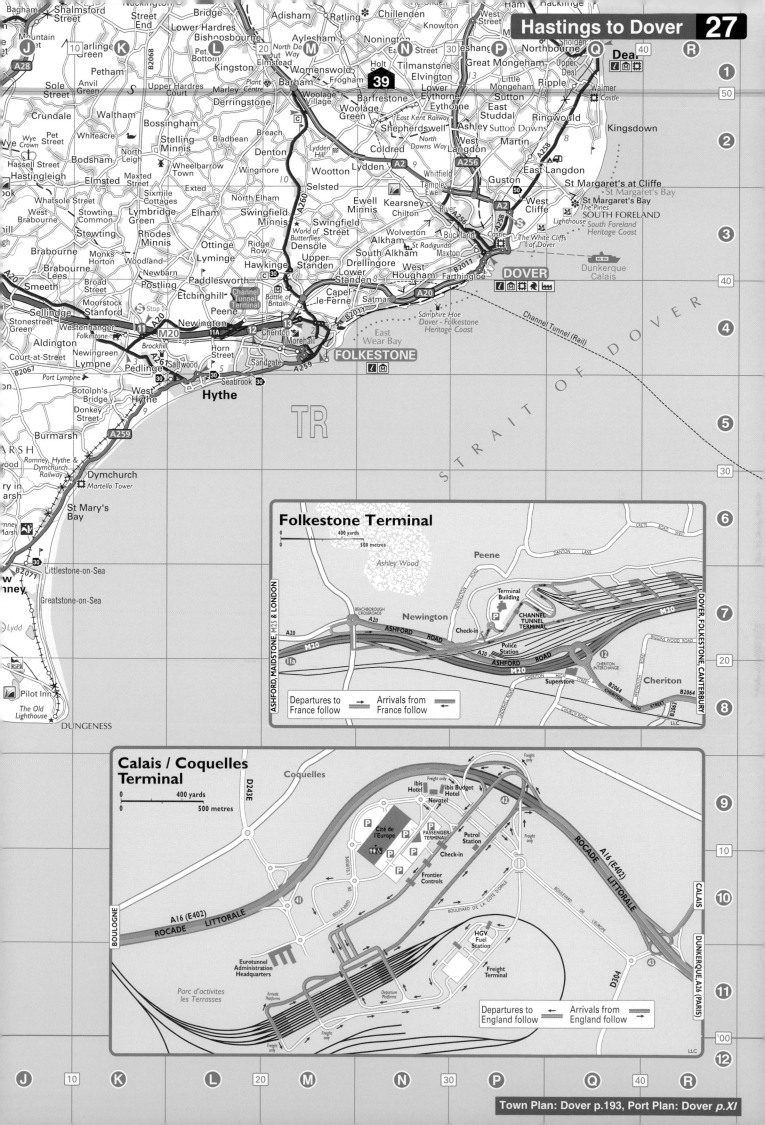

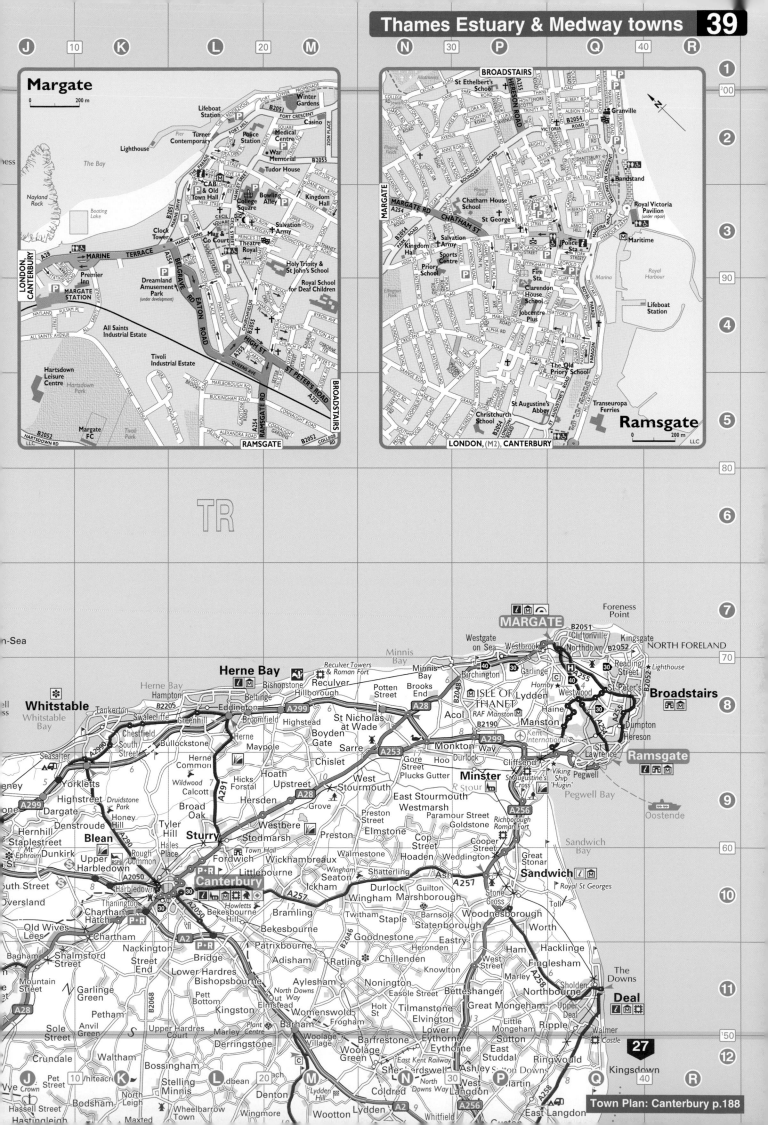

Margate

0   200 m

The Bay

Nayland Rock

Boating Lake

Lighthouse

LONDON, CANTERBURY

Premier Inn

MARGATE STATION

Hartsdown Leisure Centre

Hartsdown Park

Margate FC

Tivoli Park

Winter Gardens

Lifeboat Station

Turner Contemporary

Pier

Casino

Police Station

Medical Centre

War Memorial

Tudor House

CAB & Old Town Hall

College Square

Bowling Alley

Kingdom Hall

Clock Tower

Mag & Co Court

Theatre Royal

Salvation Army

Holy Trinity & St John's School

Royal School for Deaf Children

Dreamland Amusement Park (under development)

MARINE TERRACE

BELGRAVE RD

EATON ROAD

HIGH ST

ST PETER'S ROAD

All Saints Industrial Estate

Tivoli Industrial Estate

RAMSGATE RD

QUEENS AVE

Marlborough Road

Buckingham Road

Connaught Road

Gladstone Road

Alexandra Road

Helena Ave

College Rd

B2052

BROADSTAIRS

RAMSGATE

Ramsgate

0   200 m

BROADSTAIRS

Allotments

St Ethelbert's School

Granville

MARGATE RD

CHATHAM ST

Chatham House School

St George's

Kingdom Hall

Salvation Army

Priory School

Sports Centre

Police Sta

Fire Sta

Clarendon House School

Jobcentre Plus

The Old Priory School

St Augustine's Abbey

Christchurch School

Transeuropa Ferries

Royal Victoria Pavilion (under repair)

Maritime

Royal Harbour

Marina

Lifeboat Station

LONDON, (M2), CANTERBURY

TR

Thames Estuary map

Whitstable

Whitstable Bay

Seasalter

Yorkletts

Highstreet

Dargate

Denstroude

Hernhill

Staplestreet

Dunkirk

Mt Ephraim

Blean

Upper Harbledown

Rough Common

Harbledown

Thanington

Chartham Hatch

Chartham

Old Wives Lees

Shalmsford Street

Nackington

Street End

Lower Hardres

Bishopsbourne

Bridge

Patrixbourne

Adisham

Garlinge Green

Petham

Anvil Green

Upper Hardres Court

Kingston

Barham

Derringstone

Sole Street

Crundale

Waltham

Bossingham

Stelling Minnis

Denton

Wootton

Hassell Street

Bodsham

North Leigh

Wheelbarrow Town

Maxted

Herne Bay

Hampton

Tankerton

Swalecliffe

Greenhill

Chestfield

South Street

Bullockstone

Herne

Maypole

Herne Common

Wildwood Calcott

Tyler Hill

Broad Oak

Sturry

Hales Place

Fordwich

Westbere

Stodmarsh

Littlebourne

Ickham

Bekesbourne Hill

Bekesbourne

Womenswold

Eddington

Broomfield

Beltinge

Bishopstone

Reculver

Hillborough

Reculver Towers & Roman Fort

Highstead

Boyden Gate

Sarre

Chislet

Hoath

Upstreet

Hicks Forstal

Hersden

Grove

West Stourmouth

Preston

Wickhambreaux

Seaton

Shatterling

Wingham

Staple

Woolage Village

Barfreston

Woolage Green

East Kent Railway

Shepherdswell

Coldred

Lydden

Minnis Bay

Potten Street

Brooks End

St Nicholas at Wade

Acol

Birchington

ISLE OF THANET

RAF Manston

B2190

Kent International

Monkton Way

Gore Street

Hoo

Plucks Gutter

Durlock

Preston Street

Paramour Street

Elmstone

Westmarsh

Goldstone

Cop Street

Hoaden

Walmestone

Durlock

Wingham

Marshborough

Ash

Weddington

Twitham

Barnsole

Goodnestone

Staplenborough

Eastry

Heronden

Chillenden

Knowlton

Nonington

Easole Street

Tilmanstone

Elvington

Eythorne

Lower Eythorne

East Studdal

Sutton

Ringwould

Kingsdown

Frogham

Eastling

Elmstead

North Down Way

North Downs Way

Plant Centre

Ashley

Martin

East Langdon

Guston

Whitfield

Westgate on Sea

Westbrook

MARGATE

Garlinge

Northdown

Cliftonville

Kingsgate

NORTH FORELAND

Foreness Point

Lyddden

Westwood

Haine

Manston

Minster

R Stour

Cliffsend

St Augustine's Cross

Viking Ship 'Hugin'

Pegwell

Pegwell Bay

Oostende

Richborough Roman Fort

Great Stonar

Sandwich

Royal St Georges

Sandwich Bay

Stone Cross

Toll

Woodnesborough

Worth

Ham

Hacklinge

Finglesham

West Street

Marley

Betteshanger

Great Mongeham

Little Mongeham

Upper Deal

Ripple

Walmer Castle

Sholden

Northbourne

The Downs

Deal

St Lawrence

Dumpton

Hereson

Broadstairs

St Peter's

Ramsgate

Lydden Hill

A299

A28

A253

A256

A257

A258

A2050

A2

A290

A291

A299

A2990

B2205

B2046

B2048

B2050

B2051

B2052

B2054

B2055

B2068

Herne Bay

Canterbury

Town Plan: Canterbury p.188

27

A 60 B C 70 D E 80 F G 90 H

40

30

20

10

20

SM

Rosslare Harbour

STRUMBLE HEAD

Pen Brush

Pwll Deri

Trefasser

Manorowen

Pembrokeshire Coast Path

St Nicholas

Ynys Daullyn

Granston

Carreg Sampson

Abercastle

Panteg

Llangloffan

Jordans

Porthgain

Trefin

Mathry

16

Castle Morris

B4331

Abereiddy

Llanrhian

A487

Square & Compass

Llangloffan Fen

Letterst

Berea

Croes-goch

Treffynnon

Tretio

Treglemais

B4330

Hayscast Cross

St DAVID'S HEAD

Treleddyd-fawr

Carnhedryn

Cerbyd

River Solva

Llandeloy

Tancredston

Pont-yr-hafod

Rhodiad-y-brenin

Caer Farchell

Middle Mill

Treffgarne Owen

Hayscastle

Whitesand Bay

B4583

Bishop's Palace

Whitchurch

Tre

St David's

Nine Wells

Solva

A487

Pen-y-cwn

178

DUDWELL MT

Leweston

RAMSEY ISLAND

RSPB

Ramsey Sound

St David's Peninsula Heritage Coast

Newgale

16

Roch

Wolfsdale

Roch Gate

PEMBROKESHIRE COAST NATIONAL PARK

Simpson Cross

Cam

Rickets Head

A487

Keeston

Pembr

Nolton Haven

Nolton

Ta

St Brides Bay

St Brides Bay Heritage Coast

Pelcomb Cross

Pelcom

Lambston

Pelcomb Bridge

Druidston

Sutton

Haroldston West

Portfield Gate

B4341

Broadway

B4327

Broad Haven

Dreen Hill

A

Little Haven

Walton West

Solbury

Tiers Cross

4

Pembrokeshire Coast Path

Talbenny

14

Walwyn's Castle

St Brides

Hasguard

SKOMER ISLAND

Wooltack Point

Marloes

B4327

Sandy Haven

Thornton

St Ishmael's

Herbrandston

Steynton

Honeyboro

Waterstor

Broad Sound

Marloes and Dale Heritage Coast

Hubberston

Llanstad

SKOKHOLM ISLAND

Dale

Great Castle Head

Westdale Bay

Dale Point

Milford Haven

Milford Haven (Aberdaugleddau)

Pem D

St Anns Head

Angle

Angle Bay

Pwllcrochan

Doc

Rhoscrowther

Rosslare Harbour

B4320

Castlemartin Brook

B432

Freshwater West

B4319

10

Castlemartin

SR

Warren

Linney Head

Merri

PEMBROKESHIRE C NATIONAL PA

Pembrokeshire Coast Path

A 60 B C 70 D E 80 F G 90 H

0 1 2 3 4 5 miles
0 1 2 3 4 5 6 7 8 kilometres

Port Plan: Pembroke Dock *p.XIII*

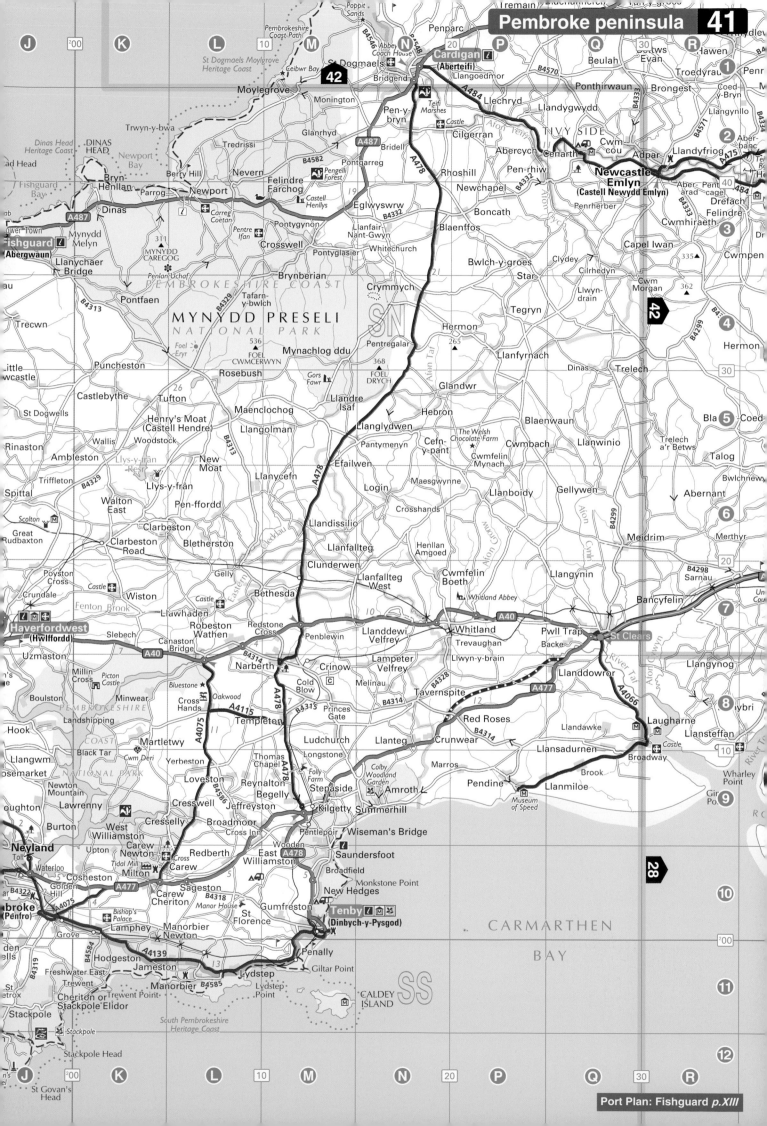

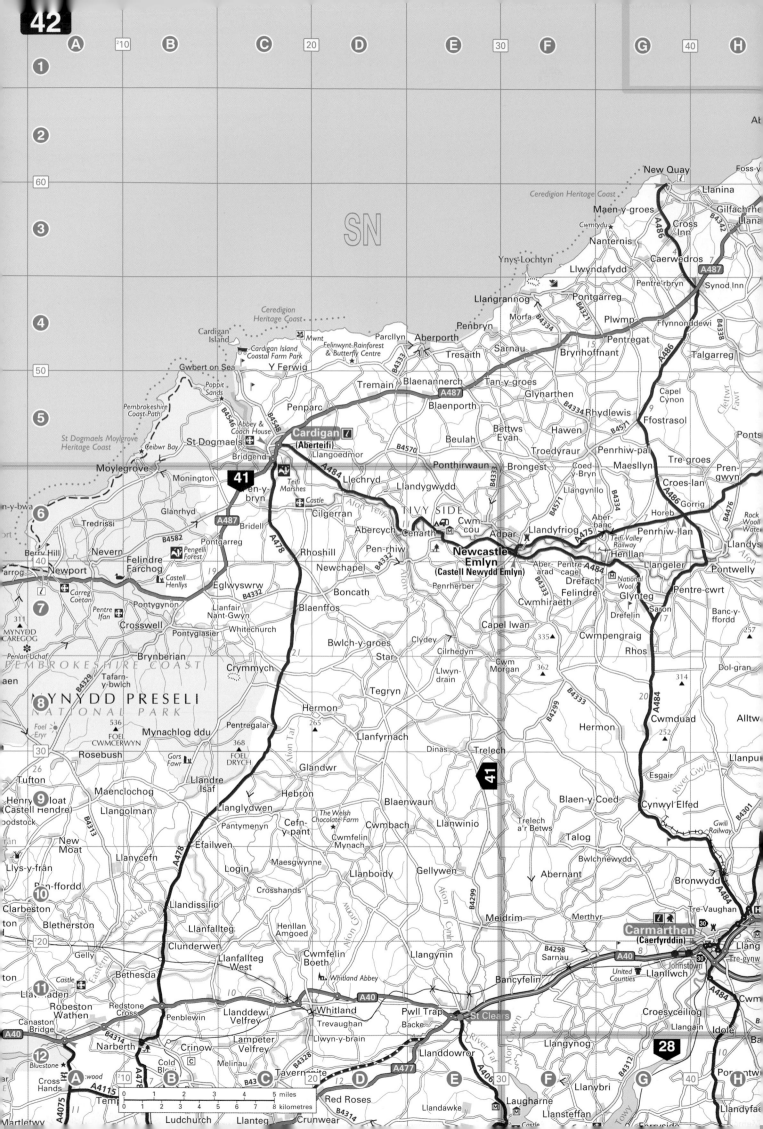

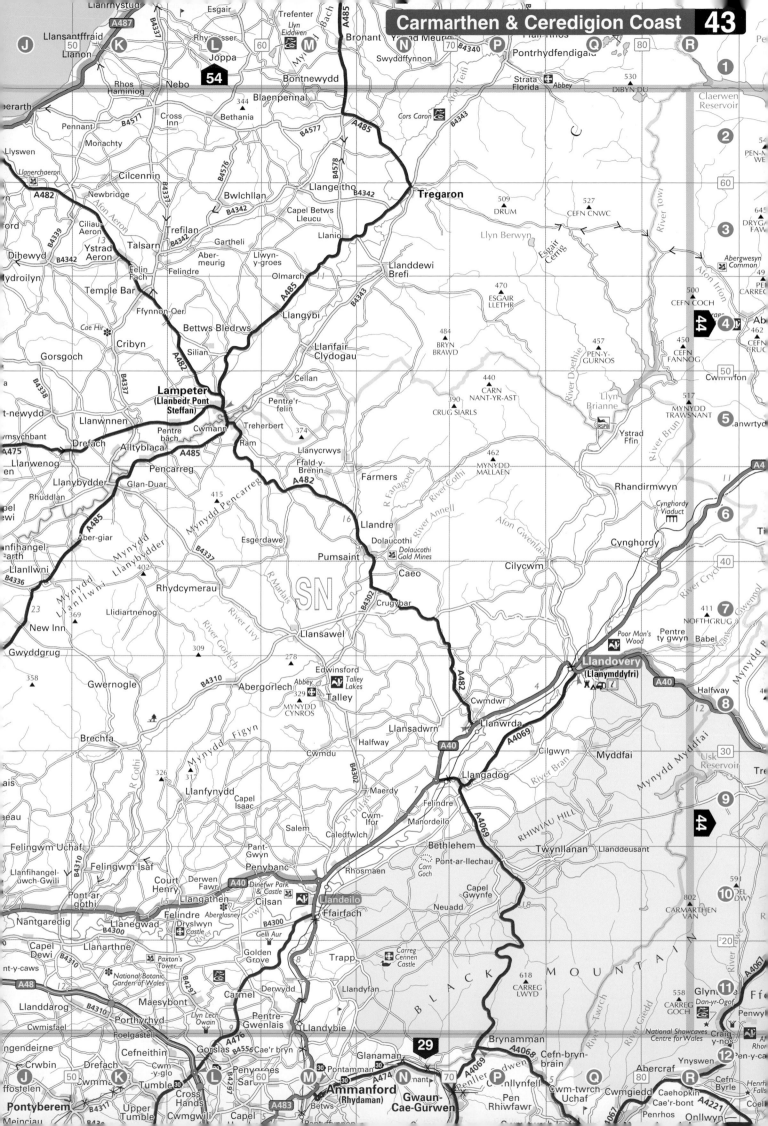

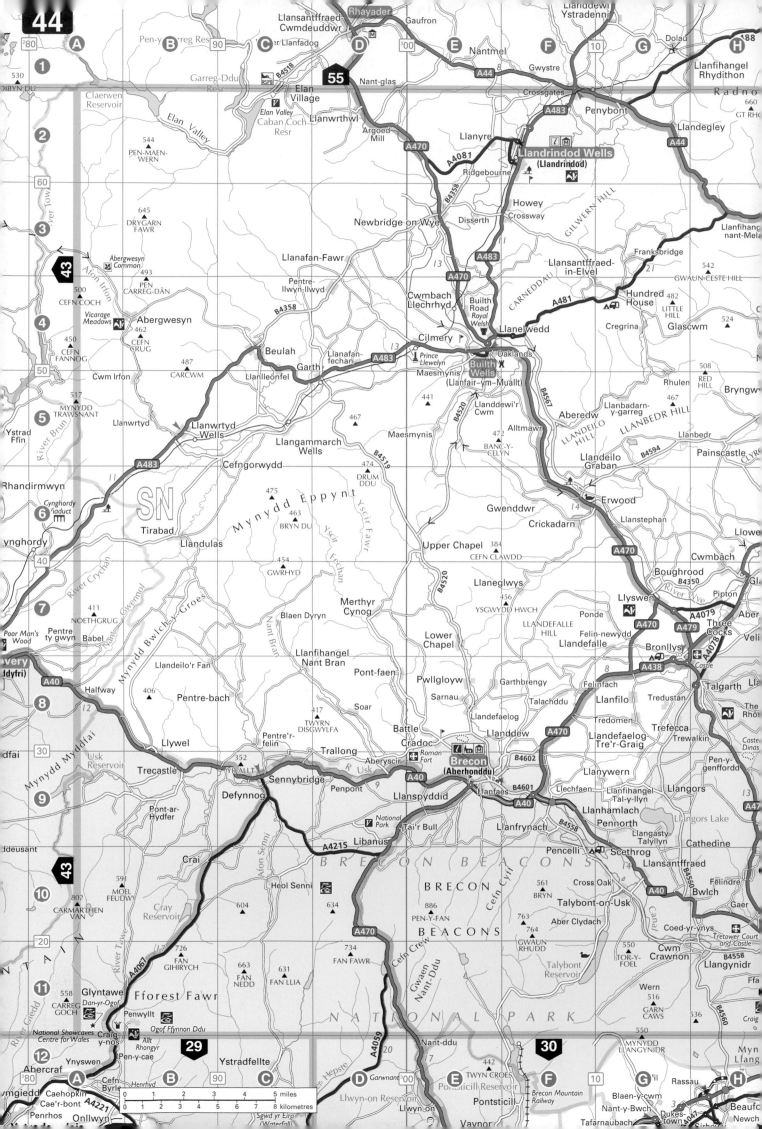

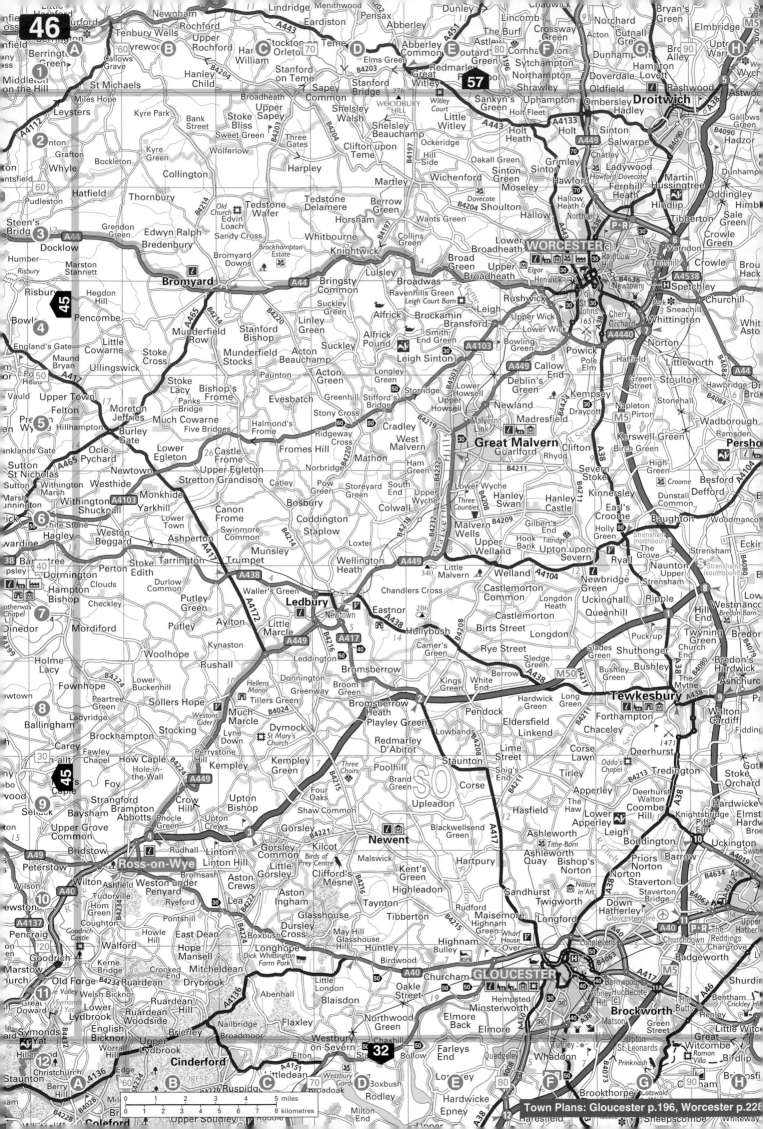

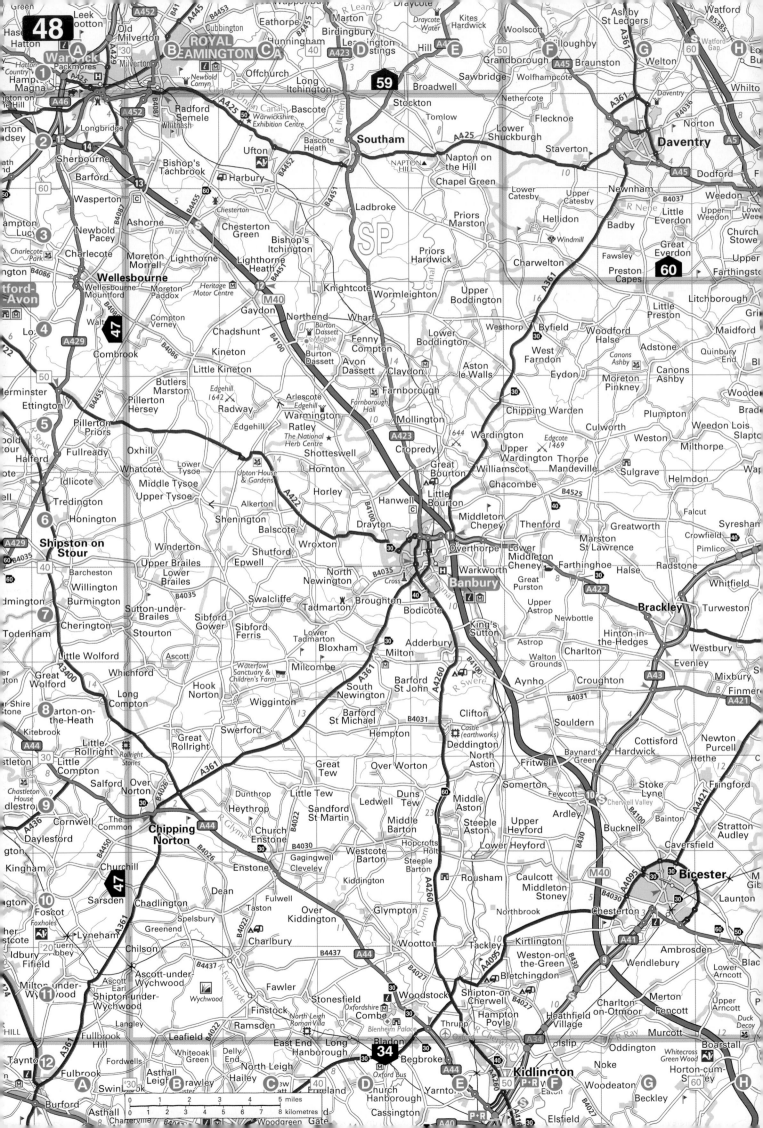

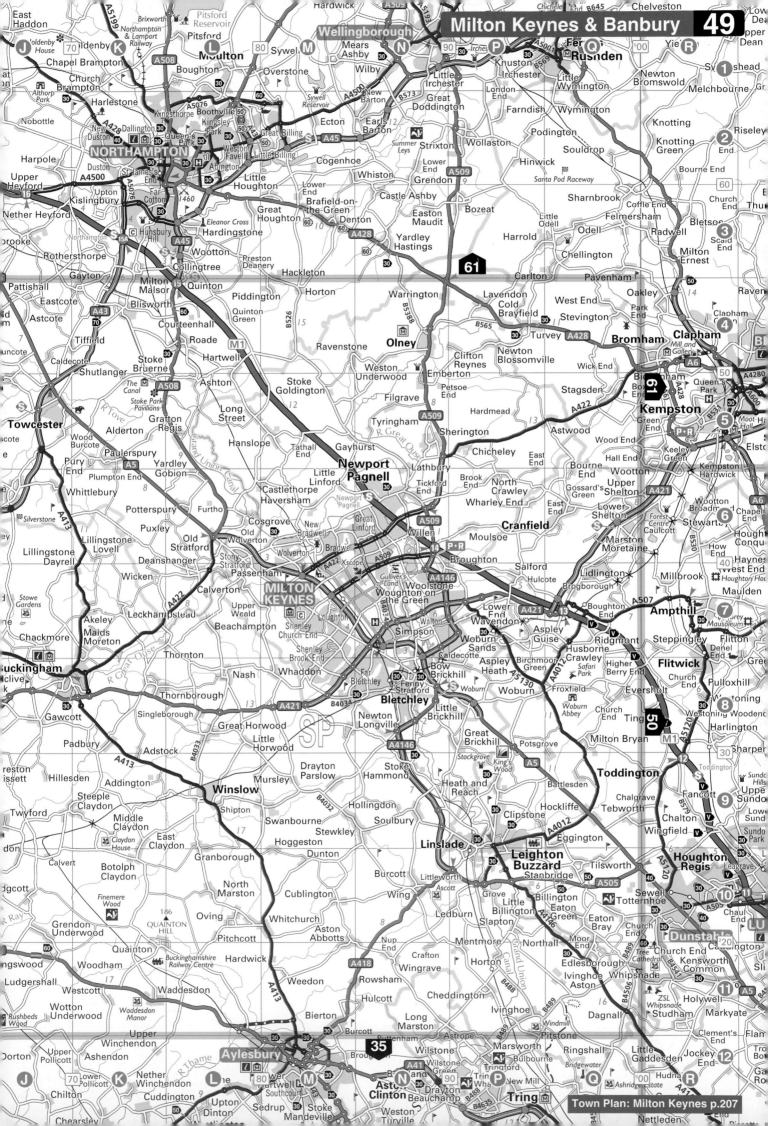

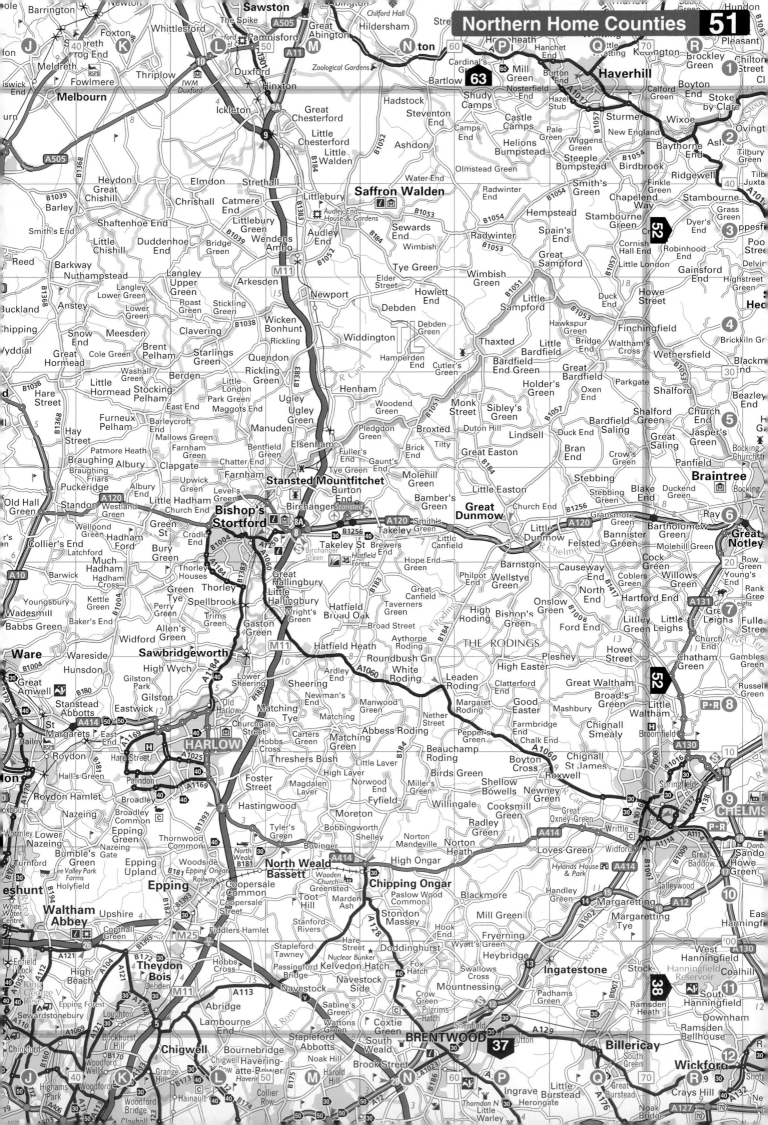

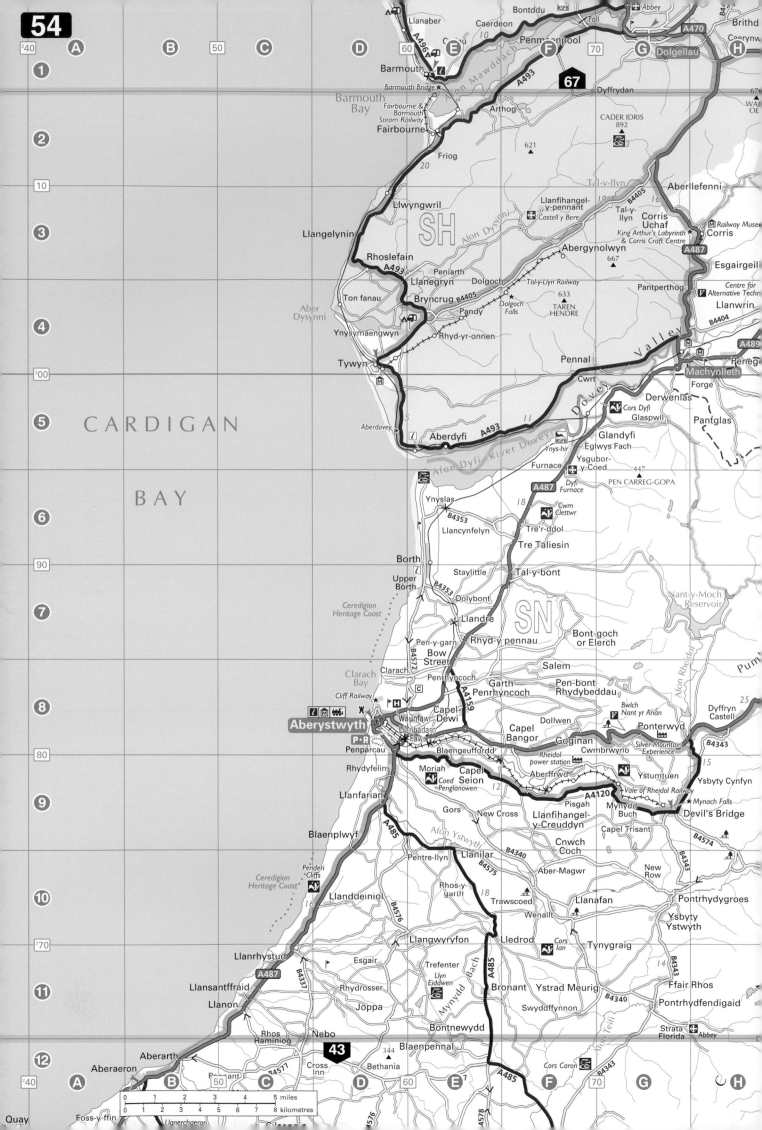

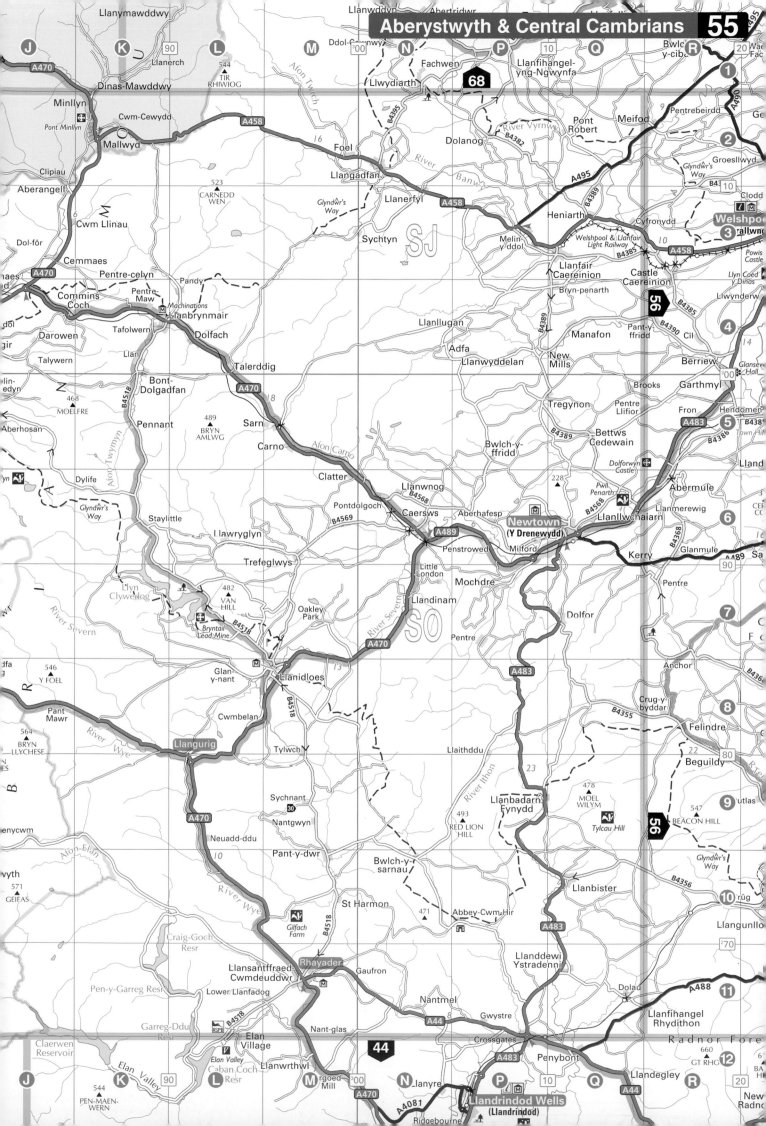

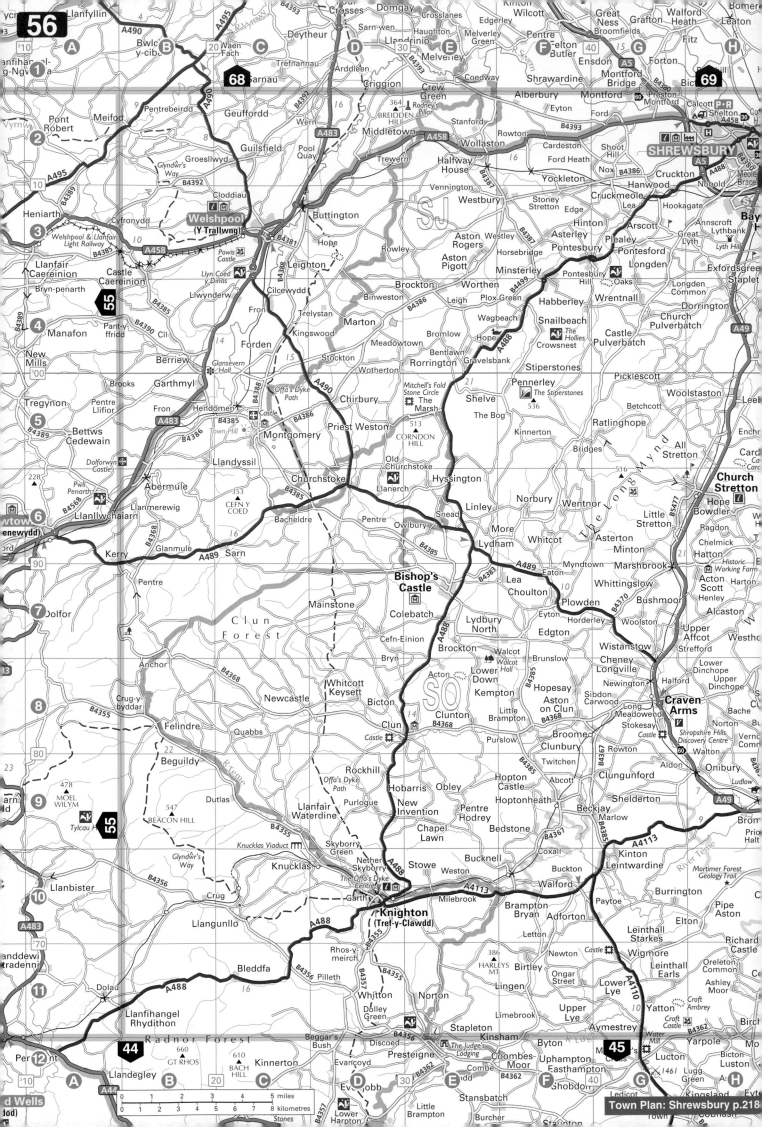

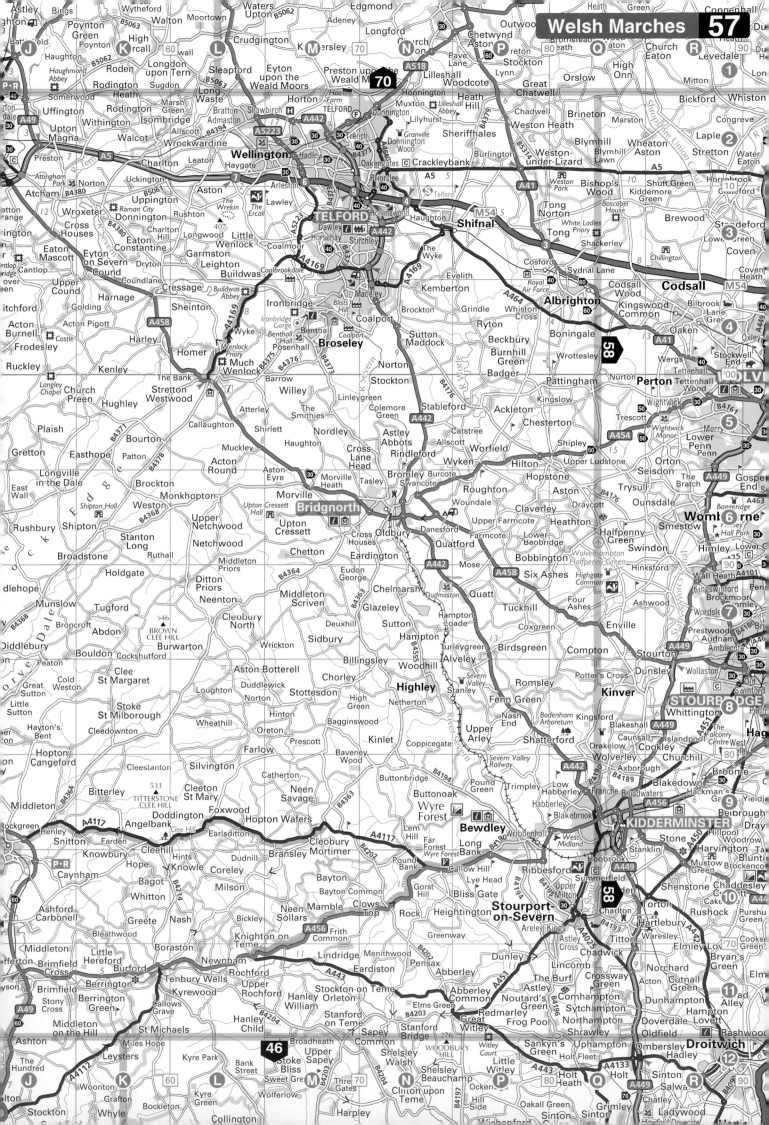

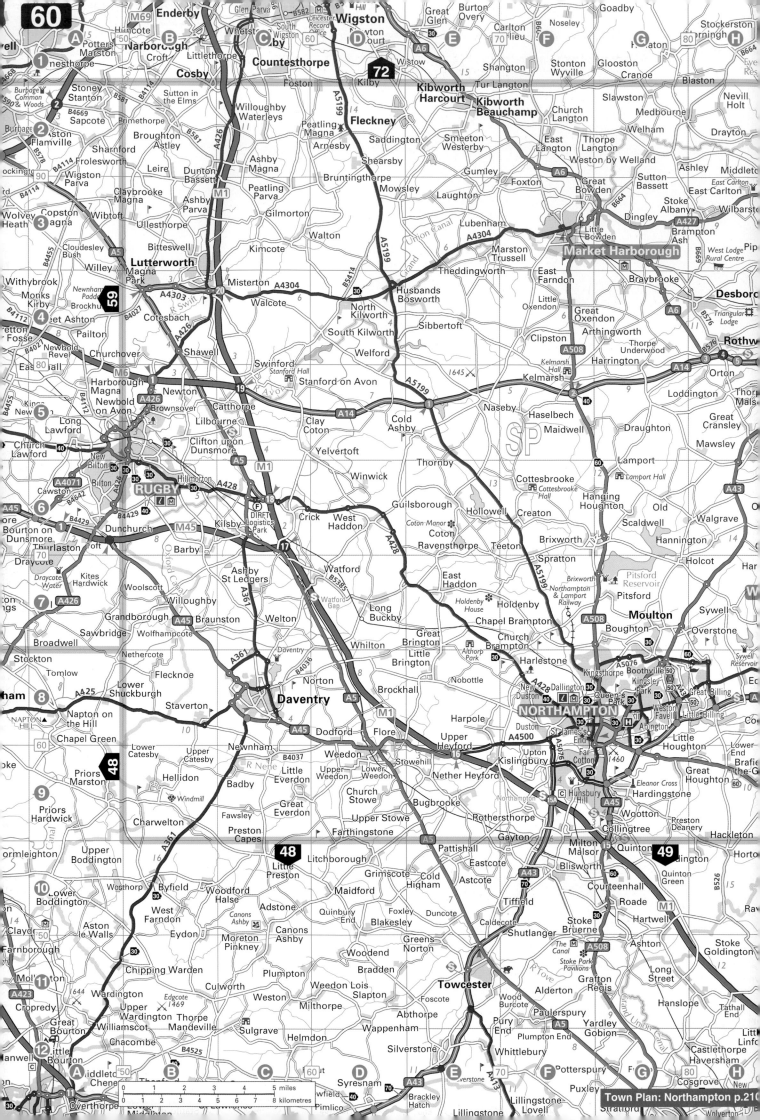

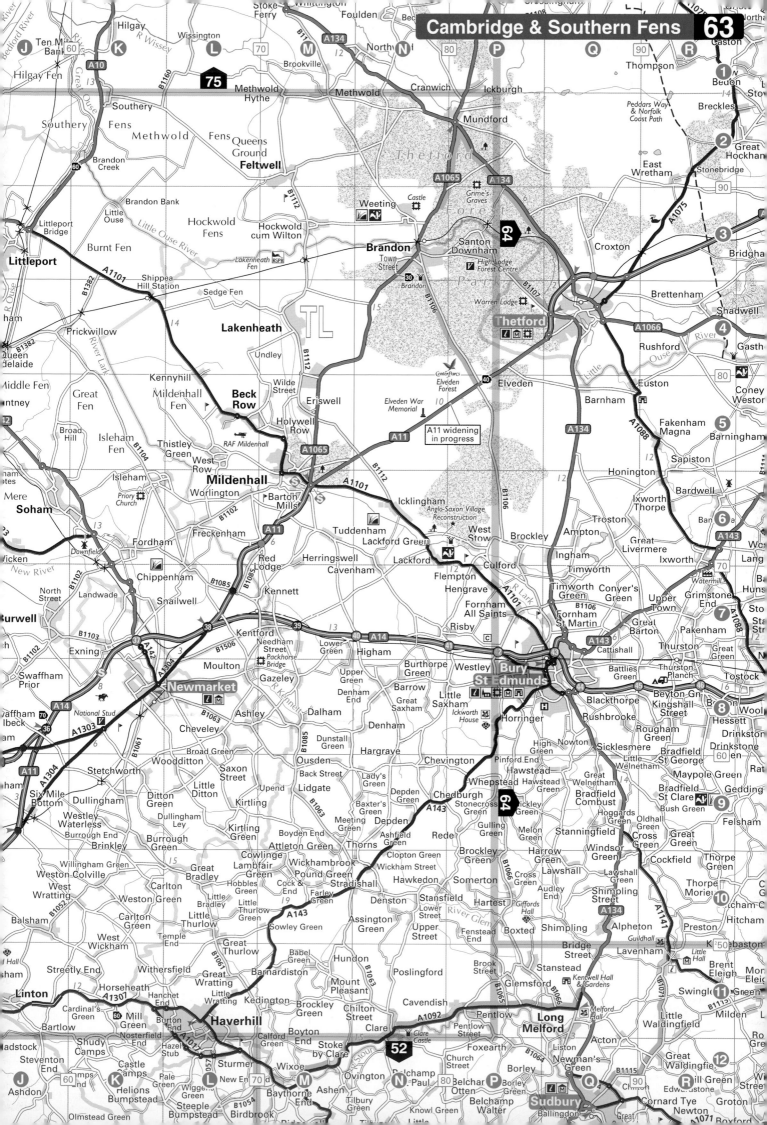

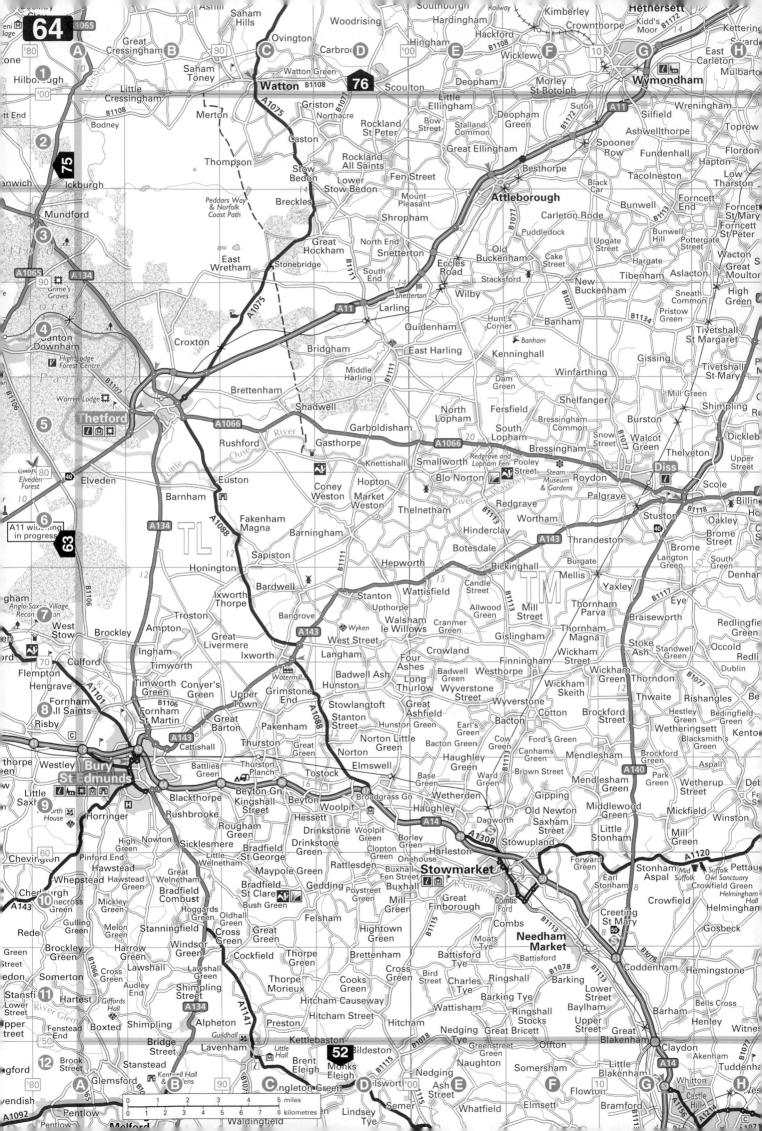

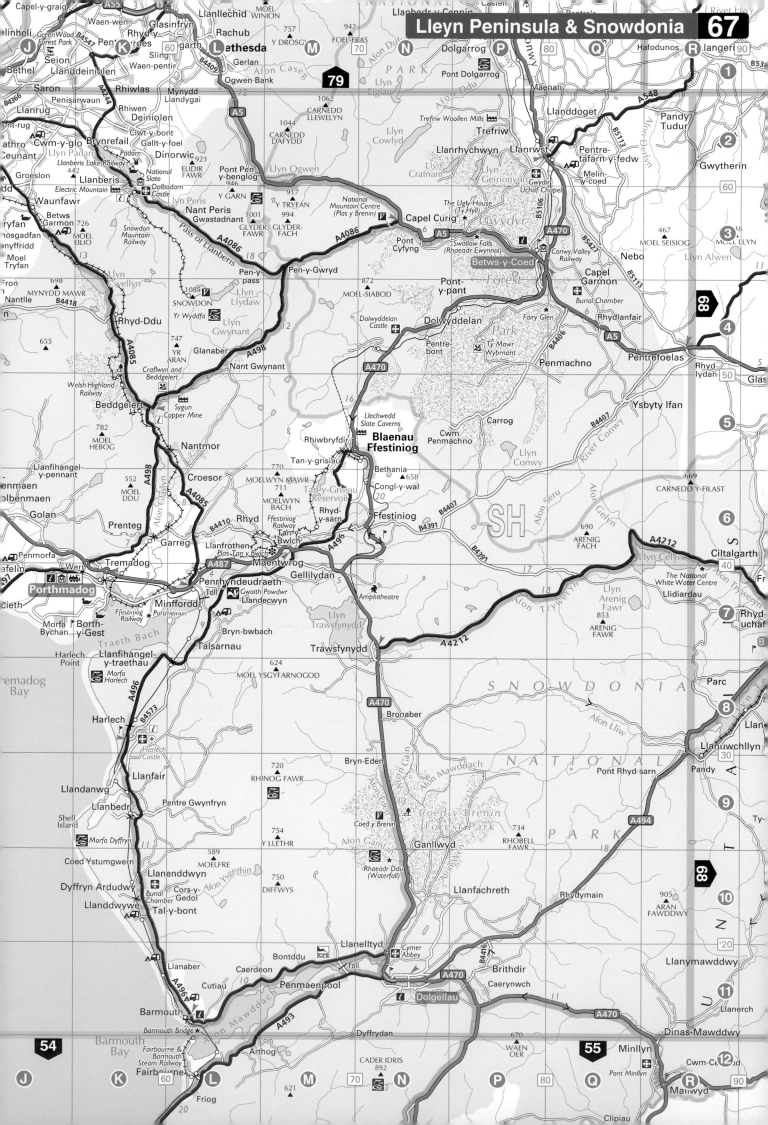

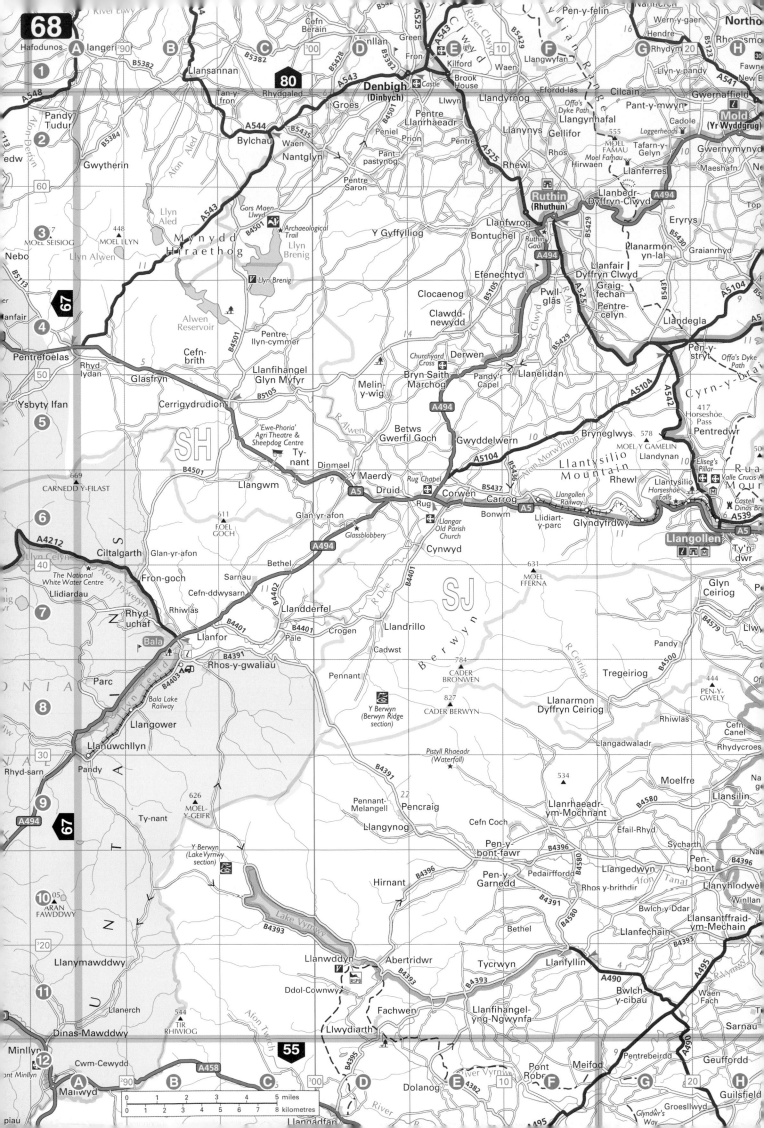

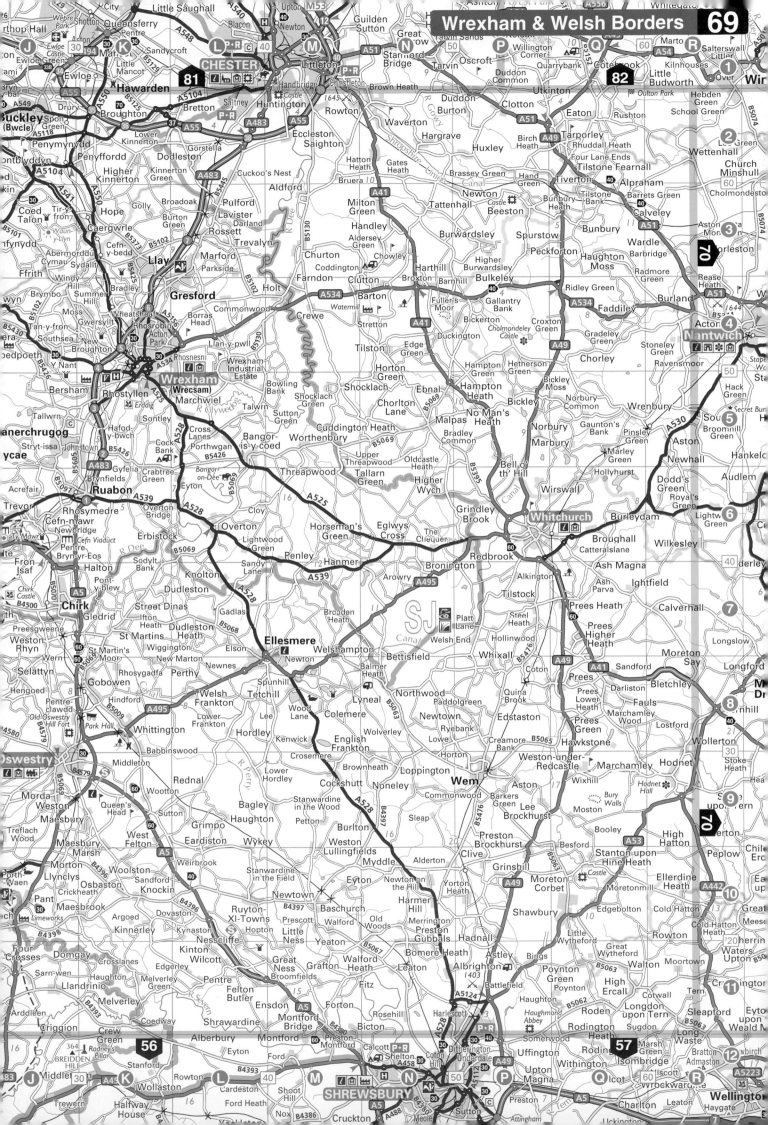

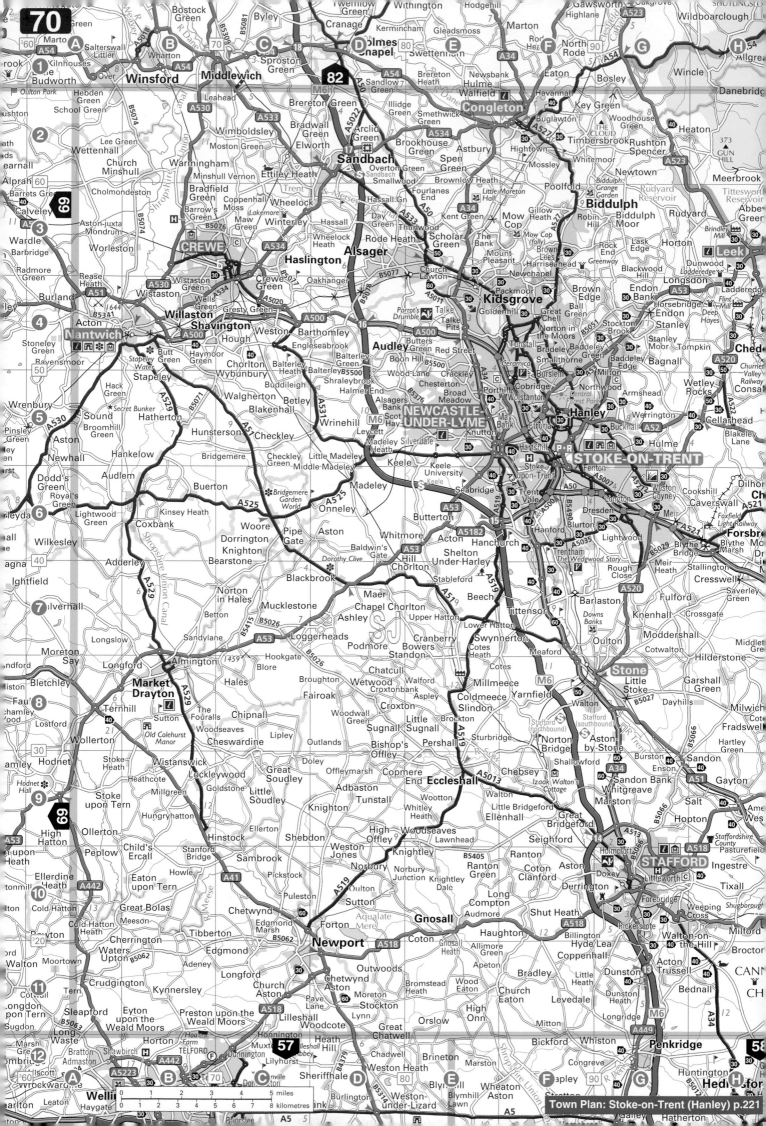

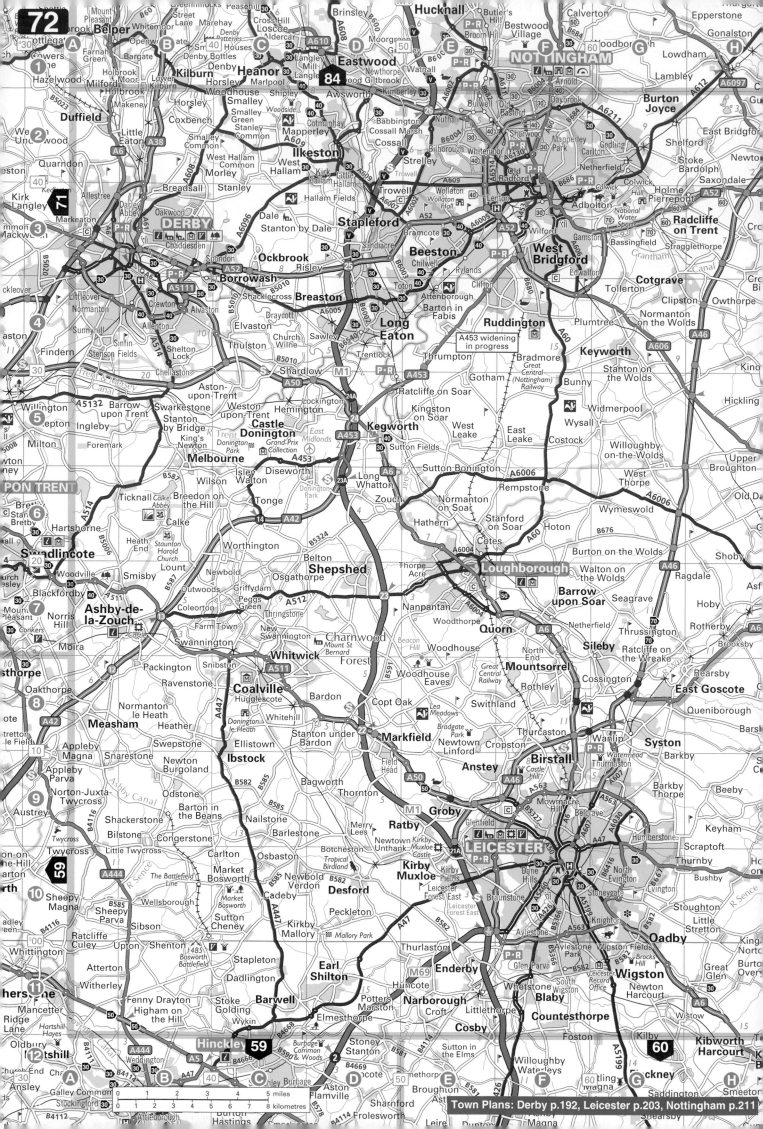

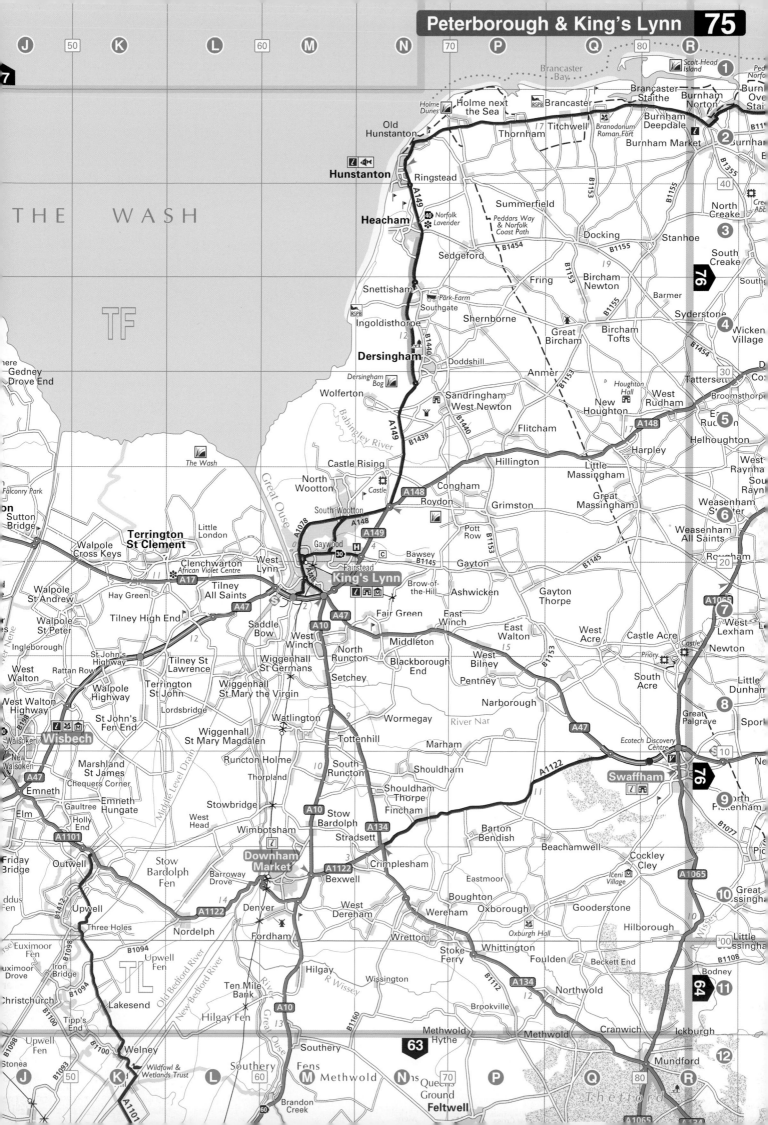

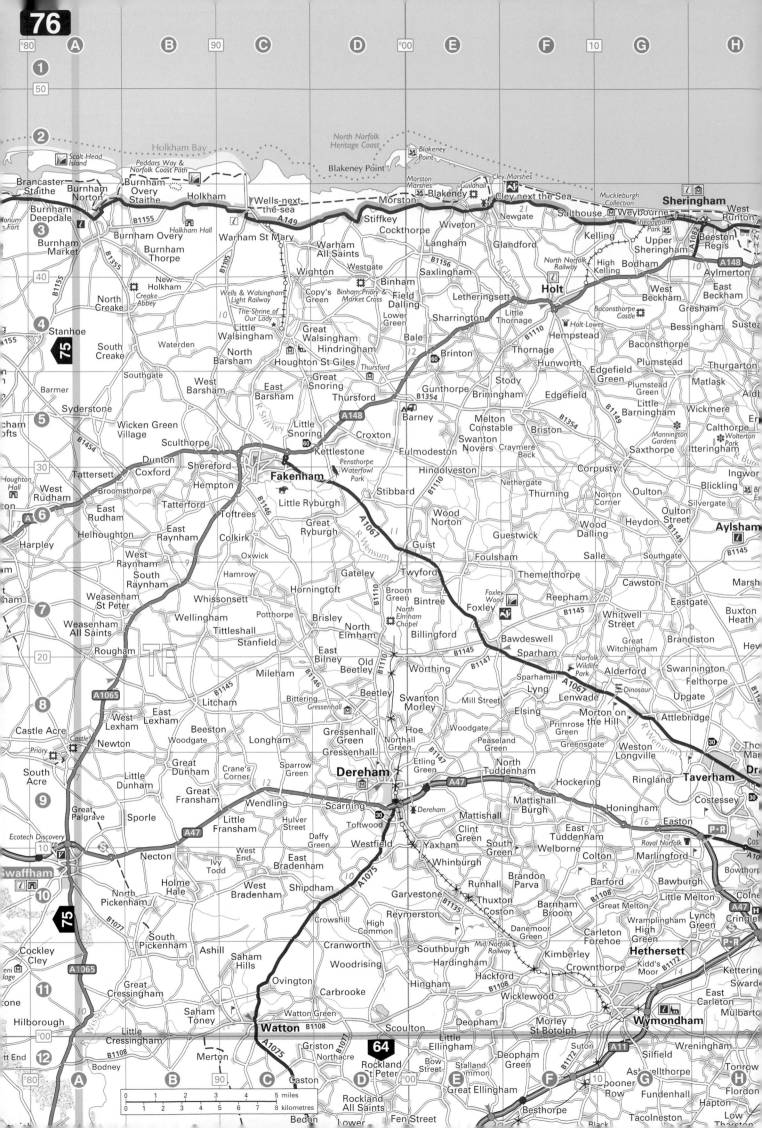

A B 20 C D 30 E F 40 G H

1

2

10

3

4

⁴00

5

90

6

7

80

8

9

⁵80

10

⁴70

11

12

²10 A B 20 C D 30 E F 40 G H

The Skerries

North Anglesey
Heritage Coast

Wylfa
Head Cemaes Porth
Wen
Bull Bay
Cemlyn
Bay
Llanbadrig Bull Bay Amlwch
Hen
Borth Cemaes Llaneilian
CARMEL HEAD Tregele Burwen Pengorf
A5025 Pentrefelin
Llanfairynghornwy Llanfechell Rhosbeirio Nebo
Bodewryd Penysarn
Swtan Folk Llanfflewyn Rhosgoch Gadfa A5025
Holyhead Llanrhyddlad Carreglefn Rhosybol Rhos
Bay 17 City
Church Llanbabo Capel Dulas
Bay Llanfaethlu Parc
Llyn Brynrefail
Dublin Alaw Llandyfrydog Din L
Llanddeusant B5111
Dún Laoghaire Gwredog Maenaddwy
(Mar-Sept) Llynnon Mill Elim
Porth Stryd-y- Llantrisant Hebron
Tywynmawr Facsen Llanerchymedd Bachau
North Stack Pen-llyn B5112 Capel
Gogarth Breakwater Llanfwrog Llyn Coch Bryn
Bay Llaingoch Llywenan ANGLESEY
RSPB Holyhead Mountain Llechcynfarwy Tregaian
Holyhead Hut Circles Holyhead Penrhos Presaddfed
South Stack Mountain Llanfachraeth Llanfigael B5109 Trefor B5111 B5110
Ellins Heritage Coast Llanynghenedl Bodedern Llangwyllog
Tower Kingsland Caergeiliog Llynfaes Oriel Rhosmei
Penrhyn Mawr Penrhos Feliw Valley A5025 Bryngwran Bodffordd Cefni Ynys Môn
Trefignath A5 Gwalchmai Reservoir Llangefr
Trearddur Bay A55 Heneglwys Llangristiolus A5 A55 A5114
B4545 K A4080 18 Anglesey Cein
Four Mile Llanfihangel Llechylched Dothan
HOLY ISLAND Bridge yn Nhowyn RSPB Cerrigceinwen A55 Llangristiolus
Llanfair-yn-Neubwll Capel Gwyn Din-Dryfol Henblas Pentre Berw
Rhoscolyn Plas Ty Newydd Pencarnisiog B4422 Gaerwen
Rhoscolyn Cymyran Llanfaelog Cerrigceinwen Capel Mawr Llanddaniel
Head Cymyran Ty Croes Bryn Du Trefdraeth Bodowyr
Bay Rhosneigr A4080 Bethel Burial Chamber
SH Barclodiad Llangadwaladr Malltraeth B4421 B4419 Brynsiency
y Gawres Aberffraw Llangaffo Castell
Porth Trecastell Anglesey Hermon A4080 Bryn Gwyn Anglesey
Aberffraw Circuit Bodorgan B4419 Sea Zoo
Bay 21 Dwyran
Aberffraw Bay Newborough Foel Farm
Heritage Coast Pen-lôn Park
Malltraeth Bay Caernarfo
Llanddwyn Island Caernarfo
Llanddwyn Castle
Bay Port Plan: Holyhead p.XI
Point Railway

Holyhead
Bay

Holyhead
(Caergybi)

0 1 2 3 4 5 miles
0 1 2 3 4 5 6 7 8 kilometres

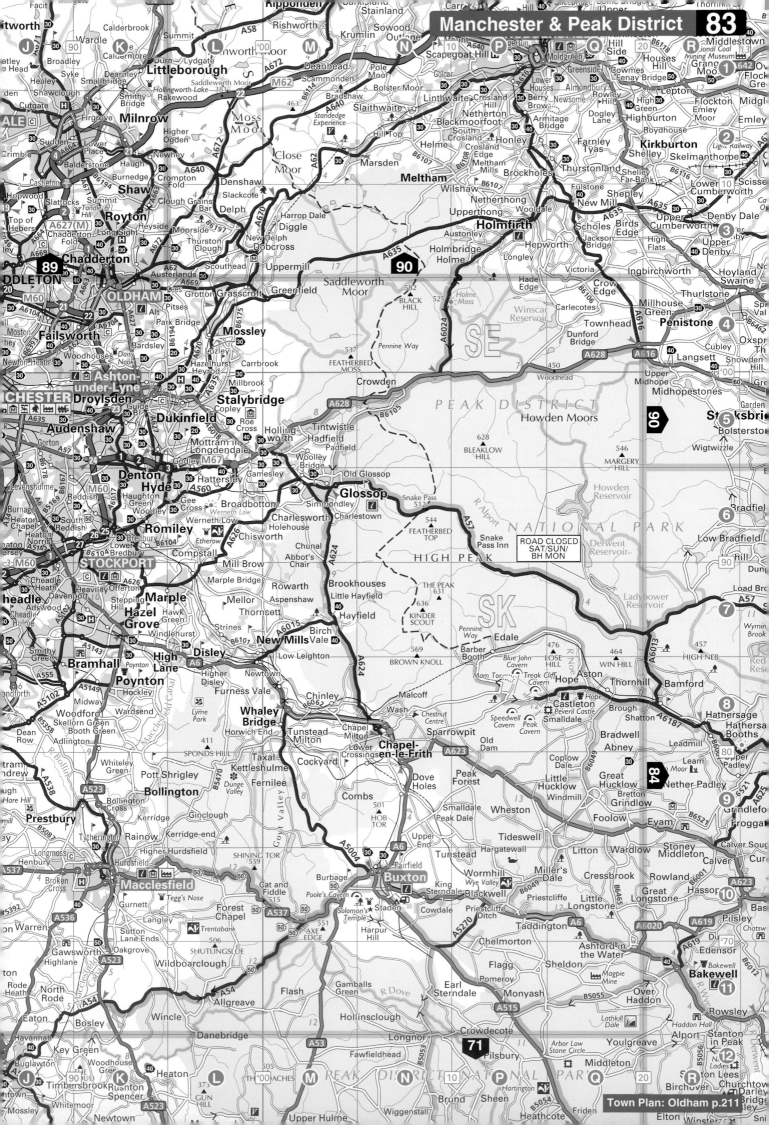

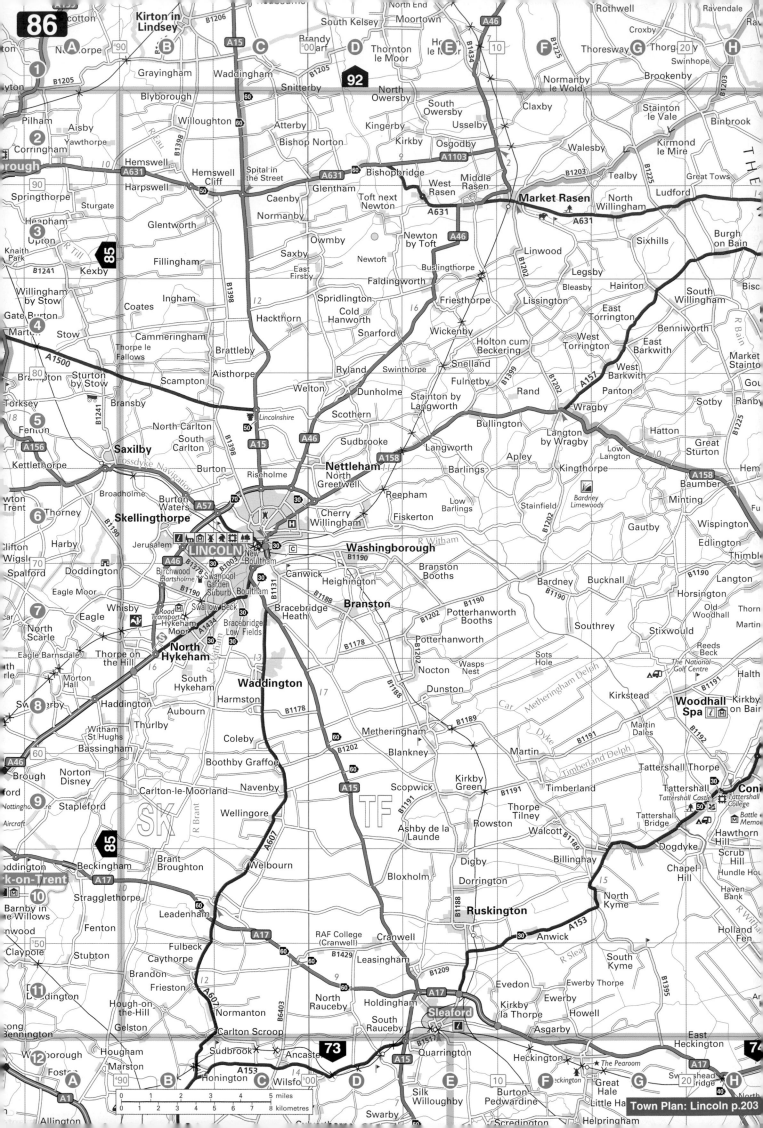

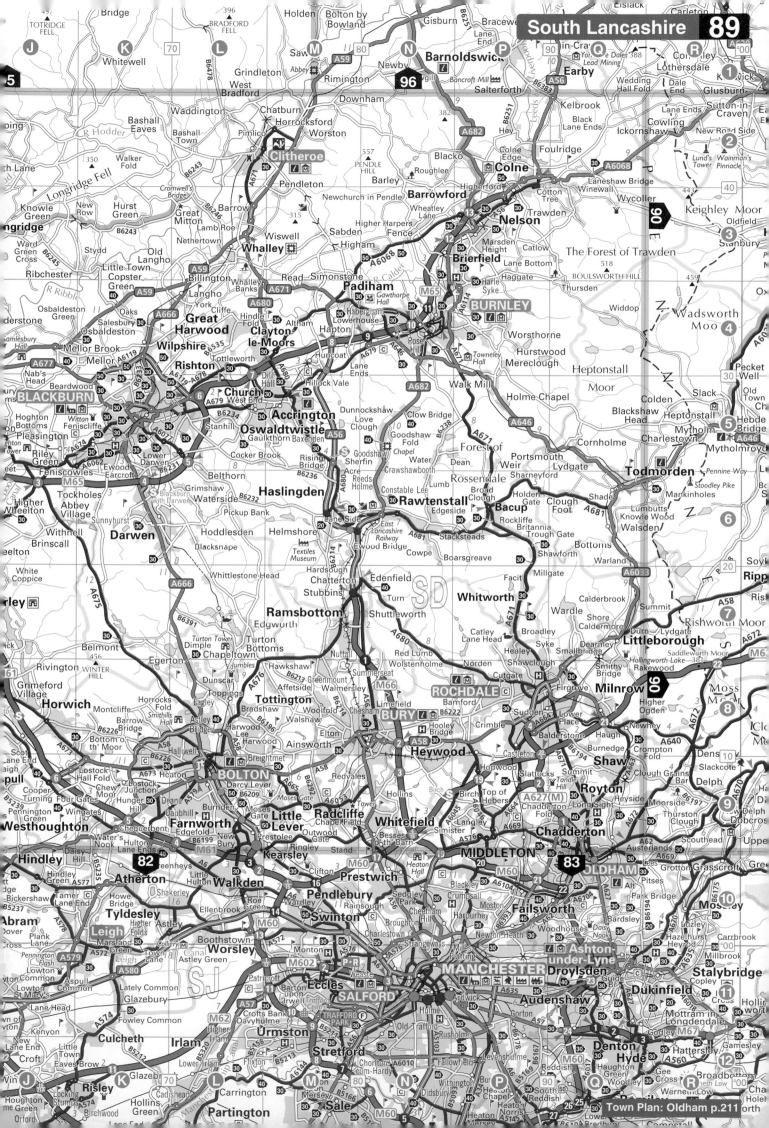

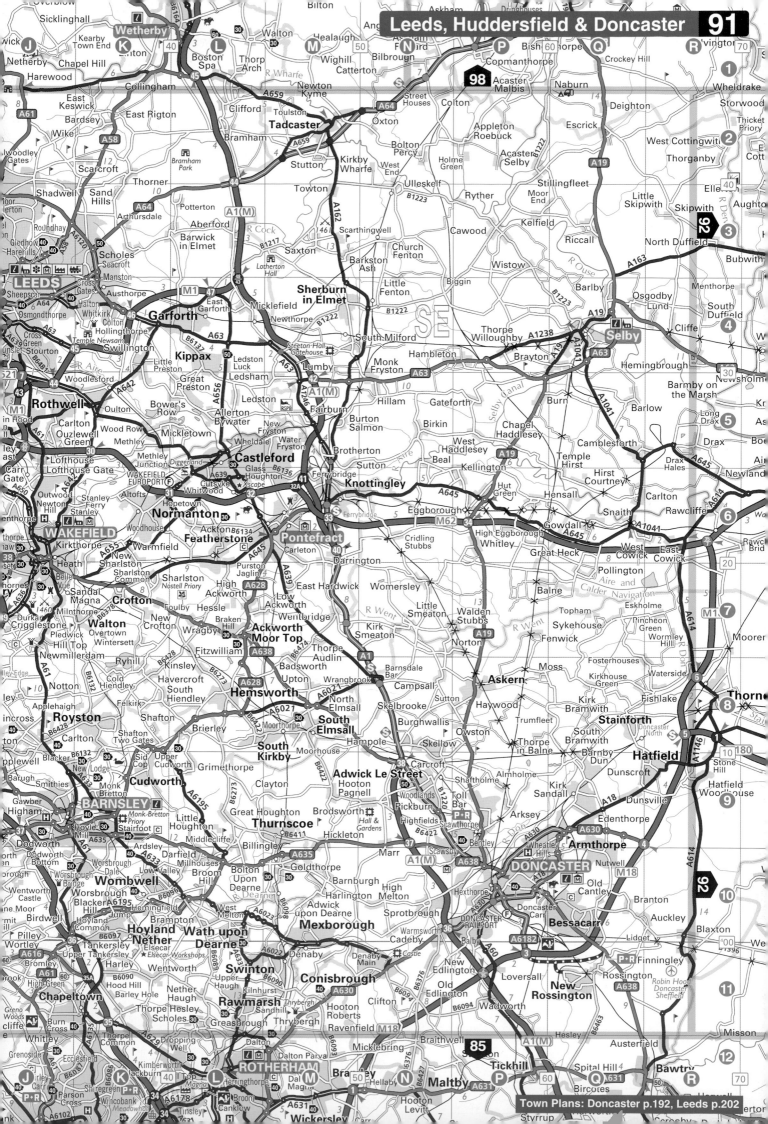

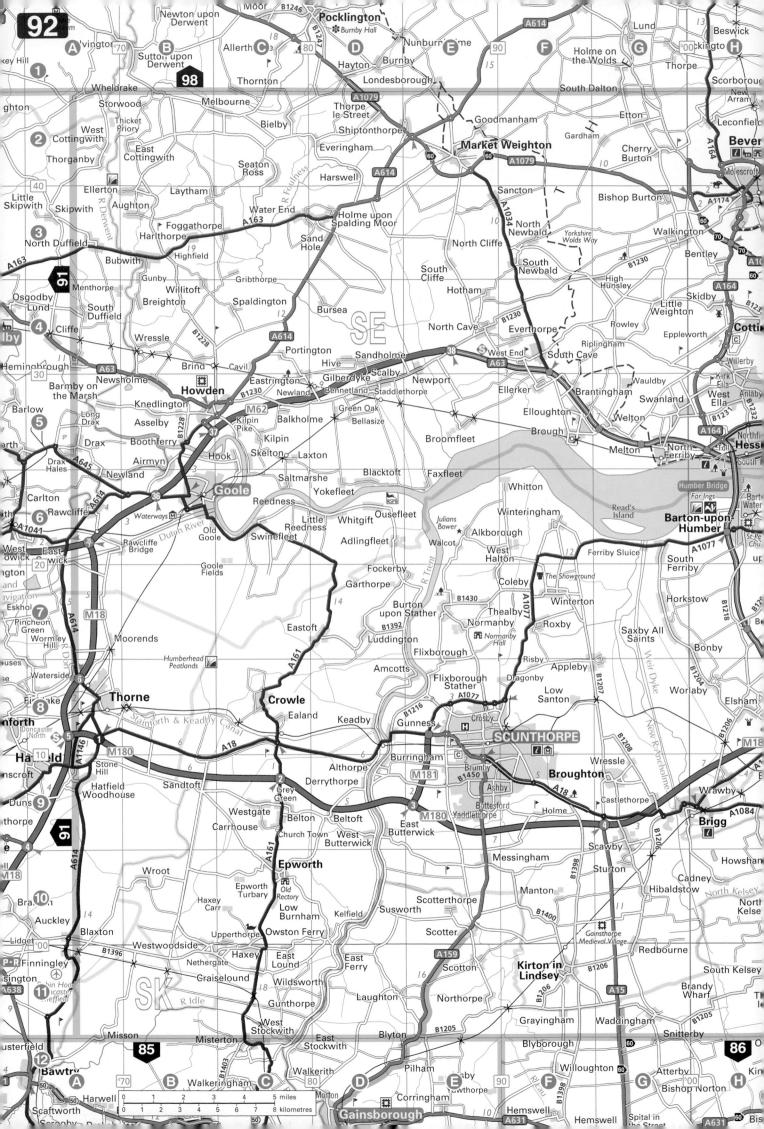

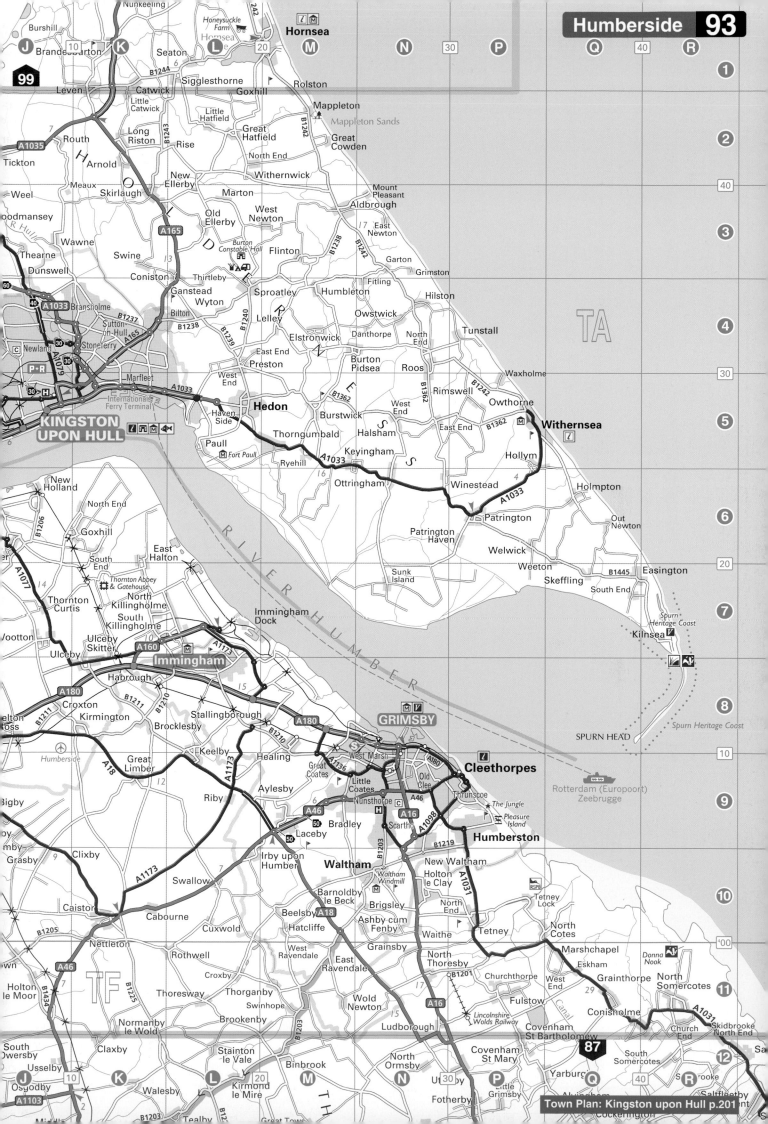

99

Burshill
Brandesburton
J
Nunkeeling
Honeysuckle Farm
Hornsea
Hornsea
Seaton
K
L
M
N
P
Q
R

Routh
Leven
Catwick
Sigglesthorne
Rolston
Goxhill

Tickton
Little Catwick
Long Riston
Rise
Little Hatfield
Great Hatfield
Mappleton
Mappleton Sands

Weel
Meaux
Arnold
New Ellerby
North End
Withernwick
Great Cowden

Thearne
Wawne
Skirlaugh
Marton
West Newton
Mount Pleasant
Aldbrough

Dunswell
Swine
Old Ellerby
Burton Constable Hall
Flinton
East Newton

Bransholme
Coniston
Thirtleby
Garton
Grimston

Newland
Sutton-on-Hull
Ganstead
Bilton
Sproatley
Humbleton
Fitling
Hilston

Stoneferry
Wyton
Lelley
Owstwick
East End
Tunstall

Marfleet
Preston
Elstronwick
Danthorpe
Burton Pidsea
Roos
Waxholme

KINGSTON UPON HULL
International Ferry Terminal
Haven Side
Hedon
Burstwick
Halsham
West End
Rimswell
Owthorne
Withernsea

Paull
Thorngumbald
Keyingham
East End
Hollym

Fort Paull
Ryehill
Ottringham
Winestead
Holmpton

New Holland
North End
Goxhill
East Halton
RIVER HUMBER
Patrington
Patrington Haven
Out Newton

Thornton Abbey & Gatehouse
North Killingholme
Immingham Dock
Sunk Island
Welwick
Weeton
Skeffling
Easington
South End

Thornton Curtis
South Killingholme
Spurn Heritage Coast
Kilnsea

Ulceby Skitter
Ulceby
Immingham
Habrough
SPURN HEAD
Spurn Heritage Coast

Croxton
Kirmington
Stallingborough
Brocklesby
GRIMSBY

Keelby
Healing
Great Coates
West Marsh
Cleethorpes

Great Limber
Riby
Aylesby
Little Coates
Old Clee
Thrunscoe

Nunsthorpe
The Jungle
Pleasure Island
Humberston

Clixby
Grasby
Bradley
Laceby
Scartho
New Waltham
Holton le Clay
Tetney Lock

Caistor
Cabourne
Irby upon Humber
Waltham
Waltham Windmill
North End
Tetney
North Cotes

Nettleton
Rothwell
Cuxwold
Hatcliffe
Barnoldby le Beck
Brigsley
Waithe
Marshchapel
Donna Nook
Grainthorpe

Holton le Moor
Thoresway
West Ravendale
Beelsby
Ashby cum Fenby
North Thoresby
West End
Churchthorpe
Fulstow
Grainthorpe
North Somercotes
Conisholme

Normanby le Wold
Croxby
East Ravendale
Grainsby
Lincolnshire Wolds Railway
Covenham St Bartholomew
Church End
Skidbrooke North End

Osgodby
Claxby
Swinhope
Brookenby
Wold Newton
Ludborough
Covenham St Mary
South Somercotes

Usselby
Walesby
Stainton le Vale
Binbrook
North Ormsby
Yarburgh
Little Grimsby

87

J
K
L
M
N
P
Q
R

Town Plan: Kingston upon Hull p.201

A · **B** · **C** · **D** · **E** · **F** · **G** · **H**

Muncaster Mill
Ravenglass and Eskdale Railway
HARTER FELL
Levers Water
Far End
Courthouse
Hawkshead
Hawkshead
Wray

Devoke Water
Seathwaite Tarn
THE OLD MAN OF CONISTON
Coniston
Roger Ground
Hill Top
Near Sawrey

Saltcoats
Roman Bath House
Muncaster
A595
100
Hall Dunnerdale
Seathwaite
Steam Yacht 'Gondola'
Bowmanstead
Torver
Bank Ground
Brantwood
Esthwaite Water
Grizedale
Grizedale Forest Park
Far Sawrey

Ravenglass
Newbiggin
Broad Oak
Waberthwaite
Ulpha
Broughton Mills
A593
Water Yeat
Blawith
A5084
High Nibthwaite
Satterthwaite
Furness Fells
Thwaite Head
Graythwaite Hall
Windermere

573 WHITFELL
Corney
Loganbeck
Beckfoot
Lower Hawthwaite
Broughton Tower
Rusland Cross
Bandrake Head
Finsthwaite
Crosslands
Stott Park Bobbin Mill

Hycemoor
Selker Bay
Hyton
Bootle
Swinside Stone Circle
Duddon Bridge
Broughton-in-Furness
Wreaks End
Lowick Bridge
Lowick
Lowick Green
Bouth
Oxen Park
Colton
Lakeside
Lakeland Motor Museum
Newby

Annaside
600 BLACK COMBE
Hallthwaites
A595
Lady Hall
Foxfield
Grizebeck
1.0
A5092
Gawthwaite
Spark Bridge
Lakeside and Haverthwaite Railway
5
Backbarrow

Whitbeck
The Green
Arnaby Bridge End
Chapels
Lowick
Penny Bridge
Haverthwaite
B60
Seatle

Gutterby Spa
Whicham
The Hill
A5093
Wall End
Kirkby-in-Furness
Beck Side
Broughton Beck
B5281
Penny Bridge
Greenodd
B5278
Low Wood
Barber Gre

Silecroft
A595
Sand Side
Soutergate
Mansriggs
3
Arrad Foot
Field Broughton
Beck Side
Gre

Kirksanton
8
Millom
Steel Green
Borwick Rails
RSPB
A595
12
Ireleth
Barrow Monument
Ulverston
Newland
Plumpton
Priory Gatehouse
Cartmel

SD
Haverigg
Haverigg Point
Askam in Furness
Pennington
Marton
A590
Swarthmoor
Canal Foot
Conishead Priory
Holker
Cark
B5278
Allithw

Sandscale Haws
South Lakes Animal Park
Lindal in Furness
Great Urswick
Little Urswick
Brow End
Bardsea
Flookburgh

North Walney
Dalton-in-Furness
Hawcoat
Newton
Scales
Baycliff
MORECAM

North Walney
BARROW-IN-FURNESS
Furness Abbey
Bow Bridge
Dendron
Stainton with Adgarley
Watermill
Gleaston
Aldingham
13
BAY

North Scale
Roose
Leece
Newbiggin

Vickerstown
A590
Barrow Island
30
Roose
A5087
Roosebeck

ISLE OF WALNEY
Biggar
Roa Island
Rampside

Sheep Island
Piel Castle
Foulney Island
Piel Island
Piel Bar

Hilpsford Point
South Walney

Douglas

Pilling Lane
Knott End-on-Sea
Fleetwood
Preesall

Rossall Point
River Wyre
B5371
Stalmine
A58

Cleveleys
Moor End
Staynall

THORNTON
Burn Naze
B5268
A585
Trunnah
40
Stanah
30
Hambleton
Sowe

Little Bispham
Norbreck
Churchtown
Earl
Mos

Port Plan: Heysham *p.XII*

| 0 | 1 | 2 | 3 | 4 | 5 miles |
| 0 | 1 2 3 4 5 6 7 | 8 kilometres |

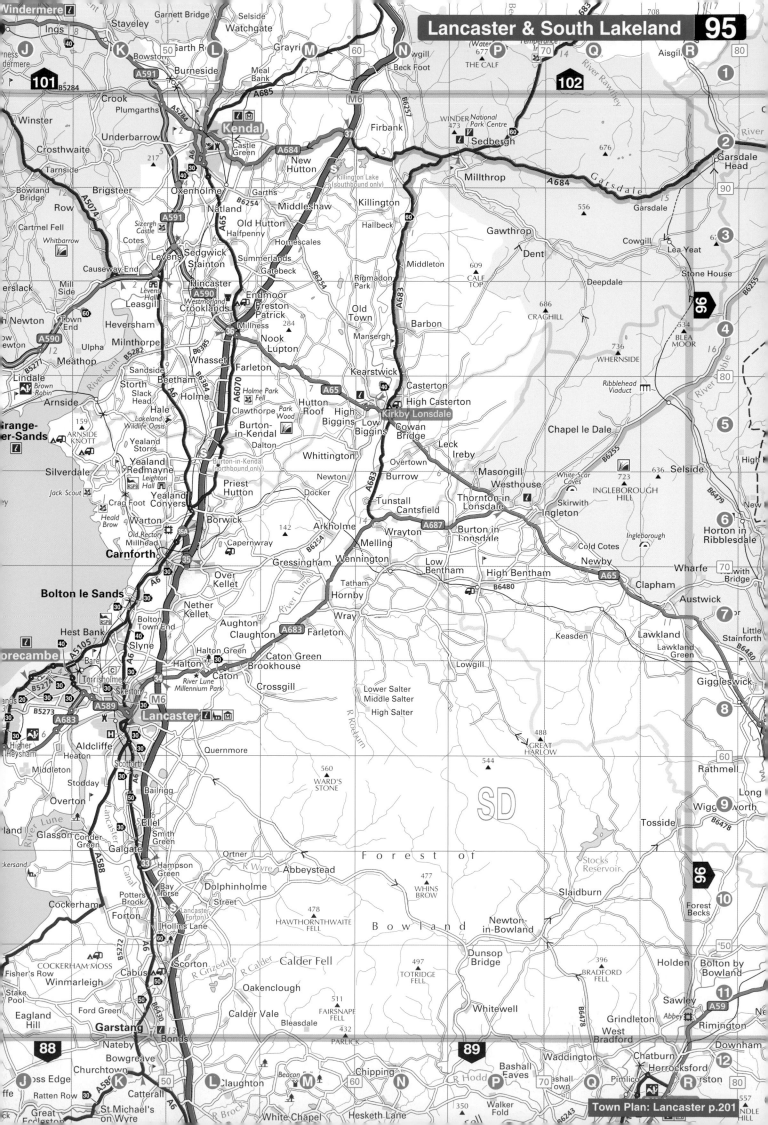

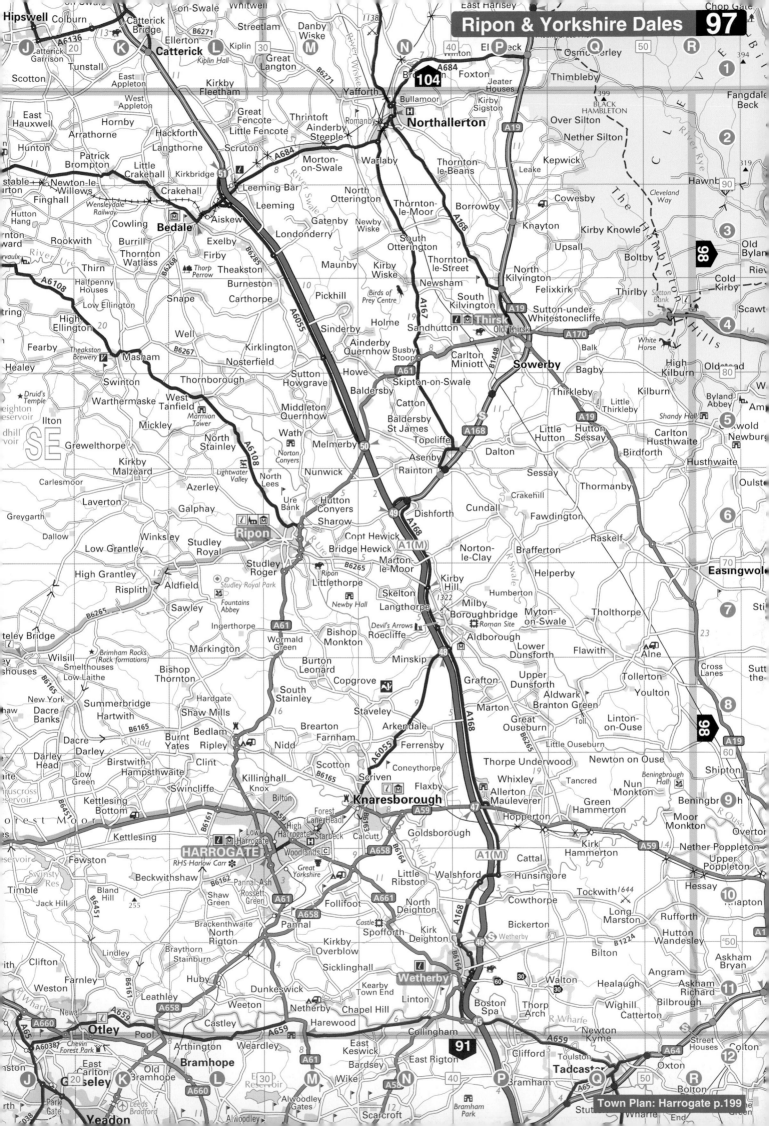

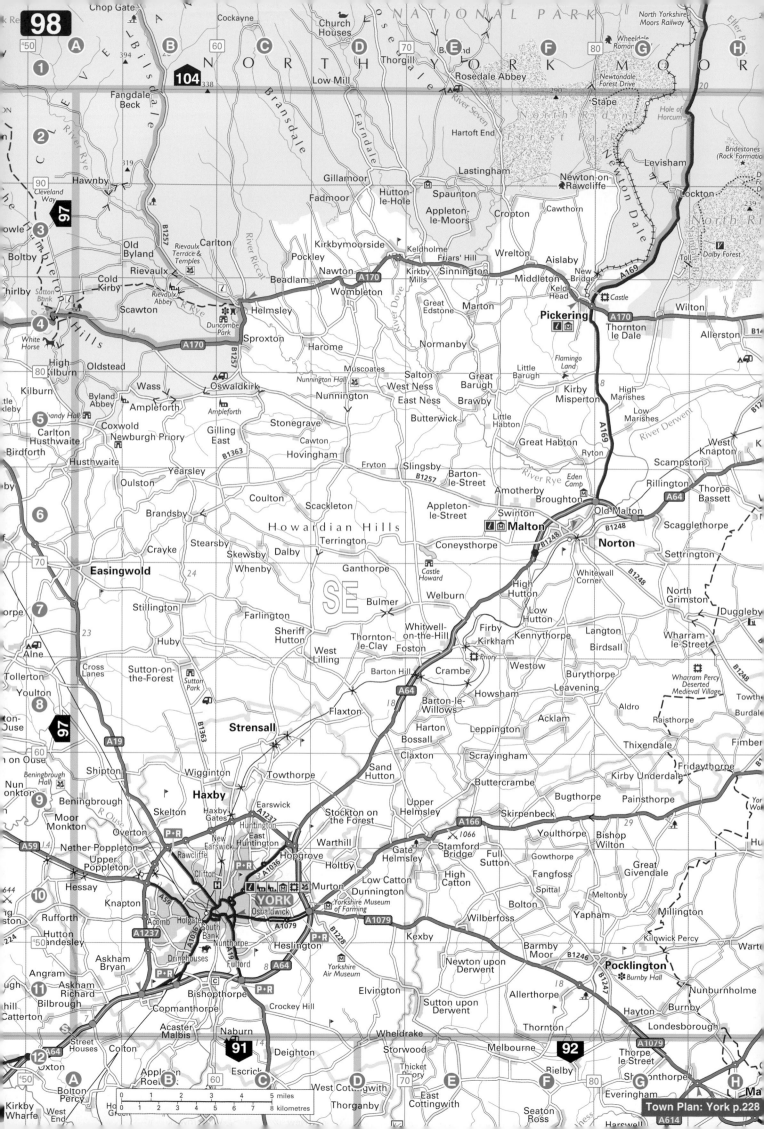

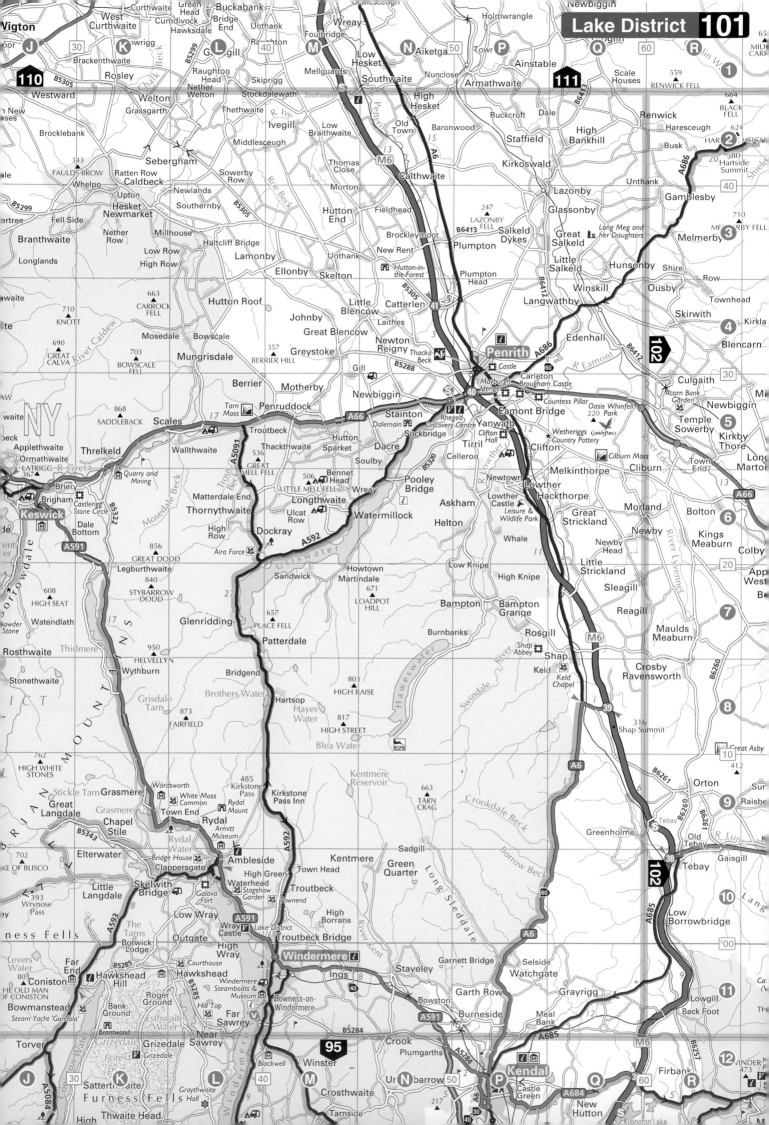

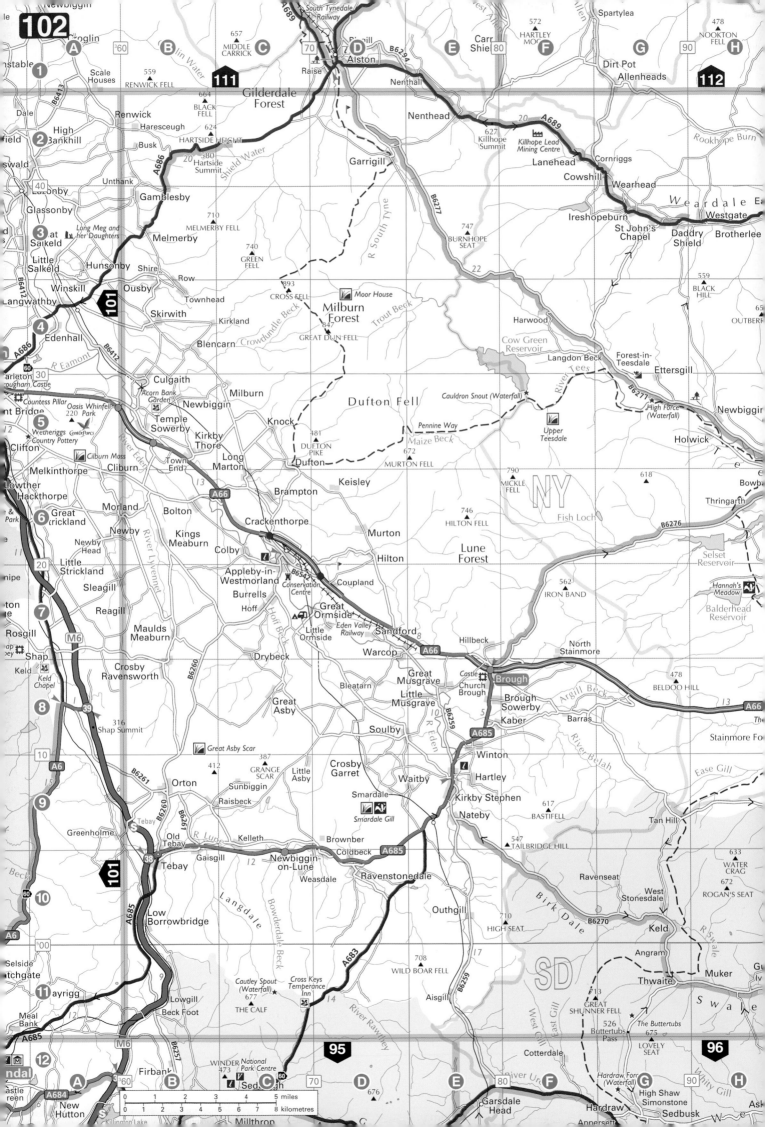

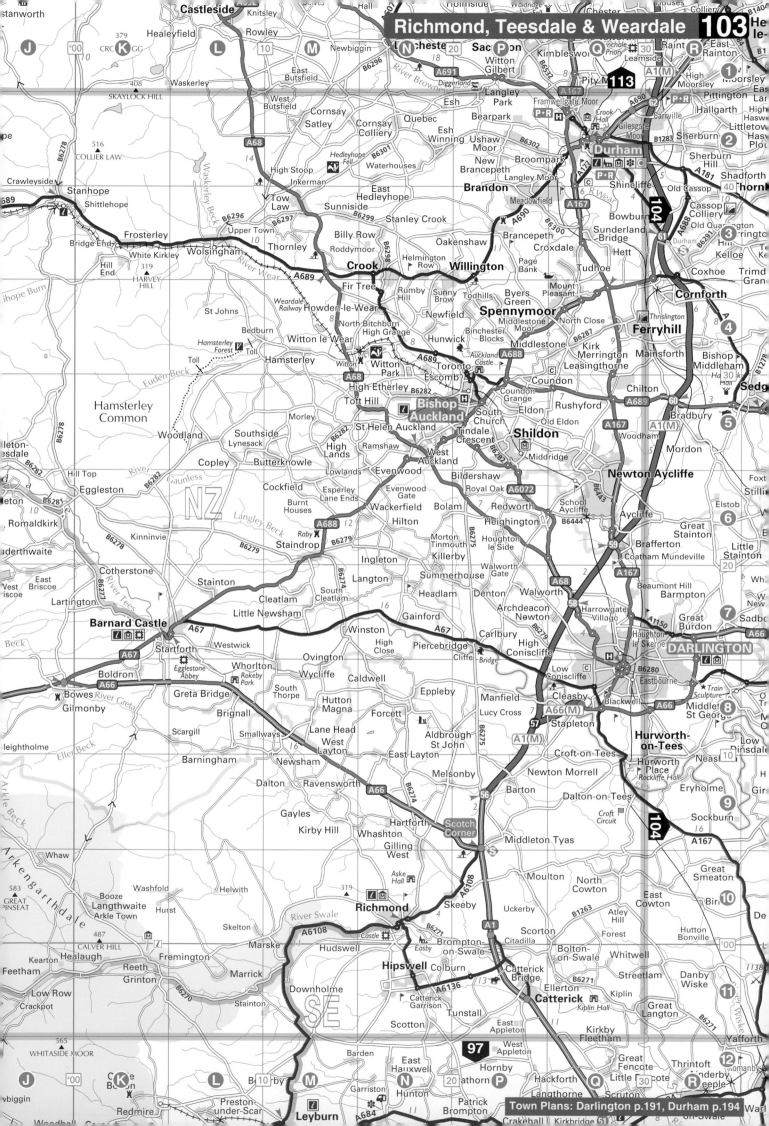

J 70 K L 80 M N 90 P Q 00 R

1
2
40
3
30
4
5
20
6
7
NZ
8
10
9
10
00
11
12

Saltburn-
by-the-
Sea
Saltburn Smugglers,
New Brotton
Brotton
Skelton
New North Kilton Carlin How Skinningrove Upton Boulby
Skelton Skelton **Loftus** Staithes
Lingdale Kilton Dalehouse Heritage Centre
Woodhill Thorpe Liverton Easington Port Mulgrave
Stanghow Mines Hinderwell North Yorkshire and
Liverton Roxby Newton Runswick Cleveland Heritage Coast
Moorsholm Handale Mulgrave Bay Kettleness Goldsborough
Gerrick Borrowby Ellerby Overdale
A171 Scaling Lythe Wyke
Moorsholm B1266 A174 Sandsend
Scaling Mickleby Sandsend
Dam 22 West East Wyke
Barnby Barnby **Whitby**
Ugthorpe Raithwaite Abbey Saltwick
The Moors Dunsley Bay
Centre 301 Stonegate Hutton Newholm
Danby Mulgrave Ruswarp
Castleton Ainthorpe Lealholm A171 Briggswath Stainsacre
River Esk Side Aislaby Sneaton High Hawsker
Lealholm Sleights Ugglebarnby Low B1447
The Egton Iburndale Hawsker Ness Point or
Green Sneatonthorpe North Cheek
Glaisdale Grosmont A169 Raw Robin Hood's Bay
dale Egton Bridge Littlebeck B1416 Raw Robin
Danby Bottom Key Green Fylingthorpe Hood's Bay
Street Old Peak or
N O R T H Y O R K M O O R S Beck Hole South Cheek
326 A171 Ravenscar
PIKE HILL Goathland 20 00
369 North Yorkshire 292
N A T I O N A L P A R K Moors Railway Staintondale TA
Rosedale Low Eller Beck Harwood Shire Horse
Thorgill Bell End Wheeldale Dale Centre Hayburn
H O R Y O R K M O O R S Roman Road Cloughton Wyke
Rosedale Abbey 290 Newtondale Newlands
Mill Forest Drive Cloughton Wyke
River Seven Stape North Riding **99** Cloughton
Lastingham Hole of Horcum
J 70 K rtoft End L 80 t M N 90 P 00 Q R Cromer Point
Bickley Broxa Bu ton A Cleveland Way
Bridestones Toll
(Rock Formation) Langdale Silpho
Levisham Dolby Hackness Suffield

J 30 K L 40 M N 50 P Q 60 R

GARWALL HILL
Forest Park
Loch Neldricken
Silver Flowe
1
St John's Town of Dalry
Garroch
Bogue
Glen Trool Lodge
Bruce Memorial
115
2
New Galloway
Glentrool Village
22
Creebank
Bargrennan
Bruce's Stone
Clatteringshaws Forest & Wildlife Centre
Drumlamford
Loch Dornal
Loch Trool
LAMACHAN HILL 716
675 LARG HILL
Clatteringshaws Loch
380 BENNAN
A762
Loch Maberry
B7027
Loch Ochiltree
440 GARLICK HILL
MILLFORE 654
Galloway
402 ROUND FELL
325 CAIRN EDWARD
3
Knowe
RSPB
Galloway Deer Range
471 FELL OF FLEET
70 ssdale
URRALL FELL 184
River Bladnoch
G A L L O W A Y
Penkill Burn
Galloway
Loch Grannoch
Loch Fleet
208 AUCHENCLOY HILL
Forest
4
Carseriggan
Challoch
R Cree
Minnigaff
710 CAIRNSMORE OF FLEET
108
Loch Skerrow
Wood Loc
Barfad
214 CULVENNAN FELL
Newton Stewart
Creebridge
Park
335 WHITE TOP OF CULREACH
Lau
5
Loch Ronald
Shennanton
A714
Kirroughtree
Big Water of Fleet
Loch Whinyeon
Tarf Water
15
B735
B733
Palnure
Carstramon Wood
Craighlaw
Kirkcowan
Baltersan
A75
Upper Ruscoe
367 BENGRAY
60
Dernaglar Loch
A75
Causeway End
7
Gem Rock
B796
Fleet Valley
6
NX
Clugston
Fell Loch
Creetown
455 CAIRNHARROW
Anwoth
Gatehouse of Fleet
B7052
Torhouse Stone Circle
18
Kirkmabreck
Cardoness Castle
B721
Littleton
THE
B733
Wigtown
Carsluith
Cairnholy Chambered Cairns
Girthon
A75
7
Castle Loch
Bladnoch
Kirwaugh
Carsluith Castle
Lennox Plunton
Tmpston
ochrum Loch
Waterof Malzie
M A C H A R S
B7005
Braehead
Orchardton Bay
Ravenshall Point
Mossyard
A755 Kirkc Mac
Culshabbin
B7005
Barrachan
B7052
B7085
Kirkinner
B7004
Culscadden
Fleet Bay
Margrie
Gledpark
50
Chapel Finian (ruin)
Elrig
Druchtag Motte
Whauphill
Little Airies
A746
Islands of Fleet
Kirkandrews
Borgue
B727
8
A747
13
Mochrum
B7085
Drumtrodden Cup & Ring
Drummoddie
Sorbie
B7052
Garlieston
Wigtown Bay
Borness
Balmangan
Drumtrodden Standing Stones
Pouton
B7004
Port William
Big Balcraig
'Wren's Egg' Standing Stones
B7021
Priory
Broughton Mains
B7004
B7063
Cruggleton Bay
Ringdoo Point
Ross
9
Barsalloch Fort
Monreith
Whithorn Story
Rispain Camp
A746
Whithorn
Portyerrock
40
Barsalloch Point
Point of Leg
A747
10
St Ninian's Cave
Kidsdale
B7004
Isle of Whithorn
St Ninian's Chapel (ruin)
Cutcloy
11
BURROW HEAD
30
12

J 30 K L 40 M N 50 P Q 60 R

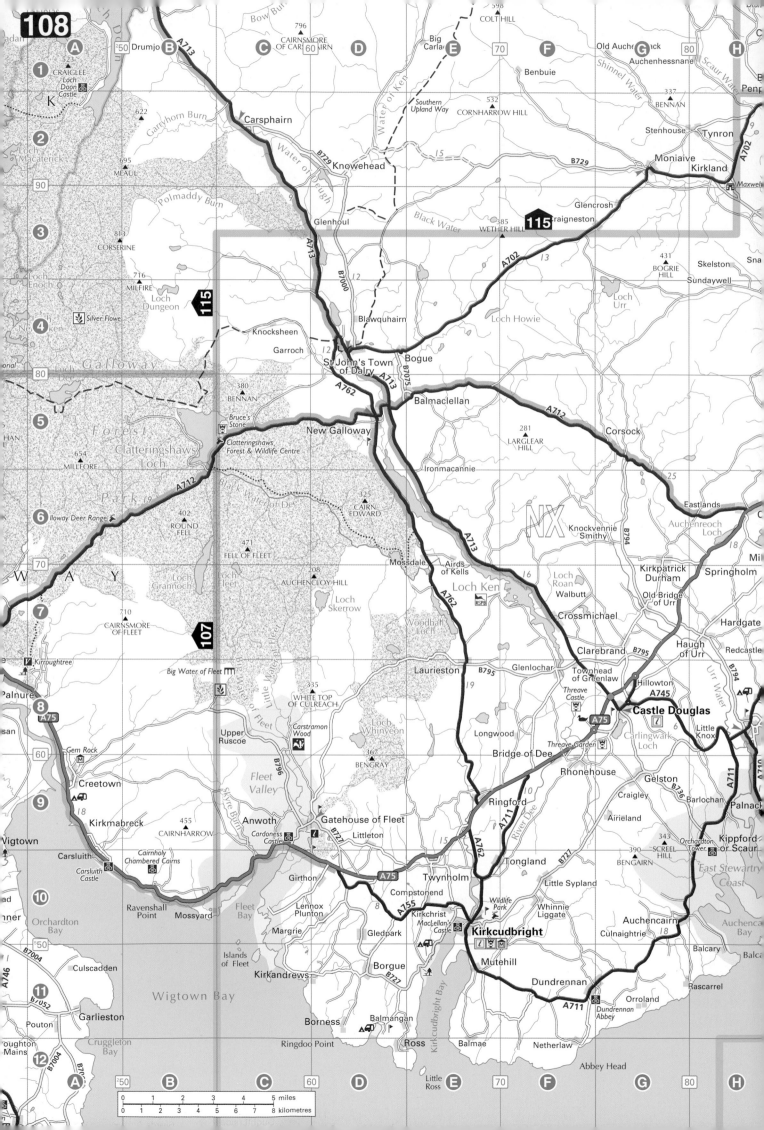

Port of Tyne

TYNEMOUTH
A193
THE NORTH
NEWCASTLE
M
MEADOW WELL
A181
PERCY MAIN
M
A187
HOWDON
Toll
A19
ROAD
Wet'n'Wild Water Park
East Howdon
Royal Quays Outlet Shopping Centre
Premier Inn
Royal Quays Marina
Check-in
TYNE VIEW
A187
TYNE TUNNEL
INTERNATIONAL PASSENGER TERMINAL
PRIORY
ROAD
B1297
Jarrow
LLC
SUNDERLAND
River Tyne

0   500 m

West Thirston
Broomhill
Red Row
Druridge Bay
J
20
Helm
K
West Chevington
L
30
Druridge Bay
M
N
40
P
Q
50
R
1
Causey Park
Stobswood
Druridge
North Northumberland Heritage Coast
Causey Park Bridge
Widdrington
Widdrington Station
Cresswell
2
Earsdon
Tritlington
Ulgham
Ellington
Fenrother
Hebron
Linton
Lynemouth
90
A1
60
Longhirst
A1068
A197
Woodhorn
Beacon Point
3
Pegswood
A197
Ashington
Woodhorn Demesne
Morpeth
Bothal
Hirst
North Seaton
Newbiggin-by-the-Sea
Wansbeck Riverside
Hepscott
A196
Sheepwash
Stakeford
Guide Post
B1334
North Seaton Colliery
River Tyne
Tranwell
Clifton
Scotland Gate
West Sleekburn
Choppington
Bomarsund
Cambois
4
Saltwick
Bedlington
East Sleekburn
North Blyth
Nedderton
B1331
B1331
Cowpen
Blyth
Stannington Station
A1068
A193
Bebside
Newsham
80
A192
East Hartford
B1505
New Delaval
Stannington
Plessey Woods
A1061
New Hartley
A193
5
Shotton
Shankhouse
A192
Seaton Sluice
River Blyth
Northumberlandia
East Cramlington
Hartley
Berwick Hill
Cramlington
B1326
A190
Seaton Delaval
St Mary's Lighthouse
6
Brenkley
Big Waters
A19
Seghill
Seaton
NZ
Dinnington
Mason
Seaton Burn
Annitsford
Holywell
B1325
B1148
Whitley Bay
Prestwick
Brunswick Village
Dudley
Burradon
Earsdon
Cullercoats
High Callerton
Hazlerigg
Wide Open
Camperdown
Backworth
Monkseaton
Woolsington
A1056
Killingworth
Shiremoor
Tynemouth
7
Black Callerton
Newcastle
B6918
Kenton Bankfoot
Forest Hall
B1317
B1505
Murton
New York
Tynemouth Priory & Castle
70
North Talbot
A1
Fawdon
A189
A191
Rising Sun
Amsterdam (IJmuiden)
A69
Gosforth
South Gosforth
Longbenton
Willington Quay
North Shields
Newburn
Kenton
A1058
Jesmond
Wallsend
Int. Ferry Terminal
SOUTH SHIELDS
Westerhope
A167
Heaton
A187
Jarrow
Tyne Tunnel
Westoe
8
B6324
NEWCASTLE UPON TYNE
Walker
A194
Hebburn
A185
Harton
Marsden Bay
Stella
Scotswood
Byker
B1313
Monkton
A1300
Marsden
Souter Lighthouse
Blaydon
Elswick
Felling
Wardley
West Boldon
Cleadon
Souter Point
Winlaton
Metro Centre
Dunston
A184
Boldon Colliery
Whitburn
Whickham
GATESHEAD
A194
A184
East Boldon
A1018
Whitburn Bay
60
Winlaton Mill
Low Fell
B1288
A194(M)
Bowes Railway & Museum
Springwell
A19
Fulwell
9
Sunniside
A692
Street Gate
A1
Team Valley
Wrekenton
Usworth
Castletown
Roker
Gibside
Marley Hill
Tanfield Railway
Lamesley
A1290
Wildfowl & Wetlands Trust
South Southwick
Monkwearmouth
Sheep Hill
Byermoor
Angel of the North
Birtley
Portobello
Hylton
SUNDERLAND
Tanfield
Beamish
B1288
A1231
South Hylton
Pennywell
A183
Hendon
Causey Arch
Kibblesworth
WASHINGTON
Penshaw Monument
A690
High Newport
Grangetown
Stanley
West Pelton
Beamish
Ouston
Fatfield
A195
Penshaw
Herrington
New Silksworth
Tunstall
Durham Heritage Coast
Catchgate
Lea
Perkinsville
River Wear
B1286
Ryhope
White-le-Head
Tanfield
A6076
High Urpeth
New Herrington
Oxhill
A693
Pelton
A693
Shiney Row
Philadelphia
A19
Seaham
Pelton Fell
Bournmoor
Newbottle
10
Lanchester
The Middles
Grange Villa
Newfield
High Dubmire
A1018
Quaking Houses
Chester-le-Street
Pelton
Houghton Gate
Houghton-le-Spring
Seaton
A693
Craghead
B6313
B1284
Parkside
South Moor
Craghead
Waldridge
Colliery Row
Dalton-le-Dale
Maiden Law
Holmside
Chester Moor
Great Lumley
West Rainton
Hetton-le-Hole
Murton
Cold Hesledon
50
11
Burnhope
Edmondsley
Plawsworth
B1404
A182
Sacriston
Nettlesworth
Finchale Priory
East Rainton
B1285
South Hetton
Hawthorn
Ornsby Hill
Witton Gilbert
Kimblesworth
Leamside
B6532
Dalton Park
A182
Langley Park
A691
Diggerland
Pity Me
High Moorsley
A19
B1432
Quebec
Esh Win
20
A167
Low Moorsley
Easington
B1280
Easington Colliery
12
Esh
A690
A1(M)
Framwellgate Moor
Crook Hall
Carrville
Hallgarth
B1283
Shotton
P+R
Little Thorpe
New Brancepeth
Bearpark
Durham
Gilesgate
Pittington
Haswell
Easington
Durham Heritage Coast
Broompark
B6302
Kepier
Littletown
Haswell Plough
J
20
K
L
M
N
50
P
Q
R

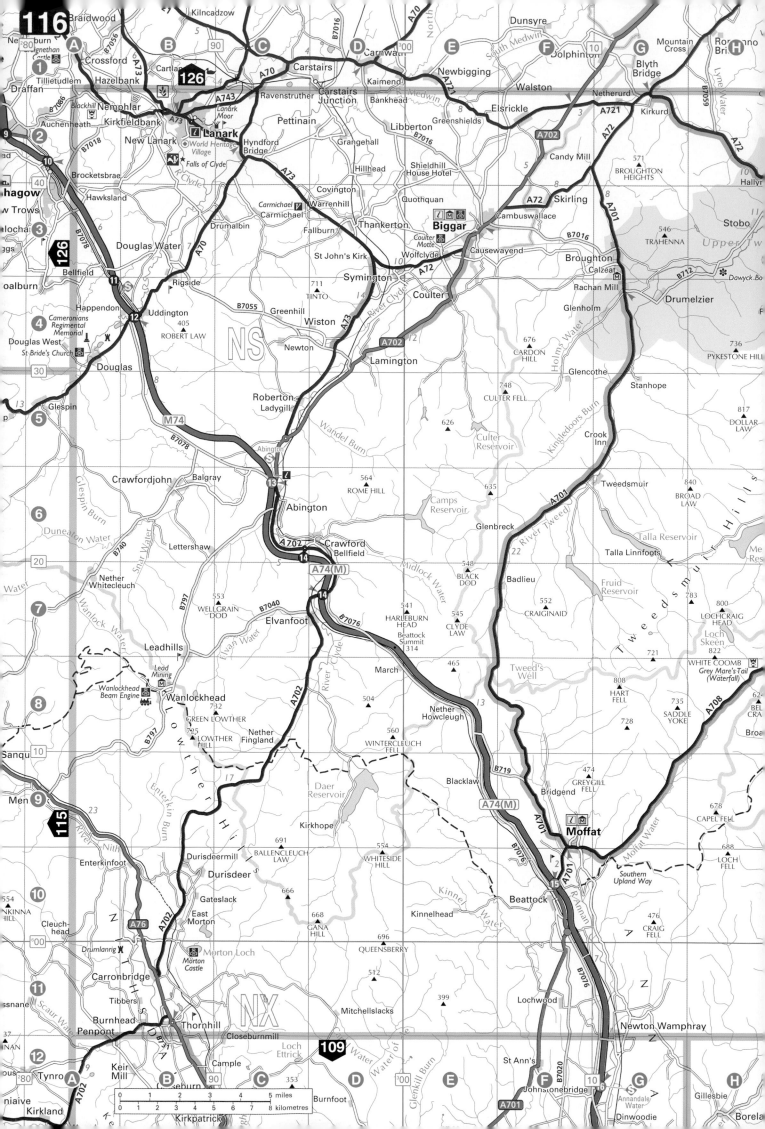

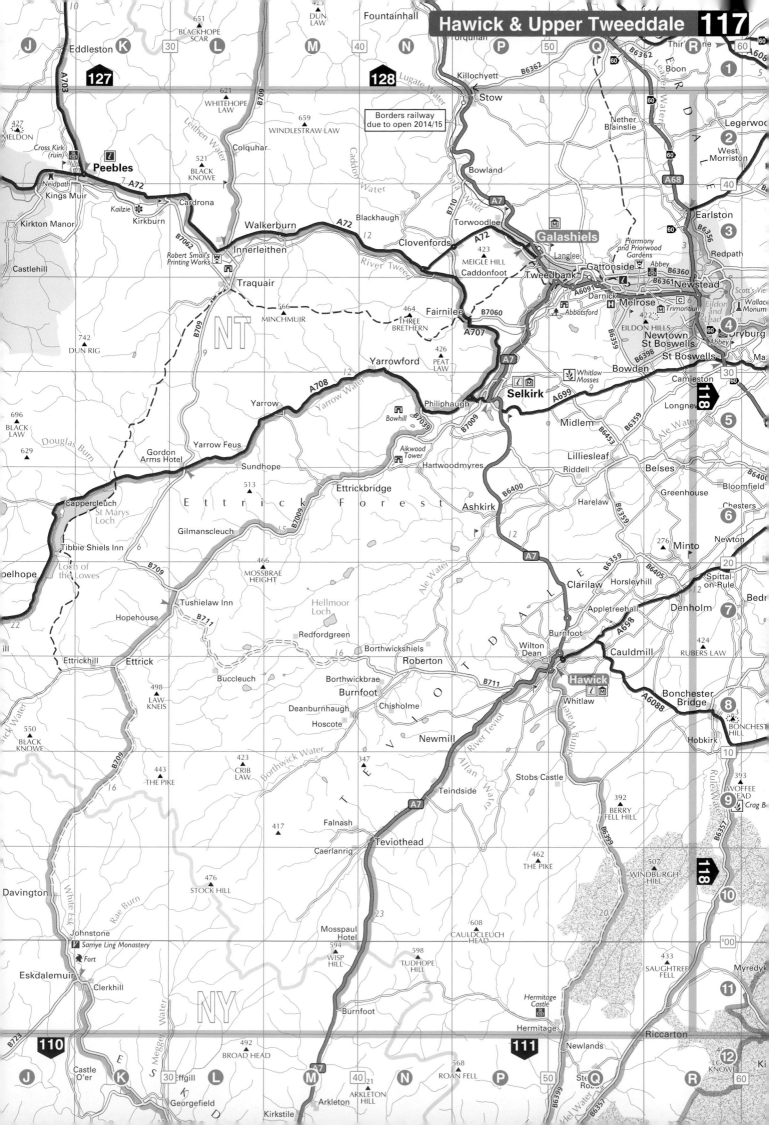

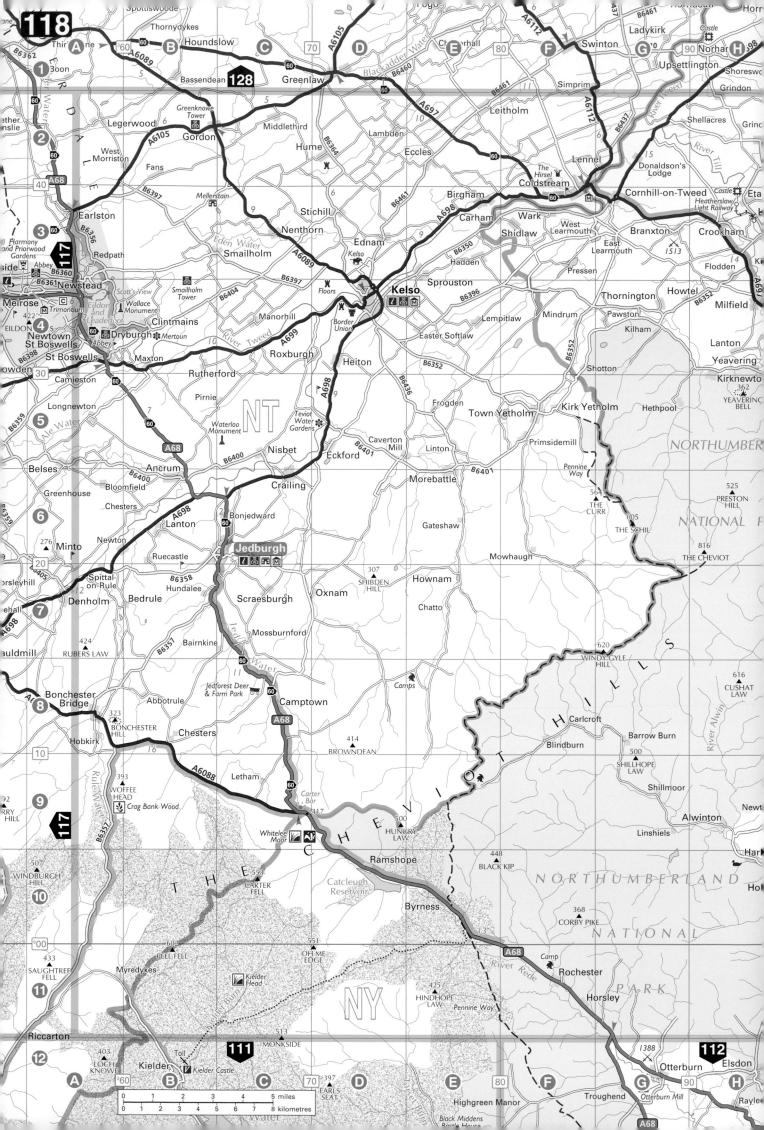

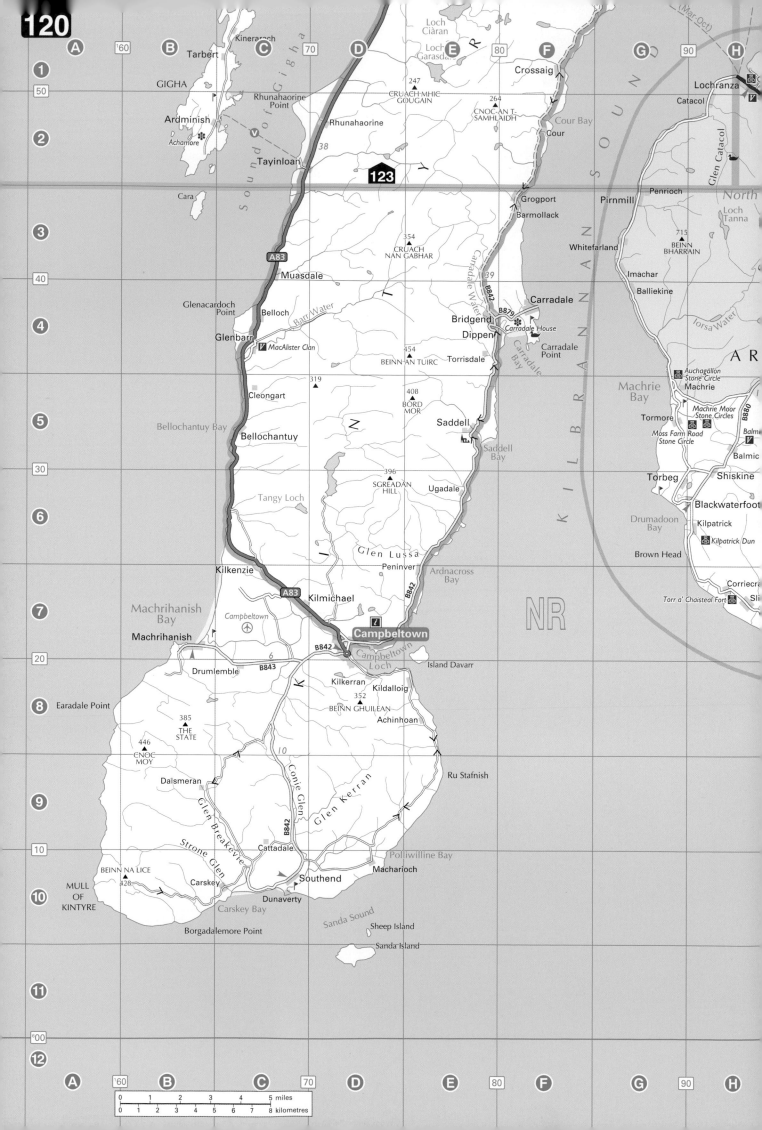

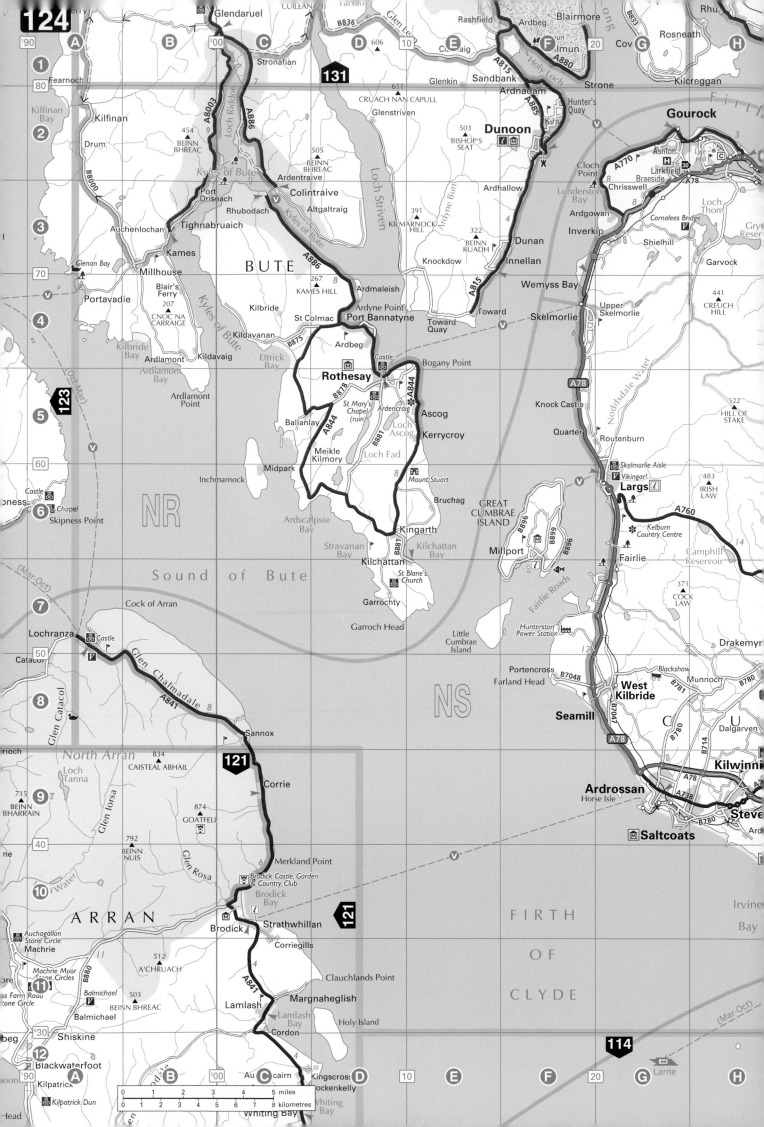

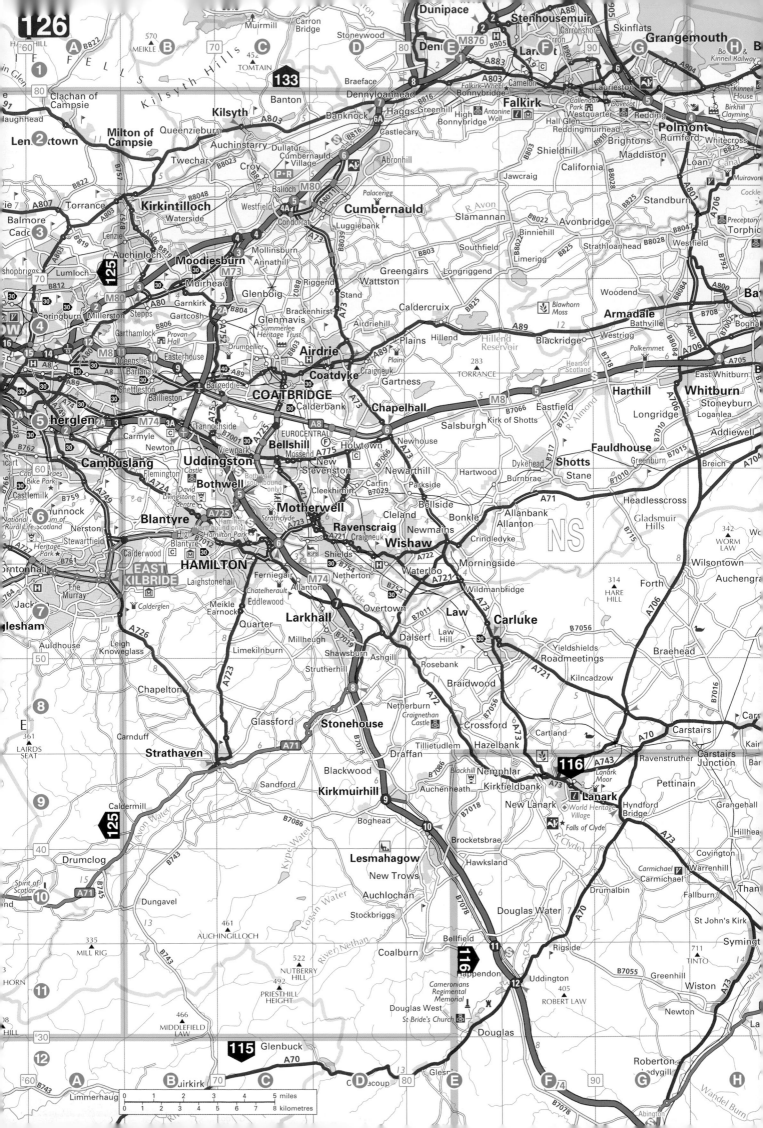

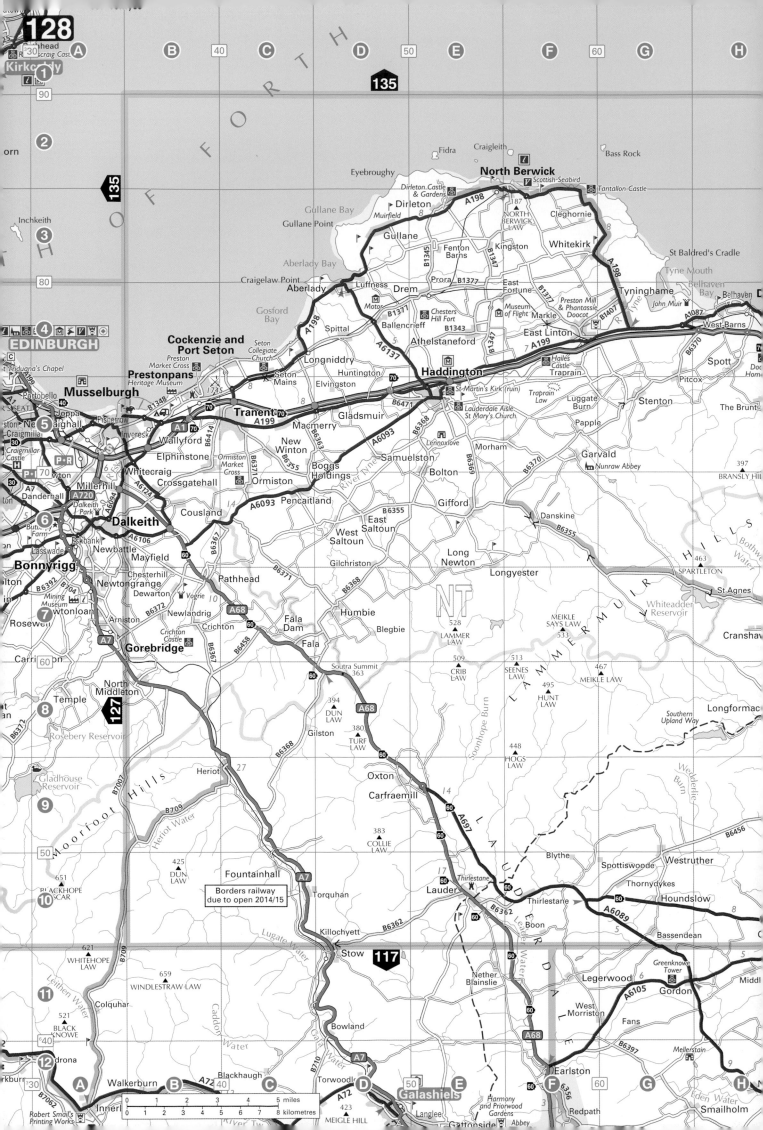

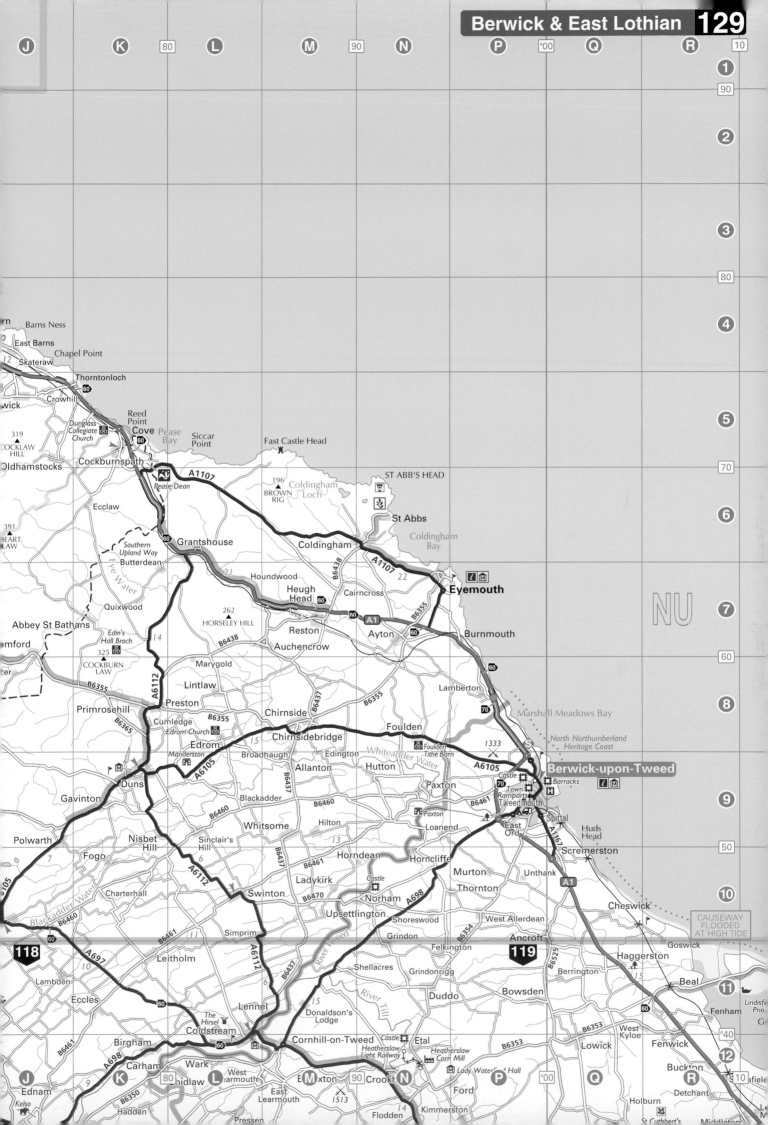

J K 80 L M 90 N P '00 Q R 10

① 90 ② ③ 80 ④ 70 ⑤ ⑥ 70 ⑦ 60 ⑧ ⑨ 50 ⑩ ⑪ 40 ⑫

Barns Ness
East Barns
Chapel Point
Skateraw
Thorntonloch
Crowhill
319
COCKLAW HILL
Oldhamstocks
Reed Point
Cove
Dunglass Collegiate Church
Cockburnspath
Pease Bay
Siccar Point
Fast Castle Head
Pease Dean
A1107
Ecclaw
196
BROWN RIG
Coldingham Loch
ST ABB'S HEAD
391
HEART LAW
Southern Upland Way
Butterdean
Eye Water
Grantshouse
60
St Abbs
Coldingham
A1107
Coldingham Bay
Quixwood
Houndwood
21
B6438
A1107 22
Eyemouth
Abbey St Bathans
Edin's Hall Broch
14
HORSELEY HILL 262
Heugh Head
60 A1
Cairncross
B6355
Ayton
60
Burnmouth
mford
325
COCKBURN LAW
B6355
A6112
Preston
Marygold
Lintlaw
B6438
Reston
Auchencrow
B5437
B6355
Lamberton
60
70
Marshall Meadows Bay
Primrosehill
B6365
Cumledge
Edrom Church
Edrom
Manderston
A6105
Chirnside
Chirnsidebridge
15
Broadhaugh
Allanton
B6437
Edington
Hutton
Foulden
Foulden Tithe Barn
Whiteadder Water
1333
North Northumberland Heritage Coast
Duns
Gavinton
Blackadder
B6460
B6460
Paxton
Paxton
B6461
A6105
Castle
70
Town Ramparts
Tweedmouth
Barracks
Berwick-upon-Tweed
Polwarth
Nisbet Hill
Fogo
Sinclair's Hill
Whitsome
Hilton
13
Horndean
Loanend
Horncliffe
East Ord
Spittal
Huds Head
Scremerston
A1167
A1
105
B6460
Charterhall
A6112
6
B6437
B6461
Ladykirk
Norham
Castle
B6470
Swinton
Upsettlington
Shoreswood
Grindon
Murton
Thornton
Unthank
A698
West Allerdean
Cheswick
CAUSEWAY FLOODED AT HIGH TIDE
118
60
A697
10
B6460
Leitholm
A6112
11
Simprim
River Tweed
Shellacres
Grindonrigg
Felkington
Duddo
Ancroft
119
B6525
Bowsden
Berrington
15
Haggerston
Goswick
Beal
Lindisf Prio
Fenham
Lambden
Eccles
B6461
Lennel
The Hirsel
Coldstream
Donaldson's Lodge
15
River Till
B6354
Lowick
West Kyloe
B6353
Fenwick
Birgham
60
Cornhill-on-Tweed
Castle
Etal
Heatherslaw Light Railway
Heatherslaw Corn Mill
Lady Waterford Hall
Ford
Buckton
Carham
A698
B6350
Wark
West Learmouth
xton
90
Crook
N
East Learmouth
1513
Kimmerston
Flodden
14
Pressen
Holburn
Detchant
Middleton
Ednam
Kelso
Hadden
J K 80 L M 90 N P '00 Q R 10
NU

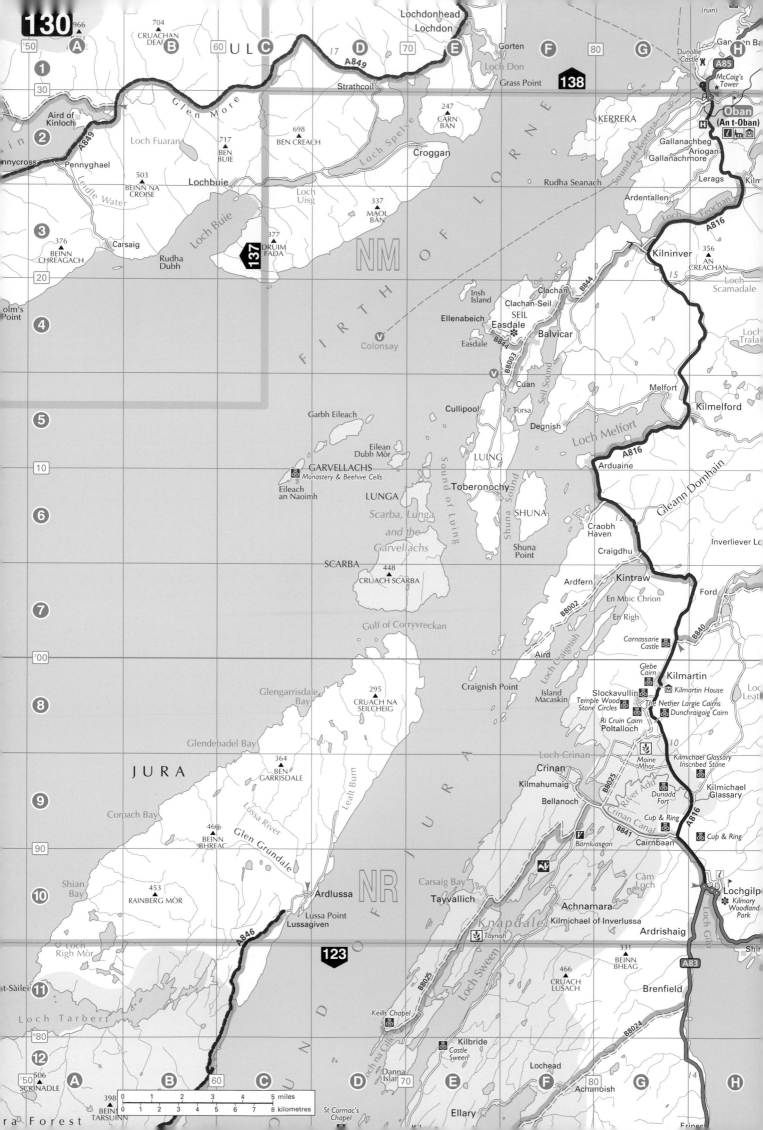

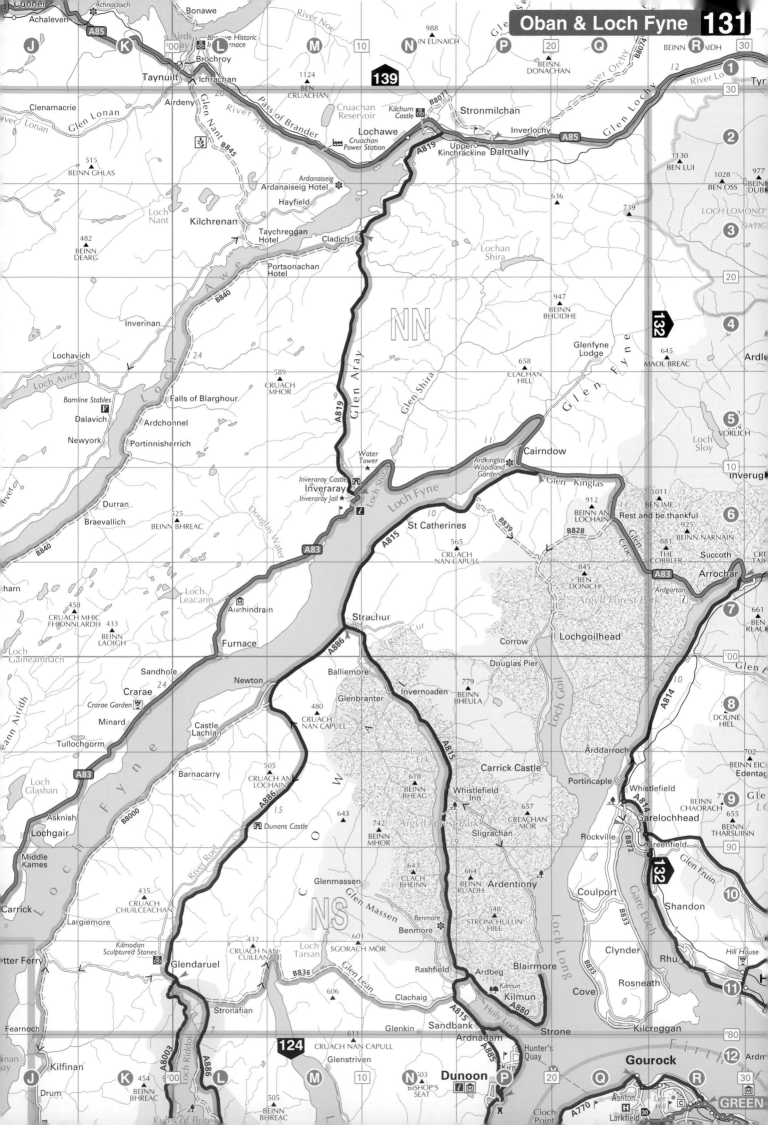

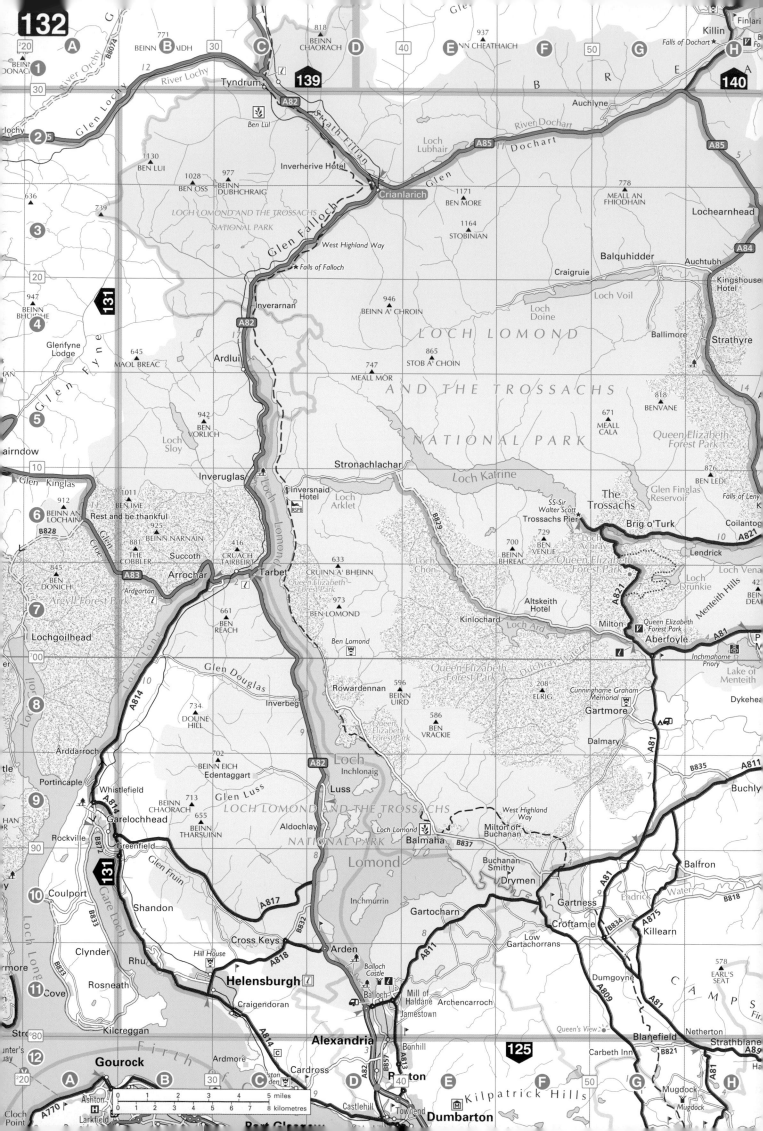

Colonsay

NL

NM

NR

COLL

TIREE

TRESHNISH
ISLES

COLONSAY

ORONSAY

IONA

Eilean Mòr
Rudha
Mòr
Rudha
Sgor-inn
Sorisdal
Bousd
Cliad
Bay
B8072
Arnabost
Grishipoll
Clabhach
B8071
Loch
Cliad
Hogh Bay
Ballyhaugh
Arinagour
Totronald
Coll
B8070
Arileod
Acha
Eilean
Ornsay
Feall
Bay
Uig
RSPB
Calgary Point
Crossapol
Bay
Rudha
Fàsachd
Gunna
Loch Breachacha
Bagh a Chaisteil
(Castlebay)
(Mar-Oct)

Rudha Port
Bhiosd
Clachan
Mor
Balephetrish
Bay
Caoles
Rudha Dubh
B8069
Loch
Bhasapoll
B8068
Ruaig
Haugh
Bay
Ballevullin
Cornoigmore
Kenovay
Gott
Bay
Kilkenneth
B8068
Tiree
Moss
Heylipoll
B8065
Scarinish
Middleton
B8065
Crossapoll
Barrapoll
Hynish Bay
Loch a
Phuill
B8067
Balemartine
Rinn
Thorbhais
Mannel
Hynish
Balephuil
Bay

Lunga

Fla

Bac Mòr or Dutchmans
Bac Beag

Eilean
Dubh
Kiloran Bay
Balnahard
Rudh' a' Geodha
COLONSAY
Kiloran
Colonsay - Oban
Kilchattan
B8087
Scalasaig
B8086
Machrins
Colonsay
B8085
Garvard
Colonsay - Port Askaig
Oronsay
Rudha
Bàn
Dubh Eilean
Eilean
Ghurdmail
ORONSAY

Iona Abbey
& Nunnery
IONA
Baile Mòr
MacLean's Cross
Sound of Oc

Soa Island
Erraid

0 1 2 3 miles
0 1 2 3 4 5 kilometres

0 1 2 3 4 5 miles
0 1 2 3 4 5 6 7 8 kilometres

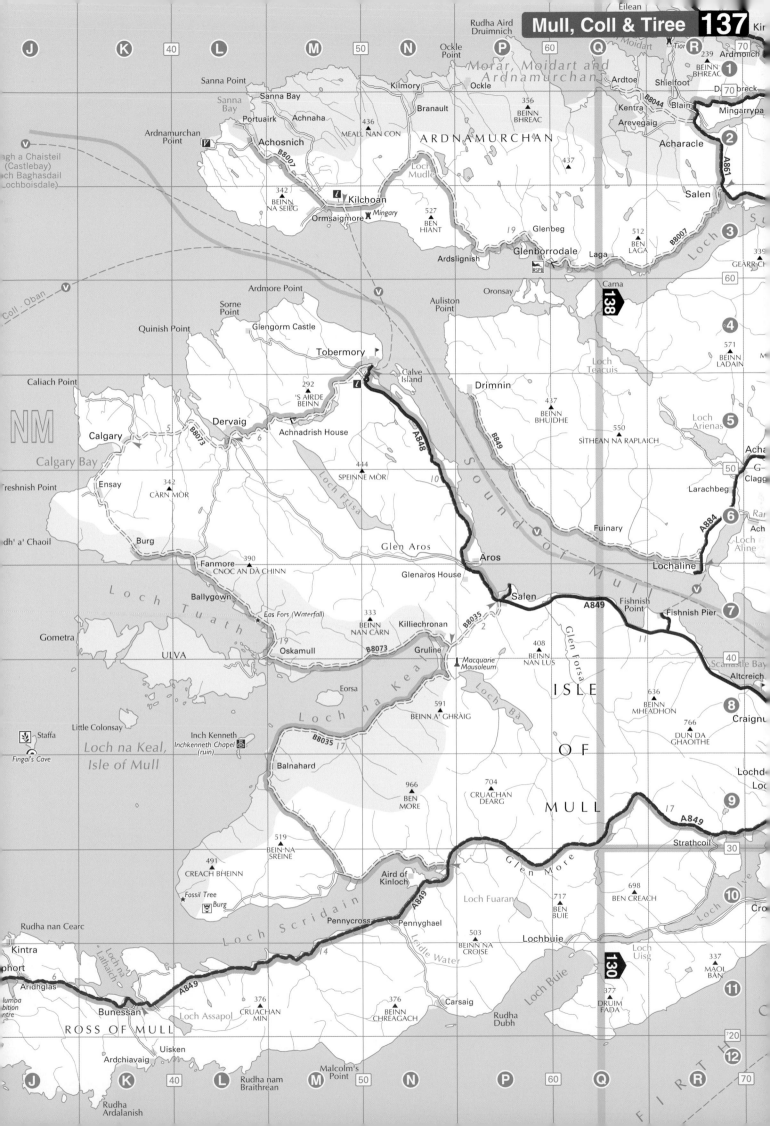

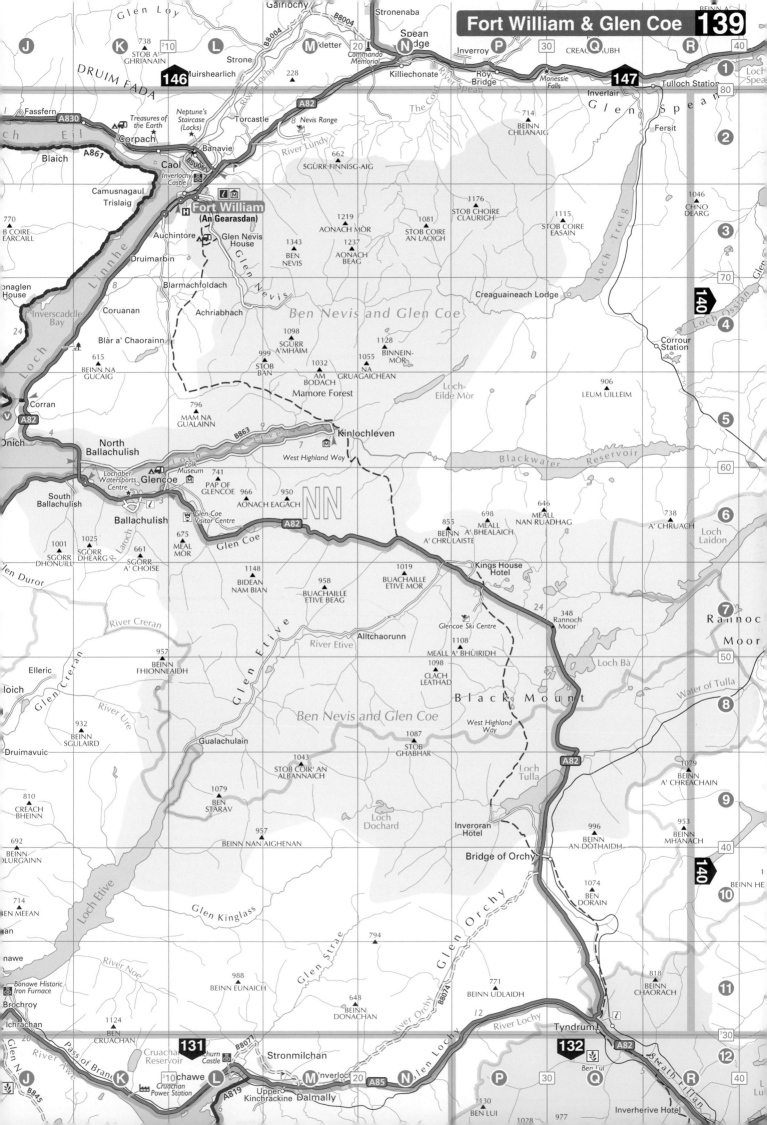

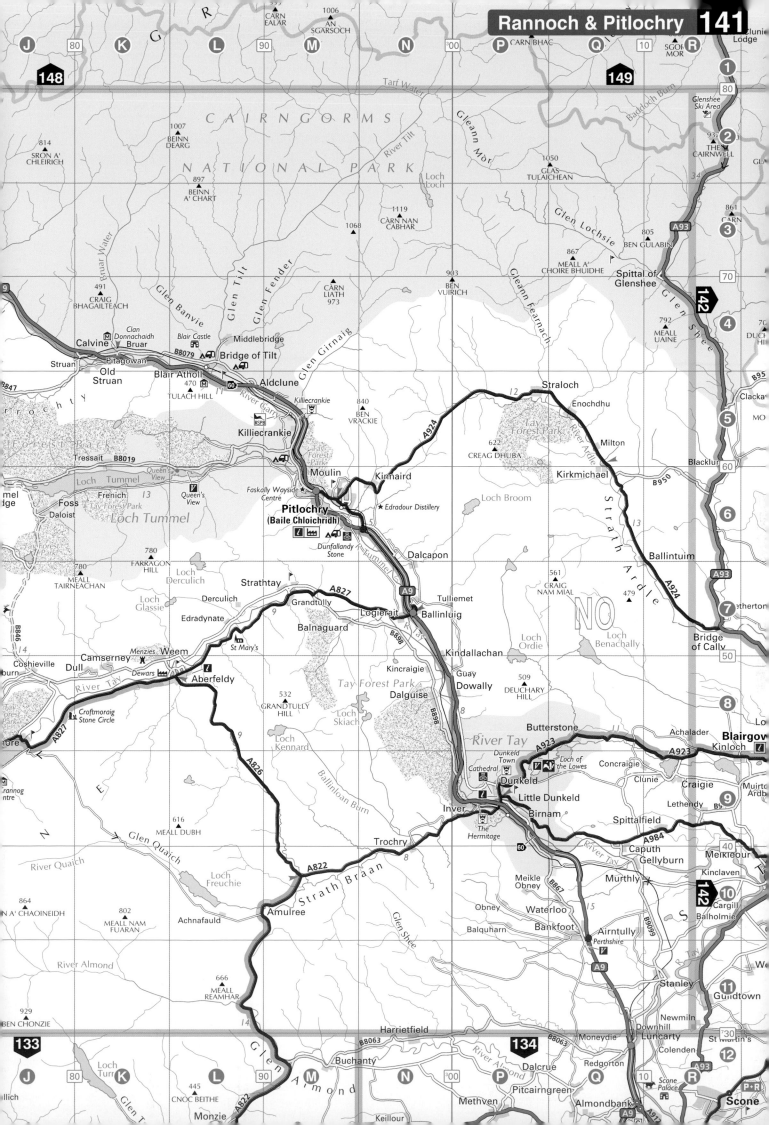

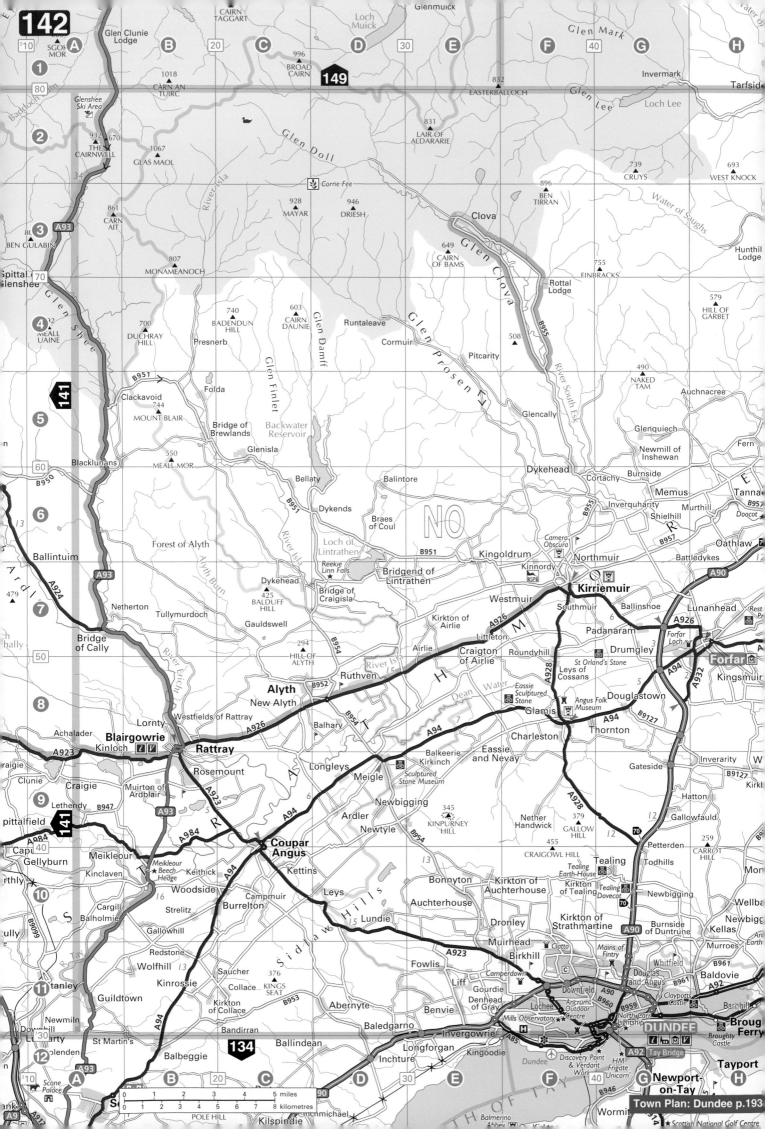

153
154

J 60 K CALPAY L CROWLIN ISLANDS 70 M N P Q 90 R

Eyre Point
Meadhonach
Eilean Mòr
Plockton
Stromeferry

isnish oint
Longay
67
Port-an-Eorr
Duirinish
1
447
BEINN RAIMH
Killilan
30

Dunan
MULLACH NA CARN
396
Pabay
27
Drumbuie
Badicaul
Balmacara
Auchtertyre
Conchra
Camas Luinie
Loch Long
2

Luib
Broadford Bay
Kyle of Lochalsh
(Caol Loch Ailse)
Skye Bridge
Lochalsh Woodland Garden
Kirkton
Nostie
Ardelve
Eilean Donan
Dornie
Bundalloch
Carndu
Loch nan Eun

Corry
Waterloo
Lower Breakish
Kyleakin
Ardelve
Keppoch

708 BEINN NA CAILLICH
732
BEINN DEORG MHOR
Harrapool
Broadford
Skulamus
Upper Breakish
SGURR A'GHAIRGID
840
Inverinate
3

orrin
14
B8083
A87
A851
SGURR NA COINNICH
732
Otter Haven
Kyle Rhea
Bernera
Galltair
603 BEINN A'CHUIRN
Letterfearn
Ratagan
20
Ault a'c Invershiel Shiel Brid

Loch Slapin
BEINN NAN CARN
300
Heast
BEN ASLÀK
605
Kylerhea
(Apr-Oct)
Glenelg Bay
Eilanreach
Glenelg
BEINN A' CHAOINICH
408
Moyle
350 Mam Ratagan
4
FIVE

Suisnish
Rudha Suisnish
Drumfearn
BEINN NA SEAMRAIG
561
Glenelg Brochs
Balvraid
Glean Beag
Glen S

Tokavaig
SGORACH BREAC
298
Duisdalemore
Isleornsay
Ornsay
Sandaig Island
BEINN SGRITHEAL
974
BEINN NAN CAORACH
773
THE SADDLE
1011
5

Ord River
Loch na Dal
17
Rudha Buidhe
Arnisdale
Glen Arnisdale
945 SGURR NA SGINE
10

arskavaig
Achnacloich
Teangue
Knock
Rudh' Ard Slisneach
SOUND OF SLEAT
Loch Hourn
Corran
614
DRUM FADA
709
6

Loch nam Uamph
Ferrindonald
Knock Bay
Inverguseran
BEINN NA CAILLICH
784
Barrisdale Bay
Kinloch Hourn

Kilmore
Kilbeg
Airor
Glen Guseran
DRUM NA CLUAIN-AIRIDHE
518
LADHAR BHEINN
1019
7

Clan Donald
Ardvasar
Calligarry
Armadale
Sandaig
KNOYDART
LUINNE BHEINN
940
Knoydart

Aird of Sleat
Sandaig Bay
Inverie
Inverie Bay
Loch an Dubh-Lochain
8

Ard Thurinish
sleat
int
Rudha Raonuill
Courteachan
Mallaigvaig
CÀRN A'GHOBHAIR
547
BEINN BHUIDHE
854
SGURR NA CICHE
1039

Mallaig (Malaig)
Glasnacardoch Bay
Loch an Nostaire
SGURR BHUIDHE
437
Tarbet
Kylesmorar
SGURR NAH-AIDE
859
Glen De

Beoraidbeg
Morar
Bracorina
Bracora
Swordland
SGARR BREAC
723
9

Glenancross
Loch Morar
Lettermorar
Meoble
AN STAC
716
Glen Pean
90

B8008 A830
Bunacaimb
CÀRN A' MHÀDAIDH-RUAIDH
503
Meoble
MEITH BHEINN
710
949 SGURR NAN COIREACHAN
964 SGT THU
146
10

Eilean Ighe
Back of Keppoch
Arisaig
SIDHEAN MOR
600
Prince Charlie's Cairn
Kinlochnanuagh
633
796 SGURR AN UTHA
11

Luinga Mhòr
Rudh' Arisaig
CRUACH DOIRE
103
Druimindarroch
Arisaig House
10
Polnish
Lochailort
Inverailort
Loch Beoriad
Loch Eilt
14
Glenfinnan Visitor Centre
Glenfinnan
80

Sound of Arisaig
Rudha Choalais
Ardnish
A830
Glenfinnan Monument
12

J 60 K 70 L M A861 N 80 P Q 90 R
Smearisary
Glenuig
ROIS-BHEINN
877
712
BEINN ODHAR BHEAG
882
allie

138

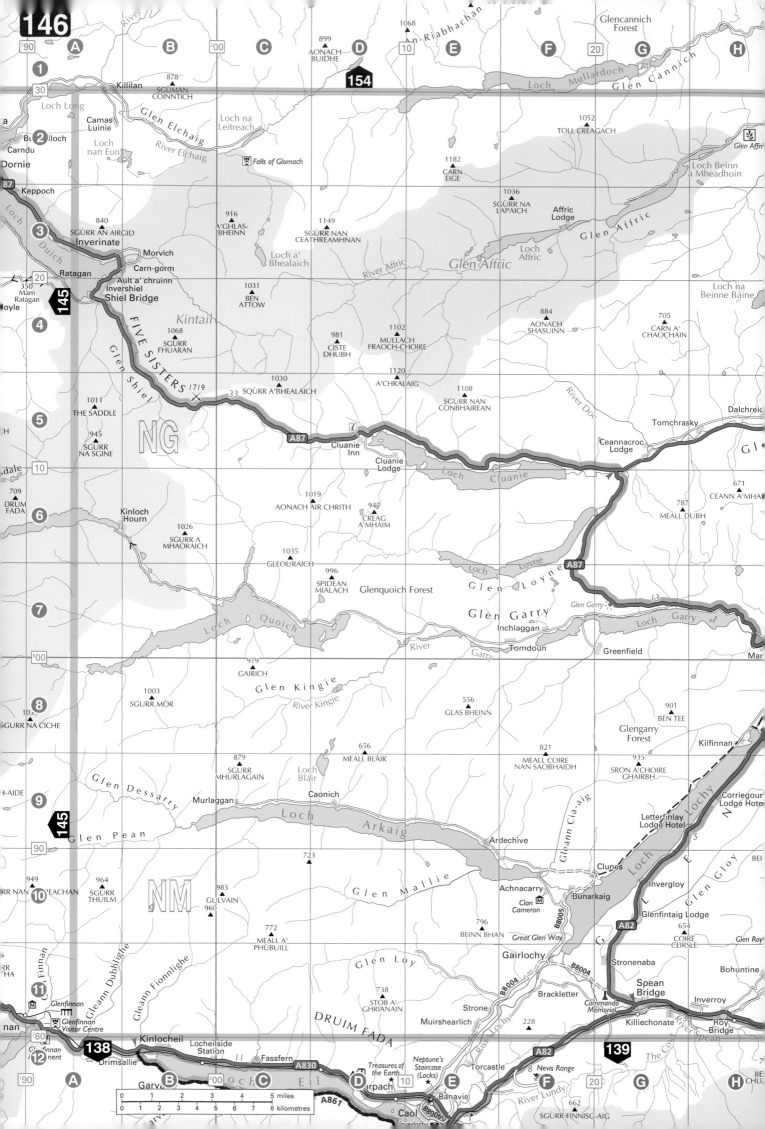

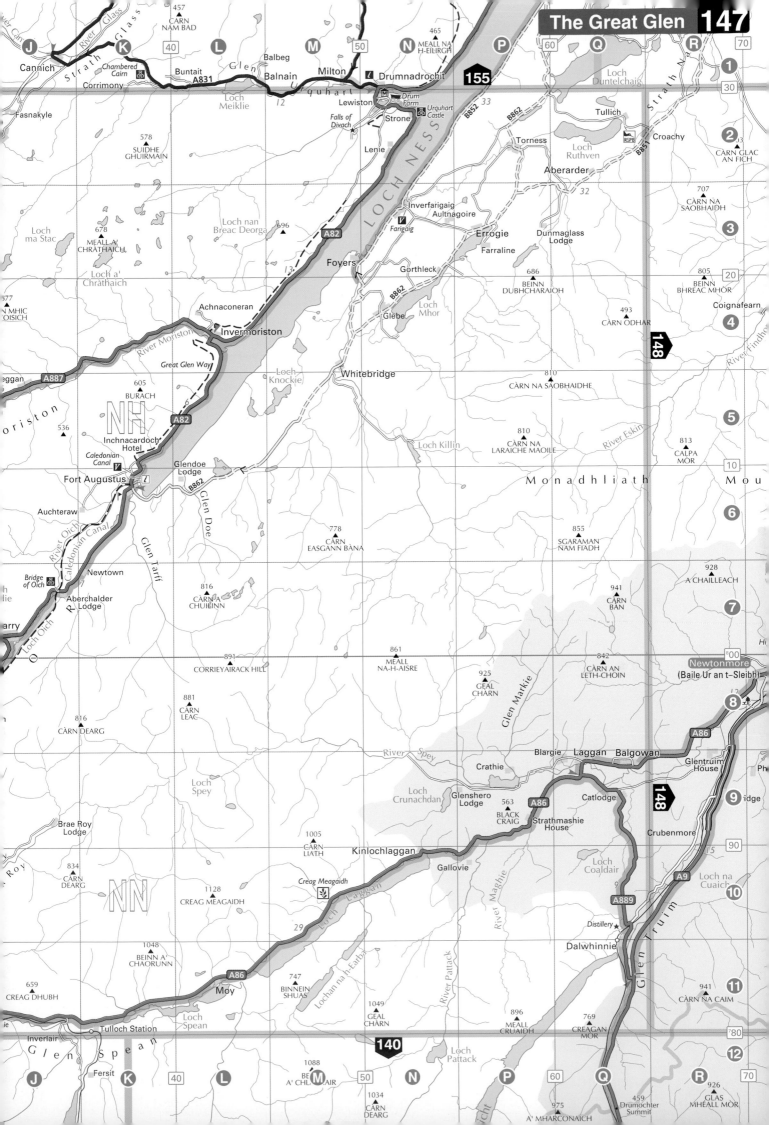

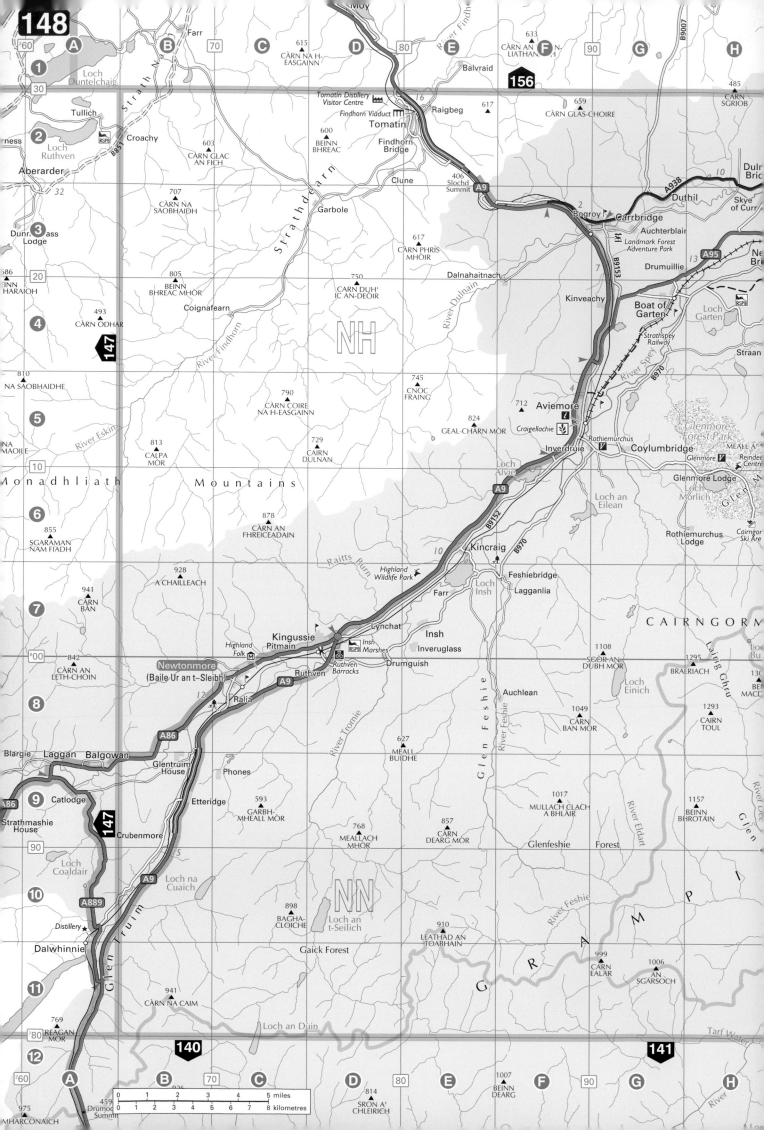

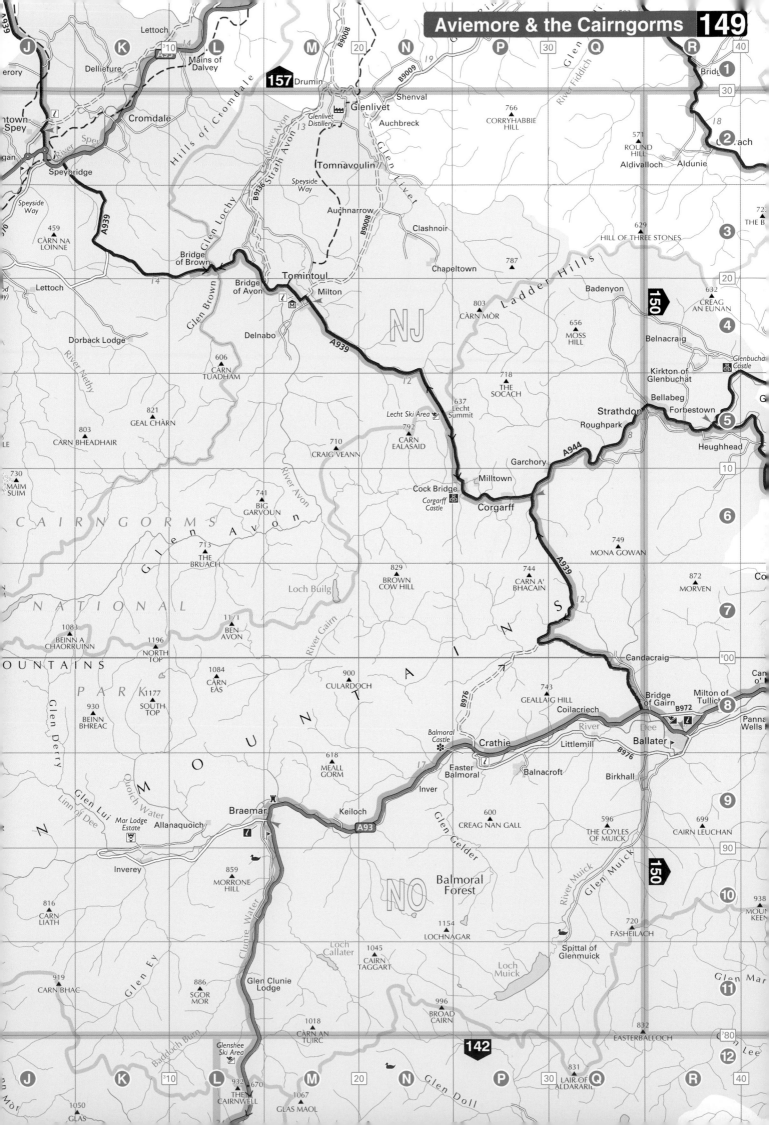

J K L M N P Q R

Lettoch
Delliefure
Mains of Dalvey
`157` Drumin

`1`

B9008
B9009

River Fiddich

`30`
`18`

`2`

Cromdale
Speyside Way
Glenlivet Distillery
Glenlivet
Shenval
Auchbreck

766 ▲
CORRYHABBIE HILL

571 ▲
ROUND HILL
Aldivalloch Aldunie

THE B

Speybridge
River Spey

Tomnavoulin

`13`
Speyside Way

629 ▲
HILL OF THREE STONES

`3`

Speyside Way
459 ▲
CÀRN NA LOINNE
A939

Glen Lochy
B9136 Strath Avon

River Avon

Auchnarrow
B9008

Clashnoir

Badenyon
`150`

632 ▲
CREAG AN EUNAN

`20`

`4`

Lettoch
Glen Brown
Bridge of Brown
`14`

Bridge of Avon
Tomintoul
Milton

Chapeltown
787 ▲

803 ▲
CÀRN MÒR

NJ

Ladder Hills

656 ▲
MOSS HILL

Belnacraig

Glenbucha[t] Castle
Kirkton of Glenbuchat

`5`

Dorback Lodge
606 ▲
CARN TUADHAM
Delnabo

A939

`12`

718 ▲
THE SOCACH

Bellabeg Forbestown
Strathdon
Roughpark

821 ▲
GEAL CHÀRN
803 ▲
CARN BHEADHAIR

710 ▲
CRAIG VEANN

792 ▲
CARN EALASAID

637 Lecht Summit
Lecht Ski Area

A944

`8`

Heughhead
`10`

730 ▲
MAIM SUIM

Garchory

`6`

CAIRNGORMS

River Avon
741 ▲
BIG GARVOUN

Glen Avon

829 ▲
BROWN COW HILL

Milltown
Cock Bridge
Corgarff Castle
Corgarff

749 ▲
MONA GOWAN

872 ▲
MORVEN

Co

NATIONAL

713 ▲
THE BRUACH

Loch Builg

744 ▲
CARN A' BHACAIN

A939

`7`

1083 ▲
BEINN A CHAORRUINN

1171 ▲
BEN AVON

N

`12`

Candacraig
`00`

OUNTAINS

1196 ▲
NORTH TOP

1084 ▲
CÀRN EÀS

900 ▲
CULARDOCH

T
B976

743 ▲
GEALLAIG HILL

Bridge of Gairn
B972

Milton of Tullich
Can o'

`8`

PARK
K 1177 ▲

930 ▲
BEINN BHREAC

1177 ▲
SOUTH TOP

Balmoral Castle

Coilacriech
Crathie
River Dee
Ballater
B976

Panna Wells

Glen Derry

Glen Lui
Linn of Dee

Quoich Water

618 ▲
MEALL GORM

Easter Balmoral
Inver
Littlemill

Balnacroft
Birkhall

`9`

N

Mar Lodge Estate
Braemar
Allanaquoich

Keiloch
A93

Glen Gelder

600 ▲
CREAG NAN GALL

596 ▲
THE COYLES OF MUICK

699 ▲
CAIRN LEUCHAN

`90`

Inverey

859 ▲
MORRONE HILL

NO

Balmoral Forest

River Muick
Glen Muick
`150`

`10`

816 ▲
CARN LIATH

Clunie Water

1154 ▲
LOCHNAGAR

720 ▲
FASHEILACH

938 ▲
MOUN KEEN

919 ▲
CARN BHAC

886 ▲
SGOR MOR

Loch Callater
1045 ▲
CAIRN TAGGART

Spittal of Glenmuick
Loch Muick

`11`

Glen Ey
Glen Clunie Lodge

1018 ▲
CÀRN AN TUIRC

996 ▲
BROAD CAIRN

832 ▲

EASTERBALLOCH
`80`

Glenshee Ski Area

`142`

Glen Mar

`12`

J K L M N P Q R

1050 ▲
GLAS

932 ▲
THE CAIRNWELL
670

1067 ▲
GLAS MAOL

Glen Doll

831 ▲
LAIR OF ALDARARIE

`30` `40`

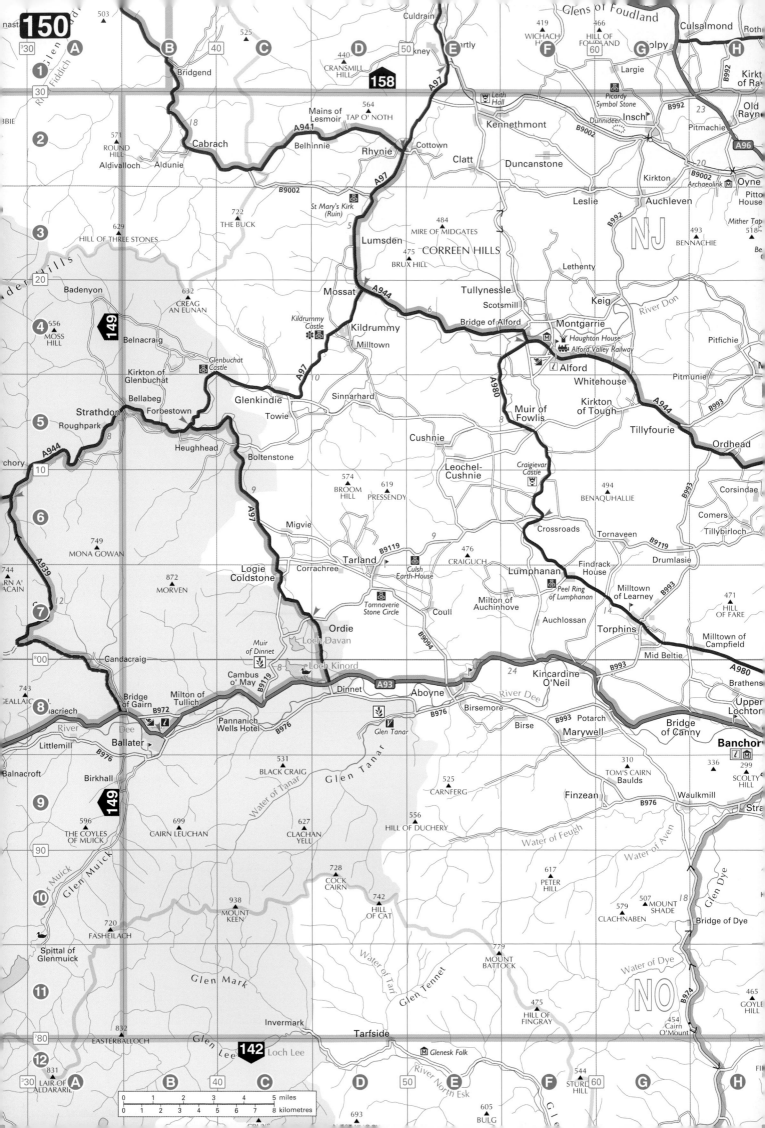

St Katherines
Barthol Chapel
Wedderlairs
Ythanbank
hedly
Ythsie
Whinnyf
J
Folla Rule
Meikle Wartle
Cross of J nton
K
80
Tulloch
L
B9170
M
Tarves
Tomb of William Forbes
159
N
Kinharrachie
P
400
Artrochie
Q
R
10
1
30
seat
Daviot
A920
Craigdam
Ellon
P·R
Kirkton of Logie Buchan
Colliestone
Kirktown of Slains
Loanhead Stone Circle
A920
Oldmeldrum
Tolquhon Castle
Esslemont
B9005
32
2
Pitmedden Garden
Pitmedden
A920
10
Logierieve
Forvie
o
ford
B9001
Carnbrogie
Housieside
B9000
B9000
Newburgh
Kirktown of Bourtie
Whiterashes
Pettymuk
B9000
Udny Green
Woodland
Tillygreig
Udny Station
Cultercullen
Foveran
A90
A975
NK
3
aiden Stone
B9170
Brandsbutt Symbol Stone
Nether Crimond
Straloch
Culterculle
Reisque
B979
Delfrigs
17
20
pel of rioch
Inverurie
A947
Newmachar
Whitecairns
Causeyend
Balmedie
Balmedie
4
Easter Aquhorthies Stone Circle
Kinmuck
B979
Belhelvie
B977
Port Elphinstone
Kinkell Church
B993
Kinmundy
Cothal
18
B977
Potterton
Burnhervie
Hatton of Fintray
B977
Dyce Symbol Stones
Blackdog
5
Kemnay
B994
Kintore
B977
Cottown
B979
Overton
Aberdeen
Dyce
B999
B997
Denmore
Craigearn
Leylodge
Blackburn
B979
A96
Stoneywood
Middleton Park
A90
30
Bridge-of-Don
P·R
Kirkwall Lerwick
V
10
Castle Fraser
16
Clinterty
70
40
Buckburn
Bankhead
40
30
A96
Old Aberdeen
6
Lyne of Skene
Skene House
B9126
Millbuie
B979
265
BRIMMOND HILL
30
40
Northfield
Kittybrewster
H
Dunecht
27
Loch of Skene
Westhill
P·R
Kingswells
Kingsford
B9119
ABERDEEN
40
Barmekin
burgh
B9119
Kirkton of Skene
Carnie
Elrick
A944
C
7
Garlogie
25
Echt
B9119
B979
Redhill
Cullerlie Stone Circle
Easter Ord
Blacktop
Ruthrieston
Torry
Nigg Bay
Landerberry
Cullerlie
B9125
Benthoul
Bieldside
Mannofield
Kincorth
A956
Nigg
Hardgate
Craigton
Milltimber
Milton of Murtle
Banchory-Devenick
40
Altens Haven
Hirn
B977
Drum Castle
18
Peterculter
Kingcausie
B9077
Charlestown
A90
Cove Bay
West Park
Myrbird
River Dee
Maryculter
Marywell
800
mfrennie
The Neuk
A93
Crathes Castle
B9077
Hillside
Auchlee
Findon
Crathes
Durris
Denside
Woodlands
70
Portlethen
Cammachmore Bay
Royal Deeside Railway
Crossroads
Cammachmore
Downies
Cookney
Netherley
Newtonhill
Skateraw
A957
B979
Muchalls
376
MONGOUR
90
Doonie Point
A90
Garron Point
Stonehaven Bay
320
HILL OF TRUSTA
70
Kirktown of Fetteresso
Stonehaven
390
LEACHIE HILL
Elfhill
Tannachie
A90
Dunnottar
Goosecruives
New Mill
70
Drumlithie
B979
Glenbervie
Mondynes
Temple of Fiddes
10
143
Crawton
Fowlsheugh Trelong Bay
enblae
B967
J
K
80
L
Kinneff
M
rline
90
N
Todhead Point
Arbuthnott

Aberdeen Harbour

ELGIN
PETERHEAD
A956
KING STREET
B886
A96
PARK STREET
BEACH BOULEVARD
ESPLANADE
500 m
A944
WESTBURN ROAD
HUTCHEON STREET
B983
B985
SKENE
B9119
B983
UNION
STREET
MARKET STREET
Victoria Dock
FERRY TERMINAL
Albert Basin
Footdee
North Pier
ABERDEEN STATION
A93
WILLOWBANK RD
STREET
Ferryhill
A956
SINCLAIR ROAD
VICTORIA ROAD
ST
River Dee
HOLBURN
B9077
WELLINGTON RD
Torry
BALNAGASK ROAD
GIRDLENESS ROAD
DRIVE
A9013
A945
RIVERSIDE
DUNDEE
LLC

Town Plan: Aberdeen p.182

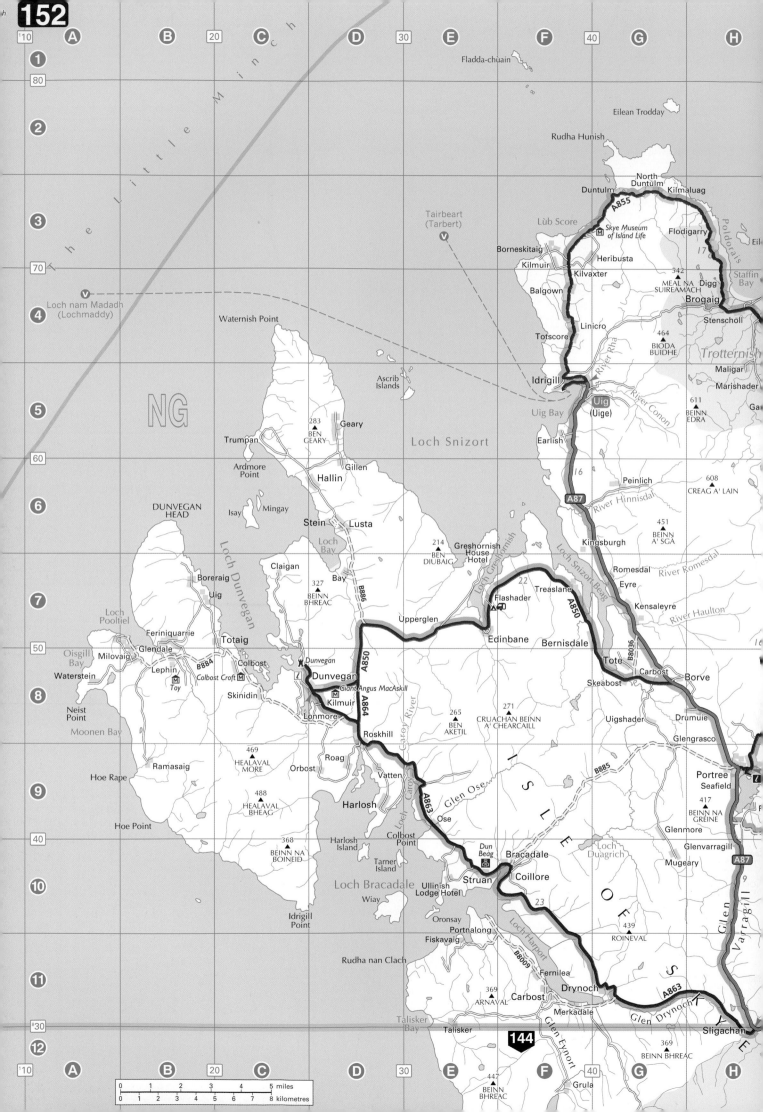

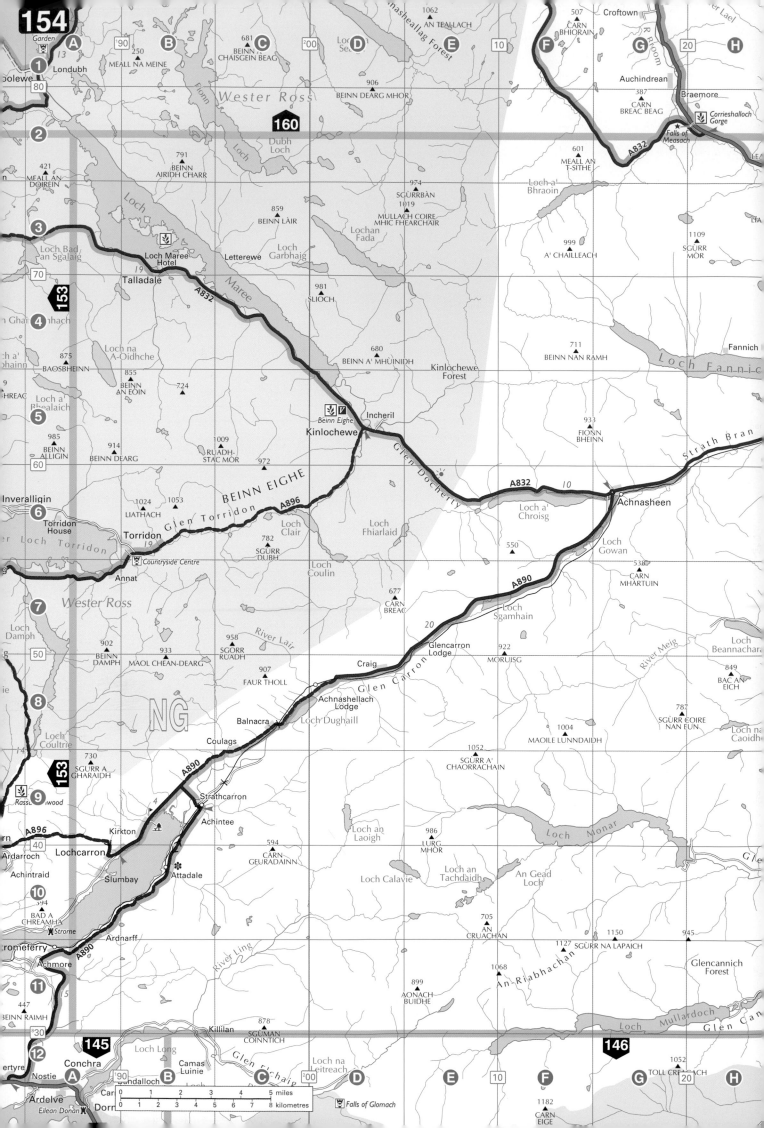

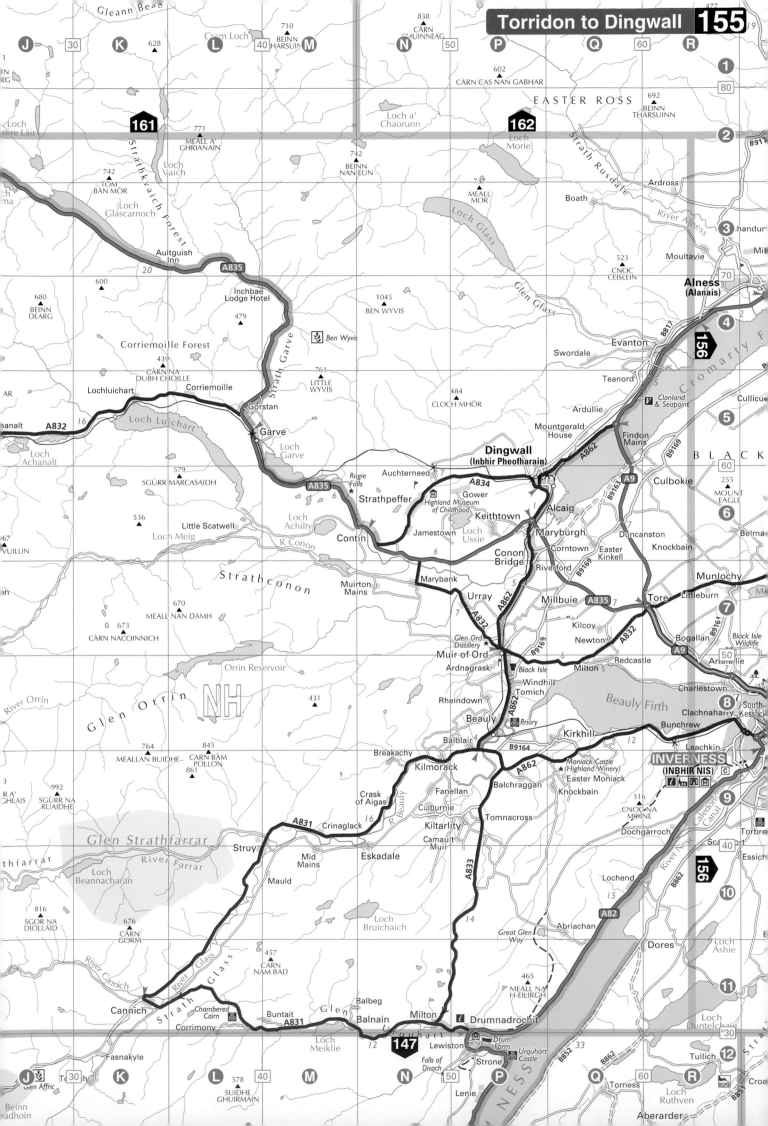

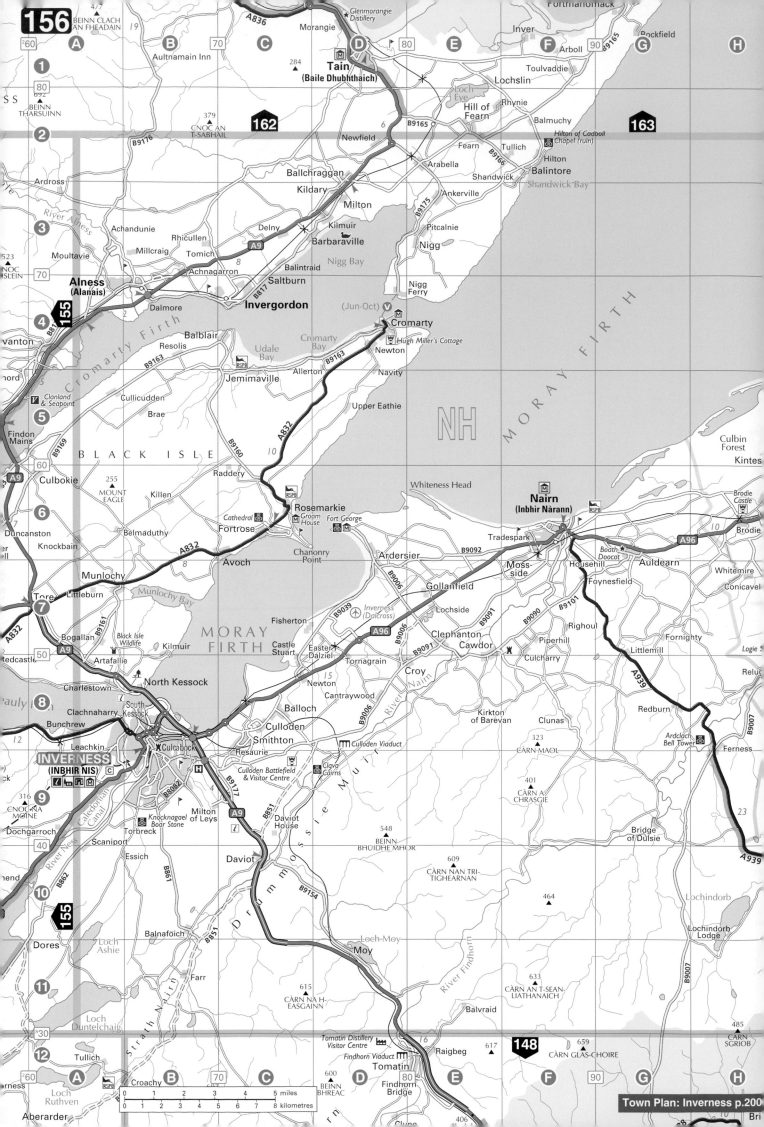

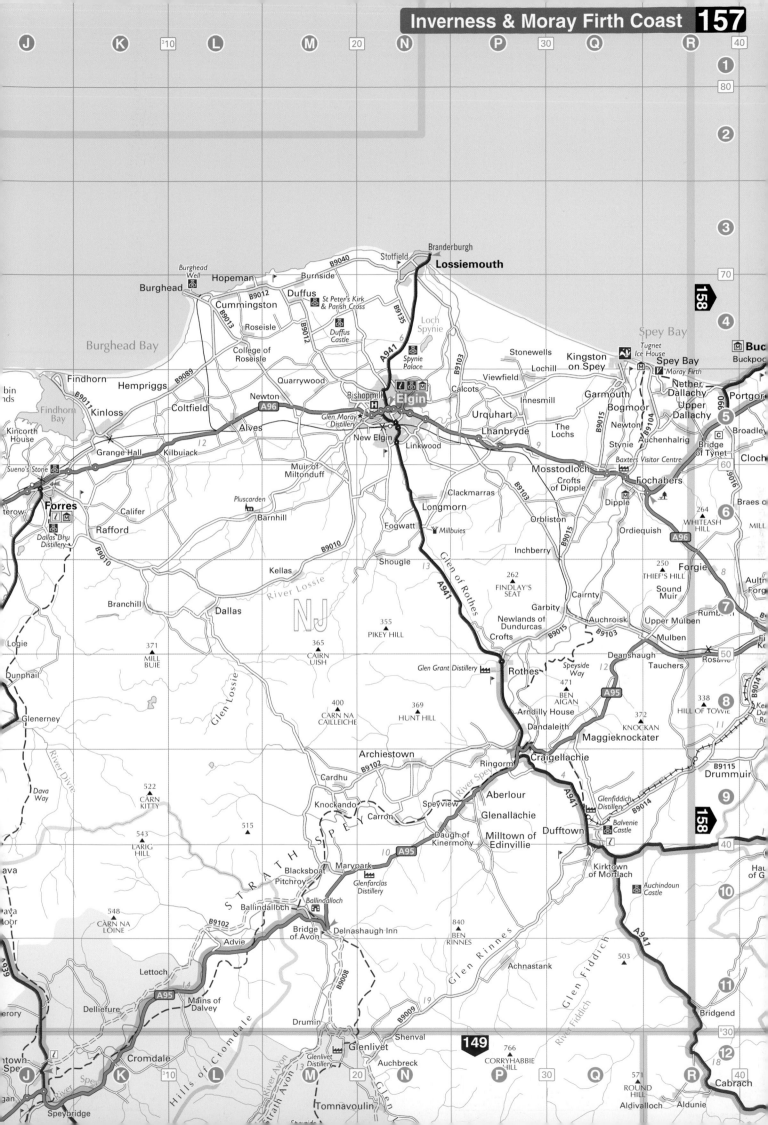

J   K ³10   L   M 20   N   P 30   Q   R 40

1   80

2

3

158   70

4

Branderburgh
Stotfield
Lossiemouth

B9040

Burnside

Burghead Well
Hopeman
Duffus
St Peter's Kirk & Parish Cross
Burghead
Cummingston
B9012
Spey Bay
Roseisle
B9012
Loch Spynie
Tugnet Ice House
Spey Bay
Bu

B9013
B9135
Duffus Castle
Stonewells
Kingston on Spey
Nether Dallachy
Upper Dallachy
Portgor

College of Roseisle
Spynie Palace
Lochill
Viewfield
Garmouth
B9015
Broadle

Findhorn
Hempriggs
B9089
Quarrywood
Newton
A96
Bishopmill
Elgin
Calcots
Innesmill
Bogmoor
Newton
Stynie
Auchenhalrig
Bridge of Tynet
Cloch

5   60 9016

Kincorth House
Kinloss
Coltfield
Alves
Glen Moray Distillery
New Elgin
Urquhart
Lhanbryde
The Lochs
Baxters Visitor Centre
Mosstodloch
Fochabers

Findhorn Bay

Forres

Sueno's Stone
Grange Hall
Kilbuiack
Linkwood
Clackmarras
Longmorn
Crofts of Dipple
B9103
Orbliston
B9015
Dipple
Ordiequish
A96
WHITEASH HILL
Braes of G
MILL

6 264

Dallas Dhu Distillery
Califer
Muir of Miltonduff
Pluscarden
Barnhill
Fogwatt
Millbuies
Inchberry
250 Forgie
THIEF'S HILL

Rafford
B9010
Kellas
Shougle
Glen of Rothes
A941
FINDLAY'S SEAT 262
Garbity
Cairnty
Newlands of Dundurcas
Auchroisk
Sound Muir
Upper Mulben
Rumbl
8

7

Branchill
Dallas
NJ
PIKEY HILL 355
13
Crofts
B9015
B9103
Mulben
Ke
Fi

Logie
371 MILL BUIE
CAIRN UISH 365
Glen Grant Distillery
Rothes
Speyside Way
Deanshaugh
Tauchers
Rosar
50

8 471 BEN AIGAN
338 HILL OF TOWIE

Dunphail
River Lossie
400 CARN NA CAILLEICHE
369 HUNT HILL
Arndilly House
12
A95
372 KNOCKAN
11

Glenerney
Glen Lossie
Dandaleith
Maggieknockater
B9115
Drummuir

9

River Divie
Archiestown
B9102
Ringorm
Craigellachie
Glenfiddich Distillery
B9014

Dava Way
Cardhu
River Spey
Aberlour
4
Balvenie Castle
158 40

Glenallachie
A941
Speyview

522 CARN KITTY
Knockando
Carron
Milltown of Edinvillie
Dufftown

10

515
Daugh of Kinermony
Kirktown of Mortlach
Auchindoun Castle
Hau of G

543 LARIG HILL
Marypark
A95
10
Blacksboat
Pitchroy

STRATHSPEY

11

548 CARN NA LOINE
Ballindalloch
Glenfarclas Distillery
Bridge of Avon
840 BEN RINNES
Glen Rinnes
Achnastank
503
A941
Bridgend

B9102
Advie
Delnashaugh Inn
Glen Fiddich

Lettoch
A95
14
Mains of Dalvey
B9008
19
12 18

Drumin
B9009
149
766 CORRYHABBIE HILL
Shenval
571 ROUND HILL
R 40 Cabrach

Cromdale
Hills of Cromdale
Glenlivet Distillery
Glenlivet
Auchbreck
Aldivalloch
Aldunie

Speybridge
River Spey
Strath Avon
13
Tomnavoulin

J   K ³10   L   M 20   N   P 30   Q   R 40

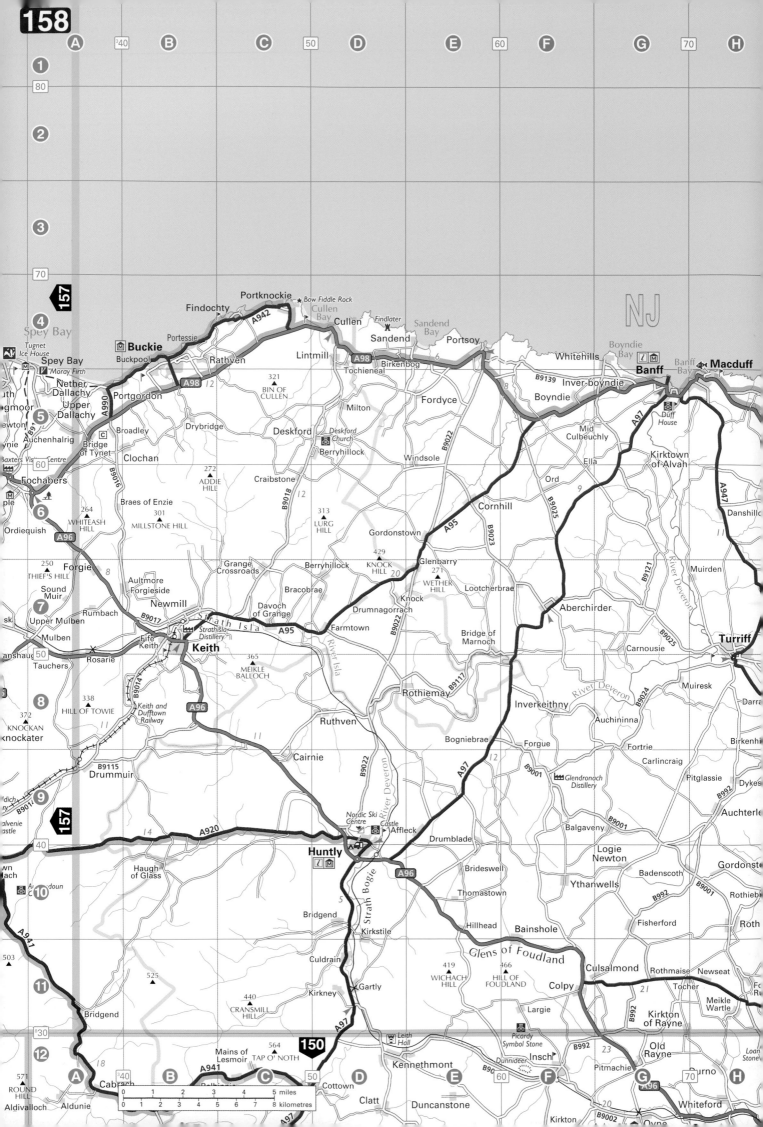

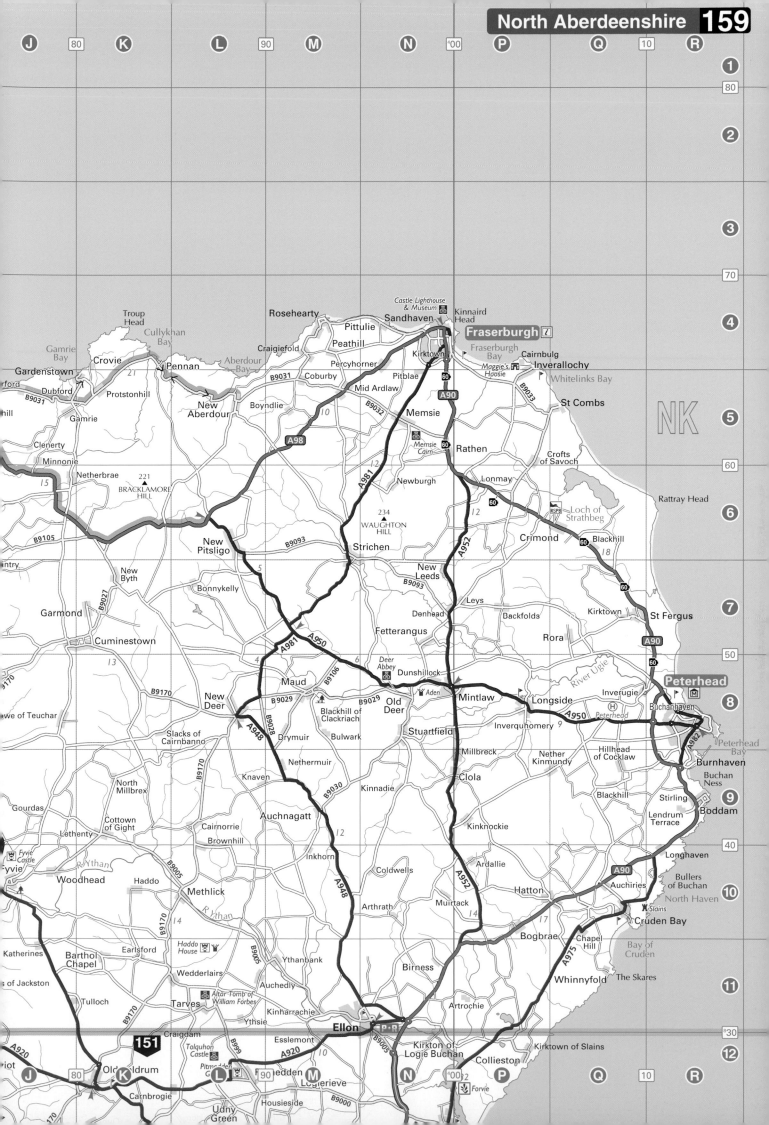

NK

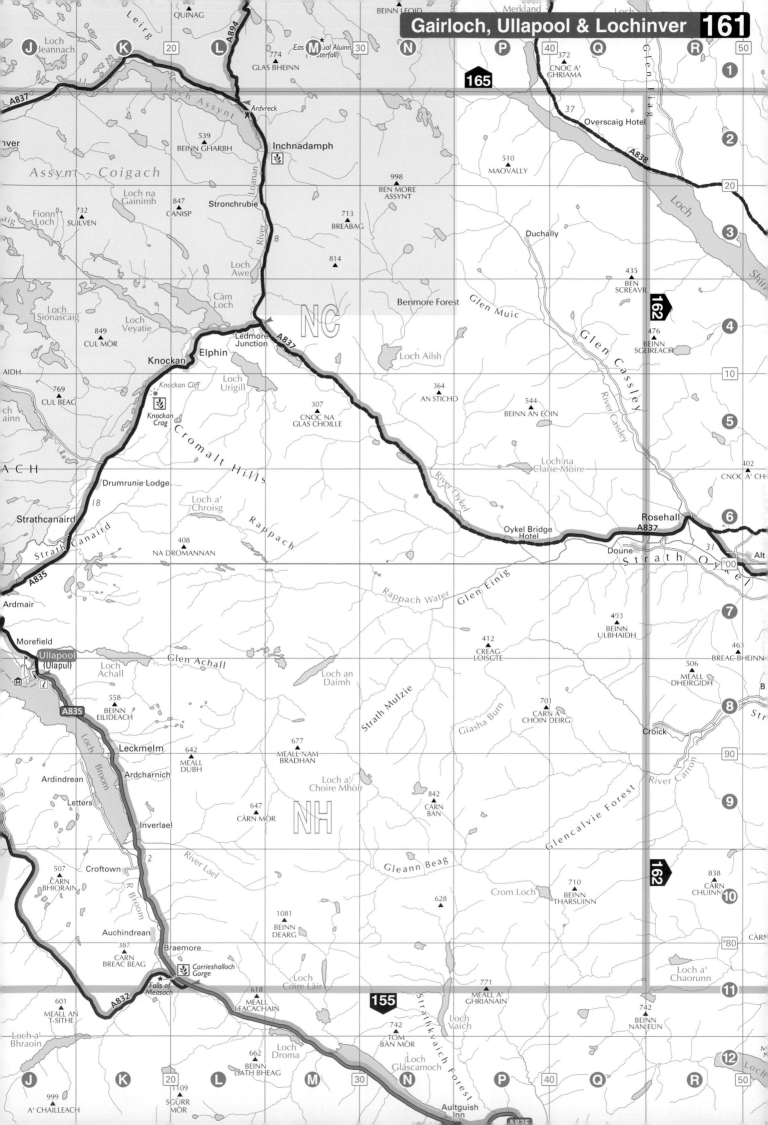

J   K   20   L   A894   M   30   N   P   40   Q   R   50

165
162
155

A837
A894
A838
A835
A832

Loch Beannach
QUINAG
Leirg
774 GLAS BHEINN
Eas ★ Mual Aluinn (Waterfall)
Merkland
BEINN LEOID
372 CNOC A' GHRIAMA
Glen Fiag
Loch

Ardvreck
Loch Assynt
539 BEINN GHARBH
Inchnadamph
Overscaig Hotel

Assynt - Coigach
847 CANISP
Stronchrubie
River Loanan
8
998 BEN MORE ASSYNT
510 MAOVALLY
Duchally
Loch Shin

Fionn Loch
732 SUILVEN
Loch na Gainimh
713 BREABAG
435 BEN SCREAVIL
162

Loch Veyatie
814
Càm Loch
Loch Awe
476 BEINN SGEIREACH

Loch Sionascaig
849 CUL MÒR
Ledmore Junction
A837
NC
Benmore Forest
Glen Muic
Glen Cassley
River Cassley
10

Knockan
Elphin
Loch Urigill
Loch Ailsh
CUL BEAG 769
Knockan Cliff
Knockan Crag
364 AN STICHD
544 BEINN AN EÒIN
402 CNOC A' CH

AIDH
ch ainn
307 CNOC NA GLAS CHOILLE
Cromalt Hills
Loch na Claise-Mòire

Drumrunie Lodge
Rappach
River Oykel
Rosehall A837
6

Strathcanaird
18
Strath Canaird
408 NA DROMANNAN
Loch a' Chroisg
Oykel Bridge Hotel
Doune
Strath Oykel
Alt

A835
Rappach Water
Glen Einig
7

Ardmair
493 BEINN ULBHAIDH
463 BREAC-BHEINN

Morefield
Glen Achall
Loch an Daimh
412 CREAG LOISGTE
506 MEALL DHEIRGIDH
8

Ullapool (Ulapul)
Loch Achall
Strath Mulzie
Giasha Burn
701 CARN A' CHOIN DEIRG
Croick
90

M
i
558 BEINN EILIDEACH
642 MEALL DUBH
677 MEALL NAM BRADHAN
River Carron
9

Leckmelm
Ardcharnich
Loch a' Choire Mhòir
842 CARN BAN
Glencalvie Forest

Letters
Ardindrean
647 CÀRN MOR
NH

Inverlael
River Lael
Gleann Beag
162
838 CÀRN CHUINN
10

Croftown
507 CÀRN BHIORAIN
R Broom
12
1081 BEINN DEARG
628
Crom Loch
710 BEINN THARSUINN

Auchindrean
387 CARN BREAC BEAG
Braemore
Corrieshalloch Gorge
771 MEALL A' GHRIANAIN
Loch a' Chaorunn
11

Loch-a' Bhraoin
601 MEALL AN T-SITHE
A832
★ Falls of Measach
618 MEALL LEACACHAIN
Loch Coire Làir
155
Loch Vaich
742 BEINN NAN EUN

662 BEINN LIATH BHEAG
Loch Droma
742 TOM BÀN MÒR
Loch Glascarnoch
Strathvaich Forest
12

J   K   20   L   30   M   30   N   P   40   Q   R   50

999 A' CHAILLEACH
1109 SGURR MÒR
Aultguish Inn
A835

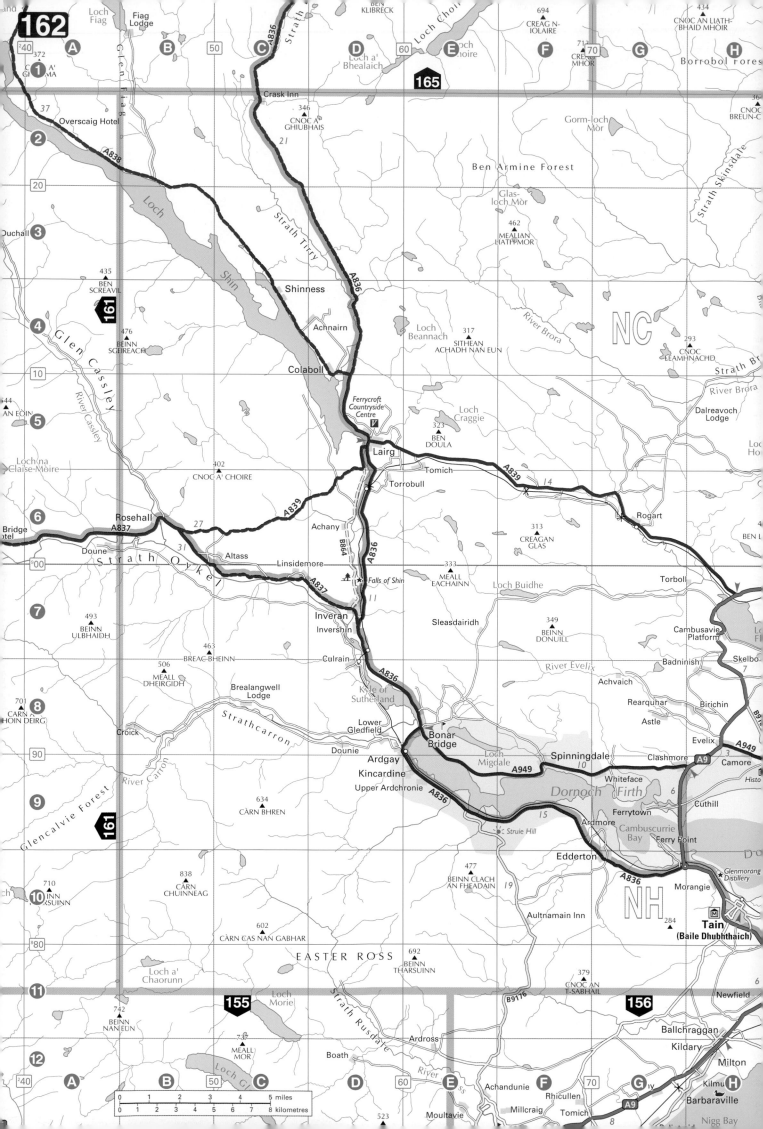

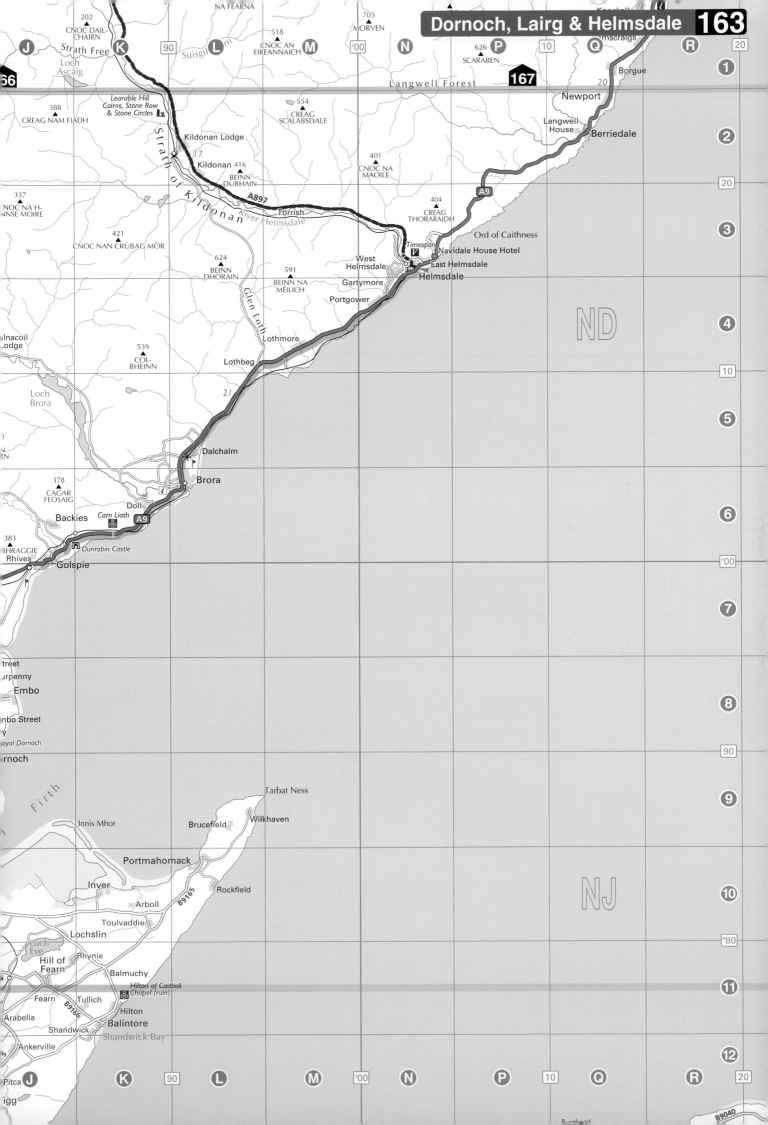

NA FEARNA

CNOC DAIL-CHAIRN 202

J K 90 Suisgil L CNOC AN EIREANNAICH M 300 N 705 MORVEN SCARABEN 626 P 10 Q smscraigs R 20

① 1

Strath Free

167

Loch Ascaig

66

Langwell Forest Borgue

20

Learable Hill Cairns, Stone Row & Stone Circles

Newport

② 2

CREAG NAM FIADH 388

Kildonan Lodge

CREAG SCALABSDALE 554

Langwell House

Berriedale

17

Strath of Kildonan

Kildonan 416 BEINN DUBHAIN

401 CNOC NA MAOILE

20

337 NOC NA H- NNSE MOIRE

A897

River Helmsdale

Torrish

404 CREAG THORARAIDH

A9

③ 3

CNOC NAN CRÙBAG MÒR 421

BEINN DHORAIN 624

Glen Loth

591 BEINN NA MÈILICH

West Helmsdale

Timespan

Gartymore

Portgower

Ord of Caithness

Navidale House Hotel

East Helmsdale

Helmsdale

ND

④ 4

Inacoil odge

539 COL-BHEINN

Lothmore

10

Lothbeg

⑤ 5

Loch Brora

21

Dalchalm

Brora

⑥ 6

378 CAGAR FEOSAIG

Doll

A9

Backies Carn Liath

383 BHRAGGIE Rhives Dunrobin Castle

300

⑦ 7

Golspie

treet urpenny

Embo

⑧ 8

nbo Street

oyal Dornoch

90

rnoch

⑨ 9

Firth

Tarbat Ness

Innis Mhor

Brucefield

Wilkhaven

Portmahomack

NJ

⑩ 10

Inver

B9165

Rockfield

Arboll

80

Toulvaddie

Lochslin

Loch Eye

Rhynie

Hilton of Cadboll Chapel (ruin)

⑪ 11

Hill of Fearn

Balmuchy

Fearn B9166 Tullich

Hilton

Arabella

Balintore

Shandwick

Ankerville

Shandwick Bay

⑫ 12

Pitca J

igg

K 90 L 300 M N P 10 Q R 20

Burghead

B9040

J 40 K L 50 M N 60 P Q 70 R
1
2
70
3
166
Ardmore Poin
Kirtomy Point M

Faraid
Head

Balnakeil
Bay

Balnakeil ⓘ
Durness
Sangomore
Keoldale
Smoo
Sangobeg

Sango
Bay
Smoo
Cave

Eilean Hoan

Whiten
Head

408 ▲
BEN HUTIG

Strathan

Rabbit
Islands

Eilean
Nan Ròn

Neave Island

Skerray

Torrisdale
Bay

Farr
Bay

Farr
Kirtom

Swordly

4

Loch
Meadaidh

423 ▲
MEALL
MEADHONACH

Loch Eriboll

Talmine

Melness
Midtown

Tongue
Bay

Achtoty
Scullomie
Torrisdale

Bettyhill

Invernaver

Achina

60
M

A838

230 ▲
BEN
ARNABOLL

A838

Laid

489 ▲
MEALL
NA CRÀ

773 ▲
EINN
NNAIDH
IE

Strath Beag

A838

31

262 ▲
DRUIM
NAN CLIAR

Kyle of Tongue

Tongue

Coldbackie

Borgie

River Borgie

13

A836

Skelpick

Skelpick Burn

Strath Naver

5

310 ▲
MEALL LEATHAD
NA CRAOIBHE

520 ▲
AN LEAN-CHÀRN

Loch Hope

Loch na
Seilg

927 ▲
BEN
HOPE

Strath More

MEALLAN
LIATH

598 ▲

Kinloch

Kyle of Tongue

318 ▲
CNOC
CRAGGIE

17

Loch
Craggie

527 ▲
BEINN
STUMANADH

Loch
Loyal

NC

213 ▲
CNOC
MALPELLY

B871

12

50

6

Loch S
7

River Hope

Loch an
Deerie

763 ▲
BEN
LOYAL

Loyal Lodge

Loch
Syre

33
MEALL
NA CU

463 ▲
FEINNE-BHEINN MHÒR

Dun Dornaigil
Broch

Glen Golly

729 ▲
SÀBHAL BEAG

656 ▲
CNOC AN
DÀIMH MÒR

557 ▲
CNOC NAN
CUILEAN

Syre

River Naver

8

Loch
Meadie

294 ▲
POLE
HILL

259 ▲
BEINN
ROSAIL

B871

40

MH

796 ▲
CÀRN
DEARG

757 ▲
CARN AN
TIONAIL

12

B873

9

Loch Coire na
Saidhe Duibhe

ch

230 ▲
MEALL A'
BHROLLAICH

Strath Naver

Loch Naver

270 ▲
BEADAIG

River Mallart

Loch
Rimsdale

Loch
nan C

Altnaharra

873 ▲
BEN
HEE

680 ▲
MEALL AN
LIATH MÒR

Loch a'
Ghorm-choire

166

Loch an
Altán F

10

613
FHEUR LOCH

472 ▲
MEALL AN
FHUARAIN

Ben Klibreck

959 ▲
BEN
KLIBRECK

Loch Choire Forest

694 ▲
CREAG N-
IOLAIRE

Loch
Truderscaig

30

Loch
Merkland

Loch
Fiag

Fiag
Lodge

A836

Strath Bagastie

Loch a'
Bhealaich

Loch
Choire

713 ▲
CREAG
MHÒR

434
CNOC AN
BHAID M

11

Borro

372 ▲
CNOC A'
GHRIAMA

37

Overscaig Hotel

A838

Glen Fiag

Crask Inn

346 ▲
CNOC A'
GHIUBHAIS

21

162

Gorm-loch
Mòr

12

510
MAOVALLY

J 40 K L 50 M 60 N P Q 70 R

Ben Armine Forest

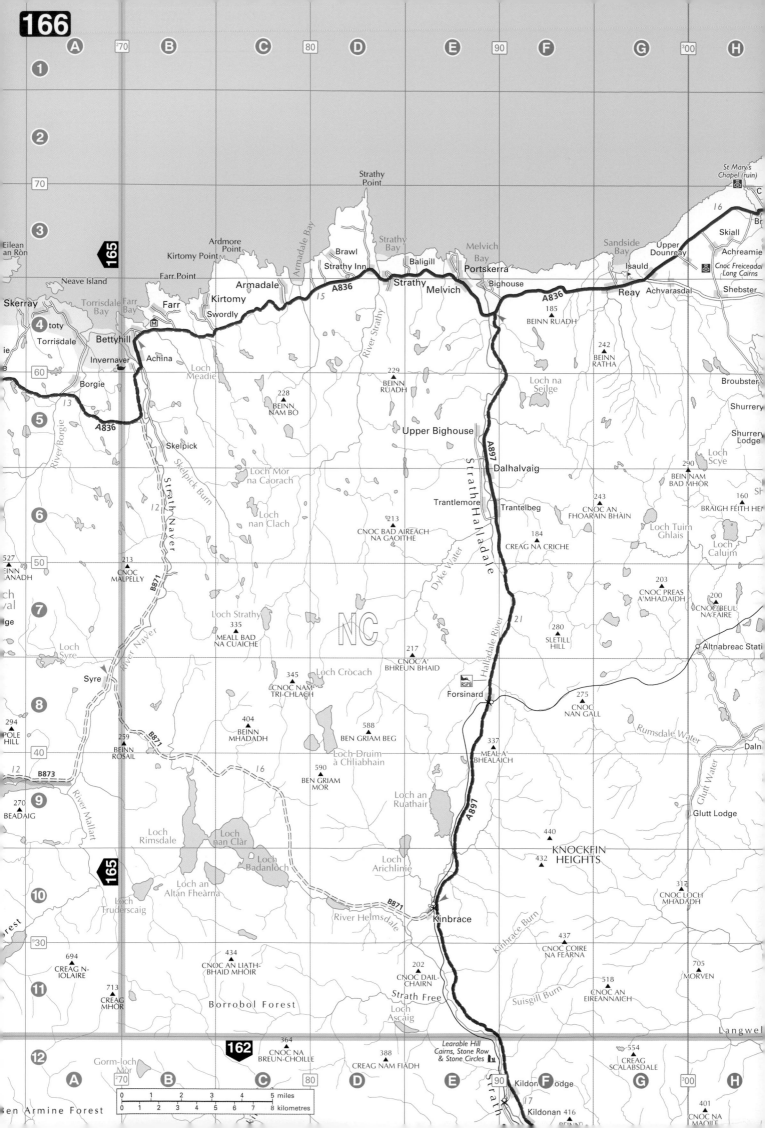

PENTLAND FIRTH

Langaton Point
Nethertown
Meil Head Uppertown
ISLAND OF STROMA
St Margaret's Hope
DUNCANSBY HEAD

DUNNET HEAD
Briga Head
Stromness
Holborn Head
Scrabster
Thurso Bay
Thurso

DUNNET HILL
Brough
St John's Loch
West Dunnet
Dunnet
Dunnet Bay
Murkle
Castlehill
Castletown
Scarfskerry
Castle of Mey
Loch Mey
Mey
Rattar
Barrock
Gills Bay
Kirkstyle
Huna
Gills
Canisbay
John o' Groats
Muckle Stack
Stacks of Duncansby
Skirza
Freswick
Freswick Bay
Ness Head

Glengolly
Westfield
Weydale
Hilliclay
Olrig House
Tain
Inkstack
Brabstermire
Greenland
Slickly
Gill Burn
Auckengill
Broch
Nybster
Brough Head

Loch Calder
Sordale
Knockdee
Roadside
Clayock
Gillock
Halcro
Bowermadden
Bower
Lyth
Sortat
Howe
Mireland
Keiss
Burn of Lyth

Scotscalder Station
Halkirk
Georgemas Junction Station
Loch Scarmclate
Kirk
Loch of Wester
Killimster
Sinclair Bay
Castle Girnigoe & Sinclair
Noss Head

Harpsdale
SPITTAL HILL
Loch Watten
Reiss
Winless
Sibster
Ackergill
Wick John o' Groats

Olgrinmore
River Thurso
Spittal
Watten
Bilbster
Haster
Milton
Janetstown
Wick
Wick Bay
Papigoe
Staxigoe

Westerdale
Mybster
Loch of Toftingall
Loch of Toftingall
Newton
Old Wick
South Head
Castle of Old Wick
Whiterow

BEINN CHÀITEAG
Loch Ruard
Loch Stemster
Badlipster
BALLHARN HILL
Grey Cairns of Camster
Tannach
Loch Hempriggs

Loch More
Loch Sand
Achavanich
Loch Rangag
STEMSTER HILL
HILL OF YARROWS
Loch of Yarrows
Thrumster
Sarclet

Loch an Thulachan
COIRE NA BEINN
Cairn o'Get
Ulbster
Whaligoe
Whaligoe Steps

CNOCAN CONACHREAG
BEN-A-CHIELT
Upper Lybster
Roster
Hill o'Many Stanes
Bruan
Mid Clyth
Halberry Head

Swiney
Occumster
Clyth Ness
Invershore
Lybster
Lybster Bay

Houstry
Landhallow
Forse
Smerral
Latheron
Latheronwheel
Janetstown
Laidhay Croft

Dunbeath Water
Knockally
Dunbeath
Ramscraigs

ARABEN
Braemore
ale Water
Borgue
Newport
163
Langwell House
riedale

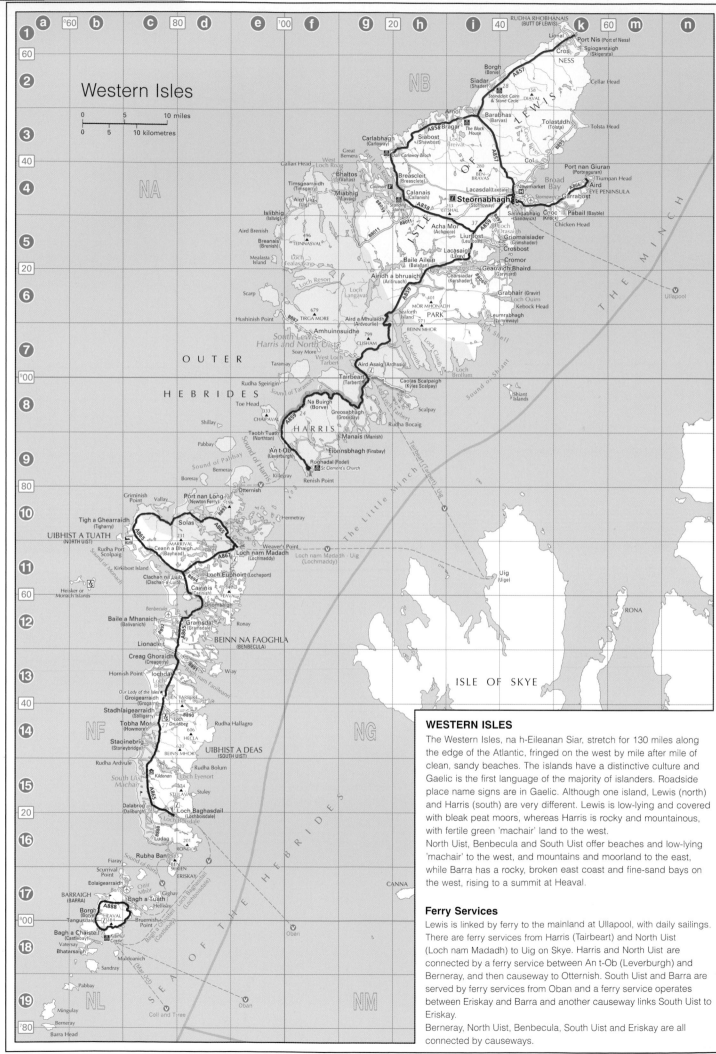

WESTERN ISLES

The Western Isles, na h-Eileanan Siar, stretch for 130 miles along the edge of the Atlantic, fringed on the west by mile after mile of clean, sandy beaches. The islands have a distinctive culture and Gaelic is the first language of the majority of islanders. Roadside place name signs are in Gaelic. Although one island, Lewis (north) and Harris (south) are very different. Lewis is low-lying and covered with bleak peat moors, whereas Harris is rocky and mountainous, with fertile green 'machair' land to the west.

North Uist, Benbecula and South Uist offer beaches and low-lying 'machair' to the west, and mountains and moorland to the east, while Barra has a rocky, broken east coast and fine-sand bays on the west, rising to a summit at Heaval.

Ferry Services

Lewis is linked by ferry to the mainland at Ullapool, with daily sailings. There are ferry services from Harris (Tairbeart) and North Uist (Loch nam Madadh) to Uig on Skye. Harris and North Uist are connected by a ferry service between An t-Ob (Leverburgh) and Berneray, and then causeway to Otternish. South Uist and Barra are served by ferry services from Oban and a ferry service operates between Eriskay and Barra and another causeway links South Uist to Eriskay.

Berneray, North Uist, Benbecula, South Uist and Eriskay are all connected by causeways.

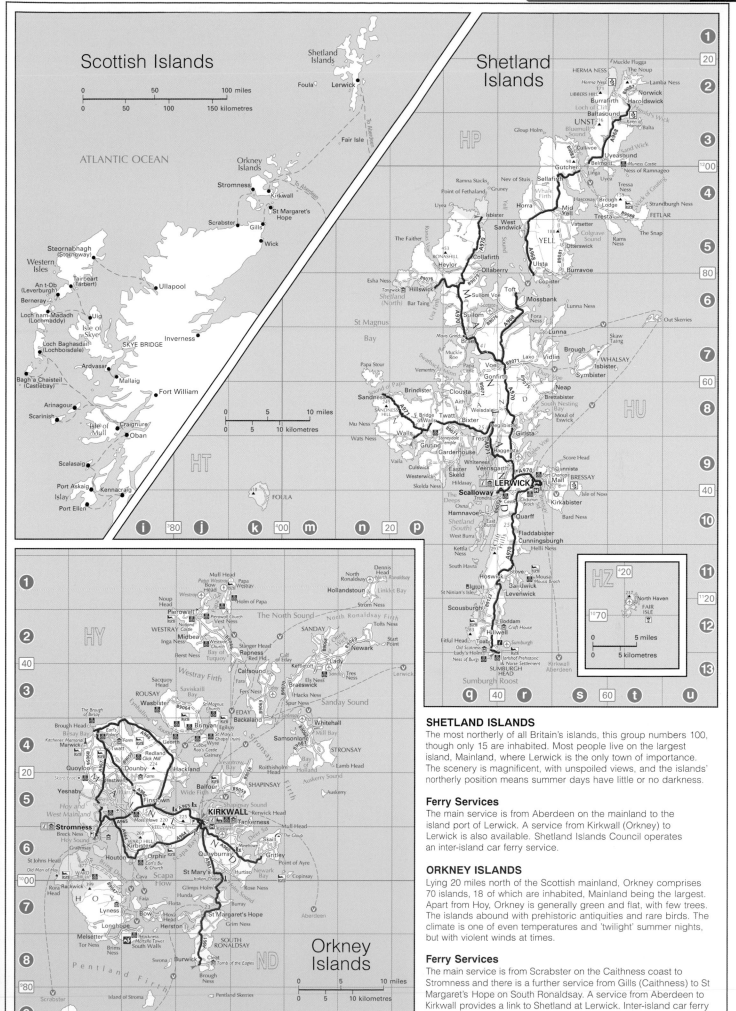

SHETLAND ISLANDS

The most northerly of all Britain's islands, this group numbers 100, though only 15 are inhabited. Most people live on the largest island, Mainland, where Lerwick is the only town of importance. The scenery is magnificent, with unspoiled views, and the islands' northerly position means summer days have little or no darkness.

Ferry Services

The main service is from Aberdeen on the mainland to the island port of Lerwick. A service from Kirkwall (Orkney) to Lerwick is also available. Shetland Islands Council operates an inter-island car ferry service.

ORKNEY ISLANDS

Lying 20 miles north of the Scottish mainland, Orkney comprises 70 islands, 18 of which are inhabited, Mainland being the largest. Apart from Hoy, Orkney is generally green and flat, with few trees. The islands abound with prehistoric antiquities and rare birds. The climate is one of even temperatures and 'twilight' summer nights, but with violent winds at times.

Ferry Services

The main service is from Scrabster on the Caithness coast to Stromness and there is a further service from Gills (Caithness) to St Margaret's Hope on South Ronaldsay. A service from Aberdeen to Kirkwall provides a link to Shetland at Lerwick. Inter-island car ferry services are also operated (advance reservations recommended).

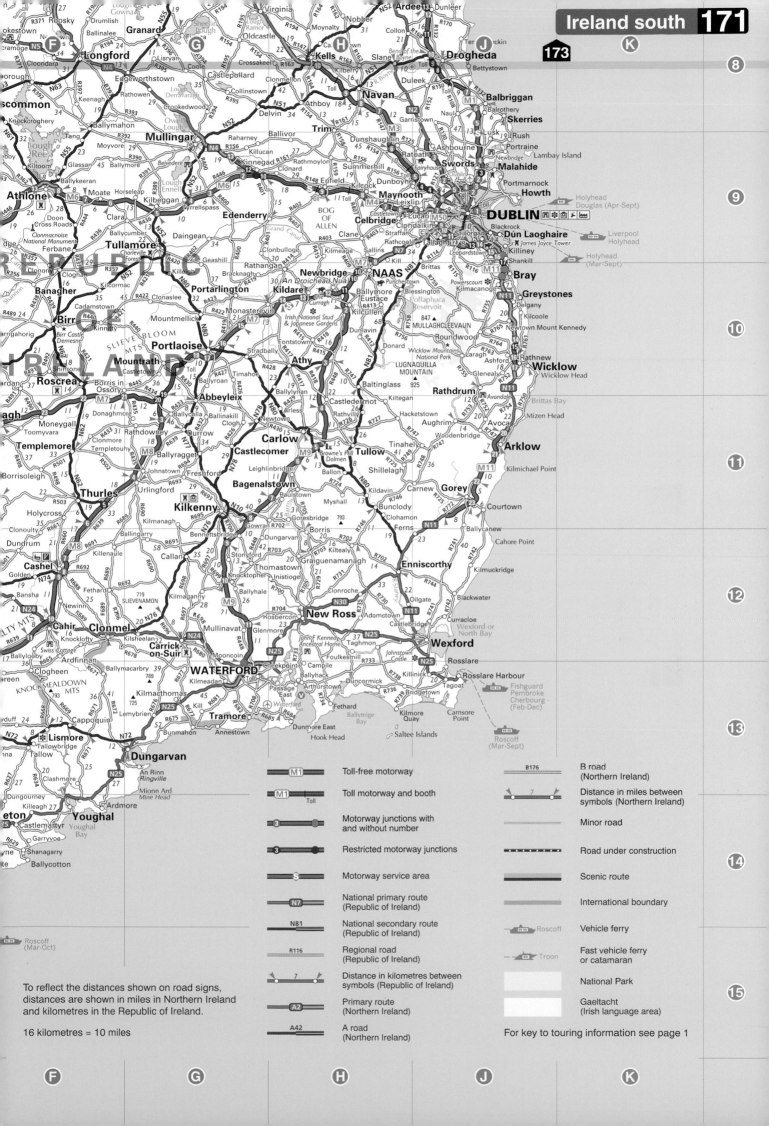

Ireland index

C12 Abbeydorney
D12 Abbeyfeale
G11 Abbeyleix
H12 Adamstown
D12 Adare
C14 Adrigole
H4 Aghadowey
E9 Ahascragh
J4 Ahoghill
B15 Allihies
B13 Anascaul
E4 An Bun Beag
E5 An Charraig
E4 An Clochán Liath
B14 An Coireán
B13 An Daingean
C9 An Fhairche
J7 Annalong
G13 Annestown
G13 An Rinn
D9 An Spidéal
J5 Antrim
D12 Ardagh
E5 Ardara
H8 Ardee
C12 Ardfert
F12 Ardfinnan
K6 Ardglass
B14 Ardgroom
F14 Ardmore
J11 Arklow
H11 Arless
H6 Armagh
J3 Armoy
H13 Arthurstown
G7 Arvagh
J9 Ashbourne
J10 Ashford
D12 Askeaton
H8 Athboy
D12 Athea
E9 Athenry
E8 Athleague
F9 Athlone
H10 Athy
G6 Augher
H6 Aughnacloy
J11 Aughrim
J11 Avoca

H11 Bagenalstown
D14 Baile Mhic Íre
H7 Bailieborough
J8 Balbriggan
D8 Balla
E7 Ballaghaderreen
D7 Ballina
E11 Ballina
E7 Ballinafad
G7 Ballinagh
G11 Ballinakill
F8 Ballinalee
G6 Ballinamallard
F7 Ballinamore
D14 Ballinascarty
E9 Ballinasloe
D8 Ballindine
D14 Ballineen
D12 Ballingarry
G12 Ballingarry
D14 Ballingeary
E14 Ballinhassig
E8 Ballinlough
D8 Ballinrobe
E15 Ballinspittle
E8 Ballintober
F5 Ballintra
H9 Ballivor
H11 Ballon
E9 Ballybaun
H7 Ballybay
F5 Ballybofey
C12 Ballybunion
J11 Ballycanew
K5 Ballycarry
J3 Ballycastle
C6 Ballycastle
J5 Ballyclare
G11 Ballycolla
B9 Ballyconneely
G7 Ballyconnell
F14 Ballycotton
F9 Ballycumber
C15 Ballydehob
D13 Ballydesmond
C12 Ballyduff
F13 Ballyduff
E7 Ballyfarnan
J4 Ballygalley
E9 Ballygar
E6 Ballygawley
H6 Ballygawley
K5 Ballygowan
H13 Ballyhack
G7 Ballyhaise
G12 Ballyhale
E8 Ballyhaunis
D8 Ballyhean
C12 Ballyheige
G8 Ballyjamesduff
F9 Ballykeeran
E12 Ballylanders
C14 Ballylickey
G3 Ballyliffin
C12 Ballylongford
F12 Ballylooby
H10 Ballylynan
F13 Ballymacarbry
F8 Ballymahon
D14 Ballymakeery
J4 Ballymena
E8 Ballymoe
H4 Ballymoney
F9 Ballymore
H10 Ballymore Eustace
E7 Ballymote
J6 Ballynahinch
J5 Ballynure

F13 Ballyporeen
G11 Ballyragget
G10 Ballyroan
H5 Ballyronan
E6 Ballysadare
F5 Ballyshannon
D10 Ballyvaughan
K5 Ballywalter
J8 Balrothery
C15 Baltimore
H10 Baltinglass
F10 Banagher
J6 Banbridge
E14 Bandon
K5 Bangor
C7 Bangor Erris
F12 Bansha
D13 Banteer
C14 Bantry
D9 Barna
B6 Béal an Mhuirthead
D14 Béal Átha an Ghaorthaidh
D9 Bearna
C13 Beaufort
F6 Belcoo
J5 Belfast
E14 Belgooly
H4 Bellaghy
F6 Belleek
B6 Belmullet
G7 Belturbet
H6 Benburb
G12 Bennettsbridge
G5 Beragh
J8 Bettystown
F10 Birr
F6 Blacklion
J9 Blackrock
J12 Blackwater
E14 Blarney
H10 Blessington
H12 Borris
F10 Borris in Ossory
F10 Borrisokane
F11 Borrisoleigh
E7 Boyle
G10 Bracknagh
J10 Bray
H13 Bridgetown
J9 Brittas
E11 Broadford
D12 Broadford
J4 Broughshane
E12 Bruff
E12 Bruree
E4 Bunbeg
H11 Bunclody
G3 Buncrana
E6 Bundoran
G13 Bunmahon
C6 Bun na hAbhna
C6 Bunnanonan
D7 Bunnyconnellan
D11 Bunratty
E13 Burnfort
H3 Bushmills
E13 Buttevant

F10 Cadamstown
E12 Caherconlish
B14 Caherdaniel
B14 Cahersiveen
F12 Cahir
H6 Caledon
G12 Callan
E9 Caltra
B13 Camp
H13 Campile
F12 Cappagh White
E11 Cappamore
F13 Cappoquin
H8 Carlanstown
J7 Carlingford
H11 Carlow
C9 Carna
G3 Carndonagh
J11 Carnew
J4 Carnlough
E7 Carracastle
F3 Carraig Airt
E5 Carrick
F3 Carrickart
K5 Carrickfergus
H7 Carrickmacross
G5 Carrickmore or
    Termon Rock
F7 Carrick-on-
    Shannon
G12 Carrick-on-Suir
F10 Carrigahorig
E14 Carrigaline
F7 Carrigallen
D14 Carriganimmy
G4 Carrigans
E14 Carrigtohill
J5 Carryduff
C9 Cashel
F12 Cashel
D8 Castlebar
J7 Castlebellingham
H7 Castleblayney
J12 Castlebridge
G11 Castlecomer
E11 Castleconnell
G5 Castlederg
H11 Castledermot
B13 Castlegregory
C13 Castleisland
C13 Castlemaine
F14 Castlemartyr
E8 Castleplunket
G8 Castlepollard
E8 Castlerea
H3 Castlerock
H6 Castleshane
G10 Castletown

B15 Castletownbere
E13 Castletownroche
D15 Castletownshend
J6 Castlewellan
B14 Cathair Dónall
C12 Causeway
G7 Cavan
H9 Celbridge
D7 Charlestown
E12 Charleville
H13 Cheekpoint
E5 Cill Charthaigh
C9 Cill Chiaráin
G5 Clady
H9 Clane
G9 Clara
D11 Clarecastle
D8 Claremorris
D10 Clarinbridge
F13 Clashmore
G4 Claudy
B9 Clifden
E6 Cliffony
G11 Clogh
F10 Cloghan
F13 Clogheen
G6 Clogher
H11 Clohamon
D15 Clonakilty
H9 Clonard
G10 Clonaslee
G9 Clonbulloge
C9 Clonbur
J9 Clondalkin
G7 Clones
E11 Clonlara
G3 Clonmany
F12 Clonmel
H8 Clonmellon
F11 Clonmore
F10 Clonony
F12 Clonoulty
H12 Clonroche
H6 Clontibret
F8 Cloondara
K6 Clough
F10 Cloughjordan
F14 Cloyne
H5 Coagh
H5 Coalisland
E14 Cobh
H3 Coleraine
G8 Collinstown
H8 Collon
E6 Collooney
K5 Comber
D9 Cong
F13 Conna
H5 Cookstown
G8 Coole
C11 Cooraclare
G7 Cootehill
E14 Cork
C9 Cornamona
C9 Corr na Móna
D10 Corrofin
E15 Courtmacsherry
J11 Courtown
J6 Craigavon
E10 Craughwell
K5 Crawfordsburn
E8 Creegs
F4 Creeslough
D12 Croagh
E4 Croithlí
E4 Crolly
G8 Crookedwood
C15 Crookhaven
D14 Crookstown
E12 Croom
H8 Crossakeel
E14 Cross Barry
E14 Crosshaven
H7 Crossmaglen
D7 Crossmolina

J5 Crumlin
D10 Crusheen
G3 Culdaff
J4 Cullybackey
J12 Curracloe
F9 Curraghboy
J4 Curry
J4 Cushendall
J3 Cushendun

G9 Daingean
J10 Delgany
G8 Delvin
G4 Derry
F6 Derrygonnelly
G6 Derrylin
H3 Dervock
B13 Dingle
J5 Doagh
K5 Donaghadee
G11 Donaghmore
H10 Donard
F5 Donegal
E13 Doneraile
C10 Doolin
E12 Doon
C11 Doonbeg
F9 Doon Cross Roads
E14 Douglas
K6 Downpatrick
F6 Dowra
H5 Draperstown
D15 Drimoleague
E14 Dripsey
J8 Drogheda
E6 Dromahair
D12 Dromcolliher
J6 Dromore
G5 Dromore
D6 Dromore West
E6 Drumcliff
H8 Drumcondra
F7 Drumkeeran
F8 Drumlish
G5 Drumod
F7 Drumquin
F7 Drumshanbo
F7 Drumsna
C12 Duagh
J9 Dublin
J8 Duleek
J9 Dunboyne
H13 Duncormick
J7 Dundalk
E14 Dunderrow
K5 Dundonald
K6 Dundrum
F12 Dundrum
F3 Dunfanaghy
H5 Dungannon
G12 Dungarvan
G13 Dungarvan
H4 Dungiven
E4 Dunglow
F14 Dungourney
E5 Dunkineely
J9 Dún Laoghaire
H10 Dunlavin
J8 Dunleer
J4 Dunloy
D14 Dunmanway
E8 Dunmore
H13 Dunmore East
J5 Dunmurry
H9 Dunshaughlin
G11 Durrow
J7 Durrus
C15 Durrus
E9 Dysart

D6 Easky
H9 Edenderry
G8 Edgeworthstown
G4 Eglinton
F8 Elphin
H6 Emyvale

H9 Enfield
D11 Ennis
H12 Enniscorthy
D14 Enniskean
F6 Enniskillen
D10 Ennistymon
F10 Eyrecourt

G4 Fahan
C13 Farranfore
E10 Feakle
F7 Fenagh
F9 Ferbane
E13 Fermoy
J12 Ferns
F12 Fethard
H13 Fethard
G8 Finnea
G6 Fintona
G6 Fivemiletown
H10 Fontstown
H12 Foulksmill
D7 Foxford
D11 Foynes
D13 Freemount
G11 Freshford
E8 Fuerty

E12 Galbally
D9 Galway
F6 Garrison
J8 Garriston
F14 Garryvoe
H4 Garvagh
G10 Geashill
J6 Gilford
D15 Glandore
E14 Glanmire
E13 Glanworth
H6 Glaslough
F9 Glassan
E5 Gleann Cholm
    Cille
J4 Glenarm
J5 Glenavy
B13 Glenbeigh
E5 Glencolumbkille
J10 Glenealy
J9 Glengarriff
H12 Glenmore
E8 Glennamaddy
E5 Glenties
D12 Glin
C9 Glinsce
C9 Glinsk
F12 Golden
C15 Goleen
H11 Goresbridge
J11 Gorey
D10 Gort
G5 Gortin
H11 Gowran
H12 Graiguenamanagh
G8 Granard
E6 Grange
J7 Greenore
K5 Greyabbey
J10 Greystones
H4 Gulladuff

H11 Hacketstown
D9 Headford
E12 Herbertstown
J6 Hillsborough
J6 Hilltown
F11 Holycross
G9 Holywood
G9 Horseleap
E12 Hospital
J9 Howth

B13 Inch
D14 Inchigeelagh
E14 Inishannon
H6 [blank]

D6 Inishcrone
H12 Inistioge
F6 Irvinestown

G11 Johnstown

D13 Kanturk
F7 Keadew
H6 Keady
B7 Keel
F8 Keenagh
J4 Kells
H8 Kells
C14 Kenmare
F5 Kesh
G9 Kilbeggan
H8 Kilberry
E14 Kilbrittain
E5 Kilcar
H9 Kilcock
D10 Kilcolgan
E9 Kilconnell
J10 Kilcoole
F10 Kilcormac
H10 Kilcullen
J7 Kilcurry
H10 Kildare
H11 Kildavin
E13 Kildorrery
D10 Kilfenora
C14 Kilgarvan
C11 Kilkee
J7 Kilkeel
D7 Kilkelly
G11 Kilkenny
C9 Kilkieran
C12 Kilkinlea Lower
H9 Kill
G13 Kill
D11 Killadysert
D6 Killala
E11 Killaloe
C13 Killarney
G7 Killashandra
F14 Killeagh
G10 Killeigh
F12 Killenaule
C11 Killimer
J10 Killimor
E10 Killinor
J9 Killiney
J13 Killinick
C13 Killorglin
K6 Killough
G9 Killucan
E5 Killybegs
K6 Killyleagh
J10 Kilmacanoge
F4 Kilmacrenan
G13 Kilmacthomas
G12 Kilmaganny
D8 Kilmaine
E12 Kilmallock
G11 Kilmanagh
G13 Kilmeadan
H9 Kilmeage
D12 Kilmeedy
D14 Kilmichael
H13 Kilmore Quay
J12 Kilmuckridge
G8 Kilnaleck
H4 Kilrea
C11 Kilrush
G12 Kilsheelan
D8 Kiltamagh
H12 Kiltealy
H11 Kiltegan
F9 Kiltoom
H7 Kingscourt
E6 Kinlough
G9 Kinnegad
F10 Kinnitty
E14 Kinsale
D10 Kinvarra
K5 Kircubbin
D8 Knock

F8 Knockcroghery
F12 Knocklofty
G12 Knocktopher

C10 Lahinch
E8 Lanesborough
J10 Laragh
K4 Larne
C14 Lauragh
F10 Laurencetown
D15 Leap
C8 Leenane
H11 Leighlinbridge
F7 Leitrim
H9 Leixlip
G13 Lemybrien
B8 Letterfrack
F4 Letterkenny
G4 Lifford
H4 Limavady
E11 Limerick
G6 Lisbellaw
J5 Lisburn
C10 Liscannor
D13 Liscarroll
D10 Lisdoonvarna
F13 Lismore
G6 Lisnaskea
G8 Lisryan
C12 Listowel
D12 Loghill
G4 Londonderry
J6 Longford
F8 Loughbrickland
H6 Loughgall
E8 Loughglinn

E10 Loughrea
C8 Louisburgh
J9 Lucan
J6 Lurgan
J9 Lusk

F3 Machair Loistche
D14 Macroom
J6 Maghera
H4 Maghera
H5 Magherafelt
G6 Maguiresbridge
J9 Malahide
C11 Málainn Mhóir
G3 Malin
E5 Malin More
E13 Mallow
F6 Manorhamilton
H6 Markethill
J4 Martinstown
H9 Maynooth
J5 Mazetown
H6 Middletown
F14 Midleton
F4 Millford
D13 Millstreet
C13 Milltown
C11 Milltown Malbay
E13 Mitchelstown
F9 Moate
F7 Mohill
H6 Monaghan
G10 Monasterevin
F11 Moneygall
H5 Moneymore
E9 Monivea

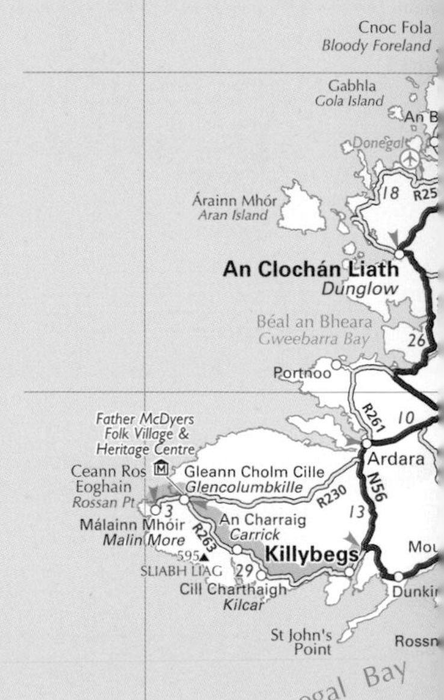

Cnoc Fola
Bloody Foreland

Gabhla
Gola Island
An B

Donegal

Árainn Mhór
Aran Island

An Clochán Liath
Dúnglow

Béal an Bheara
Gweebarra Bay

Portnoo

Father McDyers
Folk Village &
Heritage Centre

Ceann Ros
Eoghain
Rossan Pt.

Gleann Cholm Cille
Glencolumbkille

Málainn Mhóir
Malin More

An Charraig
Carrick

Kilcar

SLIABH LIAG

Cill Charthaigh
Kilcar

Killybegs

Ardara

St John's
Point

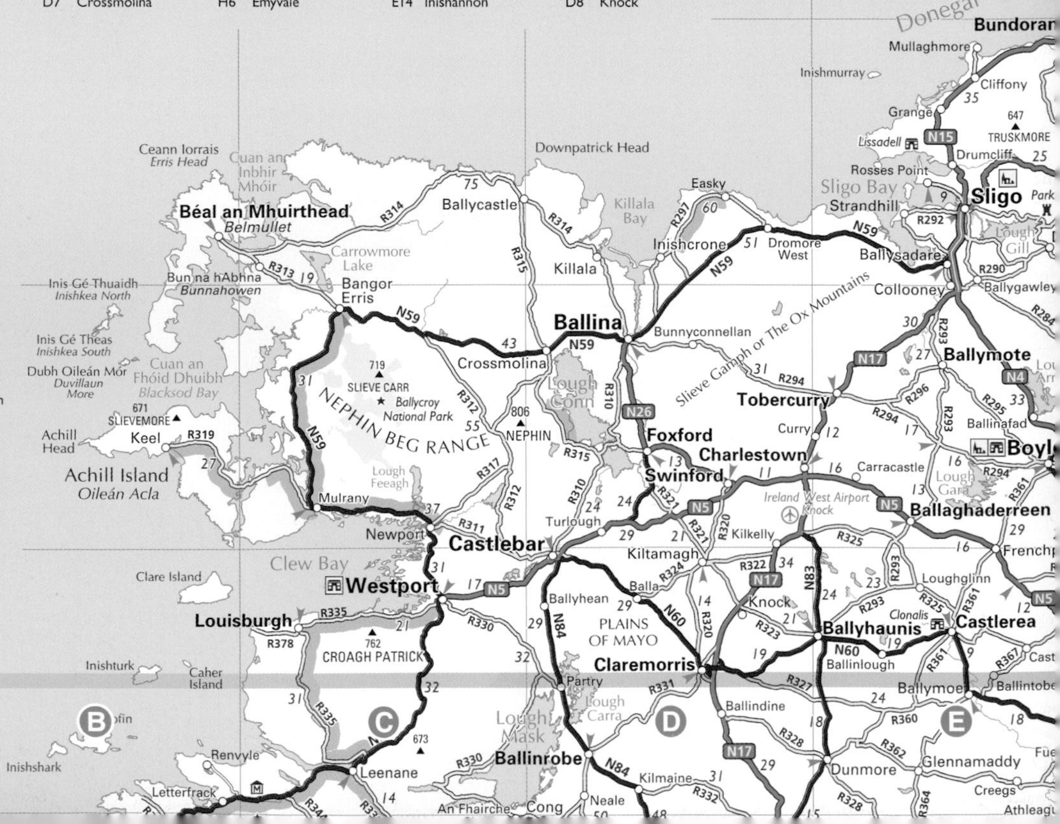

Donegal Bay

Bundoran

Mullaghmore

Inishmurray

Cliffony

Grange

Lissadell

Rosses Point

Sligo Bay

Strandhill

Sligo

TRUSKMORE
Drumcliff

Ceann Iorrais
Erris Head

Cuan an
Inbhir
Mhóir

Downpatrick Head

Easky

Inishcrone

Dromore
West

Ballysadare

Collooney

Ballygawley

Béal an Mhuirthead
Belmullet

Carrowmore
Lake

Bangor
Erris

Ballycastle

Killala
Bay

Killala

Ballina

Bunnyconnellan

Sligo Garbh or The Ox Mountains

Tobercurry

Curry

Ballymote

Ballinafad

Boyl

Inis Gé Thuaidh
Inishkea North

Bun na hAbhna
Bunnahowen

Inis Gé Theas
Inishkea South

Dubh Oileán Mór
Duvillaun
More

Cuan an Fhóid Dhuibh
Blacksod Bay

Crossmolina

Lough
Conn

NEPHIN BEG RANGE

SLIEVE CARR

Ballycroy
National Park

NEPHIN

Foxford

Charlestown

Swinford

Ireland West Airport
Knock

Ballaghaderreen

Achill
Head

SLIEVEMORE
Keel

Achill Island
Oileán Acla

Lough
Feeagh

Mulrany

Newport

Clare Island

Inishturk

Caher
Island

Clew Bay

Westport

Louisburgh

CROAGH PATRICK

Turlough

Castlebar

Kiltamagh

Kilkelly

Knock

Ballyhean

PLAINS
OF MAYO

Claremorris

Ballinlough

Ballyhaunis

Castlerea

Frenchp

Inishshark

Inishbofin

Renvyle

Letterfrack

An Fhairche Cong

Leenane

Ballinrobe

Lough
Mask

Ballindine

Kilmaine

Dunmore

Neale

Glennamaddy

Creegs

Athleag

Lough
Carra

Partry

Ballinrobe

0 10 20 miles
0 10 20 30 kilometres

G13 Mooncoin
J4 Moorfields
E9 Mountbellew Bridge
F5 Mountcharles
G10 Mountmellick
G10 Mountrath
E10 Mountshannon
G3 Moville
H6 Moy
H8 Moynalty
F9 Moyvore
C13 Muckross
G4 Muff
E6 Mullaghmore
G12 Mullinavat
G9 Mullingar
C7 Mulrany
H11 Myshall

H10 Naas
J8 Naul
H8 Navan
D8 Neale
E11 Nenagh
G7 Newbliss

H10 Newbridge
J6 Newcastle
D12 Newcastle West
F12 Newinn
D13 Newmarket
D11 Newmarket-on-Fergus
C7 Newport
E11 Newport
H12 New Ross
J6 Newry
G11 Newtown
J5 Newtownabbey
K5 Newtownards
G7 Newtownbutler
F8 Newtown Forbes
H6 Newtownhamilton
J10 Newtown Mount Kennedy
G5 Newtownstewart
H8 Nobber

E11 Ogonnelloe
H12 Oilgate
G8 Oldcastle
G5 Omagh

J7 Omeath
E12 Oola
D9 Oranmore
D8 Oughterard
E14 Ovens

E12 Pallas Green New
B14 Parknasilla
D8 Partry
H13 Passage East
E14 Passage West
E12 Patrickswell
H11 Paulstown
F5 Pettigo
G5 Plumbridge
H5 Pomeroy
H6 Portadown
H3 Portballintrae
H4 Portglenone
G10 Portlaoise
J9 Portmarnock
E4 Portnoo
J9 Portraine

E11 Portroe
H3 Portrush
H3 Portstewart
E10 Portumna
C13 Poulgorm Bridge
J6 Poyntz Pass

G9 Raharney
J5 Randalstown
H4 Rasharkin
H10 Rathangan
J9 Rathcoole
G11 Rathdowney
J10 Rathdrum
J6 Rathfriland
D12 Rathkeale
F4 Rathmelton
D13 Rathmore
H9 Rathmoylon
G4 Rathmullan
J10 Rathnew
G8 Rathowen
H11 Rathvilly
J9 Ratoath
G4 Ray

C9 Recess
B8 Renvyle
E14 Ringaskiddy
G13 Ringville
H7 Rockcorry
H12 Rosbercon
F8 Roscommon
F10 Roscrea
F3 Rosepenna
D15 Ross Carbery
E6 Rosses Point
J13 Rosslare
J13 Rosslare Harbour
G6 Rosslea
F5 Rossnowlagh
J7 Rostrevor
J10 Roundstone
J10 Roundwood
J9 Rush

C13 Scartaglin
J6 Scarva
C15 Schull
F8 Scarmoge
G5 Seskinore
F14 Shanagarry
D12 Shanagolden
J3 Shankill
D11 Shannon
F9 Shannonbridge
H7 Shercock
H11 Shillelagh
F10 Shinrone
D9 Shrule
E11 Silvermines
G5 Sion Mills
D11 Sixmilebridge
J8 Skerries
D15 Skibbereen
H8 Slane
E6 Sligo
J3 Smithborough
G4 Sneem
C11 Spanish Point
D9 Spiddal
C9 Sraith Salach

H5 Stewartstown
J9 Stillorgan
G12 Stonyford
G4 Strabane
G10 Stradbally
G7 Stradone
H9 Straffan
E6 Strandhill
K6 Strangford
F5 Stranorlar
F8 Strokestown
H9 Summerhill
F6 Swanlinbar
H4 Swatragh
D7 Swinford
J9 Swords

H12 Taghmon
J13 Tagoat
C14 Tahilla
J9 Tallaght
F13 Tallow
F13 Tallowbridge
J6 Tandragee
F9 Tang
C12 Tarbert
F11 Templemore
F11 Templetouhy
J8 Termonfeckin
F11 Thurles
G12 Thomastown
G10 Timahoe
D15 Timoleague
J11 Tinahely
F12 Tipperary

E7 Tobercurry
H4 Tobermore
F11 Toomyvara
C15 Toormore
C13 Tralee
G13 Tramore
H8 Trim
D9 Tuam
E11 Tuamgraney
D11 Tulla
G9 Tullamore
H11 Tullow
E8 Tulsk
D7 Turlough
G9 Tyrrellspass

G11 Urlingford

G8 Virginia

J7 Warrenpoint
G13 Waterford
E13 Watergrasshill
B14 Waterville
C8 Westport
J12 Wexford
E14 Whitegate
K5 Whitehead
J10 Wicklow
J11 Woodenbridge
E10 Woodford

F14 Youghal

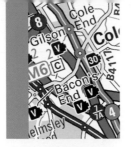

Restricted junctions

Motorway and Primary Route junctions which have access or exit restrictions are shown on the map pages thus:

M1 London - Leeds

Northbound
Access only from A1 (northbound)

Southbound
Exit only to A1 (southbound)

Northbound
Access only from A41 (northbound)

Southbound
Exit only to A41 (southbound)

Northbound
Access only from M25 (no link from A405)

Southbound
Exit only to M25 (no link from A405)

Northbound
Access only from A414

Southbound
Exit only to A414

Northbound
Exit only to M45

Southbound
Access only from M45

Northbound
Exit only to M6 (northbound)
No access restrictions

Southbound
Access only from M6
No exit restrictions

Northbound
Exit only, no access

Southbound
Access only, no exit

Northbound
Access only from A42

Southbound
No restriction

Northbound
No exit, access only

Southbound
Exit only, no access

Northbound
Exit only, no access

Southbound
Access only, no exit

Northbound
Exit only to M621

Southbound
Access only from M621

Northbound
Exit only to A1(M) (northbound)

Southbound
Access only from A1(M) (southbound)

M2 Rochester - Faversham

Westbound
No exit to A2 (eastbound)

Eastbound
No access from A2 (westbound)

M3 Sunbury - Southampton

Northeastbound
Access only from A303, no exit

Southwestbound
Exit only to A303, no access

Northbound
Exit only, no access

Southbound
Access only, no exit

Northeastbound
Access from M27 only. No exit

Southwestbound
No access to M27 (westbound)

M4 London - South Wales

Westbound
Access only from A4 (westbound)

Eastbound
Exit only to A4 (eastbound)

Westbound
Exit only to M48

Eastbound
Access only from M48

Westbound
Access only from M48

Eastbound
Exit only to M48

Westbound
Exit only, no access

Eastbound
Access only, no exit

Westbound
Exit only, no access

Eastbound
Access only, no exit

Westbound
Exit only to A48(M)

Eastbound
Access only from A48(M)

Westbound
Exit only, no access

Eastbound
No restriction

Westbound
Access only, no exit

Eastbound
No access or exit

M5 Birmingham - Exeter

Northeastbound
Access only, no exit

Southwestbound
Exit only, no access

Northeastbound
Access only from A417 (westbound)

Southwestbound
Exit only to A417 (eastbound)

Northeastbound
Exit only to M49

Southwestbound
Access only from M49

Northeastbound
No access, exit only

Southwestbound
No exit, access only

Northeastbound
No restriction

Southwestbound
Access only from A30 (westbound)

M6 Toll Motorway

See M6 Toll Motorway map on page 179

M6 Rugby - Carlisle

Northbound
Exit only to M6 Toll

Southbound
Access only from M6 Toll

Northbound
Access only from M42 (southbound)

Southbound
Exit only to M42

Northbound
Exit only, no access

Southbound
Access only, no exit

Northbound
Exit only to M54

Southbound
Access only from M54

Northbound
Access only from M6 Toll

Southbound
Exit only to M6 Toll

Northbound
No restriction

Southbound
Access only from M56 (eastbound)

Northbound
Access only, no exit

Southbound
No restriction

Northbound
Access only, no exit

Southbound
Exit only, no access

Northbound
Exit only, no access

Southbound
Access only, no exit

Northbound
No direct access, use adjacent slip road to jct 29A

Southbound
No direct exit, use adjacent slip road from jct 29A

Northbound
Acces only, no exit

Southbound
Exit only, no access

Northbound
Access only from M61

Southbound
Exit only to M61

Northbound
Exit only, no access

Southbound
Access only, no exit

Northbound
Exit only, no access

Southbound
Access only, no exit

M8 Edinburgh - Bishopton

See Glasgow District map on pages 254-255

M9 Edinburgh - Dunblane

Northwestbound
Exit only to M9 spur

Southeastbound
Access only from M9 spur

Northwestbound
Access only, no exit

Southeastbound
Exit only, no access

Northwestbound
Exit only, no access

Southeastbound
Access only, no exit

Northwestbound
Access only, no exit

Southeastbound
Exit only to A905

Northwestbound
Exit only to M876 (southwestbound)

Southeastbound
Access only from M876 (northeastbound)

M11 London - Cambridge

Northbound
Access only from A406 (eastbound)

Southbound
Exit only to A406

Northbound
Exit only, no access

Southbound
Access only, no exit

Northbound
Exit only to A11

Southbound
Access only from A11

Northbound
Exit only, no access

Southbound
Access only, no exit

Northbound
Exit only, no access

Southbound
Access only, no exit

M20 Swanley - Folkestone

Northwestbound
Staggered junction; follow signs - access only

Southeastbound
Staggered junction; follow signs - exit only

Northwestbound
Exit only to M26 (westbound)

Southeastbound
Access only from M26 (eastbound)

Northwestbound
Access only from A20

Southeastbound
For access follow signs - exit only to A20

Northwestbound
No restriction

Southeastbound
For exit follow signs

Northwestbound
Access only, no exit

Southeastbound
Exit only, no access

M23 Hooley - Crawley

Northbound
Exit only to A23 (northbound)

Southbound
Access only from A23 (southbound)

Northbound
Access only, no exit

Southbound
Exit only, no access

M25 London Orbital Motorway

See M25 London Orbital Motorway map on page 178

M26 Sevenoaks - Wrotham

Westbound
Exit only to clockwise M25 (westbound)

Eastbound
Access only from anti-clockwise M25 (eastbound)

Westbound
Access only from M20 (northwestbound)

Eastbound
Exit only to M20 (southeastbound)

M27 Cadnam - Portsmouth

Westbound
Staggered junction; follow signs - access only from M3 (southbound). Exit only to M3 (northbound)

Eastbound
Staggered junction; follow signs - access only from M3 (southbound). Exit only to M3 (northbound)

Westbound
Exit only, no access

Eastbound
Access only, no exit

Westbound
Staggered junction; follow signs - exit only to M275 (southbound)

Eastbound
Staggered junction; follow signs - access only from M275 (northbound)

M40 London - Birmingham

Northwestbound
Exit only, no access

Southeastbound
Access only, no exit

Northwestbound
Exit only, no access

Southeastbound
Access only, no exit

Northwestbound
Exit only to M40/A40

Southeastbound
Access only from M40/A40

Northwestbound
Exit only, no access

Southeastbound
Access only, no exit

Northwestbound
Access only, no exit

Southeastbound
Exit only, no access

Northwestbound
Access only, no exit

Southeastbound
Exit only, no access

M42 Bromsgrove - Measham

See Birmingham District map on pages 252-253

M45 Coventry - M1

Westbound
Access only from A45 (northbound)

Eastbound
Exit only, no access

Westbound
Access only from M1 (northbound)

Eastbound
Exit only to M1 (southbound)

M53 Mersey Tunnel - Chester

Northbound
Access only from M56 (westbound). Exit only to M56 (eastbound)

Southbound
Access only from M56 (westbound). Exit only to M56 (eastbound)

M54 Telford

Westbound
Access only from M6 (northbound)

Eastbound
Exit only to M6 (southbound)

M56 North Cheshire

For junctions 1,2,3,4 & 7 see Manchester District map on pages 256-257

Westbound
Access only, no exit

Eastbound
No access or exit

Westbound
Exit only to M53

Eastbound
Access only from M53

Westbound
No access or exit

Eastbound
No restriction

M57 Liverpool Outer Ring Road

Northwestbound
Access only, no exit

Southeastbound
Exit only, no access

Northwestbound
Access only from A580 (westbound)

Southeastbound
Exit only, no access

M58 Liverpool - Wigan

Westbound
Exit only, no access

Eastbound
Access only, no exit

M60 Manchester Orbital

See Manchester District map on pages 256-257

M61 Manchester - Preston

Northwestbound
No access or exit

Southeastbound
Exit only, no access

Northwestbound
Exit only to M6 (northbound)

Southeastbound
Access only from M6 (southbound)

M62 Liverpool - Kingston upon Hull

Westbound
Access only, no exit

Eastbound
Exit only, no access

Westbound
No access to A1(M) (southbound)

Eastbound
No restriction

M65 Preston - Colne

Northeastbound
Exit only, no access

Southwestbound
Access only, no exit

Northeastbound
Access only, no exit

Southwestbound
Exit only, no access

M66 Bury

Northbound
Exit only to A56 (northbound)

Southbound
Access only from A56 (southbound)

Northbound
Exit only, no access

Southbound
Access only, no exit

M67 Hyde Bypass

Westbound
Access only, no exit

Eastbound
Exit only, no access

Westbound
Exit only, no access

Eastbound
Access only, no exit

Westbound
Exit only, no access

Eastbound
No restriction

M69 Coventry - Leicester

Northbound
Access only, no exit

Southbound
Exit only, no access

M73 East of Glasgow

Northbound
No access from or exit to A89. No access from M8 (eastbound)

Southbound
No access from or exit to A89. No exit to M8 (westbound)

M74 and A74(M) Glasgow - Gretna

Northbound
Exit only, no access

Southbound
Access only, no exit

Northbound
Access only, no exit

Southbound
Exit only, no access

Northbound
Access only, no exit

Southbound
Exit only, no access

Northbound
No access or exit

Southbound
Access only, no exit

Northbound
No restriction

Southbound
Access only, no exit

Northbound
Access only, no exit

Southbound
Exit only, no access

Northbound
Exit only, no access

Southbound
Access only, no exit

Northbound
Exit only, no access

Southbound
Access only, no exit

M77 South of Glasgow

Northbound
No exit to M8 (westbound)

Southbound
No access from M8 (eastbound)

Northbound
Access only, no exit

Southbound
Exit only, no access

Northbound
Access only, no exit

Southbound
Exit only, no access

Northbound
Access only, no exit

Southbound
No restriction

M80 Glasgow - Stirling

For junctions 1 & 4 see Glasgow District map on pages 254-255

Northbound
Exit only, no access

Southbound
Access only, no exit

Northbound
Access only, no exit

Southbound
Exit only, no access

M90 Forth Road Bridge - Perth

Northbound
Exit only to A92 (eastbound)

Southbound
Access only from A92 (westbound)

Northbound
Access only, no exit

Southbound
Exit only, no access

Northbound
Exit only, no access

Southbound
Access only, no exit

Northbound
No access from A912
No exit to A912 (southbound)

Southbound
No access from A912 (northbound).
No exit to A912

M180 Doncaster - Grimsby

Westbound
Access only, no exit

Eastbound
Exit only, no access

M606 Bradford Spur

Northbound
Exit only, no access

Southbound
No restriction

M621 Leeds - M1

Clockwise
Access only, no exit

Anticlockwise
Exit only, no access

Clockwise
No exit or access

Anticlockwise
No restriction

Clockwise
Access only, no exit

Anticlockwise
Exit only, no access

M74 junction 5 (Glasgow)

Northbound
Access only, no exit

Southbound
Exit only, no access

Northbound
Exit only, no access

Southbound
Access only, no exit

Clockwise
Exit only, no access

Anticlockwise
Access only, no exit

Clockwise
Exit only to M1 (southbound)

Anticlockwise
Access only from M1 (northbound)

M876 Bonnybridge - Kincardine Bridge

Northeastbound
Access only from M80 (northbound)

Southwestbound
Exit only to M80 (southbound)

Northeastbound
Exit only to M9 (eastbound)

Southwestbound
Access only from M9 (westbound)

A1(M) South Mimms - Baldock

Northbound
Exit only, no access

Southbound
Access only, no exit

Northbound
No restriction

Southbound
Exit only, no access

Northbound
Access only, no exit

Southbound
No access or exit

A1(M) Pontefract - Bedale

Northbound
No access to M62 (eastbound)

Southbound
No restriction

Northbound
Access only from M1 (northbound)

Southbound
Exit only to M1 (southbound)

A1(M) Scotch Corner - Newcastle upon Tyne

Northbound
Exit only to A66(M) (eastbound)

Southbound
Access only from A66(M) (westbound)

Northbound
No access. Exit only to A194(M) & A1 (northbound)

Southbound
No exit. Access only from A194(M) & A1 (southbound)

A3(M) Horndean - Havant

Northbound
Access only from A3

Southbound
Exit only to A3

Northbound
Exit only, no access

Southbound
Access only, no exit

A48(M) Cardiff Spur

Westbound
Access only from M4 (westbound)

Eastbound
Exit only to M4 (eastbound)

Westbound
Exit only to A48 (westbound)

Eastbound
Access only from A48 (eastbound)

A66(M) Darlington Spur

Westbound
Exit only to A1(M) (southbound)

Eastbound
Access only from A1(M) (northbound)

A194(M) Newcastle upon Tyne

Northbound
Access only from A1(M) (northbound)

Southbound
Exit only to A1(M) (southbound)

A12 M25 - Ipswich

Northeastbound
Access only, no exit

Southwestbound
No restriction

Northeastbound
Exit only, no access

Southwestbound
Access only, no exit

Northeastbound
Exit only, no access

Southwestbound
Access only, no exit

Northeastbound
Access only, no exit

Southwestbound
Exit only, no access

Northeastbound
No restriction

Southwestbound
Access only, no exit

Northeastbound
Exit only, no access

Southwestbound
Access only, no exit

Northeastbound
Access only, no exit

Southwestbound
Exit only, no access

Northeastbound
Exit only, no access

Southwestbound
Access only, no exit

Northeastbound
Exit only (for Stratford St Mary and Dedham)

Southwestbound
Access only

A14 M1 Felixstowe

Westbound
Exit only to M6 & M1 (northbound)

Eastbound
Access only from M6 & M1 (southbound)

Westbound
Exit only, no access

Eastbound
Access only, no exit

Westbound
Access only from A1307

Eastbound
Exit only to A1307

Westbound
Access only, no exit

Eastbound
Exit only, no access

Westbound
Exit only to A11
Access only from A1303

Eastbound
Access only from A11

Westbound
Access only from A11

Eastbound
Exit only to A11

Westbound
Exit only, no access

Eastbound
Access only, no exit

Westbound
Access only, no exit

Eastbound
Exit only, no access

A55 Holyhead - Chester

Westbound
Exit only, no access

Eastbound
Access only, no exit

Westbound
Access only, no exit

Eastbound
Exit only, no access

Westbound
Exit only, no access

Eastbound
No access or exit.

Westbound
Exit only, no access

Eastbound
No access or exit

Westbound
Exit only, no access

Eastbound
Access only, no exit

Westbound
Exit only to A5104

Eastbound
Access only from A5104

M25 London Orbital motorway

Refer also to atlas pages 36–37 and 50–51

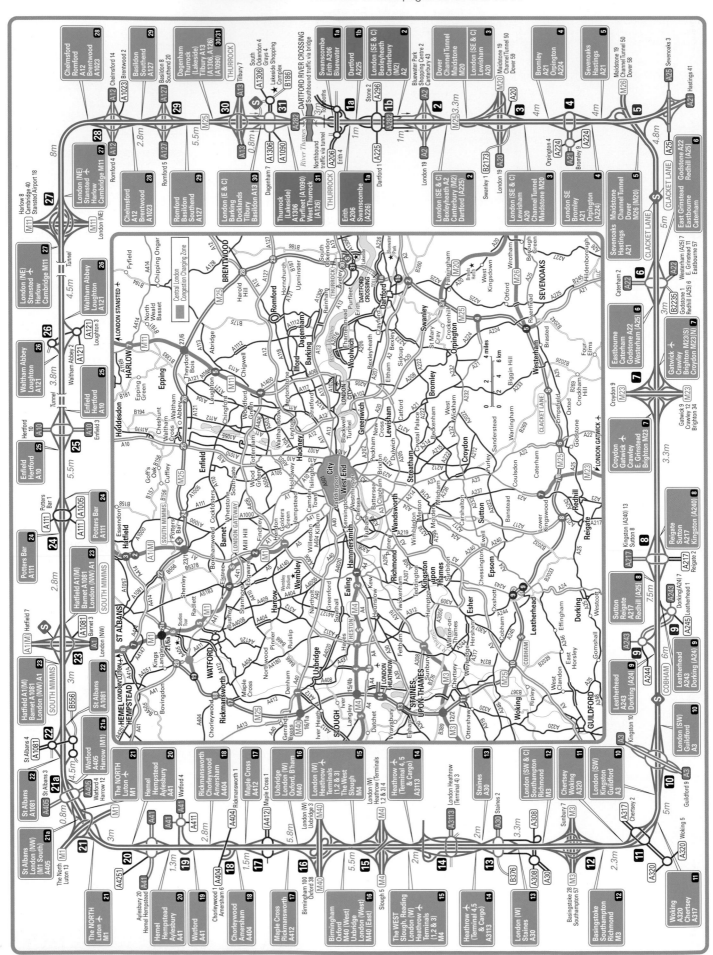

M6 Toll motorway

Refer also to atlas pages 58–59

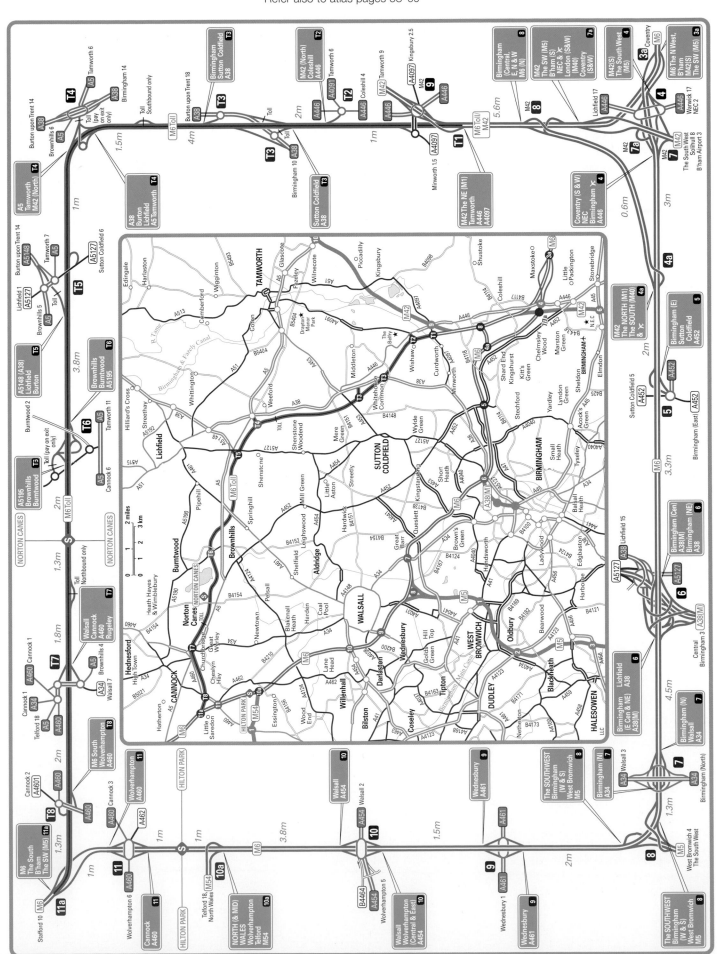

Street map symbols

Town, port and airport plans

Motorway and junction	One-way, gated/closed road	Railway station	Car park
Primary road single/dual carriageway	Restricted access road	Light rapid transit system station	Park and Ride (at least 6 days per week)
A road single/dual carriageway	Pedestrian area	Level crossing	Bus/coach station
B road single/dual carriageway	Footpath	Tramway	Hospital
Local road single/dual carriageway	Road under construction	Ferry route	24-hour Accident & Emergency hospital
Other road single/dual carriageway, minor road	Road tunnel	Airport, heliport	Petrol station, 24 hour Major suppliers only
Building of interest	Museum	Railair terminal	City wall
Ruined building	Castle	Theatre or performing arts centre	Escarpment
Tourist Information Centre	Castle mound	Cinema	Cliff lift
Visitor or heritage centre	Monument, statue	Abbey, chapel, church	River/canal, lake
World Heritage Site (UNESCO)	Post Office	Synagogue	Lock, weir
English Heritage site	Public library	Mosque	Park/sports ground
Historic Scotland site	Shopping centre	Golf Course	Cemetery
Cadw (Welsh heritage) site	Shopmobility	Racecourse	Woodland
National Trust site	Viewpoint	Nature reserve	Built-up area
National Trust Scotland site	Toilet, with facilities for the less able	Aquarium	Beach

---

Central London street map (see pages 232 - 241)

Speed camera site (fixed location) with speed limit in mph	London Underground station	Docklands Light Railway (DLR) station	
Section of road with two or more fixed camera sites; speed limit in mph	London Overground station	Central London Congestion Charging Zone	
Average speed (SPECS™) camera system with speed limit in mph	Rail interchange		

Royal Parks (opening and closing times for traffic)

Green Park	Open 5am-midnight. Constitution Hill: closed Sundays
Hyde Park	Open 5am-midnight
Regent's Park	Open 5am-dusk. Most park roads closed midnight-7am
St James's Park	Open 5am-midnight. The Mall: closed Sundays

Traffic regulations in the City of London include security checkpoints and restrict the number of entry and exit points.

Note: Oxford Street is closed to through-traffic (except buses & taxis) 7am-7pm Monday-Saturday.

Central London Congestion Charging Zone

The daily charge for driving or parking a vehicle on public roads in the Congestion Charging Zone (CCZ), during operating hours, is £10 per vehicle per day in advance or on the day of travel. Alternatively you can pay £9 by registering with CC Auto Pay, an automated payment system. Drivers can also pay the next charging day after travelling in the zone but this will cost £12. Payment permits entry, travel within and exit from the CCZ by the vehicle as often as required on that day.

The CCZ operates between 7am and 6pm, Mon–Fri only. There is no charge at weekends, on public holidays or between 25th Dec and 1st Jan inclusive.

For up to date information on the CCZ, exemptions, discounts or ways to pay, telephone 0845 900 1234, visit www.cclondon.com or write to Congestion Charging, P.O. Box 4782, Worthing BN11 9PS. Textphone users can call 020 7649 9123.

Towns, ports & airports

Aberdeen	182	Guildford	198	Plymouth	214
Basingstoke	182	Harrogate	199	Poole	216
Bath	183	Huddersfield	199	Portsmouth	215
Birmingham	184	Inverness	200	Preston	216
Blackpool	183	Ipswich	200	Ramsgate	39
Bournemouth	185	Kingston upon Hull	201	Reading	217
Bradford	185	Lancaster	201	Royal Tunbridge Wells	225
Brighton	186	Leeds	202	Salisbury	217
Bristol	186	Leicester	203	Sheffield	218
Cambridge	187	Lincoln	203	Shrewsbury	218
Canterbury	188	Liverpool	204	Southampton	219
Cardiff	188	Llandudno	79	Southend-on-Sea	220
Carlisle	189	LONDON	232-241	Stirling	220
Cheltenham	189	Luton	205	Stockton-on-Tees	221
Chester	190	Maidstone	205	Stoke-on-Trent (Hanley)	221
Colchester	190	Manchester	206	Stratford-upon-Avon	222
Coventry	191	Margate	39	Sunderland	223
Darlington	191	Middlesbrough	208	Swansea	222
Derby	192	Milton Keynes	207	Swindon	224
Doncaster	192	Newcastle upon Tyne	209	Taunton	224
Dover	193	Newport	208	Torquay	225
Dundee	193	Newquay	4	Tunbridge Wells	225
Durham	194	Northampton	210	Warwick	226
Eastbourne	194	Norwich	210	Watford	226
Edinburgh	195	Nottingham	211	Winchester	227
Exeter	196	Oldham	211	Wolverhampton	227
Glasgow	197	Oxford	212	Worcester	228
Gloucester	196	Perth	213	York	228
Great Yarmouth	198	Peterborough	213		

Central London

PADDINGTON 232	233	234	235	FINSBURY	CITY	STEPNEY 240 241
KENSINGTON 236	237	SOHO	238	239	SOUTHWARK	BERMONDSEY
CHELSEA		WESTMINSTER	KENNINGTON	

🚢 Ferry Ports

Aberdeen Harbour	151
Calais	XI
Dover, Port of	XI
Fishguard Harbour	XIII
Harwich International Port	53
Heysham Harbour	XIII
Holyhead Harbour	XIII
Liverpool Docks	XIII
Newhaven Harbour	XI
Pembroke Dock	XIII
Plymouth, Port of	X
Poole, Port of	X
Port of Tyne	113
Portsmouth Harbour	XI
Southampton, Port of	15
Weymouth Harbour	X

✈ Airports

London Heathrow	229
London Gatwick	229
London Stansted	229
London Luton	229
London City	230
Birmingham International	230
Manchester	230
East Midlands	230
Leeds Bradford International	231
Aberdeen	231
Edinburgh	231
Glasgow	231

🚇 Channel Tunnel

Folkestone Terminal	27
Calais / Coquelles Terminal	27

Aberdeen

Aberdeen is found on atlas page **151 N6**

Affleck Street	C4	Maberly Street	B1
Albert Street	A3	Marischal Street	D2
Albury Road	B4	Market Street	C3
Alford Place	A3	Nelson Street	C1
Ann Street	B1	Palmerston Road	C4
Beach Boulevard	D2	Park Street	D1
Belgrave Terrace	A2	Portland Street	C4
Berryden Road	A1	Poynernook Road	C4
Blackfriars Street	B2	Regent Quay	D3
Blaikies Quay	D3	Richmond Street	A2
Bon Accord Crescent	B4	Rose Place	A3
Bon Accord Street	B3	Rose Street	A3
Bridge Street	C3	Rosemount Place	A2
Caledonian Place	B4	Rosemount Viaduct	A2
Carmelite Street	C3	St Andrew Street	B2
Chapel Street	A3	St Clair Street	C1
Charlotte Street	B1	School Hill	C2
College Street	C3	Skene Square	B2
Constitution Street	D1	Skene Street	A3
Crimon Place	B3	Skene Terrace	B2
Crown Street	B3	South College Street	C4
Dee Street	B3	South Esplanade East	D4
Denburn Road	B2	South Mount Street	A2
Diamond Street	B3	Spa Street	B2
East North Street	D2	Springbank Street	B4
Esslemont Avenue	A2	Springbank Terrace	B4
Gallowgate	C1	Summer Street	B3
George Street	B1	Summerfield Terrace	D1
Gilcomston Park	B2	Thistle Lane	A3
Golden Square	B3	Thistle Place	A3
Gordon Street	B3	Thistle Street	A3
Great Western Road	A4	Trinity Quay	C3
Guild Street	C3	Union Bridge	B3
Hadden Street	C3	Union Grove	A4
Hanover Street	D2	Union Street	B3
Hardgate	B4	Union Terrace	B2
Harriet Street	C2	Upper Denburn	A2
Holburn Street	A4	Victoria Road	D4
Huntley Street	A3	Victoria Street	A3
Hutcheon Street	B1	View Terrace	A1
Jasmine Terrace	D1	Virginia Street	D2
John Street	B2	Wapping Street	C3
Justice Mill Lane	A4	Waverley Place	A3
King Street	C1	Wellington Place	C4
Langstane Place	B3	West North Street	C1
Leadside Road	A2	Westburn Road	A1
Loanhead Terrace	A1	Whitehall Place	A2
Loch Street	C1	Willowbank Road	A4

Basingstoke

Basingstoke is found on atlas page **22 H4**

Alencon Link	C1	London Street	C3
Allnutt Avenue	D2	Lower Brook Street	A2
Basing View	C1	Lytton Road	D3
Beaconsfield Road	C4	Market Place	B3
Bounty Rise	A4	May Place	C3
Bounty Road	A4	Montague Place	C4
Bramblys Close	A3	Mortimer Lane	A2
Bramblys Drive	A3	New Road	B3
Budd's Close	A3	New Road	C2
Castle Road	C4	New Street	B3
Chapel Hill	B1	Old Reading Road	C1
Chequers Road	C2	Penrith Road	A3
Chester Place	A4	Rayleigh Road	A2
Churchill Way	B2	Red Lion Lane	C3
Churchill Way East	D1	Rochford Road	A2
Churchill Way West	A2	St Mary's Court	C2
Church Square	B2	Sarum Hill	A3
Church Street	B2	Seal Road	C2
Church Street	B3	Solby's Road	A2
Cliddesden Road	C4	Southend Road	A2
Clifton Terrace	C1	Southern Road	B4
Cordale Road	A4	Stukeley Road	A3
Council Road	B4	Sylvia Close	B4
Crossborough Gardens	D3	Timberlake Road	B2
Crossborough Hill	D3	Victoria Street	B3
Cross Street	B3	Victory Roundabout	A1
Devonshire Place	A4	Vyne Road	B1
Eastfield Avenue	D2	Winchcombe Road	A3
Eastrop Lane	D2	Winchester Road	A4
Eastrop Roundabout	C1	Winchester Street	B3
Eastrop Way	D2	Winterthur Way	A1
Essex Road	A2	Worting Road	A3
Fairfields Road	B4	Wote Street	C3
Festival Way	C2		
Flaxfield Court	A2		
Flaxfield Road	A3		
Flaxfield Road	B3		
Frances Road	A4		
Frescade Crescent	A4		
Goat Lane	C2		
Hackwood Road	C4		
Hamelyn Road	A4		
Hardy Lane	A4		
Hawkfield Lane	A4		
Haymarket Yard	C3		
Joices Yard	B3		
Jubilee Road	B4		
London Road	D3		

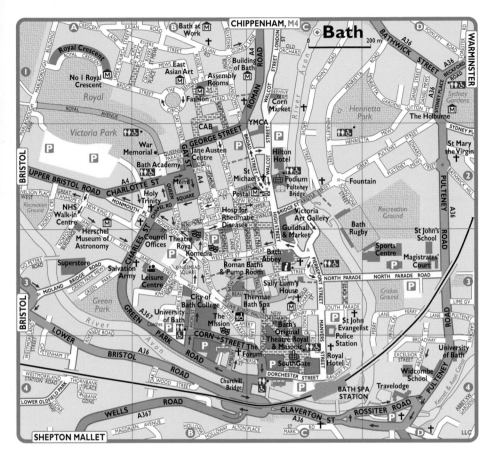

Bath

Bath is found on atlas page **20 D2**

Archway Street	D4	Lower Bristol Road	A3
Argyle Street	C2	Lower Oldfield Park	A4
Avon Street	B3	Manvers Street	C3
Bartlett Street	B1	Midland Bridge Road	A3
Barton Street	B2	Milk Street	B3
Bathwick Street	D1	Milsom Street	B2
Beauford Square	B2	Monmouth Place	A2
Beau Street	B3	Monmouth Street	B2
Beckford Road	D1	New Bond Street	B2
Bennett Street	B1	New King Street	A2
Bridge Street	C2	New Orchard Street	C3
Broad Street	C2	Norfolk Buildings	A3
Broadway	D4	North Parade	C3
Brock Street	A1	North Parade Road	D3
Chapel Road	B2	Old King Street	B2
Charles Street	A3	Oxford Row	B1
Charlotte Street	A2	Pierrepont Street	C3
Cheap Street	C3	Princes Street	B2
Cheltenham Street	A4	Pulteney Road	D2
Circus Mews	B1	Queen Square	B2
Claverton Street	C4	Queen Street	B2
Corn Street	B4	Railway Place	C4
Daniel Street	D1	Rivers Street	B1
Dorchester Street	C4	Roman Road	C1
Edward Street	D2	Rossiter Road	C4
Gay Street	B1	Royal Avenue	A1
George Street	B2	Royal Crescent	A1
Great Pulteney Street	C2	St James's Parade	B3
Great Stanhope Street	A2	St John's Road	C1
Green Park Road	A3	Saw Close	B3
Green Street	B2	Southgate Street	C4
Grove Street	C2	South Parade	C3
Guinea Lane	B1	Stall Street	C3
Henrietta Gardens	D1	Sutton Street	D1
Henrietta Mews	C2	Sydney Place	D1
Henrietta Road	C1	The Circus	B1
Henrietta Street	C2	Thornbank Place	A4
Henry Street	C3	Union Street	B2
High Street	C2	Upper Borough Walls	C2
Hot Bath Street	B3	Upper Bristol Road	A2
James Street West	B3	Upper Church Street	A1
John Street	B2	Walcot Street	C2
Julian Road	B1	Wells Road	A4
Kingsmead North	B3	Westgate Buildings	B3
Kingston Road	C3	Westgate Street	B3
Lansdown Road	B1	Westmoreland Station	
London Street	C1	Road	A4
Lower Borough Walls	B3	York Street	C3

Blackpool

Blackpool is found on atlas page **88 C3**

Abingdon Street	B1	Hornby Road	B3
Adelaide Street	B3	Hornby Road	D3
Albert Road	B3	Hull Road	B3
Albert Road	C3	Kay Street	C4
Alfred Street	C2	Kent Road	C4
Ashton Road	D4	King Street	C2
Bank Hey Street	B2	Larkhill Street	C1
Banks Street	B1	Leamington Road	D2
Belmont Avenue	C4	Leicester Road	D2
Bennett Avenue	D3	Leopold Grove	C2
Bethesda Road	C4	Lincoln Road	D2
Birley Street	B2	Livingstone Road	C3
Blenheim Avenue	D4	Lord Street	B1
Bonny Street	B4	Louise Street	C4
Buchanan Street	C1	Milbourne Street	C1
Butler Street	C1	New Bonny Street	B3
Caunce Street	D1	Palatine Road	C4
Cedar Square	C2	Palatine Road	D3
Central Drive	C4	Park Road	D2
Chapel Street	B4	Park Road	D4
Charles Street	C1	Peter Street	D2
Charnley Road	C3	Pier Street	B4
Cheapside	B2	Princess Parade	B1
Church Street	B2	Promenade	B1
Church Street	C2	Queen Street	B1
Church Street	D2	Raikes Parade	D2
Clifton Street	B2	Reads Avenue	C3
Clinton Avenue	D4	Reads Avenue	D3
Cookson Street	C2	Regent Road	C2
Coop Street	B4	Ribble Road	C4
Coronation Street	C3	Ripon Road	D3
Corporation Street	B2	Seasiders Way	B4
Dale Street	B4	Seed Street	C1
Deansgate	B2	Selbourne Road	D1
Dickson Road	B1	South King Street	C2
Edward Street	C2	Springfield Road	B1
Elizabeth Street	D1	Stanley Road	C3
Fisher Street	C1	Swainson Street	C1
Foxhall Road	B4	Talbot Road	B2
Freckleton Street	D4	Talbot Road	C1
General Street	B1	Topping Street	C2
George Street	D1	Tower Street	B2
Gorton Street	D1	Vance Road	B3
Granville Road	D2	Victoria Street	B2
Grosvenor Street	C1	Victory Road	D1
Harrison Street	D4	West Street	B2
Havelock Street	C4	Woolman Road	D4
High Street	C1	York Street	B4

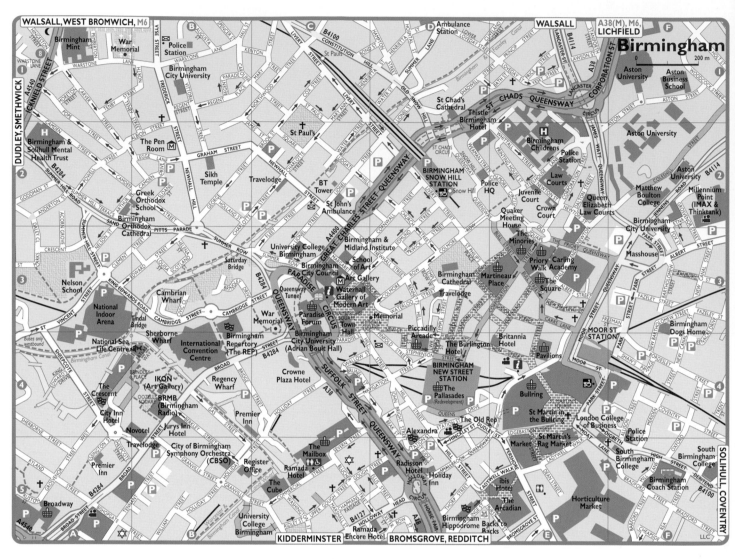

Birmingham

Birmingham is found on atlas page **58 G7**

Acorn Grove...........................A2
Albert Street..........................E3
Albert Street..........................F3
Albion Street.........................B2
Allison Street........................F4
Anderton Street.....................A2
Arthur Place..........................A2
Aston Street...........................F1
Atlas Way...............................B4
Banbury Street.......................F3
Barford Street........................F5
Bartholomew Street...............F3
Barwick Street.......................D3
Bath Street.............................E1
Beak Street............................D4
Benacre Drive.......................F4
Bennetts Hill..........................D3
Berkley Street.......................B4
Bishopgate Street..................A5
Blucher Street.......................C5
Bond Street............................C1
Bordesley Street....................D5
Bow Street.............................D5
Bradford Street......................F5
Bridge Street..........................B4
Brindley Drive........................B4
Brindley Place........................B4
Broad Street...........................A5
Bromsgrove Street................E5
Brook Street...........................C2
Brunel Street..........................C4
Bull Street..............................E3
Cambridge Street...................B3
Camden Drive........................B2
Camden Street.......................A2
Cannon Street........................D3

Caroline Street.......................B1
Carrs Lane.............................E3
Carver Street.........................A1
Chamberlain Square...............C3
Chapmans Passage................C5
Charlotte Street......................B3
Cheapside..............................F5
Cherry Street.........................D3
Church Street.........................D2
Civic Close.............................B3
Clement Street.......................A3
Cleveland Street.....................D1
Coleshill Street.......................F2
Colmore Circus
    Queensway........................E2
Colmore Row.........................D3
Commercial Street..................C5
Constitution Hill.....................C1
Cornwall Street......................D3
Corporation Street..................E1
Corporation Street..................E3
Coventry Street......................F4
Cox Street..............................C1
Dale End................................E3
Daley Close............................A3
Dalton Street..........................E2
Dean Street............................E5
Digbeth..................................E4
Dudley Street.........................D4
Eden Place.............................C3
Edgbaston Street....................E4
Edmund Street.......................D3
Edward Street........................B3
Ellis Street..............................D5
Essington Street.....................A5
Ethel Street............................D4

Etna Street.............................F2
Exeter Street..........................D5
Fazeley Street.........................F3
Fleet Street.............................C3
Fox Street...............................F3
Frederick Street.....................B1
Freeman Street......................E3
Gas Street..............................B4
George Street.........................B2
Gloucester Street...................E5
Goddman Street......................A2
Gough Street..........................C5
Graham Street........................B2
Granville Street......................B5
Great Charles Street
    Queensway........................C3
Grosvenor Street....................F2
Grosvenor Street West...........A5
Hall Street..............................B1
Hampton Street......................D1
Helena Street.........................B3
Henrietta Street......................C1
High Street.............................E4
High Street Deritend..............F5
Hill Street...............................C4
Hinckley Street.......................D4
Hingeston Street.....................A1
Holland Street........................B2
Holliday Street........................B5
Holloway Circus.....................D5
Holloway Head.......................C5
Holt Street..............................F1
Horse Fair..............................D5
Hospital Street.......................D1
Hurst Street...........................E5
Icknield Street........................A1
Inge Street.............................D5
James Street..........................B2
James Watt Queensway.........E2
Jennens Road.........................F2
John Bright Street...................D4

Kenyon Street........................B1
King Edward's Drive...............A4
King Edwards Road.................A3
Ladywell Walk........................D5
Lancaster Circus....................E1
Lancaster Street.....................E1
Lawson Street........................E1
Legge Lane.............................B2
Lighthouse Avenue.................A3
Lionel Street...........................C3
Livery Street...........................C1
Louisa Street..........................B3
Loveday Street.......................D1
Lower Loveday Street.............D1
Lower Temple Street..............D4
Ludgate Hill............................C2
Margaret Street......................C3
Marshall Street.......................C5
Martineau Way.......................E3
Mary Ann Street.....................C1
Mary Street............................C1
Meriden Street.......................F4
Mill Lane................................F5
Moat Lane..............................E4
Moor Street............................E3
Moor Street
    Queensway........................E4
Moreton Street.......................A1
Navigation Street...................D4
Needless Alley........................D3
Nelson Street.........................A3
New Bartholomew Street.......F4
New Canal Street...................F4
Newhall Hill...........................B2
Newhall Street........................C2
New Meeting Street................E3
New Street.............................D3
Newton Street........................E3
Northwood Street...................C1
Old Snow Hill........................D1
Old Square.............................E3

Oozells Square.......................B4
Oxford Street.........................F5
Paradise Circus
    Queensway........................C3
Paradise Street.......................C4
Park Street.............................E4
Pemberton Street...................A1
Pershore Street......................E5
Pinfold Street.........................D4
Pope Street............................A1
Powell Street.........................A2
Price Street............................E1
Princip Street.........................E1
Printing House Street..............E2
Queens Drive.........................D4
Queensway Tunnel.................C3
Rea Street..............................F5
Regent Parade........................B1
Regent Place..........................B1
Regent Street.........................B1
Ridley Street..........................C5
Ruston Street.........................A5
Ryland Street.........................A5
St Chads Queensway..............E1
St Jude's Pass.........................D5
St Marks Crescent..................A3
St Martin's Square..................E4
St Paul's Square.....................C1
St Philip's Place......................D3
St Vincent Street....................A3
Sand Pitts Parade...................A2
Saturday Bridge.....................B3
Scotland Street.......................C5
Severn Street.........................C5
Shadwell Street......................D1
Shaw's Passage......................F4
Sheepcote Street....................A4
Sherborne Street....................A4
Sloane Street.........................B2
Smallbrook Queensway..........D5
Snow Hill Queensway............D2

Spencer Street.......................B1
Staniforth Street.....................E1
Station Street.........................D5
Steelhouse Lane.....................E2
Stephenson Street..................D4
Suffolk Street Queensway......C4
Summer Hill Road..................A2
Summer Hill Street.................A2
Summer Hill Terrace..............A2
Summer Lane.........................D1
Summer Row..........................B3
Swallow Street.......................C4
Temple Row............................D3
Temple Row West...................D3
Temple Street.........................D3
Tenby Street...........................A1
Tenby Street North.................A1
Tennant Street.......................A5
The Priory Queensway...........E3
Thorp Street...........................D5
Tindal Bridge..........................B3
Trent Street............................F4
Union Street...........................E3
Upper Gough Street...............C5
Vesey Street...........................E1
Victoria Square......................D3
Vittoria Street........................B1
Vyse Street............................B1
Warstone Lane.......................A1
Washington Street..................C5
Waterloo Street......................D3
Water Street..........................C2
Weaman Street.......................D2
Whittall Street........................E2
William Street........................B5
Woodcock Street....................F1

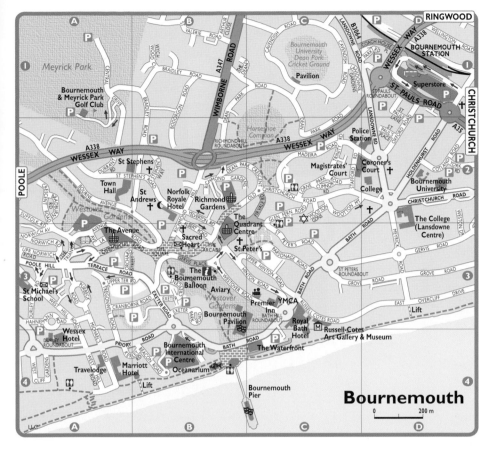

Bournemouth

Bournemouth is found on atlas page **13 J6**

Albert Road................................B3	Poole Hill A3
Arthur Close.............................B1	Priory Road...............................A4
Avenue Lane.............................A3	Purbeck Road...........................A3
Avenue Road.............................A3	Richmond Gardens................B2
Bath Road B4	Richmond Hill..........................B3
Beacon Road.............................B4	Russell Cotes Road...............C3
Bodorgon Road........................B2	St Michael's Road...................A3
Bourne Avenue A2	St Pauls Lane...........................D1
Bradburne Road.......................A2	St Paul's Place..........................D2
Braidley Road............................B1	St Pauls Road..........................D1
Cavendish Road........................C1	St Peter's Road........................C3
Central Drive............................A1	St Stephen's Road...................A2
Christchurch Road...................D2	St Valerie Road........................B1
Coach House Place D1	Stafford Road...........................C2
Commercial Road.....................A3	Stephen's Way.........................B2
Cotlands Road...........................D2	Suffolk Road.............................A2
Cranborne Road.......................A3	Terrace Road............................A3
Crescent Road..........................A2	The Arcade................................B3
Cumnor Road............................C2	The Deans.................................B1
Dean Park Crescent................B2	The Square................................B3
Dean Park Road.......................B2	The Triangle.............................A3
Durley Road..............................A3	Tregonwell Road A3
Durrant Road............................A2	Trinity Road..............................C2
East Overcliff Drive................D3	Upper Hinton Road................C3
Exeter Crescent.......................B3	Upper Norwich Road A3
Exeter Park Road.....................B3	Upper Terrace Road...............A3
Exeter Road..............................B3	Wellington Road......................D1
Fir Vale Road............................C2	Wessex Way..............................A2
Gervis Place..............................B3	West Hill Road.........................A3
Gervis Road...............................D3	Weston Drive............................D2
Glen Fern Road.........................C2	Westover Road.........................B3
Grove Road................................C3	Wimborne Road.......................B1
Hahnemann Road......................A3	Wootton Gardens....................C2
Hinton Road..............................B3	Wootton Mount.......................C2
Holdenhurst Road D2	Wychwood Close.....................B1
Kerley Road...............................A4	Yelverton Road........................B2
Lansdowne Gardens................C1	York Road..................................D2
Lansdowne Road.......................C1	
Lorne Park Road.......................C2	
Madeira Road............................C2	
Meyrick Road............................D3	
Norwich Avenue A3	
Norwich Road...........................A3	
Old Christchurch Road..........C2	
Orchard Street..........................A3	
Oxford Road..............................D2	
Park Road...................................D1	
Parsonage Road.........................C3	

Bradford

Bradford is found on atlas page **90 F4**

Aldermanbury..........................B3	Lower Kirkgate.......................C2
Bank Street...............................B2	Lumb Lane A1
Barkerend Road.......................D2	Manchester Road.....................B4
Barry Street..............................B2	Manningham Lane....................A1
Bolling Road..............................C4	Manor Row................................B1
Bolton Road...............................C2	Market Street...........................B3
Bridge Street............................C3	Midland Road............................B1
Broadway....................................C3	Morley Street...........................A4
Burnett Street...........................D2	Nelson Street............................B4
Canal Road.................................C1	North Brook Street................C1
Carlton Street...........................A3	Northgate...................................B2
Centenary Square B3	North Parade............................B1
Chandos Street..........................C4	North Street..............................B2
Chapel Street............................D3	North Wing...............................D1
Cheapside...................................B2	Otley Road.................................D1
Chester Street...........................A4	Paradise Street.........................A2
Church Bank C2	Peckover Street.......................D2
Claremont..................................A4	Piccadilly.....................................B2
Croft Street...............................C4	Pine Street.................................C2
Darfield Street...........................A1	Princes Way..............................B3
Darley Street.............................B2	Randall Well Street................A3
Drewton Road...........................A2	Rawson Road............................A2
Dryden Street...........................D4	Rawson Square.........................B2
Duke Street................................B2	Rebecca Street.........................A2
East Parade...............................D3	St Blaise Way............................C1
Edmund Street..........................A4	Sawrey Place.............................A4
Edward Street...........................C4	Senior Way................................B4
Eldon Place................................A1	Shipley Airedale Road...........C1
Filey Street................................D3	Stott Hill....................................C2
George Street............................C3	Sunbridge Road.......................A2
Godwin Street...........................B2	Sunbridge Street......................B3
Grattan Road.............................A2	Tetley Street.............................B4
Great Horton Road A4	Thornton Road.........................A3
Grove Terrace..........................A4	Trafalgar Street........................B1
Hallfield Road...........................A1	Tyrell Street..............................B3
Hall Ings....................................B4	Upper Park Gate......................D2
Hamm Strasse...........................B1	Upper Piccadilly.......................B2
Holdsworth Street...................C1	Valley Road................................C1
Houghton Place A1	Vicar Lane.................................C2
Howard Street...........................A4	Wakefield Road D4
Hustlergate...............................B3	Wapping Road D1
Infirmary Street.......................A1	Water Lane................................A2
John Street.................................B2	Wellington Street....................C2
Lansdowne Place......................A4	Westgate.....................................A2
Leeds Road................................D3	Wharf Street.............................C1
Little Horton............................A4	White Abbey Road..................A1
Little Horton Lane..................B4	Wigan Street.............................A2
Longcroft Link..........................A2	Wilton Street............................A4

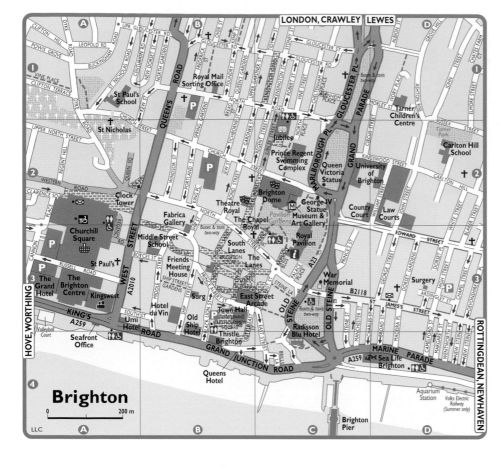

Brighton

Brighton is found on atlas page **24 H10**

Ardingley Street	D3	Madeira Place	D4
Ashton Rise	D1	Manchester Street	C4
Bartholomew Square	B3	Margaret Street	D4
Black Lion Street	B3	Marine Parade	D4
Blaker Street	D3	Market Street	B3
Bond Street	B2	Marlborough Place	C2
Boyces Street	A3	Meeting House Lane	B3
Brighton Place	B3	Middle Street	B3
Broad Street	D4	Morley Street	D1
Buckingham Road	A1	New Dorset Street	B1
Camelford Street	D4	New Road	B2
Cannon Place	A3	New Steine	D4
Carlton Hill	D2	Nile Street	B3
Centurion Road	A1	North Gardens	B1
Chapel Street	D3	North Place	C2
Charles Street	C4	North Road	B1
Cheltenham Place	C1	North Street	B2
Church Street	A1	Old Steine	C3
Church Street	B2	Portland Street	B2
Circus Street	C2	Powis Grove	A1
Clifton Hill	A1	Prince Albert Street	B3
Clifton Terrace	A1	Prince's Street	C3
Devonshire Place	D3	Queen's Gardens	B1
Dukes Lane	B3	Queen Square	A2
Duke Street	B2	Queen's Road	B2
East Street	C3	Regency Road	A2
Edward Street	C2	Regent Hill	A2
Elmore Street	D1	Regent Street	C2
Foundry Street	B1	Robert Street	C1
Frederick Street	B1	St James's Street	D3
Gardner Street	B2	St Nicholas Road	A1
George Street	D3	Ship Street Gardens	B3
Gloucester Place	C1	Spring Gardens	A2
Gloucester Road	B1	Steine Street	C4
Gloucester Street	C1	Sussex Street	D2
Grand Junction Road	B4	Sydney Street	C1
Grand Parade	C2	Tichborne Street	B2
High Street	D3	Tidy Street	C1
Ivory Place	D1	Upper Gardner Street	B1
John Street	D2	Upper Gloucester Road	B1
Jubilee Street	C2	Upper North Street	A2
Kensington Gardens	C1	Vine Street	C1
Kensington Street	C1	Wentworth Street	D4
Kew Street	B1	Western Road	A2
King's Road	A3	West Street	A3
Kingswood Street	C2	White Street	D3
Leopold Road	A1	William Street	D2
Little East Street	B4	Windsor Street	B2

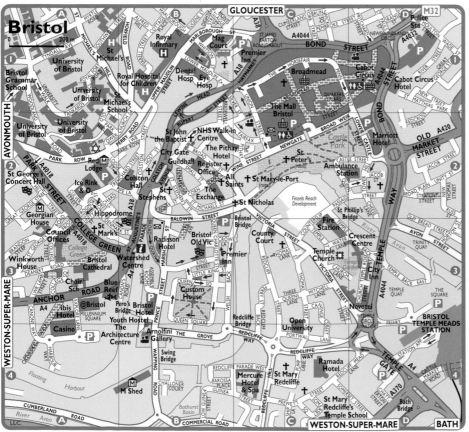

Bristol

Bristol is found on atlas page **31 Q10**

Anchor Road	A3	Passage Street	C2
Avon Street	D3	Pembroke Street	C1
Baldwin Street	B2	Penn Street	C1
Bath Bridge	D4	Pero's Bridge	B3
Bond Street	C1	Perry Road	A2
Bond Street	D2	Philadelphia Street	C2
Broadmead	C1	Portwall Lane	C4
Broad Plain	D2	Prewett Street	C4
Broad Quay	B3	Prince Street	C4
Broad Street	B2	Queen Charlotte Street	B3
Broad Weir	C2	Queen Square	B3
Canons Way	A3	Redcliffe Hill	C4
Canynge Street	C3	Redcliffe Parade West	B4
Castle Street	C2	Redcliffe Way	C4
College Green	A3	Redcliff Mead Lane	C4
Colston Avenue	B2	Redcliff Street	C3
Colston Street	B2	Royal Fort Road	A1
Commercial Road	B4	Rupert Street	B2
Corn Street	B2	St Augustine's Parade	B3
Countership	C3	St George's Road	A3
Cumberland Road	A4	St Matthias Park	D1
Deanery Road	A3	St Michael's Hill	A1
Denmark Street	A3	St Stephen's Street	B2
Explore Lane	A3	St Thomas Street	C3
Fairfax Street	C2	Small Street	B2
Ferry Street	C3	Somerset Street	C4
Friary	D3	Southwell Street	A1
Frogmore Street	A2	Tankards Close	A1
Great George Street	A3	Telephone Avenue	B3
Great George Street	D1	Temple Back	D3
Guinea Street	B4	Temple Back East	D3
Haymarket	C1	Temple Gate	D4
Hill Street	A2	Temple Street	C3
Horfield Road	B1	Temple Way	D2
Houlton Street	D1	The Grove	B4
Jacob Street	D2	The Horsefair	C1
King Street	B3	The Pithay	B2
Lewins Mead	B2	Tower Hill	D2
Lodge Street	A2	Trenchard Street	A2
Lower Castle Street	D2	Tyndall Avenue	A1
Lower Church Lane	A2	Union Street	C1
Lower Maudlin Street	B1	Upper Maudlin Street	B1
Marlborough Hill	B1	Victoria Street	C2
Marlborough Street	B1	Wapping Road	B4
Marsh Street	B3	Welsh Back	B3
Newgate	C2	Whitson Street	C1
Old Market Street	D2	Wine Street	C2
Park Street	A2	Woodland Road	A1

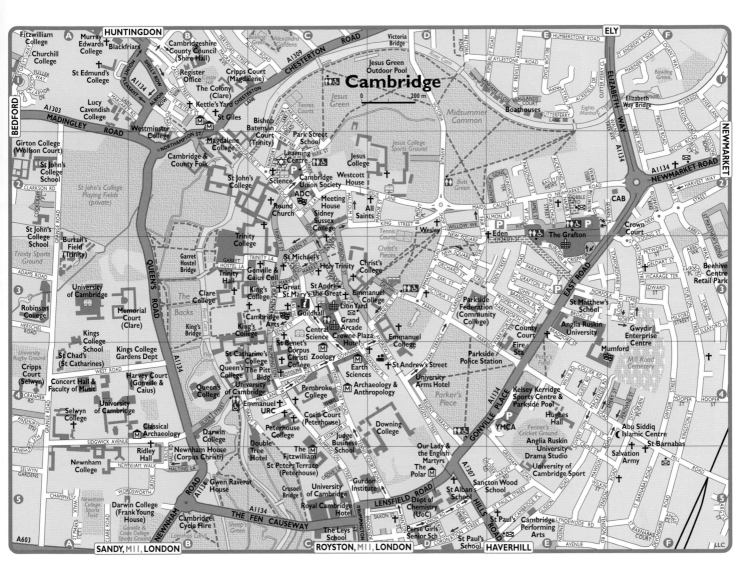

Cambridge

Cambridge is found on atlas page **62 G9**

Abbey Road	F1
Abbey Street	F2
Abbey Walk	F3
Acrefield Drive	E1
Adam and Eve Street	E3
Albion Row	B1
Alpha Road	C1
Auckland Road	E2
Aylestone Road	E1
Bailey Mews	E2
Banhams Close	D1
Beaulands Court	E1
Beche Road	F2
Belmont Place	D2
Belvoir Road	E1
Bene't Street	C3
Bentick Street	D5
Bloom Street	F3
Bradmore Street	E3
Brandon Place	E3
Bridge Street	C2
Broad Street	E3
Brookside	D5
Brunswick Gardens	E2
Brunswick Terrace	E2
Burleigh Street	E3
Cambridge Place	E5
Castle Row	B1
Castle Street	B1
Champneys Walk	A5
Chesterton Lane	B1
Chesterton Road	C1
Christchurch Street	E3
City Road	E3
Clarendon Street	D3
Cobble Yard	E2

Collier Road	E4
Coronation Street	D5
Covent Garden	E4
Crispin Place	E3
Cross Street	E4
Crusoe Bridge	B5
Cutler Ferry Close	E1
Cutterferry Lane	E1
De Freville Avenue	E1
Devonshire Road	F5
Ditchburn Place	F4
Downing Place	C4
Downing Street	C4
Drosier Road	D5
Drummer Street	D3
Earl Street	D3
East Road	E3
Eden Street	E3
Eden Street Back	E3
Edward Street	F3
Elizabeth Way	F1
Elm Street	D3
Emery Street	F4
Emmanuel Road	D3
Emmanuel Street	D3
Evening Court	E2
Fairsford Place	F3
Fair Street	D2
Fitzroy Lane	E3
Fitzroy Street	E3
Fitzwilliam Street	C4
Garret Hostel Bridge	B3
Garret Hostel Lane	B3
Geldart Street	F3
George IV Street	D5
Glisson Road	E5

Godstone Road	F2
Gonville Place	D4
Grafton Street	E3
Grange Road	A3
Grange Road	A4
Grant Place	B4
Green Street	C3
Gresham Road	E5
Guest Road	E4
Gwydir Street	F4
Harvest Way	F2
Harvey Road	E5
Hertford Street	B1
Hills Road	D5
Hobson Street	C3
Humberstone Road	E1
James Street	E2
Jesus Lane	C2
Jesus Terrace	D3
John Street	E3
Kimberley Road	E1
King's Bridge	B3
King's Parade	C3
Kingston Street	F4
King Street	D2
Lady Margaret Road	A1
Lensfield Road	D5
Logan's Way	F1
Lwr Park Street	C2
Lyndewode Road	E5
Mackenzie Road	E4
Madingley Road	A1
Magdalene Street	B2
Magrath Avenue	B1
Maids Causeway	D2
Malcolm Street	C2
Malting Lane	B5
Manhattan Drive	E1
Manor Street	D2
Mariner's Way	F1
Market Street	C3

Mawson Road	E5
Milford Street	F3
Mill Lane	C4
Mill Road	E4
Mill Street	E4
Mortimer Road	E4
Mount Pleasant	B1
Napier Street	E3
Newmarket Road	E2
Newnham Road	B5
Newnham Walk	A5
New Park Street	C2
New Square	D3
New Street	F2
Norfolk Street	E3
Norfolk Terrace	F3
Northampton Street	B2
Occupation Road	F2
Orchard Street	D3
Panton Street	D5
Paradise Street	E3
Parker Street	D3
Park Parade	C1
Parkside	D3
Park Street	C2
Park Terrace	D4
Parsonage Street	E2
Peas Hill	C3
Pembroke Street	C3
Perowne Street	F4
Petworth Street	F3
Pound Hill	B1
Priory Road	F1
Prospect Row	E3
Queen's Road	B3
Regent Street	D4
Regent Terrace	D4
River Lane	F1
Riverside	F1
St Andrew's Road	F1
St Andrew's Street	D3

St Barnabas Road	F5
St Mary's Street	C3
St Matthew's Gardens	F2
St Matthew's Street	F3
St Paul's Street	E5
St Peter's Street	B1
Salmon Lane	E2
Saxon Road	F1
Saxon Street	D5
Severn Place	F2
Shop Street	D2
Sidgwick Avenue	A4
Sidney Street	C2
Silver Street	B4
Staffordshire Street	F3
Sturton Street	F3
Sussex Street	C3
Tenison Avenue	E5
Tenison Road	E5
Tennis Court Road	C4
Tennis Court Terrace	C4
The Fen Causeway	B5
Thompson's Lane	C2
Trinity Lane	C3
Trinity Street	C2
Trumpington Street	C3
Union Road	D5
Vicarage Terrace	E3
Victoria Avenue	D1
Victoria Road	D1
Victoria Street	D3
Warkworth Street	E3
Warkworth Terrace	E3
Wellington Street	E2
West Road	A4
Wilkin Street	E5
Willis Road	E4
Willow Walk	D2
Wordsworth Grove	A5
Young Street	F3

University Colleges

Christ's College	C3
Clare College	A3
Clare College	B1
Clare College	B3
Corpus Christi College	C4
Darwin College	B4
Downing College	D4
Emmanuel College	C3
Emmanuel College	D3
Fitzwilliam College	A1
Girton College	A2
(Wolfson Court)	
Gonville & Caius College	B3
Gonville & Caius College	B4
Jesus College	C2
King's College	B3
Lucy Cavendish College	A1
Magdalene College	B2
Murray Edwards College	A1
Newnham College	A5
Pembroke College	C4
Peterhouse College	C4
Queen's College	B4
Robinson College	A3
St Catherine's College	B4
St Edmund's College	A1
St John's College	B2
Selwyn College	A4
Sidney Sussex College	C2
Trinity College	B3
Westminster College	B1

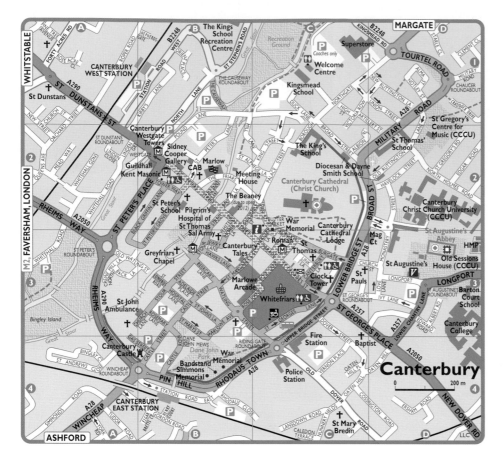

Canterbury

Canterbury is found on atlas page **39 K10**

Adelaide Place	B3	Notley Street	D1
Albert Road	D3	Nunnery Fields	C4
Albion Place	C2	Oaten Hill	C4
Alma Street	D1	Old Dover Road	C4
Artillery Street	C1	Old Ruttington Lane	D2
Beercart Lane	B3	Orchard Street	A2
Best Lane	B2	Palace Street	C2
Black Griffin Lane	A3	Parade	C3
Borough	C2	Pin Hill	B4
Broad Street	D2	Pound Lane	B2
Burgate	C3	Queens Avenue	A2
Butter Market	C2	Rheims Way	A3
Canterbury Lane	C3	Rhodaus Town	B4
Castle Row	B4	Rose Lane	B3
Castle Street	B3	Rosemary Lane	B3
Cossington Road	C4	St Alphege Lane	B2
Dover Street	C3	St Dunstans Street	A1
Duck Lane	C1	St Edmunds Road	B3
Edgar Road	D2	St George's Lane	C3
Edward Road	D3	St George's Place	C3
Ersham Road	D4	St George's Street	C3
Gas Street	A4	St Gregory's Road	D2
Gordon Road	A4	St Johns Lane	B3
Guildhall Street	B2	St Margaret's Street	B3
Havelock Street	D2	St Marys Street	B3
Hawks Lane	B3	St Peter's Grove	B3
High Street	B2	St Peter's Lane	B2
Hospital Lane	C3	St Peter's Place	A3
Ivy Lane	C3	St Peters Street	B2
Jewry Lane	B3	Station Road East	B4
King Street	B2	Station Road West	A1
Kirby's Lane	B1	Stour Street	B3
Lansdown Road	C4	Sturry Road	D1
Linden Grove	A2	Sun Street	C2
Longport	D3	The Causeway	B1
Love Lane	D3	The Friars	B2
Lower Bridge Street	C3	Tourtel Road	D1
Lower Chantry Lane	D4	Tower Way	B2
Marlowe Avenue	B3	Tudor Road	A4
Mead Way	A2	Union Street	D1
Mercery Lane	C3	Upper Bridge Street	C4
Military Road	D2	Vernon Place	C4
Mill Lane	B1	Victoria Row	C1
Monastery Street	D3	Watling Street	B3
New Dover Road	D4	Whitehall Gardens	A2
New Ruttington Lane	D1	Whitehall Road	A2
North Lane	B1	Wincheap	A4
Northgate	C1	York Road	A4

Cardiff

Cardiff is found on atlas page **30 G9**

Adam Street	D3	Museum Avenue	B1
Adams Court	D2	Museum Place	B1
Adamscroft Place	D3	Newport Road Lane	D2
Atlantic Way	D4	North Luton Place	D2
Boulevard De Nantes	B2	North Road	A1
Bridge Street	C3	Oxford Lane	D1
Brigantine Place	D4	Oxford Street	D1
Bute Street	C4	Park Grove	B1
Bute Terrace	C3	Park Lane	B1
Callaghan Square	B4	Park Place	B1
Caroline Street	B3	Park Street	A3
Castle Lane	D1	Pellett Street	C3
Castle Street	A2	Pendyris Street	A4
Central Link	D3	Quay Street	A3
Charles Street	B2	Queen Street	B2
Churchill Way	C2	Richmond Crescent	C1
City Hall Road	A1	Richmond Road	C1
City Road	D1	St Andrew's Crescent	B1
Crockherbtown Lane	B2	St Andrew's Lane	C1
Custom House Street	B4	St Andrew's Place	B1
David Street	C3	St John Street	B2
Davis Street	D3	St Mary Street	B3
Dumfries Place	C2	St Peter's Street	C1
East Bay Close	D3	Salisbury Road	C1
East Grove	D1	Sandon Street	C3
Ellen Street	D3	Saunders Road	B4
Fford Churchill	D2	Schooner Way	D4
Fitzalan Place	D2	Senghennydd Road	C1
Fitzalan Road	D2	Stuttgarter Strasse	B2
Fitzhamon Embankment	A4	The Friary	B2
Glossop Road	D1	The Hayes	B3
Greyfriars Road	B2	The Parade	D1
Guildford Street	C3	The Walk	C1
Guildhall Place	A3	Trinity Street	B3
Havelock Street	A4	Tudor Street	A4
Hayes Bridge Road	B3	Tyndall Street	D4
Heol Siarl	B2	Vere Street	D1
Herbert Street	C4	Wesley Lane	C1
High Street	B3	West Canal Wharf	C4
High Street Arcade	B2	West Grove	C1
Hills Street	B3	Westgate Street	A3
King Edward VII Avenue	A1	Wharton Street	B3
Knox Road	D2	Windsor Lane	C2
Lloyd George Avenue	C4	Windsor Place	C1
Mary Ann Street	C3	Windsor Road	D2
Mill Lane	B4	Womanby Street	A3
Moira Place	D2	Wood Street	A4
Moira Terrace	D2	Working Street	B3

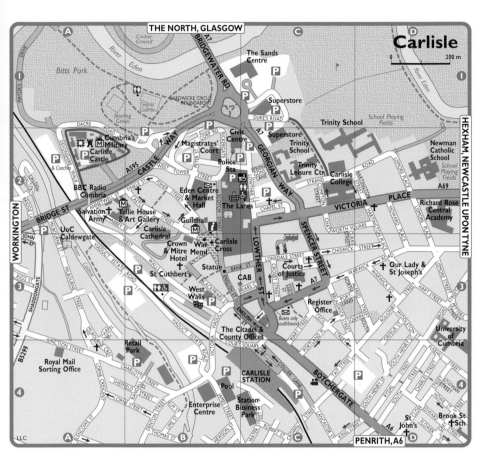

Carlisle

Carlisle is found on atlas page **110 G9**

Abbey Street	A2	Howard Place	D2
Aglionby Street	D3	Howe Street	D4
Annetwell Street	A2	James Street	B4
Bank Street	B3	John Street	A3
Blackfriars Street	B3	Junction Street	A4
Blencowe Street	A4	King Street	C4
Botchergate	C4	Lancaster Street	C4
Bridge Lane	A2	Lime Street	B4
Bridge Street	A2	Lismore Place	D2
Bridgewater Road	B1	Lismore Street	D3
Broad Street	D3	Lonsdale Street	C3
Brunswick Street	C3	Lorne Crescent	A4
Caldew Maltings	A2	Lorne Street	A4
Castle Street	B2	Lowther Street	C2
Castle Way	B2	Mary Street	C3
Cecil Street	C3	Mayor's Drive	A1
Chapel Place	A3	Milbourne Crescent	A3
Chapel Street	C2	Milbourne Street	A3
Charles Street	D4	Myddleton Street	D3
Charlotte Street	A4	North Alfred Street	D3
Chatsworth Square	C2	Orfeur Street	D3
Chiswick Street	C3	Petteril Street	D3
Close Street	D4	Peter Street	B2
Collier Lane	C4	Portland Place	C4
Compton Street	C2	Port-Land Square	C3
Corp Road	B2	Randall Street	B4
Court Square	B4	Rickergate	B2
Crosby Street	C3	Rigg Street	A3
Crown Street	C4	Robert Street	C4
Currie Street	C3	Rydal Street	D4
Dacre Road	A1	Scotch Street	B2
Denton Street	B4	Shaddongate	A3
Devonshire Walk	A2	Sheffield Street	A4
Duke's Road	C1	South Alfred Street	D3
Edward Street	D4	South Henry Street	D4
Elm Street	B4	Spencer Street	C2
English Street	B3	Spring Gardens Lane	C2
Finkle Street	B2	Strand Road	C2
Fisher Street	B2	Tait Street	C4
Flower Street	D4	Thomas Street	B4
Friars Court	C3	Viaduct Estate Road	A3
Fusehill Street	D4	Victoria Place	C2
Georgian Way	C2	Victoria Viaduct	B4
Grey Street	D4	Warwick Road	D3
Hartington Place	D2	Warwick Square	D3
Hartington Street	D2	Water Street	C4
Hart Street	D3	West Tower Street	B2
Hewson Street	B4	West Walls	B3

Cheltenham

Cheltenham is found on atlas page **46 H10**

Albion Street	C2	Montpellier Parade	B4
All Saints' Road	D2	Montpellier Spa Road	B4
Ambrose Street	B1	Montpellier Street	A4
Argyll Road	D4	Montpellier Terrace	A4
Back Montpellier Terrace	A4	Montpellier Walk	A4
Bath Road	B4	New Street	A1
Bath Street	C3	North Street	B2
Baynham Way	B1	Old Bath Road	D4
Bayshill Road	A3	Oriel Road	B3
Bayshill Villas Lane	A3	Parabola Lane	A3
Bennington Street	B1	Parabola Road	A3
Berkeley Street	C3	Park Street	A1
Burton Street	A1	Pittville Circus	D1
Carlton Street	D3	Pittville Circus Road	D1
Church Street	B2	Pittville Street	B2
Clarence Parade	B2	Portland Street	C1
Clarence Road	C1	Prestbury Road	C1
Clarence Street	B2	Priory Street	D3
College Road	C4	Promenade	B3
Crescent Terrace	B2	Queens Parade	A3
Devonshire Street	A1	Regent Street	B2
Duke Street	D3	Rodney Road	B3
Dunalley Street	B1	Royal Well	B2
Evesham Road	C1	Royal Well Lane	A2
Fairview Road	C2	St Anne's Road	D2
Fairview Street	D2	St Anne's Terrace	D2
Fauconberg Road	A3	St George's Place	A2
Glenfall Street	D1	St George's Road	A2
Grosvenor Street	C2	St George's Street	B1
Grove Street	A1	St James' Square	A2
Henrietta Street	B1	St James Street	C3
Hewlett Road	D3	St Johns Avenue	C3
High Street	A1	St Margaret's Road	B1
High Street	C2	St Paul's Street South	B1
Imperial Lane	B3	Sandford Street	C3
Imperial Square	B3	Selkirk Street	D1
Jessop Avenue	A2	Sherborne Street	C2
Keynsham Road	D4	Station Street	A1
King Street	B1	Suffolk Parade	B4
Knapp Road	A1	Swindon Road	B1
Lansdown Road	A4	Sydenham Villas Road	D3
Leighton Road	D2	Trafalgar Street	B4
London Road	D4	Union Street	D2
Malden Road	D1	Wellington Street	C3
Market Street	A1	Winchcombe Street	C2
Milsom Street	A1	Winstonian Road	D2
Monson Avenue	B1	Witcombe Place	C3
Montpellier Grove	B4	York Street	D1

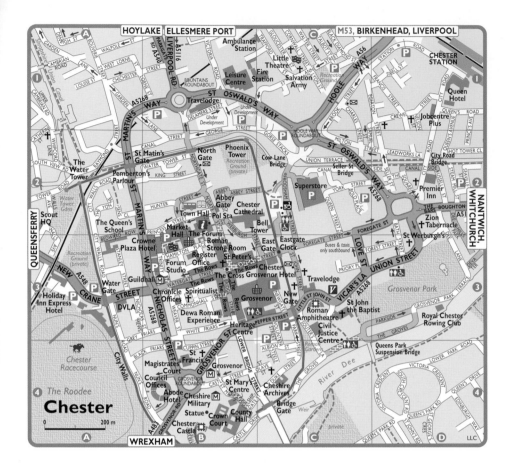

Chester

Chester is found on atlas page **81 N11**

Albion Street	C4	Nicholas Street	B3
Bath Street	D2	Northgate Street	B2
Black Diamond Street	C1	Nun's Road	A3
Boughton	D2	Parkgate Road	B1
Bouverie Street	A1	Park Street	C3
Bridge Street	B3	Pepper Street	C3
Brook Street	C1	Princess Street	B2
Canal Side	C2	Priory Place	C3
Castle Street	B4	Queen's Park Road	C4
Charles Street	C1	Queen's Road	D1
Chichester Street	A1	Queen Street	C2
City Road	D2	Raymond Street	A2
City Walls Road	A2	Russell Street	D2
Commonhall Street	B3	St Anne Street	C1
Cornwall Street	C1	St John's Road	D4
Crewel Street	D1	St John Street	C3
Cuppin Street	B4	St Martin's Way	A2
Dee Hills Park	D2	St Mary's Hill	B4
Dee Lane	D2	St Olave Street	C4
Delamere Street	B1	St Oswald's Way	B1
Duke Street	C4	St Werburgh Street	B2
Eastgate Street	B3	Samuel Street	C2
Egerton Street	C1	Seller Street	D2
Foregate Street	C2	Shipgate Street	B4
Forest Street	C3	Souter's Lane	C3
Francis Street	D1	South View Road	A2
Frodsham Street	C2	Stanley Street	A3
Garden Lane	A1	Station Road	D1
George Street	B2	Steam Mill Street	D2
Gloucester Street	C1	Steele Street	C4
Gorse Stacks	C2	Talbot Street	C1
Grosvenor Park Terrace	D3	Tower Road	A2
Grosvenor Road	B4	Trafford Street	C1
Grosvenor Street	B4	Trinity Street	B3
Hamilton Place	B3	Union Street	D3
Hoole Way	C1	Union Terrace	C2
Hunter Street	B2	Upper Cambrian Road	A1
King Street	B2	Vicar's Lane	C3
Leadworks Lane	D2	Victoria Crescent	D4
Little St John Street	C3	Victoria Road	B1
Liverpool Road	B1	Volunteer Street	C3
Lorne Street	A1	Walpole Street	A1
Love Street	C3	Walter Street	C1
Lower Bridge Street	B4	Watergate Street	B3
Lower Park Road	D4	Water Tower Street	B2
Milton Street	C2	Weaver Street	B3
New Crane Street	A3	White Friars	B3
Newgate Street	C2	York Street	C2

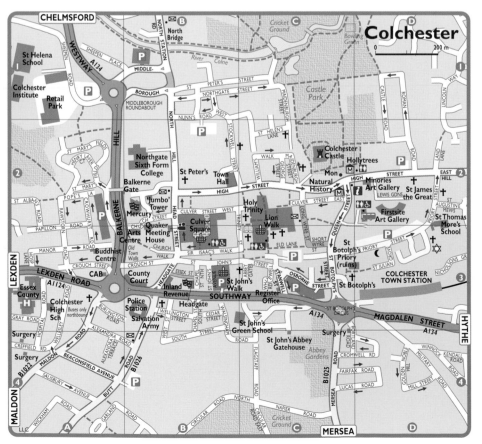

Colchester

Colchester is found on atlas page **52 G6**

Abbey Gates	C3	Middleborough	B1
Alexandra Road	A3	Military Road	D4
Alexandra Terrace	A4	Mill Street	D4
Balkerne Hill	A3	Napier Road	C4
Beaconsfield Avenue	A4	Nicholsons Green	D3
Burlington Road	A3	North Bridge	B1
Butt Road	A4	Northgate Street	B1
Castle Road	D1	North Hill	B1
Cedar Street	B3	North Station Road	B1
Chapel Street North	B3	Nunn's Road	B1
Chapel Street South	B3	Osborne Street	C3
Church Street	B3	Papillon Road	A3
Church Walk	B3	Pope's Lane	A2
Circular Road East	C4	Portland Road	C4
Circular Road North	B4	Priory Street	D3
Creffield Road	A4	Queen Street	C3
Cromwell Road	C4	Rawstorn Road	A2
Crouch Street	A3	Roman Road	D1
Crouch Street	B3	St Alban's Road	A2
Crowhurst Road	A2	St Augustine Mews	D2
Culver Street East	C2	St Botolph's Street	C3
Culver Street West	B2	St Helen's Lane	C2
East Hill	D2	St John's Avenue	B3
Essex Street	B3	St John's Street	B3
Fairfax Road	C4	St Julian Grove	D3
Flagstaff Road	C4	St Mary's Fields	A2
Garland Road	A4	St Peter's Street	B1
George Street	C2	Salisbury Avenue	A4
Golden Noble Hill	D4	Sheepen Place	A1
Gray Road	A3	Sheepen Road	A1
Headgate	B3	Short Wyre Street	C3
Head Street	B2	Sir Isaac's Walk	B3
Henry Laver Court	A2	South Street	B4
High Street	B2	Southway	B3
Hospital Road	A4	Stanwell Street	C3
Hospital Lane	A3	Trinity Street	B2
Kendall Road	D4	Walsingham Road	A4
Land Lane	D2	Wellesley Road	A4
Lewis Gardens	D2	Wellington Street	B3
Lexden Road	A3	West Stockwell Street	B1
Lincoln Way	D1	West Street	B4
Long Wyre Street	C2	Westway	A1
Lucas Road	C4	Whitewell Road	C3
Magdalen Street	D3	Wickham Road	A4
Maidenburgh Street	C1	William's Walk	C2
Maldon Road	A4	Winnock Road	D4
Manor Road	A3		
Mersea Road	C4		

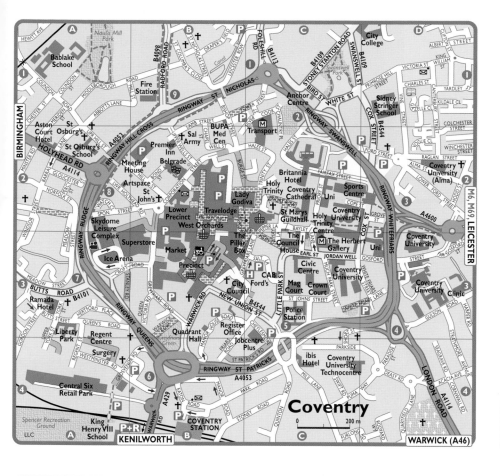

Coventry

Coventry is found on atlas page **59 M9**

Abbotts Lane	A1
Acacia Avenue	D4
Alma Street	D2
Barras Lane	A2
Bayley Lane	C2
Bird Street	C1
Bishop Street	B1
Broadgate	B2
Burge Street	B2
Butts Road	A3
Butts Street	A3
Canterbury Street	D1
Chester Street	A2
Cheylesmore	C3
Cornwall Road	D4
Corporation Street	B2
Coundon Road	A1
Cox Street	D1
Cox Street	D2
Croft Road	A3
Earl Street	C3
Eaton Road	B4
Fairfax Street	C2
Foleshill Road	C1
Gloucester Street	A2
Gosford Street	D3
Greyfriars Lane	B3
Greyfriars Road	B3
Grosvenor Road	A4
Gulson Road	D3
Hales Street	C2
Hertford Place	A3
High Street	C3
Hill Street	B2
Holyhead Road	A2
Jordan Well	C3
Lamb Street	B2
Leicester Row	B1
Little Park Street	C3
London Road	C4
Lower Ford Street	D2
Lower Holyhead Road	A2
Manor House Road	B4
Manor Road	B4
Meadow Street	A3
Meriden Street	A1
Middleborough Road	A1
Mile Lane	C4

Mill Street	A1
Much Park Street	C3
New Union Street	B3
Norfolk Street	A2
Paradise Street	D4
Park Road	B4
Parkside	C4
Primrose Hill Street	D1
Priory Row	C2
Priory Street	C2
Puma Way	C4
Quaryfield Lane	D4
Queen's Road	A3
Queen Victoria Road	B3
Quinton Road	C4
Radford Road	B1
Raglan Street	D2
Regent Street	A4
Ringway Hill Cross	A2
Ringway Queens	A3
Ringway Rudge	A3
Ringway St Nicholas	B1
Ringway St Patricks	B4
Ringway Swanswell	C1
Ringway Whitefriars	D2
St Johns Street	C3
St Nicholas Street	B1
Salt Lane	C3
Seagrave Road	D4
Spon Street	A2
Stanley Road	A3
Stoney Road	B4
Stoney Stanton Road	C1
Strathmore Avenue	D3
Swanswell Street	C1
Tower Street	B1
Trinity Street	C2
Upper Hill Street	B2
Upper Wells Street	A4
Victoria Street	D1
Vine Street	D1
Warwick Road	B3
Warwick Road	B4
Westminster Road	A4
White Friars Street	D3
White Street	C1
Windsor Street	A3
Yardley Street	D1

Darlington

Darlington is found on atlas page **103 Q8**

Abbey Road	A3
Barningham Street	B1
Bartlett Street	B1
Beaumont Street	B3
Bedford Street	C4
Beechwood Avenue	A4
Blackwellgate	B3
Bondgate	B3
Borough Road	D3
Brunswick Street	C3
Brunton Street	D4
Chestnut Street	C1
Cleveland Terrace	A4
Clifton Road	C4
Commercial Street	B2
Coniscliffe Road	A4
Corporation Road	B1
Crown Street	C2
Dodds Street	B1
Duke Street	A3
Easson Road	B1
East Mount Road	D1
East Raby Street	B3
East Street	C3
Elms Road	A2
Feethams	C4
Fife Road	A3
Four Riggs	B2
Freemans Place	C2
Gladstone Street	B2
Grange Road	B4
Greenbank Road	A1
Greenbank Road	B2
Green Street	D3
Hargreave Terrace	C4
Haughton Road	D2
High Northgate	C1
High Row	B3
Hollyhurst Road	A1
Houndgate	B3
Jack Way Steeple	D3
John Street	C1
Kendrew Street	B2
Kingston Street	B1
Langholm Crescent	A4
Larchfield Street	A3
Maude Street	A2
Neasham Road	D4

Northgate	C2
North Lodge Terrace	B2
Northumberland Street	B4
Oakdene Avenue	A4
Outram Street	A2
Parkgate	D3
Park Lane	D4
Park Place	C4
Pendower Street	B1
Pensbury Street	D4
Polam Lane	B4
Portland Place	A3
Powlett Street	B3
Priestgate	C3
Raby Terrace	B3
Russell Street	C2
St Augustine's Way	B2
St Cuthbert's Way	C2
St Cuthbert's Way	C4
St James Place	D4
Salisbury Terrace	A1
Salt Yard	B3
Scarth Street	A4
Skinnergate	B3
South Arden Street	B4
Southend Avenue	A4
Stanhope Road North	A2
Stanhope Road South	A3
Stonebridge	C3
Sun Street	B2
Swan Street	B2
Swinburne Road	A3
Trinity Road	A2
Tubwell Row	B3
Uplands Road	A3
Valley Street North	C2
Vane Terrace	A2
Victoria Embankment	C4
Victoria Road	B4
Victoria Road	C4
West Crescent	A2
West Powlett Street	A3
West Row	B3
West Street	B4
Woodland Road	A2
Yarm Road	D3

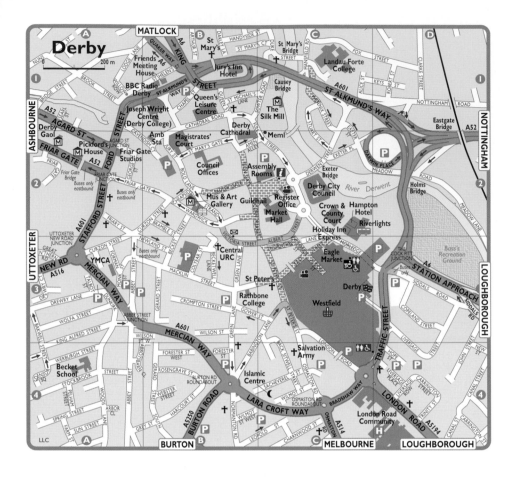

Derby

Derby is found on atlas page **72 B3**

Abbey Street	A4	King Alfred Street	A4
Agard Street	A1	King Street	B1
Albert Street	C3	Lara Croft Way	B4
Babington Lane	B4	Leopold Street	B4
Back Sitwell Street	C4	Liversage Row	D4
Becket Street	B3	Liversage Street	D3
Bold Lane	B2	Lodge Lane	A1
Bradshaw Way	C4	London Road	C3
Bramble Street	B2	Macklin Street	B3
Bridge Street	A1	Mansfield Road	C1
Brook Street	A1	Meadow Lane	D2
Burton Road	B4	Meadow Road	D2
Canal Street	D4	Mercian Way	B3
Carrington Street	D4	Morledge	C3
Cathedral Road	B1	Newland Street	A3
Cavendish Court	A2	New Road	A3
Chapel Street	B1	New Street	D4
Clarke Street	D1	Nottingham Road	D1
Copeland Street	D3	Osmaston Road	C4
Corn Market	B2	Phoenix Street	C1
Crompton Street	B3	Queen Street	B1
Curzon Street	A2	Robert Street	D1
Curzon Street	A3	Rosengrave Street	B4
Darwin Place	C2	Sacheverel Street	C4
Derwent Street	C2	Sadler Gate	B2
Drewry Lane	A3	St Alkmund's Way	C1
Duke Street	C1	St Helen's Street	B1
Dunkirk	A3	St Mary's Gate	B2
East Street	C3	St Peter's Street	C3
Exchange Street	C3	Siddals Road	D3
Exeter Place	C2	Sowter Road	C1
Exeter Street	C2	Spring Street	A4
Ford Street	A2	Stafford Street	A3
Forester Street West	B4	Station Approach	D3
Forman Street	A3	Stockbrook Street	A4
Fox Street	C1	Strand	B2
Friary Street	A2	Stuart Street	C1
Full Street	B1	Sun Street	A4
Gerard Street	B3	The Cock Pitt	D3
Gower Street	B3	Thorntree Lane	C3
Green Lane	B3	Traffic Street	D4
Grey Street	A4	Trinity Street	D4
Handyside Street	B1	Victoria Street	B2
Harcourt Street	B4	Wardwick	B2
Iron Gate	B2	Werburgh Street	A4
John Street	D4	Wilmot Street	C4
Jury Street	B2	Wolfa Street	A3
Keys Street	D1	Woods Lane	A4

Doncaster

Doncaster is found on atlas page **91 P10**

Alderson Drive	D3	Milton Walk	B4
Apley Road	B3	Montague Street	B1
Balby Road Bridge	A4	Nelson Street	B4
Beechfield Road	B3	Nether Hall Road	B1
Broxholme Lane	C1	North Bridge Road	A1
Carr House Road	C4	North Street	C4
Carr Lane	B4	Palmer Street	C4
Chamber Road	B3	Park Road	B2
Chequer Avenue	C4	Park Terrace	B2
Chequer Road	C3	Prince's Street	B2
Childers Street	C4	Priory Place	A2
Christ Church Road	B1	Prospect Place	B4
Church View	A1	Queen's Road	C1
Church Way	B1	Rainton Road	C4
Clark Avenue	C4	Ravensworth Road	C3
Cleveland Street	A4	Rectory Gardens	C1
College Road	B3	Regent Square	C2
Cooper Street	C4	Roman Road	D3
Coopers Terrace	B2	Royal Avenue	C1
Copley Road	B1	St James Street	B4
Cunningham Road	B3	St Mary's Road	C1
Danum Road	D3	St Sepulchre Gate	A2
Dockin Hill Road	B1	St Sepulchre Gate West	A3
Duke Street	A2	St Vincent Avenue	C1
East Laith Gate	B2	St Vincent Road	C1
Elmfield Road	C3	Scot Lane	B2
Exchange Street	A4	Silver Street	B2
Firbeck Road	D3	Somerset Road	B3
Frances Street	B2	South Parade	C2
Georges Gate	B2	South Street	C4
Glyn Avenue	C2	Spring Gardens	A2
Green Dyke Lane	A4	Stirling Street	B2
Grey Friars' Road	A1	Stockil Road	C4
Hall Cross Hill	C2	Theobald Avenue	C4
Hall Gate	B2	Thorne Road	C1
Hamilton Road	D4	Thorne Road	C1
Hannington Street	B1	Town Fields	C1
High Street	A2	Town Moor Avenue	D1
Highfield Road	C1	Trafford Way	A2
Jarratt Street	B4	Vaughan Avenue	C1
King's Road	C1	Waterdale	B3
Lawn Avenue	C2	Welbeck Road	D3
Lawn Road	C2	West Laith Gate	A2
Lime Tree Avenue	D4	West Street	A3
Manor Drive	D3	Whitburn Road	C3
Market Place	B2	White Rose Way	B4
Market Road	B1	Windsor Road	D1
Milbanke Street	B1	Wood Street	B2

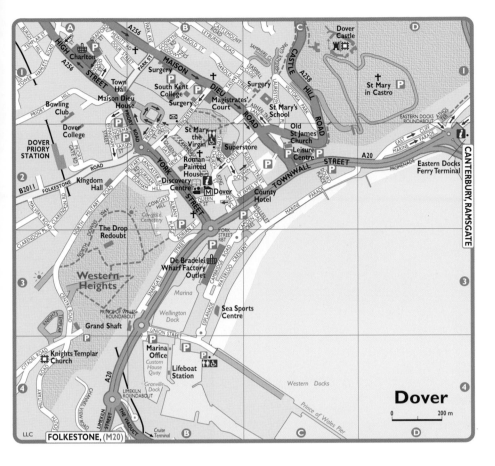

Dover

Dover is found on atlas page **27 P3**

Adrian Street...................B3	New Street...........................B2
Albany Place....................B2	Norman Street....................A2
Ashen Tree Lane................CI	North Downs Way A3
Athol Terrace...................DI	North Military Road...........A3
Biggin Street....................B2	Park Avenue......................BI
Burgh Hill........................AI	Park Street.........................BI
Cambridge Road...............B3	Pencester Road...................B2
Camden Crescent..............C2	Peter Street.......................AI
Cannon Street...................B2	Priory Gate Road...............A2
Castle Hill Road................CI	Priory Hill..........................AI
Castlemount Road.............BI	Priory Road.......................AI
Castle Street.....................B2	Priory Street......................B2
Centre Road.....................A3	Promenade.........................D2
Channel View Road...........A4	Queen's Gate......................B2
Church Street....................B2	Queen Street......................B2
Citadel Road.....................A4	Russell Street.....................B2
Clarendon Place................A3	St James Street...................B2
Clarendon Road................A2	Samphire Close...................CI
Cowgate Hill.....................B2	Saxon Street.......................A2
Crafford Street.................AI	Snargate Street...................B3
Dolphin Lane.....................B2	South Military Road...........A4
Douro Place.....................C2	Stembrook.........................B2
Dour Street......................AI	Taswell Close......................CI
Durham Close....................B2	Taswell Street.....................BI
Durham Hill......................B2	Templar Street....................AI
East Cliff..........................D2	The Viaduct.......................A4
Effingham Street................A2	Tower Hamlets Road..........AI
Esplanade.........................B3	Townwall Street.................C2
Folkestone Road................A2	Union Street.......................B3
Godwyne Close..................BI	Victoria Park......................CI
Godwyne Road..................BI	Waterloo Crescent.............B3
Harold Street....................BI	Wellesley Road...................C2
Harold Street....................BI	Wood Street......................AI
Heritage Gardens...............CI	York Street........................B2
Hewitt Road......................AI	York Street Roundabout.......B3
High Street........................AI	
King Street........................B2	
Knights Templar.................A3	
Lancaster Road..................B2	
Laureston Place.................CI	
Leyburne Road..................BI	
Limekiln Street..................A4	
Maison Dieu Road ....BI	
Malvern Road....................A2	
Marine Parade...................C2	
Marine Parade...................D2	
Military Road.....................B2	
Mill Lane..........................B2	

Dundee

Dundee is found on atlas page **142 G11**

Albert Square....................B2	Ladywell Avenue.................CI
Bank Street.......................B2	Laurel Bank........................BI
Barrack Road....................AI	Lochee Road......................AI
Barrack Road....................B2	Marketgait.........................DI
Bell Street.........................B2	Marketgait East..................CI
Blackscroft.......................DI	McDonald Street.................D2
Blinshall Street...................AI	Meadowside.......................B2
Blinshall Street...................A2	Miln Street........................A2
Bonnybank Road................CI	Murraygate........................C2
Brown Street.....................A2	Nethergate........................A4
Candle Lane......................C2	Nicoll Street......................B2
Castle Street.....................C2	North Lindsay Street B2
Chapel Street.....................C2	North Marketgait................BI
City Square.......................C3	North Victoria Road...........CI
Commercial Street..............C2	Old Hawkhill.....................A3
Constitution Crescent.........AI	Panmure Street...................B2
Constitution Road..............AI	Park Place.........................A3
Constitution Road..............B2	Perth Road........................A4
Court House Square...........A2	Princes Street....................DI
Cowgate..........................CI	Prospect Place...................BI
Cowgate..........................DI	Queen Street......................CI
Crighton Street..................C3	Rattray Street....................B2
Dens Street.......................DI	Reform Street....................B2
Dock Street.......................C3	Riverside Drive...................B4
Douglas Street...................A2	Roseangle..........................A4
Dudhope Street.................BI	St Andrews Street...............CI
Earl Grey Place..................C3	Scrimgeour Place................AI
East Dock Street................D2	Seabraes Lane....................A4
East Whale Lane.................DI	Seagate.............................C2
Euclid Crescent.................B2	Session Street....................A2
Euclid Street......................B2	Shore Terrace....................C3
Forebank Road..................CI	South Marketgait................C3
Forester Street..................A2	South Tay Street.................B3
Foundry Lane....................DI	South Victoria Dock Road...C3
Gellatly Street...................C2	South Ward Road...............B2
Greenmarket.....................B4	Sugarhouse Wynd...............CI
Guthrie Street...................A2	Tay Road Bridge.................D3
Hawkhill...........................A3	Trades Lane.......................C2
High Street........................C3	Union Street.......................B3
Hilltown...........................BI	Union Terrace....................BI
Hilltown Terrace................BI	Ward Road........................B2
Hunter Street....................A3	Weavers Yard....................DI
Infirmary Brae...................AI	West Bell Street..................A2
Johnston Street..................B2	West Marketgait.................A2
King Street........................CI	West Port..........................A3
Kirk Lane..........................CI	West Victoria Dock Road....D2
Laburn Street....................AI	Whitehall Place...................C3
	Whitehall Street..................C3

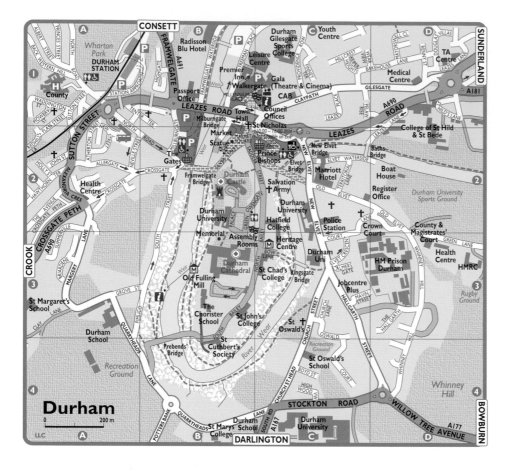

Durham

Durham is found on atlas page **103 Q2**

Albert Street	A1	Mayorswell Close	D1
Alexandria Crescent	A2	Milburngate Bridge	B1
Allergate	A2	Millburngate	B2
Atherton Street	A2	Millennium Place	B1
Back Western Hill	A1	Mowbray Street	A1
Bakehouse Lane	C1	Neville Street	A2
Baths Bridge	C2	New Elvet	C2
Bow Lane	C3	New Elvet Bridge	C2
Boyd Street	C4	New Street	A2
Briardene	A3	North Bailey	C3
Church Lane	C3	North Road	A1
Church Street	C4	Old Elvet	C2
Church Street Head	C4	Oswald Court	C3
Clay Lane	A3	Owengate	B2
Claypath	C1	Palace Green	B2
Court Lane	C3	Palmers Gate	C3
Crossgate	A2	Pelaw Rise	C1
Crossgate Peth	A3	Pimlico	A3
Douglas Villas	D1	Potters Bank	B4
Elvet Bridge	C2	Prebends' Bridge	B4
Elvet Crescent	C3	Princes' Street	A1
Elvet Waterside	C2	Providence Row	C1
Finney Terrace	C1	Quarryheads Lane	A3
Flass Street	A2	Redhills Lane	A2
Framwelgate	B1	Renny Street	D1
Framwelgate Bridge	B2	Saddler Street	B2
Framwelgate Waterside	B1	St Hild's Lane	D1
Freeman Place	B1	Silver Street	B2
Gilesgate	C1	South Bailey	B3
Green Lane	D3	South Road	C4
Grove Street	A3	South Street	B3
Hallgarth Street	C3	Station Approach	A1
Hawthorn Terrace	A2	Stockton Road	C4
Highgate	B1	Summerville	A3
High Road View	C4	Sutton Street	A2
High Street	C2	Tenter Terrace	A1
Hillcrest	C1	Territorial Lane	C2
Holly Street	A2	The Avenue	A2
John Street	A2	The Hall Garth	D3
Keiper Heights	C1	Waddington Street	A1
Kingsgate Bridge	C3	Wear View	C1
Leazes Lane	D1	Whinney Hill	D3
Leazes Lane	D2	Willow Tree Avenue	D4
Leazes Place	C1		
Leazes Road	B1		
Margery Lane	A3		
Market Square	B2		
Mavin Street	C3		

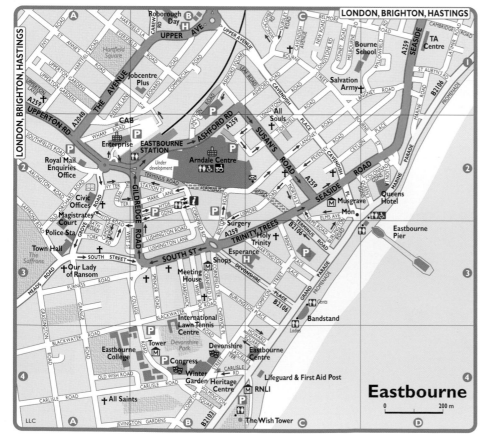

Eastbourne

Eastbourne is found on atlas page **25 P11**

Arlington Road	A2	Langney Road	D1
Ashford Road	B2	Langney Road	C2
Ashford Road	C1	Lascelles Terrace	B4
Ashford Square	B1	Latimer Road	D1
Avenue Lane	A1	Leaf Road	B1
Belmore Road	C1	Lismore Road	B2
Blackwater Road	A4	Longstone Road	C1
Bolton Road	B3	Lushington Road	B3
Bourne Street	C1	Marine Parade	D2
Burlington Place	B3	Marine Road	D1
Burlington Road	C3	Mark Lane	B2
Camden Road	A3	Meads Road	A4
Carew Road	B1	Melbourne Road	C1
Carlisle Road	A4	Old Orchard Road	A2
Carlisle Road	B4	Old Wish Road	A4
Cavendish Avenue	C1	Pevensey Road	C2
Cavendish Place	C1	Promenade	C3
Ceylon Place	C2	Queen's Gardens	D2
Chiswick Place	B3	Saffrons Road	A2
College Road	B3	St Anne's Road	A1
Colonnade Gardens	D2	St Aubyn's Road	D1
Commercial Road	B1	St Leonard's Road	B1
Compton Street	B4	Seaside	D1
Compton Street	C3	Seaside Road	C2
Cornfield Lane	B3	Southfields Road	A2
Cornfield Road	B2	South Street	A3
Cornfield Terrace	B3	South Street	B3
Devonshire Place	B3	Spencer Road	B3
Dursley Road	C1	Station Road	B2
Elms Road	C3	Susan's Road	C2
Enys Road	A1	Sutton Road	B2
Eversfield Road	A1	Sydney Road	C1
Furness Road	A3	Terminus Road	B2
Gildredge Road	B2	Terminus Road	C3
Grand Parade	C3	The Avenue	A1
Grange Road	A3	Tideswell Road	C2
Grassington Road	A3	Trinity Place	B3
Grove Road	A3	Trinity Trees	B3
Hardwick Road	B3	Upper Avenue	B1
Hartfield Lane	A1	Upperton Gardens	A1
Hartfield Road	A1	Upperton Lane	A1
Hartington Place	C3	Upperton Road	A1
Howard Square	C4	West Street	A3
Hyde Gardens	B2	West Terrace	A2
Hyde Road	A2	Willowfield Road	D1
Ivy Terrace	A2	Wilmington Square	B4
Jevington Gardens	A4	Wish Road	B3
Junction Road	B2	York Road	A3

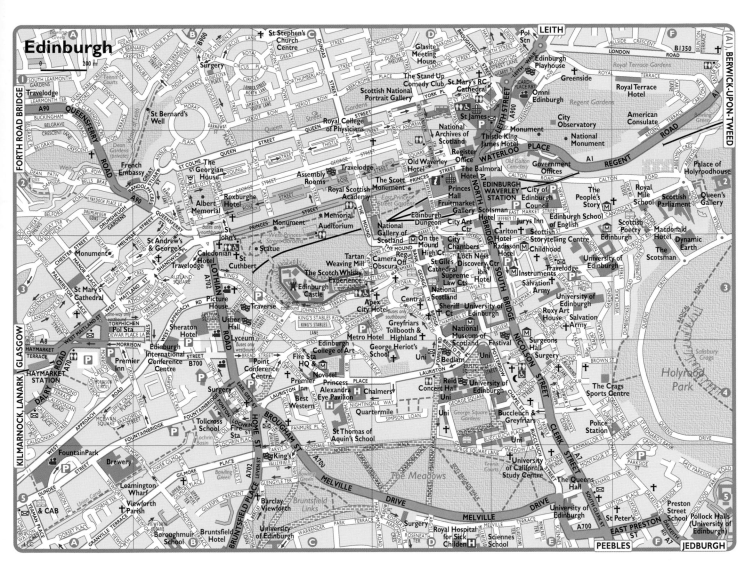

Edinburgh

Edinburgh is found on atlas page **127 P3**

Abbeyhill	F2	Charlotte Square	B2
Abercromby Place	C1	Chester Street Gardens	A3
Adam Street	E3	Circus Lane	B1
Albany Street	D1	Circus Place	B1
Ann Street	A1	Clarendon Crescent	A1
Argyle Place	D5	Clerk Street	E4
Atholl Crescent Lane	A3	Cockburn Street	D2
Bank Street	D3	Coronation Walk	C5
Belford Road	A2	Cowan's Close	E4
Belgrave Crescent	A2	Cowgate	D3
Bernard Terrace	E5	Dalkeith Road	F5
Boys Brigade Walk	D5	Dalry Road	A4
Brandfield Street	A4	Danube Street	B1
Bread Street	B4	Davie Street	E4
Bristo Place	D4	Dean Park Crescent	A1
Brougham Street	C4	Dean Street	A1
Broughton Street	D1	Dewar Place Lane	A3
Broughton Street Lane	E1	Douglas Gardens	A3
Brunton Terrace	F1	Doune Terrace	B1
Bruntsfield Place	B5	Drummond Street	E3
Buccleuch Place	D4	Dublin Street	D1
Buccleuch Street	E4	Dumbiedykes Road	F3
Caledonian Place	A4	Dunbar Street	B4
Caledonian Road	A4	Dundas Street	C1
Caledonian Street	A4	Dundee Street	A5
Calton Road	E2	Earl Grey Street	B4
Candlemaker Row	D3	Easter Road	F1
Canning Street	B3	East Market Street	E2
Canongate	E2	East Parkside	F5
Carlton Terrace	F1	East Preston Street	F5
Castle Hill	C3	Elder Street	D1
Castle Street	C2	Forrest Road	D4
Castle Terrace	B3	Forth Street	D1
Chalmers Street	C4	Fountainbridge	A4
Chambers Street	D3	Frederick Street	C2
Chapel Street	E4	Gardener's Crescent	B4
George IV Bridge	D3	Keir Street	C4
George Square	D4	Kerr Street	B1
George Square Lane	D5	King's Stables Road	B3
George Street	B2	King's Stables Road	C3
George Street	C2	Lady Lawson Street	C3
Gifford Place	E5	Lansdowne Crescent	A3
Gillespie Crescent	B5	Lauriston Gardens	C4
Gilmore Park	A5	Lauriston Place	C4
Gilmore Place	B5	Lauriston Street	C4
Gilmour Street	E4	Lawnmarket	D3
Glenfinlas Street	B2	Leamington Terrace	B5
Gloucester Lane	B1	Leith Street	E1
Granville Terrace	A5	Leith Walk	E1
Great King Street	C1	Lennox Street	A1
Great Stuart Street	B2	Leven Street	C5
Greenmarket	C3	Lochrin Place	B4
Greenside Row	E1	Lochrin Street	B4
Grindlay Street	B3	London Road	E1
Grosvenor Street	A3	Lothian Road	B3
Grove Street	A4	Lower Gilmore Place	B5
Haddon's Court	E4	Lutton Place	E5
Hanover Street	C2	Lynedoch Place Lane	A2
Haymarket Terrace	A4	Manor Place	A3
Heriot Row	C1	Marchmont Crescent	D5
Hermits Croft	F5	Marchmont Road	D5
High Street	D3	Market Street	D2
High Street	E3	Meadow Lane	E5
Hillside Crescent	E1	Melville Drive	C5
Hill Street	C2	Melville Street	A3
Holyrood Park Road	F5	Melville Terrace	D5
Holyrood Road	E3	Middle Meadow Walk	D5
Home Street	C4	Millerfield Place	D5
Hope Street	B2	Miller Row	A2
Horse Wynd	F2	Moncrieff Terrace	E5
Howden Street	E4	Montague Street	E5
Howe Street	C1	Moray Place	B1
India Place	B1	Morrison Link	A4
India Street	B1	Morrison Street	A4
Jamaica Street South Lane	B1	Mound Place	D3
Jawbone Walk	D5	Nelson Street	C1
Johnston Terrace	C3	New Street	E2
Keir Street	C4	Nicolson Square	E4
Nicolson Street	E4	St Stephen Street	B1
Nightingale Way	C4	St Vincent Street	C1
North Bridge	D2	Saunders Street	B1
North Castle Street	C2	Sciennes	E5
North Meadow Walk	C5	Semple Street	B4
North St Andrew Street	D1	Shandwick Place	B3
North St David Street	D1	Simpson Loan	D4
Northumberland Street	C1	South Bridge	E3
Oxford Street	F5	South Charlotte Street	B2
Palmerston Place	A3	South Clerk Street	E5
Panmure Place	C4	South Learmonth Gardens	A1
Pleasance	E3	South St Andrew Street	D2
Ponton Street	B4	South St David Street	D2
Potterrow	E4	Spittal Street	C4
Princes Street	C2	Stafford Street	B3
Queens Drive	F3	Tarvit Street	C5
Queensferry Road	A1	The Mound	C2
Queensferry Street	B2	Thistle Street	C2
Queen Street	B2	Torphichen Street	A3
Radical Road	F3	Union Street	E1
Ramsay Lane	C3	Upper Gilmore Place	B5
Randolph Crescent	B2	Victoria Street	D3
Randolph Lane	B2	Viewcraig Gardens	E4
Rankeillor Street	E5	Viewcraig Street	F3
Regent Road	E2	Viewforth	A5
Richmond Place	E3	Walker Street	A3
Rose Street	B2	Warrender Park Terrace	C5
Rosneath Place	D5	Waterloo Place	D2
Rothesay Place	A3	Waverley Bridge	D2
Royal Circus	B1	West Approach Road	A5
Royal Terrace	E1	West Maitland Street	A3
St Andrew Square	D1	West Nicolson Street	E4
St Bernard's Crescent	A1	West Port	C4
St Colme Street	B2	West Richmond Street	E4
St James Place	D1	West Toll Cross	B4
St Leonard's Bank	F4	William Street	A3
St Leonard's Hill	E4	Yeaman Place	A5
St Leonard's Lane	F4	York Lane	D1
St Leonard's Street	E4	York Lane	D1
St Patrick Street	E4	York Place	D1
		Young Street	B2

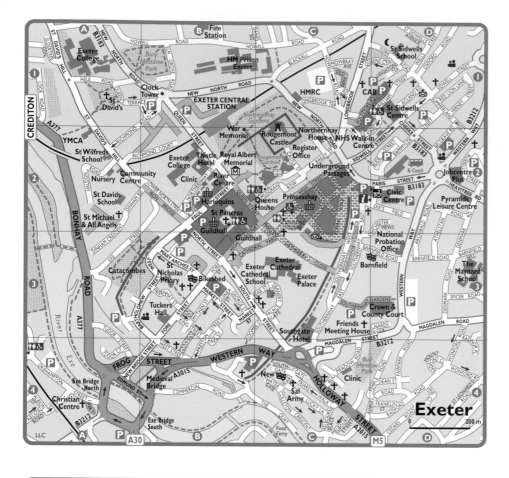

Exeter

Exeter is found on atlas page **9 M6**

Acland Road D1
Archibald Road D3
Athelstan Road D3
Bailey Street C2
Bampfylde Lane C2
Bampfylde Street D2
Barnfield Road D3
Bartholomew Street West B3
Bear Street C3
Bedford Street C2
Belgrave Road D2
Blackall Road C1
Bonhay Road A2
Bude Street D2
Bull Meadow Road C4
Castle Street C2
Cathedral Close C3
Cathedral Yard B3
Cedars Road D4
Cheeke Street D1
Chichester Mews C3
Commercial Road B4
Coombe Street B3
Deanery Place C3
Dean Street D4
Denmark Road D3
Dinham Crescent A3
Dinham Road A2
Dix's Field D2
Eastgate C2
Edmund Street A4
Elm Grove Road B1
Exe Street A3
Fairpark Road D4
Fore Street B3
Franklin Street D4
Friernhay Street B3
Frog Street A4
George Street B3
Guinea Street B3
Haldon Road A2
Heavitree Road D2
Hele Road A1
High Street C2
Holloway Street C4
Howell Road B1
Iron Bridge B2
King Street B3

King William Street D1
Longbrook Street C1
Lower North Street B2
Magdalen Road D3
Magdalen Street C4
Market Street B3
Martins Lane C2
Mary Arches Street B3
Musgrave Row C2
New Bridge Street A4
New North Road A1
Northernhay Street B2
North Street B3
Old Park Road C1
Oxford Road D1
Palace Gate C3
Paris Street D2
Paul Street B2
Preston Street B4
Princesshay C2
Queens Crescent C1
Queen's Terrace A1
Queen Street B1
Radford Road D4
Red Lion Lane D1
Richmond Court B2
Richmond Road A2
Roberts Road C4
Roman Walk C2
St David's Hill A1
Sidwell Street C2
Sidwell Street D1
Smythen Street B3
Southernhay East C3
Southernhay Gardens C3
Southernhay West C3
South Street B3
Spicer Road D3
Summerland Street D1
Temple Road D4
Tudor Court A4
Tudor Street A3
Verney Street D1
Wells Street D1
Western Way B4
West Street B4
Wonford Road D4
York Road D1

Gloucester

Gloucester is found on atlas page **46 F11**

Albert Street D4
Albion Street B4
All Saints' Road D4
Alvin Street C2
Archdeacon Street B2
Archibald Street C4
Arthur Street C4
Barbican Road B3
Barrack Square B3
Barton Street D4
Bedford Street C3
Belgrave Road C4
Berkeley Street B3
Black Dog Way C2
Blenheim Road D4
Brunswick Road B4
Brunswick Square B4
Bruton Way D3
Bull Lane B3
Castle Meads Way A2
Clarence Street C3
Clare Street B2
Commercial Road B3
Cromwell Street C4
Deans Walk C1
Eastgate Street C3
Gouda Way B1
Great Western Road D2
Greyfriars B3
Hampden Way C3
Hare Lane C2
Heathville Road D2
Henry Road D1
Henry Street D2
High Orchard Street A4
Honyatt Road D1
King Barton Street C4
Kingsholm Road C1
King's Square C3
Ladybellegate Street B3
Llanthony Road A4
London Road D2
Longsmith Street B3
Market Parade C3
Merchants' Road A4
Mercia Road B1
Metz Way D3
Millbrook Street D4

Montpellier B4
Napier Street D4
Nettleton Road C3
New Inn Lane B3
New Inn Lane C3
Norfolk Street B4
Northgate Street C3
Old Tram Road B4
Over Causeway A1
Oxford Road D1
Oxford Street D2
Park Road C4
Park Street C2
Parliament Street B3
Pembroke Street C4
Pitt Street B2
Priory Road B1
Quay Street B2
Royal Oak Road A2
Russell Street C3
St Aldate Street C2
St Catherine Street C1
St John's Lane B3
St Mark Street C1
St Mary's Square B2
St Mary's Street B2
St Michael's Square C4
St Oswald's Road B1
Sebert Street C1
Severn Road A3
Sherborne Street D2
Sinope Street D4
Southgate Street B3
Spa Road B4
Station Road C3
Swan Road C1
Sweetbriar Street C1
The Cross B3
The Oxbode C3
The Quay A2
Union Street C1
Upper Quay Street B2
Vauxhall Road D4
Wellington Street C4
Westgate Street A2
Widden Street D4
Worcester Parade C2
Worcester Street C2

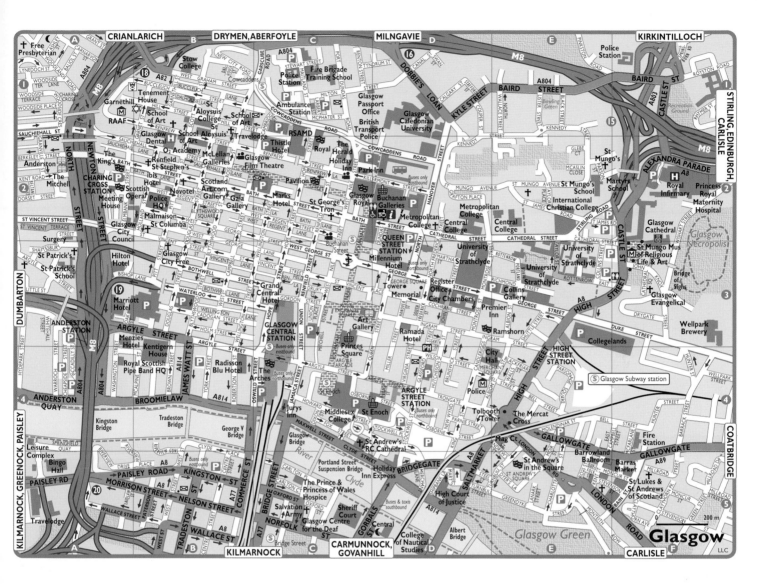

Glasgow

Glasgow is found on atlas page **125 P4**

Albert Bridge	D5	Candleriggs	D4	Garnethill Street	B1	Larbert Street	C1	Pinkston Road	E1	Stafford Street	D1
Albion Street	D4	Carlton Place	C5	Garnet Street	B2	Lister Street	E1	Pitt Street	B2	Steel Street	D5
Albion Street	E3	Carnarvon Street	A1	Garscube Road	C1	London Road	E4	Port Dundas Road	C1	Stevenson Street	F5
Alexandra Parade	F2	Castle Street	F1	Garth Street	D3	Maitland Street	C1	Portland Street Suspension		Stewart Street	C1
Anderston Quay	A4	Castle Street	F2	George Square	D3	Martha Street	D3	Bridge	C5	Stirling Road	E2
Argyle Arcade	C4	Cathedral Square	F3	George Street	E3	Mart Street	D5	Queen Street	C4	Stockwell Place	D4
Argyle Street	A3	Cathedral Street	D2	George V Bridge	B4	Maxwell Street	C4	Renfield Lane	C3	Stockwell Street	D4
Armour Street	F4	Centre Street	B5	Glasgow Bridge	C5	McAlpine Street	B4	Renfield Street	C3	Suffolk Street	E5
Ashley Street	A1	Chalmer Street	F5	Glassford Street	D4	McAslin Close	E2	Renfrew Lane	C2	Sydney Street	F4
Bain Street	F5	Charing Cross	A1	Glebe Court	E2	McFarlane Street	F4	Renfrew Street	B1	Taylor Place	E2
Baird Street	E1	Charlotte Street	E5	Gorbals Street	C5	McPhater Street	C1	Renton Street	C1	Taylor Street	E2
Baliol Street	A1	Cheapside Street	A4	Gordon Street	C3	Merchant Lane	D5	Rhymer Street	F1	Tradeston Bridge	B4
Barrack Street	F4	Claythorn Avenue	F5	Grafton Place	D2	Miller Street	D4	Richmond Street	E3	Tradeston Street	B5
Bath Lane	B2	Claythorn Park	F5	Granville Street	A2	Millroad Drive	F5	Riverview Drive	A4	Trongate	D4
Bath Street	A2	Clyde Place	B4	Greendyke Street	E5	Millroad Street	F5	Robertson Street	B4	Turnbull Street	D5
Bell Street	E4	Clyde Street	C4	Green Street	F5	Milton Street	C1	Rose Street	B2	Tyndrum Street	C1
Berkeley Street	A2	Cochrane Street	D3	Hanover Street	D3	Mitchell Street	C4	Ross Street	E5	Union Street	C3
Blackfriars Street	E4	Collins Street	E3	High Street	E4	Moir Street	E5	Rottenrow	E3	Virginia Street	D4
Black Street	E1	Commerce Street	B5	Hill Street	B1	Molendinar Street	E4	Rottenrow East	E3	Wallace Street	A5
Blythswood Square	B2	Couper Street	D1	Holland Street	B2	Moncur Street	E5	Royal Exchange Square	C3	Walls Street	E4
Blythswood Street	B3	Cowcaddens Road	C1	Holm Street	B3	Monteith Row	E5	Royston Road	F1	Warroch Street	A4
Bothwell Lane	B3	Dalhousie Lane	B1	Hope Street	C3	Montrose Street	D3	Royston Square	F1	Washington Street	A4
Bothwell Street	B3	Dixon Street	C4	Howard Street	C4	Morrison Street	A5	St Andrew's Square	E5	Waterloo Street	B3
Bridgegate	D5	Dobbie's Loan	D1	Hunter Street	F4	Nelson Street	B5	St Andrew's Street	E4	Wellington Lane	B3
Bridge of Sighs	F3	Dorset Street	A2	Hutcheson Street	D4	New City Road	B1	St James Road	E2	Wellington Street	B3
Bridge Street	C5	Douglas Street	B3	Hydepark Street	A4	Newton Street	A2	St Mungo Avenue	D2	Wellpark Street	F4
Broomielaw	B4	Drury Street	C3	Ingram Street	D3	New Wynd	D4	St Vincent Crescent	B3	West Campbell Street	B3
Brown Street	B4	Drygate	F3	Jamaica Street	C4	Norfolk Street	C5	St Vincent Place	C3	West George Lane	B2
Brunswick Street	D4	Duke Street	F3	James Watt Street	B4	North Frederick Street	D3	St Vincent Street	A2	West George Street	B2
Buccleuch Lane	B1	Dundas Street	D3	John Knox Street	F3	North Hanover Street	D3	St Vincent Terrace	A2	West Graham Street	B1
Buccleuch Street	B1	Dunlop Street	D4	John Street	D3	North Portland Street	E3	Saltmarket	D5	West Nile Street	C3
Buchanan Street	C4	Dyer's Lane	E5	Kennedy Drive	D2	North Street	A2	Sauchiehall Lane	A2	West Regent Lane	C2
Cadogan Street	B3	East Campbell Street	E4	Kennedy Street	E1	North Wallace Street	E1	Sauchiehall Street	A1	West Regent Street	B2
Calgary Street	D1	Elmbank Street	A2	Kent Road	A2	Osborne Street	C4	Sauchiehall Street	B2	West Street	B5
Cambridge Street	C1	Fox Street	C4	Kent Street	E5	Oswald Street	C4	Scott Street	B1	Wilson Street	D4
Canal Street	D1	Gallowgate	E4	Killermont Street	C2	Oxford Street	C5	Shaftesbury Street	A3	Wishart Street	F3
				Kingston Bridge	A5	Paisley Road	A5	Shipbank Lane	D5	Woodlands Road	A1
				Kingston Street	B5	Parnie Street	D4	Shuttle Street	E3	Woodside Crescent	A1
				King Street	D4	Parsonage Square	E4	South Frederick Street	D3	Woodside Terrace	A1
				Kyle Street	D1	Parson Street	E2	Springburn Road	F1	Woodside Terrace Lane	A1
				Lanark Street	E5	Paterson Street	B5	Springfield Quay	A4	York Street	B4

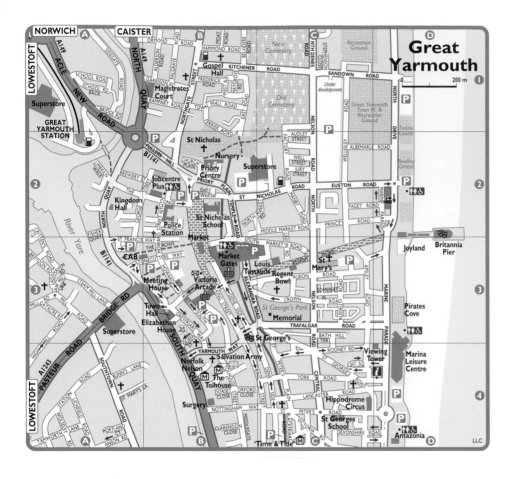

Great Yarmouth

Great Yarmouth is found on atlas page **77 Q10**

Acle New Road	A1	North Denes Road	C1
Albemarle Road	C2	North Drive	D1
Albion Road	C3	North Market Road	C2
Alderson Road	B1	North Quay	A2
Alexandra Road	B3	Northgate Street	B1
Anson Road	A4	Nottingham Way	B4
Apsley Road	C3	Ormond Road	B1
Belvidere Road	B1	Paget Road	C2
Blackfriars Road	C4	Palgrave Road	B1
Brewery Street	A2	Pasteur Road	A4
Breydon Road	A3	Prince's Road	C2
Bridge Road	A1	Priory Plain	B2
Bridge Road	A3	Queen Street	B4
Bunn's Lane	A4	Rampart Road	B1
Church Plain	B2	Regent Road	C3
Critten's Road	A3	Rodney Road	C4
Crown Road	C3	Russell Road	C3
Dene Side	B3	St Francis Way	A3
Devonshire Road	C4	St George's Road	C4
East Road	B1	St Nicholas Road	B2
Euston Road	C2	St Peter's Plain	C4
Factory Road	C2	St Peter's Road	C4
Ferrier Road	B1	Sandown Road	C1
Fishers Quay	A2	Saw Mill Lane	A3
Frederick Road	B1	School Road	A1
Fullers Hill	B2	School Road Back	A1
Garrison Road	B1	Sidegate Road	A1
Gatacre Road	A3	South Market Road	C3
George Street	A2	South Quay	B3
Greyfriars Way	B3	Southtown Road	A4
Hammond Road	B1	Station Road	A4
High Road	A3	Steam Mill Lane	A3
Howard Street North	B2	Stephenson Close	C1
Howard Street South	B3	Stonecutters Way	B3
King Street	B3	Tamworth Lane	A4
Kitchener Road	B1	Temple Road	B2
Ladyhaven Road	A3	The Conge	A2
Lancaster Road	C4	The Rows	B3
Lichfield Road	A4	Tolhouse Street	B4
Limekiln Walk	A2	Town Wall Road	B1
Manby Road	C2	Trafalgar Road	C3
Marine Parade	D3	Union Road	C3
Maygrove Road	B1	Victoria Road	C4
Middle Market Road	C2	Wellesley Road	C2
Middlegate	B4	West Road	B1
Moat Road	B1	Wolseley Road	A4
Nelson Road Central	C3	Yarmouth Way	B4
Nelson Road North	C1	York Road	C4

Guildford

Guildford is found on atlas page **23 Q5**

Abbot Road	C4	Millmead Terrace	B4
Angel Gate	B3	Mount Pleasant	A4
Artillery Road	B1	Nightingale Road	D1
Artillery Terrace	C1	North Street	B3
Bedford Road	A2	Onslow Road	C1
Bridge Street	A3	Onslow Street	B3
Bright Hill	C3	Oxford Road	C3
Brodie Road	D3	Pannells Court	C2
Bury Fields	B4	Park Street	B3
Bury Street	B4	Pewley Bank	D3
Castle Hill	C4	Pewley Fort Inner Court	D4
Castle Street	C3	Pewley Hill	C3
Chapel Street	B3	Pewley Way	D3
Chertsey Street	C2	Phoenix Court	B3
Cheselden Road	D2	Porridge Pot Alley	B4
Church Road	B1	Portsmouth Road	A4
College Road	B2	Poyle Road	D4
Commercial Road	B2	Quarry Street	B3
Dene Road	D2	Sandfield Terrace	C2
Denmark Road	D2	Semaphore Road	D3
Drummond Road	B1	South Hill	C3
Eagle Road	C1	Springfield Road	C1
Epsom Road	D2	Station Approach	D1
Falcon Road	C1	Stoke Fields	C1
Fort Road	C4	Stoke Grove	C1
Foxenden Road	D1	Stoke Road	C1
Friary Bridge	A3	Swan Lane	B3
Friary Street	B3	Sydenham Road	C3
George Road	B1	Testard Road	A3
Guildford Park Road	A2	The Bars	C2
Harvey Road	D3	The Mount	A4
Haydon Place	C2	The Shambles	B3
High Pewley	D4	Tunsgate	C3
High Street	B3	Upperton Road	A3
Jeffries Passage	C2	Victoria Road	D1
Jenner Road	D2	Walnut Tree Close	A1
Laundry Road	B2	Ward Street	C2
Leapale Lane	B2	Warwicks Bench	C4
Leapale Road	B2	Wharf Road	B1
Leas Road	B1	Wherwell Road	A3
London Road	D2	William Road	B1
Mareschal Road	A4	Wodeland Avenue	A3
Market Street	C3	Woodbridge Road	B1
Martyr Road	C2	York Road	B1
Mary Road	A1		
Millbrook	B3		
Mill Lane	B3		
Millmead	B3		

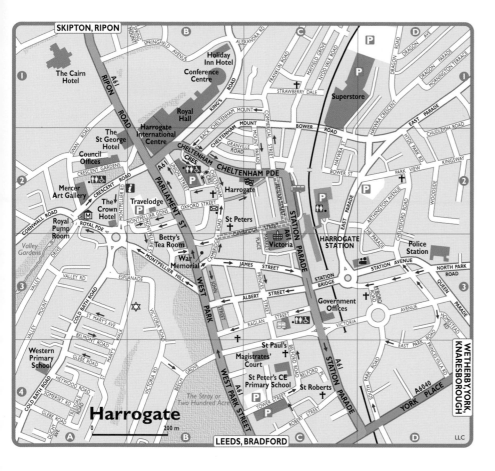

Harrogate

Harrogate is found on atlas page **97 M10**

Albert Street	C3	Montpellier Street	B2
Alexandra Road	B1	Mornington Terrace	D1
Arthington Avenue	D2	Mount Parade	C2
Back Cheltenham Mount	B2	North Park Road	D3
Beech Grove	B4	Nydd Vale Road	C1
Belford Place	C4	Oxford Street	B2
Belford Road	C4	Park View	D2
Belmont Road	A3	Parliament Street	B2
Beulah Street	C2	Princes Street	C2
Bower Road	C1	Princes Villa Road	D4
Bower Street	C2	Queen Parade	D3
Cambridge Road	B3	Raglan Street	C3
Cambridge Street	C2	Ripon Road	A1
Chelmsford Road	D3	Robert Street	C4
Cheltenham Crescent	B2	Royal Parade	A2
Cheltenham Mount	B2	St Mary's Avenue	A3
Cheltenham Parade	B2	St Mary's Walk	A4
Chudleigh Road	D2	Somerset Road	A4
Cold Bath Road	A3	South Park Road	D4
Commercial Street	C1	Springfield Avenue	B1
Cornwall Road	A2	Spring Mount	B1
Crescent Gardens	A2	Station Avenue	D3
Crescent Road	A2	Station Bridge	C3
Dragon Avenue	D1	Station Parade	C2
Dragon Parade	D1	Strawberry Dale	C1
Dragon Road	D1	Swan Road	A2
Duchy Avenue	A4	The Parade	D2
East Parade	C2	Tower Street	C4
East Park Road	D4	Treesdale Road	A4
Esplanade	A3	Union Street	B2
Franklin Road	C1	Valley Drive	A3
Glebe Road	A4	Valley Mount	A3
Granville Road	B2	Valley Road	A3
Haywra Street	C2	Victoria Avenue	C3
Heywood Road	A4	Victoria Road	B3
Homestead Road	D3	West Park	B3
Hyde Park Road	D2	West Park Street	B4
Hywra Crescent	D2	Woodside	D2
James Street	B3	York Place	D4
John Street	B3		
King's Road	B1		
Kingsway	D2		
Market Place	C3		
Marlborough Road	D3		
Mayfield Grove	C1		
Montpellier Gardens	B2		
Montpellier Hill	B3		
Montpellier Road	A2		

Huddersfield

Huddersfield is found on atlas page **90 E7**

Albion Street	B4	New North Road	A2
Alfred Street	C4	New Street	B4
Back Union Street	C1	Northgate	C1
Bankfield Road	A4	Northumberland Street	C2
Bath Street	B1	Old Leeds Road	D2
Belmont Street	A1	Old South Street	B3
Brook Street	C2	Outcote Bank	B4
Byram Street	C2	Oxford Street	C1
Cambridge Road	B1	Park Avenue	A2
Carforth Street	D4	Park Drive South	A2
Castlegate	B1	Peel Street	C4
Chancery Lane	B3	Pine Street	C2
Chapel Hill	B4	Portland Street	A2
Chapel Street	B4	Princess Street	B4
Church Street	C2	Prospect Street	A4
Clare Hill	B1	Quay Street	D2
Claremont Street	B1	Queen Street	C3
Cloth Hall Street	B3	Queen Street South	C4
Cross Church Street	C3	Queensgate	C4
Dundas Lane	B3	Railway Street	B2
Elizabeth Queen Gardens	A2	Ramsden Street	B3
Elmwood Avenue	A1	Rook Street	B1
Firth Street	D4	St Andrew's Road	D2
Fitzwilliam Street	A2	St George's Square	B2
Fitzwilliam Street	B2	St John's Road	B1
Gasworks Street	D1	St Peter's Street	C2
Great Northern Street	C1	Southgate	C2
Greenhead Road	A3	Spring Grove Street	A4
Half Moon Street	B3	Spring Street	A3
High Street	B3	Springwood Avenue	A3
Highfields Road	A1	Stadium Way	D1
John William Street	B2	Station Street	A2
King Street	C3	Trinity Street	A2
King's Mill Lane	D4	Turnbridge Road	D2
Kirkgate	C3	Union Street	C1
Leeds Road	C2	Upper George Street	A3
Lincoln Street	D3	Upperhead Row	B3
Lord Street	C2	Viaduct Street	B2
Lower Fitzwilliam Street	C1	Victoria Lane	C3
Lynton Avenue	A3	Wakefield Road	D3
Manchester Road	A4	Water Street	A3
Market Place	C3	Watergate	D2
Market Street	B3	Waverley Road	A2
Merton Street	A3	Wentworth Street	A2
Milford Street	B4	Westgate	B3
Mountjoy Road	A1	William Street	C1
New North Parade	B2	Wood Street	C2
New North Road	A1	Zetland Street	C3

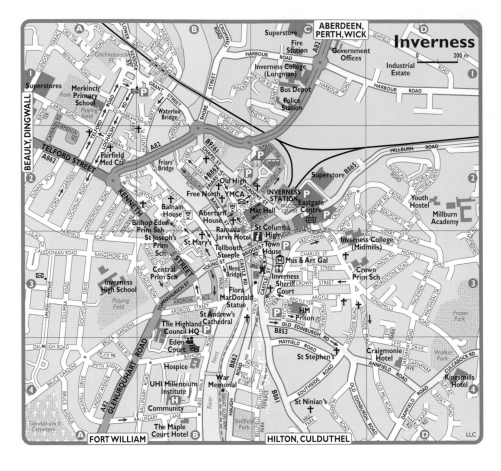

Inverness

Inverness is found on atlas page **156 B8**

Abertaff Road	D2	Glendoe Terrace	A1
Academy Street	B2	Glenurquhart Road	A4
Anderson Street	B1	Gordon Terrace	C3
Annfield Road	D4	Grant Street	B1
Ardconnel Terrace	C3	Great Glen Way	B4
Ardross Street	B3	Harbour Road	C1
Argyle Street	C3	Harris Road	D4
Argyle Terrace	C3	Harrowden Road	A2
Ballifeary Lane	A4	Haugh Road	B4
Ballifeary Road	B4	High Street	C3
Bank Street	B2	Hill Park	C4
Bellfield Terrace	C4	Hill Street	C3
Benula Road	A1	Huntly Street	B2
Bernett Road	B1	Innes Street	B1
Birnie Terrace	A1	Islay Road	D4
Bishops Road	B4	Kenneth Street	A2
Bridge Street	B3	King Street	B3
Broadstone Road	D3	Kingsmills Road	D3
Bruce Avenue	A4	Laurel Avenue	A3
Bruce Gardens	A4	Lindsay Avenue	A4
Bruce Park	A4	Lochalsh Road	A2
Burnett Road	C1	Lovat Road	D3
Caledonian Road	A3	Lower Kessock Street	A1
Cameron Road	A2	Maxwell Drive	A4
Cameron Square	A2	Mayfield Road	C4
Carse Road	A1	Midmills Road	D3
Castle Road	B3	Millburn Road	D2
Castle Street	C3	Mitchell's Lane	C3
Chapel Street	B2	Muirfield Road	C4
Charles Street	C3	Old Edinburgh Road	C3
Columba Road	A3	Park Road	A4
Crown Circus	C2	Planefield Road	B3
Crown Drive	D2	Porterfield Road	C3
Crown Road	C2	Raasay Road	D4
Crown Street	C3	Rangemore Road	A3
Culcabock Road	D4	Ross Avenue	A2
Dalneigh Road	A4	Seafield Road	D1
Damfield Road	D4	Shore Street	B1
Darnaway Road	D4	Smith Avenue	A4
Denny Street	C3	Southside Place	C3
Dochfour Drive	A3	Southside Road	C4
Dunabran Road	A1	Telford Gardens	A2
Dunain Road	A2	Telford Road	A2
Duncraig Street	B3	Telford Street	A2
Erisky Road	D4	Tomnahurich Street	B3
Fairfield Road	A3	Union Road	D3
Falcon Square	C2	Walker Road	C1
Friars' Lane	B2	Young Street	B3

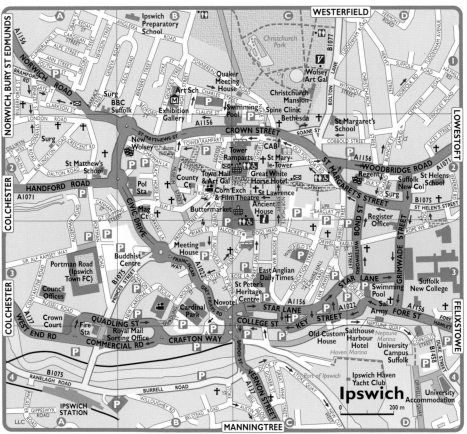

Ipswich

Ipswich is found on atlas page **53 L3**

Alderman Road	A3	London Road	A2
Anglesea Road	B1	Lower Brook Street	C3
Barrack Street	A1	Lower Orwell Street	C3
Belstead Road	B4	Museum Street	B2
Berners Street	B1	Neale Street	C1
Black Horse Lane	B2	Neptune Quay	D3
Blanche Street	D2	New Cardinal Street	B3
Bolton Lane	C1	Newson Street	A1
Bond Street	D3	Northgate Street	C2
Bramford Road	A1	Norwich Road	A1
Bridge Street	C4	Old Foundry Road	C2
Burlington Road	A2	Orchard Street	D2
Burrell Road	B4	Orford Street	A1
Cardigan Street	A1	Orwell Place	C3
Carr Street	C2	Orwell Quay	D4
Cavern Street	B3	Portman Road	A3
Cecil Road	B1	Princes Street	A3
Cemetery Road	D1	Princes Street	B3
Charles Street	B1	Quadling Street	A3
Christchurch Street	D1	Quadling Street	B3
Civic Drive	B2	Queen Street	B3
Clarkson Street	A1	Ranelagh Road	A4
Cobbold Street	C2	Redan Street	A1
College Street	C3	Russell Road	A3
Commercial Road	A4	St George's Street	B1
Constantine Road	A3	St Helen's Street	D2
Crafton Way	B4	St Margaret's Street	C2
Crown Street	B2	St Matthews Street	B2
Cumberland Street	C1	St Nicholas Street	B3
Dalton Road	A2	St Peter's Street	B3
Dock Street	C4	Silent Street	B3
Duke Street	D4	Sir Alf Ramsey Way	A3
Eagle Street	C3	Soane Street	C2
Elm Street	B2	South Street	A1
Falcon Street	B3	Star Lane	C3
Fonnereau Road	B1	Stoke Quay	C4
Foundation Street	C3	Suffolk Road	D1
Franciscan Way	B3	Tacket Street	C3
Geneva Road	A1	Tower Ramparts	B2
Great Gripping Street	A2	Tuddenham Avenue	D1
Great Whip Street	C4	Turret Lane	C3
Grey Friars Road	B3	Upper Orwell Street	C3
Grimwade Street	D3	Vernon Street	C4
Handford Road	A2	West End Road	A3
Hervey Street	D1	Westgate Street	B2
High Street	B1	Willoughby Road	B4
Key Street	C3	Wolsey Street	B3
King Street	B2	Woodbridge Road	D2

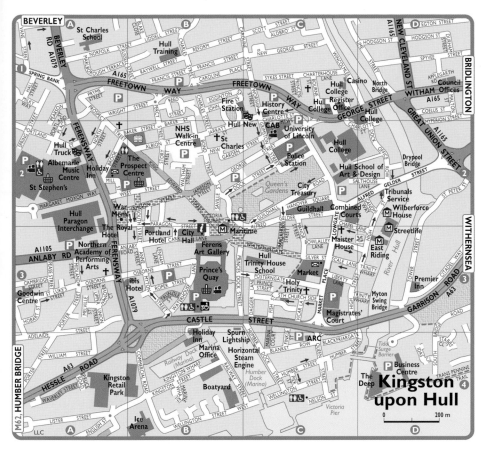

Kingston upon Hull

Kingston upon Hull is found on atlas page **93 J5**

Adelaide Street	A4	Market Place	C3
Albion Street	B2	Mill Street	A2
Alfred Gelder Street	C2	Myton Street	B3
Anlaby Road	A3	New Cleveland Street	D1
Baker Street	B2	New Garden Street	B2
Beverley Road	A1	New George Street	C1
Blackfriargate	C4	Norfolk Street	A1
Blanket Row	C4	Osborne Street	B3
Bond Street	B2	Osborne Street	A3
Brook Street	A2	Paragon Street	B2
Caroline Street	B1	Pease Street	A3
Carr Lane	B3	Percy Street	B1
Castle Street	B3	Porter Street	A3
Chapel Lane	C2	Portland Place	A2
Charles Street	B1	Portland Street	A2
Charterhouse Lane	C1	Postergate	C3
Citadel Way	D3	Princes Dock Street	B3
Commercial Road	B4	Prospect Street	A1
Dagger Lane	C3	Queen Street	C4
Dock Office Row	D2	Railway Street	B4
Dock Street	B2	Raywell Street	B1
Durham Street	D1	Reform Street	B1
Egginton Street	B1	Russell Street	A1
Ferensway	A2	St Luke's Street	A3
Freetown Way	A1	St Peter Street	D2
Gandhi Way	D2	Saville Street	B2
Garrison Road	D3	Scale Lane	C3
George Street	B2	Scott Street	C1
George Street	D1	Silver Street	C3
Great Union Street	D1	South Bridge Road	D4
Grimston Street	C2	South Church Side	C3
Guildhall Road	C2	South Street	B2
Hanover Square	C2	Spring Bank	A1
Hessle Road	A4	Spyvee Street	D1
High Street	C3	Sykes Street	C1
Hodgson Street	D1	Tower Street	D3
Humber Dock Street	C4	Upper Union Street	A3
Humber Street	C4	Victoria Square	B2
Hyperion Street	D1	Waterhouse Lane	B3
Jameson Street	B2	Wellington Street	C4
Jarratt Street	B2	Wellington Street West	B4
King Edward Street	B2	West Street	A2
Kingston Street	B4	Whitefriargate	C3
Liddell Street	B1	William Street	A4
Lime Street	C1	Wincolmlee	C1
Lister Street	A4	Witham	D1
Lowgate	C3	Worship Street	C1
Margaret Moxon Way	A2	Wright Street	A1

Lancaster

Lancaster is found on atlas page **95 K8**

Aberdeen Road	D4	Lincoln Road	A3
Aldcliffe Road	B4	Lindow Street	B4
Alfred Street	C2	Lodge Street	C2
Ambleside Road	D1	Long Marsh Lane	A2
Balmoral Road	D4	Lune Street	B1
Bath Street	D3	Market Street	B3
Blades Street	A3	Meeting House Lane	A3
Bond Street	D3	Middle Street	B3
Borrowdale Road	D2	Moor Gate	D3
Brewery Lane	C3	Moor Lane	C3
Bridge Lane	B2	Morecambe Road	B1
Brock Street	C3	Nelson Street	C3
Bulk Road	D2	North Road	C2
Bulk Street	C3	Owen Road	C1
Cable Street	B2	Park Road	D3
Castle Hill	B3	Parliament Street	C2
Castle Park	A3	Patterdale Road	D2
Caton Road	C2	Penny Street	B4
Cheapside	C3	Portland Street	B4
China Street	B3	Primrose Street	D4
Church Street	B2	Prospect Street	D4
Common Garden Street	B3	Quarry Road	C4
Dale Street	D4	Queen Street	B4
Dallas Road	B3	Regent Street	B4
Dalton Road	D2	Ridge Lane	D1
Dalton Square	C3	Ridge Street	D1
Damside Street	B2	Robert Street	C2
Derby Road	C1	Rosemary Lane	C3
De Vitre Street	C2	St George's Quay	A1
Dumbarton Road	D4	St Leonard's Gate	C3
East Road	D3	St Peter's Road	C4
Edward Street	C3	Sibsey Street	A3
Fairfield Road	A3	South Road	C4
Fenton Street	B3	Station Road	A3
Gage Street	C3	Stirling Road	D4
Garnet Street	D2	Sulyard Street	C3
George Street	C3	Sun Street	B3
Grasmere Road	D3	Thurnham Street	B4
Great John Street	C3	Troutbeck Road	D2
Gregson Road	D4	Ulleswater Road	D3
Greyhound Bridge Road	B1	West Road	A3
High Street	B4	Westbourne Road	A3
Kelsey Street	A3	Wheatfield Street	A3
Kentmere Road	D2	Williamson Road	D3
King Street	B3	Wingate-Saul Road	A3
Kingsway	C1	Wolseley Street	D2
Kirkes Road	D4	Woodville Street	D3
Langdale Road	D1	Wyresdale Road	D3

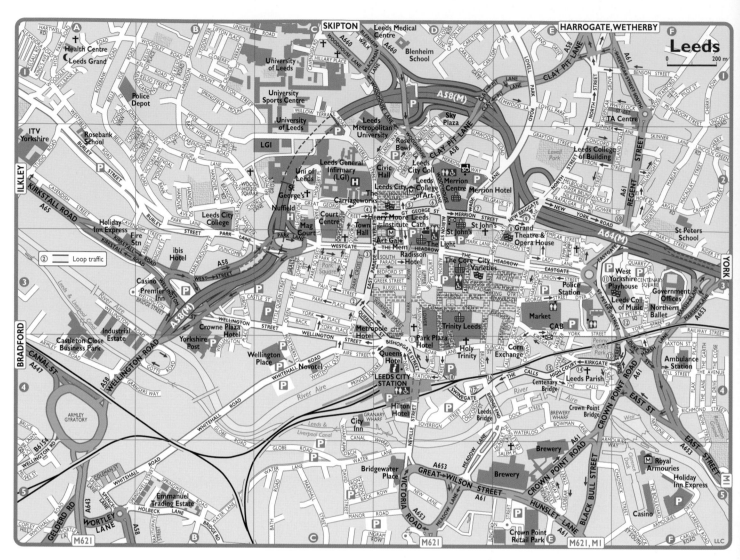

Leeds

Leeds is found on atlas page **90 H4**

Abbey Street	B3	Calverley Street	C2
Aire Street	C4	Canal Street	A4
Albion Place	D3	Canal Wharf	C4
Albion Street	D2	Carlton Carr	D1
Alexandra Road	A1	Carlton Hill	D1
Argyle Road	F2	Carlton Rise	D1
Armley Gyratory	A4	Castle Street	B3
Armley Road	A4	Cavendish Road	C1
Armouries Drive	F5	Cavendish Street	A2
Armouries Way	E4	Centenary Square	F3
Back Hyde Terrace	B2	Central Road	E3
Back Row	C5	Chadwick Street	F5
Bath Road	C5	Cherry Row	F1
Bedford Street	D3	Chorley Lane	B2
Belgrave Street	D2	City Square	D3
Belle Vue Road	A1	Claremont	B2
Belmont Grove	C2	Clarence Road	F5
Benson Street	F1	Clarendon Road	B1
Bingley Street	B3	Clay Pit Lane	D2
Bishopgate Street	D4	Cloberry Street	B1
Black Bull Street	E5	Commercial Street	D3
Blackman Lane	C1	Concord Street	E2
Blenheim Walk	C1	Consort Street	B2
Boar Lane	D4	Consort View	A1
Bowman Lane	E4	County Arcade	E3
Bow Street	F4	Cromer Terrace	B1
Brandon Road	B2	Cromwell Street	F2
Bridge End	D4	Cross Kelso Road	B1
Bridge Road	B5	Cross Stamford Street	F1
Bridge Street	E2	Crown Point Road	E5
Bridge Street	E3	Crown Street	E4
Briggate	D4	Cudbear Street	E5
Burley Street	A2	David Street	C5
Butts Court	D3	Dock Street	E4
Byron Street	E2	Duke Street	F4
Call Lane	E4	Duke Street	F4

Duncan Street	D4	Kirkgate	E3
Duncombe Street	B3	Kirkstall Road	A2
Dyer Street	E3	Lady Lane	E3
Eastgate	E3	Lands Lane	D3
East Parade	C3	Leighton Street	C2
East Street	F4	Leyland Road	F2
Elmwood Lane	E1	Lifton Place	B1
Elmwood Road	D2	Lincoln Green Road	F2
Flax Place	F4	Lisbon Street	B3
Gelderd Road	A5	Little Queen Street	C3
George Street	E3	Lovell Park Hill	E1
Globe Road	B4	Lovell Park Road	E1
Gotts Road	B4	Lower Basinghall Street	D3
Gower Street	E2	Lower Brunswick Street	E2
Grafton Street	E2	Lyddon Terrace	B1
Grangers Way	A4	Mabgate	F2
Great George Street	C2	Macaulay Street	F2
Great Wilson Street	D5	Manor Road	C5
Greek Street	D3	Mark Lane	D3
Hanover Avenue	B2	Marlborough Street	B3
Hanover Lane	B2	Marshall Street	C5
Hanover Square	B2	Marsh Lane	F4
Harewood Street	E3	Maude Street	E4
Harper Street	E3	Meadow Lane	D5
Harrison Street	E3	Melbourne Street	E2
Hartwell Road	A1	Merrion Street	D2
High Court	E4	Merrion Way	D2
Holbeck Lane	B5	Millbank Lane	A1
Hope Road	F2	Millennium Square	D2
Hunslet Road	E4	Mill Street	F4
Hunslet Road	E5	Millwright Street	F2
Hyde Park Road	A1	Mount Preston Street	B1
Hyde Street	B2	Mushroom Street	F1
Hyde Terrace	B1	Neptune Street	B4
Infirmary Street	D3	Neville Street	D4
Junction Street	D5	New Briggate	E2
Kelso Road	B1	New Lane	D5
Kendal Lane	B2	New Station Street	D4
King Edward Street	E3	New York Road	E2
King's Avenue	A1	New York Street	E3
King Street	C3	Northern Street	C4

North Street	E2	Springwell Street	B5
Oxford Place	C3	Studio Road	A2
Oxford Row	C3	Swinegate	D4
Park Cross Street	C3	Templar Street	E3
Park Lane	B2	The Avenue	F5
Park Place	C3	The Boulevard	F5
Park Row	D3	The Calls	E4
Park Square East	C3	The Headrow	D3
Park Square North	C3	Thoresby Place	C2
Park Square West	C3	Trafalgar Street	E2
Park Street	C3	Union Street	E3
Pilot Street	F1	Upper Basinghall Street	D3
Portland Crescent	D2	Vicar Lane	E3
Portland Way	D2	Victoria Road	D5
Princes Square	C4	Victoria Street	B2
Quarry Hill	F3	Victoria Terrace	B2
Quebec Street	C3	Wade Lane	D2
Queen Square	D2	Water Lane	B5
Queen Square Court	D2	Waterloo Street	E4
Queen Street	C3	Wellington Bridge Street	B3
Railway Street	F3	Wellington Road	A4
Regent Street	F2	Wellington Road	A4
Richmond Street	F4	Wellington Road	A5
Rider Street	F3	Wellington Street	A5
Rosebank Road	A1	Westfield Road	A1
St Cecilia Street	F3	Westgate	C3
St John's Road	A1	West Street	B3
St Mary's Street	F3	Wharf Approach	C4
St Paul's Street	C3	Wharf Street	E4
St Peter's Square	F3	Whitehall Quay	C4
St Peter's Street	E3	Whitehall Road	A5
Salem Place	E5	Whitehall Road	A5
Saxton Street	F4	Whitelock Street	F1
Sheepscar Grove	E1	Willow Terrace Road	C1
Sheepscar Street South	F1	Woodhouse Lane	C1
Skinner Lane	E1	Woodhouse Square	B2
South Parade	D3	Woodsley Road	A1
Sovereign Street	D4	Wortley Lane	A5
Spence Lane	A5	Wortley Lane	A5
Springfield Mount	B1	York Place	C3
Springwell Road	B5	York Street	F3

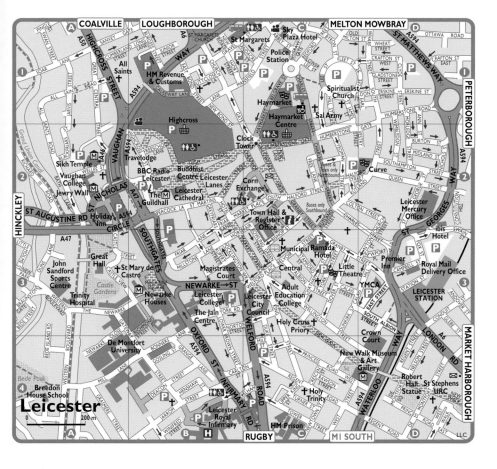

Leicester

Leicester is found on atlas page **72 F10**

Albion Street....................C3	Infirmary Road...................B4
All Saints Road.................A1	Jarrom Street....................B4
Bath Lane........................A2	Jarvis Street.....................A1
Bedford Street.................C1	King Street.......................C3
Belgrave Gate..................C1	Lee Street.......................C1
Belvoir Street..................C3	London Road....................D3
Bishop Street...................C3	Lower Brown Street..........B3
Bonners Lane...................B4	Magazine Square..............B3
Bowling Green Street........C3	Mansfield Street...............B1
Burgess Street.................B1	Market Place South...........B2
Burton Street...................D2	Market Street...................C3
Calais Hill.......................C3	Mill Lane.........................A4
Campbell Street................D3	Morledge Street................D1
Cank Street.....................B2	Newarke Street.................B3
Castle Street....................A3	New Walk.........................C3
Charles Street..................C1	Oxford Street...................B3
Chatham Street................C3	Peacock Lane....................B2
Cheapside.......................C2	Pocklington Walk..............B3
Church Gate....................B1	Princess Road East............D4
Clyde Street....................D1	Princess Road West...........C4
Colton Street...................C2	Queen Street....................D2
Conduit Street..................D3	Regent Road....................C4
Crafton Street West..........D1	Regent Street...................D4
Deacon Street..................B4	Richard III Road...............A2
De Montfort Street...........D4	Rutland Street...................C2
Dover Street....................C3	St Augustine Road............A2
Duke Street.....................C3	St George Street...............D2
Duns Lane.......................A3	St Georges Way................D2
East Bond Street Lane.......B1	St James Street.................C1
Erskine Street..................D1	St Matthews Way..............D1
Fleet Street.....................C1	St Nicholas Circle.............A2
Friar Lane.......................B3	Sanvey Gate.....................A1
Gallowtree Gate...............C2	Soar Lane........................A1
Gateway Street.................A3	South Albion Street...........D3
Granby Street...................C3	Southampton Street...........D2
Grasmere Street................A4	Southgates.......................B3
Gravel Street...................B1	Station Street...................D3
Great Central Street..........A1	The Newarke....................A3
Greyfriars.......................B2	Tower Street....................C4
Halford Street..................C2	Vaughan Way....................A2
Haymarket.......................C2	Waterloo Way..................D4
Highcross Street...............A1	Welford Road...................C3
Highcross Street...............B2	Welles Street....................A2
High Street......................B2	Wellington Street..............C3
Hill Street.......................C1	Western Boulevard.............A4
Horsefair Street...............B3	West Street......................C4
Humberstone Gate............C2	Wharf Street South............D1
Humberstone Road...........D1	Yeoman Street..................C2

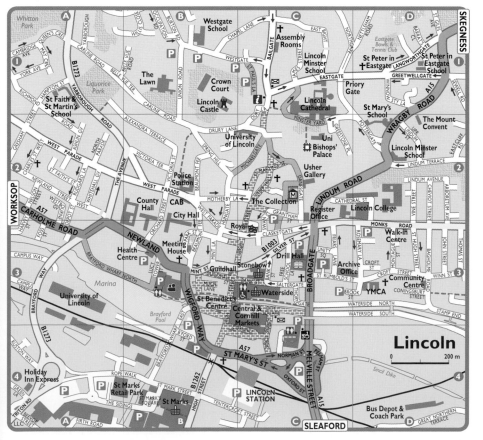

Lincoln

Lincoln is found on atlas page **86 C6**

Alexandra Terrace.............B2	Montague Street................D3
Arboretum Avenue............D2	Motherby Lane.................B2
Bagholme Road.................D3	Nelson Street...................A2
Bailgate.........................C1	Newland..........................B3
Bank Street.....................C3	Newland Street West..........A2
Beaumont Fee..................B3	Norman Street..................C4
Belle Vue Terrace.............A1	Northgate........................C1
Brayford Way...................A3	Orchard Street..................B3
Brayford Wharf East...........B4	Oxford Street...................C4
Brayford Wharf North.........A3	Park Street......................B3
Broadgate.......................C3	Pelham Street...................C4
Burton Road....................B1	Pottergate.......................D2
Carholme Road.................A2	Queen's Crescent..............A1
Carline Road...................A1	Richmond Road................A1
Cathedral Street...............C2	Rope Walk.......................A4
Chapel Lane....................B1	Rosemary Lane.................D3
Charles Street West...........A2	Rudgard Lane...................A2
Cheviot Street..................D2	St Hugh Street..................D2
City Square.....................C3	St Mark Street..................B4
Clasketgate.....................C3	St Martin's Street..............C2
Cornhill.........................B4	St Mary's Street................B4
Croft Street.....................D3	St Rumbold's Street...........C3
Danesgate.......................C2	Saltergate.......................C3
Depot Street....................A3	Silver Street....................C3
Drury Lane......................B2	Sincil Street.....................C4
East Bight.......................C1	Spring Hill.......................B2
Eastgate.........................C1	Steep Hill.......................C2
Free School Lane..............C3	Swan Street......................B2
Friars Lane......................C3	Tentercroft Street..............B4
Grantham Street...............C2	The Avenue......................A2
Greetwellgate..................D1	Thorngate.......................C3
Gresham Street.................A2	Triton Road.....................A4
Guildhall Street................B3	Union Road......................B1
Hampton Street................A1	Unity Square....................C3
High Street......................B3	Victoria Street..................B2
Hungate..........................B3	Victoria Terrace................B2
John Street......................D3	Vine Street......................D2
Langworthgate.................D1	Waterside North...............C3
Lindum Road...................C2	Waterside South...............C4
Lindum Terrace................D2	Westgate.........................B1
Lucy Tower Street.............B3	West Parade.....................A2
May Crescent..................A1	Whitehall Grove................A2
Melville Street..................C4	Wigford Way....................A3
Michaelgate.....................C2	Winnow Sty Lane..............D1
Minster Yard....................C2	Winn Street......................D3
Mint Lane.......................B3	Wragby Road...................D2
Mint Street......................B3	Yarborough Road..............A1
Monks Road....................D3	York Avenue....................A1

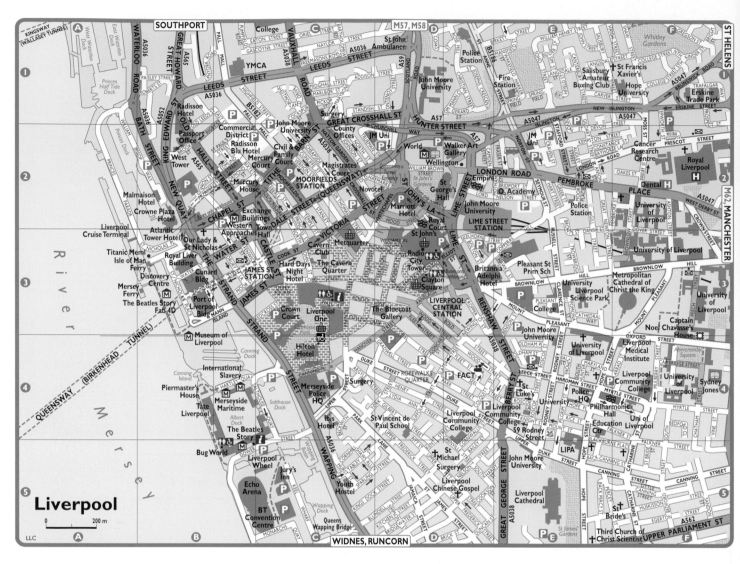

Liverpool

Liverpool is found on atlas page **81 L6**

Addison Street	C1	Chapel Street	B2
Anson Street	E2	Chatham Street	F4
Argyle Street	C4	Cheapside	C2
Arrad Street	F4	Christian Street	D1
Ashton Street	F2	Churchill Way	D2
Audley Street	E2	Church Street	C3
Back Canning Street	E5	Clarence Street	E3
Baltimore Street	E4	Cockspur Street	C1
Bath Street	B2	College Lane	C3
Beckwith Street	C4	College Street North	F1
Bedford Street South	F5	College Street South	F1
Benson Street	E3	Colquitt Street	D4
Berry Street	E4	Constance Street	E2
Bidder Street	E1	Cook Street	C3
Birkett Street	D1	Copperas Hill	E3
Bixteth Street	B2	Cornhill	C5
Blackburne Place	E5	Cornwallis Street	D5
Blundell Street	C5	Craven Street	E2
Bold Street	D3	Cropper Street	D3
Bosnett Street	D3	Crosshall Street	C2
Bridgewater Street	D5	Crown Street	F2
Bridport Street	E2	Dale Street (Queensway)	C2
Brook Street	B2	Dansie Street	E3
Brownlow Hill	E3	Daulby Street	F2
Brownlow Street	F3	Derby Square	C3
Brunswick Road	F1	Devon Street	E2
Brunswick Street	B3	Dover Street	F3
Cambridge Street	F4	Drury Lane	B3
Camden Street	D2	Duke Street	D4
Canning Place	C4	East Street	B1
Canning Street	E5	Eaton Street	B1
Canterbury Street	E1	Eberle Street	C2
Carver Street	E1	Edmund Street	B2
Castle Street	C3	Egerton Street	F5
Catharine Street	F5	Elliot Street	D3
Cathedral Way	E3	Epworth Street	F1

Erskine Street	F1
Falkner Street	E4
Fazakerley Street	B2
Fenwick Street	B3
Fleet Street	D3
Fontenoy Street	D1
Fraser Street	E2
Gascoyne Street	B1
Gerard Street	D1
Gilbert Street	D4
Gildart Street	E2
Gill Street	E2
Gower Street	B5
Gradwell Street	D4
Great Crosshall Street	C1
Great George Street	E5
Great Howard Street	B1
Great Newton Street	E2
Greek Street	E2
Gregson Street	F1
Grenville Street South	D5
Hackins Hey	C2
Hanover Street	C4
Hardman Street	E4
Harker Street	E1
Hartley Quay	B4
Hart Street	E2
Hatton Garden	C2
Hawke Street	E3
Henry Street	D4
Highfield Street	B1
Hood Street	D2
Hope Place	E4
Hope Street	E5
Hotham Street	E2
Hunter Street	D1
Huskisson Street	F5
Islington	E2
Jamaica Street	D5
James Street	B3
Johnson Street	C2

Keel Wharf	C5
Kempston Street	E2
Kent Street	D5
Kinder Street	F1
King Edward Street	B2
Kingsway (Wallasey Tunnel)	A1
Kitchen Street	D5
Knight Street	E4
Langsdale Street	E1
Leece Street	E4
Leeds Street	B1
Lime Street	D2
Liver Street	C4
London Road	D2
London Road	E2
Lord Nelson Street	D2
Lord Street	C3
Lydia Ann Street	D4
Mann Island	B3
Mansfield Street	E1
Marybone	C1
Maryland Street	E4
Midghall Street	C1
Moorfields	C2
Moor Street	B3
Moss Street	F1
Mount Pleasant	E3
Mount Street	E4
Mulberry Street	F4
Myrtle Street	E4
Naylor Street	C1
Nelson Street	D5
Newington	D4
New Islington	E1
New Quay	B2
North John Street	C3
Norton Street	E2
Old Hall Street	B2
Oldham Street	E4
Old Haymarket	C2
Old Leeds Street	B1

Ormond Street	B2
Oxford Street	F4
Paisley Street	B1
Pall Mall	B1
Paradise Street	C3
Parker Street	D3
Park Lane	C4
Parr Street	D4
Peech Street	F3
Pembroke Place	E2
Pembroke Street	F2
Percey Street	E5
Pilgrim Street	E4
Pleasant Street	E3
Pomona Street	E3
Prescot Street	F2
Princes Parade	A2
Prospect Street	F1
Queensway (Birkenhead Tunnel)	A4
Ranelagh Street	D3
Redcross Street	C3
Renshaw Street	D3
Richmond Lane	C3
Rigby Street	B2
Rodney Street	E4
Roscoe Street	E4
Rose Hill	D1
Russell Street	E3
St Anne Street	D1
St James Street	D5
St John's Lane	D2
St Josephs Crescent	D1
St Nicholas Place	B3
St Paul's Street	B2
Salisbury Street	E1
Salthouse Quay	C4
Sandon Street	F5
School Lane	C3
Scotland Road	D1
Seel Street	D4

Seymour Street	E2
Shaw Street	F1
Sir Thomas Street	C2
Skelhorne Street	D3
Slater Street	D4
Soho Street	E1
Sparling Street	C5
Springfield	E1
Stafford Street	E2
Stanley Street	C2
Strand Street	B3
Suffolk Street	D4
Tabley Street	C5
Tarleton Street	D3
Temple Street	C2
The Strand	B3
Tithe Barn Street	C2
Trafalgar Way	F1
Trowbridge Street	E3
Trueman Street	C2
Upper Duke Street	E5
Upper Frederick Street	D4
Upper Parliament Street	F5
Upper Pitt Street	D5
Vauxhall Road	C1
Vernon Street	C2
Victoria Street	C3
Wakefield Street	E1
Wall Street	C3
Wapping	C5
Waterloo Road	A1
Water Street	B3
West Derby Street	F2
Westmorland Drive	C1
Whitechapel	C3
William Henry Street	E1
William Jessop Way	A2
Williamson Square	D3
Williamson Street	D3
Wood Street	D3
York Street	C4

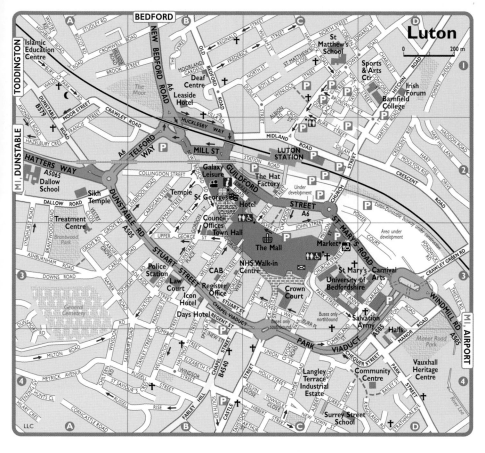

Luton

Luton is found on atlas page **50 C6**

Adelaide Street	B3	Hibbert Street	C4
Albert Road	C4	Highbury Road	A1
Alma Street	B2	High Town Road	C1
Arthur Street	C4	Hitchin Road	D1
Ashburnham Road	A3	Holly Street	C4
Biscot Road	A1	Hucklesby Way	B2
Brantwood Road	A3	Inkerman Street	B3
Brunswick Street	C1	John Street	C3
Burr Street	C2	King Street	B3
Bury Park Road	A1	Latimer Road	C4
Buxton Road	B3	Liverpool Road	B2
Cardiff Road	A3	Manor Road	D4
Cardigan Street	B2	Meyrick Avenue	A4
Castle Street	B4	Midland Road	C2
Chapel Street	B4	Mill Street	B2
Chapel Viaduct	B3	Milton Road	A4
Charles Street	D1	Moor Street	A1
Chequer Street	C4	Napier Road	A3
Chiltern Road	A4	New Bedford Road	B1
Church Street	C2	New Town Street	C3
Church Street	C3	Old Bedford Road	B1
Cobden Street	C1	Park Street	C3
Collingdon Street	B2	Park Street West	C3
Concorde Street	D1	Park Viaduct	C4
Crawley Green Road	D3	Princess Street	B3
Crawley Road	A1	Regent Street	B3
Crescent Road	D2	Reginald Street	B1
Cromwell Road	A1	Rothesay Road	A3
Cumberland Street	C4	Russell Rise	A4
Dallow Road	A2	Russell Street	B4
Dudley Street	C1	St Mary's Road	C3
Dumfries Street	B4	Salisbury Road	A4
Dunstable Road	A1	Stanley Street	B4
Farley Hill	B4	Station Road	C2
Flowers Way	C3	Strathmore Ave	D4
Frederick Street	B1	Stuart Street	B3
George Street	B3	Surrey Street	C4
George Street West	B3	Tavistock Street	B4
Gordon Street	B3	Telford Way	B2
Grove Road	A3	Upper George Street	B3
Guildford Street	B2	Vicarage Street	D3
Hart Hill Drive	D2	Waldeck Road	A1
Hart Hill Lane	D2	Wellington Street	B4
Hartley Road	D2	Wenlock Street	C1
Hastings Street	B4	Windmill Road	D3
Hatters Way	A2	Windsor Street	B4
Havelock Road	C1	Winsdon Road	A4
Hazelbury Crescent	A2	York Street	C1

Maidstone

Maidstone is found on atlas page **38 C10**

Albany Street	D1	Market Buildings	B2
Albion Place	D2	Marsham Street	C2
Allen Street	D1	Meadow Walk	D4
Ashford Road	D3	Medway Street	B3
Bank Street	B3	Melville Road	C4
Barker Road	B4	Mill Street	B3
Bedford Place	A3	Mote Avenue	D3
Bishops Way	B3	Mote Road	D3
Brewer Street	C2	Old School Place	D2
Broadway	A3	Orchard Street	C3
Broadway	B3	Padsole Lane	C3
Brunswick Street	C4	Palace Avenue	B3
Buckland Hill	A2	Princes Street	D1
Buckland Road	A2	Priory Road	C4
Camden Street	C1	Pudding Lane	B2
Chancery Lane	D3	Queen Anne Road	D2
Charles Street	A4	Reginald Road	A4
Church Street	C2	Rocky Hill	A3
College Avenue	B4	Romney Place	C3
College Road	C4	Rose Yard	B2
County Road	C1	Rowland Close	A4
Crompton Gardens	D4	St Anne Court	A2
Cromwell Road	D2	St Faith's Street	B2
Douglas Road	A4	St Luke's Avenue	D1
Earl Street	B2	St Luke's Road	D1
Elm Grove	D4	St Peters Street	A2
Fairmeadow	B1	Sandling Road	B1
Florence Road	A4	Sittingbourne Road	D1
Foley Street	D1	Square Hill Road	D3
Foster Street	C4	Stacey Street	B1
Gabriel's Hill	C3	Station Road	B1
George Street	C4	Terrace Road	A3
Greenside	D4	Tonbridge Road	A4
Hart Street	A3	Tufton Street	C2
Hastings Road	D4	Union Street	C2
Hayle Road	C4	Upper Stone Street	C4
Heathorn Street	D1	Victoria Street	A3
Hedley Street	D1	Vinters Road	D2
High Street	B3	Wat Tyler Way	C3
Holland Road	D1	Week Street	B1
James Street	C1	Well Road	C4
Jeffrey Street	C1	Westree Road	A4
King Street	C3	Wheeler Street	C1
Kingsley Road	D4	Woollett Streettt	C1
Knightrider Street	C4	Wyatt Street	C2
Lesley Place	A1		
London Road	A3		
Lower Stone Street	C3		

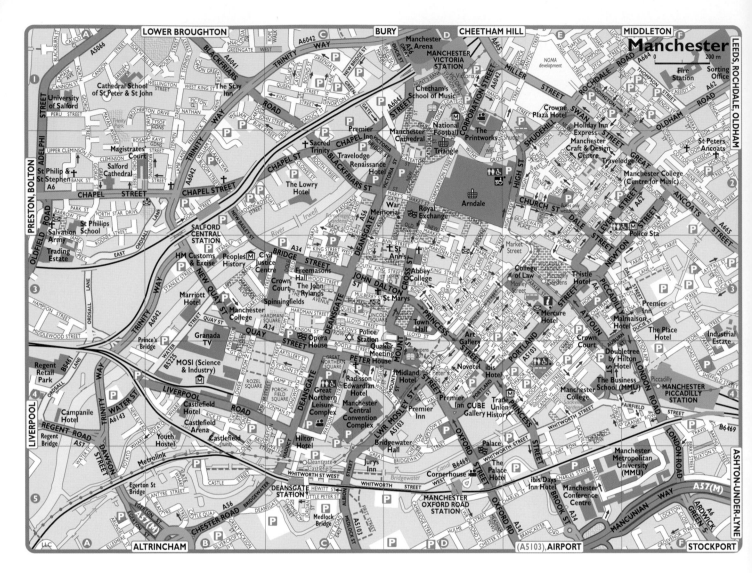

Manchester

Manchester is found on atlas page **82 H5**

Abingdon Street	E4
Addington Street	E1
Adelphi Street	A2
Albion Street	C5
Angel Street	E1
Ardwick Green South	F5
Artillery Street	C4
Atherton Street	B4
Atkinson Street	C3
Auburn Street	E4
Aytoun Street	E3
Back Piccadilly	E3
Bank Street	A2
Baring Street	F4
Barton Street	C4
Berry Street	F4
Blackfriars Road	B1
Blackfriars Street	C2
Blantyre Street	B5
Bloom Street	B2
Bloom Street	B2
Blossom Street	F2
Boad Street	F4
Boond Street	C1
Booth Street	D3
Bootle Street	C4
Brancaster Road	E5
Brazennose Street	C3
Brewer Street	F3
Bridge Street	C3
Bridgewater Place	E2
Bridgewater Street	B4
Bridgewater Viaduct	B5
Brook Street	E5
Brotherton Drive	A1
Browncross Street	B2

Browning Street	B2
Brown Street	D3
Bury Street	B1
Byrom Street	B4
Cable Street	E1
Cambridge Street	D5
Camp Street	C4
Canal Street	E4
Cannon Street	A1
Canon Green Drive	B1
Castle Street	B5
Cathedral Street	D2
Chadderton Street	F1
Chapel Street	A2
Charles Street	E5
Charlotte Street	D3
Chatham Street	E3
Cheapside	D3
Chester Road	B5
China Lane	E3
Chorlton Street	E3
Church Street	E2
City Road East	C5
Cleminson Street	A2
College Land	C2
Collier Street	C1
Commercial Street	C5
Copperas Street	E2
Cornell Street	F2
Corporation Street	D2
Cotton Street	F2
Crosskeys Street	F1
Cross Street	C2
Cross Street	D3
Dale Street	E2
Dantzic Street	E1

Dawson Street	A5
Deansgate	C4
Dickinson Street	D4
Duke Street	B4
Dulcie Street	F3
East Ordsall Lane	A3
Egerton Street	A5
Fairfield Street	F4
Faulkner Street	D4
Fennel Street	D1
Ford Street	A2
Fountain Street	D3
Frederick Street	B2
Garden Lane	B1
Gartside Street	B3
George Leigh Street	F2
George Street	D4
Gore Street	B2
Granby Row	E5
Gravel Lane	C1
Great Ancoats Street	F2
Great Bridgewater Street	C5
Great Ducie Street	D1
Great George Street	A2
Great Jackson Street	B5
Great John Street	B4
Greengate	C1
Greengate West	B1
Gun Street	F2
Hanover Street	D1
Hardman Street	C3
Hewitt Street	C5
High Street	E2
Hood Street	F2
Hope Street	E3
Houndsworth Street	F2
Hulme Street	D5
James Street	A3
Jersey Street	F2
John Dalton Street	C3
John Street	B1

John Street	E2
Joiner Street	E2
Jutland Street	F3
Kennedy Street	D3
King Street	C1
King Street	C3
King Street West	C3
Lamb Lane	B2
Laystall Street	F3
Left Bank	B3
Lena Street	F3
Lever Street	E2
Little Lever Street	E3
Little Peter Street	C5
Liverpool Road	B4
Lloyd Street	C3
London Road	F4
Long Millgate	D1
Longworth Street	C4
Lower Byrom Street	B4
Lower Mosley Street	C4
Lower Ormond Street	D5
Ludgate Street	E1
Major Street	D4
Mancunian Way	E5
Marble Street	D3
Market Street	D2
Marsden Street	D3
Marshall Street	E1
Mason Street	E1
Mayan Avenue	A1
Medlock Street	C5
Middlewood Street	A3
Miller Street	E1
Minshull Street	E3
Mirabel Street	C1
Mosley Street	D3
Mount Street	B1
Mount Street	D4
Museum Street	C4
Nathan Drive	B1

New Bailey Street	B2
New Bridge Street	C1
New Cathedral Street	D2
New Elm Road	A4
New George Street	E2
New Quay Street	B3
Newton Street	E3
New York Street	E3
Nicholas Street	D3
North George Street	A1
North Hill Street	A1
North Star Drive	A2
Norton Street	C1
Oldfield Road	A3
Oldham Road	F1
Oldham Street	E2
Ordsall Lane	A4
Oxford Road	D5
Oxford Street	D4
Pall Mall	D3
Parker Street	E3
Peru Street	A1
Peter Street	C4
Piccadilly	E3
Piccadilly Gardens	E3
Portland Street	D4
Port Street	F3
Potato Wharf	A5
Princess Street	D3
Quay Street	B3
Queen Street	C1
Queen Street	C3
Redhill Street	F2
Regent Road	A4
Reyner Street	D4
Rice Street	B4
Richmond Street	E4
Rochdale Road	E1
Rodney Street	A3
Rosamond Drive	A2
Sackville Street	E4

St Anns Square	C2
St Ann Street	C3
St James Square	C3
St James Street	D4
St Mary's Parsonage	C3
St Peter's Square	C3
St Stephen Street	B2
Store Street	F3
Sharp Street	E1
Shudehill	E2
Silk Street	A1
Simpson Street	E1
South King Street	C3
Spear Street	E3
Spring Gardens	D3
Station Approach	F3
Swan Street	E1
Tariff Street	F3
Thomas Street	E2
Thompson Street	F1
Tib Lane	D3
Tib Street	E2
Todd Street	D1
Tonman Street	C4
Travis Street	F4
Trinity Way	A4
Turner Street	E2
Victoria Bridge Street	C2
Victoria Station Approach	D1
Victoria Street	D2
Warwick Street	E2
Watson Street	C4
Well Street	D2
West King Street	C2
West Mosley Street	D3
Whitworth Street	D5
Whitworth Street West	C5
Windmill Street	C4
Withy Grove	D2
Wood Street	C3
York Street	D4

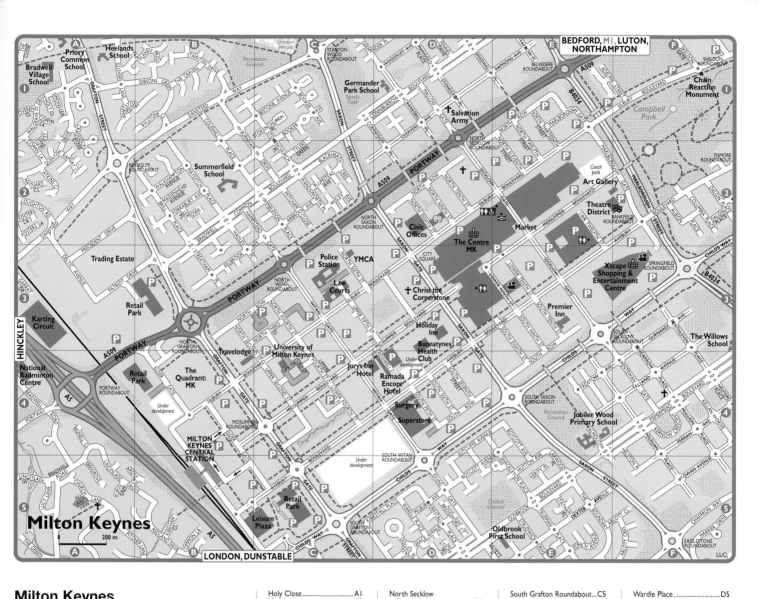

BEDFORD, MI, LUTON, NORTHAMPTON

LONDON, DUNSTABLE

Milton Keynes

Milton Keynes

Milton Keynes is found on atlas page **49 N7**

Adelphi Street	E1
Albion Place	F2
All Saints View	A5
Arbrook Avenue	C2
Ardys Court	A5
Arlott Close	E5
Arlott Crescent	F5
Atkins Close	A2
Audley Mews	A2
Avebury Boulevard	C5
Bankfield Roundabout	E2
Belvedere Roundabout	E1
Bignell Close	A4
Blackheath Crescent	C2
Booker Avenue	C1
Boycott Avenue	D5
Boycott Avenue	E4
Bradwell Common Boulevard	B2
Bradwell Road	A4
Bradwell Road	A5
Bridgeford Court	D5
Brill Place	B2
Burnham Drive	B1
Chaffron Way	F5
Childs Way	C5
Childs Way	F3
Church Lane	A5
City Square	D3
Cleavers Avenue	D1
Coleshill Place	B1
Coltsfoot Place	C1
Columbia Place	F2
Common Lane	B5
Conniburrow Boulevard	C1

Coppin Lane	A2
Craddocks Close	A1
Cranesbill Place	D1
Cresswell Lane	D3
Dalgin Place	F2
Dansteed Way	A2
Deltic Avenue	A3
Dexter Avenue	E5
Douglas Place	D5
Eaglestone Roundabout	F5
Ebbsgrove	A5
Edrich Avenue	E5
Eelbrook Avenue	B3
Elder Gate	B4
Enmore Roundabout	F2
Evans Gate	D5
Falmouth Place	E4
Fennel Drive	D1
Fishermead Boulevard	F4
Forrabury Avenue	B2
Fosters Lane	A2
Garrat Drive	A3
Germander Place	C1
Gibsons Green	B1
Glovers Lane	A1
Grace Avenue	D5
Grafton Gate	B4
Grafton Street	A1
Grafton Street	C5
Gurnards Avenue	F3
Hadley Place	B2
Hampstead Gate	B2
Harrier Drive	F5
Helford Place	F4
Helston Place	F4

Holy Close	A1
Hutton Avenue	E5
Ibistone Avenue	C1
Kellan Drive	F4
Kernow Crescent	F4
Kirkham Close	B5
Kirkstall Place	C5
Larwood Place	E5
Leasowe Place	B2
Linceslade Grove	A5
Loughton Road	A2
Lower Fourth Street	C4
Lower Ninth Street	E3
Lower Tenth Street	E3
Lower Twelfth Street	E2
Lucy Lane	A5
Maidenhead Avenue	B2
Mallow Gate	D1
Marigold Place	D1
Marlborough Gate	E1
Marlborough Gate	E2
Marlborough Street	F2
Mayditch Place	B2
Maynard Close	A2
Midsummer Boulevard	C4
Midsummer Boulevard	E2
Midsummer Roundabout	B4
Milburn Avenue	D5
Mitcham Close	C2
Mullion Place	F4
North Eighth Street	D2
North Eleventh Street	E1
North Fourth Street	C3
North Grafton Roundabout	B3
North Ninth Street	D2
North Row	B3
North Row	D2
North Saxon Roundabout	C2

North Secklow Roundabout	D1
North Second Street	B3
North Sixth Street	C3
North Tenth Street	D2
North Third Street	C3
North Thirteenth Street	E1
North Twelfth Street	E1
North Witan Roundabout	C3
Oldbrook Boulevard	E5
Overend Close	A1
Padstow Avenue	E4
Patriot Drive	A3
Pencarrow Place	F3
Pentewan Gate	F4
Perran Avenue	F4
Pitcher Lane	A5
Plumstead Avenue	C2
Polruan Place	F4
Porthleven Place	F3
Portway	A4
Portway Roundabout	A4
Precedent Drive	A3
Quinton Drive	A2
Ramsay Close	A2
Ramsons Avenue	E1
Redland Drive	B5
Rooksley Roundabout	A2
Rylstone Close	B1
Saxon Gate	D2
Saxon Street	C1
Secklow Gate	D2
Shackleton Place	E5
Sheldon Roundabout	F1
Silbury Boulevard	B4
Silbury Roundabout	B4
Simons Lea	A1
Skeldon Gate	F1
South Eighth Street	E3
South Fifth Street	D4

South Grafton Roundabout	C5
South Ninth Street	E3
South Row	D4
South Saxon Roundabout	E4
South Secklow Roundabout	F3
South Seventh Street	D4
South Sixth Street	D4
South Tenth Street	E3
South Witan Roundabout	D5
Speedwell Place	D1
Springfield Roundabout	F3
Stainton Drive	B1
Stanton Wood Roundabout	C1
Statham Place	E5
Stokenchurch Place	C1
Stonecrop Place	D1
Streatham Place	B3
Strudwick Drive	E5
Sutcliffe Avenue	D4
Talland Avenue	F4
The Boundary	A1
The Craven	B1
The Green	A5
Towan Avenue	F5
Tranlands Brigg	B1
Trueman Place	E5
Turvil End	A5
Tylers Green	C2
Tyson Place	D5
Ulyett Place	D5
Upper Fifth Street	C3
Upper Fourth Street	C4
Upper Second Street	C4
Upper Third Street	C4
Verity Place	E5
Walgrave Drive	A1
Walkhampton Avenue	B2
Wandsworth Place	C2

Wardle Place	D5
Whetstone Close	A1
Wimbledon Place	C2
Wisely Avenue	C2
Witan Gate	C3
Woodruff Avenue	D1
Yarrow Place	E1

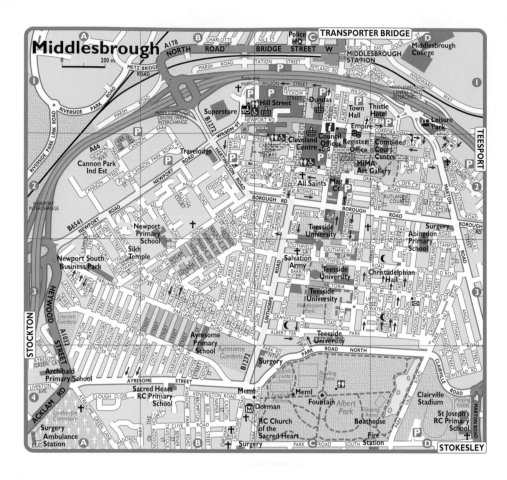

Middlesbrough

Middlesbrough is found on atlas page **104 E7**

Acklam Road	A4	Heywood Street	A3
Acton Street	C3	Kensington Road	B4
Aire Street	B4	Kildare Street	A4
Albany Street	B3	Laurel Street	D3
Albert Road	C2	Lees Road	A2
Amber Street	C2	Linthorpe Road	B4
Athol Street	B3	Longford Street	A4
Audrey Street	D3	Lorne Street	A3
Ayresome Park Road	B4	Lothian Road	D3
Ayresome Street	A4	Marsh Street	A2
Borough Road	C2	Marton Road	D2
Bretnall Street	B2	Melrose Street	D2
Bridge Street East	C1	Metz Bridge Road	A1
Bridge Street West	C1	Myrtle Street	D3
Bush Street	B4	Newlands Road	D3
Camden Street	D2	Newport Road	A2
Cannon Park Road	A2	Palm Street	D3
Cannon Park Way	A2	Park Lane	C3
Cannon Street	A2	Park Road North	C4
Carlow Street	A3	Park Road South	C4
Centre Square	C2	Park Vale Road	D4
Clairville Road	D4	Parliament Road	A3
Clarendon Road	C3	Pearl Street	C2
Clifton Street	B3	Pelham Street	C3
Corporation Road	D1	Portman Street	B3
Costa Street	B4	Princes Road	B3
Craven Street	B3	Riverside Park Road	A1
Crescent Road	A3	Ruby Street	C2
Croydon Road	D3	Russell Street	D2
Derwent Street	A2	St Pauls Road	B2
Diamond Road	B3	Southfield Road	C3
Egmont Road	D4	Station Street	C1
Emily Street	C2	Stowe Street	B3
Errol Street	C2	Tavistock Street	B4
Essex Street	A4	Tennyson Street	B3
Fairbridge Street	C2	Union Street	A3
Falmouth Street	D3	Victoria Road	C3
Finsbury Street	B3	Victoria Street	A3
Fleetham Street	B3	Warren Street	B2
Garnet Street	B2	Waterloo Road	D3
Glebe Road	B3	Waverley Street	B3
Grange Road	B2	Wembley Street	A3
Grange Road	D2	Wilson Street	B2
Granville Road	C3	Wilton Street	C3
Gresham Road	B3	Windsor Street	B2
Harewood Street	B3	Woodlands Road	C3
Harford Street	B4	Worcester Street	B4
Hartington Road	B2	Zetland Road	C1

Newport

Newport is found on atlas page **31 K7**

Albert Terrace	B3	Jones Street	B3
Allt-Yr-Yn Avenue	A2	Keynsham Avenue	C4
Bailey Street	B3	King Street	C4
Bedford Road	D2	Kingsway	C2
Blewitt Street	B3	Kingsway	C4
Bond Street	C1	Llanthewy Road	A3
Bridge Street	B2	Locke Street	B1
Bryngwyn Road	A3	Lower Dock Street	C4
Brynhyfryd Avenue	A4	Lucas Street	B1
Brynhyfryd Road	A4	Market Street	B2
Caerau Crescent	A4	Mellon Street	C4
Caerau Road	A3	Mill Street	B2
Cambrian Road	B2	North Street	B3
Caroline Street	D3	Oakfield Road	A3
Cedar Road	D2	Park Square	C4
Charles Street	C3	Pugsley Street	C1
Chepstow Road	D1	Queen's Hill	B1
Clarence Place	C1	Queen's Hill Crescent	A1
Clifton Place	B4	Queen Street	C4
Clifton Road	B4	Queensway	B2
Clyffard Crescent	A3	Risca Road	A4
Clytha Park Road	A2	Rodney Road	C2
Clytha Square	C4	Rudry Street	D1
Colts Foot Close	A1	Ruperra Lane	C4
Commercial Street	C4	Ruperra Street	D4
Corelli Street	D1	St Edward Street	B3
Corn Street	C2	St Julian Street	B4
Corporation Road	D2	St Mark's Crescent	A2
Devon Place	B2	St Mary Street	B3
Dewsland Park Road	B4	St Vincent Road	C2
Dumfries Place	D4	St Woolos Road	B3
East Street	B3	School Lane	C3
East Usk Road	C1	Serpentine Road	A2
Factory Road	B1	Skinner Street	C2
Fields Road	A2	Sorrel Drive	A1
Friars Field	B4	Spencer Road	A3
Friars Road	B4	Stow Hill	B3
Friar Street	C3	Stow Hill	B4
George Street	D4	Stow Park Avenue	A4
Godfrey Road	A2	Talbot Lane	B3
Gold Tops	A2	Tregare Street	D1
Grafton Road	C2	Tunnel Terrace	A3
Granville Lane	D4	Upper Dock Street	C2
Granville Street	D4	Upper Dock Street	C3
High Street	B3	Usk Way	D3
Hill Street	C3	Victoria Crescent	B3
John Frost Square	C3	West Street	B3
John Street	D4	York Place	A4

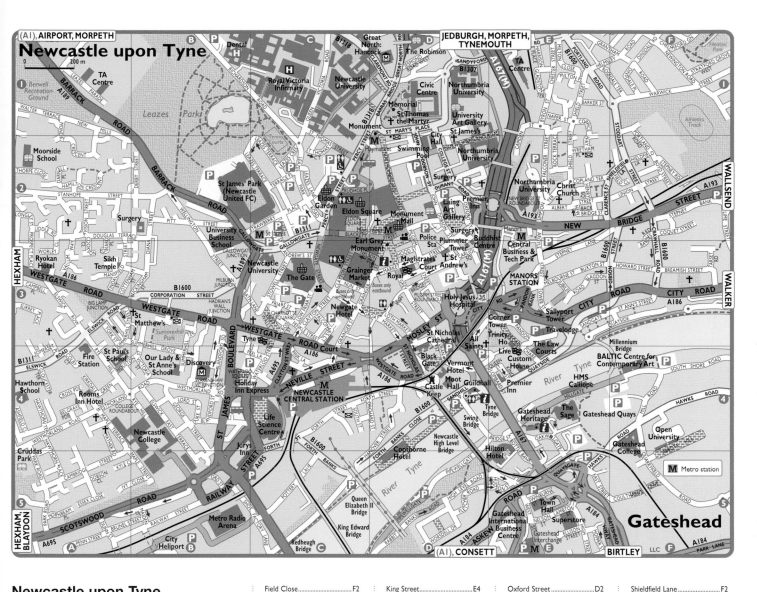

Newcastle upon Tyne

Newcastle upon Tyne is found on atlas page **113 K8**

Abbots Hill	F4	Clayton Street West	C4	Field Close	F2	King Street	E4	Oxford Street	D2	Shieldfield Lane	F2
Albert Street	E2	Colby Court	A4	Fletcher Road	D5	Kirkdale Green	A4	Pandon	E3	Shield Street	E2
Argyle Street	E2	College Roundabout	A4	Forth Banks	C4	Kyle Close	A5	Pandon Bank	E3	Shot Factory Lane	B5
Askew Road	D5	College Street	D2	Forth Banks Close	D5	Lambton Street	E4	Park Lane	F5	Simpson Terrace	E2
Avision Street	A2	Cookson Close	A3	Forth Street	C4	Leazes Crescent	C2	Park Road	A5	Somerset Place	A4
Back New Bridge Street	E2	Copland Terrace	E2	Friars Street	C3	Leazes Lane	C2	Peel Lane	B4	South Shore Road	F4
Albert Street	E2	Coppice Way	E1	Gallowgate	B2	Leazes Park Road	C2	Penn Street	A5	South Street	C4
Barker Street	E1	Coquet Street	F2	Gallowgate Junction	B3	Leazes Terrace	C2	Percy Street	C2	Stanhope Street	A2
Barrack Road	A1	Corporation Street	B3	Gateshead Highway	E5	Liddle Road	A2	Pilgrim Street	D2	Stepney Bank	F2
Barras Bridge	D1	Cottenham Street	A3	George Street	B4	Lime Street	F2	Pink Lane	C4	Stepney Lane	E3
Bath Lane	B3	Coulthards Lane	F5	Gibson Street	F3	Lombard Street	E4	Pipewellgate	D5	Stepney Road	F2
Belgrave Parade	A4	Crawhall Road	F2	Gladstone Terrace	E1	Longley Street	A2	Pitt Street	B2	Stoddart Street	F1
Big Lamp Junction	A3	Cross Parade	A4	Gloucester Terrace	A4	Lord Street	B4	Portland Road	E1	Stowell Street	C3
Blackett Street	C2	Cross Street	C3	Grainger Street	C3	Loth Market	D3	Portland Road	F1	Stratford Grove West	F1
Blagdon Street	E3	Darnell Place	A2	Grantham Road	E1	Low Friar Street	C3	Pottery Lane	C5	Strawberry Place	C2
Blandford Square	B4	Dean Street	D3	Great North Road	D1	Maiden Street	B5	Prospect Place	A2	Summerhill Grove	B3
Blandford Street	B4	Derby Street	B2	Grey Street	D3	Mansfield Street	A3	Prudhoe Place	C2	Summerhill Street	A3
Bottle Bank	E4	Diana Street	B3	Groat Market	C3	Maple Street	B5	Quarryfield Road	F5	Summerhill Terrace	B4
Boyd Street	F2	Dinsdale Place	F1	Hamilton Crescent	A2	Maple Terrace	A4	Quayside	E3	Swinburne Street	E5
Breamish Street	F3	Dinsdale Road	F1	Hanover Street	C5	Market Street	D3	Quayside	F3	Tarset Road	F2
Bridge Street	E4	Dobson Close	A5	Harrison Place	E1	Mather Road	A4	Quayside	E4	Terrace Place	C2
Broad Chare	E3	Douglas Terrace	A2	Hawks Road	E5	Melbourne Street	E3	Queen Street	E4	Thorpe Close	A2
Brunel Street	A5	Duke Street	B4	Hawthorn Place	A4	Mill Road	F4	Queen Victoria Road	C1	Tindal Street	A3
Buckingham Street	B3	Dunn Street	A5	Hawthorn Terrace	A4	Milton Close	E1	Rabbit Banks Road	D5	Tower Street	E3
Buxton Street	E3	Durant Road	D2	Helmsley Road	E1	Milton Place	E1	Railway Street	B5	Tyne Bridge	E4
Byron Street	E1	East Street	E5	Henry Square	E2	Monday Crescent	A1	Red Barnes	F2	Union Street	F2
Cambridge Street	A5	Edward Place	A3	High Bridge	D3	Mosley Street	D3	Richardson Road	B1	Vallum Way	A2
Camden Street	E2	Eldon Square	C2	High Level Road	D5	Naper Street	E1	Rock Terrace	E2	Victoria Street	B4
Campbell Place	A3	Ellison Street	E5	High Street	E5	Nelson Street	C3	Rosedale Terrace	E1	Walter Terrace	A1
Carliol Square	D3	Elswick East Terrace	B4	Hillgate	E4	Nelson Street	E5	Rye Hill	A4	Warwick Street	F1
Charlotte Square	C3	Elswick Road	A3	Hood Street	D3	Neville Street	C4	St Andrew's Street	C3	Waterloo Square	B4
Chelmsford Green	F1	Elswick Row	A3	Hopper Street	E5	New Bridge Street	E2	St Ann's Street	F3	Waterloo Street	C4
Chester Street	E1	Essex Close	A5	Hornbeam Place	A5	Newgate Street	C3	St James Boulevard	B4	Wellington Street	B2
City Road	E3	Falconar's Court	C3	Houston Street	A4	Newington Road	F1	St Mary's Place	D1	Westgate Road	A3
Claremont Road	D1	Falconer Street	E2	Howard Street	F3	New Mills	A1	St Nicholas Street	D4	Westmorland Road	A4
Clarence Street	E2	Fenkle Street	C3	Hudson Street	E5	Northumberland Road	D2	St Thomas' Court	C1	West Street	E5
Clayton Street	C3			Ivy Close	A5	Northumberland Street	D2	St Thomas' Street	C1	West Walls	C3
				Jesmond Road West	D1	Nun Street	C3	Sandgate	E3	Worley Close	A2
				John Dobson Street	D2	Oakwellgate	E4	Sandhill	D4	Worsdell Drive	D5
				Jubilee Road	E3	Orchard Street	C4	Sandyford Road	D1	Wretham Place	E2
				King Edward Bridge	C5	Ord Street	B5	Scotswood Road	A5	York Street	A3

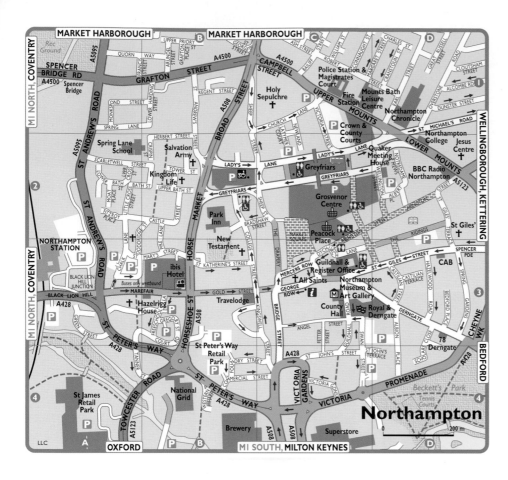

Northampton

Northampton is found on atlas page **60 G8**

Abington Street	C2	Lower Bath Street	A2
Albert Place	D2	Lower Cross Street	A2
Albion Place	D3	Lower Harding Street	B1
Angel Street	C3	Lower Mounts	D2
Arundel Street	B1	Marefair	A3
Ash Street	C1	Margaret Street	C1
Bailiff Street	C1	Market Square	C2
Black Lion Hill	A3	Mercers Row	C3
Bradshaw Street	B2	Moat Place	A2
Bridge Street	C3	Monkspond Street	A1
Broad Street	B1	Newland	C1
Campbell Street	C1	Notredame Mews	D2
Castilian Street	D3	Overstone Road	D1
Castle Street	B2	Pike Lane	B3
Chalk Lane	A3	Quorn Way	A1
Cheyne Walk	D3	Regent Street	B1
Church Lane	C1	Robert Street	C1
College Street	B2	St Andrew's Road	A2
Commercial Street	B4	St Andrew's Street	B1
Connaught Street	C1	St Giles Street	D3
Court Road	B3	St Giles' Terrace	D2
Cranstoun Street	D1	St John's Street	C4
Crispin Street	B2	St Katherine's Street	B3
Derngate	D3	St Mary's Street	A3
Doddridge Street	A3	St Michael's Road	D1
Dunster Street	D1	St Peter's Way	B4
Dychurch Lane	C3	Scarletwell Street	A2
Earl Street	D1	Scholars Close	D4
Fetter Street	C3	Sheep Street	B1
Fitzroy Place	A2	Sheep Street	C2
Foundry Street	B4	Spencer Bridge Road	A1
Francis Street	A1	Spencer Parade	D3
Freeschool Lane	B3	Spring Gardens	D3
George Row	C3	Spring Lane	A1
Gold Street	B3	Swan Street	C3
Grafton Street	A1	Tanner Street	A4
Great Russell Street	D1	The Drapery	C2
Green Street	A3	The Ridings	D2
Gregory Street	B3	Towcester Road	A4
Greyfriars	B2	Tower Street	B2
Guildhall Road	C3	Upper Bath Street	B2
Hazelwood Road	D3	Upper Mounts	C1
Herbert Street	B2	Upper Priory Street	B1
Horse Market	B3	Victoria Gardens	C4
Horseshoe Street	B3	Victoria Promenade	C4
Kingswell Street	C3	Victoria Street	C1
Lady's Lane	B2	Wellington Street	D2
Little Cross Street	A2	Western Wharf	B4

Norwich

Norwich is found on atlas page **77 J10**

All Saints Green	B4	Pottergate	A2
Bank Plain	C2	Prince of Wales Road	C2
Barn Road	A1	Princes Street	C2
Bedding Lane	C1	Quay Side	C1
Bedford Street	B2	Queens Road	B4
Ber Street	C4	Queen Street	C2
Bethel Street	A3	Rampant Horse Street	B3
Bishopgate	D1	Recorder Road	D2
Brigg Street	B3	Red Lion Street	B3
Calvert Street	B1	Riverside Road	D3
Castle Meadow	C3	Riverside Walk	D1
Cathedral Street	D2	Rose Lane	C3
Cattle Market Street	C3	Rouen Road	C3
Chantry Road	B3	Rupert Street	A4
Chapelfield East	A3	St Andrews Street	B2
Chapelfield North	A3	St Benedicts Street	A2
Chapelfield Road	A3	St Faiths Lane	D2
Cleveland Road	A3	St Georges Street	B1
Colegate	B1	St Giles Street	A2
Convent Road	A3	St Julians Alley	C4
Coslany Street	B2	St Marys Plain	B1
Cow Hill	A2	St Peters Street	B3
Davey Place	B3	St Stephens Road	B4
Dove Street	B2	St Stephens Square	A4
Duke Street	B1	St Stephens Street	B4
Elm Hill	C2	St Swithins Road	A2
Exchange Street	B2	St Verdast Street	D2
Farmers Avenue	C3	Surrey Street	B4
Ferry Lane	D2	Ten Bell Lane	A2
Fishergate	C1	Theatre Street	B3
Friars Quay	B1	Thorn Lane	C4
Gentlemans Walk	B3	Tombland	C2
Goldenball Street	C3	Unicorn Yard	A1
Grapes Hill	A2	Union Street	A4
Haymarket	B3	Unthank Road	A3
Heigham Street	A1	Upper Goat Lane	B2
King Street	C2	Upper King Street	B2
London Street	B2	Upper St Giles Street	A2
Lower Goat Lane	B2	Vauxhall Street	A3
Magdalen Street	C1	Walpole Street	A3
Market Avenue	C3	Wensum Street	C1
Mills Yard	A1	Wessex Street	A4
Mountergate	D3	Westlegate	B3
Music House Lane	D4	Westwick Street	A1
Muspole Street	B1	Wherry Road	D4
Norfolk Street	A4	Whitefriars	C1
Oak Street	A1	White Lion Street	B3
Palace Street	C1	Willow Lane	A2

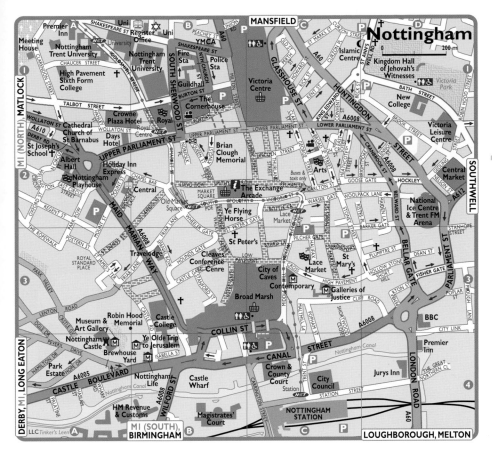

Nottingham

Nottingham is found on atlas page **72 F3**

Albert Street	B3	Lenton Road	A3
Barker Gate	D2	Lincoln Street	C2
Bath Street	D1	Lister Gate	B3
Bellar Gate	D3	London Road	D4
Belward Street	D2	Long Row	B2
Broad Street	C2	Lower Parliament Street	C2
Broadway	C3	Low Pavement	B3
Bromley Place	A2	Maid Marian Way	A2
Brook Street	D1	Market Street	B2
Burton Street	B1	Middle Hill	C3
Canal Street	C4	Milton Street	B1
Carlton Street	C2	Mount Street	A3
Carrington Street	C4	Norfolk Place	B2
Castle Boulevard	A4	North Circus Street	A2
Castle Gate	B3	Park Row	A3
Castle Road	B3	Parliament Street	D3
Chapel Bar	B2	Pelham Street	C2
Chaucer Street	A1	Peveril Drive	A4
Clarendon Street	A1	Pilcher Gate	C3
Cliff Road	C3	Popham Street	C3
Collin Street	B4	Poultry	B2
Cranbrook Street	D2	Queen Street	B2
Cumber Street	C2	Regent Street	A2
Curzon Place	C1	St Ann's Well Road	D1
Derby Road	A2	St James's Street	A3
Exchange Walk	B2	St Marks Gate	C3
Fisher Gate	D3	St Marks Street	C1
Fletcher Gate	C3	St Mary's Gate	C3
Forman Street	B1	St Peter's Gate	B3
Friar Lane	A3	Shakespeare Street	A1
Gedling Street	D2	Smithy Row	B2
George Street	C2	South Parade	B2
Glasshouse Street	C1	South Sherwood Street	B1
Goldsmith Street	A1	Spaniel Row	B3
Goose Gate	C2	Station Street	C4
Halifax Place	C3	Stoney Street	C2
Heathcote Street	C2	Talbot Street	A1
High Cross Street	C2	Thurland Street	C2
High Pavement	C3	Trent Street	C4
Hockley	D2	Upper Parliament Street	A2
Hollow Stone	D3	Victoria Street	C2
Hope Drive	A4	Warser Gate	C2
Hounds Gate	B3	Weekday Cross	C3
Howard Street	C1	Wellington Circus	A2
Huntingdon Street	C1	Wheeler Gate	B2
Kent Street	C1	Wilford Street	B4
King Edward Street	C1	Wollaton Street	A1
King Street	B2	Woolpack Lane	C2

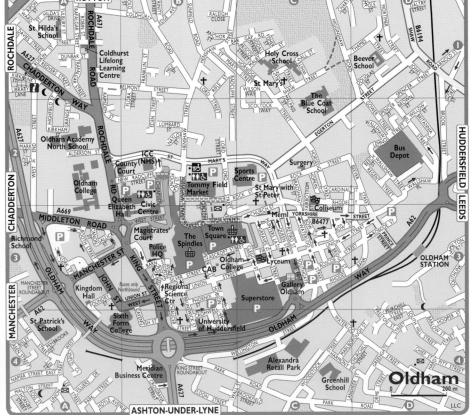

Oldham

Oldham is found on atlas page **83 K4**

Ascroft Street	B3	Mortimer Street	D1
Bar Gap Road	B1	Napier Street East	A4
Barlow Street	D4	New Radcliffe Street	A2
Barn Street	B3	Oldham Way	A3
Beever Street	D2	Park Road	B4
Bell Street	D2	Park Street	A4
Belmont Street	B1	Peter Street	B3
Booth Street	A3	Queen Street	C3
Bow Street	C3	Radcliffe Street	B1
Brook Street	D2	Raleigh Close	B1
Brunswick Street	B3	Ramsden Street	A1
Cardinal Street	C2	Regent Street	D2
Chadderton Way	A1	Rhodes Bank	C3
Chaucer Street	B3	Rhodes Street	C2
Clegg Street	C3	Rifle Street	B1
Coldhurst Road	B1	Rochdale Road	A1
Cromwell Street	B4	Rock Street	B2
Crossbank Street	B4	Roscoe Street	C3
Curzon Street	B2	Ruskin Street	A1
Dunbar Street	A1	St Hilda's Drive	A1
Eden Street	B2	St Marys Street	B1
Egerton Street	C2	St Mary's Way	B2
Firth Street	C3	Shaw Road	D1
Fountain Street	B2	Shaw Street	C1
Franklin Street	B1	Siddall Street	C1
Gower Street	D2	Silver Street	B3
Grange Street	A2	Southgate Street	C3
Greaves Street	C3	South Hill Street	D4
Greengate Street	D4	Southlink	D3
Hamilton Street	D3	Spencer Street	D2
Hardy Street	D4	Sunfield Road	B1
Harmony Street	C4	Thames Street	D1
Henshaw Street	B2	Trafalgar Street	A1
Higginshaw Road	C1	Trinity Street	B1
Highfield Street	A2	Tulbury Street	A1
High Street	B3	Union Street	B3
Hobson Street	B3	Union Street West	A4
Hooper Street	D4	Union Street West	B3
Horsedge Street	C1	Wallshaw Street	D2
John Street	A3	Wall Street	B4
King Street	B3	Ward Street	A1
Lemnos Street	D2	Waterloo Street	C3
Malby Street	C1	Wellington Street	B4
Malton Street	A4	West End Street	A2
Manchester Street	A3	West Street	B3
Market Place	B3	Willow Street	D2
Marlborough Street	C4	Woodstock Street	C4
Middleton Road	A3	Yorkshire Street	C3

Oxford

Oxford is found on atlas page **34 F3**

Abbey Road	A3	
Abingdon Road	D5	
Adelaide Street	B1	
Albert Street	A1	
Albion Place	C4	
Allam Street	A1	
Alma Place	F4	
Arthur Street	A4	
Banbury Road	C1	
Barrett Street	A4	
Bath Street	F4	
Beaumont Street	C3	
Becket Street	A3	
Beef Lane	C4	
Blackhall Road	C1	
Blue Boar Street	C4	
Bonn Square	C4	
Botley Road	A3	
Boulter Street	F4	
Brewer Street	C4	
Bridge Street	A4	
Broad Street	C3	
Broad Walk	D4	
Buckingham Street	C5	
Canal Street	A1	
Cardigan Street	A2	
Caroline Street	F4	
Castle Street	C4	
Catte Street	D3	
Circus Street	F5	
Cornmarket Street	C3	
Cowley Place	F4	
Cowley Road	F4	
Cranham Street	A1	
Cranham Terrace	A1	
Cripley Road	A3	
Cromwell Street	C5	

Dale Close	B5	
Dawson Street	F4	
East Street	A4	
Folly Bridge	C5	
Friars Wharf	C5	
George Street	B3	
George Street Mews	B3	
Gibbs Crescent	A4	
Gloucester Street	C3	
Great Clarendon Street	A2	
Hart Street	B1	
High Street	D3	
High Street	E4	
Hollybush Row	B3	
Holywell Street	D2	
Hythe Bridge Street	B3	
Iffley Road	F4	
James Street	F5	
Jericho Street	A1	
Jowett Walk	D2	
Juxon Street	A1	
Keble Road	C1	
King Edward Street	D3	
King Street	B1	
Little Clarendon Street	B2	
Littlegate Street	C4	
Longwall Street	E3	
Magdalen Bridge	E4	
Magdalen Street	C3	
Magpie Lane	D3	
Manor Place	E2	
Manor Road	E2	
Mansfield Road	D2	
Market Street	C3	
Marlborough Road	C5	
Marston Street	F5	
Merton Street	D4	

Millbank	A4	
Mill Street	A4	
Mount Street	A1	
Museum Road	C2	
Nelson Street	A2	
New College Lane	D3	
New Inn Hall Street	C3	
New Road	B3	
Norfolk Street	C4	
Observatory Street	B1	
Old Greyfriars Street	C4	
Osney Lane	A4	
Osney Lane	B4	
Osney Mead	A5	
Oxpens Road	B4	
Paradise Square	B4	
Paradise Street	B4	
Park End Street	B3	
Parks Road	C1	
Parks Road	D2	
Pembroke Street	C4	
Pike Terrace	C4	
Pusey Lane	C2	
Pusey Street	C2	
Queen's Lane	D3	
Queen Street	C4	
Radcliffe Square	D3	
Rewley Road	A2	
Rewley Road	B3	
Richmond Road	B2	
Roger Dudman Way	A3	
Rose Lane	E4	
St Aldate's	C4	
St Aldate's	D5	
St Barnabas Street	A2	
St Clement's Street	F4	
St Cross Road	E1	

St Cross Road	E2	
St Ebbes Street	C4	
St Giles	C2	
St John Street	C2	
St Michael's Street	C3	
St Thomas' Street	B4	
Savile Road	D2	
Ship Street	C3	
South Parks Road	D2	
South Street	A4	
Speedwell Street	C5	
Stockmore Street	F5	
Temple Street	F5	
Thames Street	C5	
The Plain	F4	
Tidmarsh Lane	B3	
Trinity Street	B5	
Turl Street	D3	
Turn Again Lane	C4	
Tyndale Road	F4	
Upper Fisher Row	B3	
Venables Close	A1	
Victoria Street	A1	
Walton Crescent	B2	
Walton Lane	B2	
Walton Street	B1	
Wellington Square	B2	
Wellington Street	B2	
William Lucy Way	A1	
Woodbine Place	B4	
Woodstock Road	C1	
Worcester Place	B2	
Worcester Street	B3	

University Colleges

All Souls College	D3
Balliol College	C3
Brasenose College	D3
Christ Church College	D4
Corpus Christi College	D4
Exeter College	D3
Harris Manchester College	D2
Hertford College	D3
Jesus College	C3
Keble College	C1
Linacre College	E1
Lincoln College	D3
Magdalen College	E3
Mansfield College	D2
Merton College	D4
New College	D3
Nuffield College	B3
Oriel College	D3
Pembroke College	C4
Ruskin College	B2
St Catherine's College	F2
St Cross College	C2
St Hilda's College	E5
St John's College	C2
St Peter's College	C3
Somerville College	B1
The Queen's College	D3
Trinity College	C2
University College	D3
Wadham College	D2
Worcester College	B3

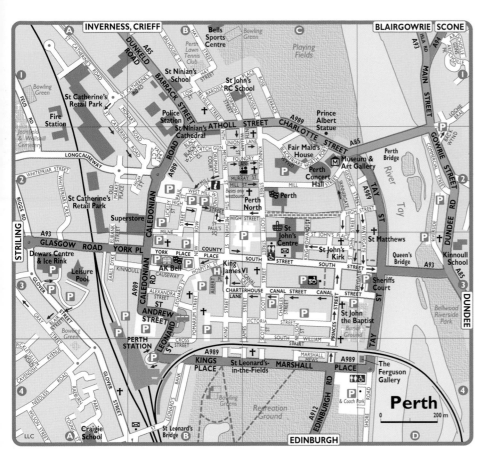

Perth

Perth is found on atlas page **134 E3**

Albert Place	B3	Melville Street	B1
Alexandra Street	B3	Mill Street	B2
Ardchoille Park	D1	Mill Street	C2
Atholl Street	B1	Milne Street	B2
Back Wynd	D2	Monart Road	A1
Balhousie Street	B1	Murray Street	B2
Barossa Place	B1	Needless Road	A4
Barrack Street	B1	New Row	B3
Blackfriars Wynd	C2	North Methven Street	B2
Black Watch Garden	B2	North Port	C2
Caledonian Road	B2	North William Street	B2
Caledonian Road	B3	Old Market Place	A2
Canal Street	C3	Paul Street	B2
Cavendish Avenue	A4	Perth Bridge	D2
Charles Street	C3	Pickletullum Road	A4
Charlotte Street	C2	Pomarium Street	B3
Charterhouse Lane	B3	Princes Street	C3
Commercial Street	D2	Queen's Bridge	D3
County Place	B3	Raeburn Park	A4
Cross Street	B4	Riggs Road	A2
Dundee Road	D3	Riverside	D3
Dunkeld Road	B1	Rose Terrace	C1
Earls Dyke	A3	St Andrew Street	B3
Edinburgh Road	C4	St Catherine's Road	A1
Feus Road	A1	St John's Place	C3
Foundry Lane	B2	St John Street	C3
George Street	C2	St Leonard's Bank	B4
Glasgow Road	A3	St Paul's Square	B2
Glover Street	A3	Scott Street	C2
Glover Street	A4	Scott Street	C3
Gowrie Street	D2	Shore Road	D4
Gray Street	A3	Skinnergate	C2
Hay Street	B1	South Methven Street	B2
High Street	B2	South Street	C3
High Street	C2	South William Street	B2
Hospital Street	B3	Speygate	D3
Isla Road	D1	Stormont Street	B1
James Street	C3	Tay Street	D2
King Edward Street	C3	Tay Street	D4
Kings Place	B4	Union Lane	B2
King Street	B3	Victoria Street	C3
Kinnoull Causeway	A3	Watergate	D2
Kinnoull Street	C2	West Mill Wynd	B2
Leonard Street	B3	Whitefriars Crescent	A2
Lochie Brae	D1	Whitefriar Street	A2
Longcauseway	A2	Wilson Street	A4
Main Street	D1	York Place	A3
Marshall Place	C4	York Place	B3

Peterborough

Peterborough is found on atlas page **74 C11**

Albert Place	B3	New Road	C1
Bishop's Road	C3	Northminster	C1
Boongate	D1	North Street	B1
Bourges Boulevard	A1	Oundle Road	B4
Bridge Street	B3	Park Road	B1
Bright Street	A1	Peet Street	B1
Broadway	B2	Pipe Lane	D2
Brook Street	C1	Priestgate	A2
Cathedral Square	B2	Rivergate	B3
Cattle Market Street	B1	River Lane	A2
Chapel Street	C1	Russell Street	A1
Church Street	B2	St John's Street	C2
Church Walk	C1	St Peters Road	B3
City Road	C2	South Street	D2
Cowgate	B2	Star Road	D2
Craig Street	B1	Station Road	A2
Crawthorne Road	C1	Thorpe Lea Road	A3
Cripple Sidings Lane	B4	Thorpe Road	A2
Cromwell Road	A1	Trinity Street	B3
Cross Street	B2	Viersen Platz	B3
Cubitt Way	B4	Vineyard Road	C3
Deacon Street	A1	Wake Road	D2
Dickens Street	D1	Wareley Road	A4
Eastfield Road	D1	Wellington Street	D1
Eastgate	D2	Wentworth Street	B3
East Station Road	C4	Westgate	A1
Embankment Road	C3		
Exchange Street	B2		
Fengate Close	D2		
Field Walk	D1		
Fitzwilliam Street	B1		
Frank Perkins Parkway	D4		
Geneva Street	B1		
Gladstone Street	A1		
Granby Street	C2		
Hereward Close	D2		
Hereward Road	D2		
King Street	B2		
Laxton Square	C2		
Lea Gardens	A3		
Lincoln Road	B1		
London Road	B4		
Long Causeway	B2		
Manor House Street	B1		
Mayor's Walk	A1		
Midgate	B2		
Morris Street	D1		
Nene Street	D2		

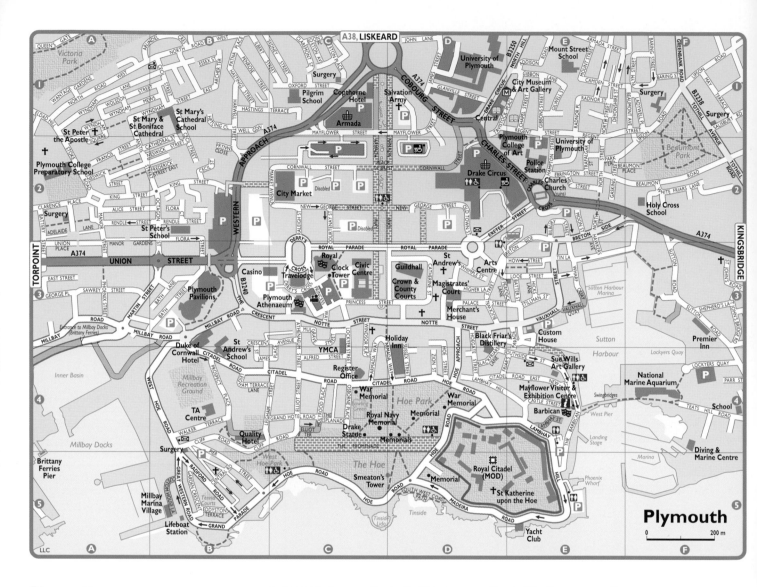

Plymouth

Plymouth is found on atlas page **6 D8**

Addison Road	E1	Claremont Street	C1
Adelaide Lane	A2	Clarence Place	A2
Alfred Street	C4	Cliff Road	B4
Alice Street	A2	Cobourg Street	D1
Anstis Street	A2	Cornwall Street	C2
Archer Terrace	B1	Courtenay Street	C3
Armada Street	E1	Crescent Avenue	B3
Armada Way	C2	Custom House Lane	B5
Armada Way	C4	Derry's Cross	C3
Arundel Crescent	A1	Devonshire Street	E1
Athenaeum Street	C3	Drake Circus	D1
Baring Street	F1	East Street	A3
Bath Lane	B3	Ebrington Street	E2
Bath Street	B3	Eddystone Terrace	B5
Batter Street	E3	Eldad Hill	A1
Battery Street	A2	Elliot Street	C4
Beaumont Avenue	F1	Elliot Terrace	C4
Beaumont Place	E2	Essex Street	B1
Beaumont Road	F2	Eton Avenue	C1
Bilbury Street	E2	Eton Place	C1
Blackfriars Lane	D4	Exeter Street	D2
Boon's Place	C1	Flora Court	B2
Breton Side	D3	Flora Street	B2
Buckwell Street	D3	Francis Street	A2
Camden Street	E1	Frederick Street East	B2
Castle Street	E4	Friar's Parade	D4
Cathedral Street	A2	Garden Crescent	B5
Catherine Street	D3	Gasking Street	E2
Cecil Street	B1	George Place	A3
Central Road	B5	Gibbon Lane	E1
Chapel Street	E1	Gibbons Street	E1
Charles Cross	E2	Gilwell Street	E1
Charles Street	D2	Glanville Street	D1
Citadel Road	B4	Grand Hotel Road	C4
Citadel Road	C4	Grand Parade	B5
Citadel Road East	D4	Great Western Road	B5

Greenbank Road	F1	Neswick Street	A2
Hampton Street	E2	New George Street	C2
Harwell Street	B1	New Street	E4
Hastings Street	B1	North Hill	E1
Hastings Terrace	B1	North Road West	A1
Hawkers Avenue	E2	North Street	E2
Hetling Close	B1	Notte Street	C3
Hicks Lane	E3	Octagon Street	B2
Higher Lane	D3	Old Town Street	D2
Hill Street	E2	Osborne Place	C4
Hoe Approach	D4	Oxford Street	C1
Hoegate Street	D3	Palace Street	D3
Hoe Road	C5	Park Terrace	E2
Hoe Street	D3	Parr Street	F4
Holyrood Place	C4	Patna Place	B1
How Street	E3	Peacock Lane	D3
Ilbert Street	B1	Penrose Street	B1
James Street	D1	Phoenix Street	A3
John Lane	D1	Pier Street	B5
King Street	A2	Place de Brest	C2
Ladywell Place	F1	Plym Street	F1
Lambhay Hill	D4	Princess Street	C3
Lambhay Street	E4	Princess Way	C3
Leigham Street	B4	Prospect Place	B4
Leigham Terrace Lane	B4	Prynne Close	B2
Lipson Road	F1	Queen's Gate	A1
Lockyers Quay	F4	Radford Road	B5
Lockyer Street	C3	Radnor Place	E1
Looe Street	D3	Radnor Street	E1
Madeira Road	D5	Raleigh Street	C2
Manor Gardens	A3	Regent Street	E1
Manor Street	A2	Rendle Street	A2
Market Avenue	C2	Royal Parade	C3
Martin Street	A3	St James Place	B4
Mayflower Street	C1	St John's Bridge Road	F3
Mayflower Street	D1	St John's Road	F3
May Terrace	F1	Salisbury Road	F1
Millbay Road	A3	Sawrey Street	A3
Moon Street	E2	Shepherd's Lane	F3
Mount Street	E1	Southside Street	D4
Mulgrave Street	C3	South West Coast Path	D5

Stillman Street	E3
Stoke Road	A2
Sussex Street	D3
Sutton Road	F3
Sydney Street	B1
Tavistock Place	D1
Teats Hill Road	F4
The Barbican	E4
The Crescent	B3
The Esplanade	C4
The Promenade	C4
Tin Lane	E3
Tothill Avenue	F1
Tothill Road	F2
Trafalgar Street	E2
Union Place	A3
Union Street	A3
Vauxhall Quay	E3
Vauxhall Street	E3
Walker Terrace	B4
Wantage Gardens	A1
Well Garden	B1
Western Approach	B2
West Hoe Road	A4
Wharf Quay	E3
Whimple Street	D3
White Friars Lane	F2
Windsor Place	C3
Wolsdon Street	A1
Wyndham Lane	A1
Wyndham Mews	A1
Wyndham Square	A1
Wyndham Street East	A1
Zion Street	D4

Portsmouth

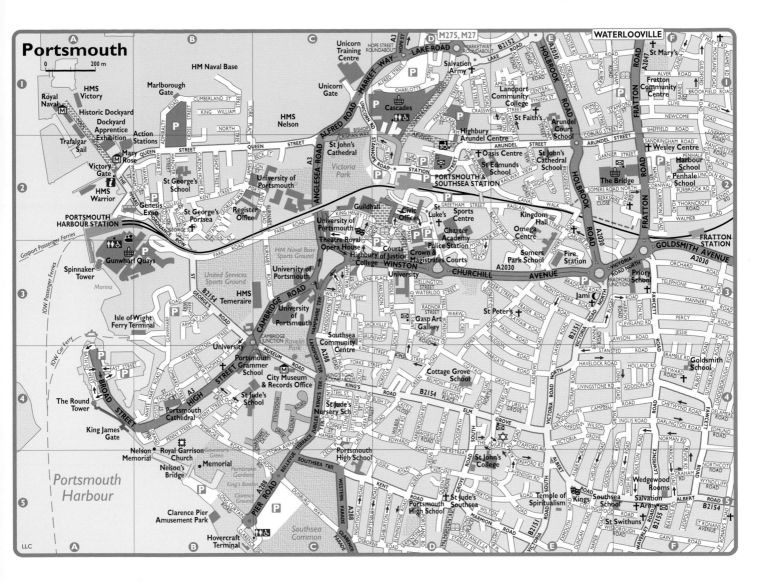

Portsmouth

Portsmouth is found on atlas page **14 H7**

Addison Road	F4	Castle Road	C4	Foster Road	E1	Lake Road	D1	Palmerston Road	D5	Stamford Street	E1
Admiralty Road	B2	Cavendish Road	E5	Fratton Road	F2	Landport Street	E1	Paradise Street	D1	Stanhope Road	D2
Albany Road	E5	Central Street	E1	Gain's Road	F5	Landport Terrace	C3	Park Road	B3	Stansted Road	E4
Albert Grove	E5	Charlotte Street	D1	Garnier Street	E2	Landsdowne Street	C3	Pelham Road	D4	Station Street	D2
Albert Road	E5	Chelsea Road	E5	Goldsmith Avenue	F3	Lawrence Road	F5	Pembroke Road	B4	Steel Street	C4
Alec Rose Lane	D3	Chester Place	E5	Gold Street	C4	Lawson Road	F3	Penhale Road	F2	Stone Street	C4
Alexandra Road	E1	Chetwynd Road	F4	Goodwood Road	E5	Leopold Street	F5	Penny Street	B4	Sussex Road	D5
Alfred Road	C1	Church Road	E1	Gordon Road	C5	Lincoln Road	F2	Percy Road	F3	Sutherland Road	F4
Alfred Street	D1	Claremont Road	F2	Great Southsea Street	C4	Little Southsea Street	C4	Pier Road	C5	Talbot Road	F4
Alver Road	F1	Clarence Parade	C5	Green Road	D4	Livingstone Road	E4	Playfair Road	E3	Telephone Road	F3
Anglesea Road	C2	Cleveland Road	F3	Greetham Street	D2	Lombard Street	B4	Portland Road	D5	Temple Street	D1
Ariel Road	F2	Clive Road	F1	Grosvenor Street	D3	Londesborough Road	F4	Purbrook Road	F2	The Hard	A2
Armory Lane	B3	Clock Street	B2	Grove Road North	D4	Lords Street	E1	Queens Crescent	D5	The Retreat	D5
Arundel Street	D2	College Street	B2	Grove Road South	D5	Lorne Road	F4	Queen Street	B2	The Thicket	D4
Arundel Street	E2	Collingwood Road	E5	Guildford Road	F1	Main Road	A1	Raglan Street	E2	Thorncroft Road	F2
Ashburton Road	D5	Commercial Road	D1	Guildhall Walk	C2	Manners Road	F4	Railway View	E2	Tottenham Road	F1
Bailey's Road	E3	Cornwall Road	F2	Gunwharf Road	B3	Margate Road	D4	Richmond Place	D5	Trevor Road	F4
Bath Square	A4	Cottage Grove	D4	Hambrook Street	C4	Market Way	C1	Rivers Street	D3	Unicorn Road	C1
Bellevue Terrace	C5	Cottage View	E2	Hampshire Terrace	C3	Marmion Road	D5	Rugby Road	E3	Upper Arundel Street	D2
Belmont Place	D4	Crasswell Street	D1	Harold Road	F5	Mary Rose Street	D2	Sackville Street	C3	Victoria Avenue	C5
Bishop Street	B2	Cross Street	B2	Havant Street	B2	Melbourne Place	C3	St Andrews Road	E4	Victoria Grove	E4
Bishop Crispian Way	C2	Cumberland Street	B1	Havelock Road	E4	Merton Road	D5	St Bartholomews Gardens	E4	Victoria Road North	E4
Blackfriars Road	E2	Curzon Howe Road	B2	Hawke Street	B2	Middle Street	D3	St Davids Road	E4	Victoria Road North	F3
Blount Road	C4	Darlington Road	F4	Hereford Road	E5	Milford Road	E2	St Edwards Road	D4	Victoria Road South	E5
Boulton Road	F5	Drummond Road	E1	Highbury Street	B4	Montgomerie Road	E3	St Faith's Road	D1	Vivash Road	F2
Bramble Road	F4	Duisburg Way	C5	High Street	B4	Moorland Road	F1	St George's Road	B3	Walmer Road	F2
Bridgeside Close	E2	Duncan Road	E5	Holbrook Road	E1	Museum Road	C4	St George's Square	B2	Warblington Street	B4
Britain Street	B2	Earlsdon Street	D3	Holland Road	F4	Napier Road	E5	St George's Way	B2	Warwick Crescent	D3
Broad Street	A4	East Street	A4	Hudson Road	E3	Nelson Road	D5	St James's Road	D3	Waterloo Street	D3
Brookfield Road	F1	Eldon Street	D4	Hyde Park Road	D3	Newcome Road	F1	St James's Street	B2	Waverley Road	F5
Brunswick Street	C3	Elm Grove	D4	Inglis Road	F4	Nightingale Road	C5	St Nicholas Street	B4	Western Parade	C5
Buckingham Street	D1	Elphinstone Road	D5	Jessie Road	F3	Norfolk Street	D4	St Paul's Road	C3	West Street	A4
Cambridge Road	C3	Exmouth Road	E5	Jubilee Terrace	C4	Norman Road	F4	St Peters Grove	E4	White Hart Road	B4
Campbell Road	E4	Fawcett Road	F3	Kent Road	D5	Olinda Street	F1	St Thomas's Street	B4	Wilson Grove	E4
Canal Walk	E2	Fawcett Road	F3	Kent Street	B2	Orchard Road	F3	Sandringham Road	F2	Wiltshire Street	C3
Carlisle Road	E2	Flint Street	C4	King Albert Street	E1	Ordnance Row	B2	Shaftesbury Road	C5	Winston Churchill Avenue	D3
				King Henry I Street	C2	Osborne Road	C5	Somers Road	D4	Wisborough Road	E5
				King's Road	C4	Outram Road	E4	Somers Road	E3	Woodpath	D4
				King's Terrace	C4	Oxford Road	F5	Somers Road North	E2	Woodville Drive	D4
				King Street	C4	Oyster Street	B4	Southsea Terrace	C5	Yarborough Road	D4
				King William Street	B1	Pains Road	E3	Stafford Road	E4	Yorke Street	C4

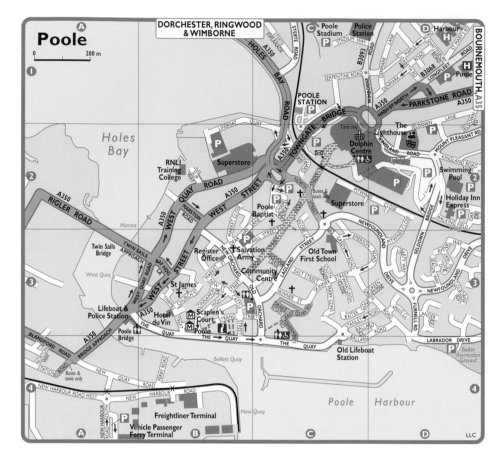

Poole

Poole is found on atlas page **12 H6**

Avenel Way	D3	New Quay Road	A4
Baiter Gardens	C3	New Street	B3
Ballard Close	C3	North Street	C2
Ballard Road	C4	Norton Way	A4
Bay Hog Lane	B3	Oak Drive	D2
Blandford Road	A3	Old Orchard	B3
Bridge Approach	A4	Parkstone Road	D1
Castle Street	B3	Perry Gardens	C3
Chapel Lane	C2	Pitwines Close	C2
Church Street	B3	Poole Bridge	A3
Cinnamon Lane	B3	Rigler Road	A2
Colborne Close	D3	St Mary's Road	D1
Dear Hay Lane	B3	Seager Way	D3
Denmark Lane	D1	Seldown Bridge	D3
Denmark Road	D1	Seldown Lane	D2
Drake Road	C3	Seldown Road	D2
Durrell Way	D3	Serpentine Road	C1
East Quay Road	C3	Shaftesbury Road	D1
East Street	C3	Skinner Street	C3
Elizabeth Road	D1	Slip Way	B2
Emerson Road	C3	South Road	C3
Ferry Road	B4	Stadium Way	C1
Fisherman's Road	C3	Stanley Road	C3
Furnell Road	D3	Sterte Esplanade	C1
Globe Lane	C2	Sterte Road	C1
Green Close	D3	Strand Street	B3
Green Road	C3	Thames Street	B3
High Street	B3	The Quay	B3
High Street North	D1	Towngate Bridge	C2
Hill Street	C3	Twin Sails Approach	A3
Holes Bay Road	C1	Twin Sails Bridge	A3
Kingland Road	D2	Vallis Close	D3
Labrador Drive	D4	Vanguard Road	A2
Lagland Street	C3	Walking Field Lane	D2
Lander Close	D3	Westons Lane	C3
Liberty Way	D3	West Quay Road	B3
Lifeboat Quay	B2	West Street	B3
Longfleet Road	D1	Whatleigh Close	C3
Maple Road	D1	Wimborne Road	D1
Market Close	B2		
Market Street	B3		
Marston Road	B2		
Mount Pleasant Road	D2		
Newfoundland Drive	C2		
New Harbour Road	A4		
New Harbour Road South	A4		
New Harbour Road West	A4		
New Orchard	B3		

Preston

Preston is found on atlas page **88 G5**

Adelphi Street	A1	Lancaster Road	C2
Arthur Street	A3	Lancaster Road North	C1
Avenham Lane	C4	Latham Street	C4
Avenham Road	C3	Lawson Street	B1
Avenham Street	C3	Leighton Street	A2
Berwick Road	C4	Lund Street	C1
Birley Street	C2	Lune Street	B3
Boltons Court	C3	Manchester Road	D3
Bow Lane	A3	Market Street	C2
Butler Street	B3	Market Street West	B2
Carlisle Road	C2	Marsh Lane	A2
Chaddock Street	C4	Maudland Bank	A1
Chapel Street	B3	Maudland Road	A1
Charlotte Street	D4	Meadow Street	C1
Cheapside	C3	Moor Lane	B1
Christ Church Street	A3	Mount Street	B3
Church Street	C3	North Road	C1
Clarendon Street	D4	Oak Street	D3
Corporation Street	B2	Ormskirk Road	D2
Corporation Street	B3	Oxford Street	C3
Craggs Row	B1	Pedder Street	A1
Cross Street	C3	Percy Street	D2
Crown Street	B1	Pitt Street	A3
Deepdale Road	D1	Pole Street	D2
Derby Street	D2	Pump Street	D1
Earl Street	C2	Queen Street	D3
East Cliff	B4	Ribblesdale Place	B4
East Street	D1	Ring Way	B2
Edmund Street	D2	Rose Street	D3
Edward Street	A2	St Austin's Road	D3
Elizabeth Street	B1	St Paul's Road	D1
Fishergate	B3	St Paul's Square	D1
Fishergate Hill	A4	St Peter's Street	D1
Fleet Street	B3	Sedgwick Street	C1
Fox Street	B3	Shepherd Street	D2
Friargate	B2	Snow Hill	B1
Fylde Road	A1	Stanleyfield Road	D1
Glover Street	C3	Starkie Street	C4
Great Avenham Street	C4	Syke Street	C3
Great Shaw Street	B2	Tithebarn Street	C2
Grimshaw Street	D2	Walker Street	B1
Guildhall Street	C3	Walton's Parade	A3
Harrington Street	B1	Ward's End	B2
Heatley Street	B2	Warwick Street	B1
Herschell Street	D4	West Cliff	A4
Holstein Street	D1	West Cliff Terrace	A4
Hopwood Street	D2	Winkley Square	B3
Jutland Street	D1		

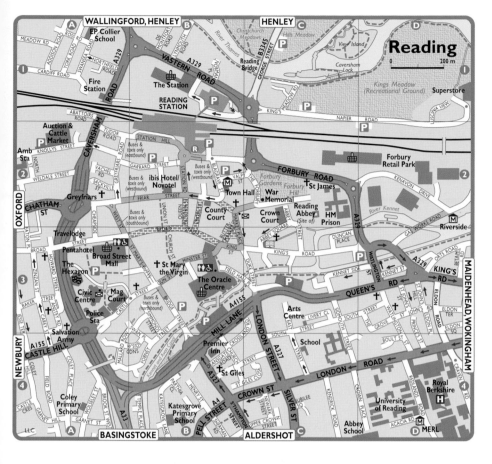

Reading

Reading is found on atlas page **35 K10**

Abbey Square	C3	King's Road	D3
Abbey Street	C2	King Street	B3
Addison Road	A1	Knollys Street	A2
Anstey Road	A3	Livery Close	C3
Baker Street	A3	London Road	C4
Blagrave Street	B2	London Street	C3
Boult Street	D4	Mallard Row	A4
Bridge Street	B3	Market Place	B2
Broad Street	A3	Mill Lane	B4
Brook Street West	A4	Minster Street	B3
Buttermarket	B3	Napier Road	C1
Cardiff Road	A1	Newark Street	C4
Carey Street	A3	Northfield Road	A1
Castle Hill	A4	Parthia Close	B4
Castle Street	A3	Pell Street	B4
Caversham Road	A2	Prince's Street	D3
Chatham Street	A2	Queen's Road	C3
Cheapside	A2	Queen Victoria Street	B2
Church Street	B3	Redlands Road	D4
Church Street	B4	Ross Road	A1
Coley Place	A4	Sackville Street	A2
Craven Road	D4	St Giles Close	B4
Crossland Road	B4	St John's Road	D3
Cross Street	B2	St Mary's Butts	B3
Crown Street	C4	Sidmouth Street	C3
Deansgate Road	B4	Silver Street	C4
Duke Street	C3	Simmonds Street	B3
Duncan Place	C3	Southampton Street	B4
East Street	C3	South Street	C3
Eldon Road	D3	Station Hill	B2
Field Road	A4	Station Road	B2
Fobney Street	B4	Swan Place	B3
Forbury Road	C2	Swansea Road	A1
Friar Street	B2	The Forbury	C2
Garnet Street	A4	Tudor Road	A2
Garrard Street	B2	Union Street	B2
Gas Works Road	D3	Upper Crown Street	C4
George Street	C1	Vachel Road	A2
Greyfriars Road	A2	Valpy Street	B2
Gun Street	B3	Vastern Road	B1
Henry Street	B4	Waterside Gardens	B4
Howard Street	A3	Watlington Street	D3
Katesgrove Lane	B4	Weldale Street	A2
Kenavon Drive	D2	West Street	A2
Kendrick Road	C4	Wolseley Street	A4
Kennet Side	C3	Yield Hall Place	B3
Kennet Street	D3	York Road	A1
King's Meadow Road	C1	Zinzan Street	A3

Salisbury

Salisbury is found on atlas page **21 M9**

Albany Road	C1	Kingsland Road	A1
Ashley Road	A1	King's Road	C1
Avon Approach	B2	Laverstock Road	D3
Bedwin Street	C2	Malthouse Lane	B3
Belle Vue Road	C2	Manor Road	D2
Blackfriars Way	C4	Marlborough Road	C1
Blue Boar Row	C3	Meadow Road	A1
Bourne Avenue	D1	Middleton Road	A1
Bourne Hill	C2	Milford Hill	D3
Bridge Street	B3	Milford Street	C3
Brown Street	C3	Mill Road	A3
Campbell Road	D1	Minster Street	B3
Castle Street	B1	Nelson Road	B1
Catherine Street	C3	New Canal	B3
Chipper Lane	C2	New Street	B3
Churchfields Road	A2	North Street	B3
Churchill Way East	D3	Park Street	D1
Churchill Way North	C1	Pennyfarthing Street	C2
Churchill Way South	C4	Queen's Road	C1
Churchill Way West	B2	Queen Street	C3
Clarendon Road	D2	Rampart Road	D3
Clifton Road	A1	Rectory Road	A3
Coldharbour Lane	A1	Rollestone Street	C2
College Street	C1	St Ann Street	C3
Cranebridge Road	B3	St Edmund's Church Street	C2
Crane Street	B3	St Mark's Avenue	D1
Devizes Road	A1	St Mark's Road	D1
Dew's Road	A3	St Paul's Road	B2
East Street	B3	Salt Lane	C2
Elm Grove	D2	Scots Lane	C2
Elm Grove Road	D2	Sidney Street	A1
Endless Street	C2	Silver Street	B3
Estcourt Road	D2	Southampton Road	D4
Exeter Street	C4	South Street	C4
Eyres Way	D4	South Western Road	A2
Fairview Road	D2	Spire View	B2
Fisherton Street	A2	Summerlock Approach	B2
Fowler's Road	D3	Tollgate Road	D4
Friary Lane	C4	Trinity Street	C3
Gas Lane	A1	Wain-A-Long Road	D1
George Street	A1	Wessex Road	B2
Gigant Street	C3	West Street	A3
Greencroft Street	C2	Wilton Road	A2
Guilder Lane	C2	Winchester Street	C3
Hamilton Road	C1	Windsor Road	B2
High Street	B3	Woodstock Road	C1
Ivy Street	C3	Wyndham Road	C1
Kelsey Road	D2	York Road	A2

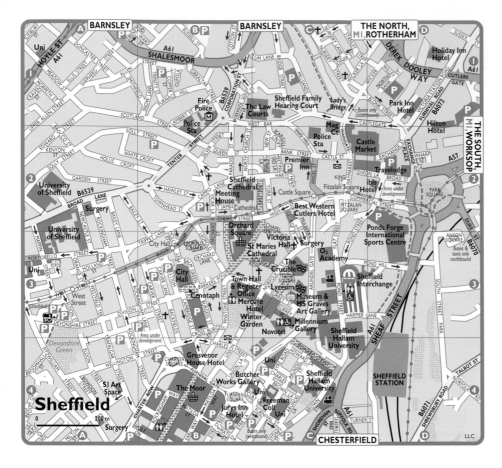

Sheffield

Sheffield is found on atlas page **84 E3**

Angel Street	C2	Howard Street	C4
Arundel Gate	C3	Hoyle Street	A1
Arundel Street	C4	King Street	C2
Backfields	B3	Lambert Street	B1
Bailey Street	A2	Leopold Street	B3
Balm Green	B3	Mappin Street	A3
Bank Street	C2	Matilda Street	B4
Barkers Pool	B3	Meetinghouse Lane	C2
Broad Lane	A2	Mulberry Street	C2
Broad Street	D2	Newcastle Street	A2
Brown Street	C4	New Street	C2
Cambridge Street	B3	Norfolk Street	C3
Campo Lane	B2	North Church Street	B2
Carver Street	B3	Orchard Street	B3
Castlegate	C1	Paradise Street	B2
Castle Street	C2	Pinstone Street	B3
Charles Street	B4	Pond Hill	C3
Charter Row	A4	Pond Street	C3
Church Street	B2	Portobello Street	A3
Commercial Street	C2	Queen Street	B2
Corporation Street	B1	Rockingham Street	A2
Cross Burgess Street	B3	St James Street	B2
Cutlers Gate	D1	Scargill Croft	C2
Derek Dooley Way	D1	Scotland Street	A1
Devonshire Street	A3	Shalesmoor	B1
Division Street	A3	Sheaf Street	D4
Dixon Lane	C2	Shoreham Street	C4
Duke Street	D2	Shrewsbury Road	D4
Exchange Street	D2	Silver Street	B2
Eyre Street	B4	Smithfield	A1
Fig Tree Lane	C2	Snig Hill	C2
Fitzwilliam Street	A4	Solly Street	A2
Flat Street	C3	Suffolk Road	C4
Furnace Hill	B1	Surrey Street	C3
Furnival Gate	B4	Talbot Street	D4
Furnival Road	D1	Tenter Street	B2
Furnival Street	C4	Townhead Street	B2
Garden Street	A2	Trafalgar Street	A4
George Street	C2	Trippet Lane	B3
Gibralter Street	B1	Union Street	B4
Harmer Lane	C3	Vicar Lane	B2
Harts Head	C2	Victoria Station Road	D1
Hawley Street	B2	Waingate	C2
Haymarket	C2	Wellington Street	A4
High Street	C2	West Bar	B2
Holland Street	A3	West Street	A3
Hollis Croft	A2	White Croft	A2
Holly Street	B3	York Street	C2

Shrewsbury

Shrewsbury is found on atlas page **56 H2**

Abbey Foregate	D3	Longner Street	B1
Albert Street	D1	Luciefelde Road	B4
Alma Street	B1	Mardol	B2
Back Lime Street	C4	Market Street	B3
Barker Street	B2	Milk Street	C3
Beacall's Lane	D1	Moreton Crescent	D4
Beeches Lane	C3	Mount Street	B1
Belle Vue Gardens	C4	Murivance	B3
Belle Vue Road	D4	Nettles Lane	B1
Belmont	B3	Newpark Road	D1
Belmont Bank	C3	New Street	A2
Benyon Street	D1	North Street	D1
Betton Street	D4	Old Coleham	D3
Bridge Street	B2	Old Potts Way	D3
Burton Street	D1	Park Avenue	A2
Butcher Row	C2	Pengrove	C4
Canonbury	A4	Pound Close	D4
Castle Foregate	C1	Pride Hill	C2
Castle Gates	C2	Princess Street	B3
Castle Street	C2	Priory Road	A2
Chester Street	C1	Quarry Place	B3
Claremont Bank	B3	Quarry View	A2
Claremont Hill	B3	Raby Crescent	C4
Claremont Street	B3	Raven Meadows	B2
Coleham Head	D3	Roushill	B2
College Hill	B3	St Chad's Terrace	B3
Copthorne Road	A2	St George's Street	A1
Coton Hill	C1	St Johns Hill	B3
Crescent Lane	B4	St Julians Friars	C3
Cross Hill	B3	St Mary's Place	C2
Darwin Gardens	A1	St Mary's Street	C2
Darwin Street	A1	St Mary's Water Lane	C2
Dogpole	C3	Salters Lane	D4
Drinkwater Street	A1	Severn Bank	D1
Fish Street	C3	Severn Street	D1
Frankwell	A2	Shop Latch	B3
Frankwell Quay	B2	Smithfield Road	B2
Greenhill Avenue	A2	Swan Hill	B3
Greyfriars Road	C4	The Dana	D1
High Street	C3	The Mount	A1
Hill's Lane	B2	The Square	B3
Howard Street	C1	Town Walls	B3
Hunter Street	B1	Victoria Avenue	A2
Kingsland Road	B4	Victoria Street	D1
Lime Street	C4	Water Lane	A2
Longden Coleham	C4	Water Street	D1
Longden Gardens	C4	West Street	D1
Longden Road	C4	Wyle Cop	C3

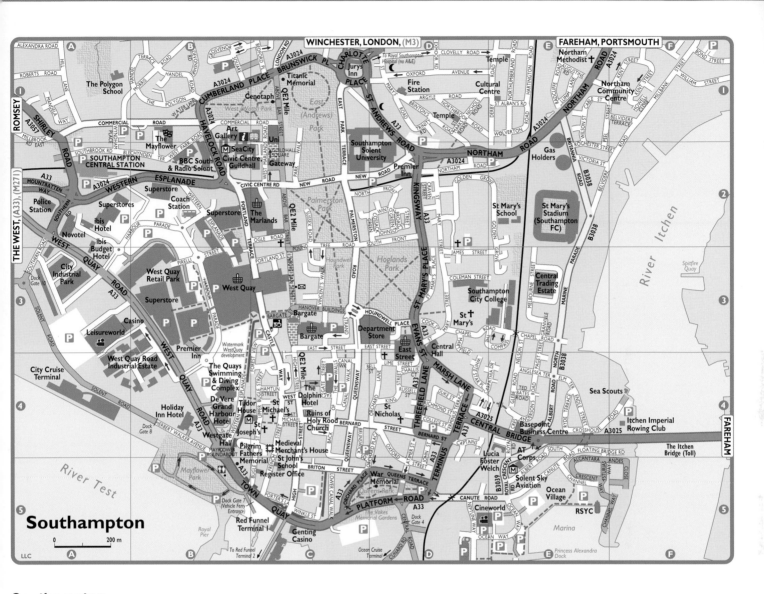

Southampton

Southampton is found on atlas page **14 D4**

Above Bar Street C1
Albert Road North E4
Albert Road South E5
Alcantara Crescent E5
Alexandra Road A1
Anderson's Road E4
Andes Close F5
Anglesea Terrace E4
Argyle Road D1
Asturias Way E5
Augustine Road E1
Back Of The Walls C4
Bargate Street C3
Bedford Place C1
Bell Street D4
Belvidere Road E2
Belvidere Terrace F1
Bernard Street C4
Blechynden Terrace B2
Bond Street F1
Brinton's Road D1
Britannia Road E1
Briton Street C5
Broad Green D2
Brunswick Place C1
Brunswick Square C4
Bugle Street C5
Cable Street E1
Canal Walk C4
Canute Road D5
Carpathia Drive D4
Castle Way C3
Central Bridge D4
Central Road D5
Challis Court D4

Channel Way E5
Chapel Road D3
Charlotte Place C1
Civic Centre Road B2
Clovelly Road D1
Coleman Street D3
College Street D4
Commercial Road A1
Cook Street D3
Cossack Green D2
Craven Street D2
Crosshouse Road E4
Cumberland Place B1
Cunard Road D5
Derby Road E1
Devonshire Road B1
Duke Street D4
Eastgate Street C4
East Park Terrace C1
East Street C3
Elm Terrace E4
Endle Street E4
Evans Street D3
Exmoor Road D1
Floating Bridge Road E4
Forest View C4
French Street C5
Glebe Road E4
Golden Grove D2
Granville Road E3
Grosvenor Square B1
Hamtun Street C4
Handel Road B1
Handel Terrace B1
Hanover Buildings C3
Harbour Parade B2

Hartington Road E1
Havelock Road B1
Herbert Walker Avenue B4
High Street C4
Hill Lane A1
Houndwell Place D3
Howell Close F1
Itchen Bridge F4
James Street D3
Johnson Street D2
John Street D5
Kent Street F1
King Street D4
Kingsway D2
Latimer Street D5
Lime Street D4
London Road C1
Lower Canal Walk C5
Lumpy Lane E1
Mandela Way A1
Marine Parade E3
Marsh Lane D4
Maryfield D3
Mayflower Roundabout B4
Melbourne Street E3
Millbank Street F1
Millbrook Road East A1
Morris Road B1
Mountbatten Way A2
Nelson Street E4
Neptune Way D5
New Road C2
Nichols Road D1
Northam Road D2
Northbrook Road D1
North Front C2

Northumberland Road E1
Ocean Way D5
Ogle Road C2
Orchard Place C5
Oxford Avenue D1
Oxford Street D4
Paget Street E4
Palmerston Road C2
Park Walk C2
Peel Street E1
Pirelli Street B3
Platform Road C5
Porter's Lane C5
Portland Street C3
Portland Terrace B2
Pound Tree Road C3
Queens Terrace D5
Queensway C4
Radcliffe Road E1
Richmond Street D4
Roberts Road A1
Rochester Street E2
Royal Crescent Road E5
Russell Street D4
Ryde Terrace E4
St Alban's Road E1
St Andrews Road D1
St Marks Road D1
St Mary's Place D3
St Mary's Road D1
St Mary Street D2
St Michael Street C4
Shirley Road A1
Solent Road A3
Southbrook Road A2
Southern Road A2

South Front C2
Strand C3
Sussex Road C2
Ted Bates Road E4
Terminus Terrace D5
The Compass D3
The Polygon B1
Threefield Lane D4
Town Quay B5
Trinity Road D1
Upper Bugle Street C4
Victoria Street E2
Vincent's Walk C3
Water Lane B1
Western Esplanade A2
Western Esplanade B4
West Marlands Road B2
West Park Road B2
West Quay Road A2
West Street C4
White Star Place D4
William Street F1
Wilson Street E1
Winkle Street C5
Winton Street D2
Wolverton Road E1
Wyndham Place A1

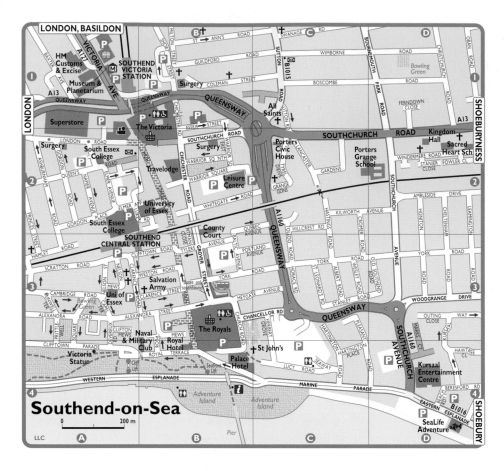

Southend-on-Sea

Southend-on-Sea is found on atlas page **38 E4**

Albert Road	C3	Kursaal Way	D4
Alexandra Road	A3	Lancaster Gardens	C2
Alexandra Street	A3	Leamington Road	D2
Ambleside Drive	D2	London Road	A2
Ashburnham Road	A2	Lucy Road	C4
Baltic Avenue	B3	Luker Road	A2
Baxter Avenue	A1	Marine Parade	C4
Beach Road	D4	Milton Street	B1
Beresford Road	D4	Napier Avenue	A2
Boscombe Road	C1	Nelson Street	A3
Bournemouth Park Road	D1	Oban Road	D1
Cambridge Road	A3	Old Southend Road	D3
Capel Terrace	A3	Outing Close	D3
Chancellor Road	B3	Pitmans Close	B2
Cheltenham Road	D2	Pleasant Road	C3
Chichester Road	B1	Portland Avenue	B3
Christchurch Road	D1	Princes Street	A2
Church Road	B3	Prittlewell Square	A3
Clarence Road	A3	Quebec Avenue	B2
Clarence Street	B3	Queen's Road	A2
Clifftown Parade	A4	Queensway	A1
Clifftown Road	B3	Royal Terrace	B4
Coleman Street	B1	Runwell Terrace	A3
Cromer Road	C2	St Ann's Road	B1
Devereux Road	A4	St Leonard's Road	C3
Eastern Esplanade	D4	Scratton Road	A3
Elmer Approach	A2	Short Street	B1
Elmer Avenue	A2	Southchurch Avenue	D2
Essex Street	B1	Southchurch Road	B2
Ferndown Close	D1	Stanier Close	D2
Fowler Close	D2	Stanley Road	C3
Gordon Place	A2	Sutton Road	C1
Gordon Road	A2	Swanage Road	C1
Grange Gardens	C2	Toledo Road	C2
Grover Street	B3	Tylers Avenue	B3
Guildford Road	B1	Tyrel Drive	C2
Hamlet Road	A3	Victoria Avenue	A1
Hartington Place	C4	Warrior Square East	B2
Hartington Road	C3	Warrior Square North	B2
Hastings Road	C2	Warrior Square	B2
Hawtree Close	D4	Wesley Road	C3
Herbert Grove	C3	Western Esplanade	A4
Heygate Avenue	B3	Weston Road	B3
High Street	B2	Whitegate Road	B2
Hillcrest Road	C2	Wimborne Road	C1
Honiton Road	D2	Windermere Road	D2
Horace Road	C3	Woodgrange Drive	D3
Kilworth Avenue	C2	York Road	B3

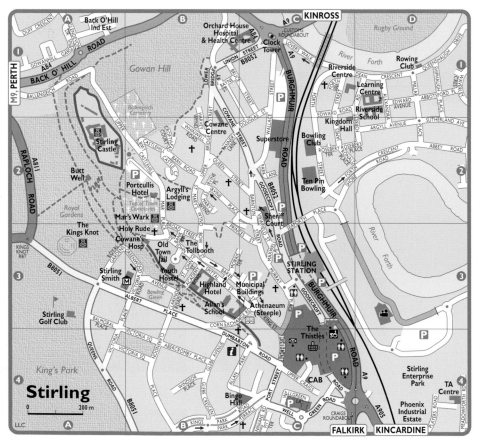

Stirling

Stirling is found on atlas page **133 M9**

Abbey Road	D2	King Street	C3
Abbotsford Place	D1	Lovers Walk	C1
Abercromby Place	B4	Lower Bridge Street	B1
Academy Road	B3	Lower Castlehill	B2
Albert Place	A3	Mar Place	B2
Alexandra Place	D1	Maxwell Place	C3
Allan Park	B4	Meadowforth Road	D4
Argyll Avenue	D2	Millar Place	D1
Back O' Hill Road	A1	Morris Terrace	B3
Baker Street	B3	Murray Place	C3
Ballengeich Road	A1	Ninians Road	C4
Balmoral Place	A3	Park Lane	C2
Bank Street	B3	Park Terrace	B4
Barn Road	B2	Pitt Terrace	C4
Barnton Street	C2	Players Road	D4
Bayne Street	B1	Port Street	C4
Bow Street	B3	Princes Street	B3
Broad Street	B3	Queenshaugh Drive	D1
Bruce Street	B1	Queens Road	A4
Burghmuir Road	C1	Queen Street	B2
Castle Court	B2	Raploch Road	A2
Clarendon Place	B4	Ronald Place	C2
Clarendon Road	B3	Rosebery Place	C2
Corn Exchange Road	B3	Rosebery Terrace	C2
Cowane Street	B1	Royal Gardens	A3
Craigs Roundabout	C4	St John Street	B3
Crofthead Court	B2	St Mary's Wynd	B2
Customs Roundabout	C1	Seaforth Place	C3
Dean Crescent	D1	Shiphaugh Place	D1
Douglas Street	C2	Shore Road	C2
Duff Crescent	A1	Spittal Street	B3
Dumbarton Road	B4	Sutherland Avenue	D2
Edward Avenue	D2	Tannery Lane	B2
Edward Road	C1	Union Street	B1
Forrest Road	D2	Upper Bridge Street	B2
Forth Crescent	C2	Upper Castlehill	A2
Forth Street	C1	Upper Craigs	C4
Forth View	C1	Victoria Place	A4
Glebe Avenue	B4	Victoria Road	B3
Glebe Crescent	B4	Victoria Square	A4
Glendevon Drive	A1	Viewfield Street	C2
Goosecroft Road	C2	Wallace Street	C2
Gowanhill Gardens	A1	Waverley Crescent	D1
Greenwood Avenue	A3	Wellgreen Lane	C4
Harvey Wynd	B1	Wellgreen Road	C4
Irvine Place	B2	Whinwell Road	B2
James Street	C2	Windsor Place	B4
Kings Park Road	B4		

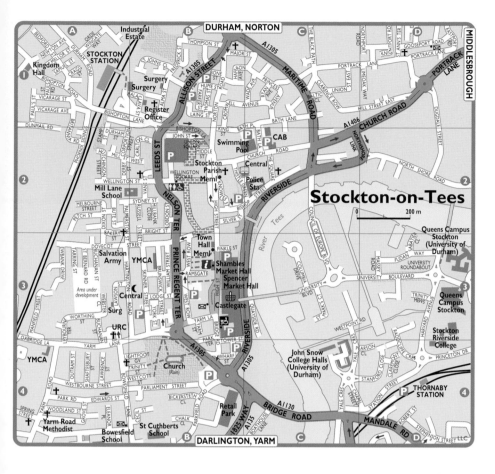

Stockton-on-Tees

Stockton-on-Tees is found on atlas page **104 D7**

1825 Way	B4	Massey Road	D3
Allison Street	B1	Melbourne Street	A2
Alma Street	B1	Middle Street	B2
Bath Lane	C1	Mill Street West	A2
Bedford Street	A1	Nelson Terrace	B2
Bishop Street	B2	North Shore Road	D2
Bishopton Lane	A1	Northport Road	D1
Bishopton Road	A1	Northshore Link	C2
Bowesfield Lane	A4	Norton Road	B1
Bridge Road	B3	Palmerston Street	A2
Bridge Road	C4	Park Road	A4
Bright Street	B2	Park Terrace	C3
Britannia Road	A1	Parkfield Road	B4
Brunswick Street	B3	Parliament Street	B4
Bute Street	A2	Portrack Lane	D1
Church Road	D1	Prince Regent Terrace	B3
Clarence Row	C1	Princess Avenue	C1
Corporation Street	A2	Princeton Drive	D4
Council of Europe		Quayside Road	C3
Boulevard	C2	Raddcliffe Crescent	D3
Cromwell Avenue	B1	Ramsgate	B3
Dixon Street	A2	Riverside	C4
Dovecot Street	A3	Russell Street	B2
Dugdale Street	D1	St Paul's Street	A1
Durham Road	A1	Silver Street	B2
Durham Street	A2	Skinner Street	B3
Edwards Street	A4	Station Street	D4
Farrer Street	B1	Sydney Street	B2
Finkle Street	C3	The Square	D2
Frederick Street	B1	Thistle Green	C2
Fudan Way	D3	Thomas Street	B1
Gooseport Road	D1	Thompson Street	B1
Hartington Road	A3	Tower Street	B4
Harvard Avenue	D3	Union Street East	C1
High Street	B2	University Boulevard	C3
Hill Street East	D1	Vane Street	B2
Hume Street	B1	Vicarage Street	A1
Hutchinson Street	A2	Wellington Street	A2
John Street	B2	West Row	B3
King Street	B2	Westbourne Street	A4
Knightport Road	D1	Westpoint Road	C3
Knowles Street	C2	Wharf Road	B4
Laing Street	B1	William Street	B4
Leeds Street	B2	Woodland Street	A4
Lobdon Street	B2	Worthing Street	A3
Lodge Street	B3	Yale Crescent	C4
Mandale Road	D4	Yarm Lane	A4
Maritime Road	C1	Yarm Road	A4

Stoke-on-Trent (Hanley)

Stoke-on-Trent (Hanley) is found on atlas page **70 F5**

Albion Street	B3	Lichfield Street	C3
Bagnall Street	B3	Linfield Road	D2
Balfour Street	D3	Lower Mayer Street	D1
Baskerville Road	D1	Lowther Street	A1
Bathesda Street	B4	Ludlow Street	D3
Bernard Street	C4	Malam Street	B1
Bethesda Street	B3	Marsh Street	B2
Birch Terrace	C3	Marsh Street North	B2
Botteslow Street	C3	Marsh Street South	B3
Broad Street	B3	Mayer Street	C1
Broom Street	C1	Mersey Street	B3
Brunswick Street	B3	Milton Street	A4
Bryan Street	B1	Mount Pleasant	A4
Bucknall New Road	C2	Mynors Street	D1
Bucknall Old Road	D2	New Hall Street	B2
Cardiff Grove	B4	Ogden Road	C4
Century Street	A1	Old Hall Street	C3
Charles Street	C3	Old Town Road	C1
Cheapside	B3	Pall Mall	B2
Chelwood Street	A1	Percy Street	C2
Clough Street	A3	Piccadilly	B3
Clyde Street	A4	Portland Street	A1
Commercial Road	D3	Potteries Way	B1
Denbigh Street	A1	Quadrant Road	B2
Derby Street	C4	Regent Road	C4
Dyke Street	D2	Rutland Street	A1
Eastwood Road	C4	St John Street	D1
Eaton Street	D2	St Luke Street	D3
Etruria Road	A2	Sampson Street	B1
Festing Street	C1	Sheaf Street	A4
Foundry Street	B2	Slippery Lane	A4
Garth Street	C2	Snow Hill	A4
Gilman Street	C3	Stafford Street	B2
Goodson Street	C2	Sun Street	A4
Grafton Street	C1	Tontine Street	C3
Hanover Street	B1	Town Road	C2
Harley Street	C4	Trafalgar Street	B1
Hillchurch	C2	Trinity Street	B2
Hillcrest Street	C2	Union Street	B1
Hinde Street	B4	Upper Hillchurch Street	C2
Hope Street	B1	Upper Huntbach Street	C2
Hordley Street	C3	Warner Street	B3
Huntbach Street	C2	Waterloo Street	D3
Jasper Street	C4	Well Street	D3
Jervis Street	D1	Wellington Road	D3
John Bright Street	D1	Wellington Street	D3
John Street	B3	Yates Street	A4
Keelings Road	D1	York Street	B1

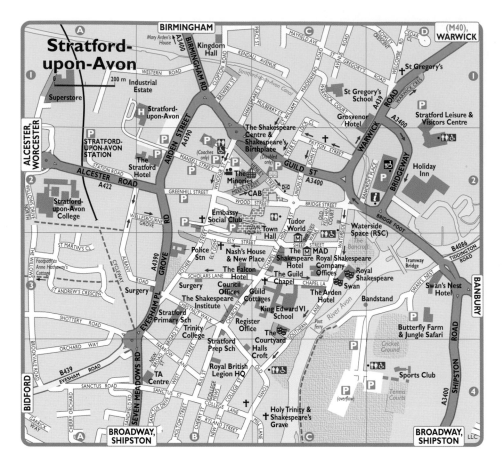

Stratford-upon-Avon

Stratford-upon-Avon is found on atlas page **47 P3**

Albany Road	A3	Old Red Hen Court	C2
Alcester Road	A2	Old Town	C4
Arden Street	B2	Orchard Way	A4
Avenue Road	C1	Payton Street	C2
Bancroft Place	C2	Percy Street	C1
Birmingham Road	B1	Rother Street	B3
Brewery Street	B1	Rowley Crescent	D1
Bridge Foot	D2	Ryland Street	B4
Bridge Street	C2	St Andrew's Crescent	A3
Bridgeway	D2	St Gregory's Road	C1
Broad Street	B4	St Martin's Close	A3
Brookvale Road	A4	Sanctus Drive	B4
Bull Street	B4	Sanctus Road	A4
Cedar Close	D1	Sanctus Street	B4
Chapel Lane	C3	Sandfield Road	A4
Chapel Street	C3	Scholars Lane	B3
Cherry Orchard	A4	Seven Meadows Road	A4
Cherry Street	A4	Shakespeare Street	B1
Chestnut Walk	B3	Sheep Street	C3
Church Street	B3	Shipston Road	D4
Clopton Road	B1	Shottery Road	A3
College Lane	B4	Shrieves Walk	C3
College Mews	B4	Southern Lane	C3
College Street	B4	Station Road	A2
Ely Gardens	B3	Swan's Nest	D3
Ely Street	B3	The Willows	A3
Evesham Place	B3	Tiddington Road	D3
Evesham Road	A4	Town Square	B2
Garrick Way	A4	Tramway Bridge	D3
Great William Street	C1	Tyler Street	C2
Greenhill Street	B2	Union Street	C2
Grove Road	B3	Warwick Court	C1
Guild Street	C2	Warwick Crescent	D1
Henley Street	B2	Warwick Road	C2
High Street	C3	Waterside	C3
Holtom Street	B4	Welcombe Road	D1
John Street	C2	Wellesbourne Grove	B2
Kendall Avenue	B1	Western Road	B1
Lock Close	C2	West Street	B4
Maidenhead Road	C1	Willows Drive North	A2
Mansell Street	B2	Windsor Street	B2
Mayfield Avenue	C1	Wood Street	B2
Meer Street	B2		
Mill Lane	C4		
Mulberry Street	C1		
Narrow Lane	B4		
New Broad Street	B4		
New Street	B4		

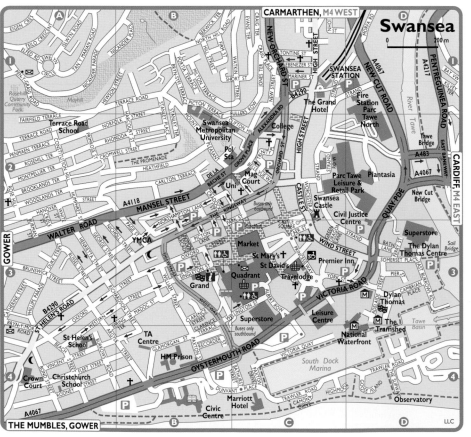

Swansea

Swansea is found on atlas page **29 J6**

Adelaide Street	D3	New Orchard Street	C1
Alexandra Road	C2	New Street	C1
Argyle Street	A4	Nicander Parade	A1
Bath Lane	D3	Nicholl Street	A3
Beach Street	A4	Norfolk Street	A2
Bond Street	A4	North Hill Road	B1
Brunswick Street	A3	Northampton Lane	B2
Burrows Road	A4	Orchard Street	C2
Caer Street	C3	Oxford Street	A3
Carlton Terrace	B2	Oystermouth Road	B4
Castle Street	C2	Page Street	B3
Catherine Street	A3	Park Street	B3
Clarence Street	B3	Paxton Street	B4
Clifton Hill	C2	Pentreguinea Road	D1
Constituion Hill	A2	Pen-Y-Graig Road	A1
Cradock Street	B2	Picton Lane	B3
Craig Place	C1	Pier Street	D3
Cromwell Street	A2	Primrose Street	A2
De La Beche Street	B2	Princess Way	C3
Dillwyn Street	B3	Quay Parade	D2
Duke Street	A3	Recorder Street	B4
Dunvant Place	B4	Rhondda Street	A2
East Bank Way	D2	Richardson Street	A3
East Burrows Road	D3	Rodney Street	A4
Ebenezer Street	C1	Rose Hill	A2
Elfed Road	A1	Russel Street	A3
Ferry Street	D3	St Helen's Road	A3
Firm Street	B1	Short Street	C4
Fleet Street	A4	Singleton Street	B3
George Street	A3	Somerset Place	D3
Glamorgan Street	B4	Strand	C1
Green Lane Dragon	C3	Tan Y Marian Road	A1
Grove Place	C2	Teilo Crescent	A1
Hanover Street	A2	Terrace Road	A2
Harcourt Street	B2	The Kingsway	B2
Heathfield	B2	Tontine Street	C1
Henrietta Street	A3	Trawler Road	C4
Hewson Street	A1	Victoria Quay	C4
High Street	C2	Victoria Road	C3
Hill Street	B1	Vincent Street	A4
Humphrey Street	A2	Walter Road	A3
Islwyn Road	A1	Watkin Street	C1
Llewelyn Circle	A1	Wellington Street	C3
Madoc Street	B3	West Way	B3
Mansel Street	B2	Western Street	A4
Mariner Street	C1	William Street	B3
Mount Pleasant	B2	Wind Street	C3
New Cut Road	D1	York Street	C3

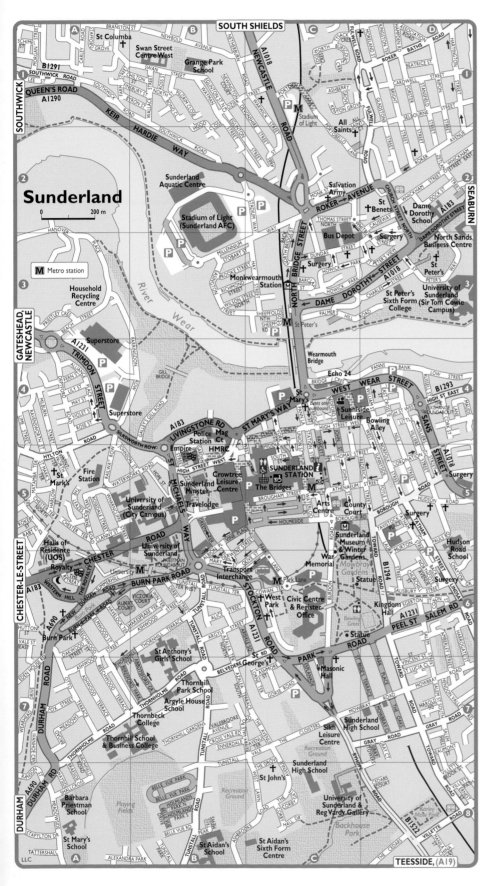

Sunderland

Sunderland is found on atlas page **113 N9**

Abbotsford Green	B7	Meadowside	A8
Abbs Street	C2	Middle Street	C5
Albion Place	B6	Milburn Street	A4
Alice Street	B6	Millennium Way	B3
Alliance Place	A4	Monk Street	C2
Amberley Street	D6	Moreland Street	D1
Argyle Square	B6	Morgan Street	A1
Argyle Street	B6	Mowbray Road	D7
Ashbrooke Road	B8	Netherburn Road	B1
Ashmore Street	C7	Newbold Avenue	B1
Ashwood Street	A7	Newcastle Road	C1
Ashwood Terrace	A7	New Durham Road	A6
Association Road	D1	Nile Street	D4
Athenaeum Street	C5	Norfolk Street	D5
Azalea Terrace North	B6	North Bridge Street	C3
Azalea Terrace South	B7	Northcote Avenue	D6
Back North Bridge Street	C3	North Street	B1
Beach Street	A3	Oakwood Street	A6
Beaumont Street	D7	Olive Street	B6
Bedford Street	C4	Otto Terrace	A7
Beechwood Street	A6	Palmer's Hill Road	C3
Beechwood Terrace	A7	Panns Bank	D4
Belvedere Road	B7	Park Lane	C5
Beresford Park	A7	Park Place	D6
Birchfield Road	A7	Park Road	C6
Borough Road	D5	Pauls Road	D5
Bridge Crescent	C4	Peel Street	D6
Bridge Street	C4	Portobello Lane	C1
Briery Vale Road	C7	Queen's Road	A1
Bright Street	D1	Railway Row	A5
Brooke Street	B3	Ravensworth Street	A4
Brougham Street	C5	Richmond Street	B3
Burdon Road	C5	Ripon Street	D1
Burn Park Road	B6	Roker Avenue	C2
Cardwell Street	D1	Roker Baths Road	D1
Carley Road	A1	Rosedale Street	A5
Charles Street	D3	Ross Street	B1
Chester Road	A6	Russell Street	D4
Churchill Street	D6	Ryhope Road	C7
Church Street North	D2	St Bede's Terrace	D7
Clanny Street	A5	St Mary's Way	C3
Cork Street	D4	St Michaels Way	B5
Coronation Street	D5	St Peter's View	D3
Cowan Terrace	C6	St Thomas' Street	C5
Cross Vale Road	B7	Salem Road	D6
Crozier Street	B1	Salem Street	D6
Dame Dorothy Street	C3	Salem Street South	D7
Deptford Road	A4	Salisbury Street	D6
Derby Street	B6	Sans Street	D4
Derwent Street	B6	Selbourne Street	D1
Devonshire Street	B1	Shakespeare Terrace	A6
Dock Street	D2	Shallcross	A8
Dundas Street	C3	Sheepfolds Road	C3
Durham Road	A7	Silksworth Row	A4
Easington Street	B3	South Street	C5
East Cross Street	D4	Southwick Road	A1
Eden House Road	A7	Stadium Way	C2
Egerton Street	D6	Stansfield Street	D1
Eglinton Street	B1	Station Street	C4
Eglinton Street North	B1	Stobart Street	B3
Elmwood Street	A6	Stockton Road	C6
Ennerdale	B7	Swan Street	B1
Farm Street	A1	Tatham Street	D5
Farringdon Row	B4	Tatham Street Back	D5
Fawcett Street	C4	The Avenue	C7
Forster Street	D1	The Cloisters	C7
Fox Street	A7	The Royalty	A6
Foyle Street	D5	Thomas Street North	C2
Frederick Street	D5	Thornhill Terrace	B6
Fulwell Road	C1	Thornholme Road	A7
Galley's Gill Road	B4	Toward Road	D5
Gladstone Street	D1	Trimdon Street	A4
Gorse Road	C7	Tunstall Road	B7
Gray Road	D7	Tunstall Terrace	B6
Green Terrace	B5	Tunstall Terrace West	B6
Hampden Road	D1	Tunstall Vale	B8
Hanover Place	A2	Union Street	C4
Harlow Street	A5	Valebrooke Avenue	B7
Harrogate Street	D6	Villette Road	D8
Hartington Street	D1	Villiers Street	D4
Havelock Terrace	A6	Vine Place	B5
Hay Street	C3	Wallace Street	B1
Hendon Valley Road	D7	Warwick Street	C1
High Street East	D4	Waterloo Place	C5
High Street West	B5	Waterworks Road	A5
Holmeside	C5	Wayman Street	B1
Hope Street	B5	Wearhead Drive	A7
Howick Park	C3	Westbourne Road	A5
Hudson Road	D5	Western Hill	A6
Hylton Road	A5	West Lawn	C8
Johnson Street	A5	West Street	C5
John Street	C4	West Sunniside	D4
Keir Hardie Way	A1	West Wear Street	C4
Laura Street	D5	Wharncliffe Street	A5
Lime Street	A4	Whickham Street	D2
Lindsay Road	D6	Whickham Street East	D2
Little Villiers Street	D4	Whitburn Street	D3
Livingstone Road	B4	William Street	D4
Low Street	D4	Wilson Street North	B3
Mary Street	B6	York Street	C4
Mauds Lane	D4	Zetland Street	D2

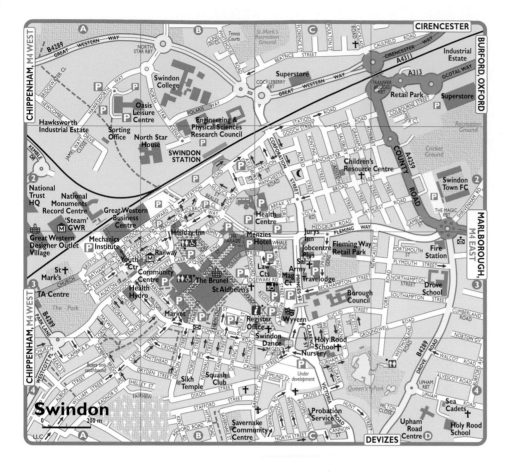

Swindon

Swindon is found on atlas page **33 M8**

Albion Street	A4	Islington Street	C3
Alfred Street	C2	John Street	B3
Ashford Road	B4	King Street	B3
Aylesbury Street	B2	London Street	A3
Bathurst Road	C2	Manchester Road	C2
Beckhampton Street	C3	Market Street	B3
Bridge Street	B2	Maxwell Street	A3
Bristol Street	A3	Medgbury Road	C2
Broad Street	C2	Milford Street	B2
Cambria Bridge Road	A4	Milton Road	B3
Canal Walk	B3	Morley Street	B3
Carfax Street	C2	Morse Street	B4
Carr Street	B3	Newcastle Street	D3
Chester Street	A3	Newcombe Drive	A1
Church Place	A3	Newhall Street	B4
Cirencester Way	D1	Northampton Street	D3
Clarence Street	C3	North Star Avenue	B1
College Street	B3	Ocotal Way	D1
Commercial Road	B3	Park Lane	A3
Corporation Street	C2	Plymouth Street	D3
County Road	D2	Polaris Way	B1
Crombey Street	B4	Ponting Street	C2
Curtis Street	A4	Portsmouth Street	D3
Deacon Street	B4	Princes Street	C3
Dixon Street	B4	Prospect Hill	C4
Dover Street	C4	Queen Street	B3
Dowling Street	B4	Radnor Street	A4
Drove Road	D4	Regent Place	C3
Dryden Street	A4	Regent Street	B3
Eastcott Hill	C4	Rosebery Street	C2
East Street	B2	Salisbury Street	C2
Edgeware Road	B3	Sanford Street	B3
Elmina Road	C1	Sheppard Street	B2
Emlyn Square	A3	Southampton Street	D3
Euclid Street	C3	Stafford Street	B4
Faringdon Road	A3	Stanier Street	B4
Farnsby Street	B3	Station Road	B2
Fleet Street	B2	Swindon Road	C4
Fleming Way	C3	Tennyson Street	A3
Gladstone Street	C2	Theobald Street	A3
Gooch Street	C2	Victoria Road	C4
Graham Street	C2	Villett Street	B3
Great Western Way	A1	Westcott Place	A4
Groundwell Road	C3	Western Street	C4
Havelock Street	B3	Whitehead Street	B4
Hawksworth Way	A1	Whitney Street	B4
Haydon Street	C2	William Street	A4
Holbrook Way	B2	York Road	D3

Taunton

Taunton is found on atlas page **18 H10**

Albemarle Road	B2	Northfield Road	A3
Alfred Street	D3	North Street	B3
Alma Street	C4	Obridge Road	C1
Belvedere Road	B2	Obridge Viaduct	D2
Billetfield	C4	Old Pig Market	B4
Billet Street	C4	Parkfield Road	A4
Bridge Street	B2	Park Street	A4
Canal Road	B2	Paul Street	B4
Cann Street	A4	Plais Street	C1
Canon Street	C3	Portland Street	A3
Castle Street	A4	Priorswood Road	B1
Cheddon Road	B1	Priory Avenue	D1
Chip Lane	A1	Priory Bridge Road	C2
Church Street	D4	Queen Street	D4
Clarence Street	A3	Railway Street	B1
Cleveland Street	A3	Ranmer Road	C3
Compass Hill	A4	Raymond Street	A1
Critchard Way	D2	Rupert Street	A1
Cyril Street	A1	St Andrew's Road	B1
Deller's Wharf	B2	St Augustine Street	C3
Duke Street	C3	St James Street	B3
Eastbourne Road	C3	St John's Road	A4
Eastleigh Road	D4	Samuels Court	A1
East Reach	D3	South Road	C4
East Street	C4	South Street	D4
Fore Street	B4	Staplegrove Road	A2
Fowler Street	A1	Station Road	B2
French Weir Avenue	A2	Stephen Street	C3
Gloucester Road	C3	Stephen Way	C3
Grays Street	D3	Tancred Street	C3
Greenway Avenue	A1	The Avenue	A2
Gyffarde Street	C3	The Bridge	B3
Hammet Street	B4	The Crescent	B4
Haydon Road	C2	The Triangle	C1
Herbert Street	B1	Thomas Street	B1
High Street	B4	Toneway	D2
Hugo Street	C3	Tower Street	B4
Hurdle Way	C4	Trinity Road	D4
Laburnum Street	C3	Trinity Street	D4
Lambrook Road	D2	Upper High Street	A4
Lansdowne Road	C1	Victoria Gate	D3
Leslie Avenue	A1	Victoria Street	D3
Linden Grove	A2	Viney Street	D4
Lower Middle Street	B3	Wellington Road	A4
Magdalene Street	B4	Wilfred Road	C3
Mary Street	B4	William Street	B1
Maxwell Street	A1	Winchester Street	C2
Middle Street	B3	Wood Street	B3

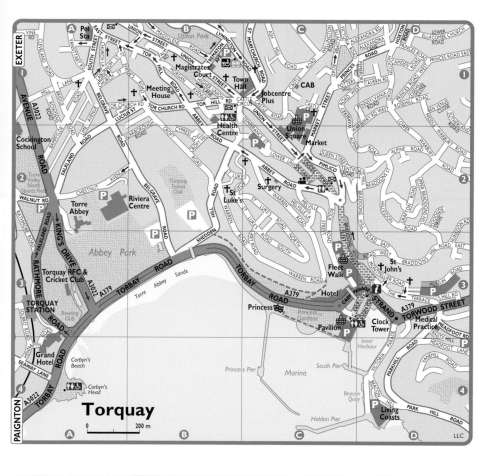

Torquay

Torquay

Torquay is found on atlas page **7 N6**

Abbey Road	B1	Middle Warbury Road	D1
Alexandra Road	C1	Mill Lane	A1
Alpine Road	C2	Montpellier Road	D3
Ash Hill Road	C1	Morgan Avenue	B1
Avenue Road	A1	Museum Road	D3
Bampfylde Road	A2	Palm Road	B1
Beacon Hill	D4	Parkhill Road	D4
Belgrave Road	A1	Pembroke Road	C1
Braddons Hill Road East	D3	Pennsylvania Road	D1
Braddons Hill Road West	C2	Pimlico	C2
Braddons Street	D2	Potters Hill	C1
Bridge Road	A1	Princes Road	C1
Camden Road	D1	Queen Street	C2
Cary Parade	C3	Rathmore Road	A2
Cary Road	C3	Rock Road	C2
Castle Lane	C1	Rosehill Road	D1
Castle Road	C1	St Efride's Road	A1
Cavern Road	D1	St Luke's Road	B2
Chestnut Avenue	A2	St Marychurch Road	C1
Church Lane	A1	Scarborough Road	B2
Church Street	A1	Seaway Lane	A4
Cleveland Road	A1	Shedden Hill Road	B3
Croft Hill	B2	Solbro Road	A3
Croft Road	B2	South Hill Road	D3
East Street	A1	South Street	A1
Ellacombe Road	C1	Stentiford Hill Road	C2
Falkland Road	A2	Strand	D3
Fleet Street	C3	Sutherland Road	D1
Grafton Road	D2	Temperance Street	C2
Hennapyn Road	A4	The Terrace	D3
Higher Union Lane	B1	Torbay Road	A4
Hillesdon Road	D2	Tor Church Road	A1
Hoxton Road	D1	Tor Hill Road	B1
Hunsdon Road	D3	Torwood Street	D3
King's Drive	A3	Trematon Ave	D3
Laburnum Street	A1	Trinity Hill	D3
Lime Avenue	A2	Union Street	B1
Lower Ellacombe Church		Upper Braddons Hill	D2
Road	D1	Vanehill Road	D4
Lower Union Lane	C2	Vansittart Road	A1
Lower Warbury Road	D2	Vaughan Parade	C3
Lucius Street	A1	Victoria Parade	D4
Lymington Road	B1	Victoria Road	C1
Magdalene Road	B1	Vine Road	A1
Market Street	C2	Walnut Road	A2
Meadfoot Lane	D4	Warberry Road West	C1
Melville Lane	C2	Warren Road	B2
Melville Street	C2	Wellington Road	C1

Tunbridge Wells (Royal)

Tunbridge Wells (Royal) is found on atlas page **25 N3**

Albert Street	C1	High Street	B4
Arundel Road	C4	Lansdowne Road	C2
Bayhall Road	D2	Lime Hill Road	B1
Belgrave Road	C1	Linden Park Road	A4
Berkeley Road	B4	Little Mount Sion	B4
Boyne Park	A1	London Road	A2
Buckingham Road	C4	Lonsdale Gardens	B2
Calverley Gardens	C3	Madeira Park	B4
Calverley Park	C2	Major York's Road	A4
Calverley Park Gardens	D2	Meadow Road	B1
Calverley Road	C2	Molyneux Park Road	A1
Calverley Street	C1	Monson Road	C1
Cambridge Gardens	D4	Monson Way	B2
Cambridge Street	D3	Mount Edgcumbe Road	A3
Camden Hill	D3	Mount Ephraim	A2
Camden Park	D3	Mount Ephraim Road	B1
Camden Road	C1	Mountfield Gardens	C3
Carlton Road	D2	Mountfield Road	C3
Castle Road	A2	Mount Pleasant Avenue	B2
Castle Street	B3	Mount Pleasant Road	B2
Chapel Place	B4	Mount Sion	B4
Christchurch Avenue	B3	Nevill Street	B4
Church Road	A2	Newton Road	B1
Civic Way	B2	Norfolk Road	C4
Claremont Gardens	C4	North Street	D2
Claremont Road	C4	Oakfield Court Road	D3
Clarence Road	B2	Park Street	D3
Crescent Road	B2	Pembury Road	D2
Culverden Street	B1	Poona Road	C4
Dale Street	C1	Prince's Street	D3
Dudley Road	B1	Prospect Road	D3
Eden Road	B4	Rock Villa Road	B1
Eridge Road	A4	Royal Chase	A1
Farmcombe Lane	C4	St James' Road	D1
Farmcombe Road	C4	Sandrock Road	D1
Ferndale	D1	Somerville Gardens	A1
Frant Road	A4	South Green	B3
Frog Lane	B4	Station Approach	B3
Garden Road	C1	Stone Street	D1
Garden Street	C1	Sutherland Road	C3
George Street	D3	Tunnel Road	C1
Goods Station Road	B1	Upper Grosvenor Road	B1
Grecian Road	C4	Vale Avenue	B3
Grosvenor Road	B1	Vale Road	B3
Grove Hill Gardens	C3	Victoria Road	C1
Grove Hill Road	C3	Warwick Park	B4
Guildford Road	C3	Wood Street	C1
Hanover Road	B1	York Road	B2

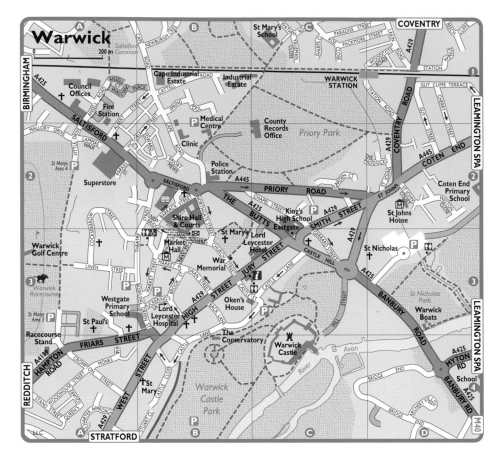

Warwick

Warwick is found on atlas page **59 L11**

Albert Street	A2	Packmore Street	C1
Ansell Court	A1	Paradise Street	C1
Ansell Road	A1	Parkes Street	A2
Archery Fields	D4	Priory Mews	B2
Back Lane	B3	Priory Road	C2
Banbury Road	D3	Puckering's Lane	B3
Barrack Street	B2	Queen's Square	A4
Beech Cliffe	D1	Roe Close	C1
Bowling Green Street	B3	St Johns	D2
Bridge End	D4	St Johns Court	D2
Brook Street	B3	Saltisford	A1
Cape Road	B1	Sharpe Close	C1
Castle Close	B4	Smith Street	C2
Castle Hill	C3	Spring Pool	B1
Castle Lane	B4	Stand Street	A4
Castle Street	B3	Station Avenue	D1
Cattell Road	B1	Station Road	D1
Chapel Street	C2	Stuart Close	B4
Charter Approach	A4	Swan Street	B3
Cherry Street	D1	Theatre Street	B3
Church Street	B3	The Butts	B2
Cocksparrow Street	A3	The Paddocks	D2
Coten End	D2	Trueman Close	C1
Coventry Road	D2	Victoria Street	A2
Crompton Street	A4	Vittle Drive	A2
Edward Street	B2	Wallwin Place	A1
Friars Street	A4	Wathen Road	C1
Garden Court	C2	Weston Close	D2
Gerrard Street	C3	West Street	A4
Guy Cliffe Terrace	D1	Woodcote Road	D1
Guy Street	D1	Woodhouse Street	A4
Hampton Road	A4		
High Street	B3		
Jury Street	B3		
Lakin Road	D1		
Lammas Walk	A2		
Linen Street	A3		
Mallory Drive	A2		
Market Place	B3		
Market Street	B3		
Mill Street	C3		
Monks Way	A4		
Myton Road	D4		
New Bridge	B2		
Newburgh Crescent	B1		
New Street	B3		
Northgate Street	B2		
Old Square	B3		

Watford

Watford is found on atlas page **50 D11**

Addiscombe Road	B3	Market Street	B4
Albert Road North	B2	Marlborough Road	B3
Albert Road South	B2	Merton Road	B3
Alexandra Road	A1	Mildred Avenue	A3
Anglian Close	D1	Monica Close	D1
Beechen Grove	C3	Nascot Street	B1
Brocklesbury Close	D2	New Road	D4
Burton Avenue	A4	New Street	C3
Cassiobury Drive	A2	Orphanage Road	C1
Cassio Road	A3	Park Avenue	A3
Charter Way	C3	Peace Prospect	A2
Chester Road	A4	Percy Road	B3
Chester Street	A4	Pretoria Road	A4
Clarendon Road	C1	Prince Street	C2
Cross Street	C2	Queen's Road	C2
Denmark Road	A1	Queen Street	C3
Derby Road	C3	Radlett Road	D2
Duke Street	C2	Raphael Drive	D1
Durban Road East	A4	Reeds Crescent	C1
Durban Road West	A4	Rickmansworth Road	A3
Earl Street	C3	Rosslyn Road	B3
Ebury Road	D2	St Albans Road	B1
Essex Road	A1	St John's Road	B1
Estcourt Road	C2	St Mary's Road	B4
Exchange Road	B3	St Pauls Way	D1
Farraline Road	B4	Shady Lane	B1
Feranley Street	B4	Shaftesbury Road	D2
Francis Street	B3	Smith Street	C4
Franklin Road	B1	Sotheron Road	C2
Gartlet Road	C2	Southsea Avenue	A4
Gaumont Approach	B2	Stanley Road	C3
George Street	C4	Station Road	B1
Gladstone Road	D3	Stephenson Way	D3
Granville Road	C4	Sutton Road	C2
Grosvenor Road	C3	The Avenue	A1
Halsey Road	B2	The Broadway	C3
Harwoods Road	A4	The Crescent	C4
Hempstead Road	A1	The Parade	B2
High Street	C3	Upton Road	B3
Hyde Road	A2	Vicarage Road	B4
Keele Close	C1	Water Lane	D4
King Street	C4	Wellington Road	B1
Lady's Close	C4	Wellstone Street	B3
Link Road	D1	Westland Road	B1
Loates Lane	C3	West Street	B1
Lord Street	C3	Whippendell Road	A4
Lower High Street	D4	Wiggenhall Road	B4
Malden Road	A1	Woodford Road	C1

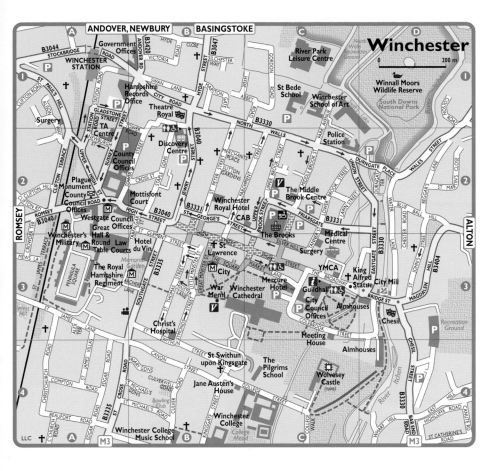

Winchester

Winchester is found on atlas page **22 E9**

Alex Terrace	A3	Market Lane	C3
Alison Way	A1	Marston Gate	B1
Andover Road	B1	Merchants Place	B2
Archery Lane	A3	Mews Lane	A3
Bar End Road	D4	Middle Brook Street	C2
Beaufort Road	A4	Minster Lane	B3
Beggar's Lane	D2	Newburgh Street	A2
Blue Ball Hill	D2	North Walls	B1
Bridge Street	D3	Parchment Street	B2
Canon Street	B4	Park Avenue	C2
Canute Road	D4	Romsey Road	A2
Chesil Street	D3	St Clement Street	B2
Chester Road	D2	St Cross Road	A4
Christchurch Road	A4	St George's Street	B2
City Road	B1	St James' Lane	A3
Clifton Hill	A2	St James Terrace	A3
Clifton Road	A1	St James' Villas	A4
Clifton Terrace	A2	St John's Street	D3
Colebrook Street	C3	St Martin's Close	D2
College Street	B4	St Michael's Gardens	B4
College Walk	C4	St Michael's Road	B4
Colson Road	D1	St Paul's Hill	A1
Compton Road	A4	St Peter Street	B2
Cross Street	B2	St Swithun Street	B3
Crowder Terrace	A3	St Thomas Street	B3
Culver Road	B4	Silchester Way	B1
Culverwell Gardens	B4	Silver Hill	C3
Durngate Place	D2	Southgate Street	B3
Durngate Terrace	D2	Staple Gardens	B2
Eastgate Street	D3	Station Road	A1
East Hill	D4	Stockbridge Road	A1
Edgar Road	A4	Sussex Street	A2
Friarsgate	C2	Sutton Gardens	B2
Friary Gardens	B4	Swan Lane	B1
Gladstone Street	A1	Symonds Street	B3
Gordon Road	C1	Tanner Street	C3
Great Minster Street	B3	The Broadway	C3
Highcliffe Road	D4	The Square	B3
High Street	B2	Tower Road	A1
Hyde Abbey Road	B1	Tower Street	A2
Hyde Close	B1	Trafalgar Street	B3
Hyde Street	B1	Union Street	C2
Jewry Street	B2	Upper Brook Street	C2
Kingsgate Street	B4	Upper High Street	A2
Lawn Street	C2	Victoria Road	B1
Little Minster Street	B3	Wales Street	D2
Lower Brook Street	C2	Water Lane	D3
Magdalen Hill	D3	Wharf Hill	D4

Wolverhampton

Wolverhampton is found on atlas page **58 D5**

Alexander Street	A3	Park Road East	B1
Bath Avenue	A1	Park Road West	A2
Bath Road	A2	Peel Street	B3
Bell Street	B3	Penn Road	B4
Bilston Road	D3	Piper's Row	D2
Bilston Street	C3	Pitt Street	B3
Birch Street	B2	Powlett Street	D4
Broad Street	C2	Princess Street	C2
Castle Street	C3	Queen Square	B2
Chapel Ash	A3	Queen Street	C2
Church Lane	B4	Raby Street	D4
Church Street	B4	Raglan Street	A3
Clarence Road	B2	Railway Drive	D2
Clarence Street	B2	Red Lion Street	B2
Cleveland Road	D4	Retreat Street	A4
Cleveland Street	B3	Ring Road St Andrews	A2
Corn Hill	D2	Ring Road St Davids	D2
Culwell Street	D1	Ring Road St Georges	C4
Dale Street	A4	Ring Road St Johns	B4
Darlington Street	B3	Ring Road St Marks	B3
Dudley Road	C4	Ring Road St Patricks	C1
Dudley Street	C2	Ring Road St Peters	B2
Fold Street	B3	Russell Street	A4
Fryer Street	C2	St John's Square	C4
Garrick Street	C3	St Mark's Road	A3
George's Parade	C3	St Mark's Street	A3
Graiseley Street	A4	Salop Street	B3
Great Brickkiln Street	A4	School Street	B3
Great Western Street	C1	Skinner Street	B3
Grimstone Street	D1	Snow Hill	C3
Herrick Street	A3	Stafford Street	C1
Horseley Fields	D2	Stephenson Street	A3
Hospital Street	D4	Stewart Street	B4
Lansdown Road	A1	Summer Row	B3
Lever Street	C4	Sutherland Place	D4
Lichfield Street	C2	Temple Street	B3
Little's Lane	C1	Thomas Street	B4
Long Street	C2	Tower Street	C3
Lord Street	A3	Vicarage Road	D4
Mander Street	A4	Victoria Street	B3
Market Street	C3	Waterloo Road	B1
Merridale Street	A4	Wednesfield Road	D1
Middle Cross	D3	Westbury Street	B2
Mitre Fold	B2	Whitemore Hill	B1
Molineux Street	B1	Whitmore Street	C2
New Hampton Road East	A1	Worcester Street	B4
North Street	B2	Wulfruna Street	C2
Park Avenue	A1	Zoar Street	A4

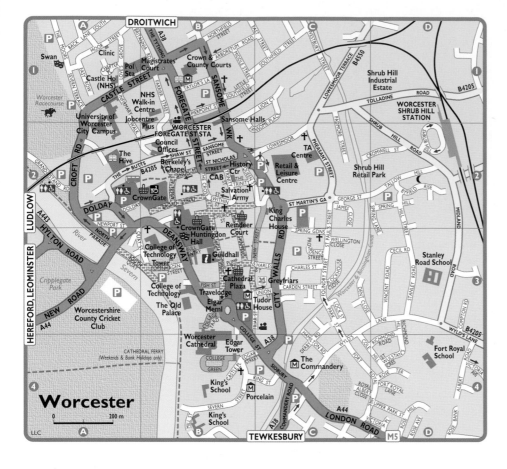

Worcester

Worcester is found on atlas page **46 G4**

Albert Road	D4	Middle Street	B1
Angel Street	B2	Midland Road	D2
Arboretum Road	B1	Mill Street	B4
Back Lane South	A1	Moor Street	A1
Blockhouse Close	C3	Newport Street	A2
Britannia Road	A1	New Road	A3
Broad Street	B2	New Street	C3
Byfield Rise	D2	Northfield Street	B1
Carden Street	C3	North Parade	A3
Castle Street	A1	Padmore Street	C1
Cathedral Ferry	A4	Park Street	C2
Cecil Road	D3	Pheasant Street	C2
Charles Street	C3	Pierpoint Street	B1
Charter Place	A1	Providence Street	C3
Church Street	B2	Pump Street	B3
City Walls Road	C3	Quay Street	A3
Cole Hill	C4	Queen Street	B2
College Street	B3	Richmond Road	D4
Commandery Road	C4	Rose Hill	D4
Compton Road	D3	Rose Terrace	D4
Copenhagen Street	B3	St Martin's Gate	C2
Croft Road	A2	St Nicholas Street	B2
Cromwell Street	D2	St Paul's Street	C3
Deansway	B3	St Swithin Street	B2
Dent Close	C3	Sansome Walk	B1
Derby Road	C4	Severn Street	B4
Dolday	A2	Severn Terrace	A1
East Street	B1	Shaw Street	B2
Edgar Street	B4	Shrub Hill Road	D2
Farrier Street	B1	Sidbury	C4
Fish Street	B3	Southfield Street	C1
Foregate Street	B1	Spring Hill	D2
Fort Royal Hill	C4	Stanley Road	D3
Foundry Street	C3	Tallow Hill	D2
Friar Street	C3	Taylor's Lane	B1
George Street	C2	The Butts	A2
Grandstand Road	A2	The Cross	B2
Hamilton Road	C3	The Moors	A1
High Street	B3	The Shambles	B2
Hill Street	D2	The Tything	B1
Hylton Road	A3	Tolladine Road	C1
King Street	B4	Trinity Street	B2
Little Southfield Street	B1	Union Street	C3
Lock Street	C3	Upper Park Street	D4
London Road	C4	Vincent Road	D3
Love's Grove	A1	Wellington Close	C3
Lowesmoor	C2	Westbury Street	C1
Lowesmoor Terrace	C1	Wyld's Lane	C4

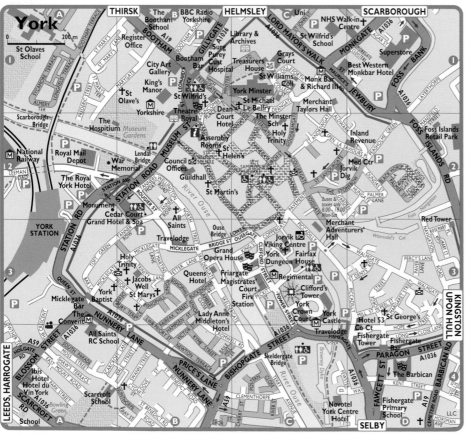

York

York is found on atlas page **98 C10**

Aldwark	C2	Lower Ousegate	C3
Barbican Road	D4	Lower Priory Street	B3
Bishopgate Street	B4	Low Petergate	C2
Bishophill Senior	B3	Margaret Street	D3
Black Horse Lane	D2	Market Street	C2
Blake Street	B2	Micklegate	A3
Blossom Street	A4	Minster Yard	B1
Bootham	B1	Monkgate	C1
Bridge Street	B3	Museum Street	B2
Buckingham Street	B3	Navigation Road	D3
Cemetery Road	D4	New Street	B2
Church Street	C2	North Street	B2
Clifford Street	C3	Nunnery Lane	A3
College Street	C1	Ogleforth	C1
Colliergate	C2	Palmer Lane	D2
Coney Street	B2	Palmer Street	D2
Coppergate	C3	Paragon Street	D4
Cromwell Road	B4	Parliament Street	C2
Davygate	B2	Pavement	C2
Deangate	C1	Peasholme Green	D2
Dove Street	B4	Percy's Lane	D3
Duncombe Place	B2	Piccadilly	C3
Dundas Street	D2	Price's Lane	B4
Fairfax Street	B3	Priory Street	C3
Fawcett Street	D4	Queen Street	A3
Feasegate	C2	Rougier Street	B2
Fetter Lane	B3	St Andrewgate	C2
Finkle Street	C2	St Denys' Road	D3
Fishergate	C4	St Leonard's Place	B1
Foss Bank	D1	St Martins Lane	B3
Fossgate	C2	St Maurice's Road	C1
Foss Islands Road	D2	St Saviourgate	C2
George Street	D3	St Saviours Place	C2
Gillygate	B1	Scarcroft Road	A4
Goodramgate	C2	Shambles	C2
Hampden Street	B4	Skeldergate	B3
High Ousegate	C3	Spen Lane	C2
High Petergate	B1	Spurriergate	B2
Holgate Road	A4	Station Road	A3
Hope Street	D4	Stonegate	B2
Hungate	D2	Swinegate	C2
Jewbury	D1	The Stonebow	C2
Kent Street	D4	Toft Green	A3
King Street	C3	Tower Street	C3
Kyme Street	B4	Trinity Lane	B3
Lendal	B2	Victor Street	B4
Long Close Lane	D4	Walmgate	D3
Lord Mayor's Walk	C1	Wellington Road	B2

Major airports

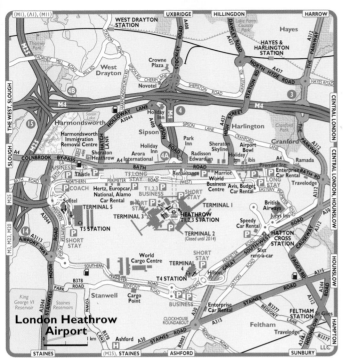

London Heathrow Airport – 16 miles west of London

Telephone: 0844 335 1801 or visit *www.heathrowairport.com*
Parking: short-stay, long-stay and business parking is available.
For booking and charges tel: 0844 335 1000
Public Transport: coach, bus, rail and London Underground.
There are several 4-star and 3-star hotels within easy reach of the airport.
Car hire facilities are available.

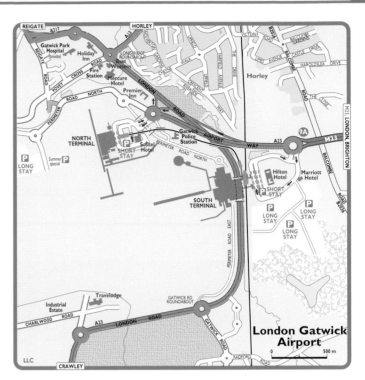

London Gatwick Airport – 35 miles south of London

Telephone: 0844 892 0322 or visit *www.gatwickairport.com*
Parking: short and long-stay parking is available at both the North and South terminals.
For booking and charges tel: 0844 811 8311
Public Transport: coach, bus and rail.
There are several 4-star and 3-star hotels within easy reach of the airport.
Car hire facilities are available.

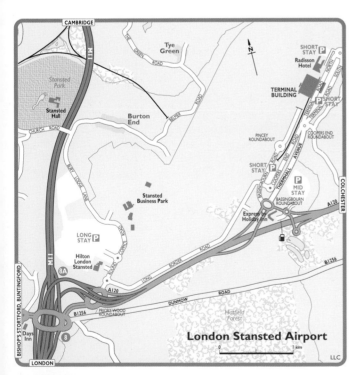

London Stansted Airport – 36 miles north east of London

Telephone: 0844 335 1803 or visit *www.stanstedairport.com*
Parking: short, mid and long-stay open-air parking is available.
For booking and charges tel: 0844 335 1000
Public Transport: coach, bus and direct rail link to London on the Stansted Express.
There are several hotels within easy reach of the airport.
Car hire facilities are available.

London Luton Airport – 33 miles north of London

Telephone: 01582 405 100 or visit *www.london-luton.co.uk*
Parking: short-term, mid-term and long-stay parking is available.
For booking and charges tel: 0845 303 7397
Public Transport: coach, bus and rail.
There are several hotels within easy reach of the airport.
Car hire facilities are available.

Major airports

London City Airport – 7 miles east of London

Telephone: 020 7646 0088 or visit *www.londoncityairport.com*
Parking: short and long-stay open-air parking is available.
For booking and charges tel: 0844 332 1237
Public Transport: easy access to the rail network, Docklands Light Railway and the London Underground.
There are 5-star, 4-star and 3-star hotels within easy reach of the airport.
Car hire facilities are available.

Birmingham International Airport – 8 miles east of Birmingham

Telephone: 0871 222 0072 or visit *www.birminghamairport.co.uk*
Parking: short, mid-term and long-stay parking is available.
For booking and charges tel: 0871 222 0072
Public Transport: Air-Rail Link service operates every 2 minutes to and from Birmingham International Railway Station & Interchange.
There is one 3-star hotel adjacent to the airport and several 4 and 3-star hotels within easy reach of the airport. Car hire facilities are available.

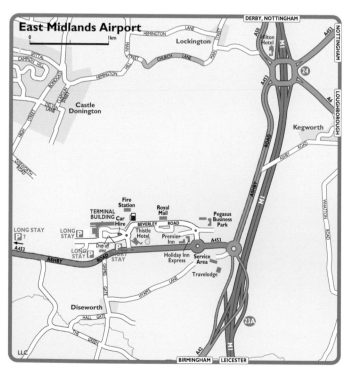

East Midlands Airport – 15 miles south west of Nottingham, next to the M1 at junctions 23A and 24

Telephone: 0871 919 9000 or visit *www.eastmidlandsairport.com*
Parking: short and long-stay parking is available.
For booking and charges tel: 0871 310 3300
Public Transport: bus and coach services to major towns and cities in the East Midlands.
There are several 3-star hotels within easy reach of the airport.
Car hire facilities are available.

Manchester Airport – 10 miles south of Manchester

Telephone: 0871 271 0711 or visit *www.manchesterairport.co.uk*
Parking: short and long-stay parking is available.
For booking and charges tel: 0871 310 2200
Public Transport: coach, bus and rail.
There are several 4-star and 3-star hotels within easy reach of the airport.
Car hire facilities are available.

Major airports

Leeds Bradford International Airport – 7 miles north east of Bradford and 9 miles north west of Leeds

Telephone: 0871 288 2288 or visit *www.leedsbradfordairport.co.uk*
Parking: short, mid-term and long-stay parking is available.
For booking and charges tel: 0844 414 3295
Public Transport: bus service operates every 30 minutes from Bradford, Leeds and Otley.
There are several 4-star and 3-star hotels within easy reach of the airport.
Car hire facilities are available.

Aberdeen Airport – 7 miles north west of Aberdeen

Telephone: 0844 481 6666 or visit *www.aberdeenairport.com*
Parking: short and long-stay parking is available.
For booking and charges tel: 0844 335 1000
Public Transport: regular bus service to central Aberdeen.
There are several 4-star and 3-star hotels within easy reach of the airport.
Car hire facilities are available.

Edinburgh Airport – 7 miles west of Edinburgh

Telephone: 0844 481 8989 or visit *www.edinburghairport.com*
Parking: short and long-stay parking is available.
For booking and charges tel: 0844 770 3040
Public Transport: regular bus services to central Edinburgh.
There are several 4-star and 3-star hotels within easy reach of the airport.
Car hire facilities are available.

Glasgow Airport – 8 miles west of Glasgow

Telephone: 0844 481 5555 or visit *www.glasgowairport.com*
Parking: short and long-stay parking is available.
For booking and charges tel: 0844 335 1000
Public Transport: regular coach services operate direct to central Glasgow and Edinburgh.
There are several 3-star hotels within easy reach of the airport.
Car hire facilities are available.

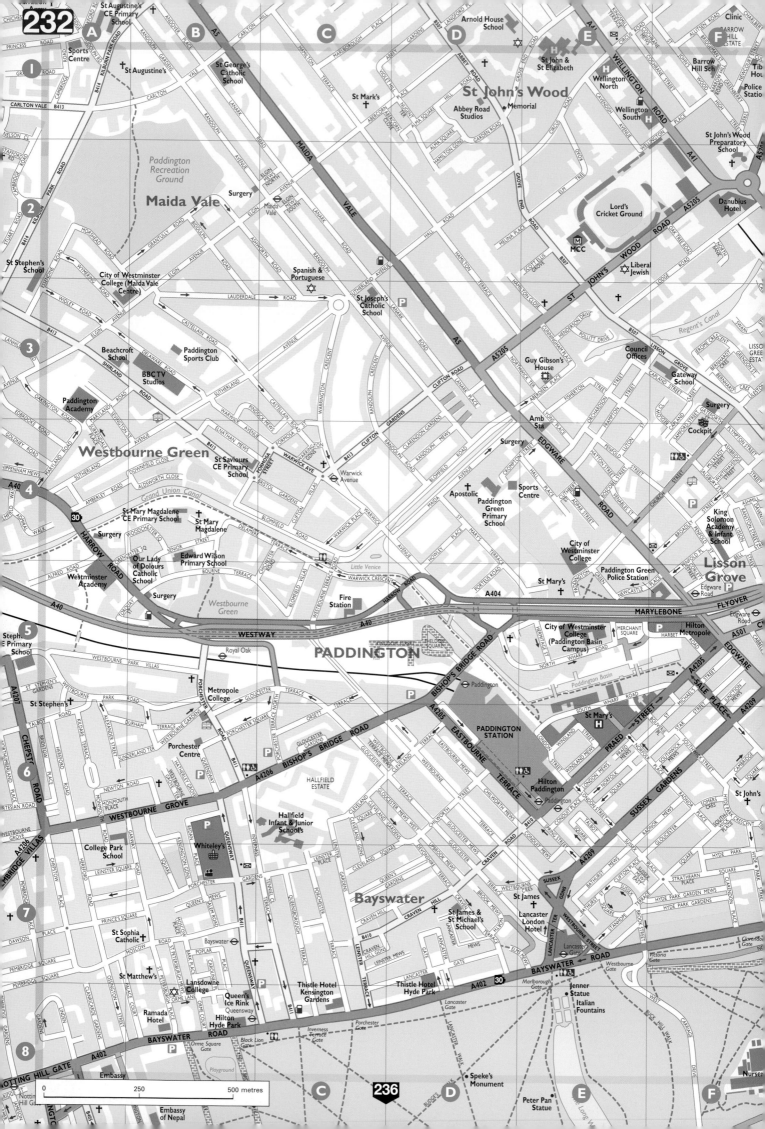

A B C D E F

Bishopsgate

Old Spitalfields
Market

Christ Church

Christ Church
School

Police
Station

Brady Arts &
Community
Centre

WHITECHAPEL
STATION

1

Liverpool
Street Station

Bishopsgate
Institute

Royal London

London Churchill
College

Pinnacle
(Bishopsgate
Tower)

The Gherkin

Petticoat Lane
Market

East End
Community
School

Canon
Barnett
School

Whitechapel
Gallery

London
Metropolitan
University

London Muslim
Centre

East London
Mosque

London
College

Barts & The London
School of Medicine
& Dentistry

City University
London

2

St Helen's

Travelodge

Whitechapel
Bell Foundry

Kobi Nazrul
Primary School

Queen Mary
Innovation Centre

Madani Girls
School

Guildhall College

235

Lloyd's

Sir John
Cass's
Prim Sch

London
Metropolitan
University

Aldgate
East

Icon College
of Technology

London
School of
Commerce
& IT

London
Metropolitan
University

Beckett
College

Mulberry Sports
& Leisure Centre

Mulberry School
for Girls

Watney
Market

3

Lloyd's of
Shipping

English
Martyrs
Catholic
School

Police
Station

City of London
College

Harry Gosling
Primary School

Surgery

Bigland Green
Primary School

Islamic Sixth
Form College

Guild Church
of St Margaret
Pattens

FENCHURCH
STREET
STATION

Travelodge

Premier
Inn

Travelodge

Whitechapel

Shapla Primary
School

St Paul's
Primary School

St George
in the East

Latifiah Girls
School

Swimming
Pool

The Grange
Hotel

Ten
Trinity
Square

Trinity
House

London
Metropolitan
University

SHORTER ST

ROYAL MINT STREET

Whitechapel
Estate

Swimming
Pool

St George in the East

4

Custom House

All Hallows
by the Tower

TOWER HILL

Tower of London

Tower Bridge
House

EAST SMITHFIELD

Thomas
More Square

St George in the East

News International

Tobacco
Dock

St Peter's
Primary
School

Sugar Quay

Tower Millennium
Pier

5

HMS
Belfast

Hay's
Galleria

Southwark
Crown
Court

MORE LONDON

The
Scoop

City Hall

Tower Hotel

St Katharine
Pier

Tower
Bridge

Hermitage
School

John Orwell
Sports Centre

Wapping

Hilton
Hotel

Unicorn
Theatre

River Thames

Alderman
Stairs

The Captain
Kidd

6

CRUCIFIX LA

London
City Mission

Magistrates'
Court

TOOLEY STREET

Design

BUTLER'S
WHARF

JAVA
WHARF

Police
Station

239

Tower Bridge
Primary School

TANNER ST

ST SAVIOURS
WHARF

JAMAICA
WHARF

Fire Station

CHAMBERS
WHARF

St Michael's
Catholic
School

Cherry Garden
Pier

King's
Stairs

7

Premier
Inn

Most Holy
Trinity

St Joseph's RC
Primary School

ARNOLD
ESTATE

JAMAICA ROAD

Royal Marines
Reserves (City
of London)

St James
CE Primary
School

Riverside
Primary
School

JAMAICA ROAD

BERMONDSEY

Bosco
College

8

Grange
Primary
School

Bermondsey
Square Hotel

Buddhist
Centre

Discovery
Business Park

Southwark
College

Southwark
Park

0   250   500 metres

A B C D E F

Central London street index

In this index, street and station names are listed in alphabetical order and written in full, but may be abbreviated on the map.
Each entry is followed by its Postcode District and then the page number and grid reference to the square in which the name is found.
Names are asterisked (*) in the index where there is insufficient space to show them on the map.

A

Abbey Gardens NW8 .... 232 C1
Abbey Orchard Street SW1P ... 238 B4
Abbey Road NW8 .... 232 D1
Abbey Street SE1 .... 240 B7
Abchurch Lane EC4N 235 L7
Abercorn Close NW8 .... 232 C1
Abercorn Place NW8 .... 232 C1
Aberdeen Place NW8 .... 232 E3
Aberdour Street SE1 .... 239 M5
Abingdon Road W8 .... 236 A4
Abingdon Street SW1P 238 C3
Abingdon Villas W8 .... 236 A4
Ackroyd Drive E3 .... 241 L1
Acorn Walk SE16 .... 241 K5
Acton Street WC1X 234 E2
Adam and Eve Mews W8 .... 236 A3
Adam's Row W1K 233 K8
Adam Street WC2N 234 D8
Addle Hill EC4V 235 H7
Adelina Grove E1 .... 240 F1
Adeline Place WC1B 234 B5
Adler Street E1 .... 240 D2
Admiral Place SE16 .... 241 K5
Admiral Walk W9 .... 232 A4
Adpar Street W2 .... 232 E4
Agar Street WC2N 234 D8
Agdon Street EC1V 235 H3
Agnes Street E14 .... 241 L2
Ainsty Street SE16 .... 241 G6
Air Street W1B 234 A8
Alaska Street SE1 .... 238 F2
Albany Road SE5 .... 239 L8
Albany Street NW1 .... 233 L1
Albemarle Street W1S 233 L8
Albemarle Way EC1V 235 H4
Alberta Street SE17 .... 239 H6
Albert Bridge SW3 .... 237 G8
Albert Embankment SE1 .... 238 D7
Albert Gardens E1 .... 241 H3
Albert Gate SW1X 237 H2
Albert Place W8 .... 236 C3
Albion Gate W2 .... 233 G7
Albion Place EC1M 235 H4
Albion Street SE16 .... 241 G7
Albion Street W2 .... 233 G7
Aldenham Street NW1 .... 234 A1
Aldermanbury EC2V 235 K6
Alderney Mews SE1 .... 239 K4
Alderney Street SW1V 237 L6
Aldford Street W1K 233 J8
Aldgate EC3M 240 B3
Aldgate ⊖ EC3N 240 B2
Aldgate East ⊖ E1 .... 240 D2
Aldgate High Street EC3N 240 B3
Aldsworth Close W9 .... 232 B4
Aldwych WC2E 234 E7
Alexander Place SW7 .... 236 F5
Alexander Street W2 .... 232 A6
Alexandra Gate SW7 .... 236 E3
Alfred Mews WC1E 234 B4
Alfred Place WC1E 234 B4
Alfred Road W2 .... 232 A5
Alice Street SE1 .... 239 M4
Alie Street E1 .... 240 C3
Allen Street W8 .... 236 A4
Allhallows Lane EC4R 235 L8
Allington Street SW1E 237 L4
Allitsen Road NW8 .... 232 F1
Allsop Place NW1 .... 233 H4
Alma Square NW8 .... 232 D1
Alpha Place SW3 .... 237 G8
Alsace Road SE17 .... 239 M7
Alscot Road SE1 .... 240 C8
Alvey Street SE17 .... 239 M6
Ambergate Street SE17 .... 239 H7
Amberley Road W9 .... 232 A4
Ambrosden Avenue SW1P 238 A4
Amelia Street SE17 .... 239 J6
America Square EC3N 240 B3
America Street SE1 .... 239 J2
Ampton Street WC1X 234 E2
Amwell Street EC1R 234 F2
Anchorage Point E14 .... 241 M6
Andover Place NW6 .... 232 B1
Angel ⊖ N1 .... 235 G1
Angel Junction N1 .... 235 G1
Angel Lane EC4R 235 L8
Angel Street EC1A 235 J6
Ann Moss Way SE16 .... 240 F8
Ann's Close SW1X 237 J3
Ansdell Street W8 .... 236 B4
Antill Terrace E1 .... 241 H2
Antizan Street E1 .... 240 B2
Apple Tree Yard SW1Y 234 A8
Appold Street EC2A 235 M4
Apsley Gate W1J 237 J2
Aquinas Street SE1 .... 239 G1
Arbour Square E1 .... 241 H2
Archangels SE16 .... 241 J7
Archer Street W1B 234 B7
Arch Street SE1 .... 239 J4
Arden Estate N1 .... 235 M1
Argyle Square WC1H 234 D2
Argyle Street WC1H 234 D2
Argyll Road W8 .... 236 A3
Argyll Street W1F 233 M6
Arlington Street SW1A 237 M1
Arlington Way EC1R 235 G2
Arne Street WC2H 234 D6
Arnhem Place E14 .... 241 M8
Arnold Estate N1 .... 240 C7
Arnside Street SE17 .... 239 K8
Artesian Road W11 .... 232 A6
Arthur Street EC4V 235 L7

Artichoke Hill E1W 240 E4
Artillery Lane E1 .... 240 A1
Artillery Row SW1P 238 B4
Arundel Street WC2R 234 F7
Ashbridge Street NW8 .... 232 F4
Ashburn Gardens SW7 .... 236 C5
Ashburn Place SW7 .... 236 C5
Ashby Street EC1V 235 H2
Ashfield Street E1 .... 240 E2
Ashford Street N1 .... 235 M2
Ashley Place SW1P 237 M4
Ashmill Street NW1 .... 232 F4
Ashmole Street SW8 .... 238 F8
Ashworth Road W9 .... 232 B2
Assam Street E1 .... 240 C2
Assembly Place E1 .... 241 G1
Astell Street SW3 .... 237 G6
Aston Street E14 .... 241 K1
Astwood Mews SW7 .... 236 C5
Atherstone Mews SW7 .... 236 D5
Atterbury Street SW1P 238 C6
Attneave Street WC1X 234 F3
Augustus Street NW1 .... 233 L1
Aulton Place SE11 .... 239 G7
Austin Friars EC2N 235 L6
Australia Gate SW1A 237 M3
Austral Street SE11 .... 239 H5
Aveline Street SE11 .... 238 F7
Ave Maria Lane EC1A 235 H6
Avenue Dock Hill SE16 .... 241 J6
Avery Farm Row SW1W 237 K6
Avery Row W1K 233 L7
Aybrook Street W1U 233 J5
Aylesbury Road SE17 .... 239 L7
Aylesbury Street EC1R 235 H4
Aylesford Street SW1V 238 B7
Aylward Street E1 .... 241 G2
Ayres Street SE1 .... 239 K2

B

Babmaes Street SW1Y 234 B8
Bache's Street N1 .... 235 L2
Back Church Lane E1 .... 240 D3
Back Hill EC1R 235 G4
Bacon Grove SE1 .... 240 B8
Bainbridge Street WC1A 234 C6
Bakers Mews W1U 233 J6
Baker's Row EC1R 235 G4
Baker Street NW1 .... 233 H4
Baker Street W1U 233 J5
Baker Street ⊖ NW1 .... 233 H4
Balcombe Street NW1 .... 233 G3
Balderton Street W1K 233 J7
Baldwin's Gardens EC1N 234 F5
Baldwin Street EC1V 235 L2
Bale Road E1 .... 241 J1
Balfe Street N1 .... 234 D1
Balfour Mews W1K 233 K8
Balfour Place W1K 233 J8
Balfour Street SE17 .... 239 K5
Baltic Street East EC1Y 235 J3
Baltic Street West EC1Y 235 J4
Bank ⊖ EC2R 235 L6
Bank End SE1 .... 239 K1
Bankside SE1 .... 239 J1
Banner Street EC1Y 235 K3
Banyard Road SE16 .... 240 E8
Barbican ⊖ EC1A 235 J4
Barbican Estate EC2Y 235 J5
Barge House Street SE1 .... 239 G1
Bark Place W2 .... 232 B7
Barkston Gardens SW5 .... 236 B6
Barley Corn Way E14 .... 241 L4
Barlow/Congreve
        Estate SE17 .... 239 M5
Barlow Place W1J 233 L7
Barlow Street SE17 .... 239 L5
Barnardo Street E1 .... 241 H3
Barnby Street NW1 .... 234 A1
Barnes Street E14 .... 241 J2
Barnham Street SE1 .... 240 A6
Baron's Place SE1 .... 239 G3
Baron Street N1 .... 235 G1
Barrett Street W1U 233 K6
Barrow Hill Estate NW8 .... 232 F1
Barrow Hill Road NW8 .... 232 F1
Barter Street WC1A 234 D5
Bartholomew Close EC1A 235 J5
Bartholomew Lane EC2R 235 L6
Bartholomew Street SE1 ...... 239 L5
Bartlett Court EC4A 235 C6
Barton Street SW1P 238 C4
Basil Street SW3 .... 237 H4
Basin Approach E14 .... 241 K3
Basinghall Lane EC2V 235 K5
Basinghall Street EC2V 235 K5
Bastwick Street EC1V 235 J3
Bateman's Buildings W1D 234 B6
Bateman Street W1D 234 B6
Bath Street EC1V 235 K2
Bath Terrace SE1 .... 239 J4
Bathurst Mews W2 .... 232 E7
Bathurst Street W2 .... 232 E7
Battle Bridge Lane SE1 .... 239 M1
Batty Street E1 .... 240 D2
Bayley Street WC1B 234 B5
Baylis Road SE1 .... 238 F3
Bayswater ⊖ W2 .... 232 B7
Bayswater Road W2 .... 232 D7
Baythorne Street E3 .... 241 L1
Beaconsfield Road SE17 ...... 239 M7
Beak Street W1F 234 A7
Bear Gardens SE1 .... 239 J1
Bear Lane SE1 .... 239 H1

Beauchamp Place SW3 .... 237 G4
Beaufort Gardens SW3 .... 237 G4
Beaufort Street SW3 .... 236 E8
Beaumont Place W1T 234 A3
Beaumont Street W1G 233 K4
Beccles Street E14 .... 241 M3
Beckett Street SE1 .... 239 L3
Beckway Street SE17 .... 239 M6
Bedale Street SE1 .... 239 L1
Bedford Avenue WC1B 234 C5
Bedfordbury WC2N 234 C7
Bedford Gardens W8 .... 236 A2
Bedford Place WC1N 234 D4
Bedford Row WC1R 234 E4
Bedford Square WC1B 234 B5
Bedford Street WC2E 234 D7
Bedford Way WC1H 234 C3
Bedlow Close NW8 .... 232 F3
Beech Street EC2Y 235 J4
Beeston Place SW1W 237 L4
Belgrave Mews North * SW1X .. 237 J3
Belgrave Mews South * SW1X . 237 K4
Belgrave Place SW1X 237 J4
Belgrave Road SW1V 237 L5
Belgrave Road SW1V 238 A6
Belgrave Square SW1X 237 J3
Belgrave Street E1 .... 241 J2
Belgrove Street WC1H 234 D2
Bell Lane E1 .... 240 B1
Bell Street NW1 .... 232 F4
Bell Yard WC2A 234 F6
Belvedere Road SE1 .... 238 E2
Benjamin Street EC1M 235 H4
Ben Jonson Road E1 .... 241 J1
Bennett Street SW1A 237 M1
Ben Smith Way SE16 .... 240 D7
Benson Quay E1W 240 F4
Bentinck Mews W1U 233 K6
Bentinck Street W1U 233 K6
Bere Street E1W 241 H3
Bergen Square SE16 .... 241 K8
Berkeley Mews W1H 233 H6
Berkeley Square W1J 233 L8
Berkeley Street W1J 233 L8
Bermondsey ⊖ ⊖ SE16 .... 240 E7
Bermondsey Spa SE16 .... 240 C8
Bermondsey Square SE1 ...... 240 A8
Bermondsey Street SE1 .... 240 A6
Bermondsey Wall East SE16 ... 240 E7
Bermondsey Wall
        Estate SE16 .... 240 D7
Bermondsey Wall West SE16 .. 240 C6
Bernard Street WC1N 234 D4
Berners Mews W1T 234 A5
Berners Place W1F 234 A6
Berners Street W1T 234 A5
Bernhardt Crescent NW8 ..... 232 F3
Berryfield Road SE17 .... 239 J6
Berry Street EC1V 235 H3
Berwick Street W1F 234 A6
Bessborough Gardens SW1V .. 238 B6
Bessborough Street SW1V 238 B6
Betterton Street WC2H 234 D6
Bevenden Street N1 .... 235 L2
Bevin Close SE16 .... 241 J5
Bevington Street SE16 .... 240 D7
Bevin Way WC1X 234 F1
Bevis Marks EC3A 240 A2
Bewley Street E1 .... 240 F3
Bickenhall Street W1U 233 H4
Bidborough Street WC1H 234 C2
Biddulph Road W9 .... 232 B2
Bigland Street E1 .... 240 E3
Billiter Square EC3M 240 A3
Billiter Street EC3M 240 A3
Bina Gardens SW5 .... 236 C6
Bingham Place W1U 233 J4
Binney Street W1K 233 K7
Birchfield Street E14 .... 241 M3
Birchin Lane EC3V 235 L7
Birdcage Walk SW1H 238 A3
Birde Lane EC4Y 235 H6
Bird Street W1C 233 K6
Birkenhead Street N1 .... 234 D1
Bishop's Bridge Road W2 ..... 232 C6
Bishopsgate EC2M 240 A2
Bishops Square E1 .... 240 B1
Bishop's Terrace SE11 .... 239 G5
Bittern Street SE1 .... 239 J3
Blackall Street EC2A 235 M3
Blackburne's Mews W1K 233 J7
Blackfriars ⮕ ⊖ EC4V 235 H7
Blackfriars Bridge EC4V 235 H8
Black Friars Lane EC4V 235 H7
Blackfriars Road SE1 .... 239 H3
Blackhorse Court SE1 .... 239 L4
Black Lion Gate W2 .... 232 B8
Black Prince Road SE11 ...... 238 E6
Blackwood Street SE17 .... 239 K6
Blandford Street W1U 233 H5
Blenheim Street W1S 233 L7
Bletchley Street N1 .... 235 K1
Blomfield Road W9 .... 232 C4
Blomfield Street EC2M 235 M5
Blomfield Villas W2 .... 232 C5
Bloomfield Terrace SW1W 237 J6
Bloomsbury Square WC1A 234 D5
Bloomsbury Street WC1B 234 C5
Bloomsbury Way WC1A 234 C5
Blount Street E14 .... 241 K2
Blue Ball Yard SW1A 237 M1
Bohn Road E1 .... 241 J1
Bolsover Street W1W 233 L4
Bolton Gardens SW5 .... 236 B6
Bolton Street W1J 237 L1
Bond Street ⊖ W1C 233 K6
Bondway SW8 .... 238 D8
Bonhill Street EC2A 235 L4

Bonnington Square SW8 ...... 238 E8
Boot Street N1 .... 235 M2
Borough ⊖ SE1 .... 239 K3
Borough High Street SE1 ..... 239 K3
Borough Road SE1 .... 239 H3
Boscobel Place SW1W 237 K5
Boscobel Street NW8 .... 232 E4
Boss Street SE1 .... 240 B6
Boston Place NW1 .... 233 G3
Botolph Lane EC3R 235 M7
Boundary Lane SE17 .... 239 K8
Boundary Row SE1 .... 239 G2
Bourdon Street W1K 233 L7
Bourlet Close W1W 233 M5
Bourne Estate EC1N 234 F4
Bourne Street SW1W 237 J6
Bourne Terrace W2 .... 232 B5
Bouverie Place W2 .... 232 F6
Bouverie Street EC4Y 235 G6
Bowland Yard * SW1X 237 J3
Bow Lane EC4M 235 K7
Bowling Green Lane EC1R 235 G3
Bowling Green Place SE1 ..... 239 L2
Bowling Green Street SE11 ... 238 F8
Bowling Green Walk N1 .... 235 M2
Bowsell Street WC1N 234 D4
Bow Street WC2E 234 D7
Boyd Street E1 .... 240 D3
Boyfield Street SE1 .... 239 H3
Boyle Street W1S 233 M7
Boyson Road SE17 .... 239 K8
Brackland Terrace SW3 .... 237 H6
Brackley Street EC1Y 235 J4
Bradenham Close SE17 .... 239 K8
Brad Street SE1 .... 239 G2
Braganza Street SE17 .... 239 H7
Braham Street E1 .... 240 C3
Bramerton Street SW3 .... 236 F7
Bramham Gardens SW5 ...... 236 B6
Branch Road E14 .... 241 J3
Brandon Estate SE17 .... 239 H8
Brandon Street SE17 .... 239 K6
Brangton Road SE11 .... 238 F7
Bray Crescent SE16 .... 241 H6
Bray Place SW3 .... 237 H6
Bread Street EC4M 235 K7
Bream's Buildings EC4A 234 F6
Brechin Place SW7 .... 236 D6
Breezer's Hill E1W 240 D4
Brendon Street W1H 233 G5
Bressenden Place SW1W 237 L4
Brettell Street SE17 .... 239 L7
Brewers Green SW1H 238 A3
Brewer Street W1F 234 A7
Brewhouse Lane E1W 240 F6
Brewhouse Walk SE16 .... 241 J5
Brick Court WC2R 234 F7
Brick Lane E1 .... 240 C1
Brick Street W1J 237 K2
Bridewell Place EC4V 235 H7
Bridgeman Street NW8 .... 232 F1
Bridge Place SW1V 237 L5
Bridgeport Place E1W 240 D4
Bridge Street EC4V 235 J7
Bridge Street SW1A 238 D3
Bridgewater Street EC2Y 235 J4
Bridgeway Street NW1 .... 234 A1
Bridle Lane W1F 234 A7
Bridstow Place W2 .... 232 A6
Brightlingsea Place E14 .... 241 L4
Brill Place NW1 .... 234 C1
Briset Street EC1M 235 H4
Bristol Gardens W9 .... 232 B4
Britannia Street WC1X 234 E2
Britannia Walk N1 .... 235 L2
Britannia Way N1 .... 235 K1
Britten Street SW3 .... 236 F7
Britton Street EC1M 235 H4
Broadbent Street W1K 233 L7
Broadgate Circle EC2M 235 M5
Broadley Street NW8 .... 232 F4
Broadley Terrace NW1 .... 232 F4
Broadstone Place W1U 233 J5
Broad Walk NW1 .... 233 K1
Broad Walk W2 .... 233 H7
Broadwall SE1 .... 239 G1
Broadway SW1H 238 B4
Broadwick Street W1F 234 A7
Brockham Street SE1 .... 239 K4
Brodlove Lane E1W 241 H3
Bromley Street E1 .... 241 J2
Brompton Road SW3 .... 237 G4
Brompton Road SW7 .... 236 F5
Brompton Square SW3 .... 237 G4
Bronti Close SE17 .... 239 K7
Brook Drive SE11 .... 239 G5
Brooke Street EC1N 234 F5
Brook Gate W2 .... 233 H8
Brook Mews North W2 .... 232 D7
Brook's Mews W1K 233 K7
Brook Street W1K 233 K7
Brook Street W2 .... 232 E7
Brown Heart Gardens W1K ... 233 K7
Browning Mews W1G 233 K5
Browning Street SE17 .... 239 K6
Brownlow Mews WC1N 234 E4
Brownlow Street WC1V 234 E5
Brown Street W1H 233 G6
Brunel Road SE16 .... 241 G6
Brune Street E1 .... 240 B1
Brunswick Close SE16 .... 241 G8
Brunswick Gardens W8 .... 236 A1
Brunswick Place N1 .... 235 L2
Brunswick Quay SE16 .... 241 J8
Brunswick Square WC1N 234 D3
Brunton Place E14 .... 241 K3
Brushfield Street E1 .... 240 B1

Bruton Lane W1J 233 L8
Bruton Place W1J 233 L7
Bruton Street W1J 233 L8
Bryan Road SE16 .... 241 K6
Bryanstone Mews West W1H . 233 G5
Bryanston Mews East W1H ... 233 H5
Bryanston Place W1H 233 G5
Bryanston Square W1H 233 H5
Bryanston Street W1C 233 H7
Buck Hill Walk W2 .... 232 E8
Buckingham Gate SW1E 237 M3
Buckingham Mews SW1E 237 M3
Buckingham Palace
        Road SW1W 237 L5
Buckingham Place SW1E 237 M4
Buckland Street N1 .... 235 L1
Buckle Street E1 .... 240 C2
Buckters Rents SE16 .... 241 J5
Budge's Walk W2 .... 236 D2
Bulleid Way SW1V 237 L5
Bulstrode Street W1U 233 K5
Bunhill Row EC1Y 235 L3
Burdett Estate E14 .... 241 M1
Burdett Road E14 .... 241 L2
Burdett Street SE1 .... 238 F3
Burgess Street E14 .... 241 M1
Burge Street SE1 .... 239 L4
Burlington Arcade W1J 233 M8
Burlington Gardens W1S 233 M8
Burnhouse Place SW1W 237 J6
Burnsall Street SW3 .... 237 G7
Burnside Close SE16 .... 241 J5
Burrell Street SE1 .... 239 H1
Burslem Street E1 .... 240 D3
Burton Grove SE17 .... 239 L7
Burton Street WC1H 234 C3
Burwood Place W2 .... 233 G6
Bury Close SE16 .... 241 H5
Bury Court EC3A 240 A2
Bury Place WC1A 234 D5
Bury Street EC3A 240 A2
Bury Street SW1Y 238 A1
Bury Walk SW3 .... 236 F6
Bushell Street E1W 240 D5
Bush Lane EC4V 235 L7
Butcher Row E14 .... 241 J3
Bute Street SW7 .... 236 E5
Butler Place SW1H 238 B4
Butler's Wharf SE1 .... 240 C6
Buttesland Street N1 .... 235 L2
Byefield Close SE16 .... 241 K6
Bylands Close SE16 .... 241 J5
Byng Place WC1E 234 B4
Byng Street E14 .... 241 M6
Byward Street EC3R 240 A4
Bywater Place SE16 .... 241 K5
Bywater Street SW3 .... 237 G6

C

Cabbell Street NW1 .... 232 F5
Cable Street E1 .... 240 F3
Cadiz Street SE17 .... 239 K7
Cadogan Gardens SW3 .... 237 H5
Cadogan Gate SW1X 237 H5
Cadogan Lane SW1X 237 J4
Cadogan Place SW1X 237 J4
Cadogan Square SW1X 237 H5
Cadogan Street SW3 .... 237 G6
Caledonian Road N1 .... 234 D1
Caledonia Street N1 .... 234 D1
Cale Street SW3 .... 236 F6
Callow Street SW3 .... 236 D7
Calshot Street N1 .... 234 E1
Calthorpe Street WC1X 234 E3
Cambridge Circus WC2H 234 C7
Cambridge Gardens NW6 .... 232 A1
Cambridge Gate NW1 .... 233 L3
Cambridge Road NW6 .... 232 A1
Cambridge Road NW6 .... 232 A2
Cambridge Square W2 .... 232 F6
Cambridge Street SW1V 237 L6
Cambridge Terrace NW1 ...... 233 L2
Cambridge Terrace
        Mews NW1 .... 233 L3
Camdenhurst Street E14 ...... 241 K2
Camera Place SW10 .... 236 D8
Camomile Street EC3A 240 A2
Campden Grove W8 .... 236 A2
Campden Hill Road W8 .... 236 A2
Campden Street W8 .... 236 A1
Camperdown Street E1 .... 240 C3
Canada Estate SE16 .... 241 G7
Canada Gate SW1A 237 M3
Canada Street SE16 .... 241 H7
Canada Water ⊖ ⊖ SE16 ..... 241 H7
Canada Wharf SE16 .... 241 L5
Canal Street SE5 .... 239 L8
Canary Riverside E14 .... 241 L4
Candle Street E1 .... 241 K1
Canning Place W8 .... 236 C4
Cannon Drive E14 .... 241 M4
Cannon Street EC4N 235 K7
Cannon Street ⮕ ⊖ EC4R 235 L7
Cannon Street Road E1 .... 240 E3
Canon Beck Road SE16 .... 241 G6
Canon Row SW1A 238 D3
Canton Street E14 .... 241 M3
Capeners Close * SW1X 237 J3
Capland Street NW8 .... 232 E3
Capper Street WC1E 234 A4
Capstan Way SE16 .... 241 K5
Carbis Road E14 .... 241 L2
Carburton Street W1W 233 L4
Cardigan Street SE11 .... 238 F6
Cardington Street NW1 .... 234 A2

Carey Street - Fanshaw Street 243

Carey Street WC2A 234 F6
Carlisle Avenue EC3N 240 B3
Carlisle Lane SE1 238 F4
Carlisle Place SW1P 237 M5
Carlisle Street W1D 234 B6
Carlos Place W1K 233 K7
Carlton Gardens SW1Y 238 B2
Carlton Hill NW6 232 B1
Carlton House Terrace SW1Y 238 B1
Carlton Street W1J 237 L1
Carlton Vale NW6 232 A1
Carlton Vale NW6 232 B1
Carlyle Square SW3 236 F7
Carmelite Street EC4Y 235 G7
Carnaby Street W1F 233 M7
Caroline Place W2 232 B7
Caroline Street E1 241 H3
Caroline Terrace SW1W 237 J5
Carpenter Street W1K 233 K7
Carrington Street W1J 237 L1
Carr Street E14 241 K1
Carteret Street SW1H 238 B3
Carter Lane EC4V 235 H7
Carter Place SE17 239 K7
Carter Street SE17 239 J7
Carthusian Street EC1M 235 J4
Carting Lane WC2R 234 D8
Cartwright Gardens WC1H 234 C2
Cartwright Street E1 240 C4
Casey Close NW8 232 F3
Casson Street E1 240 C1
Castellain Road W9 232 B3
Castlebrook Close SE11 239 G5
Castle Lane SW1E 237 M4
Catesby Street SE17 239 L6
Cathay Street SE16 240 F7
Cathcart Road SW10 236 C8
Cathedral Walk SW1E 237 M4
Catherine Place SW1E 237 M4
Catherine Street WC2E 234 D7
Cato Street W1H 233 G5
Causton Street SW1P 238 B6
Cavell Street E1 240 F1
Cavendish Avenue NW8 232 E1
Cavendish Place W1G 233 L6
Cavendish Square W1G 233 L6
Cavendish Street N1 235 L1
Caversham Street SW3 237 G8
Caxton Street SW1H 238 B4
Cayton Street EC1V 235 K2
Centaur Street SE1 238 F4
Central Street EC1V 235 J2
Chadwell Street EC1R 235 G1
Chadwick Street SW1P 238 B4
Chagford Street NW1 233 H4
Chalton Street NW1 234 B1
Chambers Street SE16 240 D7
Chamber Street E1 240 C3
Chambers Wharf SE16 240 D6
Chancel Street SE1 239 H1
Chancery Lane WC2A 234 F5
Chancery Lane ⊖ WC1V 234 F5
Chandos Place WC2N 234 C8
Chandos Street W1G 233 L5
Chantry Square W8 236 B4
Chapel Market N1 234 F1
Chapel Street NW1 232 F5
Chapel Street SW1X 237 K3
Chaplin Close SE1 239 G3
Chapman Street E1 240 E3
Chapter Road SE17 239 H7
Chapter Street SW1P 238 B6
Chargrove Close SE16 241 H6
Charing Cross ⇌ ⊖ WC2N 238 D1
Charing Cross Road WC2H 234 B6
Charing Cross Road WC2N 234 C8
Charlbert Street NW8 232 F1
Charles II Street SW1Y 234 B8
Charles Square N1 235 M2
Charles Street W1J 237 K1
Charleston Street SE17 239 K6
Charlotte Road EC2A 235 M3
Charlotte Street W1T 234 A4
Charlwood Place SW1V 238 A6
Charlwood Street SW1V 237 M7
Charlwood Street SW1V 238 A6
Charrington Street NW1 234 B1
Charterhouse Square EC1M 235 H4
Charterhouse Street EC1M 235 G5
Chart Street N1 235 L2
Chaseley Street E14 241 J2
Chatham Street SE17 239 L5
Cheapside EC2V 235 K6
Chelsea Bridge SW1W 237 K8
Chelsea Bridge Road SW1W 237 J7
Chelsea Embankment SW3 237 G8
Chelsea Manor Gardens SW3 236 F7
Chelsea Manor Street SW3 237 G7
Chelsea Park Gardens SW3 236 E8
Chelsea Square SW3 236 E7
Cheltenham Terrace SW3 237 H6
Chenies Mews WC1E 234 B4
Chenies Street WC1E 234 B4
Cheniston Gardens W8 236 A4
Chepstow Place W2 232 A7
Chepstow Road W2 232 A6
Chequer Street EC1Y 235 K3
Cherbury Street N1 235 L1
Cherry Garden Street SE16 240 E7
Chesham Close SW1X 237 J4
Chesham Place SW1X 237 J4
Chesham Street SW1X 237 J4
Chester Close SW1X 237 K3
Chester Close North NW1 233 L2
Chester Close South NW1 233 L2
Chesterfield Gardens W1J 237 K1
Chesterfield Hill W1J 233 K8
Chesterfield Street W1J 237 K1
Chester Gate NW1 233 L2
Chester Mews SW1X 237 K3
Chester Place NW1 233 L1
Chester Road NW1 233 K2
Chester Row SW1W 237 K5
Chester Square SW1W 237 K5
Chester Square Mews SW1W 237 K4
Chester Street SW1X 237 K4
Chester Terrace NW1 233 L2
Chester Way SE11 239 G6
Cheval Place SW7 237 G4
Cheval Street E14 241 M7
Cheyne Gardens SW3 237 G8
Cheyne Row SW3 236 F8
Cheyne Walk SW3 236 F8
Chicheley Street SE1 238 E2
Chichester Road NW6 232 A1
Chichester Road W2 232 C5
Chichester Street SW1V 238 A7
Chicksand Street E1 240 C1
Chigwell Hill E1W 240 E4
Child's Place SW5 236 A5
Child's Street SW5 236 A5
Chiltern Street W1U 233 J4
Chilworth Mews W2 232 D6
Chilworth Street W2 232 D6
China Hall Mews SE16 241 G8
Chippenham Mews W9 232 A4
Chiswell Street EC1Y 235 K4
Chitty Street W1T 234 A4
Christchurch Street SW3 237 G8
Christian Street E1 240 D3
Christina Street EC2A 235 M3
Christopher Close SE16 241 H6
Christopher Street EC2A 235 L4
Chudleigh Street E1 241 H2
Chumleigh Street SE5 239 M8
Churchill Gardens Road SW1V 237 L7
Church Street NW8 232 F4
Church Way NW1 234 B2
Churchyard Row SE1 239 H5
Churton Place SW1V 238 A6
Churton Street SW1V 238 A6
Circus Road NW8 232 E1
Cirencester Square W2 232 A5
City Garden Row N1 235 J1
City Road EC1V 235 J1
City Road EC1Y 235 L3
City Thameslink ⇌ EC4M 235 H6
Clabon Mews SW1X 237 H5
Clack Street SE16 241 G7
Clanricarde Gardens W2 232 A8
Claremont Square N1 234 F1
Clarence Gardens NW1 233 L2
Clarence Mews SE16 241 G6
Clarendon Gardens W9 232 D4
Clarendon Gate W2 232 F7
Clarendon Place W2 232 F7
Clarendon Street SW1V 237 L6
Clareville Grove SW7 236 D6
Clareville Street SW7 236 D6
Clarges Mews W1J 237 L1
Clarges Street W1J 237 L1
Clark Street E1 240 F2
Claverton Street SW1V 238 A7
Clave Street E1W 240 F5
Clay Street W1U 233 H5
Clayton Street SE11 238 F8
Cleaver Square SE11 239 G7
Cleaver Street SE11 239 G7
Clegg Street E1W 240 F5
Clemence Street E14 241 L2
Clements Lane EC4N 235 L7
Clement's Road SE16 240 E8
Clenston Mews W1H 233 H6
Clere Street EC2A 235 L3
Clerkenwell Grove EC1R 235 G4
Clerkenwell Lane EC1R 235 G3
Clerkenwell Road EC1M 235 G4
Cleveland Gardens W2 232 C6
Cleveland Mews W1T 233 M4
Cleveland Place SW1Y 238 A1
Cleveland Row SW1A 238 A2
Cleveland Square W2 232 C6
Cleveland Street W1T 233 M4
Cleveland Terrace W2 232 D6
Clifford Street W1S 233 M7
Clifton Gardens W9 232 C4
Clifton Place SE16 241 G6
Clifton Place W2 232 E7
Clifton Road W9 232 D3
Clifton Street EC2A 235 M3
Clifton Villas W9 232 C4
Clink Street SE1 239 K1
Clipper Close SE16 241 H6
Clipstone Mews W1W 233 M4
Clipstone Street W1W 233 L4
Cliveden Place SW1W 237 J5
Cloak Lane EC4R 235 K7
Cloth Fair EC1A 235 J5
Cloth Street EC1A 235 J5
Cluny Place SE1 240 A8
Cobb Street E1 240 B2
Cobourg Street NW1 234 A2
Coburg Close SW1P 238 A5
Cochrane Mews NW8 232 E1
Cochrane Street NW8 232 E1
Cock Lane EC1A 235 H5
Cockspur Street SW1Y 238 C1
Codling Close * E1W 240 D5
Coin Street SE1 239 G1
Coke Street E1 240 D2
Colbeck Mews SW7 236 C6
Colebrook Row N1 235 H1
Coleherne Road SW10 236 B7
Coleman Street EC2R 235 L6
Cole Street SE1 239 K3
Coley Street WC1X 234 F3
College Hill EC4R 235 K7
College Street EC4R 235 K7
Collett Road SE16 240 D8
Collier Street N1 234 E1
Collingham Gardens SW5 236 B6
Collingham Place SW5 236 B5
Collingham Road SW5 236 B5
Colnbrook Street SE1 239 H4
Colombo Street SE1 239 H1
Colonnade WC1N 234 D4
Coltman Street E14 241 K2
Commercial Road E1 240 D2
Commercial Road E14 241 K3
Commercial Street E1 240 B1
Compton Street EC1V 235 H3
Concert Hall Approach SE1 238 E2
Conder Street E14 241 K2
Conduit Mews W2 232 E6
Conduit Place W2 232 E6
Conduit Street W1S 233 L7
Congreve Street SE17 239 M5
Connaught Close W2 232 F7
Connaught Place W2 233 G7
Connaught Square W2 233 G6
Connaught Street W2 233 G6
Cons Street SE1 239 G2
Constitution Hill SW1A 237 L3
Content Street SE17 239 K5
Conway Street W1T 233 M4
Cookham Crescent SE16 241 H6
Cook's Road SE17 239 H8
Coombs Street N1 235 J1
Cooper's Lane Estate NW1 234 B1
Cooper's Road EC3N 240 B3
Copenhagen Place E14 241 L2
Cope Place W8 236 A4
Copley Court SE17 239 J8
Copley Street E1 241 H2
Copperfield Road E3 241 K1
Copperfield Street SE1 239 J2
Copthall Avenue EC2R 235 L6
Coptic Street WC1A 234 C5
Coral Street SE1 239 G3
Coram Street WC1H 234 C3
Cork Square E1W 240 E5
Cork Street W1S 233 M8
Corlett Street NW1 232 F4
Cornhill EC3V 235 L6
Cornwall Gardens SW7 236 C4
Cornwall Mews South SW7 236 C5
Cornwall Road SE1 238 F1
Cornwall Road SE1 239 G2
Cornwall Street E1 240 E3
Cornwall Terrace Mews NW1 233 H4
Cornwood Drive E1 241 G2
Coronet Street N1 235 M2
Corporation Row EC1R 235 G3
Corsham Street N1 235 L2
Cosser Street SE1 238 F4
Cosway Street NW1 233 G4
Cottage Place SW3 236 F4
Cottesmore Gardens W8 236 B4
Cottons Lane SE1 239 M1
Coulson Street SW3 237 H6
Counter Street SE1 239 M1
County Street SE1 239 K5
Courtenay Square SE11 238 F7
Courtenay Street SE11 238 F6
Courtfield Gardens SW5 236 B5
Courtfield Road SW7 236 C5
Court Street E1 240 E1
Cousin Lane SE1 235 K8
Covent Garden WC2E 234 D7
Covent Garden ⊖ WC2E 234 D7
Coventry Street W1D 234 B8
Cowcross Street EC1M 235 H4
Cowper Street EC2A 235 L3
Crail Row SE17 239 L5
Cramer Street W1U 233 J5
Crampton Street SE17 239 J6
Cranbourn Street WC2H 234 C7
Cranleigh Street NW1 234 A1
Cranley Gardens SW7 236 D6
Cranley Mews SW7 236 D6
Cranley Place SW7 236 E6
Cranston Estate N1 235 L1
Cranwood Street EC1V 235 L2
Craven Hill W2 232 C7
Craven Hill W2 232 D7
Craven Hill Gardens W2 232 C7
Craven Road W2 232 D7
Craven Street WC2N 238 D1
Craven Terrace W2 232 D7
Crawford Passage EC1R 235 G3
Crawford Place W1H 233 G5
Crawford Street W1H 233 G5
Creechurch Lane EC3A 240 A3
Creed Lane EC4V 235 H7
Cresswell Place SW10 236 D6
Cressy Place E1 241 G1
Crestfield Street WC1H 234 D2
Crimscott Street SE1 240 A8
Crispin Street E1 240 B1
Cromer Street WC1H 234 D2
Crompton Street W2 232 D4
Cromwell Place SW7 236 E5
Cromwell Road SW5 236 B5
Cromwell Road SW7 236 E5
Crondall Court N1 235 M1
Crondall Street N1 235 L1
Cropley Street N1 235 K1
Crosby Row SE1 239 L3
Cross Lane EC3R 240 A4
Crosswall EC3N 240 B3
Crowder Street E1 240 E3
Crucifix Lane SE1 240 A6
Cruikshank Street WC1X 234 F1
Crutched Friars EC3N 240 A3
Cuba Street E14 241 M6
Cubitt Street WC1X 234 E2
Culford Gardens SW3 237 H6
Culling Road SE16 240 F7
Cullum Street EC3M 235 M7
Culross Street W1K 233 J8
Culworth Street NW8 232 F1
Cumberland Gardens WC1X 234 F2
Cumberland Gate W2 233 G7
Cumberland Market NW1 233 L2
Cumberland Street SW1V 237 L6
Cumberland Terrace NW1 233 K1
Cumberland Terrace
Mews NW1 233 L1
Cumberland Wharf SE16 241 G6
Cumming Street N1 234 E1
Cundy Street SW1W 237 K6
Cunningham Place NW8 232 E3
Cureton Street SW1P 238 C6
Curlew Street SE1 240 B6
Cursitor Street EC4A 234 F6
Curtain Road EC2A 235 M3
Curtain Road EC2A 235 M4
Curzon Gate W2 237 K2
Curzon Street W1J 237 K1
Cuthbert Street W2 232 E4
Cutler Street EC3A 240 A2
Cynthia Street N1 234 F1
Cypress Place W1T 234 A4
Cyrus Street EC1V 235 H3

D

Dacre Street SW1H 238 B3
Dakin Place E1 241 J1
Dallington Street EC1V 235 H3
Damien Street E1 240 F2
Dane Street WC1R 234 E5
Dansey Place W1D 234 B7
Dante Road SE11 239 H5
Danvers Street SW3 236 F8
D'Arblay Street W1F 234 A6
Dartford Street SE17 239 K8
Dartmouth Street SW1H 238 B3
Darwin Street SE17 239 L5
Date Street SE17 239 K7
Davenant Street E1 240 D1
Daventry Street NW1 232 F4
Davidge Street SE1 239 H3
Davies Mews W1K 233 K7
Davies Street W1K 233 K7
Dawes Street SE17 239 L6
Dawson Place W2 232 A7
Deacon Way SE17 239 J5
Deal Porters Way SE16 241 G8
Deal Street E1 240 D1
Dean Bradley Street SW1P 238 C5
Dean Close SE16 241 H6
Deancross Street E1 240 F3
Deanery Street W1K 237 K1
Dean Farrar Street SW1H 238 B3
Dean Ryle Street SW1P 238 C5
Dean's Buildings SE17 239 L6
Dean Stanley Street SW1P 238 C4
Dean Street W1D 234 B6
Dean Yard SW1P 238 C4
Decima Street SE1 239 M4
Deck Close SE16 241 J6
Defoe Close SE16 241 K7
Delamere Terrace W2 232 B4
De Laune Street SE17 239 H7
Delaware Road W9 232 B3
Dellow Street E1 240 F3
Delverton Road SE17 239 H7
Denbigh Place SW1V 237 M6
Denman Street W1D 234 B7
Denmark Street WC2H 234 C6
Denny Close SE11 239 G6
Denyer Street SW3 237 G5
Derby Gate SW1A 238 D3
Derby Street W1J 237 K1
Dering Street W1S 233 L6
Derry Street W8 236 B3
De Vere Gardens W8 236 C3
Deverell Street SE1 239 L4
Devonport Street E1 241 G3
Devonshire Close W1G 233 K4
Devonshire Mews South W1G 233 K4
Devonshire Mews West W1G 233 K4
Devonshire Place W1G 233 K4
Devonshire Place Mews W1G 233 K4
Devonshire Row EC2M 240 A2
Devonshire Square EC2M 240 A2
Devonshire Street W1G 233 K4
Devonshire Terrace W2 232 D7
De Walden Street W1G 233 K5
Dickens Estate SE16 240 D7
Dickens Square SE1 239 K4
Dilke Street SW3 237 H8
Dingley Place EC1V 235 K2
Dingley Road EC1V 235 J2
Discovery Walk E1W 240 E5
Disney Place SE1 239 K2
Distaff Lane EC4V 235 J7
Distin Street SE11 238 F6
Dockhead SE1 240 C7
Dockley Road SE16 240 D8
Dock Street E1 240 D4
Doddington Grove SE17 239 H7
Doddington Place SE17 239 H8
Dodson Street SE1 239 G3
Dod Street E14 241 M2
Dolben Street SE1 239 H2
Dolland Street SE11 238 E7
Dolphin Square SW1V 238 A7
Dolphin Square SW1V 238 B7
Dombey Street WC1N 234 E4
Dominion Street EC2A 235 L5
Donegal Street N1 234 F1
Dongola Road E1 241 J1
Donne Place SW3 237 G5
Doon Street SE1 238 F1
Dora Street E14 241 L2
Doric Way NW1 234 B2
Dorset Rise EC4Y 235 G7
Dorset Square NW1 233 H4
Dorset Street W1U 233 H5
Doughty Mews WC1N 234 E3
Doughty Street WC1N 234 E3
Douglas Street SW1P 238 B6
Douro Place W8 236 C3
Douthwaite Square * E1W 240 D5
Dovehouse Street SW3 236 E6
Dover Street W1J 237 L1
Dover Street W1S 233 L8
Dowgate Hill EC4R 235 K7
Downfield Close W9 232 B4
Downing Street SW1A 238 C2
Down Street W1J 237 K2
Downtown Road SE16 241 K6
D'Oyley Street SW1X 237 J5
Draco Street SE17 239 J8
Drake Close SE16 241 H6
Draycott Avenue SW3 237 G5
Draycott Place SW3 237 H6
Draycott Terrace SW3 237 H5
Drayson Mews W8 236 A3
Drayton Gardens SW10 236 D6
Druid Street SE1 240 A6
Druid Street SE1 240 B6
Drummond Crescent NW1 234 B2
Drummond Road SE16 240 E8
Drummond Street NW1 234 A3
Drury Lane WC2B 234 D6
Dryden Court SE11 239 G5
Dryden Street WC2B 234 D6
Duchess Mews W1G 233 L5
Duchess Street W1B 233 L5
Duchy Street SE1 239 G1
Duckett Street E1 241 J1
Duck Lane W1F 234 B6
Dufferin Street EC1Y 235 K4
Duke of Wellington
Place SW1W 237 K3
Duke of York Square SW3 237 H6
Duke of York Street SW1Y 234 A8
Duke Shore Wharf E14 241 K4
Duke's Lane W8 236 A2
Duke's Place EC3A 240 B2
Duke's Road WC1H 234 C2
Duke Street W1K 233 K7
Duke Street W1U 233 J6
Duke Street Hill SE1 239 L1
Duke Street St James's SW1Y 238 A1
Dunbar Wharf E14 241 L4
Duncannon Street WC2N 234 C8
Duncan Terrace N1 235 H1
Dundee Street E1W 240 E5
Dundee Wharf E14 241 L4
Dunelm Street E1 241 H2
Dunlop Place SE16 240 C8
Dunraven Street W1K 233 H7
Dunster Court EC3R 240 A3
Duplex Ride SW1X 237 H3
Durand's Wharf SE16 241 L6
Durham Row E1 241 J1
Durham Street SE11 238 E7
Durham Terrace W2 232 A6
Dyott Street WC1A 234 C6
Dysart Street EC2A 235 M4

E

Eagle Close EC1M 235 H4
Eagle Street WC1R 234 E5
Eardley Crescent SW5 236 A7
Earlham Street WC2H 234 C7
Earl's Court ⇌ ⊖ SW5 236 A6
Earl's Court Gardens SW5 236 B6
Earl's Court Road SW5 236 A6
Earl's Court Square SW5 236 A6
Earlstoke Street EC1V 235 H2
Earl Street EC2A 235 M4
Earnshaw Street WC2H 234 C6
East Arbour Street E1 241 H2
Eastbourne Mews W2 232 D6
Eastbourne Terrace W2 232 D6
Eastcastle Street W1W 234 A6
Eastcheap EC3M 235 M7
Eastfield Street E14 241 K1
East India Dock Road E14 241 M3
East Lane SE16 240 D6
Easton Street WC1X 234 F3
East Poultry Avenue EC1A 235 H5
East Road N1 235 L2
East Smithfield E1W 240 C4
East Street SE17 239 L6
Eaton Close SW1W 237 J5
Eaton Gate SW1W 237 J5
Eaton Lane SW1W 237 L4
Eaton Mews North SW1W 237 J5
Eaton Mews South SW1W 237 K5
Eaton Mews West SW1W 237 K5
Eaton Place SW1X 237 J4
Eaton Row SW1W 237 K4
Eaton Square SW1W 237 K5
Eaton Terrace SW1W 237 J5
Ebbisham Drive SW8 238 E8
Ebury Bridge SW1W 237 K6
Ebury Bridge Road SW1W 237 K7
Ebury Mews SW1W 237 K5
Ebury Square SW1W 237 K6
Ebury Street SW1W 237 K5
Eccleston Bridge SW1W 237 L5
Eccleston Mews SW1X 237 K4
Eccleston Place SW1W 237 L5
Eccleston Square SW1V 237 L6
Eccleston Street SW1X 237 K4
Edbrooke Road W9 232 A3
Edge Street W8 236 A1
Edgware Road W2 232 F5
Edgware Road ⊖ NW1 232 F5
Edinburgh Gate SW1X 237 H3
Edith Grove SW10 236 C8
Edwards Mews W1H 233 J6
Egerton Crescent SW3 236 F5
Egerton Gardens SW3 236 F5
Egerton Terrace SW3 237 G4
Eglington Court SE17 239 J7
Elba Place SE17 239 K5
Eldon Place EC2M 235 L5
Eldon Road W8 236 B4
Eleanor Close SE16 241 H6
Elephant & Castle SE1 239 J4
Elephant & Castle ⇌ ⊖ SE1 239 J5
Elephant Lane SE16 240 F6
Elephant Road SE17 239 J5
Elf Row E1W 241 G3
Elgar Street SE16 241 K7
Elgin Avenue W9 232 B2
Elgin Mews North W9 232 C2
Elgin Mews South W9 232 C2
Elia Mews N1 235 H1
Elia Street N1 235 H1
Elim Estate SE1 239 M3
Elim Street SE1 239 M3
Elizabeth Street SW1W 237 K5
Ellen Street E1 240 D3
Elliott's Row SE11 239 H5
Ellis Street SW1X 237 J5
Elmfield Way W9 232 A4
Elm Park Gardens SW10 236 E7
Elm Park Lane SW3 236 E7
Elm Park Road SW3 236 E8
Elm Place SW7 236 E7
Elms Mews W2 232 D7
Elm Street WC1X 234 F4
Elm Tree Road NW8 232 E2
Elnathan Mews W9 232 B4
Elsa Street E1 241 J1
Elsted Street SE17 239 L6
Elvaston Mews SW7 236 D4
Elvaston Place SW7 236 D4
Elverton Street SW1P 238 B5
Ely Place EC1N 235 G5
Elystan Place SW3 237 G6
Elystan Street SW3 236 F6
Embankment ⊖ WC2N 238 D1
Embankment Gardens SW3 237 H8
Embankment Place WC2N 238 D1
Emba Street SE16 240 D7
Emerald Street WC1N 234 E4
Emerson Street SE1 239 J1
Emery Hill Street SW1P 238 A5
Emery Street SE1 239 G3
Emperor's Gate SW7 236 C5
Empire Square SE1 239 L3
Empress Place SW6 236 A7
Endell Street WC2H 234 C6
Endsleigh Gardens WC1H 234 B3
Endsleigh Place WC1H 234 B3
Endsleigh Street WC1H 234 B3
Enford Street W1H 233 G5
English Grounds SE1 239 M1
Enid Street SE16 240 C8
Ennismore Gardens SW7 236 F3
Ennismore Gardens
Mews SW7 236 F3
Ennismore Mews SW7 236 F3
Ennismore Street SW7 236 F4
Enny Street SE11 239 G6
Ensign Street E1 240 D4
Epworth Street EC2A 235 L3
Erasmus Street SW1P 238 C6
Errol Street EC1Y 235 K4
Essendine Road W9 232 A3
Essex Street WC2R 234 F7
Essex Villas W8 236 A3
Europa Place EC1V 235 J2
Euston ⇌ ⊖ ⊖ NW1 234 B2
Euston Road NW1 234 B3
Euston Square NW1 234 B2
Euston Square ⊖ NW1 234 A3
Euston Street NW1 234 A3
Evelyn Gardens SW7 236 D7
Evelyn Way N1 235 L1
Eversholt Street NW1 234 A1
Everton Buildings NW1 233 M2
Ewer Street SE1 239 J2
Ewhurst Close E1 241 G1
Exchange Square EC2A 235 M4
Exeter Street WC2E 234 D7
Exhibition Road SW7 236 E3
Exmouth Market EC1R 235 G3
Exon Street SE17 239 M6
Exton Street SE1 238 F2
Eyre Street Hill EC1R 234 F4

F

Fairclough Street E1 240 D3
Fair Street SE1 240 B6
Falmouth Road SE1 239 K4
Fann Street EC1M 235 J4
Fanshaw Street N1 235 M1

Fareham Street W1D 234 B6
Farmer Street W8 .... 236 A1
Farm Lane SW6 .... 236 A8
Farm Street W1K 233 K8
Farnham Place SE1 .... 239 J1
Farrance Street E14 .... 241 M3
Farringdon ≥ ⊖ EC1M 235 G4
Farringdon Lane EC1R 235 G4
Farringdon Road EC1R 234 F3
Farringdon Street EC1M 235 H5
Farrins Rents SE16 .... 241 J5
Farrow Place SE16 .... 241 K7
Farthing Fields * E1W 240 F5
Fashion Street E1 .... 240 B1
Faunce Street SE17 .... 239 H7
Fawcett Street SW10 .... 236 C8
Featherstone Street EC1Y 235 L3
Fenchurch Avenue EC3M 240 A3
Fenchurch Buildings EC3M 240 A3
Fenchurch Place EC3M 240 A3
Fenchurch Street ≥ EC3M 240 A3
Fendall Street SE1 .... 240 B8
Fenning Street SE1 .... 239 M2
Fentiman Road SW8 .... 238 D8
Fernsbury Street WC1X 234 F2
Fetter Lane EC4A 235 G6
Fieldgate Street E1 .... 240 D2
Fielding Street SE17 .... 239 J7
Field Street WC1X 234 E1
Finborough Road SW10 .... 236 B8
Finch Lane EC3V 235 L6
Finland Street SE16 .... 241 K8
Finsbury Circus EC2M 235 L5
Finsbury Estate EC1R 235 G3
Finsbury Market EC2A 235 M4
Finsbury Square EC2A 235 L4
Finsbury Street EC2Y 235 L4
First Street SW3 .... 237 G5
Fishermans Drive SE16 .... 241 J4
Fisher Street WC1R 234 D5
Fisherton Street NW8 .... 232 E3
Fish Street Hill EC3R 235 L7
Fitzalan Street SE11 .... 238 F5
Fitzhardinge Street W1H 233 J6
Fitzroy Square W1T 233 M4
Fitzroy Street W1T 233 M4
Flamborough Street E14 .... 241 J3
Flank Street E1 .... 240 C4
Flaxman Terrace WC1H 234 C3
Fleet Street EC4A 235 G6
Fleming Road SE17 .... 239 H8
Fletcher Street E1 .... 240 D3
Flint Street SE17 .... 239 L6
Flitcroft Street WC2H 234 C6
Flockton Street SE16 .... 240 D7
Flood Street SW3 .... 237 G7
Flood Walk SW3 .... 237 G7
Floral Street WC2E 234 D7
Forbes Street E1 .... 240 D3
Fordham Street E1 .... 240 D2
Ford Square E1 .... 240 F2
Fore Street EC2Y 235 K5
Formosa Street W9 .... 232 C4
Forset Street W1H 233 G6
Forsyth Gardens SE17 .... 239 H8
Fort Street E1 .... 240 B1
Fortune Street EC1Y 235 K4
Foster Lane EC2V 235 J6
Foulis Terrace SW7 .... 236 E6
Foundry Close SE16 .... 241 J5
Fournier Street E1 .... 240 B1
Fowey Close E1W 240 E5
Frampton Street NW8 .... 232 E4
Francis Street SW1P 238 A5
Frankland Close SE16 .... 240 F8
Franklin's Row SW3 .... 237 H6
Frazier Street SE1 .... 239 G3
Frean Street SE16 .... 240 C8
Frederick Close W2 .... 233 G7
Frederick Street WC1X 234 E2
Frederic Mews * SW1X 237 J3
Freemantle Street SE17 .... 239 M6
Friend Street EC1V 235 H2
Frith Street W1D 234 B6
Fulbourne Street E1 .... 240 E1
Fulford Street SE16 .... 240 F7
Fulham Road SW10 .... 236 D8
Fulham Road SW3 .... 236 F6
Furnival Street EC4A 234 F5
Fynes Street SW1P 238 B5

G

Gabriel's Wharf SE1 .... 239 G1
Gainsford Street SE1 .... 240 B6
Galleon Close SE16 .... 241 G6
Galsworthy Avenue E14 .... 241 K2
Galway Street EC1V 235 K2
Gambia Street SE1 .... 239 H2
Garden Road NW8 .... 232 D1
Garden Row SE1 .... 239 H4
Garden Street E1 .... 241 H1
Garden Walk EC2A 235 M3
Gard Street EC1V 235 J2
Garford Street E14 .... 241 M4
Garnault Place EC1R 235 G3
Garnet Street E1W 240 F4
Garrett Street EC1Y 235 K3
Garrick Street WC2E 234 C7
Garterway SE16 .... 241 H7
Garway Road W2 .... 232 B6
Gataker Street * SE16 .... 240 E8
Gate Mews SW7 .... 236 F3
Gateforth Street NW8 .... 232 F3
Gate Mews NW1 .... 233 L3
Gatesborough Street * EC2A 235 M3
Gate Street WC2A 234 E5
Gatliff Road SW1W 237 K7
Gaunt Street SE1 .... 239 J4
Gayfere Street SW1P 238 C4
Gaywood Street SE1 .... 239 H4
Gaza Street SE17 .... 239 H7
Gedling Place SE1 .... 240 C7
Gee Street EC1V 235 J3
George Mathers
        Road SE11 .... 239 H5
George Row SE16 .... 240 C7
George Street W1H 233 H6
George Yard W1K 233 K7
Geraldine Street SE11 .... 239 H4
Gerald Road SW1W 237 K5
Gerrard Street W1D 234 B7
Gerridge Street SE1 .... 239 G3
Gertrude Street SW10 .... 236 D8
Gibson Road SE11 .... 238 E5
Gilbert Place WC1A 234 C5
Gilbert Street SE11 .... 239 G5

Gilbert Street W1K 233 K7
Gildea Street W1W 233 L5
Gillingham Street SW1V 237 M5
Gill Street E14 .... 241 L3
Gilston Road SW10 .... 236 D7
Giltspur Street EC1A 235 H5
Gladstone Street SE1 .... 239 H4
Glamis Place E1W 241 G4
Glamis Road E1W 241 G4
Glasgow Terrace SW1V 237 M7
Glasshill Street SE1 .... 239 J3
Glasshouse Street W1B 234 A8
Glasshouse Walk SE11 .... 238 D7
Glebe Place SW3 .... 236 F7
Gledhow Road SW5 .... 236 C6
Glentworth Street NW1 .... 233 H4
Globe Pond Road SE16 .... 241 J5
Globe Street SE1 .... 239 K3
Gloucester Court * EC3R 240 A4
Gloucester Gardens W2 .... 232 C6
Gloucester Mews W2 .... 232 D6
Gloucester Mews West W2 .... 232 C6
Gloucester Place NW1 .... 233 H3
Gloucester Place W1U 233 H5
Gloucester Place
        Mews W1U 233 H5
Gloucester Road SW7 .... 236 C4
Gloucester Road SW7 .... 236 D6
Gloucester Road SW7 .... 236 C5
Gloucester Square W2 .... 232 F6
Gloucester Street SW1V 237 M7
Gloucester Terrace W2 .... 232 B5
Gloucester Terrace W2 .... 232 D6
Gloucester Walk W8 .... 236 A2
Gloucester Way EC1R 235 G2
Glyn Street SE11 .... 238 E7
Godfrey Street SW3 .... 237 G6
Goding Street SE11 .... 238 D7
Godliman Street EC4V 235 J7
Godwin Close N1 .... 235 K1
Golden Jubilee
        Bridge WC2N 238 D1
Golden Lane EC1Y 235 J4
Golden Square W1F 234 A7
Golding Street E1 .... 240 E3
Goldney Road W9 .... 232 A4
Goldsmith Street EC2V 235 K6
Gomm Road SE16 .... 241 G8
Goodge Place W1T 234 A5
Goodge Street W1T 234 A5
Goodge Street W1T 234 B5
Goodwin Close SE16 .... 240 C8
Gordon Place W8 .... 236 A2
Gordon Square WC1H 234 B3
Gordon Street WC1H 234 B3
Gore Street SW7 .... 236 D4
Goring Street * EC3A 240 A2
Gosfield Street W1W 233 L5
Goslett Yard WC2H 234 B6
Goswell Road EC1V 235 H1
Gough Street WC1X 234 F3
Coulston Street E1 .... 240 B2
Gower Mews WC1E 234 B5
Gower Place NW1 .... 234 A3
Gower Street WC1E 234 B3
Gower's Walk E1 .... 240 D2
Gracechurch Street EC3V 235 M7
Grafton Place NW1 .... 234 B2
Grafton Street W1S 233 L8
Grafton Way W1T 234 A4
Graham Street N1 .... 235 J1
Graham Terrace SW1W 237 J6
Granby Terrace NW1 .... 233 M1
Grand Avenue EC1A 235 H5
Grange Road SE1 .... 240 B8
Grange Walk SE1 .... 240 B8
Grange Yard SE1 .... 240 B8
Grantully Road W9 .... 232 B2
Granville Place W1H 233 J6
Granville Road NW6 .... 232 A1
Granville Square WC1X 234 F2
Grape Street WC2H 234 C6
Gravel Lane E1 .... 240 B2
Gray's Inn Road WC1X 234 D2
Gray's Inn Square WC1R 234 F5
Gray Street SE1 .... 239 G3
Great Castle Street W1G 233 L6
Great Central Street NW1 ...... 233 G4
Great Chapel Street W1D 234 B6
Great College Street SW1P 238 C4
Great Cumberland
        Place W1H 233 H6
Great Dover Street SE1 .... 239 K3
Great Eastern Street EC2A 235 M3
Great George Street SW1P 238 C3
Great Guildford Street SE1 .... 239 J1
Great James Street WC1N 234 E4
Great Marlborough
        Street W1F 233 M7
Great Maze Pond SE1 .... 239 L2
Great New Portland
        Street WC2H 234 C7
Greatorex Street E1 .... 240 D1
Great Ormond Street WC1N 234 D4
Great Percy Street WC1X 234 F2
Great Peter Street SW1P 238 B4
Great Portland Street W1W 233 L4
Great Portland Street ⊖ W1W ... 233 L4
Great Pulteney Street W1F 234 A7
Great Queen Street WC2B 234 D6
Great Russell Street WC1B 234 C5
Great Scotland Yard SW1A 238 C1
Great Smith Street SW1P 238 C4
Great Suffolk Street SE1 ...... 239 H2
Great Sutton Street EC1V 235 H4
Great Swan Alley EC2R 235 L6
Great Titchfield
        Street W1W 233 M4
Great Tower Street EC3M 235 M7
Great Tower Street EC3R 240 A4
Great Winchester
        Street EC2N 235 L6
Great Windmill
        Street W1D 234 B7
Greek Street W1D 234 B6
Greenacre Square SE16 .... 241 J6
Green Bank E1W 240 E5
Greenberry Street NW8 .... 232 F1
Greencoat Place SW1P 238 A4
Green Coat Row SW1P 238 A4
Greenfield Road E1 .... 240 D1
Greenham Close SE1 .... 238 F3
Green Park ⊖ W1J 237 M1
Green Street W1K 233 J7
Greenwell Street W1W 233 L4
Greet Street SE1 .... 239 G2
Grenade Street E14 .... 241 L4
Grendon Street NW8 .... 232 F4
Grenville Place SW7 .... 236 C5
Gresham Street EC2V 235 J6
Gresse Street W1T 234 B5

Greville Street EC1N 235 G5
Greycoat Place SW1P 238 B4
Greycoat Street SW1P 238 B4
Grigg's Place SE1 .... 240 A8
Grosvenor Bridge SW8 .... 237 L8
Grosvenor Crescent SW1X 237 J3
Grosvenor Crescent
        Mews SW1X 237 J3
Grosvenor Gardens SW1W 237 L4
Grosvenor Gardens Mews
        East SW1W 237 L4
Grosvenor Gardens Mews
        North SW1W 237 L4
Grosvenor Gardens Mews
        South * SW1W 237 L4
Grosvenor Gate W2 .... 233 H8
Grosvenor Hill W1K 233 L7
Grosvenor Place SW1X 237 K3
Grosvenor Road SW1V 237 L8
Grosvenor Square W1K 233 J7
Grosvenor Street W1K 233 K7
Grosvenor Terrace SE5 .... 239 J8
Grove End Road NW8 .... 232 D2
Guildhouse Street SW1V 237 M5
Guilford Street WC1N 234 D4
Guinness Square SE1 .... 239 M5
Gulliver Street SE16 .... 241 K8
Gunpowder Square EC4A 235 G6
Gun Street E1 .... 240 B1
Gunthorpe Street E1 .... 240 C2
Gutter Lane EC2V 235 J6
Guy Street SE1 .... 239 L3

H

Haberdasher Street N1 .... 235 L2
Haddonhall Estate SE1 .... 239 M4
Hainton Close E1 .... 240 F3
Halcrow Street * E1 .... 240 F2
Half Moon Street W1J 237 L1
Halford Road SW6 .... 236 A8
Halkin Place SW1X 237 J4
Halkin Street SW1X 237 K3
Hallam Street W1W 233 L5
Halley Street E14 .... 241 K1
Hallfield Estate W2 .... 232 C6
Hall Place W2 .... 232 E4
Hall Road NW8 .... 232 D2
Hall Street EC1V 235 H2
Halpin Place SE17 .... 239 M6
Halsey Street SW3 .... 237 G5
Hamilton Close NW8 .... 232 D2
Hamilton Close SE16 .... 241 K7
Hamilton Gardens NW8 .... 232 D2
Hamilton Place W1J 237 K2
Hamilton Terrace NW8 .... 232 C1
Hamlet Way SE1 .... 239 L3
Hammett Street EC3N 240 B4
Hampden Close NW1 .... 234 B1
Hampden Gurney
        Street W1H 233 H6
Hampstead Road NW1 .... 233 M2
Hampton Street SE17 .... 239 J6
Hanbury Street E1 .... 240 C1
Hand Court WC1V 234 E5
Handel Street WC1N 234 D3
Hankey Place SE1 .... 239 L3
Hannibal Road E1 .... 241 G1
Hanover Place WC2E 234 D6
Hanover Square W1S 233 L6
Hanover Street W1S 233 L7
Hans Crescent SW3 .... 237 H3
Hanson Street W1W 233 M4
Hans Place SW1X 237 H4
Hans Road SW3 .... 237 G4
Hans Street SW1X 237 H4
Hanway Place W1T 234 B6
Hanway Street W1T 234 B6
Harbet Road W2 .... 232 F5
Harbour Street WC1N 234 E4
Harcourt Street W1H 233 G5
Harcourt Terrace SW10 .... 236 C7
Hardinge Street E1W 241 G3
Hardwick Street EC1R 235 G2
Hardwidge Street SE1 .... 239 M2
Hardy Close SE16 .... 241 H6
Harewood Place W1G 233 L6
Harewood Row NW1 .... 233 G4
Harewoood Avenue NW1 .... 233 G4
Harford Street E1 .... 241 J1
Harleyford Road SE11 .... 238 E8
Harley Gardens SW10 .... 236 D7
Harley Street W1G 233 K4
Harmsworth Street SE17 .... 239 G7
Harold Estate SE1 .... 240 A8
Harper Road SE1 .... 239 K4
Harriet Street SW1X 237 H3
Harriet Walk SW1X 237 H3
Harrington Gardens SW7 .... 236 C6
Harrington Road SW7 .... 236 E5
Harrington Square NW1 .... 233 M1
Harrington Street NW1 .... 233 M1
Harrison Street WC1H 234 D2
Harrowby Street W1H 233 G6
Harrow Place E1 .... 240 B2
Harrow Road W2 .... 232 A4
Hart Street EC3R 240 A3
Hasker Street SW3 .... 237 G5
Hastings Street WC1H 234 C2
Hatfields SE1 .... 239 G1
Hatherley Grove W2 .... 232 B6
Hatteraick Road SE16 .... 241 G6
Hatton Garden EC1N 235 G4
Hatton Street W2 .... 232 E4
Hatton Wall EC1N 235 G4
Havering Street E1 .... 241 H3
Haverstock Street N1 .... 235 J1
Hawke Place * SE16 .... 241 H6
Haydon Street EC3N 240 B3
Hayes Place NW1 .... 233 G4
Hay Hill W1J 233 L8
Hayles Street SE11 .... 239 H5
Haymarket SW1Y 234 B8
Hayne Street EC1A 235 J4
Hay's Lane SE1 .... 239 M1
Hay's Mews W1J 233 L8
Haywood Place EC1R 235 H3
Headfort Place SW1X 237 K3
Head Street E1 .... 241 H2
Hearnshaw Street E14 .... 241 K2
Hearn Street EC2A 235 M4
Heathcote Street WC1N 234 E3
Heddon Street W1S 233 M7
Heddon Street W1S 234 A7
Hedger Street SE11 .... 239 H5
Heiron Street SE17 .... 239 J8
Hellings Street E1 .... 240 D5
Helmet Row EC1V 235 K3
Helsinki Square SE16 .... 241 L8
Henderson Drive NW8 .... 232 E3

Heneage Lane EC3A 240 A3
Heneage Street E1 .... 240 C1
Henrietta Place W1G 233 L6
Henrietta Street WC2E 234 D7
Henriques Street E1 .... 240 D2
Henshaw Street SE17 .... 239 L5
Herbal Hill EC1R 235 G4
Herbert Crescent SW1X 237 H4
Herbrand Street WC1H 234 C3
Hercules Road SE1 .... 238 F4
Hereford Road W2 .... 232 A6
Hereford Square SW7 .... 236 D6
Hermitage Street W2 .... 232 E5
Hermitage Wall E1W 240 D5
Hermit Street EC1V 235 H2
Heron Place SE16 .... 241 K5
Heron Quay E14 .... 241 M5
Herrick Street SW1P 238 C6
Hertford Street W1J 237 K2
Hertsmere Road E14 .... 241 M4
Hesper Mews SW5 .... 236 B6
Hessel Street E1 .... 240 E3
Hewett Street EC2A 235 M3
Heygate Estate SE17 .... 239 J5
Heygate Street SE17 .... 239 J5
Hide Place SW1P 238 B6
High Holborn WC1V 234 E5
High Street
        Kensington ⊖ W8 ...... 236 A3
Hildyard Road SW6 .... 236 A8
Hilliards Court E1W 240 F5
Hillingdon Street SE17 .... 239 J8
Hill Road NW8 .... 232 D1
Hills Place W1F 233 M6
Hill Street W1J 233 K8
Hinde Street W1U 233 K6
Hind Grove E14 .... 241 M3
Hindgrove Area E14 .... 241 M3
Hithe Grove SE16 .... 241 G8
Hobart Place SW1W 237 K4
Hobury Street SW10 .... 236 D8
Hogarth Road SW5 .... 236 B6
Holbein Mews SW1W 237 J6
Holbein Place SW1W 237 J6
Holborn EC1N 235 G5
Holborn ⊖ WC2B 234 E5
Holborn Viaduct EC1A 235 G5
Holford Road WC1X 234 F2
Holland Street SE1 .... 239 H1
Holland Street W8 .... 236 A3
Hollen Street W1F 234 A6
Holles Street W1C 233 L6
Hollywood Road SW10 .... 236 C8
Holyoak Road SE11 .... 239 H5
Holyrood Street SE1 .... 239 M2
Holyrood Street SE1 .... 240 A6
Holywell Row EC2A 235 M4
Homefield Street * N1 .... 235 M1
Homer Row W1H 233 G5
Homer Street W1H 233 G5
Hooper Street E1 .... 240 D3
Hopetown Street E1 .... 240 C1
Hopkins Street W1F 234 A7
Hopton Street SE1 .... 239 H1
Hopwood Road SE17 .... 239 L8
Hornton Place W8 .... 236 A3
Hornton Street W8 .... 236 A2
Horse & Dolphin Yard W1D 234 B7
Horseferry Road E14 .... 241 J3
Horseferry Road SW1P 238 B4
Horse Guards
        Avenue SW1A 238 C2
Horse Guards Parade SW1A 238 C2
Horse Guards Road SW1A 238 C2
Horselydown Lane SE1 .... 240 B6
Horsley Street SE17 .... 239 K8
Hosier Lane EC1A 235 H5
Hothfield Place SE16 .... 241 G8
Hotspur Street SE11 .... 238 F6
Houghton Street WC2A 234 E6
Houndsditch EC3A 240 A2
Howick Place SW1E 238 A4
Howland Street W1T 234 A4
Howland Way SE16 .... 241 K7
Howley Place W2 .... 232 D4
Hoxton Square N1 .... 235 M2
Hoxton Street N1 .... 235 M1
Hugh Mews SW1V 237 L6
Hugh Street SW1V 237 L6
Hugh Street SW1V 237 L6
Hull Close SE16 .... 241 J6
Hull Street EC1V 235 J2
Hungerford Bridge SE1 .... 238 E1
Hunter Close SE1 .... 239 M4
Hunter Street WC1N 234 D3
Huntley Street WC1E 234 A4
Huntsman Street SE17 .... 239 M6
Huntsworth Mews NW1 .... 233 H3
Hurley Crescent SE16 .... 241 H6
Hutching's Street E14 .... 241 M7
Hutton Street EC4Y 235 G7
Hyde Park Corner W1J 237 K2
Hyde Park Corner ⊖ W1J 237 K2
Hyde Park Court ⊖ SW7 .... 236 D3
Hyde Park Crescent W2 .... 232 F6
Hyde Park Garden
        Mews W2 .... 232 F7
Hyde Park Gardens W2 .... 232 F7
Hyde Park Gate SW7 .... 236 C3
Hyde Park Gate SW7 .... 236 C3
Hyde Park Square W2 .... 232 F7
Hyde Park Street W2 .... 232 F7

I

Idol Lane EC3R 235 M7
Ifield Road SW10 .... 236 B8
Iliffe Street SE17 .... 239 J6
Iliffe Yard SE17 .... 239 J6
Imperial College Road SW7 ..... 236 D4
India Street EC3N 240 B3
Ingestre Place W1F 234 A7
Inglebert Street EC1R 234 F2
Ingram Close SE11 .... 238 E5
Inner Circle NW1 .... 233 J2
Inverness Terrace W2 .... 232 B6
Inverness Terrace Gate W2 ..... 232 C8
Invicta Plaza SE1 .... 239 H1
Inville Road SE17 .... 239 L7
Ironmonger Lane EC2V 235 K6
Ironmonger Row EC1V 235 K2
Irving Street WC2N 234 C7
Isambard Place SE16 .... 241 G6
Island Row E14 .... 241 K3
Iverna Court W8 .... 236 A4
Iverna Gardens W8 .... 236 A4
Ives Street SW3 .... 237 G5
Ivor Place NW1 .... 233 G4
Ixworth Place SW3 .... 236 F6

Heneage Lane EC3A — section J:

J

Jacob Street SE1 .... 240 C6
Jamaica Gate SE16 .... 241 F8
Jamaica Road SE16 .... 240 C7
Jamaica Road SE16 .... 240 E7
Jamaica Street E1 .... 241 G2
Jamaica Wharf SE1 .... 240 C6
James Street W1U 233 K6
James Street WC2E 234 D7
Jameson Street W8 .... 236 A1
Janeway Street SE16 .... 240 D7
Jardine Road E1W 241 J4
Java Wharf SE1 .... 240 C6
Jay Mews SW7 .... 236 D3
Jermyn Street SW1Y 234 A8
Jerome Crescent NW8 .... 232 F3
Jewery Street EC3N 240 B3
Joan Street SE1 .... 239 G2
Jockey's Fields WC1R 234 E4
Johanna Street SE1 .... 238 F3
John Adam Street WC2N 234 D8
John Carpenter Street EC4Y 235 G7
John Felton Road SE16 .... 240 D7
John Fisher Street E1 .... 240 C4
John Islip Street SW1P 238 C5
John Prince's Street W1G 233 L6
John Roll Way SE16 .... 240 D7
John Ruskin Street SE5 .... 239 J8
John Slip Street SW1P 238 C6
John's Mews WC1N 234 E4
Johnson's Place SW1V 238 A7
Johnson Street E1 .... 241 G3
John Street WC1N 234 E4
Joiner Street SE1 .... 239 L1
Jonathan Street SE11 .... 238 E6
Jubilee Place SW3 .... 237 G6
Jubilee Street E1 .... 241 G2
Jubilee Walk W8 .... 236 B1
Judd Street WC1H 234 C2
Junction Mews W2 .... 232 F5
Juxon Street SE11 .... 238 E5

K

Katherine Close SE16 .... 241 H5
Kean Street WC2B 234 E6
Keel Close SE16 .... 241 H5
Keeley Street WC2B 234 E6
Keeton's Road SE16 .... 240 E7
Kell Street SE1 .... 239 H3
Kelso Place W8 .... 236 B4
Kemble Street WC2B 234 E6
Kempsford Gardens SW5 .... 236 A7
Kempsford Road SE11 .... 239 G6
Kendall Place W1U 233 J5
Kendal Street W2 .... 233 G6
Kennet Street E1W 240 D5
Kenning Street SE16 .... 241 G6
Kennings Way SE11 .... 239 G7
Kennington ⊖ SE11 .... 239 H7
Kennington Lane SE11 .... 239 G6
Kennington Oval SE11 .... 238 E8
Kennington Park
        Gardens SE11 .... 239 G8
Kennington Park Place SE11 .... 239 G7
Kennington Park Road SE11 ..... 239 G7
Kennington Road SE1 .... 238 F4
Kennington Road SE11 .... 239 G5
Kennnington Oval SE11 .... 238 F8
Kenrick Place W1U 233 J5
Kensington Church
        Street W8 .... 236 A1
Kensington Court W8 .... 236 B3
Kensington Gardens
        Square W2 .... 232 B6
Kensington Gate W8 .... 236 C4
Kensington Gore SW7 .... 236 D3
Kensington High Street W8 ..... 236 A4
Kensington Palace
        Gardens W8 .... 236 B1
Kensington Palace
        Gardens W8 .... 236 B2
Kensington Place W8 .... 236 A1
Kensington Road SW7 .... 237 G3
Kensington Road W8 .... 236 B3
Kensington Square W8 .... 236 B3
Kenton Street WC1H 234 C3
Kenway Road SW5 .... 236 A6
Keystone Close N1 .... 234 D1
Keyworth Street SE1 .... 239 H4
Kilburn Park Road NW6 .... 232 A2
Kildare Terrace W2 .... 232 A6
Killick Street N1 .... 234 E1
Kinburn Street SE16 .... 241 H6
Kinder Street E1 .... 240 E2
King & Queen Wharf SE16 .... 241 H5
King and Queen Street SE17 .... 239 K6
King Charles Street SW1A 238 C2
Kingdom Street W2 .... 232 C5
King Edward Street EC1A 235 J6
King Edward Walk SE1 .... 239 G4
King James Street SE1 .... 239 H3
Kingly Street W1F 233 M7
King's Arms Yard EC2R 235 L6
King's Bench Street SE1 .... 239 H2
Kingscote Street EC4V 235 H7
King's Cross ≥ N1C 234 C2
King's Cross Road WC1X 234 E2
King's Cross
        St Pancras ⊖ N1C 234 D1
King's Head Yard SE1 .... 239 L1
King's Mews WC1N 234 E4
Kingsmill Terrace NW8 .... 232 E1
King Square EC1V 235 J2
King's Road SW3 .... 236 E8
King's Scholars
        Passage SW1P 237 M5
King's Stairs Close SE16 ...... 240 F6
King Street WC2E 234 D7
King Street SW1Y 238 A1
King Street EC2V 235 K6
Kingsway WC2B 234 E6
King William Street EC4N 235 L7
Kinnerton Place
        North * SW1X 237 J3
Kinnerton Place
        South * SW1X 237 J3
Kinnerton Street SW1X 237 J3
Kinnerton Yard * SW1X 237 J3
Kipling Estate SE1 .... 239 L3
Kipling Street SE1 .... 239 L3
Kirby Estate SE16 .... 240 D7
Kirby Grove SE1 .... 239 M3
Kirby Street EC1N 235 G4
Knaresborough Place SW5 .... 236 B5
Knightrider Street EC4V 235 H7

Knightsbridge SW1X 237 H3
Knightsbridge ⊖ SW3 237 H3
Knox Street W1H 233 H4
Kynance Mews SW7 236 C4
Kynance Place SW7 236 C4

L

Lackington Street EC2A 235 L4
Lafone Street SE1 240 B6
Lagado Mews SE16 241 H5
Lambeth Bridge SW1P 238 D5
Lambeth High Street SE1 238 D5
Lambeth Hill EC4V 235 J7
Lambeth North ⊖ SE1 238 F3
Lambeth Palace Road SE1 238 E4
Lambeth Road SE1 238 E4
Lambeth Walk SE11 238 F5
Lamb's Conduit
   Street WC1N 234 E4
Lamb's Passage EC1Y 235 K4
Lamb Street E1 240 B1
Lamb Way SE1 240 A7
Lamlash Street SE11 239 H5
Lanark Place W9 232 D3
Lanark Road W9 232 D3
Lancaster Gate W2 232 D8
Lancaster Gate W2 232 D7
Lancaster Gate ⊖ W2 232 E7
Lancaster Mews W2 232 D7
Lancaster Place WC2E 234 E7
Lancaster Street SE1 239 H3
Lancaster Terrace W2 232 E7
Lancaster Walk W2 232 D8
Lancelot Place SW7 237 G3
Lancing Street NW1 234 B2
Lanesborough
   Place * SW1X 237 J3
Langdale Street E1 240 E3
Langford Place NW8 232 D1
Langham Place W1B 233 L5
Langham Street W1 233 L5
Langham Street W1W 233 M5
Langley Lane SW8 238 D8
Langley Street WC2H 234 C7
Langton Close WC1X 234 E3
Lanhill Road W9 232 A3
Lansdowne Place SE1 239 L4
Lant Street SE1 239 J3
Larcom Street SE17 239 K6
Lauderdale Road W9 232 B3
Laud Street SE11 238 E7
Launcelot Street SE1 238 F3
Launceston Place W8 236 C4
Laurence Pountney
   Lane EC4V 235 L7
Lavender Road SE16 241 K5
Lavender Wharf SE16 241 K4
Lavington Street SE1 239 J1
Lawn Lane SW8 238 D8
Lawrence Street SW3 236 F8
Lawrence Wharf SE16 241 L6
Law Street SE1 239 L4
Laxton Place NW1 233 L3
Laystall Street EC1R 234 F4
Leadenhall Place EC3A 240 A3
Leadenhall Street EC3V 235 M6
Leake Street SE1 238 E2
Leather Lane EC1N 235 G4
Leathermarket Street SE1 239 M3
Leeke Street WC1X 234 E2
Lees Place W1K 233 J7
Leicester Square WC2H 234 B7
Leicester Square ⊖ WC2H 234 C7
Leicester Street WC2H 234 B7
Leigh Street WC1H 234 C3
Leinster Gardens W2 232 C6
Leinster Mews W2 232 C7
Leinster Place W2 232 C7
Leinster Square W2 232 A7
Leinster Terrace W2 232 C7
Leman Street E1 240 C3
Lennox Gardens SW1X 237 G4
Lennox Gardens Mews SW1X 237 G4
Leonard Street EC2A 235 L3
Leopold Estate E3 241 M1
Leopold Street E3 241 L1
Leroy Street SE1 239 M5
Lever Street EC1V 235 J2
Lewisham Street SW1H 238 B3
Lexham Gardens W8 236 A5
Lexham Mews W8 236 A5
Lexington Street W1F 234 A7
Leyden Street E1 240 B2
Leydon Close SE16 241 H5
Library Street SE1 239 H3
Lidlington Place NW1 234 A1
Lilestone Street NW8 232 F4
Lilley Close E1W 240 D5
Lillie Road SW6 236 A4
Lillie Yard W14 236 A7
Limeburner Lane EC4M 235 H6
Lime Close E1W 240 D5
Limehouse Causeway E14 241 L4
Limehouse Link E14 241 L3
Limehouse ⇌ ⊖ E1 241 J3
Limerston Street SW10 236 D8
Lime Street EC3M 235 M7
Lincoln's Inn Fields WC2A 234 E6
Linden Gardens W2 232 A8
Lindley Street E1 240 F1
Lindsay Square SW1V 238 B7
Lindsey Street EC1A 235 H4
Linhope Street NW1 233 G3
Linsey Street SE16 240 D8
Lisle Street WC2H 234 B7
Lisson Green Estate NW8 232 F3
Lisson Grove NW1 232 D4
Lisson Grove NW8 232 F3
Lisson Street NW1 232 F4
Litchfield Street WC2H 234 C7
Little Argyll Street W1F 233 M6
Little Britain EC1A 235 J5
Little Chester Street SW1X 237 K4
Little George Street SW1P 238 C3
Little Marlborough
   Street W1F 234 A7
Little New Street EC4A 235 G6
Little Portland Street W1G 233 M5
Little Russell Street WC1A 234 C5
Little St James's Street SW1A 237 M2
Little Sanctuary SW1A 238 C3
Little Somerset Street E1 240 B3
Little Titchfield Street W1W 233 M5
Liverpool Grove SE17 239 K7
Liverpool Road N1 235 G1
Liverpool Street ⇌ ⊖ EC2M 235 M5
Lizard Street EC1V 235 K3
Llewellyn Street SE16 240 D7

Lloyd Baker Street WC1X 234 F2
Lloyd's Avenue EC3N 240 B3
Lloyd Square WC1X 234 F2
Lloyds Row EC1R 235 G2
Lloyd's Street WC1X 234 F2
Locksley Estate E14 241 M1
Locksley Street E14 241 L1
Lockyer Street SE1 239 L3
Lodge Road NW8 232 F3
Loftie Street SE16 240 D7
Logan Place W8 236 A5
Lolesworth Close E1 240 B1
Lollard Street SE11 238 F5
Lollard Street SE11 238 F6
Loman Street SE1 239 J2
Lomas Street E1 240 D1
Lombard Lane EC4Y 235 G6
Lombard Street EC3V 235 L7
London Bridge EC4R 235 L8
London Bridge ⇌ ⊖ SE1 239 L1
London Bridge Street SE1 239 L1
London Mews W2 232 E6
London Road SE1 239 H4
London Street EC3R 240 A3
London Street W2 232 E6
London Wall EC2M 235 K5
Long Acre WC2E 234 D7
Longford Street NW1 233 L3
Long Lane EC1A 235 J5
Long Lane SE1 239 L3
Longmoore Street SW1V 237 M5
Longridge Road SW5 236 A5
Longville Road SE11 239 H5
Long Walk SE1 240 A8
Long Yard WC1N 234 E4
Lord North Street SW1P 238 C4
Lorenzo Street WC1X 234 E1
Lorrimore Road SE17 239 J8
Lorrimore Square SE17 239 H8
Lothbury EC2R 235 L6
Loughborough Street SE11 238 F7
Lovat Lane EC3R 235 M7
Love Lane EC2V 235 K6
Lovell Place SE16 241 K7
Lowell Street E14 241 L1
Lower Belgrave
   Street SW1W 237 K4
Lower Grosvenor
   Place SW1W 237 L4
Lower James Street W1F 234 A7
Lower John Street W1F 234 A7
Lower Marsh SE1 238 F3
Lower Road SE16 241 G7
Lower Sloane Street SW1W 237 J6
Lower Thames Street EC3R 240 A4
Lowndes Close * SW1X 237 J4
Lowndes Place SW1X 237 J4
Lowndes Square SW1X 237 H3
Lowndes Street SW1X 237 J4
Lucan Place SW3 236 F5
Lucey Road SE16 240 C8
Ludgate Circus EC4M 235 H6
Ludgate Hill EC4M 235 H6
Luke Street EC2A 235 M3
Lukin Street E1 241 G1
Lumley Street W1K 233 K7
Lupus Street SW1V 237 L7
Lupus Street SW1V 238 B7
Luton Street NW8 232 E4
Luxborough Street W1U 233 J4
Lyall Mews SW1X 237 J4
Lyall Street SW1X 237 J4
Lyons Place NW8 232 E3
Lytham Street SE17 239 K7

M

Macclesfield Road EC1V 235 J2
Macclesfield Street * W1D 234 B7
Mace Close E1W 240 E5
Macklin Street WC2B 234 D6
Mackworth Street NW1 233 M2
Macleod Street SE17 239 K7
Maddox Street W1S 233 M7
Magdalen Street SE1 239 M2
Magee Street SE11 238 F8
Maguire Street SE1 240 C6
Maida Avenue W9 232 D4
Maida Vale W9 232 C2
Maida Vale ⊖ W9 232 C2
Maiden Lane SE1 239 K1
Maiden Lane WC2E 234 D7
Major Road SE16 240 D7
Makins Street SW3 237 G6
Malet Street WC1E 234 B4
Mallord Street SW3 236 E8
Mallory Street NW8 232 F3
Mallow Street EC1Y 235 L3
Malta Street EC1V 235 H3
Maltby Street SE1 240 B7
Manchester Square W1U 233 J6
Manchester Street W1U 233 J5
Manciple Street SE1 239 L3
Mandeville Place W1U 233 K6
Manette Street W1D 234 B6
Manilla Street E14 241 M6
Manningford Close EC1V 235 H2
Manor Place SE17 239 J7
Manresa Road SW3 236 F7
Mansell Street E1 240 C3
Mansfield Mews W1G 233 K5
Mansfield Street W1G 233 L5
Mansion House ⊖ EC4V 235 K7
Manson Mews SW7 236 D5
Manson Place SW7 236 D6
Mapleleaf Square SE16 241 J6
Maples Place E1 240 F1
Maple Street W1T 233 M4
Marble Arch ⊖ W1C 233 H7
Marchmont Street WC1H 234 C3
Margaret Street W1W 233 L6
Margaretta Terrace SW3 236 F7
Margery Street WC1X 234 F3
Marigold Street SE16 240 D7
Marine Street SE16 240 C7
Market Mews W1J 237 K1
Market Place W1W 233 M6
Markham Square SW3 237 G6
Markham Street SW3 237 G6
Mark Lane EC3R 240 A4
Marlborough Gate SE1 232 E7
Marlborough Place NW8 232 C1
Marlborough Road SW1A 238 A2
Marlborough Street SW3 236 F6
Marloes Road W8 236 B4
Marlow Way SE16 241 J6
Maroon Street E14 241 M1
Marshall Street W1F 234 A7
Marshalsea Road SE1 239 J2

Marsham Street SW1P 238 C5
Marsh Wall E14 241 M5
Martha's Buildings EC1V 235 K3
Martha Street E1 241 F3
Martin Lane EC4V 235 L7
Maryland Road W9 232 A4
Marylands Road W9 232 A4
Marylebone ⇌ ⊖ NW1 233 G4
Marylebone
   High Street W1U 233 K5
Marylebone Lane W1U 233 K6
Marylebone Road NW1 233 G4
Marylebone Street W1G 233 K5
Marylee Way SE11 238 F6
Masjid Lane E14 241 M2
Mason Street SE17 239 M5
Massinger Street SE17 239 M6
Masters Street E1 241 J1
Matlock Street E14 241 J2
Matthew Parker
   Street SW1H 238 C3
Maunsel Street SW1P 238 B5
Mayfair Place W1J 237 L1
Mayflower Street SE16 240 F7
Mayford Estate N1 235 K1
Mayford Street E1 234 A1
Maynards Quay E1W 240 F4
May's Street WC2E 234 C8
McAuley Close SE1 238 F4
McLeod's Mews SW7 236 C5
Meadcroft Road SE11 238 F8
Meadcroft Road SE11 239 H8
Meadow Road SW8 238 E8
Meadow Row SE1 239 J5
Mead Row SE1 238 F4
Meakin Estate SE1 239 M4
Mecklenburgh
   Square WC1N 234 E3
Medway Street SW1P 238 B5
Meeting House Alley E1W 240 E5
Melcombe Place NW1 233 G4
Melcombe Street W1U 233 H4
Melina Place NW8 232 D2
Melior Place SE1 239 M2
Melior Street SE1 239 M2
Melton Street NW1 234 A2
Memorial Gates SW1W 237 K3
Mepham Street SE1 238 F2
Mercer Street WC2H 234 C7
Merchant Square W2 232 E5
Mermaid Court SE1 239 K2
Merrick Square SE1 239 K4
Merrington Road SW6 236 A8
Merrow Street SE17 239 L7
Methley Street SE11 239 G7
Meymott Street SE1 239 G2
Micawber Street N1 235 K1
Micklethwaite Lane SW6 236 A8
Middlesex Street E1 240 A1
Middlesex Street E1 240 B2
Middle Street EC1A 235 J5
Middle Temple WC2R 234 F7
Middle Temple Lane EC4Y 234 F7
Middleton Drive SE16 241 H6
Midland Road NW1 234 C1
Midship Close SE16 241 H6
Milborne Grove SW10 236 D7
Milcote Street SE1 239 H3
Miles Street SW8 238 D8
Milford Lane WC2R 234 F7
Milk Street EC2V 235 K6
Milk Yard E1W 241 G4
Millbank SW1P 238 D4
Millennium Bridge SE1 235 J8
Millennium Harbour E14 241 M6
Milligan Street E14 241 L4
Millman Mews WC1N 234 F4
Millman Street WC1N 234 E4
Mill Place E14 241 K3
Millstream Road SE1 240 B7
Mill Street SE1 240 C6
Mill Street W1S 233 L7
Milner Street SW3 237 G5
Milton Street EC2Y 235 K4
Milverton Street SE11 239 G7
Mincing Lane EC3M 240 A4
Minera Mews SW1W 237 J5
Minories EC3N 240 B3
Mitchell Street EC1V 235 J3
Mitre Road SE1 239 G2
Mitre Street EC3A 240 A3
Molyneux Street W1H 233 G5
Monck Street SW1P 238 C4
Monkton Street SE11 239 G5
Monkwell Square EC2Y 235 K5
Monmouth Place W2 232 A6
Monmouth Road W2 232 A6
Monmouth Street WC2H 234 C6
Montague Close SE1 239 L1
Montague Place EC3R 234 C5
Montague Street WC1B 234 C5
Montagu Mansions W1U 233 H5
Montagu Mews North W1H 233 H5
Montagu Mews West W1H 233 H6
Montagu Place W1H 233 H5
Montagu Row W1U 233 H5
Montagu Square W1H 233 H5
Montagu Street W1H 233 H6
Montford Place SE11 238 F7
Monthorpe Road SE1 240 C1
Montpelier Square SW7 237 G3
Montpelier Street SW7 237 G3
Montpelier Walk SW7 237 G3
Montrose Place SW1X 237 J3
Monument ⊖ EC4R 235 L7
Monument Street EC3R 235 L7
Monument Street EC3R 235 M7
Monza Street E1W 241 G4
Moodkee Street SE16 241 G7
Moore Street SW3 237 H5
Moorfields EC2Y 235 L5
Moorgate EC2Y 235 L5
Moorgate ⇌ ⊖ EC2Y 235 L5
Moor Lane EC2Y 235 K5
Moor Street W1D 234 C7
Mora Street EC1V 235 K2
Morecambe Street SE17 239 K6
Moreland Street EC1V 235 H2
Moreton Place SW1V 238 A6
Moreton Street SW1V 238 B6
Moreton Terrace SW1V 238 A6
Morgan's Lane SE1 239 M2
Morgan's Lane SE1 240 A5
Morley Street SE1 239 G3
Mornington Crescent NW1 233 M1
Mornington Place NW1 233 L1
Mornington Terrace NW1 233 L1
Morocco Street SE1 239 M3
Morpeth Terrace SW1P 237 M5
Morris Street E1 240 F3
Morshead Road W9 232 A2

Mortimer Market WC1E 234 A4
Mortimer Street W1T 234 A5
Mortimer Street W1W 233 M5
Morton Place SE1 238 F4
Morwell Street WC1B 234 B5
Moscow Place W2 232 B7
Moscow Road W2 232 B7
Mossop Street SW3 237 G5
Motcomb Street SW1X 237 J4
Mount Gate W2 236 E2
Mount Mills EC1V 235 J3
Mount Pleasant WC1X 234 F4
Mount Row W1K 233 K8
Mount Street W1K 233 K8
Mount Street Mews W1K 233 K8
Mount Terrace E1 240 E1
Moxon Street W1U 233 J5
Mulberry Street E1 240 D2
Mulberry Walk SW3 236 E8
Mulready Street NW8 232 F4
Mundy Street N1 235 M2
Munster Square NW1 233 L3
Munton Road SE17 239 K5
Murphy Street SE1 238 F3
Murray Grove N1 235 K1
Musbury Street E1 241 G2
Muscovy Street EC3N 240 A4
Museum Street WC1A 234 C5
Myddelton Passage EC1R 235 G2
Myddelton Square EC1R 235 G1
Myddelton Street EC1R 235 G3
Myrdle Street E1 240 D2

N

Naoroji Street WC1X 234 F2
Napier Grove N1 235 K1
Narrow Street E14 241 K4
Nash Street NW1 233 L2
Nassau Street W1W 233 M5
Nathaniel Close * E1 240 C2
Neal Street WC2H 234 C6
Neckinger SE1 240 C8
Needleman Street SE16 241 H7
Nelson Close NW6 232 A1
Nelson Place N1 235 H1
Nelson Square SE1 239 H2
Nelson Street E1 240 E2
Nelson Terrace N1 235 H1
Neptune Street SE16 241 G7
Nesham Street E1W 240 D4
Netherton Grove SW10 236 D8
Netley Street NW1 233 M2
Nevern Place SW5 236 A6
Nevern Square SW5 236 A6
Neville Street SW7 236 E6
Newark Street E1 240 E2
New Atlas Wharf E14 241 M8
New Bond Street W1S 233 L7
New Bond Street W1S 233 L8
New Bridge Street EC4V 235 H6
New Broad Street EC2M 235 M5
New Burlington
   Street W1S 233 M7
Newburn Street SE11 238 F7
Newbury Street EC1A 235 J5
Newcastle Place W2 232 E5
New Cavendish Street W1G 233 K5
New Change EC4M 235 J6
New Church Road SE5 239 L8
Newcomen Street SE1 239 K2
Newcourt Street NW8 232 F1
Newell Street E14 241 L3
New Fetter Lane EC4A 235 G6
Newgate Street EC1A 235 H6
New Goulston Street E1 240 B2
Newham's Row SE1 240 A7
Newington Butts SE1 239 H6
Newington Causeway SE1 239 J4
New Kent Road SE1 239 K5
Newlands Quay E1W 240 F4
Newman Street W1T 234 A5
New North Place EC2A 235 M3
New North Road N1 235 L1
New North Street WC1N 234 D4
New Oxford Street WC1A 234 C6
Newport Street SE11 238 E5
New Quebec Street W1H 233 H6
New Ride SW7 236 E3
New Road E1 240 E2
New Row WC2N 234 C7
New Spring Gardens
   Walk SE1 238 D7
New Square WC2A 234 F6
New Street EC2M 240 A2
New Street Square EC4A 235 G6
Newton Road W2 232 A6
Newton Street WC2B 234 D5
New Union Street EC2Y 235 K5
Nicholas Lane EC3V 235 L7
Nicholson Street SE1 239 H1
Nightingale Place SW10 236 D8
Nile Street N1 235 K2
Nine Elms Lane SW8 238 C8
Noble Street EC2V 235 J6
Noel Road N1 235 J1
Noel Street W1F 234 A6
Norbiton Road E14 241 L2
Norfolk Crescent W2 233 G6
Norfolk Place W2 232 E6
Norfolk Square W2 232 E6
Norman Street EC1V 235 J3
Norris Street SW1Y 234 B8
Northampton Road EC1R 235 G3
Northampton Square EC1V 235 H2
North Audley Street W1K 233 J7
North Bank NW8 232 F2
Northburgh Street EC1V 235 H3
North Carriage Drive W2 232 F7
Northdown Street N1 234 D1
Northey Street E14 241 K4
North Gower Street NW1 234 A2
Northington Street WC1N 234 E4
North Mews WC1N 234 E4
North Ride W2 233 G7
North Row W1K 233 J7
North Tenter Street E1 240 C3
North Terrace SW3 236 F5
Northumberland
   Alley EC3N 240 B3
Northumberland
   Avenue WC2N 238 C1
Northumberland Place W2 232 A6
Northumberland
   Street WC2N 238 C1
North Wharf Road W2 232 E5
Northwick Terrace NW8 232 D3
Norway Gate SE16 241 K7
Norway Place E14 241 L3

Norwich Street EC4A 234 F5
Nottingham Place W1U 233 J4
Nottingham Street W1U 233 J4
Notting Hill Gate W11 232 A8
Notting Hill Gate ⊖ W11 236 A1
Nugent Terrace NW8 232 D1
Nutford Place W1H 233 G6

O

Oakden Street SE11 239 G5
Oakington Road W9 232 A3
Oak Lane E14 241 L3
Oakley Close EC1V 235 H1
Oakley Gardens SW3 237 G8
Oakley Square NW1 234 A1
Oakley Street SW3 236 F8
Oak Tree Road NW8 232 F2
Oat Lane EC2V 235 J5
Occupation Road SE17 239 J6
Ocean Square E1 241 J1
Odessa Street SE16 241 L7
Ogle Street W1W 233 M5
Old Bailey EC4M 235 H6
Old Barrack Yard SW1X 237 J3
Old Bond Street W1S 233 M8
Old Broad Street EC2N 235 M6
Old Brompton Road SW5 236 B6
Old Brompton Road SW7 236 D6
Old Burlington Street W1S 233 M7
Oldbury Place W1U 233 J4
Old Castle Street E1 240 B2
Old Cavendish Street W1G 233 L6
Old Church Road E1 241 H2
Old Church Street SW3 236 E7
Old Compton Street W1D 234 B7
Old Court Place W8 236 B3
Old Gloucester Street WC1N 234 D4
Old Jamaica Road SE16 240 C7
Old Jewry EC2R 235 K6
Old Kent Road SE1 239 M5
Old Marylebone Road NW1 233 G5
Old Montague Street E1 240 C1
Old North Street WC1X 234 D4
Old Paradise Street SE11 238 E5
Old Park Lane W1J 237 K2
Old Pye Street SW1P 238 B4
Old Queen Street SW1H 238 B3
Old Square WC2A 234 F6
Old Street EC1V 235 J3
Old Street ⇌ ⊖ EC1Y 235 L3
Old Street Junction EC1Y 235 L3
Oliver's Yard EC1Y 235 L3
Olney Road SE17 239 J8
O'Meara Street SE1 239 K2
Omega Place N1 234 D1
Onega Gate SE16 241 J8
Ongar Road SW6 236 A8
Onslow Gardens SW7 236 D6
Onslow Square SW7 236 E5
Onslow Square SW7 236 E6
Ontario Street SE1 239 J4
Ontario Way E14 241 M4
Opal Street SE11 239 H6
Orange Place SE16 241 G8
Orange Square SW1W 237 K6
Orange Street E1W 240 D5
Orange Street WC2H 234 B8
Orb Street SE17 239 L6
Orchardson Street NW8 232 E4
Orchard Street W1H 233 J6
Ordehall Street WC1N 234 E4
Orient Street SE11 239 H5
Orme Court W2 232 B8
Orme Lane W2 232 B8
Orme Square Gate W2 232 B8
Ormond Close WC1N 234 D4
Ormonde Gate SW3 237 H7
Ormond Yard SW1Y 234 A8
Orsett Street SE11 238 E6
Orsett Terrace W2 232 C6
Orton Street E1W 240 D5
Osbert Street SW1V 238 B6
Osborn Street E1 240 C2
Oslo Square SE16 241 K7
Osnaburgh Street NW1 233 L3
Osnaburgh Terrace NW1 233 L3
Ossington Buildings W1U 233 J5
Ossington Street W2 232 A7
Ossulston Street NW1 234 B1
Oswin Street SE11 239 H5
Othello Close SE11 239 H6
Otto Street SE17 239 H8
Outer Circle NW1 233 H3
Outer Circle NW1 233 K1
Oval ⊖ SE11 238 F8
Oval Way SE11 238 E7
Ovington Square SW3 237 G4
Ovington Street SW3 237 G5
Owen Street EC1V 235 G1
Oxendon Street SW1Y 234 B8
Oxford Circus ⊖ W1B 233 M6
Oxford Road NW6 232 A1
Oxford Square W2 232 F6
Oxford Street W1C 233 L6
Oxford Street WC1A 234 A6

P

Pace Place E1 240 E3
Pacific Wharf SE16 241 H5
Paddington ⇌ ⊖ W2 232 D6
Paddington Green W2 232 E5
Paddington Street W1U 233 J5
Pageant Crescent SE16 241 K5
Page Street SW1P 238 B5
Paget Street EC1V 235 H2
Pakenham Street WC1X 234 E3
Palace Avenue W8 236 B2
Palace Court W2 232 A7
Palace Gardens Terrace W8 236 A1
Palace Gate W8 236 C3
Palace Green W8 236 B2
Palace Place SW1E 237 M4
Palace Street SW1E 237 M4
Pall Mall SW1Y 238 A1
Pall Mall East SW1Y 234 B8
Palmer Street SW1H 238 B3
Pancras Lane EC4N 235 K6
Panton Street SW1Y 234 B8
Paradise Street SE16 240 E7
Paradise Walk SW3 237 H8
Pardoner Street SE1 239 L4
Pardon Street EC1V 235 H3
Parfett Street E1 240 D2
Paris Garden SE1 239 G1
Park Crescent W1B 233 K4

Street	Grid
Parker's Row SE1	240 C7
Parker Street WC2B	234 D6
Park Lane W1K	233 H7
Park Lane W2	233 J1
Park Place SW1A	237 M1
Park Road NW1	233 H3
Park Square East NW1	233 L3
Park Square Mews NW1	233 K3
Park Square West NW1	233 K3
Park Street SE1	239 K1
Park Street W1K	233 J7
Park Village East NW1	233 L1
Park Walk SW10	236 D8
Park West Place W2	233 G6
Parliament Street SW1A	238 C2
Parry Street SW8	238 D8
Passmore Street SW1W	237 J6
Paternoster Square	235 J6
Pater Street W8	236 A4
Pattina Walk SE16	241 K5
Paul Street EC2A	235 M3
Paultons Square SW3	236 E8
Paveley Street NW1	233 G3
Pavilion Road SW1X	237 H3
Pavilion Street SW1X	237 H4
Paxton Terrace SW1V	237 L7
Peabody Avenue SW1V	237 L7
Peabody Estate SE1	239 J1
Peacock Street SE17	239 J6
Pearl Street E1W	240 F5
Pearman Street SE1	239 G3
Pear Tree Court EC1R	235 G3
Peartree Lane E1W	241 G4
Pear Tree Street EC1V	235 J3
Peel Street W8	236 A1
Peerless Street EC1V	235 K2
Pelham Crescent SW7	236 F6
Pelham Place SW7	236 F5
Pelham Street SW7	236 F5
Pelier Street SE17	239 K8
Pemberton Row EC4A	235 G6
Pembridge Gardens W2	232 A8
Pembridge Place W2	232 A7
Pembridge Square W2	232 A7
Pembridge Villas W11	232 A7
Pembroke Close SW1X	237 J3
Penang Street E1W	240 F5
Penfold Place NW8	232 F5
Penfold Street NW8	232 E4
Pennant Mews W8	236 B5
Pennington Street E1W	240 D4
Pennyfields E14	241 M4
Penrose Grove SE17	239 J7
Penrose Street SE17	239 J7
Penryn Road SE16	240 E7
Penton Place SE17	239 H6
Penton Rise WC1X	234 E2
Penton Street N1	234 F1
Pentonville Road N1	234 E1
Penywern Road SW5	236 A6
Pepper Street SE1	239 J2
Pepys Street EC3N	240 A4
Percival Street EC1V	235 H3
Percy Circus WC1X	234 F2
Percy Street W1T	234 B5
Perkin's Rent SW1P	238 B4
Petersham Mews SW7	236 D4
Petersham Place SW7	236 C4
Peter Street W1F	234 B7
Peto Place NW1	233 L3
Petticoat Lane E1	240 B2
Petty France SW1H	238 A3
Petty Wales EC3R	240 A4
Petyward SW3	237 G6
Phelp Street SE17	239 L7
Phene Street SW3	237 G8
Phillimore Walk W8	236 A3
Philpot Lane EC3M	235 M7
Philpot Street E1	240 E2
Phipp's Mews SW1W	237 L5
Phipp Street EC2A	235 M3
Phoenix Place WC1X	234 F3
Phoenix Road NW1	234 B1
Phoenix Street WC2H	234 C6
Piccadilly W1J	237 L2
Piccadilly Arcade SW1Y	237 M1
Piccadilly Circus W1B	234 A8
Piccadilly Circus W1J	234 B8
Pickard Street EC1V	235 J2
Picton Place W1U	233 K6
Pier Head E1W	240 E6
Pigott Street E14	241 M3
Pilgrimage Street SE1	239 L3
Pimlico SW1V	238 B6
Pimlico Road SW1W	237 J6
Pinchin Street E1	240 D3
Pindar Street EC2A	235 M4
Pindock Mews W9	232 B3
Pine Street EC1R	235 G3
Pitfield Street N1	235 M1
Pitsea Street E1	241 H3
Pitt's Head Mews W1J	237 K2
Pitt Street W8	236 A2
Pixley Street E14	241 L2
Platina Street * EC2A	235 L3
Plover Way SE16	241 K8
Plumbers Row E1	240 D2
Plumtree Court EC4A	235 G5
Plympton Street NW8	232 F4
Pocock Street SE1	239 H2
Poland Street W1F	234 A6
Pollen Street W1S	233 L7
Pollitt Drive NW8	232 E3
Polperrom SE1	239 G5
Polygon Road NW1	234 B1
Pond Place SW3	236 F6
Ponler Street E1	240 E3
Ponsonby Place SW1P	238 C7
Ponsonby Terrace SW1P	238 C7
Ponton Road SW1V	238 B8
Pont Street SW1X	237 H4
Poolmans Street SE16	241 H6
Pope Street SE1	240 B7
Poplar Place W2	232 B7
Poppin's Court EC4A	235 H6
Porchester Gardens W2	232 B7
Porchester Gate W2	232 C8
Porchester Place W2	233 G6
Porchester Road W2	232 B5
Porchester Square W2	232 B6
Porchester Terrace W2	232 C7
Porchester Terrace North W2	232 C6
Porlock Street SE1	239 L3
Porter Street NW1	233 H4
Porteus Road W2	232 D5
Portland Place W1B	233 L4
Portland Place W1B	233 L5
Portland Square E1W	240 E5
Portland Street SE17	239 L7
Portman Close W1H	233 J6
Portman Mews South W1H	233 J6
Portman Square W1H	233 J6
Portman Street W1H	233 J6
Portpool Lane EC1N	234 F4
Portsea Place W2	233 G6
Portsmouth Street WC2A	234 E6
Portsoken Street E1	240 B3
Portugal Street WC2A	234 E6
Potier Street SE1	239 L4
Potters Fields SE1	240 B6
Pottery Street SE16	240 E7
Poultry EC2V	235 K6
Powis Place WC1N	234 D4
Praed Mews W2	232 E6
Praed Street W2	232 E6
Pratt Walk SE1	238 E5
Premier Place E14	241 M4
Prescot Street E1	240 C3
Preston Close SE1	239 M5
Price's Street SE1	239 H1
Prideaux Place WC1X	234 F2
Primrose Street EC2A	240 A1
Prince Albert Road NW8	232 F1
Prince Consort Road SW7	236 D3
Princelet Street E1	240 C1
Prince of Wales Gate SW7	236 F3
Princes Arcade SW1Y	234 A8
Prince's Gardens SW7	236 E3
Prince's Gate Mews SW7	236 E4
Princes Riverside Road SE16	241 H5
Prince's Square W2	232 A7
Princess Road NW6	232 A1
Princess Street SE1	239 H4
Princes Street W1B	233 L6
Prince's Street EC2R	235 L6
Princeton Street WC1R	234 E5
Prioress Street SE1	239 L4
Priory Green Estate N1	234 E1
Priory Walk SW10	236 D7
Proctor Street WC1V	234 E5
Prospect Place E1W	241 G5
Prospect Street SE16	240 E7
Provident Court W1K	233 J7
Provost Street N1	235 L1
Prusom Street E1W	240 F5
Pudding Lane EC3R	235 M7
Pumphouse Mews E1	240 D3
Purbrook Street SE1	240 A7
Purcell Street N1	235 M1
Purchese Street NW1	234 B1

Q

Street	Grid
Quebec Way SE16	241 J7
Queen Anne's Gate SW1H	238 B3
Queen Ann Street W1G	233 K5
Queen Elizabeth Street SE1	240 B6
Queen Mother Gate W2	237 J2
Queensborough Terrace W2	232 C7
Queensbury Place SW7	236 E5
Queen's Gardens SW7	232 C7
Queen's Gate SW7	236 D3
Queen's Gate Gardens SW7	236 D5
Queen's Gate Mews SW7	236 D4
Queen's Gate Place SW7	236 D4
Queen's Gate Place Mews SW7	236 D4
Queen's Gate Terrace SW7	236 C4
Queen's Head Yard SE1	239 L2
Queen's Mews W2	232 B7
Queen Square WC1N	234 D4
Queen's Row SE17	239 K7
Queen Street EC4N	235 K7
Queen Street W1J	237 L1
Queen Street Place EC4R	235 K7
Queen's Walk SE1	240 A5
Queen's Walk SW1A	237 M2
Queensway W2	232 B6
Queensway W2	232 B8
Queen Victoria Street EC4V	235 J7
Quick Street N1	235 H1

R

Street	Grid
Raby Street E14	241 K2
Radcliffe Road SE1	240 B8
Radcot Street SE11	239 G7
Radnor Mews W2	232 E6
Radnor Place W2	232 F6
Radnor Street EC1V	235 K3
Radnor Walk SW3	237 G7
Railway Approach SE1	239 L1
Railway Avenue SE16	241 G6
Railway Street N1	234 D1
Raine Street E1W	240 F5
Ralston Street SW3	237 H7
Ramillies Place W1F	233 M6
Ramillies Street W1F	233 M6
Rampart Street E1	240 E2
Rampayne Street SW1V	238 B6
Randall Road SE11	238 D6
Randall Row SE11	238 E6
Randolph Avenue W9	232 B1
Randolph Crescent W9	232 C3
Randolph Gardens NW6	232 B1
Randolph Mews W9	232 D4
Randolph Road W9	232 C4
Ranelagh Grove SW1W	237 K6
Ranelagh Road SW1V	238 A7
Rangoon Street * EC3N	240 B3
Ranston Street NW8	232 F4
Raphael Street SW7	237 G3
Ratcliffe Cross Street E1W	241 J3
Ratcliffe Lane E14	241 J3
Rathbone Place W1T	234 B5
Rathbone Street W1T	234 A5
Raven Row E1	240 F1
Ravensdon Street SE11	239 G7
Ravey Street EC2A	235 M3
Rawlings Street SW3	237 G5
Rawstone Street EC1V	235 H2
Ray Street EC1R	235 G4
Reardon Place E1W	240 F5
Reardon Street E1W	240 E5
Rectory Square E1	241 H1
Redan Place W2	232 B6
Redburn Street SW3	237 G7
Redcastle Close E1W	241 G4
Redcliffe Gardens SW10	236 B7
Redcliffe Mews SW10	236 C8
Redcliffe Place SW10	236 C8
Redcliffe Road SW10	236 D7
Redcliffe Square SW10	236 B8
Redcliffe Street SW10	236 B8
Redcross Way SE1	239 K2
Redesdale Street SW3	237 G7
Redfield Lane SW5	236 A5
Redhill Street NW1	233 L1
Red Lion Row SE5	239 K8
Red Lion Square WC1R	234 E5
Red Lion Street WC2B	234 E5
Redman's Road E1	241 G1
Red Place W1K	233 J7
Redriff Road SE16	241 J8
Reedworth Street SE11	239 G6
Reeves Mews W1K	233 J8
Regal Close E1	240 D1
Regan Way N1	235 M1
Regency Street SW1P	238 B5
Regent Place W1B	234 A7
Regent's Park W1B	233 L4
Regent's Park Estate NW1	233 L2
Regent Square WC1H	234 D2
Regent Street W1Y	234 B8
Regent Street W1S	233 M7
Relton Mews SW7	237 G4
Remington Street N1	235 H1
Remnant Street WC2A	234 E6
Renforth Street SE16	241 G7
Renfrew Road SE11	239 H5
Rennie Street SE1	239 H1
Rephidim Street SE1	239 M4
Repton Street E14	241 K2
Reveley Square SE16	241 K7
Rex Place W1K	233 J8
Rhodeswell Road E14	241 L1
Rich Street E14	241 M3
Rickett Street SW6	236 A8
Ridgemount Street WC1E	234 B4
Ridgemount Gardens WC1E	234 B4
Riding House Street W1W	233 M5
Riley Road SE1	240 B7
Risborough Street SE1	239 J2
Risdon Street SE16	241 G7
Rissinghill Street N1	234 F1
River Street EC1R	234 F2
Rivington Street EC2A	235 M3
Robert Adam Street W1U	233 J6
Roberts Close SE16	241 J7
Robert Street NW1	233 L2
Rochester Row SW1P	238 A5
Rochester Street SW1P	238 B5
Rockingham Street SE1	239 J4
Rocliffe Street N1	235 H1
Roding Mews E1W	240 D5
Rodmarton Street W1U	233 H5
Rodney Place SE17	239 K5
Rodney Road SE17	239 K5
Rodney Street N1	234 E1
Roger Street WC1N	234 E4
Roland Gardens SW7	236 D6
Roland Way SE17	239 L7
Romford Street E1	240 E1
Romilly Street W1D	234 B7
Romney Street SW1P	238 C5
Rood Lane EC3M	235 M7
Ropemaker Road SE16	241 K7
Ropemaker Street EC2Y	235 L4
Roper Lane SE1	240 B7
Rope Street SE16	241 K8
Rope Walk Gardens E1	240 E2
Rosary Gardens SW7	236 D6
Roscoe Street EC1Y	235 K3
Rose Alley SE1	235 K8
Rosebery Avenue EC1R	234 F3
Rosemoor Street SW3	237 G6
Rose Street WC2E	234 C7
Rossmore Road NW1	233 G3
Rotary Street SE1	239 H3
Rotherhithe SE16	241 G6
Rotherhithe Street SE16	241 G6
Rotherhithe Street SE16	241 J4
Rotherhithe Tunnel SE16	241 H5
Rothsay Street SE1	239 M4
Rotten Row W2	236 F2
Rouel Road SE16	240 C8
Roupell Street SE1	239 G2
Royal Avenue SW3	237 H6
Royal Hospital Road SW3	237 H7
Royal Mint Street E1	240 C4
Royal Oak W2	232 B5
Royal Oak Yard SE1	240 A7
Royal Road SE17	239 H8
Royal Street SE1	238 E3
Rudolph Road NW6	232 A1
Rugby Street WC1N	234 E4
Rum Close E1W	240 F4
Rupack Street SE16	240 F7
Rupert Street W1D	234 B7
Rushworth Street SE1	239 H2
Russell Court SW1A	238 A2
Russell Square WC1B	234 C4
Russell Square WC1B	234 D4
Russell Street WC2B	234 D7
Russia Dock Road SE16	241 K6
Rutherford Street SW1P	238 B5
Rutland Gardens SW7	237 G3
Rutland Gate SW7	236 F3
Rutland Mews SW7	236 F4
Rutland Street SW7	237 G4
Ryder Street SW1Y	238 A1

S

Street	Grid
Sackville Street W1S	234 A8
Saffron Hill EC1N	235 G4
Saffron Street EC1N	235 G4
Sail Street SE11	238 F5
St Agnes Place SE11	239 G8
St Alban's Grove W8	236 B4
St Alban's Street SW1Y	234 B8
St Alphage Garden EC2Y	235 K5
St Andrews Hill EC4V	235 H7
St Andrew's Place NW1	233 L3
St Andrew Street EC4A	235 G5
St Anne's Court W1F	234 B6
St Ann's Street SW1P	238 C4
St Anselm's Place W1K	233 K7
St Barnabas Street SW1W	237 K6
St Botolph Street EC3N	240 B2
St Bride Street EC4A	235 G6
St Chad's Street WC1H	234 D2
St Clare Street EC3N	240 B3
St Clements Lane WC2A	234 E6
St Cross Street EC1N	235 G4
St Dunstan's Hill EC3R	235 M8
St Dunstan's Lane EC3R	235 M7
St Elmos Road SE16	241 J7
St Ermin's Hill SW1H	238 B3
St George's Circus SE1	239 H3
St George's Drive SW1V	237 M6
St George's Lane * EC3R	235 M7
St George's Road SE1	239 G4
St George's Square SW1V	238 B7
St George Street W1S	233 L7
St Giles High Street WC2H	234 C6
St Helen's Place EC3A	235 M6
St James Market * SW1Y	234 B8
St James's Park SW1H	238 B3
St James's Place SW1A	237 M2
St James's Road SE16	240 D8
St James's Square SW1Y	238 A1
St James Way N1	235 G3
St John's Lane EC1M	235 H4
St John's Place EC1M	235 H4
St John's Square EC1V	235 H4
St John Street EC1V	235 H2
St John's Wood High Street NW8	232 F1
St John's Wood Road NW8	232 E3
St Katharine's Way E1W	240 C5
St Leonard's Terrace SW3	237 H7
St Loo Avenue SW3	237 G8
St Luke's Close EC1V	235 K3
St Luke's Street SW3	236 F6
St Manningtree E1	240 C3
St Mark Street E1	240 C3
St Martin's Lane WC2N	234 C7
St Martin's le Grand EC1A	235 J6
St Mary at Hill EC3R	235 M8
St Mary Axe EC3A	240 A3
St Mary Church Street SE16	240 F7
St Mary's Gardens SE11	239 G5
St Mary's Terrace W2	232 D4
St Mary's Walk SE11	239 G5
St Matthew Street SW1P	238 B4
St Michael's Street W2	232 F6
St Olav's Square SE16	240 F7
St Oswald's Place SE11	238 E7
St Pancras International ⇌ N1C	234 C1
St Paul's EC1A	235 J6
St Paul's Avenue SE16	241 J5
St Paul's Churchyard EC4M	235 J6
St Paul's Way E3	241 L1
St Petersburgh Mews W2	232 B7
St Petersburgh Place W2	232 B7
St Saviours Wharf SE1	240 C6
St Stephen's Gardens W2	232 A5
St Swithin's Lane EC4N	235 L7
St Thomas Street SE1	239 L2
St Vincent Street W1U	233 J5
Salamanca Street SE1	238 D6
Sale Place W2	232 F5
Salisbury Court EC4Y	235 G6
Salisbury Place W1H	233 H4
Salisbury Street NW8	232 F4
Salmon Lane E14	241 J2
Salter Road SE16	241 J5
Salter Street E14	241 M4
Samford Street NW8	232 F4
Sampson Street E1W	240 D5
Sancroft Street SE11	238 F6
Sandford Row SE17	239 L6
Sandland Street WC1R	234 E5
Sandpiper Close SE16	241 L6
Sandwich Street WC1H	234 C2
Sandy's Row E1	240 B1
Sans Walk EC1R	235 G3
Sardinia Street WC2A	234 E6
Savage Gardens EC3N	240 B3
Savile Row W1S	233 M7
Savoy Hill WC2R	234 E8
Savoy Place WC2R	234 D8
Savoy Street WC2E	234 E7
Sawyer Street SE1	239 J2
Scala Street W1T	234 A5
Scandrett Street E1W	240 E5
Scarborough Street E1	240 C3
Scarsdale Villas W8	236 A4
Schooner Close * SE16	241 K6
Scoresby Street SE1	239 H2
Scotch House Junction SW1X	237 H3
Scotland Place SW1A	238 C1
Scott Ellis Grove NW8	232 E2
Scott Lidgett Crescent SE16	240 D7
Scrutton Street EC2A	235 M3
Seaford Street WC1H	234 D2
Seagrave Road SW6	236 A8
Searles Road SE1	239 L5
Sebastian Street EC1V	235 H2
Secker Street SE1	238 F2
Sedan Way SE17	239 M6
Sedding Street SW1X	237 J5
Seddon Street WC1X	234 E3
Sekforde Street EC1R	235 H3
Selsey Street E14	241 M1
Selwood Place SW7	236 E6
Semley Place SW1W	237 K6
Senior Street W2	232 B4
Senrab Street E1	241 H1
Serle Street WC2A	234 F6
Serpentine Bridge W2	236 E1
Serpentine Road W2	236 F2
Seth Street SE16	241 G7
Settles Street E1	240 D2
Seven Dials WC2H	234 C6
Seville Street SW1X	237 H3
Sevington Street W9	232 A3
Seward Street EC1V	235 J3
Seymour Mews W1H	233 J6
Seymour Place W1H	233 G5
Seymour Street W1H	233 H6
Seymour Street W2	233 G7
Seymour Walk SW10	236 C7
Shad Thames SE1	240 B6
Shad Thames SE1	240 C6
Shadwell E1	240 F3
Shadwell Gardens E1	240 F3
Shaftesbury Avenue WC2H	234 C6
Shaftesbury Street N1	235 K1
Shand Street SE1	240 A6
Sharsted Street SE17	239 H7
Shaw Crescent E14	241 K2
Shawfield Street SW3	237 G7
Sheffield Terrace W8	236 A2
Sheldon Square W2	232 D5
Shelmerdine Close E3	241 M1
Shelton Street WC2H	234 D6
Shepherdess Walk N1	235 K1
Shepherd Street W1J	237 K1
Sheraton Street W1F	234 B6
Sherborne Lane EC4N	235 L7
Ship and Mermaid Row SE1	239 M2
Shipwright Road SE16	241 K7
Shirland Road W9	232 A3
Shoe Lane EC4A	235 G5
Shorter Street EC3N	240 B4
Shorts Gardens WC2H	234 C6
Short Street SE1	239 G2
Shoulder of Mutton Alley E14	241 K4
Shouldham Street W1H	233 G5
Shroton Street NW1	232 F4
Siddons Lane W1H	233 H4
Sidmouth Street WC1N	234 D3
Sidney Square E1	240 F2
Sidney Street E1	240 F1
Silex Street SE1	239 H3
Silk Street EC2Y	235 K4
Silver Walk SE16	241 K5
Silvester Street SE1	239 K3
Singer Street EC2A	235 L3
Skinner Place * SW1W	237 J6
Skinners Lane EC4V	235 K7
Skinner Street EC1R	235 G3
Slippers Place SE16	240 F8
Sloane Avenue SW3	237 G6
Sloane Court SW3	237 J6
Sloane Court East SW3	237 J6
Sloane Gardens SW1W	237 J6
Sloane Square SW1W	237 J5
Sloane Square ⊖ SW1W	237 J5
Sloane Street SW1X	237 H3
Sloane Terrace SW1X	237 J5
Smeaton Street E1W	240 E5
Smithfield Street EC1A	235 H5
Smith Square SW1P	238 C4
Smith Street SW3	237 G7
Smith Terrace SW3	237 G7
Smithy Street E1	241 G1
Snowden Street EC2A	235 M4
Snow Hill EC1A	235 H5
Snowsfields SE1	239 L2
Soho Square W1D	234 B6
Soho Street W1D	234 B6
Somerford Way SE16	241 K7
Somers Crescent W2	232 F6
Somerstown Estate NW1	234 A1
Sondes Street SE17	239 L7
South & West Africa Gate SW1A	238 A3
Southall Place SE1	239 L3
Southampton Buildings WC2A	234 F5
Southampton Place WC1A	234 D5
Southampton Row WC1B	234 D4
Southampton Street WC2E	234 D7
South Audley Street W1K	233 K8
South Carriage Drive SW1X	237 H3
South Carriage Drive SW7	236 F3
South Eaton Place SW1W	237 J5
Southern Street N1	234 E1
South Kensington ⊖ SW7	236 E4
South Kensington ⊖ SW7	236 E5
South Lambeth Road SW8	238 D8
South Molton Lane W1K	233 K7
South Molton Street W1K	233 K7
South Parade SW3	236 E7
South Place EC2M	235 L5
South Sea Street SE16	241 L8
South Square WC1R	234 F5
South Street W1K	237 J1
South Tenter Street E1	240 C3
South Terrace SW7	236 F5
Southwark ⊖ SE1	239 H2
Southwark Bridge SE1	235 K8
Southwark Bridge Road SE1	239 J3
Southwark Park Road SE16	240 E8
Southwark Street SE1	239 H1
Southwell Gardens SW7	236 C5
South Wharf Road W2	232 E6
Southwick Mews W2	232 F6
Southwick Place W2	232 F6
Southwick Street W2	232 F6
Sovereign Close E1W	240 F4
Sovereign Crescent SE16	241 J4
Spanish Place W1U	233 J5
Spa Road SE16	240 C8
Spear Mews SW5	236 A6
Spelman Street E1	240 C1
Spence Close SE16	241 K7
Spencer Street EC1V	235 H2
Spenser Street SW1E	238 A4
Spert Street E14	241 J4
Spital Square E1	240 A1
Spring Gardens SW1A	238 C1
Spring Street W2	232 E6
Spurgeon Street SE1	239 L4
Spur Road SE1	238 F3
Stables Way SE11	238 F7
Stable Yard Road SW1A	238 A2
Stacey Street WC2H	234 C6
Stafford Place SW1E	238 A3
Stafford Road NW6	232 A2
Stafford Street W1S	233 M8
Stafford Terrace W8	236 A3
Stainer Street SE1	239 L2
Stainsby Road E14	241 M2
Stalham Street SE16	240 F8
Stamford Street SE1	239 G1
Stanford Place SE1	239 M6
Stanford Road W8	236 B4
Stanhope Close * SE16	241 H6
Stanhope Gardens SW7	236 D5
Stanhope Gate W1K	237 K1
Stanhope Mews W7	236 D5
Stanhope Mews East SW7	236 D5
Stanhope Mews West SW7	236 D5
Stanhope Place W2	233 G7
Stanhope Place Gate W2	233 G7
Stanhope Row W1J	237 K1
Stanhope Street NW1	233 M1
Stanhope Terrace W2	232 E7
Stannary Street SE11	239 G7
Staples Close SE16	241 J5
Staple Street SE1	239 L3
Starcross Street NW1	234 A2
Star Street W2	232 F6
Station Approach Road SE1	238 F3
Stave Yard Road SE16	241 J5
Stead Street SE17	239 K6
Steedman Street SE17	239 J6
Steel's Lane E1	241 G3
Steeres Way SE16	241 K7
Stephenson Way NW1	234 A3
Stephen Street W1T	234 B5
Stepney Green E1	241 H1
Stepney High Street E1	241 J1
Stepney Way E1	240 E1
Sterling Street SW7	237 G4
Stevedore Street E1W	240 E5
Stevens Street SE1	240 B7
Steward Street * E1	240 B1
Stewart's Grove SW3	236 F6
Stew Lane EC4V	235 J7
Stillington Street SW1P	238 A5
Stockholm Way E1W	240 D5

Stocks Place E14 241 M3
Stone Buildings WC2A 234 F5
Stonecutter Street EC4A 235 G6
Stoney Lane E1 240 B2
Stoney Street SE1 239 K1
Stopford Road SE17 239 J7
Store Street WC1E 234 B5
Storey's Gate SW1H 238 C3
Storks Road SE16 240 D8
Stoughton Close SE11 238 E6
Stourcliffe Street W1H 233 G6
Strafford Street E14 241 M6
Strand WC2R 234 D8
Stratford Place W1C 233 K6
Stratford Road W8 236 A5
Strathearn Place W2 232 F7
Stratton Street W1J 237 L1
Strype Street E1 240 B2
Stuart Road NW6 232 A2
Stukeley Street WC2B 234 D6
Sturgeon Road SE17 239 J7
Sturge Street SE1 239 J3
Sturt Street N1 235 K1
Stutfield Street E1 240 D3
Sudley Street N1 235 H1
Sudrey Street SE1 239 J3
Suffolk Lane EC4V 235 L7
Suffolk Street SW1Y 234 B8
Sugar Quay Walk EC3R 240 A4
Sullivan Road SE11 239 G5
Summercourt Road E1 241 G2
Summer Place SW7 236 E6
Summers Street EC1R 234 F4
Sumner Street SE1 239 J1
Sunderland Terrace W2 232 A6
Sun Passage SE16 240 D8
Sun Street EC2M 235 M4
Surrendale Place W9 232 A4
Surrey Quays Road SE16 241 H7
Surrey Row SE1 239 H2
Surrey Square SE17 239 M6
Surrey Street WC2E 234 E7
Surrey Water Road SE16 241 H6
Sussex Gardens W2 232 E6
Sussex Mews East W2 232 E7
Sussex Place NW1 233 H3
Sussex Place W2 232 E6
Sussex Square W2 232 E7
Sussex Street SW1V 237 L7
Sutherland Avenue W9 232 A4
Sutherland Row SW1V 237 L6
Sutherland Square SE17 239 J7
Sutherland Street SW1V 237 L7
Sutton Row W1D 234 B6
Sutton Street E1 241 G3
Suttons Way EC1Y 235 K4
Swain Street NW8 232 F3
Swallow Place W1B 233 L6
Swallow Street W1B 234 A8
Swan Lane EC4R 235 L8
Swan Mead SE1 239 M4
Swan Road SE16 241 G6
Swan Street SE1 239 K3
Swan Walk SW3 237 H8
Swedenborg Gardens E1 240 E4
Sweeney Crescent SE1 240 C7
Swinton Street WC1X 234 E2
Sydney Street SW3 236 F6
Symons Street SW3 237 H6

T
Tabard Gardens Estate SE1 239 L3
Tabard Street SE1 239 L3
Tabernacle Street EC2A 235 L3
Tachbrook Street SW1V 238 A6
Talbot Road W2 232 A6
Talbot Square W2 232 E6
Tallis Street EC4Y 235 G7
Tamworth Street SW6 236 A8
Tanner Street SE1 240 A7
Taplow Street N1 235 K1
Tarling Street E1 240 F3
Tarver Road SE17 239 H7
Tatum Street SE17 239 M6
Taunton Place NW1 233 G3
Tavistock Place WC1H 234 C3
Tavistock Square WC1H 234 C3
Tavistock Street WC2E 234 D7
Taviton Street WC1H 234 B3
Teak Close SE16 241 K6
Tedworth Square SW3 237 G7
Telford Terrace SW1V 237 M7
Temeraire Street SE16 241 G6
Temple ⊖ WC2R 234 F7
Temple Avenue EC4Y 235 G7
Temple Lane EC4Y 235 G7
Temple Place WC2R 234 F7
Templeton Place SW5 236 A5
Tench Street E1W 240 E5
Tenniel Close W2 232 C7
Tennis Street SE1 239 L2
Tenterden Street W1S 233 L6
Tenterground E1 240 B1
Teredo Street SE16 241 J8
Terminus Place SW1V 237 L4
Thame Road SE16 241 H6
Thanet Street WC1H 234 C2
Thavies Inn EC4A 235 G6
Thayer Street W1U 233 K5
The Arches WC2N 234 D8
The Boltons SW10 236 C7
The Broad Walk W2 232 B8
The Broad Walk W8 236 C2
The Cut SE1 239 G2
The Flower Walk W2 236 D3
The Grange SE1 240 B8
The Highway E1W 240 E4
The Little Boltons SW10 236 C7
The Mall SW1A 238 B2
The Mitre E14 241 L3
Theobald's Road WC1X 234 E4
Theobald Street SE1 239 L5
The Vale SW3 236 E8
Thirleby Road SW1P 238 A4
Thomas More Street E1W 240 D4
Thomas Road E14 241 M2
Thoresby Street N1 235 K1
Thorney Street SW1P 238 C5
Thornton Place W1H 233 H4
Thrale Street SE1 239 K1
Thrawl Street E1 240 C1
Threadneedle Street EC2R 235 L6
Three Colt Street E14 241 L3
Three Oak Lane SE1 240 B6
Throgmorton Avenue EC2N 235 L6
Throgmorton Street EC2N 235 L6
Thurland Road SE16 240 D8

Thurloe Place SW7 236 F5
Thurloe Square SW7 236 F5
Thurloe Street SW7 236 E5
Thurlow Street SE17 239 M7
Tichbourne Row W2 232 F6
Tiller Road E14 241 M8
Tillman Street E1 240 E3
Tilney Street W1J 237 K1
Timber Pond Road SE16 241 J6
Tinsley Road E1 241 G1
Tinworth Street SE11 238 D6
Tisdall Place SE17 239 L6
Tite Street SW3 237 H8
Tiverton Street SE1 239 J4
Token House Yard EC2R 235 L6
Tolmer's Square NW1 234 A3
Tomlin's Terrace E14 241 K2
Tonbridge Street WC1H 234 D2
Tooley Street SE1 239 L1
Tooley Street SE1 240 B6
Tor Gardens W8 236 A2
Torquay Street W2 232 A5
Torrens Street EC1V 235 G1
Torrington Place E1W 240 D5
Torrington Place WC1E 234 B4
Torrington Square WC1E 234 B4
Tothill Street SW1H 238 B3
Tottenham Court Road W1T 234 A4
Tottenham Court Road ⊖ W1D 234 B6
Tottenham Street W1T 234 A5
Toulmin Street SE1 239 J3
Tower Bridge ⊖ SE1 240 B5
Tower Bridge Approach EC3N 240 B5
Tower Bridge Road SE1 240 A7
Tower Bridge Wharf E1W 240 C5
Tower Gateway ⊖ EC3N 240 B4
Tower Hill EC3N 240 B4
Tower Hill ⊖ EC3N 240 B4
Tower Place EC3R 240 A4
Tower Street WC2H 234 C7
Townsend Street SE17 239 M5
Toynbee Street E1 240 B1
Trafalgar Gardens E1 241 H1
Trafalgar Square WC2N 238 C1
Trafalgar Street SE17 239 L7
Transept Street NW1 232 F5
Trebeck Street W1J 237 L1
Trebovir Road SW5 236 A6
Tregunter Road SW10 236 C7
Trenton Road SE16 240 E8
Tresham Crescent NW8 232 F3
Trevor Place SW7 237 G3
Trevor Square SW7 237 G3
Trevor Street SW7 237 G3
Trinidad Street E14 241 M4
Trinity Church Square SE1 239 K3
Trinity Square EC3N 240 B4
Trinity Street SE1 239 K3
Trump Street EC2V 235 K6
Tudor Street EC4Y 235 G7
Tufton Street SW1P 238 C4
Tunnel Road SE16 241 G6
Turks Row SW3 237 J6
Turner's Road E3 241 L2
Turner Street E1 240 E2
Turnmill Street EC1N 235 G4
Turpentine Lane SW1V 237 L7
Turquand Street SE17 239 K6
Tyers Gate SE1 239 M3
Tyers Street SE11 238 E7
Tyers Terrace SE11 238 E7
Tyron Street SW3 237 H6
Tysoe Street EC1R 235 G3

U
Udall Street SW1P 238 A5
Ufford Street SE1 239 G3
Ulster Place NW1 233 K4
Umberston Street E1 240 E2
Undershaft EC3A 240 A2
Underwood Road N1 235 K2
Underwood Street N1 235 K1
Union Street SE1 239 H2
University Street WC1E 234 A4
Upbrook Mews W2 232 D6
Upper Belgrave Street SW1X 237 K4
Upper Berkeley Street W1H 233 H6
Upper Brook Street W1K 233 J7
Upper Cheyne Row SW3 236 F8
Upper Grosvenor Street W1K 233 J8
Upper Ground SE1 238 F1
Upper Harley Street NW1 233 K3
Upper James Street W1F 234 A7
Upper John Street W1F 234 A7
Upper Marsh SE1 238 E3
Upper Montagu Street W1H 233 H5
Upper St Martin's WC2H 234 C7
Upper Tachbrook Street SW1V 238 A5
Upper Thames Street EC4V 235 J7
Upper Wimpole Street W1K 233 K4
Upper Woburn Place WC1H 234 C2
Urlwin Street SE5 239 J8
Uxbridge Street W8 236 A1

V
Valentine Place SE1 239 G3
Vandon Passage SW1H 238 A3
Vandon Street SW1H 238 A4
Vandy Street EC2A 235 M4
Varden Street E1 240 E2
Varndell Street NW1 233 M2
Vauban Street SE16 240 C8
Vaughan Street SE16 241 L7
Vaughan Way E1W 240 D5
Vauxhall ⊖ SW8 238 D7
Vauxhall Bridge SW1V 238 D7
Vauxhall Bridgefoot SE1 238 D7
Vauxhall Bridge Road SW1V 237 M5
Vauxhall Cross SE1 238 D7
Vauxhall Grove SW8 238 D8
Vauxhall Street SE11 238 E6
Vauxhall Walk SE11 238 E6
Venables Street W2 232 E4
Vere Street W1G 233 K6
Vernon Place WC1A 234 D5
Vernon Rise WC1X 234 E2
Verulam Street WC1X 234 F4

Vestry Street N1 235 L2
Victoria ⊖ ⊖ SW1V 237 L5
Victoria Embankment SW1A 238 D2
Victoria Embankment WC2R 234 F7
Victoria Gate W2 232 F7
Victoria Road W8 236 C4
Victoria Square SW1W 237 L4
Victoria Street SW1E 237 L4
Victory Place SE17 239 K5
Victory Way SE16 241 K7
Vigo Street W1S 233 M8
Villa Street SE17 239 L7
Villiers Street WC2N 234 D8
Vincent Close SE16 241 K7
Vincent Square SW1P 238 B5
Vincent Street SW1P 238 B5
Vincent Terrace N1 235 H1
Vince Street EC1V 235 L2
Vine Court E1 240 D1
Vine Hill EC1R 234 F4
Vine Lane SE1 240 A6
Vine Street EC3N 240 B3
Violet Hill NW8 232 C1
Virgil Street SE1 238 F4
Virginia Street E1W 240 D4
Viscount Street EC2Y 235 J4

W
Wadding Street SE17 239 K6
Wakefield Street WC1H 234 D3
Wakeling Street E14 241 J3
Wakley Street EC1V 235 H2
Walbrook EC4N 235 L7
Walcorde Avenue SE17 239 K6
Walcot Square SE11 239 G5
Walden Street E1 240 E2
Wallwood Street E14 241 M1
Walnut Tree Walk SE11 238 F5
Walpole Street SW3 237 H6
Walter Terrace E1 241 H2
Walton Place SW3 237 H4
Walton Street SW3 237 G4
Walworth Place SE17 239 K7
Walworth Road SE17 239 J5
Wandsworth Road SW8 238 C8
Wansey Street SE17 239 J6
Wapping ⊖ E1W 240 F5
Wapping High Street E1W 240 E6
Wapping Lane E1W 240 F4
Wapping Wall E1W 241 G5
Warden's Grove SE1 239 J2
Wardour Street W1F 234 B6
Warner Street EC1R 234 F4
Warren Street E1 233 M4
Warren Street ⊖ NW1 233 M3
Warrington Crescent W9 232 C3
Warrington Gardens W9 232 C4
Warwick Avenue W9 232 B3
Warwick Avenue ⊖ W9 232 C4
Warwick Crescent W2 232 C5
Warwick House Street SW1Y 238 B1
Warwick Lane EC4M 235 H6
Warwick Place W9 232 C4
Warwick Road SW5 236 A6
Warwick Row SW1E 237 L4
Warwick Square SW1V 237 M6
Warwick Street W1B 234 A7
Warwick Way SW1V 237 L6
Waterhouse Square EC1N 234 F5
Waterloo ⊖ ⊖ SE1 238 F2
Waterloo Bridge SE1 238 F1
Waterloo Bridge WC2R 234 E8
Waterloo East ⊖ SE1 239 G2
Waterloo Place SW1Y 238 B1
Waterloo Road SE1 238 F1
Waterloo Road SE1 239 G2
Waterman Way E1W 240 E5
Waterside Close SE16 240 D8
Watling Street EC4N 235 K7
Watney Street E1 240 F3
Watts Street E1 240 E5
Waveney Close E1W 240 D5
Waverton Street W1J 233 K8
Weavers Lane SE1 240 A6
Webber Row SE1 239 G3
Webber Street SE1 239 H3
Webb Street SE1 240 A8
Webster Road SE16 240 D8
Weigh House Street W1K 233 K7
Welbeck Street W1G 233 K5
Welbeck Way W1G 233 K6
Welland Mews E1W 240 E5
Wellclose Square E1 240 D4
Wellesley Street E1 241 H2
Wellesley Terrace N1 235 K2
Wellington Square SW3 237 H6
Wellington Place NW8 232 E2
Wellington Road NW8 232 E1
Wellington Street WC2E 234 D7
Wells Mews W1T 234 A5
Wells Street W1T 234 A5
Wells Way SE5 239 M8
Wenlock Road N1 235 K1
Wenlock Street N1 235 K1
Wentworth Street E1 240 B2
Werrington Street NW1 234 A1
Wesley Street W1G 233 K5
West Arbour Street E1 241 G2
Westbourne Crescent W2 232 D7
Westbourne Gardens W2 232 B6
Westbourne Gate W2 232 E7
Westbourne Grove W2 232 A6
Westbourne Grove Terrace W2 232 B6
Westbourne Park Road W2 232 A5
Westbourne Park Villas W2 232 A5
Westbourne Street W2 232 E7
Westbourne Terrace W2 232 D6
Westbourne Terrace Mews W2 232 C6
Westbourne Terrace Road W2 232 C5
West Brompton ⊖ ⊖ ⊖ SW5 236 A7
West Carriage Drive W2 236 F2
Westcott Road SE17 239 H8
West Cromwell Road SW5 236 A5
Western Place SE16 241 G6
Westferry ⊖ E14 241 M4
Westferry Circus E14 241 M5
Westferry Road E14 241 M5
West Gardens E1 240 F4
Westgate Terrace SW10 236 B7
West Halkin Street SW1X 237 J4
West India Avenue E14 241 M5
West India Dock Road E14 241 M3
Westland Place N1 235 K2

West Lane SE16 240 E7
Westminster ⊖ SW1A 238 D3
Westminster Bridge SE1 238 D3
Westminster Bridge Road SE1 238 F3
Westmoreland Place SW1V 237 L7
Westmoreland Road SE17 239 K8
Westmoreland Street W1G 233 K5
Westmoreland Terrace SW1V 237 L7
Weston Rise WC1X 234 E1
Weston Street SE1 239 M2
Weston Street SE1 239 M3
Westport Street E1 241 H2
West Poultry Avenue EC1A 235 H5
West Road SW3 237 H7
West Smithfield EC1A 235 H5
West Square SE11 239 H4
West Street WC2H 234 C7
West Tenter Street E1 240 C3
West Warwick Place SW1V 237 M6
Westway W2 232 B5
Wetherby Gardens SW5 236 C6
Weyhill Road E1 240 D2
Weymouth Mews W1G 233 L5
Weymouth Street W1G 233 K5
Wharfdale Road N1 234 D1
Wharfedale Street SW10 236 B7
Wharf Road N1 235 J1
Wharton Street WC1X 234 F2
Wheatley Street W1G 233 K5
Whetstone Park WC2A 234 E5
Whidborne Street WC1H 234 D2
Whiskin Street EC1R 235 G2
Whitcomb Street WC2H 234 B8
Whitechapel ⊖ ⊖ ⊖ E1 240 E1
Whitechapel Estate E1 240 C4
Whitechapel High Street E1 240 C2
Whitechapel Road E1 240 D1
Whitecross Street EC1Y 235 K3
Whitefriars Street EC4Y 235 G6
Whitehall SW1A 238 C2
Whitehall Court SW1A 238 D2
Whitehall Place SW1A 238 D1
White Hart Street SE11 239 G6
White Hart Yard SE1 239 L2
Whitehaven Street NW8 232 F4
Whitehead's Grove SW3 237 G6
White Horse Lane E1 241 H1
Whitehorse Road E1 241 J1
Whitehorse Road E1 241 J3
White Horse Street W1J 237 L1
White Kennett Street E1 240 B2
White Lion Hill EC4V 235 H7
White Lion Street N1 234 F1
White's Grounds SE1 240 A7
White's Row E1 240 B1
White Tower Way E1 241 J1
Whitfield Place W1T 234 A4
Whitfield Street W1T 234 A4
Whitgift Street SE11 238 E5
Whittaker Street SW1W 237 J6
Whittlesey Street SE1 239 G2
Wicker Street E1 240 E3
Wickham Close E1 241 G1
Wickham Street SE11 238 E7
Wicklow Street WC1X 234 E2
Widegate Street E1 240 A1
Widley Road W9 232 A3
Wigmore Place W1G 233 K5
Wigmore Street W1U 233 K6
Wigton Place SE11 239 G7
Wilbraham Place SW1X 237 J5
Wild Court WC2B 234 E6
Wild's Rents SE1 239 M4
Wild Street WC2B 234 D6
Wilfred Street SW1E 237 M4
Wilkes Street E1 240 B1
William IV Street WC2N 234 C8
William Mews SW1X 237 H3
William Road NW1 233 M3
Willow Place SW1P 238 A5
Willow Street EC2A 235 M3
Wilmington Square WC1X 234 F3
Wilmington Street WC1X 234 F2
Wilson Grove SE16 240 E7
Wilson Street EC2A 235 L4
Wilton Crescent SW1X 237 J3
Wilton Mews SW1X 237 K4
Wilton Place SW1X 237 J3
Wilton Road SW1V 237 L4
Wilton Row SW1X 237 J3
Wilton Street SW1X 237 K4
Wimpole Mews W1G 233 K5
Wimpole Street W1G 233 K5
Winchester Street SW1V 237 L6
Winchester Walk SE1 239 K1
Wincott Street SE11 239 G5
Windmill Road SE11 238 F7
Windmill Street W1T 234 B5
Windrose Close SE16 241 H6
Windsor Terrace N1 235 K1
Wine Close E1W 240 F5
Winnett Street W1D 234 B7
Winsland Mews W2 232 E6
Winsland Street W2 232 E6
Winsley Street W1W 234 A6
Winthrop Street E1 240 E1
Woburn Place WC1H 234 C3
Woburn Square WC1H 234 C4
Wodeham Gardens E1 240 E1
Wolfe Crescent SE16 241 H7
Wolseley Street SE1 240 C6
Woodbridge Street EC1R 235 G3
Woodchester Square W9 232 A4
Woodfall Street SW3 237 H7
Woodland Crescent SE16 241 H7
Woodseer Street E1 240 C1
Woods Mews W1K 233 J7
Woods Place SE1 240 A8
Woodstock Street W1C 233 K6
Wood Street EC2V 235 K6
Woolaston Close SE1 239 J5
Wooler Street SE17 239 L7
Wooton Street SE1 239 G2
Worgan Street SE11 238 E6
Worgan Street SE16 241 H8
Wormwood Street EC2M 235 M5
Worship Street EC2A 235 M4
Wren Street WC1X 234 E3
Wright's Lane W8 236 A3
Wyatt Close SE16 241 L7
Wyclif Street EC1V 235 H2
Wymering Road W9 232 A2
Wynard Street SE11 238 F7
Wyndham Place W1H 233 H5
Wyndham Street W1H 233 G4
Wynnstay Gardens W8 236 A4
Wynyat Street EC1V 235 H2
Wythburn Place W1H 233 H6

Y
Yalding Road SE16 240 C8
Yardley Street WC1X 234 F2
Yeomans Row SW3 237 G4
York Boulevard WC2N 234 D8
York Bridge NW1 233 J3
York Gate NW1 233 J4
York Road SE1 238 E2
York Square E14 241 J2
York Street W1H 233 G5
York Terrace East NW1 233 J4
York Terrace West NW1 233 J4
York Way N1 234 D1

Z
Zoar Street SE1 239 J1

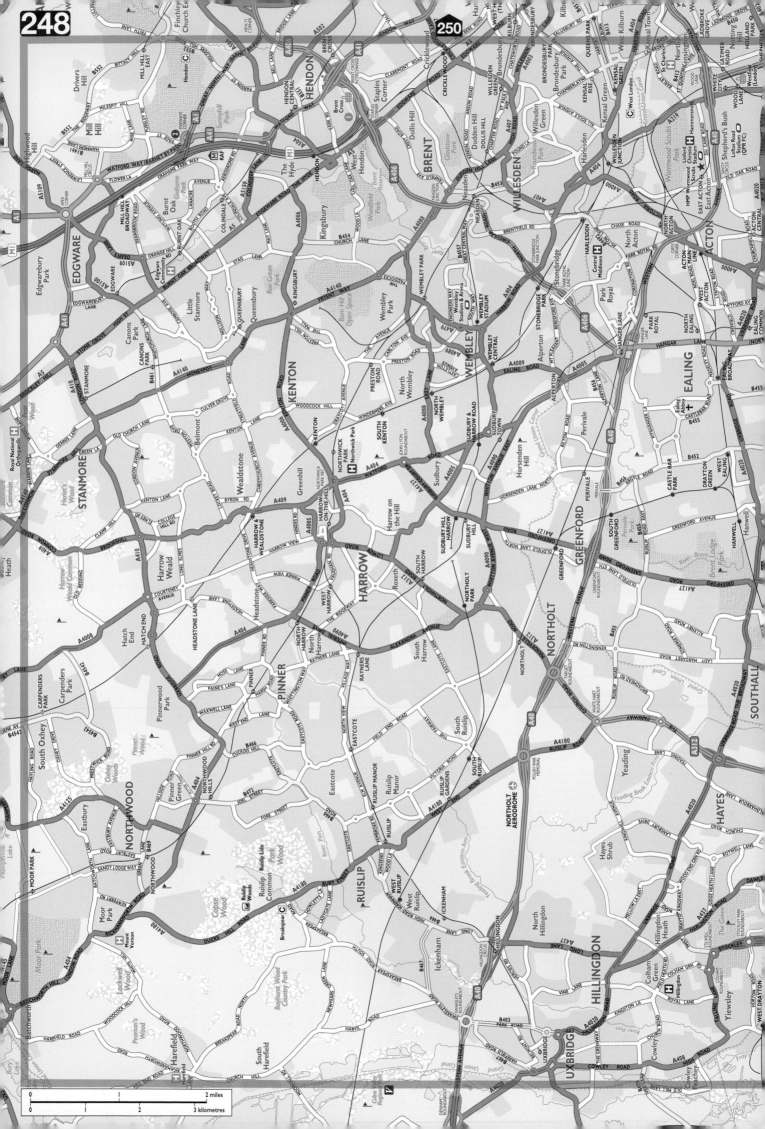

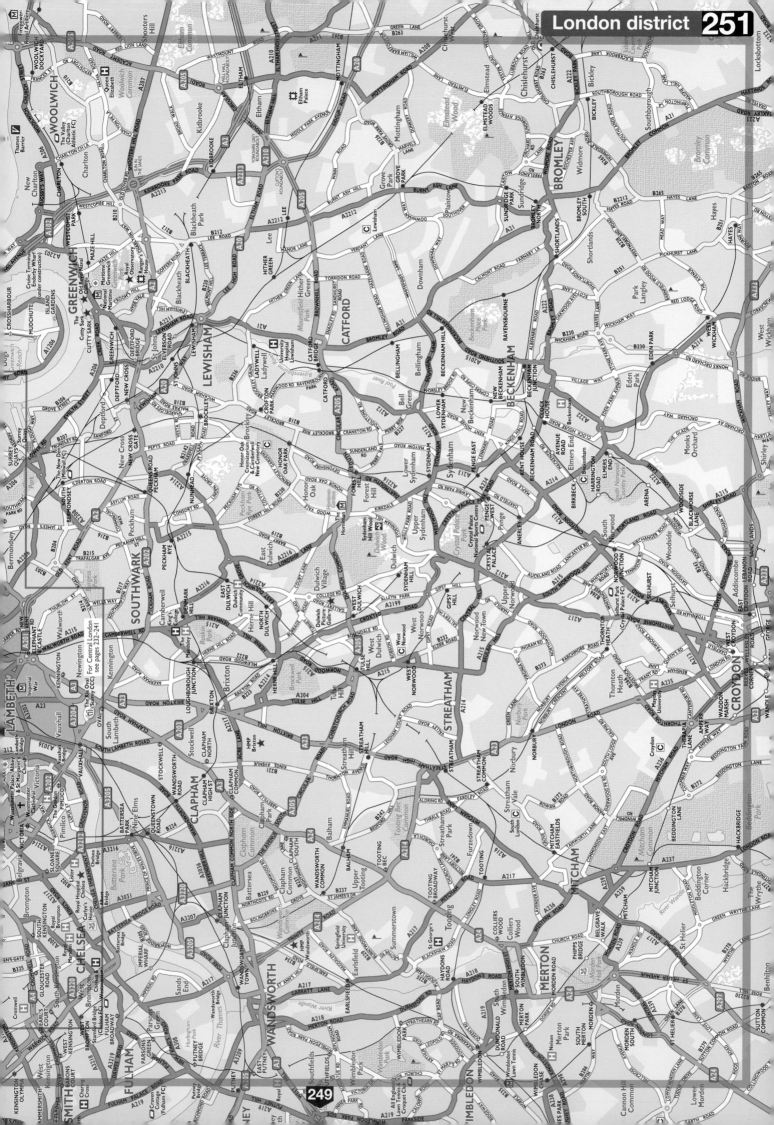

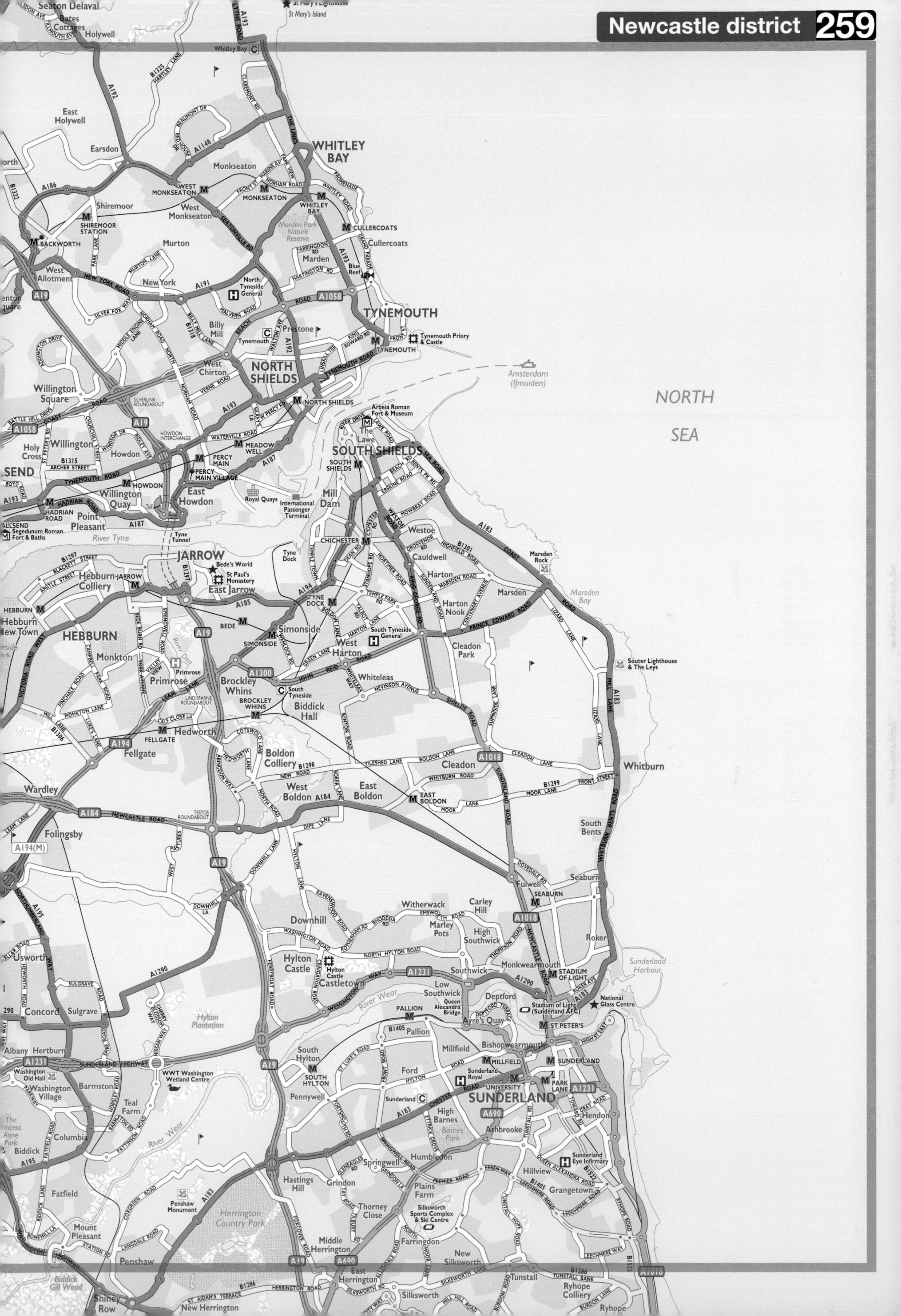

NORTH SEA

WHITLEY BAY

TYNEMOUTH

NORTH SHIELDS

SOUTH SHIELDS

JARROW

HEBBURN

SUNDERLAND

Seaton Delaval
Bates Cottages
Holywell
St Mary's Lighthouse
St Mary's Island
Whitley Bay
East Holywell
Earsdon
Monkseaton
West Monkseaton
Shiremoor
Shiremoor Station
Murton
Backworth
West Allotment
New York
Benton Square
Willington Square
Holy Cross
Willington
Howdon
Battle Hill Drive
Silverlink Roundabout
Howdon Interchange
SEND
Percy Main
Meadow Well
East Howdon
Willington Quay
Point Pleasant
Segedunum Roman Fort & Baths
Tyne Tunnel
River Tyne
Marden Park Nature Reserve
Marden
Cullercoats
Blue Reef
Prestone
Tynemouth
West Chirton
Tynemouth Priory & Castle
Amsterdam (IJmuiden)
Billy Mill
Royal Quays
International Passenger Terminal
Arbeia Roman Fort & Museum
The Lawe
Mill Dam
Westoe
Chichester
Cauldwell
Harton
Tyne Dock
Bede's World
St Paul's Monastery
East Jarrow
Hebburn-Jarrow Colliery
Hebburn New Town
Monkton
Primrose
Brockley Whins
Simonside
Bede
West Harton
South Tyneside General
Harton Nook
Marsden
Marsden Rock
Marsden Bay
Souter Lighthouse & The Leys
Whiteleas
Cleadon Park
Hedworth
Fellgate
Fellgate
Wardley
Boldon Colliery
Biddick Hall
South Tyneside
Cleadon
Whitburn
Folingsby
West Boldon
East Boldon
East Boldon
South Bents
Downhill
Witherwack
Carley Hill
Marley Pots
High Southwick
Seaburn
Seaburn
Roker
Usworth
Hylton Castle
Castletown
Southwick
Monkwearmouth
Stadium of Light
Sunderland Harbour
Concord
Sulgrave
Hylton Plantation
Low Southwick
Queen Alexandra Bridge
Deptford
Stadium of Light (Sunderland AFC)
National Glass Centre
St Peter's
Albany
Hertburn
Washington Old Hall
Sunderland Highway
WWT Washington Wetland Centre
South Hylton
South Hylton
Pallion
Pallion
Ayre's Quay
Millfield
Bishopwearmouth
Millfield
Sunderland
Park Lane
Ford
Sunderland Royal
University
Hendon
Pennywell
Sunderland
High Barnes
Barnes Park
Ashbrooke
Sunderland Eye Infirmary
Barmston
Washington Village
Teal Farm
Columbia
Biddick
Fatfield
Mount Pleasant
Penshaw
Penshaw Monument
Herrington Country Park
Springwell
Humbledon
Hillview
Grangetown
Grindon
Plains Farm
Hastings Hill
Thorney Close
Middle Herrington
Silksworth Sports Complex & Ski Centre
Farringdon
New Silksworth
Shiney Row
New Herrington
East Herrington
Silksworth
Tunstall
Ryhope Colliery
Ryhope
Biddick Gill Wood

Index to place names

This index lists places appearing in the main-map section of the atlas in alphabetical order. The reference following each name gives the atlas page number and grid reference of the square in which the place appears. The map shows counties, unitary authorities and administrative areas, together with a list of the abbreviated name forms used in the index. The top 100 places of tourist interest are indexed in **red** (or **green** if a World Heritage site), motorway service areas in **blue,** airports in blue *italic* and National Parks in green *italic*.

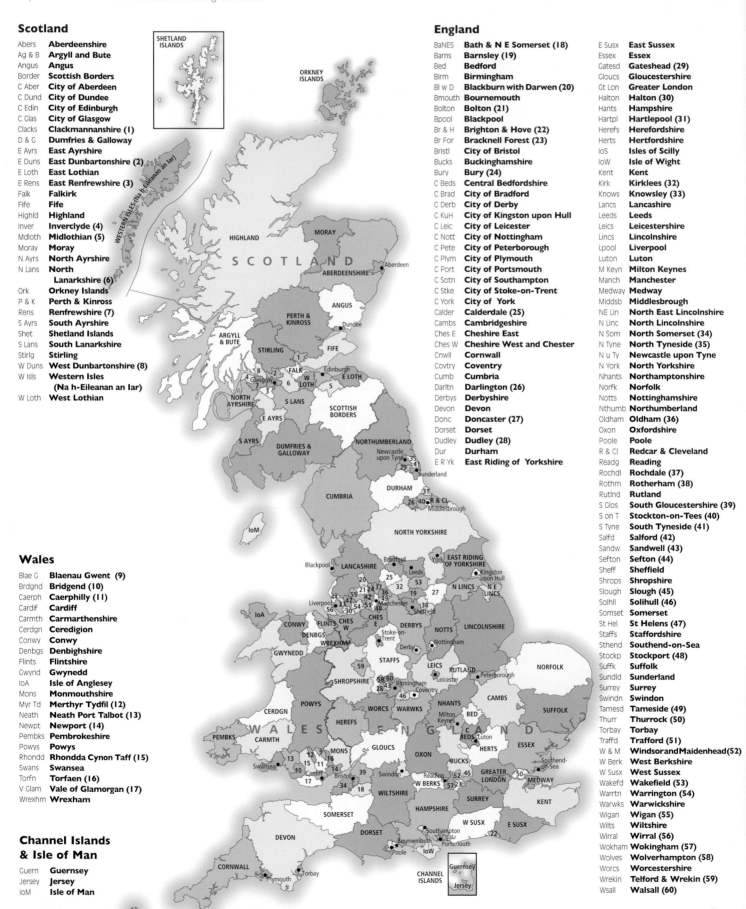

Scotland

Abers	**Aberdeenshire**
Ag & B	**Argyll and Bute**
Angus	**Angus**
Border	**Scottish Borders**
C Aber	**City of Aberdeen**
C Dund	**City of Dundee**
C Edin	**City of Edinburgh**
C Glas	**City of Glasgow**
Clacks	**Clackmannanshire (1)**
D & G	**Dumfries & Galloway**
E Ayrs	**East Ayrshire**
E Duns	**East Dunbartonshire (2)**
E Loth	**East Lothian**
E Rens	**East Renfrewshire (3)**
Falk	**Falkirk**
Fife	**Fife**
Highld	**Highland**
Inver	**Inverclyde (4)**
Mdloth	**Midlothian (5)**
Moray	**Moray**
N Ayrs	**North Ayrshire**
N Lans	**North Lanarkshire (6)**
Ork	**Orkney Islands**
P & K	**Perth & Kinross**
Rens	**Renfrewshire (7)**
S Ayrs	**South Ayrshire**
Shet	**Shetland Islands**
S Lans	**South Lanarkshire**
Stirlg	**Stirling**
W Duns	**West Dunbartonshire (8)**
W Isls	**Western Isles (Na h-Eileanan an Iar)**
W Loth	**West Lothian**

Wales

Blae G	**Blaenau Gwent (9)**
Brdgnd	**Bridgend (10)**
Caerph	**Caerphilly (11)**
Cardif	**Cardiff**
Carmth	**Carmarthenshire**
Cerdgn	**Ceredigion**
Conwy	**Conwy**
Denbgs	**Denbighshire**
Flints	**Flintshire**
Gwynd	**Gwynedd**
IoA	**Isle of Anglesey**
Mons	**Monmouthshire**
Myr Td	**Merthyr Tydfil (12)**
Neath	**Neath Port Talbot (13)**
Newpt	**Newport (14)**
Pembks	**Pembrokeshire**
Powys	**Powys**
Rhondd	**Rhondda Cynon Taff (15)**
Swans	**Swansea**
Torfn	**Torfaen (16)**
V Glam	**Vale of Glamorgan (17)**
Wrexhm	**Wrexham**

Channel Islands & Isle of Man

Guern	**Guernsey**
Jersey	**Jersey**
IoM	**Isle of Man**

England

BaNES	**Bath & N E Somerset (18)**
Barns	**Barnsley (19)**
Bed	**Bedford**
Birm	**Birmingham**
Bl w D	**Blackburn with Darwen (20)**
Bmouth	**Bournemouth**
Bolton	**Bolton (21)**
Bpool	**Blackpool**
Br & H	**Brighton & Hove (22)**
Br For	**Bracknell Forest (23)**
Bristl	**City of Bristol**
Bucks	**Buckinghamshire**
Bury	**Bury (24)**
C Beds	**Central Bedfordshire**
C Brad	**City of Bradford**
C Derb	**City of Derby**
C KuH	**City of Kingston upon Hull**
C Leic	**City of Leicester**
C Nott	**City of Nottingham**
C Pete	**City of Peterborough**
C Plym	**City of Plymouth**
C Port	**City of Portsmouth**
C Sotn	**City of Southampton**
C Stke	**City of Stoke-on-Trent**
C York	**City of York**
Calder	**Calderdale (25)**
Cambs	**Cambridgeshire**
Ches E	**Cheshire East**
Ches W	**Cheshire West and Chester**
Cnwll	**Cornwall**
Covtry	**Coventry**
Cumb	**Cumbria**
Darltn	**Darlington (26)**
Derbys	**Derbyshire**
Devon	**Devon**
Donc	**Doncaster (27)**
Dorset	**Dorset**
Dudley	**Dudley (28)**
Dur	**Durham**
E R Yk	**East Riding of Yorkshire**

E Susx	**East Sussex**
Essex	**Essex**
Gatesd	**Gateshead (29)**
Gloucs	**Gloucestershire**
Gt Lon	**Greater London**
Halton	**Halton (30)**
Hants	**Hampshire**
Hartpl	**Hartlepool (31)**
Herefs	**Herefordshire**
Herts	**Hertfordshire**
IoS	**Isles of Scilly**
IoW	**Isle of Wight**
Kent	**Kent**
Kirk	**Kirklees (32)**
Knows	**Knowsley (33)**
Lancs	**Lancashire**
Leeds	**Leeds**
Leics	**Leicestershire**
Lincs	**Lincolnshire**
Lpool	**Liverpool**
Luton	**Luton**
M Keyn	**Milton Keynes**
Manch	**Manchester**
Medway	**Medway**
Middsb	**Middlesbrough**
NE Lin	**North East Lincolnshire**
N Linc	**North Lincolnshire**
N Som	**North Somerset (34)**
N Tyne	**North Tyneside (35)**
N u Ty	**Newcastle upon Tyne**
N York	**North Yorkshire**
Nhants	**Northamptonshire**
Norfk	**Norfolk**
Notts	**Nottinghamshire**
Nthumb	**Northumberland**
Oldham	**Oldham (36)**
Oxon	**Oxfordshire**
Poole	**Poole**
R & Cl	**Redcar & Cleveland**
Readg	**Reading**
Rochdl	**Rochdale (37)**
Rothm	**Rotherham (38)**
Rutlnd	**Rutland**
S Glos	**South Gloucestershire (39)**
S on T	**Stockton-on-Tees (40)**
S Tyne	**South Tyneside (41)**
Salfd	**Salford (42)**
Sandw	**Sandwell (43)**
Sefton	**Sefton (44)**
Sheff	**Sheffield**
Shrops	**Shropshire**
Slough	**Slough (45)**
Solhll	**Solihull (46)**
Somset	**Somerset**
St Hel	**St Helens (47)**
Staffs	**Staffordshire**
Sthend	**Southend-on-Sea**
Stockp	**Stockport (48)**
Suffk	**Suffolk**
Sundld	**Sunderland**
Surrey	**Surrey**
Swindn	**Swindon**
Tamesd	**Tameside (49)**
Thurr	**Thurrock (50)**
Torbay	**Torbay**
Traffd	**Trafford (51)**
W & M	**Windsor and Maidenhead (52)**
W Berk	**West Berkshire**
W Susx	**West Sussex**
Wakefd	**Wakefield (53)**
Warrtn	**Warrington (54)**
Warwks	**Warwickshire**
Wigan	**Wigan (55)**
Wilts	**Wiltshire**
Wirral	**Wirral (56)**
Wokham	**Wokingham (57)**
Wolves	**Wolverhampton (58)**
Worcs	**Worcestershire**
Wrekin	**Telford & Wrekin (59)**
Wsall	**Walsall (60)**

Abbas Combe - Anslow Gate 261

A

Abbas Combe Somset 20 D10
Abberley Worcs 57 P11
Abberley Common Worcs 57 N11
Abberton Essex 52 H8
Abberton Worcs 47 J4
Abberwick Nthumb 119 M8
Abbess Roding Essex 51 N8
Abbey Devon 10 C2
Abbey-Cwm-Hir Powys 55 P10
Abbeydale Sheff 84 D4
Abbey Dore Herefs 45 M8
Abbey Green Staffs 70 H3
Abbey Hill Somset 19 J11
Abbey St Bathans Border 129 K7
Abbeystead Lancs 95 M10
Abbey Town Cumb 110 C10
Abbey Village Lancs 89 J6
Abbey Wood Gt Lon 37 L5
Abbotrule Border 118 B8
Abbots Bickington Devon 16 F9
Abbots Bromley Staffs 71 K10
Abbotsbury Dorset 11 M7
Abbot's Chair Derbys 83 M6
Abbots Deuglie P & K 134 E5
Abbotsham Devon 16 G6
Abbotskerswell Devon 7 M5
Abbots Langley Herts 50 C10
Abbotsleigh Devon 7 L9
Abbots Leigh N Som 31 P10
Abbotsley Cambs 62 B9
Abbots Morton Worcs 47 K3
Abbots Ripton Cambs 62 B5
Abbot's Salford Warwks 47 L4
Abbotstone Hants 22 G8
Abbotswood Hants 22 C10
Abbots Worthy Hants 22 E8
Abbotts Ann Hants 22 B6
Abbott Street Dorset 12 G4
Abcott Shrops 56 F9
Abdon Shrops 57 K7
Abenhall Gloucs 46 C11
Aberaeron Cerdgn 43 J2
Aberaman Rhondd 30 D4
Aberangell Gwynd 55 J2
Aber-arad Carmth 42 F6
Aberarder Highld 147 Q2
Aberargie P & K 134 F4
Aberarth Cerdgn 43 J2
Aberavon Neath 29 K7
Aber-banc Cerdgn 42 G6
Aberbargoed Caerph 30 G4
Aberbeeg Blae G 30 H4
Abercanaid Myr Td 30 E4
Abercarn Caerph 30 H6
Abercastle Pembks 40 G4
Abercegir Powys 55 J4
Aberchalder Lodge Highld 147 J7
Aberchirder Abers 158 F7
Aber Clydach Powys 44 G10
Abercraf Powys 29 M2
Abercregan Neath 29 M5
Abercwmboi Rhondd 30 D5
Abercych Pembks 41 P2
Abercynon Rhondd 30 E6
Aberdalgie P & K 134 D3
Aberdare Rhondd 30 D4
Aberdaron Gwynd 66 B9
Aberdeen C Aber 151 N6
Aberdeen Airport C Aber 151 M5
Aberdeen Crematorium C Aber 151 M6
Aberdesach Gwynd 66 G4
Aberdour Fife 134 F10
Aberdulais Neath 29 L5
Aberdyfi Gwynd 54 E5
Aberedw Powys 44 F5
Abereiddy Pembks 40 E4
Abererch Gwynd 66 F7
Aberfan Myr Td 30 E4
Aberfeldy P & K 141 L8
Aberffraw IoA 78 F11
Aberffrwd Cerdgn 54 F9
Aberford Leeds 91 L3
Aberfoyle Stirlg 132 G7
Abergarw Brdgnd 29 P8
Abergarwed Neath 29 M4
Abergavenny Mons 31 J2
Abergele Conwy 80 C9
Aber-giar Carmth 43 K6
Abergorlech Carmth 43 L8
Abergwesyn Powys 44 B4
Abergwili Carmth 42 H10
Abergwydol Powys 54 H4
Abergwynfi Neath 29 N5
Abergwyngregyn Gwynd 79 M10
Abergynolwyn Gwynd 54 F3
Aberhafesp Powys 55 P6
Aberhosan Powys 55 J5
Aberkenfig Brdgnd 29 N8
Aberlady E Loth 128 D4
Aberlemno Angus 143 J6
Aberllefenni Gwynd 54 H3
Aberllynfi Powys 44 H7
Aberlour Moray 157 P9
Aber-Magwr Cerdgn 54 F10
Aber-meurig Cerdgn 43 L3
Abermorddu Flints 69 K3
Abermule Powys 56 B6
Abernant Carmth 42 F10
Aber-nant Rhondd 30 D4
Abernethy P & K 134 F4
Abernyte P & K 142 D11
Aberporth Cerdgn 42 E4
Abersoch Gwynd 66 E9
Abersychan Torfn 31 J4
Aberthin V Glam 30 D10
Abertillery Blae G 30 H4
Abertridwr Caerph 30 F7
Abertridwr Powys 68 D11
Abertysswg Caerph 30 F3
Aberuthven P & K 134 B4
Aberyscir Powys 44 D9
Aberystwyth Cerdgn 54 D8
Aberystwyth Crematorium Cerdgn 54 E8
Abingdon-on-Thames Oxon 34 E5
Abinger Common Surrey 36 D11
Abinger Hammer Surrey 36 C11
Abington Nhants 60 G8
Abington S Lans 116 C6
Abington Pigotts Cambs 50 H2
Abington Services S Lans 116 C6
Abingworth W Susx 24 D7
Ab Kettleby Leics 73 J6
Ab Lench Worcs 47 K4
Ablington Gloucs 33 M3
Ablington Wilts 21 N5
Abney Derbys 83 Q8
Above Church Staffs 71 J4
Aboyne Abers 150 E8
Abram Wigan 82 D4
Abriachan Highld 155 Q10
Abridge Essex 51 L11
Abronhill N Lans 126 D2
Abson S Glos 32 D10
Abthorpe Nhants 48 H5
Aby Lincs 87 M5
Acaster Malbis C York 98 B11
Acaster Selby N York 91 P2
Accrington Lancs 89 M5
Accrington Crematorium Lancs 89 M5
Acha Ag & B 136 F5
Achahoish Ag & B 123 N4
Achalader P & K 141 R8
Achaleven Ag & B 138 G11
Acha Mor W Isls 168 i5
Achanalt Highld 155 J5
Achandunie Highld 156 A3
Achany Highld 162 D6
Acharacle Highld 138 B4
Acharn Highld 138 C7
Acharn P & K 141 J9
Achavanich Highld 167 L8
Achduart Highld 160 G6
Achfary Highld 164 G9
A'Chill Highld 144 C6
Achiltibuie Highld 160 G5
Achina Highld 166 B4
Achinhoan Ag & B 120 E8
Achintee Highld 154 B9
Achintraid Highld 153 Q10
Achmelvich Highld 160 H2
Achmore Highld 153 R11
Achmore W Isls 168 i5
Achnacarnin Highld 164 B10
Achnacarry Highld 146 F10
Achnacloich Highld 145 J6
Achnaconeran Highld 147 L4
Achnacroish Ag & B 138 F9
Achnadrish House Ag & B 137 M5
Achnafauld P & K 141 L10
Achnagarron Highld 156 B3
Achnaha Highld 137 M2
Achnahaird Highld 160 G4
Achnairn Highld 162 D4
Achnalea Highld 138 F5
Achnamara Ag & B 130 F10
Achnasheen Highld 154 G6
Achnashellach Lodge Highld 154 D8
Achnastank Moray 157 P11
Achosnich Highld 137 L2
Achranich Highld 138 C8
Achreamie Highld 166 H3
Achriabhach Highld 139 L4
Achriesgill Highld 164 G6
Achtoty Highld 165 Q4
Achurch Nhants 61 M4
Achvaich Highld 162 G8
Achvarasdal Highld 166 G4
Ackergill Highld 167 Q6
Acklam Middsb 104 E7
Acklam N York 98 F8
Ackleton Shrops 57 P5
Acklington Nthumb 119 P10
Ackton Wakefd 91 L6
Ackworth Moor Top Wakefd 91 L7
Acle Norfk 77 N9
Acock's Green Birm 58 H8
Acol Kent 39 P8
Acomb C York 98 B10
Acomb Nthumb 112 D7
Acombe Somset 10 D2
Aconbury Herefs 45 Q8
Acre Lancs 89 M6
Acrefair Wrexhm 69 J6
Acton Ches E 70 A4
Acton Dorset 12 G9
Acton Gt Lon 36 F4
Acton Shrops 56 E8
Acton Staffs 70 E6
Acton Suffk 52 E2
Acton Worcs 58 B11
Acton Beauchamp Herefs 46 C4
Acton Bridge Ches W 82 C9
Acton Burnell Shrops 57 J4
Acton Green Herefs 46 C4
Acton Park Wrexhm 69 K4
Acton Pigott Shrops 57 J4
Acton Round Shrops 57 L5
Acton Scott Shrops 56 H7
Acton Trussell Staffs 70 G11
Acton Turville S Glos 32 F8
Adbaston Staffs 70 D9
Adber Dorset 19 Q10
Adbolton Notts 72 F3
Adderbury Oxon 48 E7
Adderley Shrops 70 B7
Adderstone Nthumb 119 M4
Addiewell W Loth 126 H5
Addingham C Brad 96 G11
Addington Bucks 49 K9
Addington Gt Lon 37 J8
Addington Kent 37 Q9
Addiscombe Gt Lon 36 H7
Addlestone Surrey 36 C8
Addlestonemoor Surrey 36 C7
Addlethorpe Lincs 87 P7
Adeney Wrekin 70 B11
Adeyfield Herts 50 C9
Adfa Powys 55 P4
Adforton Herefs 56 G10
Adisham Kent 39 M11
Adlestrop Gloucs 47 P9
Adlingfleet E R Yk 92 D6
Adlington Ches E 83 K8
Adlington Lancs 89 J8
Admaston Staffs 71 J10
Admaston Wrekin 57 L2
Admington Warwks 47 P5
Adpar Cerdgn 42 F6
Adsborough Somset 19 J9
Adscombe Somset 18 G7
Adstock Bucks 49 K9
Adstone Nhants 48 G4
Adswood Stockp 83 J7
Adversane W Susx 24 C6
Advie Highld 157 L11
Adwalton Leeds 90 G5
Adwell Oxon 35 J5
Adwick Le Street Donc 91 N9
Adwick upon Dearne Donc 91 M10
Ae D & G 109 L3
Ae Bridgend D & G 109 M3
Afan Forest Park Neath 29 N5
Affetside Bury 89 M8
Affleck Abers 158 E9
Affpuddle Dorset 12 D6
Affric Lodge Highld 146 F3
Afon-wen Flints 80 G10
Afton Devon 7 L6
Afton IoW 13 P7
Agecroft Crematorium Salfd 82 H4
Agglethorpe N York 96 G3
Aigburth Lpool 81 M7
Aike E R Yk 99 L11
Aiketgate Cumb 111 J11
Aikhead Cumb 110 D11
Aikton Cumb 110 E10
Ailby Lincs 87 M5
Ailey Herefs 45 L5
Ailsworth C Pete 74 B11
Ainderby Quernhow N York 97 M4
Ainderby Steeple N York 97 M2
Aingers Green Essex 53 K7
Ainsdale Sefton 88 C8
Ainsdale-on-Sea Sefton 88 B8
Ainstable Cumb 111 K11
Ainsworth Bury 89 M8
Ainthorpe N York 105 K9
Aintree Sefton 81 M5
Ainville W Loth 127 L5
Aird Ag & B 130 F7
Aird D & G 106 E5
Aird W Isls 168 k4
Aird a Mhulaidh W Isls 168 g6
Aird Asaig W Isls 168 g7
Aird Dhubh Highld 153 N9
Airdeny Ag & B 131 K2
Aird of Kinloch Ag & B 137 N10
Aird of Sleat Highld 145 J7
Airdrie N Lans 126 D4
Airdriehill N Lans 126 D4
Airds of Kells D & G 108 E6
Aird Uig W Isls 168 f4
Airidh a bhruaich W Isls 168 h6
Airieland D & G 108 G9
Airlie Angus 142 E7
Airmyn E R Yk 92 B6
Airntully P & K 141 Q10
Airor Highld 145 M6
Airth Falk 133 Q10
Airton N York 96 D9
Aisby Lincs 73 Q3
Aisby Lincs 85 Q2
Aisgill Cumb 102 E11
Aish Devon 6 H6
Aish Devon 7 L7
Aisholt Somset 18 G7
Aiskew N York 97 L3
Aislaby N York 98 F3
Aislaby N York 105 N9
Aislaby S on T 104 D8
Aisthorpe Lincs 86 B4
Aith Shet 169 q8
Akeld Nthumb 119 J5
Akeley Bucks 49 K7
Akenham Suffk 53 K2
Albaston Cnwll 5 Q7
Alberbury Shrops 56 F2
Albourne W Susx 24 G7
Albourne Green W Susx 24 G7
Albrighton Shrops 57 Q4
Albrighton Shrops 69 N11
Alburgh Norfk 65 K4
Albury Herts 51 K6
Albury Oxon 35 J3
Albury Surrey 36 B11
Albury End Herts 51 K6
Albury Heath Surrey 36 C11
Alby Hill Norfk 76 H5
Alcaig Highld 155 Q6
Alcaston Shrops 56 H7
Alcester Warwks 47 L3
Alcester Lane End Birm 58 G8
Alciston E Susx 25 M9
Alcombe Somset 18 C5
Alcombe Wilts 32 F11
Alconbury Cambs 61 Q5
Alconbury Weston Cambs 61 Q5
Aldborough N York 97 P7
Aldborough Norfk 76 H5
Aldbourne Wilts 33 Q9
Aldbrough E R Yk 93 M3
Aldbrough St John N York 103 P8
Aldbury Herts 35 Q2
Aldcliffe Lancs 95 K8
Aldclune P & K 141 L5
Aldeburgh Suffk 65 P10
Aldeby Norfk 65 N3
Aldenham Herts 50 D11
Alderbury Wilts 21 N9
Aldercar Derbys 84 F11
Alderford Norfk 76 G8
Alderholt Dorset 13 K2
Alderley Gloucs 32 E6
Alderley Edge Ches E 82 H9
Aldermans Green Covtry 59 N8
Aldermaston W Berk 34 G11
Alderminster Warwks 47 P5
Alder Moor Staffs 71 N9
Aldersey Green Ches W 69 N3
Aldershot Hants 23 N4
Alderton Gloucs 47 K8
Alderton Nhants 49 K5
Alderton Shrops 69 N10
Alderton Suffk 53 P3
Alderton Wilts 32 F8
Alderwasley Derbys 71 Q4
Aldfield N York 97 L7
Aldford Ches W 69 M3
Aldgate Rutlnd 73 P10
Aldham Essex 52 F6
Aldham Suffk 52 J2
Aldingbourne W Susx 15 P5
Aldingham Cumb 94 F6
Aldington Kent 27 J4
Aldington Worcs 47 L6
Aldington Corner Kent 27 J4
Aldivalloch Moray 150 B2
Aldochlay Ag & B 132 D9
Aldon Shrops 56 G9
Aldoth Cumb 109 P11
Aldreth Cambs 62 F6
Aldridge Wsall 58 G4
Aldringham Suffk 65 N9
Aldro N York 98 G8
Aldsworth Gloucs 33 N3
Aldsworth W Susx 15 L5
Aldunie Moray 150 B2
Aldwark Derbys 84 B9
Aldwark N York 97 Q8
Aldwick W Susx 15 P7
Aldwincle Nhants 61 M4
Aldworth W Berk 34 G9
Alexandria W Duns 125 K2
Aley Somset 18 G7
Alfardisworthy Devon 16 D9
Alfington Devon 10 C5
Alfold Surrey 24 B4
Alfold Bars W Susx 24 B4
Alfold Crossways Surrey 24 B3
Alford Abers 150 F4
Alford Lincs 87 N5
Alford Somset 20 B8
Alford Crematorium Lincs 87 M5
Alfreton Derbys 84 F9
Alfrick Worcs 46 D4
Alfrick Pound Worcs 46 D4
Alfriston E Susx 25 M10
Algarkirk Lincs 74 E3
Alhampton Somset 20 B8
Alkborough N Linc 92 E6
Alkerton Gloucs 32 E3
Alkerton Oxon 48 C6
Alkham Kent 27 N3
Alkington Shrops 69 P7
Alkmonton Derbys 71 M7
Allaleigh Devon 7 L8
Allanaquoich Abers 149 L9
Allanbank N Lans 126 E6
Allanton Border 129 M9
Allanton N Lans 126 E6
Allanton S Lans 126 C7
Allaston Gloucs 32 B4
Allbrook Hants 22 E10
All Cannings Wilts 21 L2
Allendale Nthumb 112 B9
Allen End Warwks 59 J5
Allenheads Nthumb 112 C11
Allensford Dur 112 G10
Allen's Green Herts 51 L7
Allensmore Herefs 45 P7
Allenton C Derb 72 B4
Aller Devon 17 P6
Aller Somset 19 M9
Allerby Cumb 100 E3
Allercombe Devon 9 P6
Allerford Somset 18 B5
Allerston N York 98 H4
Allerthorpe E R Yk 98 F11
Allerton C Brad 90 E4
Allerton Highld 156 D4
Allerton Lpool 81 M7
Allerton Bywater Leeds 91 L5
Allerton Mauleverer N York 97 P9
Allesley Covtry 59 M8
Allestree C Derb 72 A3
Allet Common Cnwll 3 K4
Allexton Leics 73 L10
Allgreave Ches E 83 L11
Allhallows Medway 38 D6
Allhallows-on-Sea Medway 38 D6
Alligin Shuas Highld 153 Q6
Allimore Green Staffs 70 F11
Allington Dorset 11 K6
Allington Kent 38 C10
Allington Lincs 73 M2
Allington Wilts 21 L2
Allington Wilts 21 P7
Allington Wilts 32 G9
Allithwaite Cumb 94 H5
Alloa Clacks 133 P9
Allonby Cumb 100 E2
Allostock Ches W 82 F10
Alloway S Ayrs 114 F4
Allowenshay Somset 10 H2
All Saints South Elmham Suffk 65 L5
Allscott Shrops 57 N5
Allscott Wrekin 57 L2
All Stretton Shrops 56 H5
Alltami Flints 81 K11
Alltchaorunn Highld 139 M7
Alltmawr Powys 44 F5
Alltwalis Carmth 42 H8
Alltwen Neath 29 K4
Alltyblaca Cerdgn 43 K5
Allweston Dorset 11 P2
Allwood Green Suffk 64 E7
Almeley Herefs 45 L4
Almeley Wooton Herefs 45 L4
Almer Dorset 12 F5
Almholme Donc 91 P9
Almington Staffs 70 C8
Almodington W Susx 15 M7
Almondbank P & K 134 D2
Almondbury Kirk 90 F8
Almondsbury S Glos 32 B8
Alne N York 97 Q7
Alness Highld 156 B4
Alnham Nthumb 119 J8
Alnmouth Nthumb 119 P8
Alnwick Nthumb 119 N8
Alperton Gt Lon 36 E4
Alphamstone Essex 52 E4
Alpheton Suffk 64 B11
Alphington Devon 9 M6
Alpington Norfk 77 K11
Alport Derbys 84 B8
Alpraham Ches E 69 Q3
Alresford Essex 53 J7
Alrewas Staffs 59 J2
Alsager Ches E 70 D3
Alsagers Bank Staffs 70 D5
Alsop en le Dale Derbys 71 M4
Alston Cumb 111 P11
Alston Devon 10 G4
Alstone Gloucs 47 J8
Alstone Somset 19 K5
Alstonefield Staffs 71 L3
Alston Sutton Somset 19 M4
Alswear Devon 17 N7
Alt Oldham 83 K4
Altandhu Highld 160 F4
Altarnun Cnwll 5 L5
Altass Highld 162 C6
Altcreich Ag & B 138 B10
Altgaltraig Ag & B 124 C3
Altham Lancs 89 M4
Althorne Essex 38 F2
Althorpe N Linc 92 D9
Altnabreac Station Highld 166 H7
Altnaharra Highld 165 N9
Altofts Wakefd 91 K6
Alton Derbys 84 E8
Alton Hants 23 K7
Alton Staffs 71 K6
Alton Wilts 21 N5
Alton Barnes Wilts 21 M2
Alton Pancras Dorset 11 Q4
Alton Priors Wilts 21 M2
Alton Towers Staffs 71 K6
Altrincham Traffd 82 G7
Altrincham Crematorium Traffd 82 F7
Altskeith Hotel Stirlg 132 F7
Alva Clacks 133 P8
Alvanley Ches W 81 P10
Alvaston C Derb 72 B4
Alvechurch Worcs 58 F10
Alvecote Warwks 59 K4
Alvediston Wilts 21 J10
Alveley Shrops 57 P8
Alverdiscott Devon 17 J6
Alverstoke Hants 14 H7
Alverstone IoW 14 G9
Alverthorpe Wakefd 91 J6
Alverton Notts 73 K2
Alves Moray 157 L5
Alvescot Oxon 33 Q4
Alveston S Glos 32 B7
Alveston Warwks 47 P3
Alvingham Lincs 87 L2
Alvington Gloucs 32 B4
Alwalton C Pete 74 B11
Alwinton Nthumb 118 H9
Alwoodley Leeds 90 H2
Alwoodley Gates Leeds 91 J2
Alyth P & K 142 C8
Ambergate Derbys 84 D10
Amber Hill Lincs 86 H11
Amberley Gloucs 32 G4
Amberley W Susx 24 B8
Amber Row Derbys 84 E9
Amberstone E Susx 25 N8
Amble Nthumb 119 Q10
Amblecote Dudley 58 C7
Ambler Thorn C Brad 90 D5
Ambleside Cumb 101 L10
Ambleston Pembks 41 K5
Ambrosden Oxon 48 H11
Amcotts N Linc 92 E8
America Cambs 62 F5
Amersham Bucks 35 Q5
Amersham Common Bucks 35 Q5
Amersham Old Town Bucks 35 Q5
Amersham on the Hill Bucks 35 Q5
Amerton Staffs 70 H9
Amesbury Wilts 21 N6
Amhuinnsuidhe W Isls 168 f7
Amington Staffs 59 K4
Amisfield Town D & G 109 M4
Amlwch IoA 78 G6
Ammanford Carmth 28 H2
Amotherby N York 98 E6
Ampfield Hants 22 D10
Ampleforth N York 98 B5
Ampney Crucis Gloucs 33 L4
Ampney St Mary Gloucs 33 L4
Ampney St Peter Gloucs 33 L4
Amport Hants 22 B6
Ampthill C Beds 50 B3
Ampton Suffk 64 B7
Amroth Pembks 41 N9
Amulree P & K 141 L10
Amwell Herts 50 E8
Anaheilt Highld 138 E5
Ancaster Lincs 73 P2
Anchor Shrops 56 B7
Ancroft Nthumb 129 P11
Ancrum Border 118 B6
Ancton W Susx 15 Q6
Anderby Lincs 87 P5
Andersea Somset 19 K8
Andersfield Somset 18 H8
Anderson Dorset 12 E5
Anderton Ches W 82 D9
Anderton Cnwll 6 C8
Andover Hants 22 C5
Andoversford Gloucs 47 K11
Andreas IoM 80 f2
Anelog Gwynd 66 B9
Anerley Gt Lon 36 H7
Anfield Lpool 81 M6
Anfield Crematorium Lpool 81 M6
Angarrack Cnwll 2 F6
Angarrick Cnwll 3 K6
Angelbank Shrops 57 K9
Angersleigh Somset 18 G11
Angerton Cumb 110 D9
Angle Pembks 40 G10
Anglesey IoA 78 G8
Angmering W Susx 24 C10
Angram N York 97 R11
Angram N York 102 G11
Angrouse Cnwll 2 H10
Anick Nthumb 112 D7
Ankerville Highld 156 E3
Ankle Hill Leics 73 K7
Anlaby E R Yk 92 H5
Anmer Norfk 75 P5
Anmore Hants 15 J4
Annan D & G 110 C7
Annandale Water Services D & G 109 P2
Annaside Cumb 94 B3
Annat Highld 154 A7
Annathill N Lans 126 C3
Anna Valley Hants 22 C6
Annbank S Ayrs 114 H3
Anne Hathaway's Cottage Warwks 47 N4
Annesley Notts 84 H10
Annesley Woodhouse Notts 84 G10
Annfield Plain Dur 113 J10
Anniesland C Glas 125 N4
Annitsford N Tyne 113 L6
Annscroft Shrops 56 H3
Ansdell Lancs 88 C5
Ansford Somset 20 B8
Ansley Warwks 59 M6
Anslow Staffs 71 N9
Anslow Gate Staffs 71 M10

262 Anslow Lees - Bacheldre

Anslow Lees Staffs 71 N10
Ansteadbrook Surrey 23 P8
Anstey Hants 23 K6
Anstey Herts 51 K4
Anstey Leics 72 F9
Anstruther Fife 135 P7
Ansty W Susx 24 G6
Ansty Warwks 59 P8
Ansty Wilts 21 J9
Ansty Cross Dorset 12 C4
Anthill Common Hants 14 H4
Anthonys Surrey 36 B8
Anthorn Cumb 110 C9
Antingham Norfk 77 K5
An t-Ob W Isls 168 f9
Anton's Gowt Lincs 87 K11
Antony Cnwll 5 Q11
Antrobus Ches W 82 D9
Anvil Corner Devon 16 F11
Anvil Green Kent 27 K2
Anwick Lincs 86 F10
Anwoth D & G 108 C9
Aperfield Gt Lon 37 K9
Apes Dale Worcs 58 E10
Apethorpe Nhants 73 Q11
Apeton Staffs 70 F11
Apley Lincs 86 F5
Apperknowle Derbys 84 E5
Apperley Gloucs 46 G9
Apperley Bridge C Brad 90 F3
Apperley Dene Nthumb 112 G9
Appersett N York 96 C2
Appin Ag & B 138 G8
Appleby N Linc 92 G8
Appleby-in-Westmorland Cumb 102 C6
Appleby Magna Leics 59 M3
Appleby Parva Leics 59 M3
Appleby Street Herts 50 H10
Applecross Highld 153 N9
Appledore Devon 9 Q2
Appledore Devon 16 H5
Appledore Kent 26 G6
Appledore Heath Kent 26 G5
Appleford Oxon 34 F6
Applegarth Town D & G 109 P4
Applehaigh Wakefd 91 K8
Appleshaw Hants 22 B5
Applethwaite Cumb 101 J5
Appleton Halton 81 Q7
Appleton Oxon 34 D4
Appleton Warrtn 82 D8
Appleton-le-Moors N York 98 E3
Appleton-le-Street N York 98 E6
Appleton Roebuck N York 91 P2
Appleton Thorn Warrtn 82 D8
Appleton Wiske N York 104 C10
Appletreehall Border 117 Q7
Appletreewick N York 96 G8
Appley Somset 18 E10
Appley Bridge Lancs 88 G9
Apse Heath IoW 14 G10
Apsley End C Beds 50 D4
Apuldram W Susx 15 M6
Arabella Highld 156 E2
Arbirlot Angus 143 L9
Arboll Highld 163 K10
Arborfield Wokham 35 L11
Arborfield Cross Wokham 35 L11
Arbourthorne Sheff 84 E3
Arbroath Angus 143 L9
Arbuthnott Abers 143 P2
Arcadia Kent 26 E4
Archddu Carmth 28 D4
Archdeacon Newton Darltn 103 Q7
Archencarroch W Duns 132 E11
Archiestown Moray 157 N9
Archirondel Jersey 11 c1
Arclid Green Ches E 70 D2
Ardallie Abers 159 P10
Ardanaiseig Hotel Ag & B 131 M3
Ardaneaskan Highld 153 Q10
Ardarroch Highld 153 Q10
Ardbeg Ag & B 122 F10
Ardbeg Ag & B 124 D4
Ardbeg Ag & B 131 P11
Ardcharnich Highld 161 K9
Ardchiavaig Ag & B 137 K12
Ardchonnel Ag & B 131 K5
Ardchullarie More Stirlg 132 H5
Arddarroch Ag & B 131 Q9
Arddleen Powys 69 J11
Ardechive Highld 146 E9
Ardeer N Ayrs 124 H9
Ardeley Herts 50 H5
Ardelve Highld 145 Q2
Arden Ag & B 132 D11
Ardens Grafton Warwks 47 M4
Ardentallen Ag & B 130 G3
Ardentinny Ag & B 131 P10
Ardentraive Ag & B 124 C3
Ardeonaig Stirlg 140 G10
Ardersier Highld 156 D7
Ardessie Highld 160 H9
Ardfern Ag & B 130 G7
Ardfernal Ag & B 123 J5
Ardgay Highld 162 D8
Ardgour Highld 139 J5
Ardgowan Inver 124 G3
Ardhallow Ag & B 124 F3
Ardhasig W Isls 168 g7
Ardheslaig Highld 153 P6
Ardindrean Highld 161 K9
Ardingly W Susx 24 H5
Ardington Oxon 34 D7
Ardington Wick Oxon 34 D7
Ardlamont Ag & B 124 B4
Ardleigh Essex 53 J6
Ardleigh Heath Essex 52 H5
Ardler P & K 142 D9
Ardley Oxon 48 F9
Ardley End Essex 51 M8
Ardlui Ag & B 132 C4
Ardlussa Ag & B 130 C10
Ardmair Highld 161 J7
Ardmaleish Ag & B 124 D4
Ardminish Ag & B 123 K10
Ardmolich Highld 138 C3
Ardmore Ag & B 125 J2
Ardmore Highld 162 G9
Ardnadam Ag & B 131 P11
Ardnagrask Highld 155 P8
Ardnarff Highld 154 A10
Ardnastang Highld 138 E5
Ardpatrick Ag & B 123 N8
Ardrishaig Ag & B 130 H10
Ardross Highld 155 R3
Ardrossan N Ayrs 124 G9
Ardsley Barns 91 K9
Ardsley East Leeds 91 J5
Ardslignish Highld 137 P3
Ardtalla Ag & B 122 G9
Ardtoe Highld 138 A3
Arduaine Ag & B 130 F5
Ardullie Highld 155 Q5
Ardvasar Highld 145 K7
Ardvorlich P & K 133 J3
Ardvourlie W Isls 168 g6
Ardwell D & G 106 F8
Ardwick Manch 83 J5
Areley Kings Worcs 57 P10
Arevegaig Highld 138 B4
Arford Hants 23 M7
Argoed Caerph 30 G5
Argoed Shrops 69 K10
Argoed Mill Powys 44 D2
Argos Hill E Susx 25 N5
Argyll Forest Park Ag & B 131 Q7
Aribruach W Isls 168 h6
Aridhglas Ag & B 137 J11
Arileod Ag & B 136 F5
Arinagour Ag & B 136 G4
Ariogan Ag & B 130 H2
Arisaig Highld 145 L10
Arisaig House Highld 145 L11
Arkendale N York 97 N8
Arkesden Essex 51 L4
Arkholme Lancs 95 M6
Arkleby Cumb 100 F3
Arkleton D & G 110 G2
Arkle Town N York 103 K10
Arkley Gt Lon 50 F11
Arksey Donc 91 P9
Arkwright Town Derbys 84 F6
Arle Gloucs 46 H10
Arlecdon Cumb 100 D7
Arlescote Warwks 48 C5
Arlesey C Beds 50 E3
Arleston Wrekin 57 M2
Arley Ches E 82 E8
Arley Warwks 59 L6
Arlingham Gloucs 32 D2
Arlington Devon 17 L3
Arlington E Susx 25 M9
Arlington Gloucs 33 M3
Arlington Beccott Devon 17 L3
Armadale Highld 145 K7
Armadale Highld 166 C4
Armadale W Loth 126 G4
Armaside Cumb 100 G5
Armathwaite Cumb 111 K11
Arminghall Norfk 77 K11
Armitage Staffs 71 K11
Armitage Bridge Kirk 90 E8
Armley Leeds 90 H4
Armscote Warwks 47 P6
Armshead Staffs 70 G5
Armston Nhants 61 N3
Armthorpe Donc 91 Q10
Arnabost Ag & B 136 G3
Arnaby Cumb 94 D4
Arncliffe N York 96 D6
Arncliffe Cote N York 96 D6
Arncroach Fife 135 N6
Arndilly House Moray 157 P8
Arne Dorset 12 G7
Arnesby Leics 60 D2
Arngask P & K 134 E5
Arnisdale Highld 145 P5
Arnish Highld 153 K8
Arniston Mdloth 127 Q5
Arnol W Isls 168 i3
Arnold E R Yk 93 K2
Arnold Notts 85 J11
Arnprior Stirlg 133 J9
Arnside Cumb 95 K5
Aros Ag & B 137 P6
Arowry Wrexhm 69 N7
Arrad Foot Cumb 94 G4
Arram E R Yk 92 H2
Arran N Ayrs 120 H4
Arrathorne N York 97 K2
Arreton IoW 14 F9
Arrina Highld 153 N6
Arrington Cambs 62 D10
Arrochar Ag & B 132 B7
Arrow Warwks 47 L3
Arrowfield Top Worcs 58 F10
Arscott Shrops 56 G3
Artafallie Highld 156 A8
Arthington Leeds 90 H2
Arthingworth Nhants 60 G4
Arthog Gwynd 54 E2
Arthrath Abers 159 N10
Arthursdale Leeds 91 K3
Artrochie Abers 159 P11
Arundel W Susx 24 B9
Asby Cumb 100 E6
Ascog Ag & B 124 E5
Ascot W & M 35 P11
Ascott Warwks 48 B8
Ascott Earl Oxon 48 B11
Ascott-under-Wychwood Oxon 48 B11
Asenby N York 97 N5
Asfordby Leics 73 J7
Asfordby Hill Leics 73 J7
Asgarby Lincs 86 F11
Asgarby Lincs 87 K7
Ash Devon 7 L9
Ash Devon 17 J10
Ash Dorset 12 E2
Ash Kent 37 P8
Ash Kent 39 N10
Ash Somset 19 J10
Ash Somset 19 N10
Ash Surrey 23 P4
Ashampstead W Berk 34 G9
Ashampstead Green W Berk 34 G9
Ashbocking Suffk 64 H11
Ashbourne Derbys 71 M5
Ashbrittle Somset 18 E10
Ashburnham Place E Susx 25 Q8
Ashburton Devon 7 K4
Ashbury Devon 8 D5
Ashbury Oxon 33 Q7
Ashby N Linc 92 E9
Ashby by Partney Lincs 87 M7
Ashby cum Fenby NE Lin 93 N10
Ashby de la Launde Lincs 86 E9
Ashby-de-la-Zouch Leics 72 B7
Ashby Folville Leics 73 J8
Ashby Magna Leics 60 C2
Ashby Parva Leics 60 B3
Ashby Puerorum Lincs 87 K6
Ashby St Ledgers Nhants 60 C7
Ashby St Mary Norfk 77 L11
Ashchurch Gloucs 46 H8
Ashcombe Devon 9 M9
Ashcombe N Som 19 K2
Ashcott Somset 19 M7
Ashdon Essex 51 N2
Ashe Hants 22 F4
Asheldham Essex 52 G11
Ashen Essex 52 B3
Ashendon Bucks 35 K2
Asheridge Bucks 35 P4
Ashfield Hants 22 C11
Ashfield Herefs 46 A10
Ashfield Stirlg 133 M7
Ashfield cum Thorpe Suffk 65 J9
Ashfield Green Suffk 63 N9
Ashfield Green Suffk 65 K7
Ashfold Crossways W Susx 24 F5
Ashford Devon 6 H9
Ashford Devon 17 J4
Ashford Kent 26 H3
Ashford Surrey 36 C6
Ashford Bowdler Shrops 57 J10
Ashford Carbonell Shrops 57 J10
Ashford Hill Hants 22 G2
Ashford in the Water Derbys 83 Q11
Ashgill S Lans 126 D7
Ash Green Surrey 23 P5
Ash Green Warwks 59 M8
Ashill Devon 10 B2
Ashill Norfk 76 B11
Ashill Somset 19 K11
Ashingdon Essex 38 E3
Ashington Nthumb 113 L3
Ashington Poole 12 H5
Ashington Somset 19 Q10
Ashington W Susx 24 D7
Ashkirk Border 117 P6
Ashlett Hants 14 E6
Ashleworth Gloucs 46 F9
Ashleworth Quay Gloucs 46 F9
Ashley Cambs 63 L8
Ashley Ches E 82 G8
Ashley Devon 17 M9
Ashley Dorset 13 K4
Ashley Gloucs 32 H6
Ashley Hants 13 N5
Ashley Hants 22 C8
Ashley Kent 27 P2
Ashley Nhants 60 G2
Ashley Staffs 70 D7
Ashley Wilts 32 F11
Ashley Green Bucks 35 Q3
Ashleyhay Derbys 71 P4
Ashley Heath Dorset 13 K4
Ashley Moor Herefs 56 H11
Ash Magna Shrops 69 Q7
Ashmansworth Hants 22 D3
Ashmansworthy Devon 16 E8
Ashmead Green Gloucs 32 E5
Ashmill Devon 5 P2
Ash Mill Devon 17 P7
Ashmore Dorset 20 H11
Ashmore Green W Berk 34 F11
Ashorne Warwks 48 B3
Ashover Derbys 84 D8
Ashover Hay Derbys 84 D8
Ashow Warwks 59 M10
Ash Parva Shrops 69 Q7
Ashperton Herefs 46 B6
Ashprington Devon 7 L7
Ash Priors Somset 18 G9
Ashreigney Devon 17 L9
Ash Street Suffk 52 H2
Ashtead Surrey 36 E9
Ash Thomas Devon 9 P2
Ashton C Pete 74 B9
Ashton Ches W 81 Q11
Ashton Cnwll 2 G8
Ashton Devon 9 L8
Ashton Hants 22 F11
Ashton Herefs 45 Q2
Ashton Inver 124 G2
Ashton Nhants 49 L5
Ashton Nhants 61 N3
Ashton Somset 19 M5
Ashton Common Wilts 20 G3
Ashton Hill Wilts 20 H3
Ashton-in-Makerfield Wigan 82 C5
Ashton Keynes Wilts 33 K6
Ashton under Hill Worcs 47 J7
Ashton-under-Lyne Tamesd 83 K5
Ashton upon Mersey Traffd 82 G6
Ashurst Hants 13 P2
Ashurst Kent 25 M3
Ashurst Lancs 88 F9
Ashurst W Susx 24 E7
Ashurstwood W Susx 25 K3
Ash Vale Surrey 23 N4
Ashwater Devon 5 P2
Ashwell Herts 50 G3
Ashwell Rutlnd 73 M8
Ashwell Somset 19 L11
Ashwell End Herts 50 G2
Ashwellthorpe Norfk 64 G2
Ashwick Somset 20 B5
Ashwicken Norfk 75 P7
Ashwood Staffs 58 C7
Askam in Furness Cumb 94 E5
Askern Donc 91 P8
Askerswell Dorset 11 L6
Askett Bucks 35 M3
Askham Cumb 101 P6
Askham Notts 85 M6
Askham Bryan C York 98 B11
Askham Richard C York 98 A11
Asknish Ag & B 131 J9
Askrigg N York 96 D2
Askwith N York 97 J11
Aslackby Lincs 74 A4
Aslacton Norfk 64 H3
Aslockton Notts 73 J3
Asney Somset 19 N7
Aspall Suffk 64 H9
Aspatria Cumb 100 F2
Aspenden Herts 51 J5
Aspenshaw Derbys 83 M7
Asperton Lincs 74 E3
Aspley Staffs 70 E8
Aspley Guise C Beds 49 P7
Aspley Heath C Beds 49 P8
Aspley Heath Warwks 58 G10
Aspull Wigan 89 J9
Aspull Common Wigan 82 D5
Asselby E R Yk 92 B5
Asserby Lincs 87 N5
Asserby Turn Lincs 87 N5
Assington Suffk 52 F4
Assington Green Suffk 63 N10
Astbury Ches E 70 E2
Astcote Nhants 49 J4
Asterby Lincs 87 J5
Asterley Shrops 56 F3
Asterton Shrops 56 F6
Asthall Oxon 33 Q2
Asthall Leigh Oxon 34 B2
Astle Highld 162 G8
Astley Shrops 69 P11
Astley Warwks 59 M7
Astley Wigan 82 F4
Astley Worcs 57 P11
Astley Abbots Shrops 57 N5
Astley Bridge Bolton 89 L8
Astley Cross Worcs 57 Q11
Astley Green Wigan 82 F5
Aston Birm 58 G7
Aston Ches E 69 R5
Aston Ches W 82 C9
Aston Derbys 83 Q8
Aston Flints 81 L11
Aston Herefs 45 P2
Aston Herts 50 G6
Aston Oxon 34 B4
Aston Rothm 84 G3
Aston Shrops 57 Q6
Aston Shrops 69 P9
Aston Staffs 70 D6
Aston Staffs 70 F10
Aston Wokham 35 L8
Aston Wrekin 57 L3
Aston Abbotts Bucks 49 M10
Aston Botterell Shrops 57 L8
Aston-by-Stone Staffs 70 G8
Aston Cantlow Warwks 47 M2
Aston Clinton Bucks 35 N2
Aston Crews Herefs 46 C10
Aston Cross Gloucs 46 H8
Aston End Herts 50 G6
Aston-Eyre Shrops 57 M6
Aston Fields Worcs 58 E11
Aston Flamville Leics 59 Q6
Aston Heath Ches W 82 C9
Aston Ingham Herefs 46 C10
Aston juxta Mondrum Ches E 70 A3
Aston le Walls Nhants 48 E4
Aston Magna Gloucs 47 N7
Aston Munslow Shrops 57 J7
Aston on Clun Shrops 56 F8
Aston Pigott Shrops 56 E3
Aston Rogers Shrops 56 E3
Aston Rowant Oxon 35 K5
Aston Sandford Bucks 35 L3
Aston Somerville Worcs 47 K7
Aston-sub-Edge Gloucs 47 M6
Aston Tirrold Oxon 34 G7
Aston-upon-Trent Derbys 72 C5
Aston Upthorpe Oxon 34 G7
Astrop Nhants 48 F7
Astrope Herts 35 N2
Astwick C Beds 50 F3
Astwith Derbys 84 F8
Astwood M Keyn 49 Q5
Astwood Worcs 58 D11
Astwood Bank Worcs 47 K2
Astwood Crematorium Worcs 46 G3
Aswarby Lincs 73 R3
Aswardby Lincs 87 L6
Atcham Shrops 57 J3
Atch Lench Worcs 47 K4
Athelhampton Dorset 12 C6
Athelington Suffk 65 J7
Athelney Somset 19 K9
Athelstaneford E Loth 128 E4
Atherfield Green IoW 14 E11
Atherington Devon 17 K7
Atherington W Susx 24 B10
Atherstone Somset 19 L11
Atherstone Warwks 59 M5
Atherstone on Stour Warwks 47 P4
Atherton Wigan 82 E4
Atley Hill N York 103 Q10
Atlow Derbys 71 N5
Attadale Highld 154 B10
Attenborough Notts 72 E4
Atterby Lincs 86 C2
Attercliffe Sheff 84 E3
Atterley Shrops 57 L5
Atterton Leics 72 B11
Attleborough Norfk 64 E2
Attleborough Warwks 59 N6
Attlebridge Norfk 76 G8
Attleton Green Suffk 63 M10
Atwick E R Yk 99 P10
Atworth Wilts 32 G11
Auberrow Herefs 45 P5
Aubourn Lincs 86 B8
Auchbreck Moray 149 N2
Auchedly Abers 159 L11
Auchenblae Abers 143 N2
Auchenbowie Stirlg 133 M10
Auchencairn D & G 108 G10
Auchencairn D & G 109 L4
Auchencairn N Ayrs 121 K6
Auchencrow Border 129 M7
Auchendinny Mdloth 127 P5
Auchengray S Lans 126 H7
Auchenhalrig Moray 157 R5
Auchenheath S Lans 126 E9
Auchenhessnane D & G 115 R8
Auchenlochan Ag & B 124 B3
Auchenmade N Ayrs 125 K8
Auchenmalg D & G 106 H7
Auchentiber N Ayrs 125 K8
Auchindrain Ag & B 131 L7
Auchindrean Highld 161 K10
Auchininna Abers 158 G8
Auchinleck E Ayrs 115 L3
Auchinloch N Lans 126 B3
Auchinstarry N Lans 126 C2
Auchintore Highld 139 K3
Auchiries Abers 159 Q10
Auchlean Highld 148 F8
Auchlee Abers 151 M8
Auchleven Abers 150 G3
Auchlochan S Lans 126 E10
Auchlossan Abers 150 F7
Auchlyne Stirlg 132 G2
Auchmillan E Ayrs 115 K2
Auchmithie Angus 143 M9
Auchmuirbridge Fife 134 G7
Auchnacree Angus 142 H5
Auchnagatt Abers 159 M9
Auchnarrow Moray 149 N3
Auchnotteroch D & G 106 C5
Auchroisk Moray 157 Q7
Auchterarder P & K 133 Q5
Auchteraw Highld 147 K6
Auchterblair Highld 148 G3
Auchtercairn Highld 153 Q2
Auchterderran Fife 134 G8
Auchterhouse Angus 142 E10
Auchterless Abers 158 H9
Auchtermuchty Fife 134 G5
Auchterneed Highld 155 N6
Auchtertool Fife 134 G9
Auchtertyre Highld 145 P2
Auchtubh Stirlg 132 H3
Auckengill Highld 167 Q3
Auckley Donc 91 Q10
Audenshaw Tamesd 83 K5
Audlem Ches E 70 B6
Audley Staffs 70 D4
Audley End Essex 51 M3
Audley End Essex 52 D4
Audley End Suffk 64 B11
Audley End House & Gardens Essex 51 M3
Audmore Staffs 70 E10
Audnam Dudley 58 C7
Aughertree Cumb 101 J3
Aughton E R Yk 92 B3
Aughton Lancs 88 D9
Aughton Lancs 95 M7
Aughton Rothm 84 G3
Aughton Wilts 21 P3
Aughton Park Lancs 88 E9
Auldearn Highld 156 G6
Aulden Herefs 45 P4
Auldgirth D & G 109 K3
Auldhouse S Lans 125 Q7
Ault a' chruinn Highld 146 A3
Aultbea Highld 160 D9
Aultgrishin Highld 160 A9
Aultguish Inn Highld 155 L3
Ault Hucknall Derbys 84 G7
Aultmore Moray 158 B7
Aultnagoire Highld 147 N3
Aultnamain Inn Highld 162 F10
Aunby Lincs 73 Q8
Aunk Devon 9 P4
Aunsby Lincs 73 Q3
Aust S Glos 31 Q7
Austendike Lincs 74 E6
Austerfield Donc 85 L2
Austerlands Oldham 90 B9
Austhorpe Leeds 91 K4
Austonley Kirk 90 E9
Austrey Warwks 59 L3
Austwick N York 95 R7
Authorpe Lincs 87 L4
Authorpe Row Lincs 87 P6
Avebury Wilts 33 M11
Avebury Trusloe Wilts 33 L11
Aveley Thurr 37 N4
Avening Gloucs 32 G5
Averham Notts 85 N10
Aveton Gifford Devon 6 H9
Aviemore Highld 148 F5
Avington W Berk 34 C11
Avoch Highld 156 C6
Avon Hants 13 K5
Avonbridge Falk 126 G3
Avon Dassett Warwks 48 D4
Avonmouth Bristl 31 P9
Avonwick Devon 7 J7
Awbridge Hants 22 B10
Awkley S Glos 31 Q7
Awliscombe Devon 10 C4
Awre Gloucs 32 D3
Awsworth Notts 72 D2
Axborough Worcs 58 C9
Axbridge Somset 19 M4
Axford Hants 22 H6
Axford Wilts 33 P10
Axminster Devon 10 F5
Axmouth Devon 10 F6
Axton Flints 80 G8
Aycliffe Dur 103 Q6
Aydon Nthumb 112 F7
Aylburton Gloucs 32 B4
Ayle Nthumb 111 P11
Aylesbeare Devon 9 P6
Aylesbury Bucks 35 M2
Aylesby NE Lin 93 M9
Aylesford Kent 38 B10
Aylesham Kent 39 M11
Aylestone C Leic 72 F10
Aylestone Park C Leic 72 F10
Aylmerton Norfk 76 H4
Aylsham Norfk 76 H6
Aylton Herefs 46 C7
Aylworth Gloucs 47 M10
Aymestrey Herefs 56 G11
Aynho Nhants 48 F8
Ayot Green Herts 50 F8
Ayot St Lawrence Herts 50 E7
Ayot St Peter Herts 50 F7
Ayr S Ayrs 114 F3
Aysgarth N York 96 F3
Ayshford Devon 18 D11
Ayside Cumb 94 H4
Ayston Rutlnd 73 M10
Aythorpe Roding Essex 51 N7
Ayton Border 129 N7
Azerley N York 97 L6

B

Babbacombe Torbay 7 N5
Babbington Notts 72 D2
Babbinswood Shrops 69 K9
Babbs Green Herts 51 J7
Babcary Somset 19 Q9
Babel Carmth 44 A7
Babel Green Suffk 63 M11
Babell Flints 80 H10
Babeny Devon 8 G9
Bablock Hythe Oxon 34 D4
Babraham Cambs 62 H10
Babworth Notts 85 L4
Bachau IoA 78 G8
Bache Shrops 56 H8
Bacheldre Powys 56 C6

Bachelor's Bump - Bearley Cross 263

Bachelor's Bump E Susx 26 D9
Backaland Ork 169 e3
Backbarrow Cumb 94 H4
Backe Carmth 41 Q7
Backfolds Abers 159 P7
Backford Ches W 81 M10
Backford Cross Ches W 81 M10
Backies Highld 163 J6
Back of Keppoch Highld 145 L10
Back o' th' Brook Staffs 71 K4
Back Street Suffk 63 M9
Backwell N Som 31 N11
Backworth N Tyne 113 M6
Bacon's End Solhll 59 J7
Baconsthorpe Norfk 76 G4
Bacton Herefs 45 M8
Bacton Norfk 77 L5
Bacton Suffk 64 F8
Bacton Green Suffk 64 E8
Bacup Lancs 89 P6
Badachro Highld 153 P3
Badbury Swindn 33 N8
Badby Nhants 60 C9
Badcall Highld 164 E8
Badcall Highld 164 F5
Badcaul Highld 160 G8
Baddeley Edge C Stke 70 G4
Baddeley Green C Stke 70 G4
Baddesley Clinton Warwks 59 K10
Baddesley Ensor Warwks 59 L5
Baddidarrach Highld 160 H2
Baddinsgill Border 127 L7
Badenscoth Abers 158 G10
Badenyon Abers 149 Q4
Badgall Cnwll 5 L4
Badgeney Cambs 74 H11
Badger Shrops 57 P5
Badger's Cross Cnwll 2 D7
Badgers Mount Kent 37 L8
Badgeworth Gloucs 46 H11
Badgworth Somset 19 L4
Badharlick Cnwll 5 M4
Badicaul Highld 145 N2
Badingham Suffk 65 L8
Badlesmere Kent 38 H11
Badlieu Border 116 F7
Badlipster Highld 167 M7
Badluachrach Highld 160 F8
Badninish Highld 162 H8
Badrallach Highld 160 H8
Badsey Worcs 47 L6
Badshot Lea Surrey 23 N5
Badsworth Wakefd 91 M8
Badwell Ash Suffk 64 D8
Badwell Green Suffk 64 E8
Bagber Dorset 12 C2
Bagby N York 97 Q4
Bag Enderby Lincs 87 L6
Bagendon Gloucs 33 K3
Bagginswood Shrops 57 M8
Baggrow Cumb 100 G2
Bagh a Chaisteil W Isls 168 b18
Bagham Kent 39 J11
Bagh a Tuath W Isls 168 c17
Bagillt Flints 81 J9
Baginton Warwks 59 M10
Baglan Neath 29 K6
Bagley Leeds 90 G3
Bagley Shrops 69 M9
Bagley Somset 19 N5
Bagmore Hants 23 J6
Bagnall Staffs 70 G4
Bagnor W Berk 34 E11
Bagot Shrops 57 K10
Bagshot Surrey 23 P2
Bagshot Wilts 34 B11
Bagstone S Glos 32 C7
Bagthorpe Notts 84 G10
Bagworth Leics 72 C9
Bagwy Llydiart Herefs 45 N9
Baildon C Brad 90 F3
Baildon Green C Brad 90 E3
Baile Ailein W Isls 168 h5
Baile a Mhanaich W Isls 168 c12
Baile Mor Ag & B 136 H11
Bailey Green Hants 23 J9
Baileyhead Cumb 111 K5
Bailiff Bridge Calder 90 E5
Baillieston C Glas 126 B5
Bailrigg Lancs 95 K9
Bainbridge N York 96 D2
Bainshole Abers 158 F10
Bainton C Pete 74 A9
Bainton E R Yk 99 K10
Bainton Oxon 48 G9
Baintown Fife 135 K7
Bairnkine Border 118 C7
Baker's End Herts 51 J7
Baker Street Thurr 37 P4
Bakewell Derbys 84 B7
Bala Gwynd 68 B7
Balallan W Isls 168 h5
Balbeg Highld 155 M11
Balbeggie P & K 134 F2
Balblair Highld 155 P8
Balblair Highld 156 C4
Balby Donc 91 P10
Balcary D & G 108 H11
Balchraggan Highld 155 P9
Balchreick Highld 164 E4
Balcombe W Susx 24 H4
Balcombe Lane W Susx 24 H4
Balcomie Links Fife 135 Q6
Baldersby N York 97 N5
Baldersby St James N York 97 N5
Balderstone Lancs 89 J4
Balderstone Rochdl 89 Q8
Balderton Notts 85 P10
Baldhu Cnwll 3 K5
Baldinnie Fife 135 L5
Baldinnies P & K 134 C4
Baldock Herts 50 F4
Baldock Services Herts 50 F3
Baldovie C Dund 142 H11
Baldrine IoM 80 f5
Baldslow E Susx 26 D9
Baldwin IoM 80 e5
Baldwinholme Cumb 110 F10
Baldwin's Gate Staffs 70 D7
Baldwin's Hill W Susx 25 J3
Bale Norfk 76 E4
Baledgarno P & K 142 D11
Balemartine Ag & B 136 B7
Balerno C Edin 127 M4
Balfarg Fife 134 H7
Balfield Angus 143 J4
Balfour Ork 169 d5
Balfron Stirlg 132 G10
Balgaveny Abers 158 G9
Balgonar Fife 134 C9
Balgowan D & G 106 F9
Balgowan Highld 147 Q9
Balgown Highld 152 F4
Balgracie D & G 106 C5
Balgray S Lans 116 B6
Balham Gt Lon 36 G6
Balhary P & K 142 D8
Balholmie P & K 142 A10
Baligill Highld 166 E3
Balintore Angus 142 D6
Balintore Highld 156 F2
Balintraid Highld 156 C3
Balivanich W Isls 168 c12
Balk N York 97 Q4
Balkeerie Angus 142 E9
Balkholme E R Yk 92 C5
Ballabeg IoM 80 c7
Ballachulish Highld 139 K6
Ballafesson IoM 80 b7
Ballajora IoM 80 g3
Ballakilpheric IoM 80 b7
Ballamodha IoM 80 c7
Ballanlay Ag & B 124 C5
Ballantrae S Ayrs 114 A11
Ballards Gore Essex 38 F3
Ballards Green Warwks 59 L6
Ballasalla IoM 80 c7
Ballater Abers 150 B8
Ballaugh IoM 80 d3
Ballchraggan Highld 156 D2
Ballencrieff E Loth 128 D4
Ballevullin Ag & B 136 B6
Ball Green C Stke 70 F4
Ball Haye Green Staffs 70 H3
Ball Hill Hants 22 D2
Ballidon Derbys 71 N4
Balliekine N Ayrs 120 G4
Balliemore Ag & B 131 N8
Balligmorrie S Ayrs 114 D9
Ballimore Stirlg 132 G4
Ballindalloch Moray 157 M10
Ballindean P & K 134 H2
Ballingdon Suffk 52 E3
Ballinger Common Bucks 35 P4
Ballingham Herefs 46 A8
Ballingry Fife 134 F8
Ballinluig P & K 141 N7
Ballinshoe Angus 142 G7
Ballintuim P & K 141 R6
Balloch Highld 156 C8
Balloch N Lans 126 C3
Balloch P & K 133 N4
Balloch S Ayrs 114 F8
Balloch W Duns 132 D11
Balls Cross W Susx 23 Q9
Balls Green E Susx 25 L3
Ball's Green Gloucs 32 G5
Ballygown Ag & B 137 L7
Ballygrant Ag & B 122 E6
Ballyhaugh Ag & B 136 F4
Balmacara Highld 145 P2
Balmaclellan D & G 108 E5
Balmae D & G 108 E12
Balmaha Stirlg 132 E9
Balmalcolm Fife 135 J6
Balmangan D & G 108 D11
Balmedie Abers 151 P4
Balmer Heath Shrops 69 M8
Balmerino Fife 135 K3
Balmerlawn Hants 13 P4
Balmichael N Ayrs 120 H5
Balmoral Castle Grounds Abers 149 P9
Balmore E Duns 125 P3
Balmuchy Highld 163 K11
Balmule Fife 134 G10
Balmullo Fife 135 L3
Balnacoil Lodge Highld 163 J4
Balnacra Highld 154 C8
Balnacroft Abers 149 P9
Balnafoich Highld 156 B10
Balnaguard P & K 141 M7
Balnahard Ag & B 136 c2
Balnahard Ag & B 137 M9
Balnain Highld 155 M11
Balnakeil Highld 165 J3
Balne N York 91 P7
Balquharn P & K 141 P10
Balquhidder Stirlg 132 G3
Balsall Common Solhll 59 K9
Balsall Heath Birm 58 G8
Balsall Street Solhll 59 K9
Balscote Oxon 48 C6
Balsham Cambs 63 J10
Baltasound Shet 169 t3
Balterley Staffs 70 D4
Balterley Green Staffs 70 D4
Balterley Heath Staffs 70 C4
Baltersan D & G 107 M5
Baltonsborough Somset 19 P8
Balvicar Ag & B 130 F4
Balvraid Highld 145 P4
Balvraid Highld 156 E11
Balwest Cnwll 2 F7
Bamber Bridge Lancs 88 H5
Bamber's Green Essex 51 N6
Bamburgh Nthumb 119 N4
Bamburgh Castle Nthumb 119 N3
Bamford Derbys 84 B4
Bamford Rochdl 89 P8
Bampton Cumb 101 P7
Bampton Devon 18 C10
Bampton Oxon 34 B4
Bampton Grange Cumb 101 P7
Banavie Highld 139 L2
Banbury Oxon 48 E6
Banbury Crematorium Oxon 48 E6
Bancffosfelen Carmth 28 E2
Banchory Abers 150 H8
Banchory-Devenick Abers 151 N7
Bancycapel Carmth 28 D2
Bancyfelin Carmth 42 F11
Banc-y-ffordd Carmth 42 H7
Bandirran P & K 142 C11
Bandrake Head Cumb 94 G3
Banff Abers 158 G5
Bangor Gwynd 79 K10
Bangor Crematorium Gwynd 79 K10
Bangor-is-y-coed Wrexhm 69 L5
Bangors Cnwll 5 L2
Bangor's Green Lancs 88 D9
Bangrove Suffk 64 C7
Banham Norfk 64 F4
Bank Hants 13 N3
Bankend D & G 109 M7
Bankfoot P & K 141 Q10
Bankglen E Ayrs 115 L5
Bank Ground Cumb 101 K11
Bankhead C Aber 151 N6
Bankhead S Lans 116 D2
Bank Newton N York 96 D10
Banknock Falk 126 D2
Banks Cumb 111 L8
Banks Lancs 88 D6
Banks Green Worcs 58 E11
Bankshill D & G 110 C4
Bank Street Worcs 46 B2
Bank Top Calder 90 E6
Bank Top Lancs 88 G9
Banningham Norfk 77 J6
Bannister Green Essex 51 Q6
Bannockburn Stirlg 133 N9
Banstead Surrey 36 G9
Bantham Devon 6 H10
Banton N Lans 126 C2
Banwell N Som 19 L3
Bapchild Kent 38 F9
Bapton Wilts 21 J7
Barabhas W Isls 168 i3
Barassie S Ayrs 125 J11
Barbaraville Highld 156 C3
Barber Booth Derbys 83 P8
Barber Green Cumb 94 H4
Barbieston S Ayrs 114 H4
Barbon Cumb 95 N4
Barbridge Ches E 69 R3
Barbrook Devon 17 N2
Barby Nhants 60 B6
Barcaldine Ag & B 138 H9
Barcheston Warwks 47 Q7
Barclose Cumb 110 H8
Barcombe E Susx 25 K8
Barcombe Cross E Susx 25 K7
Barcroft C Brad 90 C3
Barden N York 96 H2
Barden Park Kent 37 N11
Bardfield End Green Essex 51 P4
Bardfield Saling Essex 51 Q5
Bardney Lincs 86 F7
Bardon Leics 72 C8
Bardon Mill Nthumb 111 Q8
Bardowie E Duns 125 P3
Bardown E Susx 25 Q5
Bardrainney Inver 125 J3
Bardsea Cumb 94 G6
Bardsey Leeds 91 K2
Bardsey Island Gwynd 66 A10
Bardsley Oldham 83 K4
Bardwell Suffk 64 C7
Bare Lancs 95 K8
Bareppa Cnwll 3 K8
Barfad D & G 107 K4
Barford Norfk 76 G10
Barford Warwks 47 Q2
Barford St John Oxon 48 D8
Barford St Martin Wilts 21 L8
Barford St Michael Oxon 48 D8
Barfrestone Kent 39 N11
Bargate Derbys 84 E11
Bargeddie N Lans 126 B5
Bargoed Caerph 30 G5
Bargrennan D & G 107 L2
Barham Cambs 61 P5
Barham Kent 39 M11
Barham Suffk 64 G11
Barham Crematorium Kent 27 M2
Bar Hill Cambs 62 E8
Barholm Lincs 74 A8
Barkby Leics 72 G9
Barkby Thorpe Leics 72 G9
Barkers Green Shrops 69 P9
Barkestone-le-Vale Leics 73 K4
Barkham Wokham 35 L11
Barking Gt Lon 37 K4
Barking Suffk 64 F11
Barkingside Gt Lon 37 K3
Barking Tye Suffk 64 F11
Barkisland Calder 90 D7
Barkla Shop Cnwll 3 J3
Barkston Lincs 73 N2
Barkston Ash N York 91 M3
Barkway Herts 51 J3
Barlanark C Glas 126 B5
Barlaston Staffs 70 F7
Barlavington W Susx 23 Q11
Barlborough Derbys 84 G5
Barlby N York 91 Q4
Barlestone Leics 72 C9
Barley Herts 51 K3
Barley Lancs 89 N2
Barleycroft End Herts 51 K5
Barley Hole Rothm 91 K11
Barleythorpe Rutlnd 73 L9
Barling Essex 38 F4
Barlings Lincs 86 E6
Barlochan D & G 108 H9
Barlow Derbys 84 D6
Barlow Gatesd 113 J8
Barlow N York 91 Q5
Barmby Moor E R Yk 98 F11
Barmby on the Marsh E R Yk 92 A5
Barmer Norfk 75 R4
Barming Heath Kent 38 B10
Barmollack Ag & B 120 F3
Barmouth Gwynd 67 L11
Barmpton Darltn 104 B7
Barmston E R Yk 99 P9
Barnaby Green Suffk 65 P5
Barnacarry Ag & B 131 L9
Barnack C Pete 74 A9
Barnacle Warwks 59 N8
Barnard Castle Dur 103 L7
Barnard Gate Oxon 34 D2
Barnardiston Suffk 63 M11
Barnbarroch D & G 108 H9
Barnburgh Donc 91 M10
Barnby Suffk 65 P4
Barnby Dun Donc 91 Q9
Barnby in the Willows Notts 85 Q10
Barnby Moor Notts 85 L4
Barncorkrie D & G 106 E10
Barnehurst Gt Lon 37 L5
Barnes Gt Lon 36 F5
Barnes Street Kent 37 P11
Barnet Gt Lon 50 F11
Barnetby le Wold N Linc 93 J9
Barnet Gate Gt Lon 50 F11
Barney Norfk 76 D5
Barnham Suffk 64 B6
Barnham W Susx 15 Q6
Barnham Broom Norfk 76 F10
Barnhead Angus 143 M6
Barnhill C Dund 142 H11
Barnhill Ches W 69 N4
Barnhill Moray 157 L6
Barnhills D & G 106 C3
Barningham Dur 103 L8
Barningham Suffk 64 D6
Barnoldby le Beck NE Lin 93 M10
Barnoldswick Lancs 96 C11
Barnsdale Bar Donc 91 N8
Barns Green W Susx 24 D5
Barnsley Barns 91 J9
Barnsley Gloucs 33 L4
Barnsley Crematorium Barns 91 K9
Barnsole Kent 39 N10
Barnstaple Devon 17 K5
Barnston Essex 51 P7
Barnston Wirral 81 K8
Barnstone Notts 73 J3
Barnt Green Worcs 58 F10
Barnton C Edin 127 M3
Barnton Ches W 82 D10
Barnwell All Saints Nhants 61 M4
Barnwell St Andrew Nhants 61 N4
Barnwood Gloucs 46 G11
Baron's Cross Herefs 45 P3
Baronwood Cumb 101 P2
Barr S Ayrs 114 E9
Barra W Isls 168 b17
Barra Airport W Isls 168 c17
Barrachan D & G 107 L8
Barraigh W Isls 168 b17
Barrapoll Ag & B 136 A7
Barras Cumb 102 F8
Barrasford Nthumb 112 D6
Barregarrow IoM 80 d4
Barrets Green Ches E 69 Q3
Barrhead E Rens 125 M6
Barrhill S Ayrs 114 D11
Barrington Cambs 62 E11
Barrington Somset 19 L11
Barripper Cnwll 2 G6
Barrmill N Ayrs 125 K7
Barrock Highld 167 N2
Barrow Gloucs 46 G10
Barrow Lancs 89 L3
Barrow Rutlnd 73 M7
Barrow Shrops 57 M4
Barrow Somset 20 D8
Barrow Suffk 63 N8
Barroway Drove Norfk 75 L10
Barrow Bridge Bolton 89 K8
Barrow Burn Nthumb 118 G8
Barrowby Lincs 73 M3
Barrowden Rutlnd 73 N10
Barrowford Lancs 89 P3
Barrow Gurney N Som 31 P11
Barrow Haven N Linc 93 J6
Barrow Hill Derbys 84 F5
Barrow-in-Furness Cumb 94 E7
Barrow Island Cumb 94 D7
Barrow Nook Lancs 81 N4
Barrow's Green Ches E 70 B3
Barrow Street Wilts 20 F8
Barrow-upon-Humber N Linc 93 J6
Barrow upon Soar Leics 72 F7
Barrow upon Trent Derbys 72 B5
Barrow Vale BaNES 20 B2
Barry Angus 143 J11
Barry V Glam 30 F11
Barry Island V Glam 30 F11
Barsby Leics 72 H8
Barsham Suffk 65 M4
Barston Solhll 59 K9
Bartestree Herefs 45 R6
Barthol Chapel Abers 159 K11
Bartholomew Green Essex 52 B7
Barthomley Ches E 70 D4
Bartley Hants 13 P2
Bartley Green Birm 58 F8
Bartlow Cambs 63 J11
Barton Cambs 62 F9
Barton Ches W 69 M4
Barton Gloucs 47 L9
Barton Herefs 45 K3
Barton Lancs 88 D9
Barton Lancs 88 G3
Barton N York 103 P9
Barton Oxon 34 G3
Barton Torbay 7 N5
Barton Warwks 47 M4
Barton Bendish Norfk 75 P9
Barton End Gloucs 32 F5
Barton Green Staffs 71 M11
Barton Hartshorn Bucks 48 H8
Barton Hill N York 98 E8
Barton in Fabis Notts 72 E4
Barton in the Beans Leics 72 B9
Barton-le-Clay C Beds 50 C4
Barton-le-Street N York 98 E6
Barton-le-Willows N York 98 E8
Barton Mills Suffk 63 M6
Barton-on-Sea Hants 13 M6
Barton-on-the-Heath Warwks 47 Q8
Barton St David Somset 19 P8
Barton Seagrave Nhants 61 J5
Barton Stacey Hants 22 D6
Barton Town Devon 17 M3
Barton Turf Norfk 77 M7
Barton-under-Needwood Staffs 71 M11
Barton-upon-Humber N Linc 92 H6
Barton upon Irwell Salfd 82 G5
Barton Waterside N Linc 92 H6
Barugh Barns 91 J9
Barugh Green Barns 91 J9
Barvas W Isls 168 i3
Barway Cambs 63 J5
Barwell Leics 72 C11
Barwick Devon 17 K10
Barwick Herts 51 J7
Barwick Somset 11 M2
Barwick in Elmet Leeds 91 L3
Baschurch Shrops 69 M10
Bascote Warwks 48 D2
Bascote Heath Warwks 48 C2
Base Green Suffk 64 E9
Basford Green Staffs 70 H4
Bashall Eaves Lancs 89 K2
Bashall Town Lancs 89 L2
Bashley Hants 13 M5
Basildon Essex 38 B4
Basildon & District Crematorium Essex 38 C4
Basingstoke Hants 22 H4
Basingstoke Crematorium Hants 22 G5
Baslow Derbys 84 C6
Bason Bridge Somset 19 K5
Bassaleg Newpt 31 J7
Bassendean Border 128 G10
Bassenthwaite Cumb 100 H4
Bassett C Sotn 22 D11
Bassingbourn Cambs 50 H2
Bassingfield Notts 72 G3
Bassingham Lincs 86 B9
Bassingthorpe Lincs 73 P5
Bassus Green Herts 50 H5
Basted Kent 37 P9
Baston Lincs 74 B8
Bastwick Norfk 77 N8
Batch Somset 19 K3
Batchworth Herts 36 C2
Batchworth Heath Herts 36 C2
Batcombe Dorset 11 N4
Batcombe Somset 20 C7
Bate Heath Ches E 82 E9
Batford Herts 50 D7
Bath BaNES 20 D2
Bathampton BaNES 32 E11
Bathealton Somset 18 E10
Batheaston BaNES 32 E11
Bathford BaNES 32 E11
Bathgate W Loth 126 H4
Bathley Notts 85 N9
Bathpool Cnwll 5 M7
Bathpool Somset 19 J9
Bath Side Essex 53 N5
Bathville W Loth 126 G4
Bathway Somset 19 Q4
Batley Kirk 90 G6
Batsford Gloucs 47 N8
Batson Devon 7 J11
Battersby N York 104 G9
Battersea Gt Lon 36 G5
Battisborough Cross Devon 6 F9
Battisford Suffk 64 F11
Battisford Tye Suffk 64 E11
Battle E Susx 26 C8
Battle Powys 44 E8
Battleborough Somset 19 K4
Battledown Gloucs 47 J10
Battledykes Angus 142 H6
Battlefield Shrops 69 P11
Battle of Britain Memorial Flight Visitor Centre Lincs 86 H9
Battlesbridge Essex 38 C3
Battlesden C Beds 49 Q9
Battleton Somset 18 B9
Battlies Green Suffk 64 C9
Battramsley Cross Hants 13 P5
Batt's Corner Hants 23 M6
Baughton Worcs 46 G6
Baughurst Hants 22 G2
Baulds Abers 150 G9
Baulking Oxon 34 B6
Baumber Lincs 86 H6
Baunton Gloucs 33 K4
Baveney Wood Shrops 57 M9
Baverstock Wilts 21 K8
Bawburgh Norfk 76 H10
Bawdeswell Norfk 76 E7
Bawdrip Somset 19 K7
Bawdsey Suffk 53 P3
Bawsey Norfk 75 N6
Bawtry Donc 85 K2
Baxenden Lancs 89 M5
Baxterley Warwks 59 L5
Baxter's Green Suffk 63 N9
Bay Highld 152 D7
Bayble W Isls 168 k4
Baybridge Hants 22 F10
Baybridge Nthumb 112 E10
Baycliff Cumb 94 F6
Baydon Wilts 33 Q9
Bayford Herts 50 H9
Bayford Somset 20 D9
Bayhead W Isls 168 c11
Bay Horse Lancs 95 K10
Bayley's Hill Kent 37 M10
Baylham Suffk 64 G11
Baynard's Green Oxon 48 F9
Baysdale Abbey N York 104 H9
Baysham Herefs 45 R9
Bayston Hill Shrops 56 H3
Baythorne End Essex 52 B3
Bayton Worcs 57 M10
Bayton Common Worcs 57 N10
Bayworth Oxon 34 E4
Beach S Glos 32 D10
Beachampton Bucks 49 L7
Beachamwell Norfk 75 Q9
Beachley Gloucs 31 Q6
Beachy Head E Susx 25 N11
Beacon Devon 10 D3
Beacon End Essex 52 G7
Beacon Hill E Susx 25 M4
Beacon Hill Kent 26 D5
Beacon Hill Notts 85 P10
Beacon Hill Surrey 23 N7
Beacon's Bottom Bucks 35 L5
Beaconsfield Bucks 35 P6
Beaconsfield Services Bucks 35 Q7
Beadlam N York 98 D4
Beadlow C Beds 50 D3
Beadnell Nthumb 119 P5
Beaford Devon 17 K8
Beal N York 91 N5
Beal Nthumb 119 L2
Bealbury Cnwll 5 P8
Bealsmill Cnwll 5 P6
Beam Hill Staffs 71 N9
Beamhurst Staffs 71 K7
Beaminster Dorset 11 K4
Beamish Dur 113 K10
Beamsley N York 96 G10
Bean Kent 37 N6
Beanacre Wilts 32 H11
Beanley Nthumb 119 L7
Beardon Devon 8 D8
Beardwood Bl w D 89 K5
Beare Devon 9 N4
Beare Green Surrey 24 E2
Bearley Warwks 47 N2
Bearley Cross Warwks 47 N2

Bearpark Dur 103 P2
Bearsden E Duns 125 N3
Bearsted Kent 38 D10
Bearstone Shrops 70 C7
Bearwood Birm 58 F7
Bearwood Herefs 45 M3
Bearwood Poole 12 H5
Beattock D & G 116 F10
Beauchamp Roding
Essex 51 N9
Beauchief Sheff 84 D4
Beaudesert Warwks 59 J11
Beaufort Blae G 30 G2
Beaulieu Hants 14 C6
Beaulieu Road Station
Hants 13 P3
Beauly Highld 155 P8
Beaumaris IoA 79 L9
Beaumont Cumb 110 F9
Beaumont Essex 53 L7
Beaumont Jersey 11 b2
Beaumont Hill Darltn 103 Q7
Beausale Warwks 59 K10
Beauworth Hants 22 G9
Beaworthy Devon 8 C5
Beazley End Essex 52 B6
Bebington Wirral 81 L8
Bebside Nthumb 113 L4
Beccles Suffk 65 N4
Becconsall Lancs 88 F6
Beckbury Shrops 57 P4
Beckenham Gt Lon 37 J7
Beckenham
Crematorium Gt Lon 37 J7
Beckermet Cumb 100 D9
Beckett End Norfk 75 Q11
Beckfoot Cumb 94 D3
Beckfoot Cumb 100 G10
Beck Foot Cumb 102 B11
Beckfoot Cumb 109 N11
Beckford Worcs 47 J7
Beckhampton Wilts 33 L11
Beck Hole N York 105 M10
Beckingham Lincs 85 Q10
Beckingham Notts 85 N3
Beckington Somset 20 F4
Beckjay Shrops 56 F9
Beckley E Susx 26 E7
Beckley Hants 13 M5
Beckley Oxon 34 G2
Beck Row Suffk 63 L5
Becks C Brad 96 F11
Beck Side Cumb 94 E4
Beck Side Cumb 94 H4
Beckton Gt Lon 37 K4
Beckwithshaw N York 97 L10
Becontree Gt Lon 37 L3
Becquet Vincent Jersey 11 b1
Bedale N York 97 L3
Bedburn Dur 103 L4
Bedchester Dorset 20 G11
Beddau Rhondd 30 E7
Beddgelert Gwynd 67 K5
Beddingham E Susx 25 K9
Beddington Gt Lon 36 H7
Beddington Corner
Gt Lon 36 G7
Bedfield Suffk 65 J8
Bedfield Little Green
Suffk 65 J8
Bedford Bed 61 M11
Bedford Crematorium
Bed 61 N10
Bedgebury Cross Kent 26 B5
Bedham W Susx 24 B6
Bedhampton Hants 15 K5
Bedingfield Suffk 64 H8
Bedingfield Green Suffk 64 H8
Bedlam N York 97 L8
Bedlington Nthumb 113 L4
Bedlinog Myr Td 30 E4
Bedminster Bristl 31 Q10
Bedminster Down Bristl 31 Q10
Bedmond Herts 50 C10
Bednall Staffs 70 H11
Bedrule Border 118 B7
Bedstone Shrops 56 F9
Bedwas Caerph 30 G7
Bedwellty Caerph 30 G4
Bedworth Warwks 59 N7
Bedworth Woodlands
Warwks 59 M7
Beeby Leics 72 H9
Beech Hants 23 J7
Beech Staffs 70 F7
Beech Hill W Berk 23 J2
Beechingstoke Wilts 21 L3
Beedon W Berk 34 E9
Beedon Hill W Berk 34 E9
Beeford E R Yk 99 N10
Beeley Derbys 84 C7
Beelsby NE Lin 93 M10
Beenham W Berk 34 G11
Beenham's Heath W & M 35 M9
Beeny Cnwll 5 J3
Beer Devon 10 E7
Beer Somset 19 M8
Beercrocombe Somset 19 K10
Beer Hackett Dorset 11 N2
Beesands Devon 7 L10
Beesby Lincs 87 N4
Beeson Devon 7 L10
Beeston C Beds 61 Q11
Beeston Ches W 69 P3
Beeston Leeds 90 H4
Beeston Norfk 76 C8
Beeston Notts 72 E3
Beeston Regis Norfk 76 H3
Beeswing D & G 109 J7
Beetham Cumb 95 K5
Beetham Somset 10 F2
Beetley Norfk 76 D8
Began Cardif 30 H8
Begbroke Oxon 34 E2
Begdale Cambs 75 J9
Begelly Pembks 41 M9
Beggarington Hill Leeds 90 H6
Beggar's Bush Powys 45 K2
Beguildy Powys 56 B9
Beighton Norfk 77 M10
Beighton Sheff 84 F4
Beinn Na Faoghla W Isls 168 d12
Beith N Ayrs 125 K7
Bekesbourne Kent 39 L10
Bekesbourne Hill Kent 39 L10
Belaugh Norfk 77 K8
Belbroughton Worcs 58 D9
Belchalwell Dorset 12 C3
Belchalwell Street
Dorset 12 C3

Belchamp Otten Essex 52 D3
Belchamp St Paul Essex 52 C3
Belchamp Walter Essex 52 D3
Belchford Lincs 87 J5
Belford Nthumb 119 M4
Belgrave C Leic 72 F9
Belhelvie Abers 151 N4
Belhinnie Abers 150 D2
Bellabeg Abers 150 B5
Bellamore Herefs 45 M6
Bellanoch Ag & B 130 F9
Bellasize E R Yk 92 D5
Bellaty Angus 142 C6
Bell Bar Herts 50 G9
Bell Busk N York 96 D9
Belleau Lincs 87 M5
Bellerby N York 96 H2
Bellever Devon 8 G9
Belle Vue Cumb 110 G9
Belle Vue Wakefd 91 J7
Bellfield S Lans 116 D6
Bellfield S Lans 126 E11
Bell Heath Worcs 58 D9
Bell Hill Hants 23 K10
Bellingdon Bucks 35 P3
Bellingham Nthumb 112 B4
Belloch Ag & B 120 C4
Bellochantuy Ag & B 120 C5
Bell o' th' Hill Ches W 69 P5
Bellows Cross Dorset 13 J2
Bells Cross Suffk 64 H11
Bellshill N Lans 126 C5
Bellshill Nthumb 119 M4
Bellside N Lans 126 E6
Bellsquarry W Loth 127 J4
Bells Yew Green E Susx 25 N3
Belluton BaNES 20 B2
Belmaduthy Highld 156 A6
Belmesthorpe Rutlnd 73 Q8
Belmont Bl w D 89 K7
Belmont Gt Lon 36 G8
Belmont S Ayrs 114 F4
Belmont Shet 169 s3
Belnacraig Abers 150 B4
Belowda Cnwll 4 D9
Belper Derbys 84 D11
Belper Lane End Derbys 84 D11
Belph Derbys 84 H5
Belsay Nthumb 112 G5
Belses Border 117 R5
Belsford Devon 7 K7
Belsize Herts 50 B10
Belstead Suffk 53 K3
Belstone Devon 8 F6
Belthorn Lancs 89 L6
Beltinge Kent 39 L8
Beltingham Nthumb 111 Q8
Beltoft N Linc 92 D9
Belton Leics 72 C6
Belton Lincs 73 N3
Belton N Linc 92 C9
Belton Norfk 77 P11
Belton Rutlnd 73 L10
Beltring Kent 37 Q11
Belvedere Gt Lon 37 L5
Belvoir Leics 73 L4
Belvoir Castle Leics 73 L4
Bembridge IoW 14 H9
Bemerton Wilts 21 M8
Bempton E R Yk 99 P6
Benacre Suffk 65 Q5
Benbecula Airport W Isls 168 c12
Benbecula W Isls 168 d12
Benbuie D & G 115 P8
Benderloch Ag & B 138 G10
Benenden Kent 26 D5
Benfieldside Dur 112 G10
Bengates Norfk 77 L6
Bengeo Herts 50 H8
Bengeworth Worcs 47 K6
Benhall Green Suffk 65 M9
Benhall Street Suffk 65 M9
Benholm Abers 143 Q4
Beningbrough N York 98 A9
Benington Herts 50 G6
Benington Lincs 87 L11
Benington Sea End Lincs 87 M11
Benllech IoA 79 J8
Benmore Ag & B 131 N10
Bennacott Cnwll 5 M3
Bennan N Ayrs 121 J7
Bennet Head Cumb 101 M6
Bennetland E R Yk 92 D5
Bennett End Bucks 35 L5
Ben Nevis Highld 139 M3
Benniworth Lincs 86 H4
Benover Kent 26 B2
Ben Rhydding C Brad 96 H11
Benslie N Ayrs 125 J9
Benson Oxon 34 H6
Bentfield Green Essex 51 M5
Benthall Shrops 57 M4
Benthoul C Aber 151 L7
Bentlawn Shrops 56 E4
Bentley Donc 91 P9
Bentley E R Yk 92 H3
Bentley Hants 23 L6
Bentley Suffk 53 K4
Bentley Warwks 59 L5
Bentley Crematorium
Essex 51 N11
Bentley Heath Herts 50 G11
Bentley Heath Solhll 59 J9
Benton Devon 17 M4
Bentpath D & G 110 F2
Bentwichen Devon 17 N5
Bentworth Hants 23 J6
Benvie Angus 142 K11
Benville Dorset 11 L4
Benwick Cambs 62 D2
Beoley Worcs 58 G11
Beoraidbeg Highld 145 L9
Bepton W Susx 23 N11
Berden Essex 51 L5
Berea Pembks 40 E4
Bere Alston Devon 6 C5
Bere Ferrers Devon 6 D6
Berepper Cnwll 2 H9
Bere Regis Dorset 12 D6
Bergh Apton Norfk 77 L11
Berhill Somset 19 M7
Berinsfield Oxon 34 G5
Berkeley Gloucs 32 C5
Berkeley Heath Gloucs 32 C5
Berkeley Road Gloucs 32 D4
Berkhamsted Herts 35 Q3
Berkley Somset 20 F5

Berkswell Solhll 59 K9
Bermondsey Gt Lon 36 H5
Bermuda Warwks 59 N7
Bernera Highld 145 P3
Bernisdale Highld 152 G7
Berrick Prior Oxon 34 H6
Berrick Salome Oxon 34 H6
Berriedale Highld 163 Q2
Berrier Cumb 101 L5
Berriew Powys 56 B4
Berrington Nthumb 119 K2
Berrington Shrops 57 J3
Berrington Worcs 57 K11
Berrington Green Worcs 57 K11
Berrow Somset 19 J4
Berrow Worcs 46 E8
Berrow Green Worcs 46 E3
Berry Brow Kirk 90 E8
Berry Cross Devon 16 H9
Berry Down Cross Devon 17 K3
Berry Hill Gloucs 31 Q2
Berry Hill Pembks 41 L2
Berryhillock Moray 158 D5
Berryhillock Moray 158 D7
Berrynarbor Devon 17 K2
Berry Pomeroy Devon 7 L6
Berry's Green Gt Lon 37 K9
Bersham Wrexhm 69 K5
Berthengam Flints 80 G9
Berwick E Susx 25 M9
Berwick Bassett Wilts 33 L10
Berwick Hill Nthumb 113 J5
Berwick St James Wilts 21 L7
Berwick St John Wilts 20 H10
Berwick St Leonard Wilts 20 H8
Berwick-upon-Tweed
Nthumb 129 P9
Bescaby Leics 73 L5
Bescar Lancs 88 D8
Besford Shrops 69 Q9
Besford Worcs 46 H6
Bessacarr Donc 91 Q10
Bessels Leigh Oxon 34 E4
Besses o' th' Barn Bury 89 N9
Bessingby E R Yk 99 P7
Bessingham Norfk 76 H4
Bestbeech Hill E Susx 25 P4
Besthorpe Norfk 64 F2
Besthorpe Notts 85 P8
Bestwood Village Notts 85 J11
Beswick E R Yk 99 L11
Betchcott Shrops 56 G5
Betchworth Surrey 36 F10
Bethania Cerdgn 43 L2
Bethania Gwynd 67 N6
Bethel Gwynd 68 C7
Bethel Gwynd 79 J11
Bethel IoA 78 F10
Bethel Powys 68 F10
Bethersden Kent 26 F3
Bethesda Gwynd 79 L11
Bethesda Pembks 41 L7
Bethlehem Carmth 43 N9
Bethnal Green Gt Lon 36 H4
Betley Staffs 70 D5
Betsham Kent 37 P6
Betteshanger Kent 39 P11
Bettiscombe Dorset 10 H4
Bettisfield Wrexhm 69 N7
Betton Shrops 70 B7
Betton Strange Shrops 57 J3
Bettws Newpt 31 J6
Bettws Bledrws Cerdgn 43 L4
Bettws Cedewain Powys 55 Q5
Bettws Evan Cerdgn 42 F5
Bettws-Newydd Mons 31 L3
Bettyhill Highld 166 B4
Betws Brdgnd 29 N7
Betws Carmth 28 H2
Betws Garmon Gwynd 67 J3
Betws Gwerfil Goch
Denbgs 68 D5
Betws-y-Coed Conwy 67 P3
Betws-yn-Rhos Conwy 80 C10
Beulah Cerdgn 42 E5
Beulah Powys 44 C4
Bevendean Br & H 24 H9
Bevercotes Notts 85 L6
Beverley E R Yk 92 H3
Beverston Gloucs 32 G6
Bevington Gloucs 32 C4
Bewaldeth Cumb 100 H4
Bewcastle Cumb 111 L6
Bewdley Worcs 57 P9
Bewerley N York 97 J7
Bewholme E R Yk 99 P11
Bewlbridge Kent 25 Q4
Bexhill E Susx 26 B10
Bexley Gt Lon 37 L5
Bexleyheath Gt Lon 37 L5
Bexleyhill W Susx 23 P9
Bexon Kent 38 E10
Bexwell Norfk 75 M10
Beyton Suffk 64 C9
Beyton Green Suffk 64 C9
Bhaltos W Isls 168 f4
Bhatarsaigh W Isls 168 b18
Bibstone S Glos 32 C6
Bibury Gloucs 33 M3
Bicester Oxon 48 G10
Bickenhill Solhll 59 J8
Bicker Lincs 74 D3
Bicker Bar Lincs 74 D3
Bicker Gauntlet Lincs 74 D3
Bickershaw Wigan 82 D4
Bickerstaffe Lancs 81 N4
Bickerton Ches E 69 P4
Bickerton Devon 7 L11
Bickerton N York 97 Q10
Bickerton Nthumb 119 J10
Bickford Staffs 58 C2
Bickington Devon 7 L4
Bickington Devon 17 J3
Bickleigh Devon 6 E6
Bickleigh Devon 9 M3
Bickleton Devon 17 J5
Bickley Ches W 69 P5
Bickley Gt Lon 37 K6
Bickley N York 99 J2
Bickley Worcs 57 N9
Bickley Moss Ches W 69 P5
Bicknacre Essex 52 C11
Bicknoller Somset 18 F7
Bicknor Kent 38 E10
Bickton Hants 13 K2
Bicton Herefs 45 P2
Bicton Shrops 56 D8
Bicton Shrops 69 M11
Bidborough Kent 25 N2
Bidden Hants 23 K5

Biddenden Kent 26 E4
Biddenden Green Kent 26 E3
Biddenham Bed 61 M10
Biddestone Wilts 32 G10
Biddisham Somset 19 L4
Biddlesden Bucks 48 H7
Biddlestone Nthumb 119 J9
Biddulph Staffs 70 F3
Biddulph Moor Staffs 70 G3
Bideford Devon 16 H6
Bidford-on-Avon Warwks 47 M4
Bidston Wirral 81 K6
Bielby E R Yk 92 C2
Bieldside C Aber 151 M7
Bierley IoW 14 F11
Bierton Bucks 49 M11
Big Balcraig D & G 107 L8
Bigbury Devon 6 H9
Bigbury-on-Sea Devon 6 H10
Bigby Lincs 93 J9
Big Carlae D & G 115 N8
Biggar Cumb 94 D7
Biggar S Lans 116 E3
Biggin Derbys 71 M3
Biggin Derbys 71 P5
Biggin N York 91 N4
Biggin Hill Gt Lon 37 K9
Biggin Hill Airport Gt Lon 37 K8
Biggleswade C Beds 50 E2
Bigholms D & G 110 F3
Bighouse Highld 166 E4
Bighton Hants 22 H8
Biglands Cumb 110 E10
Bignor W Susx 15 Q4
Big Pit Blaenavon (WHS)
Torfn 30 H4
Bigrigg Cumb 100 D8
Big Sand Highld 160 B11
Bigton Shet 169 q11
Bilborough C Nott 72 E2
Bilbrook Somset 18 D6
Bilbrook Staffs 58 C4
Bilbrough N York 98 A11
Bilbster Highld 167 N6
Bildershaw Dur 103 P6
Bildeston Suffk 52 G2
Billacott Cnwll 5 M3
Billericay Essex 37 Q2
Billesdon Leics 73 J10
Billesley Warwks 47 M3
Billingborough Lincs 74 B4
Billinge St Hel 82 B4
Billingford Norfk 64 H6
Billingford Norfk 76 E7
Billingham S on T 104 E6
Billinghay Lincs 86 G10
Billingley Barns 91 L10
Billingshurst W Susx 24 C5
Billingsley Shrops 57 N8
Billington C Beds 49 P10
Billington Lancs 89 L3
Billington Staffs 70 F10
Billockby Norfk 77 N9
Billy Row Dur 103 N3
Bilsborrow Lancs 88 G3
Bilsby Lincs 87 N5
Bilsham W Susx 15 Q6
Bilsington Kent 26 H5
Bilsthorpe Notts 85 L8
Bilsthorpe Moor Notts 85 L8
Bilston Mdloth 127 P5
Bilston Wolves 58 E5
Bilstone Leics 72 B9
Bilting Kent 27 J2
Bilton E R Yk 93 L4
Bilton N York 97 M9
Bilton N York 97 Q11
Bilton Nthumb 119 P8
Bilton Warwks 59 Q10
Bilton Banks Nthumb 119 P8
Binbrook Lincs 86 H2
Binchester Blocks Dur 103 P4
Bincombe Dorset 11 P8
Binegar Somset 20 B5
Bines Green W Susx 24 E7
Binfield Br For 35 M10
Binfield Heath Oxon 35 K9
Bingfield Nthumb 112 E6
Bingham Notts 73 J2
Bingham's Melcombe
Dorset 12 C4
Bingley C Brad 90 E3
Bings Shrops 69 P11
Binham Norfk 76 D4
Binley Covtry 59 N9
Binley Hants 22 D4
Binley Woods Warwks 59 N9
Binnegar Dorset 12 E7
Binniehill Falk 126 F3
Binscombe Surrey 23 Q6
Binsey Oxon 34 E3
Binstead IoW 14 G8
Binsted Hants 23 L6
Binsted W Susx 15 Q5
Binton Warwks 47 M4
Bintree Norfk 76 E7
Binweston Shrops 56 E4
Birch Essex 52 F8
Birch Rochdl 89 P9
Bircham Newton Norfk 75 Q4
Bircham Tofts Norfk 75 Q4
Birchanger Essex 51 M6
Birchanger Green
Services Essex 51 M6
Birch Cross Staffs 71 L8
Birchencliffe Kirk 90 E7
Birchendale Herefs 56 H11
Bircher Herefs 45 P2
Birchfield Birm 58 G6
Birch Green Essex 52 F8
Birch Green Herts 50 G8
Birch Green Worcs 46 G5
Birchgrove Cardif 30 G9
Birchgrove Swans 29 K5
Birchgrove W Susx 25 K5
Birch Heath Ches W 69 P2
Birch Hill Ches W 81 Q10
Birchington Kent 39 P8
Birchley Heath Warwks 59 L6
Birchmoor Warwks 59 L4
Birchmoor Green C Beds 49 Q8
Birchover Derbys 84 B8
Birch Services Rochdl 89 N9
Birch Vale Derbys 83 M7
Birchwood Lincs 86 B7
Birchwood Somset 10 E2
Birchwood Warrtn 82 E6
Bircotes Notts 85 K2
Birdbrook Essex 52 B3
Birdforth N York 97 Q5
Birdham W Susx 15 M6

Birdingbury Warwks 59 P11
Birdlip Gloucs 32 H2
Birdoswald Cumb 111 M7
Birdsall N York 98 G5
Birds Edge Kirk 90 G4
Birds Green Essex 51 N9
Birdsgreen Shrops 57 P7
Birdsmoorgate Dorset 10 H4
Bird Street Suffk 64 E11
Birdwell Barns 91 J10
Birdwood Gloucs 46 D11
Birgham Border 118 E3
Birichin Highld 162 H9
Birkacre Lancs 88 H8
Birkby N York 104 B10
Birkdale Sefton 88 C8
Birkenbog Abers 158 C4
Birkenhead Wirral 81 L7
Birkenhills Abers 158 H8
Birkenshaw Kirk 90 G5
Birkhall Abers 149 Q9
Birkhill Angus 142 F11
Birkhill D & G 117 J7
Birkholme Lincs 73 P6
Birkin N York 91 N5
Birks Leeds 90 H5
Birkshaw Nthumb 111 Q7
Birley Herefs 45 P4
Birley Carr Sheff 84 D2
Birling Kent 37 Q8
Birling Nthumb 119 P9
Birling Gap E Susx 25 N11
Birlingham Worcs 46 H6
Birmingham Birm 58 G7
Birmingham Airport
Solhll 59 J8
Birnam P & K 141 P9
Birness Abers 159 N11
Birse Abers 150 E8
Birsemore Abers 150 E8
Birstall Kirk 90 G5
Birstall Leics 72 F9
Birstwith N York 97 K9
Birthorpe Lincs 74 B4
Birtley Gatesd 113 L9
Birtley Herefs 56 F11
Birtley Nthumb 112 C5
Birtley Crematorium
Gatesd 113 L9
Birts Street Worcs 46 E7
Bisbrooke Rutlnd 73 M11
Biscathorpe Lincs 86 H4
Biscovey Cnwll 3 R3
Bisham W & M 35 M7
Bishampton Worcs 47 J4
Bish Mill Devon 17 N6
Bishop Auckland Dur 103 P4
Bishopbridge Lincs 86 D2
Bishopbriggs E Duns 125 N4
Bishop Burton E R Yk 92 G3
Bishop Middleham Dur 104 B4
Bishopmill Moray 157 N5
Bishop Monkton N York 97 M7
Bishop Norton Lincs 86 C2
Bishopsbourne Kent 39 L11
Bishops Cannings Wilts 21 K2
Bishop's Castle Shrops 56 E7
Bishop's Caundle Dorset 11 P2
Bishop's Cleeve Gloucs 47 J9
Bishop's Frome Herefs 46 C5
Bishops Gate Surrey 35 Q10
Bishop's Green Essex 51 P7
Bishop's Green Hants 22 F2
Bishops Hull Somset 18 H10
Bishop's Itchington
Warwks 48 C3
Bishops Lydeard Somset 18 G9
Bishop's Norton Gloucs 46 F10
Bishop's Nympton
Devon 17 P7
Bishop's Offley Staffs 70 D9
Bishop's Stortford Herts 51 L6
Bishop's Sutton Hants 22 H8
Bishop's Tachbrook
Warwks 48 B2
Bishop's Tawton Devon 17 K6
Bishopsteignton Devon 7 P3
Bishopstoke Hants 22 E11
Bishopston Swans 28 G7
Bishopstone Bucks 35 M2
Bishopstone E Susx 25 L10
Bishopstone Herefs 45 N6
Bishopstone Kent 39 M8
Bishopstone Swindn 33 N3
Bishopstone Wilts 21 L9
Bishopstrow Wilts 20 G6
Bishop Sutton BaNES 19 Q3
Bishop's Waltham Hants 22 G11
Bishopswood Somset 10 F2
Bishop's Wood Staffs 58 B3
Bishopsworth Bristl 31 Q11
Bishop Thornton N York 97 L8
Bishopthorpe C York 98 B11
Bishopton Darltn 104 C6
Bishopton Rens 125 L3
Bishopton Warwks 47 N3
Bishop Wilton E R Yk 98 F9
Bishton Newpt 31 L7
Bishton Staffs 71 J10
Bisley Gloucs 32 H3
Bisley Surrey 23 Q3
Bisley Camp Surrey 23 P3
Bispham Bpool 88 C2
Bispham Green Lancs 88 F8
Bissoe Cnwll 3 K5
Bisterne Hants 13 L4
Bitchet Green Kent 37 N10
Bitchfield Lincs 73 P5
Bittadon Devon 17 J3
Bittering Norfk 76 C8
Bitterley Shrops 57 K9
Bitterne C Sotn 14 E4
Bitteswell Leics 60 B3
Bitton S Glos 32 C11
Bix Oxon 35 K8
Bixter Shet 169 Q8
Blaby Leics 72 F11
Blackadder Border 129 J9
Blackawton Devon 7 L8
Blackbeck Cumb 100 D9
Blackborough Devon 10 D3
Blackborough End Norfk 75 N7
Black Bourton Oxon 33 Q4
Blackboys E Susx 25 M6
Blackbrook Derbys 84 D11
Blackbrook St Hel 82 B5
Blackbrook Staffs 70 D7
Blackbrook Surrey 36 E11
Blackburn Abers 151 L5

Blackburn - Boyton Cross 265

Blackburn Bl w D 89 K5
Blackburn Rothm 84 E2
Blackburn W Loth 126 H4
Blackburn with Darwen Services Bl w D 89 K6
Black Callerton N u Ty 113 J7
Black Car Norfk 64 F2
Black Corner W Susx 24 G3
Blackcraig E Ayrs 115 M6
Black Crofts Ag & B 138 G11
Black Cross Cnwll 4 E9
Blackden Heath Ches E 82 G10
Blackdog Abers 151 P5
Black Dog Devon 9 K3
Blackdown Devon 8 D9
Blackdown Dorset 10 H4
Blackdyke Cumb 109 P10
Blacker Barns 91 J9
Blacker Hill Barns 91 K10
Blackfen Gt Lon 37 L6
Blackfield Hants 14 D6
Blackford Cumb 110 G8
Blackford P & K 133 P6
Blackford Somset 19 M5
Blackford Somset 20 C9
Blackfordby Leics 72 A7
Blackgang IoW 14 E11
Blackhall C Edin 127 M2
Blackhall Dur 104 E3
Blackhall Colliery Dur 104 E3
Blackhall Mill Gatesd 112 H9
Blackhaugh Border 117 N3
Blackheath Essex 52 H7
Blackheath Gt Lon 37 J5
Blackheath Sandw 58 E7
Blackheath Suffk 65 N7
Blackheath Surrey 36 B11
Black Heddon Nthumb 112 G5
Blackhill Abers 159 Q6
Blackhill Abers 159 Q9
Blackhill Dur 112 G10
Blackhill of Clackriach Abers 159 M8
Blackhorse Devon 9 N6
Blackjack Lincs 74 E3
Blackland Wilts 33 K11
Black Lane Ends Lancs 89 Q2
Blacklaw D & G 116 E9
Blackley Manch 83 J4
Blackley Crematorium Manch 82 H4
Blacklunans P & K 142 A5
Blackmarstone Herefs 45 Q7
Blackmill Brdgnd 29 P7
Blackmoor Hants 23 L8
Black Moor Leeds 90 H3
Blackmoor N Som 19 N2
Blackmoorfoot Kirk 90 D8
Blackmore Essex 51 P10
Blackmore End Essex 52 B5
Blackmore End Herts 50 E7
Blackness Falk 127 K2
Blacknest Hants 23 L6
Blacknest W & M 35 Q11
Black Notley Essex 52 C7
Blacko Lancs 89 P2
Black Pill Swans 28 H6
Blackpool Bpool 88 C3
Blackpool Devon 5 L4
Blackpool Devon 7 M9
Blackpool Airport Lancs 88 C4
Blackpool Gate Cumb 111 K5
Blackridge W Loth 126 F4
Blackrock Cnwll 2 H7
Blackrock Mons 30 H2
Blackrod Bolton 89 J8
Blacksboat Moray 157 M10
Blackshaw D & G 109 M7
Blackshaw Head Calder 90 B5
Blacksmith's Green Suffk 64 G8
Blacksnape Bl w D 89 L6
Blackstone W Susx 24 F7
Black Street Suffk 65 Q4
Black Tar Pembks 41 J9
Blackthorn Oxon 48 H11
Blackthorpe Suffk 64 C9
Blacktoft E R Yk 92 D6
Blacktop C Aber 151 M7
Black Torrington Devon 8 C3
Blackwall Derbys 71 P5
Blackwater Cnwll 3 J4
Blackwater Hants 23 M3
Blackwater IoW 14 F9
Blackwater Somset 19 J11
Blackwaterfoot N Ayrs 120 H6
Blackwell Cumb 110 H10
Blackwell Darltn 103 Q8
Blackwell Derbys 83 P10
Blackwell Derbys 84 F9
Blackwell Warwks 47 P6
Blackwell Worcs 58 E10
Blackwellsend Green Gloucs 46 E9
Blackwood Caerph 30 G5
Blackwood D & G 109 K3
Blackwood S Lans 126 D9
Blackwood Hill Staffs 70 G3
Blacon Ches W 81 M11
Bladbean Kent 27 L2
Bladnoch D & G 107 M7
Bladon Oxon 34 E2
Bladon Somset 19 M10
Blaenannerch Cerdgn 42 D5
Blaenau Ffestiniog Gwynd 67 N5
Blaenavon Torfn 31 J3
Blaen Dyryn Powys 44 C7
Blaenffos Pembks 41 N3
Blaengarw Brdgnd 29 P6
Blaengeuffordd Cerdgn 54 E8
Blaengwrach Neath 29 N3
Blaengwynfi Neath 29 N5
Blaenllechau Rhondd 30 D5
Blaenpennal Cerdgn 43 M2
Blaenplwyf Cerdgn 54 D9
Blaenporth Cerdgn 42 E5
Blaenrhondda Rhondd 29 P5
Blaenwaun Carmth 41 P5
Blaen-y-Coed Carmth 42 F9
Blaen-y-cwm Blae G 30 F2
Blaenycwm Cerdgn 55 J9
Blaen-y-cwm Rhondd 29 P5
Blagdon N Som 19 P3
Blagdon Somset 18 H11
Blagdon Torbay 7 M6
Blagdon Hill Somset 18 H11
Blagill Cumb 111 P11
Blaguegate Lancs 88 F9
Blaich Highld 139 J2
Blain Highld 138 B4
Blaina Blae G 30 H3
Blair Atholl P & K 141 L4
Blair Drummond Stirlg 133 L8
Blairgowrie P & K 142 B8
Blairhall Fife 134 B10
Blairingone P & K 134 B8
Blairlogie Stirlg 133 N8
Blairmore Ag & B 131 P11
Blairmore Highld 164 E5
Blair's Ferry Ag & B 124 B4
Blaisdon Gloucs 46 D11
Blakebrook Worcs 57 Q9
Blakedown Worcs 58 C9
Blake End Essex 52 B7
Blakeley Lane Staffs 70 H5
Blakemere Ches W 82 C10
Blakemere Herefs 45 M6
Blakemore Devon 7 K6
Blakenall Heath Wsall 58 F4
Blakeney Gloucs 32 C3
Blakeney Norfk 76 E3
Blakenhall Ches E 70 C5
Blakenhall Wolves 58 D5
Blakeshall Worcs 58 B8
Blakesley Nhants 48 H4
Blanchland Nthumb 112 E10
Blandford Camp Dorset 12 F3
Blandford Forum Dorset 12 E3
Blandford St Mary Dorset 12 E3
Bland Hill N York 97 K10
Blanefield Stirlg 125 N2
Blankney Lincs 86 E8
Blantyre S Lans 126 B6
Blar a' Chaorainn Highld 139 L4
Blargie Highld 147 Q9
Blarmachfoldach Highld 139 K4
Blashford Hants 13 L3
Blaston Leics 73 L11
Blatherwycke Nhants 73 P11
Blawith Cumb 94 F3
Blawquhairn D & G 108 D4
Blaxhall Suffk 65 M10
Blaxton Donc 91 R10
Blaydon Gatesd 113 J8
Bleadney Somset 19 N5
Bleadon N Som 19 K3
Bleak Street Somset 20 E8
Blean Kent 39 K9
Bleasby Lincs 86 F4
Bleasby Notts 85 M11
Bleasdale Lancs 95 M11
Bleatarn Cumb 102 D8
Bleathwood Herefs 57 K10
Blebocraigs Fife 135 L4
Bleddfa Powys 56 C11
Bledington Gloucs 47 P10
Bledlow Bucks 35 L4
Bledlow Ridge Bucks 35 L5
Bleet Wilts 20 G3
Blegbie E Loth 128 D7
Blencarn Cumb 102 B4
Blencogo Cumb 110 C11
Blendworth Hants 15 K4
Blennerhasset Cumb 100 G2
Bletchingdon Oxon 48 F11
Bletchingley Surrey 36 H10
Bletchley M Keyn 49 N8
Bletchley Shrops 69 R8
Bletherston Pembks 41 L6
Bletsoe Bed 61 M9
Blewbury Oxon 34 F7
Blickling Norfk 76 H6
Blidworth Notts 85 J9
Blidworth Bottoms Notts 85 J10
Blindburn Nthumb 118 F8
Blindcrake Cumb 100 F4
Blindley Heath Surrey 37 J11
Blisland Cnwll 5 J7
Blissford Hants 13 L2
Bliss Gate Worcs 57 N10
Blisworth Nhants 49 K4
Blithbury Staffs 71 K11
Blitterlees Cumb 109 P10
Blockley Gloucs 47 N8
Blofield Norfk 77 L10
Blofield Heath Norfk 77 L9
Blo Norton Norfk 64 E6
Bloomfield Border 118 A6
Blore Staffs 70 C8
Blore Staffs 71 L5
Blounce Hants 23 K5
Blounts Green Staffs 71 K8
Blowick Sefton 88 D7
Bloxham Oxon 48 D7
Bloxholm Lincs 86 E10
Bloxwich Wsall 58 E4
Bloxworth Dorset 12 E6
Blubberhouses N York 97 J9
Blue Anchor Cnwll 4 E10
Blue Anchor Somset 18 D6
Blue Bell Hill Kent 38 B9
Blue John Cavern Derbys 83 P8
Blundellsands Sefton 81 L5
Blundeston Suffk 65 Q2
Blunham C Beds 61 Q10
Blunsdon St Andrew Swindn 33 M7
Bluntington Worcs 58 D10
Bluntisham Cambs 62 E6
Blunts Cnwll 5 N9
Blunts Green Warwks 58 H11
Blurton C Stke 70 F6
Blyborough Lincs 86 B2
Blyford Suffk 65 N6
Blymhill Staffs 57 Q2
Blymhill Lawn Staffs 57 Q2
Blyth Notts 85 K3
Blyth Nthumb 113 M4
Blyth Bridge Border 127 L8
Blythburgh Suffk 65 N6
Blyth Crematorium Nthumb 113 M4
Blythe Border 128 F10
Blythe Bridge Staffs 70 H6
Blythe End Warwks 59 K6
Blythe Marsh Staffs 70 H6
Blyton Lincs 85 Q2
Boarhills Fife 135 P5
Boarhunt Hants 14 H5
Boarley Kent 38 C10
Boarsgreave Lancs 89 N6
Boarshead E Susx 25 M4
Boar's Head Wigan 88 H9
Boars Hill Oxon 34 E4
Boarstall Bucks 34 H2
Boasley Cross Devon 8 D6
Boath Highld 155 Q3
Boat of Garten Highld 148 G4
Bobbing Kent 38 E8
Bobbington Staffs 57 Q6
Bobbingworth Essex 51 M9
Bocaddon Cnwll 5 K10
Bocking Essex 52 C7
Bocking Churchstreet Essex 52 C6
Bockleton Worcs 46 A2
Boconnoc Cnwll 5 J9
Boddam Abers 159 R9
Boddam Shet 169 q12
Boddington Gloucs 46 G9
Bodedern IoA 78 E8
Bodelwyddan Denbgs 80 E9
Bodenham Herefs 45 Q4
Bodenham Wilts 21 N9
Bodenham Moor Herefs 45 Q4
Bodewryd IoA 78 G6
Bodfari Denbgs 80 F10
Bodffordd IoA 78 G9
Bodfuan Gwynd 66 E7
Bodham Norfk 76 G3
Bodiam E Susx 26 C6
Bodiam Castle E Susx 26 C6
Bodicote Oxon 48 E7
Bodieve Cnwll 4 F7
Bodinnick Cnwll 5 J11
Bodle Street Green E Susx 25 Q8
Bodmin Cnwll 4 H8
Bodmin Moor Cnwll 5 K6
Bodnant Garden NT Conwy 79 Q10
Bodney Norfk 64 A2
Bodorgan IoA 78 F11
Bodsham Kent 27 K2
Bodwen Cnwll 4 G9
Bodymoor Heath Warwks 59 J5
Bogallan Highld 156 A7
Bogbrae Abers 159 P10
Bogend S Ayrs 125 L11
Boggs Holdings E Loth 128 C5
Boghall Mdloth 127 N4
Boghall W Loth 126 H4
Boghead S Lans 126 D9
Bogmoor Moray 157 R5
Bogmuir Abers 143 L3
Bogniebrae Abers 158 E8
Bognor Regis W Susx 15 P7
Bogroy Highld 148 G3
Bogue D & G 108 D4
Bohetherick Cnwll 5 Q8
Bohortha Cnwll 3 M7
Bohuntine Highld 146 H11
Bojewyan Cnwll 2 B7
Bokiddick Cnwll 4 H9
Bolam Dur 103 N6
Bolam Nthumb 112 H4
Bolberry Devon 6 H11
Bold Heath St Hel 82 B7
Boldmere Birm 58 H6
Boldon Colliery S Tyne 113 M8
Boldre Hants 13 P5
Boldron Dur 103 K8
Bole Notts 85 N3
Bolehill Derbys 84 C9
Bole Hill Derbys 84 D6
Bolenowe Cnwll 2 H6
Bolham Devon 18 C11
Bolham Water Devon 10 D2
Bolingey Cnwll 3 K3
Bollington Ches E 83 K9
Bollington Cross Ches E 83 K9
Bollow Gloucs 32 D2
Bolney W Susx 24 G6
Bolnhurst Bed 61 N9
Bolshan Angus 143 L7
Bolsover Derbys 84 G6
Bolster Moor Kirk 90 D7
Bolsterstone Sheff 90 H11
Boltby N York 97 Q3
Boltenstone Abers 150 C5
Bolter End Bucks 35 L6
Bolton Bolton 89 L9
Bolton Cumb 102 B6
Bolton E Loth 128 E6
Bolton E R Yk 98 F10
Bolton Nthumb 119 M8
Bolton Abbey N York 96 G10
Bolton Bridge N York 96 G10
Bolton by Bowland Lancs 96 A11
Boltonfellend Cumb 111 J7
Boltongate Cumb 100 H2
Bolton le Sands Lancs 95 K7
Bolton Low Houses Cumb 100 H2
Bolton New Houses Cumb 100 H2
Bolton-on-Swale N York 103 Q11
Bolton Percy N York 91 N2
Bolton Town End Lancs 95 K7
Bolton Upon Dearne Barns 91 M10
Bolventor Cnwll 5 K6
Bomarsund Nthumb 113 L4
Bomere Heath Shrops 69 N11
Bonar Bridge Highld 162 E8
Bonawe Ag & B 139 J11
Bonby N Linc 92 H7
Boncath Pembks 41 P3
Bonchester Bridge Border 118 A8
Bonchurch IoW 14 G11
Bondleigh Devon 8 G4
Bonds Lancs 88 F2
Bonehill Devon 8 H9
Bonehill Staffs 59 J4
Bo'ness Falk 134 C11
Boney Hay Staffs 58 F2
Bonhill W Duns 125 K2
Boningale Shrops 57 Q4
Bonjedward Border 118 C6
Bonkle N Lans 126 E6
Bonnington Angus 143 K10
Bonnington Kent 27 J4
Bonnybank Fife 135 K7
Bonnybridge Falk 126 E2
Bonnykelly Abers 159 L7
Bonnyrigg Mdloth 127 Q4
Bonnyton Angus 142 E10
Bonsall Derbys 84 C9
Bonshaw Tower D & G 110 D6
Bont Mons 45 M11
Bontddu Gwynd 67 M11
Bont-Dolgadfan Powys 55 K4
Bont-goch or Elerch Cerdgn 54 F7
Bonthorpe Lincs 87 N6
Bontnewydd Cerdgn 54 E11
Bontnewydd Gwynd 66 H3
Bontuchel Denbgs 68 E3
Bonvilston V Glam 30 E10
Bonwm Denbgs 68 F6
Bon-y-maen Swans 29 J5
Boode Devon 17 J4
Booker Bucks 35 M6
Booley Shrops 69 Q9
Boon Border 128 F10
Boon Hill Staffs 70 E4
Boorley Green Hants 14 F4
Boosbeck R & Cl 105 J7
Boose's Green Essex 52 D5
Boot Cumb 100 G10
Booth Calder 90 C5
Boothby Graffoe Lincs 86 C9
Boothby Pagnell Lincs 73 P4
Boothferry E R Yk 92 B5
Booth Green Ches E 83 K8
Boothstown Salfd 82 F4
Booth Town Calder 90 D5
Boothville Nhants 60 G8
Bootle Cumb 94 C3
Bootle Sefton 81 L5
Boots Green Ches W 82 G10
Boot Street Suffk 53 M2
Booze N York 103 K10
Boraston Shrops 57 L11
Bordeaux Guern 10 c1
Borden Kent 38 E9
Borden W Susx 23 M10
Border Cumb 110 C10
Border Forest Park 111 M4
Borders Crematorium Border 117 R4
Bordley N York 96 D7
Bordon Camp Hants 23 L7
Boreham Essex 52 C10
Boreham Wilts 20 G6
Boreham Street E Susx 25 Q8
Borehamwood Herts 50 E11
Boreland D & G 110 C2
Boreraig Highld 152 B7
Boreton Shrops 57 J3
Borgh W Isls 168 b17
Borgh W Isls 168 j2
Borgie Highld 165 Q5
Borgue D & G 108 D11
Borgue Highld 167 K11
Borley Essex 52 D3
Borley Green Essex 52 D3
Borley Green Suffk 64 D9
Borneskitaig Highld 152 F3
Borness D & G 108 D11
Boroughbridge N York 97 N7
Borough Green Kent 37 P9
Borras Head Wrexhm 69 L4
Borrowash Derbys 72 C4
Borrowby N York 97 P3
Borrowby N York 105 L7
Borrowstoun Falk 134 B11
Borstal Medway 38 B8
Borth Cerdgn 54 E6
Borthwickbrae Border 117 N8
Borthwickshiels Border 117 N7
Borth-y-Gest Gwynd 67 K7
Borve Highld 152 G8
Borve W Isls 168 b17
Borve W Isls 168 f8
Borve W Isls 168 j2
Borwick Lancs 95 L6
Borwick Lodge Cumb 101 K11
Borwick Rails Cumb 94 D5
Bosavern Cnwll 2 B7
Bosbury Herefs 46 C6
Boscarne Cnwll 4 G8
Boscastle Cnwll 4 H3
Boscombe Bmouth 13 K6
Boscombe Wilts 21 P7
Boscoppa Cnwll 3 Q3
Bosham W Susx 15 M6
Bosham Hoe W Susx 15 M6
Bosherston Pembks 41 J12
Boskednan Cnwll 2 C7
Boskenna Cnwll 2 C9
Bosley Ches E 83 K11
Bosoughan Cnwll 4 D9
Bossall N York 98 E8
Bossiney Cnwll 4 H4
Bossingham Kent 27 L2
Bossington Somset 18 A5
Bostock Green Ches W 82 E11
Boston Lincs 74 F2
Boston Crematorium Lincs 87 K11
Boston Spa Leeds 97 P11
Boswarthan Cnwll 2 C7
Boswinger Cnwll 3 P5
Botallack Cnwll 2 B7
Botany Bay Gt Lon 50 G11
Botcheston Leics 72 D10
Botesdale Suffk 64 E6
Bothal Nthumb 113 K3
Bothampstead W Berk 34 F9
Bothamsall Notts 85 L6
Bothel Cumb 100 G3
Bothenhampton Dorset 11 K6
Bothwell S Lans 126 C6
Bothwell Services S Lans 126 C6
Botley Bucks 35 Q4
Botley Hants 14 F4
Botley Oxon 34 E3
Botolph Claydon Bucks 49 K10
Botolphs W Susx 24 E9
Botolph's Bridge Kent 27 K5
Bottesford Leics 73 L3
Bottesford N Linc 92 E9
Bottisham Cambs 62 H8
Bottomcraig Fife 135 K3
Bottom of Hutton Lancs 88 F5
Bottom o' th' Moor Bolton 89 K8
Bottoms Calder 89 Q6
Bottoms Cnwll 2 B9
Botts Green Warwks 59 K6
Botusfleming Cnwll 5 Q9
Botwnnog Gwynd 66 D8
Bough Beech Kent 37 L11
Boughrood Powys 44 G7
Boughspring Gloucs 31 Q5
Boughton Nhants 60 G7
Boughton Norfk 75 P10
Boughton Notts 85 L7
Boughton Aluph Kent 26 H2
Boughton End C Beds 49 Q7
Boughton Green Kent 38 C11
Boughton Malherbe Kent 26 E2
Boughton Monchelsea Kent 38 C11
Boughton Street Kent 39 J10
Boulby R & Cl 105 L7
Boulder Clough Calder 90 C6
Bouldnor IoW 14 C9
Bouldon Shrops 57 J7
Boulmer Nthumb 119 Q8
Boulston Pembks 41 J8
Boultham Lincs 86 C7
Bourn Cambs 62 D9
Bourne Lincs 74 A6
Bournebridge Essex 37 M2
Bournebrook Birm 58 F8
Bourne End Bed 61 M8
Bourne End Bucks 35 N7
Bourne End C Beds 49 Q6
Bourne End Herts 50 B9
Bournemouth Bmouth 13 J6
Bournemouth Airport Dorset 13 K5
Bournemouth Crematorium Bmouth 13 K6
Bournes Green Gloucs 32 H4
Bournes Green Sthend 38 F4
Bournheath Worcs 58 E10
Bournmoor Dur 113 M10
Bournstream Gloucs 32 D6
Bournville Birm 58 F8
Bourton Dorset 20 E8
Bourton N Som 19 L2
Bourton Oxon 33 P7
Bourton Shrops 57 K5
Bourton Wilts 21 K2
Bourton on Dunsmore Warwks 59 P10
Bourton-on-the-Hill Gloucs 47 N8
Bourton-on-the-Water Gloucs 47 N10
Bousd Ag & B 136 H3
Boustead Hill Cumb 110 E9
Bouth Cumb 94 G3
Bouthwaite N York 96 H6
Bouts Worcs 47 K3
Boveney Bucks 35 P9
Boveridge Dorset 13 J2
Bovey Tracey Devon 9 K9
Bovingdon Herts 50 B10
Bovingdon Green Bucks 35 M7
Bovinger Essex 51 M9
Bovington Dorset 12 D7
Bovington Camp Dorset 12 D7
Bow Cumb 110 F9
Bow Devon 7 L7
Bow Devon 8 H4
Bow Gt Lon 37 J4
Bow Ork 169 c7
Bowbank Dur 102 H6
Bow Brickhill M Keyn 49 P8
Bowbridge Gloucs 32 G3
Bowburn Dur 104 B3
Bowcombe IoW 14 E9
Bowd Devon 10 C6
Bowden Border 117 R4
Bowden Devon 7 L9
Bowden Hill Wilts 32 H11
Bowdon Traffd 82 G7
Bower Highld 167 M4
Bower Ashton Bristl 31 Q10
Bowerchalke Wilts 21 K10
Bowerhill Wilts 20 H2
Bower Hinton Somset 19 N11
Bower House Tye Suffk 52 G3
Bowermadden Highld 167 M4
Bowers Staffs 70 E7
Bowers Gifford Essex 38 C4
Bowershall Fife 134 D9
Bower's Row Leeds 91 L5
Bowes Dur 103 J8
Bowgreave Lancs 88 F2
Bowhouse D & G 109 M7
Bowithick Cnwll 5 K5
Bowker's Green Lancs 81 N4
Bowland Border 117 P2
Bowland Bridge Cumb 95 J3
Bowley Herefs 45 Q4
Bowley Town Herefs 45 Q4
Bowlhead Green Surrey 23 P7
Bowling C Brad 90 F4
Bowling W Duns 125 L3
Bowling Bank Wrexhm 69 L5
Bowling Green Worcs 46 F4
Bowmanstead Cumb 101 K11
Bowmore Ag & B 122 D8
Bowness-on-Solway Cumb 110 D8
Bowness-on-Windermere Cumb 101 M11
Bow of Fife Fife 135 J5
Bowriefauld Angus 143 J8
Bowscale Cumb 101 L4
Bowsden Nthumb 119 J2
Bowston Cumb 101 N11
Bow Street Cerdgn 54 E7
Bow Street Norfk 64 E2
Bowthorpe Norfk 76 H10
Box Gloucs 32 G4
Box Wilts 32 F11
Boxbush Gloucs 32 D2
Boxbush Gloucs 46 C10
Box End Bed 61 M11
Boxford Suffk 52 G3
Boxford W Berk 34 D10
Boxgrove W Susx 15 P5
Box Hill Surrey 36 E10
Boxley Kent 38 C10
Boxmoor Herts 50 B9
Box's Shop Cnwll 16 C11
Boxted Essex 52 G5
Boxted Essex 52 H5
Boxted Suffk 64 A11
Boxted Cross Essex 52 H5
Boxwell Gloucs 32 F6
Boxworth Cambs 62 D8
Boxworth End Cambs 62 E7
Boyden End Suffk 63 M9
Boyden Gate Kent 39 M8
Boylestone Derbys 71 M7
Boyndie Abers 158 F5
Boyndlie Abers 159 M5
Boynton E R Yk 99 N7
Boysack Angus 143 L8
Boys Hill Dorset 11 P2
Boythorpe Derbys 84 E7
Boyton Cnwll 5 N3
Boyton Suffk 53 Q2
Boyton Wilts 21 J7
Boyton Cross Essex 51 P9

Boyton End Suffk 52 B3
Bozeat Nhants 61 K9
Braaid IoM 80 d6
Brabling Green Suffk 65 K9
Brabourne Kent 27 K3
Brabourne Lees Kent 27 J3
Brabstermire Highld 167 P3
Bracadale Highld 152 F10
Braceborough Lincs 74 A8
Bracebridge Heath Lincs 86 C7
Bracebridge Low Fields Lincs 86 C7
Braceby Lincs 73 Q3
Bracewell Lancs 96 C11
Brackenfield Derbys 84 E9
Brackenhirst N Lans 126 B6
Brackenthwaite Cumb 110 E11
Brackenthwaite N York 97 L10
Bracklesham W Susx 15 M7
Brackletter Highld 146 F11
Brackley Nhants 48 G7
Brackley Hatch Nhants 48 H6
Bracknell Br For 35 N11
Braco P & K 133 N6
Bracobrae Moray 158 D7
Bracon Ash Norfk 64 H2
Bracora Highld 145 M9
Bracorina Highld 145 M9
Bradaford Devon 5 P3
Bradbourne Derbys 71 N4
Bradbury Dur 104 B5
Bradden Nhants 48 H5
Braddock Cnwll 5 K10
Bradeley C Stke 70 F4
Bradenham Bucks 35 M5
Bradenstoke Wilts 33 K9
Bradfield Devon 9 Q3
Bradfield Essex 53 K5
Bradfield Norfk 77 K5
Bradfield Sheff 84 C2
Bradfield W Berk 34 H10
Bradfield Combust Suffk 64 B10
Bradfield Green Ches E 70 B3
Bradfield Heath Essex 53 K5
Bradfield St Clare Suffk 64 C10
Bradfield St George Suffk 64 C10
Bradford C Brad 90 F4
Bradford Cnwll 5 J6
Bradford Devon 16 G10
Bradford Nthumb 112 G5
Bradford Nthumb 119 N4
Bradford Abbas Dorset 11 M2
Bradford Leigh Wilts 20 F2
Bradford-on-Avon Wilts 20 F2
Bradford-on-Tone Somset 18 G10
Bradford Peverell Dorset 11 P6
Bradiford Devon 17 K5
Brading IoW 14 H9
Bradley Derbys 71 N5
Bradley Hants 22 H6
Bradley Kirk 90 F6
Bradley N York 96 F4
Bradley NE Lin 93 M9
Bradley Staffs 70 F11
Bradley Wolves 58 E5
Bradley Worcs 47 J2
Bradley Wrexhm 69 K4
Bradley Common Ches W 69 P5
Bradley Green Somset 19 J7
Bradley Green Warwks 59 L4
Bradley Green Worcs 47 J2
Bradley in the Moors Staffs 71 K6
Bradley Stoke S Glos 32 B8
Bradmore Notts 72 F4
Bradney Somset 19 K7
Bradninch Devon 9 N4
Bradninch Devon 17 L5
Bradnop Staffs 71 J3
Bradnor Green Herefs 45 K3
Bradpole Dorset 11 K6
Bradshaw Bolton 89 L8
Bradshaw Calder 90 D5
Bradshaw Kirk 90 D8
Bradstone Devon 5 P5
Bradwall Green Ches E 70 D2
Bradwell Derbys 83 Q8
Bradwell Devon 17 J3
Bradwell Essex 52 D7
Bradwell M Keyn 49 M6
Bradwell Norfk 77 Q11
Bradwell Crematorium Staffs 70 F5
Bradwell-on-Sea Essex 52 H10
Bradwell Waterside Essex 52 G10
Bradworthy Devon 16 E9
Brae Highld 156 B5
Brae Shet 169 q7
Braeface Falk 133 M11
Braehead Angus 143 M7
Braehead D & G 107 M7
Braehead S Lans 126 H7
Braemar Abers 149 M9
Braemore Highld 161 K11
Braemore Highld 167 J11
Brae Roy Lodge Highld 147 J9
Braeside Inver 124 G3
Braes of Coul Angus 142 D6
Braes of Enzie Moray 158 A6
Braeswick Ork 169 f3
Braevallich Ag & B 131 K6
Brafferton Darltn 103 Q6
Brafferton N York 97 P6
Brafield-on-the-Green Nhants 60 H9
Bragar W Isls 168 h3
Bragbury End Herts 50 G6
Braidwood S Lans 126 E8
Brailsford Derbys 71 P6
Brailsford Green Derbys 71 P6
Brain's Green Gloucs 32 C3
Braintree Essex 52 C7
Braiseworth Suffk 64 G7
Braishfield Hants 22 C9
Braithwaite C Brad 90 C2
Braithwaite Cumb 100 H6
Braithwell Donc 84 H4
Braken Hill Wakefd 91 L7
Bramber W Susx 24 E8
Brambridge Hants 22 E10
Bramcote Notts 72 E3
Bramcote Warwks 59 P7
Bramcote Crematorium Notts 72 E3
Bramdean Hants 22 H9
Bramerton Norfk 77 K11

Bramfield Herts 50 G7
Bramfield Suffk 65 M7
Bramford Suffk 53 K2
Bramhall Stockp 83 J8
Bramham Leeds 91 L2
Bramhope Leeds 90 H2
Bramley Hants 23 J3
Bramley Leeds 90 G3
Bramley Rothm 84 G2
Bramley Surrey 24 B2
Bramley Corner Hants 22 H3
Bramley Green Hants 23 J3
Bramley Head N York 96 H9
Bramling Kent 39 M10
Brampford Speke Devon 9 M5
Brampton Cambs 62 B6
Brampton Cumb 102 C6
Brampton Cumb 111 K8
Brampton Lincs 85 P5
Brampton Norfk 77 J7
Brampton Rothm 91 L10
Brampton Suffk 65 N5
Brampton Abbotts Herefs 46 B9
Brampton Ash Nhants 60 G3
Brampton Bryan Herefs 56 F10
Brampton-en-le-Morthen Rothm 84 G3
Bramshall Staffs 71 K8
Bramshaw Hants 21 Q11
Bramshill Hants 23 K2
Bramshott Hants 23 M8
Bramwell Somset 19 M9
Branault Highld 137 N2
Brancaster Norfk 75 Q2
Brancaster Staithe Norfk 75 Q2
Brancepeth Dur 103 P3
Branchill Moray 157 K7
Brand End Lincs 87 L11
Branderburgh Moray 157 N3
Brandesburton E R Yk 99 N11
Brandeston Suffk 65 J9
Brand Green Gloucs 46 D9
Brandis Corner Devon 16 G11
Brandiston Norfk 76 G7
Brandon Dur 103 P2
Brandon Lincs 86 B11
Brandon Nthumb 119 K7
Brandon Suffk 63 N3
Brandon Warwks 59 P9
Brandon Bank Norfk 63 K3
Brandon Creek Norfk 63 K2
Brandon Parva Norfk 76 F10
Brandsby N York 98 B6
Brandy Wharf Lincs 92 H11
Brane Cnwll 2 C8
Bran End Essex 51 Q5
Branksome Poole 12 H6
Branksome Park Poole 13 J6
Bransbury Hants 22 D6
Bransby Lincs 85 Q5
Branscombe Devon 10 D7
Bransford Worcs 46 E4
Bransgore Hants 13 L5
Bransholme C KuH 93 K4
Bransley Shrops 57 M9
Branson's Cross Worcs 58 G10
Branston Leics 73 L5
Branston Lincs 86 D7
Branston Staffs 71 N10
Branston Booths Lincs 86 E7
Branstone IoW 14 G10
Brant Broughton Lincs 86 B10
Brantham Suffk 53 K5
Branthwaite Cumb 100 E6
Branthwaite Cumb 101 J3
Brantingham E R Yk 92 F5
Branton Donc 91 Q10
Branton Nthumb 119 K7
Branton Green N York 97 P8
Branxton Nthumb 118 G3
Brassey Green Ches W 69 P2
Brassington Derbys 71 N4
Brasted Kent 37 L9
Brasted Chart Kent 37 L10
Brathens Abers 150 H8
Bratoft Lincs 87 N8
Brattleby Lincs 86 B4
Bratton Somset 18 B5
Bratton Wilts 20 H4
Bratton Wrekin 57 L2
Bratton Clovelly Devon 8 C6
Bratton Fleming Devon 17 L4
Bratton Seymour Somset 20 C9
Braughing Herts 51 J5
Braughing Friars Herts 51 K6
Braunston Nhants 60 B7
Braunston Rutlnd 73 L9
Braunstone Leics 72 F10
Braunton Devon 16 H4
Brawby N York 98 E5
Brawl Highld 166 D3
Braworth N York 104 F9
Bray W & M 35 P9
Braybrooke Nhants 60 G4
Braydon Wilts 33 K7
Braydon Brook Wilts 33 J6
Braydon Side Wilts 33 K7
Brayford Devon 17 M5
Bray's Hill E Susx 25 Q8
Bray Shop Cnwll 5 N7
Braystones Cumb 100 D9
Braythorn N York 97 K11
Brayton N York 91 Q4
Braywick W & M 35 N9
Braywoodside W & M 35 N9
Brazacott Cnwll 5 M3
Breach Kent 27 L2
Breach Kent 38 D8
Breachwood Green Herts 50 E6
Breaden Heath Shrops 69 M7
Breadsall Derbys 72 B3
Breadstone Gloucs 32 D4
Breadward Herefs 45 K4
Breage Cnwll 2 G8
Breakachy Highld 155 N9
Breakspear Crematorium Gt Lon 36 C3
Brealangwell Lodge Highld 162 C6
Bream Gloucs 32 B3
Breamore Hants 21 N11
Brean Somset 19 J3
Breanais W Isls 168 e5
Brearley Calder 90 C5
Brearton N York 97 M8
Breascleit W Isls 168 h4
Breasclete W Isls 168 h4

Breaston Derbys 72 D4
Brechfa Carmth 43 K8
Brechin Angus 143 L5
Breckles Norfk 64 D3
Brecon Powys 44 E9
Brecon Beacons National Park Powys 44 E10
Bredbury Stockp 83 K6
Brede E Susx 26 D8
Bredenbury Herefs 46 B3
Bredfield Suffk 65 K11
Bredgar Kent 38 E9
Bredhurst Kent 38 C9
Bredon Worcs 46 H7
Bredon's Hardwick Worcs 46 H7
Bredon's Norton Worcs 46 H7
Bredwardine Herefs 45 K6
Breedon on the Hill Leics 72 C6
Breich W Loth 126 H5
Breightmet Bolton 89 L9
Breighton E R Yk 92 B4
Breinton Herefs 45 P7
Bremhill Wilts 33 J10
Bremridge Devon 17 M6
Brenchley Kent 25 Q2
Brendon Devon 16 H2
Brendon Devon 17 P2
Brendon Hill Somset 18 D8
Brenfield Ag & B 123 P3
Brenish W Isls 168 e5
Brenkley N u Ty 113 K5
Brent Eleigh Suffk 52 F2
Brentford Gt Lon 36 E5
Brentingby Leics 73 K7
Brent Knoll Somset 19 K4
Brent Mill Devon 6 H7
Brent Pelham Herts 51 K4
Brentwood Essex 37 N2
Brenzett Kent 26 H6
Brenzett Green Kent 26 H6
Brereton Staffs 71 K11
Brereton Green Ches E 70 D2
Brereton Heath Ches E 82 H11
Brereton Hill Staffs 71 K11
Bressay Shet 169 s9
Bressingham Norfk 64 F5
Bressingham Common Norfk 64 F5
Bretby Derbys 71 P10
Bretby Crematorium Derbys 71 P10
Bretford Warwks 59 P9
Bretforton Worcs 47 L6
Bretherton Lancs 88 F5
Brettabister Shet 169 r8
Brettenham Norfk 64 C5
Brettenham Suffk 64 D11
Bretton Derbys 84 B5
Bretton Flints 69 L2
Brewers End Essex 51 N6
Brewer Street Surrey 36 H10
Brewood Staffs 58 C3
Briantspuddle Dorset 12 D6
Brick End Essex 51 N5
Brickendon Herts 50 H9
Bricket Wood Herts 50 D10
Brick Houses Sheff 84 D4
Brickkiln Green Essex 52 B5
Bricklehampton Worcs 47 J6
Bride IoM 80 f1
Bridekirk Cumb 100 F4
Bridell Pembks 41 N2
Bridestowe Devon 8 D7
Brideswell Abers 158 E10
Bridford Devon 8 K7
Bridge Kent 39 L11
Bridge End Cumb 94 D4
Bridge End Cumb 110 G11
Bridge End Devon 6 H9
Bridge End Dur 103 K3
Bridge End Essex 51 Q4
Bridge End Lincs 74 B3
Bridgefoot Cumb 100 E5
Bridge Green Essex 51 L3
Bridgehampton Somset 19 Q10
Bridge Hewick N York 97 M6
Bridgehill Dur 112 G10
Bridgehouse Gate N York 97 J7
Bridgemary Hants 14 G6
Bridgemere Ches E 70 C5
Bridgend Abers 158 D10
Bridgend Ag & B 120 C4
Bridgend Ag & B 122 D7
Bridgend Angus 143 L4
Bridgend Brdgnd 29 P9
Bridgend Cerdgn 42 C5
Bridgend Cumb 101 M8
Bridgend D & G 116 F9
Bridgend Devon 6 F9
Bridgend Fife 135 K5
Bridgend Moray 158 A11
Bridgend P & K 134 E3
Bridgend W Loth 127 J2
Bridgend of Lintrathen Angus 142 D7
Bridge of Alford Abers 150 F4
Bridge of Allan Stirlg 133 M4
Bridge of Avon Moray 149 M3
Bridge of Avon Moray 157 M10
Bridge of Balgie P & K 140 E8
Bridge of Brewlands Angus 142 B5
Bridge of Brown Highld 149 L3
Bridge of Cally P & K 142 A7
Bridge of Canny Abers 150 H8
Bridge of Craigisla Angus 142 D7
Bridge of Dee D & G 108 F8
Bridge of Don C Aber 151 N6
Bridge of Dulsie Highld 156 G9
Bridge of Dye Abers 150 H10
Bridge of Earn P & K 134 E4
Bridge of Ericht P & K 140 D6
Bridge of Feugh Abers 151 J9
Bridge of Forss Highld 166 H3
Bridge of Gairn Abers 150 B8
Bridge of Gaur P & K 140 D6
Bridge of Marnoch Abers 158 E7
Bridge of Orchy Ag & B 139 P10
Bridge of Tilt P & K 141 L4
Bridge of Tynet Moray 158 A5
Bridge of Walls Shet 169 p8
Bridge of Weir Rens 125 K4
Bridge Reeve Devon 17 M9
Bridgerule Devon 16 D11
Bridges Shrops 56 F5
Bridge Sollers Herefs 45 N6
Bridge Street Suffk 52 E2

Bridgetown Cnwll 5 N4
Bridgetown Somset 18 B8
Bridge Trafford Ches W 81 P10
Bridge Yate S Glos 32 C10
Bridgham Norfk 64 D4
Bridgnorth Shrops 57 N6
Bridgwater Somset 19 J7
Bridgwater Services Somset 19 K8
Bridlington E R Yk 99 P7
Bridport Dorset 11 K6
Bridstow Herefs 46 A10
Brierfield Lancs 89 N3
Brierley Barns 91 L8
Brierley Gloucs 46 B11
Brierley Herefs 45 P3
Brierley Hill Dudley 58 D7
Brierton Hartpl 104 E4
Briery Cumb 101 J6
Brigg N Linc 92 H9
Briggate Norfk 77 L6
Briggswath N York 105 N9
Brigham Cumb 100 E4
Brigham Cumb 101 J6
Brigham E R Yk 99 M10
Brighouse Calder 90 E6
Brighstone IoW 14 D10
Brightgate Derbys 84 C9
Brighthampton Oxon 34 C4
Brightholmlee Sheff 90 H11
Brightley Devon 8 F5
Brightling E Susx 25 Q6
Brightlingsea Essex 53 J8
Brighton Br & H 24 H10
Brighton Cnwll 3 N3
Brighton le Sands Sefton 81 L5
Brightons Falk 126 G2
Brightwalton W Berk 34 D9
Brightwalton Green W Berk 34 D9
Brightwalton Holt W Berk 34 D9
Brightwell Suffk 53 N3
Brightwell Baldwin Oxon 35 J5
Brightwell-cum-Sotwell Oxon 34 G6
Brightwell Upperton Oxon 35 J6
Brignall Dur 103 L8
Brig o'Turk Stirlg 132 G6
Brigsley NE Lin 93 N10
Brigsteer Cumb 95 K3
Brigstock Nhants 61 K3
Brill Bucks 35 J2
Brill Cnwll 3 J8
Brilley Herefs 45 K5
Brimfield Herefs 57 J11
Brimfield Cross Herefs 57 J11
Brimington Derbys 84 F6
Brimley Devon 9 K9
Brimpsfield Gloucs 32 H2
Brimpton W Berk 22 G2
Brimpton Common W Berk 22 G2
Brimscombe Gloucs 32 G4
Brimstage Wirral 81 L8
Brincliffe Sheff 84 D4
Brind E R Yk 92 B4
Brindham Somset 19 P7
Brindister Shet 169 p8
Brindle Lancs 88 H6
Brineton Staffs 57 Q2
Bringhurst Leics 60 H2
Bringsty Common Herefs 46 D3
Brington Cambs 61 N5
Briningham Norfk 76 E5
Brinkely Notts 85 M10
Brinkhill Lincs 87 L6
Brinkley Cambs 63 K10
Brinklow Warwks 59 P9
Brinkworth Wilts 33 K8
Brinscall Lancs 89 J6
Brinscombe Somset 19 M4
Brinsea N Som 19 M2
Brinsley Notts 84 G11
Brinsop Herefs 45 N6
Brinsworth Rothm 84 F3
Brinton Norfk 76 E4
Brinyan Ork 169 d4
Brisco Cumb 110 H10
Brisley Norfk 76 C7
Brislington Bristl 32 B10
Brissenden Green Kent 26 F4
Bristol Bristl 31 Q10
Bristol Airport N Som 31 P11
Bristol Zoo Gardens Bristl 31 Q10
Briston Norfk 76 F5
Brisworthy Devon 6 F5
Britannia Lancs 89 P5
Britford Wilts 21 N9
Brithdir Caerph 30 F4
Brithdir Gwynd 67 P11
British Legion Village Kent 38 B10
Briton Ferry Neath 29 K6
Britwell Salome Oxon 35 J6
Brixham Torbay 7 N7
Brixton Devon 6 F8
Brixton Gt Lon 36 H5
Brixton Deverill Wilts 20 G7
Brixworth Nhants 60 F6
Brize Norton Oxon 33 Q3
Brize Norton Airport Oxon 33 Q3
Broad Alley Worcs 58 C11
Broad Blunsdon Swindn 33 M6
Broadbottom Tamesd 83 L6
Broadbridge W Susx 15 M5
Broadbridge Heath W Susx 24 D4
Broad Campden Gloucs 47 N7
Broad Carr Calder 90 D7
Broad Chalke Wilts 21 K9
Broad Clough Lancs 89 P6
Broadclyst Devon 9 N5
Broadfield Inver 125 J3
Broadfield Pembks 41 M10
Broadford Highld 145 K3
Broad Ford Kent 26 B4
Broadford Bridge W Susx 24 C6
Broadgairhill Border 117 J7
Broadgrass Green Suffk 64 D9
Broad Green Cambs 63 L8
Broad Green Essex 52 E7
Broad Green Worcs 46 E3
Broad Green Worcs 58 D11
Broadhaugh Border 129 M9

Broad Haven Pembks 40 G8
Broadheath Traffd 82 G7
Broadheath Worcs 57 M11
Broadhembury Devon 10 L5
Broadhempston Devon 7 L5
Broad Hill Cambs 63 J5
Broad Hinton Wilts 33 M9
Broadholme Lincs 85 Q6
Broadland Row E Susx 26 D8
Broadlay Carmth 28 C3
Broad Layings Hants 22 E5
Broadley Essex 51 K9
Broadley Lancs 89 P7
Broadley Moray 158 A5
Broadley Common Essex 51 K9
Broad Marston Worcs 47 M5
Broadmayne Dorset 12 B7
Broad Meadow Staffs 70 E5
Broadmere Hants 22 H5
Broadmoor Gloucs 46 B11
Broadmoor Pembks 41 L9
Broadnymett Devon 8 H4
Broad Oak Cumb 94 C2
Broadoak Dorset 11 J5
Broad Oak E Susx 25 P6
Broad Oak E Susx 26 D8
Broadoak Gloucs 32 C2
Broad Oak Hants 23 L4
Broad Oak Herefs 45 P10
Broad Oak Kent 39 L9
Broad Oak St Hel 82 B5
Broadoak Wrexhm 69 L3
Broad Road Suffk 65 K6
Broad's Green Essex 51 Q8
Broadstairs Kent 39 Q8
Broadstone Mons 31 P4
Broadstone Poole 12 H5
Broadstone Shrops 57 J7
Broad Street E Susx 26 E8
Broad Street Essex 51 N4
Broad Street Kent 27 K3
Broad Street Kent 38 D10
Broad Street Medway 38 C7
Broad Street Wilts 21 M3
Broad Street Green Essex 52 E10
Broad Town Wilts 33 L9
Broadwas Worcs 46 E3
Broadwater Herts 50 F5
Broadwater W Susx 24 D10
Broadwaters Worcs 58 C9
Broadway Carmth 28 C3
Broadway Pembks 40 G8
Broadway Somset 19 K11
Broadway Suffk 65 M6
Broadway Worcs 47 L7
Broadwell Gloucs 31 Q2
Broadwell Gloucs 47 P9
Broadwell Oxon 33 Q4
Broadwell Warwks 59 Q11
Broadwey Dorset 11 P8
Broadwindsor Dorset 11 J4
Broadwood Kelly Devon 8 H4
Broadwoodwidger Devon 5 Q4
Brobury Herefs 45 L6
Brochel Highld 153 K8
Brochroy Ag & B 139 J11
Brock Lancs 88 G2
Brockamin Worcs 46 E4
Brockbridge Hants 22 H11
Brockdish Norfk 65 J5
Brockencote Worcs 58 C10
Brockenhurst Hants 13 M4
Brocketsbrae S Lans 126 E10
Brockford Green Suffk 64 G8
Brockford Street Suffk 64 G8
Brockhall Nhants 60 D8
Brockham Surrey 36 E11
Brockhampton Gloucs 46 H9
Brockhampton Gloucs 47 K10
Brockhampton Hants 15 K5
Brockhampton Herefs 46 A8
Brockhampton Estate NT Herefs 46 C3
Brockhampton Green Dorset 11 Q3
Brockholes Kirk 90 F8
Brockhurst Derbys 84 D8
Brockhurst Warwks 59 Q8
Brocklebank Cumb 101 K2
Brocklesby Lincs 93 K8
Brockley N Som 31 N11
Brockley Suffk 64 C9
Brockley Green Suffk 63 N11
Brockley Green Suffk 64 A11
Brockleymoor Cumb 101 N3
Brockmoor Dudley 58 D7
Brockscombe Devon 8 C5
Brock's Green Hants 22 F2
Brockton Shrops 56 E4
Brockton Shrops 56 H5
Brockton Shrops 57 K6
Brockton Shrops 57 N4
Brockton Staffs 70 E8
Brockweir Gloucs 31 P4
Brockwood Park Hants 22 H9
Brockworth Gloucs 46 G11
Brocton Cnwll 4 E5
Brocton Staffs 70 H11
Brodick N Ayrs 121 J4
Brodie Moray 156 H6
Brodsworth Donc 91 N9
Brogaig Highld 152 G4
Brogborough C Beds 49 Q7
Brokenborough Wilts 32 H7
Broken Cross Ches E 83 J10
Broken Cross Ches W 82 E10
Brokerswood Wilts 20 F4
Bromborough Wirral 81 M8
Brome Suffk 64 G6
Brome Street Suffk 64 G6
Bromeswell Suffk 65 L11
Bromfield Cumb 110 C11
Bromfield Shrops 56 H9
Bromham Bed 61 M10
Bromham Wilts 33 J11
Bromley Barns 91 J11
Bromley Dudley 58 D7
Bromley Gt Lon 37 K7
Bromley Shrops 57 N5
Bromley Common Gt Lon 37 K7
Bromley Cross Essex 53 J6
Bromley Green Kent 26 E4
Bromlow Shrops 56 E4
Brompton Medway 38 C7
Brompton N York 104 C11

Brompton-by-Sawdon N York....99 J4
Brompton-on-Swale N York....103 P11
Brompton Ralph Somset....18 E8
Brompton Regis Somset....18 C8
Bromsash Herefs....46 C10
Bromsberrow Gloucs....46 D8
Bromsberrow Heath Gloucs....46 D8
Bromsgrove Worcs....58 E10
Bromstead Heath Staffs....70 D6
Bromyard Herefs....46 C4
Bromyard Downs Herefs....46 C4
Bronaber Gwynd....67 N8
Bronant Cerdgn....54 E11
Broncroft Shrops....57 J7
Brongest Cerdgn....42 F5
Bronington Wrexhm....69 N7
Bronllys Powys....44 G8
Bronwydd Carmth....42 H10
Bronydd Powys....45 J5
Bronygarth Shrops....69 J7
Bron-y-Nant Crematorium Conwy....79 Q9
Brook Carmth....41 Q9
Brook Hants....13 N2
Brook Hants....22 B9
Brook IoW....14 C10
Brook Kent....27 J3
Brook Surrey....23 P7
Brook Surrey....36 C11
Brooke Norfk....65 K2
Brooke Rutlnd....73 L9
Brookenby Lincs....93 M11
Brook End Bed....61 N8
Brook End C Beds....61 Q11
Brook End Cambs....61 N6
Brook End M Keyn....49 P6
Brookfield Rens....125 L5
Brookhampton Oxon....34 H5
Brookhampton Somset....20 B9
Brook Hill Hants....13 N2
Brook House Denbgs....80 F11
Brookhouse Lancs....95 L8
Brookhouse Rothm....84 H3
Brookhouse Green Ches E....70 E2
Brookhouses Derbys....83 M7
Brookland Kent....26 G6
Brooklands Traffd....82 G6
Brookmans Park Herts....50 F10
Brooks Powys....55 Q5
Brooksby Leics....72 H7
Brooks End Kent....39 N8
Brooks Green W Susx....24 D6
Brook Street Essex....37 N2
Brook Street Kent....26 F7
Brook Street Suffk....52 D2
Brook Street W Susx....24 H5
Brookthorpe Gloucs....32 F2
Brookville Norfk....75 P11
Brookwood Surrey....23 Q3
Broom C Beds....50 E2
Broom Rothm....84 F2
Broom Warwks....47 L4
Broome Norfk....65 M3
Broome Shrops....56 G8
Broome Worcs....58 D9
Broomedge Warrtn....82 F7
Broome Park Nthumb....119 M8
Broomer's Corner W Susx....24 D6
Broomershill W Susx....24 C7
Broomfield Essex....52 B9
Broomfield Kent....30 D11
Broomfield Kent....39 L8
Broomfield Somset....18 H8
Broomfields Shrops....69 M11
Broomfleet E R Yk....92 E5
Broom Green Norfk....76 D7
Broomhall W & M....35 Q11
Broomhaugh Nthumb....112 F8
Broom Hill Barns....91 L10
Broom Hill Dorset....12 H4
Broom Hill Notts....84 H11
Broomhill Nthumb....119 P10
Broom Hill Worcs....58 D9
Broomhill Green Ches E....70 A5
Bromley Nthumb....112 F8
Broompark Dur....103 P2
Broom's Green Gloucs....46 D8
Broomsthorpe Norfk....76 A6
Broom Street Kent....38 H9
Brora Highld....163 L6
Broseley Shrops....57 M4
Brotherlee Bar Lincs....74 F4
Brotherlee Dur....102 H3
Brothertoft Lincs....87 J11
Brotherton N York....91 M5
Brotton R & Cl....105 J7
Broubster Highld....166 H5
Brough Cumb....102 E8
Brough Derbys....83 Q8
Brough E R Yk....92 F5
Brough Highld....167 M2
Brough Notts....85 P9
Brough Shet....169 s7
Broughall Shrops....69 Q6
Brough Lodge Shet....169 s4
Brough Sowerby Cumb....102 E8
Broughton Border....116 G3
Broughton Bucks....35 M2
Broughton Cambs....62 C5
Broughton Flints....69 K2
Broughton Hants....22 B8
Broughton Lancs....88 G4
Broughton M Keyn....49 N7
Broughton N Linc....92 G9
Broughton N York....96 D10
Broughton N York....98 F6
Broughton Nhants....60 H5
Broughton Oxon....48 C7
Broughton Salfd....82 H4
Broughton Staffs....70 D8
Broughton V Glam....29 P10
Broughton Astley Leics....60 B2
Broughton Beck Cumb....94 F4
Broughton Gifford Wilts....20 G2
Broughton Green Worcs....47 J2
Broughton Hackett Worcs....46 H4
Broughton-in-Furness Cumb....94 E3
Broughton Mains D & G....107 N8
Broughton Mills Cumb....94 E3
Broughton Moor Cumb....100 E4
Broughton Poggs Oxon....33 Q4
Broughton Tower Cumb....94 E3
Broughty Ferry C Dund....142 H11

Brow End Cumb....94 F6
Brownber Cumb....102 D9
Brown Candover Hants....22 G7
Brown Edge Lancs....88 D8
Brown Edge Staffs....70 G4
Brown Heath Ches W....69 N2
Brownheath Shrops....69 N9
Brownhill Abers....159 L9
Brownhills Fife....135 N4
Brownhills Wsall....58 F3
Brownieside Nthumb....119 N6
Browninghill Green Hants....22 G3
Brown Lees Staffs....70 F3
Brownlow Heath Ches E....70 E2
Brownrigg Cumb....100 D8
Brownrigg Cumb....110 C10
Brownsea Island Dorset....12 H7
Brown's Green Birm....58 G6
Brownsham Devon....16 D6
Browns Hill Gloucs....32 G4
Brownsover Warwks....60 B5
Brownston Devon....6 H8
Brown Street Suffk....64 F9
Brow-of-the-Hill Norfk....75 N7
Browston Green Norfk....77 P11
Broxa N York....99 J2
Broxbourne Herts....51 J9
Broxburn E Loth....128 H4
Broxburn W Loth....127 K3
Broxfield Nthumb....119 P7
Broxted Essex....51 N5
Broxton Ches W....69 N4
Broyle Side E Susx....25 L8
Bruan Highld....167 P9
Bruar P & K....141 K4
Brucefield Highld....163 L9
Bruchag Ag & B....124 E6
Bruera Ches W....69 M2
Bruern Abbey Oxon....47 Q10
Bruichladdich Ag & B....122 C7
Bruisyard Suffk....65 L8
Bruisyard Street Suffk....65 L8
Brumby N Linc....92 F9
Brund Staffs....71 L2
Brundall Norfk....77 L10
Brundish Suffk....65 K8
Brundish Street Suffk....65 K7
Brunery Highld....138 C3
Brunion Cnwll....2
Brunslow Shrops....56 F8
Brunswick Village N u Ty....113 K6
Bruntcliffe Leeds....90 H5
Bruntingthorpe Leics....60 D3
Brunton Fife....135 J3
Brunton Nthumb....119 P6
Brunton Wilts....21 P3
Brushford Devon....17 M10
Brushford Somset....18 B9
Bruton Somset....20 C7
Bryan's Green Worcs....58 C11
Bryanston Dorset....12 E3
Bryant's Bottom Bucks....35 M5
Brydekirk D & G....110 C6
Bryher IoS....2 b2
Brymbo Wrexhm....69 J4
Brympton Somset....19 P11
Bryn Carmth....28 F4
Bryn Ches W....82 D10
Bryn Neath....29 M6
Bryn Shrops....56 D7
Bryn Wigan....82 C4
Brynamman Carmth....29 K2
Brynberian Pembks....41 M3
Brynbryddan Neath....29 L6
Bryn-bwbach Gwynd....67 L7
Bryncae Rhondd....30 C8
Bryncethin Brdgnd....29 P8
Bryncir Gwynd....66 H6
Bryn-coch Neath....29 K5
Bryncroes Gwynd....66 C8
Bryncrug Gwynd....54 E4
Bryn Du IoA....78 E10
Bryn-Eden Gwynd....67 N9
Bryneglwys Denbgs....68 F5
Brynfields Wrexhm....69 K6
Brynford Flints....80 H10
Bryn Gates Wigan....82 C4
Bryn Golau Rhondd....30 D7
Bryngwran IoA....78 F9
Bryngwyn Mons....31 L3
Bryngwyn Powys....44 H5
Bryn-Henllan Pembks....41 K3
Brynhoffnant Cerdgn....42 F4
Bryning Lancs....88 E5
Brynithel Blae G....30 H4
Brynmawr Blae G....30 G2
Bryn-mawr Gwynd....66 C8
Brynmenyn Brdgnd....29 P8
Brynmill Swans....28 H6
Brynna Rhondd....30 C8
Bryn-penarth Powys....55 Q4
Brynrefail Gwynd....67 K2
Brynrefail IoA....78 H7
Brynsadler Rhondd....30 D8
Bryn Saith Marchog Denbgs....68 E4
Brynsiencyn IoA....78 H11
Brynteg IoA....78 H8
Bryn-y-bal Flints....69 J2
Bryn-y-Maen Conwy....79 Q9
Bryn-yr-Eos Wrexhm....69 J4
Bualintur Highld....144 F3
Buarth-draw Flints....80 H9
Bubbenhall Warwks....59 N10
Bubwith E R Yk....92 B3
Buccleuch Border....117 L8
Buchanan Smithy Stirlg....132 F10
Buchanhaven Abers....159 R8
Buchanty P & K....133 Q2
Buchany Stirlg....133 L7
Buchlyvie Stirlg....132 H9
Buckabank Cumb....110 G11
Buckden Cambs....61 Q7
Buckden N York....96 D5
Buckenham Norfk....77 M10
Buckerell Devon....10 C4
Buckfast Devon....7 J5
Buckfastleigh Devon....7 J5
Buckhaven Fife....135 K8
Buckholt Mons....45 Q11
Buckhorn Devon....5 P2
Buckhorn Weston Dorset....20 E10
Buckhurst Hill Essex....37 K2
Buckie Moray....158 B4
Buckingham Bucks....49 J8
Buckland Bucks....35 N2
Buckland Devon....6 H10

Buckland Gloucs....47 L7
Buckland Hants....13 P5
Buckland Herts....51 J4
Buckland Kent....27 P3
Buckland Oxon....34 B5
Buckland Surrey....36 F10
Buckland Brewer Devon....16 G7
Buckland Common Bucks....35 P3
Buckland Dinham Somset....20 E4
Buckland Filleigh Devon....16 H10
Buckland in the Moor Devon....7 J4
Buckland Monachorum Devon....6 D5
Buckland Newton Dorset....11 P3
Buckland Ripers Dorset....11 P8
Buckland St Mary Somset....10 F2
Buckland-Tout-Saints Devon....7 K9
Bucklebury W Berk....34 G10
Bucklers Hard Hants....14 D6
Bucklesham Suffk....53 M3
Buckley Flints....69 J2
Buckley Green Warwks....59 J11
Bucklow Hill Ches E....82 F8
Buckminster Leics....73 M6
Bucknall C Stke....70 G5
Bucknall Lincs....86 F7
Bucknell Oxon....48 G9
Bucknell Shrops....56 F10
Buckpool Moray....158 B4
Bucksburn C Aber....151 M6
Buck's Cross Devon....16 F7
Bucks Green W Susx....24 C4
Buckshaw Village Lancs....88 H6
Bucks Hill Herts....50 C10
Bucks Horn Oak Hants....23 M6
Buck's Mills Devon....16 F7
Buckton E R Yk....99 P6
Buckton Herefs....56 F10
Buckton Nthumb....119 L3
Buckworth Cambs....61 P5
Budby Notts....85 K7
Budd's Cross Devon....16 C10
Budge's Shop Cnwll....5 N10
Budlake Devon....9 N5
Budle Nthumb....119 N3
Budleigh Salterton Devon....9 Q8
Budlett's Common E Susx....25 L6
Budock Water Cnwll....3 K7
Buerton Ches E....70 B6
Bugbrooke Nhants....60 E9
Bugford Devon....7 L8
Buglawton Ches E....70 F2
Bugle Cnwll....4 G10
Bugley Dorset....20 E10
Bugthorpe E R Yk....98 F9
Buildwas Shrops....57 L4
Builth Road Powys....44 E4
Builth Wells Powys....44 E4
Bulbourne Herts....35 P2
Bulbridge Wilts....21 L8
Bulby Lincs....73 R5
Bulford Wilts....21 N6
Bulford Camp Wilts....21 N6
Bulkeley Ches E....69 P4
Bulkington Warwks....59 N7
Bulkington Wilts....20 H3
Bulkworthy Devon....16 F9
Bullamoor N York....97 N2
Bull Bay IoA....78 G6
Bullbridge Derbys....84 E10
Bullbrook Br For....35 N11
Bullen's Green Herts....50 F9
Bulley Gloucs....46 E11
Bullgill Cumb....100 E3
Bullinghope Herefs....45 Q7
Bullington Hants....22 E6
Bullington Lincs....86 E5
Bullockstone Kent....39 L8
Bull's Green Herts....50 G7
Bull's Green Norfk....65 N3
Bulmer Essex....52 D3
Bulmer N York....98 D7
Bulmer Tye Essex....52 D4
Bulphan Thurr....37 P3
Bulstone Devon....10 D7
Bulstrode Herts....50 B10
Bulverhythe E Susx....26 C10
Bulwark Abers....159 M8
Bulwell C Nott....72 F2
Bulwick Nhants....61 L2
Bumble's Green Essex....51 K9
Bunacaimb Highld....145 L10
Bunarkaig Highld....146 F10
Bunbury Ches E....69 Q3
Bunbury Heath Ches E....69 Q3
Bunchrew Highld....155 R8
Bundalloch Highld....145 Q2
Bunessan Ag & B....137 K11
Bungay Suffk....65 L4
Bunker's Hill Lincs....87 J10
Bunnahabhain Ag & B....122 F5
Bunny Notts....72 F5
Buntait Highld....155 M11
Buntingford Herts....51 J5
Bunwell Norfk....64 G3
Bunwell Hill Norfk....64 G3
Bupton Derbys....71 N7
Burbage Derbys....83 M10
Burbage Leics....59 P6
Burbage Wilts....21 P2
Burcher Herefs....45 L2
Burchett's Green E Susx....25 Q4
Burchett's Green W & M....35 M8
Burcombe Wilts....21 L8
Burcot Oxon....34 G5
Burcot Worcs....58 E10
Burcote Shrops....57 N5
Burcott Bucks....49 M11
Burcott Bucks....49 N10
Burdale N York....98 H8
Bures Essex....52 F5
Burford Oxon....33 Q2
Burford Shrops....57 K11
Burg Ag & B....137 K6
Burgate Suffk....64 F6
Burgates Hants....23 L8
Burge End Herts....50 D4
Burgess Hill W Susx....24 H7
Burgh Suffk....65 J11
Burgh by Sands Cumb....110 F9

Burgh Castle Norfk....77 P10
Burghclere Hants....22 E2
Burghead Moray....157 L4
Burghfield W Berk....35 J11
Burghfield Common W Berk....35 J11
Burgh Heath Surrey....36 F9
Burgh Hill E Susx....26 B6
Burghill Herefs....45 P6
Burgh Island Devon....6 G10
Burgh le Marsh Lincs....87 P7
Burgh next Aylsham Norfk....77 J6
Burgh on Bain Lincs....86 H3
Burgh St Margaret Norfk....77 N9
Burgh St Peter Norfk....65 P3
Burghwallis Donc....91 N8
Burham Kent....38 B9
Buriton Hants....23 K11
Burland Ches E....69 R4
Burlawn Cnwll....4 F7
Burleigh Gloucs....32 G4
Burlescombe Devon....18 E11
Burleston Dorset....12 C6
Burlestone Devon....7 L9
Burley Hants....13 M4
Burley Rutlnd....73 M8
Burley Shrops....56 H8
Burleydam Ches E....69 R6
Burley Gate Herefs....46 A5
Burley in Wharfedale C Brad....97 J11
Burley Lawn Hants....13 M4
Burley Street Hants....13 M4
Burley Wood Head C Brad....90 F2
Burlingham Green Norfk....77 M9
Burlingjobb Powys....45 K3
Burlington Shrops....57 P2
Burlton Shrops....69 N9
Burmarsh Kent....27 K5
Burmington Warwks....47 Q7
Burn N York....91 P5
Burnage Manch....83 J6
Burnaston Derbys....71 P8
Burnbanks Cumb....101 P7
Burnbrae N Lans....126 F6
Burnby E R Yk....98 G11
Burn Cross Sheff....91 J11
Burndell W Susx....15 Q6
Burnden Bolton....89 L9
Burnedge Rochdl....89 Q8
Burneside Cumb....101 P11
Burneston N York....97 M4
Burnett BaNES....32 C11
Burnfoot Border....117 N8
Burnfoot Border....117 Q7
Burnfoot D & G....109 L2
Burnfoot D & G....110 F3
Burnfoot D & G....117 M11
Burnfoot P & K....134 B7
Burnham Bucks....35 P8
Burnham N Linc....93 J7
Burnham Deepdale Norfk....75 R2
Burnham Green Herts....50 G7
Burnham Market Norfk....76 A3
Burnham Norton Norfk....76 A3
Burnham-on-Crouch Essex....38 F2
Burnham-on-Sea Somset....19 K5
Burnham Overy Norfk....76 A3
Burnham Overy Staithe Norfk....76 A3
Burnham Thorpe Norfk....76 B3
Burnhaven Abers....159 R9
Burnhead D & G....116 B11
Burnhervie Abers....151 J4
Burnhill Green Staffs....57 P4
Burnhope Dur....113 J11
Burnhouse N Ayrs....125 K7
Burniston N York....99 L2
Burnley Lancs....89 N4
Burnley Crematorium Lancs....89 N4
Burnmouth Border....129 P7
Burn Naze Lancs....88 C2
Burn of Cambus Stirlg....133 L7
Burnopfield Dur....113 J9
Burnrigg Cumb....111 J9
Burnsall N York....96 F8
Burnside Angus....142 G6
Burnside Angus....143 J7
Burnside Fife....134 F6
Burnside Moray....157 M4
Burnside W Loth....127 K2
Burnside of Duntrune Angus....142 G11
Burntcommon Surrey....36 B10
Burntheath Derbys....71 N8
Burnt Heath Essex....53 J6
Burnt Hill W Berk....34 G10
Burnthouse Cnwll....3 K6
Burnt Houses Dur....103 M6
Burntisland Fife....134 G10
Burnt Oak E Susx....25 M5
Burntwood Staffs....58 G3
Burntwood Green Staffs....58 G3
Burnt Yates N York....97 L8
Burnworthy Somset....18 G11
Burpham Surrey....36 B10
Burpham W Susx....24 B9
Burradon N Tyne....113 L6
Burradon Nthumb....119 J9
Burrafirth Shet....169 t2
Burras Cnwll....2 H7
Burraton Cnwll....5 Q8
Burravoe Shet....169 s5
Burrells Cumb....102 C7
Burrelton P & K....142 C10
Burridge Devon....17 K4
Burridge Hants....14 F4
Burrill N York....97 K3
Burringham N Linc....92 D9
Burrington Devon....17 L8
Burrington Herefs....56 G10
Burrington N Som....19 N3
Burrough End Cambs....63 K9
Burrough Green Cambs....63 K9
Burrough on the Hill Leics....73 K8
Burrow Lancs....95 N6
Burrow Somset....18 B6
Burrow Bridge Somset....19 L8
Burrowhill Surrey....35 Q2
Burrows Cross Surrey....36 C11
Burry Swans....28 E6
Burry Green Swans....28 E6
Burry Port Carmth....28 D4

Burscough Lancs....88 E8
Burscough Bridge Lancs....88 E8
Bursea E R Yk....92 D4
Burshill E R Yk....99 M11
Bursledon Hants....14 E5
Burslem C Stke....70 F5
Burstall Suffk....53 L3
Burstock Dorset....11 J4
Burston Norfk....64 G5
Burston Staffs....70 G8
Burstow Surrey....24 H2
Burstwick E R Yk....93 M5
Burtersett N York....96 C3
Burtholme Cumb....111 K8
Burthorpe Green Suffk....63 N8
Burthwaite Cumb....110 H11
Burthy Cnwll....4 E10
Burtle Hill Somset....19 L6
Burtoft Lincs....74 E3
Burton Ches W....69 P2
Burton Ches W....81 L10
Burton Dorset....11 P6
Burton Dorset....13 L6
Burton Lincs....86 C6
Burton Nthumb....119 N4
Burton Pembks....41 J9
Burton Somset....11 L2
Burton Somset....18 G6
Burton Wilts....20 F8
Burton Wilts....32 F9
Burton Agnes E R Yk....99 N8
Burton Bradstock Dorset....11 K7
Burton Coggles Lincs....73 P5
Burton Constable Hall E R Yk....93 L3
Burton Dassett Warwks....48 C4
Burton End Essex....51 M6
Burton End Suffk....63 L11
Burton Fleming E R Yk....99 M6
Burton Green Warwks....59 L9
Burton Green Wrexhm....69 K3
Burton Hastings Warwks....59 P7
Burton-in-Kendal Cumb....95 L5
Burton-in-Kendal Services Cumb....95 L5
Burton in Lonsdale N York....95 P6
Burton Joyce Notts....72 G2
Burton Latimer Nhants....61 K6
Burton Lazars Leics....73 K7
Burton Leonard N York....97 M8
Burton on the Wolds Leics....72 F6
Burton Overy Leics....72 H11
Burton Pedwardine Lincs....74 B2
Burton Pidsea E R Yk....93 M4
Burton Salmon N York....91 M5
Burton's Green Essex....52 D6
Burton upon Stather N Linc....92 E7
Burton upon Trent Staffs....71 N10
Burton Waters Lincs....86 B6
Burtonwood Warrtn....82 C6
Burtonwood Services Warrtn....82 C6
Burwardsley Ches W....69 P3
Burwarton Shrops....57 L7
Burwash E Susx....25 Q6
Burwash Common E Susx....25 P6
Burwash Weald E Susx....25 Q6
Burwell Cambs....63 J7
Burwell Lincs....87 L5
Burwen IoA....78 G6
Burwick Ork....169 d8
Bury Bury....89 N8
Bury Cambs....62 C4
Bury Somset....18 B9
Bury W Susx....24 B8
Bury End C Beds....50 D3
Bury Green Herts....51 L6
Bury St Edmunds Suffk....64 B9
Burythorpe N York....98 F8
Busby E Rens....125 P6
Busby Stoop N York....97 N4
Buscot Oxon....33 P5
Bush Abers....143 P4
Bush Cnwll....16 C10
Bush Bank Herefs....45 P4
Bushbury Wolves....58 D4
Bushbury Crematorium Wolves....58 D4
Bushby Leics....72 H10
Bushey Herts....50 D11
Bushey Heath Herts....36 D2
Bush Green Norfk....65 J4
Bush Green Suffk....64 C10
Bush Hill Park Gt Lon....50 H11
Bushley Worcs....46 G8
Bushley Green Worcs....46 G8
Bushmead Bed....61 P8
Bushmoor Shrops....56 G7
Bushton Wilts....33 L9
Busk Cumb....102 B2
Buslingthorpe Lincs....86 E3
Bussage Gloucs....32 G4
Bussex Somset....19 L7
Butcher's Cross E Susx....25 N5
Butcombe N Som....19 P2
Bute Ag & B....124 C4
Butleigh Somset....19 P8
Butleigh Wootton Somset....19 P8
Butler's Cross Bucks....35 M3
Butler's Hill Notts....84 H11
Butlers Marston Warwks....48 B4
Butley Suffk....65 M11
Butley High Corner Suffk....53 Q2
Buttercrambe N York....98 E9
Butterden Border....129 K7
Butterknowle Dur....103 M5
Butterleigh Devon....9 N3
Butterley Derbys....84 F10
Buttermere Cumb....100 G7
Buttermere Wilts....22 B2
Butters Green Staffs....70 E4
Buttershaw C Brad....90 E5
Butterstone P & K....141 P8
Butterton Staffs....70 E6
Butterton Staffs....71 K3
Butterwick Dur....104 C4
Butterwick Lincs....87 L11
Butterwick N York....98 H5
Butterwick N York....99 K6
Butt Green Ches E....70 B4
Buttington Powys....56 C3
Buttonbridge Shrops....57 N9
Buttonoak Shrops....57 P9
Buttsash Hants....14 D5

Buttsbear Cross Cnwll 16 D11
Butt's Green Essex 52 C11
Buxhall Suffk 64 E10
Buxhall Fen Street Suffk ..64 E10
Buxted E Susx 25 L6
Buxton Derbys 83 N10
Buxton Norfk 77 J7
Buxton Heath Norfk 76 H7
Bwlch Powys 44 H10
Bwlchgwyn Wrexhm 69 J4
Bwlchllan Cerdgn 43 L3
Bwlchnewydd Carmth 42 G10
Bwlchtocyn Gwynd 66 E9
Bwlch-y-cibau Powys 68 G11
Bwlch-y-Ddar Powys 68 G10
Bwlchyfadfa Cerdgn 42 H5
Bwlch-y-ffridd Powys 55 P5
Bwlch-y-groes Pembks 41 P3
Bwlchymyrdd Swans 28 G5
Bwlch-y-sarnau Powys 55 N10
Byermoor Gatesd 113 J9
Byers Green Dur 103 P4
Byfield Nhants 48 F4
Byfleet Surrey 36 C8
Byford Herefs 45 M6
Bygrave Herts 50 G3
Byker N u Ty 113 L8
Byland Abbey N York 98 A5
Bylchau Conwy 68 C2
Byley Ches W 82 F11
Bynea Carmth 28 F5
Byrness Nthumb 118 E10
Bystock Devon 9 P8
Bythorn Cambs 61 N5
Byton Herefs 45 M2
Bywell Nthumb 112 F8
Byworth W Susx 23 Q10

C

Cabbacott Devon 16 G7
Cabourne Lincs 93 K10
Cabrach Ag & B 122 G7
Cabrach Moray 150 B2
Cabus Lancs 95 K11
Cackle Street E Susx 25 L5
Cackle Street E Susx 25 Q7
Cackle Street E Susx 26 D8
Cadbury Devon 9 M3
Cadbury Barton Devon 17 M8
Cadder E Duns 125 Q3
Caddington C Beds 50 C7
Caddonfoot Border 117 P3
Cadeby Donc 91 N10
Cadeby Leics 72 C10
Cadeleigh Devon 9 M3
Cade Street E Susx 25 P6
Cadgwith Cnwll 3 J11
Cadham Fife 134 H7
Cadishead Salfd 82 F6
Cadle Swans 28 H5
Cadley Lancs 88 G4
Cadley Wilts 21 P4
Cadley Wilts 33 P11
Cadmore End Bucks 35 L6
Cadnam Hants 13 P2
Cadney N Linc 92 H10
Cadole Flints 68 H2
Cadoxton V Glam 30 F11
Cadoxton Juxta-Neath
  Neath 29 L5
Cadwst Denbgs 68 D7
Caeathro Gwynd 67 J2
Caehopkin Powys 29 M2
Caenby Lincs 86 C3
Caeo Carmth 43 N6
Caerau Brdgnd 29 N6
Caerau Cardif 30 F9
Cae'r-bont Powys 29 M2
Cae'r bryn Carmth 28 G2
Caerdeon Gwynd 67 M11
Caer Farchell Pembks 40 E5
Caergeiliog IoA 78 E9
Caergwrle Flints 69 K3
Caerhun Conwy 79 P10
Caerlanrig Border 117 M10
Caerleon Newpt 31 K6
Caerleon Roman Fortress
  & Baths Newpt 31 K6
Caernarfon Gwynd 66 H2
Caernarfon Castle WHS
  Gwynd 66 H2
Caerphilly Caerph 30 G7
Caersws Powys 55 N6
Caerwedros Cerdgn 42 G3
Caerwent Mons 31 N6
Caerwys Flints 80 G10
Caerynwch Gwynd 67 P11
Caggle Street Mons 45 M11
Caim IoA 79 L8
Cairinis W Isls 168 d11
Cairnbaan Ag & B 130 G9
Cairnbulg Abers 159 P4
Cairncross Border 129 M7
Cairncurran Inver 125 J3
Cairndow Ag & B 131 Q5
Cairneyhill Fife 134 C10
Cairngarroch D & G 106 E8
Cairngorms
  National Park Moray ..149 K7
Cairnie Abers 158 C9
Cairnorrie Abers 159 L9
Cairnryan D & G 106 E4
Cairnty Moray 157 Q7
Caister-on-Sea Norfk 77 Q9
Caistor Lincs 93 K10
Caistor St Edmund Norfk ..77 J11
Cakebole Worcs 58 C10
Cake Street Norfk 64 F3
Calais Street Suffk 52 G4
Calanais W Isls 168 h4
Calbourne IoW 14 D9
Calceby Lincs 87 L5
Calcot Flints 80 H10
Calcot Gloucs 33 L2
Calcot W Berk 35 J10
Calcots Moray 157 P5
Calcott Kent 39 L9
Calcott Shrops 56 G2
Calcutt N York 97 M9
Calcutt Wilts 33 M6
Caldbeck Cumb 101 K2
Caldbergh N York 96 G3
Caldecote Cambs 61 P3
Caldecote Cambs 61 D9
Caldecote Herts 50 E4
Caldecote Nhants 49 J4

Caldecote Highfields
  Cambs 62 E9
Caldecott Nhants 61 L7
Caldecott Oxon 34 E5
Caldecott Rutlnd 61 J2
Caldecotte M Keyn 49 N7
Calder Cumb 100 D10
Calderbank N Lans 126 D5
Calder Bridge Cumb 100 D9
Calderbrook Rochdl 89 Q7
Caldercruix N Lans 126 E4
Calder Grove Wakefd 91 J7
Caldermill S Lans 126 B9
Caldermore Rochdl 89 Q7
Calder Vale Lancs 95 L11
Calderwood S Lans 126 B6
Caldey Island Pembks 41 M11
Caldicot Mons 31 N7
Caldmore Wsall 58 F5
Caldwell N York 103 N8
Caldy Wirral 81 J7
Caledfwlch Carmth 43 N9
Calenick Cnwll 3 L5
Calford Green Suffk 63 M11
Calfsound Ork 169 e3
Calgary Ag & B 137 K5
Califer Moray 157 K6
California Falk 126 G2
California Norfk 77 Q8
California Cross Devon 7 J7
Calke Derbys 72 B6
Callakille Highld 153 M6
Callander Stirlg 133 J6
Callanish W Isls 168 h4
Callaughton Shrops 57 L5
Callestick Cnwll 3 K3
Calligarry Highld 145 K7
Calligarry Highld 145 K7
Callingwood Staffs 71 M10
Callow Herefs 45 P8
Callow End Worcs 46 F4
Callow Hill Wilts 33 K8
Callow Hill Worcs 47 K2
Callow Hill Worcs 57 N10
Callows Grave Worcs 57 K11
Calmore Hants 13 P2
Calmsden Gloucs 33 K3
Calne Wilts 33 J10
Calow Derbys 84 F6
Calshot Hants 14 E6
Calstock Cnwll 6 C5
Calstone Wellington
  Wilts 33 K11
Calthorpe Norfk 76 H5
Calthorpe Street Norfk ..77 N6
Calthwaite Cumb 101 N2
Calton N York 96 D9
Calton Staffs 71 L5
Calveley Ches E 69 Q3
Calver Derbys 84 B6
Calverhall Shrops 69 R7
Calver Hill Herefs 45 M5
Calverleigh Devon 9 M2
Calverley Leeds 90 G3
Calver Sough Derbys 84 B6
Calvert Bucks 49 J10
Calverton M Keyn 49 L7
Calverton Notts 85 K11
Calvine P & K 141 K4
Calvo Cumb 109 P10
Calzeat Border 116 G3
Cam Gloucs 32 E5
Camasachoire Highld 138 D5
Camasine Highld 138 D5
Camas Luinie Highld 146 A2
Camastianavaig Highld ..153 J10
Camault Muir Highld 155 P9
Camber E Susx 26 G8
Camberley Surrey 23 N2
Camberwell Gt Lon 36 H5
Camblesforth N York 91 Q5
Cambo Nthumb 112 F3
Cambois Nthumb 113 M4
Camborne Cnwll 2 G5
Cambourne Cambs 62 D9
Cambridge Cambs 62 G9
Cambridge Gloucs 32 D4
Cambridge Airport
  Cambs 62 G9
Cambridge City
  Crematorium Cambs ..62 E8
Cambrose Cnwll 2 H4
Cambus Clacks 133 P9
Cambusavie Platform
  Highld 162 H7
Cambusbarron Stirlg 133 M9
Cambuskenneth Stirlg ..133 N9
Cambuslang S Lans 125 Q5
Cambus o' May Abers 150 C8
Cambuswallace S Lans ..116 E3
Camden Town Gt Lon 36 G4
Cameley BaNES 20 B3
Camelford Cnwll 5 J5
Camelon Falk 133 P11
Camerory Highld 157 J11
Camer's Green Worcs 46 E7
Camerton BaNES 20 C3
Camerton Cumb 100 D4
Camghouran P & K 140 E6
Camieston Border 117 R4
Cammachmore Abers 151 N8
Cammeringham Lincs 86 B4
Camore Highld 162 H9
Campbeltown Ag & B 120 D7
Campbeltown Airport
  Ag & B 120 C7
Camperdown N Tyne 113 L6
Cample D & G 109 J2
Campmuir P & K 142 C10
Camps W Loth 127 K4
Campsall Donc 91 N8
Campsea Ash Suffk 65 L10
Camps End Cambs 51 P2
Campton C Beds 50 D3
Camptown Border 118 C8
Camrose Pembks 40 H6
Camserney P & K 141 K8
Camusnagaul Highld 139 K3
Camusnagaul Highld 160 H9
Camusteel Highld 153 N9
Camusterrach Highld 153 N9
Canada Hants 21 Q11
Canal Foot Cumb 94 G5
Canaston Bridge Pembks ..41 L7
Candacraig Abers 149 Q8
Candlesby Lincs 87 N7
Candle Street Suffk 64 E7
Candover Green Shrops ..57 J3
Candy Mill Border 116 F2

Cane End Oxon 35 J9
Canewdon Essex 38 F3
Canford Bottom Dorset ..12 H4
Canford Cliffs Poole 13 J7
Canford Crematorium
  Bristl 31 Q9
Canford Heath Poole 12 H6
Canford Magna Poole 12 H5
Canhams Green Suffk 64 F8
Canisbay Highld 167 Q2
Canklow Rothm 84 F2
Canley Covtry 59 M9
Canley Crematorium
  Covtry 59 M9
Cann Dorset 20 G10
Canna Highld 144 B6
Cannich Highld 155 K11
Cannington Somset 19 J7
Canning Town Gt Lon 37 K4
Cannock Staffs 58 E2
Cannock Chase Staffs 70 H11
Cannock Wood Staffs 58 F2
Cannon Bridge Herefs 45 N6
Canonbie D & G 110 G5
Canon Frome Herefs 46 B6
Canon Pyon Herefs 45 P5
Canons Ashby Nhants 48 G4
Canonstown Cnwll 2 E6
Canterbury Kent 39 K10
Canterbury Cathedral
  Kent 39 L10
Cantley Norfk 77 M11
Cantlop Shrops 57 J3
Canton Cardif 30 G9
Cantraywood Highld 156 D8
Cantsfield Lancs 95 N6
Canvey Island Essex 38 C5
Canwick Lincs 86 C7
Canworthy Water Cnwll 5 L3
Caol Highld 139 L2
Caolas Scalpaigh W Isls ..168 h8
Caoles Ag & B 136 D6
Caonich Highld 146 D9
Capel Kent 25 P2
Capel Surrey 24 E2
Capel Bangor Cerdgn 54 F8
Capel Betws Lleucu
  Cerdgn 43 M3
Capel Coch IoA 78 H8
Capel Curig Conwy 67 N3
Capel Cynon Cerdgn 42 G5
Capel Dewi Carmth 43 J10
Capel Dewi Cerdgn 43 J8
Capel-Dewi Cerdgn 54 E8
Capel Garmon Conwy 67 Q3
Capel Green Suffk 53 Q2
Capel Gwyn Carmth 43 J10
Capel Gwyn IoA 78 E9
Capel Gwynfe Carmth 43 P10
Capel Hendre Carmth 28 G2
Capel Isaac Carmth 43 L9
Capel Iwan Carmth 41 Q3
Capel le Ferne Kent 27 N4
Capelles Guern 10 c1
Capel Llanilltern Cardif ..30 E9
Capel Mawr IoA 78 G10
Capel Parc IoA 78 G7
Capel St Andrew Suffk 53 Q2
Capel St Mary Suffk 53 J4
Capel Seion Cerdgn 54 E9
Capel Trisant Cerdgn 54 G9
Capeluchaf Gwynd 66 G5
Capelulo Conwy 79 N9
Capel-y-ffin Powys 45 K8
Capel-y-graig Gwynd 79 J11
Capenhurst Ches W 81 M10
Capernwray Lancs 95 L6
Capheaton Nthumb 112 F4
Caplaw E Rens 125 L6
Capon's Green Suffk 65 K8
Cappercleuch Border 117 J6
Capstone Medway 38 C8
Capton Devon 7 L8
Capton Somset 18 E7
Caputh P & K 141 Q9
Caradon Town Cnwll 5 M7
Carbeth Inn Stirlg 125 N2
Carbis Cnwll 4 G10
Carbis Bay Cnwll 2 E6
Carbost Highld 152 F11
Carbost Highld 152 G8
Carbrook Sheff 84 E3
Carbrooke Norfk 76 C11
Carburton Notts 85 K6
Carclaze Cnwll 3 Q3
Car Colston Notts 73 J2
Carcroft Donc 91 N9
Cardenden Fife 134 G8
Cardeston Shrops 56 F2
Cardewlees Cumb 110 G10
Cardiff Cardif 30 G9
Cardiff Airport V Glam 30 E11
Cardiff Gate Services
  Cardif 30 H8
Cardiff West Services
  Cardif 30 E9
Cardigan Cerdgn 42 C5
Cardinal's Green Cambs ..63 K11
Cardington Bed 61 N11
Cardington Shrops 57 J5
Cardinham Cnwll 5 J8
Cardrain D & G 106 F11
Cardrona Border 117 L3
Cardross D & G 125 J2
Cardross Crematorium
  Ag & B 125 J2
Cardryne D & G 106 F11
Cardurnock Cumb 110 D9
Careby Lincs 73 Q7
Careston Angus 143 J5
Carew Pembks 41 K10
Carew Cheriton Pembks ..41 K10
Carew Newton Pembks 41 K10
Carey Herefs 45 R8
Carfin N Lans 126 D5
Carfraemill Border 128 C3
Cargate Green Norfk 77 M9
Cargenbridge D & G 109 L5
Cargill P & K 142 B10
Cargo Cumb 110 G9
Cargreen Cnwll 6 C6
Cargurrel Cnwll 3 M6
Carham Nthumb 118 E3
Carhampton Somset 18 D6
Carharrack Cnwll 3 J5
Carie P & K 140 F6
Carinish W Isls 168 d11
Carisbrooke IoW 14 E9
Cark Cumb 94 H5

Carkeel Cnwll 5 Q9
Carlabhagh W Isls 168 h3
Carland Cross Cnwll 3 M3
Carlbury Darltn 103 P7
Carlby Lincs 73 Q8
Carlcroft Nthumb 118 F8
Carleen Cnwll 2 G7
Carlesmoor N York 97 K6
Carleton Cumb 100 D9
Carleton Cumb 101 P5
Carleton Cumb 110 H10
Carleton Lancs 88 C3
Carleton N York 96 E11
Carleton Wakefd 91 M6
Carleton Crematorium
  Bpool 88 C3
Carleton Forehoe Norfk ..76 F10
Carleton Rode Norfk 64 G3
Carleton St Peter Norfk ..77 L11
Carlidnack Cnwll 3 K8
Carlincraig Abers 158 G9
Carlingcott BaNES 20 C3
Carlin How R & Cl 105 K7
Carlisle Cumb 110 G9
Carlisle Airport Cumb 111 J8
Carlisle Crematorium
  Cumb 110 G10
Carloggas Cnwll 4 D8
Carlops Border 127 M6
Carloway W Isls 168 h3
Carlton Barns 91 K8
Carlton Bed 61 L9
Carlton Cambs 63 K10
Carlton Leeds 91 J5
Carlton Leics 72 B10
Carlton N York 91 Q6
Carlton N York 96 C3
Carlton N York 98 C3
Carlton Notts 72 G2
Carlton S on T 104 C6
Carlton Suffk 65 M9
Carlton Colville Suffk 65 Q4
Carlton Curlieu Leics 72 H11
Carlton Green Cambs 63 K10
Carlton Husthwaite
  N York 97 Q5
Carlton-in-Cleveland
  N York 104 F10
Carlton in Lindrick Notts ..85 J4
Carlton-le-Moorland
  Lincs 86 B9
Carlton Miniott N York 97 N4
Carlton-on-Trent Notts 85 N8
Carlton Scroop Lincs 86 B11
Carluke S Lans 126 F6
Carlyon Bay Cnwll 3 R3
Carmacoup S Lans 115 Q2
Carmarthen Carmth 42 H10
Carmel Carmth 43 L11
Carmel Flints 80 H9
Carmel Gwynd 66 H4
Carmichael S Lans 116 C3
Carmountside
  Crematorium C Stke ..70 G5
Carmunnock C Glas 125 P6
Carmyle C Glas 125 Q5
Carmyllie Angus 143 J9
Carnaby E R Yk 99 N7
Carnbee Fife 135 N6
Carnbo P & K 134 D7
Carn Brea Cnwll 2 H5
Carnbrogie Abers 151 M2
Carndu Highld 145 Q2
Carnduff S Lans 126 B8
Carne Cnwll 3 K9
Carne Cnwll 3 N6
Carne Cnwll 3 M6
Carnell E Ayrs 125 M11
Carnewas Cnwll 4 D8
Carnforth Lancs 95 K6
Carn-gorm Highld 146 B3
Carnhedryn Pembks 40 F5
Carnhell Green Cnwll 2 G6
Carnie Abers 151 L6
Carnkie Cnwll 2 H5
Carnkie Cnwll 3 J7
Carnkief Cnwll 3 K3
Carno Powys 55 M5
Carnock Fife 134 C10
Carnon Downs Cnwll 3 K5
Carnousie Abers 158 G7
Carnoustie Angus 143 K11
Carnsmerry Cnwll 4 G10
Carnwath S Lans 126 H8
Carnyorth Cnwll 2 B7
Carol Green Solhll 59 L9
Carpalla Cnwll 3 P3
Carperby N York 96 F3
Carr Rothm 84 H2
Carradale Ag & B 120 F4
Carrbridge Highld 148 G3
Carrbrook Tamesd 83 L4
Carrefour Jersey 11 b1
Carreglefn IoA 78 F7
Carr Gate Wakefd 91 J6
Carrhouse N Linc 92 C9
Carrick Ag & B 131 J10
Carrick Castle Ag & B 131 P9
Carriden Falk 134 C11
Carrington Lincs 87 K9
Carrington Mdloth 127 Q5
Carrington Traffd 82 F6
Carrog Conwy 67 P5
Carrog Denbgs 68 F6
Carron Falk 133 P11
Carron Moray 157 N9
Carronbridge D & G 116 B11
Carron Bridge Stirlg 133 L11
Carronshore Falk 133 P11
Carrow Hill Mons 31 M7
Carr Shield Nthumb 112 B11
Carrutherstown D & G 109 P6
Carr Vale Derbys 84 G7
Carrville Dur 104 B2
Carsaig Ag & B 137 N11
Carseriggan D & G 107 K4
Carsethorn D & G 109 L9
Carshalton Gt Lon 36 G8
Carsington Derbys 71 P4
Carskey Ag & B 120 C10
Carsluith D & G 107 N7
Carsphairn D & G 115 J11
Carstairs S Lans 126 G8
Carstairs Junction S Lans ..126 H8
Carswell Marsh Oxon 34 B5
Carter's Clay Hants 22 B10
Carters Green Essex 51 M8
Carterton Oxon 33 Q3

Carterway Heads
  Nthumb 112 F10
Carthew Cnwll 4 G10
Carthorpe N York 97 M4
Cartington Nthumb 119 K10
Cartland S Lans 126 F8
Cartmel Cumb 94 H5
Cartmel Fell Cumb 95 J3
Carway Carmth 28 E3
Carwinley Cumb 110 H6
Cashe's Green Gloucs 32 F3
Cashmoor Dorset 12 G3
Cassington Oxon 34 E2
Cassop Colliery Dur 104 B3
Castallack Cnwll 2 D8
Castel Guern 10 b2
Castell Conwy 79 P11
Castell-y-bwch Torfn 31 J6
Casterton Cumb 95 N5
Castle Cnwll 4 H10
Castle Acre Norfk 75 R7
Castle Ashby Nhants 61 J9
Castlebay W Isls 168 b18
Castle Bolton N York 96 F3
Castle Bromwich Solhll ..58 H7
Castle Bytham Lincs 73 P7
Castlebythe Pembks 41 K5
Castle Caereinion Powys ..56 B3
Castle Camps Cambs 51 P2
Castle Carrock Cumb 111 K9
Castlecary Falk 126 D2
Castle Cary Somset 20 B8
Castle Combe Wilts 32 F9
Castle Donington Leics ..72 C5
Castle Douglas D & G 108 G8
Castle Eaton Swindn 33 M5
Castle Eden Dur 104 D3
Castle End C Pete 74 D11
Castleford Wakefd 91 L5
Castle Frome Herefs 46 C5
Castle Gate Cnwll 2 D7
Castle Green Cumb 95 L3
Castle Green Surrey 23 Q2
Castle Gresley Derbys 71 N11
Castle Hedingham Essex ..52 C4
Castlehill Border 117 J3
Castlehill Highld 167 M3
Castle Hill Kent 25 Q2
Castle Hill Suffk 53 K2
Castlehill W Duns 125 K2
Castle Kennedy D & G 106 F6
Castle Lachlan Ag & B 131 L8
Castlemartin Pembks 40 H11
Castlemilk C Glas 125 P6
Castle Morris Pembks 40 H4
Castlemorton Worcs 46 E7
Castlemorton Common
  Worcs 46 E7
Castle O'er D & G 110 D2
Castle Pulverbatch
  Shrops 56 G4
Castlerigg Stone Circle
  Cumb 101 J6
Castle Rising Norfk 75 N6
Castleside Dur 112 G11
Castle Stuart Highld 156 C8
Castlethorpe M Keyn 49 M6
Castlethorpe N Linc 92 G9
Castleton Border 111 K3
Castleton Derbys 83 Q8
Castleton N York 105 J9
Castleton Newpt 31 J8
Castleton Rochdl 89 P8
Castletown Dorset 11 P10
Castletown Highld 167 M3
Castletown IoM 80 c8
Castletown Sundld 113 N9
Castley N York 97 L11
Caston Norfk 64 D2
Castor C Pete 74 B11
Caswell Bay Swans 28 G7
Catacol N Ayrs 123 R10
Cat and Fiddle Derbys 83 M10
Catbrain S Glos 31 Q8
Catbrook Mons 31 P4
Catch Flints 81 J10
Catchall Cnwll 2 C8
Catchem's Corner Solhll ..59 L9
Catchgate Dur 113 J10
Catcliffe Rothm 84 F3
Catcomb Wilts 33 K9
Catcott Somset 19 L7
Catcott Burtle Somset 19 M6
Caterham Surrey 36 H9
Catfield Norfk 77 M7
Catfield Common Norfk ..77 N7
Catford Gt Lon 37 J6
Catforth Lancs 88 F3
Cathcart C Glas 125 P5
Cathedine Powys 44 G9
Catherine-de-Barnes
  Solhll 59 J8
Catherine Slack C Brad ..90 D4
Catherington Hants 15 J4
Catherston Leweston
  Dorset 10 H6
Catherton Shrops 57 M9
Catisfield Hants 14 G5
Catley Herefs 46 C6
Catley Lane Head Rochdl ..89 P7
Catlodge Highld 147 Q9
Catlow Lancs 89 N4
Catlowdy Cumb 111 J5
Catmere End Essex 51 L3
Catmore W Berk 34 E8
Caton Devon 7 J4
Caton Lancs 95 L8
Caton Green Lancs 95 M7
Cator Court Devon 8 C7
Catrine E Ayrs 115 K2
Cat's Ash Newpt 31 L6
Catsfield E Susx 26 B9
Catsfield Stream E Susx ..26 B9
Catsgore Somset 19 P9
Catsham Somset 19 Q8
Catshill Worcs 58 E10
Catstree Shrops 57 N5
Cattadale Ag & B 120 C9
Cattal N York 97 P10
Cattawade Suffk 53 K5
Catterall Lancs 88 F2
Catterick N York 103 P11
Catterick Bridge N York ..103 P11
Catterick Garrison
  N York 103 N11
Catterlen Cumb 101 N4
Catterline Abers 143 Q2
Catterton N York 97 R11

Catteshall - Church Enstone 269

Catteshall Surrey 23 Q6
Catthorpe Leics 60 C5
Cattishall Suffk 64 B8
Cattistock Dorset 11 M5
Catton N York 97 N5
Catton Nthumb 112 B9
Catwick E R Yk 99 N11
Catworth Cambs 61 N6
Caudle Green Gloucs 32 H2
Caulcott C Beds 50 B2
Caulcott Oxon 48 F10
Cauldcots Angus 143 M8
Cauldhame Stirlg 133 J9
Cauldmill Border 117 Q7
Cauldon Staffs 71 K5
Cauldon Lowe Staffs 71 K5
Cauldwell Derbys 71 P11
Caulkerbush D & G 109 K9
Caulside D & G 110 H4
Caundle Marsh Dorset 11 P2
Caunsall Worcs 58 C8
Caunton Notts 85 M8
Causeway Hants 23 K10
Causeway End Cumb 95 K3
Causeway End D & G 107 M6
Causeway End Essex 51 Q7
Causewayend S Lans 116 E3
Causewayhead Cumb 109 P10
Causewayhead Stirlg 133 N8
Causeyend Abers 151 N4
Causey Park Nthumb 113 J2
Causey Park Bridge Nthumb 113 J2
Cavendish Suffk 63 P11
Cavenham Suffk 63 N6
Caversfield Oxon 48 G9
Caversham Readg 35 K10
Caverswall Staffs 70 H6
Caverton Mill Border 118 D5
Cavil E R Yk 92 C4
Cawdor Highld 156 E7
Cawkwell Lincs 87 J5
Cawood N York 91 P3
Cawsand Cnwll 6 C8
Cawston Norfk 76 G7
Cawston Warwks 59 Q10
Cawthorn N York 98 F3
Cawthorne Barns 90 H9
Cawton N York 98 C5
Caxton Cambs 62 D9
Caxton End Cambs 62 D9
Caxton Gibbet Cambs 62 C8
Caynham Shrops 57 K10
Caythorpe Lincs 86 B11
Caythorpe Notts 85 L11
Cayton N York 99 M4
Ceann a Bhaigh W Isls 168 c11
Ceannacroc Lodge Highld 146 G5
Cearsiadar W Isls 168 i5
Ceciliford Mons 31 P4
Cefn Newpt 31 J7
Cefn Berain Conwy 80 D11
Cefn-brith Conwy 68 B4
Cefn-bryn-brain Carmth 29 K2
Cefn Byrle Powys 29 M2
Cefn Canel Powys 68 H8
Cefn Coch Powys 68 F9
Cefn-coed-y-cymmer Myr Td 30 D3
Cefn Cribwr Brdgnd 29 N8
Cefn Cross Brdgnd 29 N8
Cefn-ddwysarn Gwynd 68 C7
Cefn-Einion Shrops 56 D7
Cefneithin Carmth 28 G2
Cefngorwydd Powys 44 C5
Cefn-mawr Wrexhm 69 J6
Cefnpennar Rhondd 30 D4
Cefn-y-bedd Flints 69 K3
Cefn-y-pant Carmth 41 N5
Ceint IoA 78 H9
Cellan Cerdgn 43 M5
Cellardyke Fife 135 P7
Cellarhead Staffs 70 H5
Celleron Cumb 101 N5
Celynen Caerph 30 H5
Cemaes IoA 78 F6
Cemmaes Powys 55 J3
Cemmaes Road Powys 55 J4
Cenarth Cerdgn 41 Q2
Cerbyd Pembks 40 F5
Ceres Fife 135 L5
Cerne Abbas Dorset 11 P4
Cerney Wick Gloucs 33 L5
Cerrigceinwen IoA 78 G10
Cerrigydrudion Conwy 68 C5
Cess Norfk 77 N8
Ceunant Gwynd 67 J2
Chaceley Gloucs 46 G8
Chacewater Cnwll 3 K5
Chackmore Bucks 49 J7
Chacombe Nhants 48 E6
Chadbury Worcs 47 K5
Chadderton Oldham 89 Q9
Chadderton Fold Oldham 89 Q9
Chaddesden C Derb 72 B3
Chaddesley Corbett Worcs 58 C10
Chaddlehanger Devon 8 C9
Chaddleworth W Berk 34 D9
Chadlington Oxon 48 B10
Chadshunt Warwks 48 B4
Chadwell Leics 73 K6
Chadwell Shrops 57 P2
Chadwell End Bed 61 N7
Chadwell Heath Gt Lon 37 L3
Chadwell St Mary Thurr 37 P5
Chadwick Worcs 58 B11
Chadwick End Solhll 59 K10
Chadwick Green St Hel 82 B5
Chaffcombe Somset 10 H2
Chafford Hundred Thurr 37 P5
Chagford Devon 8 H7
Chailey E Susx 25 J7
Chainbridge Cambs 74 H10
Chainhurst Kent 26 B2
Chalbury Dorset 12 H3
Chalbury Common Dorset 12 H3
Chaldon Surrey 36 H9
Chale IoW 14 E11
Chale Green IoW 14 E11
Chalfont Common Bucks 36 B2
Chalfont St Giles Bucks 35 Q6
Chalfont St Peter Bucks 36 B2
Chalford Gloucs 32 G4
Chalford Oxon 35 K4
Chalford Wilts 20 G4
Chalgrave C Beds 50 B5
Chalgrove Oxon 34 H5
Chalk Kent 37 Q6
Chalk End Essex 51 P8
Chalkhouse Green Oxon 35 K9
Chalkway Somset 10 H3
Chalkwell Kent 38 E9
Challaborough Devon 6 H10
Challacombe Devon 17 M3
Challoch D & G 107 L4
Challock Kent 38 H11
Chalmington Dorset 11 M4
Chalton C Beds 50 B5
Chalton C Beds 61 P10
Chalton Hants 23 K11
Chalvey Slough 35 Q9
Chalvington E Susx 25 M9
Chambers Green Kent 26 F3
Chandler's Cross Herts 50 C11
Chandlers Cross Worcs 46 E7
Chandler's Ford Hants 22 D11
Channel's End Bed 61 P9
Chanterlands Crematorium C KuH 93 J4
Chantry Somset 20 D5
Chantry Suffk 53 K3
Chapel Cumb 100 H4
Chapel Fife 134 H9
Chapel Allerton Leeds 91 J3
Chapel Allerton Somset 19 M4
Chapel Amble Cnwll 4 F6
Chapel Brampton Nhants 60 F7
Chapelbridge Cambs 62 C2
Chapel Chorlton Staffs 70 E7
Chapel Cross E Susx 25 P6
Chapel End Bed 61 P9
Chapel End C Beds 50 C2
Chapel End Cambs 61 P4
Chapel End Warwks 59 M6
Chapelend Way Essex 52 B4
Chapel-en-le-Frith Derbys 83 N8
Chapel Field Bury 89 M9
Chapelgate Lincs 74 H6
Chapel Green Warwks 48 E2
Chapel Green Warwks 59 L7
Chapel Haddlesey N York 91 P5
Chapelhall N Lans 126 D5
Chapel Hill Abers 159 Q10
Chapel Hill Lincs 86 H10
Chapel Hill Mons 31 P5
Chapel Hill N York 97 M11
Chapelhope Border 117 J7
Chapelknowe D & G 110 F6
Chapel Lawn Shrops 56 E9
Chapel le Dale N York 95 Q5
Chapel Leigh Somset 18 F9
Chapel Milton Derbys 83 N8
Chapel of Garioch Abers 151 J3
Chapel Rossan D & G 106 F9
Chapel Row E Susx 25 P8
Chapel Row Essex 52 C11
Chapel Row W Berk 34 G11
Chapels Cumb 94 E4
Chapel St Leonards Lincs 87 Q6
Chapel Stile Cumb 101 K9
Chapelton Angus 143 L8
Chapelton Devon 17 K6
Chapelton S Lans 126 B8
Chapeltown Bl w D 89 L7
Chapel Town Cnwll 4 D10
Chapeltown Moray 149 N3
Chapeltown Sheff 91 K11
Chapmanslade Wilts 20 F5
Chapmans Well Devon 5 P3
Chapmore End Herts 50 H7
Chappel Essex 52 E6
Charaton Cnwll 5 N8
Chard Somset 10 G3
Chard Junction Somset 10 G4
Chardleigh Green Somset 10 G2
Chardstock Devon 10 G4
Charfield S Glos 32 D6
Chargrove Gloucs 46 H11
Charing Kent 26 G2
Charing Crematorium Kent 26 G2
Charing Heath Kent 26 F2
Charing Hill Kent 38 G11
Charingworth Gloucs 47 N7
Charlbury Oxon 48 C11
Charlcombe BaNES 32 D11
Charlcutt Wilts 33 J9
Charlecote Warwks 47 Q3
Charlemont Sandw 58 F6
Charles Devon 17 M5
Charleshill Surrey 23 N6
Charleston Angus 142 F8
Charlestown C Aber 151 N7
Charlestown C Brad 90 F3
Charlestown Calder 90 B5
Charlestown Cnwll 3 Q3
Charlestown Derbys 83 M6
Charlestown Dorset 11 P9
Charlestown Fife 134 D11
Charlestown Highld 153 Q3
Charlestown Highld 156 A8
Charlestown Salfd 82 H4
Charles Tye Suffk 64 E11
Charlesworth Derbys 83 M6
Charlinch Somset 18 H7
Charlottetown Fife 134 H5
Charlton Gt Lon 37 K5
Charlton Hants 22 C5
Charlton Herts 50 E5
Charlton Nhants 48 F7
Charlton Nthumb 112 B4
Charlton Oxon 34 D7
Charlton Somset 19 J9
Charlton Somset 20 B6
Charlton Somset 20 C4
Charlton Surrey 36 C7
Charlton W Susx 15 N4
Charlton Wilts 20 H10
Charlton Wilts 33 J7
Charlton Worcs 47 K5
Charlton Worcs 58 B10
Charlton Wrekin 57 K2
Charlton Abbots Gloucs 47 K10
Charlton Adam Somset 19 P9
Charlton All Saints Wilts 21 N10
Charlton Down Dorset 11 P5
Charlton Hill Shrops 57 K3
Charlton Horethorne Somset 20 C10
Charlton Kings Gloucs 47 J10
Charlton Mackrell Somset 19 P9
Charlton Marshall Dorset 12 F4
Charlton Musgrove Somset 20 D9
Charlton-on-Otmoor Oxon 48 G11
Charlton on the Hill Dorset 12 E4
Charlton St Peter Wilts 21 M3
Charlwood Hants 23 J8
Charlwood Surrey 24 F2
Charminster Dorset 11 P6
Charmouth Dorset 10 H6
Charndon Bucks 49 J10
Charney Bassett Oxon 34 C6
Charnock Green Lancs 88 H7
Charnock Richard Lancs 88 H7
Charnock Richard Crematorium Lancs 88 H7
Charnock Richard Services Lancs 88 G7
Charsfield Suffk 65 K10
Chart Corner Kent 38 C11
Charter Alley Hants 22 G3
Charterhall Border 129 K10
Charterhouse Somset 19 N3
Chartershall Stirlg 133 M9
Charterville Allotments Oxon 34 B2
Chartham Kent 39 K11
Chartham Hatch Kent 39 K10
Chart Hill Kent 26 C2
Chartridge Bucks 35 P4
Chart Sutton Kent 26 D2
Chartway Street Kent 38 D11
Charvil Wokham 35 L9
Charwelton Nhants 60 B9
Chase Terrace Staffs 58 F3
Chasetown Staffs 58 F3
Chastleton Oxon 47 P9
Chasty Devon 16 E11
Chatburn Lancs 89 M2
Chatcull Staffs 70 D8
Chatham Caerph 30 H7
Chatham Medway 38 C8
Chatham Green Essex 52 B8
Chathill Nthumb 119 N5
Chatley Worcs 46 G2
Chatsworth House Derbys 84 C6
Chattenden Medway 38 C7
Chatter End Essex 51 L5
Chatteris Cambs 62 E3
Chatterton Lancs 89 M7
Chattisham Suffk 53 J3
Chatto Border 118 E7
Chatton Nthumb 119 L5
Chaul End C Beds 50 C6
Chawleigh Devon 17 N9
Chawley Oxon 34 E4
Chawston Bed 61 Q9
Chawton Hants 23 K7
Chaxhill Gloucs 32 D2
Chazey Heath Oxon 35 J9
Cheadle Staffs 71 J6
Cheadle Stockp 83 J7
Cheadle Heath Stockp 83 J7
Cheadle Hulme Stockp 83 J7
Cheam Gt Lon 36 F8
Cheapside W & M 35 P11
Chearsley Bucks 35 K2
Chebsey Staffs 70 F9
Checkendon Oxon 35 J8
Checkley Ches E 70 C5
Checkley Herefs 46 A7
Checkley Staffs 71 J7
Checkley Green Ches E 70 C5
Chedburgh Suffk 63 N9
Cheddar Somset 19 N4
Cheddington Bucks 49 P11
Cheddleton Staffs 70 H4
Cheddleton Heath Staffs 70 H4
Cheddon Fitzpaine Somset 18 H9
Chedglow Wilts 32 H6
Chedgrave Norfk 65 M2
Chedington Dorset 11 K3
Chediston Suffk 65 M6
Chediston Green Suffk 65 M6
Chedworth Gloucs 33 L2
Chedzoy Somset 19 K7
Cheeseman's Green Kent 26 H4
Cheetham Hill Manch 82 H4
Cheldon Devon 8 H2
Chelford Ches E 82 H10
Chellaston C Derb 72 B4
Chellington Bed 61 L9
Chelmarsh Shrops 57 N7
Chelmick Shrops 56 H6
Chelmondiston Suffk 53 M4
Chelmorton Derbys 83 P11
Chelmsford Essex 52 B10
Chelmsford Crematorium Essex 51 Q9
Chelmsley Wood Solhll 59 J7
Chelsea Gt Lon 36 G5
Chelsfield Gt Lon 37 L8
Chelsham Surrey 37 J9
Chelston Somset 18 G10
Chelsworth Suffk 52 G2
Cheltenham Gloucs 46 H10
Cheltenham Crematorium Gloucs 47 J10
Chelveston Nhants 61 L7
Chelvey N Som 31 N11
Chelwood BaNES 20 B2
Chelwood Common E Susx 25 K5
Chelwood Gate E Susx 25 K4
Chelworth Wilts 33 J6
Chelworth Lower Green Wilts 33 L6
Chelworth Upper Green Wilts 33 L6
Cheney Longville Shrops 56 G8
Chenies Bucks 50 B11
Chepstow Mons 31 P6
Chequerbent Bolton 89 K9
Chequers Corner Norfk 75 J9
Cherhill Wilts 33 K10
Cherington Gloucs 32 H5
Cherington Warwks 47 Q7
Cheriton Devon 17 N2
Cheriton Hants 22 G9
Cheriton Kent 27 M4
Cheriton Swans 28 E6
Cheriton Bishop Devon 9 J6
Cheriton Fitzpaine Devon 9 L3
Cheriton or Stackpole Elidor Pembks 41 J11
Cherrington Wrekin 70 B11
Cherry Burton E R Yk 92 G2
Cherry Hinton Cambs 62 G9
Cherry Orchard Worcs 46 G4
Cherry Willingham Lincs 86 D6
Chertsey Surrey 36 B7
Cherwell Valley Services Oxon 48 F9
Cheselbourne Dorset 12 C5
Chesham Bucks 35 Q4
Chesham Bury 89 N8
Chesham Bois Bucks 35 Q5
Cheshunt Herts 51 J10
Chesil Beach Dorset 11 N9
Chesley Kent 38 E9
Cheslyn Hay Staffs 58 E3
Chessetts Wood Warwks 59 J10
Chessington Gt Lon 36 E8
Chessington World of Adventures Gt Lon 36 E8
Chester Ches W 81 N11
Chesterblade Somset 20 C6
Chester Cathedral Ches W 81 N11
Chester Crematorium Ches W 81 M11
Chesterfield Derbys 84 E6
Chesterfield Staffs 58 G3
Chesterfield Crematorium Derbys 84 E6
Chesterfield Services Derbys 84 F8
Chesterhill Mdloth 128 B7
Chester-le-Street Dur 113 L10
Chester Moor Dur 113 L11
Chesters Border 118 B6
Chesters Border 118 B8
Chester Services Ches W 81 P10
Chesterton Cambs 62 G8
Chesterton Cambs 74 B11
Chesterton Gloucs 33 K4
Chesterton Oxon 48 G10
Chesterton Shrops 57 P5
Chesterton Staffs 70 E5
Chesterton Green Warwks 48 C3
Chesterwood Nthumb 112 B7
Chester Zoo Ches W 81 N10
Chestfield Kent 39 K8
Chestnut Street Kent 38 E9
Cheston Devon 6 H7
Cheswardine Shrops 70 C8
Cheswick Nthumb 129 Q10
Cheswick Green Solhll 58 H9
Chetnole Dorset 11 N3
Chettiscombe Devon 9 N2
Chettisham Cambs 62 H4
Chettle Dorset 12 G2
Chetton Shrops 57 M6
Chetwode Bucks 48 H9
Chetwynd Wrekin 70 C10
Chetwynd Aston Wrekin 70 D11
Cheveley Cambs 63 L8
Chevening Kent 37 L9
Cheverton IoW 14 E10
Chevington Suffk 63 N9
Cheviot Hills 118 E9
Chevithorne Devon 18 C11
Chew Magna BaNES 19 Q2
Chew Moor Bolton 89 K9
Chew Stoke BaNES 19 Q2
Chewton Keynsham BaNES 32 C11
Chewton Mendip Somset 19 Q4
Chichacott Devon 8 F5
Chicheley M Keyn 49 P5
Chichester W Susx 15 N6
Chichester Crematorium W Susx 15 N5
Chickerell Dorset 11 N8
Chickering Suffk 65 J6
Chicklade Wilts 20 H8
Chickward Herefs 45 K4
Chidden Hants 23 J11
Chiddingfold Surrey 23 Q7
Chiddingly E Susx 25 M8
Chiddingstone Kent 37 M12
Chiddingstone Causeway Kent 37 M11
Chideock Dorset 11 J6
Chidham W Susx 15 L6
Chidswell Kirk 90 H6
Chieveley W Berk 34 E10
Chignall St James Essex 51 Q8
Chignall Smealy Essex 51 Q8
Chigwell Essex 37 K2
Chigwell Row Essex 37 L2
Chilbolton Hants 22 C6
Chilcomb Hants 22 F9
Chilcombe Dorset 11 L6
Chilcompton Somset 20 B4
Chilcote Leics 59 L2
Childer Thornton Ches W 81 M9
Child Okeford Dorset 12 D2
Childrey Oxon 34 C7
Child's Ercall Shrops 70 B9
Childswickham Worcs 47 L7
Childwall Lpool 81 N7
Childwick Bury Herts 50 D8
Childwick Green Herts 50 D8
Chilfrome Dorset 11 M5
Chilgrove W Susx 15 M4
Chilham Kent 39 J11
Chilla Devon 8 B4
Chillaton Devon 8 B8
Chillenden Kent 39 N11
Chillerton IoW 14 E10
Chillesford Suffk 65 M11
Chillingham Nthumb 119 L5
Chillington Devon 7 K10
Chillington Somset 10 H2
Chilmark Wilts 21 J8
Chilmington Green Kent 26 G3
Chilson Oxon 48 B11
Chilsworthy Cnwll 5 Q7
Chilsworthy Devon 16 E10
Chiltern Green C Beds 50 D7
Chiltern Hills 35 L5
Chilterns Crematorium Bucks 35 P5
Chilthorne Domer Somset 19 P11
Chilton Bucks 35 J2
Chilton Devon 9 L4
Chilton Dur 103 Q5
Chilton Kent 27 N3
Chilton Oxon 34 E7
Chilton Suffk 52 E3
Chilton Candover Hants 22 G6
Chilton Cantelo Somset 19 Q10
Chilton Foliat Wilts 34 B10
Chilton Polden Somset 19 L6
Chilton Street Suffk 63 N11
Chilton Trinity Somset 19 J7
Chilwell Notts 72 E3
Chilworth Hants 22 D11
Chilworth Surrey 36 B11
Chimney Oxon 34 C4
Chineham Hants 23 J3
Chingford Gt Lon 37 J2
Chinley Derbys 83 M8
Chinnor Oxon 35 L4
Chipchase Castle Nthumb 112 C5
Chipnall Shrops 70 C8
Chippenham Cambs 63 L7
Chippenham Wilts 32 H10
Chipperfield Herts 50 B10
Chipping Herts 51 J4
Chipping Lancs 89 J2
Chipping Campden Gloucs 47 N7
Chipping Hill Essex 52 D8
Chipping Norton Oxon 48 B9
Chipping Ongar Essex 51 N10
Chipping Sodbury S Glos 32 D8
Chipping Warden Nhants 48 E5
Chipstable Somset 18 D9
Chipstead Kent 37 M9
Chipstead Surrey 36 G9
Chirbury Shrops 56 D5
Chirk Wrexhm 69 J7
Chirnside Border 129 M8
Chirnsidebridge Border 129 M8
Chirton Wilts 21 L3
Chisbury Wilts 33 Q11
Chiselborough Somset 11 K2
Chiseldon Swindn 33 N8
Chiselhampton Oxon 34 G5
Chisholme Border 117 N8
Chislehurst Gt Lon 37 K6
Chislet Kent 39 M9
Chisley Calder 90 C5
Chiswell Green Herts 50 D10
Chiswick Gt Lon 36 F5
Chiswick End Cambs 62 E11
Chisworth Derbys 83 L6
Chitcombe E Susx 26 D7
Chithurst W Susx 23 M10
Chittering Cambs 62 G7
Chitterne Wilts 21 J6
Chittlehamholt Devon 17 M7
Chittlehampton Devon 17 L6
Chittoe Wilts 33 J11
Chivelstone Devon 7 K11
Chivenor Devon 17 J5
Chlenry D & G 106 F5
Chobham Surrey 23 Q2
Cholderton Wilts 21 P6
Cholesbury Bucks 35 P3
Chollerford Nthumb 112 D6
Chollerton Nthumb 112 D6
Cholmondeston Ches E 70 A3
Cholsey Oxon 34 G7
Cholstrey Herefs 45 P3
Chop Gate N York 104 G11
Choppington Nthumb 113 L4
Chopwell Gatesd 112 H9
Chorley Ches E 69 Q4
Chorley Lancs 88 H7
Chorley Shrops 57 M8
Chorley Staffs 58 G2
Chorleywood Herts 50 B11
Chorleywood West Herts 50 B11
Chorlton Ches E 70 C4
Chorlton-cum-Hardy Manch 82 H6
Chorlton Lane Ches W 69 N5
Choulton Shrops 56 F7
Chowley Ches W 69 N3
Chrishall Essex 51 K3
Chrisswell Inver 124 G3
Christchurch Cambs 75 J11
Christchurch Dorset 13 L6
Christchurch Gloucs 31 Q2
Christchurch Newpt 31 K7
Christian Malford Wilts 33 J9
Christleton Ches W 81 N11
Christmas Common Oxon 35 K6
Christon N Som 19 L3
Christon Bank Nthumb 119 P6
Christow Devon 9 K7
Christ's Hospital W Susx 24 D5
Chuck Hatch E Susx 25 L4
Chudleigh Devon 9 L9
Chudleigh Knighton Devon 9 K9
Chulmleigh Devon 17 M9
Chunal Derbys 83 M6
Church Lancs 89 L5
Churcham Gloucs 46 E11
Church Aston Wrekin 70 C11
Church Brampton Nhants 60 F7
Church Brough Cumb 102 E8
Church Broughton Derbys 71 N8
Church Cove Cnwll 3 J11
Church Crookham Hants 23 M4
Churchdown Gloucs 46 G11
Church Eaton Staffs 70 E11
Church End Bed 61 N9
Church End Bed 61 P9
Church End Bucks 35 K3
Church End C Beds 49 Q10
Church End C Beds 49 Q8
Church End C Beds 50 B4
Church End C Beds 50 B7
Church End C Beds 50 E3
Church End C Beds 61 Q10
Church End Cambs 61 N6
Church End Cambs 62 B4
Church End Cambs 62 D5
Church End Cambs 62 G9
Churchend Essex 38 H3
Church End Essex 51 P6
Church End Essex 52 B6
Church End Essex 52 B8
Church End Gloucs 46 G7
Church End Gt Lon 36 F2
Church End Herts 50 D8
Church End Herts 50 G4
Church End Herts 51 K6
Church End Lincs 74 D4
Church End Lincs 93 R11
Church End Warwks 59 K6
Church End Warwks 59 L6
Church Enstone Oxon 48 C9

270 Church Fenton - Comberton

Church Fenton N York 91 N3
Churchfield Sandw 58 F6
Churchgate Herts 50 H10
Churchgate Street Essex 51 L8
Church Green Devon 10 D5
Church Gresley Derbys 71 P11
Church Hanborough Oxon 34 D2
Church Hill Staffs 58 F2
Church Houses N York 105 J11
Churchill Devon 10 F4
Churchill Devon 17 K3
Churchill N Som 19 M3
Churchill Oxon 47 Q10
Churchill Worcs 46 H4
Churchill Worcs 58 C9
Churchinford Somset 10 E2
Church Knowle Dorset 12 F8
Church Laneham Notts 85 P5
Church Langton Leics 60 F2
Church Lawford Warwks 59 Q9
Church Lawton Ches E 70 E3
Church Leigh Staffs 71 J7
Church Lench Worcs 47 K4
Church Mayfield Staffs 71 M6
Church Minshull Ches E 70 B2
Church Norton W Susx 15 N7
Churchover Warwks 60 B4
Church Preen Shrops 57 J5
Church Pulverbatch Shrops 56 G4
Churchstanton Somset 10 D2
Churchstoke Powys 56 D6
Churchstow Devon 7 J9
Church Stowe Nhants 60 D9
Church Street Essex 52 C3
Church Street Kent 38 B7
Church Street Suffk 65 P5
Church Stretton Shrops 56 H6
Churchthorpe Lincs 93 P11
Churchtown Bpool 88 C2
Churchtown Cnwll 4 H6
Churchtown Derbys 84 C8
Churchtown Devon 17 M3
Churchtown IoM 80 f3
Churchtown Lancs 88 F2
Church Town N Linc 92 C9
Churchtown Sefton 88 D7
Church Village Rhondd 30 E7
Church Warsop Notts 85 J7
Church Wilne Derbys 72 C4
Churnsike Lodge Nthumb 111 N5
Churston Ferrers Torbay 7 N7
Churt Surrey 23 N7
Churton Ches W 69 M3
Churwell Leeds 90 H5
Chwilog Gwynd 66 G7
Chyandour Cnwll 2 D7
Chyanvounder Cnwll 2 H9
Chyeowling Cnwll 3 K5
Chysauster Cnwll 2 D7
Chyvarloe Cnwll 2 H9
Cil Powys 56 B4
Cilcain Flints 80 H11
Cilcennin Cerdgn 43 K2
Cilcewydd Powys 56 C4
Cilfrew Neath 29 L4
Cilfynydd Rhondd 30 E6
Cilgerran Pembks 41 N2
Cilgwyn Carmth 43 P9
Cilgwyn Gwynd 66 H4
Ciliau-Aeron Cerdgn 43 K3
Cilmaengwyn Neath 29 K3
Cilmery Powys 44 E4
Cilrhedyn Pembks 41 Q4
Cilsan Carmth 43 L10
Ciltalgarth Gwynd 68 A6
Cilycwm Carmth 43 Q7
Cimla Neath 29 L5
Cinderford Gloucs 32 C2
Cinder Hill Wolves 58 D6
Cippenham Slough 35 Q8
Cirencester Gloucs 33 K4
Citadilla N York 103 P11
City Gt Lon 36 H4
City V Glam 30 C9
City Airport Gt Lon 37 K4
City Dulas IoA 78 H7
City of Bath BaNES 20 E2
City of London Crematorium Gt Lon 37 K3
Clabhach Ag & B 136 F4
Clachaig Ag & B 131 N11
Clachan Ag & B 123 N8
Clachan Ag & B 130 F4
Clachan Ag & B 138 F9
Clachan Highld 153 J10
Clachan-a-Luib W Isls 168 d11
Clachan Mor Ag & B 136 B6
Clachan na Luib W Isls 168 d11
Clachan of Campsie E Duns 125 Q2
Clachan-Seil Ag & B 130 F4
Clachnaharry Highld 156 A8
Clachtoll Highld 164 B11
Clackavoid P & K 142 A5
Clacket Lane Services Surrey 37 K10
Clackmannan Clacks 133 Q9
Clackmarras Moray 157 N6
Clacton-on-Sea Essex 53 L8
Cladich Ag & B 131 M3
Cladswell Worcs 47 L3
Claggan Highld 138 C8
Claigan Highld 152 C7
Clandown BaNES 20 C3
Clanfield Hants 23 J11
Clanfield Oxon 33 Q4
Clannaborough Devon 8 H4
Clanville Hants 22 B5
Clanville Somset 20 B8
Claonaig Ag & B 123 Q8
Clapgate Dorset 12 H4
Clapgate Herts 51 K6
Clapham Bed 61 M10
Clapham Devon 9 L7
Clapham Gt Lon 36 G5
Clapham N York 95 Q7
Clapham W Susx 24 C9
Clapham Green Bed 61 M10
Clap Hill Kent 27 J4
Clappersgate Cumb 101 L10
Clapton Somset 11 J3
Clapton Somset 20 B4
Clapton-in-Gordano N Som 31 N10
Clapton-on-the-Hill Gloucs 47 N11
Clapworthy Devon 17 M7
Clarach Cerdgn 54 E8
Claravale Gatesd 112 H8
Clarbeston Pembks 41 L6
Clarbeston Road Pembks 41 K6
Clarborough Notts 85 M4
Clare Suffk 63 N11
Clarebrand D & G 108 G7
Clarencefield D & G 109 N7
Clarewood Nthumb 112 F7
Clarilaw Border 117 Q7
Clark's Green Surrey 24 E3
Clarkston E Rens 125 P6
Clashmore Highld 162 G9
Clashmore Highld 164 B10
Clashnessie Highld 164 C10
Clashnoir Moray 149 N3
Clathy P & K 134 B3
Clathymore P & K 134 C3
Clatt Abers 150 E2
Clatter Powys 55 M6
Clatterford End Essex 51 P8
Clatworthy Somset 18 E8
Claughton Lancs 88 G2
Claughton Lancs 95 M7
Claughton Wirral 81 L7
Clavelshay Somset 19 J8
Claverdon Warwks 59 J11
Claverham N Som 31 N11
Clavering Essex 51 L4
Claverley Shrops 57 P6
Claverton BaNES 20 E2
Claverton Down BaNES 20 E2
Clawdd-coch V Glam 30 E9
Clawdd-newydd Denbgs 68 E4
Clawthorpe Cumb 95 L5
Clawton Devon 5 P2
Claxby Lincs 86 F2
Claxby Lincs 87 N6
Claxton N York 98 D9
Claxton Norfk 77 L11
Claybrooke Magna Leics 59 Q7
Clay Common Suffk 65 P5
Clay Coton Nhants 60 C5
Clay Cross Derbys 84 E8
Claydon Oxon 48 E5
Claydon Suffk 53 K2
Clay End Herts 50 H6
Claygate D & G 110 G5
Claygate Kent 26 B3
Claygate Surrey 36 E8
Claygate Cross Kent 37 P9
Clayhall Gt Lon 37 K2
Clayhanger Devon 18 D10
Clayhanger Wsall 58 F4
Clayhidon Devon 18 G11
Clayhill E Susx 26 D7
Clayhill Hants 13 P3
Clayhithe Cambs 62 H8
Clayock Highld 167 L5
Claypit Hill Cambs 62 E10
Claypits Gloucs 32 E3
Claypole Lincs 85 P11
Claythorpe Lincs 87 M5
Clayton C Brad 90 E4
Clayton Donc 91 M9
Clayton W Susx 24 G8
Clayton Green Lancs 88 H6
Clayton-le-Moors Lancs 89 M4
Clayton-le-Woods Lancs 88 H6
Clayton West Kirk 90 H8
Clayworth Notts 85 M3
Cleadale Highld 144 G10
Cleadon S Tyne 113 N8
Clearbrook Devon 6 E5
Clearwell Gloucs 31 Q3
Clearwell Meend Gloucs 31 Q3
Cleasby N York 103 Q8
Cleat Ork 169 d8
Cleatlam Dur 103 M7
Cleator Cumb 100 D8
Cleator Moor Cumb 100 D7
Cleckheaton Kirk 90 F5
Cleedownton Shrops 57 K8
Cleehill Shrops 57 K9
Cleekhimin N Lans 126 D6
Clee St Margaret Shrops 57 K8
Cleestanton Shrops 57 K9
Cleethorpes NE Lin 93 P9
Cleeton St Mary Shrops 57 L9
Cleeve N Som 31 N11
Cleeve Oxon 34 H8
Cleeve Hill Gloucs 47 J9
Cleeve Prior Worcs 47 L5
Cleghornie E Loth 128 F3
Clehonger Herefs 45 N7
Cleish P & K 134 D8
Cleland N Lans 126 D6
Clement's End C Beds 50 B8
Clement Street Kent 37 M6
Clenamacrie Ag & B 131 J2
Clench Common Wilts 33 N11
Clenchwarton Norfk 75 L6
Clenerty Abers 159 J5
Clent Worcs 58 D9
Cleobury Mortimer Shrops 57 M9
Cleobury North Shrops 57 L7
Cleongart Ag & B 120 C5
Clephanton Highld 156 E7
Clerkhill D & G 117 K11
Cleuch-head D & G 115 R7
Clevancy Wilts 33 L9
Clevedon N Som 31 M10
Cleveley Oxon 48 C10
Cleveleys Lancs 88 C2
Cleverton Wilts 33 J7
Clewer Somset 19 M4
Cley next the Sea Norfk 76 E3
Cliburn Cumb 101 Q6
Cliddesden Hants 22 H5
Cliff Warwks 59 K5
Cliffe Lancs 89 L4
Cliffe Medway 38 B6
Cliffe N York 91 R4
Cliffe N York 103 P7
Cliff End E Susx 26 E9
Cliffe Woods Medway 38 B7
Clifford Herefs 45 J5
Clifford Leeds 91 L2
Clifford Chambers Warwks 47 N4
Clifford's Mesne Gloucs 46 D10
Cliffsend Kent 39 P9
Clifton Bristl 31 Q10
Clifton C Beds 50 E3
Clifton C Nott 72 E4
Clifton C York 98 B10
Clifton Calder 90 F6
Clifton Cumb 101 P5
Clifton Derbys 71 M6
Clifton Devon 17 L3
Clifton Donc 91 N11
Clifton Lancs 88 F4
Clifton N York 97 J11
Clifton Nthumb 113 K4
Clifton Oxon 48 E8
Clifton Salfd 82 G4
Clifton Worcs 46 F5
Clifton Campville Staffs 59 L2
Clifton Hampden Oxon 34 F5
Clifton Reynes M Keyn 49 P4
Clifton upon Dunsmore Warwks 60 B5
Clifton upon Teme Worcs 46 D2
Cliftonville Kent 39 Q7
Climping W Susx 15 Q6
Clink Somset 20 E5
Clint N York 97 L9
Clinterty C Aber 151 L5
Clint Green Norfk 76 E9
Clintmains Border 118 B4
Clipiau Gwynd 55 J2
Clippesby Norfk 77 N9
Clipsham Rutlnd 73 P7
Clipston Nhants 60 F4
Clipston Notts 72 G4
Clipstone C Beds 49 P9
Clipstone Notts 85 J8
Clitheroe Lancs 89 L2
Clive Shrops 69 P10
Clixby Lincs 93 J10
Cloatley Wilts 33 J6
Clocaenog Denbgs 68 E4
Clochan Moray 158 B5
Clock Face St Hel 82 B6
Cloddiau Powys 56 C3
Clodock Herefs 45 L9
Cloford Somset 20 D6
Clola Abers 159 P9
Clophill C Beds 50 C3
Clopton Nhants 61 N4
Clopton Suffk 65 J11
Clopton Corner Suffk 65 J11
Clopton Green Suffk 63 N10
Clopton Green Suffk 64 D10
Clos du Valle Guern 10 c1
Closeburn D & G 109 J2
Closeburnmill D & G 109 K2
Closeclark IoM 80 c6
Closworth Somset 11 M2
Clothall Herts 50 G4
Clotton Ches W 69 P2
Cloudesley Bush Warwks 59 Q7
Clouds Herefs 46 A7
Clough Oldham 89 Q9
Clough Foot Calder 89 Q6
Clough Head Calder 90 D7
Cloughton N York 99 L2
Cloughton Newlands N York 105 R11
Clousta Shet 169 q8
Clova Angus 142 E3
Clovelly Devon 16 E7
Clovenfords Border 117 P3
Clovulin Highld 139 J5
Clow Bridge Lancs 89 N5
Clowne Derbys 84 G5
Clows Top Worcs 57 N10
Cloy Wrexhm 69 L6
Cluanie Inn Highld 146 D5
Cluanie Lodge Highld 146 D5
Clubworthy Cnwll 5 M3
Clugston D & G 107 L6
Clun Shrops 56 E8
Clunas Highld 156 F8
Clunbury Shrops 56 F8
Clunderwen Carmth 41 M7
Clune Highld 148 D2
Clunes Highld 146 F10
Clungunford Shrops 56 F9
Clunie P & K 141 R9
Clunton Shrops 56 E8
Cluny Fife 134 G8
Clutton BaNES 20 B3
Clutton Ches W 69 N4
Clutton Hill BaNES 20 B3
Clwt-y-bont Gwynd 67 K2
Clydach Mons 30 H2
Clydach Swans 29 J4
Clydach Vale Rhondd 30 C6
Clydebank W Duns 125 M3
Clydebank Crematorium W Duns 125 M3
Clydey Pembks 41 Q3
Clyffe Pypard Wilts 33 L9
Clynder Ag & B 131 Q11
Clyne Neath 29 M4
Clynnog-fawr Gwynd 66 G5
Clyro Powys 45 J6
Clyst Honiton Devon 9 N6
Clyst Hydon Devon 9 P4
Clyst St George Devon 9 N7
Clyst St Lawrence Devon 9 P4
Clyst St Mary Devon 9 N6
Cnoc W Isls 168 j4
Cnwch Coch Cerdgn 54 F10
Coad's Green Cnwll 5 M6
Coal Aston Derbys 84 E5
Coalbrookvale Blae G 30 G3
Coalburn S Lans 126 E11
Coalburns Gatesd 112 H8
Coaley Gloucs 32 E4
Coalhill Essex 38 C2
Coalmoor Wrekin 57 M3
Coalpit Heath S Glos 32 C8
Coal Pool Wsall 58 F5
Coalport Wrekin 57 M4
Coalsnaughton Clacks 133 Q8
Coal Street Suffk 65 J7
Coaltown of Balgonie Fife 134 H8
Coaltown of Wemyss Fife 135 J8
Coalville Leics 72 C8
Coanwood Nthumb 111 N9
Coat Somset 19 N10
Coatbridge N Lans 126 C4
Coatdyke N Lans 126 C4
Coate Swindn 33 N8
Coate Wilts 21 K2
Coates Cambs 74 F11
Coates Gloucs 33 J4
Coates Lincs 86 B4
Coates Notts 85 P4
Coates W Susx 23 Q11
Coatham R & Cl 104 G5
Coatham Mundeville Darltn 103 Q6
Cobbaton Devon 17 L6
Coberley Gloucs 47 J11
Cobhall Common Herefs 45 P7
Cobham Kent 37 Q7
Cobham Surrey 36 D8
Cobham Services Surrey 36 D9
Coblers Green Essex 51 Q7
Cobley Dorset 21 K10
Cobnash Herefs 45 P2
Cobo Guern 10 b1
Cobridge C Stke 70 F5
Coburby Abers 159 M5
Cock Alley Derbys 84 F6
Cockayne N York 104 H11
Cockayne Hatley C Beds 62 C11
Cock Bank Wrexhm 69 L5
Cock Bevington Warwks 47 L4
Cock Bridge Abers 149 P6
Cockburnspath Border 129 K5
Cock Clarks Essex 52 D11
Cock & End Suffk 63 M10
Cockenzie and Port Seton E Loth 128 C4
Cocker Bar Lancs 88 G6
Cocker Brook Lancs 89 L5
Cockerham Lancs 95 K10
Cockermouth Cumb 100 F4
Cockernhoe Herts 50 D6
Cockersdale Leeds 90 G5
Cockett Swans 28 H6
Cockfield Dur 103 M6
Cockfield Suffk 64 C11
Cockfosters Gt Lon 50 G11
Cock Green Essex 51 Q7
Cocking W Susx 23 N11
Cocking Causeway W Susx 23 N11
Cockington Torbay 7 M6
Cocklake Somset 19 M5
Cockley Beck Cumb 100 H10
Cockley Cley Norfk 75 Q10
Cock Marling E Susx 26 E8
Cockpole Green Wokham 35 L8
Cocks Cnwll 3 K3
Cockshutford Shrops 57 K7
Cockshutt Shrops 69 M9
Cock Street Kent 38 C11
Cockthorpe Norfk 76 D3
Cockwells Cnwll 2 E7
Cockwood Devon 9 N8
Cockwood Somset 18 H6
Cockyard Derbys 83 M9
Cockyard Herefs 45 N8
Coddenham Suffk 64 G11
Coddington Ches W 69 N3
Coddington Herefs 46 D6
Coddington Notts 85 P10
Codford St Mary Wilts 21 J7
Codford St Peter Wilts 21 J7
Codicote Herts 50 F7
Codmore Hill W Susx 24 C6
Codnor Derbys 84 F11
Codrington S Glos 32 D9
Codsall Staffs 58 C4
Codsall Wood Staffs 58 B4
Coedely Rhondd 30 D7
Coedkernew Newpt 31 J8
Coed Morgan Mons 31 L2
Coedpoeth Wrexhm 69 J4
Coed Talon Flints 69 J3
Coedway Powys 69 K11
Coed-y-Bryn Cerdgn 42 G5
Coed-y-caerau Newpt 31 L6
Coed-y-paen Mons 31 K5
Coed-yr-ynys Powys 44 H10
Coed Ystumgwern Gwynd 67 K10
Coelbren Powys 29 N2
Coffinswell Devon 7 M5
Coffle End Bed 61 M9
Cofton Devon 9 N8
Cofton Hackett Worcs 58 F9
Cogan V Glam 30 G10
Cogenhoe Nhants 60 H8
Cogges Oxon 34 C3
Coggeshall Essex 52 E7
Coggin's Mill E Susx 25 N5
Coignafearn Highld 148 C4
Coilacriech Abers 149 Q8
Coilantogle Stirlg 132 H6
Coillore Highld 152 F10
Coity Brdgnd 29 P8
Col W Isls 168 j4
Colaboll Highld 162 D4
Colan Cnwll 4 D9
Colaton Raleigh Devon 10 B7
Colbost Highld 152 C8
Colburn N York 103 N11
Colby Cumb 102 C6
Colby IoM 80 b7
Colby Norfk 77 J5
Colchester Essex 52 G6
Colchester Crematorium Essex 52 G7
Cold Ash W Berk 34 F11
Cold Ashby Nhants 60 E5
Cold Ashton S Glos 32 E10
Cold Aston Gloucs 47 M11
Coldbackie Highld 165 P4
Coldbeck Cumb 102 D10
Cold Blow Pembks 41 M8
Cold Brayfield M Keyn 49 P4
Cold Cotes N York 95 Q6
Coldean Br & H 24 H9
Coldeast Devon 7 L4
Colden Calder 90 B5
Colden Common Hants 22 E10
Coldfair Green Suffk 65 N9
Coldham Cambs 74 H10
Cold Hanworth Lincs 86 D4
Coldharbour Cnwll 3 K4
Coldharbour Devon 9 Q2
Coldharbour Gloucs 31 Q4
Cold Harbour Herts 50 D7
Cold Harbour Oxon 34 H9
Coldharbour Surrey 24 D2
Cold Harbour Wilts 20 G5
Cold Hatton Wrekin 70 A10
Cold Hatton Heath Wrekin 70 A10
Cold Hesledon Dur 113 P11
Cold Hiendley Wakefd 91 K8
Cold Higham Nhants 49 J4
Coldingham Border 129 N6
Cold Kirby N York 98 A4
Coldmeece Staffs 70 F8
Cold Newton Leics 73 J9
Cold Northcott Cnwll 5 L4
Cold Norton Essex 52 E11
Cold Overton Leics 73 L8
Coldred Kent 27 N2
Coldridge Devon 17 M10
Coldstream Border 118 F3
Coldwaltham W Susx 24 B7
Coldwell Herefs 45 N7
Coldwells Abers 159 N10
Cold Weston Shrops 57 K8
Cole Somset 20 C8
Colebatch Shrops 56 E7
Colebrook C Plym 6 E7
Colebrook Devon 9 P3
Colebrooke Devon 9 J5
Coleby Lincs 86 C8
Coleby N Linc 92 E7
Cole End Warwks 59 K7
Coleford Devon 9 J4
Coleford Gloucs 31 Q2
Coleford Somset 20 C5
Coleford Water Somset 18 F8
Colegate End Norfk 64 H4
Cole Green Herts 50 G8
Cole Green Herts 51 K4
Cole Henley Hants 22 E4
Colehill Dorset 12 H4
Coleman Green Herts 50 E8
Coleman's Hatch E Susx 25 K4
Colemere Shrops 69 M8
Colemore Hants 23 K8
Colemore Green Shrops 57 N5
Colenden P & K 134 E2
Coleorton Leics 72 C7
Colerne Wilts 32 F10
Colesbourne Gloucs 33 K2
Cole's Cross Devon 7 K9
Coles Cross Dorset 10 H4
Colesden Bed 61 P9
Coles Green Suffk 53 K3
Coleshill Bucks 35 P5
Coleshill Oxon 33 P6
Coleshill Warwks 59 K7
Colestocks Devon 10 B4
Coley BaNES 19 Q3
Colgate W Susx 24 F4
Colinsburgh Fife 135 M7
Colinton C Edin 127 N4
Colintraive Ag & B 124 C3
Colkirk Norfk 76 C6
Coll Ag & B 136 G4
Collace P & K 142 C11
Collafirth Shet 169 q5
Coll Airport Ag & B 136 F4
Collaton Devon 7 J11
Collaton St Mary Torbay 7 M6
College of Roseisle Moray 157 L4
College Town Br For 23 N2
Collessie Fife 134 H5
Colleton Mills Devon 17 M8
Collier Row Gt Lon 37 M2
Collier's End Herts 51 J6
Collier's Green E Susx 26 C7
Colliers Green Kent 26 C4
Collier Street Kent 26 B2
Colliery Row Sundld 113 M11
Collieston Abers 151 Q2
Collin D & G 109 M5
Collingbourne Ducis Wilts 21 P4
Collingbourne Kingston Wilts 21 P3
Collingham Leeds 97 N11
Collingham Notts 85 P8
Collington Herefs 46 B2
Collingtree Nhants 60 G9
Collins Green Warrtn 82 C6
Collins Green Worcs 46 D3
Colliston Angus 143 L8
Colliton Devon 10 B4
Collyweston Nhants 73 P10
Colmonell S Ayrs 114 B10
Colmworth Bed 61 P9
Colnbrook Slough 36 B5
Colne Cambs 62 E5
Colne Lancs 89 P3
Colne Bridge Kirk 90 F6
Colne Edge Lancs 89 P2
Colne Engaine Essex 52 D5
Colney Norfk 76 H10
Colney Heath Herts 50 F9
Colney Street Herts 50 E10
Coln Rogers Gloucs 33 L3
Coln St Aldwyns Gloucs 33 M3
Coln St Dennis Gloucs 33 L2
Colonsay Ag & B 136 b2
Colonsay Airport Ag & B 136 b3
Colpy Abers 158 F11
Colquhar Border 117 L2
Colquite Cnwll 4 H7
Colscott Devon 16 F9
Colsterdale N York 96 H4
Colsterworth Lincs 73 N6
Colston Bassett Notts 73 J4
Coltfield Moray 157 L5
Colt Hill Hants 23 L4
Coltishall Norfk 77 K8
Colton Cumb 94 G3
Colton Leeds 91 K4
Colton N York 91 N2
Colton Norfk 76 G10
Colton Staffs 71 J10
Colt's Hill Kent 25 P2
Columbjohn Devon 9 N5
Colva Powys 44 H4
Colvend D & G 109 J10
Colwall Herefs 46 E6
Colwell Nthumb 112 E5
Colwich Staffs 71 J10
Colwick Notts 72 G2
Colwinston V Glam 29 P9
Colworth W Susx 15 P6
Colwyn Bay Conwy 80 B9
Colyford Devon 10 F6
Colyton Devon 10 E6
Combe Devon 7 J11
Combe Herefs 45 L2
Combe Oxon 48 D11
Combe W Berk 22 C2
Combe Almer Dorset 12 G5
Combe Common Surrey 23 P7
Combe Down BaNES 20 E2
Combe Fishacre Devon 7 L5
Combe Florey Somset 18 G8
Combe Hay BaNES 20 D3
Combeinteignhead Devon 7 N4
Combe Martin Devon 17 K2
Combe Raleigh Devon 10 D4
Comberbach Ches W 82 D9
Comberford Staffs 59 J3
Comberton Cambs 62 E9
Comberton Herefs 56 H11

Combe St Nicholas
Somset.........10 G2
Combpyne Devon.........10 F6
Cambridge Staffs.........71 K7
Combrook Warwks.........48 B4
Combs Derbys.........83 M9
Combs Suffk.........64 E10
Combs Ford Suffk.........64 E10
Combwich Somset.........19 J6
Comers Abers.........150 H6
Comhampton Worcs.........58 B11
Commercial End Cambs.........63 J8
Commins Coch Powys.........55 J4
Commondale N York.........105 J8
Common Edge Bpool.........88 C4
Common End Cumb.........100 D6
Common Moor Cnwll.........5 L8
Common Platt Wilts.........33 M7
Commonside Ches W.........82 B10
Commonside Derbys.........71 N6
Common Side Derbys.........84 D5
Commonwood Shrops.........69 N9
Commonwood Wrexhm.........69 L4
Compass Somset.........19 J8
Compstall Stockp.........83 L6
Compstonend D & G.........108 G10
Compton Devon.........7 M6
Compton Hants.........22 B9
Compton Hants.........22 E9
Compton Staffs.........57 Q8
Compton Surrey.........23 Q5
Compton W Berk.........34 F8
Compton W Susx.........15 L4
Compton Wilts.........21 M4
Compton Abbas Dorset.........20 G11
Compton Abdale Gloucs.........47 L11
Compton Bassett Wilts.........33 K10
Compton Beauchamp
Oxon.........33 Q7
Compton Bishop Somset.........19 L3
Compton Chamberlayne Wilts.........21 K9
Compton Dando BaNES.........20 B2
Compton Dundon
Somset.........19 N8
Compton Durville
Somset.........19 M11
Compton Greenfield
S Glos.........31 Q8
Compton Martin BaNES.........19 P3
Compton Pauncefoot
Somset.........20 B9
Compton Valence Dorset.........11 M6
Compton Verney Warwks.........48 B4
Comrie Fife.........134 C10
Comrie P & K.........133 M3
Conaglen House Highld.........139 J4
Conchra Highld.........145 Q2
Concraigie P & K.........141 Q9
Conder Green Lancs.........95 K9
Conderton Worcs.........47 J7
Condicote Gloucs.........47 N9
Condorrat N Lans.........126 C3
Condover Shrops.........56 H3
Coney Hill Gloucs.........46 G11
Coneyhurst Common
W Susx.........24 D6
Coneysthorpe N York.........98 E6
Coneythorpe N York.........97 N9
Coney Weston Suffk.........64 D6
Conford Hants.........23 M8
Congdon's Shop Cnwll.........5 M6
Congerstone Leics.........72 B9
Congham Norfk.........75 P6
Congleton Ches E.........70 F2
Congl-y-wal Gwynd.........67 N6
Congresbury N Som.........19 M2
Congreve Staffs.........58 D2
Conheath D & G.........109 L7
Conicavel Moray.........156 H7
Coningsby Lincs.........86 H9
Conington Cambs.........61 Q3
Conington Cambs.........62 D7
Conisbrough Donc.........91 N11
Conisholme Lincs.........93 R11
Coniston Cumb.........101 K11
Coniston E R Yk.........93 L3
Coniston Cold N York.........96 D10
Conistone N York.........96 E7
Connah's Quay Flints.........81 K11
Connel Ag & B.........138 G10
Connel Park E Ayrs.........115 M5
Connor Downs Cnwll.........2 F6
Conon Bridge Highld.........155 P6
Cononley N York.........96 E11
Consall Staffs.........70 H5
Consett Dur.........112 H10
Constable Burton N York.........97 J2
Constable Lee Lancs.........89 N6
Constantine Cnwll.........3 J8
Constantine Bay Cnwll.........4 D7
Contin Highld.........155 N6
Conwy Conwy.........79 P9
Conyer Kent.........38 G9
Conyer's Green Suffk.........64 B8
Cooden E Susx.........26 B10
Cookbury Devon.........16 G10
Cookbury Wick Devon.........16 F10
Cookham W & M.........35 N7
Cookham Dean W & M.........35 N7
Cookham Rise W & M.........35 N7
Cookhill Worcs.........47 L3
Cookley Suffk.........65 L6
Cookley Worcs.........58 B8
Cookley Green Oxon.........35 J6
Cookney Abers.........151 M9
Cooksbridge E Susx.........25 K8
Cooksey Green Worcs.........58 D11
Cook's Green Essex.........53 L8
Cooks Green Suffk.........64 D11
Cookshill Staffs.........70 G6
Cooksland Cnwll.........4 H8
Cookson Green Ches W.........82 C10
Coolham W Susx.........24 D6
Cooling Medway.........38 C6
Cooling Street Medway.........38 B7
Coombe Cnwll.........2 D6
Coombe Cnwll.........3 L5
Coombe Cnwll.........4 G6
Coombe Devon.........7 N4
Coombe Devon.........9 K8
Coombe Devon.........10 C6
Coombe Gloucs.........32 E6
Coombe Hants.........23 J10
Coombe Wilts.........21 M4
Coombe Bissett Wilts.........21 M8
Coombe Cellars Devon.........7 N4
Coombe Cross Hants.........23 J10
Coombe Hill Gloucs.........46 G9

Coombe Keynes Dorset.........12 D8
Coombe Pafford Torbay.........7 N5
Coombes W Susx.........24 E9
Coombes-Moor Herefs.........45 M2
Coombe Street Somset.........20 E8
Coombeswood Dudley.........58 E7
Coopersale Common
Essex.........51 L10
Coopersale Street Essex.........51 L10
Cooper's Corner Kent.........37 L11
Coopers Green E Susx.........25 L6
Coopers Green Herts.........50 E9
Cooper Street Kent.........39 P9
Cooper Turning Bolton.........89 J9
Cootham W Susx.........24 C8
Copdock Suffk.........53 K3
Copford Green Essex.........52 F7
Copgrove N York.........97 M8
Copister Shet.........169 r6
Cople Bed.........61 P11
Copley Calder.........90 D6
Copley Dur.........103 L5
Copley Tamesd.........83 L5
Coplow Dale Derbys.........83 Q9
Copmanthorpe C York.........98 B11
Copmere End Staffs.........70 E9
Copp Lancs.........88 E3
Coppathorne Cnwll.........16 C11
Coppenhall Staffs.........70 G11
Coppenhall Moss Ches E.........70 C3
Copperhouse Cnwll.........2 F6
Coppicegate Shrops.........57 N8
Coppingford Cambs.........61 Q5
Coppins Corner Kent.........26 F2
Copplestone Devon.........9 J4
Coppull Lancs.........88 H8
Coppull Moor Lancs.........88 H8
Copsale W Susx.........24 E6
Copster Green Lancs.........89 K4
Copston Magna Warwks.........59 Q7
Cop Street Kent.........39 N9
Copthall Green Essex.........51 K10
Copt Heath Solhll.........59 J9
Copt Hewick N York.........97 M6
Copthorne Cnwll.........5 M3
Copthorne W Susx.........24 H3
Copt Oak Leics.........72 D8
Copy's Green Norfk.........76 C4
Coram Street Suffk.........52 H3
Corbets Tey Gt Lon.........37 N3
Corbiere Jersey.........11 a2
Corbridge Nthumb.........112 E8
Corby Nhants.........61 J3
Corby Glen Lincs.........73 Q6
Corby Hill Cumb.........111 J9
Cordon N Ayrs.........121 K5
Cordwell Derbys.........84 D5
Coreley Shrops.........57 L10
Cores End Bucks.........35 P7
Corfe Somset.........18 H11
Corfe Castle Dorset.........12 G8
Corfe Mullen Dorset.........12 G5
Corfton Shrops.........56 H7
Corgarff Abers.........149 P6
Corhampton Hants.........22 H10
Corks Pond Kent.........25 Q2
Corley Warwks.........59 M7
Corley Ash Warwks.........59 L7
Corley Moor Warwks.........59 L8
Corley Services Warwks.........59 M7
Cormuir Angus.........142 F4
Cornard Tye Suffk.........52 F3
Corndon Devon.........8 G7
Corner Row Lancs.........88 E4
Corney Cumb.........94 C2
Cornforth Dur.........104 B4
Cornhill Abers.........158 E6
Cornhill-on-Tweed
Nthumb.........118 J3
Cornholme Calder.........89 Q5
Cornish Hall End Essex.........51 Q3
Cornoigmore Ag & B.........136 B6
Cornsay Dur.........103 M2
Cornsay Colliery Dur.........103 N2
Corntown Highld.........155 N6
Corntown V Glam.........29 P9
Cornwell Oxon.........47 Q9
Cornwood Devon.........6 G7
Cornworthy Devon.........7 L7
Corpach Highld.........139 K2
Corpusty Norfk.........76 G6
Corrachree Abers.........150 D7
Corran Highld.........139 J5
Corran Highld.........145 P6
Corrany IoM.........80 g4
Corrie D & G.........110 D3
Corrie N Ayrs.........121 K3
Corriecravie N Ayrs.........120 H7
Corriegills N Ayrs.........121 K4
Corriegour Lodge Hotel
Highld.........146 H9
Corriemoille Highld.........155 L5
Corrimony Highld.........155 L11
Corringham Lincs.........85 Q2
Corringham Thurr.........38 B5
Corris Gwynd.........54 H3
Corris Uchaf Gwynd.........54 G3
Corrow Ag & B.........131 P7
Corry Highld.........145 K3
Corscombe Devon.........8 F5
Corscombe Dorset.........11 L3
Corse Gloucs.........46 E9
Corse Lawn Gloucs.........46 F8
Corsham Wilts.........32 G10
Corsindae Abers.........150 H6
Corsley Wilts.........20 F5
Corsley Heath Wilts.........20 F5
Corsock D & G.........108 G5
Corston BaNES.........32 C11
Corston Wilts.........33 H8
Corstorphine C Edin.........127 M3
Cors-y-Gedol Gwynd.........67 L10
Corton Suffk.........65 Q2
Corton Wilts.........21 H6
Corton Denham Somset.........20 B10
Coruanan Highld.........139 K4
Corwen Denbgs.........68 G6
Coryates Dorset.........11 N7
Coryton Devon.........8 C8
Coryton Thurr.........38 B5
Cosby Leics.........72 E11
Coseley Dudley.........58 D6
Cosford Shrops.........57 Q3
Cosgrove Nhants.........49 L6
Cosham C Port.........15 J5
Cosheston Pembks.........41 K10
Coshieville P & K.........141 J8

Cossall Notts.........72 D2
Cossall Marsh Notts.........72 D2
Cossington Leics.........72 G8
Cossington Somset.........19 L6
Costessey Norfk.........76 H9
Costock Notts.........72 F5
Coston Leics.........73 L6
Coston Norfk.........76 F10
Cote Oxon.........34 C4
Cote Somset.........19 K6
Cotebrook Ches W.........82 C11
Cotehill Cumb.........111 J10
Cotes Cumb.........95 K3
Cotes Leics.........72 F6
Cotes Staffs.........70 E8
Cotesbach Leics.........60 B4
Cotes Heath Staffs.........70 E8
Cotford St Luke Somset.........18 G9
Cotgrave Notts.........72 G3
Cothal Abers.........151 M4
Cotham Notts.........85 N11
Cothelstone Somset.........18 G9
Cotherstone Dur.........103 K7
Cothill Oxon.........34 E5
Cotleigh Devon.........10 E4
Cotmanhay Derbys.........72 C2
Coton Cambs.........62 F9
Coton Nhants.........60 E6
Coton Shrops.........69 P8
Coton Staffs.........59 J4
Coton Staffs.........70 E10
Coton Staffs.........70 H5
Coton Clanford Staffs.........70 F10
Coton Hayes Staffs.........70 H8
Coton Hill Shrops.........56 H2
Coton in the Clay Staffs.........71 M9
Coton in the Elms
Derbys.........71 N11
Coton Park Derbys.........71 P11
Cotswolds.........33 J3
Cott Devon.........7 K6
Cottage End Hants.........22 D6
Cottam Lancs.........88 G4
Cottam Notts.........85 P5
Cottenham Cambs.........62 F7
Cotterdale N York.........96 B2
Cottered Herts.........50 H5
Cotteridge Birm.........58 F8
Cotterstock Nhants.........61 M2
Cottesbrooke Nhants.........60 F6
Cottesmore Rutlnd.........73 N8
Cottingham E R Yk.........92 H4
Cottingham Nhants.........60 H2
Cottingley C Brad.........90 E3
Cottingley Hall
Crematorium Leeds.........90 H4
Cottisford Oxon.........48 G8
Cotton Suffk.........64 F8
Cotton End Bed.........61 N11
Cotton Tree Lancs.........89 Q3
Cottown Abers.........150 E2
Cottown Abers.........151 K4
Cottown of Gight Abers.........159 K9
Cotts Devon.........6 C5
Cotwall Wrekin.........69 N11
Cotwalton Staffs.........70 G8
Couch's Mill Cnwll.........5 K4
Coughton Herefs.........46 A10
Coughton Warwks.........47 L2
Coulaghailtro Ag & B.........123 M6
Coulags Highld.........154 C9
Coulderton Cumb.........100 C9
Coull Abers.........150 E7
Coulport Ag & B.........131 Q10
Coulsdon Gt Lon.........36 G9
Coulston Wilts.........21 J4
Coulter S Lans.........116 E4
Coultershaw Bridge
W Susx.........23 Q11
Coultings Somset.........18 H6
Coulton N York.........98 C6
Coultra Fife.........135 K3
Cound Shrops.........57 K3
Coundlane Shrops.........57 K4
Coundon Dur.........103 P5
Coundon Grange Dur.........103 P5
Countersett N York.........96 D3
Countess Wilts.........21 N6
Countess Cross Essex.........52 E5
Countess Wear Devon.........9 M7
Countesthorpe Leics.........72 F11
Countisbury Devon.........17 N2
Coupar Angus P & K.........142 C10
Coup Green Lancs.........88 H5
Coupland Cumb.........102 D7
Coupland Nthumb.........118 H4
Cour Ag & B.........123 P10
Court-at-Street Kent.........27 J4
Courteachan Highld.........145 L8
Courteenhall Nhants.........49 L4
Court Henry Carmth.........43 L10
Coursland Essex.........38 H3
Courtway Somset.........18 H8
Cousland Mdloth.........128 B6
Cousley Wood E Susx.........25 Q4
Cove Ag & B.........131 Q11
Cove Border.........129 K5
Cove Devon.........18 C11
Cove Hants.........23 N3
Cove Highld.........160 C8
Cove Bay C Aber.........151 P7
Cove Bottom Suffk.........65 P6
Covehithe Suffk.........65 Q5
Coven Staffs.........58 D3
Coveney Cambs.........62 G4
Covenham St
Bartholomew Lincs.........87 K2
Covenham St Mary Lincs.........87 K2
Coven Heath Staffs.........58 D3
Coventry Covtry.........59 M9
Coventry Airport Warwks.........59 N10
Coverack Cnwll.........3 K10
Coverack Bridges Cnwll.........2 H7
Coverham N York.........96 H3
Covington Cambs.........61 N6
Covington S Lans.........116 E3
Cowan Bridge Lancs.........95 N5
Cowbech E Susx.........25 N8
Cowbit Lincs.........74 E7
Cowbridge V Glam.........30 C10
Cowdale Derbys.........83 N10
Cowden Kent.........25 L2
Cowdenbeath Fife.........134 F9
Cowden Pound Kent.........25 L2
Cowden Station Kent.........25 L2
Cowers Lane Derbys.........71 Q5
Cowes IoW.........14 E7
Cowesby N York.........97 Q3
Cowesfield Green Wilts.........21 Q10
Cowfold W Susx.........24 F6

Cowgill Cumb.........95 R3
Cow Green Suffk.........64 F8
Cowhill S Glos.........32 B6
Cowie Stirlg.........133 N10
Cowlam E R Yk.........99 K7
Cowley Devon.........9 M5
Cowley Gloucs.........33 J2
Cowley Gt Lon.........36 C4
Cowley Oxon.........34 F4
Cowling Lancs.........88 H7
Cowling N York.........90 B2
Cowling N York.........97 K3
Cowlinge Suffk.........63 M10
Cowmes Kirk.........90 F7
Cowpe Lancs.........89 N6
Cowpen Nthumb.........113 L4
Cowpen Bewley S on T.........104 E6
Cowplain Hants.........15 J4
Cowshill Dur.........102 G2
Cowslip Green N Som.........19 N2
Cowthorpe N York.........97 P10
Coxall Herefs.........56 F10
Coxbank Ches E.........70 B6
Coxbench Derbys.........72 B2
Coxbridge Somset.........19 P7
Cox Common Suffk.........65 N5
Coxford Cnwll.........5 K2
Coxford Norfk.........76 B6
Coxgreen Staffs.........57 Q7
Coxheath Kent.........38 B11
Coxhoe Dur.........104 B3
Coxley Somset.........19 P6
Coxley Wakefd.........90 H7
Coxley Wick Somset.........19 P6
Coxpark Cnwll.........5 Q7
Coxtie Green Essex.........51 N11
Coxwold N York.........98 A5
Coychurch Brdgnd.........29 P9
Coychurch
Crematorium Brdgnd.........29 P8
Coylton S Ayrs.........114 H4
Coylumbridge Highld.........148 G5
Coytrahen Brdgnd.........29 N7
Crabbs Cross Worcs.........58 F11
Crab Orchard Dorset.........13 J3
Crabtree W Susx.........24 F5
Crabtree Green Wrexhm.........69 K6
Crackenthorpe Cumb.........102 C6
Crackington Haven
Cnwll.........5 J2
Crackley Staffs.........70 E4
Crackley Warwks.........59 L10
Crackleybank Shrops.........57 P2
Crackpot N York.........103 J11
Cracoe N York.........96 E8
Craddock Devon.........10 B2
Cradle End Herts.........51 L6
Cradley Dudley.........58 D7
Cradley Herefs.........46 D5
Cradley Heath Sandw.........58 D7
Cradoc Powys.........44 D8
Crafthole Cnwll.........5 P11
Crafton Bucks.........49 N11
Crag Foot Lancs.........95 K6
Craggan Highld.........149 J2
Cragg Hill Leeds.........90 G3
Craghead Dur.........113 K10
Crai Powys.........44 B10
Craibstone Moray.........158 C6
Craichie Angus.........143 J8
Craig Angus.........143 M6
Craig Highld.........154 D8
Craigbank E Ayrs.........115 L5
Craigburn Border.........127 N7
Craigcefnparc Swans.........29 J4
Craigcleuch D & G.........110 F3
Craigdam Abers.........159 K11
Craigdhu Ag & B.........130 G6
Craigearn Abers.........151 J5
Craigellachie Moray.........157 P9
Craigend P & K.........134 E3
Craigend Rens.........125 M3
Craigendoran Ag & B.........132 C11
Craigends Rens.........125 L4
Craighlaw D & G.........107 K5
Craighouse Ag & B.........122 H6
Craigie P & K.........141 R9
Craigie S Ayrs.........125 L11
Craigiefold Abers.........159 M4
Craigley D & G.........108 G9
Craig Llangiwg Neath.........29 K4
Craiglockhart C Edin.........127 N3
Craigmillar C Edin.........127 Q3
Craignant Shrops.........69 J7
Craigneston D & G.........115 Q10
Craigneuk N Lans.........126 D4
Craigneuk N Lans.........126 D4
Craignure Ag & B.........138 C10
Craigo Angus.........143 M5
Craig Penllyn V Glam.........30 C9
Craigrothie Fife.........135 K5
Craigruie Stirlg.........132 F3
Craig's End Essex.........52 B4
Craigton Angus.........143 J10
Craigton C Aber.........151 L7
Craigton E Rens.........125 M7
Craigton Crematorium
C Glas.........125 N5
Craigton of Airlie Angus.........142 E7
Craig-y-Duke Neath.........29 K4
Craig-y-nos Powys.........44 A11
Crail Fife.........135 Q6
Crailing Border.........118 C6
Craiselound N Linc.........92 C11
Crakehall N York.........97 K3
Crakehill N York.........97 P6
Crambe N York.........98 E8
Cramlington Nthumb.........113 L5
Cramond C Edin.........127 M2
Cramond Bridge C Edin.........127 M2
Crammport Hants.........22 C10
Cranage Ches E.........82 G11
Cranberry Staffs.........70 E7
Cranborne Dorset.........13 J2
Cranbourne Br For.........35 P10
Cranbrook Devon.........9 N6
Cranbrook Gt Lon.........36 D5
Cranbrook Common
Kent.........26 C4
Crane Moor Barns.........91 J10
Crane's Corner Norfk.........76 C9
Cranfield C Beds.........49 Q6
Cranford Devon.........16 E7
Cranford Gt Lon.........36 D5
Cranford St Andrew
Nhants.........61 K5
Cranford St John Nhants.........61 K5
Cranham Gloucs.........32 G2
Cranham Gt Lon.........37 N3
Cranhill Warwks.........47 M4

Crank St Hel.........81 Q5
Cranleigh Surrey.........24 C3
Cranmer Green Suffk.........64 E7
Cranmore IoW.........14 C8
Cranmore Somset.........20 C6
Cranoe Leics.........73 K11
Cransford Suffk.........65 L9
Cranshaws Border.........128 H7
Cranstal IoM.........80 g1
Cranswick E R Yk.........99 L10
Crantock Cnwll.........4 C10
Cranwell Lincs.........86 D11
Cranwich Norfk.........63 N3
Cranworth Norfk.........76 D11
Craobh Haven Ag & B.........130 F6
Crapstone Devon.........6 E5
Crarae Ag & B.........131 K8
Crask Inn Highld.........162 C2
Crask of Aigas Highld.........155 N9
Craster Nthumb.........119 Q7
Craswall Herefs.........45 K8
Crateford Staffs.........58 D3
Cratfield Suffk.........65 L6
Crathes Abers.........151 K8
Crathes Castle Abers.........151 J8
Crathie Abers.........149 P8
Crathie Highld.........147 P9
Crathorne N York.........104 D9
Craven Arms Shrops.........56 G8
Crawcrook Gatesd.........112 H8
Crawford Lancs.........81 P4
Crawford S Lans.........116 D6
Crawfordjohn S Lans.........116 B6
Crawley Hants.........22 D8
Crawley Oxon.........34 B2
Crawley W Susx.........24 G3
Crawley Down W Susx.........24 H3
Crawleyside Dur.........103 J2
Crawshawbooth Lancs.........89 N5
Crawton Abers.........143 R2
Craxe's Green Essex.........52 F8
Cray N York.........96 D5
Crayford Gt Lon.........37 M5
Crayke N York.........98 B6
Craymere Beck Norfk.........76 F5
Crays Hill Essex.........38 B3
Cray's Pond Oxon.........34 H8
Craythorne Staffs.........71 N9
Craze Lowman Devon.........9 N2
Crazies Hill Wokham.........35 L8
Creacombe Devon.........17 Q8
Creagan Ag & B.........138 H9
Creag Ghoraidh W Isls.........168 c13
Creagorry W Isls.........168 c13
Creaguaineach Lodge
Highld.........139 Q4
Creamore Bank Shrops.........69 P8
Creaton Nhants.........60 F6
Creca D & G.........110 D6
Credenhill Herefs.........45 P6
Crediton Devon.........9 K4
Creebank D & G.........107 K2
Creebridge D & G.........107 M4
Creech Dorset.........12 F8
Creech Heathfield
Somset.........19 J9
Creech St Michael
Somset.........19 J9
Creed Cnwll.........3 N4
Creekmouth Gt Lon.........37 L4
Creeksea Essex.........38 F2
Creeting St Mary Suffk.........64 F10
Creeton Lincs.........73 Q6
Creetown D & G.........107 N6
Cregneash IoM.........80 a8
Cregny Baa IoM.........80 e5
Cregrina Powys.........44 G4
Creich Fife.........135 J3
Creigiau Cardif.........30 E8
Cremyll Cnwll.........6 D8
Cressage Shrops.........57 K4
Cressbrook Derbys.........83 Q10
Cresselly Pembks.........41 L9
Cressex Bucks.........35 M6
Cressing Essex.........52 C7
Cresswell Nthumb.........113 L2
Cresswell Pembks.........41 L9
Cresswell Staffs.........70 H7
Creswell Derbys.........84 H6
Creswell Green Staffs.........58 G2
Cretingham Suffk.........65 J9
Cretshengan Ag & B.........123 M6
Crewe Ches E.........70 C3
Crewe Ches E.........69 M4
Crewe Crematorium
Ches E.........70 C3
Crewe Green Ches E.........70 C3
Crew Green Powys.........69 K11
Crewkerne Somset.........11 J3
Crews Hill Station Gt Lon.........50 H10
Crewton C Derb.........72 B4
Crianlarich Stirlg.........132 D2
Cribyn Cerdgn.........43 K4
Criccieth Gwynd.........66 H7
Crich Derbys.........84 D10
Crich Carr Derbys.........84 D10
Crichton Mdloth.........128 B7
Crick Mons.........31 N6
Crick Nhants.........60 C6
Crickadarn Powys.........44 F6
Cricket St Thomas
Somset.........10 H3
Crickheath Shrops.........69 J10
Crickhowell Powys.........45 J11
Cricklade Wilts.........33 L6
Cricklewood Gt Lon.........36 F3
Cridling Stubbs N York.........91 N6
Crieff P & K.........133 P3
Criggan Cnwll.........4 G9
Criggion Powys.........69 J11
Crigglestone Wakefd.........91 J7
Crimble Rochdl.........89 P8
Crimond Abers.........159 Q6
Crimplesham Norfk.........75 N10
Crimscote Warwks.........47 P5
Crinaglack Highld.........155 M9
Crinan Ag & B.........130 F9
Cringleford Norfk.........76 H10
Cringles C Brad.........96 F11
Crinow Pembks.........41 M8
Cripplesease Cnwll.........2 E6
Cripp's Corner E Susx.........26 C7
Croachy Highld.........148 B2
Croanford Cnwll.........4 G7
Crockenhill Kent.........37 M7
Crocker End Oxon.........35 K7
Crockerhill W Susx.........15 P5
Crockernwell Devon.........9 J6

Crocker's Ash Herefs 45 Q11
Crockerton Wilts 20 G6
Crocketford D & G 108 H6
Crockey Hill C York 98 C11
Crockham Hill Kent 37 K10
Crockhurst Street Kent 37 H11
Crock Street Somset 10 G2
Croeserw Neath 29 N5
Croes-goch Pembks 40 F4
Croes-lan Cerdgn 42 G6
Croesor Gwynd 67 L6
Croesyceiliog Carmth 42 H11
Croesyceiliog Torfn 31 K5
Croes-y-mwyalch Torfn 31 K6
Croes-y-pant Mons 31 K4
Croft Leics 72 E11
Croft Lincs 87 P8
Croft Warrtn 82 D6
Croftamie Stirlg 132 F10
Crofton Cumb 110 F10
Crofton Wakefd 91 K7
Crofton Wilts 21 Q2
Croft-on-Tees N York 103 Q9
Croftown Highld 161 K10
Crofts Moray 157 P7
Crofts Bank Traffd 82 G5
Crofts of Dipple Moray 157 Q6
Crofts of Savoch Abers 159 P5
Crofty Swans 28 F6
Crogen Gwynd 68 D7
Croggan Ag & B 130 E2
Croglin Cumb 111 L11
Croick Highld 162 B8
Cromarty Highld 156 D4
Crombie Fife 134 D11
Cromdale Highld 149 K2
Cromer Herts 50 G5
Cromer Norfk 77 J3
Cromford Derbys 84 C9
Cromhall S Glos 32 C6
Cromhall Common
    S Glos 32 C7
Cromor W Isls 168 j5
Crompton Fold Oldham 89 Q9
Cromwell Notts 85 N8
Cronberry E Ayrs 115 M3
Crondall Hants 23 L5
Cronkbourne IoM 80 e6
Cronk-y-Voddy IoM 80 d4
Cronton Knows 81 P7
Crook Cumb 101 N11
Crook Dur 103 N3
Crookdake Cumb 100 G2
Crooke Wigan 88 H9
Crooked End Gloucs 46 B11
Crookedholm E Ayrs 125 M10
Crooked Soley Wilts 34 B10
Crookes Sheff 84 D3
Crookhall Dur 112 H10
Crookham Nthumb 118 H3
Crookham W Berk 22 F2
Crookham Village Hants 23 L4
Crook Inn Border 116 G5
Crooklands Cumb 95 L4
Crook of Devon P & K 134 C7
Cropper Derbys 71 N7
Cropredy Oxon 48 E5
Cropston Leics 72 F8
Cropthorne Worcs 47 J5
Cropton N York 98 F3
Cropwell Bishop Notts 72 H3
Cropwell Butler Notts 72 H3
Cros W Isls 168 k1
Crosbost W Isls 168 i5
Crosby Cumb 100 E3
Crosby IoM 80 d6
Crosby N Linc 92 E8
Crosby Sefton 81 L5
Crosby Garret Cumb 102 D9
Crosby Ravensworth
    Cumb 102 B8
Crosby Villa Cumb 100 E3
Croscombe Somset 19 Q6
Crosemere Shrops 69 M9
Crosland Edge Kirk 90 E8
Crosland Hill Kirk 90 E8
Cross Somset 19 M4
Crossaig Ag & B 123 P9
Crossapol Ag & B 136 B7
Cross Ash Mons 45 N11
Cross-at-Hand Kent 26 C2
Crossbush W Susx 24 B9
Crosscanonby Cumb 100 E3
Cross Coombe Cnwll 3 J4
Crossdale Street Norfk 77 J4
Cross End Bed 61 N4
Cross End Essex 52 E5
Crossens Sefton 88 D6
Cross Flatts C Brad 90 E2
Crossford Fife 134 D10
Crossford S Lans 126 E8
Crossgate Cnwll 5 N4
Crossgate Lincs 74 D5
Crossgate Staffs 70 G7
Crossgatehall E Loth 128 B6
Crossgates E Ayrs 25 K9
Crossgates Fife 134 E10
Cross Gates Leeds 91 K4
Crossgates N York 99 L4
Crossgates Powys 44 F2
Crossgill Lancs 95 M8
Cross Green Devon 5 P4
Cross Green Leeds 91 J4
Cross Green Suffk 58 D3
Cross Green Suffk 64 A11
Cross Green Suffk 64 D11
Cross Hands Carmth 28 G2
Crosshands Carmth 41 N6
Crosshands E Ayrs 125 M11
Cross Hands Pembks 41 L8
Cross Hill Derbys 84 F11
Crosshill Fife 134 F8
Crosshill S Ayrs 114 F6
Cross Hills N York 96 F11
Crosshouse E Ayrs 125 K10
Cross Houses Shrops 57 J3
Cross Houses Shrops 57 M6
Cross in Hand E Susx 25 N6
Cross Inn Cerdgn 42 G3
Cross Inn Cerdgn 43 K2
Cross Inn Pembks 41 M9
Cross Inn Rhondd 30 E8
Cross Keys Ag & B 132 C10
Crosskeys Caerph 30 H6
Cross Keys Wilts 32 G10
Crosskirk Highld 166 H3
Crosslands Cumb 94 G3

Cross Lane IoW 14 F9
Cross Lane Head Shrops 57 N5
Cross Lanes Cnwll 2 H9
Cross Lanes Cnwll 3 K5
Cross Lanes N York 98 A8
Crosslanes Shrops 69 K11
Cross Lanes Wrexhm 69 L5
Crosslee Rens 125 L4
Crossmichael D & G 108 F7
Cross Oak Powys 44 G10
Cross of Jackston Abers 158 H11
Cross o' th' hands
    Derbys 71 P5
Crosspost W Susx 24 G6
Crossroads Abers 150 F6
Crossroads Abers 151 K9
Cross Street Suffk 64 H6
Crosston Angus 143 J6
Cross Town Ches E 82 G9
Crossway Mons 45 N11
Crossway Powys 44 F3
Crossway Green Mons 31 P6
Crossway Green Worcs 58 B10
Crossways Dorset 12 C7
Crosswell Pembks 41 M4
Crosthwaite Cumb 95 J2
Croston Lancs 88 F7
Crostwick Norfk 77 K8
Crostwight Norfk 77 L6
Crouch Kent 37 P9
Crouch Kent 39 J10
Crouch End Gt Lon 36 H3
Croucheston Wilts 21 L9
Crouch Hill Dorset 11 Q2
Crough House Green
    Kent 37 K11
Croughton Nhants 48 F8
Crovie Abers 159 K4
Crow Hants 13 L4
Crowan Cnwll 2 G7
Crowborough E Susx 25 M4
Crowborough Town
    E Susx 25 M4
Crowcombe Somset 18 F7
Crowdecote Derbys 83 P11
Crowden Derbys 83 N5
Crowden Devon 8 C5
Crowdhill Hants 22 E10
Crowdleham Kent 37 N9
Crow Edge Barns 83 Q4
Crowell Oxon 35 K5
Crowfield Nhants 48 H6
Crowfield Suffk 64 G10
Crowfield Green Suffk 64 G10
Crowgate Street Norfk 77 L7
Crow Green Essex 51 N11
Crowhill E Loth 129 J5
Crow Hill Herefs 46 B9
Crowhole Derbys 84 D5
Crowhurst E Susx 26 C9
Crowhurst Surrey 37 J11
Crowhurst Lane End
    Surrey 37 J11
Crowland Lincs 74 D8
Crowland Suffk 64 E7
Crowlas Cnwll 2 E7
Crowle N Linc 92 C8
Crowle Worcs 46 H3
Crowle Green Worcs 46 H3
Crowmarsh Gifford
    Oxon 34 H7
Crown Corner Suffk 65 K7
Crownhill C Plym 6 D7
Crownhill Crematorium
    M Keyn 49 M7
Crownpits Surrey 23 Q6
Crownthorpe Norfk 76 F11
Crowntown Cnwll 2 G7
Crows-an-Wra Cnwll 2 B8
Crow's Green Essex 51 Q5
Crowshill Norfk 76 D10
Crow's Nest Cnwll 5 M8
Crowsnest Shrops 56 F4
Crowthorne Wokham 23 M2
Crowton Ches W 82 C10
Croxall Staffs 59 J2
Croxby Lincs 93 L11
Croxdale Dur 103 Q3
Croxden Staffs 71 K7
Croxley Green Herts 50 C11
Croxteth Lpool 81 N6
Croxton Cambs 62 B8
Croxton N Linc 93 J8
Croxton Norfk 64 B4
Croxton Norfk 76 D5
Croxton Staffs 70 D8
Croxtonbank Staffs 70 D8
Croxton Green Ches E 69 Q4
Croxton Kerrial Leics 73 L5
Croy Highld 156 D8
Croy N Lans 126 C2
Croyde Devon 16 G4
Croyde Bay Devon 16 G4
Croydon Cambs 62 D11
Croydon Gt Lon 36 H7
Croydon Crematorium
    Gt Lon 36 H7
Crubenmore Highld 148 B9
Cruckmeole Shrops 56 G3
Cruckton Shrops 56 G2
Cruden Bay Abers 159 Q10
Crudgington Wrekin 70 A11
Crudwell Wilts 33 J4
Cruft Devon 8 D5
Crug Powys 56 B10
Crugmeer Cnwll 4 E6
Crugybar Carmth 43 N7
Crug-y-byddar Powys 56 B9
Crumlin Caerph 30 H5
Crumplehorn Cnwll 5 L11
Crumpsall Manch 82 H4
Crundale Kent 27 J2
Crundale Pembks 41 J7
Crunwear Pembks 41 N8
Cruwys Morchard Devon 9 L2
Crux Easton Hants 22 D3
Cruxton Dorset 11 N5
Crwbin Carmth 28 E2
Cryers Hill Bucks 35 N5
Crymmych Pembks 41 N4
Crynant Neath 29 L4
Crystal Palace Gt Lon 36 H6
Cuaig Highld 153 N6
Cuan Ag & B 130 F5
Cubbington Warwks 59 M11
Cubert Cnwll 4 B10
Cubley Barns 90 G10
Cublington Bucks 49 M10

Cublington Herefs 45 N7
Cuckfield W Susx 24 H5
Cucklington Somset 20 E9
Cuckney Notts 85 J6
Cuckoo Bridge Lincs 74 D6
Cuckoo's Corner Hants 23 K6
Cuckoo's Nest Ches W 69 L2
Cuddesdon Oxon 34 G4
Cuddington Bucks 35 K2
Cuddington Ches W 82 C10
Cuddington Heath
    Ches W 69 N5
Cuddy Hill Lancs 88 F3
Cudham Gt Lon 37 K9
Cudliptown Devon 8 D9
Cudnell Bmouth 13 J5
Cudworth Barns 91 K9
Cudworth Somset 10 H2
Cuerdley Cross Warrtn 82 B7
Cufaude Hants 23 J3
Cuffley Herts 50 H11
Cuil Highld 138 H6
Culbokie Highld 155 R6
Culbone Somset 17 Q2
Culburnie Highld 155 N9
Culcabock Highld 156 B9
Culcharry Highld 156 F7
Culcheth Warrtn 82 E6
Culdrain Abers 158 D11
Culduie Highld 153 N9
Culford Suffk 64 A7
Culgaith Cumb 102 B5
Culham Oxon 34 F5
Culkein Highld 164 B10
Culkein Drumbeg Highld 164 D10
Culkerton Gloucs 32 H5
Cullen Moray 158 D4
Cullercoats N Tyne 113 N6
Cullerlie Abers 151 K7
Cullicudden Highld 156 A5
Cullingworth C Brad 90 D3
Cuillin Hills Highld 144 G3
Cullipool Ag & B 130 E5
Cullivoe Shet 169 s3
Culloden Highld 156 C8
Cullompton Devon 9 P3
Cullompton Services
    Devon 9 P3
Culm Davy Devon 18 F11
Culmington Shrops 56 H8
Culmstock Devon 10 C2
Culnacraig Highld 160 H6
Culnaightrie D & G 108 G10
Culnaknock Highld 153 J5
Culpho Suffk 53 M2
Culrain Highld 162 D8
Culross Fife 134 B10
Culroy S Ayrs 114 F5
Culsalmond Abers 158 G11
Culscadden D & G 107 N8
Culshabbin D & G 107 K7
Culswick Shet 169 p4
Cultercullen Abers 151 N3
Cults C Aber 151 M7
Culverstone Green Kent 37 P8
Culverthorpe Lincs 73 Q2
Culworth Nhants 48 F5
Culzean Castle &
    Country Park S Ayrs 114 D5
Cumbernauld N Lans 126 D3
Cumbernauld Village
    N Lans 126 D2
Cumberworth Lincs 87 P6
Cumdivock Cumb 110 F11
Cuminestown Abers 159 K7
Cumledge Border 129 K8
Cummersdale Cumb 110 G10
Cummertrees D & G 109 P7
Cummingston Moray 157 L4
Cumnock E Ayrs 115 L3
Cumnor Oxon 34 E4
Cumrew Cumb 111 J10
Cumrue D & G 109 N3
Cumwhinton Cumb 111 J10
Cumwhitton Cumb 111 K10
Cundall N York 97 P6
Cunninghamhead N Ayrs 125 K9
Cunningsburgh Shet 169 r10
Cupar Fife 135 K5
Cupar Muir Fife 135 K5
Curbar Derbys 84 C6
Curbridge Hants 14 F4
Curbridge Oxon 34 B3
Curdridge Hants 14 F4
Curdworth Warwks 59 J6
Curland Somset 19 J11
Curling Tye Green Essex 52 E10
Curridge W Berk 34 E10
Currie C Edin 127 M4
Curry Mallet Somset 19 K10
Curry Rivel Somset 19 L9
Curteis Corner Kent 26 E4
Curtisden Green Kent 26 B3
Curtisknowle Devon 7 J6
Cury Cnwll 2 H9
Cushnie Abers 150 E5
Cushuish Somset 18 G8
Cusop Herefs 45 J6
Cutcloy D & G 107 N11
Cutcombe Somset 18 B7
Cutgate Rochdl 89 P8
Cuthill Highld 162 H9
Cutiau Gwynd 67 L11
Cutler's Green Essex 51 N4
Cutmadoc Cnwll 4 H9
Cutmere Cnwll 5 N9
Cutnall Green Worcs 58 C11
Cutsdean Gloucs 47 L8
Cutsyke Wakefd 91 L6
Cutthorpe Derbys 84 D6
Cuttivett Cnwll 5 P9
Cuxham Oxon 35 J5
Cuxton Medway 38 B8
Cuxwold Lincs 93 L10
Cwm Blae G 30 G3
Cwm Denbgs 80 F9
Cwmafan Neath 29 L6
Cwmaman Rhondd 30 D5
Cwmann Carmth 43 L5
Cwmavon Torfn 31 J4
Cwm-bach Carmth 28 A4
Cwmbach Carmth 41 Q5
Cwmbach Powys 44 H7
Cwmbach Rhondd 30 D5
Cwmbach Llechrhyd
    Powys 44 D3
Cwmbelan Powys 55 L9
Cwmbran Torfn 31 J6
Cwmbrwyno Cerdgn 54 G8
Cwm Capel Carmth 28 E3
Cwmcarn Caerph 30 H6

Cwmcarvan Mons 31 N3
Cwm-celyn Blae G 30 H3
Cwm-Cewydd Gwynd 55 K2
Cwm-cou Cerdgn 41 Q2
Cwm Crawnon Powys 44 G11
Cwmdare Rhondd 30 C4
Cwmdu Carmth 43 M8
Cwmdu Powys 44 H10
Cwmdu Swans 28 H6
Cwmduad Carmth 42 G8
Cwm Dulais Swans 28 H4
Cwmdwr Carmth 43 P8
Cwmfelin Brdgnd 29 N7
Cwmfelin Myr Td 30 E4
Cwmfelin Boeth Carmth 41 N7
Cwmfelinfach Caerph 30 G6
Cwmfelin Mynach
    Carmth 41 P6
Cwmffrwd Carmth 42 H11
Cwmgiedd Powys 29 L2
Cwmgorse Carmth 29 K2
Cwmgwili Carmth 28 G2
Cwmgwrach Neath 29 M3
Cwmhiraeth Carmth 42 F7
Cwm-Ifor Carmth 43 N9
Cwm Irfon Powys 44 B5
Cwmisfael Carmth 43 J11
Cwm Llinau Powys 55 J3
Cwmllynfell Neath 29 K2
Cwmmawr Carmth 28 F2
Cwm Morgan Carmth 41 Q4
Cwmparc Rhondd 29 P5
Cwmpengraig Carmth 42 G7
Cwm Penmachno Conwy 67 P4
Cwmpennar Rhondd 30 D4
Cwmrhos Powys 44 H10
Cwmrhydyceirw Swans 29 J5
Cwmsychbant Cerdgn 43 J5
Cwmtillery Blae G 30 H3
Cwm-twrch Isaf Powys 29 L2
Cwm-twrch Uchaf
    Powys 29 L2
Cwm-y-glo Carmth 28 G2
Cwm-y-glo Gwynd 67 K2
Cwmyoy Mons 45 K10
Cwmystwyth Cerdgn 54 H10
Cwrt Gwynd 54 F5
Cwrt-newydd Cerdgn 43 J5
Cwrt-y-gollen Powys 45 J11
Cyfronydd Powys 55 Q3
Cylibebyll Neath 29 K4
Cymau Flints 69 J3
Cymer Neath 29 N5
Cymmer Rhondd 30 D6
Cynghordy Carmth 43 R6
Cynheidre Carmth 28 E3
Cynonville Neath 29 M5
Cynwyd Denbgs 68 E6
Cynwyl Elfed Carmth 42 G9

D

Daccombe Devon 7 N5
Dacre Cumb 101 N5
Dacre N York 97 J8
Dacre Banks N York 97 J8
Daddry Shield Dur 102 G3
Dadford Bucks 49 J7
Dadlington Leics 72 C11
Dafen Carmth 28 F4
Daffy Green Norfk 76 D10
Dagenham Gt Lon 37 M4
Daglingworth Gloucs 33 J3
Dagnall Bucks 49 Q11
Dagworth Suffk 64 E9
Dailly S Ayrs 114 E7
Dainton Devon 7 M5
Dairsie Fife 135 L4
Daisy Hill Bolton 82 E4
Daisy Hill Leeds 90 H5
Dalabrog W Isls 168 c15
Dalavich Ag & B 131 K5
Dalbeattie D & G 108 H8
Dalblair E Ayrs 115 N4
Dalbury Derbys 71 P8
Dalby IoM 80 b6
Dalby Lincs 87 M7
Dalby N York 98 C6
Dalcapon P & K 141 N7
Dalchalm Highld 163 L5
Dalchreichart Highld 146 H5
Dalchruin P & K 133 L4
Dalcrue P & K 134 C2
Dalderby Lincs 87 J7
Dalditch Devon 9 P8
Daldowie Crematorium
    C Glas 126 B5
Dale Cumb 101 P2
Dale Derbys 72 C3
Dale Pembks 40 F9
Dale Bottom Cumb 101 J6
Dale End Derbys 84 B8
Dale End N York 96 E11
Dale Hill E Susx 26 B5
Dalehouse N York 105 L7
Dalelia Highld 138 C4
Dalgarven N Ayrs 124 H8
Dalgety Bay Fife 134 F11
Dalgig E Ayrs 115 L5
Dalginross P & K 133 M3
Dalguise P & K 141 N8
Dalhalvaig Highld 166 E6
Dalham Suffk 63 M8
Daliburgh W Isls 168 c15
Dalkeith Mdloth 127 Q4
Dallas Moray 157 L7
Dallinghoo Suffk 65 K10
Dallington E Susx 25 Q7
Dallington Nhants 60 F8
Dallow N York 97 J6
Dalmally Ag & B 131 N2
Dalmary Stirlg 132 G8
Dalmellington E Ayrs 115 J4
Dalmeny C Edin 127 L2
Dalmore Highld 156 B4
Dalmuir W Duns 125 M3
Dalnabreck Highld 138 C4
Dalnacardoch P & K 140 F3
Dalnahaitnach Highld 148 H4
Dalnaspidal P & K 140 F2
Dalnawillan Lodge
    Highld 166 H10
Daloist P & K 141 J6
Dalqueich P & K 134 D7
Dalquhairn S Ayrs 114 F4
Dalreavoch Lodge
    Highld 162 H5
Dalry N Ayrs 124 H9
Dalrymple E Ayrs 114 G5

Dalserf S Lans 126 D7
Dalsmeran Ag & B 120 B9
Dalston Gt Lon 36 H4
Dalston Cumb 110 G10
Dalswinton D & G 109 M3
Dalton D & G 109 P4
Dalton Lancs 88 F9
Dalton N York 97 P5
Dalton N York 103 M9
Dalton Nthumb 112 H10
Dalton Rothm 84 G3
Dalton-in-Furness Cumb 94 E5
Dalton-le-Dale Dur 113 P11
Dalton Magna Rothm 84 G2
Dalton-on-Tees N York 103 Q9
Dalton Parva Rothm 84 G2
Dalton Piercy Hartpl 104 E4
Dalveich Stirlg 133 J3
Dalwhinnie Highld 147 Q11
Dalwood Devon 10 E4
Damask Green Herts 50 G5
Damerham Hants 21 M11
Damgate Norfk 77 N10
Dam Green Norfk 64 E4
Danaway Kent 38 E9
Danbury Essex 52 C10
Danby N York 105 K9
Danby Bottom N York 105 J10
Danby Wiske N York 104 B11
Dandaleith Moray 157 M9
Danderhall Mdloth 127 Q4
Danebridge Ches E 83 L11
Dane End Herts 50 H6
Danegate E Susx 25 M4
Danehill E Susx 25 K5
Dane Hills C Leic 72 F9
Danemoor Green Norfk 76 F10
Danesford Shrops 57 N6
Danesmoor Derbys 84 F8
Dane Street Kent 39 J11
Daniel's Water Kent 26 G3
Danshillock Abers 158 H6
Danskine E Loth 128 E5
Danthorpe E R Yk 93 N4
Danzey Green Warwks 58 H11
Dapple Heath Staffs 71 J9
Darby Green Hants 23 M3
Darcy Lever Bolton 89 L9
Dardy Powys 45 J11
Daren-felen Mons 30 H2
Darenth Kent 37 N6
Daresbury Halton 82 C8
Darfield Barns 91 L10
Darfoulds Notts 85 J5
Dargate Kent 39 J9
Darite Cnwll 5 M8
Darland Medway 38 C8
Darland Wrexhm 69 L3
Darlaston Wsall 58 E5
Darlaston Green Wsall 58 E5
Darley N York 97 K9
Darley Abbey C Derb 72 B3
Darley Bridge Derbys 84 C8
Darley Dale Derbys 84 C8
Darley Green Solhll 59 J10
Darleyhall Herts 50 D6
Darley Head N York 97 J9
Darlingscott Warwks 47 P6
Darlington Darltn 103 Q8
Darlington
    Crematorium Darltn 103 Q8
Darliston Shrops 69 Q8
Darlton Notts 85 N6
Darnford Staffs 58 H3
Darnick Border 117 Q4
Darowen Powys 55 J3
Darra Abers 158 H8
Darracott Devon 16 G4
Darracott Devon 16 H4
Darras Hall Nthumb 113 J7
Darrington Wakefd 91 M7
Darsham Suffk 65 N9
Darshill Somset 20 B6
Dartford Kent 37 N6
Dartington Devon 7 K6
Dartmeet Devon 6 H4
Dartmoor National Park
    Devon 8 G9
Dartmouth Devon 7 M8
Darton Barns 91 J8
Darvel E Ayrs 125 P10
Darwell Hole E Susx 25 Q7
Darwen Bl w D 89 K6
Datchet W & M 35 Q9
Datchworth Herts 50 G7
Datchworth Green Herts 50 G7
Daubhill Bolton 89 L9
Daugh of Kinermony
    Moray 157 N9
Dauntsey Wilts 33 J8
Dava Highld 157 J10
Davenham Ches W 82 E10
Davenport Stockp 83 K7
Davenport Green Ches E 82 H8
Davenport Green Traffd 82 H7
Daventry Nhants 60 C8
Davidson's Mains C Edin 127 N2
Davidstow Cnwll 5 K4
Davington D & G 117 J10
Davington Hill Kent 38 H9
Daviot Abers 151 J2
Daviot Highld 156 C10
Daviot House Highld 156 C9
Davis's Town E Susx 25 M7
Davoch of Grange Moray 158 C7
Davyhulme Traffd 82 G5
Daw End Wsall 58 F4
Dawesgreen Surrey 36 F11
Dawley Wrekin 57 M3
Dawlish Devon 9 N9
Dawlish Warren Devon 9 N9
Dawn Conwy 80 B10
Daws Green Somset 18 G9
Daws Heath Essex 38 D4
Daw's House Cnwll 5 N5
Dawsmere Lincs 74 H4
Daybrook Notts 85 J11
Day Green Ches E 70 D3
Dayhills Staffs 70 F8
Dayhouse Bank Worcs 58 E9
Daylesford Gloucs 47 P9
Ddol Flints 80 G10
Ddol-Cownwy Powys 68 D11
Deal Kent 39 Q11
Dean Cumb 100 E5
Dean Devon 7 L2
Dean Devon 8 G3
Dean Devon 17 N2

Dean Dorset 21 J11
Dean Hants 22 D8
Dean Hants 22 G11
Dean Lancs 89 P5
Dean Oxon 48 B10
Dean Somset 20 C6
Dean Bottom Kent 37 N7
Deanburnhaugh Border 117 M5
Deancombe Devon 7 J6
Dean Court Oxon 34 E3
Deane Bolton 89 K9
Deane Hants 22 H4
Dean End Dorset 21 J11
Dean Head Barns 90 H10
Deanland Dorset 21 J11
Deanlane End W Susx 15 K4
Dean Prior Devon 7 J6
Deanraw Nthumb 112 B8
Dean Row Ches E 83 J8
Deans W Loth 127 J4
Deanscales Cumb 100 E5
Deanshanger Nhants 49 L7
Deanshaugh Moray 157 R7
Deanston Stirlg 133 L7
Dean Street Kent 38 B11
Dearham Cumb 100 E3
Dearnley Rochdl 89 Q7
Debach Suffk 65 J11
Debden Essex 51 K11
Debden Essex 51 N4
Debden Green Essex 51 N4
Debenham Suffk 64 H9
Deblin's Green Worcs 46 F5
Dechmont W Loth 127 J3
Dechmont Road W Loth 127 J4
Deddington Oxon 48 E8
Dedham Essex 53 J5
Dedham Heath Essex 53 J5
Dedworth W & M 35 P9
Deene Nhants 61 K2
Deenethorpe Nhants 61 L2
Deepcar Sheff 90 H11
Deepcut Surrey 23 P3
Deepdale Cumb 95 Q4
Deepdale N York 96 C5
Deeping Gate C Pete 74 B9
Deeping St James Lincs 74 C9
Deeping St Nicholas Lincs 74 D7
Deerhurst Gloucs 46 G8
Deerhurst Walton Gloucs 46 G9
Deerton Street Kent 38 G9
Defford Worcs 46 H6
Defynnog Powys 44 C9
Deganwy Conwy 79 P9
Degnish Ag & B 130 F5
Deighton C York 91 Q2
Deighton N York 104 C10
Deiniolen Gwynd 67 K2
Delabole Cnwll 4 H5
Delamere Ches W 82 C11
Delfrigs Abers 151 P3
Delley Devon 17 J7
Delliefure Highld 157 K11
Dell Quay W Susx 15 M6
Delly End Oxon 34 C2
Delnabo Moray 149 M4
Delnashaugh Inn Moray 157 M10
Delny Highld 156 C3
Delph Oldham 90 B9
Delves Dur 112 H11
Delvin End Essex 52 C4
Dembleby Lincs 73 Q3
Demelza Cnwll 4 F9
Denaby Donc 91 M11
Denaby Main Donc 91 M11
Denbies Surrey 36 D10
Denbigh Denbgs 80 F11
Denbrae Fife 135 K4
Denbury Devon 7 L5
Denby Derbys 84 E11
Denby Bottles Derbys 84 E11
Denby Dale Kirk 90 G9
Denchworth Oxon 34 C6
Dendron Cumb 94 E6
Denel End C Beds 50 B3
Denfield P & K 134 B2
Denford Nhants 61 L5
Dengie Essex 52 G11
Denham Bucks 36 B3
Denham Suffk 63 N8
Denham Suffk 64 H7
Denham End Suffk 63 N8
Denham Green Bucks 36 B3
Denham Green Suffk 64 H7
Denhead Abers 159 N7
Denhead Fife 135 M5
Denhead of Gray C Dund 142 F11
Denholm Border 117 R7
Denholme C Brad 90 D4
Denholme Clough C Brad 90 D4
Denio Gwynd 66 F7
Denmead Hants 15 J4
Denmore C Aber 151 N5
Denne Park W Susx 24 E6
Dennington Suffk 65 K8
Denny Falk 133 N11
Dennyloanhead Falk 133 N11
Den of Lindores Fife 134 H4
Denshaw Oldham 90 B8
Denside Abers 151 L8
Densole Kent 27 M3
Denston Suffk 63 N10
Denstone Staffs 71 K6
Denstroude Kent 39 K9
Dent Cumb 95 Q3
Denton Cambs 61 Q3
Denton Darltn 103 P7
Denton E Susx 25 L10
Denton Kent 27 M2
Denton Kent 37 Q6
Denton Lincs 73 M4
Denton N York 96 H11
Denton Nhants 60 H9
Denton Norfk 65 K4
Denton Oxon 34 G4
Denton Tamesd 83 K5
Denver Norfk 75 M10
Denwick Nthumb 119 P8
Deopham Norfk 76 E11
Deopham Green Norfk 64 E2
Depden Suffk 63 N9
Depden Green Suffk 63 N9
Deptford Gt Lon 37 J5
Deptford Wilts 21 K7
Derby C Derb 72 B3
Derby Devon 17 K5
Derbyhaven IoM 80 c8
Derculich P & K 141 L7

Dereham Norfk 76 D9
Deri Caerph 30 F4
Derril Devon 16 E11
Derringstone Kent 27 M2
Derrington Staffs 70 F10
Derry Hill Wilts 33 J10
Derrythorpe N Linc 92 D9
Dersingham Norfk 75 N4
Dervaig Ag & B 137 L5
Derwen Denbgs 68 E4
Derwen Fawr Carmth 43 L10
Derwenlas Powys 54 G5
Derwent Water Cumb 101 J6
Derwydd Carmth 43 M11
Desborough Nhants 60 H4
Desford Leics 72 D10
Deskford Moray 158 D5
Detchant Nthumb 119 L3
Detling Kent 38 C10
Deuxhill Shrops 57 M7
Devauden Mons 31 N5
Devil's Bridge Cerdgn 54 C9
Devitts Green Warwks 59 L6
Devizes Wilts 21 K2
Devonport C Plym 6 D8
Devonside Clacks 133 Q8
Devoran Cnwll 3 K6
Dewarton Mdloth 128 B7
Dewlish Dorset 12 C5
Dewsbury Kirk 90 G6
Dewsbury Moor Kirk 90 G6
Dewsbury Moor Crematorium Kirk 90 G6
Deytheur Powys 68 H11
Dial N Som 31 P11
Dial Green W Susx 23 P9
Dial Post W Susx 24 E7
Dibberford Dorset 11 K4
Dibden Hants 14 D5
Dibden Purlieu Hants 14 D5
Dickens Heath Solhll 58 H9
Dickleburgh Norfk 64 H5
Didbrook Gloucs 47 L8
Didcot Oxon 34 F6
Didcot Railway Centre Oxon 34 F6
Diddington Cambs 61 Q8
Diddlebury Shrops 57 J7
Didley Herefs 45 P8
Didling W Susx 23 M11
Didmarton Gloucs 32 F7
Didsbury Manch 82 H6
Didworthy Devon 6 H6
Digby Lincs 86 E10
Digg Highld 152 H4
Diggle Oldham 90 C9
Digmoor Lancs 88 F9
Digswell Herts 50 F7
Digswell Water Herts 50 G8
Dihewyd Cerdgn 43 J3
Dilham Norfk 77 L6
Dilhorne Staffs 70 H6
Dill Hall Lancs 89 M5
Dillington Cambs 61 P7
Dilston Nthumb 112 E8
Dilton Wilts 20 G5
Dilton Marsh Wilts 20 F5
Dilwyn Herefs 45 N4
Dimple Bolton 89 L7
Dimple Derbys 84 C8
Dinas Carmth 41 Q4
Dinas Cnwll 4 E7
Dinas Gwynd 66 D6
Dinas Pembks 41 K3
Dinas Rhondd 30 D6
Dinas Dinlle Gwynd 66 C3
Dinas-Mawddwy Gwynd 67 R11
Dinas Powys V Glam 30 G10
Dinder Somset 19 Q6
Dinedor Herefs 45 Q7
Dingestow Mons 31 N2
Dingle Lpool 81 M7
Dingleden Kent 26 D5
Dingley Nhants 60 G3
Dingwall Highld 155 P6
Dinmael Conwy 68 D6
Dinnet Abers 150 D8
Dinnington N u Ty 113 K6
Dinnington Rothm 84 H3
Dinnington Somset 11 J2
Dinorwic Gwynd 67 K2
Dinton Bucks 35 L2
Dinton Wilts 21 K8
Dinwoodie D & G 109 P2
Dinworthy Devon 16 E8
Dipford Somset 18 H10
Dipley Hants 23 K3
Dippen Ag & B 120 F4
Dippen N Ayrs 121 K7
Dippenhall Surrey 23 M5
Dippermill Devon 8 B3
Dippertown Devon 8 B8
Dipple Moray 157 Q6
Dipple S Ayrs 114 C4
Diptford Devon 7 J7
Dipton Dur 113 J10
Diptonmill Nthumb 112 D8
Dirleton E Loth 128 E3
Dirt Pot Nthumb 112 C11
Discoed Powys 45 K2
Diseworth Leics 72 D6
Dishforth N York 97 N6
Disley Ches E 83 L8
Diss Norfk 64 G5
Disserth Powys 44 E3
Distington Cumb 100 D6
Distington Hall Crematorium Cumb 100 D6
Ditchampton Wilts 21 L8
Ditcheat Somset 20 B7
Ditchingham Norfk 65 L3
Ditchling E Susx 24 H7
Ditherington Shrops 57 J2
Ditteridge Wilts 32 F11
Dittisham Devon 7 M7
Ditton Kent 38 B10
Ditton Green Cambs 63 L9
Ditton Priors Shrops 57 L7
Dixton Gloucs 47 J8
Dixton Mons 31 P2
Dizzard Cnwll 5 K2
Dobcross Oldham 90 B9
Dobwalls Cnwll 5 L8
Doccombe Devon 9 J7
Dochgarroch Highld 155 N9
Docker Lancs 95 M6
Docking Norfk 75 N4
Docklow Herefs 45 R3

Dockray Cumb 101 L6
Dockray Cumb 110 E11
Dodbrooke Devon 7 J10
Doddinghurst Essex 51 N11
Doddington Cambs 62 F2
Doddington Kent 38 F10
Doddington Lincs 85 Q6
Doddington Nthumb 119 J4
Doddington Shrops 57 L9
Doddiscombsleigh Devon 9 L7
Dodd's Green Ches E 69 R6
Doddshill Norfk 75 N4
Doddy Cross Cnwll 5 N9
Dodford Nhants 60 D8
Dodford Worcs 58 D10
Dodington S Glos 32 E8
Dodington Somset 18 G6
Dodleston Ches W 69 L2
Dodscott Devon 17 J8
Dodside E Rens 125 N7
Dod's Leigh Staffs 71 J8
Dodworth Barns 91 J10
Dodworth Bottom Barns 91 J10
Dodworth Green Barns 91 J10
Doe Bank Birm 58 H5
Doe Lea Derbys 84 G7
Dogdyke Lincs 86 H9
Dogley Lane Kirk 90 F8
Dogmersfield Hants 23 L4
Dogridge Wilts 33 L7
Dogsthorpe C Pete 74 C10
Dog Village Devon 9 N5
Dolanog Powys 55 P2
Dolau Powys 55 Q11
Dolaucothi Carmth 43 N6
Dolbenmaen Gwynd 67 J6
Doley Staffs 70 C9
Dolfach Powys 55 L4
Dol-for Powys 55 J3
Dolfor Powys 55 Q7
Dolgarrog Conwy 79 P11
Dolgellau Gwynd 67 N11
Dolgoch Gwynd 54 F4
Dol-gran Carmth 42 H8
Doll Highld 163 K6
Dollar Clacks 134 B8
Dollarfield Clacks 134 B8
Dolley Green Powys 56 D11
Dollwen Cerdgn 54 F8
Dolphin Flints 80 H10
Dolphinholme Lancs 95 L10
Dolphinton S Lans 127 L8
Dolton Devon 17 K9
Dolwen Conwy 80 B10
Dolwyddelan Conwy 67 N4
Dolybont Cerdgn 54 E7
Dolyhir Powys 45 J3
Domgay Powys 69 J11
Donaldson's Lodge Nthumb 118 G2
Doncaster Donc 91 P10
Doncaster Carr Donc 91 P10
Doncaster North Services Donc 91 R8
Donhead St Andrew Wilts 20 H10
Donhead St Mary Wilts 20 H10
Donibristle Fife 134 F10
Doniford Somset 18 E6
Donington Lincs 74 D3
Donington on Bain Lincs 86 H4
Donington Park Services Leics 72 D5
Donington Southing Lincs 74 D4
Donisthorpe Leics 59 M2
Donkey Street Kent 27 K5
Donkey Town Surrey 23 P2
Donnington Gloucs 47 N9
Donnington Herefs 46 D8
Donnington Shrops 57 K3
Donnington W Berk 34 E11
Donnington W Susx 15 N6
Donnington Wrekin 57 N2
Donnington Wood Wrekin 57 N2
Donyatt Somset 10 G2
Doomsday Green W Susx 24 E5
Doonfoot S Ayrs 114 F4
Dorback Lodge Highld 149 K4
Dorchester Dorset 11 P6
Dorchester Oxon 34 G6
Dordon Warwks 59 L4
Dore Sheff 84 D4
Dores Highld 155 Q11
Dorking Surrey 36 E11
Dorking Tye Suffk 52 F4
Dormans Land Surrey 25 K2
Dormans Park Surrey 25 J2
Dormington Herefs 46 A6
Dormston Worcs 47 J3
Dorn Gloucs 47 P8
Dorney Bucks 35 P9
Dornie Highld 145 Q2
Dornoch Highld 162 H9
Dornock D & G 110 D7
Dorrery Highld 167 J5
Dorridge Solhll 59 J10
Dorrington Lincs 86 E10
Dorrington Shrops 56 H4
Dorrington Shrops 70 C6
Dorsington Warwks 47 M5
Dorstone Herefs 45 L6
Dorton Bucks 35 J2
Dosthill Staffs 59 K5
Dothan IoA 78 F10
Dottery Dorset 11 K5
Doublebois Cnwll 5 K9
Doughton Gloucs 32 G6
Douglas IoM 80 e6
Douglas S Lans 116 A4
Douglas and Angus C Dund 142 G11
Douglas Borough Crematorium IoM 80 e6
Douglas Pier Ag & B 131 P8
Douglastown Angus 142 G8
Douglas Water S Lans 116 B3
Douglas West S Lans 126 A4
Doulting Somset 20 B6
Dounby Ork 169 b4
Doune Highld 161 J6
Doune Highld 133 L7
Dounepark S Ayrs 114 C8
Dounie Highld 162 D9
Dousland Devon 6 F6
Dovaston Shrops 69 J9
Dove Green Notts 84 G10
Dove Holes Derbys 83 N9

Dovenby Cumb 100 E4
Dover Kent 27 P3
Dover Wigan 82 D4
Dover Castle Kent 27 P3
Dovercourt Essex 53 M5
Doverdale Worcs 58 C11
Doveridge Derbys 71 L8
Doversgreen Surrey 36 G11
Dowally P & K 141 P8
Dowbridge Lancs 88 E4
Dowdeswell Gloucs 47 K11
Dowlais Myr Td 30 E3
Dowland Devon 17 K9
Dowlish Ford Somset 10 H2
Dowlish Wake Somset 10 H2
Down Ampney Gloucs 33 L5
Downderry Cnwll 5 N11
Downe Gt Lon 37 K8
Downend Gloucs 32 F5
Downend IoW 14 F9
Downend S Glos 32 C9
Downend W Berk 34 E9
Downfield C Dund 142 F11
Downgate Cnwll 5 M7
Downgate Cnwll 5 P7
Downham Essex 38 B2
Downham Gt Lon 37 J6
Downham Lancs 89 M2
Downham Market Norfk 75 M10
Down Hatherley Gloucs 46 G10
Downhead Somset 19 Q9
Downhead Somset 20 C5
Downhill Cnwll 4 D8
Downhill P & K 134 D2
Downholland Cross Lancs 88 D9
Downholme N York 103 M11
Downicarey Devon 5 P3
Downies Abers 151 N9
Downing Flints 80 H9
Downley Bucks 35 M5
Down St Mary Devon 8 H4
Downs Crematorium Br & H 24 H9
Downside Somset 20 B4
Downside Somset 20 B6
Downside Surrey 36 D9
Down Thomas Devon 6 E8
Downton Hants 13 N6
Downton Wilts 21 N10
Dowsby Lincs 74 B5
Dowsdale Lincs 74 E8
Doxey Staffs 70 F10
Doxford Nthumb 119 N6
Doynton S Glos 32 D10
Draethen Caerph 30 H7
Draffan S Lans 126 D8
Dragonby N Linc 92 F8
Dragons Green W Susx 24 D6
Drakeholes Notts 85 M2
Drakelow Worcs 57 Q8
Drakemyre N Ayrs 124 H7
Drakes Broughton Worcs 46 H5
Drakewalls Cnwll 6 C4
Draughton N York 96 F10
Draughton Nhants 60 G5
Drax N York 92 A5
Drax Hales N York 91 R5
Draycote Warwks 59 P10
Draycot Foliat Swindn 33 N9
Draycott Derbys 72 C4
Draycott Gloucs 47 N7
Draycott Shrops 57 Q6
Draycott Somset 19 N4
Draycott Somset 19 Q10
Draycott Worcs 46 G5
Draycott in the Clay Staffs 71 M9
Draycott in the Moors Staffs 70 H6
Drayford Devon 9 J2
Drayton C Port 15 J5
Drayton Leics 60 H2
Drayton Lincs 74 D3
Drayton Norfk 76 H9
Drayton Oxon 34 E6
Drayton Oxon 48 D5
Drayton Somset 19 M10
Drayton Somset 58 D9
Drayton Bassett Staffs 59 J4
Drayton Beauchamp Bucks 35 P2
Drayton Manor Park Staffs 59 J4
Drayton Parslow Bucks 49 M9
Drayton St Leonard Oxon 34 G5
Drebley N York 96 G9
Dreemskerry IoM 80 g3
Dreen Hill Pembks 40 H8
Drefach Carmth 28 F2
Drefach Carmth 42 G7
Drefach Cerdgn 43 J5
Drefelin Carmth 42 G7
Dreghorn N Ayrs 125 K10
Drellingore Kent 27 M3
Drem E Loth 128 E4
Dresden C Stke 70 G6
Drewsteignton Devon 8 H6
Driby Lincs 87 L6
Driffield E R Yk 99 L9
Driffield Gloucs 33 L5
Driffield Cross Roads Gloucs 33 L5
Drift Cnwll 2 C8
Drigg Cumb 100 E11
Drighlington Leeds 90 G5
Drimnin Highld 137 P5
Drimpton Dorset 11 J4
Drimsallie Highld 138 H2
Dringhouses C York 98 B11
Drinkstone Suffk 64 D9
Drinkstone Green Suffk 64 D9
Drive End Dorset 11 M3
Driver's End Herts 50 F6
Drointon Staffs 71 J9
Droitwich Worcs 46 G2
Dron P & K 134 E4
Dronfield Derbys 84 E5
Dronfield Woodhouse Derbys 84 D5
Drongan E Ayrs 114 H4
Dronley Angus 142 E10
Droop Dorset 12 C3
Dropping Well Rothm 84 E2
Droxford Hants 22 H11
Droylsden Tamesd 83 K5
Druid Denbgs 68 D6
Druidston Pembks 40 G7

Druimarbin Highld 139 K3
Druimavuic Ag & B 139 J8
Druimdrishaig Ag & B 123 M5
Druimindarroch Highld 145 L11
Drum Ag & B 124 A2
Drum P & K 134 C7
Drumalbin S Lans 116 C3
Drumbeg Highld 164 D10
Drumblade Abers 158 E9
Drumbreddon D & G 106 C9
Drumbuie Highld 153 P11
Drumburgh Cumb 110 E9
Drumburn D & G 109 J10
Drumchapel C Glas 125 N3
Drumchastle P & K 140 G6
Drumclog S Lans 125 Q10
Drumeldrie Fife 135 L7
Drumelzier Border 116 G4
Drumfearn Highld 145 L4
Drumfrennie Abers 151 J8
Drumguish Highld 148 D7
Drumin Moray 157 M11
Drumjohn D & G 115 K8
Drumlamford S Ayrs 107 J2
Drumlasie Abers 150 G6
Drumleaning Cumb 110 E10
Drumlemble Ag & B 120 C8
Drumlithie Abers 151 K11
Drummoddie D & G 107 L8
Drummore D & G 106 F10
Drummuir Moray 158 A9
Drumnadrochit Highld 155 P11
Drumnaglaur D & G 106 F10
Drumnagorrach Moray 158 D7
Drumpark D & G 109 J5
Drumrunie Lodge Highld 161 K6
Drumshang S Ayrs 114 E5
Drumuie Highld 152 H8
Drumuillie Highld 148 G3
Drumvaich Stirlg 133 K7
Drunzie P & K 134 E6
Druridge Nthumb 119 Q11
Drury Flints 69 J2
Drybeck Cumb 102 C7
Drybridge Moray 158 B5
Drybridge N Ayrs 125 K10
Drybrook Gloucs 46 B11
Dryburgh Border 118 A4
Dry Doddington Lincs 85 Q11
Dry Drayton Cambs 62 E8
Drymen Stirlg 132 F10
Drymuir Abers 159 M8
Drynoch Highld 152 G11
Dry Sandford Oxon 34 E4
Dryslwyn Carmth 43 L10
Dubford Abers 159 J5
Dublin Suffk 64 H8
Duchally Highld 161 P3
Duck End Bed 50 C2
Duck End Cambs 62 B8
Duck End Essex 51 Q4
Duck End Essex 51 Q5
Duckend Green Essex 52 B7
Duckington Ches W 69 N4
Ducklington Oxon 34 C3
Duck's Cross Bed 61 P9
Duddenhoe End Essex 51 L3
Duddingston C Edin 127 P3
Duddington Nhants 73 P10
Duddlestone Somset 18 H10
Duddleswell E Susx 25 L5
Duddlewick Shrops 57 M8
Duddo Nthumb 118 H2
Duddon Ches W 69 P2
Duddon Bridge Cumb 94 D3
Duddon Common Ches W 81 Q11
Dudleston Shrops 69 K7
Dudleston Heath Shrops 69 L7
Dudley Dudley 58 D6
Dudley N Tyne 113 L6
Dudley Hill C Brad 90 F4
Dudley Port Sandw 58 E6
Dudnill Shrops 57 L10
Dudsbury Dorset 13 J5
Dudswell Herts 35 Q3
Duffield Derbys 72 A2
Duffryn Neath 29 M5
Dufftown Moray 157 Q9
Duffus Moray 157 M4
Dufton Cumb 102 C5
Duggleby N York 98 H7
Duirinish Highld 153 P11
Duisdalemore Highld 145 M5
Duisky Highld 139 J2
Dukestown Blae G 30 F2
Duke Street Essex 53 J3
Dukinfield Tamesd 83 K5
Dukinfield Crematorium Tamesd 83 K5
Dulas IoA 78 H7
Dulcote Somset 19 Q6
Dulford Devon 9 Q3
Dull P & K 141 K8
Dullatur N Lans 126 C2
Dullingham Cambs 63 K9
Dullingham Ley Cambs 63 K9
Dulnain Bridge Highld 148 H3
Duloe Bed 61 Q8
Duloe Cnwll 5 L10
Dulverton Somset 18 C9
Dulwich Gt Lon 36 H6
Dumbarton W Duns 125 K3
Dumbleton Gloucs 47 K7
Dumfries D & G 109 L5
Dumgoyne Stirlg 132 G11
Dummer Hants 22 G5
Dumpton Kent 39 Q8
Dun Angus 143 M6
Dunalastair P & K 140 H6
Dunan Ag & B 124 F3
Dunan Highld 145 J2
Dunan P & K 140 C6
Dunaverty Ag & B 120 C10
Dunball Somset 19 K6
Dunbar E Loth 128 H4
Dunbeath Highld 167 L11
Dunbeg Ag & B 138 F11
Dunblane Stirlg 133 M7
Dunbog Fife 134 H4
Dunbridge Hants 22 B9
Duncanston Highld 155 Q6
Duncanstone Abers 150 F2
Dunchideock Devon 9 L7
Dunchurch Warwks 59 Q10
Duncote Nhants 49 J4
Duncow D & G 109 L4

Duncrievie P & K 134 E6
Duncton W Susx 23 Q11
Dundee C Dund 142 G11
Dundee Airport C Dund 135 K2
Dundee Crematorium
 C Dund 142 F11
Dundon Somset 19 N8
Dundonald S Ayrs 125 K11
Dundonnell Highld 160 H9
Dundraw Cumb 110 D11
Dundreggan Highld 147 J5
Dundrennan D & G 108 F11
Dundry N Som 31 Q11
Dunecht Abers 151 K6
Dunfermline Fife 134 D10
Dunfermline
 Crematorium Fife 134 E10
Dunfield Gloucs 33 M5
Dunford Bridge Barns 83 Q4
Dungate Kent 38 F10
Dungavel S Lans 126 B10
Dunge Wilts 20 G4
Dungeness Kent 27 J8
Dungworth Sheff 84 C3
Dunham Notts 85 P6
Dunham-on-the-Hill
 Ches W 81 P10
Dunhampstead Worcs 46 H2
Dunhampton Worcs 58 B11
Dunham Town Traffd 82 F7
Dunham Woodhouses
 Traffd 82 F7
Dunholme Lincs 86 D5
Dunino Fife 135 N5
Dunipace Falk 133 N11
Dunkeld P & K 141 P9
Dunkerton BaNES 20 D3
Dunkeswell Devon 10 C3
Dunkeswick N York 97 M11
Dunkirk Ches W 81 M10
Dunkirk Kent 39 J10
Dunkirk S Glos 32 E7
Dunkirk Wilts 21 J2
Dunk's Green Kent 37 P10
Dunlappie Angus 143 K4
Dunley Hants 22 E4
Dunley Worcs 57 P11
Dunlop E Ayrs 125 L8
Dunmaglass Highld 147 P3
Dunmere Cnwll 4 G8
Dunmore Falk 133 P10
Dunnet Highld 167 M2
Dunnichen Angus 143 J8
Dunning P & K 134 C5
Dunnington C York 98 D10
Dunnington E R Yk 99 P10
Dunnington Warwks 47 L4
Dunnockshaw Lancs 89 N5
Dunn Street Kent 38 C9
Dunoon Ag & B 124 F2
Dunphail Moray 157 J8
Dunragit D & G 106 G6
Duns Border 129 K9
Dunsa Derbys 84 B6
Dunsby Lincs 74 B5
Dunscar Bolton 89 L8
Dunscore D & G 109 J4
Dunscroft Donc 91 Q9
Dunsdale R & Cl 104 H7
Dunsden Green Oxon 35 K9
Dunsdon Devon 16 E10
Dunsfold Surrey 24 B3
Dunsford Devon 9 K7
Dunshalt Fife 134 G5
Dunshillock Abers 159 N8
Dunsill Notts 84 G8
Dunsley N York 105 N8
Dunsley Staffs 58 C8
Dunsmore Bucks 35 N3
Dunsop Bridge Lancs 95 P11
Dunstable C Beds 50 B6
Dunstall Staffs 71 M10
Dunstall Common Worcs 46 G6
Dunstall Green Suffk 63 M8
Dunstan Nthumb 119 P7
Dunstan Steads Nthumb 119 P6
Dunster Somset 18 C6
Duns Tew Oxon 48 E9
Dunston Gatesd 113 K8
Dunston Lincs 86 E8
Dunston Norfk 77 J11
Dunston Staffs 70 G11
Dunstone Devon 6 F8
Dunstone Devon 8 H9
Dunston Heath Staffs 70 G11
Dunsville Donc 91 Q9
Dunswell E R Yk 93 J3
Dunsyre S Lans 127 K8
Dunterton Devon 5 P6
Dunthrop Oxon 48 C9
Duntisbourne Abbots
 Gloucs 33 J3
Duntisbourne Leer
 Gloucs 33 J3
Duntisbourne Rouse
 Gloucs 33 J3
Duntish Dorset 11 P3
Duntocher W Duns 125 M3
Dunton Bucks 49 M10
Dunton C Beds 50 F2
Dunton Norfk 76 B5
Dunton Bassett Leics 60 B2
Dunton Green Kent 37 M9
Dunton Wayletts Essex 37 Q2
Duntulm Highld 152 G3
Dunure S Ayrs 114 E4
Dunvant Swans 28 G6
Dunvegan Highld 152 D8
Dunwich Suffk 65 P7
Dunwood Staffs 70 G3
Durdar Cumb 110 H10
Durgan Cnwll 3 K8
Durham Dur 103 Q2
Durham Cathedral Dur 103 Q2
Durham Crematorium
 Dur 103 Q2
Durham Services Dur 104 B3
Durham Tees Valley
 Airport S on T 104 C8
Durisdeer D & G 116 B10
Durisdeermill D & G 116 B10
Durkar Wakefd 91 J7
Durleigh Somset 19 J7
Durley Hants 22 F11
Durley Wilts 21 P2
Durley Street Hants 22 F11
Durlock Kent 39 N10
Durlock Kent 39 P9
Durlow Common Herefs 46 B7
Durn Rochdl 89 Q7

Durness Highld 165 K3
Durno Abers 151 J2
Duror Highld 138 H6
Durran Ag & B 131 K6
Durrington W Susx 24 D9
Durrington Wilts 21 N6
Durris Abers 151 K8
Dursley Gloucs 32 E5
Dursley Cross Gloucs 46 C10
Durston Somset 19 J9
Durweston Dorset 12 E3
Duston Nhants 60 F8
Duthil Highld 148 G3
Dutlas Powys 56 C9
Duton Hill Essex 51 P5
Dutson Cnwll 5 N4
Dutton Ches W 82 C9
Duxford Cambs 62 G11
Duxford Oxon 34 C5
Dwygyfylchi Conwy 79 N9
Dwyran IoA 78 G11
Dyce C Aber 151 M5
Dyer's End Essex 52 B4
Dyfatty Carmth 28 E4
Dyffrydan Gwynd 54 F2
Dyffryn Brdgnd 29 N6
Dyffryn Myr Td 30 E4
Dyffryn V Glam 30 E10
Dyffryn Ardudwy Gwynd 67 K10
Dyffryn Castell Cerdgn 54 H8
Dyffryn Cellwen Neath 29 N2
Dyke Lincs 74 B6
Dyke Moray 156 H6
Dykehead Angus 142 C7
Dykehead Angus 142 F6
Dykehead N Lans 126 F6
Dykehead Stirlg 132 H8
Dykelands Abers 143 N4
Dykends Angus 142 D6
Dykeside Abers 143 H9
Dylife Powys 55 K6
Dymchurch Kent 27 K6
Dymock Gloucs 46 D8
Dyrham S Glos 32 D9
Dysart Fife 135 J9
Dyserth Denbgs 80 F9

E

Eachway Worcs 58 E9
Eachwick Nthumb 112 H6
Eagland Hill Lancs 95 J11
Eagle Lincs 85 Q7
Eagle Barnsdale Lincs 85 Q7
Eagle Moor Lincs 85 Q7
Eaglescliffe S on T 104 D7
Eaglesfield Cumb 100 E5
Eaglesfield D & G 110 D6
Eaglesham E Rens 125 P7
Eagley Bolton 89 L8
Eairy IoM 80 c6
Eakring Notts 85 L8
Ealand N Linc 92 C8
Ealing Gt Lon 36 E4
Eals Nthumb 111 N9
Eamont Bridge Cumb 101 P5
Earby Lancs 96 D11
Earcroft Bl w D 89 K6
Eardington Shrops 57 N6
Eardisland Herefs 45 N3
Eardisley Herefs 45 L5
Eardiston Shrops 69 L9
Eardiston Worcs 57 M11
Earith Cambs 62 E5
Earle Nthumb 119 J5
Earlestown St Hel 82 C5
Earley Wokham 35 K10
Earlham Norfk 76 H10
Earlham Crematorium
 Norfk 77 J10
Earlish Highld 152 F5
Earls Barton Nhants 61 J8
Earls Colne Essex 52 E6
Earls Common Worcs 47 J3
Earl's Croome Worcs 46 G6
Earlsditton Shrops 57 L9
Earlsdon Covtry 59 M9
Earl's Down E Susx 25 P7
Earlsferry Fife 135 M7
Earlsfield Gt Lon 36 G6
Earlsford Abers 159 K11
Earl's Green Suffk 64 E8
Earlsheaton Kirk 90 H6
Earl Shilton Leics 72 D11
Earl Soham Suffk 65 J9
Earl Sterndale Derbys 83 N11
Earlston Border 117 R3
Earlston E Ayrs 125 L10
Earl Stonham Suffk 64 G10
Earlswood Surrey 36 G11
Earlswood Warwks 58 H10
Earlswood Common
 Mons 31 N6
Earnley W Susx 15 M7
Earnshaw Bridge Lancs 88 G6
Earsdon N Tyne 113 M6
Earsdon Nthumb 113 J2
Earsham Norfk 65 L4
Earswick C York 98 C9
Eartham W Susx 15 P5
Earthcott S Glos 32 C7
Easby N York 104 G9
Easdale Ag & B 130 E4
Easebourne W Susx 23 P10
Easenhall Warwks 59 Q9
Eashing Surrey 23 P6
Easington Bucks 35 J2
Easington Dur 104 D2
Easington E R Yk 93 Q7
Easington Nthumb 119 M4
Easington Oxon 35 J5
Easington R & Cl 105 K7
Easington Colliery Dur 104 D2
Easington Lane Sundld 113 N11
Easingwold N York 98 A7
Easole Street Kent 39 N11
Eassie and Nevay Angus 142 E9
East Aberthaw V Glam 30 D11
East Allington Devon 7 K9
East Anstey Devon 17 R6
East Anton Hants 22 C5
East Appleton N York 103 P11
East Ashey IoW 14 G9
East Ashling W Susx 15 M5
East Aston Hants 22 D5
East Ayton N York 99 K3
East Balsdon Cnwll 5 M2
East Bank Blae G 30 H3

East Barkwith Lincs 86 G4
East Barming Kent 38 B11
East Barnby N York 105 M8
East Barnet Gt Lon 50 G11
East Barns E Loth 129 J4
East Barsham Norfk 76 C5
East Beckham Norfk 76 H4
East Bedfont Gt Lon 36 C6
East Bergholt Suffk 53 J5
East Bierley Kirk 90 F5
East Bilney Norfk 76 D8
East Blatchington E Susx 25 L10
East Bloxworth Dorset 12 E6
East Boldon S Tyne 113 N8
East Boldre Hants 14 C6
East Bolton Nthumb 119 M6
Eastbourne Darltn 104 B8
Eastbourne E Susx 25 P11
Eastbourne
 Crematorium E Susx 25 P10
East Bower Somset 19 K7
East Bradenham Norfk 76 C10
East Brent Somset 19 K4
Eastbridge Suffk 65 P8
East Bridgford Notts 72 H2
East Briscoe Dur 103 J7
Eastbrook V Glam 30 G10
East Buckland Devon 17 M5
East Budleigh Devon 9 Q8
Eastburn C Brad 90 C2
Eastburn E R Yk 99 K9
East Burnham Bucks 35 Q8
East Burton Dorset 12 D7
Eastbury Herts 36 C2
Eastbury W Berk 34 B9
East Butsfield Dur 112 H11
East Butterwick N Linc 92 D9
Eastby N York 96 F10
East Calder W Loth 127 K4
East Carleton Norfk 76 H11
East Carlton Leics 60 G2
East Carlton Nhants 60 H3
East Chaldon (Chaldon
 Herring) Dorset 12 C8
East Challow Oxon 34 C7
East Charleton Devon 7 K10
East Chelborough
 Dorset 11 M3
East Chiltington E Susx 25 J7
East Chinnock Somset 11 K2
East Chisenbury Wilts 21 M4
Eastchurch Kent 38 G7
East Clandon Surrey 36 C10
East Claydon Bucks 49 K9
East Clevedon N Som 31 M10
East Coker Somset 11 L2
Eastcombe Gloucs 32 G4
Eastcombe Somset 18 G8
East Compton Somset 20 B6
East Cornworthy Devon 7 L7
East Cote Cumb 109 P9
Eastcote Gt Lon 36 D3
Eastcote Nhants 49 J4
Eastcote Solhll 59 J9
Eastcott Cnwll 16 D8
Eastcott Wilts 21 K3
East Cottingwith E R Yk 92 B2
Eastcourt Wilts 21 P2
Eastcourt Wilts 33 J6
East Cowes IoW 14 F8
East Cowick E R Yk 91 R6
East Cowton N York 104 B10
East Cramlington
 Nthumb 113 L6
East Cranmore Somset 20 C6
East Creech Dorset 12 F8
East Curthwaite Cumb 110 F11
East Dean E Susx 25 N11
East Dean Gloucs 46 C10
East Dean Hants 21 Q9
East Dean W Susx 15 P4
East Devon
 Crematorium Devon 9 Q5
Eastdown Devon 7 L9
East Down Devon 17 L3
East Drayton Notts 85 N5
East Dulwich Gt Lon 36 H5
East Dundry N Som 31 Q11
East Ella C KuH 93 J5
East End Bed 61 P9
East End C Beds 49 Q6
East End E R Yk 93 L4
East End E R Yk 93 N5
Eastend Essex 38 F3
East End Essex 51 K8
East End Hants 14 C7
East End Hants 22 D2
East End Herts 51 L5
East End Kent 26 D4
East End Kent 38 G7
East End M Keyn 49 P6
East End N Som 31 N10
East End Oxon 48 C11
East End Somset 20 C5
East End Suffk 53 K4
East Molesey Surrey 36 D7
Eastmoor Norfk 75 P10
East Morden Dorset 12 F6
East Morton C Brad 90 D2
East Morton D & G 116 B10
East Ness N York 98 D5
East Newton E R Yk 93 N3
Eastney C Port 15 J7
Eastnor Herefs 46 D7
East Norton Leics 73 K10
Eastoft N Linc 92 D7
East Ogwell Devon 7 L2
Easton Cambs 61 P6
Easton Cumb 110 E9
Easton Devon 8 H7
Easton Dorset 11 P10
Easton Hants 22 F8
Easton Lincs 73 N5
Easton Norfk 76 H9
Easton Somset 19 P5
Easton Suffk 65 L10
Easton W Berk 34 D10
Easton Wilts 32 G9
Easton Grey Wilts 32 G7
Easton-in-Gordano
 N Som 31 P9
Easton Maudit Nhants 61 J9
Easton-on-the-Hill
 Nhants 73 Q10
Easton Royal Wilts 21 P2
East Orchard Dorset 20 F11
East Ord Nthumb 129 P9
East Panson Devon 5 P3
East Parley Dorset 13 J5
East Peckham Kent 37 Q11
East Pennard Somset 19 Q7
East Pennard Somset 19 Q7
East Perry Cambs 61 Q7
East Portlemouth Devon 7 K11
East Prawle Devon 7 K11
East Preston W Susx 24 C10
East Pulham Dorset 11 Q3

East Guldeford E Susx 26 F7
East Haddon Nhants 60 E7
East Hagbourne Oxon 34 F7
East Halton N Linc 93 K7
East Ham Gt Lon 37 K4
Eastham Wirral 81 M8
Eastham Ferry Wirral 81 M8
Easthampstead Park
 Crematorium Br For 35 M11
Easthampton Herefs 45 N2
East Hanney Oxon 34 D6
East Hanningfield Essex 52 C11
East Hardwick Wakefd 91 M7
East Harling Norfk 64 D4
East Harlsey N York 104 D11
East Harnham Wilts 21 M9
East Harptree BaNES 19 Q3
East Hartburn S on T 104 D7
East Hartford Nthumb 113 L5
East Harting W Susx 23 L11
East Hatch Wilts 20 H9
East Hatley Cambs 62 C10
East Hauxwell N York 97 J2
East Haven Angus 143 K10
Eastheath Wokham 35 L11
East Heckington Lincs 74 C2
East Hedleyhope Dur 103 N2
East Helmsdale Highld 163 N3
East Hendred Oxon 34 D7
East Heslerton N York 99 J5
East Hewish N Som 19 M2
East Hoathly E Susx 25 M7
East Holme Dorset 12 E7
Easthope Shrops 57 K5
Easthorpe Essex 52 F7
Easthorpe Notts 85 M10
East Horrington Somset 19 Q5
East Horsley Surrey 36 C10
East Horton Nthumb 119 K4
East Howe Bmouth 13 J5
East Huntington C York 98 C9
East Huntspill Somset 19 K5
East Hyde C Beds 50 D7
East Ilkerton Devon 17 N2
East Ilsley W Berk 34 E8
Eastington Devon 8 H3
Eastington Gloucs 32 E3
Eastington Gloucs 33 M2
East Keal Lincs 87 L8
East Kennett Wilts 33 M11
East Keswick Leeds 91 K2
East Kilbride S Lans 125 Q7
East Kimber Devon 8 C5
East Kirkby Lincs 87 K8
East Knighton Dorset 12 D7
East Knowstone Devon 17 Q7
East Knoyle Wilts 20 G8
East Lambrook Somset 19 N11
East Lancashire
 Crematorium Bury 89 M9
Eastlands D & G 108 H6
East Langdon Kent 27 P2
East Langton Leics 60 F2
East Lavant W Susx 15 N5
East Lavington W Susx 23 P11
Eastleach Martin Gloucs 33 P4
Eastleach Turville Gloucs 33 N3
East Leake Notts 72 F5
East Learmouth Nthumb 118 G3
East Leigh Devon 6 H8
East Leigh Devon 7 K7
East Leigh Devon 8 G3
Eastleigh Devon 16 H6
Eastleigh Hants 22 E11
East Lexham Norfk 76 B8
Eastling Kent 38 G10
East Linton E Loth 128 F4
East Liss Hants 23 L9
East Lockinge Oxon 34 D7
East London
 Crematorium Gt Lon 37 J4
East Lound N Linc 92 C11
East Lulworth Dorset 12 E8
East Lutton N York 99 J7
East Lydeard Somset 18 G9
East Lydford Somset 19 Q8
East Malling Kent 38 B10
East Malling Heath Kent 37 Q9
East Marden W Susx 15 M4
East Markham Notts 85 M6
East Martin Hants 21 L11
East Marton N York 96 F10
East Meon Hants 23 J10
East Mere Devon 18 C11
East Mersea Essex 52 H9
East Midlands Airport
 Leics 72 D5

East Putford Devon 16 F8
East Quantoxhead
 Somset 18 F6
East Rainham Medway 38 D8
East Rainton Sundld 113 M11
East Ravendale NE Lin 93 M11
East Raynham Norfk 76 B6
Eastrea Cambs 74 E11
East Riding
 Crematorium E R Yk 99 L7
Eastriggs D & G 110 D7
East Rigton Leeds 91 K2
Eastrington E R Yk 92 D4
East Rolstone N Som 19 L2
Eastrop Swindn 33 P6
East Rounton N York 104 D10
East Rudham Norfk 76 A6
East Runton Norfk 76 H3
East Ruston Norfk 77 L6
Eastry Kent 39 P11
East Saltoun E Loth 128 D6
Eastshaw W Susx 23 N10
East Sheen Gt Lon 36 F6
East Shefford W Berk 34 C10
East Sleekburn Nthumb 113 L4
East Somerton Norfk 77 P8
East Stockwith Lincs 85 N2
East Stoke Dorset 12 E7
East Stoke Notts 85 N11
East Stour Dorset 20 F10
East Stourmouth Kent 39 N9
East Stowford Devon 17 L6
East Stratton Hants 22 F6
East Studdal Kent 27 P2
East Sutton Kent 26 D2
East Taphouse Cnwll 5 K9
East-the-Water Devon 16 H6
East Thirston Nthumb 119 N10
East Tilbury Thurr 37 Q5
East Tisted Hants 23 K8
East Torrington Lincs 86 F4
East Tuddenham Norfk 76 F9
East Tytherley Hants 21 Q9
East Tytherton Wilts 33 J10
East Village Devon 9 K3
Eastville Bristl 32 B10
Eastville Lincs 87 M9
East Wall Shrops 57 K5
East Walton Norfk 75 P7
East Water Somset 19 P4
East Week Devon 8 G6
Eastwell Leics 73 K5
East Wellow Hants 22 B10
East Wemyss Fife 135 J8
East Whitburn W Loth 126 H4
Eastwick Herts 51 K8
East Wickham Gt Lon 37 L5
East Williamston
 Pembks 41 L10
East Winch Norfk 75 N7
East Winterslow Wilts 21 P8
East Wittering W Susx 15 L7
East Witton N York 96 H3
Eastwood Notts 84 G11
Eastwood Sthend 38 E4
East Woodburn Nthumb 112 D3
Eastwood End Cambs 62 F2
East Woodhay Hants 22 D2
East Woodlands Somset 20 E6
East Worldham Hants 23 L7
East Wretham Norfk 64 C3
East Youlstone Devon 16 D8
Eathorpe Warwks 59 N11
Eaton Ches E 83 J11
Eaton Ches W 69 Q2
Eaton Leics 73 K5
Eaton Norfk 77 J10
Eaton Notts 85 M5
Eaton Oxon 34 D4
Eaton Shrops 56 H7
Eaton Shrops 57 J7
Eaton Bishop Herefs 45 N7
Eaton Bray C Beds 49 Q10
Eaton Constantine
 Shrops 57 K3
Eaton Ford Cambs 61 Q9
Eaton Green C Beds 49 Q10
Eaton Hastings Oxon 33 Q5
Eaton Mascott Shrops 57 J3
Eaton Socon Cambs 61 Q9
Eaton upon Tern Shrops 70 B10
Eaves Brow Warrtn 82 D6
Eaves Green Solhll 59 L8
Ebberston N York 98 H4
Ebbesborne Wake Wilts 21 J10
Ebbw Vale Blae G 30 G3
Ebchester Dur 112 H9
Ebdon N Som 19 L2
Ebford Devon 9 N7
Ebley Gloucs 32 F3
Ebnal Ches W 69 N5
Ebnall Herefs 45 N3
Ebrington Gloucs 47 N6
Ebsworthy Devon 8 D6
Ecchinswell Hants 22 E3
Ecclaw Border 129 K6
Ecclefechan D & G 110 C6
Eccles Border 118 E3
Eccles Kent 38 B9
Eccles Salfd 82 G5
Eccles Crematorium
 Salfd 82 F5
Ecclesfield Sheff 84 E2
Eccles Green Herefs 45 M5
Eccleshall Staffs 70 E9
Eccleshill C Brad 90 F3
Ecclesmachan W Loth 127 K3
Eccles on Sea Norfk 77 N6
Eccles Road Norfk 64 E4
Eccleston Ches W 69 M2
Eccleston Lancs 88 G7
Eccleston St Hel 81 P5
Eccleston Green Lancs 88 G7
Echt Abers 151 J6
Eckford Border 118 D5
Eckington Derbys 84 F5
Eckington Worcs 46 H6
Ecton Nhants 60 H8
Ecton Staffs 71 K3
Edale Derbys 83 P7
Eday Ork 169 e3
Eday Airport Ork 169 e3
Edburton W Susx 24 F8
Edderside Cumb 109 P11
Edderton Highld 162 G10
Eddington Kent 39 L8
Eddleston Border 127 N3
Eddlewood S Lans 126 C7
Edenbridge Kent 37 K11

Edenfield - Farthing Street 275

Edenfield Lancs 89 N7
Edenhall Cumb 101 Q4
Edenham Lincs 73 R6
Eden Mount Cumb 95 J5
Eden Park Gt Lon 37 J7
Eden Project Cnwll 3 Q3
Edensor Derbys 84 B7
Edentaggart Ag & B 132 C9
Edenthorpe Donc 91 Q9
Edern Gwynd 66 D7
Edgarley Somset 19 P7
Edgbaston Birm 58 G8
Edgcombe Cnwll 3 J7
Edgcott Bucks 49 J10
Edgcott Somset 17 Q4
Edge Gloucs 32 F3
Edge Shrops 56 F3
Edgebolton Shrops 69 Q10
Edge End Gloucs 31 Q2
Edgefield Norfk 76 F5
Edgefield Green Norfk 76 F5
Edgefold Bolton 89 L9
Edge Green Ches W 69 N4
Edgehill Warwks 48 C5
Edgerley Shrops 69 L11
Edgerton Kirk 90 E7
Edgeside Lancs 89 N6
Edgeworth Gloucs 32 H3
Edgeworthy Devon 9 K2
Edginswell Torbay 7 M5
Edgiock Worcs 47 K2
Edgmond Wrekin 70 C11
Edgmond Marsh Wrekin 70 C10
Edgton Shrops 56 F7
Edgware Gt Lon 36 E2
Edgworth Bl w D 89 L7
Edinbane Highld 152 E7
Edinburgh C Edin 127 P3
Edinburgh Airport C Edin 127 L3
Edinburgh Castle C Edin 127 P3
Edinburgh Royal Botanic Gardens C Edin 127 N2
Edinburgh Zoo C Edin 127 N3
Edingale Staffs 59 K2
Edingham D & G 108 H8
Edingley Notts 85 L9
Edingthorpe Norfk 77 L5
Edingthorpe Green Norfk 77 L5
Edington Border 129 M9
Edington Nthumb 113 J4
Edington Somset 19 L7
Edington Wilts 20 H4
Edington Burtle Somset 19 L6
Edingworth Somset 19 L4
Edistone Devon 16 D7
Edithmead Somset 19 K5
Edith Weston RutInd 73 N9
Edlesborough Bucks 49 Q11
Edlingham Nthumb 119 M9
Edlington Lincs 86 H6
Edmond Castle Cumb 111 J9
Edmondsham Dorset 13 J2
Edmondsley Dur 113 K11
Edmondthorpe Leics 73 M7
Edmonton Cnwll 4 F7
Edmonton Gt Lon 36 H2
Edmundbyers Dur 112 F10
Ednam Border 118 D3
Ednaston Derbys 71 N6
Edradynate P & K 141 L7
Edrom Border 129 L8
Edstaston Shrops 69 P8
Edstone Warwks 47 N2
Edvin Loach Herefs 46 C3
Edwalton Notts 72 F3
Edwardstone Suffk 52 F3
Edwardsville Myr Td 30 E5
Edwinsford Carmth 43 M8
Edwinstowe Notts 85 K7
Edworth C Beds 50 F2
Edwyn Ralph Herefs 46 B3
Edzell Angus 143 L4
Edzell Woods Abers 143 L4
Efail-fach Neath 29 L5
Efail Isaf Rhondd 30 E8
Efailnewydd Gwynd 66 F7
Efail-Rhyd Powys 68 G9
Efailwen Carmth 41 M5
Efenechtyd Denbgs 68 F3
Effgill D & G 110 F2
Effingham Surrey 36 D10
Efflinch Staffs 71 M11
Efford Devon 9 L4
Efford Crematorium C Plym 6 E7
Egbury Hants 22 D4
Egdean W Susx 23 Q10
Egerton Bolton 89 L8
Egerton Kent 26 F2
Egerton Forstal Kent 26 E2
Eggborough N York 91 P6
Eggbuckland C Plym 6 E7
Eggesford Devon 17 M9
Eggington C Beds 49 Q9
Egginton Derbys 71 P9
Egglescliffe S on T 104 D8
Eggleston Dur 103 J6
Egham Surrey 36 B6
Egham Wick Surrey 35 Q10
Egleton RutInd 73 M9
Eglingham Nthumb 119 M7
Egloshayle Cnwll 4 G7
Egloskerry Cnwll 5 M4
Eglwysbach Conwy 79 Q10
Eglwys-Brewis V Glam 30 D11
Eglwys Cross Wrexhm 69 N6
Eglwys Fach Cerdgn 54 F5
Eglwyswrw Pembks 41 M3
Egmanton Notts 85 M7
Egremont Cumb 100 D8
Egremont Wirral 81 L6
Egton N York 105 M9
Egton Bridge N York 105 M10
Egypt Bucks 35 Q7
Egypt Hants 22 E6
Eigg Highld 144 G10
Eight Ash Green Essex 52 F6
Eilanreach Highld 145 P4
Eisteddfa Gurig Cerdgn 54 H8
Elan Valley Powys 44 B2
Elan Village Powys 44 C2
Elberton S Glos 32 B7
Elbridge W Susx 15 P6
Elburton C Plym 6 E8
Elcombe Swindn 33 M8
Elcot W Berk 34 C11
Eldernell Cambs 74 F11
Eldersfield Worcs 46 E8
Elderslie Rens 125 L5
Elder Street Essex 51 N4
Eldon Dur 103 P5
Eldwick C Brad 90 E2
Elfhill Abers 151 L10
Elford Nthumb 119 N4
Elford Staffs 59 J2
Elgin Moray 157 N5
Elgol Highld 144 H5
Elham Kent 27 L3
Elie Fife 135 M7
Elilaw Nthumb 119 J9
Elim IoA 78 F8
Eling Hants 14 C4
Elkesley Notts 85 L5
Elkstone Gloucs 33 J2
Ella Abers 158 F6
Ellacombe Torbay 7 N6
Elland Calder 90 E6
Elland Lower Edge Calder 90 E6
Ellary Ag & B 123 M4
Ellastone Staffs 71 L6
Ellel Lancs 95 K9
Ellemford Border 129 J7
Ellenabeich Ag & B 130 E4
Ellenborough Cumb 100 D3
Ellenbrook Salfd 82 F4
Ellenhall Staffs 70 E9
Ellen's Green Surrey 24 C3
Ellerbeck N York 104 D11
Ellerby N York 105 L8
Ellerdine Heath Wrekin 69 R10
Ellerhayes Devon 9 N4
Elleric Ag & B 139 J8
Ellerker E R Yk 92 F5
Ellers N York 90 C2
Ellerton E R Yk 92 B3
Ellerton N York 103 Q11
Ellerton Shrops 70 C9
Ellesborough Bucks 35 M3
Ellesmere Shrops 69 L8
Ellesmere Port Ches W 81 N9
Ellingham Hants 13 K3
Ellingham Norfk 65 M3
Ellingham Nthumb 119 N5
Ellingstring N York 97 J4
Ellington Cambs 61 Q6
Ellington Nthumb 113 L2
Ellington Thorpe Cambs 61 Q6
Elliots Green Somset 20 E5
Ellisfield Hants 22 H5
Ellishader Highld 153 J4
Ellistown Leics 72 C8
Ellon Abers 159 N11
Ellonby Cumb 101 M3
Ellough Suffk 65 N4
Elloughton E R Yk 92 F5
Ellwood Gloucs 31 Q3
Elm Cambs 75 J9
Elmbridge Worcs 58 D11
Elmdon Essex 51 L3
Elmdon Solhll 59 J8
Elmdon Heath Solhll 59 J8
Elmer W Susx 15 Q6
Elmers End Gt Lon 37 J7
Elmer's Green Lancs 88 G9
Elmesthorpe Leics 72 D11
Elm Green Essex 52 C10
Elmhurst Staffs 58 H2
Elmley Castle Worcs 47 J6
Elmley Lovett Worcs 58 C11
Elmore Gloucs 46 E11
Elmore Back Gloucs 46 E11
Elm Park Gt Lon 37 M3
Elmscott Devon 16 C7
Elmsett Suffk 53 J2
Elms Green Worcs 57 N11
Elmstead Heath Essex 53 J7
Elmstead Market Essex 53 J7
Elmstead Row Essex 53 J7
Elmsted Kent 27 K3
Elmstone Kent 39 N9
Elmstone Hardwicke Gloucs 46 H9
Elmswell E R Yk 99 K9
Elmswell Suffk 64 D9
Elmton Derbys 84 H6
Elphin Highld 161 L4
Elphinstone E Loth 128 B6
Elrick Abers 151 L6
Elrig D & G 107 K8
Elrington Nthumb 112 C8
Elsdon Nthumb 112 D2
Elsecar Barns 91 K11
Elsenham Essex 51 M5
Elsfield Oxon 34 F2
Elsham N Linc 92 H8
Elsing Norfk 76 F8
Elslack N York 96 D11
Elson Hants 14 H6
Elson Shrops 69 L7
Elsrickle S Lans 116 F2
Elstead Surrey 23 P6
Elsted W Susx 23 M11
Elsthorpe Lincs 73 R6
Elstob Dur 104 B6
Elston Lancs 88 H4
Elston Notts 85 N11
Elston Wilts 21 L6
Elstone Devon 17 M8
Elstow Bed 61 N11
Elstree Herts 50 E11
Elstronwick E R Yk 93 M4
Elswick Lancs 88 E3
Elswick N u Ty 113 K8
Elsworth Cambs 62 D8
Elterwater Cumb 101 K10
Eltham Gt Lon 37 K6
Eltham Crematorium Gt Lon 37 K6
Eltisley Cambs 62 C9
Elton Bury 89 M8
Elton Cambs 61 N2
Elton Ches W 81 P9
Elton Derbys 84 B8
Elton Gloucs 32 D2
Elton Herefs 56 H10
Elton Notts 73 K3
Elton S on T 104 D7
Elton Green Ches W 81 P10
Eltringham Nthumb 112 G8
Elvanfoot S Lans 116 D7
Elvaston Derbys 72 C4
Elveden Suffk 63 P4
Elvetham Heath Hants 23 M3
Elvingston E Loth 128 D5
Elvington C York 98 E11
Elvington Kent 39 N11
Elwell Devon 17 M5
Elwick Hartpl 104 E4
Elwick Nthumb 119 M3
Elworth Ches E 70 C2
Elworthy Somset 18 E8
Ely Cambs 62 H4
Ely Cardif 30 F9
Emberton M Keyn 49 N5
Embleton Cumb 100 G4
Embleton Dur 104 D5
Embleton Nthumb 119 P6
Embo Highld 163 J8
Emborough Somset 20 B4
Embo Street Highld 163 J8
Embsay N York 96 F10
Emery Down Hants 13 N3
Emley Kirk 90 G8
Emley Moor Kirk 90 G8
Emmbrook Wokham 35 M11
Emmer Green Readg 35 K9
Emmett Carr Derbys 84 G5
Emmington Oxon 35 K4
Emneth Norfk 75 J9
Emneth Hungate Norfk 75 K9
Empingham RutInd 73 N9
Empshott Hants 23 L8
Empshott Green Hants 23 K8
Emstrey Crematorium Shrops 57 J2
Emsworth Hants 15 K5
Enborne W Berk 34 D11
Enborne Row W Berk 22 D2
Enchmarsh Shrops 57 J5
Enderby Leics 72 E11
Endmoor Cumb 95 L4
Endon Staffs 70 G4
Endon Bank Staffs 70 G4
Enfield Gt Lon 51 J11
Enfield Crematorium Gt Lon 50 H11
Enfield Lock Gt Lon 51 J11
Enfield Wash Gt Lon 51 J11
Enford Wilts 21 M4
Engine Common S Glos 32 C8
England's Gate Herefs 45 Q4
Englefield W Berk 34 H10
Englefield Green Surrey 35 Q10
Engleseabrook Ches E 70 D4
English Bicknor Gloucs 46 A11
Englishcombe BaNES 20 D2
English Frankton Shrops 69 N9
Engollan Cnwll 4 D7
Enham-Alamein Hants 22 C5
Enmore Somset 18 H7
Enmore Green Dorset 20 G10
Ennerdale Bridge Cumb 100 E7
Enniscaven Cnwll 4 F10
Enochdhu P & K 141 Q5
Ensay Ag & B 137 K6
Ensbury Bmouth 13 J5
Ensdon Shrops 69 M11
Ensis Devon 17 K6
Enson Staffs 70 G9
Enstone Oxon 48 C10
Enterkinfoot D & G 116 B10
Enterpen N York 104 E9
Enville Staffs 58 B7
Eolaigearraidh W Isls 168 c17
Epney Gloucs 32 E2
Epperstone Notts 85 L11
Epping Essex 51 L10
Epping Green Essex 51 K9
Epping Green Herts 50 G9
Epping Upland Essex 51 K10
Eppleby N York 103 N8
Eppleworth E R Yk 92 H4
Epsom Surrey 36 F8
Epwell Oxon 48 C6
Epworth N Linc 92 C10
Epworth Turbary N Linc 92 C10
Erbistock Wrexhm 69 L6
Erdington Birm 58 H6
Eridge Green E Susx 25 N3
Eridge Station E Susx 25 M4
Erines Ag & B 123 Q4
Eriska Ag & B 138 G9
Eriskay W Isls 168 c17
Eriswell Suffk 63 M5
Erith Gt Lon 37 M5
Erlestoke Wilts 21 J4
Ermington Devon 6 G8
Erpingham Norfk 76 H5
Erriottwood Kent 38 F10
Errogie Highld 147 P3
Errol P & K 134 G3
Erskine Rens 125 M3
Ervie D & G 106 D4
Erwarton Suffk 53 M5
Erwood Powys 44 F6
Eryholme N York 104 B9
Eryrys Denbgs 68 H3
Escalls Cnwll 2 B8
Escomb Dur 103 N4
Escott Somset 18 E7
Escrick N York 91 Q2
Esgair Carmth 42 G9
Esgair Cerdgn 54 D11
Esgairgeiliog Powys 54 H3
Esgerdawe Carmth 43 M6
Esgyryn Conwy 79 Q9
Esh Dur 103 N2
Esher Surrey 36 D8
Esholt C Brad 90 F2
Eshott Nthumb 119 P11
Eshton N York 96 D9
Esh Winning Dur 103 N2
Eskadale Highld 155 N9
Eskbank Mdloth 127 Q4
Eskdale Green Cumb 100 F10
Eskdalemuir D & G 117 K11
Eskham Lincs 93 Q11
Eskholme Donc 91 Q7
Esperley Lane Ends Dur 103 M6
Esprick Lancs 88 E3
Essendine RutInd 73 Q8
Essendon Herts 50 G9
Essich Highld 156 A10
Essington Staffs 58 E4
Esslemont Abers 151 N2
Eston R & Cl 104 F7
Etal Nthumb 118 H3
Etchilhampton Wilts 21 K2
Etchingham E Susx 26 B6
Etchinghill Kent 27 L4
Etchinghill Staffs 71 J11
Etchingwood E Susx 25 M6
Etling Green Norfk 76 E9
Etloe Gloucs 32 C3
Eton W & M 35 Q9
Eton Wick W & M 35 P9
Etruria C Stke 70 F5
Etteridge Highld 148 B9
Ettersgill Dur 102 G5
Ettiley Heath Ches E 70 C2
Ettingshall Wolves 58 D5
Ettington Warwks 47 Q5
Etton C Pete 74 B9
Etton E R Yk 92 G2
Ettrick Border 117 K8
Ettrickbridge Border 117 M6
Ettrickhill Border 117 K8
Etwall Derbys 71 P8
Eudon George Shrops 57 M7
Euston Suffk 64 B6
Euximoor Drove Cambs 75 J11
Euxton Lancs 88 H7
Evancoyd Powys 45 K2
Evanton Highld 155 R4
Evedon Lincs 86 E11
Evelith Shrops 57 N3
Evelix Highld 162 H8
Evenjobb Powys 45 K2
Evenley Nhants 48 G8
Evenlode Gloucs 47 P9
Evenwood Dur 103 N6
Evenwood Gate Dur 103 N6
Evercreech Somset 20 B7
Everingham E R Yk 92 D2
Everleigh Wilts 21 P4
Everley N York 99 K3
Eversholt C Beds 49 Q8
Evershot Dorset 11 M4
Eversley Hants 23 L2
Eversley Cross Hants 23 L2
Everthorpe E R Yk 92 F4
Everton C Beds 62 B10
Everton Hants 13 N6
Everton Lpool 81 L6
Everton Notts 85 L2
Evertown D & G 110 G5
Evesbatch Herefs 46 C5
Evesham Worcs 47 K6
Evington C Leic 72 G10
Ewden Village Sheff 90 H11
Ewell Surrey 36 F8
Ewell Minnis Kent 27 N3
Ewelme Oxon 34 H6
Ewen Gloucs 33 K5
Ewenny V Glam 29 P9
Ewerby Lincs 86 F11
Ewerby Thorpe Lincs 86 F11
Ewhurst Surrey 24 C2
Ewhurst Green E Susx 26 C7
Ewhurst Green Surrey 24 C3
Ewloe Flints 81 L11
Ewloe Green Flints 81 K11
Ewood Bl w D 89 K5
Ewood Bridge Lancs 89 M6
Eworthy Devon 8 B5
Ewshot Hants 23 M5
Ewyas Harold Herefs 45 M9
Exbourne Devon 8 F4
Exbridge Somset 18 B10
Exbury Hants 14 D6
Exceat E Susx 25 M11
Exelby N York 97 L3
Exeter Devon 9 M6
Exeter Airport Devon 9 N6
Exeter & Devon Crematorium Devon 9 M6
Exeter Services Devon 9 N6
Exford Somset 17 R4
Exfordsgreen Shrops 56 H3
Exhall Warwks 47 M3
Exhall Warwks 59 N7
Exlade Street Oxon 35 J8
Exley Head C Brad 90 C2
Exminster Devon 9 M7
Exmoor National Park Somset 17 R4
Exmouth Devon 9 P8
Exning Suffk 63 K7
Exted Kent 27 L3
Exton Devon 9 N7
Exton Hants 22 H10
Exton RutInd 73 N8
Exton Somset 18 B8
Exwick Devon 9 M6
Eyam Derbys 84 B5
Eydon Nhants 48 F5
Eye C Pete 74 D10
Eye Herefs 45 P2
Eye Suffk 64 G7
Eye Green C Pete 74 D10
Eye Kettleby Leics 73 J7
Eyemouth Border 129 N7
Eyeworth C Beds 62 C11
Eyhorne Street Kent 38 D11
Eyke Suffk 65 L11
Eynesbury Cambs 61 Q9
Eynsford Kent 37 M7
Eynsham Oxon 34 D3
Eype Dorset 11 J6
Eyre Highld 152 G7
Eythorne Kent 27 N2
Eyton Herefs 45 P2
Eyton Shrops 56 F7
Eyton Shrops 56 F7
Eyton Shrops 69 M10
Eyton Wrexhm 69 L6
Eyton on Severn Shrops 57 K3
Eyton upon the Weald Moors Wrekin 57 M2

F

Faccombe Hants 22 C3
Faceby N York 104 E10
Fachwen Powys 68 D11
Facit Lancs 89 P7
Fackley Notts 84 G8
Faddiley Ches E 69 Q4
Fadmoor N York 98 D3
Faerdre Swans 29 J4
Fagwyr Swans 29 J4
Faifley W Duns 125 M3
Failand N Som 31 P10
Failford S Ayrs 115 J2
Failsworth Oldham 83 J4
Fairbourne Gwynd 54 E2
Fairburn N York 91 M5
Fairfield Derbys 83 N10
Fairfield Kent 26 G6
Fairfield Worcs 58 D9
Fairford Gloucs 33 N4
Fairford Park Gloucs 33 N4
Fairgirth D & G 109 J9
Fair Green Norfk 75 N7
Fairhaven Lancs 88 C5
Fair Isle Shet 169 t12
Fairlands Surrey 23 Q4
Fairlie N Ayrs 124 G7
Fairlight E Susx 26 E9
Fairmile Devon 10 B5
Fairmile Surrey 36 D8
Fairnilee Border 117 P4
Fair Oak Hants 22 E11
Fairoak Staffs 70 D8
Fair Oak Green Hants 23 J2
Fairseat Kent 37 P8
Fairstead Essex 52 C8
Fairstead Norfk 75 M6
Fairstead Norfk 77 K7
Fairwarp E Susx 25 L5
Fairwater Cardif 30 F9
Fairy Cross Devon 16 G7
Fakenham Norfk 76 C6
Fakenham Magna Suffk 64 C6
Fala Mdloth 128 C7
Fala Dam Mdloth 128 C7
Falcut Nhants 48 G6
Faldingworth Lincs 86 E4
Faldouet Jersey 11 c2
Falfield S Glos 32 C6
Falkenham Suffk 53 N4
Falkirk Falk 133 P11
Falkirk Crematorium Falk 133 P11
Falkland Fife 134 H6
Fallburn S Lans 116 D3
Fallgate Derbys 84 E8
Fallin Stirlg 133 N9
Fallodon Nthumb 119 N6
Fallowfield Manch 83 J6
Fallowfield Nthumb 112 D7
Falls of Blarghour Ag & B 131 K5
Falmer E Susx 25 J9
Falmouth Cnwll 3 L7
Falnash Border 117 M9
Falsgrave N York 99 L3
Falstone Nthumb 111 P3
Fanagmore Highld 164 E7
Fancott C Beds 50 B5
Fanellan Highld 155 N9
Fangdale Beck N York 98 B2
Fangfoss E R Yk 98 F10
Fanmore Ag & B 137 L7
Fannich Lodge Highld 154 H4
Fans Border 118 B2
Far Bletchley M Keyn 49 N8
Farcet Cambs 62 B2
Far Cotton Nhants 60 G9
Farden Shrops 57 K9
Fareham Hants 14 G5
Far End Cumb 101 K11
Farewell Staffs 58 G2
Far Forest Worcs 57 N9
Farforth Lincs 87 K5
Far Green Gloucs 32 E4
Faringdon Oxon 33 Q5
Farington Lancs 88 G5
Farlam Cumb 111 L9
Farleigh N Som 31 P11
Farleigh Surrey 37 J8
Farleigh Hungerford Somset 20 F3
Farleigh Wallop Hants 22 H5
Farlesthorpe Lincs 87 N6
Farleton Cumb 95 L4
Farleton Lancs 95 M7
Farley Derbys 84 C8
Farley Staffs 71 K6
Farley Wilts 21 P9
Farley Green Suffk 63 M10
Farley Green Surrey 36 C11
Farley Hill Wokham 23 K2
Farleys End Gloucs 32 E2
Farlington C Port 15 J5
Farlington N York 98 C7
Farlow Shrops 57 L8
Farmborough BaNES 20 C2
Farmbridge End Essex 51 P8
Farmcote Gloucs 47 L9
Farmcote Shrops 57 P6
Farmers Carmth 43 M6
Farmington Gloucs 47 M11
Farmoor Oxon 34 E3
Far Moor Wigan 82 B4
Farms Common Cnwll 2 H7
Farm Town Leics 72 B7
Farmtown Moray 158 D7
Farnah Green Derbys 84 D11
Farnborough Gt Lon 37 K8
Farnborough Hants 23 N4
Farnborough W Berk 34 D8
Farnborough Warwks 48 D5
Farnborough Park Hants 23 N3
Farnborough Street Hants 23 N3
Farncombe Surrey 23 Q6
Farndish Bed 61 K8
Farndon Ches W 69 M4
Farndon Notts 85 N10
Farne Islands Nthumb 119 Q3
Farnell Angus 143 L6
Farnham Dorset 21 J11
Farnham Essex 51 L6
Farnham N York 97 M8
Farnham Suffk 65 M9
Farnham Surrey 23 M5
Farnham Common Bucks 35 Q7
Farnham Green Essex 51 L5
Farnham Royal Bucks 35 Q8
Farningham Kent 37 M7
Farnley Leeds 90 H4
Farnley N York 97 K11
Farnley Tyas Kirk 90 F8
Farnsfield Notts 85 K9
Farnworth Bolton 89 L9
Farnworth Halton 81 Q7
Far Oakridge Gloucs 32 H4
Farr Highld 148 E7
Farr Highld 156 B11
Farr Highld 166 B4
Farraline Highld 147 P3
Farringdon Devon 9 P6
Farrington Gurney BaNES 20 B3
Far Sawrey Cumb 101 L11
Farsley Leeds 90 G3
Farther Howegreen Essex 52 D11
Farthing Green Kent 26 D2
Farthinghoe Nhants 48 F7
Farthingloe Kent 27 N3
Farthingstone Nhants 48 H4
Farthing Street Gt Lon 37 K8

Fartown Kirk....90 F7
Fartown Leeds....90 G4
Farway Devon....10 D5
Fasnacloich Ag & B....139 J8
Fasnakyle Highld....147 J2
Fassfern Highld....139 J2
Fatfield Sundld....113 L10
Faugh Cumb....111 K10
Fauld Staffs....71 M9
Fauldhouse W Loth....126 G5
Faulkbourne Essex....52 C8
Faulkland Somset....20 D4
Fauls Shrops....69 Q8
Faversham Kent....38 H9
Fawdington N York....97 P6
Fawdon N u Ty....113 K7
Fawdon Nthumb....119 K7
Fawfieldhead Staffs....71 K2
Fawkham Green Kent....37 N7
Fawler Oxon....48 C11
Fawley Bucks....35 L7
Fawley Hants....14 E6
Fawley W Berk....34 C8
Fawley Chapel Herefs....46 A9
Fawnog Flints....81 J11
Fawsley Nhants....60 C9
Faxfleet E R Yk....92 E6
Faygate W Susx....24 F4
Fazakerley Lpool....81 M5
Fazeley Staffs....59 K4
Fearby N York....97 J4
Fearn Highld....156 E2
Fearnan P & K....140 H9
Fearnbeg Highld....153 N6
Fearnhead Warrtn....82 D6
Fearnmore Highld....153 N5
Fearnoch Ag & B....124 A2
Featherstone Staffs....58 D3
Featherstone Wakefd....91 L6
Feckenham Worcs....47 K2
Feering Essex....52 E7
Feetham N York....103 J11
Feizor N York....96 A7
Felbridge Surrey....25 J3
Felbrigg Norfk....77 J4
Felcourt Surrey....25 J2
Felden Herts....50 B10
Felindre Carmth....42 G7
Felindre Carmth....43 L10
Felindre Carmth....43 P9
Felindre Cerdgn....43 L3
Felindre Powys....44 H10
Felindre Powys....56 B8
Felindre Swans....28 H4
Felindre Farchog Pembks....41 M3
Felin Fach Cerdgn....43 K3
Felinfach Powys....44 F8
Felinfoel Carmth....28 F4
Felingwm Isaf Carmth....43 K10
Felingwm Uchaf Carmth....43 K10
Felin-newydd Powys....44 G7
Felixkirk N York....97 Q4
Felixstowe Suffk....53 P5
Felixstowe Ferry Suffk....53 P4
Felkington Nthumb....118 H2
Felkirk Wakefd....91 K8
Felling Gatesd....113 L8
Fell Lane C Brad....90 C2
Fell Side Cumb....101 K3
Felmersham Bed....61 L9
Felmingham Norfk....77 K6
Felpham W Susx....15 P7
Felsham Suffk....64 C10
Felsted Essex....51 Q6
Feltham Gt Lon....36 D6
Felthamhill Surrey....36 C6
Felthorpe Norfk....76 H8
Felton Herefs....46 A5
Felton N Som....31 P11
Felton Nthumb....119 N10
Felton Butler Shrops....69 L11
Feltwell Norfk....63 M2
Fenay Bridge Kirk....90 F7
Fence Lancs....89 N3
Fence Rothm....84 F3
Fence Houses Sundld....113 M11
Fencott Oxon....48 G11
Fendike Corner Lincs....87 N8
Fen Ditton Cambs....62 G8
Fen Drayton Cambs....62 D7
Fen End Lincs....74 D6
Fen End Solhll....59 K10
Fenham Nthumb....119 L2
Feniscliffe Bl w D....89 K5
Feniscowles Bl w D....89 J5
Feniton Devon....10 C5
Fenland Crematorium Cambs....62 F2
Fenn Green Shrops....57 P8
Fenn Street Medway....38 C6
Fenny Bentley Derbys....71 M5
Fenny Bridges Devon....10 C5
Fenny Compton Warwks....48 C4
Fenny Drayton Leics....72 B11
Fenny Stratford M Keyn....49 N8
Fenrother Nthumb....113 J2
Fenstanton Cambs....62 D7
Fenstead End Suffk....63 P10
Fen Street Norfk....64 D2
Fen Street Suffk....64 H9
Fenton C Stke....70 F6
Fenton Cambs....62 D5
Fenton Cumb....111 K9
Fenton Lincs....85 P5
Fenton Lincs....85 Q10
Fenton Notts....85 N4
Fenton Nthumb....119 J4
Fenton Barns E Loth....128 E3
Fenwick Donc....91 P7
Fenwick E Ayrs....125 M9
Fenwick Nthumb....112 G6
Fenwick Nthumb....119 L2
Feock Cnwll....3 L6
Feolin Ferry Ag & B....122 F6
Fergushill N Ayrs....125 J9
Feriniquarrie Highld....152 B7
Fermain Bay Guern....10 c2
Fern Angus....142 H5
Ferndale Rhondd....30 C5
Ferndown Dorset....13 J4
Ferness Highld....156 H8
Fernham Oxon....33 Q6
Fernhill Heath Worcs....46 G3
Fernhurst W Susx....23 N9
Fernie Fife....135 J4
Ferniegair S Lans....126 C6
Fernilea Highld....152 F11
Fernilee Derbys....83 M9
Fernwood Notts....85 P10

Ferrensby N York....97 N8
Ferriby Sluice N Linc....92 G6
Ferrindonald Highld....145 L6
Ferring W Susx....24 C10
Ferrybridge Wakefd....91 M6
Ferrybridge Services Wakefd....91 M6
Ferryden Angus....143 N6
Ferryhill Dur....103 Q4
Ferry Point Highld....162 G9
Ferryside Carmth....28 C2
Ferrytown Highld....162 G9
Fersfield Norfk....64 F5
Fersit Highld....139 R2
Feshiebridge Highld....148 F7
Fetcham Surrey....36 D9
Fetlar Shet....169 t4
Fetterangus Abers....159 N7
Fettercairn Abers....143 M3
Fewcott Oxon....48 F9
Fewston N York....97 J10
Ffairfach Carmth....43 M10
Ffair Rhos Cerdgn....54 G11
Ffald-y-Brenin Carmth....43 M6
Ffawyddog Powys....45 J11
Ffestiniog Gwynd....67 N6
Ffestiniog Railway Gwynd....67 M6
Ffordd-las Denbgs....68 F2
Fforest Carmth....28 G4
Fforest Mons....45 K10
Fforest Fach Swans....28 H5
Fforest Goch Neath....29 K4
Ffostrasol Cerdgn....42 G5
Ffynnonddewi Cerdgn....42 G4
Ffynnongroyw Flints....80 G8
Ffynnon-Oer Cerdgn....43 K4
Fiag Lodge Highld....165 L11
Fickleshole Surrey....37 J8
Fiddington Gloucs....46 H8
Fiddington Somset....18 H6
Fiddleford Dorset....12 D2
Fiddlers Green Cnwll....4 C10
Fiddlers Hamlet Essex....51 L10
Field Staffs....71 J8
Field Broughton Cumb....94 H4
Field Dalling Norfk....76 E4
Fieldhead Cumb....101 N3
Field Head Leics....72 D9
Fifehead Magdalen Dorset....20 E10
Fifehead Neville Dorset....12 C2
Fifehead St Quintin Dorset....12 C2
Fife Keith Moray....158 B7
Fifield Oxon....47 P11
Fifield W & M....35 P9
Fifield Wilts....21 M4
Figheldean Wilts....21 N5
Filands Wilts....32 H7
Filby Norfk....77 P9
Filey N York....99 N4
Filgrave M Keyn....49 N5
Filkins Oxon....33 P4
Filleigh Devon....8 H2
Filleigh Devon....17 M6
Fillingham Lincs....86 B3
Fillongley Warwks....59 L7
Filmore Hill Hants....23 J9
Filton S Glos....32 B9
Fimber E R Yk....98 H8
Finavon Angus....142 H6
Fincham Norfk....75 N9
Finchampstead Wokham....23 L2
Fincharn Ag & B....131 J7
Finchdean Hants....15 K4
Finchingfield Essex....51 Q4
Finchley Gt Lon....36 G2
Findern Derbys....71 Q8
Findhorn Moray....157 J5
Findhorn Bridge Highld....148 E2
Findochty Moray....158 C4
Findo Gask P & K....134 C4
Findon Abers....151 N8
Findon W Susx....24 D9
Findon Mains Highld....155 R5
Findrack House Abers....150 G7
Finedon Nhants....61 K6
Fineshade Nhants....73 P11
Fingal Street Suffk....65 J8
Fingask P & K....134 F2
Fingest Bucks....35 L6
Finghall N York....97 J3
Fingland Cumb....110 E9
Fingland D & G....115 Q4
Fingringhoe Essex....52 H7
Finkle Green Essex....52 B3
Finkle Street Barns....91 J11
Finlarig Stirlg....140 E11
Finmere Oxon....48 H8
Finnart P & K....140 D6
Finningham Suffk....64 F8
Finningley Donc....91 R11
Finsbay W Isls....168 f9
Finstall Worcs....58 E10
Finsthwaite Cumb....94 H3
Finstock Oxon....48 C11
Finstown Ork....169 c5
Fintry Abers....159 J7
Fintry Stirlg....133 J10
Finzean Abers....150 G9
Fionnphort Ag & B....137 J11
Fionnsbhagh W Isls....168 f9
Firbank Cumb....95 N2
Firbeck Rothm....85 J3
Firby N York....97 L3
Firby N York....98 E7
Firgrove Rochdl....89 Q8
Firle E Susx....25 L9
Firsby Lincs....87 N8
Firsdown Wilts....21 P8
Fir Tree Dur....103 M4
Fishbourne IoW....14 G8
Fishbourne W Susx....15 M6
Fishbourne Roman Palace W Susx....15 M5
Fishburn Dur....104 C4
Fishcross Clacks....133 P8
Fisher W Susx....15 N6
Fisherford Abers....158 G10
Fisherrow E Loth....127 Q3
Fisher's Pond Hants....22 E10
Fisher's Row Lancs....95 J11
Fisherstreet W Susx....23 P8
Fisherton Highld....156 C7
Fisherton S Ayrs....114 E4
Fisherton de la Mere Wilts....21 K7

Fisherwick Staffs....59 J3
Fishery Estate W & M....35 N8
Fishguard Pembks....41 J3
Fishlake Donc....91 R8
Fishleigh Devon....8 D3
Fishmere End Lincs....74 E3
Fishnish Pier Ag & B....138 B9
Fishpond Bottom Dorset....10 H5
Fishponds Bristl....32 B9
Fishtoft Lincs....74 G2
Fishtoft Drove Lincs....87 K11
Fishwick Lancs....88 H5
Fiskavaig Highld....152 E11
Fiskerton Lincs....86 D6
Fiskerton Notts....85 M10
Fitling E R Yk....93 N4
Fittleton Wilts....21 M5
Fittleworth W Susx....24 B7
Fitton End Cambs....74 H8
Fitz Shrops....69 M11
Fitzhead Somset....18 F9
Fitzroy Somset....18 G9
Fitzwilliam Wakefd....91 L7
Five Ash Down E Susx....25 L6
Five Ashes E Susx....25 N5
Five Bells Somset....18 E6
Five Bridges Herefs....46 B5
Fivecrosses Ches W....82 B9
Fivehead Somset....19 L10
Five Lanes Mons....31 M6
Five Oak Green Kent....37 P11
Five Oaks Jersey....11 c2
Five Oaks W Susx....24 C5
Five Roads Carmth....28 E3
Five Wents Kent....38 D11
Flack's Green Essex....52 C9
Flackwell Heath Bucks....35 N7
Fladbury Worcs....47 J5
Fladdabister Shet....169 r10
Flagg Derbys....83 P11
Flamborough E R Yk....99 Q6
Flamborough Head E R Yk....99 R6
Flamingo Land Theme Park N York....98 F5
Flamstead Herts....50 C8
Flansham W Susx....15 Q6
Flanshaw Wakefd....91 J6
Flappit Spring C Brad....90 D3
Flasby N York....96 D9
Flash Staffs....83 M11
Flashader Highld....152 E7
Flaunden Herts....50 B10
Flawborough Notts....73 K2
Flawith N York....97 Q7
Flax Bourton N Som....31 P11
Flaxby N York....97 N9
Flaxley Gloucs....46 C11
Flaxmere Ches W....82 C10
Flaxpool Somset....18 F7
Flaxton N York....98 D8
Fleckney Leics....60 D2
Flecknoe Warwks....60 B8
Fledborough Notts....85 P6
Fleet Dorset....11 N8
Fleet Hants....15 K6
Fleet Hants....23 M4
Fleet Lincs....74 G6
Fleet Air Arm Museum Somset....19 Q10
Fleetend Hants....14 F5
Fleet Hargate Lincs....74 G6
Fleet Services Hants....23 L3
Fleetwood Lancs....94 G11
Flemingston V Glam....30 D11
Flemington S Lans....126 B6
Flempton Suffk....63 P7
Fletcher Green Kent....37 M11
Fletchersbridge Cnwll....5 J8
Fletchertown Cumb....100 H2
Fletching E Susx....25 K6
Fleur-de-lis Caerph....30 G5
Flexbury Cnwll....16 C10
Flexford Surrey....23 P4
Flimby Cumb....100 D4
Flimwell E Susx....26 B5
Flint Flints....81 J10
Flintham Notts....85 M11
Flint Mountain Flints....81 J10
Flinton E R Yk....93 M3
Flint's Green Solhll....59 L8
Flishinghurst Kent....26 C4
Flitcham Norfk....75 P5
Flitton C Beds....50 C3
Flitwick C Beds....50 B4
Flixborough N Linc....92 E8
Flixborough Stather N Linc....92 E8
Flixton N York....99 L5
Flixton Suffk....65 L4
Flixton Traffd....82 F6
Flockton Kirk....90 G8
Flockton Green Kirk....90 H7
Flodden Nthumb....118 H3
Flodigarry Highld....152 H3
Flookburgh Cumb....94 H5
Flordon Norfk....64 H2
Flore Nhants....60 D8
Flotterton Nthumb....119 J10
Flowers Green E Susx....25 P8
Flowton Suffk....53 J2
Flushdyke Wakefd....90 H6
Flushing Cnwll....3 L7
Fluxton Devon....10 B6
Flyford Flavell Worcs....47 J3
Fobbing Thurr....38 B5
Fochabers Moray....157 Q6
Fochriw Caerph....30 F3
Fockerby N Linc....92 E7
Foddington Somset....19 Q9
Foel Powys....55 M2
Foelgastell Carmth....28 F2
Foel y Dyffryn Brdgnd....29 N6
Foggathorpe E R Yk....92 C3
Fogo Border....129 K10
Fogwatt Moray....157 N6
Foindle Highld....164 E7
Folda Angus....142 B5
Fole Staffs....71 J7
Foleshill Covtry....59 N8
Folke Dorset....11 P2
Folkestone Kent....27 M4
Folkingham Lincs....73 R4
Folkington E Susx....25 N10
Folksworth Cambs....61 P3
Folkton N York....99 M5
Folla Rule Abers....158 H11
Follifoot N York....97 M10
Folly Gate Devon....8 E6

Folly Hill Surrey....23 M5
Fonmon V Glam....30 D11
Fonthill Bishop Wilts....20 H8
Fonthill Gifford Wilts....20 H8
Fontmell Magna Dorset....20 G11
Fontmell Parva Dorset....12 D2
Fontwell W Susx....15 P5
Font-y-gary V Glam....30 D11
Foolow Derbys....83 Q9
Foots Cray Gt Lon....37 L6
Forbestown Abers....150 B5
Forcett N York....103 N8
Ford Ag & B....130 H7
Ford Bucks....35 L3
Ford Derbys....84 F4
Ford Devon....6 G8
Ford Devon....8 K10
Ford Devon....16 G7
Ford Gloucs....47 L9
Ford Nthumb....118 H3
Ford Somset....56 G2
Ford Somset....18 E9
Ford Somset....19 Q4
Ford Staffs....71 K4
Ford W Susx....15 Q6
Ford Wilts....21 N8
Ford Wilts....32 F9
Forda Devon....8 D6
Fordcombe Kent....25 M2
Fordell Fife....134 F10
Forden Powys....56 C4
Ford End Essex....51 Q7
Forder Green Devon....7 K5
Ford Green Lancs....95 K11
Fordham Cambs....63 K6
Fordham Essex....52 F6
Fordham Norfk....75 M11
Fordham Heath Essex....52 F6
Ford Heath Shrops....56 G2
Fordingbridge Hants....13 K2
Fordon E R Yk....99 L5
Fordoun Abers....143 N2
Ford's Green Suffk....64 F8
Fordstreet Essex....52 F6
Ford Street Somset....18 G11
Fordton Devon....9 K5
Fordwells Oxon....34 B2
Fordwich Kent....39 L10
Fordyce Abers....158 E5
Forebridge Staffs....70 G10
Foremark Derbys....72 A5
Forest Guern....10 b2
Forest N York....103 Q10
Forest Becks Lancs....96 A10
Forestburn Gate Nthumb....119 L11
Forest Chapel Ches E....83 L10
Forest Gate Gt Lon....37 K3
Forest Green Surrey....24 D2
Forest Hall N Tyne....113 L7
Forest Head Cumb....111 L9
Forest Hill Oxon....34 G3
Forest-in-Teesdale Dur....102 G4
Forest Lane Head N York....97 M9
Forest Mill Clacks....134 B9
Forest of Dean Gloucs....32 C6
Forest Park Crematorium Gt Lon....37 L2
Forest Row E Susx....25 K4
Forest Side IoW....14 E9
Forestside W Susx....15 L4
Forest Town Notts....85 J8
Forfar Angus....142 H7
Forgandenny P & K....134 D4
Forge Powys....54 H5
Forge Hammer Torfn....31 J5
Forge Side Torfn....30 H3
Forgie Moray....158 A7
Forgieside Moray....158 B7
Forgue Abers....158 F8
Forhill Worcs....58 G9
Formby Sefton....88 C9
Forncett End Norfk....64 G3
Forncett St Mary Norfk....64 H3
Forncett St Peter Norfk....64 H3
Fornham All Saints Suffk....64 A8
Fornham St Martin Suffk....64 B8
Fornighty Highld....156 G7
Forres Moray....157 J6
Forsbrook Staffs....70 H6
Forse Highld....167 M10
Forshaw Heath Warwks....58 G10
Forsinard Highld....166 E8
Forston Dorset....11 P5
Fort Augustus Highld....147 K6
Forteviot P & K....134 D4
Forth S Lans....126 G7
Forthampton Gloucs....46 G8
Fort Hommet Guern....10 b1
Fortingall P & K....140 H8
Fort le Marchant Guern....10 c1
Forton Hants....22 D6
Forton Lancs....95 K10
Forton Shrops....69 M11
Forton Somset....10 G3
Forton Staffs....70 D10
Fortrie Abers....158 G8
Fortrose Highld....156 C6
Fortuneswell Dorset....11 P10
Fort William Highld....139 L3
Forty Green Bucks....35 P6
Forty Hill Gt Lon....50 H11
Forward Green Suffk....64 G10
Fosbury Wilts....22 B3
Foscot Oxon....47 P10
Foscote Nhants....49 J5
Fosdyke Lincs....74 F4
Fosdyke Bridge Lincs....74 F4
Foss P & K....141 J6
Fossebridge Gloucs....33 L2
Fosterhouses Donc....91 R8
Foster Street Essex....51 L9
Foston Derbys....71 M8
Foston Leics....60 D2
Foston Lincs....73 M2
Foston N York....98 D7
Foston on the Wolds E R Yk....99 M9
Fotherby Lincs....87 K2
Fothergill Cumb....100 D4
Fotheringhay Nhants....61 N2
Foula Shet....169 k10
Foulbridge Cumb....110 H11
Foulby Wakefd....91 K7
Foulden Border....129 N8
Foulden Norfk....75 Q11
Foul End Warwks....59 K6
Foul Mile E Susx....25 P7

Foulness Island Essex....38 G3
Foulon Vale Crematorium Guern....10 b2
Foulridge Lancs....89 P2
Foulsham Norfk....76 E7
Fountainhall Border....128 C10
Four Ashes Solhll....59 J9
Four Ashes Staffs....57 Q5
Four Ashes Staffs....58 D3
Four Ashes Suffk....64 E7
Four Cabots Guern....10 b2
Four Crosses Powys....69 J11
Four Crosses Staffs....58 E3
Four Elms Kent....37 L11
Four Foot Somset....19 Q8
Four Forks Somset....18 H7
Four Gates Bolton....89 J9
Four Gotes Cambs....75 J7
Four Lane End Barns....90 H10
Four Lane Ends Ches W....69 Q2
Four Lanes Cnwll....2 H7
Fourlanes End Ches E....70 E3
Four Marks Hants....23 J7
Four Mile Bridge IoA....78 D9
Four Oaks Birm....58 H5
Four Oaks E Susx....26 E7
Four Oaks Gloucs....46 C9
Four Oaks Solhll....59 K8
Fourpenny Highld....163 J8
Four Points W Berk....34 G9
Four Roads Carmth....28 D3
Four Shire Stone Warwks....47 P8
Fourstones Nthumb....112 C7
Four Throws Kent....26 C6
Four Wents Kent....37 P10
Fovant Wilts....21 K9
Foveran Abers....151 P3
Fowey Cnwll....5 J11
Fowley Common Warrtn....82 E5
Fowlhall Kent....37 Q11
Fowlis Angus....142 E11
Fowlis Wester P & K....133 Q3
Fowlmere Cambs....62 F11
Fownhope Herefs....46 A8
Foxbar Rens....125 M5
Foxcombe Devon....8 C7
Fox Corner Surrey....23 Q4
Foxcote Gloucs....47 K11
Foxcote Somset....20 D3
Foxdale IoM....80 c6
Foxearth Essex....52 D3
Foxendown Kent....37 P7
Foxfield Cumb....94 E3
Foxham Wilts....33 J9
Fox Hatch Essex....51 N11
Foxhills Hants....13 P2
Foxhole Cnwll....3 P3
Foxholes N York....99 L6
Foxhunt Green E Susx....25 M7
Foxley Nhants....48 H4
Foxley Norfk....76 E7
Foxley Wilts....32 G7
Foxlydiate Worcs....58 F11
Fox Street Essex....52 H6
Foxt Staffs....71 J5
Foxton Cambs....62 F11
Foxton Dur....104 C6
Foxton Leics....60 F3
Foxton N York....104 D11
Foxup N York....96 C5
Foxwist Green Ches W....82 D11
Foxwood Shrops....57 L9
Foy Herefs....46 A9
Foyers Highld....147 M3
Foynesfield Highld....156 F7
Fraddam Cnwll....2 F7
Fraddon Cnwll....4 E10
Fradley Staffs....59 J2
Fradswell Staffs....70 H8
Fraisthorpe E R Yk....99 P8
Framfield E Susx....25 L6
Framingham Earl Norfk....77 K11
Framingham Pigot Norfk....77 K11
Framlingham Suffk....65 K9
Frampton Dorset....11 N5
Frampton Lincs....74 F3
Frampton Cotterell S Glos....32 C8
Frampton Mansell Gloucs....32 H4
Frampton on Severn Gloucs....32 D3
Frampton West End Lincs....74 F2
Framsden Suffk....64 H10
Framwellgate Moor Dur....103 Q2
Franche Worcs....57 Q9
Frandley Ches W....82 D9
Frankaborough Devon....5 P3
Frankby Wirral....81 J7
Frankfort Norfk....77 L7
Franklands Gate Herefs....45 Q5
Frankley Worcs....58 E8
Frankley Services Worcs....58 E8
Franksbridge Powys....44 G3
Frankton Warwks....59 P10
Frant E Susx....25 N3
Fraserburgh Abers....159 N4
Frating Essex....53 J7
Frating Green Essex....53 J7
Fratton C Port....15 J6
Freathy Cnwll....5 P11
Freckenham Suffk....63 L6
Freckleton Lancs....88 E5
Freebirch Derbys....84 D6
Freeby Leics....73 L7
Freefolk Hants....22 E5
Freehay Staffs....71 J6
Freeland Oxon....34 D2
Freethorpe Norfk....77 N10
Freethorpe Common Norfk....77 N10
Freiston Lincs....74 G2
Fremington Devon....17 J5
Fremington N York....103 K11
Frenchay S Glos....32 B9
Frenchbeer Devon....8 G7
French Street Kent....37 L10
Frenich P & K....141 K6
Frensham Surrey....23 M6
Freshfield Sefton....88 B9
Freshford Wilts....20 E2
Freshwater IoW....13 P7
Freshwater Bay IoW....13 P7
Freshwater East Pembks....41 K11
Fressingfield Suffk....65 K6
Freston Suffk....53 L4
Freswick Highld....167 Q3
Fretherne Gloucs....32 D2

Frettenham - Godwinscroft 277

Frettenham Norfk 77 J8
Freuchie Fife 134 H6
Freystrop Pembks 41 J8
Friar Park Sandw 58 F6
Friar's Gate E Susx 25 L4
Friars' Hill N York 98 E3
Friar Waddon Dorset 11 N7
Friday Bridge Cambs 75 J10
Friday Street Suffk 65 J10
Friday Street Suffk 65 L11
Friday Street Suffk 65 M9
Friday Street Surrey 36 D11
Fridaythorpe E R Yk 98 H9
Friden Derbys 71 M2
Friendly Calder 90 D6
Friern Barnet Gt Lon 36 G2
Friesthorpe Lincs 86 E4
Frieston Lincs 86 B11
Frieth Bucks 35 L6
Friezeland Notts 84 G10
Frilford Oxon 34 D5
Frilsham W Berk 34 F10
Frimley Surrey 23 N3
Frimley Green Surrey 23 N3
Frindsbury Medway 38 B8
Fring Norfk 75 P4
Fringford Oxon 48 H9
Frinsted Kent 38 E10
Frinton-on-Sea Essex 53 M7
Friockheim Angus 143 K8
Friog Gwynd 54 E2
Frisby on the Wreake Leics 72 H7
Friskney Lincs 87 N9
Friskney Eaudike Lincs 87 N9
Friston E Susx 25 N11
Friston Suffk 65 N9
Fritchley Derbys 84 E10
Fritham Hants 13 M2
Frith Bank Lincs 87 K11
Frith Common Worcs 57 M11
Frithelstock Devon 16 H8
Frithelstock Stone Devon 16 H8
Frithend Hants 23 M7
Frithsden Herts 50 B9
Frithville Lincs 87 K10
Frittenden Kent 26 D3
Frittiscombe Devon 7 L10
Fritton Norfk 65 J3
Fritton Norfk 77 P11
Fritwell Oxon 48 F9
Frizinghall C Brad 90 E3
Frizington Cumb 100 D7
Frocester Gloucs 32 E4
Frodesley Shrops 57 J4
Frodsham Ches W 81 Q9
Frogden Border 118 E5
Frog End Cambs 62 E11
Frog End Cambs 62 H9
Froggatt Derbys 84 B5
Froghall Staffs 71 J5
Frogham Hants 13 L2
Frogham Kent 39 N11
Frogmore Devon 7 K10
Frognall Lincs 74 C8
Frogpool Cnwll 3 K5
Frog Pool Worcs 57 Q11
Frogwell Cnwll 5 N8
Frolesworth Leics 60 B2
Frome Somset 20 E5
Frome St Quintin Dorset 11 M4
Fromes Hill Herefs 46 C5
Fron Denbgs 80 F11
Fron Gwynd 66 F7
Fron Gwynd 67 J4
Fron Powys 56 B5
Fron Powys 56 C4
Froncysyllte Denbgs 69 J6
Fron-goch Gwynd 68 B7
Fron Isaf Wrexhm 69 J6
Frostenden Suffk 65 P5
Frosterley Dur 103 K3
Froxfield C Beds 49 Q8
Froxfield Wilts 33 Q11
Froxfield Green Hants 23 K9
Fryern Hill Hants 22 D10
Fryerning Essex 51 P10
Fryton N York 98 D6
Fuinary Highld 137 Q6
Fulbeck Lincs 86 B10
Fulbourn Cambs 62 H9
Fulbrook Oxon 33 Q2
Fulflood Hants 22 E8
Fulford C York 98 C11
Fulford Somset 18 H9
Fulford Staffs 70 H7
Fulham Gt Lon 36 G5
Fulking W Susx 24 F8
Fullaford Devon 17 M4
Fullarton N Ayrs 125 J10
Fuller's End Essex 51 M5
Fuller's Moor Ches W 69 N4
Fuller Street Essex 52 B8
Fuller Street Kent 37 N9
Fullerton Hants 22 C7
Fulletby Lincs 87 J6
Fullready Warwks 47 Q5
Full Sutton E R Yk 98 E9
Fullwood E Ayrs 125 L7
Fulmer Bucks 35 Q7
Fulmodeston Norfk 76 D5
Fulnetby Lincs 86 E5
Fulney Lincs 74 E6
Fulstone Kirk 90 F9
Fulstow Lincs 93 P11
Fulwell Oxon 48 C10
Fulwell Sundld 113 N9
Fulwood Lancs 88 G4
Fulwood Notts 84 G9
Fulwood Sheff 84 D3
Fulwood Somset 18 H10
Fundenhall Norfk 64 H2
Funtington W Susx 15 M5
Funtley Hants 14 G5
Funtullich P & K 133 M2
Furley Devon 10 F4
Furnace Ag & B 131 L7
Furnace Carmth 28 F4
Furnace Cerdgn 54 F5
Furnace End Warwks 59 K6
Furner's Green E Susx 25 K5
Furness Vale Derbys 83 M8
Furneux Pelham Herts 51 K5
Further Quarter Kent 26 E4
Furtho Nhants 49 L6
Furzehill Devon 17 N2
Furzehill Dorset 12 H4
Furzehills Lincs 87 J6
Furzeley Corner Hants 15 J4
Furze Platt W & M 35 N8
Furzley Hants 21 Q11
Fyfett Somset 10 E2
Fyfield Essex 51 N9
Fyfield Hants 21 Q5
Fyfield Oxon 34 D5
Fyfield Wilts 21 N2
Fyfield Wilts 33 M11
Fyfield Bavant Wilts 21 K9
Fylingthorpe N York 105 P10
Fyning W Susx 23 M10
Fyvie Abers 159 J10

G

Gabroc Hill E Ayrs 125 M7
Gaddesby Leics 72 H8
Gaddesden Row Herts 50 C8
Gadfa IoA 78 H7
Gadgirth S Ayrs 114 H3
Gadlas Shrops 69 L7
Gaer Powys 44 H10
Gaer-llwyd Mons 31 M5
Gaerwen IoA 78 H10
Gagingwell Oxon 48 D9
Gailes N Ayrs 125 J10
Gailey Staffs 58 D2
Gainford Dur 103 N7
Gainsborough Lincs 85 P3
Gainsford End Essex 52 B4
Gairloch Highld 153 Q2
Gairlochy Highld 146 F11
Gairneybridge P & K 134 E8
Gaisgill Cumb 102 B9
Gaitsgill Cumb 110 G11
Galashiels Border 117 P3
Galgate Lancs 95 K9
Galhampton Somset 20 B9
Gallanachbeg Ag & B 130 G2
Gallanachmore Ag & B 130 G2
Gallantry Bank Ches E 69 P4
Gallatown Fife 134 H9
Galley Common Warwks 59 M6
Galleywood Essex 52 B11
Gallovie Highld 147 P10
Galloway Forest Park 114 H10
Gallowfauld Angus 142 G9
Gallowhill P & K 142 B10
Gallows Green Essex 52 F6
Gallows Green Worcs 46 H2
Gallowstree Common Oxon 35 J8
Galltair Highld 145 P3
Gallt-y-foel Gwynd 67 K2
Gally Hill Hants 23 M4
Gallypot Street E Susx 25 L3
Galmpton Devon 6 H10
Galmpton Torbay 7 M7
Galphay N York 97 L6
Galston E Ayrs 125 N10
Gamballs Green Staffs 83 M11
Gamblesby Cumb 102 B3
Gambles Green Essex 52 C9
Gamelsby Cumb 110 E10
Gamesley Derbys 83 M6
Gamlingay Cambs 62 B10
Gamlingay Cinques Cambs 62 B10
Gamlingay Great Heath Cambs 62 B10
Gammersgill N York 96 G4
Gamrie Abers 159 J5
Gamston Notts 72 F3
Gamston Notts 85 M5
Ganarew Herefs 45 Q11
Ganavan Bay Ag & B 138 F11
Gang Cnwll 5 N8
Ganllwyd Gwynd 67 N10
Gannachy Angus 143 K3
Ganstead E R Yk 93 K4
Ganthorpe N York 98 D6
Ganton N York 99 K5
Ganwick Corner Herts 50 G11
Gappah Devon 9 L9
Garbity Moray 157 Q7
Garboldisham Norfk 64 E5
Garbole Highld 148 D3
Garchory Abers 149 Q5
Garden City Flints 81 L11
Gardeners Green Wokham 35 M11
Gardenstown Abers 159 K5
Garden Village Sheff 90 H11
Garderhouse Shet 169 q9
Gardham E R Yk 92 G2
Gare Hill Somset 20 E6
Garelochhead Ag & B 131 Q9
Garford Oxon 34 D5
Garforth Leeds 91 L4
Gargrave N York 96 D10
Gargunnock Stirlg 133 L9
Garizim Conwy 79 M9
Garlic Street Norfk 65 J5
Garlieston D & G 107 N8
Garlinge Kent 39 P8
Garlinge Green Kent 39 K11
Garlogie Abers 151 K6
Garmond Abers 159 K7
Garmouth Moray 157 Q5
Garmston Shrops 57 L3
Garnant Carmth 29 J2
Garn-Dolbenmaen Gwynd 66 H6
Garnett Bridge Cumb 101 P11
Garnfadryn Gwynd 66 D8
Garnkirk N Lans 126 B4
Garnswllt Swans 28 H3
Garn-yr-erw Torfn 30 H3
Garrabost W Isls 168 k4
Garrallan E Ayrs 115 K4
Garras Cnwll 3 J9
Garreg Gwynd 67 L6
Garrigill Cumb 102 D2
Garriston N York 97 J2
Garroch D & G 108 C4
Garrochtrie D & G 106 F10
Garrochty Ag & B 124 D7
Garros Highld 152 H5
Garsdale Cumb 95 Q3
Garsdale Head Cumb 96 A2
Garsdon Wilts 33 J7
Garshall Green Staffs 70 H8
Garsington Oxon 34 G4
Garstang Lancs 95 K11
Garston Herts 50 D10
Garston Lpool 81 N8
Gartachossan Ag & B 122 D7
Gartcosh N Lans 126 B4
Garth Brdgnd 29 N6
Garth Mons 31 K6
Garth Powys 44 D5
Garth Powys 56 D10
Garth Wrexhm 69 J6
Garthamlock C Glas 126 B4
Garthbrengy Powys 44 E8
Gartheli Cerdgn 43 L3
Garthmyl Powys 56 B5
Garthorpe Leics 73 L6
Garthorpe N Linc 92 D7
Garth Penrhyncoch Cerdgn 54 E8
Garth Row Cumb 101 P11
Garths Cumb 95 L3
Gartly Abers 158 D11
Gartmore Stirlg 132 G8
Gartness N Lans 126 D5
Gartness Stirlg 132 G10
Gartocharn W Duns 132 E10
Garton E R Yk 93 N3
Garton-on-the-Wolds E R Yk 99 K9
Gartymore Highld 163 N4
Garvald E Loth 128 F5
Garvan Highld 138 H2
Garvard Ag & B 136 b3
Garve Highld 155 L5
Garvellachs Ag & B 130 D5
Garvestone Norfk 76 E10
Garvock Inver 124 H3
Garway Herefs 45 P10
Garway Common Herefs 45 P10
Garway Hill Herefs 45 N9
Garyvard W Isls 168 i6
Gasper Wilts 20 E8
Gastard Wilts 32 G11
Gasthorpe Norfk 64 D5
Gaston Green Essex 51 L7
Gatcombe IoW 14 E9
Gatebeck Cumb 95 L3
Gate Burton Lincs 85 P4
Gateford Notts 85 J4
Gateforth N York 91 P5
Gatehead E Ayrs 125 K10
Gate Helmsley N York 98 D9
Gatehouse Nthumb 111 Q3
Gatehouse of Fleet D & G 108 C9
Gateley Norfk 76 D7
Gatenby N York 97 M3
Gatesgarth Cumb 100 G7
Gateshaw Border 118 E6
Gateshead Gatesd 113 L8
Gates Heath Ches W 69 N2
Gateside Angus 142 G9
Gateside E Rens 125 M6
Gateside Fife 134 F6
Gateside N Ayrs 125 K7
Gateslack D & G 116 B10
Gathurst Wigan 88 G9
Gatley Stockp 82 H7
Gatton Surrey 36 G10
Gattonside Border 117 Q3
Gatwick Airport W Susx 24 G2
Gaufron Powys 55 M11
Gaulby Leics 72 H10
Gauldry Fife 135 K3
Gauldswell P & K 142 C7
Gaulkthorn Lancs 89 M5
Gaultree Norfk 75 J9
Gaunton's Bank Ches E 69 Q5
Gaunt's Common Dorset 12 H3
Gaunt's End Essex 51 N5
Gautby Lincs 86 G6
Gavinton Border 129 K9
Gawber Barns 91 J9
Gawcott Bucks 49 J8
Gawsworth Ches E 83 J11
Gawthorpe Wakefd 90 H6
Gawthrop Cumb 95 P3
Gawthwaite Cumb 94 F4
Gay Bowers Essex 52 C11
Gaydon Warwks 48 C4
Gayhurst M Keyn 49 M5
Gayle N York 96 C3
Gayles N York 103 M9
Gay Street W Susx 24 C6
Gayton Nhants 49 K4
Gayton Norfk 75 P7
Gayton Staffs 70 H9
Gayton Wirral 81 K8
Gayton le Marsh Lincs 87 M4
Gayton Thorpe Norfk 75 P7
Gaywood Norfk 75 M6
Gazeley Suffk 63 M8
Gear Cnwll 3 J9
Gearraidh Bhaird W Isls 168 i6
Geary Highld 152 D5
Gedding Suffk 64 C10
Geddington Nhants 61 J4
Gedling Notts 72 G2
Gedney Lincs 74 H6
Gedney Broadgate Lincs 74 H6
Gedney Drove End Lincs 75 J5
Gedney Dyke Lincs 74 H5
Gedney Hill Lincs 74 F8
Gee Cross Tamesd 83 L6
Geeston Rutlnd 73 P10
Geldeston Norfk 65 M3
Gelli Rhondd 30 C6
Gelli Torfn 31 J6
Gellifor Denbgs 68 F2
Gelligaer Caerph 30 F5
Gelligroes Caerph 30 G6
Gelligron Neath 29 K4
Gellilydan Gwynd 67 M7
Gellinudd Neath 29 K4
Gelly Pembks 41 L7
Gellyburn P & K 141 Q10
Gellywen Carmth 41 Q6
Gelston D & G 108 G9
Gelston Lincs 86 B11
Gembling E R Yk 99 N9
Gentleshaw Staffs 58 G2
Georgefield D & G 110 E2
George Green Bucks 35 Q8
Georgeham Devon 16 H4
Georgemas Junction Station Highld 167 L5
George Nympton Devon 17 N7
Georgetown Blae G 30 G3
Georgia Cnwll 2 D6
Georth Ork 169 c4
Gerlan Gwynd 79 L11
Germansweek Devon 8 B6
Germoe Cnwll 2 F8
Gerrans Cnwll 3 M6
Gerrards Cross Bucks 36 B3
Gerrick R & Cl 105 K8
Gestingthorpe Essex 52 D4
Geuffordd Powys 56 C2
Gib Hill Ches W 82 D9
Gibraltar Lincs 87 Q9
Gibsmere Notts 85 M11
Giddeahall Wilts 32 G10
Giddy Green Dorset 12 D7
Gidea Park Gt Lon 37 M2
Gidleigh Devon 8 G7
Giffnock E Rens 125 P6
Gifford E Loth 128 E6
Giffordtown Fife 134 H5
Giggleswick N York 96 B8
Gigha Ag & B 123 K10
Gilberdyke E R Yk 92 D5
Gilbert's End Worcs 46 F6
Gilbert Street Hants 22 H8
Gilchriston E Loth 128 D6
Gilcrux Cumb 100 F3
Gildersome Leeds 90 G5
Gildingwells Rothm 85 J3
Gilesgate Moor Dur 103 Q2
Gileston V Glam 30 D11
Gilfach Caerph 30 G5
Gilfach Goch Brdgnd 30 C6
Gilfachrheda Cerdgn 42 H3
Gilgarran Cumb 100 D6
Gill Cumb 101 M5
Gillamoor N York 98 D3
Gillan Cnwll 3 K8
Gillen Highld 152 D6
Gillesbie D & G 110 C2
Gilling East N York 98 C5
Gillingham Dorset 20 F9
Gillingham Medway 38 C8
Gillingham Norfk 65 N3
Gilling West N York 103 N9
Gillock Highld 167 M5
Gillow Heath Staffs 70 F3
Gills Highld 167 P2
Gill's Green Kent 26 C5
Gilmanscleuch Border 117 L6
Gilmerton C Edin 127 P4
Gilmerton P & K 133 P3
Gilmonby Dur 103 J8
Gilmorton Leics 60 C3
Gilroes Crematorium C Leic 72 F9
Gilsland Nthumb 111 M7
Gilson Warwks 59 J7
Gilstead C Brad 90 E3
Gilston Border 128 C8
Gilston Herts 51 K8
Gilston Park Herts 51 K8
Giltbrook Notts 84 G11
Gilwern Mons 30 H2
Gimingham Norfk 77 K4
Ginclough Ches E 83 L9
Gingers Green E Susx 25 P8
Gipping Suffk 64 F9
Gipsey Bridge Lincs 87 J11
Girdle Toll N Ayrs 125 J9
Girlington C Brad 90 E4
Girlsta Shet 169 r8
Girsby N York 104 C9
Girtford C Beds 61 Q11
Girthon D & G 108 D10
Girton Cambs 62 F8
Girton Notts 85 P7
Girvan S Ayrs 114 C8
Gisburn Lancs 96 B11
Gisleham Suffk 65 Q4
Gislingham Suffk 64 F7
Gissing Norfk 64 G4
Gittisham Devon 10 C5
Gladestry Powys 45 J3
Gladsmuir E Loth 128 D5
Glais Swans 29 K4
Glaisdale N York 105 L9
Glamis Angus 142 F8
Glanaber Gwynd 67 L4
Glanafon Pembks 41 J7
Glanaman Carmth 29 J2
Glandford Norfk 76 E3
Glan-Duar Carmth 43 K6
Glandwr Pembks 41 N5
Glan-Dwyfach Gwynd 66 H6
Glandyfi Cerdgn 54 F5
Glangrwyney Powys 45 J11
Glanllynfi Brdgnd 29 N6
Glanmule Powys 56 B6
Glanrhyd Pembks 41 M2
Glan-rhyd Powys 29 L3
Glanton Nthumb 119 L8
Glanton Pike Nthumb 119 L8
Glanvilles Wootton Dorset 11 P3
Glan-y-don Flints 80 H9
Glan-y-llyn Rhondd 30 F8
Glan-y-nant Powys 55 L8
Glan-yr-afon Gwynd 68 B6
Glan-yr-afon Gwynd 68 D6
Glan-yr-afon IoA 79 L8
Glan-yr-afon Swans 28 H3
Glapthorn Nhants 61 M2
Glapwell Derbys 84 G7
Glasbury Powys 44 H7
Glascoed Denbgs 80 D10
Glascoed Mons 31 K4
Glascote Staffs 59 K4
Glascwm Powys 44 H4
Glasfryn Conwy 68 B4
Glasgow C Glas 125 P4
Glasgow Airport Rens 125 M4
Glasgow Science Centre C Glas 125 P4
Glasinfryn Gwynd 79 K11
Glasnacardoch Bay Highld 145 L8
Glasnakille Highld 144 H5
Glaspwll Powys 54 G5
Glassenbury Kent 26 C4
Glassford S Lans 126 C8
Glass Houghton Wakefd 91 L6
Glasshouse Gloucs 46 D10
Glasshouse Hill Gloucs 46 D10
Glasshouses N York 97 J8
Glasson Cumb 110 E8
Glasson Lancs 95 J9
Glassonby Cumb 101 Q3
Glasterlaw Angus 143 K7
Glaston Rutlnd 73 M10
Glastonbury Somset 19 P7
Glatton Cambs 61 Q3
Glazebrook Warrtn 82 E6
Glazebury Warrtn 82 E5
Glazeley Shrops 57 N7
Gleadless Sheff 84 E4
Gleadsmoss Ches E 82 H11
Gleaston Cumb 94 F6
Glebe Highld 147 N4
Gledhow Leeds 91 J3
Gledpark D & G 108 D10
Gledrid Shrops 69 K7
Glemsford Suffk 52 D2
Glenallachie Moray 157 P9
Glenancross Highld 145 L9
Glenaros House Ag & B 137 P7
Glen Auldyn IoM 80 f3
Glenbarr Ag & B 120 C4
Glenbarry Abers 158 E7
Glenbeg Highld 137 P3
Glenbervie Abers 151 K11
Glenboig N Lans 126 C4
Glenborrodale Highld 137 Q3
Glenbranter Ag & B 131 N8
Glenbreck Border 116 F6
Glenbrittle House Highld 144 F3
Glenbuck E Ayrs 115 P2
Glencally Angus 142 F5
Glencaple D & G 109 L7
Glencarron Lodge Highld 154 E7
Glencarse P & K 134 F3
Glen Clunie Lodge Abers 149 L11
Glencoe Highld 139 L6
Glencothe Border 116 F5
Glencraig Fife 134 F9
Glencrosh D & G 115 Q10
Glendale Highld 152 B8
Glendaruel Ag & B 131 K11
Glendevon P & K 134 B7
Glendoe Lodge Highld 147 L6
Glendoick P & K 134 G3
Glenduckie Fife 134 H4
Glenegedale Ag & B 122 D9
Glenelg Highld 145 P4
Glenerney Moray 157 J8
Glenfarg P & K 134 E5
Glenfield Leics 72 E9
Glenfinnan Highld 145 R11
Glenfintaig Lodge Highld 146 G10
Glenfoot P & K 134 F4
Glenfyne Lodge Ag & B 131 Q4
Glengarnock N Ayrs 125 J7
Glengolly Highld 167 K3
Glengorm Castle Ag & B 137 L4
Glengrasco Highld 152 G9
Glenholm Border 116 G4
Glenhoul D & G 115 M10
Glenisla Angus 142 C5
Glenkin Ag & B 131 N11
Glenkindie Abers 150 C5
Glenlivet Moray 149 M2
Glenlochar D & G 108 F8
Glenlomond P & K 134 F7
Glenluce D & G 106 G6
Glenmassen Ag & B 131 N10
Glenmavis N Lans 126 D4
Glen Maye IoM 80 b6
Glen Mona IoM 80 g4
Glenmore Highld 152 G9
Glenmore Lodge Highld 148 H6
Glen Nevis House Highld 139 L3
Glenochil Clacks 133 P8
Glen Parva Leics 72 F11
Glenquiech Angus 142 G5
Glenralloch Ag & B 123 Q6
Glenridding Cumb 101 L7
Glenrothes Fife 134 H7
Glenshero Lodge Highld 147 P9
Glenstriven Ag & B 124 D2
Glentham Lincs 86 D2
Glen Trool Lodge D & G 114 H11
Glentrool Village D & G 107 L2
Glentruim House Highld 148 B9
Glentworth Lincs 86 B3
Glenuig Highld 138 B2
Glenvarragill Highld 152 H10
Glen Vine IoM 80 d6
Glenwhilly D & G 106 G3
Glespin S Lans 115 R2
Glewstone Herefs 45 R10
Glinton C Pete 74 C9
Glooston Leics 73 K11
Glossop Derbys 83 M6
Gloster Hill Nthumb 119 Q10
Gloucester Gloucs 46 F11
Gloucester Crematorium Gloucs 46 G11
Gloucestershire Airport Gloucs 46 G10
Glusburn N York 96 F11
Glutt Lodge Highld 166 H9
Gluvian Cnwll 4 E9
Glympton Oxon 48 D10
Glynarthen Cerdgn 42 F5
Glyn Ceiriog Wrexhm 68 H7
Glyncorrwg Neath 29 N5
Glynde E Susx 25 L9
Glyndebourne E Susx 25 L8
Glyndyfrdwy Denbgs 68 F6
Glynneath Neath 29 N3
Glynn Valley Crematorium Cnwll 4 H8
Glyntaff Rhondd 30 E7
Glyntaff Crematorium Rhondd 30 E7
Glyntawe Powys 44 A11
Glynteg Carmth 42 G7
Gnosall Staffs 70 E10
Gnosall Heath Staffs 70 E10
Goadby Leics 73 K11
Goadby Marwood Leics 73 K5
Goatacre Wilts 33 K9
Goatham Green E Susx 26 D7
Goathill Dorset 20 C11
Goathland N York 105 M10
Goathurst Somset 19 J8
Goathurst Common Kent 37 L10
Goat Lees Kent 26 H2
Gobowen Shrops 69 K8
Godalming Surrey 23 Q6
Goddard's Corner Suffk 65 K8
Goddard's Green Kent 26 D5
Godford Cross Devon 10 C4
Godington Oxon 48 H9
Godley Tamesd 83 L5
Godmanchester Cambs 62 B6
Godmanstone Dorset 11 P5
Godmersham Kent 39 J11
Godney Somset 19 N6
Godolphin Cross Cnwll 2 G7
Godre'r-graig Neath 29 L3
Godshill Hants 21 N11
Godshill IoW 14 F10
Godstone Staffs 71 J8
Godstone Surrey 37 J10
Godsworthy Devon 8 D9
Godwinscroft Hants 13 L5

278 Goetre - Grisling Common

Goetre Mons 31 K3
Goff's Oak Herts 50 H10
Gofilon Mons 31 J2
Gogar C Edin 127 M3
Goginan Cerdgn 54 F8
Golan Gwynd 67 J6
Golant Cnwll 5 J11
Golberdon Cnwll 5 N7
Golborne Wigan 82 D5
Golcar Kirk 90 D7
Goldcliff Newpt 31 L8
Golden Cross E Susx 25 M8
Golden Green Kent 37 P11
Golden Grove Carmth 43 L11
Goldenhill C Stke 70 F4
Golden Hill Pembks 41 J10
Golden Pot Hants 23 K6
Golden Valley Derbys 84 F10
Golders Green Gt Lon 36 F3
Golders Green Crematorium Gt Lon 36 G3
Goldfinch Bottom W Berk 22 F2
Goldhanger Essex 52 F10
Gold Hill Cambs 62 H2
Gold Hill Dorset 12 D2
Golding Shrops 57 J4
Goldington Bed 61 N10
Goldsborough N York 97 N9
Goldsborough N York 105 M8
Golds Green Sandw 58 E6
Goldsithney Cnwll 2 E7
Goldstone Kent 39 N9
Goldstone Shrops 70 C9
Goldsworth Park Surrey 23 Q3
Goldthorpe Barns 91 M10
Goldworthy Devon 16 F7
Golford Kent 26 C4
Golford Green Kent 26 C4
Gollanfield Highld 156 E7
Gollinglith Foot N York 96 H4
Golly Wrexhm 69 K3
Golsoncott Somset 18 D7
Golspie Highld 163 J6
Gomeldon Wilts 21 N7
Gomersal Kirk 90 G5
Gomshall Surrey 36 C11
Gonalston Notts 85 L11
Gonerby Hill Foot Lincs 73 N3
Gonfirth Shet 169 q7
Goodameavy Devon 6 E6
Good Easter Essex 51 P8
Gooderstone Norfk 75 Q10
Goodleigh Devon 17 L5
Goodmanham E R Yk 92 E2
Goodmayes Gt Lon 37 L3
Goodnestone Kent 38 H9
Goodnestone Kent 39 N11
Goodrich Herefs 45 R11
Goodrich Castle Herefs 46 A11
Goodrington Torbay 7 M7
Goodshaw Lancs 89 N5
Goodshaw Fold Lancs 89 N5
Goodstone Devon 7 K4
Goodwick Pembks 40 H3
Goodworth Clatford Hants 22 C6
Goodyers End Warwks 59 M7
Goole E R Yk 92 B6
Goole Fields E R Yk 92 C6
Goom's Hill Worcs 47 K4
Goonbell Cnwll 3 J4
Goonhavern Cnwll 3 K3
Goonvrea Cnwll 3 J4
Goosecruives Abers 151 K11
Gooseford Devon 8 G6
Goose Green Essex 53 K6
Goose Green Kent 26 D4
Goose Green Kent 37 P10
Goose Green S Glos 32 C10
Goose Green W Susx 24 D7
Goose Green Wigan 82 C4
Gooseham Cnwll 16 C8
Gooseham Mill Cnwll 16 C8
Goosehill Green Worcs 46 H2
Goose Pool Herefs 45 P7
Goosey Oxon 34 C6
Goosnargh Lancs 88 H3
Goostrey Ches E 82 G10
Gordano Services N Som 31 P9
Gorddinog Conwy 79 M10
Gordon Border 118 B2
Gordon Arms Hotel Border 117 L5
Gordonstown Abers 158 E6
Gordonstown Abers 158 H10
Gore Powys 45 K3
Gorebridge Mdloth 127 Q5
Gorefield Cambs 74 H8
Gore Pit Essex 52 E8
Gores Wilts 21 M3
Gore Street Kent 39 N8
Gorey Jersey 11 c2
Goring Oxon 34 H8
Goring-by-Sea W Susx 24 D10
Goring Heath Oxon 35 J9
Gorleston on Sea Norfk 77 Q11
Gornal Wood Crematorium Dudley 58 D6
Gorrachie Abers 158 H6
Gorran Churchtown Cnwll 3 P5
Gorran Haven Cnwll 3 Q5
Gorran High Lanes Cnwll 3 P5
Gorrig Cerdgn 42 H6
Gors Cerdgn 54 E9
Gorsedd Flints 80 H9
Gorse Hill Swindn 33 N7
Gorseinon Swans 28 G5
Gorseybank Derbys 71 P4
Gorsgoch Cerdgn 43 J4
Gorslas Carmth 28 G2
Gorsley Gloucs 46 C9
Gorsley Common Herefs 46 C9
Gorstage Ches W 82 D10
Gorstan Highld 155 L5
Gorstella Ches W 69 L2
Gorst Hill Worcs 57 N10
Gorsty Hill Staffs 71 L9
Gorten Ag & B 138 C11
Gorthleck Highld 147 N3
Gorton Manch 83 J5
Gosbeck Suffk 64 H10
Gosberton Lincs 74 D4
Gosberton Clough Lincs 74 C5
Gosfield Essex 52 C6
Gosford Devon 10 C5
Gosforth Cumb 100 E10
Gosforth N u Ty 113 K7
Gosling Street Somset 19 P8
Gosmore Herts 50 E5
Gospel End Staffs 58 C6
Gospel Green W Susx 23 P8
Gosport Hants 14 H7
Gossard's Green C Beds 49 Q6
Gossington Gloucs 32 D4
Goswick Nthumb 119 L2
Gotham Notts 72 E4
Gotherington Gloucs 47 J9
Gotton Somset 18 H9
Goudhurst Kent 26 B4
Goulceby Lincs 87 J5
Gourdas Abers 159 J9
Gourdie C Dund 142 F11
Gourdon Abers 143 Q3
Gourock Inver 124 G2
Govan C Glas 125 N4
Goveton Devon 7 K9
Gowdall E R Yk 91 Q6
Gower Highld 155 P6
Gower Swans 28 F6
Gowerton Swans 28 G5
Gowkhall Fife 134 D10
Gowthorpe E R Yk 98 F10
Goxhill E R Yk 93 L2
Goxhill N Linc 93 K6
Grabhair W Isls 168 i6
Graby Lincs 74 A5
Grade Cnwll 3 J11
Gradeley Green Ches E 69 Q4
Graffham W Susx 23 P11
Grafham Cambs 61 Q7
Grafham Surrey 24 B2
Grafton Herefs 45 P7
Grafton N York 97 P8
Grafton Oxon 33 Q4
Grafton Shrops 69 M11
Grafton Worcs 46 A2
Grafton Worcs 47 J7
Grafton Flyford Worcs 47 J3
Grafton Regis Nhants 49 L5
Grafton Underwood Nhants 61 K4
Grafty Green Kent 26 E2
Graianrhyd Denbgs 68 H3
Graig Conwy 79 Q10
Graig Denbgs 80 F10
Graig-fechan Denbgs 68 F4
Grain Medway 38 E6
Grains Bar Oldham 90 B9
Grainsby Lincs 93 N11
Grainthorpe Lincs 93 Q11
Grampound Cnwll 3 N4
Grampound Road Cnwll 3 N3
Gramsdal W Isls 168 d12
Gramsdale W Isls 168 d12
Granborough Bucks 49 L9
Granby Notts 73 K3
Grandborough Warwks 59 Q11
Grand Chemins Jersey 11 c2
Grandes Rocques Guern 10 b1
Grand Prix Collection Donington Leics 72 C5
Grandtully P & K 141 M7
Grange Cumb 101 J7
Grange Medway 38 C8
Grange P & K 134 H2
Grange Wirral 81 J7
Grange Crossroads Moray 158 C7
Grange Hall Moray 157 K5
Grangehall S Lans 116 D2
Grange Hill Essex 37 K2
Grangemill Derbys 84 B9
Grange Moor Kirk 90 G7
Grangemouth Falk 133 Q11
Grange of Lindores Fife 134 H4
Grange-over-Sands Cumb 95 J5
Grangepans Falk 134 C11
Grangetown R & Cl 104 F6
Grangetown Sundld 113 P10
Grange Villa Dur 113 K10
Gransmoor E R Yk 99 N9
Gransmore Green Essex 51 Q6
Granston Pembks 40 G4
Grantchester Cambs 62 F9
Grantham Lincs 73 N3
Grantham Crematorium Lincs 73 N3
Granton C Edin 127 N2
Grantown-on-Spey Highld 149 J2
Grantsfield Herefs 45 Q2
Grantshouse Border 129 L6
Grappenhall Warrtn 82 D7
Grasby Lincs 93 J10
Grasmere Cumb 101 K9
Grasscroft Oldham 83 L4
Grassendale Lpool 81 M7
Grassgarth Cumb 101 K2
Grass Green Essex 52 B4
Grassington N York 96 F8
Grassmoor Derbys 84 F7
Grassthorpe Notts 85 N7
Grateley Hants 21 Q6
Gratwich Staffs 71 J8
Graveley Cambs 62 C8
Graveley Herts 50 F5
Gravelly Hill Birm 58 H6
Gravelsbank Shrops 56 E4
Graveney Kent 39 J9
Gravesend Kent 37 Q6
Gravir W Isls 168 i6
Grayingham Lincs 92 F11
Grayrigg Cumb 101 Q11
Grays Thurr 37 P5
Grayshott Hants 23 N7
Grayson Green Cumb 100 C5
Grayswood Surrey 23 P8
Graythorpe Hartpl 104 F5
Grazeley Wokham 35 J11
Greasbrough Rothm 91 L11
Greasby Wirral 81 K7
Greasley Notts 84 G11
Great Abington Cambs 62 H11
Great Addington Nhants 61 L5
Great Alne Warwks 47 M3
Great Altcar Lancs 88 C9
Great Amwell Herts 51 J8
Great Asby Cumb 102 C8
Great Ashfield Suffk 64 D8
Great Ayton N York 104 G8
Great Baddow Essex 52 B11
Great Badminton S Glos 32 F8
Great Bardfield Essex 51 Q4
Great Barford Bed 61 P10
Great Barr Sandw 58 F5
Great Barrington Gloucs 33 P2
Great Barrow Ches W 81 P11
Great Barton Suffk 64 B8
Great Barugh N York 98 E5
Great Bavington Nthumb 112 E4
Great Bealings Suffk 53 M2
Great Bedwyn Wilts 21 Q2
Great Bentley Essex 53 K7
Great Billing Nhants 60 H8
Great Bircham Norfk 75 Q4
Great Blakenham Suffk 64 G11
Great Blencow Cumb 101 N4
Great Bolas Wrekin 70 A10
Great Bookham Surrey 36 D10
Great Bosullow Cnwll 2 C7
Great Bourton Oxon 48 E5
Great Bowden Leics 60 F3
Great Bradley Suffk 63 L10
Great Braxted Essex 52 E9
Great Bricett Suffk 64 E11
Great Brickhill Bucks 49 P8
Great Bridgeford Staffs 70 F9
Great Brington Nhants 60 E7
Great Bromley Essex 53 J6
Great Broughton Cumb 100 E4
Great Broughton N York 104 F9
Great Budworth Ches W 82 E9
Great Burdon Darltn 104 B7
Great Burstead Essex 37 Q2
Great Busby N York 104 F9
Great Canfield Essex 51 N7
Great Carlton Lincs 87 M3
Great Casterton Rutlnd 73 Q9
Great Chalfield Wilts 20 G2
Great Chart Kent 26 G3
Great Chatwell Staffs 57 P2
Great Chell C Stke 70 F4
Great Chesterford Essex 51 M2
Great Cheverell Wilts 21 J4
Great Chishill Cambs 51 K3
Great Clacton Essex 53 L8
Great Cliffe Wakefd 91 J7
Great Clifton Cumb 100 D5
Great Coates NE Lin 93 M9
Great Comberton Worcs 47 J6
Great Comp Kent 37 P9
Great Corby Cumb 111 J10
Great Cornard Suffk 52 E3
Great Cowden E R Yk 93 M2
Great Coxwell Oxon 33 Q6
Great Cransley Nhants 60 H5
Great Cressingham Norfk 76 B11
Great Crosthwaite Cumb 101 J6
Great Cubley Derbys 71 M7
Great Cumbrae Island N Ayrs 124 F6
Great Dalby Leics 73 J8
Great Doddington Nhants 61 J8
Great Doward Herefs 45 Q11
Great Dunham Norfk 76 B9
Great Dunmow Essex 51 P6
Great Durnford Wilts 21 M7
Great Easton Essex 51 P5
Great Easton Leics 60 H2
Great Eccleston Lancs 88 E2
Great Edstone N York 98 E4
Great Ellingham Norfk 64 E2
Great Elm Somset 20 D5
Great Everdon Nhants 60 C9
Great Eversden Cambs 62 E10
Great Fencote N York 97 L2
Greatfield Wilts 33 L7
Great Finborough Suffk 64 E10
Greatford Lincs 74 A8
Great Fransham Norfk 76 B9
Great Gaddesden Herts 50 B8
Greatgate Staffs 71 K7
Great Gidding Cambs 61 P4
Great Givendale E R Yk 98 G10
Great Glemham Suffk 65 L9
Great Glen Leics 72 H11
Great Gonerby Lincs 73 M3
Great Gransden Cambs 62 C9
Great Green Cambs 50 G2
Great Green Norfk 65 K4
Great Green Suffk 64 C10
Great Green Suffk 64 C8
Great Habton N York 98 F5
Great Hale Lincs 74 B2
Great Hallingbury Essex 51 M7
Greatham Hants 23 L8
Greatham Hartpl 104 E5
Greatham W Susx 24 B7
Great Hampden Bucks 35 M4
Great Harrowden Nhants 61 J6
Great Harwood Lancs 89 L4
Great Haseley Oxon 34 H4
Great Hatfield E R Yk 93 L2
Great Haywood Staffs 70 H10
Great Heck N York 91 P6
Great Henny Essex 52 E4
Great Hinton Wilts 20 H3
Great Hockham Norfk 64 D3
Great Holland Essex 53 M8
Great Hollands Br For 35 N11
Great Horkesley Essex 52 G5
Great Hormead Herts 51 K5
Great Horton C Brad 90 E4
Great Horwood Bucks 49 L8
Great Houghton Barns 91 L9
Great Houghton Nhants 60 G9
Great Hucklow Derbys 83 Q9
Great Kelk E R Yk 99 N9
Great Kimble Bucks 35 M3
Great Kingshill Bucks 35 N5
Great Langdale Cumb 101 J9
Great Langton N York 103 Q11
Great Leighs Essex 52 B8
Great Limber Lincs 93 K9
Great Linford M Keyn 49 N6
Great Livermere Suffk 64 B7
Great Longstone Derbys 84 B6
Great Lumley Dur 113 L11
Great Lyth Shrops 56 H3
Great Malvern Worcs 46 E5
Great Maplestead Essex 52 D5
Great Marton Bpool 88 C3
Great Massingham Norfk 75 Q6
Great Melton Norfk 76 G10
Great Meols Wirral 81 J6
Great Milton Oxon 34 H4
Great Missenden Bucks 35 N4
Great Mitton Lancs 89 L3
Great Mongeham Kent 39 Q11
Great Moulton Norfk 64 H3
Great Munden Herts 51 J6
Great Musgrave Cumb 102 E8
Great Ness Shrops 69 L11
Great Notley Essex 52 B7
Great Oak Mons 31 L2
Great Oakley Essex 53 L6
Great Oakley Nhants 61 J3
Great Offley Herts 50 D5
Great Ormside Cumb 102 D7
Great Orton Cumb 110 F10
Great Ouseburn N York 97 P8
Great Oxendon Nhants 60 F4
Great Oxney Green Essex 51 Q9
Great Palgrave Norfk 76 A9
Great Pattenden Kent 26 B3
Great Paxton Cambs 62 B8
Great Plumpton Lancs 88 D4
Great Plumstead Norfk 77 L9
Great Ponton Lincs 73 N4
Great Potheridge Devon 17 J9
Great Preston Leeds 91 L5
Great Purston Nhants 48 F7
Great Raveley Cambs 62 C4
Great Rissington Gloucs 47 N11
Great Rollright Oxon 48 B8
Great Rudbaxton Pembks 41 J6
Great Ryburgh Norfk 76 D6
Great Ryle Nthumb 119 K8
Great Ryton Shrops 56 H4
Great Saling Essex 51 Q5
Great Salkeld Cumb 101 Q3
Great Sampford Essex 51 P3
Great Saredon Staffs 58 E3
Great Saughall Ches W 81 M11
Great Saxham Suffk 63 N8
Great Shefford W Berk 34 C9
Great Shelford Cambs 62 G10
Great Smeaton N York 104 B10
Great Snoring Norfk 76 C5
Great Somerford Wilts 33 J8
Great Soudley Shrops 70 C9
Great Stainton Darltn 104 B6
Great Stambridge Essex 38 E3
Great Staughton Cambs 61 P8
Great Steeping Lincs 87 M8
Great Stoke S Glos 32 B8
Great Stonar Kent 39 P10
Greatstone-on-Sea Kent 27 J7
Great Strickland Cumb 101 Q6
Great Stukeley Cambs 62 B6
Great Sturton Lincs 86 H5
Great Sutton Ches W 81 M9
Great Sutton Shrops 57 J8
Great Swinburne Nthumb 112 D5
Great Tew Oxon 48 D9
Great Tey Essex 52 E6
Great Thurlow Suffk 63 L10
Great Torrington Devon 16 H8
Great Tosson Nthumb 119 K10
Great Totham Essex 52 E9
Great Totham Essex 52 E9
Great Tows Lincs 86 H2
Great Urswick Cumb 94 F6
Great Wakering Essex 38 F4
Great Waldingfield Suffk 52 F3
Great Walsingham Norfk 76 C4
Great Waltham Essex 51 Q8
Great Warford Ches E 82 H9
Great Warley Essex 37 N2
Great Washbourne Gloucs 47 J8
Great Weeke Devon 8 H7
Great Weldon Nhants 61 K3
Great Welnetham Suffk 64 B10
Great Wenham Suffk 53 J4
Great Whittington Nthumb 112 F6
Great Wigborough Essex 52 G8
Great Wilbraham Cambs 63 J9
Great Wishford Wilts 21 L7
Great Witchingham Norfk 76 G7
Great Witcombe Gloucs 32 H2
Great Witley Worcs 57 P11
Great Wolford Warwks 47 Q8
Greatworth Nhants 48 G6
Great Wratting Suffk 63 L11
Great Wymondley Herts 50 F5
Great Wyrley Staffs 58 E3
Great Wytheford Shrops 69 Q11
Great Yarmouth Norfk 77 Q10
Great Yarmouth Crematorium Norfk 77 Q11
Great Yeldham Essex 52 C4
Grebby Lincs 87 M7
Greeba IoM 80 d5
Green Denbgs 80 F11
Green Bank Cumb 94 H4
Greenburn W Loth 126 G5
Greencroft Hall Dur 113 J11
Green Cross Surrey 23 N7
Green Down Somset 19 Q4
Green End Bed 61 M11
Green End Bed 61 N8
Green End Bed 61 P10
Green End Bed 61 P8
Green End Cambs 61 Q4
Green End Cambs 62 B6
Green End Cambs 62 E9
Green End Cambs 62 G7
Green End Cambs 62 G8
Green End Herts 50 G4
Green End Herts 50 H4
Green End Herts 50 H6
Greenend Oxon 48 B10
Green End Warwks 59 L7
Greenfield Ag & B 131 Q9
Greenfield C Beds 50 C4
Greenfield Flints 80 H9
Greenfield Highld 146 G7
Greenfield Oldham 83 L4
Greenfield Oxon 35 K6
Greenford Gt Lon 36 D4
Greengairs N Lans 126 D3
Greengates C Brad 90 F3
Greengill Cumb 100 F3
Greenhalgh Lancs 88 E3
Greenham Somset 18 E10
Greenham W Berk 34 E11
Green Hammerton N York 97 Q9
Greenhaugh Nthumb 111 Q3
Green Head Cumb 110 G11
Greenhead Nthumb 111 N7
Green Heath Staffs 58 E2
Greenheys Salfd 82 F4
Greenhill D & G 109 P5
Greenhill Falk 126 E2
Greenhill Herefs 46 D5
Greenhill Kent 39 L8
Greenhill S Lans 116 C4
Green Hill Wilts 33 L7
Greenhillocks Derbys 84 F11
Greenhithe Kent 37 N5
Greenholm E Ayrs 125 N10
Greenholme Cumb 101 Q9
Greenhouse Border 117 R6
Greenhow Hill N York 96 H8
Greenland Highld 167 M3
Greenland Sheff 84 E3
Greenlands Bucks 35 L7
Green Lane Devon 9 J9
Green Lane Worcs 47 L2
Greenlaw Border 129 J10
Greenlea D & G 109 M5
Greenloaning P & K 133 N6
Green Moor Barns 90 H11
Greenmount Bury 89 M8
Green Oak E R Yk 92 D5
Greenock Inver 124 H2
Greenock Crematorium Inver 124 H2
Greenodd Cumb 94 G4
Green Ore Somset 19 Q4
Green Quarter Cumb 101 N10
Greensgate Norfk 76 G8
Greenshields S Lans 116 E2
Greenside Gatesd 112 H8
Greenside Kirk 90 F7
Greens Norton Nhants 49 J5
Greenstead Essex 52 H6
Greenstead Green Essex 52 D6
Greensted Essex 51 M10
Green Street E Susx 26 C9
Green Street Gloucs 46 G11
Green Street Herts 50 E11
Green Street Herts 51 L6
Green Street Worcs 46 G5
Green Street Green Gt Lon 37 L8
Green Street Green Kent 37 N6
Greenstreet Green Suffk 52 H2
Green Tye Herts 51 K7
Greenway Gloucs 46 D8
Greenway Somset 19 K10
Greenway V Glam 30 E10
Greenway Worcs 57 N10
Greenwich Gt Lon 37 J5
Greet Gloucs 47 K8
Greete Shrops 57 K10
Greetham Lincs 87 K6
Greetham Rutlnd 73 N8
Greetland Calder 90 D6
Gregson Lane Lancs 88 H5
Greinton Somset 19 M7
Grenaby IoM 80 c7
Grendon Nhants 61 J8
Grendon Warwks 59 L5
Grendon Green Herefs 46 A3
Grendon Underwood Bucks 49 J10
Grenofen Devon 6 D4
Grenoside Sheff 84 D2
Grenoside Crematorium Sheff 84 D2
Greosabhagh W Isls 168 g8
Gresford Wrexhm 69 K4
Gresham Norfk 76 H4
Greshornish House Hotel Highld 152 E7
Gressenhall Norfk 76 D8
Gressenhall Green Norfk 76 D8
Gressingham Lancs 95 M7
Gresty Green Ches E 70 C4
Greta Bridge Dur 103 L8
Gretna D & G 110 F7
Gretna Green D & G 110 F7
Gretna Services D & G 110 F7
Gretton Gloucs 47 K8
Gretton Nhants 61 J2
Gretton Shrops 57 J5
Grewelthorpe N York 97 K5
Grey Friars Suffk 65 P7
Greygarth N York 97 J6
Grey Green N Linc 92 C9
Greylake Somset 19 L8
Greyrigg D & G 109 N3
Greys Green Oxon 35 K8
Greysouthen Cumb 100 E5
Greystoke Cumb 101 M4
Greystone Angus 143 J9
Greywell Hants 23 K4
Gribb Dorset 10 H4
Gribthorpe E R Yk 92 C3
Griff Warwks 59 N7
Griffithstown Torfn 31 J5
Griffydam Leics 72 C7
Griggs Green Hants 23 M8
Grimeford Village Lancs 89 J8
Grimesthorpe Sheff 84 E3
Grimethorpe Barns 91 L9
Grimley Worcs 46 F2
Grimmet S Ayrs 114 F5
Grimoldby Lincs 87 L3
Grimpo Shrops 69 L9
Grimsargh Lancs 88 H4
Grimsby NE Lin 93 N8
Grimsby Crematorium NE Lin 93 N9
Grimscote Nhants 49 J4
Grimscott Cnwll 16 D10
Grimshader W Isls 168 j5
Grimshaw Bl w D 89 L6
Grimshaw Green Lancs 88 F8
Grimsthorpe Lincs 73 Q6
Grimston E R Yk 93 N3
Grimston Leics 72 H6
Grimston Norfk 75 P6
Grimstone Dorset 11 N6
Grimstone End Suffk 64 C8
Grinacombe Moor Devon 5 Q3
Grindale E R Yk 99 N6
Grindle Shrops 57 P4
Grindleford Derbys 84 B5
Grindleton Lancs 95 R11
Grindley Brook Shrops 69 P6
Grindlow Derbys 83 Q9
Grindon Nthumb 118 H2
Grindon S on T 104 C5
Grindon Staffs 71 K4
Grindon Hill Nthumb 112 B7
Grindonrigg Nthumb 118 H2
Gringley on the Hill Notts 85 M2
Grinsdale Cumb 110 G9
Grinshill Shrops 69 P10
Grinton N York 103 K11
Griomaisiader W Isls 168 j5
Griomsaigh W Isls 168 d12
Grishipoll Ag & B 136 F4
Grisling Common E Susx 25 K6

Gristhorpe - Hartpury 279

Gristhorpe N York 99 M4
Griston Norfk 64 C2
Gritley Ork 169 e6
Grittenham Wilts 33 K8
Grittleton Wilts 32 G8
Grizebeck Cumb 94 E4
Grizedale Cumb 94 G2
Groby Leics 72 E9
Groes Conwy 68 D2
Groes-faen Rhondd 30 E8
Groesffordd Gwynd 66 D7
Groesffordd Marli Denbgs 80 E10
Groesllwyd Powys 56 C2
Groeslon Gwynd 66 H3
Groeslon Gwynd 67 J2
Groes-Wen Caerph 30 F7
Grogarry W Isls 168 c14
Grogport Ag & B 120 F3
Groigearraidh W Isls 168 c14
Gromford Suffk 65 M10
Gronant Flints 80 F8
Groombridge E Susx 25 M3
Grosebay W Isls 168 g8
Grosmont Mons 45 N10
Grosmont N York 105 M9
Groton Suffk 52 G3
Grotton Oldham 83 L4
Grouville Jersey 11 c2
Grove Bucks 49 P10
Grove Dorset 11 P10
Grove Kent 39 M9
Grove Notts 85 M5
Grove Oxon 34 D6
Grove Pembks 41 J10
Grove Green Kent 38 C10
Grovenhurst Kent 26 B3
Grove Park Gt Lon 37 K6
Grovesend S Glos 32 C7
Grovesend Swans 28 G4
Grubb Street Kent 37 N7
Gruinard Highld 160 E9
Gruinart Ag & B 122 C6
Grula Highld 144 E2
Gruline Ag & B 137 N7
Grumbla Cnwll 2 C8
Grundisburgh Suffk 65 J11
Gruting Shet 169 p9
Gualachulain Highld 139 L8
Guanockgate Lincs 74 G8
Guardbridge Fife 135 M4
Guarlford Worcs 46 F5
Guay P & K 141 P8
Guernsey Guern 10 b2
Guernsey Airport Guern 10 b2
Guestling Green E Susx 26 E9
Guestling Thorn E Susx 26 E8
Guestwick Norfk 76 F6
Guide Bridge Tamesd 83 K5
Guide Post Nthumb 113 L3
Guilden Morden Cambs 50 G2
Guilden Sutton Ches W 81 N11
Guildford Surrey 23 Q5
Guildford Crematorium Surrey 23 Q5
Guildstead Kent 38 D9
Guildtown P & K 142 A11
Guilsborough Nhants 60 E6
Guilsfield Powys 56 C2
Guilton Kent 39 N10
Guiltreehill S Ayrs 114 G5
Guineaford Devon 17 K4
Guisborough R & Cl 104 H7
Guiseley Leeds 90 F2
Guist Norfk 76 E6
Guiting Power Gloucs 47 L10
Gullane E Loth 128 D3
Gulling Green Suffk 64 A10
Gulval Cnwll 2 D7
Gulworthy Devon 6 D4
Gumfreston Pembks 41 M10
Gumley Leics 60 E3
Gummow's Shop Cnwll 4 D10
Gunby E R Yk 92 B3
Gunby Lincs 73 N6
Gunby Lincs 87 N7
Gundleton Hants 22 H8
Gun Green Kent 26 C5
Gun Hill E Susx 25 N8
Gun Hill Warwks 59 L7
Gunn Devon 17 L5
Gunnerside N York 103 J11
Gunnerton Nthumb 112 D6
Gunness N Linc 92 D8
Gunnislake Cnwll 6 C4
Gunnista Shet 169 s9
Gunthorpe C Pete 74 C10
Gunthorpe N Linc 92 D11
Gunthorpe Norfk 76 E5
Gunthorpe Notts 72 H2
Gunton Suffk 65 Q2
Gunwalloe Cnwll 2 H9
Gupworthy Somset 18 C8
Gurnard IoW 14 E7
Gurnett Ches E 83 K10
Gurney Slade Somset 20 B5
Gurnos Powys 29 L3
Gushmere Kent 38 H10
Gussage All Saints Dorset 12 H2
Gussage St Andrew Dorset 12 G2
Gussage St Michael Dorset 12 G2
Guston Kent 27 P3
Gutcher Shet 169 s4
Guthrie Angus 143 K7
Guyhirn Cambs 74 H10
Guyhirn Gull Cambs 74 G10
Guy's Marsh Dorset 20 F10
Guyzance Nthumb 119 P10
Gwaenysgor Flints 80 F8
Gwalchmai IoA 78 F9
Gwastadnant Gwynd 67 L3
Gwaun-Cae-Gurwen Carmth 29 J2
Gwbert on Sea Cerdgn 42 C4
Gwealavellan Cnwll 2 G5
Gweek Cnwll 3 J8
Gwehelog Mons 31 L4
Gwenddwr Powys 44 F6
Gwennap Cnwll 3 J5
Gwent Crematorium Mons 31 K5
Gwenter Cnwll 3 J10
Gwernaffield Flints 81 J11
Gwernesney Mons 31 M4
Gwernogle Carmth 43 K8
Gwernymynydd Flints 68 H2
Gwersyllt Wrexhm 69 K4
Gwespyr Flints 80 G8
Gwindra Cnwll 3 P3
Gwinear Cnwll 2 F6
Gwithian Cnwll 2 F5
Gwredog IoA 78 G7
Gwrhay Caerph 30 G5
Gwyddelwern Denbgs 68 E5
Gwyddgrug Carmth 43 J7
Gwynfryn Wrexhm 69 J4
Gwystre Powys 55 P11
Gwytherin Conwy 68 A2
Gyfelia Wrexhm 69 K5
Gyrn-goch Gwynd 66 G5

H

Habberley Shrops 56 F4
Habberley Worcs 57 Q9
Habergham Lancs 89 N4
Habertoft Lincs 87 P7
Habin W Susx 23 M10
Habrough NE Lin 93 K8
Hacconby Lincs 74 B5
Haceby Lincs 73 Q3
Hacheston Suffk 65 L10
Hackbridge Gt Lon 36 G7
Hackenthorpe Sheff 84 F4
Hackford Norfk 76 F11
Hackforth N York 97 K2
Hack Green Ches E 70 A5
Hackland Ork 169 c4
Hackleton Nhants 60 H9
Hacklinge Kent 39 P11
Hackman's Gate Worcs 58 C9
Hackness N York 99 K2
Hackness Somset 19 K5
Hackney Gt Lon 36 H4
Hackthorn Lincs 86 C4
Hackthorpe Cumb 101 P6
Hacton Gt Lon 37 N3
Hadden Border 118 E3
Haddenham Bucks 35 K3
Haddenham Cambs 62 G5
Haddington E Loth 128 E5
Haddington Lincs 86 B8
Haddiscoe Norfk 65 N2
Haddo Abers 159 K10
Haddon Cambs 61 P2
Hade Edge Kirk 83 P4
Hadfield Derbys 83 M5
Hadham Cross Herts 51 K7
Hadham Ford Herts 51 K6
Hadleigh Essex 38 D4
Hadleigh Suffk 52 H3
Hadleigh Heath Suffk 52 G3
Hadley Worcs 46 G2
Hadley Wrekin 57 M2
Hadley End Staffs 71 L10
Hadley Wood Gt Lon 50 G11
Hadlow Kent 37 P10
Hadlow Down E Susx 25 M6
Hadnall Shrops 69 P10
Hadrian's Wall Nthumb 112 E7
Hadstock Essex 51 N2
Hadzor Worcs 46 H2
Haffenden Quarter Kent 26 E3
Hafodunos Conwy 80 B11
Hafod-y-bwch Wrexhm 69 K5
Hafod-y-coed Blae G 30 H4
Hafodyrynys Caerph 30 H5
Haggate Lancs 89 P3
Haggbeck Cumb 111 J6
Haggersta Shet 169 q9
Haggerston Nthumb 119 K2
Haggington Hill Devon 17 K2
Haggs Falk 126 D2
Hagley Herefs 45 R6
Hagley Worcs 58 D8
Hagmore Green Suffk 52 G4
Hagnaby Lincs 87 K8
Hagnaby Lincs 87 N5
Hagworthingham Lincs 87 K7
Haigh Wigan 89 J9
Haighton Green Lancs 88 H4
Haile Cumb 100 D9
Hailes Gloucs 47 K8
Hailey Herts 51 J8
Hailey Oxon 34 C2
Hailey Oxon 34 H7
Hailsham E Susx 25 N9
Hail Weston Cambs 61 Q8
Hainault Gt Lon 37 L2
Haine Kent 39 Q8
Hainford Norfk 77 J8
Hainton Lincs 86 G4
Hainworth C Brad 90 D3
Haisthorpe E R Yk 99 N8
Hakin Pembks 40 G9
Halam Notts 85 L10
Halbeath Fife 134 E10
Halberton Devon 9 P2
Halcro Highld 167 M4
Hale Cumb 95 L5
Hale Halton 81 P8
Hale Hants 21 N11
Hale Somset 20 D9
Hale Surrey 23 M5
Hale Traffd 82 G7
Hale Bank Halton 81 P8
Halebarns Traffd 82 G7
Hale Green E Susx 25 N8
Hale Nook Lancs 88 D2
Hales Norfk 65 M2
Hales Staffs 70 C8
Halesgate Lincs 74 F5
Hales Green Derbys 71 M6
Halesowen Dudley 58 E8
Hales Place Kent 39 K10
Hale Street Kent 37 Q11
Halesville Essex 38 F3
Halesworth Suffk 65 M6
Halewood Knows 81 P7
Halford Devon 7 L4
Halford Shrops 56 G8
Halford Warwks 47 Q5
Halfpenny Cumb 95 L3
Halfpenny Green Staffs 58 B6
Halfpenny Houses N York 97 K4
Halfway Carmth 43 M8
Halfway Carmth 44 A8
Halfway Sheff 84 F4
Halfway W Berk 34 D11
Halfway Bridge W Susx 23 P10
Halfway House Shrops 56 E2
Halfway Houses Kent 38 F7
Halifax Calder 90 D5
Halket E Ayrs 125 L7
Halkirk Highld 167 K5
Halkyn Flints 81 J10
Hall E Rens 125 L7
Hallam Fields Derbys 72 D3
Halland E Susx 25 L7
Hallaton Leics 73 K11
Hallatrow BaNES 20 B3
Hallbankgate Cumb 111 L9
Hallbeck Cumb 95 N3
Hall Cliffe Wakefd 90 H7
Hall Cross Lancs 88 E4
Hall Dunnerdale Cumb 100 H11
Hallen S Glos 31 Q8
Hall End Bed 61 M11
Hall End C Beds 50 C3
Hallfield Gate Derbys 84 E9
Hallgarth Dur 104 B2
Hall Glen Falk 126 F2
Hall Green Birm 58 H8
Hallin Highld 152 D6
Halling Medway 38 B9
Hallington Lincs 87 K3
Hallington Nthumb 112 E5
Halliwell Bolton 89 K8
Halloughton Notts 85 L10
Hallow Worcs 46 F3
Hallow Heath Worcs 46 F3
Hallsands Devon 7 L11
Hall's Green Essex 51 K9
Hall's Green Herts 50 G5
Hallthwaites Cumb 94 D3
Hallworthy Cnwll 5 K4
Hallyne Border 116 H2
Halmer End Staffs 70 D5
Halmond's Frome Herefs 46 C5
Halmore Gloucs 32 D4
Halnaker W Susx 15 P5
Halsall Lancs 88 D8
Halse Nhants 48 G6
Halse Somset 18 F9
Halsetown Cnwll 2 E6
Halsham E R Yk 93 N5
Halsinger Devon 17 J4
Halstead Essex 52 D5
Halstead Kent 37 L8
Halstead Leics 73 K9
Halstock Dorset 11 L3
Halsway Somset 18 F7
Haltcliff Bridge Cumb 101 L3
Haltemprice Crematorium E R Yk 92 H4
Haltham Lincs 86 H8
Haltoft End Lincs 87 L11
Halton Bucks 35 N3
Halton Halton 82 B8
Halton Lancs 95 L8
Halton Leeds 91 K4
Halton Nthumb 112 E7
Halton Wrexhm 69 K7
Halton East N York 96 F10
Halton Fenside Lincs 87 M8
Halton Gill N York 96 C5
Halton Green Lancs 95 L7
Halton Holegate Lincs 87 M7
Halton Lea Gate Nthumb 111 M9
Halton Quay Cnwll 5 Q8
Halton Shields Nthumb 112 F7
Halton West N York 96 B10
Haltwhistle Nthumb 111 P8
Halvergate Norfk 77 N10
Halwell Devon 7 K8
Halwill Devon 8 B5
Halwill Junction Devon 8 B4
Ham Devon 10 E4
Ham Gloucs 32 C5
Ham Gloucs 47 J10
Ham Gt Lon 36 E6
Ham Kent 39 P11
Ham Somset 19 J9
Ham Somset 20 C5
Ham Wilts 22 B2
Hambleden Bucks 35 L7
Hambledon Hants 14 H4
Hambledon Surrey 23 Q7
Hamble-le-Rice Hants 14 E5
Hambleton Lancs 88 D2
Hambleton N York 91 P4
Hambleton Moss Side Lancs 88 D2
Hambridge Somset 19 L10
Hambrook S Glos 32 B9
Hambrook W Susx 15 L5
Ham Common Dorset 20 F9
Hameringham Lincs 87 K7
Hamerton Cambs 61 P5
Ham Green Herefs 46 E6
Ham Green Kent 26 E6
Ham Green Kent 38 D8
Ham Green N Som 31 P9
Ham Green Worcs 47 K2
Ham Hill Kent 37 Q8
Hamilton S Lans 126 C6
Hamilton Services S Lans 126 C6
Hamlet Dorset 11 M3
Hamlins E Susx 25 N9
Hammerpot W Susx 24 C9
Hammersmith Gt Lon 36 F5
Hammerwich Staffs 58 G3
Hammerwood E Susx 25 K3
Hammond Street Herts 50 H10
Hammoon Dorset 12 D2
Hamnavoe Shet 169 q10
Hampden Park E Susx 25 P10
Hamperden End Essex 51 N4
Hampnett Gloucs 47 L11
Hampole Donc 91 N8
Hampreston Dorset 13 J5
Hampsfield Cumb 95 J4
Hampson Green Lancs 95 K10
Hampstead Gt Lon 36 G3
Hampstead Norreys W Berk 34 F9
Hampsthwaite N York 97 L9
Hampton C Pete 61 Q2
Hampton Devon 10 F5
Hampton Gt Lon 36 D7
Hampton Kent 39 L8
Hampton Shrops 57 N7
Hampton Swindn 33 N6
Hampton Worcs 47 K6
Hampton Bishop Herefs 45 R7
Hampton Court Palace Gt Lon 36 E7
Hampton Fields Gloucs 32 G5
Hampton Green Ches W 69 P5
Hampton Heath Ches W 69 P5
Hampton in Arden Solhll 59 K8
Hampton Loade Shrops 57 N7
Hampton Lovett Worcs 58 C11
Hampton Lucy Warwks 47 Q3
Hampton Magna Warwks 59 L11
Hampton on the Hill Warwks 47 Q2
Hampton Poyle Oxon 48 F11
Hampton Wick Gt Lon 36 E7
Hamptworth Wilts 21 P11
Hamrow Norfk 76 C7
Hamsey E Susx 25 K8
Hamsey Green Surrey 37 J9
Hamstall Ridware Staffs 71 L11
Hamstead Birm 58 G6
Hamstead IoW 14 D8
Hamstead Marshall W Berk 34 D11
Hamsterley Dur 103 M4
Hamsterley Dur 112 H9
Hamstreet Kent 26 H5
Ham Street Somset 19 Q8
Hamwood N Som 19 L3
Hamworthy Poole 12 G6
Hanbury Staffs 71 M9
Hanbury Worcs 47 J2
Hanby Lincs 73 Q4
Hanchet End Suffk 63 K11
Hanchurch Staffs 70 E6
Handa Island Highld 164 D7
Handale R & Cl 105 K7
Hand and Pen Devon 9 P5
Handbridge Ches W 81 N11
Handcross W Susx 24 G5
Handforth Ches E 83 J8
Hand Green Ches W 69 P2
Handley Ches W 69 N3
Handley Derbys 84 E8
Handley Green Essex 51 Q10
Handsacre Staffs 71 K11
Handsworth Birm 58 F7
Handsworth Sheff 84 F3
Handy Cross Bucks 35 N6
Hanford C Stke 70 F6
Hanford Dorset 12 D2
Hanging Heaton Kirk 90 H6
Hanging Houghton Nhants 60 G6
Hanging Langford Wilts 21 K7
Hangleton Br & H 24 G9
Hangleton W Susx 24 C10
Hanham S Glos 32 B10
Hankelow Ches E 70 B5
Hankerton Wilts 33 J6
Hankham E Susx 25 P9
Hanley C Stke 70 F5
Hanley Castle Worcs 46 F6
Hanley Child Worcs 57 M11
Hanley Swan Worcs 46 F6
Hanley William Worcs 57 M11
Hanlith N York 96 C8
Hanmer Wrexhm 69 N7
Hannaford Devon 17 L6
Hannah Lincs 87 N5
Hannington Hants 22 F3
Hannington Nhants 60 H6
Hannington Swindn 33 N6
Hannington Wick Swindn 33 N5
Hanscombe End C Beds 50 D4
Hanslope M Keyn 49 M5
Hanthorpe Lincs 74 A6
Hanwell Gt Lon 36 E5
Hanwell Oxon 48 D6
Hanwood Shrops 56 G3
Hanworth Gt Lon 36 D6
Hanworth Norfk 76 H4
Happendon S Lans 116 B4
Happisburgh Norfk 77 M5
Happisburgh Common Norfk 77 M6
Hapsford Ches W 81 P10
Hapton Lancs 89 M4
Hapton Norfk 64 H2
Harberton Devon 7 K7
Harbertonford Devon 7 K7
Harbledown Kent 39 K10
Harborne Birm 58 F8
Harborough Magna Warwks 59 Q9
Harbottle Nthumb 118 H10
Harbourneford Devon 7 J6
Harbours Hill Worcs 58 E11
Harbridge Hants 13 K2
Harbridge Green Hants 13 K2
Harbury Warwks 48 C3
Harby Leics 73 J4
Harby Notts 85 Q6
Harcombe Devon 9 L8
Harcombe Devon 10 D6
Harcombe Bottom Devon 10 G5
Harden C Brad 90 D3
Harden Wsall 58 F4
Hardenhuish Wilts 32 H10
Hardgate Abers 151 K7
Hardgate D & G 108 H7
Hardgate N York 97 L8
Hardgate W Duns 125 N3
Hardham W Susx 24 B7
Hardhorn Lancs 88 D3
Hardingham Norfk 76 E11
Hardingstone Nhants 60 G9
Hardington Somset 20 D4
Hardington Mandeville Somset 11 L2
Hardington Marsh Somset 11 L3
Hardington Moor Somset 11 L2
Hardisworthy Devon 16 C7
Hardley Hants 14 D5
Hardley Street Norfk 77 M11
Hardmead M Keyn 49 P5
Hardraw N York 96 C2
Hardsough Lancs 89 M6
Hardstoft Derbys 84 F8
Hardway Hants 14 H6
Hardway Somset 20 D8
Hardwick Bucks 49 M11
Hardwick Cambs 62 E9
Hardwick Nhants 60 H7
Hardwick Norfk 65 J4
Hardwick Oxon 34 C3
Hardwick Oxon 48 G9
Hardwick Rothm 84 G3
Hardwick Wsall 58 G5
Hardwicke Gloucs 32 E2
Hardwicke Gloucs 46 H9
Hardy's Green Essex 52 F7
Harebeating E Susx 25 N8
Hareby Lincs 87 K7
Hare Croft C Brad 90 D3
Harefield Gt Lon 36 C2
Hare Green Essex 53 K6
Hare Hatch Wokham 35 M9
Harehill Derbys 71 M7
Harehills Leeds 91 J4
Harehope Nthumb 119 L6
Harelaw Border 117 Q6
Harelaw D & G 110 H5
Harelaw Dur 113 J10
Hareplain Kent 26 D4
Haresceugh Cumb 102 B2
Harescombe Gloucs 32 F2
Haresfield Gloucs 32 F2
Harestock Hants 22 E8
Hare Street Essex 51 K9
Hare Street Essex 51 M10
Hare Street Herts 51 J5
Harewood Leeds 97 M11
Harewood End Herefs 45 Q9
Harford Devon 6 G7
Hargate Norfk 64 G3
Hargatewall Derbys 83 P9
Hargrave Ches W 69 N2
Hargrave Nhants 61 M6
Hargrave Suffk 63 N9
Harker Cumb 110 G8
Harkstead Suffk 53 L5
Harlaston Staffs 59 K2
Harlaxton Lincs 73 M4
Harlech Gwynd 67 K8
Harlescott Shrops 69 N11
Harlesden Gt Lon 36 F4
Harlesthorpe Derbys 84 G5
Harleston Devon 7 K9
Harleston Norfk 65 J5
Harleston Suffk 64 E9
Harlestone Nhants 60 F8
Harle Syke Lancs 89 P3
Harley Rothm 91 K11
Harley Shrops 57 K4
Harlington C Beds 50 B4
Harlington Donc 91 M10
Harlington Gt Lon 36 C5
Harlosh Highld 152 D9
Harlow Essex 51 K8
Harlow Hill Nthumb 112 G7
Harlthorpe E R Yk 92 B3
Harlton Cambs 62 E10
Harlyn Cnwll 4 D6
Harman's Cross Dorset 12 G8
Harmby N York 96 H3
Harmer Green Herts 50 G7
Harmer Hill Shrops 69 N10
Harmondsworth Gt Lon 36 C5
Harmston Lincs 86 C8
Harnage Shrops 57 K4
Harnham Nthumb 112 G4
Harnhill Gloucs 33 L4
Harold Hill Gt Lon 37 M2
Haroldston West Pembks 40 G7
Haroldswick Shet 169 t2
Harold Wood Gt Lon 37 N2
Harome N York 98 C4
Harpenden Herts 50 D8
Harpford Devon 10 B6
Harpham E R Yk 99 M8
Harpley Norfk 75 Q5
Harpley Worcs 46 C2
Harpole Nhants 60 E8
Harpsdale Highld 167 K5
Harpsden Oxon 35 L8
Harpswell Lincs 86 B3
Harpurhey Manch 83 J4
Harpur Hill Derbys 83 N10
Harraby Cumb 110 H10
Harracott Devon 17 K6
Harrapool Highld 145 L3
Harrietfield P & K 134 B2
Harrietsham Kent 38 E11
Harringay Gt Lon 36 H3
Harrington Cumb 100 C5
Harrington Lincs 87 L6
Harrington Nhants 60 G4
Harringworth Nhants 73 N11
Harris W Isls 168 f8
Harriseahead Staffs 70 F3
Harriston Cumb 100 G2
Harrogate N York 97 M10
Harrogate Crematorium N York 97 M10
Harrold Bed 61 K9
Harrop Dale Oldham 90 C9
Harrow Gt Lon 36 E3
Harrowbarrow Cnwll 5 Q7
Harrowden Bed 61 N11
Harrowgate Village Darltn 103 Q7
Harrow Green Suffk 64 B11
Harrow on the Hill Gt Lon 36 E3
Harrow Weald Gt Lon 36 E2
Harston Cambs 62 F10
Harston Leics 73 L4
Harswell E R Yk 92 D2
Hart Hartpl 104 E4
Hartburn Nthumb 112 G3
Hartburn S on T 104 D7
Hartest Suffk 64 A11
Hartfield E Susx 25 L3
Hartford Cambs 62 C6
Hartford Ches W 82 D10
Hartford Somset 18 C9
Hartfordbridge Hants 23 L3
Hartford End Essex 51 Q7
Hartforth N York 103 N9
Hartgrove Dorset 20 F11
Harthill Ches W 69 N3
Harthill N Lans 126 G5
Harthill Rothm 84 G4
Hartington Derbys 71 L2
Hartington Nthumb 112 F3
Hartland Devon 16 D7
Hartland Quay Devon 16 C7
Hartlebury Worcs 58 B10
Hartlepool Hartpl 104 F4
Hartlepool Crematorium Hartpl 104 F4
Hartley Cumb 102 E9
Hartley Kent 26 C5
Hartley Kent 37 P7
Hartley Nthumb 113 M5
Hartley Green Kent 37 P7
Hartley Green Staffs 70 H9
Hartley Wespall Hants 23 J3
Hartley Wintney Hants 23 L3
Hartlip Kent 38 D9
Hartoft End N York 98 E2
Harton N York 98 E8
Harton S Tyne 113 N7
Harton Shrops 56 H7
Hartpury Gloucs 46 E10

Hartshead Kirk 90 F6
Hartshead Moor Services Calder 90 F6
Hartshill C Stke 70 F5
Hartshill Warwks 59 M6
Hartshorne Derbys 71 Q10
Hartside Nthumb 119 J7
Hartsop Cumb 101 M8
Hart Station Hartpl 104 E3
Hartswell Somset 18 E9
Hartwell Nhants 49 L4
Hartwith N York 97 K8
Hartwood N Lans 126 E6
Hartwoodmyres Border 117 N6
Harvel Kent 37 Q8
Harvington Worcs 47 L5
Harvington Worcs 58 C10
Harwell Notts 85 L2
Harwell Oxon 34 E7
Harwich Essex 53 N5
Harwood Bolton 89 L8
Harwood Dur 102 F4
Harwood Dale N York 105 Q11
Harwood Lee Bolton 89 L8
Harwood Park Crematorium Herts 50 G6
Harworth Notts 85 K2
Hasbury Dudley 58 E8
Hascombe Surrey 24 B3
Haselbech Nhants 60 F5
Haselbury Plucknett Somset 11 K2
Haseley Warwks 59 K11
Haseley Green Warwks 59 K11
Haseley Knob Warwks 59 K10
Haselor Warwks 47 M3
Hasfield Gloucs 46 F9
Hasguard Pembks 40 G9
Haskayne Lancs 88 D9
Hasketon Suffk 65 J11
Hasland Derbys 84 E7
Haslemere Surrey 23 P8
Haslingden Lancs 89 M6
Haslingfield Cambs 62 F10
Haslington Ches E 70 C3
Hassall Ches E 70 D3
Hassall Green Ches E 70 D3
Hassell Street Kent 27 J2
Hassingham Norfk 77 M10
Hassness Cumb 100 G7
Hassocks W Susx 24 H7
Hassop Derbys 84 B6
Haste Hill Surrey 23 P8
Haster Highld 167 P6
Hasthorpe Lincs 87 N7
Hastingleigh Kent 27 J2
Hastings E Susx 26 D10
Hastings Somset 19 K11
Hastings Borough Crematorium E Susx 26 D9
Hastingwood Essex 51 L9
Hastoe Herts 35 P3
Haswell Dur 104 C2
Haswell Plough Dur 104 C2
Hatch C Beds 61 Q11
Hatch Beauchamp Somset 19 K10
Hatch End Bed 61 N8
Hatch End Gt Lon 36 D2
Hatchet Gate Hants 14 C6
Hatching Green Herts 50 D8
Hatchmere Ches W 82 C10
Hatcliffe NE Lin 93 M10
Hatfield Donc 91 R9
Hatfield Herefs 46 A3
Hatfield Herts 50 F9
Hatfield Worcs 46 G4
Hatfield Broad Oak Essex 51 M7
Hatfield Heath Essex 51 M7
Hatfield Peverel Essex 52 C9
Hatfield Woodhouse Donc 92 A9
Hatford Oxon 34 B6
Hatherden Hants 22 B4
Hatherleigh Devon 8 D4
Hathern Leics 72 E6
Hatherop Gloucs 33 N3
Hathersage Derbys 84 B4
Hathersage Booths Derbys 84 B4
Hatherton Ches E 70 B5
Hatherton Staffs 58 E2
Hatley St George Cambs 62 C10
Hatt Cnwll 5 Q9
Hattersley Tamesd 83 L6
Hattingley Hants 22 H7
Hatton Abers 159 Q10
Hatton Angus 142 H9
Hatton Derbys 71 N8
Hatton Gt Lon 36 C5
Hatton Lincs 86 G5
Hatton Shrops 56 H6
Hatton Warrtn 82 C8
Hatton Warwks 59 K11
Hatton Heath Ches W 69 N2
Hatton of Fintray Abers 151 L4
Haugh E Ayrs 115 J2
Haugh Lincs 87 M5
Haugh Rochdl 89 Q8
Haugham Lincs 87 K4
Haughhead E Duns 125 Q2
Haugh Head Nthumb 119 K5
Haughley Suffk 64 E9
Haughley Green Suffk 64 E9
Haugh of Glass Moray 158 B10
Haugh of Urr D & G 108 H7
Haughs of Kinnaird Angus 143 L6
Haughton Notts 85 L6
Haughton Powys 69 K11
Haughton Shrops 57 M5
Haughton Shrops 57 N3
Haughton Shrops 69 L9
Haughton Shrops 69 Q11
Haughton Staffs 70 F10
Haughton Green Tamesd 83 K6
Haughton le Skerne Darltn 104 B7
Haughton Moss Ches E 69 Q3
Haultwick Herts 50 H6
Haunton Staffs 59 K2
Hauxton Cambs 62 F10
Hautes Croix Jersey 11 b1
Havannah Ches E 70 F2
Havant Hants 15 K5
Haven Herefs 45 N4
Haven Bank Lincs 86 H10
Haven Side E R Yk 93 L5
Havenstreet IoW 14 G8

Havercroft Wakefd 91 K8
Haverfordwest Pembks 41 J7
Haverhill Suffk 63 L11
Haverigg Cumb 94 D5
Havering-atte-Bower Gt Lon 37 M2
Haversham M Keyn 49 M6
Haverthwaite Cumb 94 G4
Haverton Hill S on T 104 E6
Havyat N Som 19 N2
Hawarden Flints 81 L11
Hawbridge Worcs 46 H5
Hawbush Green Essex 52 C7
Hawcoat Cumb 94 E6
Hawen Cerdgn 42 F5
Hawe's Green Norfk 65 J2
Hawford Worcs 46 F2
Hawick Border 117 Q8
Hawkchurch Devon 10 G4
Hawkedon Suffk 63 N10
Hawkenbury Kent 26 D2
Hawkeridge Wilts 20 G4
Hawkerland Devon 9 Q7
Hawkesbury S Glos 32 E7
Hawkesbury Warwks 59 N8
Hawkesbury Upton S Glos 32 E7
Hawkes End Covtry 59 L8
Hawk Green Stockp 83 L7
Hawkhill Nthumb 119 P8
Hawkhurst Kent 26 C5
Hawkhurst Common E Susx 25 M7
Hawkinge Kent 27 M4
Hawkinge Crematorium Kent 27 M3
Hawkley Hants 23 K9
Hawkley Wigan 82 C4
Hawkridge Somset 17 R5
Hawksdale Cumb 110 G11
Hawkshaw Bury 89 M7
Hawkshead Cumb 101 L11
Hawkshead Hill Cumb 101 K11
Hawksland S Lans 116 A3
Hawkspur Green Essex 51 Q4
Hawkstone Shrops 69 Q8
Hawkswick N York 96 E6
Hawksworth Leeds 90 F2
Hawksworth Notts 73 K2
Hawkwell Essex 38 E3
Hawkwell Nthumb 112 G6
Hawley Hants 23 N3
Hawley Kent 37 M6
Hawling Gloucs 47 L10
Hawnby N York 98 A3
Haworth C Brad 90 C3
Hawridge Bucks 35 P3
Hawstead Suffk 64 B10
Hawstead Green Suffk 64 B10
Hawthorn Dur 113 P11
Hawthorn Hants 23 J8
Hawthorn Rhondd 30 E7
Hawthorn Hill Br For 35 N10
Hawthorn Hill Lincs 86 H9
Hawthorpe Lincs 73 Q5
Hawton Notts 85 N10
Haxby C York 98 C9
Haxby Gates C York 98 C9
Haxey N Linc 92 C11
Haxey Carr N Linc 92 C10
Haxted Surrey 37 K11
Haxton Wilts 21 M5
Hay Cnwll 3 P3
Hay Cnwll 4 F7
Haycombe Crematorium BaNES 20 D2
Haydock St Hel 82 C5
Haydon BaNES 20 C4
Haydon Dorset 20 C11
Haydon Somset 19 J10
Haydon Bridge Nthumb 112 B8
Haydon Wick Swindn 33 M7
Haye Cnwll 5 P7
Hayes Gt Lon 36 C4
Hayes Gt Lon 37 K7
Hayes End Gt Lon 36 C4
Hayfield Ag & B 131 M3
Hayfield Derbys 83 M7
Haygate Wrekin 57 L2
Hay Green Norfk 75 K7
Hayhillock Angus 143 J9
Hayle Cnwll 2 F6
Hayley Green Dudley 58 E8
Hayling Island Hants 15 K6
Haymoor Green Ches E 70 B4
Hayne Devon 9 J7
Hayne Devon 18 C11
Haynes (Church End) C Beds 50 C2
Haynes (Northwood End) C Beds 50 C2
Haynes (Silver End) C Beds 50 D2
Haynes (West End) C Beds 50 C2
Hay-on-Wye Powys 45 J6
Hayscastle Pembks 40 G5
Hayscastle Cross Pembks 40 H5
Haysden Kent 37 N11
Hay Street Herts 51 J5
Hayton Cumb 100 F2
Hayton Cumb 111 K9
Hayton E R Yk 98 G11
Hayton Notts 85 M4
Hayton's Bent Shrops 57 J8
Haytor Vale Devon 9 J9
Haytown Devon 16 F9
Haywards Heath W Susx 24 H6
Haywood Donc 91 P8
Haywood Herefs 45 P8
Haywood Oaks Notts 85 K9
Hazards Green E Susx 25 Q8
Hazelbank S Lans 126 E8
Hazelbury Bryan Dorset 12 B3
Hazeleigh Essex 52 D11
Hazeley Hants 23 K3
Hazelford Notts 85 M11
Hazel Grove Stockp 83 K7
Hazelhurst Tamesd 83 L4
Hazelslade Staffs 58 F2
Hazel Street Kent 25 Q3
Hazel Stub Suffk 51 Q2
Hazelton Walls Fife 135 J3
Hazelwood Derbys 84 D11
Hazlemere Bucks 35 N5
Hazlerigg N u Ty 113 K6
Hazles Staffs 71 J3

Hazleton Gloucs 47 L11
Heacham Norfk 75 N3
Headbourne Worthy Hants 22 E8
Headbrook Herefs 45 K3
Headcorn Kent 26 D3
Headingley Leeds 90 H3
Headington Oxon 34 F3
Headlam Dur 103 N7
Headlesscross N Lans 126 G6
Headless Cross Worcs 58 F11
Headley Hants 22 F2
Headley Hants 23 M7
Headley Surrey 36 F10
Headley Down Hants 23 M7
Headley Heath Worcs 58 G9
Headon Devon 16 F11
Headon Notts 85 M5
Heads Nook Cumb 111 K10
Heage Derbys 84 E10
Healaugh N York 97 R11
Healaugh N York 103 K11
Heald Green Stockp 82 H7
Heale Devon 17 L2
Heale Somset 18 H10
Heale Somset 19 L9
Healey N York 97 J4
Healey Nthumb 112 F9
Healey Rochdl 89 P7
Healey Wakefd 90 H7
Healeyfield Dur 112 G11
Healing NE Lin 93 M8
Heamoor Cnwll 2 D7
Heanor Derbys 84 F11
Heanton Punchardon Devon 17 J4
Heapham Lincs 85 Q3
Hearn Hants 23 M7
Heart of England Crematorium Warwks 59 N6
Heart of Scotland Services N Lans 126 G5
Hearts Delight Kent 38 E9
Heasley Mill Devon 17 N5
Heast Highld 145 K4
Heath Derbys 84 G7
Heath Wakefd 91 K6
Heath and Reach C Beds 49 P9
Heath Common W Susx 24 C7
Heathcote Derbys 71 L2
Heathcote Shrops 70 B9
Heath End Bucks 35 N5
Heath End Hants 22 D2
Heath End Leics 72 B6
Heath End Warwks 47 P2
Heather Leics 72 B8
Heathfield Devon 9 K9
Heathfield E Susx 25 N6
Heathfield N York 96 H7
Heathfield Somset 18 G9
Heathfield Village Oxon 48 F11
Heath Green Worcs 58 G10
Heath Hall D & G 109 L5
Heath Hayes & Wimblebury Staffs 58 F2
Heath Hill Shrops 57 P2
Heath House Somset 19 M5
Heathrow Airport Gt Lon 36 C5
Heathstock Devon 10 E4
Heathton Shrops 57 Q6
Heath Town Wolves 58 D5
Heathwaite N York 104 E10
Heatley Staffs 71 K9
Heaton Bolton 89 K8
Heaton C Brad 90 E3
Heaton Lancs 95 J8
Heaton N u Ty 113 L7
Heaton Staffs 70 H2
Heaton Chapel Stockp 83 J6
Heaton Mersey Stockp 83 J6
Heaton Norris Stockp 83 J6
Heaton's Bridge Lancs 88 E8
Heaverham Kent 37 N9
Heaviley Stockp 83 K7
Heavitree Devon 9 M6
Hebburn S Tyne 113 M8
Hebden N York 96 F8
Hebden Bridge Calder 90 B5
Hebden Green Ches W 82 D11
Hebing End Herts 50 H6
Hebron Carmth 41 N5
Hebron IoA 78 H8
Hebron Nthumb 113 J3
Heckfield Hants 23 K3
Heckfield Green Suffk 64 H6
Heckfordbridge Essex 52 F7
Heckington Lincs 74 B2
Heckmondwike Kirk 90 G6
Heddington Wilts 33 J11
Heddon-on-the-Wall Nthumb 112 H7
Hedenham Norfk 65 L3
Hedge End Hants 14 E4
Hedgerley Bucks 35 Q7
Hedgerley Green Bucks 35 Q7
Hedging Somset 19 K9
Hedley on the Hill Nthumb 112 G9
Hednesford Staffs 58 E2
Hedon E R Yk 93 L5
Hedsor Bucks 35 P7
Hegdon Hill Herefs 46 A4
Heglibister Shet 169 q8
Heighington Darltn 103 P6
Heighington Lincs 86 D7
Heightington Worcs 57 P10
Heiton Border 118 D4
Hele Devon 7 J4
Hele Devon 9 N4
Hele Devon 17 J2
Hele Somset 18 G10
Helebridge Cnwll 16 C11
Hele Lane Devon 9 J2
Helensburgh Ag & B 132 B11
Helenton S Ayrs 125 K11
Helford Cnwll 3 K8
Helford Passage Cnwll 3 K8
Helhoughton Norfk 76 B6
Helions Bumpstead Essex 51 Q2
Hellaby Rothm 84 H2
Helland Cnwll 4 H7
Hellandbridge Cnwll 4 H7
Hell Corner W Berk 22 C2
Hellescott Cnwll 5 M4
Hellesdon Norfk 77 J9
Hellesveor Cnwll 2 E5
Hellidon Nhants 60 B9
Hellifield N York 96 C9

Hellingly E Susx 25 N8
Hellington Norfk 77 L11
Helm Nthumb 119 N11
Helmdon Nhants 48 G6
Helme Kirk 90 D8
Helmingham Suffk 64 H10
Helmington Row Dur 103 N3
Helmsdale Highld 163 N10
Helmshore Lancs 89 M6
Helmsley N York 98 C4
Helperby N York 97 P7
Helperthorpe N York 99 K5
Helpringham Lincs 74 B2
Helpston C Pete 74 B9
Helsby Ches W 81 P9
Helsey Lincs 87 P6
Helston Cnwll 2 H9
Helstone Cnwll 4 H5
Helton Cumb 101 P6
Helwith N York 103 L10
Helwith Bridge N York 96 B7
Hemblington Norfk 77 L9
Hembridge Somset 19 Q7
Hemel Hempstead Herts 50 C9
Hemerdon Devon 6 F7
Hemingbrough N York 91 R4
Hemingby Lincs 86 H6
Hemingfield Barns 91 K10
Hemingford Abbots Cambs 62 C6
Hemingford Grey Cambs 62 C6
Hemingstone Suffk 64 G11
Hemington Leics 72 D5
Hemington Nhants 61 N3
Hemington Somset 20 D4
Hemley Suffk 53 N3
Hemlington Middsb 104 F8
Hempholme E R Yk 99 M10
Hempnall Norfk 65 J3
Hempnall Green Norfk 65 J3
Hempriggs Moray 157 L5
Hempstead Essex 51 P3
Hempstead Medway 38 C9
Hempstead Norfk 76 G4
Hempstead Norfk 77 N6
Hempsted Gloucs 46 F11
Hempton Norfk 76 C6
Hempton Oxon 48 D8
Hemsby Norfk 77 P8
Hemswell Lincs 86 B2
Hemswell Cliff Lincs 86 B3
Hemsworth Wakefd 91 L8
Hemyock Devon 10 C2
Henbury Bristl 31 Q9
Henbury Ches E 83 J10
Hendomen Powys 56 C5
Hendon Gt Lon 36 F3
Hendon Sundld 113 P9
Hendon Crematorium Gt Lon 36 F2
Hendra Cnwll 3 J6
Hendra Cnwll 4 G6
Hendre Brdgnd 29 P8
Hendre Flints 80 H11
Hendre Mons 31 N2
Hendy Carmth 28 G4
Heneglwys IoA 78 G9
Henfield W Susx 24 F7
Henford Devon 5 P3
Henghurst Kent 26 G4
Hengoed Caerph 30 G6
Hengoed Powys 45 J4
Hengoed Shrops 69 J8
Hengrave Suffk 63 P7
Henham Essex 51 M5
Heniarth Powys 55 Q3
Henlade Somset 19 J10
Henley Dorset 11 P4
Henley Gloucs 46 H11
Henley Shrops 56 H7
Henley Shrops 57 J9
Henley Somset 19 M8
Henley Suffk 64 H11
Henley W Susx 23 N9
Henley Green Covtry 59 N8
Henley-in-Arden Warwks 59 J11
Henley-on-Thames Oxon 35 L8
Henley Park Surrey 23 P4
Henley's Down E Susx 26 B9
Henley Street Kent 37 Q7
Henllan Cerdgn 42 G6
Henllan Denbgs 80 E11
Henllan Amgoed Carmth 41 N7
Henllys Torfn 31 J6
Henlow C Beds 50 E3
Hennock Devon 9 J8
Henny Street Essex 52 E4
Henryd Conwy 79 P10
Henry's Moat (Castell Hendre) Pembks 41 K5
Hensall N York 91 P6
Henshaw Nthumb 111 Q8
Hensingham Cumb 100 C7
Henstead Suffk 65 P4
Hensting Hants 22 E10
Henstridge Somset 20 D11
Henstridge Ash Somset 20 D10
Henstridge Marsh Somset 20 D10
Henton Oxon 35 L4
Henton Somset 19 N5
Henwick Worcs 46 F3
Henwood Cnwll 5 M7
Henwood Oxon 34 A4
Heol-las Swans 29 J5
Heol Senni Powys 44 C10
Heol-y-Cyw Brdgnd 29 P8
Hepburn Nthumb 119 L6
Hepple Nthumb 119 J10
Hepscott Nthumb 113 K4
Heptonstall Calder 90 B5
Hepworth Kirk 90 F9
Hepworth Suffk 64 D7
Herbrandston Pembks 40 G9
Hereford Herefs 45 Q7
Hereford Crematorium Herefs 45 P6
Hereson Kent 39 Q8
Heribusta Highld 152 H3
Heriot Border 128 C9
Hermiston C Edin 127 M3
Hermitage Border 117 Q11
Hermitage Dorset 11 P3
Hermitage W Berk 34 F10
Hermitage W Susx 15 L5
Hermon Carmth 42 G8
Hermon IoA 78 E11
Hermon Pembks 41 P4

Herne Kent 39 L8
Herne Bay Kent 39 L8
Herne Common Kent 39 L8
Herne Hill Gt Lon 36 H6
Herne Pound Kent 37 Q10
Herner Devon 17 K6
Hernhill Kent 39 J9
Herodsfoot Cnwll 5 L9
Heronden Kent 39 N11
Herongate Essex 37 P2
Heronsford S Ayrs 114 B11
Heronsgate Herts 36 B2
Herriard Hants 23 J5
Herringfleet Suffk 65 P2
Herring's Green Bed 50 C2
Herringswell Suffk 63 M6
Herringthorpe Rothm 84 F2
Herrington Sundld 113 N10
Hersden Kent 39 M9
Hersham Cnwll 16 D10
Hersham Surrey 36 D8
Herstmonceux E Susx 25 P8
Herston Dorset 12 H9
Herston Ork 169 d7
Hertford Herts 50 H8
Hertford Heath Herts 51 J8
Hertingfordbury Herts 50 H8
Hesket Bank Lancs 88 E6
Hesketh Lane Lancs 89 J2
Hesket Newmarket Cumb 101 K3
Heskin Green Lancs 88 G7
Hesleden Dur 104 D3
Hesleden N York 96 C6
Hesley Donc 85 K2
Hesleyside Nthumb 112 B4
Heslington C York 98 C10
Hessay C York 97 R10
Hessenford Cnwll 5 N10
Hessett Suffk 64 C9
Hessle E R Yk 92 H5
Hessle Wakefd 91 L7
Hest Bank Lancs 95 K7
Hestley Green Suffk 64 H8
Heston Gt Lon 36 D5
Heston Services Gt Lon 36 D5
Hestwall Ork 169 b5
Heswall Wirral 81 K8
Hethe Oxon 48 G9
Hethersett Norfk 76 G11
Hethersgill Cumb 111 J7
Hetherside Cumb 110 H6
Hetherson Green Ches W 69 P4
Hethpool Nthumb 118 G5
Hett Dur 103 Q3
Hetton N York 96 E9
Hetton-le-Hole Sundld 113 N11
Hetton Steads Nthumb 119 K3
Heugh Nthumb 112 G6
Heughhead Abers 150 B5
Heveningham Suffk 65 L7
Hever Kent 37 L11
Heversham Cumb 95 K4
Hevingham Norfk 76 H7
Hewas Water Cnwll 3 N4
Hewelsfield Gloucs 31 Q4
Hewenden C Brad 90 D3
Hewish N Som 19 M2
Hewish Somset 11 J3
Hewood Dorset 10 H4
Hexham Nthumb 112 D8
Hextable Kent 37 M6
Hexthorpe Donc 91 P10
Hexton Herts 50 D4
Hexworthy Cnwll 5 P5
Hexworthy Devon 6 H4
Hey Lancs 89 P2
Heybridge Essex 51 P11
Heybridge Essex 52 E10
Heybridge Basin Essex 52 E10
Heybrook Bay Devon 6 D9
Heydon Cambs 51 K3
Heydon Norfk 76 G6
Heydour Lincs 73 Q3
Heyhead Manch 82 H7
Hey Houses Lancs 88 C5
Heylipoll Ag & B 136 B7
Heylor Shet 169 p5
Heyrod Tamesd 83 L5
Heysham Lancs 95 J8
Heyshaw N York 97 J8
Heyshott W Susx 23 N11
Heyside Oldham 89 Q9
Heytesbury Wilts 20 H6
Heythrop Oxon 48 B9
Heywood Rochdl 89 P8
Heywood Wilts 20 G4
Hibaldstow N Linc 92 G10
Hickleton Donc 91 M9
Hickling Norfk 77 N7
Hickling Notts 72 H5
Hickling Green Norfk 77 N7
Hickling Heath Norfk 77 N7
Hickmans Green Kent 39 J10
Hicks Forstal Kent 39 L9
Hickstead W Susx 24 G6
Hidcote Bartrim Gloucs 47 N6
Hidcote Boyce Gloucs 47 N6
High Ackworth Wakefd 91 L7
Higham Barns 91 J9
Higham Derbys 84 E9
Higham Kent 37 P11
Higham Kent 38 B7
Higham Lancs 89 N3
Higham Suffk 52 H5
Higham Suffk 63 M7
Higham Dykes Nthumb 112 H5
Higham Ferrers Nhants 61 L7
Higham Gobion C Beds 50 D4
Higham Hill Gt Lon 37 J2
Higham on the Hill Leics 72 B11
Highampton Devon 8 C4
Highams Park Gt Lon 37 J2
High Angerton Nthumb 112 G3
High Ardwell D & G 106 D7
High Auldgirth D & G 109 K3
High Bankhill Cumb 101 Q2
High Beach Essex 51 K11
High Bentham N York 95 P7
High Bewaldeth Cumb 100 H4
High Bickington Devon 17 L8
High Biggins Cumb 95 N5
High Blantyre S Lans 126 B6
High Bonnybridge Falk 126 E2
High Borrans Cumb 101 M10
High Bradley N York 96 F11
High Bray Devon 17 M5
Highbridge Hants 22 E10

Highbridge - Hopton Cangeford 281

Highbridge Somset 19 K5
Highbrook W Susx 23 J4
High Brooms Kent 25 N2
High Bullen Devon 17 J7
Highburton Kirk 90 F8
Highbury Gt Lon 36 H3
Highbury Somset 20 C5
High Buston Nthumb 119 P9
High Callerton Nthumb 113 J6
High Casterton Cumb 95 N5
High Catton E R Yk 98 E10
Highclere Hants 22 D3
Highcliffe Dorset 13 M6
High Close Dur 103 N7
High Cogges Oxon 34 C3
High Common Norfk 76 D10
High Coniscliffe Darltn 103 P7
High Crosby Cumb 111 J9
High Cross Cnwll 3 J8
High Cross E Ayrs 125 L8
High Cross Hants 23 K9
High Cross Herts 51 J7
Highcross Lancs 88 C3
High Cross W Susx 24 F7
High Cross Warwks 59 K11
High Drummore D & G 106 F10
High Dubmire Sundld 113 M11
High Easter Essex 51 P8
High Eggborough N York 91 P6
High Ellington N York 97 J4
Higher Alham Somset 20 C6
Higher Ansty Dorset 12 C4
Higher Ballam Lancs 88 D4
Higher Bartle Lancs 88 G4
Higher Berry End C Beds 49 Q8
Higher Bockhampton Dorset 12 B6
Higher Brixham Torbay 7 N8
Higher Burrowton Devon 9 P5
Higher Burwardsley Ches W 69 P3
High Ercall Wrekin 69 Q11
Higher Chillington Somset 10 H2
Higher Clovelly Devon 16 E7
Highercombe Somset 18 B8
Higher Coombe Dorset 11 L6
Higher Disley Ches E 83 L8
Higher Folds Wigan 82 E4
Higherford Lancs 89 P2
Higher Gabwell Devon 7 N5
Higher Halstock Leigh Dorset 11 L3
Higher Harpers Lancs 89 N3
Higher Heysham Lancs 95 J8
Higher Hurdsfield Ches E 83 K10
Higher Irlam Salfd 82 F5
Higher Kingcombe Dorset 11 L5
Higher Kinnerton Flints 69 K2
Higher Marston Ches W 82 E9
Higher Muddiford Devon 17 K4
Higher Nyland Dorset 20 D10
Higher Ogden Rochdl 90 B8
Higher Pentire Cnwll 2 H8
Higher Penwortham Lancs 88 G5
Higher Prestacott Devon 5 P2
Higher Studfold N York 96 B6
Higher Town Cnwll 3 L5
Higher Town Cnwll 4 G9
Higher Town IoS 2 c1
Higher Tregantle Cnwll 5 Q11
Higher Walton Lancs 88 H5
Higher Walton Warrtn 82 C7
Higher Wambrook Somset 10 F3
Higher Waterston Dorset 11 Q5
Higher Whatcombe Dorset 12 D4
Higher Wheelton Lancs 89 J6
Higher Whitley Ches W 82 D8
Higher Wincham Ches W 82 E9
Higher Wraxhall Dorset 11 M4
Higher Wych Ches W 69 N6
High Etherley Dur 103 N5
High Ferry Lincs 87 L11
Highfield E R Yk 92 B3
Highfield Gatesd 112 H9
Highfield N Ayrs 125 J7
Highfields Donc 91 N9
High Flats Kirk 90 G9
High Garrett Essex 52 C6
Highgate E Susx 25 K4
Highgate Gt Lon 36 G3
Highgate Kent 26 C5
High Grange Dur 103 N4
High Grantley N York 97 K7
High Green Cumb 101 M10
High Green Kirk 90 G8
High Green Norfk 64 H4
High Green Norfk 76 G10
High Green Sheff 91 J11
High Green Shrops 57 N8
High Green Suffk 64 B9
High Green Worcs 46 G5
Highgreen Manor Nthumb 112 B2
High Halden Kent 26 E4
High Halstow Medway 38 C6
High Ham Somset 19 M8
High Harrington Cumb 100 D5
High Harrogate N York 97 M9
High Haswell Dur 104 C2
High Hatton Shrops 69 R10
High Hauxley Nthumb 119 Q10
High Hawsker N York 105 P9
High Hesket Cumb 101 N2
High Hoyland Barns 90 H9
High Hunsley E R Yk 92 G3
High Hurstwood E Susx 25 L5
High Hutton N York 98 F7
High Ireby Cumb 100 H3
High Kelling Norfk 76 G3
High Kilburn N York 97 R5
High Killerby N York 99 M4
High Knipe Cumb 101 P7
High Lands Dur 103 M5
Highland Wildlife Park Highld 148 E7
Highlane Ches E 83 J11
Highlane Derbys 84 F4
High Lane Stockp 83 L7
High Lanes Cnwll 2 F6
High Laver Essex 51 M9
Highlaws Cumb 109 P11
Highleadon Gloucs 46 E10
High Legh Ches E 82 F8
Highleigh W Susx 15 M7
High Leven S on T 104 E8
Highley Shrops 57 N8
High Littleton BaNES 20 B3
High Lorton Cumb 100 G5
High Marishes N York 98 G5
High Marnham Notts 85 P6
High Melton Donc 91 N10
High Mickley Nthumb 112 G8
Highmoor Cumb 110 E11
Highmoor Oxon 35 K8
Highmoor Cross Oxon 35 K8
Highmoor Hill Mons 31 N7
High Moorsley Sundld 113 M11
Highnam Gloucs 46 E11
Highnam Green Gloucs 46 E10
High Newport Sundld 113 N10
High Newton Cumb 95 J4
High Nibthwaite Cumb 94 F3
High Offley Staffs 70 D9
High Ongar Essex 51 N10
High Onn Staffs 70 E11
High Park Corner Essex 52 H7
High Pennyvenie E Ayrs 115 J6
High Post Wilts 21 N7
Highridge N Som 31 Q11
High Roding Essex 51 P7
High Row Cumb 101 L3
High Row Cumb 101 L6
High Salter Lancs 95 N8
High Salvington W Susx 24 D9
High Scales Cumb 110 C11
High Seaton Cumb 100 D4
High Shaw N York 96 C2
High Side Cumb 100 H4
High Spen Gatesd 112 H9
Highstead Kent 39 M8
Highsted Kent 38 F9
High Stoop Dur 103 M2
High Street Cnwll 3 P3
High Street Kent 26 B5
Highstreet Kent 39 J9
High Street Suffk 65 N10
High Street Suffk 65 N7
Highstreet Green Essex 52 C5
Highstreet Green Surrey 23 Q7
Hightae D & G 109 N5
Highter's Heath Birm 58 G9
High Throston Hartpl 104 E4
Hightown Ches E 70 F2
Hightown Hants 13 L4
Hightown Sefton 81 L4
High Town Staffs 58 E2
Hightown Green Suffk 64 D10
High Toynton Lincs 87 J7
High Trewhitt Nthumb 119 K9
High Urpeth Dur 113 K10
High Valleyfield Fife 134 C10
High Warden Nthumb 112 D7
Highway Herefs 45 P5
Highway Wilts 33 K10
Highweek Devon 7 L4
High Westwood Dur 112 H9
Highwood Staffs 71 K8
Highwood Hill Gt Lon 36 F2
High Woolaston Gloucs 31 Q5
High Worsall N York 104 C9
Highworth Swindn 33 P6
High Wray Cumb 101 L11
High Wych Herts 51 L8
High Wycombe Bucks 35 N6
Hilborough Norfk 75 R10
Hilcote Derbys 84 G9
Hilcott Wilts 21 M3
Hildenborough Kent 37 N11
Hilden Park Kent 37 N11
Hildersham Cambs 62 H11
Hilderstone Staffs 70 H8
Hilderthorpe E R Yk 99 P7
Hilfield Dorset 11 N3
Hilgay Norfk 75 M11
Hill S Glos 32 B5
Hill Warwks 59 Q11
Hillam N York 91 N5
Hillbeck Cumb 102 E7
Hillborough Kent 39 M8
Hill Brow Hants 23 L9
Hillbutts Dorset 12 G4
Hill Chorlton Staffs 70 D7
Hillclifflane Derbys 71 P5
Hill Common Norfk 77 N7
Hill Common Somset 18 F9
Hill Deverill Wilts 20 G6
Hilldyke Lincs 87 K11
Hill End Dur 103 K3
Hill End Fife 134 C8
Hillend Fife 134 E11
Hill End Gloucs 46 H7
Hillend Mdloth 127 P4
Hillend N Lans 126 E4
Hillend Swans 28 D6
Hillersland Gloucs 31 Q2
Hillerton Devon 8 H5
Hillesden Bucks 49 J9
Hillesley Gloucs 32 E7
Hillfarrance Somset 18 G10
Hill Green Kent 38 D9
Hillgrove W Susx 23 P9
Hillhampton Herefs 46 A5
Hillhead Abers 158 E10
Hillhead Devon 7 N8
Hill Head Hants 14 F6
Hillhead S Lans 116 D2
Hillhead of Cocklaw Abers 159 Q9
Hilliard's Cross Staffs 59 J2
Hilliclay Highld 167 L4
Hillingdon Gt Lon 36 C4
Hillington C Glas 125 N5
Hillington Norfk 75 P5
Hillis Corner IoW 14 E8
Hillmorton Warwks 60 B6
Hillock Vale Lancs 89 M5
Hill of Beath Fife 134 F9
Hill of Fearn Highld 163 J11
Hillowton D & G 108 G8
Hillpool Worcs 58 C9
Hillpound Hants 22 G11
Hill Ridware Staffs 71 K11
Hillside Abers 151 N8
Hillside Angus 143 N5
Hillside Devon 7 J6
Hill Side Kirk 90 F7
Hill Side Worcs 46 E2
Hills Town Derbys 84 G7
Hillstreet Hants 22 B11
Hillswick Shet 169 p6
Hill Top Dur 103 J6
Hill Top Hants 14 D6
Hill Top Kirk 90 D8
Hill Top Rothm 84 E2
Hill Top Sandw 58 E6
Hill Top Wakefd 91 J7
Hillwell Shet 169 q12
Hilmarton Wilts 33 K9
Hilperton Wilts 20 G3
Hilperton Marsh Wilts 20 G3
Hilsea C Port 15 J6
Hilston E R Yk 93 N4
Hiltingbury Hants 22 D10
Hilton Border 129 M9
Hilton Cambs 62 C7
Hilton Cumb 102 D6
Hilton Derbys 71 N8
Hilton Dorset 12 C4
Hilton Dur 103 N6
Hilton Highld 156 F2
Hilton S on T 104 E8
Hilton Shrops 57 P5
Hilton Park Services Staffs 58 E4
Himbleton Worcs 46 H3
Himley Staffs 58 C6
Hincaster Cumb 95 L4
Hinchley Wood Surrey 36 E7
Hinckley Leics 59 P6
Hinderclay Suffk 64 E6
Hinderwell N York 105 L7
Hindford Shrops 69 K8
Hindhead Surrey 23 N7
Hindle Fold Lancs 89 L4
Hindley Nthumb 112 F9
Hindley Wigan 82 D4
Hindley Green Wigan 82 D4
Hindlip Worcs 46 G3
Hindolveston Norfk 76 E6
Hindon Wilts 20 H8
Hindringham Norfk 76 D4
Hingham Norfk 76 E11
Hinksford Staffs 58 C7
Hinstock Shrops 70 B9
Hintlesham Suffk 53 J3
Hinton Gloucs 32 C4
Hinton Hants 13 M5
Hinton Herefs 45 L7
Hinton S Glos 32 D9
Hinton Shrops 56 G3
Hinton Shrops 57 M8
Hinton Admiral Hants 13 M5
Hinton Ampner Hants 22 H9
Hinton Blewett BaNES 19 Q3
Hinton Charterhouse BaNES 20 E3
Hinton Green Worcs 47 K6
Hinton-in-the-Hedges Nhants 48 G7
Hinton Marsh Hants 22 G9
Hinton Martell Dorset 12 H3
Hinton on the Green Worcs 47 K6
Hinton Parva Swindn 33 P8
Hinton St George Somset 11 J2
Hinton St Mary Dorset 20 E11
Hinton Waldrist Oxon 34 C5
Hints Shrops 57 L10
Hints Staffs 59 J4
Hinwick Bed 61 K8
Hinxhill Kent 26 H3
Hinxton Cambs 62 G11
Hinxworth Herts 50 F2
Hipperholme Calder 90 E5
Hipsburn Nthumb 119 P8
Hipswell N York 103 N11
Hirn Abers 151 J7
Hirnant Powys 68 D10
Hirst Nthumb 113 L3
Hirst Courtney N York 91 Q6
Hirwaen Denbgs 68 F2
Hirwaun Rhondd 30 C3
Hiscott Devon 17 J6
Histon Cambs 62 F8
Hitcham Suffk 64 D11
Hitcham Causeway Suffk 64 D11
Hitcham Street Suffk 64 D11
Hitchin Herts 50 E5
Hither Green Gt Lon 37 J6
Hittisleigh Devon 8 H5
Hive E R Yk 92 D4
Hixon Staffs 71 J9
Hoaden Kent 39 N10
Hoar Cross Staffs 71 L10
Hoarwithy Herefs 45 Q9
Hoath Kent 39 M9
Hoathly Kent 25 Q3
Hobarris Shrops 56 E9
Hobbles Green Suffk 63 M10
Hobbs Cross Essex 51 L11
Hobbs Cross Essex 51 L8
Hobkirk Border 118 A8
Hobland Hall Norfk 77 Q11
Hobsick Notts 84 G11
Hobson Dur 113 J9
Hoby Leics 72 H7
Hoccombe Somset 18 F9
Hockering Norfk 76 F9
Hockerton Notts 85 M9
Hockley Ches E 83 K8
Hockley Covtry 59 L9
Hockley Essex 38 D3
Hockley Staffs 59 K4
Hockley Heath Solhll 59 J10
Hockliffe C Beds 49 Q9
Hockwold cum Wilton Norfk 63 M3
Hockworthy Devon 18 D11
Hoddesdon Herts 51 J9
Hoddlesden Bl w D 89 L6
Hoddom Cross D & G 110 C6
Hoddom Mains D & G 110 C6
Hodgehill Ches E 82 H11
Hodgeston Pembks 41 K11
Hodnet Shrops 69 R9
Hodsock Notts 85 K3
Hodsoll Street Kent 37 P8
Hodson Swindn 33 N8
Hodthorpe Derbys 84 H5
Hoe Hants 22 G11
Hoe Norfk 76 D8
Hoe Gate Hants 14 H4
Hoff Cumb 102 C7
Hogben's Hill Kent 38 H10
Hoggards Green Suffk 64 B10
Hoggeston Bucks 49 M10
Hoggrill's End Warwks 59 K6
Hog Hill E Susx 26 E8
Hoghton Lancs 89 J5
Hoghton Bottoms Lancs 89 J5
Hognaston Derbys 71 N4
Hogsthorpe Lincs 87 P6
Holbeach Lincs 74 G6
Holbeach Bank Lincs 74 G5
Holbeach Clough Lincs 74 G5
Holbeach Drove Lincs 74 F8
Holbeach Hurn Lincs 74 G5
Holbeach St Johns Lincs 74 G7
Holbeach St Mark's Lincs 74 G4
Holbeach St Matthew Lincs 74 H4
Holbeck Notts 84 H6
Holbeck Woodhouse Notts 84 H6
Holberrow Green Worcs 47 K3
Holbeton Devon 6 G8
Holborn Gt Lon 36 H4
Holborough Kent 38 B9
Holbrook Derbys 72 B2
Holbrook Sheff 84 F4
Holbrook Suffk 53 L4
Holbrook Moor Derbys 84 E11
Holbrooks Covtry 59 M8
Holburn Nthumb 119 K3
Holbury Hants 14 D6
Holcombe Devon 7 P4
Holcombe Somset 20 C5
Holcombe Rogus Devon 18 E11
Holcot Nhants 60 G7
Holden Lancs 96 A11
Holdenby Nhants 60 E7
Holden Gate Calder 89 P6
Holder's Green Essex 51 P5
Holdgate Shrops 57 K7
Holdingham Lincs 86 E11
Holditch Dorset 10 G4
Holdsworth Calder 90 D5
Holehouse Derbys 83 M6
Hole-in-the-Wall Herefs 46 B9
Holemoor Devon 16 G10
Hole Street W Susx 24 D8
Holford Somset 18 G6
Holgate C York 98 B10
Holker Cumb 94 H5
Holkham Norfk 76 B3
Holkham Hall Norfk 76 B3
Hollacombe Devon 16 F11
Holland Fen Lincs 86 H11
Holland Lees Lancs 88 G9
Holland-on-Sea Essex 53 L8
Hollandstoun Ork 169 g1
Hollee D & G 110 E7
Hollesley Suffk 53 Q3
Hollicombe Torbay 7 M6
Hollingbourne Kent 38 D10
Hollingbury Br & H 24 H9
Hollingdon Bucks 49 N9
Hollingthorpe Leeds 91 K4
Hollington Derbys 71 N7
Hollington Staffs 71 K7
Hollingworth Tamesd 83 M5
Hollinlane Ches E 82 H8
Hollins Bury 89 N9
Hollins Derbys 84 D6
Hollins Staffs 70 H5
Hollinsclough Staffs 83 N11
Hollins End Sheff 84 E4
Hollins Green Warrtn 82 E6
Hollins Lane Lancs 95 K10
Hollinswood Wrekin 57 N3
Hollinwood Shrops 69 P7
Hollinwood Crematorium Oldham 83 K4
Hollingrove E Susx 25 Q6
Hollocombe Devon 17 L9
Holloway Derbys 84 D9
Holloway Gt Lon 36 H3
Holloway Wilts 20 G8
Hollowell Nhants 60 E6
Hollowmoor Heath Ches W 81 P11
Hollows D & G 110 G5
Hollybush Caerph 30 G4
Hollybush E Ayrs 114 G4
Hollybush Herefs 46 E7
Holly End Norfk 75 J9
Holly Green Worcs 46 G6
Hollyhurst Ches E 69 Q6
Hollym E R Yk 93 P5
Hollywood Worcs 58 G9
Holmbridge Kirk 90 E9
Holmbury St Mary Surrey 24 D2
Holmbush Cnwll 3 Q3
Holmcroft Staffs 70 G10
Holme Cambs 61 Q3
Holme Cumb 95 L5
Holme Kirk 90 E9
Holme N Linc 92 F9
Holme N York 97 N4
Holme Notts 85 P9
Holme Chapel Lancs 89 P5
Holme Green N York 91 P2
Holme Hale Norfk 76 B10
Holme Lacy Herefs 45 R7
Holme Marsh Herefs 45 L4
Holme next the Sea Norfk 75 P2
Holme on the Wolds E R Yk 99 K11
Holme Pierrepont Notts 72 G3
Holmer Herefs 45 Q6
Holmer Green Bucks 35 P5
Holme St Cuthbert Cumb 109 P11
Holmes Chapel Ches E 82 G11
Holmesfield Derbys 84 D5
Holmes Hill E Susx 25 M8
Holmeswood Lancs 88 E7
Holmethorpe Surrey 36 G10
Holme upon Spalding Moor E R Yk 92 D3
Holmewood Derbys 84 F7
Holmfield Calder 90 D5
Holmfirth Kirk 90 E9
Holmhead E Ayrs 115 L3
Holmpton E R Yk 93 Q6
Holmrook Cumb 100 E11
Holmsford Bridge Crematorium N Ayrs 125 K10
Holmshurst E Susx 25 P5
Holmside Dur 113 K11
Holmwrangle Cumb 111 K11
Holne Devon 7 J5
Holnest Dorset 11 P3
Holnicote Somset 18 B5
Holsworthy Devon 16 E11
Holsworthy Beacon Devon 16 F10
Holt Dorset 12 H4
Holt Norfk 76 F4
Holt Wilts 20 G2
Holt Worcs 46 F2
Holt Wrexhm 69 M4
Holtby C York 98 D10
Holt End Worcs 58 G11
Holt Fleet Worcs 46 F2
Holt Green Lancs 88 D9
Holt Heath Dorset 13 J4
Holt Heath Worcs 46 F2
Holton Oxon 34 H3
Holton Somset 20 C9
Holton Suffk 65 N6
Holton cum Beckering Lincs 86 F4
Holton Heath Dorset 12 F6
Holton Hill E Susx 25 Q5
Holton le Clay Lincs 93 N10
Holton le Moor Lincs 93 J11
Holton St Mary Suffk 53 J4
Holt Street Kent 39 N11
Holtye E Susx 25 L3
Holway Flints 80 H9
Holwell Dorset 11 P2
Holwell Herts 50 E4
Holwell Leics 73 J6
Holwell Oxon 33 P3
Holwick Dur 102 H5
Holworth Dorset 12 C8
Holybourne Hants 23 K6
Holy Cross Worcs 58 D9
Holyfield Essex 51 J10
Holyhead IoA 78 C8
Holy Island IoA 78 D8
Holy Island Nthumb 119 M2
Holymoorside Derbys 84 D7
Holyport W & M 35 N9
Holystone Nthumb 119 J10
Holytown N Lans 126 D5
Holytown Crematorium N Lans 126 D5
Holywell C Beds 50 B7
Holywell Cambs 62 D6
Holywell Cnwll 4 B10
Holywell Dorset 11 M4
Holywell Flints 80 H9
Holywell Nthumb 113 M6
Holywell Warwks 59 K11
Holywell Green Calder 90 D7
Holywell Lake Somset 18 F10
Holywell Row Suffk 63 M5
Holywood D & G 109 K4
Holywood Village D & G 109 L5
Homer Shrops 57 L4
Homer Green Sefton 81 L4
Homersfield Suffk 65 K4
Homescales Cumb 95 M3
Hom Green Herefs 46 A10
Homington Wilts 21 M9
Honeyborough Pembks 40 H9
Honeybourne Worcs 47 M6
Honeychurch Devon 8 F4
Honey Hill Kent 39 K9
Honeystreet Wilts 21 M2
Honey Tye Suffk 52 G4
Honiley Warwks 59 K10
Honing Norfk 77 L6
Honingham Norfk 76 G9
Honington Lincs 73 N2
Honington Suffk 64 C7
Honington Warwks 47 Q6
Honiton Devon 10 D4
Honley Kirk 90 E8
Honnington Wrekin 70 C11
Honor Oak Crematorium Gt Lon 37 J6
Hoo Kent 39 N9
Hoobrook Worcs 58 B10
Hood Green Barns 91 J10
Hood Hill Rothm 91 K11
Hooe C Plym 6 E8
Hooe E Susx 25 Q8
Hoo End Herts 50 E6
Hoo Green Ches E 82 F8
Hoohill Bpool 88 C3
Hook Cambs 62 F2
Hook Devon 10 G3
Hook E R Yk 92 C5
Hook Gt Lon 36 E8
Hook Hants 14 F5
Hook Hants 23 K4
Hook Pembks 41 J8
Hook Wilts 33 L8
Hookagate Shrops 56 H3
Hook Bank Worcs 46 F6
Hooke Dorset 11 L4
Hook End Essex 51 N10
Hookgate Staffs 70 C7
Hook Green Kent 25 Q3
Hook Green Kent 37 P6
Hook Norton Oxon 48 C8
Hook Street Gloucs 32 C5
Hook Street Wilts 33 L8
Hookway Devon 9 L5
Hookwood Surrey 24 G2
Hooley Surrey 36 G9
Hooley Bridge Rochdl 89 P8
Hoo Meavy Devon 6 E5
Hoo St Werburgh Medway 38 C7
Hooton Ches W 81 M9
Hooton Levitt Rothm 84 H2
Hooton Pagnell Donc 91 M9
Hooton Roberts Rothm 91 M11
Hopcrofts Holt Oxon 48 E9
Hope Derbys 83 Q8
Hope Devon 6 H10
Hope Flints 69 K3
Hope Powys 56 D3
Hope Shrops 56 E4
Hope Shrops 57 K10
Hope Staffs 71 L4
Hope Bowdler Shrops 56 H6
Hope End Green Essex 51 N6
Hopehouse Border 117 K7
Hopeman Moray 157 L4
Hope Mansell Herefs 46 B11
Hopesay Shrops 56 F8
Hopetown Wakefd 91 K6
Hope under Dinmore Herefs 45 Q4
Hopgrove C York 98 C10
Hopperton N York 97 P9
Hop Pole Lincs 74 C8
Hopsford Warwks 59 P8
Hopstone Shrops 57 P6
Hopton Derbys 71 P4
Hopton Shrops 69 L10
Hopton Staffs 70 G9
Hopton Suffk 64 D6
Hopton Cangeford Shrops 57 J8

Hopton Castle Shrops....56 F9
Hoptonheath Shrops....56 F9
Hopton on Sea Norfk....65 Q2
Hopton Wafers Shrops....57 L9
Hopwas Staffs....59 J4
Hopwood Rochdl....89 P9
Hopwood Worcs....58 F9
Hopwood Park Services Worcs....58 F10
Horam E Susx....25 N7
Horbling Lincs....74 B3
Horbury Wakefd....90 H7
Horcott Gloucs....33 N4
Horden Dur....104 D2
Horderley Shrops....56 G7
Hordle Hants....13 N5
Hordley Shrops....69 L8
Horeb Carmth....28 E3
Horeb Cerdgn....42 G6
Horfield Bristl....31 Q9
Horham Suffk....65 J7
Horkesley Heath Essex....52 G6
Horkstow N Linc....92 G7
Horley Oxon....48 D6
Horley Surrey....24 G2
Hornblotton Green Somset....19 Q8
Hornby Lancs....95 M7
Hornby N York....97 K2
Hornby N York....104 C9
Horncastle Lincs....87 J7
Hornchurch Gt Lon....37 M3
Horncliffe Nthumb....129 N10
Horndean Border....129 N10
Horndean Hants....15 K4
Horndon Devon....8 D8
Horndon on the Hill Thurr....37 Q4
Horne Surrey....24 H2
Horner Somset....18 B5
Horne Row Essex....52 C11
Horners Green Suffk....52 G3
Horney Common E Susx....25 L5
Horn Hill Bucks....36 B2
Horning Norfk....77 L8
Horninghold Leics....73 L11
Horninglow Staffs....71 N9
Horningsea Cambs....62 G8
Horningsham Wilts....20 F6
Horningtoft Norfk....76 C7
Horningtops Cnwll....5 M9
Hornsbury Somset....10 G2
Hornsby Cumb....111 K10
Hornsbygate Cumb....111 K10
Horns Cross Devon....16 F7
Horns Cross E Susx....26 D7
Hornsea E R Yk....99 P11
Hornsey Gt Lon....36 H3
Horn's Green Gt Lon....37 L9
Horn Street Kent....27 L4
Hornton Oxon....48 C5
Horpit Swindn....33 P8
Horra Shet....169 r4
Horrabridge Devon....6 E5
Horringer Suffk....64 A9
Horringford IoW....14 F9
Horrocks Fold Bolton....89 L8
Horrocksford Lancs....89 M2
Horsacott Devon....17 J5
Horsebridge Devon....5 Q6
Horsebridge E Susx....25 N8
Horsebridge Hants....22 B8
Horsebridge Shrops....56 F3
Horsebridge Staffs....70 H4
Horsebrook Staffs....58 C2
Horsecastle N Som....31 M11
Horsedown Cnwll....2 G7
Horsegate Lincs....74 C8
Horsehay Wrekin....57 M3
Horseheath Cambs....63 K11
Horsehouse N York....96 F4
Horsell Surrey....23 Q3
Horseman's Green Wrexhm....69 M6
Horsenden Bucks....35 L4
Horsey Norfk....77 P7
Horsey Somset....19 K7
Horsey Corner Norfk....77 P7
Horsford Norfk....76 H8
Horsforth Leeds....90 G3
Horsham W Susx....24 E4
Horsham Worcs....46 D3
Horsham St Faith Norfk....77 J8
Horsington Lincs....86 G7
Horsington Somset....20 D10
Horsley Derbys....72 B2
Horsley Gloucs....32 F5
Horsley Nthumb....112 G7
Horsley Nthumb....118 F11
Horsley Cross Essex....53 K6
Horsleycross Street Essex....53 K6
Horsley-Gate Derbys....84 D5
Horsleyhill Border....117 Q7
Horsley's Green Bucks....35 L6
Horsley Woodhouse Derbys....72 B2
Horsmonden Kent....26 B3
Horspath Oxon....34 G3
Horstead Norfk....77 K8
Horsted Keynes W Susx....25 J5
Horton Bucks....49 P11
Horton Dorset....12 H3
Horton Lancs....96 C10
Horton Nhants....49 M4
Horton S Glos....32 E8
Horton Shrops....69 N9
Horton Somset....10 G2
Horton Staffs....70 H3
Horton Surrey....36 E8
Horton Swans....28 E7
Horton W & M....36 B5
Horton Wilts....21 K2
Horton Wrekin....57 M2
Horton Cross Somset....19 K11
Horton-cum-Studley Oxon....34 G2
Horton Green Ches W....69 N5
Horton Heath Hants....22 E11
Horton in Ribblesdale N York....96 B6
Horton Kirby Kent....37 N7
Horwich Bolton....89 J8
Horwich End Derbys....83 M8
Horwood Devon....17 J6
Hoscar Lancs....88 F8
Hoscote Border....117 M8
Hose Leics....73 J5
Hosey Hill Kent....37 L10
Hosh P & K....133 P3

Hoswick Shet....169 r11
Hotham E R Yk....92 E4
Hothfield Kent....26 G3
Hoton Leics....72 F6
Hott Nthumb....111 Q3
Hough Ches E....70 C4
Hough Ches E....83 J9
Hougham Lincs....73 M2
Hough End Leeds....90 G4
Hough Green Halton....81 P7
Hough-on-the-Hill Lincs....86 B11
Houghton Cambs....62 C6
Houghton Cumb....110 H9
Houghton Hants....22 B8
Houghton Nthumb....112 H7
Houghton Pembks....41 J9
Houghton W Susx....24 B8
Houghton Conquest C Beds....50 B2
Houghton Gate Dur....113 M10
Houghton Green E Susx....26 F7
Houghton Green Warrtn....82 D6
Houghton le Side Darltn....103 P6
Houghton-le-Spring Sundld....113 M11
Houghton on the Hill Leics....72 H10
Houghton Regis C Beds....50 B6
Houghton St Giles Norfk....76 C4
Hound Green Hants....23 K3
Houndslow Border....128 G10
Houndsmoor Somset....18 F9
Houndwood Border....129 L7
Hounslow Gt Lon....36 D5
Househill Highld....156 F6
Houses Hill Kirk....90 F7
Housieside Abers....151 M2
Houston Rens....125 L4
Houstry Highld....167 L10
Houton Ork....169 c6
Hove Br & H....24 G10
Hove Edge Calder....90 E6
Hoveringham Notts....85 L11
Hoveton Norfk....77 L8
Hovingham N York....98 D5
Howbrook Barns....91 J11
How Caple Herefs....46 B8
Howden E R Yk....92 B5
Howden-le-Wear Dur....103 N4
Howe Highld....167 P4
Howe IoM....80 a8
Howe N York....97 N4
Howe Norfk....65 K2
Howe Bridge Wigan....82 E4
Howe Bridge Crematorium Wigan....82 E4
Howe Green Essex....52 B11
Howegreen Essex....52 D11
Howell Lincs....86 F11
How End C Beds....50 B2
Howe of Teuchar Abers....159 J8
Howes D & G....110 C7
Howe Street Essex....51 Q4
Howe Street Essex....51 Q8
Howey Powys....44 F3
Howgate Cumb....100 C6
Howgate Mdloth....127 N6
Howgill Lancs....96 B11
Howick Nthumb....119 Q7
Howle Wrekin....70 B10
Howle Hill Herefs....46 B10
Howlett End Essex....51 N4
Howley Somset....10 F3
How Mill Cumb....111 K9
Howmore W Isls....168 c14
Hownam Border....118 E7
Howrigg Cumb....110 F11
Howsham N Linc....92 H10
Howsham N York....98 E8
Howtel Nthumb....118 G4
Howt Green Kent....38 E8
Howton Herefs....45 N9
Howtown Cumb....101 M7
Howwood Rens....125 K5
Hoxne Suffk....64 H6
Hoy Ork....169 b7
Hoylake Wirral....81 J7
Hoyland Common Barns....91 K10
Hoyland Nether Barns....91 K10
Hoyland Swaine Barns....90 H10
Hoyle W Susx....23 P11
Hoyle Mill Barns....91 K9
Hubberholme N York....96 D5
Hubberston Pembks....40 G9
Hubbert's Bridge Lincs....74 E2
Huby N York....97 L11
Huby N York....98 B7
Huccaby Devon....6 H4
Hucclecote Gloucs....46 G11
Hucking Kent....38 D10
Hucknall Notts....84 H11
Huddersfield Kirk....90 E7
Huddersfield Crematorium Kirk....90 E6
Huddington Worcs....46 H3
Hudnall Herts....50 B8
Hudswell N York....103 M10
Huggate E R Yk....98 H9
Hugglescote Leics....72 C8
Hughenden Valley Bucks....35 N5
Hughley Shrops....57 K5
Hugh Town IoS....2 c2
Huish Devon....17 J9
Huish Wilts....21 M2
Huish Champflower Somset....18 E9
Huish Episcopi Somset....19 M9
Hulcote C Beds....49 P7
Hulcott Bucks....35 N11
Hulham Devon....9 P8
Hulland Derbys....71 N5
Hulland Ward Derbys....71 P5
Hullavington Wilts....32 G8
Hullbridge Essex....38 D2
Hull, Kingston upon C KuH....93 J5
Hulme Manch....82 H5
Hulme Staffs....70 G5
Hulme Warrtn....82 D6
Hulme End Staffs....71 L3
Hulme Walfield Ches E....82 H11
Hulse Heath Ches E....82 F8
Hulton Lane Ends Bolton....89 K9
Hulverstone IoW....14 C10
Hulver Street Norfk....76 C9
Hulver Street Suffk....65 P4
Humber Devon....9 L9
Humber Herefs....45 P4
Humberside Airport N Linc....93 J8

Humberston NE Lin....93 P9
Humberstone C Leic....72 G9
Humberton N York....97 P7
Humbie E Loth....128 D7
Humbleton E R Yk....93 M4
Humbleton Nthumb....119 J5
Humby Lincs....73 Q4
Hume Border....118 D2
Humshaugh Nthumb....112 D6
Huna Highld....167 Q2
Huncoat Lancs....89 M4
Huncote Leics....72 E11
Hundalee Border....118 B7
Hundall Derbys....84 E5
Hunderthwaite Dur....103 J6
Hundleby Lincs....87 L7
Hundle Houses Lincs....86 H10
Hundleton Pembks....41 J10
Hundon Suffk....63 M11
Hundred End Lancs....88 E6
Hundred House Powys....44 G4
Hungarton Leics....72 H9
Hungerford Hants....13 L2
Hungerford Somset....18 D6
Hungerford W Berk....34 B11
Hungerford Newtown W Berk....34 C10
Hunger Hill Bolton....89 K9
Hunger Hill Lancs....88 G8
Hungerstone Herefs....45 N7
Hungerton Lincs....73 M5
Hungryhatton Shrops....70 B9
Hunmanby N York....99 M5
Hunningham Warwks....59 N11
Hunnington Worcs....58 E8
Hunsbury Hill Nhants....60 F9
Hunsdon Herts....51 K8
Hunsingore N York....97 P10
Hunslet Leeds....91 J4
Hunsonby Cumb....101 Q3
Hunstanton Norfk....75 N2
Hunstanworth Dur....112 D11
Hunsterson Ches E....70 B5
Hunston Suffk....64 D8
Hunston W Susx....15 N6
Hunston Green Suffk....64 D8
Hunstrete BaNES....20 B2
Hunsworth Kirk....90 F5
Hunt End Worcs....47 K2
Hunter's Inn Devon....17 M2
Hunter's Quay Ag & B....124 F2
Huntham Somset....19 K9
Hunthill Lodge Angus....142 H3
Huntingdon Cambs....62 B6
Huntingfield Suffk....65 L7
Huntingford Dorset....20 F9
Huntington C York....98 C9
Huntington Ches W....69 M2
Huntington E Loth....128 D5
Huntington Herefs....45 K4
Huntington Herefs....45 P6
Huntington Staffs....58 E2
Huntley Gloucs....46 D11
Huntly Abers....158 D10
Hunton Hants....22 E6
Hunton Kent....26 B2
Hunton N York....97 J2
Hunton Bridge Herts....50 C10
Hunt's Corner Norfk....64 F4
Huntscott Somset....18 B6
Hunt's Cross Lpool....81 N7
Hunts Green Bucks....35 N4
Hunts Green Warwks....59 J5
Huntsham Devon....18 D10
Huntshaw Devon....17 J7
Huntshaw Cross Devon....17 J7
Huntspill Somset....19 K5
Huntstile Somset....19 J8
Huntworth Somset....19 K8
Hunwick Dur....103 N4
Hunworth Norfk....76 F4
Hurcott Somset....19 L11
Hurdcott Wilts....21 N8
Hurdsfield Ches E....83 K10
Hurley W & M....35 M8
Hurley Warwks....59 K5
Hurley Bottom W & M....35 M8
Hurley Common Warwks....59 K5
Hurlford E Ayrs....125 M10
Hurlston Green Lancs....88 D8
Hurn Dorset....13 K5
Hurn's End Lincs....87 M11
Hursley Hants....22 D9
Hurst Dorset....12 C6
Hurst N York....103 K10
Hurst Somset....19 N11
Hurst Wokham....35 L10
Hurstbourne Priors Hants....22 D5
Hurstbourne Tarrant Hants....22 C4
Hurst Green E Susx....26 B6
Hurst Green Essex....53 J8
Hurst Green Lancs....89 K3
Hurst Green Surrey....37 J10
Hurst Hill Dudley....58 D6
Hurstley Herefs....45 M5
Hurstpierpoint W Susx....24 G7
Hurst Wickham W Susx....24 G7
Hurstwood Lancs....89 P4
Hurtiso Ork....169 e6
Hurtmore Surrey....23 P5
Hurworth Burn Dur....104 D4
Hurworth-on-Tees Darltn....104 B9
Hurworth Place Darltn....103 Q9
Hury Dur....103 J7
Husbands Bosworth Leics....60 D4
Husborne Crawley C Beds....49 Q7
Husthwaite N York....97 R6
Hutcherleigh Devon....7 K8
Hutcliffe Wood Crematorium Sheff....84 D4
Hut Green N York....91 P6
Huthwaite Notts....84 G9
Huttoft Lincs....87 P5
Hutton Border....129 N9
Hutton Cumb....101 M5
Hutton E R Yk....99 L10
Hutton Essex....51 P11
Hutton Lancs....88 F5
Hutton N Som....19 L3
Hutton Bonville N York....104 B10
Hutton Buscel N York....99 K4
Hutton Conyers N York....97 M6
Hutton Cranswick E R Yk....99 L10
Hutton End Cumb....101 N3
Hutton Hang N York....97 J3

Hutton Henry Dur....104 D3
Hutton-le-Hole N York....98 E2
Hutton Lowcross R & Cl....104 G8
Hutton Magna Dur....103 M8
Hutton Mulgrave N York....105 M9
Hutton Roof Cumb....95 M5
Hutton Roof Cumb....101 L4
Hutton Rudby N York....104 E9
Hutton Sessay N York....97 Q5
Hutton Wandesley N York....97 R10
Huxham Devon....9 M5
Huxham Green Somset....19 Q7
Huxley Ches W....69 P2
Huyton Knows....81 N6
Hycemoor Cumb....94 B3
Hyde Gloucs....32 G4
Hyde Hants....13 L2
Hyde Tamesd....83 K6
Hyde End Wokham....35 K11
Hyde Heath Bucks....35 P4
Hyde Lea Staffs....70 G11
Hydestile Surrey....23 Q6
Hykeham Moor Lincs....86 B7
Hyndford Bridge S Lans....116 C2
Hynish Ag & B....136 B8
Hyssington Powys....56 E6
Hystfield Gloucs....32 C5
Hythe Hants....14 D5
Hythe Kent....27 L5
Hythe Somset....19 M4
Hythe End W & M....36 B6
Hyton Cumb....94 B3

I

Ibberton Dorset....12 C3
Ible Derbys....84 B9
Ibsley Hants....13 L3
Ibstock Leics....72 C9
Ibstone Bucks....35 L6
Ibthorpe Hants....22 C4
Iburndale N York....105 N9
Ibworth Hants....22 G4
Icelton N Som....31 L11
Ichrachan Ag & B....139 J11
Ickburgh Norfk....75 R11
Ickenham Gt Lon....36 C3
Ickford Bucks....34 H3
Ickham Kent....39 M10
Ickleford Herts....50 E4
Icklesham E Susx....26 E8
Ickleton Cambs....51 L2
Icklingham Suffk....63 N6
Ickornshaw N York....90 B2
Ickwell Green C Beds....61 Q11
Ickworth Suffk....63 P8
Icomb Gloucs....47 P10
Idbury Oxon....47 P11
Iddesleigh Devon....17 K10
Ide Devon....9 L4
Ideford Devon....9 L9
Ide Hill Kent....37 L10
Iden E Susx....26 F7
Iden Green Kent....26 B4
Iden Green Kent....26 D5
Idle C Brad....90 F3
Idless Cnwll....3 L4
Idlicote Warwks....47 Q6
Idmiston Wilts....21 N7
Idole Carmth....42 H11
Idridgehay Derbys....71 P5
Idrigill Highld....152 F5
Idstone Oxon....33 Q8
Iffley Oxon....34 F4
Ifield W Susx....24 G3
Ifold W Susx....23 R4
Iford Bmouth....13 K6
Iford E Susx....25 K9
Ifton Mons....31 N7
Ifton Heath Shrops....69 K7
Ightfield Shrops....69 Q7
Ightham Kent....37 N9
Iken Suffk....65 N10
Ilam Staffs....71 L4
Ilchester Somset....19 P10
Ilderton Nthumb....119 K6
Ilford Gt Lon....37 K3
Ilford Somset....19 L11
Ilfracombe Devon....17 J2
Ilkeston Derbys....72 D2
Ilketshall St Andrew Suffk....65 M4
Ilketshall St John Suffk....65 M4
Ilketshall St Lawrence Suffk....65 M5
Ilketshall St Margaret Suffk....65 M4
Ilkley C Brad....96 H11
Illand Cnwll....5 M6
Illey Dudley....58 E8
Illidge Green Ches E....70 D2
Illingworth Calder....90 D5
Illogan Cnwll....2 H5
Illston on the Hill Leics....73 J11
Ilmer Bucks....35 L3
Ilmington Warwks....47 P6
Ilminster Somset....10 H2
Ilsington Devon....9 J9
Ilsington Dorset....12 C6
Ilston Swans....28 G6
Ilton N York....97 J5
Ilton Somset....19 L11
Imachar N Ayrs....120 G3
Immingham NE Lin....93 M8
Immingham Dock NE Lin....93 L7
Impington Cambs....62 F8
Ince Ches W....81 P9
Ince Blundell Sefton....81 L4
Ince-in-Makerfield Wigan....82 C4
Inchbae Lodge Hotel Highld....155 M4
Inchbare Angus....143 L4
Inchberry Moray....157 Q6
Incheril Highld....154 D5
Inchinnan Rens....125 M4
Inchlaggan Highld....146 F7
Inchmichael P & K....134 G2
Inchnacardoch Hotel Highld....147 K5
Inchnadamph Highld....161 M2
Inchture P & K....134 F2
Inchvuilt Highld....154 H10
Inchyra P & K....134 F3
Indian Queens Cnwll....4 E10
Ingate Place Suffk....65 N4
Ingatestone Essex....51 P11

Ingbirchworth Barns....90 G9
Ingerthorpe N York....97 L7
Ingestre Staffs....70 H10
Ingham Lincs....86 B4
Ingham Norfk....77 M6
Ingham Suffk....64 B7
Ingham Corner Norfk....77 M6
Ingleborough Norfk....75 J7
Ingleby Derbys....72 A5
Ingleby Arncliffe N York....104 D10
Ingleby Barwick S on T....104 D8
Ingleby Cross N York....104 E10
Ingleby Greenhow N York....104 G9
Ingleigh Green Devon....8 F3
Inglesbatch BaNES....20 D2
Inglesham Swindn....33 P5
Ingleston D & G....109 L7
Ingleton Dur....103 N6
Ingleton N York....95 P6
Inglewhite Lancs....88 G3
Ingoe Nthumb....112 F6
Ingol Lancs....88 G4
Ingoldisthorpe Norfk....75 N4
Ingoldmells Lincs....87 Q7
Ingoldsby Lincs....73 Q5
Ingram Nthumb....119 K7
Ingrave Essex....37 P2
Ingrow C Brad....90 D3
Ings Cumb....101 M11
Ingst S Glos....31 Q7
Ingthorpe Rutlnd....73 P9
Ingworth Norfk....76 H6
Inkberrow Worcs....47 K3
Inkerman Dur....103 M3
Inkhorn Abers....159 M10
Inkpen W Berk....22 C2
Inkstack Highld....167 N2
Inmarsh Wilts....20 H2
Innellan Ag & B....124 F3
Innerleithen Border....117 L3
Innerleven Fife....135 K7
Innermessan D & G....106 E5
Innerwick E Loth....129 J5
Innesmill Moray....157 P5
Insch Abers....150 G2
Insh Highld....148 E7
Inskip Lancs....88 F3
Inskip Moss Side Lancs....88 F3
Instow Devon....16 H5
Insworke Cnwll....6 C8
Intake Sheff....84 E4
Inver Abers....149 N9
Inver Highld....163 K10
Inver P & K....141 P9
Inverailort Highld....145 N11
Inveralligin Highld....153 Q6
Inverallochy Abers....159 P4
Inveran Highld....162 D7
Inveraray Ag & B....131 M6
Inverarish Highld....153 K10
Inverarity Angus....142 H9
Inverarnan Stirlg....132 C4
Inverasdale Highld....160 C10
Inverbeg Ag & B....132 C8
Inverbervie Abers....143 Q3
Inver-boyndie Abers....158 G5
Invercreran House Hotel Ag & B....139 J8
Inverdruie Highld....148 F5
Inveresk E Loth....127 Q3
Inveresragan Ag & B....138 H10
Inverewe Garden Highld....160 D10
Inverey Abers....149 K10
Inverfarigaig Highld....147 N3
Inverfolla Ag & B....138 H9
Invergarry Highld....147 J7
Invergeldie P & K....133 L2
Invergloy Highld....146 G10
Invergordon Highld....156 C4
Invergowrie P & K....142 E11
Inverguseran Highld....145 M6
Inverhadden P & K....140 G6
Inverherive Hotel Stirlg....132 D2
Inverie Highld....145 N7
Inverinan Ag & B....131 K4
Inverinate Highld....145 R3
Inverkeilor Angus....143 M8
Inverkeithing Fife....134 E11
Inverkeithny Abers....158 F8
Inverkip Inver....124 G3
Inverkirkaig Highld....160 H3
Inverlael Highld....161 K9
Inverlair Highld....139 Q2
Inverleven Lodge Ag & B....130 H4
Inverlochy Highld....131 P2
Invermark Angus....150 C11
Invermoriston Highld....147 L4
Invernaver Highld....166 B4
Inverness Highld....156 B8
Inverness Crematorium Highld....156 A9
Inverness Dalcross Airport Highld....156 D7
Invernoaden Ag & B....131 N8
Inveroran Hotel Ag & B....139 P9
Inverquharity Angus....142 G6
Inverquhomery Abers....159 P8
Inverroy Highld....146 H11
Inversanda Highld....138 G6
Invershiel Highld....145 A4
Invershin Highld....162 D7
Invershore Highld....167 N6
Inversnaid Hotel Stirlg....132 C6
Inverugie Abers....159 Q8
Inveruglas Ag & B....132 C6
Inveruglass Highld....148 E7
Inverurie Abers....151 K3
Inwardleigh Devon....8 F3
Inworth Essex....52 E8
Iochdar W Isls....168 c13
Iona Ag & B....136 H10
Iping W Susx....23 N10
Ipplepen Devon....7 L5
Ipsden Oxon....34 H7
Ipstones Staffs....71 J5
Ipswich Suffk....53 L3
Ipswich Crematorium Suffk....53 L2
Irby Wirral....81 K8
Irby in the Marsh Lincs....87 N8
Irby upon Humber NE Lin....93 L10
Irchester Nhants....61 K7
Ireby Cumb....100 H3
Ireby Lancs....95 P5
Ireland C Beds....50 D2
Ireleth Cumb....94 E5
Ireshopeburn Dur....102 H3
Ireton Wood Derbys....71 P5

Irlam Salfd 82 F6
Irnham Lincs 73 Q5
Iron Acton S Glos 32 C8
Iron Bridge Cambs 75 J11
Ironbridge Wrekin 57 M4
Ironbridge Gorge Shrops 57 M4
Iron Cross Warwks 47 L4
Ironmacannie D & G 108 E5
Irons Bottom Surrey 36 F11
Ironville Derbys 84 F10
Irstead Norfk 77 M7
Irthington Cumb 111 J8
Irthlingborough Nhants 61 K6
Irton N York 99 L4
Irvine N Ayrs 125 J10
Irvine Maritime Centre N Ayrs 125 J10
Isauld Highld 166 G3
Isbister Shet 169 q4
Isbister Shet 169 s7
Isfield E Susx 25 K7
Isham Nhants 61 J6
Isington Hants 23 L6
Islandpool Worcs 58 C8
Islay Ag & B 122 E4
Islay Airport Ag & B 122 D9
Isle Abbotts Somset 19 L10
Isle Brewers Somset 19 L10
Isleham Cambs 63 K6
Isle of Dogs Gt Lon 37 J5
Isle of Grain Medway 38 E6
Isle of Lewis W Isls 168 i4
Isle of Man IoM 80 e4
Isle of Man Ronaldsway Airport IoM 80 c8
Isle of Mull Ag & B 137 Q8
Isle of Purbeck Dorset 12 H8
Isle of Sheppey Kent 38 G8
Isle of Skye Highld 152 G10
Isle of Thanet Kent 39 P8
Isle of Walney Cumb 94 D7
Isle of Whithorn D & G 107 N10
Isle of Wight IoW 14 F9
Isle of Wight Crematorium IoW 14 F9
Isleornsay Highld 145 M5
Isles of Scilly St Mary's Airport IoS 2 c2
Islesteps D & G 109 L4
Islet Village Guern 10 C1
Isleworth Gt Lon 36 E5
Isley Walton Leics 72 C6
Islibhig W Isls 168 f5
Islington Gt Lon 36 H4
Islington Crematorium Gt Lon 36 G2
Islip Nhants 61 L5
Islip Oxon 34 F2
Islivig W Isls 168 f5
Isombridge Wrekin 57 L2
Istead Rise Kent 37 P6
Itchen Abbas Hants 22 F8
Itchen Stoke Hants 22 G8
Itchingfield W Susx 24 D5
Itchington S Glos 32 C7
Itteringham Norfk 76 G5
Itton Devon 8 G5
Itton Mons 31 N5
Itton Common Mons 31 N5
Ivegill Cumb 101 M2
Ivelet N York 102 H11
Iver Bucks 36 B4
Iver Heath Bucks 36 B4
Iveston Dur 112 H10
Ivinghoe Bucks 49 P11
Ivinghoe Aston Bucks 49 Q11
Ivington Herefs 45 P3
Ivington Green Herefs 45 P3
Ivybridge Devon 6 G7
Ivychurch Kent 26 H6
Ivy Cross Dorset 20 G10
Ivy Hatch Kent 37 N10
Ivy Todd Norfk 76 B10
Iwade Kent 38 F8
Iwerne Courtney or Shroton Dorset 12 E2
Iwerne Minster Dorset 12 E2
IWM Duxford Cambs 62 G11
Ixworth Suffk 64 C7
Ixworth Thorpe Suffk 64 C7

J

Jack Green Lancs 88 H5
Jack Hill N York 97 J10
Jack-in-the-Green Devon 9 P5
Jack's Bush Hants 21 Q7
Jacksdale Notts 84 F10
Jackson Bridge Kirk 90 F9
Jackton S Lans 125 P7
Jacobstow Cnwll 5 K2
Jacobstowe Devon 8 E4
Jacobs Well Surrey 36 B10
Jameston Pembks 41 L11
Jamestown Highld 155 N6
Jamestown W Duns 132 D11
Janetstown Highld 167 L10
Janets-town Highld 167 Q6
Jardine Hall D & G 109 P3
Jarrow S Tyne 113 M8
Jarvis Brook E Susx 25 M5
Jasper's Green Essex 52 B6
Jawcraig Falk 126 E2
Jaywick Essex 53 L9
Jealott's Hill Br For 35 N10
Jeater Houses N York 97 P2
Jedburgh Border 118 B6
Jeffreyston Pembks 41 L9
Jemimaville Highld 156 C4
Jerbourg Guern 10 c2
Jersey Jersey 11 b1
Jersey Airport Jersey 11 a2
Jersey Crematorium Jersey 11 b1
Jersey Marine Neath 29 K6
Jerusalem Lincs 86 D4
Jesmond N u Ty 113 L7
Jevington E Susx 25 N10
Jingle Street Mons 31 N2
Jockey End Herts 50 B8
Jodrell Bank Ches E 82 G10
Johnby Cumb 101 M4
John Lennon Airport Lpool 81 N8
John o' Groats Highld 167 Q2
John's Cross E Susx 26 B7
Johnshaven Abers 143 P4
Johnson's Street Norfk 77 M8

Johnston Pembks 40 H8
Johnstone D & G 117 J10
Johnstone Rens 125 L5
Johnstonebridge D & G 109 P2
Johnstown Carmth 42 G11
Johnstown Wrexhm 69 K5
Joppa C Edin 127 Q3
Joppa Cerdgn 54 D11
Joppa S Ayrs 114 H4
Jordans Bucks 35 Q6
Jordanston Pembks 40 H4
Jordanthorpe Sheff 84 E4
Joyden's Wood Kent 37 M6
Jubilee Corner Kent 26 D2
Jump Barns 91 K10
Jumper's Town E Susx 25 L4
Juniper Nthumb 112 D9
Juniper Green C Edin 127 M4
Jura Ag & B 122 H3
Jurby IoM 80 e2
Jurston Devon 8 G8

K

Kaber Cumb 102 E8
Kaimend S Lans 126 H8
Kames Ag & B 124 B3
Kames E Ayrs 115 N2
Kea Cnwll 3 L5
Keadby N Linc 92 D8
Keal Cotes Lincs 87 L8
Kearby Town End N York 97 M11
Kearsley Bolton 82 G4
Kearsley Nthumb 112 F5
Kearsney Kent 27 N3
Kearstwick Cumb 95 N5
Kearton N York 103 J11
Keasden N York 95 Q7
Keaton Devon 6 G7
Keckwick Halton 82 C8
Keddington Lincs 87 K3
Keddington Corner Lincs 87 L3
Kedington Suffk 63 N11
Kedleston Derbys 71 Q6
Keelby Lincs 93 L8
Keele Staffs 70 E5
Keele Services Staffs 70 E6
Keele University Staffs 70 E5
Keeley Green Bed 61 M11
Keelham C Brad 90 D4
Keeston Pembks 40 H7
Keevil Wilts 20 H3
Kegworth Leics 72 D5
Kehelland Cnwll 2 G5
Keig Abers 150 G4
Keighley C Brad 90 D2
Keighley Crematorium C Brad 90 C3
Keilarsbrae Clacks 133 P9
Keillour P & K 134 B2
Keiloch Abers 149 M9
Keils Ag & B 122 H6
Keinton Mandeville Somset 19 P8
Keir Mill D & G 109 J2
Keirsleywell Row Nthumb 111 Q10
Keisby Lincs 73 Q5
Keisley Cumb 102 D6
Keiss Highld 167 P4
Keith Moray 158 B7
Keithick P & K 142 C10
Keithock Angus 143 L5
Keithtown Highld 155 P6
Kelbrook Lancs 89 Q2
Kelby Lincs 73 Q2
Keld Cumb 101 Q8
Keld N York 102 G10
Keld Head N York 98 F4
Keldholme N York 98 E3
Kelfield N Linc 92 D10
Kelfield N York 91 P3
Kelham Notts 85 N9
Kelhead D & G 109 P7
Kellacott Devon 5 Q4
Kellamergh Lancs 88 E5
Kellas Angus 142 H10
Kellas Moray 157 M7
Kellaton Devon 7 L11
Kelleth Cumb 102 C9
Kelling Norfk 76 F3
Kellington N York 91 P6
Kelloe Dur 104 B3
Kelloholm D & G 115 P5
Kells Cumb 100 C7
Kelly Devon 5 P6
Kelly Bray Cnwll 5 P7
Kelmarsh Nhants 60 F5
Kelmscott Oxon 33 P5
Kelsale Suffk 65 M8
Kelsall Ches W 81 Q11
Kelshall Herts 50 H3
Kelsick Cumb 110 C10
Kelso Border 118 D4
Kelstedge Derbys 84 D8
Kelstern Lincs 86 H3
Kelsterton Flints 81 K10
Kelston BaNES 32 D11
Keltneyburn P & K 141 J8
Kelton D & G 109 L6
Kelty Fife 134 E9
Kelvedon Essex 52 E8
Kelvedon Hatch Essex 51 N11
Kelynack Cnwll 2 B8
Kemacott Devon 17 M2
Kemback Fife 135 L5
Kemberton Shrops 57 N4
Kemble Gloucs 33 J5
Kemerton Worcs 47 J7
Kemeys Commander Mons 31 K4
Kemnay Abers 151 J4
Kempe's Corner Kent 26 H2
Kempley Gloucs 46 C9
Kempley Green Gloucs 46 C9
Kempsey Worcs 46 G5
Kempsford Gloucs 33 N5
Kemps Green Warwks 58 H10
Kempshott Hants 22 H4
Kempston Bed 61 M11
Kempston Hardwick Bed 50 B2
Kempton Shrops 56 F8
Kemp Town Br & H 24 H10
Kemsing Kent 37 N9
Kemsley Kent 38 F8
Kemsley Street Kent 38 D9

Kenardington Kent 26 G5
Kenchester Herefs 45 N6
Kencot Oxon 33 Q4
Kendal Cumb 95 L2
Kenderchurch Herefs 45 N9
Kendleshire S Glos 32 C9
Kenfig Brdgnd 29 M8
Kenfig Hill Brdgnd 29 M8
Kenilworth Warwks 59 L10
Kenley Gt Lon 36 H8
Kenley Shrops 57 K4
Kenmore Highld 153 P6
Kenmore P & K 141 J9
Kenn Devon 9 M7
Kenn N Som 31 M11
Kennacraig Ag & B 123 P7
Kennards House Cnwll 5 N4
Kenneggy Cnwll 2 F8
Kennerleigh Devon 9 J4
Kennessee Green Sefton 81 M4
Kennet Clacks 133 Q9
Kennethmont Abers 150 E2
Kennett Cambs 63 L7
Kennford Devon 9 M7
Kenninghall Norfk 64 E4
Kennington Kent 26 H2
Kennington Oxon 34 F4
Kennoway Fife 135 K7
Kenny Somset 19 K11
Kennyhill Suffk 63 L5
Kennythorpe N York 98 F7
Kenovay Ag & B 136 B6
Kensaleyre Highld 152 G7
Kensington Gt Lon 36 G5
Kensworth Common C Beds 50 B7
Kentallen Highld 139 L4
Kent and Sussex Crematorium Kent 25 N3
Kentchurch Herefs 45 N9
Kentford Suffk 63 M7
Kent Green Ches E 70 E3
Kent International Airport Kent 39 P8
Kentisbeare Devon 9 L3
Kentisbury Devon 17 L3
Kentisbury Ford Devon 17 L3
Kentish Town Gt Lon 36 G4
Kentmere Cumb 101 N10
Kenton Devon 9 M7
Kenton Gt Lon 36 E3
Kenton N u Ty 113 K7
Kenton Suffk 64 H8
Kenton Bankfoot N u Ty 113 K7
Kentra Highld 138 B4
Kents Bank Cumb 94 H5
Kent's Green Gloucs 46 D10
Kent's Oak Hants 22 B10
Kent Street E Susx 26 C8
Kent Street Kent 37 Q10
Kenwick Shrops 69 M8
Kenwyn Cnwll 3 L4
Kenyon Warrtn 82 D5
Keoldale Highld 165 J3
Keppoch Highld 145 Q3
Kepwick N York 97 Q2
Keresley Covtry 59 M8
Kermincham Ches E 82 H11
Kernborough Devon 7 K10
Kerne Bridge Herefs 46 A11
Kerrera Ag & B 130 G2
Kerridge Ches E 83 K9
Kerridge-end Ches E 83 K9
Kerris Cnwll 2 C8
Kerry Powys 55 Q6
Kerrycroy Ag & B 124 E5
Kersall Notts 85 M8
Kerscott Devon 17 L6
Kersey Suffk 52 H3
Kersey Tye Suffk 52 G3
Kersey Upland Suffk 52 G3
Kershader W Isls 168 i5
Kershopefoot Cumb 111 J4
Kersoe Worcs 47 J6
Kerswell Devon 10 B4
Kerswell Green Worcs 46 G5
Kerthen Wood Cnwll 2 F7
Kesgrave Suffk 53 M2
Kessingland Suffk 65 Q4
Kessingland Beach Suffk 65 Q4
Kestle Cnwll 3 P4
Kestle Mill Cnwll 4 C10
Keston Gt Lon 37 K8
Keswick Cumb 101 J6
Keswick Norfk 77 J11
Ketsby Lincs 87 L5
Kettering Nhants 61 J5
Kettering Crematorium Nhants 61 J5
Ketteringham Norfk 76 H11
Kettins P & K 142 C10
Kettlebaston Suffk 64 D11
Kettlebridge Fife 135 J6
Kettlebrook Staffs 59 K4
Kettleburgh Suffk 65 K9
Kettle Green Herts 51 K7
Kettleholm D & G 109 P5
Kettleness N York 105 M7
Kettleshulme Ches E 83 L9
Kettlesing N York 97 L9
Kettlesing Bottom N York 97 K9
Kettlestone Norfk 76 D5
Kettlethorpe Lincs 85 P5
Kettletoft Ork 169 f3
Kettlewell N York 96 E6
Ketton Rutlnd 73 P10
Kew Gt Lon 36 E5
Kewstoke N Som 19 K2
Kexbrough Barns 91 J9
Kexby C York 98 E10
Kexby Lincs 85 Q3
Key Green Ches E 70 F2
Key Green N York 105 M10
Keyham Leics 72 H9
Keyhaven Hants 13 P6
Keyingham E R Yk 93 M5
Keymer W Susx 24 H7
Keynsham BaNES 32 C11
Keysoe Bed 61 N8
Keysoe Row Bed 61 N8
Keyston Cambs 61 M5
Key Street Kent 38 E9
Keyworth Notts 72 G4
Kibbear Somset 18 H10
Kibblesworth Gatesd 113 K9
Kibworth Beauchamp Leics 60 E2
Kibworth Harcourt Leics 60 E2

Kidbrooke Gt Lon 37 K5
Kidburngill Cumb 100 E6
Kiddemore Green Staffs 58 C3
Kidderminster Worcs 58 B9
Kiddington Oxon 48 D10
Kidd's Moor Norfk 76 G11
Kidlington Oxon 34 E2
Kidmore End Oxon 35 J9
Kidsdale D & G 107 M10
Kidsgrove Staffs 70 E4
Kidstones N York 96 E4
Kidwelly Carmth 28 D3
Kiel Crofts Ag & B 138 G10
Kielder Nthumb 111 M2
Kiells Ag & B 122 F6
Kilbarchan Rens 125 L5
Kilbeg Highld 145 L6
Kilberry Ag & B 123 M7
Kilbirnie N Ayrs 125 J7
Kilbride Ag & B 123 M4
Kilbride Ag & B 124 C4
Kilbuiack Moray 157 K5
Kilburn Derbys 84 E11
Kilburn Gt Lon 36 F4
Kilburn N York 97 R5
Kilby Leics 72 G11
Kilchamaig Ag & B 123 P7
Kilchattan Ag & B 124 E7
Kilchattan Ag & B 136 b2
Kilcheran Ag & B 138 E10
Kilchoan Highld 137 M3
Kilchoman Ag & B 122 B7
Kilchrenan Ag & B 131 L3
Kilconquhar Fife 135 M7
Kilcot Gloucs 46 C9
Kilcoy Highld 155 Q7
Kilcreggan Ag & B 131 Q11
Kildale N York 104 H9
Kildalloig Ag & B 120 E8
Kildary Highld 156 D3
Kildavaig Ag & B 124 B4
Kildavanan Ag & B 124 C4
Kildonan Highld 163 L2
Kildonan N Ayrs 121 K7
Kildonan Lodge Highld 163 L2
Kildonnan Highld 144 G10
Kildrochet House D & G 106 E6
Kildrummy Abers 150 D4
Kildwick N York 96 F11
Kilfinan Ag & B 124 A2
Kilfinnan Highld 146 H8
Kilford Denbgs 80 F11
Kilgetty Pembks 41 M9
Kilgrammie S Ayrs 114 E7
Kilgwrrwg Common Mons 31 N5
Kilham E R Yk 99 M8
Kilham Nthumb 118 G4
Kilkenneth Ag & B 136 A7
Kilkenzie Ag & B 120 C7
Kilkerran Ag & B 120 D8
Kilkhampton Cnwll 16 D9
Killamarsh Derbys 84 G4
Killay Swans 28 H6
Killean Stirlg 132 G10
Killen Highld 156 B6
Killerby Darltn 103 N7
Killerton Devon 9 N4
Killichonan P & K 140 D6
Killiechonate Highld 146 G11
Killiechronan Ag & B 137 N7
Killiecrankie P & K 141 M5
Killilan Highld 154 B11
Killimster Highld 167 P5
Killin Stirlg 140 E11
Killinghall N York 97 L9
Killington Cumb 95 N3
Killington Devon 17 M2
Killington Lake Services Cumb 95 M2
Killingworth N Tyne 113 L6
Killiow Cnwll 3 L5
Killochyett Border 128 D10
Kilmacolm Inver 125 K3
Kilmahog Stirlg 133 J6
Kilmahumaig Ag & B 130 F9
Kilmaluag Highld 152 G3
Kilmany Fife 135 K3
Kilmarnock E Ayrs 125 L10
Kilmartin Ag & B 130 G8
Kilmaurs E Ayrs 125 L9
Kilmelford Ag & B 130 H5
Kilmersdon Somset 20 C4
Kilmeston Hants 22 G9
Kilmichael Ag & B 120 C7
Kilmichael Glassary Ag & B 130 H9
Kilmichael of Inverlussa Ag & B 130 F10
Kilmington Devon 10 F5
Kilmington Wilts 20 E7
Kilmington Common Wilts 20 E7
Kilmington Street Wilts 20 E7
Kilmorack Highld 155 N9
Kilmore Ag & B 130 H2
Kilmore Highld 145 L6
Kilmory Ag & B 123 M5
Kilmory Highld 137 N1
Kilmory N Ayrs 121 J7
Kilmuir Highld 152 D8
Kilmuir Highld 152 F3
Kilmuir Highld 156 B8
Kilmuir Highld 156 D3
Kilnave Ag & B 122 C5
Kilncadzow S Lans 126 E8
Kilndown Kent 26 C4
Kiln Green Wokham 35 M9
Kilnhill Cumb 100 H4
Kilnhouses Ches W 82 D11
Kilnhurst Rothm 91 M11
Kiln Pit Hill Nthumb 112 F9
Kilnsea E R Yk 93 R7
Kilnsey N York 96 E7
Kilnwick E R Yk 99 K11
Kilnwick Percy E R Yk 98 G11
Kiloran Ag & B 136 b2
Kilpatrick N Ayrs 121 H6
Kilpeck Herefs 45 N8
Kilpin E R Yk 92 C5
Kilpin Pike E R Yk 92 C5
Kilrenny Fife 135 P7
Kilsby Nhants 60 C6
Kilspindie P & K 134 G2
Kilstay D & G 106 F10
Kilsyth N Lans 126 C2
Kiltarlity Highld 155 P9
Kilton R & Cl 105 K7

Kilton Thorpe R & Cl 105 J7
Kilvaxter Highld 152 F4
Kilve Somset 18 F6
Kilvington Notts 73 L2
Kilwinning N Ayrs 125 J9
Kimberley Norfk 76 F11
Kimberley Notts 72 D2
Kimberworth Rothm 84 F2
Kimblesworth Dur 113 L11
Kimble Wick Bucks 35 M3
Kimbolton Cambs 61 P7
Kimbolton Herefs 45 Q2
Kimcote Leics 60 C3
Kimmeridge Dorset 12 F9
Kimmerston Nthumb 119 J3
Kimpton Hants 21 Q5
Kimpton Herts 50 E7
Kimworthy Devon 16 E9
Kinbrace Highld 166 E10
Kinbuck Stirlg 133 M6
Kincaple Fife 135 M4
Kincardine Fife 133 Q10
Kincardine Highld 162 E9
Kincardine O'Neil Abers 150 F8
Kinclaven P & K 142 B10
Kincorth C Aber 151 N7
Kincorth House Moray 157 J5
Kincraig Highld 148 E6
Kincraigie P & K 141 N8
Kindallachan P & K 141 N8
Kinerarach Ag & B 123 L9
Kineton Gloucs 47 L9
Kineton Warwks 48 B4
Kinfauns P & K 134 F3
Kingarth Ag & B 124 D6
King Arthur's Labyrinth Gwynd 54 H3
Kingcausie Abers 151 M8
Kingcoed Mons 31 M3
Kingerby Lincs 86 E2
Kingford Devon 16 D10
Kingham Oxon 47 Q10
Kingholm Quay D & G 109 L6
Kinghorn Fife 134 H10
Kinglassie Fife 134 G8
Kingoldrum Angus 142 E6
Kingoodie P & K 135 J2
King's Acre Herefs 45 P6
Kingsand Cnwll 6 C8
Kingsash Bucks 35 N3
Kingsbarns Fife 135 P5
Kingsbridge Devon 7 J10
Kingsbridge Somset 18 C7
King's Bridge Swans 28 G5
Kingsburgh Highld 152 F6
Kingsbury Gt Lon 36 E3
Kingsbury Warwks 59 K5
Kingsbury Episcopi Somset 19 M10
King's Caple Herefs 45 R9
Kingsclere Hants 22 F3
King's Cliffe Nhants 73 Q11
Kingscote Gloucs 32 F5
Kingscott Devon 17 J8
King's Coughton Warwks 47 L3
Kingscross N Ayrs 121 K6
Kingsdon Somset 19 P9
Kingsdown Kent 27 Q2
Kingsdown Swindn 33 N7
Kingsdown Wilts 32 F11
Kingsdown Crematorium Swindn 33 N7
Kingseat Fife 134 E9
Kingsey Bucks 35 K3
Kingsfold W Susx 24 E3
Kingsford C Aber 151 M6
Kingsford E Ayrs 125 L8
Kingsford Worcs 57 Q8
Kingsgate Kent 39 Q7
Kings Green Gloucs 46 E8
Kingshall Street Suffk 64 C9
Kingsheanton Devon 17 K4
King's Heath Birm 58 G8
King's Hill Kent 37 Q9
King's Hill Wsall 58 E5
Kings House Hotel Highld 139 P7
Kingshouse Hotel Stirlg 132 H3
Kingshurst Solhll 59 J7
Kingside Hill Cumb 110 C10
Kingskerswell Devon 7 M5
Kingskettle Fife 135 J6
Kingsland Dorset 11 K5
Kingsland Herefs 45 N2
Kingsland IoA 78 D8
Kings Langley Herts 50 C9
Kingsley Ches W 82 C10
Kingsley Hants 23 L7
Kingsley Staffs 71 J5
Kingsley Green W Susx 23 N8
Kingsley Park Nhants 60 G8
Kingslow Shrops 57 P5
King's Lynn Norfk 75 M6
Kings Meaburn Cumb 102 B6
Kingsmead Hants 14 G4
King's Mills Guern 10 b2
King's Moss St Hel 81 Q4
Kingsmuir Angus 142 H8
Kings Muir Border 117 K3
Kingsmuir Fife 135 N6
Kings Newnham Warwks 59 Q9
King's Newton Derbys 72 B5
Kingsnorth Kent 26 H4
King's Norton Birm 58 G9
King's Norton Leics 72 H10
King's Nympton Devon 17 M9
Kings Ripton Cambs 62 C5
King's Somborne Hants 22 C8
King's Stag Dorset 11 Q2
King's Stanley Gloucs 32 F4
King's Sutton Nhants 48 E7
Kingstanding Birm 58 G6
Kingsteignton Devon 7 M4
King's Sterndale Derbys 83 N10
Kingsthorne Herefs 45 P8
Kingsthorpe Nhants 60 G8
Kingston Cambs 62 D9
Kingston Cnwll 5 P6
Kingston Devon 6 G9
Kingston Devon 9 Q7
Kingston Dorset 11 Q4
Kingston Dorset 12 G7
Kingston E Loth 128 E3
Kingston Hants 13 K4
Kingston IoW 14 E10
Kingston Kent 27 L11
Kingston W Susx 24 C10
Kingston Bagpuize Oxon 34 D5

Place	County	Page	Grid
Kingston Blount	Oxon	35	K5
Kingston Deverill	Wilts	20	F7
Kingstone	Herefs	45	N7
Kingstone	Somset	10	H2
Kingstone	Staffs	71	K9
Kingstone Winslow	Oxon	33	Q7
Kingston Lisle	Oxon	34	B7
Kingston near Lewes	E Susx	9	J9
Kingston on Soar	Notts	72	E5
Kingston on Spey	Moray	157	Q4
Kingston Russell	Dorset	11	M6
Kingston St Mary	Somset	18	H9
Kingston Seymour	N Som	31	M11
Kingston Stert	Oxon	35	K4
Kingston upon Hull	C KuH	93	J5
Kingston upon Thames	Gt Lon	36	E7
Kingston upon Thames Crematorium	Gt Lon	36	E7
Kingstown	Cumb	110	G9
King's Walden	Herts	50	E6
Kingswear	Devon	7	M8
Kingswells	C Aber	151	M6
Kings Weston	Bristl	31	P9
Kingswinford	Dudley	58	C7
Kingswood	Bucks	49	J11
Kingswood	Gloucs	32	D6
Kingswood	Kent	38	D11
Kingswood	Powys	56	C4
Kingswood	S Glos	32	B10
Kingswood	Somset	18	F7
Kingswood	Surrey	36	F9
Kingswood	Warwks	59	J10
Kingswood Brook	Warwks	59	J10
Kingswood Common	Herefs	45	K4
Kingswood Common	Staffs	58	B4
Kings Worthy	Hants	22	E8
Kingthorpe	Lincs	86	F5
Kington	Herefs	45	K3
Kington	S Glos	32	B6
Kington	Worcs	47	J3
Kington Langley	Wilts	32	H9
Kington Magna	Dorset	20	E10
Kington St Michael	Wilts	32	H9
Kingussie	Highld	148	D7
Kingweston	Somset	19	P8
Kinharrachie	Abers	159	M11
Kinharvie	D & G	109	K7
Kinknockie	Abers	159	P9
Kinleith	C Edin	127	M4
Kinlet	Shrops	57	N8
Kinloch	Highld	144	F8
Kinloch	Highld	164	H10
Kinloch	Highld	165	N6
Kinloch	P & K	142	A9
Kinlochard	Stirlg	132	F7
Kinlochbervie	Highld	164	F5
Kinlocheil	Highld	138	H2
Kinlochewe	Highld	154	D5
Kinloch Hourn	Highld	146	B6
Kinlochlaggan	Highld	147	N10
Kinlochleven	Highld	139	M5
Kinlochmoidart	Highld	138	C3
Kinlochnanuagh	Highld	145	M11
Kinloch Rannoch	P & K	140	G6
Kinloss	Moray	157	K5
Kinmel Bay	Conwy	80	D8
Kinmuck	Abers	151	L4
Kinmundy	Abers	151	M4
Kinnabus	Ag & B	122	C11
Kinnadie	Abers	159	N9
Kinnaird	P & K	141	N6
Kinneff	Abers	143	Q2
Kinnelhead	D & G	116	E10
Kinnell	Angus	143	L7
Kinnerley	Shrops	69	K10
Kinnersley	Herefs	45	L5
Kinnersley	Worcs	46	G6
Kinnerton	Powys	45	J2
Kinnerton	Shrops	56	F5
Kinnerton Green	Flints	69	K2
Kinnesswood	P & K	134	F7
Kinninvie	Dur	103	L6
Kinnordy	Angus	142	F6
Kinoulton	Notts	72	H4
Kinross	P & K	134	E7
Kinrossie	P & K	142	B11
Kinross Services	P & K	134	E7
Kinsbourne Green	Herts	50	D7
Kinsey Heath	Ches E	70	B6
Kinsham	Herefs	56	F11
Kinsham	Worcs	46	H7
Kinsley	Wakefd	91	L8
Kinson	Bmouth	13	J5
Kintail	Highld	146	B4
Kintbury	W Berk	34	C11
Kintessack	Moray	157	J5
Kintillo	P & K	134	E4
Kinton	Herefs	56	G10
Kinton	Shrops	69	L11
Kintore	Abers	151	K4
Kintour	Ag & B	122	G9
Kintra	Ag & B	122	D10
Kintra	Ag & B	137	J10
Kintraw	Ag & B	130	G7
Kintyre	Ag & B	120	D4
Kinveachy	Highld	148	G4
Kinver	Staffs	58	B8
Kiplin	N York	103	Q11
Kippax	Leeds	91	L4
Kippen	Stirlg	133	J9
Kippford or Scaur	D & G	108	H10
Kipping's Cross	Kent	25	P2
Kirbister	Ork	169	c6
Kirby Bedon	Norfk	77	K10
Kirby Bellars	Leics	73	J7
Kirby Cane	Norfk	65	M3
Kirby Corner	Covtry	59	L9
Kirby Cross	Essex	53	M7
Kirby Fields	Leics	72	E10
Kirby Grindalythe	N York	99	J7
Kirby Hill	N York	97	N7
Kirby Hill	N York	103	M9
Kirby Knowle	N York	97	Q3
Kirby le Soken	Essex	53	M7
Kirby Misperton	N York	98	F5
Kirby Muxloe	Leics	72	E10
Kirby Sigston	N York	97	P2
Kirby Underdale	E R Yk	98	G9
Kirby Wiske	N York	97	N4
Kirdford	W Susx	24	B5
Kirk	Highld	167	N5
Kirkabister	Shet	169	r10
Kirkandrews	D & G	108	D11
Kirkandrews upon Eden	Cumb	110	G9
Kirkbampton	Cumb	110	F9
Kirkbean	D & G	109	L9
Kirk Bramwith	Donc	91	Q8
Kirkbride	Cumb	110	D9
Kirkbridge	N York	97	L2
Kirkbuddo	Angus	143	J9
Kirkburn	Border	117	K3
Kirkburn	E R Yk	99	K9
Kirkburton	Kirk	90	F8
Kirkby	Knows	81	N5
Kirkby	Lincs	86	E2
Kirkby	N York	104	F9
Kirkby Fleetham	N York	97	L2
Kirkby Green	Lincs	86	E9
Kirkby in Ashfield	Notts	84	G9
Kirkby-in-Furness	Cumb	94	E4
Kirkby la Thorpe	Lincs	86	E11
Kirkby Lonsdale	Cumb	95	N5
Kirkby Malham	N York	96	C8
Kirkby Mallory	Leics	72	D10
Kirkby Malzeard	N York	97	K6
Kirkby Mills	N York	98	E3
Kirkbymoorside	N York	98	D3
Kirkby on Bain	Lincs	86	H8
Kirkby Overblow	N York	97	M11
Kirkby Stephen	Cumb	102	E9
Kirkby Thore	Cumb	102	B5
Kirkby Underwood	Lincs	73	R5
Kirkby Wharf	N York	91	N2
Kirkby Woodhouse	Notts	84	G10
Kirkcaldy	Fife	134	H9
Kirkcaldy Crematorium	Fife	134	H9
Kirkcambeck	Cumb	111	K7
Kirkchrist	D & G	108	E10
Kirkcolm	D & G	106	D4
Kirkconnel	D & G	115	P5
Kirkconnell	D & G	109	L7
Kirkcowan	D & G	107	K5
Kirkcudbright	D & G	108	E10
Kirkdale	Lpool	81	L6
Kirk Deighton	N York	97	N10
Kirk Ella	E R Yk	92	H5
Kirkfieldbank	S Lans	116	B2
Kirkgunzeon	D & G	109	J7
Kirk Hallam	Derbys	72	D2
Kirkham	Lancs	88	E4
Kirkham	N York	98	E7
Kirkhamgate	Wakefd	90	H6
Kirk Hammerton	N York	97	Q9
Kirkharle	Nthumb	112	F4
Kirkhaugh	Nthumb	111	N11
Kirkheaton	Kirk	90	F7
Kirkheaton	Nthumb	112	F5
Kirkhill	Highld	155	Q8
Kirkhope	S Lans	116	D9
Kirkhouse	Cumb	111	L9
Kirkhouse Green	Donc	91	Q8
Kirkibost	Highld	145	J4
Kirkinch	P & K	142	E9
Kirkinner	D & G	107	M7
Kirkintilloch	E Duns	126	B3
Kirk Ireton	Derbys	71	P4
Kirkland	Cumb	100	E7
Kirkland	Cumb	102	B4
Kirkland	D & G	109	M3
Kirkland	D & G	115	P5
Kirkland	D & G	115	R9
Kirkland Guards	Cumb	100	G3
Kirk Langley	Derbys	71	P7
Kirkleatham	R & Cl	104	G6
Kirklevington	S on T	104	D9
Kirkley	Suffk	65	Q3
Kirklington	N York	97	M4
Kirklington	Notts	85	L9
Kirklinton	Cumb	110	H7
Kirkliston	C Edin	127	L3
Kirkmabreck	D & G	107	N6
Kirkmaiden	D & G	106	F10
Kirk Merrington	Dur	103	Q4
Kirk Michael	IoM	80	d3
Kirkmichael	P & K	141	Q6
Kirkmichael	S Ayrs	114	F6
Kirkmuirhill	S Lans	126	D9
Kirknewton	Nthumb	118	H4
Kirknewton	W Loth	127	L4
Kirkney	Abers	158	D11
Kirk of Shotts	N Lans	126	E5
Kirkoswald	Cumb	101	Q2
Kirkoswald	S Ayrs	114	D6
Kirkpatrick	D & G	109	K2
Kirkpatrick Durham	D & G	108	G6
Kirkpatrick-Fleming	D & G	110	E6
Kirk Sandall	Donc	91	Q9
Kirksanton	Cumb	94	C4
Kirk Smeaton	N York	91	N7
Kirkstall	Leeds	90	H3
Kirkstead	Lincs	86	G8
Kirkstile	Abers	158	D10
Kirkstile	D & G	110	G2
Kirkstone Pass Inn	Cumb	101	M9
Kirkstyle	Highld	167	P2
Kirkthorpe	Wakefd	91	K6
Kirkton	Abers	150	G2
Kirkton	D & G	109	L4
Kirkton	Fife	135	K2
Kirkton	Highld	145	P2
Kirkton	Highld	154	B4
Kirkton	P & K	134	B4
Kirkton Manor	Border	117	J3
Kirkton of Airlie	Angus	142	E7
Kirkton of Auchterhouse	Angus	142	E10
Kirkton of Barevan	Highld	156	E8
Kirkton of Collace	P & K	142	B11
Kirkton of Glenbuchat	Abers	150	B4
Kirkton of Logie Buchan	Abers	151	P2
Kirkton of Menmuir	Angus	143	J5
Kirkton of Monikie	Angus	143	J10
Kirkton of Rayne	Abers	158	G11
Kirkton of Skene	Abers	151	L6
Kirkton of Strathmartine	Angus	142	F10
Kirkton of Tealing	Angus	142	G10
Kirkton of Tough	Abers	150	G5
Kirktown	Abers	159	N4
Kirktown	Abers	159	Q7
Kirktown of Alvah	Abers	158	G5
Kirktown of Bourtie	Abers	151	L2
Kirktown of Fetteresso	Abers	151	M10
Kirktown of Mortlach	Moray	157	Q10
Kirktown of Slains	Abers	151	Q2
Kirkurd	Border	116	G2
Kirkwall	Ork	169	d5
Kirkwall Airport	Ork	169	d6
Kirkwhelpington	Nthumb	112	E4
Kirk Yetholm	Border	118	F5
Kirmington	N Linc	93	K8
Kirmond le Mire	Lincs	86	G2
Kirn	Ag & B	124	F2
Kirriemuir	Angus	142	F7
Kirstead Green	Norfk	65	K2
Kirtlebridge	D & G	110	D6
Kirtling	Cambs	63	L9
Kirtling Green	Cambs	63	L9
Kirtlington	Oxon	48	E11
Kirtomy	Highld	166	B4
Kirton	Lincs	74	F3
Kirton	Notts	85	L7
Kirton	Suffk	53	N3
Kirton End	Lincs	74	E2
Kirtonhill	W Duns	125	K2
Kirton Holme	Lincs	74	E2
Kirton in Lindsey	N Linc	92	F11
Kirwaugh	D & G	107	M7
Kishorn	Highld	153	Q10
Kislingbury	Nhants	60	E9
Kitebrook	Warwks	47	P8
Kite Green	Warwks	59	J11
Kites Hardwick	Warwks	59	Q11
Kitleigh	Cnwll	5	L2
Kitt Green	Wigan	88	G9
Kittisford	Somset	18	E10
Kittle	Swans	28	G7
Kitt's Green	Birm	59	J7
Kittybrewster	C Aber	151	N6
Kitwood	Hants	23	J8
Kivernoll	Herefs	45	P8
Kiveton Park	Rothm	84	G4
Knaith	Lincs	85	P4
Knaith Park	Lincs	85	P3
Knap Corner	Dorset	20	F10
Knaphill	Surrey	23	Q3
Knapp	Somset	19	K9
Knapp Hill	Hants	22	D10
Knapthorpe	Notts	85	M9
Knapton	C York	98	B10
Knapton	N York	98	H5
Knapton	Norfk	77	L5
Knapton Green	Herefs	45	N4
Knapwell	Cambs	62	D8
Knaresborough	N York	97	N9
Knarsdale	Nthumb	111	N10
Knaven	Abers	159	L9
Knayton	N York	97	P3
Knebworth	Herts	50	G5
Knedlington	E R Yk	92	B5
Kneesall	Notts	85	M8
Kneesworth	Cambs	50	H2
Kneeton	Notts	85	M11
Knelston	Swans	28	E7
Knenhall	Staffs	70	G7
Knettishall	Suffk	64	D5
Knightacott	Devon	17	M4
Knightcote	Warwks	48	D4
Knightley	Staffs	70	E9
Knightley Dale	Staffs	70	E10
Knighton	C Leic	72	G10
Knighton	Devon	6	E9
Knighton	Dorset	11	N2
Knighton	Poole	12	H5
Knighton	Powys	56	D10
Knighton	Somset	18	G6
Knighton	Staffs	70	C6
Knighton	Staffs	70	D9
Knighton	Wilts	33	Q10
Knighton on Teme	Worcs	57	L11
Knightsbridge	Gloucs	46	G9
Knightsmill	Cnwll	4	H5
Knightwick	Worcs	46	D3
Knill	Herefs	45	K2
Knipton	Leics	73	L4
Knitsley	Dur	112	H11
Kniveton	Derbys	71	N4
Knock	Cumb	102	C5
Knock	Highld	145	L6
Knock	Moray	158	D7
Knock	W Isls	168	j4
Knockally	Highld	167	K11
Knockan	Highld	161	L4
Knockando	Moray	157	M9
Knockbain	Highld	155	Q9
Knockbain	Highld	156	A6
Knock Castle	N Ayrs	124	F5
Knockdee	Highld	167	L4
Knockdow	Ag & B	124	E3
Knockdown	Wilts	32	F7
Knockeen	S Ayrs	114	F8
Knockenkelly	N Ayrs	121	K6
Knockentiber	E Ayrs	125	L10
Knockhall	Kent	37	N6
Knockholt	Kent	37	L9
Knockholt Pound	Kent	37	L9
Knockin	Shrops	69	K10
Knockinlaw	E Ayrs	125	L10
Knockmill	Kent	37	N8
Knocknain	D & G	106	C5
Knockrome	Ag & B	123	J5
Knocksharry	IoM	80	c4
Knocksheen	D & G	108	C2
Knockvennie Smithy	D & G	108	G6
Knodishall	Suffk	65	N9
Knodishall Common	Suffk	65	N9
Knole	Somset	19	N9
Knole Park	S Glos	31	Q8
Knolls Green	Ches E	82	H9
Knolton	Wrexhm	69	L7
Knook	Wilts	20	H6
Knossington	Leics	73	L9
Knott End-on-Sea	Lancs	94	H11
Knotting	Bed	61	M8
Knotting Green	Bed	61	M8
Knottingley	Wakefd	91	N6
Knotty Ash	Lpool	81	N6
Knotty Green	Bucks	35	P6
Knowbury	Shrops	57	K9
Knowe	D & G	107	K3
Knowehead	D & G	115	M9
Knoweside	S Ayrs	114	E5
Knowle	Bristl	32	B10
Knowle	Devon	9	J4
Knowle	Devon	9	P3
Knowle	Devon	9	Q8
Knowle	Devon	16	H4
Knowle	Shrops	57	K10
Knowle	Solhll	59	J9
Knowle	Somset	18	C6
Knowle Cross	Devon	9	P5
Knowlefield	Cumb	110	H9
Knowle Green	Lancs	89	J3
Knowle Hill	Surrey	35	Q11
Knowle St Giles	Somset	10	G2
Knowle Village	Hants	14	G5
Knowle Wood	Calder	89	Q6
Knowl Green	Essex	52	C3
Knowl Hill	W & M	35	M9
Knowlton	Dorset	12	H3
Knowlton	Kent	39	N11
Knowsley	Knows	81	N5
Knowsley Safari Park	Knows	81	P6
Knowstone	Devon	17	Q7
Knox	N York	97	L9
Knox Bridge	Kent	26	C3
Knucklas	Powys	56	D10
Knuston	Nhants	61	K7
Knutsford	Ches E	82	G9
Knutsford Services	Ches E	82	F9
Knutton	Staffs	70	E5
Krumlin	Calder	90	D7
Kuggar	Cnwll	3	J10
Kyleakin	Highld	145	L2
Kyle of Lochalsh	Highld	145	N2
Kylerhea	Highld	145	N3
Kylesku	Highld	164	F10
Kylesmorar	Highld	145	P9
Kyles Scalpay	W Isls	168	h8
Kylestrome	Highld	164	F10
Kynaston	Herefs	46	B7
Kynaston	Shrops	69	L10
Kynnersley	Wrekin	70	B11
Kyre Green	Worcs	46	B2
Kyre Park	Worcs	46	B2
Kyrewood	Worcs	57	K11
Kyrle	Somset	18	E10

L

Place	County	Page	Grid
La Bellieuse	Guern	10	b2
Lacasaigh	W Isls	168	i5
Lacasdal	W Isls	168	j4
Laceby	NE Lin	93	M9
Lacey Green	Bucks	35	M4
Lach Dennis	Ches W	82	F10
Lackenby	R & Cl	104	G7
Lackford	Suffk	63	N6
Lackford Green	Suffk	63	N6
Lacock	Wilts	32	H11
Ladbroke	Warwks	48	D3
Ladderedge	Staffs	70	H4
Laddingford	Kent	37	Q11
Lade Bank	Lincs	87	L10
Ladock	Cnwll	3	M3
Lady	Ork	169	f2
Ladybank	Fife	135	J6
Ladycross	Cnwll	5	N4
Ladygill	S Lans	116	C5
Lady Hall	Cumb	94	D3
Ladykirk	Border	129	K10
Ladyridge	Herefs	46	A8
Lady's Green	Suffk	63	N9
Ladywood	Birm	58	G7
Ladywood	Worcs	46	G2
La Fontenelle	Guern	10	c1
La Fosse	Guern	10	b2
Lag	D & G	109	J3
Laga	Highld	138	A5
Lagavulin	Ag & B	122	F10
Lagg	N Ayrs	121	J7
Laggan	Highld	146	H8
Laggan	Highld	147	Q9
Lagganlia	Highld	148	F7
La Greve	Guern	10	c1
La Greve de Lecq	Jersey	11	a1
La Hougue Bie	Jersey	11	c2
La Houguette	Guern	10	b2
Laid	Highld	165	K5
Laide	Highld	160	E8
Laig	Highld	144	G10
Laigh Clunch	E Ayrs	125	M8
Laigh Fenwick	E Ayrs	125	M9
Laigh Glenmuir	E Ayrs	115	M3
Laighstonehall	S Lans	126	C7
Laindon	Essex	37	Q3
Lairg	Highld	162	D5
Laisterdyke	C Brad	90	F4
Laithes	Cumb	101	N4
Lake	Devon	8	D7
Lake	Devon	17	K5
Lake	IoW	14	G10
Lake	Poole	12	G6
Lake	Wilts	21	M7
Lake District National Park	Cumb	100	H9
Lakenheath	Suffk	63	M4
Laker's Green	Surrey	24	B3
Lakesend	Norfk	75	K11
Lakeside	Cumb	94	H3
Laleham	Surrey	36	C7
Laleston	Brdgnd	29	N9
Lamanva	Cnwll	3	K7
Lamarsh	Essex	52	E4
Lamas	Norfk	77	J7
Lambden	Border	118	D2
Lamberhurst	Kent	25	Q3
Lamberhurst Down	Kent	25	Q3
Lamberton	Border	129	P8
Lambeth	Gt Lon	36	H5
Lambeth Crematorium	Gt Lon	36	G6
Lambfair Green	Suffk	63	M10
Lambley	Notts	85	K11
Lambley	Nthumb	111	N9
Lambourn	W Berk	34	B9
Lambourne End	Essex	37	L2
Lambourn Woodlands	W Berk	34	B9
Lamb Roe	Lancs	89	L3
Lambs Green	W Susx	24	F3
Lambston	Pembks	40	H7
Lamellion	Cnwll	5	M9
Lamerton	Devon	5	Q5
Lamesley	Gatesd	113	L9
Lamington	S Lans	116	D4
Lamlash	N Ayrs	121	K5
Lamonby	Cumb	101	M3
Lamorick	Cnwll	4	G9
Lamorna	Cnwll	2	C9
Lamorran	Cnwll	3	M5
Lampen	Cnwll	5	K8
Lampeter	Cerdgn	43	L5
Lampeter Velfrey	Pembks	41	N8
Lamphey	Pembks	41	K10
Lamplugh	Cumb	100	E6
Lamport	Nhants	60	G6
Lamyatt	Somset	20	C7
Lana	Devon	5	M7
Lana	Devon	16	E10
Lanark	S Lans	116	B2
Lancaster	Lancs	95	K8
Lancaster & Morecambe Crematorium	Lancs	95	K8
Lancaster Services (Forton)	Lancs	95	L10
Lancaut	Gloucs	31	P5
Lanchester	Dur	113	J11
Lancing	W Susx	24	E10
L'Ancresse	Guern	10	c1
Landbeach	Cambs	62	G7
Landcross	Devon	16	H7
Landerberry	Abers	151	J7
Landford	Wilts	21	Q11
Land-hallow	Highld	167	L10
Landican Crematorium	Wirral	81	K7
Landimore	Swans	28	E6
Landkey	Devon	17	K5
Landore	Swans	29	J5
Landrake	Cnwll	5	P9
Landscove	Devon	7	K5
Land's End	Cnwll	2	A8
Land's End	Cnwll	2	A8
Land's End Airport	Cnwll	2	A8
Landshipping	Pembks	41	K8
Landue	Cnwll	5	P6
Landulph	Cnwll	6	C6
Landwade	Suffk	63	K7
Lane	Cnwll	4	C9
Laneast	Cnwll	5	L5
Lane Bottom	Lancs	89	P3
Lane End	Bucks	35	M6
Lane End	Cnwll	4	G8
Lane End	Hants	22	G9
Lane End	Kent	37	N6
Lane End	Lancs	96	C11
Lane End	Warrtn	82	E6
Lane End	Wilts	20	F5
Lane Ends	Derbys	71	N8
Lane Ends	Lancs	89	M4
Lane Ends	N York	90	B2
Lane Green	Staffs	58	C4
Laneham	Notts	85	P5
Lanehead	Dur	102	F2
Lane Head	Dur	103	M8
Lanehead	Nthumb	111	Q3
Lane Head	Wigan	82	D5
Lane Head	Wsall	58	E4
Lane Heads	Lancs	88	E3
Laneshaw Bridge	Lancs	89	Q2
Lane Side	Lancs	89	M6
Langaford	Devon	5	Q2
Langaller	Somset	19	J9
Langar	Notts	73	J4
Langbank	Rens	125	K3
Langbar	N York	96	G10
Langbaurgh	N York	104	G8
Langcliffe	N York	96	B8
Langdale End	N York	99	J3
Langdon	Cnwll	5	N4
Langdon Beck	Dur	102	G4
Langdown	Hants	14	D5
Langdyke	Fife	135	J7
Langenhoe	Essex	52	H8
Langford	C Beds	50	E2
Langford	Devon	9	P4
Langford	Essex	52	D10
Langford	N Som	19	N2
Langford	Notts	85	P9
Langford	Oxon	33	P4
Langford Budville	Somset	18	F10
Langham	Dorset	20	E8
Langham	Essex	52	H5
Langham	Norfk	76	E3
Langham	Rutlnd	73	L8
Langham	Suffk	64	D8
Langho	Lancs	89	L4
Langholm	D & G	110	G3
Langland	Swans	28	H7
Langlee	Border	117	Q3
Langley	Ches E	83	K10
Langley	Derbys	84	F11
Langley	Gloucs	47	K9
Langley	Hants	14	D6
Langley	Herts	50	F6
Langley	Kent	38	D11
Langley	Nthumb	112	M9
Langley	Oxon	47	Q11
Langley	Rochdl	89	P9
Langley	Slough	36	B5
Langley	Somset	18	E9
Langley	W Susx	23	M9
Langley	Warwks	47	N2
Langley Burrell	Wilts	32	H9
Langley Castle	Nthumb	112	B8
Langley Common	Derbys	71	P7
Langley Green	Derbys	71	P7
Langley Green	Essex	52	E7
Langley Green	Warwks	47	N2
Langley Lower Green	Essex	51	K4
Langley Marsh	Somset	18	E9
Langley Mill	Derbys	84	F11
Langley Moor	Dur	103	Q2
Langley Park	Dur	113	K11
Langley Street	Norfk	77	M11
Langley Upper Green	Essex	51	K4
Langney	E Susx	25	P10
Langold	Notts	85	J3
Langore	Cnwll	5	M4
Langport	Somset	19	M9
Langrick	Lincs	87	J11
Langridge	BaNES	32	D11
Langridgeford	Devon	17	K7
Langrigg	Cumb	110	C11
Langrish	Hants	23	K10
Langsett	Barns	90	G10
Langside	P & K	133	N5
Langstone	Hants	15	K6
Langstone	Newpt	31	L7
Langthorne	N York	97	L3
Langthorpe	N York	97	N7
Langthwaite	N York	103	K9
Langtoft	E R Yk	99	L7

Langtoft Lincs......74 B8
Langton Dur......103 N7
Langton Lincs......86 H7
Langton Lincs......87 L6
Langton N York......98 F7
Langton by Wragby
  Lincs......86 F5
Langton Green Kent......25 M3
Langton Green Suffk......64 G7
Langton Herring Dorset......11 N8
Langton Long
  Blandford Dorset......12 F3
Langton Matravers
  Dorset......12 H9
Langtree Devon......16 H8
Langtree Week Devon......16 H8
Langwathby Cumb......101 Q4
Langwell House Highld......163 Q2
Langwith Derbys......84 H7
Langwith Junction
  Derbys......84 H7
Langworth Lincs......86 E5
Lanhydrock House &
  Gardens Cnwll......4 H9
Lanivet Cnwll......4 G9
Lanjeth Cnwll......3 P3
Lank Cnwll......4 H6
Lanlivery Cnwll......4 H10
Lanner Cnwll......3 J6
Lanoy Cnwll......5 M6
Lanreath Cnwll......5 K10
Lansallos Cnwll......5 K11
Lanteglos Cnwll......4 H5
Lanteglos Highway
  Cnwll......5 J11
Lanton Border......118 B6
Lanton Nthumb......118 H4
La Passee Guern......10 b1
Lapford Devon......8 H3
Laphroaig Ag & B......122 E10
Lapley Staffs......58 C2
La Pulente Jersey......11 a2
Lapworth Warwks......59 J10
Larachbeg Highld......138 B8
Larbert Falk......133 P11
Larbreck Lancs......88 E2
Largie Abers......158 F11
Largiemore Ag & B......131 J4
Largoward Fife......135 M6
Largs N Ayrs......124 C6
Largybeg N Ayrs......121 K7
Largymore N Ayrs......121 K7
Larkbeare Devon......9 Q5
Larkfield Inver......124 G2
Larkfield Kent......38 B10
Larkhall S Lans......126 D7
Larkhill Wilts......21 M6
Larling Norfk......64 D4
La Rocque Jersey......11 c2
La Rousaillerie Guern......10 b1
Lartington Dur......103 K7
Lasborough Gloucs......32 F6
Lasham Hants......23 J6
Lashbrook Devon......8 B3
Lashbrook Devon......16 C10
Lashenden Kent......26 D3
Lask Edge Staffs......70 G3
Lasswade Mdloth......127 Q4
Lastingham N York......98 E2
Latcham Somset......19 M5
Latchford Herts......51 J6
Latchford Oxon......35 J4
Latchingdon Essex......52 E11
Latchley Cnwll......5 Q7
Lately Common Warrtn......82 E5
Lathbury M Keyn......49 N6
Latheron Highld......167 M10
Latheronwheel Highld......167 L10
Lathones Fife......135 M6
Latimer Bucks......50 B11
Latteridge S Glos......32 C8
Lattiford Somset......20 C9
Latton Wilts......33 L5
Lauder Border......128 E10
Laugharne Carmth......28 B2
Laughterton Lincs......85 P5
Laughton E Susx......25 L8
Laughton Leics......60 E3
Laughton Lincs......74 A4
Laughton Lincs......92 D11
Laughton-en-le-
  Morthen Rothm......84 H3
Launcells Cnwll......16 C10
Launcells Cross Cnwll......16 D10
Launceston Cnwll......5 N5
Launton Oxon......48 H10
Laurencekirk Abers......143 N3
Laurieston D & G......108 G2
Laurieston Falk......126 G2
Lavendon M Keyn......49 P4
Lavenham Suffk......52 F2
Lavernock V Glam......30 G11
Laversdale Cumb......111 J8
Laverstock Wilts......21 N8
Laverstoke Hants......22 E5
Laverton Gloucs......47 L7
Laverton N York......97 K6
Laverton Somset......20 E4
La Villette Guern......10 b2
Lavister Wrexhm......69 L3
Law S Lans......126 E7
Lawers P & K......140 G10
Lawford Essex......53 J5
Lawford Somset......18 F7
Law Hill S Lans......126 E7
Lawhitton Cnwll......5 P5
Lawkland N York......95 N7
Lawkland Green N York......96 A7
Lawley Wrekin......57 M3
Lawnhead Staffs......70 E9
Lawns Wood
  Crematorium Leeds......90 H4
Lawrenny Pembks......41 K9
Lawshall Suffk......64 B11
Lawshall Green Suffk......64 B11
Lawton Herefs......45 N3
Laxay W Isls......168 i5
Laxdale W Isls......168 j4
Laxey IoM......80 f5
Laxfield Suffk......65 K7
Laxford Bridge Highld......164 F7
Laxo Shet......169 r7
Laxton E R Yk......92 C5
Laxton Nhants......73 P11
Laxton Notts......85 M7
Laycock C Brad......90 C2
Layer Breton Essex......52 F8
Layer-de-la-Haye Essex......52 G7
Layer Marney Essex......52 F8
Layham Suffk......52 H3

Layland's Green W Berk......34 C11
Laymore Dorset......10 H4
Layter's Green Bucks......35 Q6
Laytham E R Yk......92 B3
Laythes Cumb......110 D9
Lazenby R & Cl......104 G7
Lazonby Cumb......101 P3
Lea Derbys......84 D9
Lea Herefs......46 C10
Lea Lincs......85 P3
Lea Shrops......56 F7
Lea Shrops......56 G3
Lea Wilts......33 J7
Leachkin Highld......156 A9
Leadburn Border......127 N6
Leadenham Lincs......86 B10
Leaden Roding Essex......51 N8
Leadgate Dur......112 H10
Leadgate Nthumb......112 H9
Leadhills S Lans......116 B7
Leadingcross Green Kent......38 E11
Leadmill Derbys......84 B4
Leafield Oxon......48 B11
Leagrave Luton......50 C6
Leahead Ches W......70 B2
Lea Heath Staffs......71 J9
Leake N York......97 P2
Leake Common Side
  Lincs......87 L10
Lealholm N York......105 L9
Lealholm Side N York......105 L9
Lealt Highld......153 J5
Leam Derbys......84 B5
Lea Marston Warwks......59 K6
Leamington Hastings
  Warwks......59 P11
Leamington Spa Warwks......59 M11
Leamside Dur......113 M11
Leap Cross E Susx......25 N8
Leasgill Cumb......95 K4
Leasingham Lincs......86 E11
Leasingthorne Dur......103 Q4
Leatherhead Surrey......36 E9
Leathley N York......97 K11
Leaton Shrops......69 N11
Leaton Wrekin......57 L2
Lea Town Lancs......88 F4
Leaveland Kent......38 H11
Leavenheath Suffk......52 G4
Leavening N York......98 F3
Leaves Green Gt Lon......37 K8
Lea Yeat Cumb......95 R3
Lebberston N York......99 M4
Le Bigard Guern......10 b2
Le Bourg Guern......10 b2
Le Bourg Jersey......11 c2
Lechlade on Thames
  Gloucs......33 P5
Lecht Gruinart Ag & B......122 C6
Leck Lancs......95 N5
Leckbuie P & K......140 H9
Leckford Hants......22 C7
Leckhampstead Bucks......49 K7
Leckhampstead W Berk......34 D9
Leckhampstead Thicket
  W Berk......34 D9
Leckhampton Gloucs......46 H11
Leckmelm Highld......161 K9
Leckwith V Glam......30 G10
Leconfield E R Yk......92 H2
Ledaig Ag & B......138 G10
Ledburn Bucks......49 P10
Ledbury Herefs......46 D7
Leddington Gloucs......46 C8
Ledgemoor Herefs......45 N4
Ledicot Herefs......45 N2
Ledmore Junction
  Highld......161 L4
Ledsham Ches W......81 M10
Ledsham Leeds......91 M5
Ledston Leeds......91 L5
Ledstone Devon......7 J9
Ledston Luck Leeds......91 L4
Ledwell Oxon......48 D9
Lee Devon......16 H2
Lee Gt Lon......37 J5
Lee Hants......22 C11
Lee Shrops......69 M8
Leebotwood Shrops......56 H5
Lee Brockhurst Shrops......69 P9
Leece Cumb......94 E7
Lee Chapel Essex......37 Q3
Lee Clump Bucks......35 P4
Lee Common Bucks......35 P4
Leeds Kent......38 D11
Leeds Leeds......90 H4
Leeds Bradford Airport
  Leeds......90 G2
Leeds Castle Kent......38 D11
Leedstown Cnwll......2 G7
Lee Green Ches E......70 B3
Leek Staffs......70 H3
Leek Wootton Warwks......59 L11
Lee Mill Devon......6 F7
Leeming C Brad......90 C4
Leeming N York......97 L3
Leeming Bar N York......97 L3
Lee Moor Devon......6 F6
Lee-on-the-Solent Hants......14 G6
Lees C Brad......90 C3
Lees Derbys......71 P7
Lees Oldham......83 L4
Lees Green Derbys......71 P7
Leesthorpe Leics......73 K8
Lee Street Surrey......24 G2
Leeswood Flints......69 J2
Leetown P & K......134 G3
Leftwich Ches W......82 E10
Legar Powys......45 J11
Legbourne Lincs......87 L4
Legburthwaite Cumb......101 K7
Legerwood Border......118 A2
Legoland W & M......35 P10
Le Gron Guern......10 b2
Legsby Lincs......86 F3
Le Haguais Jersey......11 c2
Le Hocq Jersey......11 c2
Leicester C Leic......72 F10
Leicester Forest East
  Leics......72 E10
Leicester Forest East
  Services Leics......72 E10
Leigh Devon......17 N9
Leigh Dorset......11 N3
Leigh Gloucs......46 G9
Leigh Kent......37 M11
Leigh Shrops......56 F4
Leigh Surrey......36 F11
Leigh Wigan......82 E5
Leigh Wilts......33 L6

Leigh Worcs......46 E4
Leigh Beck Essex......38 D5
Leigh Delamere Wilts......32 G9
Leigh Delamere
  Services Wilts......32 G9
Leigh Green Kent......26 F5
Leigh Knoweglass S Lans......125 Q7
Leighland Chapel
  Somset......18 D7
Leigh-on-Sea Sthend......38 D4
Leigh Park Dorset......12 H5
Leigh Sinton Worcs......46 E4
Leighswood Wsall......58 G4
Leighterton Gloucs......32 F6
Leighton N York......97 J5
Leighton Powys......56 C3
Leighton Shrops......57 L3
Leighton Somset......20 D6
Leighton Bromswold
  Cambs......61 P5
Leighton Buzzard C Beds......49 P9
Leigh upon Mendip
  Somset......20 C5
Leigh Woods N Som......31 Q10
Leinthall Earls Herefs......56 G11
Leinthall Starkes Herefs......56 G11
Leintwardine Herefs......56 G10
Leire Leics......60 B3
Leiston Suffk......65 N9
Leith C Edin......127 P2
Leitholm Border......118 G3
Lelant Cnwll......2 E7
Lelley E R Yk......93 M4
Lem Hill Worcs......57 N9
Lempitlaw Border......118 E4
Lemreway W Isls......168 i6
Lemsford Herts......50 F8
Lenchwick Worcs......47 K5
Lendalfoot S Ayrs......114 C9
Lendrick Stirlg......132 H6
Lendrum Terrace Abers......159 R9
Lenham Kent......38 E11
Lenham Heath Kent......26 F2
Lenie Highld......147 N2
Lennel Border......118 G2
Lennox Plunton D & G......108 D10
Lennoxtown E Duns......125 Q2
Lent Bucks......35 P8
Lenton C Nott......72 F3
Lenton Lincs......73 Q4
Lenwade Norfk......76 F8
Lenzie E Duns......126 B3
Leochel-Cushnie Abers......150 F4
Leomansley Staffs......58 H3
Leominster Herefs......45 P3
Leonard Stanley Gloucs......32 F4
Leoville Jersey......11 a1
Lepe Hants......14 D7
Lephin Highld......152 B8
Leppington N York......98 F8
Lepton Kirk......90 G7
Lerags Ag & B......130 H2
L'Eree Guern......10 a2
Lerryn Cnwll......5 J10
Lerwick Shet......169 r9
Les Arquets Guern......10 b2
Lesbury Nthumb......119 P8
Les Hubits Guern......10 c2
Leslie Abers......150 F3
Leslie Fife......134 H7
Les Lohiers Guern......10 b2
Lesmahagow S Lans......126 E10
Les Murchez Guern......10 b2
Lesnewth Cnwll......5 J3
Les Nicolles Guern......10 b2
Les Quartiers Guern......10 c1
Les Quennevais Jersey......11 a2
Les Sages Guern......10 b2
Lessingham Norfk......77 M6
Lessonhall Cumb......110 D10
Lestowder Cnwll......3 K9
Leswalt D & G......106 D5
L'Etacq Jersey......11 a1
Letchmore Heath Herts......50 E11
Letchworth Garden City
  Herts......50 F4
Letcombe Bassett Oxon......34 C8
Letcombe Regis Oxon......34 C7
Letham Angus......143 J8
Letham Border......118 C9
Letham Falk......133 P10
Letham Fife......135 J5
Letham Grange Angus......143 L8
Lethendy P & K......142 A9
Lethenty Abers......150 F3
Lethenty Abers......159 K9
Letheringham Suffk......65 K10
Letheringsett Norfk......76 F4
Lettaford Devon......8 H8
Letterewe Highld......154 C3
Letterfearn Highld......145 Q3
Letterfinlay Lodge
  Hotel Highld......146 H9
Lettermorar Highld......145 M10
Letters Highld......161 K9
Lettershaw S Lans......116 B6
Letterston Pembks......40 H5
Lettoch Highld......149 J4
Lettoch Highld......157 L11
Letton Herefs......45 L5
Letton Herefs......56 F10
Lett's Green Kent......37 L9
Letty Green Herts......50 G8
Letwell Rothm......85 J3
Leuchars Fife......135 M3
Leumrabhagh W Isls......168 i6
Leurbost W Isls......168 i5
Levalsa Meor Cnwll......3 Q4
Level's Green Essex......51 L6
Leven E R Yk......99 N11
Leven Fife......135 K7
Levens Cumb......95 K3
Levens Green Herts......51 J6
Levenshulme Manch......83 J6
Levenwick Shet......169 r11
Leverburgh W Isls......168 f9
Leverington Cambs......74 H8
Leverstock Green Herts......50 C9
Leverton Lincs......87 M11
Le Villocq Guern......10 b1
Levington Suffk......53 M4
Levisham N York......98 G2
Lewannick Cnwll......5 M5
Lewdown Devon......5 P4
Lewes E Susx......25 K8
Leweston Pembks......40 H6
Lewisham Gt Lon......37 J6

Lewisham Crematorium
  Gt Lon......37 J6
Lewiston Highld......147 N2
Lewistown Brdgnd......29 P7
Lewis Wych Herefs......45 L3
Lewknor Oxon......35 K5
Leworthy Devon......16 E11
Leworthy Devon......17 M4
Lewson Street Kent......38 G9
Lewth Lancs......88 F3
Lewtrenchard Devon......5 P4
Lexden Essex......52 G6
Lexworthy Somset......19 J7
Ley Cnwll......5 K8
Leybourne Kent......37 Q9
Leyburn N York......96 H2
Leycett Staffs......70 D5
Leygreen Herts......50 E6
Ley Hill Bucks......35 Q4
Leyland Lancs......88 G6
Leyland Green St Hel......82 C4
Leylodge Abers......151 K5
Leys Abers......159 P7
Leys P & K......142 D10
Leysdown-on-Sea Kent......38 H7
Leysmill Angus......143 L8
Leys of Cossans Angus......142 F8
Leysters Herefs......45 R2
Leyton Gt Lon......37 J3
Leytonstone Gt Lon......37 J3
Lezant Cnwll......5 N6
Lezerea Cnwll......2 H7
Lhanbryde Moray......157 P5
Libanus Powys......44 D9
Libberton S Lans......116 D2
Liberton C Edin......127 P4
Lichfield Staffs......58 H3
Lickey Worcs......58 E9
Lickey End Worcs......58 E10
Lickey Rock Worcs......58 E10
Lickfold W Susx......23 P9
Liddaton Green Devon......8 C8
Liddesdale Highld......138 D6
Liddington Swindn......33 P8
Lidgate Derbys......84 D5
Lidgate Suffk......63 M9
Lidget Donc......91 R10
Lidgett Notts......85 K7
Lidham Hill E Susx......26 D8
Lidlington C Beds......49 Q7
Lidsing Kent......38 C9
Liff Angus......142 E11
Lifford Birm......58 G8
Lifton Devon......5 P4
Liftondown Devon......5 P4
Lighthorne Warwks......48 B3
Lighthorne Heath
  Warwks......48 C3
Lightwater Surrey......23 P2
Lightwood C Stke......70 G6
Lightwood Green Ches E......70 A6
Lightwood Green
  Wrexhm......69 L6
Lilbourne Nhants......60 C5
Lilburn Tower Nthumb......119 K6
Lilleshall Wrekin......70 C11
Lilley Herts......50 D5
Lilley W Berk......34 D9
Lilliesleaf Border......117 Q5
Lillingstone Dayrell
  Bucks......49 K7
Lillingstone Lovell Bucks......49 K6
Lillington Dorset......11 N2
Lilliput Poole......12 H7
Lilstock Somset......18 G5
Lilyhurst Shrops......57 N2
Limbrick Lancs......89 J7
Limbury Luton......50 C6
Limebrook Herefs......56 F11
Limefield Bury......89 N8
Limekilnburn S Lans......126 C7
Limekilns Fife......134 D11
Limerigg Falk......126 F3
Limerstone IoW......14 D10
Limestone Brae Nthumb......111 Q11
Lime Street Worcs......46 F8
Limington Somset......19 P10
Limmerhaugh E Ayrs......115 M2
Limpenhoe Norfk......77 M11
Limpley Stoke Wilts......20 E2
Limpsfield Surrey......37 K10
Limpsfield Chart Surrey......37 K10
Linby Notts......84 H10
Linchmere W Susx......23 N8
Lincluden D & G......109 L5
Lincoln Lincs......86 C6
Lincoln Crematorium
  Lincs......86 C6
Lincomb Worcs......57 Q11
Lincombe Devon......7 J10
Lincombe Devon......16 H2
Lindale Cumb......95 J4
Lindal in Furness Cumb......94 E5
Lindfield W Susx......24 H5
Lindford Hants......23 M7
Lindley Kirk......90 E7
Lindley N York......97 K11
Lindow End Ches E......82 H9
Lindridge Worcs......57 M11
Lindsell Essex......51 P5
Lindsey Suffk......52 G2
Lindsey Tye Suffk......52 G2
Liney Somset......19 L7
Linford Hants......13 L3
Linford Thurr......37 Q5
Lingbob C Brad......90 D3
Lingdale R & Cl......105 J7
Lingen Herefs......56 F11
Lingfield Surrey......25 J2
Lingwood Norfk......77 M10
Linicro Highld......152 F4
Linkend Worcs......46 F8
Linkenholt Hants......22 C3
Linkhill Kent......26 D6
Linkinhorne Cnwll......5 N7
Linktown Fife......134 H9
Linkwood Moray......157 N5
Linley Shrops......56 F6
Linley Green Herefs......46 C4
Linleygreen Shrops......57 M5
Linlithgow W Loth......126 H2
Linshiels Nthumb......118 G9
Linsidemore Highld......162 C7
Linslade C Beds......49 P9
Linstead Parva Suffk......65 L6
Linstock Cumb......110 H9
Linthurst Worcs......58 E10
Linthwaite Kirk......90 E8
Lintlaw Border......129 L8
Lintmill Moray......158 D4

Linton Border......118 E5
Linton Cambs......63 J11
Linton Derbys......71 P11
Linton Herefs......46 C9
Linton Kent......38 C11
Linton Leeds......97 N11
Linton N York......96 E8
Linton Nthumb......113 L2
Linton Heath Derbys......71 P11
Linton Hill Herefs......46 C10
Linton-on-Ouse N York......97 Q3
Linwood Hants......13 L3
Linwood Lincs......86 F3
Linwood Rens......125 L5
Lionacleit W Isls......168 c13
Lional W Isls......168 k1
Lions Green E Susx......25 N7
Liphook Hants......23 M8
Lipley Shrops......70 C8
Liscard Wirral......81 K6
Liscombe Somset......18 A8
Liskeard Cnwll......5 M9
Lismore Ag & B......138 G9
Liss Hants......23 L9
Lissett E R Yk......99 N9
Liss Forest Hants......23 L9
Lissington Lincs......86 F4
Liston Essex......52 E3
Lisvane Cardif......30 G8
Liswerry Newpt......31 K7
Litcham Norfk......76 B8
Litchard Brdgnd......29 P8
Litchborough Nhants......48 H4
Litchfield Hants......22 E4
Litherland Sefton......81 L5
Litlington Cambs......50 H2
Litlington E Susx......25 M10
Little Abington Cambs......62 H11
Little Addington Nhants......61 L6
Little Airies D & G......107 M8
Little Almshoe Herts......50 F5
Little Alne Warwks......47 M2
Little Altcar Sefton......88 C9
Little Amwell Herts......51 J8
Little Asby Cumb......102 C9
Little Aston Staffs......58 G5
Little Atherfield IoW......14 E11
Little Ayton N York......104 G8
Little Baddow Essex......52 C10
Little Badminton S Glos......32 F8
Little Bampton Cumb......110 E9
Little Bardfield Essex......51 Q4
Little Barford Bed......61 Q9
Little Barningham Norfk......76 G5
Little Barrington Gloucs......33 P2
Little Barrow Ches W......81 P11
Little Barugh N York......98 F5
Little Bavington Nthumb......112 H4
Little Bealings Suffk......53 M2
Littlebeck N York......105 N10
Little Bedwyn Wilts......33 Q11
Little Bentley Essex......53 K6
Little Berkhamsted
  Herts......50 G9
Little Billing Nhants......60 H8
Little Billington C Beds......49 P10
Little Birch Herefs......45 Q8
Little Bispham Bpool......88 C2
Little Blakenham Suffk......53 K2
Little Blencow Cumb......101 N4
Little Bloxwich Wsall......58 F4
Little Bognor W Susx......24 B6
Little Bolehill Derbys......71 P4
Little Bollington Ches E......82 F7
Little Bookham Surrey......36 D10
Littleborough Devon......9 K4
Littleborough Notts......85 P4
Littleborough Rochdl......89 Q7
Littlebourne Kent......39 M10
Little Bourton Oxon......48 E6
Little Bowden Leics......60 F3
Little Bradley Suffk......63 L10
Little Brampton Herefs......45 L2
Little Brampton Shrops......56 F8
Little Braxted Essex......52 D9
Little Brechin Angus......143 K5
Littlebredy Dorset......11 M7
Little Brickhill M Keyn......49 P8
Little Bridgeford Staffs......70 F9
Little Brington Nhants......60 E8
Little Bromley Essex......53 J6
Little Broughton Cumb......100 E4
Little Budworth Ches W......82 C11
Littleburn Highld......156 A7
Little Burstead Essex......37 Q2
Littlebury Essex......51 M3
Littlebury Green Essex......51 L3
Little Bytham Lincs......73 Q7
Little Canfield Essex......51 N6
Little Carlton Lincs......87 L3
Little Carlton Notts......85 N9
Little Casterton Rutlnd......73 Q9
Little Catwick E R Yk......93 K2
Little Catworth Cambs......61 P6
Little Cawthorpe Lincs......87 L4
Little Chalfont Bucks......35 Q5
Little Chart Kent......26 H2
Little Chesterford Essex......51 M2
Little Cheveney Kent......26 B3
Little Cheverell Wilts......21 J4
Little Chishill Cambs......51 K3
Little Clacton Essex......53 L8
Little Clanfield Oxon......33 Q4
Little Clifton Cumb......100 E5
Little Coates NE Lin......93 M9
Little Comberton Worcs......47 J6
Little Common E Susx......26 B10
Little Comp Kent......37 P9
Little Compton Warwks......47 Q8
Little Corby Cumb......111 J9
Little Cornard Suffk......52 F4
Littlecott Wilts......21 M4
Little Cowarne Herefs......46 B4
Little Coxwell Oxon......33 Q6
Little Crakehall N York......97 K2
Little Cransley Nhants......60 H5
Little Cressingham Norfk......76 B11
Little Crosby Sefton......81 L4
Little Crosthwaite Cumb......100 H5
Little Cubley Derbys......71 M7
Little Dalby Leics......73 K8
Littledean Gloucs......32 C3
Little Dewchurch Herefs......45 Q8
Little Ditton Cambs......63 L9
Little Doward Herefs......45 Q11
Littledown Hants......22 B3
Little Dunham Norfk......76 B9
Little Dunkeld P & K......141 P9

Little Dunmow Essex....51 Q6
Little Durnford Wilts....21 M8
Little Easton Essex....51 P6
Little Eaton Derbys....72 B2
Little Ellingham Norfk....64 E2
Little Elm Somset....20 D5
Little Everdon Nhants....60 C9
Little Eversden Cambs....62 E10
Little Faringdon Oxon....33 P4
Little Fencote N York....97 L2
Little Fenton N York....91 N3
Little Fransham Norfk....76 C9
Little Gaddesden Herts....35 Q2
Little Garway Herefs....45 N10
Little Gidding Cambs....61 P4
Little Glemham Suffk....65 L10
Little Gorsley Herefs....46 C10
Little Gransden Cambs....62 C9
Little Green Notts....73 J2
Little Green Somset....20 D5
Little Grimsby Lincs....87 K2
Little Gringley Notts....85 M4
Little Habton N York....98 E5
Little Hadham Herts....51 K6
Little Hale Lincs....74 B2
Little Hallam Derbys....72 D2
Little Hallingbury Essex....51 M7
Littleham Devon....9 P8
Littleham Devon....16 G7
Little Hampden Bucks....35 N4
Littlehampton W Susx....24 B10
Little Hanford Dorset....12 D2
Little Harrowden Nhants....61 J6
Little Haseley Oxon....34 H4
Little Hatfield E R Yk....93 L2
Little Hautbois Norfk....77 K7
Little Haven Pembks....40 G8
Littlehaven W Susx....24 E4
Little Hay Staffs....58 H4
Little Hayfield Derbys....83 M7
Little Haywood Staffs....71 J10
Little Heath Staffs....70 F11
Little Heath W Berk....35 J10
Littlehempston Devon....7 L6
Little Hereford Herefs....57 K11
Little Horkesley Essex....52 G5
Little Hormead Herts....51 K5
Little Horsted E Susx....25 L7
Little Horton C Brad....90 F4
Little Horton Wilts....21 K2
Little Horwood Bucks....49 L8
Little Houghton Barns....91 L9
Little Houghton Nhants....60 H9
Littlehoughton Nthumb....119 P7
Little Hucklow Derbys....83 Q9
Little Hulton Salfd....82 H4
Little Hungerford W Berk....34 F10
Little Hutton N York....97 Q5
Little Irchester Nhants....61 K7
Little Kelk E R Yk....99 M9
Little Keyford Somset....20 E5
Little Kimble Bucks....35 M3
Little Kineton Warwks....48 B4
Little Kingshill Bucks....35 N5
Little Knox D & G....108 H8
Little Langdale Cumb....101 K10
Little Langford Wilts....21 K7
Little Laver Essex....51 M9
Little Leigh Ches W....82 D9
Little Leighs Essex....52 B8
Little Lever Bolton....89 M9
Little Linford M Keyn....49 M6
Little Load Somset....19 N10
Little London Bucks....34 H2
Little London Cambs....74 H11
Little London E Susx....25 N6
Little London Essex....51 L5
Little London Essex....51 Q3
Little London Gloucs....46 D11
Little London Hants....22 C5
Little London Hants....22 H3
Little London Leeds....90 G3
Little London Lincs....74 D6
Little London Lincs....74 H6
Little London Lincs....87 K6
Little London Norfk....75 L6
Little London Powys....55 N7
Little Longstone Derbys....83 Q10
Little Madeley Staffs....70 D5
Little Malvern Worcs....46 E6
Little Mancot Flints....81 L11
Little Maplestead Essex....52 D5
Little Marcle Herefs....46 C7
Little Marland Devon....17 J9
Little Marlow Bucks....35 N7
Little Massingham Norfk....75 Q6
Little Melton Norfk....76 H10
Littlemill Abers....149 Q8
Littlemill Highld....156 G7
Little Mill Mons....31 K4
Little Milton Oxon....34 H4
Little Missenden Bucks....35 P5
Little Mongeham Kent....39 P11
Littlemoor Derbys....84 E8
Littlemoor Somset....19 K8
Littlemore Oxon....34 F4
Little Musgrave Cumb....102 E8
Little Ness Shrops....69 M11
Little Neston Ches W....81 K9
Little Newcastle Pembks....41 J5
Little Newsham Dur....103 M7
Little Norton Somset....19 N11
Little Oakley Essex....53 M6
Little Oakley Nhants....61 J3
Little Odell Bed....61 L9
Little Offley Herts....50 D5
Little Ormside Cumb....102 D7
Little Orton Cumb....110 G9
Little Ouse Cambs....63 K3
Little Ouseburn N York....97 P8
Littleover C Derb....72 A4
Little Oxendon Nhants....60 F4
Little Packington Warwks....59 K8
Little Pattenden Kent....26 B2
Little Paxton Cambs....61 Q8
Little Petherick Cnwll....4 E7
Little Plumpton Lancs....88 D4
Little Plumstead Norfk....77 L9
Little Ponton Lincs....73 N4
Littleport Cambs....63 J3
Littleport Bridge Cambs....63 J3
Little Posbrook Hants....14 F6
Little Potheridge Devon....17 J9
Little Preston Leeds....91 K4
Little Preston Nhants....48 G4
Littler Ches W....82 D11
Little Raveley Cambs....62 C5
Little Reedness E R Yk....92 D6
Little Ribston N York....97 N10
Little Rissington Gloucs....47 N11
Little Rollright Oxon....47 Q8
Little Rowsley Derbys....84 C7
Little Ryburgh Norfk....76 D6
Little Ryle Nthumb....119 K8
Little Ryton Shrops....56 H4
Little Salkeld Cumb....101 Q3
Little Sampford Essex....51 Q4
Little Sandhurst Br For....23 M2
Little Saredon Staffs....58 D3
Little Saughall Ches W....81 M11
Little Saxham Suffk....63 P8
Little Scatwell Highld....155 L6
Little Shelford Cambs....62 G10
Little Shrewley Warwks....59 K11
Little Silver Devon....9 M3
Little Singleton Lancs....88 D3
Little Skipwith N York....91 R3
Little Smeaton N York....91 N7
Little Snoring Norfk....76 D5
Little Sodbury S Glos....32 E8
Little Sodbury End S Glos....32 D8
Little Somborne Hants....22 C8
Little Somerford Wilts....33 J8
Little Soudley Shrops....70 C9
Little Stainforth N York....96 B2
Little Stainton Darltn....104 B6
Little Stanney Ches W....81 N10
Little Staughton Bed....61 P8
Little Steeping Lincs....87 M8
Littlestone-on-Sea Kent....27 J7
Little Stonham Suffk....64 G9
Little Stretton Leics....72 H10
Little Stretton Shrops....56 G6
Little Strickland Cumb....101 Q7
Little Stukeley Cambs....62 B5
Little Sugnall Staffs....70 E8
Little Sutton Ches W....81 M9
Little Sutton Shrops....57 J8
Little Swinburne Nthumb....112 D5
Little Sypland D & G....108 F10
Little Tew Oxon....48 C9
Little Tey Essex....52 E7
Little Thetford Cambs....62 H5
Little Thirkleby N York....97 Q5
Little Thornage Norfk....76 F4
Little Thornton Lancs....88 D2
Little Thorpe Dur....104 D2
Littlethorpe Leics....72 E11
Littlethorpe N York....97 M7
Little Thurlow Suffk....63 L10
Little Thurlow Green Suffk....63 L10
Little Thurrock Thurr....37 P5
Littleton Angus....142 E7
Littleton BaNES....19 Q2
Littleton Ches W....81 N11
Littleton D & G....108 D9
Littleton Dorset....12 E4
Littleton Hants....22 E8
Littleton Somset....19 N8
Littleton Surrey....23 Q5
Littleton Surrey....36 C7
Littleton Drew Wilts....32 F8
Littleton-on-Severn S Glos....31 Q7
Littleton Pannell Wilts....21 K4
Little Torrington Devon....16 H8
Little Totham Essex....52 E9
Little Town Cumb....100 H7
Littletown Dur....104 B2
Little Town Lancs....89 K3
Little Town Warrtn....82 D6
Little Twycross Leics....72 A9
Little Urswick Cumb....94 F6
Little Wakering Essex....38 F4
Little Walden Essex....51 M2
Little Waldingfield Suffk....52 F2
Little Walsingham Norfk....76 C4
Little Waltham Essex....52 B9
Little Warley Essex....37 P2
Little Washbourne Gloucs....47 J8
Little Weighton E R Yk....92 G4
Little Weldon Nhants....61 K3
Little Welnetham Suffk....64 B10
Little Welton Lincs....87 K3
Little Wenham Suffk....53 J4
Little Wenlock Wrekin....57 L3
Little Weston Somset....20 B9
Little Whitefield IoW....14 G9
Little Whittingham Green Suffk....65 K6
Little Whittington Nthumb....112 E7
Littlewick Green W & M....35 M9
Little Wilbraham Cambs....62 H9
Littlewindsor Dorset....11 J4
Little Witcombe Gloucs....46 H11
Little Witley Worcs....46 E2
Little Wittenham Oxon....34 G6
Little Wolford Warwks....47 Q7
Littlewood Staffs....58 E3
Little Woodcote Gt Lon....36 G8
Littleworth Bucks....49 N10
Littleworth Oxon....34 B5
Littleworth Staffs....58 F2
Littleworth Staffs....70 G10
Littleworth W Susx....24 E6
Littleworth Worcs....46 G4
Littleworth Worcs....47 J2
Littleworth Common Bucks....35 P7
Little Wratting Suffk....63 L11
Little Wymington Bed....61 L8
Little Wymondley Herts....50 F5
Little Wyrley Staffs....58 F3
Little Wytheford Shrops....69 Q11
Little Yeldham Essex....52 C4
Littley Green Essex....51 Q7
Litton Derbys....83 Q9
Litton N York....96 D6
Litton Somset....19 Q4
Litton Cheney Dorset....11 L6
Liurbost W Isls....168 I5
Liverpool Lpool....81 L6
Liversedge Kirk....90 F6
Liverton Devon....7 K9
Liverton R & Cl....105 K7
Liverton Mines R & Cl....105 K7
Liverton Street Kent....38 E11
Livingston W Loth....127 K4
Livingston Village W Loth....127 J4
Lixwm Flints....80 H10
Lizard Cnwll....3 J11
Llaingoch IoA....78 C8
Llaithddu Powys....55 P8
Llan Powys....55 K4
Llanaber Gwynd....67 L11
Llanaelhaearn Gwynd....66 F6
Llanafan Cerdgn....54 F10
Llanafan-Fawr Powys....44 D3
Llanafan-fechan Powys....44 D4
Llanallgo IoA....79 J7
Llanarmon Gwynd....66 G7
Llanarmon Dyffryn Ceiriog Wrexhm....68 G8
Llanarmon-yn-Ial Denbgs....68 G3
Llanarth Cerdgn....42 H3
Llanarth Mons....31 L2
Llanarthne Carmth....43 K11
Llanasa Flints....80 G8
Llanbabo IoA....78 F7
Llanbadarn Fawr Cerdgn....54 E8
Llanbadarn Fynydd Powys....55 P9
Llanbadarn-y-garreg Powys....44 G5
Llanbadoc Mons....31 L5
Llanbadrig IoA....78 F6
Llanbeder Newpt....31 L6
Llanbedr Gwynd....67 K9
Llanbedr Powys....44 G5
Llanbedr Powys....45 J10
Llanbedr-Dyffryn-Clwyd Denbgs....68 F3
Llanbedrgoch IoA....79 J8
Llanbedrog Gwynd....66 E8
Llanbedr-y-Cennin Conwy....79 P10
Llanberis Gwynd....67 K2
Llanbethery V Glam....30 D11
Llanbister Powys....55 Q10
Llanblethian V Glam....30 C10
Llanboidy Carmth....41 P6
Llanbradach Caerph....30 F6
Llanbrynmair Powys....55 K4
Llancadle V Glam....30 D11
Llancarfan V Glam....30 D10
Llancayo Mons....31 L4
Llancloudy Herefs....45 P10
Llandaff Cardif....30 G9
Llandanwg Gwynd....67 K9
Llandarcy Neath....29 K5
Llandawke Carmth....41 Q8
Llanddaniel Fab IoA....78 H10
Llanddarog Carmth....43 K11
Llanddeiniol Cerdgn....54 D10
Llanddeiniolen Gwynd....79 J11
Llandderfel Gwynd....68 C7
Llanddeusant Carmth....43 Q10
Llanddeusant IoA....78 E7
Llanddew Powys....44 E8
Llanddewi Swans....28 E7
Llanddewi Brefi Cerdgn....43 N3
Llanddewi'r Cwm Powys....44 E5
Llanddewi Rhydderch Mons....31 L2
Llanddewi Velfrey Pembks....41 M7
Llanddewi Ystradenni Powys....55 Q11
Llanddoget Conwy....67 Q2
Llanddona IoA....79 K9
Llanddowror Carmth....41 Q8
Llanddulas Conwy....80 C9
Llanddwywe Gwynd....67 K10
Llanddyfnan IoA....79 J9
Llandecwyn Gwynd....67 L7
Llandefaelog Powys....44 E8
Llandefaelog-Tre'r-Graig Powys....44 G9
Llandefalle Powys....44 G7
Llandegfan IoA....79 K10
Llandegla Denbgs....68 G4
Llandegley Powys....44 G2
Llandegveth Mons....31 K5
Llandegwning Gwynd....66 D9
Llandeilo Carmth....43 M10
Llandeilo Graban Powys....44 F6
Llandeilo'r Fan Powys....44 B8
Llandeloy Pembks....40 G5
Llandenny Mons....31 M4
Llandevaud Newpt....31 M6
Llandevenny Mons....31 M7
Llandinabo Herefs....45 Q9
Llandinam Powys....55 N7
Llandissilio Pembks....41 M6
Llandogo Mons....31 P4
Llandough V Glam....30 C10
Llandough V Glam....30 G10
Llandovery Carmth....43 Q8
Llandow V Glam....29 P10
Llandre Carmth....43 N6
Llandre Cerdgn....54 E7
Llandre Isaf Pembks....41 M5
Llandrillo Denbgs....68 D7
Llandrillo-yn-Rhos Conwy....79 Q8
Llandrindod Wells Powys....44 F2
Llandrinio Powys....69 J11
Llandudno Conwy....79 P8
Llandudno Junction Conwy....79 P9
Llandulas Powys....44 B6
Llandwrog Gwynd....66 H3
Llandybie Carmth....43 M11
Llandyfaelog Carmth....28 D2
Llandyfan Carmth....43 M11
Llandyfriog Cerdgn....42 F6
Llandyfrydog IoA....78 G7
Llandygai Gwynd....79 K10
Llandygwydd Cerdgn....41 P2
Llandynan Denbgs....68 G5
Llandyrnog Denbgs....80 G11
Llandyssil Powys....56 B5
Llandysul Cerdgn....42 H6
Llanedeyrn Cardif....30 H8
Llanedi Carmth....28 G3
Llaneglwys Powys....44 F7
Llanegryn Gwynd....54 E3
Llanegwad Carmth....43 K10
Llaneilian IoA....78 H6
Llanelian-yn-Rhôs Conwy....80 B9
Llanelidan Denbgs....68 F4
Llanelieu Powys....44 H8
Llanellen Mons....31 K2
Llanelli Carmth....28 F4
Llanelli Crematorium Carmth....28 F4
Llanelltyd Gwynd....67 N11
Llanelly Mons....30 H2
Llanelwedd Powys....44 E4
Llanenddwyn Gwynd....67 K10
Llanengan Gwynd....66 D9
Llanerch Gwynd....68 A11
Llanerch Powys....56 E6
Llanerchymedd IoA....78 G8
Llanerfyl Powys....55 N3
Llanfachraeth IoA....78 E8
Llanfachreth Gwynd....67 P10
Llanfaelog IoA....78 E10
Llanfaelrhys Gwynd....66 C9
Llanfaes Powys....44 E9
Llanfaes IoA....79 L9
Llanfaethlu IoA....78 E7
Llanfair Gwynd....67 K9
Llanfair Caereinion Powys....55 Q3
Llanfair Clydogau Cerdgn....43 M4
Llanfair Dyffryn Clwyd Denbgs....68 F3
Llanfairfechan Conwy....79 M10
Llanfair Kilgeddin Mons....31 L3
Llanfair-Nant-Gwyn Pembks....41 N3
Llanfair P G IoA....79 J10
Llanfair Talhaiarn Conwy....80 C10
Llanfair Waterdine Shrops....56 C9
Llanfairynghornwy IoA....78 E6
Llanfair-yn-Neubwll IoA....78 E10
Llanfallteg Carmth....41 N6
Llanfallteg West Carmth....41 N6
Llanfarian Cerdgn....54 D9
Llanfechain Powys....68 G10
Llanfechell IoA....78 F6
Llanferres Denbgs....68 G2
Llanfflewyn IoA....78 F7
Llanfigael IoA....78 E8
Llanfihangel-ar-arth Carmth....43 J7
Llanfihangel Glyn Myfyr Conwy....68 C5
Llanfihangel Nant Bran Powys....44 C8
Llanfihangel-nant-Melan Powys....44 H3
Llanfihangel Rhydithon Powys....56 B11
Llanfihangel Rogiet Mons....31 N7
Llanfihangel Tal-y-llyn Powys....44 G9
Llanfihangel-uwch-Gwili Carmth....43 J10
Llanfihangel-y-Creuddyn Cerdgn....54 F9
Llanfihangel-yng-Ngwynfa Powys....68 E11
Llanfihangel yn Nhowyn IoA....78 E9
Llanfihangel-y-pennant Gwynd....54 F3
Llanfihangel-y-pennant Gwynd....67 J6
Llanfihangel-y-traethau Gwynd....67 K8
Llanfilo Powys....44 G8
Llanfoist Mons....31 J2
Llanfor Gwynd....68 B7
Llanfrechfa Torfn....31 K6
Llanfrothen Gwynd....67 L6
Llanfrynach Powys....44 F9
Llanfwrog Denbgs....68 F3
Llanfwrog IoA....78 D8
Llanfyllin Powys....68 F11
Llanfynydd Carmth....43 L9
Llanfynydd Flints....69 J3
Llanfyrnach Pembks....41 P4
Llangadfan Powys....55 N2
Llangadog Carmth....43 P9
Llangadwaladr IoA....78 F11
Llangadwaladr Powys....68 G8
Llangaffo IoA....78 G11
Llangain Carmth....42 G11
Llangammarch Wells Powys....44 C5
Llangan V Glam....30 C9
Llangarron Herefs....45 Q10
Llangasty-Talyllyn Powys....44 G9
Llangathen Carmth....43 L10
Llangattock Powys....45 J11
Llangattock Lingoed Mons....45 M10
Llangattock-Vibon-Avel Mons....45 P11
Llangedwyn Powys....68 G10
Llangefni IoA....78 H9
Llangeinor Brdgnd....29 P7
Llangeitho Cerdgn....43 M3
Llangeler Carmth....42 G7
Llangelynin Gwynd....54 D3
Llangendeirne Carmth....28 E2
Llangennech Carmth....28 G4
Llangennith Swans....28 D6
Llangenny Powys....45 J11
Llangernyw Conwy....80 B11
Llangian Gwynd....66 D9
Llangiwg Neath....29 K3
Llangloffan Pembks....40 H4
Llanglydwen Carmth....41 N5
Llangoed IoA....79 L9
Llangoedmor Cerdgn....42 D5
Llangollen Denbgs....68 H6
Llangolman Pembks....41 M5
Llangors Powys....44 G9
Llangovan Mons....31 N3
Llangower Gwynd....68 B8
Llangrannog Cerdgn....42 F4
Llangristiolus IoA....78 G10
Llangrove Herefs....45 Q11
Llangua Mons....45 M9
Llangunllo Powys....56 C10
Llangunnor Carmth....42 H10
Llangurig Powys....55 L9
Llangwm Conwy....68 C6
Llangwm Mons....31 M5
Llangwm Pembks....41 J9
Llangwnnadl Gwynd....66 C8
Llangwyfan Denbgs....80 G11
Llangwyllog IoA....78 H8
Llangwyryfon Cerdgn....54 D10
Llangybi Cerdgn....43 M4
Llangybi Gwynd....66 G6
Llangybi Mons....31 L5
Llangyfelach Swans....28 H5
Llangynhafal Denbgs....68 F2
Llangynidr Powys....44 H11
Llangynin Carmth....41 Q7
Llangynllo Cerdgn....42 G6
Llangynog Carmth....28 B2
Llangynog Powys....68 E9
Llangynwyd Brdgnd....29 N7
Llanhamlach Powys....44 F9
Llanharan Rhondd....30 D9
Llanharry Rhondd....30 D8
Llanhennock Mons....31 L6
Llanhilleth Blae G....30 H4
Llanidan IoA....78 H10
Llanidloes Powys....55 M8
Llaniestyn Gwynd....66 D9
Llanigon Powys....45 J7
Llanilar Cerdgn....54 E9
Llanilid Rhondd....30 C8
Llanina Cerdgn....42 H3
Llanio Cerdgn....43 M3
Llanishen Cardif....30 G8
Llanishen Mons....31 N4
Llanllechid Gwynd....79 L11
Llanlleonfel Powys....44 C4
Llanllowell Mons....31 L5
Llanllugan Powys....55 P4
Llanllwch Carmth....42 G11
Llanllwchaiarn Powys....55 Q6
Llanllwni Carmth....43 J7
Llanllyfni Gwynd....66 H4
Llanmadoc Swans....28 D6
Llanmaes V Glam....30 C11
Llanmartin Newpt....31 L7
Llanmerewig Powys....56 B6
Llanmihangel V Glam....30 C10
Llanmiloe Carmth....41 P9
Llanmorlais Swans....28 F6
Llannefydd Conwy....80 D10
Llannon Carmth....28 F3
Llannor Gwynd....66 F7
Llanon Cerdgn....54 C11
Llanover Mons....31 K3
Llanpumsaint Carmth....42 H9
Llanrhaeadr-ym-Mochnant Powys....68 F9
Llanrhian Pembks....40 F4
Llanrhidian Swans....28 E6
Llanrhos Conwy....79 P8
Llanrhychwyn Conwy....67 P2
Llanrhyddlad IoA....78 E7
Llanrhystud Cerdgn....54 C11
Llanrothal Herefs....45 P11
Llanrug Gwynd....67 J2
Llanrumney Cardif....30 H7
Llanrwst Conwy....67 Q2
Llansadurnen Carmth....41 Q8
Llansadwrn Carmth....43 N8
Llansadwrn IoA....79 K9
Llansaint Carmth....28 C3
Llansamlet Swans....29 J5
Llansanffraid Glan Conwy Conwy....79 Q9
Llansannan Conwy....80 C11
Llansannor V Glam....30 C9
Llansantffraed Powys....44 G10
Llansantffraed-Cwmdeuddwr Powys....55 M11
Llansantffraed-in-Elvel Powys....44 F4
Llansantffraid Cerdgn....54 C11
Llansantffraid-ym-Mechain Powys....68 H10
Llansawel Carmth....43 M7
Llansilin Powys....68 H9
Llansoy Mons....31 M4
Llanspyddid Powys....44 E9
Llanstadwell Pembks....40 H10
Llansteffan Carmth....28 C2
Llanstephan Powys....44 G6
Llantarnam Torfn....31 K6
Llanteg Pembks....41 N8
Llanthewy Skirrid Mons....45 L11
Llanthony Mons....45 K9
Llantilio-Crossenny Mons....31 L2
Llantilio Pertholey Mons....45 L11
Llantrisant IoA....78 F8
Llantrisant Mons....31 L5
Llantrisant Rhondd....30 D8
Llantrithyd V Glam....30 D10
Llantwit Fardre Rhondd....30 E7
Llantwit Major V Glam....30 C11
Llantysilio Denbgs....68 G6
Llanuwchllyn Gwynd....68 A8
Llanvaches Newpt....31 M6
Llanvair Discoed Mons....31 M6
Llanvapley Mons....31 L2
Llanvetherine Mons....45 M11
Llanveynoe Herefs....45 L8
Llanvihangel Crucorney Mons....45 L10
Llanvihangel Gobion Mons....31 K3
Llanvihangel-Ystern-Llewern Mons....31 M2
Llanwarne Herefs....45 Q9
Llanwddyn Powys....68 D11
Llanwenarth Mons....31 J2
Llanwenog Cerdgn....43 J5
Llanwern Newpt....31 L7
Llanwinio Carmth....41 Q5
Llanwnda Gwynd....66 H3
Llanwnda Pembks....40 H4
Llanwnnen Cerdgn....43 K5
Llanwnog Powys....55 N5
Llanwonno Rhondd....30 D5
Llanwrda Carmth....43 P8
Llanwrin Powys....54 H4
Llanwrthwl Powys....44 D2
Llanwrtyd Powys....44 B5
Llanwrtyd Wells Powys....44 B5
Llanwyddelan Powys....55 P4
Llanyblodwel Shrops....68 H10
Llanybri Carmth....28 B2
Llanybydder Carmth....43 K6
Llanycefn Pembks....41 L6
Llanychaer Bridge Pembks....41 J3
Llanycrwys Carmth....43 M5
Llanymawddwy Gwynd....68 B11
Llanymynech Powys....69 J10
Llanynghenedl IoA....78 E8
Llanynys Denbgs....68 F2
Llan-y-pwll Wrexhm....69 L4
Llanyre Powys....44 E2
Llanystumdwy Gwynd....66 H7
Llanywern Powys....44 G9
Llawhaden Pembks....41 L7
Llawnt Shrops....68 H8
Llawryglyn Powys....55 L6
Llay Wrexhm....69 K3
Llechcynfarwy IoA....78 F8
Llechfaen Powys....44 F9
Llechrhyd Caerph....30 F3

Llechryd - Ludworth 287

Llechryd Cerdgn 41 P2
Llechylched IoA 78 E9
Lledrod Cerdgn 54 E10
Lleyn Peninsula Gwynd 66 E7
Llidiardau Gwynd 68 A7
Llidiartnenog Carmth 43 K7
Llidiart-y-parc Denbgs 68 F6
Llithfaen Gwynd 66 F6
Lloc Flints 80 G9
Llowes Powys 44 H6
Llwydcoed Rhondd 30 C4
Llwydcoed Crematorium Rhondd 30 C3
Llwydiarth Powys 68 D11
Llwyn Denbgs 68 E2
Llwyncelyn Cerdgn 42 H3
Llwyndafydd Cerdgn 42 G3
Llwynderw Powys 56 C4
Llwyn-drain Pembks 41 Q4
Llwyn-du Mons 45 K11
Llwyndyrys Gwynd 66 F6
Llwyngwril Gwynd 54 D3
Llwynhendy Carmth 28 F5
Llwynmawr Wrexhm 68 H7
Llwyn-on Myr Td 30 D2
Llwyn-y-brain Carmth 41 N8
Llwyn-y-groes Cerdgn 43 L3
Llwynypia Rhondd 30 C6
Llynclys Shrops 69 J10
Llynfaes IoA 78 G9
Llyn-y-pandy Flints 81 J11
Llysfaen Conwy 80 B9
Llyswen Cerdgn 43 J2
Llyswen Powys 44 G7
Llysworney V Glam 30 C10
Llys-y-frân Pembks 41 K6
Llywel Powys 44 B8
Load Brook Sheff 84 C3
Loan Falk 126 H2
Loanend Nthumb 129 N9
Loanhead Mdloth 127 P4
Loaningfoot D & G 109 L9
Loans S Ayrs 125 J11
Lobb Devon 16 H4
Lobhillcross Devon 8 C7
Lochailort Highld 145 N11
Lochaline Highld 138 B9
Lochans D & G 106 E6
Locharbriggs D & G 109 L4
Lochavich Ag & B 131 J4
Lochawe Ag & B 131 N2
Loch Baghasdail W Isls 168 c16
Lochboisdale W Isls 168 c16
Lochbuie Ag & B 137 Q10
Lochcarron Highld 154 A10
Lochdon Ag & B 138 C11
Lochdonhead Ag & B 138 C11
Lochead Ag & B 123 N4
Lochearnhead Stirlg 132 H3
Lochee C Dund 142 F11
Locheilside Station Highld 138 H2
Lochend Highld 155 Q10
Locheport W Isls 168 d11
Loch Euphoirt W Isls 168 d11
Lochfoot D & G 109 J6
Lochgair Ag & B 131 J9
Lochgelly Fife 134 F9
Lochgilphead Ag & B 130 H10
Lochgoilhead Ag & B 131 Q7
Lochieheads Fife 134 H5
Lochill Moray 157 P5
Lochindorb Lodge Highld 156 H10
Lochinver Highld 160 H2
Loch Lomond and The Trossachs National Park Stirlg 132 E5
Lochluichart Highld 155 K5
Lochmaben D & G 109 N4
Lochmaddy W Isls 168 e11
Loch Maree Hotel Highld 154 B3
Loch nam Madadh W Isls 168 e11
Loch Ness Highld 147 N2
Lochore Fife 134 F8
Lochranza N Ayrs 124 A7
Lochside Abers 143 N5
Lochside D & G 109 L5
Lochside Highld 156 E7
Lochslin Highld 163 J10
Lochton S Ayrs 107 J2
Lochty Angus 143 J5
Lochty Fife 135 N6
Lochuisge Highld 138 D6
Lochwinnoch Rens 125 K6
Lochwood D & G 116 F11
Lockengate Cnwll 4 G9
Lockerbie D & G 109 P4
Lockeridge Wilts 33 M11
Lockerley Hants 22 B9
Locking N Som 19 L3
Locking Stumps Warrtn 82 D6
Lockington E R Yk 99 K11
Lockington Leics 72 D5
Lockleywood Shrops 70 B9
Locksbottom Gt Lon 37 K7
Locksgreen IoW 14 D8
Locks Heath Hants 14 F5
Lockton N York 98 G3
Loddington Leics 73 K10
Loddington Nhants 60 H5
Loddiswell Devon 7 J9
Loddon Norfk 65 M2
Lode Cambs 62 H8
Lode Heath Solhll 59 J8
Loders Dorset 11 K6
Lodge Hill Crematorium Birm 58 F8
Lodsworth W Susx 23 P10
Lofthouse Leeds 91 J5
Lofthouse N York 96 H6
Lofthouse Gate Wakefd 91 J6
Loftus R & Cl 105 K7
Logan E Ayrs 115 L3
Loganbeck Cumb 94 D2
Loganlea W Loth 126 H5
Loggerheads Staffs 70 C7
Logie Angus 143 M5
Logie Fife 135 L3
Logie Moray 157 J7
Logie Coldstone Abers 150 C7
Logie Newton Abers 158 G10
Logie Pert Angus 143 M5
Logierait P & K 141 N7
Logierieve Abers 151 N2
Login Carmth 41 N6
Lolworth Cambs 62 E8
Lonbain Highld 153 M7
Londesborough E R Yk 98 H11
London Gt Lon 36 G5
London Apprentice Cnwll 3 Q4
London Beach Kent 26 E4
London Colney Herts 50 E10
Londonderry N York 97 M3
London End Nhants 61 K7
London Gateway Services Gt Lon 36 E2
Londonthorpe Lincs 73 P3
Londubh Highld 160 D10
Lonemore Highld 153 P2
Long Ashton N Som 31 P10
Long Bank Worcs 57 P10
Long Bennington Lincs 73 L2
Longbenton N Tyne 113 L7
Longborough Gloucs 47 N9
Long Bredy Dorset 11 M6
Longbridge Birm 58 F9
Longbridge Warwks 47 Q2
Longbridge Deverill Wilts 20 G6
Long Buckby Nhants 60 D7
Longburgh Cumb 110 F9
Longburton Dorset 11 N2
Long Cause Devon 7 K6
Long Clawson Leics 73 J5
Longcliffe Derbys 84 B9
Longcombe Devon 7 L7
Long Common Hants 14 F4
Long Compton Staffs 70 F10
Long Compton Warwks 47 Q8
Longcot Oxon 33 Q6
Long Crendon Bucks 35 J3
Long Crichel Dorset 12 G2
Longcroft Cumb 110 D9
Longcross Surrey 35 Q11
Longden Shrops 56 G3
Longden Common Shrops 56 G3
Long Ditton Surrey 36 E7
Longdon Staffs 58 G2
Longdon Worcs 46 F7
Longdon Green Staffs 58 G2
Longdon Heath Worcs 46 F7
Longdon upon Tern Wrekin 69 R11
Longdown Devon 9 L6
Longdowns Cnwll 3 J7
Long Drax N York 92 A5
Long Duckmanton Derbys 84 F6
Long Eaton Derbys 72 D4
Longfield Kent 37 P7
Longford Covtry 59 N8
Longford Derbys 71 N7
Longford Gloucs 46 F10
Longford Gt Lon 36 C5
Longford Kent 37 M9
Longford Shrops 70 A8
Longford Wrekin 70 C11
Longforgan P & K 134 H2
Longformacus Border 128 H8
Longframlington Nthumb 119 M10
Long Green Ches W 81 P10
Long Green Worcs 46 F8
Longham Dorset 13 J5
Longham Norfk 76 C8
Long Hanborough Oxon 34 D2
Longhaven Abers 159 R10
Long Hedges Lincs 87 L11
Longhirst Nthumb 113 K3
Longhope Gloucs 46 C11
Longhope Ork 169 c7
Longhorsley Nthumb 112 H2
Longhoughton Nthumb 119 P7
Long Itchington Warwks 59 P11
Longlands Cumb 101 J3
Longlane Derbys 71 N7
Long Lawford Warwks 59 Q9
Longleat Safari & Adventure Park Wilts 20 F6
Longlevens Gloucs 46 G11
Longley Calder 90 D6
Longley Kirk 90 E9
Longley Green Worcs 46 D4
Longleys P & K 142 D9
Long Load Somset 19 N10
Longmanhill Abers 158 H5
Long Marston Herts 49 N11
Long Marston N York 97 R10
Long Marston Warwks 47 N5
Long Marton Cumb 102 C6
Long Meadowend Shrops 56 G8
Long Melford Suffk 52 E2
Longmoor Camp Hants 23 L8
Longmorn Moray 157 N6
Longmoss Ches E 83 J10
Long Newnton Gloucs 32 H6
Longnewton Border 118 A5
Long Newton E Loth 128 E7
Longnewton S on T 104 C7
Longney Gloucs 32 E2
Longniddry E Loth 128 C4
Longnor Shrops 56 H4
Longnor Staffs 71 K2
Longparish Hants 22 D5
Longpark Cumb 110 H8
Long Preston N York 96 B9
Longridge Lancs 89 J3
Longridge Staffs 70 G11
Longridge W Loth 126 G5
Longriggend N Lans 126 E3
Long Riston E R Yk 93 K2
Longrock Cnwll 2 E7
Longsdon Staffs 70 H4
Longshaw Wigan 82 B4
Longside Abers 159 P8
Long Sight Oldham 89 Q9
Longslow Shrops 70 B7
Longstanton Cambs 62 E7
Longstock Hants 22 C7
Longstone Pembks 41 M9
Longstowe Cambs 62 D10
Long Stratton Norfk 64 H3
Long Street M Keyn 49 L5
Longstreet Wilts 21 M4
Long Sutton Hants 23 K5
Long Sutton Lincs 74 H6
Long Sutton Somset 19 N9
Longthorpe C Pete 74 C11
Long Thurlow Suffk 64 E8
Longthwaite Cumb 101 M6
Longton C Stke 70 G6
Longton Lancs 88 F5
Longtown Cumb 110 G7
Longtown Herefs 45 L9
Longueville Jersey 11 c2
Longville in the Dale Shrops 57 J6
Long Waste Wrekin 69 R11
Long Whatton Leics 72 D6
Longwick Bucks 35 L3
Long Wittenham Oxon 34 F6
Longwitton Nthumb 112 G3
Longwood D & G 108 F8
Longwood Shrops 57 L3
Longworth Oxon 34 C5
Longyester E Loth 128 E7
Lon-las Swans 29 K5
Lonmay Abers 159 P6
Lonmore Highld 152 D8
Looe Cnwll 5 M11
Loose Kent 38 C11
Loosebeare Devon 8 H3
Loosegate Lincs 74 F5
Loosley Row Bucks 35 M4
Lootcherbrae Abers 158 F7
Lopcombe Corner Wilts 21 Q7
Lopen Somset 11 J2
Loppington Shrops 69 N9
Lorbottle Nthumb 119 K9
Lordington W Susx 15 L5
Lordsbridge Norfk 75 L8
Lords Wood Medway 38 C9
Lornty P & K 142 B8
Loscoe Derbys 84 F11
Loscombe Dorset 11 K5
Lossiemouth Moray 157 N3
Lostford Shrops 69 R8
Lost Gardens of Heligan Cnwll 3 P4
Lostock Gralam Ches W 82 E10
Lostock Green Ches W 82 E10
Lostock Hall Lancs 88 G5
Lostock Hall Fold Bolton 89 K9
Lostock Junction Bolton 89 K9
Lostwithiel Cnwll 5 J10
Lothbeg Highld 163 L4
Lothersdale N York 96 E11
Lothmore Highld 163 M4
Loudwater Bucks 35 P6
Loughborough Leics 72 E7
Loughborough Crematorium Leics 72 E7
Loughor Swans 28 G5
Loughton Essex 51 K11
Loughton M Keyn 49 M7
Loughton Shrops 57 L8
Lound Lincs 73 R7
Lound Notts 85 L3
Lound Suffk 65 Q2
Lounston Devon 9 J9
Lount Leics 72 B7
Louth Lincs 87 K3
Love Clough Lancs 89 N5
Lovedean Hants 15 J4
Lover Wilts 21 P10
Loversall Donc 91 P11
Loves Green Essex 51 P10
Lovesome Hill N York 104 C11
Loveston Pembks 41 L9
Lovington Somset 19 Q8
Low Ackworth Wakefd 91 M7
Low Angerton Nthumb 112 G4
Lowbands Gloucs 46 E8
Low Barbeth D & G 106 D4
Low Barlings Lincs 86 E6
Low Bell End N York 105 K11
Low Bentham N York 95 N7
Low Biggins Cumb 95 N5
Low Borrowbridge Cumb 102 B10
Low Bradfield Sheff 84 C2
Low Bradley N York 96 F11
Low Braithwaite Cumb 101 M2
Low Burnham N Linc 92 C10
Low Buston Nthumb 119 P9
Lowca Cumb 100 C6
Low Catton E R Yk 98 E10
Low Coniscliffe Darltn 103 Q8
Low Crosby Cumb 110 H9
Lowdham Notts 85 L11
Low Dinsdale Darltn 104 B8
Lowe Shrops 69 N8
Lowe Hill Staffs 70 H3
Low Ellington N York 97 K4
Lower Aisholt Somset 18 H7
Lower Ansty Dorset 12 C4
Lower Apperley Gloucs 46 G9
Lower Arncott Oxon 48 H11
Lower Ashton Devon 9 K8
Lower Assendon Oxon 35 K8
Lower Ballam Lancs 88 D4
Lower Bartle Lancs 88 F4
Lower Basildon W Berk 34 H9
Lower Bearwood Herefs 45 M3
Lower Beeding W Susx 24 F5
Lower Benefield Nhants 61 L3
Lower Bentley Worcs 58 E11
Lower Beobridge Shrops 57 P6
Lower Birchwood Derbys 84 F10
Lower Boddington Nhants 48 E4
Lower Boscaswell Cnwll 2 B7
Lower Bourne Surrey 23 M6
Lower Brailes Warwks 48 B7
Lower Breakish Highld 145 L3
Lower Bredbury Stockp 83 K6
Lower Broadheath Worcs 46 F3
Lower Broxwood Herefs 45 M4
Lower Buckenhill Herefs 46 B8
Lower Bullingham Herefs 45 Q7
Lower Burgate Hants 21 N11
Lower Burrowton Devon 9 P5
Lower Burton Herefs 45 N3
Lower Caldecote C Beds 61 Q11
Lower Cam Gloucs 32 D4
Lower Canada N Som 19 L3
Lower Catesby Nhants 60 B9
Lower Chapel Powys 44 E7
Lower Chicksgrove Wilts 21 J9
Lower Chute Wilts 22 B4
Lower Clapton Gt Lon 36 H3
Lower Clent Worcs 58 D9
Lower Creedy Devon 9 K4
Lower Crossings Derbys 83 M8
Lower Cumberworth Kirk 90 G9
Lower Darwen Bl w D 89 K5
Lower Dean Bed 61 N7
Lower Denby Kirk 90 G9
Lower Diabaig Highld 153 P5
Lower Dicker E Susx 25 N8
Lower Dinchope Shrops 56 H8
Lower Down Shrops 56 E8
Lower Dunsforth N York 97 P8
Lower Egleton Herefs 46 B5
Lower Elkstone Staffs 71 K3
Lower Ellastone Staffs 71 L6
Lower End Bucks 35 J3
Lower End M Keyn 49 P7
Lower End Nhants 60 H9
Lower End Nhants 61 J8
Lower Everleigh Wilts 21 N4
Lower Exbury Hants 14 D7
Lower Eythorne Kent 27 N2
Lower Failand N Som 31 P10
Lower Farringdon Hants 23 K7
Lower Feltham Gt Lon 36 C6
Lower Fittleworth W Susx 24 B7
Lower Foxdale IoM 80 c6
Lower Frankton Shrops 69 L8
Lower Freystrop Pembks 41 J8
Lower Froyle Hants 23 L6
Lower Gabwell Devon 7 N5
Lower Gledfield Highld 162 D8
Lower Godney Somset 19 N6
Lower Gornal Dudley 58 D6
Lower Gravenhurst C Beds 50 D3
Lower Green Herts 50 E4
Lower Green Herts 51 K4
Lower Green Kent 25 N2
Lower Green Kent 25 P2
Lower Green Norfk 76 D4
Lower Green Staffs 58 D3
Lower Green Suffk 63 M7
Lower Hacheston Suffk 65 L10
Lower Halliford Surrey 36 C7
Lower Halstock Leigh Dorset 11 L3
Lower Halstow Kent 38 E8
Lower Hamworthy Poole 12 G6
Lower Hardres Kent 39 L11
Lower Harpton Herefs 45 K2
Lower Hartlip Kent 38 D9
Lower Hartshay Derbys 84 E10
Lower Hartwell Bucks 35 L2
Lower Hatton Staffs 70 E7
Lower Hawthwaite Cumb 94 E3
Lower Hergest Herefs 45 K3
Lower Heyford Oxon 48 E10
Lower Heysham Lancs 95 J8
Lower Higham Kent 38 B7
Lower Holbrook Suffk 53 L4
Lower Hordley Shrops 69 L9
Lower Horncroft W Susx 24 B7
Lowerhouse Lancs 89 N4
Lower Houses Kirk 90 F7
Lower Howsell Worcs 46 E5
Lower Irlam Salfd 82 F6
Lower Kilburn Derbys 72 B2
Lower Kilcott Gloucs 32 E7
Lower Killeyan Ag & B 122 C11
Lower Kingcombe Dorset 11 M5
Lower Kingswood Surrey 36 F10
Lower Kinnerton Ches W 69 K2
Lower Langford N Som 19 N2
Lower Largo Fife 135 L7
Lower Leigh Staffs 71 J7
Lower Lemington Gloucs 47 P8
Lower Llanfadog Powys 55 M11
Lower Lovacott Devon 17 J6
Lower Loxhore Devon 17 L4
Lower Lydbrook Gloucs 46 A11
Lower Lye Herefs 56 G11
Lower Machen Newpt 30 H7
Lower Maes-coed Herefs 45 L8
Lower Mannington Dorset 13 J4
Lower Marston Somset 20 E6
Lower Meend Gloucs 31 Q4
Lower Merridge Somset 18 H8
Lower Middleton Cheney Nhants 48 F6
Lower Milton Somset 19 P5
Lower Moor Worcs 47 J5
Lower Morton S Glos 32 B6
Lower Nazeing Essex 51 J9
Lower Norton Warwks 47 P2
Lower Nyland Dorset 20 E10
Lower Penarth V Glam 30 G11
Lower Penn Staffs 58 C5
Lower Pennington Hants 13 P6
Lower Penwortham Lancs 88 G5
Lower Peover Ches E 82 F10
Lower Place Rochdl 89 Q8
Lower Pollicott Bucks 35 K2
Lower Quinton Warwks 47 N5
Lower Rainham Medway 38 D8
Lower Raydon Suffk 52 H4
Lower Roadwater Somset 18 D7
Lower Salter Lancs 95 N8
Lower Seagry Wilts 33 J8
Lower Sheering Essex 51 L8
Lower Shelton C Beds 49 Q6
Lower Shiplake Oxon 35 L9
Lower Shuckburgh Warwks 48 E2
Lower Slaughter Gloucs 47 N10
Lower Soothill Kirk 90 H6
Lower Soudley Gloucs 32 C3
Lower Standen Kent 27 M3
Lower Stanton St Quintin Wilts 32 H8
Lower Stoke Medway 38 D6
Lower Stone Gloucs 32 C6
Lower Stonnall Staffs 58 G4
Lower Stow Bedon Norfk 64 D3
Lower Street Dorset 12 D5
Lower Street E Susx 26 B9
Lower Street Norfk 77 K4
Lower Street Suffk 63 N10
Lower Street Suffk 64 G11
Lower Stretton Warrtn 82 D8
Lower Stroud Dorset 11 K5
Lower Sundon C Beds 50 C5
Lower Swanwick Hants 14 E5
Lower Swell Gloucs 47 N9
Lower Tadmarton Oxon 48 D7
Lower Tale Devon 9 Q4
Lower Tean Staffs 71 J7
Lower Thurlton Norfk 65 N2
Lower Town Cnwll 2 H8
Lower Town Devon 7 J4
Lower Town Herefs 46 B6
Lower Town Pembks 41 J3
Lower Trebullett Cnwll 5 N6
Lower Treluswell Cnwll 3 K6
Lower Tysoe Warwks 48 B5
Lower Ufford Suffk 65 K11
Lower Upcott Devon 9 L8
Lower Upham Hants 22 F11
Lower Upnor Medway 38 C7
Lower Vexford Somset 18 F7
Lower Walton Warrtn 82 D7
Lower Waterston Dorset 12 B5
Lower Weare Somset 19 M4
Lower Weedon Nhants 60 D9
Lower Welson Herefs 45 K4
Lower Westmancote Worcs 46 H7
Lower Whatcombe Dorset 12 D4
Lower Whatley Somset 20 D5
Lower Whitley Ches W 82 D9
Lower Wick Gloucs 32 D5
Lower Wick Worcs 46 F4
Lower Wield Hants 22 H6
Lower Willingdon E Susx 25 N10
Lower Withington Ches E 82 H11
Lower Woodend Bucks 35 M7
Lower Woodford Wilts 21 M7
Lower Wraxhall Dorset 11 M4
Lower Wyche Worcs 46 E6
Lower Wyke C Brad 90 F5
Lowesby Leics 73 J9
Lowestoft Suffk 65 Q3
Loweswater Cumb 100 F6
Low Fell Gatesd 113 L9
Lowfield Heath W Susx 24 G3
Low Gartachorrans Stirlg 132 F10
Low Gate Nthumb 112 D8
Low Gettbridge Cumb 111 K9
Lowgill Cumb 102 B11
Lowgill Lancs 95 P8
Low Grantley N York 97 K6
Low Green N York 97 K9
Low Habberley Worcs 57 Q9
Low Ham Somset 19 M9
Low Harrogate N York 97 L9
Low Hawsker N York 105 P9
Low Hesket Cumb 111 J11
Low Hutton N York 98 F7
Lowick Cumb 94 F3
Lowick Nhants 61 L4
Lowick Nthumb 119 K3
Lowick Bridge Cumb 94 F3
Lowick Green Cumb 94 F3
Low Knipe Cumb 101 P7
Low Laithe N York 97 J8
Lowlands Dur 103 M5
Lowlands Torfn 31 J5
Low Langton Lincs 86 G5
Low Leighton Derbys 83 M7
Low Lorton Cumb 100 G5
Low Marishes N York 98 G5
Low Marnham Notts 85 P7
Low Middleton Nthumb 119 M3
Low Mill N York 105 J11
Low Moor C Brad 90 F5
Low Moorsley Sundld 113 M11
Low Moresby Cumb 100 C6
Low Newton Cumb 95 J4
Low Row Cumb 100 G2
Low Row Cumb 101 L3
Low Row Cumb 111 L8
Low Row N York 103 J11
Low Salchrie D & G 106 D4
Low Santon N Linc 92 F8
Lowsonford Warwks 59 J11
Low Street Norfk 77 L7
Low Street Thurr 37 Q5
Low Tharston Norfk 64 H2
Lowther Cumb 101 P6
Lowther Castle Cumb 101 P6
Lowthorpe E R Yk 99 M8
Lowton Devon 8 G4
Lowton Somset 18 G11
Lowton Wigan 82 D5
Lowton Common Wigan 82 D5
Lowton St Mary's Wigan 82 D5
Low Torry Fife 134 C10
Low Toynton Lincs 87 J6
Low Valley Barns 91 L10
Low Wood Cumb 94 G4
Low Worsall N York 104 C9
Low Wray Cumb 101 L10
Loxbeare Devon 18 B11
Loxhill Surrey 24 B3
Loxhore Devon 17 L4
Loxhore Cott Devon 17 L4
Loxley Warwks 47 Q4
Loxley Green Staffs 71 K8
Loxter Herefs 46 D6
Loxton N Som 19 L3
Loxwood W Susx 24 B4
Loyal Lodge Highld 165 P7
Lubenham Leics 60 F3
Lucasgate Lincs 87 M11
Lucas Green Surrey 23 P2
Luccombe Somset 18 B6
Luccombe Village IoW 14 G11
Lucker Nthumb 119 N4
Luckett Cnwll 5 P7
Lucking Street Essex 52 D5
Luckington Wilts 32 F8
Lucklawhill Fife 135 L3
Lucknam Wilts 32 F10
Luckwell Bridge Somset 18 B7
Lucton Herefs 45 N2
Lucy Cross N York 103 P8
Ludag W Isls 168 c16
Ludborough Lincs 93 N11
Ludbrook Devon 6 H8
Ludchurch Pembks 41 M8
Luddenden Calder 90 C5
Luddenden Foot Calder 90 C5
Luddenham Court Kent 38 G9
Luddesdown Kent 37 Q7
Luddington N Linc 92 D7
Luddington Warwks 47 N4
Luddington in the Brook Nhants 61 P4
Ludford Lincs 86 G3
Ludford Shrops 57 J10
Ludgershall Bucks 49 J11
Ludgershall Wilts 21 Q4
Ludgvan Cnwll 2 E7
Ludham Norfk 77 M8
Ludlow Shrops 57 J9
Ludney Somset 10 H2
Ludwell Wilts 20 H10
Ludworth Dur 104 C2

288 Luffenhall - Meerbrook

Luffenhall Herts 50 G5
Luffincott Devon 5 N3
Luffness E Loth 128 D4
Lugar E Ayrs 115 L3
Luggate Burn E Loth 128 F5
Lugg Green Herefs 45 N2
Luggiebank N Lans 126 D3
Lugton E Ayrs 125 L7
Lugwardine Herefs 45 R6
Luib Highld 145 J2
Luing Ag & B 130 E5
Lulham Herefs 45 N6
Lullington Derbys 59 K2
Lullington E Susx 25 M10
Lullington Somset 20 E4
Lulsgate Bottom N Som 31 P11
Lulsley Worcs 46 D3
Lulworth Camp Dorset 12 D8
Lumb Calder 90 C6
Lumb Lancs 89 N6
Lumbutts Calder 90 B6
Lumby N York 91 M4
Lumloch E Duns 125 Q3
Lumphanan Abers 150 F7
Lumphinnans Fife 134 F9
Lumsden Abers 150 D3
Lunan Angus 143 M7
Lunanhead Angus 142 H7
Luncarty P & K 134 D2
Lund E R Yk 99 K11
Lund N York 91 R4
Lundie Angus 142 D10
Lundin Links Fife 135 L7
Lundin Mill Fife 135 L7
Lundy Devon 16 A2
Lundy Green Norfk 65 J3
Lunga Ag & B 130 E6
Lunna Shet 169 r7
Lunsford Kent 37 Q9
Lunsford's Cross E Susx 26 B9
Lunt Sefton 81 L4
Luntley Herefs 45 M3
Luppitt Devon 10 D3
Lupridge Devon 7 J8
Lupset Wakefd 91 J7
Lupton Cumb 95 M4
Lurgashall W Susx 23 P9
Lurley Devon 18 B11
Lusby Lincs 87 K7
Luscombe Devon 7 K7
Luson Devon 6 G8
Luss Ag & B 132 D9
Lussagiven Ag & B 130 C10
Lusta Highld 152 D6
Lustleigh Devon 9 J8
Luston Herefs 45 P2
Luthermuir Abers 143 M4
Luthrie Fife 135 J4
Lutley Dudley 58 D8
Luton Devon 9 M9
Luton Devon 10 B4
Luton Luton 50 C6
Luton Medway 38 C8
Luton Airport Luton 50 D6
Lutterworth Leics 60 B4
Lutton Devon 6 F7
Lutton Devon 6 H6
Lutton Lincs 74 H5
Lutton Nhants 61 P3
Luxborough Somset 18 C7
Luxulyan Cnwll 4 H10
Luzley Tamesd 83 L4
Lybster Highld 167 M9
Lydbury North Shrops 56 E7
Lydcott Devon 17 M4
Lydd Kent 26 H7
Lydd Airport Kent 27 J7
Lydden Kent 27 N2
Lydden Kent 39 Q8
Lyddington Rutlnd 73 M11
Lydeard St Lawrence Somset 18 F8
Lyde Green Hants 23 K3
Lydford Devon 8 D7
Lydford on Fosse Somset 19 Q8
Lydgate Calder 89 Q5
Lydgate Rochdl 90 B7
Lydham Shrops 56 E6
Lydiard Green Wilts 33 L7
Lydiard Millicent Wilts 33 L7
Lydiard Tregoze Swindn 33 M8
Lydiate Sefton 81 M4
Lydiate Ash Worcs 58 E9
Lydlinch Dorset 12 B2
Lydney Gloucs 32 B4
Lydstep Pembks 41 L11
Lye Dudley 58 D8
Lye Cross N Som 19 N2
Lye Green Bucks 35 Q4
Lye Green E Susx 25 M4
Lye Green Warwks 59 J11
Lye Head Worcs 57 P10
Lye's Green Wilts 20 F5
Lyford Oxon 34 C6
Lymbridge Green Kent 27 K3
Lyme Regis Dorset 10 G6
Lyminge Kent 27 L3
Lymington Hants 13 P5
Lyminster W Susx 24 B10
Lymm Warrtn 82 E7
Lympne Kent 27 K4
Lympsham Somset 19 K4
Lympstone Devon 9 N8
Lynbridge Devon 17 N2
Lynchat Highld 148 D7
Lynch Green Norfk 76 H10
Lyndhurst Hants 13 P3
Lyndon Rutlnd 73 N10
Lyndon Green Birm 58 H7
Lyne Border 117 J2
Lyne Surrey 36 B7
Lyneal Shrops 69 M8
Lyne Down Herefs 46 B8
Lyneham Devon 9 L9
Lyneham Oxon 47 Q10
Lyneham Wilts 33 K9
Lyneham Airport Wilts 33 K9
Lyneholmford Cumb 111 K6
Lynemouth Nthumb 113 L2
Lyne of Skene Abers 151 K5
Lynesack Dur 103 L5
Lyness Ork 169 c7
Lyng Norfk 76 F8
Lyng Somset 19 K9
Lynmouth Devon 17 N2
Lynn Staffs 58 G4
Lynn Wrekin 70 D11
Lynsted Kent 38 F9
Lynstone Cnwll 16 C10
Lynton Devon 17 N2
Lyon's Gate Dorset 11 P3
Lyonshall Herefs 45 L3
Lytchett Matravers Dorset 12 F5
Lytchett Minster Dorset 12 G6
Lyth Highld 167 N4
Lytham Lancs 88 D5
Lytham St Anne's Lancs 88 C5
Lythbank Shrops 56 H3
Lythe N York 105 M8
Lythmore Highld 167 J3

M

Mabe Burnthouse Cnwll 3 K7
Mablethorpe Lincs 87 P4
Macclesfield Ches E 83 K10
Macclesfield Crematorium Ches E 83 K10
Macduff Abers 158 H5
Macharioch Ag & B 120 D10
Machen Caerph 30 H7
Machrie N Ayrs 120 G5
Machrihanish Ag & B 120 B7
Machrins Ag & B 136 b3
Machynlleth Powys 54 G4
Machynys Carmth 28 F5
Mackworth Derbys 71 Q7
Macmerry E Loth 128 C5
Maddaford Devon 8 D6
Madderty P & K 134 B3
Maddington Wilts 21 L6
Maddiston Falk 126 G2
Madehurst W Susx 15 Q4
Madeley Staffs 70 D6
Madeley Wrekin 57 M4
Madeley Heath Staffs 70 D5
Madford Devon 10 C2
Madingley Cambs 62 E8
Madley Herefs 45 N7
Madresfield Worcs 46 F5
Madron Cnwll 2 D7
Maenaddwyn IoA 78 H8
Maenan Conwy 79 P11
Maenclochog Pembks 41 L5
Maendy V Glam 30 D9
Maenporth Cnwll 3 K8
Maentwrog Gwynd 67 M6
Maen-y-groes Cerdgn 42 G3
Maer Cnwll 16 C10
Maer Staffs 70 D7
Maerdy Carmth 43 N9
Maerdy Rhondd 30 C5
Maesbrook Shrops 69 K10
Maesbury Shrops 69 K9
Maesbury Marsh Shrops 69 K9
Maes-glas Newpt 31 J7
Maesgwynne Carmth 41 P6
Maeshafn Denbgs 68 H2
Maesllyn Cerdgn 42 G6
Maesmynis Powys 44 E5
Maesmynis Powys 44 E5
Maesteg Brdgnd 29 N6
Maesybont Carmth 43 L11
Maesycwmmer Caerph 30 G6
Magdalen Laver Essex 51 M9
Maggieknockater Moray 157 Q8
Maggots End Essex 51 L5
Magham Down E Susx 25 P8
Maghull Sefton 81 M4
Magna Park Leics 60 B4
Magor Mons 31 M7
Magor Services Mons 31 M7
Maidenbower W Susx 24 G3
Maiden Bradley Wilts 20 F7
Maidencombe Torbay 7 N5
Maidenhayne Devon 10 F5
Maiden Head N Som 31 Q11
Maidenhead W & M 35 N8
Maiden Law Dur 113 J11
Maiden Newton Dorset 11 M5
Maidens S Ayrs 114 D6
Maiden's Green Br For 35 P10
Maidenwell Lincs 87 K5
Maiden Wells Pembks 41 J11
Maidford Nhants 48 H4
Maids Moreton Bucks 49 K7
Maidstone Kent 38 C10
Maidstone Services Kent 38 D10
Maidwell Nhants 60 F5
Mail Shet 169 r9
Maindee Newpt 31 K7
Mainland Ork 169 d6
Mainland Shet 169 r8
Mainsforth Dur 104 B4
Mains of Balhall Angus 143 J5
Mains of Balnakettle Abers 143 L3
Mains of Dalvey Highld 157 L11
Mains of Haulkerton Abers 143 N3
Mains of Lesmoir Abers 150 D2
Mains of Melgunds Angus 143 J6
Mainsriddle D & G 109 K9
Mainstone Shrops 56 D7
Maisemore Gloucs 46 F10
Major's Green Worcs 58 H9
Makeney Derbys 72 B2
Malborough Devon 7 J11
Malcoff Derbys 83 N8
Malden Rushett Gt Lon 36 E8
Maldon Essex 52 E10
Malham N York 96 D8
Maligar Highld 152 H5
Mallaig Highld 145 L8
Mallaigvaig Highld 145 L8
Malleny Mills C Edin 127 M4
Mallows Green Essex 51 L5
Malltraeth IoA 78 G11
Mallwyd Gwynd 55 K2
Malmesbury Wilts 32 H7
Malmsmead Devon 17 P2
Malpas Ches W 69 N5
Malpas Cnwll 3 L5
Malpas Newpt 31 K6
Malswick Gloucs 46 D10
Maltby Lincs 87 K4
Maltby Rothm 84 H2
Maltby S on T 104 E8
Maltby le Marsh Lincs 87 N4
Malting Green Essex 52 G7
Maltman's Hill Kent 26 F3
Malton N York 98 F6
Malvern Hills 46 E6
Malvern Link Worcs 46 E5
Malvern Wells Worcs 46 E6
Mamble Worcs 57 M10
Mamhilad Mons 31 K4
Manaccan Cnwll 3 K9
Manafon Powys 55 Q4
Manais W Isls 168 g9
Manaton Devon 9 J8
Manby Lincs 87 L3
Mancetter Warwks 59 M5
Manchester Manch 82 H5
Manchester Airport Manch 82 H8
Mancot Flints 81 L11
Mandally Highld 146 H7
Manderston House Border 129 L9
Manea Cambs 62 G3
Maney Birm 58 H5
Manfield N York 103 P8
Mangerton Dorset 11 K5
Mangotsfield S Glos 32 C9
Mangrove Green Herts 50 D6
Manhay Cnwll 2 H7
Manish W Isls 168 g9
Mankinholes Calder 90 B6
Manley Ches W 81 Q10
Manmoel Caerph 30 G4
Mannel Ag & B 136 B7
Manningford Bohune Wilts 21 M3
Manningford Bruce Wilts 21 M3
Manningham C Brad 90 E3
Manning's Heath W Susx 24 F5
Mannington Dorset 13 J3
Manningtree Essex 53 K5
Mannofield C Aber 151 N7
Manorbier Pembks 41 L11
Manorbier Newton Pembks 41 K10
Manordeilo Carmth 43 N9
Manorhill Border 118 C4
Manorowen Pembks 40 H3
Manor Park Gt Lon 37 K3
Manor Park Crematorium Gt Lon 37 K3
Mansell Gamage Herefs 45 M6
Mansell Lacy Herefs 45 N5
Mansergh Cumb 95 N4
Mansfield E Ayrs 115 M5
Mansfield Notts 84 H8
Mansfield & District Crematorium Notts 84 H9
Mansfield Woodhouse Notts 84 H8
Mansriggs Cumb 94 F4
Manston Dorset 20 F11
Manston Kent 39 P8
Manston Leeds 91 K4
Manswood Dorset 12 G3
Manthorpe Lincs 73 N3
Manthorpe Lincs 73 R7
Manton N Linc 92 F10
Manton Notts 85 K5
Manton Rutlnd 73 M10
Manton Wilts 33 N11
Manuden Essex 51 L5
Manwood Green Essex 51 M8
Maperton Somset 20 C9
Maplebeck Notts 85 M8
Maple Cross Herts 36 B2
Mapledurham Oxon 35 J9
Mapledurwell Hants 23 J4
Maplehurst W Susx 24 E6
Maplescombe Kent 37 N8
Mapleton Derbys 71 M5
Mapleton Kent 37 L11
Mapperley Derbys 72 C2
Mapperley Park C Nott 72 F2
Mapperton Dorset 11 L5
Mappleborough Green Warwks 58 G11
Mappleton E R Yk 93 M2
Mapplewell Barns 91 J8
Mappowder Dorset 12 B3
Marazanvose Cnwll 3 K3
Marazion Cnwll 2 E7
Marbury Ches E 69 Q5
March Cambs 74 H11
March S Lans 116 D8
Marcham Oxon 34 E5
Marchamley Shrops 69 Q9
Marchamley Wood Shrops 69 Q8
Marchington Staffs 71 L8
Marchington Woodlands Staffs 71 L9
Marchros Gwynd 66 E9
Marchwiel Wrexhm 69 L5
Marchwood Hants 14 C4
Marcross V Glam 29 P11
Marden Herefs 45 Q5
Marden Kent 26 B3
Marden Wilts 21 L3
Marden Ash Essex 51 N10
Marden Beech Kent 26 B3
Mardens Hill E Susx 25 M4
Marden Thorn Kent 26 C3
Mardlebury Herts 50 G7
Mardy Mons 45 L11
Marefield Leics 73 J9
Mareham le Fen Lincs 87 J8
Mareham on the Hill Lincs 87 J7
Marehay Derbys 84 E11
Marehill W Susx 24 C7
Maresfield E Susx 25 L6
Marfleet C KuH 93 K5
Marford Wrexhm 69 L3
Margam Neath 29 L7
Margam Crematorium Neath 29 L7
Margaret Marsh Dorset 20 F11
Margaret Roding Essex 51 N8
Margaretting Essex 51 Q10
Margaretting Tye Essex 51 Q10
Margate Kent 39 Q7
Margnaheglish N Ayrs 121 K5
Margrie D & G 108 C10
Margrove Park R & Cl 105 J7
Marham Norfk 75 P9
Marhamchurch Cnwll 16 C11
Marholm C Pete 74 B10
Marian-glas IoA 79 J8
Mariansleigh Devon 17 N7
Marine Town Kent 38 F7
Marionburgh Abers 151 J6
Marishader Highld 152 H5
Maristow Devon 6 D6
Marjoriebanks D & G 109 N4
Mark Somset 19 L5
Markbeech Kent 25 L2
Markby Lincs 87 N5
Mark Causeway Somset 19 L5
Mark Cross E Susx 25 N4
Markeaton C Derb 72 A3
Markeaton Crematorium C Derb 72 A3
Market Bosworth Leics 72 C10
Market Deeping Lincs 74 B8
Market Drayton Shrops 70 B8
Market Harborough Leics 60 F3
Market Lavington Wilts 21 K4
Market Overton Rutlnd 73 M7
Market Rasen Lincs 86 F3
Market Stainton Lincs 86 H5
Market Warsop Notts 85 J7
Market Weighton E R Yk 92 E2
Market Weston Suffk 64 D6
Markfield Leics 72 D9
Markham Caerph 30 G4
Markham Moor Notts 85 M6
Markinch Fife 134 H7
Markington N York 97 L7
Markle E Loth 128 F4
Marksbury BaNES 20 C2
Mark's Corner IoW 14 E8
Marks Tey Essex 52 F7
Markwell Cnwll 5 P10
Markyate Herts 50 C7
Marlborough Wilts 33 N11
Marlbrook Herefs 45 Q4
Marlbrook Worcs 58 E10
Marlcliff Warwks 47 L4
Marldon Devon 7 M6
Marle Green E Susx 25 N7
Marlesford Suffk 65 L10
Marley Kent 39 L11
Marley Kent 39 P11
Marley Green Ches E 69 Q5
Marley Hill Gatesd 113 K9
Marlingford Norfk 76 G10
Marloes Pembks 40 E9
Marlow Bucks 35 M7
Marlow Herefs 56 G9
Marlow Bottom Bucks 35 M7
Marlpit Hill Kent 37 K11
Marlpits E Susx 25 L5
Marlpits E Susx 26 B9
Marlpool Derbys 84 F11
Marnhull Dorset 20 E11
Marple Stockp 83 L7
Marple Bridge Stockp 83 L7
Marr Donc 91 N9
Marrick N York 103 L11
Marros Carmth 41 P9
Marsden Kirk 90 C8
Marsden S Tyne 113 N8
Marsden Height Lancs 89 P3
Marsett N York 96 D3
Marsh Bucks 35 M3
Marsh C Brad 90 C3
Marsh Devon 10 F2
Marshall's Heath Herts 50 E8
Marshalswick Herts 50 E9
Marsham Norfk 76 H7
Marsh Baldon Oxon 34 G5
Marsh Benham W Berk 34 D11
Marshborough Kent 39 P10
Marshbrook Shrops 56 G7
Marshchapel Lincs 93 Q11
Marsh Farm Luton 50 C5
Marshfield Newpt 31 J8
Marshfield S Glos 32 E10
Marshgate Cnwll 5 K3
Marsh Gibbon Bucks 48 H10
Marsh Green Devon 9 P6
Marsh Green Kent 25 K2
Marsh Green Wrekin 57 L2
Marshland St James Norfk 75 K9
Marsh Lane Derbys 84 F5
Marsh Lane Gloucs 31 Q3
Marshside Sefton 88 D7
Marsh Street Somset 18 C6
Marshwood Dorset 10 H5
Marske N York 103 M10
Marske-by-the-Sea R & Cl 104 H6
Marsland Green Wigan 82 E5
Marston Ches W 82 E9
Marston Herefs 45 M3
Marston Lincs 73 M2
Marston Oxon 34 F3
Marston Staffs 58 B2
Marston Staffs 70 G9
Marston Warwks 59 K6
Marston Wilts 21 J3
Marston Green Solhll 59 J7
Marston Jabbet Warwks 59 N7
Marston Magna Somset 19 Q10
Marston Meysey Wilts 33 M5
Marston Montgomery Derbys 71 L7
Marston Moretaine C Beds 49 Q6
Marston on Dove Derbys 71 N9
Marston St Lawrence Nhants 48 F6
Marston Stannett Herefs 45 R3
Marston Trussell Nhants 60 E3
Marstow Herefs 45 R11
Marsworth Bucks 35 P2
Marten Wilts 21 Q2
Marthall Ches E 82 G9
Martham Norfk 77 P8
Martin Hants 21 L11
Martin Kent 27 P2
Martin Lincs 86 F9
Martin Lincs 86 H7
Martindale Cumb 101 M7
Martin Dales Lincs 86 G8
Martin Drove End Hants 21 L10
Martinhoe Devon 17 M2
Martin Hussingtree Worcs 46 G2
Martinscroft Warrtn 82 E7
Martinstown Dorset 11 N7
Martlesham Suffk 53 M2
Martlesham Heath Suffk 53 M2
Martletwy Pembks 41 K8
Martley Worcs 46 E2
Martock Somset 19 N11
Marton Ches E 83 J11
Marton Ches W 82 D11
Marton Cumb 94 E5
Marton E R Yk 93 L3
Marton E R Yk 99 Q7
Marton Lincs 85 P4
Marton Middsb 104 F7
Marton N York 97 P8
Marton N York 98 E4
Marton Shrops 56 D4
Marton Warwks 59 P11
Marton-le-Moor N York 97 N6
Martyr's Green Surrey 36 C9
Martyr Worthy Hants 22 F8
Marwick Ork 169 b4
Marwood Devon 17 J4
Marybank Highld 155 N7
Maryburgh Highld 155 P6
Maryculter Abers 151 M8
Marygold Border 129 L8
Maryhill C Glas 125 P4
Maryhill Crematorium C Glas 125 P4
Marykirk Abers 143 M4
Maryland Mons 31 P3
Marylebone Gt Lon 36 G4
Marylebone Wigan 88 H9
Marypark Moray 157 M10
Maryport Cumb 100 D3
Maryport D & G 106 F11
Marystow Devon 8 B8
Mary Tavy Devon 8 D9
Maryton Angus 143 M6
Marywell Abers 150 F8
Marywell Abers 151 N8
Marywell Angus 143 M9
Masham N York 97 K4
Mashbury Essex 51 Q8
Mason N u Ty 113 K6
Masongill N York 95 P5
Masonhill Crematorium S Ayrs 114 G3
Mastin Moor Derbys 84 G5
Matching Essex 51 M8
Matching Green Essex 51 M8
Matching Tye Essex 51 M8
Matfen Nthumb 112 F6
Matfield Kent 25 Q2
Mathern Mons 31 P6
Mathon Herefs 46 D5
Mathry Pembks 40 G4
Matlask Norfk 76 H5
Matlock Derbys 84 D9
Matlock Bank Derbys 84 D8
Matlock Bath Derbys 84 C9
Matlock Dale Derbys 84 C9
Matson Gloucs 46 G11
Matterdale End Cumb 101 L6
Mattersey Notts 85 L3
Mattersey Thorpe Notts 85 L3
Mattingley Hants 23 K3
Mattishall Norfk 76 F9
Mattishall Burgh Norfk 76 F9
Mauchline E Ayrs 115 J2
Maud Abers 159 M8
Maufant Jersey 11 c1
Maugersbury Gloucs 47 P9
Maughold IoM 80 g3
Mauld Highld 155 M10
Maulden C Beds 50 C3
Maulds Meaburn Cumb 102 B7
Maunby N York 97 N3
Maund Bryan Herefs 45 R4
Maundown Somset 18 E9
Mautby Norfk 77 P9
Mavesyn Ridware Staffs 71 K11
Mavis Enderby Lincs 87 L7
Mawbray Cumb 109 N11
Mawdesley Lancs 88 F8
Mawdlam Brdgnd 29 M8
Mawgan Cnwll 3 J8
Mawgan Porth Cnwll 4 D8
Maw Green Ches E 70 C3
Mawla Cnwll 3 J4
Mawnan Cnwll 3 K8
Mawnan Smith Cnwll 3 K8
Mawsley Nhants 60 H5
Mawthorpe Lincs 87 N6
Maxey C Pete 74 B9
Maxstoke Warwks 59 K7
Maxted Street Kent 27 K3
Maxton Border 118 B4
Maxton Kent 27 P3
Maxwell Town D & G 109 L5
Maxworthy Cnwll 5 M3
Mayals Swans 28 H7
May Bank Staffs 70 F5
Maybole S Ayrs 114 E6
Maybury Surrey 36 B9
Mayes Green Surrey 24 D3
Mayfield E Susx 25 N5
Mayfield Mdloth 128 B7
Mayfield Staffs 71 M5
Mayford Surrey 23 Q3
May Hill Gloucs 46 D10
Mayland Essex 52 F11
Maylandsea Essex 52 F11
Maynard's Green E Susx 25 N7
Maypole Birm 58 G9
Maypole Kent 39 M9
Maypole Mons 45 P11
Maypole Green Norfk 65 N2
Maypole Green Suffk 64 C10
Maypole Green Suffk 65 K8
May's Green Oxon 35 K8
May's Green Surrey 36 C9
Mead Devon 16 C8
Meadgate BaNES 20 C3
Meadle Bucks 35 M3
Meadowfield Dur 103 P3
Meadowtown Shrops 56 E4
Meadwell Devon 5 Q5
Meaford Staffs 70 F7
Meal Bank Cumb 101 P11
Mealrigg Cumb 109 P11
Mealsgate Cumb 100 H2
Meanwood Leeds 90 H3
Mearbeck N York 96 B8
Meare Somset 19 N6
Meare Green Somset 19 J10
Meare Green Somset 19 K9
Mearns E Rens 125 N6
Mears Ashby Nhants 60 H7
Measham Leics 72 A8
Meathop Cumb 95 J4
Meaux E R Yk 93 J3
Meavy Devon 6 E5
Medbourne Leics 60 H2
Meddon Devon 16 D8
Meden Vale Notts 85 J7
Medlam Lincs 87 K9
Medlar Lancs 88 E3
Medmenham Bucks 35 M8
Medomsley Dur 112 H10
Medstead Hants 23 J7
Medway Crematorium Kent 38 B9
Medway Services Medway 38 D9
Meerbrook Staffs 70 H2

Meer Common Herefs....45 M4
Meesden Herts....51 K4
Meeson Wrekin....70 A10
Meeth Devon....17 J10
Meeting Green Suffk....63 M9
Meeting House Hill Norfk....77 L6
Meidrim Carmth....41 Q6
Meifod Powys....56 B2
Meigle P & K....142 D9
Meikle Carco D & G....115 Q5
Meikle Earnock S Lans....126 C7
Meikle Kilmory Ag & B....124 D5
Meikle Obney P & K....141 P10
Meikleour P & K....142 B10
Meikle Wartle Abers....158 H11
Meinciau Carmth....28 E2
Meir C Stke....70 G6
Meir Heath Staffs....70 G6
Melbourn Cambs....51 J2
Melbourne Derbys....72 B5
Melbourne E R Yk....92 C2
Melbur Cnwll....3 N3
Melbury Devon....16 F8
Melbury Abbas Dorset....20 G10
Melbury Bubb Dorset....11 M3
Melbury Osmond Dorset....11 M3
Melbury Sampford
  Dorset....11 M3
Melchbourne Bed....61 M7
Melcombe Bingham
  Dorset....12 C4
Meldon Devon....8 E6
Meldon Nthumb....112 H4
Meldon Park Nthumb....112 H3
Meldreth Cambs....62 E11
Meldrum Stirlg....133 L8
Melfort Ag & B....130 G5
Meliden Denbgs....80 F8
Melinau Pembks....41 N8
Melin-byrhedyn Powys....55 J5
Melincourt Neath....29 M4
Melin-y-coed Conwy....67 Q2
Melin-y-ddol Powys....55 P3
Melin-y-wig Denbgs....68 D5
Melkinthorpe Cumb....101 Q5
Melkridge Nthumb....111 P8
Melksham Wilts....20 H2
Mellangoose Cnwll....2 H8
Mell Green W Berk....34 E9
Mellguards Cumb....110 H11
Melling Lancs....95 M6
Melling Sefton....81 M4
Melling Mount Sefton....81 N4
Mellis Suffk....64 F7
Mellon Charles Highld....160 C8
Mellon Udrigle Highld....160 D7
Mellor Lancs....89 K4
Mellor Stockp....83 L7
Mellor Brook Lancs....89 J4
Mells Somset....20 D5
Mells Suffk....65 N6
Melmerby Cumb....102 B3
Melmerby N York....96 G3
Melmerby N York....97 M5
Melness Highld....165 N4
Melon Green Suffk....64 A10
Melplash Dorset....11 K5
Melrose Border....117 Q4
Melsetter Ork....169 b8
Melsonby N York....103 N9
Meltham Kirk....90 E8
Meltham Mills Kirk....90 E8
Melton E R Yk....92 G5
Melton Suffk....65 K11
Meltonby E R Yk....98 F10
Melton Constable Norfk....76 F5
Melton Mowbray Leics....73 K7
Melton Ross N Linc....93 J8
Melvaig Highld....160 A9
Melverley Shrops....69 K11
Melverley Green Shrops....69 K11
Melvich Highld....166 E4
Membury Devon....10 F4
Membury Services
  W Berk....34 B9
Memsie Abers....159 N5
Memus Angus....142 G6
Menabilly Cnwll....4 H11
Menagissey Cnwll....3 J4
Menai Bridge IoA....79 K10
Mendham Suffk....65 K5
Mendip Crematorium
  Somset....19 Q6
Mendip Hills....19 P4
Mendlesham Suffk....64 G8
Mendlesham Green
  Suffk....64 F7
Menheniot Cnwll....5 M9
Menithwood Worcs....57 N11
Mennock D & G....115 R6
Menston C Brad....90 F2
Menstrie Clacks....133 P8
Menthorpe N York....92 B4
Mentmore Bucks....49 P11
Meoble Highld....145 N10
Meole Brace Shrops....56 H2
Meonstoke Hants....22 H11
Meopham Kent....37 P7
Meopham Green Kent....37 P7
Meopham Station Kent....37 P7
Mepal Cambs....62 F4
Meppershall C Beds....50 D3
Merbach Herefs....45 L5
Mere Ches E....82 F8
Mere Wilts....20 F8
Mere Brow Lancs....88 E7
Mereclough Lancs....89 P4
Mere Green Birm....58 H5
Mere Green Worcs....47 J2
Mere Heath Ches W....82 E10
Meresborough Medway....38 D9
Mereworth Kent....37 Q10
Meriden Solhll....59 K8
Merkadale Highld....152 F11
Merley Poole....12 H5
Merlin's Bridge Pembks....40 H8
Merrington Shrops....69 N10
Merrion Pembks....40 H11
Merriott Somset....11 J2
Merrivale Devon....8 D9
Merrow Surrey....36 B10
Merry Field Hill Dorset....12 H4
Merryhill Herts....36 C5
Merryhill Wolves....58 C5
Merry Lees Leics....72 D9
Merrymeet Cnwll....5 M8
Mersea Island Essex....52 H7
Mersham Kent....27 J3
Merstham Surrey....36 G10
Merston W Susx....15 N6

Merstone IoW....14 F9
Merther Cnwll....3 M5
Merthyr Carmth....42 G10
Merthyr Cynog Powys....44 D7
Merthyr Dyfan V Glam....30 F11
Merthyr Mawr Brdgnd....29 N9
Merthyr Tydfil Myr Td....30 D3
Merthyr Vale Myr Td....30 E5
Merton Devon....17 J9
Merton Gt Lon....36 G6
Merton Norfk....64 C2
Merton Oxon....48 G11
Meshaw Devon....17 P8
Messing Essex....52 E8
Messingham N Linc....92 E10
Metfield Suffk....65 K5
Metherell Cnwll....5 Q8
Metheringham Lincs....86 E8
Methil Fife....135 K8
Methilhill Fife....135 K7
Methley Leeds....91 K5
Methley Junction Leeds....91 K5
Methlick Abers....159 L10
Methven P & K....134 C2
Methwold Norfk....63 M2
Methwold Hythe Norfk....63 M2
Mettingham Suffk....65 M4
Metton Norfk....76 J4
Mevagissey Cnwll....3 Q5
Mexborough Donc....91 M10
Mey Highld....167 N2
Meyllteyrn Gwynd....66 C8
Meysey Hampton
  Gloucs....33 M4
Miabhig W Isls....168 f4
Miavaig W Isls....168 f4
Michaelchurch Herefs....45 Q9
Michaelchurch Escley
  Herefs....45 L8
Michaelchurch-on-
  Arrow Powys....45 J4
Michaelstone-y-Fedw
  Newpt....30 H8
Michaelston-le-Pit
  V Glam....30 G10
Michaelstow Cnwll....4 H6
Michaelwood Services
  Gloucs....32 D5
Michelcombe Devon....6 H5
Micheldever Hants....22 F7
Micheldever Station
  Hants....22 F6
Michelmersh Hants....22 B9
Mickfield Suffk....64 G9
Micklebring Donc....84 H2
Mickleby N York....105 M8
Micklefield Leeds....91 L4
Micklefield Green Herts....50 B11
Mickleham Surrey....36 E10
Mickleover C Derb....71 Q8
Micklethwaite C Brad....90 E2
Micklethwaite Cumb....110 E10
Mickleton Dur....103 J5
Mickleton Gloucs....47 N6
Mickletown Leeds....91 L5
Mickle Trafford Ches W....81 N11
Mickley Derbys....84 D5
Mickley N York....97 L5
Mickley Green Suffk....64 A10
Mickley Square Nthumb....112 G8
Mid Ardlaw Abers....159 M5
Midbea Ork....169 d2
Mid Beltie Abers....150 G7
Mid Bockhampton
  Dorset....13 L5
Mid Calder W Loth....127 K4
Mid Clyth Highld....167 N9
Mid Culbuachy Abers....158 G5
Middle Assendon Oxon....35 K7
Middle Aston Oxon....48 E9
Middle Barton Oxon....48 D9
Middlebie D & G....110 D5
Middlebridge P & K....141 L4
Middle Chinnock Somset....11 K2
Middle Claydon Bucks....49 K9
Middlecliffe Barns....91 L9
Middlecott Devon....8 H7
Middle Duntisbourne
  Gloucs....33 J3
Middleham N York....96 H3
Middle Handley Derbys....84 F5
Middle Harling Norfk....64 D4
Middlehill Cnwll....5 M8
Middlehill Wilts....32 F11
Middlehope Shrops....56 H7
Middle Kames Ag & B....131 J10
Middle Littleton Worcs....47 L5
Middle Madeley Staffs....70 D5
Middle Maes-coed
  Herefs....45 L8
Middlemarsh Dorset....11 P3
Middle Mayfield Staffs....71 L6
Middle Mill Pembks....40 F5
Middlemore Devon....6 D4
Middle Quarter Kent....26 E4
Middle Rasen Lincs....86 E3
Middle Rocombe Devon....7 N5
Middle Salter Lancs....95 N8
Middlesbrough Middsb....104 E7
Middlesceugh Cumb....101 M2
Middleshaw Cumb....95 M3
Middlesmoor N York....96 G6
Middle Stoford Somset....18 G10
Middle Stoke Medway....38 D6
Middlestone Moor Dur....103 P4
Middle Stoughton
  Somset....19 M5
Middlestown Wakefd....90 H7
Middle Street Gloucs....32 E4
Middle Taphouse Cnwll....5 K9
Middlethird Border....118 C2
Middleton Ag & B....136 A7
Middleton Cumb....95 N3
Middleton Derbys....71 M2
Middleton Derbys....84 C9
Middleton Essex....52 E4
Middleton Hants....22 D6
Middleton Herefs....57 J11
Middleton Lancs....95 J9
Middleton Leeds....91 J5
Middleton N York....96 H11
Middleton N York....98 F3
Middleton Nhants....60 H3
Middleton Norfk....75 N7
Middleton Nthumb....112 G4
Middleton Nthumb....119 M3
Middleton P & K....134 E6
Middleton Rochdl....89 P9
Middleton Shrops....57 J9

Middleton Shrops....69 K9
Middleton Suffk....65 N8
Middleton Swans....28 D7
Middleton Warwks....59 J5
Middleton Cheney
  Nhants....48 E6
Middleton Crematorium
  Rochdl....89 P10
Middleton Green Staffs....70 H7
Middleton Hall Nthumb....119 J5
Middleton-in-Teesdale
  Dur....102 H5
Middleton Moor Suffk....65 N8
Middleton One Row
  Darltn....104 C8
Middleton-on-Leven
  N York....104 E9
Middleton-on-Sea
  W Susx....15 Q6
Middleton on the Hill
  Herefs....45 Q2
Middleton on the Wolds
  E R Yk....99 J11
Middleton Park C Aber....151 N5
Middleton Priors Shrops....57 L6
Middleton Quernhow
  N York....97 M5
Middleton St George
  Darltn....104 B8
Middleton Scriven
  Shrops....57 M7
Middleton Stoney Oxon....48 F10
Middleton Tyas N York....103 P9
Middletown N Som....31 N10
Middle Town IoS....2 b3
Middletown N Som....31 N10
Middletown Powys....56 E2
Middle Tysoe Warwks....48 B6
Middle Wallop Hants....21 Q7
Middlewich Ches E....82 F11
Middle Winterslow Wilts....21 P8
Middlewood Cnwll....5 M6
Middlewood Herefs....45 K6
Middle Woodford Wilts....21 M7
Middlewood Green Suffk....64 F9
Middleyard E Ayrs....125 N11
Middle Yard Gloucs....32 F4
Middlezoy Somset....19 L8
Middridge Dur....103 P5
Midford BaNES....20 E2
Midge Hall Lancs....88 G6
Midgeholme Cumb....111 M9
Midgham W Berk....34 G11
Midgley Calder....90 C5
Midgley Wakefd....90 H8
Mid Holmwood Surrey....36 E11
Midhopestones Sheff....90 G11
Midhurst W Susx....23 N10
Mid Lavant W Susx....15 N5
Midlem Border....117 Q5
Mid Mains Highld....155 M10
Midney Somset....19 N9
Midpark Ag & B....124 C6
Midsomer Norton
  BaNES....20 C4
Midtown Highld....165 N4
Midville Lincs....87 L9
Mid Warwickshire
  Crematorium Warwks....48 B3
Midway Ches E....83 K8
Mid Yell Shet....169 s4
Migvie Abers....150 C6
Milborne Port Somset....20 C11
Milborne St Andrew
  Dorset....12 D5
Milborne Wick Somset....20 C10
Milbourne Nthumb....112 H5
Milbourne Wilts....33 J7
Milburn Cumb....102 C5
Milbury Heath S Glos....32 C6
Milby N York....97 P7
Milcombe Oxon....48 D8
Milden Suffk....52 G2
Mildenhall Suffk....63 M6
Mildenhall Wilts....33 P11
Milebrook Powys....56 E10
Milebush Kent....26 C2
Mile Elm Wilts....33 J11
Mile End Essex....52 G6
Mile End Gloucs....31 Q2
Mile End Suffk....65 L4
Mileham Norfk....76 C8
Mile Oak Br & H....24 F9
Mile Oak Kent....25 Q2
Mile Oak Staffs....59 J4
Miles Hope Herefs....45 R2
Milesmark Fife....134 D10
Miles Platting Manch....83 J5
Mile Town Kent....38 F7
Milfield Nthumb....118 H4
Milford Derbys....84 E11
Milford Devon....16 C7
Milford Powys....55 P6
Milford Staffs....70 H10
Milford Surrey....23 P6
Milford Haven Pembks....40 H9
Milford on Sea Hants....13 N6
Milkwall Gloucs....31 Q3
Millais Jersey....11 a1
Milland W Susx....23 M9
Milland Marsh W Susx....23 M9
Mill Bank Calder....90 C6
Millbeck Cumb....101 J5
Millbreck Abers....159 P9
Millbridge Surrey....23 M6
Millbrook C Beds....50 B3
Millbrook C Sotn....14 C4
Millbrook Cnwll....6 C8
Millbrook Cnwll....11 b2
Millbrook Tamesd....83 L5
Mill Brow Stockp....83 L7
Millbuie Abers....151 K6
Millbuie Highld....155 Q7
Millcombe Devon....7 L9
Mill Common Norfk....77 L11
Mill Common Suffk....65 N5
Millcorner E Susx....26 D7
Millcraig Highld....156 B3
Mill Cross Devon....7 J6
Milldale Staffs....71 L4
Mill End Bucks....35 L7
Mill End Cambs....62 D4
Millend Gloucs....32 D5
Mill End Herts....51 H4
Millerhill Mdloth....127 Q4
Miller's Dale Derbys....83 P10
Millers Green Derbys....71 P4
Miller's Green Essex....51 N4
Millerston C Glas....125 Q4
Millerston Lancs....89 P4
Millgate Lancs....89 P5

Mill Green Cambs....63 K11
Mill Green Essex....51 P10
Mill Green Herts....50 F8
Mill Green Lincs....74 D6
Mill Green Norfk....64 G5
Mill Green Shrops....70 B9
Mill Green Staffs....58 G4
Mill Green Staffs....71 K10
Mill Green Suffk....52 G3
Mill Green Suffk....64 D10
Mill Green Suffk....64 G9
Mill Green Suffk....65 L9
Millhalf Herefs....45 K5
Millhayes Devon....10 E4
Millhead Lancs....95 K6
Millheugh S Lans....126 C7
Mill Hill E Susx....25 P9
Mill Hill Gt Lon....36 F2
Millhouse Ag & B....124 B4
Millhouse Cumb....101 L3
Millhousebridge D & G....109 P3
Millhouse Green Barns....90 G10
Millhouses Barns....91 L10
Millhouses Sheff....84 D4
Milliken Park Rens....125 L5
Millin Cross Pembks....41 J8
Millington E R Yk....98 G10
Millmeece Staffs....70 E8
Millness Cumb....95 L4
Mill of Drummond P & K....133 N4
Mill of Haldane W Duns....132 D11
Millom Cumb....94 D4
Millook Cnwll....5 K2
Millpool Cnwll....2 F7
Millpool Cnwll....5 J7
Millport N Ayrs....124 F7
Mill Side Cumb....95 J4
Mill Street Kent....37 Q9
Mill Street Norfk....76 F8
Mill Street Suffk....64 F7
Millthorpe Derbys....84 D5
Millthrop Cumb....95 P2
Milltimber C Aber....151 M7
Milltown Abers....149 P6
Milltown Abers....150 D4
Milltown Cnwll....5 J10
Milltown D & G....110 F5
Milltown Derbys....84 E8
Milltown Devon....17 K4
Milltown of Campfield
  Abers....150 H7
Milltown of Edinvillie
  Moray....157 P9
Milltown of Learney
  Abers....150 G7
Milnathort P & K....134 E7
Milngavie E Duns....125 P3
Milnrow Rochdl....89 Q8
Milnthorpe Cumb....95 K4
Milnthorpe Wakefd....91 J7
Milovaig Highld....152 B8
Milson Shrops....57 L10
Milstead Kent....38 F10
Milston Wilts....21 N5
Milthorpe Nhants....48 G5
Milton C Stke....70 G4
Milton Cambs....62 G8
Milton Cumb....111 L8
Milton D & G....106 H7
Milton D & G....108 H6
Milton Derbys....71 Q9
Milton Highld....153 N9
Milton Highld....155 N11
Milton Highld....155 Q8
Milton Highld....156 D3
Milton Highld....167 P6
Milton Inver....125 K4
Milton Kent....37 Q6
Milton Moray....149 M4
Milton Moray....158 D5
Milton N Som....19 K2
Milton Newpt....31 L7
Milton Notts....85 M6
Milton Oxon....34 E6
Milton Oxon....48 E7
Milton P & K....141 Q6
Milton Pembks....41 K10
Milton Somset....19 N10
Milton Stirlg....132 G7
Milton Stirlg....125 L3
Milton Abbas Dorset....12 D4
Milton Abbot Devon....5 Q6
Milton Bridge Mdloth....127 P5
Milton Bryan C Beds....49 Q8
Milton Clevedon Somset....20 C7
Milton Damerel Devon....16 F9
Milton End Gloucs....32 D2
Milton End Gloucs....33 M4
Milton Ernest Bed....61 M9
Milton Green Ches W....69 N3
Milton Hill Oxon....34 G6
Milton Keynes M Keyn....49 N7
Milton Lilbourne Wilts....21 N2
Milton Malsor Nhants....60 F9
Milton Morenish P & K....140 F10
Milton of Auchinhove
  Abers....150 F7
Milton of Balgonie Fife....135 J7
Milton of Buchanan
  Stirlg....132 E9
Milton of Campsie
  E Duns....126 B2
Milton of Leys Highld....156 B9
Milton of Murtle C Aber....151 M7
Milton of Tullich Abers....150 B8
Milton on Stour Dorset....20 E9
Milton Regis Kent....38 F9
Milton Street E Susx....25 M10
Milton-under-
  Wychwood Oxon....47 Q11

Minnigaff D & G....107 M4
Minnis Bay Kent....39 N8
Minnonie Abers....159 J5
Minshull Vernon Ches E....70 B2
Minskip N York....97 N8
Minstead Hants....13 N2
Minsted W Susx....23 N10
Minster Kent....38 G7
Minster Kent....39 P9
Minsterley Shrops....56 F3
Minster Lovell Oxon....34 B2
Minsterworth Gloucs....46 E11
Minterne Magna Dorset....11 P4
Minterne Parva Dorset....11 P4
Minting Lincs....86 G6
Mintlaw Abers....159 N8
Mintlyn Crematorium
  Norfk....75 N7
Minto Border....117 R6
Minton Shrops....56 G6
Minwear Pembks....41 K8
Minworth Birm....59 J6
Mirehouse Cumb....100 C7
Mireland Highld....167 P4
Mirfield Kirk....90 G7
Miserden Gloucs....32 H3
Miskin Rhondd....30 D5
Miskin Rhondd....30 D8
Misson Notts....85 L2
Misterton Leics....60 C4
Misterton Notts....85 N2
Misterton Somset....11 K3
Mistley Essex....53 K5
Mistley Heath Essex....53 K5
Mitcham Gt Lon....36 G7
Mitcheldean Gloucs....46 C11
Mitchell Cnwll....3 M3
Mitchellslacks D & G....116 D11
Mitchel Troy Mons....31 N2
Mitford Nthumb....113 J3
Mithian Cnwll....3 J3
Mitton Staffs....70 F11
Mixbury Oxon....48 H8
Mixenden Calder....90 D5
Moats Tye Suffk....64 E10
Mobberley Ches E....82 G9
Mobberley Staffs....71 J6
Moccas Herefs....45 M6
Mochdre Conwy....79 Q9
Mochdre Powys....55 P7
Mochrum D & G....107 K8
Mockbeggar Hants....13 L3
Mockbeggar Kent....26 B2
Mockerkin Cumb....100 E6
Modbury Devon....6 H8
Moddershall Staffs....70 G7
Moelfre IoA....79 J7
Moelfre Powys....68 G9
Moel Tryfan Gwynd....67 J3
Moffat D & G....116 F9
Moggerhanger C Beds....61 P11
Moira Leics....71 Q11
Molash Kent....38 H11
Mol-chlach Highld....144 G5
Mold Flints....68 H2
Moldgreen Kirk....90 F7
Molehill Green Essex....51 N6
Molehill Green Essex....52 B7
Molescroft E R Yk....92 H2
Molesden Nthumb....112 H4
Molesworth Cambs....61 N5
Molland Devon....17 Q6
Mollington Ches W....81 M10
Mollington Oxon....48 D5
Mollinsburn N Lans....126 C3
Monachty Cerdgn....43 K2
Mondynes Abers....143 P2
Monewden Suffk....65 J10
Moneydie P & K....134 C2
Moneyrow Green W & M....35 N9
Moniaive D & G....115 Q3
Monifieth Angus....142 H11
Monikie Angus....142 H10
Monimail Fife....134 H5
Monington Pembks....41 M2
Monk Bretton Barns....91 K9
Monken Hadley Gt Lon....50 F11
Monk Fryston N York....91 N5
Monkhide Herefs....46 B6
Monkhill Cumb....110 F9
Monkhopton Shrops....57 L6
Monkland Herefs....45 P3
Monkleigh Devon....16 H7
Monknash V Glam....29 P10
Monkokehampton
  Devon....8 E3
Monkseaton N Tyne....113 M6
Monks Eleigh Suffk....52 G2
Monk's Gate W Susx....24 F5
Monks Heath Ches E....82 H10
Monk Sherborne Hants....22 H3
Monks Horton Kent....27 K3
Monksilver Somset....18 E7
Monks Kirby Warwks....59 Q8
Monk Soham Suffk....65 J8
Monkspath Solhll....58 H9
Monks Risborough
  Bucks....35 M4
Monksthorpe Lincs....87 M7
Monk Street Essex....51 P5
Monkswood Mons....31 K4
Monkton Devon....10 D4
Monkton Kent....39 N9
Monkton S Ayrs....114 G2
Monkton S Tyne....113 M8
Monkton V Glam....29 N7
Monkton Combe BaNES....20 E2
Monkton Deverill Wilts....20 G7
Monkton Farleigh Wilts....32 F11
Monkton Heathfield
  Somset....19 J9
Monkton Up Wimborne
  Dorset....12 H2
Monkton Wyld Dorset....10 F5
Monkwearmouth Sundld....113 N9
Monkwood Hants....23 J8
Monmore Green Wolves....58 D5
Monmouth Mons....31 P2
Monnington on Wye
  Herefs....45 M6
Monreith D & G....107 L9
Montacute Somset....19 N11
Montcliffe Bolton....89 K8
Montford Shrops....69 M2
Montford Bridge Shrops....69 M11
Montgarrie Abers....150 D4
Montgomery Powys....56 D5
Monton Salfd....82 G5
Montrose Angus....143 N6
Mont Saint Guern....10 b2

Monxton Hants 22 B6
Monyash Derbys 83 Q11
Monymusk Abers 150 H4
Monzie P & K 133 P2
Moodiesburn N Lans 126 B3
Moonzie Fife 135 J4
Moor Allerton Leeds 91 J3
Moorbath Dorset 11 J5
Moorby Lincs 87 J8
Moorcot Herefs 45 M3
Moor Crichel Dorset 12 G3
Moordown Bmouth 13 J6
Moore Halton 82 C8
Moor End C Beds 49 Q10
Moor End Calder 90 D5
Moor End Devon 17 M10
Moorend Gloucs 32 D4
Moor End Lancs 88 D2
Moor End N York 91 Q3
Moorends Donc 92 A7
Moorgreen Hants 22 E11
Moor Green Herts 50 H5
Moorgreen Notts 84 G11
Moorhall Derbys 84 D6
Moorhampton Herefs 45 M5
Moorhead C Brad 90 E3
Moor Head Leeds 90 G5
Moorhouse Cumb 110 E10
Moorhouse Cumb 110 F9
Moorhouse Donc 91 M8
Moorhouse Notts 85 N7
Moorhouse Bank Surrey 37 K10
Moorland Somset 19 K8
Moorlinch Somset 19 L7
Moor Monkton N York 97 R9
Moor Row Cumb 100 D8
Moor Row Cumb 110 D11
Moorsholm R & Cl 105 J8
Moorside Dorset 20 E11
Moor Side Lancs 88 E4
Moor Side Lancs 88 F3
Moorside Leeds 90 G3
Moor Side Lincs 87 J9
Moorside Oldham 89 Q9
Moorstock Kent 27 K4
Moor Street Birm 58 E8
Moor Street Medway 38 D8
Mooreswater Cnwll 5 L9
Moorthorpe Wakefd 91 M8
Moortown Devon 6 E4
Moortown Hants 13 L4
Moortown IoW 14 D10
Moortown Leeds 90 H3
Moortown Lincs 93 J11
Moortown Wrekin 69 R11
Morangie Highld 162 H10
Morar Highld 145 L9
Moray Crematorium Moray 158 A5
Morborne Cambs 61 P2
Morchard Bishop Devon 9 J3
Morcombelake Dorset 11 J6
Morcott Rutlnd 73 N10
Morda Shrops 69 J9
Morden Dorset 12 F5
Morden Gt Lon 36 G7
Mordiford Herefs 45 R7
Mordon Dur 104 B5
More Shrops 56 E6
Morebath Devon 18 C9
Morebattle Border 118 E6
Morecambe Lancs 95 J8
Moredon Swindn 33 M7
Morefield Highld 161 J7
Morehall Kent 27 M4
Moreleigh Devon 7 K8
Morenish P & K 140 F10
Moresby Parks Cumb 100 C7
Morestead Hants 22 F9
Moreton Dorset 12 D7
Moreton Essex 51 M9
Moreton Herefs 45 Q2
Moreton Oxon 35 J4
Moreton Staffs 70 D11
Moreton Staffs 71 L9
Moreton Wirral 81 K7
Moreton Corbet Shrops 69 Q10
Moretonhampstead Devon 9 J7
Moreton-in-Marsh Gloucs 47 P8
Moreton Jeffries Herefs 46 B5
Moretonmill Shrops 69 Q10
Moreton Morrell Warwks 48 B3
Moreton on Lugg Herefs 45 Q5
Moreton Paddox Warwks 48 B4
Moreton Pinkney Nhants 48 G5
Moreton Say Shrops 70 A8
Moreton Valence Gloucs 32 E3
Morfa Cerdgn 42 F4
Morfa Bychan Gwynd 67 J7
Morfa Dinlle Gwynd 66 G3
Morfa Glas Neath 29 N3
Morfa Nefyn Gwynd 66 D6
Morganstown Cardif 30 F8
Morgan's Vale Wilts 21 N10
Morham E Loth 128 F5
Moriah Cerdgn 54 E9
Morland Cumb 102 B6
Morley Ches E 82 H8
Morley Derbys 72 B2
Morley Dur 103 M5
Morley Leeds 90 H5
Morley Green Ches E 82 H8
Morley St Botolph Norfk 64 F2
Mornick Cnwll 5 N7
Morningside C Edin 127 N3
Morningside N Lans 126 E6
Morningthorpe Norfk 65 J3
Morpeth Nthumb 113 J3
Morphie Abers 143 N5
Morrey Staffs 71 L11
Morridge Side Staffs 71 J4
Morriston Swans 29 J5
Morston Norfk 76 E3
Mortehoe Devon 16 H2
Morthen Rothm 84 G3
Mortimer W Berk 23 J2
Mortimer Common W Berk 35 J11
Mortimer's Cross Herefs 45 N2
Mortimer West End Hants 22 H2
Mortlake Gt Lon 36 F5
Mortlake Crematorium Gt Lon 36 E5
Morton Cumb 101 N3
Morton Cumb 110 G10
Morton Derbys 84 F8
Morton IoW 14 H9

Morton Lincs 74 A6
Morton Lincs 85 P2
Morton Notts 85 M10
Morton Shrops 69 J10
Morton Hall Lincs 85 Q8
Mortonhall Crematorium C Edin 127 P4
Morton-on-Swale N York 97 M2
Morton on the Hill 76 G8
Morton Tinmouth Dur 103 N6
Morvah Cnwll 2 C6
Morval Cnwll 5 M10
Morvich Highld 146 B3
Morville Shrops 57 M6
Morville Heath Shrops 57 M6
Morwellham Quay Devon 6 C5
Morwenstow Cnwll 16 C8
Mosborough Sheff 84 F4
Moscow E Ayrs 125 M9
Mose Shrops 57 P6
Mosedale Cumb 101 L4
Moseley Birm 58 G8
Moseley Wolves 58 D5
Moseley Worcs 46 F3
Moses Gate Bolton 89 L9
Moss Ag & B 136 B7
Moss Donc 91 P8
Moss Wrexhm 69 K4
Mossat Abers 150 D4
Mossbank Shet 169 r6
Moss Bank St Hel 81 Q5
Mossbay Cumb 100 C5
Mossblown S Ayrs 114 H3
Mossbrow Traffd 82 F7
Mossburnford Border 118 C7
Mossdale D & G 108 E6
Mossdale E Ayrs 115 J7
Moss Edge Lancs 88 E2
Moss End Ches E 82 E9
Mossend N Lans 126 C5
Mosser Mains Cumb 100 F5
Mossley Ches E 70 F2
Mossley Tamesd 83 L4
Mosspaul Hotel Border 117 M11
Moss Side Cumb 110 C10
Moss-side Highld 156 F6
Moss Side Lancs 88 D4
Moss Side Sefton 81 M4
Mosstodloch Moray 157 Q6
Mossyard D & G 107 P7
Mossy Lea Lancs 88 G8
Mosterton Dorset 11 K3
Moston Manch 83 J4
Moston Shrops 69 Q9
Moston Green Ches E 70 C2
Mostyn Flints 80 H8
Motcombe Dorset 20 G9
Mothecombe Devon 6 G9
Motherby Cumb 101 M5
Motherwell N Lans 126 C6
Motspur Park Gt Lon 36 F7
Mottingham Gt Lon 37 K6
Mottisfont Hants 22 B9
Mottistone IoW 14 D10
Mottram in Longdendale Tamesd 83 L5
Mottram St Andrew Ches E 83 J9
Mouilpied Guern 10 b2
Mouldsworth Ches W 81 Q10
Moulin P & K 141 M6
Moulsecoomb Br & H 24 H9
Moulsford Oxon 34 G8
Moulsoe M Keyn 49 P6
Moultavie Highld 156 A3
Moulton Ches W 82 E11
Moulton Lincs 74 F6
Moulton N York 103 P10
Moulton Nhants 60 G7
Moulton Suffk 63 L8
Moulton V Glam 30 E11
Moulton Chapel Lincs 74 E7
Moulton St Mary Norfk 77 M10
Moulton Seas End Lincs 74 F5
Mount Cnwll 4 B10
Mount Cnwll 5 J8
Mount Kirk 90 D7
Mountain C Brad 90 D4
Mountain Ash Rhondd 30 D5
Mountain Cross Border 127 M8
Mountain Street Kent 39 J11
Mount Ambrose Cnwll 3 J5
Mount Bures Essex 52 F5
Mountfield E Susx 26 B7
Mountgerald House Highld 155 Q4
Mount Hawke Cnwll 3 J4
Mount Hermon Cnwll 2 H10
Mountjoy Cnwll 4 D9
Mount Lothian Mdloth 127 P6
Mountnessing Essex 51 P11
Mounton Mons 31 P6
Mount Pleasant Ches E 70 E3
Mount Pleasant Derbys 71 P11
Mount Pleasant Derbys 84 D11
Mount Pleasant Dur 103 Q4
Mount Pleasant E R Yk 93 N3
Mount Pleasant E Susx 25 K7
Mount Pleasant Norfk 64 D3
Mount Pleasant Suffk 63 M11
Mount Pleasant Worcs 47 K2
Mountsett Crematorium Dur 113 J10
Mountsorrel Leics 72 F8
Mount Sorrel Wilts 21 K10
Mount Tabor Calder 90 D5
Mousehill Surrey 23 P6
Mousehole Cnwll 2 D8
Mouswald D & G 109 N6
Mow Cop Ches E 70 F3
Mowhaugh Border 118 F6
Mowmacre Hill C Leic 72 F9
Mowsley Leics 60 D3
Moy Highld 147 L11
Moy Highld 156 D11
Moyle Highld 145 Q4
Moylegrove Pembks 41 M2
Muasdale Ag & B 120 C3
Muchalls Abers 151 N9
Much Birch Herefs 45 Q8
Much Cowarne Herefs 46 B5
Much Dewchurch Herefs 45 P8
Muchelney Somset 19 M10
Muchelney Ham Somset 19 M10
Much Hadham Herts 51 K7
Much Hoole Lancs 88 F6
Much Hoole Town Lancs 88 F6
Muchlarnick Cnwll 5 L10
Much Marcle Herefs 46 C8

Much Wenlock Shrops 57 L5
Muck Highld 144 F12
Mucking Thurr 37 Q4
Muckingford Thurr 37 Q5
Muckleburgh Collection Norfk 76 G3
Muckleford Dorset 11 N6
Mucklestone Staffs 70 C7
Muckley Shrops 57 L5
Muckton Lincs 87 L4
Muddiford Devon 17 K4
Muddles Green E Susx 25 M8
Mudeford Dorset 13 L6
Mudford Somset 19 Q11
Mudford Sock Somset 19 Q11
Mudgley Somset 19 N5
Mud Row Kent 38 H7
Mugdock Stirlg 125 P2
Mugeary Highld 152 G10
Mugginton Derbys 71 P6
Muggintonlane End Derbys 71 P6
Muggleswick Dur 112 F11
Muirden Abers 158 H7
Muirdrum Angus 143 K10
Muiresk Abers 158 G8
Muirhead Angus 142 E11
Muirhead Fife 134 H6
Muirhead N Lans 126 B4
Muirkirk E Ayrs 115 N2
Muirmill Stirlg 133 L11
Muir of Fowlis Abers 150 F5
Muir of Miltonduff Moray 157 M6
Muir of Ord Highld 155 P7
Muirshearlich Highld 146 E11
Muirtack Abers 159 N10
Muirton P & K 133 Q5
Muirton Mains Highld 155 N7
Muirton of Ardblair P & K 142 B9
Muker N York 102 H11
Mulbarton Norfk 76 H11
Mulben Moray 157 R7
Mulfra Cnwll 2 D7
Mull Ag & B 137 Q9
Mullacott Cross Devon 17 J3
Mullion Cnwll 2 H10
Mullion Cove Cnwll 2 H10
Mumby Lincs 87 P6
Munderfield Row Herefs 46 B4
Munderfield Stocks Herefs 46 C4
Mundesley Norfk 77 L4
Mundford Norfk 63 P2
Mundham Norfk 65 L2
Mundon Hill Essex 52 E11
Mundy Bois Kent 26 F2
Mungrisdale Cumb 101 L4
Munlochy Highld 156 A7
Munnoch N Ayrs 124 H8
Munsley Herefs 46 C6
Munslow Shrops 57 J7
Murchington Devon 8 G7
Murcot Worcs 47 L6
Murcott Oxon 48 G11
Murcott Wilts 33 J6
Murkle Highld 167 L3
Murlaggan Highld 146 C9
Murrell Green Hants 23 K3
Murroes Angus 142 H10
Murrow Cambs 74 G9
Mursley Bucks 49 M9
Murston Kent 38 F9
Murthill Angus 142 H6
Murthly P & K 141 R10
Murton C York 98 C10
Murton Cumb 102 D6
Murton Dur 113 N11
Murton N Tyne 113 M6
Murton Nthumb 129 P10
Musbury Devon 10 F6
Muscoates N York 98 D5
Musselburgh E Loth 127 Q3
Muston Leics 73 L3
Muston N York 99 M5
Mustow Green Worcs 58 C10
Muswell Hill Gt Lon 36 G3
Mutehill D & G 108 E11
Mutford Suffk 65 P4
Muthill P & K 133 P4
Mutterton Devon 9 P3
Muxton Wrekin 57 N2
Mybster Highld 167 L6
Myddfai Carmth 43 Q8
Myddle Shrops 69 N10
Mydroilyn Cerdgn 43 J3
Myerscough Lancs 88 F3
Mylor Cnwll 3 L6
Mylor Bridge Cnwll 3 L6
Mynachlog ddu Pembks 41 M4
Myndd-llan Flints 80 H10
Myndtown Shrops 56 F7
Mynydd-bach Mons 31 N6
Mynydd-Bach Swans 29 J5
Mynydd Buch Cerdgn 54 G9
Mynyddgarreg Carmth 28 D3
Mynydd Isa Flints 69 J2
Mynydd Llandygai Gwynd 79 L11
Mynytho Gwynd 66 E8
Myrebird Abers 151 J8
Myredykes Border 118 A11
Mytchett Surrey 23 N3
Mytholm Calder 90 B5
Mytholmroyd Calder 90 C5
Mythop Lancs 88 C4
Myton-on-Swale N York 97 P7

N

Naast Highld 160 C10
Nab's Head Lancs 89 J5
Na Buirgh W Isls 168 f8
Naburn C York 98 B11
Naccolt Kent 27 J3
Nackington Kent 39 L11
Nacton Suffk 53 M3
Nafferton E R Yk 99 M9
Nag's Head Gloucs 32 G5
Nailbridge Gloucs 46 B11
Nailsbourne Somset 18 H9
Nailsea N Som 31 N10
Nailstone Leics 72 C9
Nailsworth Gloucs 32 F5

Nairn Highld 156 F6
Nalderswood Surrey 36 F11
Nancegollan Cnwll 2 G7
Nancledra Cnwll 2 D6
Nanhoron Gwynd 66 D8
Nannerch Flints 80 H11
Nanpantan Leics 72 E7
Nanpean Cnwll 4 F10
Nanquidno Cnwll 2 B8
Nanstallon Cnwll 4 G8
Nant-ddu Powys 30 D2
Nanternis Cerdgn 42 G5
Nantgaredig Carmth 43 J10
Nantgarw Rhondd 30 F7
Nant-glas Powys 55 M11
Nantglyn Denbgs 68 D2
Nantgwyn Powys 55 M9
Nant Gwynant Gwynd 67 L4
Nantile Gwynd 67 J4
Nantmawr Shrops 69 J10
Nantmel Powys 55 N11
Nantmor Gwynd 67 L5
Nant Peris Gwynd 67 L3
Nant-y-Bwch Blae G 30 F2
Nant-y-caws Carmth 43 J11
Nant-y-derry Mons 31 K3
Nantyffyllon Brdgnd 29 M6
Nant-y-gollen Shrops 68 H9
Nantyglo Blae G 30 G2
Nant-y-moel Brdgnd 29 P6
Nant-y-pandy Conwy 79 M10
Naphill Bucks 35 M5
Napleton Worcs 46 G5
Nappa N York 96 C10
Napton on the Hill Warwks 48 E2
Narberth Pembks 41 M8
Narborough Leics 72 E11
Narborough Norfk 75 P8
Narkurs Cnwll 5 N10
Nasareth Gwynd 66 H5
Naseby Nhants 60 E5
Nash Bucks 49 L8
Nash Gt Lon 37 K8
Nash Herefs 45 L2
Nash Newpt 31 K8
Nash Shrops 57 L10
Nash End Worcs 57 N8
Nash Lee Bucks 35 M3
Nash's Green Hants 23 J5
Nash Street Kent 37 P7
Nassington Nhants 73 R11
Nastend Gloucs 32 E3
Nasty Herts 51 J6
Nateby Cumb 102 E9
Nateby Lancs 88 F2
National Memorial Arboretum Staffs 59 J2
National Motor Museum (Beaulieu) Hants 14 C6
National Space Science Centre C Leic 72 F9
Natland Cumb 95 L3
Naughton Suffk 52 H2
Naunton Gloucs 47 M10
Naunton Worcs 46 G7
Naunton Beauchamp Worcs 47 J4
Navenby Lincs 86 C9
Navestock Essex 51 M11
Navestock Side Essex 51 N11
Navidale House Hotel Highld 163 N3
Navity Highld 156 D5
Nawton N York 98 D4
Nayland Suffk 52 G5
Nazeing Essex 51 K9
Nazeing Gate Essex 51 K9
Neacroft Hants 13 L5
Neal's Green Warwks 59 M8
Neap Shet 169 s8
Near Cotton Staffs 71 K5
Near Sawrey Cumb 101 L11
Neasden Gt Lon 36 F3
Neasham Darltn 104 B8
Neath Neath 29 L5
Neatham Hants 23 K6
Neatishead Norfk 77 L7
Nebo Cerdgn 54 C11
Nebo Conwy 67 Q3
Nebo Gwynd 66 H4
Nebo IoA 78 H6
Necton Norfk 76 B10
Nedd Highld 164 D10
Nedderton Nthumb 113 K4
Nedging Suffk 52 G2
Nedging Tye Suffk 52 H2
Needham Norfk 65 J5
Needham Market Suffk 64 F10
Needham Street Suffk 63 M7
Needingworth Cambs 62 D6
Neen Savage Shrops 57 M9
Neen Sollars Shrops 57 M10
Neenton Shrops 57 L7
Nefyn Gwynd 66 E6
Neilston E Rens 125 M6
Nelson Caerph 30 F5
Nelson Lancs 89 P3
Nemphlar S Lans 116 B2
Nempnett Thrubwell BaNES 19 P2
Nenthall Cumb 111 Q11
Nenthead Cumb 102 E2
Nenthorn Border 118 C3
Neopardy Devon 9 J5
Nep Town W Susx 24 F7
Nercwys Flints 68 H2
Nereabolls Ag & B 122 B8
Nerston S Lans 125 Q6
Nesbit Nthumb 119 J4
Nesfield N York 96 G11
Ness Ches W 81 L9
Ness Botanic Gardens Ches W 81 L9
Nesscliffe Shrops 69 L11
Neston Ches W 81 K9
Neston Wilts 32 G11
Netchwood Shrops 57 L6
Nether Alderley Ches E 82 H9
Netheravon Wilts 21 M5
Nether Blainslie Border 117 Q2
Netherbrae Abers 159 J6
Nether Broughton Leics 72 H5
Netherburn S Lans 126 D8
Netherbury Dorset 11 K5
Netherby Cumb 110 G6
Netherby N York 97 M11
Nether Cerne Dorset 11 P5
Nethercleuch D & G 109 P3

Nether Compton Dorset 19 Q11
Nethercote Warwks 60 B8
Nethercott Devon 5 P2
Nethercott Devon 16 H4
Nether Crimond Abers 151 L3
Nether Dallachy Moray 157 R5
Netherend Gloucs 31 Q4
Nether Exe Devon 9 M4
Netherfield E Susx 26 B8
Netherfield Leics 72 F7
Netherfield Notts 72 G2
Nether Fingland S Lans 116 C8
Nethergate N Linc 92 C11
Nethergate Norfk 76 F6
Netherhampton Wilts 21 M9
Nether Handley Derbys 84 F5
Nether Handwick Angus 142 F9
Nether Haugh Rothm 91 L11
Netherhay Dorset 11 J3
Nether Headon Notts 85 M9
Nether Heage Derbys 84 E10
Nether Heyford Nhants 60 E9
Nether Howcleugh S Lans 116 E8
Nether Kellet Lancs 95 L7
Nether Kinmundy Abers 159 Q9
Netherland Green Staffs 71 L8
Nether Langwith Notts 84 H6
Netherlaw D & G 108 F12
Netherley Abers 151 M9
Nethermill D & G 109 M3
Nethermuir Abers 159 M9
Netherne-on-the-Hill Surrey 36 G9
Netheroyd Hill Kirk 90 E7
Nether Padley Derbys 84 B5
Netherplace E Rens 125 N6
Nether Poppleton C York 98 B10
Nether Row Cumb 101 K3
Netherseal Derbys 59 L2
Nether Silton N York 97 Q2
Nether Skyborry Shrops 56 D10
Nether Stowey Somset 18 G7
Nether Street Essex 51 N8
Netherstreet Wilts 21 J2
Netherthong Kirk 90 E9
Netherthorpe Derbys 84 F6
Netherton Angus 143 J6
Netherton Devon 7 M4
Netherton Dudley 58 D7
Netherton Hants 22 C3
Netherton Herefs 45 Q9
Netherton Kirk 90 E8
Netherton N Lans 126 D7
Netherton Nthumb 119 J9
Netherton Oxon 34 D5
Netherton P & K 142 A7
Netherton Shrops 57 N8
Netherton Stirlg 125 P2
Netherton Wakefd 90 H7
Netherton Worcs 47 J6
Nethertown Cumb 100 C9
Nethertown Highld 167 Q1
Nethertown Lancs 89 L3
Nethertown Staffs 71 L11
Netherurd Border 116 G2
Nether Wallop Hants 22 B7
Nether Wasdale Cumb 100 F10
Nether Welton Cumb 110 G11
Nether Westcote Gloucs 47 P10
Nether Whitacre Warwks 59 K6
Nether Whitecleuch S Lans 116 A7
Nether Winchendon Bucks 35 K2
Netherwitton Nthumb 112 G2
Nethy Bridge Highld 149 J3
Netley Hants 14 E5
Netley Marsh Hants 13 P2
Nettlebed Oxon 35 J7
Nettlebridge Somset 20 B5
Nettlecombe Dorset 11 L5
Nettlecombe IoW 14 F11
Nettleden Herts 50 B8
Nettleham Lincs 86 D5
Nettlestead Kent 37 Q10
Nettlestead Green Kent 37 Q10
Nettlestone IoW 14 H8
Nettlesworth Dur 113 L11
Nettleton Lincs 93 K10
Nettleton Wilts 32 F9
Nettleton Shrub Wilts 32 F9
Netton Devon 6 F9
Netton Wilts 21 M7
Neuadd Carmth 43 P10
Neuadd-ddu Powys 55 L9
Nevendon Essex 38 C3
Nevern Pembks 41 L2
Nevill Holt Leics 60 H2
New Abbey D & G 109 L7
New Aberdour Abers 159 L5
New Addington Gt Lon 37 J8
Newall Leeds 97 J11
New Alresford Hants 22 G8
New Alyth P & K 142 C8
Newark C Pete 74 D10
Newark Ork 169 g2
Newark-on-Trent Notts 85 N10
New Arram E R Yk 92 H2
Newarthill N Lans 126 D6
New Ash Green Kent 37 P7
New Balderton Notts 85 P10
Newbarn Kent 27 L3
New Barn Kent 37 P7
New Barnet Gt Lon 50 G11
New Barton Nhants 61 J7
Newbattle Mdloth 127 Q4
New Bewick Nthumb 119 L6
Newbie D & G 110 C7
Newbiggin Cumb 94 B2
Newbiggin Cumb 94 F7
Newbiggin Cumb 101 N5
Newbiggin Cumb 102 B5
Newbiggin Cumb 111 L11
Newbiggin Dur 102 H5
Newbiggin Dur 112 H11
Newbiggin N York 96 F3
Newbiggin N York 96 F3
Newbiggin-by-the-Sea Nthumb 113 M3
Newbigging Angus 142 D9
Newbigging Angus 142 G10
Newbigging Angus 142 H10
Newbigging S Lans 127 J8
Newbiggin-on-Lune Cumb 102 D10
New Bilton Warwks 59 Q9
Newbold Derbys 84 E6
Newbold Leics 72 C7

Newbold on Avon
Warwks............................59 Q9
Newbold on Stour
Warwks............................47 P5
Newbold Pacey Warwks....47 Q3
Newbold Revel Warwks......59 Q8
Newbold Verdon Leics......72 C10
New Bolingbroke Lincs......87 K9
Newborough C Pete..........74 D9
Newborough IoA................78 G11
Newborough Staffs............71 L8
Newbottle Nhants.............48 F7
Newbottle Sundld...........113 M10
New Boultham Lincs..........86 C6
Newbourne Suffk..............53 N3
New Bradwell M Keyn.........49 M6
New Brampton Derbys........84 E6
New Brancepeth Dur.........103 P2
Newbridge C Edin............127 L3
Newbridge Caerph.............30 H5
Newbridge Cerdgn.............43 K3
Newbridge Cnwll.................2 C7
Newbridge Cnwll.................3 K5
Newbridge D & G...............109 K6
Newbridge Hants..............21 Q11
Newbridge IoW..................14 D9
New Bridge N York.............98 G3
Newbridge Oxon................34 D4
Newbridge Wrexhm............69 J6
Newbridge Green Worcs.....46 F7
Newbridge-on-Usk Mons......31 L6
Newbridge on Wye
Powys.............................44 E3
New Brighton Flints............81 K11
New Brighton Wirral...........81 L6
New Brinsley Notts............84 G10
New Brotton R & Cl...........105 J4
Newbrough Nthumb..........112 C7
New Broughton Wrexhm......69 K4
New Buckenham Norfk........64 G3
Newbuildings Devon.............9 J4
Newburgh Abers..............151 P2
Newburgh Abers..............159 N6
Newburgh Fife................134 G4
Newburgh Lancs................88 F8
Newburgh Priory N York.....98 A5
Newburn N u Ty...............113 J7
New Bury Bolton................82 F4
Newbury Somset...............20 C5
Newbury W Berk.................34 E11
Newbury Wilts...................20 F6
Newbury Park Gt Lon..........37 K3
Newby Cumb...................101 Q6
Newby Lancs....................96 B11
Newby N York...................95 Q7
Newby N York...................99 L2
Newby N York..................104 F8
Newby Bridge Cumb...........94 H3
Newby Cross Cumb...........110 G10
Newby East Cumb............111 J9
Newby Head Cumb...........101 Q6
New Byth Abers...............159 K7
Newby West Cumb...........110 G10
Newby Wiske N York..........97 N3
Newcastle Mons................45 N11
Newcastle Shrops..............56 D8
Newcastle Airport
Nthumb............................113 J6
Newcastle Emlyn
Carmth............................42 F6
Newcastleton Border........111 J3
Newcastle-under-Lyme
Staffs..............................70 E5
Newcastle upon Tyne
N u Ty.............................113 K8
Newchapel Pembks............41 P3
Newchapel Staffs...............70 F4
Newchapel Surrey.............25 J2
Newchurch Blae G.............30 G2
Newchurch Herefs.............45 M4
Newchurch IoW..................14 G9
Newchurch Kent................27 J5
Newchurch Mons................31 N5
Newchurch Powys..............45 J4
Newchurch Staffs...............71 L10
Newchurch in Pendle
Lancs..............................89 N3
New Costessey Norfk........76 H9
New Cowper Cumb...........109 P10
Newcraighall C Edin..........127 Q3
New Crofton Wakefd..........91 K7
New Cross Cerdgn.............54 E9
New Cross Gt Lon...............37 J5
New Cross Somset.............19 M11
New Cumnock E Ayrs........115 M5
New Cut E Susx..................26 D8
New Deer Abers...............159 L8
New Delaval Nthumb.........113 L5
New Delph Oldham............90 B9
New Denham Bucks............36 B4
Newdigate Surrey..............24 E2
New Duston Nhants...........60 F8
New Earswick C York..........98 C9
New Eastwood Notts..........84 G11
New Edlington Donc...........91 N11
New Elgin Moray...............157 N5
New Ellerby E R Yk.............93 L3
Newell Green Br For...........35 N10
New Eltham Gt Lon.............37 K6
New End Worcs..................47 L2
Newenden Kent..................26 D6
New England C Pete...........74 C10
New England Essex............52 B3
Newent Gloucs...................46 D9
New Farnley Leeds.............90 H4
New Ferry Wirral................81 L7
Newfield Dur...................103 P4
Newfield Dur...................113 K10
Newfield Highld...............156 D2
New Fletton C Pete............74 C11
New Forest
National Park Hants...........13 N3
Newfound Hants.................22 G4
New Fryston Wakefd...........91 M5
Newgale Pembks................40 G6
New Galloway D & G.........108 D5
Newgate Norfk...................76 E3
Newgate Street Herts.........51 H9
New Gilston Fife...............135 L6
New Grimsby IoS.................2 b1
Newhall Ches E..................69 R5
Newhall Derbys..................71 P10
Newham Nthumb...............119 N5
New Hartley Nthumb.........113 M5
Newhaven C Edin..............127 P2
Newhaven Derbys..............71 M2
Newhaven E Susx...............25 K10
New Haw Surrey.................36 C8
New Hedges Pembks...........41 M10
New Herrington Sundld.....113 M10**

Newhey Rochdl...................89 Q8
New Holkham Norfk...........76 B4
New Holland N Linc.............93 J6
Newholm N York...............105 N8
New Houghton Derbys.......84 G7
New Houghton Norfk..........75 Q5
New Houses N York............96 B6
New Houses Wigan.............82 C4
New Hutton Cumb...............95 M2
New Hythe Kent..................38 B10
Newick E Susx....................25 K6
Newingreen Kent................27 K4
Newington Kent..................27 L4
Newington Kent..................38 E9
Newington Oxon.................34 H5
Newington Shrops..............56 G8
Newington Bagpath
Gloucs.............................32 F6
New Inn Carmth..................43 J7
New Inn Torfn.....................31 K5
New Invention Shrops.........56 D9
New Lakenham Norfk..........77 J10
New Lanark S Lans............116 B2
Newland C KuH...................93 J4
Newland Cumb...................94 G5
Newland E R Yk..................92 D5
Newland Gloucs.................31 Q3
Newland N York..................92 A6
Newland Oxon...................34 C3
Newland Somset................17 Q4
Newland Worcs...................46 E5
Newlandrig Mdloth.............128 B7
Newlands Border...............111 K2
Newlands Cumb................101 K3
Newlands Nthumb.............112 G9
Newlands of Dundurcas
Moray..............................157 P7
New Lane Lancs..................88 E8
New Lane End Warrtn.........82 D6
New Langholm D & G.........110 G4
New Leake Lincs..................87 M9
New Leeds Abers...............159 N7
New Lodge Barns................91 K9
New Longton Lancs.............88 G5
New Luce D & G.................106 G5
Newlyn Cnwll........................2 D8
Newlyn East Cnwll...............4 C10
Newmachar Abers.............151 M4
New Malden Gt Lon.............36 F7
Newman's End Essex.........51 M8
Newman's Green Suffk......52 E3
Newmarket Suffk................63 K8
Newmarket W Isls.............168 j4
New Marske R & Cl...........104 H6
New Marston Oxon..............34 F3
New Marton Shrops............69 K8
New Mill Abers..................151 K11
Newmill Border..................117 P8
New Mill Cnwll......................2 D7
New Mill Herts.....................35 P2
New Mill Kirk.......................90 F9
Newmill Moray....................158 B7
Newmillerdam Wakefd.........91 J7
Newmill of Inshewan
Angus.............................142 G5
Newmills C Edin................127 M4
New Mills Cnwll.....................3 M3
New Mills Derbys.................83 M7
Newmills Fife....................134 C10
Newmills Mons...................31 P3
New Mills Powys..................55 P4
Newmiln P & K..................142 A11
Newmilns E Ayrs...............125 N10
New Mistley Essex..............53 K5
New Moat Pembks..............41 L5
Newnes Shrops...................69 L8
Newney Green Essex..........51 Q9
Newnham Gloucs.................32 C2
Newnham Hants..................23 K4
Newnham Herts...................50 F3
Newnham Kent....................38 G10
Newnham Nhants................60 C9
Newnham Worcs..................57 L11
New Ollerton Notts.............85 L7
New Oscott Birm.................58 G6
New Pitsligo Abers............159 L6
New Polzeath Cnwll..............4 E6
Newport Cnwll......................5 N4
Newport Dorset...................12 B5
Newport E R Yk...................92 E4
Newport Essex....................51 M4
Newport Gloucs...................32 D5
Newport Highld..................163 Q2
Newport IoW.......................14 F9
Newport Newpt....................31 K7
Newport Norfk.....................77 Q8
Newport Pembks.................41 L3
Newport Wrekin...................70 C11
Newport-on-Tay Fife..........135 L2
Newport Pagnell M Keyn....49 N6
Newport Pagnell
Services M Keyn...................49 N6
Newpound Common
W Susx............................24 C5
New Prestwick S Ayrs........114 F3
New Quay Cerdgn................42 G3
Newquay Cnwll.....................4 C9
New Quay Essex..................52 H7
Newquay Airport Cnwll..........4 D9
New Rackheath Norfk..........77 K9
New Radnor Powys..............45 J2
New Rent Cumb.................101 N3
New Ridley Nthumb...........112 G9
New Road Side N York.........90 B2
New Romney Kent...............27 J7
New Rossington Donc........91 Q11
New Row Cerdgn..................54 G10
New Row Lancs....................89 J3
New Sauchie Clacks...........133 P9
Newsbank Ches E................82 H11
Newseat Abers...................158 H11
Newsham Lancs...................88 G3
Newsham N York..................97 N4
Newsham N York.................103 M8
Newsham Nthumb..............113 M5
New Sharlston Wakefd........91 K7
Newsholme E R Yk..............92 B5
Newsholme Lancs................96 B11
New Shoreston Nthumb.....119 N4
New Silksworth Sundld......113 N10
New Skelton R & Cl...........105 J7
Newsome Kirk......................90 F8
New Somerby Lincs.............73 N3
New Southgate
Crematorium Gt Lon...........36 G2
New Springs Wigan.............88 H9
Newstead Border...............117 R4**

Newstead Notts..................84 H10
Newstead Nthumb.............119 N5
New Stevenston N Lans.....126 D6
New Street Herefs..............45 L3
New Swannington Leics.......72 C7
Newthorpe N York...............91 M4
Newton Ag & B..................131 L8
Newton Border..................118 B6
Newton Brdgnd....................29 M9
Newton C Beds....................50 F2
Newton Cambs....................62 F11
Newton Cambs....................74 H8
Newton Cardif.....................30 H9
Newton Ches W...................69 P3
Newton Ches W...................81 N11
Newton Ches W...................82 B9
Newton Cumb......................94 E6
Newton Derbys....................84 F9
Newton Herefs....................45 L8
Newton Herefs....................45 Q4
Newton Herefs....................56 F11
Newton Highld...................155 Q7
Newton Highld...................156 C8
Newton Highld...................156 D4
Newton Highld...................167 P7
Newton Lancs.....................88 C3
Newton Lancs.....................95 M6
Newton Lancs.....................95 Q3
Newton Mdloth...................127 Q4
Newton Moray....................157 M5
Newton Moray....................157 Q5
Newton N York.....................98 H6
Newton Nhants....................61 J4
Newton Norfk.......................76 A8
Newton Notts.......................85 H2
Newton Nthumb.................112 F8
Newton Nthumb.................118 H9
Newton S Lans...................116 C4
Newton S Lans...................116 B5
Newton Sandw.....................58 F6
Newton Shrops.....................69 M8
Newton Somset...................18 F7
Newton Staffs......................71 J9
Newton Suffk.......................52 F3
Newton W Loth...................127 K2
Newton Warwks...................60 B5
Newton Wilts.......................21 P10
Newton Abbot Devon............7 M4
Newton Arlosh Cumb..........110 D9
Newton Aycliffe Dur...........103 Q6
Newton Bewley Hartpl........104 E5
Newton Blossomville
M Keyn............................49 P4
Newton Bromswold
Nhants............................61 L7
Newton Burgoland Leics.....72 B9
Newton-by-the-Sea
Nthumb............................119 P5
Newton by Toft Lincs..........86 D3
Newton Ferrers Cnwll...........5 N8
Newton Ferrers Devon..........6 F9
Newton Ferry W Isls...........168 d10
Newton Flotman Norfk.........65 J2
Newtongrange Mdloth........127 Q5
Newton Green Mons............31 P6
Newton Harcourt Leics........72 G11
Newton Heath Manch..........83 J4
Newtonhill Abers...............151 N9
Newton Hill Wakefd.............91 J6
Newton-in-Bowland
Lancs..............................95 P10
Newton Kyme N York..........91 M2
Newton-le-Willows
N York.............................97 K3
Newton-le-Willows
St Hel..............................82 C5
Newtonloan Mdloth...........127 Q5
Newton Longville Bucks.......49 M8
Newton Mearns E Rens.....125 N6
Newtonmill Angus.............143 L5
Newtonmore Highld..........148 D7
Newton Morrell N York.......103 P9
Newton Mountain
Pembks............................41 J9
Newton Mulgrave
N York............................105 L7
Newton of Balcanquhal
P & K..............................134 F5
Newton of Balcormo
Fife.................................135 N7
Newton on Ouse N York......97 R9
Newton-on-Rawcliffe
N York..............................98 G2
Newton on the Hill
Shrops.............................69 N10
Newton-on-the-Moor
Nthumb............................119 N9
Newton on Trent Lincs........85 P6
Newton Poppleford
Devon...............................10 B7
Newton Purcell Oxon...........48 H8
Newton Regis Warwks.........59 L3
Newton Reigny Cumb.........101 N4
Newton St Cyres Devon.........9 L5
Newton St Faith Norfk.........77 J8
Newton St Loe BaNES..........20 D2
Newton St Petrock
Devon...............................16 G9
Newton Solney Derbys........71 P9
Newton Stacey Hants.........22 D6
Newton Stewart D & G.......107 M4
Newton Tony Wilts..............21 P6
Newton Tracey Devon.........17 J6
Newton under
Roseberry R & Cl..............104 G8
Newton Underwood
Nthumb............................112 H3
Newton upon Derwent
E R Yk.............................98 E11
Newton Valence Hants.........23 K8
Newton Wamphray
D & G.............................109 P2
Newton with Scales
Lancs..............................88 F4
Newtown Blae G...................30 G3
Newtown Ches W.................82 B9
Newtown Cnwll.....................3 G3
Newtown Cnwll.....................5 M6
Newtown Cumb...................101 M6
Newtown Cumb...................109 P11
Newtown Cumb....................110 G8
Newtown Cumb...................111 K8
Newtown D & G...................115 Q5
Newtown Derbys...................83 L5
Newtown Devon.....................9 Q5
Newtown Devon....................17 P6**

Newtown Dorset...................11 K4
New Town Dorset.................12 G3
New Town Dorset.................21 J11
New Town Dorset.................21 J11
New Town E Susx.................25 L6
Newtown Gloucs...................32 C4
Newtown Hants....................13 N3
Newtown Hants....................14 H4
Newtown Hants....................22 E2
Newtown Herefs...................45 P3
Newtown Herefs...................45 Q8
Newtown Herefs...................46 B5
Newtown Herefs...................46 D7
Newtown Highld.................147 K7
Newtown IoW.......................14 D8
Newtown Lancs....................88 G7
Newtown Nthumb...............119 H8
Newtown Nthumb...............119 K10
Newtown Nthumb...............119 K5
Newtown Poole....................12 H6
Newtown Powys....................55 Q6
Newtown Rhondd.................30 E5
Newtown Shrops..................69 M10
Newtown Shrops..................69 N8
Newtown Somset.................10 F2
Newtown Staffs....................58 E4
Newtown Staffs....................70 G2
Newtown Wigan...................82 C4
Newtown Wilts......................20 H9
Newtown Wilts......................21 Q2
New Town Wilts....................33 Q10
Newtown Worcs....................46 G3
Newtown Worcs....................58 D9
Newtown-in-St Martin
Cnwll.................................3 J9
Newtown Linford Leics.........72 E9
Newtown of Beltrees
Rens...............................125 K6
Newtown St Boswells
Border.............................117 R4
Newtown Unthank Leics......72 D10
New Tredegar Caerph..........30 F4
New Trows S Lans.............126 E10
New Tupton Derbys.............84 E7
Newtyle Angus...................142 D9
New Walsoken Cambs.........75 J9
New Waltham NE Lin...........93 N10
New Whittington Derbys......84 E5
New Winton E Loth.............128 C5
New Yatt Oxon.....................34 C2
Newyears Green Gt Lon.......36 C3
New York Lincs....................86 H9
New York N Tyne................113 M6
New York N York..................97 J8
Nextend Herefs...................45 L3
Neyland Pembks..................41 J9
Niarbyl IoM..........................80 b6
Nibley Gloucs.......................32 C3
Nibley Gloucs.......................32 C8
Nibley S Glos.......................32 C8
Nibley Green Gloucs............32 D5
Nicholashayne Devon..........18 F11
Nicholaston Swans..............28 F7
Nickies Hill Cumb...............111 K7
Nidd N York..........................97 M8
Nigg C Aber........................151 N7
Nigg Highld........................156 E3
Nigg Ferry Highld...............156 D4
Nimlet BaNES.......................32 D10
Ninebanks Nthumb............111 Q10
Nine Elms Swindn...............33 M7
Nine Wells Pembks.............40 E6
Ninfield E Susx.....................26 B9
Ningwood IoW......................14 C9
Nisbet Border.....................118 C5
Nisbet Hill Border...............129 K9
Niton IoW.............................14 F11
Nitshill C Glas...................125 N5
Noah's Ark Kent...................37 N9
Noak Bridge Essex...............37 Q2
Noak Hill Gt Lon...................37 M2
Noblethorpe Barns..............90 H9
Nobottle Nhants...................60 E8
Nocton Lincs.........................86 E8
Nogdam End Norfk..............77 M11
Noke Oxon............................34 F2
Nolton Pembks......................40 G7
Nolton Haven Pembks..........40 G7
No Man's Heath Ches W......69 P5
No Man's Heath Warwks......59 L3
No Man's Land Cnwll............5 M10
Nomansland Devon...............9 K2
Nomansland Wilts................21 Q11
Noneley Shrops....................69 N9
Nonington Kent....................39 N11
Nook Cumb...........................95 L4
Nook Cumb..........................111 J5
Norbiton Gt Lon...................36 E7
Norbreck Bpool....................88 C2
Norbridge Herefs.................46 D6
Norbury Ches E....................69 Q5
Norbury Derbys.....................71 L6
Norbury Gt Lon.....................36 H7
Norbury Shrops....................56 F6
Norbury Staffs......................70 D10
Norbury Common
Ches E..............................69 Q5
Norbury Junction Staffs......70 D10
Norchard Worcs....................58 B11
Norcott Brook Ches W.........82 D8
Norcross Lancs.....................88 C2
Nordelph Norfk.....................75 L10
Norden Rochdl......................89 P8
Nordley Shrops......................57 M5
Norfolk Broads Norfk...........77 N10
Norham Nthumb..................129 N10
Norland Town Calder...........90 D6
Norley Ches W......................82 C10
Norleywood Hants................14 C7
Norlington E Susx.................25 K8
Normanby Lincs....................86 C3
Normanby N Linc..................92 E7
Normanby N York..................98 E4
Normanby R & Cl................104 F7
Normanby le Wold Lincs.....93 K11
Norman Cross Cambs..........61 Q2
Normandy Surrey.................23 P4
Norman's Bay E Susx..........25 Q9
Norman's Green Devon..........9 Q5
Normanton C Derb................72 A4
Normanton Leics...................73 L2
Normanton Lincs..................86 B11
Normanton Notts..................85 M10
Normanton Rutlnd................73 N9
Normanton Wakefd...............91 K6
Normanton Wilts...................21 M6
Normanton le Heath
Leics................................72 B8**

Normanton on Soar
Notts...............................72 E6
Normanton on the
Wolds Notts......................72 G4
Normanton on Trent
Notts...............................85 N7
Normoss Lancs.....................88 C3
Norney Surrey.......................23 P6
Norrington Common
Wilts................................20 G2
Norris Green Cnwll.................5 Q3
Norris Green Lpool...............81 M6
Norris Hill Leics....................72 A7
Norristhorpe Kirk..................90 F6
Northacre Norfk....................64 D2
Northall Bucks......................49 Q10
Northallerton N York............97 N2
Northall Green Norfk............76 D9
Northam C Sotn....................14 D4
Northam Devon.....................16 H6
Northampton Nhants............60 G8
Northampton Worcs..............58 B11
North Anston Rothm.............84 H4
North Ascot Br For...............35 P11
North Aston Oxon..................48 E5
Northaw Herts......................50 G10
Northay Somset....................10 F3
North Baddesley Hants.........22 C10
North Ballachulish
Highld.............................139 K5
North Barrow Somset...........20 B9
North Barsham Norfk............76 C4
North Benfleet Essex............38 C4
North Bersted W Susx...........15 P6
North Berwick E Loth..........128 E3
North Bitchburn Dur...........103 N4
North Blyth Nthumb.............113 M4
North Boarhunt Hants..........14 H4
North Bockhampton
Dorset..............................13 L5
Northborough C Pete............74 C9
Northbourne Kent..................39 P11
North Bovey Devon.................8 H8
North Bradley Wilts..............20 G3
North Brentor Devon...............8 C8
North Brewham Somset........20 D7
North Bridge Surrey..............23 Q7
Northbridge Street
E Susx...............................26 B7
Northbrook Hants..................22 F7
Northbrook Oxon..................48 E10
North Brook End Cambs.......50 G2
North Buckland Devon...........16 H3
North Burlingham Norfk.......77 M10
North Cadbury Somset.........20 B9
North Carlton Lincs..............86 B5
North Carlton Notts..............85 J4
North Cave E R Yk................92 E4
North Cerney Gloucs............33 K3
North Chailey E Susx...........25 J6
Northchapel W Susx.............23 Q9
North Charford Hants...........21 N11
North Charlton Nthumb.......119 N6
North Cheam Gt Lon.............36 F7
North Cheriton Somset........20 C9
North Chideock Dorset..........11 J6
Northchurch Herts.................35 Q3
North Cliffe E R Yk................92 E3
North Clifton Notts...............85 P6
North Close Dur..................103 Q4
North Cockerington
Lincs................................87 L2
North Connel Ag & B..........138 G11
North Cornelly Brdgnd..........29 M8
North Corner Cnwll................3 K10
North Cotes Lincs.................93 P10
Northcott Devon......................5 N3
Northcott Devon....................10 B2
Northcott Devon....................10 C3
North Country Cnwll...............2 H5
Northcourt Oxon...................34 E5
North Cove Suffk...................65 P4
North Cowton N York...........103 Q10
North Crawley M Keyn..........49 P6
North Cray Gt Lon.................37 L6
North Creake Norfk...............76 B4
North Curry Somset...............19 K9
North Dalton E R Yk..............99 J10
North Deighton N York.........97 N10
North Devon
Crematorium Devon.............17 J5
Northdown Kent....................39 Q7
North Downs.........................38 F10
North Duffield N York...........92 A3
North Duntulm Highld.........152 G3
North East Surrey
Crematorium Gt Lon...........36 F7
Northedge Derbys.................84 E7
North Elham Kent..................27 L3
North Elkington Lincs...........87 J2
North Elmham Nthumb.........76 D7
North Elmsall Wakefd...........91 M8
Northend Bucks.....................35 K6
North End C Port...................15 J6
North End Cumb..................110 F9
North End Dorset...................12 F9
North End E R Yk...................93 L2
North End E R Yk...................93 N4
North End Essex....................51 Q7
North End Hants....................21 M11
North End Hants....................22 G9
North End Leics.....................72 F7
North End Lincs.....................74 D2
North End Lincs.....................87 M3
North End Lincs.....................92 H11
North End N Linc...................93 K6
North End N Som...................31 M11
North End Nhants..................61 L7
North End Norfk.....................64 D3
North End Nthumb...............119 M10
North End Sefton...................81 L4
North End W Susx..................15 Q6
North End W Susx..................24 D9
Northend Warwks..................48 C4
Northenden Manch................82 H7
Northend Woods Bucks........35 P7
North Erradale Highld.........160 A10
North Evington C Leic..........72 G10
North Fambridge Essex........38 E2
North Ferriby E R Yk.............92 G5
Northfield Birm.....................58 F9
Northfield C Aber.................151 N6
Northfield E R Yk...................92 H5
Northfields Lincs...................73 Q8
Northfleet Kent......................37 P6
North Frodingham
E R Yk.............................99 N10
North Gorley Hants................13 L2
North Green Norfk.................65 J4**

Place	County	Page	Grid
North Green	Suffk	65	L9
North Green	Suffk	65	M8
North Greetwell	Lincs	86	D6
North Grimston	N York	98	G7
North Halling	Medway	38	B8
North Hayling	Hants	15	K6
North Hazelrigg	Nthumb	119	L4
North Heasley	Devon	17	N5
North Heath	W Susx	24	C6
North Hele	Devon	18	D10
North Hill	Cnwll	5	M6
North Hillingdon	Gt Lon	36	C4
North Hinksey Village	Oxon	34	E3
North Holmwood	Surrey	36	E11
North Huish	Devon	7	J7
North Hykeham	Lincs	86	B7
Northiam	E Susx	26	D7
Northill	C Beds	61	P11
Northington	Gloucs	32	D3
Northington	Hants	22	G7
North Kelsey	Lincs	92	H10
North Kessock	Highld	156	B8
North Killingholme	N Linc	93	K7
North Kilvington	N York	97	P3
North Kilworth	Leics	60	D4
North Kingston	Hants	13	L4
North Kyme	Lincs	86	G10
North Landing	E R Yk	99	Q6
Northlands	Lincs	87	K10
Northleach	Gloucs	33	M2
North Lee	Bucks	35	M3
North Lees	N York	97	L6
Northleigh	Devon	10	D5
Northleigh	Devon	17	L5
North Leigh	Kent	27	K2
North Leigh	Oxon	34	C2
North Leverton with Habblesthorpe	Notts	85	N4
Northlew	Devon	8	D5
North Littleton	Worcs	47	L5
Northload Bridge	Somset	19	N7
North Lopham	Norfk	64	E5
North Luffenham	Rutlnd	73	N10
North Marden	W Susx	23	M11
North Marston	Bucks	49	L10
North Middleton	Mdloth	128	B8
North Middleton	Nthumb	119	J6
North Millbrex	Abers	159	K9
North Milmain	D & G	106	E7
North Molton	Devon	17	N6
North Moreton	Oxon	34	G7
Northmuir	Angus	142	F7
North Mundham	W Susx	15	N6
North Muskham	Notts	85	N9
North Newbald	E R Yk	92	F3
North Newington	Oxon	48	D6
North Newnton	Wilts	21	M3
North Newton	Somset	18	K8
Northney	Hants	15	K6
North Nibley	Gloucs	32	D5
North Oakley	Hants	22	F4
North Ockendon	Gt Lon	37	N3
Northolt	Gt Lon	36	D4
Northop	Flints	81	J11
Northop Hall	Flints	81	K11
North Ormesby	Middsb	104	F7
North Ormsby	Lincs	87	J2
Northorpe	Kirk	90	G6
Northorpe	Lincs	74	A7
Northorpe	Lincs	74	D3
Northorpe	Lincs	92	E11
North Otterington	N York	97	N3
Northover	Somset	19	N7
Northover	Somset	19	P10
North Owersby	Lincs	86	E2
Northowram	Calder	90	E5
North Perrott	Somset	11	K3
North Petherton	Somset	19	J8
North Petherwin	Cnwll	5	M4
North Pickenham	Norfk	76	B10
North Piddle	Worcs	47	J4
North Poorton	Dorset	11	L5
Northport	Dorset	12	F7
North Poulner	Hants	13	L3
North Queensferry	Fife	134	E11
North Radworthy	Devon	17	P5
North Rauceby	Lincs	86	D11
Northrepps	Norfk	77	J4
North Reston	Lincs	87	L4
North Rigton	N York	97	L11
North Ripley	Hants	13	L5
North Rode	Ches E	83	J11
North Ronaldsay	Ork	169	g1
North Ronaldsay Airport	Ork	169	g1
North Row	Cumb	100	H4
North Runcton	Norfk	75	M7
North Scale	Cumb	94	D7
North Scarle	Lincs	85	P7
North Seaton	Nthumb	113	L3
North Seaton Colliery	Nthumb	113	L3
North Shian	Ag & B	138	G9
North Shields	N Tyne	113	N7
North Shoebury	Sthend	38	F4
North Shore	Bpool	88	C3
North Side	C Pete	74	E11
North Side	Cumb	100	C5
North Skelton	R & Cl	105	J7
North Somercotes	Lincs	93	R11
North Stainley	N York	97	L5
North Stainmore	Cumb	102	F8
North Stifford	Thurr	37	P4
North Stoke	BaNES	32	D11
North Stoke	Oxon	34	H7
North Stoke	W Susx	24	B8
North Street	Cambs	63	J7
North Street	Hants	21	N11
North Street	Hants	22	H8
North Street	Kent	38	H10
North Street	Medway	38	D7
North Street	W Berk	34	H10
North Sunderland	Nthumb	119	P4
North Tamerton	Cnwll	5	N2
North Tawton	Devon	8	G4
North Third	Stirlg	133	M10
North Thoresby	Lincs	93	N11
North Togston	Nthumb	119	P10
Northton	W Isls	168	e9
North Town	Devon	17	J10
North Town	Somset	19	Q6
North Town	W & M	35	N8
North Tuddenham	Norfk	76	F9
North Uist	W Isls	168	c10
Northumberland National Park	Nthumb	118	G10
North Walbottle	N u Ty	113	J7
North Walsham	Norfk	77	K5
North Waltham	Hants	22	G5
North Warnborough	Hants	23	K4
Northway	Somset	18	F9
Northway	Swans	28	G7
North Weald Bassett	Essex	51	L10
North Wheatley	Notts	85	N3
North Whilborough	Devon	7	M5
Northwich	Ches W	82	E10
North Wick	BaNES	31	Q11
Northwick	S Glos	31	Q7
Northwick	Somset	19	L5
Northwick	Worcs	46	F3
North Widcombe	BaNES	19	Q3
North Willingham	Lincs	86	G3
North Wingfield	Derbys	84	F7
North Witham	Lincs	73	N6
Northwold	Norfk	75	Q11
Northwood	C Stke	70	F5
Northwood	Derbys	84	C8
Northwood	Gt Lon	36	C2
Northwood	IoW	14	E8
Northwood	Shrops	69	N8
Northwood Green	Gloucs	46	D11
North Wootton	Dorset	11	P2
North Wootton	Norfk	75	M6
North Wootton	Somset	19	Q6
North Wraxall	Wilts	32	F9
North Wroughton	Swindn	33	M8
North York Moors National Park	N York	105	K10
Norton	Donc	91	N7
Norton	E Susx	25	L10
Norton	Gloucs	32	G10
Norton	Halton	82	C8
Norton	Herts	50	F4
Norton	IoW	13	P7
Norton	Mons	45	N10
Norton	N Som	19	K2
Norton	N York	98	F6
Norton	Nhants	60	C8
Norton	Notts	85	J6
Norton	Powys	56	E11
Norton	S on T	104	D6
Norton	Sheff	84	E4
Norton	Shrops	56	H8
Norton	Shrops	57	K3
Norton	Shrops	57	L8
Norton	Shrops	57	N4
Norton	Suffk	64	D8
Norton	Swans	28	H7
Norton	W Susx	15	P5
Norton	Wilts	32	G8
Norton	Worcs	46	G4
Norton	Worcs	47	K5
Norton Bavant	Wilts	20	H6
Norton Bridge	Staffs	70	F8
Norton Canes	Staffs	58	F3
Norton Canes Services	Staffs	58	F3
Norton Canon	Herefs	45	M5
Norton Corner	Norfk	76	F6
Norton Disney	Lincs	85	Q9
Norton Ferris	Wilts	20	E7
Norton Fitzwarren	Somset	18	G9
Norton Green	IoW	13	P7
Norton Hawkfield	BaNES	19	Q2
Norton Heath	Essex	51	P10
Norton in Hales	Shrops	70	C7
Norton in the Moors	C Stke	70	F4
Norton-Juxta-Twycross	Leics	59	M3
Norton-le-Clay	N York	97	P6
Norton Lindsey	Warwks	47	P2
Norton Little Green	Suffk	64	D8
Norton Malreward	BaNES	20	B2
Norton Mandeville	Essex	51	N10
Norton St Philip	Somset	20	E3
Norton Subcourse	Norfk	65	N2
Norton sub Hamdon	Somset	19	N11
Norton Wood	Herefs	45	M5
Norwell	Notts	85	N8
Norwell Woodhouse	Notts	85	M8
Norwich	Norfk	77	J10
Norwich Airport	Norfk	77	J9
Norwich Cathedral	Norfk	77	J10
Norwich (St Faith) Crematorium	Norfk	77	J8
Norwick	Shet	169	t2
Norwood	Clacks	133	P9
Norwood	Derbys	84	G4
Norwood	Kent	27	J5
Norwood End	Essex	51	N9
Norwood Green	Calder	90	E5
Norwood Green	Gt Lon	36	D5
Norwood Hill	Surrey	24	F2
Norwoodside	Cambs	74	H11
Noseley	Leics	73	J11
Noss Mayo	Devon	6	F9
Nosterfield	N York	97	L4
Nosterfield End	Cambs	51	P2
Nostie	Highld	145	Q2
Notgrove	Gloucs	47	M10
Nottage	Brdgnd	29	M9
Notter	Cnwll	5	P9
Nottingham	C Nott	72	F3
Nottington	Dorset	11	P8
Notton	Wakefd	91	J8
Notton	Wilts	32	H11
Nounsley	Essex	52	C9
Noutard's Green	Worcs	57	Q11
Nowton	Suffk	64	B9
Nox	Shrops	56	G2
Nuffield	Oxon	35	J7
Nunburnholme	E R Yk	98	G11
Nuncargate	Notts	84	H10
Nunclose	Cumb	111	J11
Nuneaton	Warwks	59	N6
Nuneham Courtenay	Oxon	34	G5
Nunhead	Gt Lon	36	H5
Nunkeeling	E R Yk	99	N11
Nun Monkton	N York	97	R9
Nunney	Somset	20	D5
Nunney Catch	Somset	20	D6
Nunnington	Herefs	45	R6
Nunnington	N York	98	D5
Nunsthorpe	NE Lin	93	N9
Nunthorpe	C York	98	C10
Nunthorpe	Middsb	104	F8
Nunthorpe Village	Middsb	104	F8
Nunton	Wilts	21	N9
Nunwick	N York	97	M6
Nunwick	Nthumb	112	C6
Nupdown	S Glos	32	B5
Nup End	Bucks	49	N11
Nupend	Gloucs	32	E3
Nuptown	Br For	35	N10
Nursling	Hants	22	C11
Nursted	Hants	23	L10
Nursteed	Wilts	21	K2
Nurton	Staffs	58	B5
Nutbourne	W Susx	15	L5
Nutbourne	W Susx	24	C7
Nutfield	Surrey	36	H10
Nuthall	Notts	72	E2
Nuthampstead	Herts	51	K4
Nuthurst	W Susx	24	E5
Nutley	E Susx	25	K5
Nutley	Hants	22	H6
Nuttall	Bury	89	M7
Nutwell	Donc	91	Q10
Nybster	Highld	167	Q4
Nyetimber	W Susx	15	N7
Nyewood	W Susx	23	M10
Nymet Rowland	Devon	17	N10
Nymet Tracey	Devon	8	H4
Nympsfield	Gloucs	32	F4
Nynehead	Somset	18	F10
Nythe	Somset	19	M8
Nyton	W Susx	15	P5

O

Place	County	Page	Grid
Oadby	Leics	72	G10
Oad Street	Kent	38	E9
Oakall Green	Worcs	46	F2
Oakamoor	Staffs	71	J6
Oakbank	W Loth	127	K4
Oak Cross	Devon	8	D5
Oakdale	Caerph	30	G5
Oake	Somset	18	G9
Oaken	Staffs	58	C4
Oakenclough	Lancs	95	L11
Oakengates	Wrekin	57	N2
Oakenholt	Flints	81	K10
Oakenshaw	Dur	103	N3
Oakenshaw	Kirk	90	F5
Oakerthorpe	Derbys	84	E10
Oakford	Cerdgn	43	J3
Oakford	Devon	18	B10
Oakfordbridge	Devon	18	B10
Oakgrove	Ches E	83	K11
Oakham	Rutlnd	73	M9
Oakhanger	Ches E	70	D4
Oakhanger	Hants	23	L7
Oakhill	Somset	20	B5
Oakhurst	Kent	37	N10
Oakington	Cambs	62	F8
Oaklands	Powys	44	E4
Oakle Street	Gloucs	46	E11
Oakley	Bed	61	M10
Oakley	Bucks	34	H2
Oakley	Fife	134	C10
Oakley	Hants	22	G4
Oakley	Oxon	35	L4
Oakley	Poole	12	H5
Oakley	Suffk	65	H6
Oakley Green	W & M	35	P9
Oakley Park	Powys	55	M7
Oakridge	Gloucs	32	H4
Oaks	Lancs	89	K4
Oaks	Shrops	56	G4
Oaksey	Wilts	33	J6
Oaks Green	Derbys	71	M8
Oakshaw Ford	Cumb	111	K5
Oakshott	Hants	23	K9
Oakthorpe	Leics	59	M2
Oak Tree	Darltn	104	C8
Oakwood	C Derb	72	B3
Oakwood	Nthumb	112	D7
Oakworth	C Brad	90	C3
Oare	Kent	38	H9
Oare	Somset	17	P2
Oare	Wilts	21	N2
Oasby	Lincs	73	Q3
Oath	Somset	19	L9
Oathlaw	Angus	142	H6
Oatlands Park	Surrey	36	C7
Oban	Ag & B	130	H2
Oban Airport	Ag & B	138	C10
Obley	Shrops	56	E9
Oborne	Dorset	20	C11
Obthorpe	Lincs	74	A8
Occold	Suffk	64	H7
Occumster	Highld	167	N9
Ochiltree	E Ayrs	115	K3
Ockbrook	Derbys	72	C3
Ocker Hill	Sandw	58	E6
Ockeridge	Worcs	46	E2
Ockham	Surrey	36	C9
Ockle	Highld	137	P1
Ockley	Surrey	24	D2
Ocle Pychard	Herefs	46	A5
Octon	E R Yk	99	L7
Odcombe	Somset	19	P11
Odd Down	BaNES	20	D2
Oddingley	Worcs	46	H3
Oddington	Gloucs	47	P9
Oddington	Oxon	48	G11
Odell	Bed	61	L9
Odham	Devon	8	C4
Odiham	Hants	23	K4
Odsal	C Brad	90	F5
Odsey	Cambs	50	G3
Odstock	Wilts	21	M9
Odstone	Leics	72	B9
Offchurch	Warwks	59	N11
Offenham	Worcs	47	L5
Offerton	Stockp	83	K7
Offerton	Sundld	113	M9
Offham	E Susx	25	K8
Offham	Kent	37	Q9
Offham	W Susx	24	B9
Offleymarsh	Staffs	70	D9
Offord Cluny	Cambs	62	B7
Offord D'Arcy	Cambs	62	B7
Offton	Suffk	53	J2
Offwell	Devon	10	D5
Ogbourne Maizey	Wilts	33	N10
Ogbourne St Andrew	Wilts	33	N10
Ogbourne St George	Wilts	33	P10
Ogden	Calder	90	D4
Ogle	Nthumb	112	H5
Oglet	Lpool	81	N8
Ogmore	V Glam	29	N9
Ogmore-by-Sea	V Glam	29	N9
Ogmore Vale	Brdgnd	29	P6
Ogwen Bank	Gwynd	79	L11
Okeford Fitzpaine	Dorset	12	D2
Okehampton	Devon	8	E5
Oker Side	Derbys	84	C8
Okewood Hill	Surrey	24	D3
Olchard	Devon	9	L3
Old	Nhants	60	G6
Old Aberdeen	C Aber	151	N6
Old Alresford	Hants	22	G8
Oldany	Highld	164	C10
Old Auchenbrack	D & G	115	Q3
Old Basford	C Nott	72	F2
Old Basing	Hants	23	J4
Old Beetley	Norfk	76	D8
Oldberrow	Warwks	58	H11
Old Bewick	Nthumb	119	L6
Old Bolingbroke	Lincs	87	L7
Old Bramhope	Leeds	90	G2
Old Brampton	Derbys	84	D6
Old Bridge of Urr	D & G	108	G7
Old Buckenham	Norfk	64	F3
Old Burghclere	Hants	22	E3
Oldbury	Kent	37	N9
Oldbury	Sandw	58	E7
Oldbury	Shrops	57	N6
Oldbury	Warwks	59	M6
Oldbury Naite	S Glos	32	B6
Oldbury-on-Severn	S Glos	32	B6
Oldbury on the Hill	Gloucs	32	F7
Old Byland	N York	98	B3
Old Cantley	Donc	91	Q10
Old Cassop	Dur	104	B3
Old Castle	Brdgnd	29	P9
Oldcastle	Mons	45	L10
Oldcastle Heath	Ches W	69	N5
Old Catton	Norfk	77	J9
Old Churchstoke	Powys	56	D6
Old Clee	NE Lin	93	N9
Old Cleeve	Somset	18	D6
Old Clipstone	Notts	85	K8
Old Colwyn	Conwy	80	B9
Oldcotes	Notts	85	J3
Old Dailly	S Ayrs	114	D8
Old Dalby	Leics	72	H6
Old Dam	Derbys	83	P9
Old Deer	Abers	159	N8
Old Ditch	Somset	19	P5
Old Edlington	Donc	91	N11
Old Eldon	Dur	103	P5
Old Ellerby	E R Yk	93	L3
Old Felixstowe	Suffk	53	P4
Oldfield	C Brad	90	C3
Oldfield	Worcs	46	F2
Old Fletton	C Pete	74	C11
Oldford	Somset	20	E4
Old Forge	Herefs	45	R11
Old Furnace	Herefs	45	P10
Old Glossop	Derbys	83	M6
Old Goole	E R Yk	92	B6
Old Grimsby	IoS	2	b1
Old Hall Green	Herts	51	J6
Oldhall Green	Suffk	64	B10
Old Hall Street	Norfk	77	L5
Oldham	Oldham	83	K4
Oldhamstocks	E Loth	129	J5
Old Harlow	Essex	51	L8
Old Heath	Essex	52	H7
Old Hunstanton	Norfk	75	N2
Old Hurst	Cambs	62	D5
Old Hutton	Cumb	95	M3
Old Kea	Cnwll	3	L5
Old Kilpatrick	W Duns	125	M3
Old Knebworth	Herts	50	F6
Old Lakenham	Norfk	77	J10
Oldland	S Glos	32	C10
Old Langho	Lancs	89	L3
Old Laxey	IoM	80	f5
Old Leake	Lincs	87	M10
Old Malton	N York	98	F6
Oldmeldrum	Abers	151	L2
Oldmill	Cnwll	5	P7
Old Milverton	Warwks	59	L11
Oldmixon	N Som	19	K3
Old Newton	Suffk	64	F9
Old Quarrington	Dur	104	B3
Old Radford	C Nott	72	F2
Old Radnor	Powys	45	K3
Old Rayne	Abers	150	H2
Old Romney	Kent	26	H7
Old Shoreham	W Susx	24	F9
Oldshoremore	Highld	164	F5
Old Soar	Kent	37	P10
Old Sodbury	S Glos	32	E8
Old Somerby	Lincs	73	P4
Oldstead	N York	98	A5
Old Stratford	Nhants	49	L6
Old Struan	P & K	141	K4
Old Swarland	Nthumb	119	N10
Old Swinford	Dudley	58	D8
Old Tebay	Cumb	102	B9
Old Thirsk	N York	97	P4
Old Town	Calder	90	C5
Old Town	Cumb	95	M4
Old Town	Cumb	101	N2
Old Town	E Susx	25	N11
Old Town	IoS	2	c2
Old Trafford	Traffd	82	H5
Old Tupton	Derbys	84	E7
Oldwall	Cumb	111	J8
Oldwalls	Swans	28	E6
Old Warden	C Beds	50	D2
Oldways End	Somset	17	R7
Old Weston	Cambs	61	N5
Old Wick	Highld	167	Q7
Old Windsor	W & M	35	Q10
Old Wives Lees	Kent	39	J11
Old Woking	Surrey	36	B9
Old Wolverton	M Keyn	49	N6
Old Woodhall	Lincs	86	H7
Old Woods	Shrops	69	N10
Olgrinmore	Highld	167	J6
Olive Green	Staffs	71	L11
Oliver's Battery	Hants	22	E9
Ollaberry	Shet	169	q5
Ollach	Highld	153	J10
Ollerton	Ches E	82	G9
Ollerton	Notts	85	L7
Ollerton	Shrops	70	A9
Olmarch	Cerdgn	43	M3
Olmstead Green	Cambs	51	P3
Olney	M Keyn	49	N4
Olrig House	Highld	167	L3
Olton	Solhll	58	H8
Olveston	S Glos	32	B7
Ombersley	Worcs	46	F2
Ompton	Notts	85	L7
Once Brewed	Nthumb	111	P7
Onchan	IoM	80	e6
Onecote	Staffs	71	J3
Onehouse	Suffk	64	E10
Onen	Mons	31	M2
Ongar Street	Herefs	56	F11
Onibury	Shrops	56	H9
Onich	Highld	139	J5
Onllwyn	Neath	29	M2
Onneley	Staffs	70	D6
Onslow Green	Essex	51	Q7
Onslow Village	Surrey	23	Q5
Onston	Ches W	82	C10
Openwoodgate	Derbys	84	E11
Opinan	Highld	153	N3
Orbliston	Moray	157	Q6
Orbost	Highld	152	D9
Orby	Lincs	87	N7
Orchard Portman	Somset	18	H10
Orcheston	Wilts	21	L5
Orcop	Herefs	45	P9
Orcop Hill	Herefs	45	P9
Ord	Abers	158	F6
Ordhead	Abers	150	H5
Ordie	Abers	150	D7
Ordiequish	Moray	157	Q6
Ordley	Nthumb	112	D9
Ordsall	Notts	85	M5
Ore	E Susx	26	D9
Oreleton Common	Herefs	56	H11
Oreton	Shrops	57	M8
Orford	Suffk	65	N11
Orford	Warrtn	82	D6
Organford	Dorset	12	F6
Orgreave	Staffs	71	L11
Orkney Islands	Ork	169	d6
Orlestone	Kent	26	H5
Orleton	Herefs	56	H11
Orleton	Worcs	57	N11
Orlingbury	Nhants	61	J6
Ormathwaite	Cumb	101	J5
Ormesby	R & Cl	104	F7
Ormesby St Margaret	Norfk	77	P9
Ormesby St Michael	Norfk	77	P9
Ormiscaig	Highld	160	B9
Ormiston	E Loth	128	C6
Ormsaigmore	Highld	137	M3
Ormsary	Ag & B	123	M5
Ormskirk	Lancs	88	E9
Ornsby Hill	Dur	113	J10
Oronsay	Ag & B	136	b4
Orphir	Ork	169	c6
Orpington	Gt Lon	37	L7
Orrell	Sefton	81	L5
Orrell	Wigan	82	B4
Orrell Post	Wigan	88	G9
Orrisdale	IoM	80	d3
Orroland	D & G	108	G11
Orsett	Thurr	37	P4
Orslow	Staffs	70	E11
Orston	Notts	73	K2
Orthwaite	Cumb	101	J4
Ortner	Lancs	95	L10
Orton	Cumb	102	B9
Orton	Nhants	60	H5
Orton	Staffs	58	C5
Orton Longueville	C Pete	74	C11
Orton-on-the-Hill	Leics	59	M4
Orton Rigg	Cumb	110	F10
Orton Waterville	C Pete	74	C11
Orwell	Cambs	62	E10
Osbaldeston	Lancs	89	J4
Osbaldeston Green	Lancs	89	J4
Osbaldwick	C York	98	C10
Osbaston	Leics	72	C10
Osbaston	Shrops	69	K10
Osborne	IoW	14	F8
Osborne House	IoW	14	F8
Osbournby	Lincs	73	R3
Oscroft	Ches W	81	Q11
Ose	Highld	152	E9
Osgathorpe	Leics	72	C7
Osgodby	Lincs	86	E2
Osgodby	N York	91	Q4
Osgodby	N York	99	M4
Oskaig	Highld	153	J10
Oskamull	Ag & B	137	M7
Osmaston	Derbys	71	M6
Osmington	Dorset	11	P8
Osmington Mills	Dorset	12	B8
Osmondthorpe	Leeds	91	J4
Osmotherley	N York	104	E11
Osney	Oxon	34	E3
Ospringe	Kent	38	H9
Ossett	Wakefd	90	H6
Ossington	Notts	85	N8
Ostend	Essex	38	F2
Osterley	Gt Lon	36	E5
Oswaldkirk	N York	98	C5
Oswaldtwistle	Lancs	89	L5
Oswestry	Shrops	69	J9
Otford	Kent	37	M9
Otham	Kent	38	C11
Otham Hole	Kent	38	D11
Othery	Somset	19	L8
Otley	Leeds	97	H3
Otley	Suffk	65	K10
Otley Green	Suffk	65	J10
Otterbourne	Hants	22	E10
Otterburn	N York	96	C9
Otterburn	Nthumb	112	C2
Otter Ferry	Ag & B	131	L1
Otterham	Cnwll	5	K3
Otterhampton	Somset	18	H6
Otterham Quay	Kent	38	E9
Otterham Station	Cnwll	5	K3
Otternish	W Isls	168	e10
Ottershaw	Surrey	36	B8
Otterswick	Shet	169	s5
Otterton	Devon	10	B7
Otterwood	Hants	14	D6
Ottery St Mary	Devon	10	C5
Ottinge	Kent	27	L3
Ottringham	E R Yk	93	L6
Oughterby	Cumb	110	E9
Oughtershaw	N York	96	E5

Place	County	Page	Grid
Oughterside	Cumb	100	F2
Oughtibridge	Sheff	84	D2
Oughtrington	Warrtn	82	E7
Oulston	N York	98	A6
Oulton	Cumb	110	D10
Oulton	Leeds	91	K5
Oulton	Norfk	76	G6
Oulton	Staffs	70	D10
Oulton	Staffs	70	G7
Oulton	Suffk	65	Q3
Oulton Broad	Suffk	65	Q3
Oulton Street	Norfk	76	H6
Oundle	Nhants	61	M3
Ounsdale	Staffs	58	C6
Ousby	Cumb	102	B4
Ousden	Suffk	63	M9
Ousefleet	E R Yk	92	D6
Ouston	Dur	113	L10
Outchester	Nthumb	119	M4
Out Elmstead	Kent	39	M11
Outgate	Cumb	101	L11
Outhgill	Cumb	102	E10
Outhill	Warwks	58	H11
Outlands	Staffs	70	D8
Outlane	Kirk	90	D7
Out Newton	E R Yk	93	Q6
Out Rawcliffe	Lancs	88	E2
Outwell	Norfk	75	K10
Outwick	Hants	21	M11
Outwood	Surrey	36	H11
Outwood	Wakefd	91	J6
Outwood Gate	Bury	89	M9
Outwoods	Leics	72	C7
Outwoods	Staffs	70	D11
Ouzlewell Green	Leeds	91	J5
Ovenden	Calder	90	D5
Over	Cambs	62	E6
Over	Ches W	82	D11
Over	Gloucs	46	F11
Over	S Glos	31	Q8
Over Burrows	Derbys	71	P7
Overbury	Worcs	47	J7
Overcombe	Dorset	11	P8
Over Compton	Dorset	19	Q11
Overdale Crematorium Bolton		89	K9
Over End	Cambs	61	N2
Overgreen	Derbys	84	D6
Over Green	Warwks	59	J6
Over Haddon	Derbys	84	B7
Over Kellet	Lancs	95	L7
Over Kiddington	Oxon	48	D10
Overleigh	Somset	19	N7
Overley	Staffs	71	M11
Over Monnow	Mons	31	P2
Over Norton	Oxon	48	B9
Over Peover	Ches E	82	G10
Overpool	Ches W	81	M9
Overscaig Hotel	Highld	161	Q2
Overseal	Derbys	71	P11
Over Silton	N York	97	P2
Oversland	Kent	39	J10
Oversley Green	Warwks	47	L3
Overstone	Nhants	60	G7
Over Stowey	Somset	18	G7
Overstrand	Norfk	77	J3
Over Stratton	Somset	19	M11
Overstreet	Wilts	21	L7
Over Tabley	Ches E	82	F9
Overthorpe	Nhants	48	E6
Overton	C Aber	151	M5
Overton	Ches W	81	Q9
Overton	Hants	22	F5
Overton	Lancs	95	J9
Overton	N York	91	B9
Overton	Shrops	57	J10
Overton	Swans	28	E7
Overton	Wakefd	90	H7
Overton	Wrexhm	69	L6
Overton Bridge	Wrexhm	69	L6
Overton Green	Ches E	70	E2
Overtown	Lancs	95	N5
Overtown	N Lans	126	E7
Overtown	Swindn	33	N9
Overtown	Wakefd	91	K7
Over Wallop	Hants	21	Q7
Over Whitacre	Warwks	59	L6
Over Woodhouse	Derbys	84	G6
Over Worton	Oxon	48	D9
Overy	Oxon	34	G6
Oving	Bucks	49	L10
Oving	W Susx	15	P6
Ovingdean	Br & H	25	J10
Ovingham	Nthumb	112	G8
Ovington	Dur	103	M8
Ovington	Essex	52	C3
Ovington	Hants	22	G8
Ovington	Norfk	76	C11
Ovington	Nthumb	112	G8
Ower	Hants	14	E6
Ower	Hants	22	B11
Owermoigne	Dorset	12	C7
Owlbury	Shrops	56	E6
Owlerton	Sheff	84	D3
Owlpen	Gloucs	32	E5
Owl's Green	Suffk	65	K8
Owlsmoor	Br For	23	M2
Owlswick	Bucks	35	L3
Owmby	Lincs	86	D3
Owmby	Lincs	93	J10
Owslebury	Hants	22	F10
Owston	Donc	91	P8
Owston	Leics	73	K9
Owston Ferry	N Linc	92	D10
Owstwick	E R Yk	93	N4
Owthorne	E R Yk	93	P5
Owthorpe	Notts	72	H4
Owton Manor	Hartpl	104	E5
Oxborough	Norfk	75	P10
Oxbridge	Dorset	11	K5
Oxcombe	Lincs	87	K5
Oxcroft	Derbys	84	G6
Oxen End	Essex	51	Q5
Oxenholme	Cumb	95	L3
Oxenhope	C Brad	90	C4
Oxen Park	Cumb	94	G3
Oxenpill	Somset	19	M6
Oxenton	Gloucs	47	J8
Oxenwood	Wilts	22	B3
Oxenton	Oxon	34	F3
Oxford Airport	Oxon	48	E11
Oxford Crematorium	Oxon	34	G3
Oxford Services	Oxon	34	H4
Oxhey	Herts	50	D11
Oxhill	Dur	113	J10
Oxhill	Warwks	48	B5
Oxley	Wolves	58	D4
Oxley Green	Essex	52	F9
Oxley's Green	E Susx	25	M6
Oxlode	Cambs	62	G3
Oxnam	Border	118	C7
Oxnead	Norfk	77	J7
Oxshott	Surrey	36	D8
Oxshott Heath	Surrey	36	D8
Oxspring	Barns	90	H10
Oxted	Surrey	37	J10
Oxton	Border	128	D9
Oxton	N York	91	N2
Oxton	Notts	85	K10
Oxwich	Swans	28	E7
Oxwich Green	Swans	28	E7
Oxwick	Norfk	76	C6
Oykel Bridge Hotel	Highld	161	P6
Oyne	Abers	150	H2
Oystermouth	Swans	28	H7
Ozleworth	Gloucs	32	E6

P

Place	County	Page	Grid
Pabail	W Isls	168	k4
Packers Hill	Dorset	11	Q2
Packington	Leics	72	B8
Packmoor	C Stke	70	F4
Packmores	Warwks	59	L11
Padanaram	Angus	142	G7
Padbury	Bucks	49	K8
Paddington	Gt Lon	36	G4
Paddington	Warrtn	82	D7
Paddlesworth	Kent	27	L4
Paddlesworth	Kent	37	Q8
Paddock Wood	Kent	25	Q2
Paddolgreen	Shrops	69	P8
Padfield	Derbys	83	M5
Padgate	Warrtn	82	D7
Padham's Green	Essex	51	P11
Padiham	Lancs	89	M4
Padside	N York	97	J9
Padstow	Cnwll	4	E6
Padworth	W Berk	34	H11
Page Bank	Dur	103	P3
Pagham	W Susx	15	N7
Paglesham	Essex	38	F3
Paignton	Torbay	7	M6
Pailton	Warwks	59	Q8
Paine's Cross	E Susx	25	P6
Painleyhill	Staffs	71	J8
Painscastle	Powys	44	H5
Painshawfield	Nthumb	112	G8
Painsthorpe	E R Yk	98	G9
Painswick	Gloucs	32	G3
Painter's Forstal	Kent	38	G10
Paisley	Rens	125	M5
Paisley Woodside Crematorium	Rens	125	M5
Pakefield	Suffk	65	Q3
Pakenham	Suffk	64	C8
Pale	Gwynd	68	C7
Pale Green	Essex	51	Q2
Palestine	Hants	21	Q6
Paley Street	W & M	35	N9
Palfrey	Wsall	58	F5
Palgrave	Suffk	64	G6
Pallington	Dorset	12	C6
Palmersbridge	Cnwll	5	K6
Palmers Green	Gt Lon	36	H2
Palmerston	E Ayrs	115	K4
Palmerston	V Glam	30	F11
Palnackie	D & G	108	H9
Palnure	D & G	107	N5
Palterton	Derbys	84	G7
Pamber End	Hants	22	H3
Pamber Green	Hants	22	H3
Pamber Heath	Hants	22	H2
Pamington	Gloucs	46	H8
Pamphill	Dorset	12	G4
Pampisford	Cambs	62	G11
Panborough	Somset	19	N5
Panbride	Angus	143	K10
Pancrasweek	Devon	16	D10
Pancross	V Glam	30	D11
Pandy	Caerph	30	G7
Pandy	Gwynd	68	E4
Pandy	Gwynd	68	A10
Pandy	Mons	45	L10
Pandy	Powys	55	J8
Pandy	Wrexhm	68	G7
Pandy'r Capel	Denbgs	68	E4
Pandy Tudur	Conwy	67	R2
Panfield	Essex	52	B6
Pangbourne	W Berk	34	H9
Pangdean	W Susx	24	H8
Panks Bridge	Herefs	46	B5
Pannal	N York	97	M10
Pannal Ash	N York	97	L10
Pannanich Wells Hotel	Abers	150	C8
Pant	Shrops	69	J10
Pantasaph	Flints	80	H9
Panteg	Pembks	40	H4
Pantersbridge	Cnwll	5	J10
Pant Glas	Gwynd	66	H5
Pantglas	Powys	54	H5
Pant-Gwyn	Carmth	43	L9
Pant-lasau	Swans	29	J4
Pant Mawr	Powys	55	J8
Panton	Lincs	86	G5
Pant-pastynog	Denbgs	68	D2
Pantperthog	Gwynd	54	G4
Pant-y-dwr	Powys	55	M10
Pant-y-ffridd	Powys	56	B4
Pantyffynnon	Carmth	28	H2
Pantygaseg	Torfn	31	J5
Pant-y-gog	Brdgnd	29	P6
Pantymenyn	Carmth	41	M5
Pant-y-mwyn	Flints	68	G2
Panxworth	Norfk	77	M9
Papa Westray Airport	Ork	169	d1
Papcastle	Cumb	100	F4
Papigoe	Highld	167	Q6
Papple	E Loth	128	F5
Papplewick	Notts	84	H10
Papworth Everard	Cambs	62	C8
Papworth St Agnes	Cambs	62	C8
Par	Cnwll	3	R3
Paramour Street	Kent	39	N9
Parbold	Lancs	88	F8
Parbrook	Somset	19	Q7
Parbrook	W Susx	24	C5
Parc	Gwynd	68	A8
Parc Gwyn Crematorium	Pembks	41	M8
Parclyn	Cerdgn	42	D4
Parc Seymour	Newpt	31	M6
Pardshaw	Cumb	100	E6
Parham	Suffk	65	L9
Park	D & G	109	K2
Park	Nthumb	111	N8
Park Bottom	Cnwll	2	H5
Park Bridge	Tamesd	83	K4
Park Corner	E Susx	25	M3
Park Corner	Oxon	35	J7
Park Corner	W & M	35	N8
Park Crematorium	Lancs	88	D5
Park End	Bed	49	Q4
Park End	Nthumb	112	C5
Parkers Green	Kent	37	P11
Parkeston	Essex	53	M5
Parkeston Quay	Essex	53	M5
Park Farm	Kent	26	H4
Parkgate	Ches W	81	K9
Parkgate	Cumb	110	D10
Parkgate	D & G	109	M3
Parkgate	E Susx	26	B9
Parkgate	Essex	51	Q5
Park Gate	Hants	14	F5
Parkgate	Kent	26	E5
Park Gate	Kent	37	M8
Parkgate	Leeds	90	F2
Park Gate	Surrey	24	F2
Park Gate	Worcs	58	D10
Park Green	Essex	51	L5
Park Green	Suffk	64	G9
Parkgrove Crematorium	Angus	143	L8
Parkhall	W Duns	125	M3
Parkham	Devon	16	F7
Parkham Ash	Devon	16	F7
Park Head	Derbys	84	E10
Park Hill	Gloucs	31	Q5
Parkhouse	Mons	31	P4
Parkmill	Swans	28	F7
Park Royal	Gt Lon	36	E4
Parkside	Dur	113	P11
Parkside	N Lans	126	E6
Parkside	Wrexhm	69	L3
Parkstone	Poole	12	H6
Park Street	Herts	50	D10
Park Street	W Susx	24	D4
Park Wood Crematorium	Calder	90	E6
Parley Green	Dorset	13	K5
Parmoor	Bucks	35	L7
Parndon	Essex	51	K9
Parndon Wood Crematorium	Essex	51	K9
Parracombe	Devon	17	M2
Parrog	Pembks	41	L3
Parson Cross	Sheff	84	D2
Parson Drove	Cambs	74	G9
Parson's Heath	Essex	52	H6
Parson's Hill	Derbys	71	P9
Partick	C Glas	125	N4
Partington	Traffd	82	F6
Partney	Lincs	87	M7
Parton	Cumb	100	C6
Partridge Green	W Susx	24	D7
Partrishow	Powys	45	K10
Parwich	Derbys	71	M4
Paslow Wood Common	Essex	51	N10
Passenham	Nhants	49	L7
Passfield	Hants	23	M8
Passingford Bridge	Essex	51	M11
Paston	C Pete	74	C10
Paston	Norfk	77	L5
Pasturefields	Staffs	70	H10
Patchacott	Devon	8	C5
Patcham	Br & H	24	H9
Patchetts Green	Herts	50	D11
Patching	W Susx	24	C9
Patchole	Devon	17	L3
Patchway	S Glos	32	B8
Pateley Bridge	N York	97	J7
Paternoster Heath	Essex	52	F8
Pathe	Somset	19	L8
Pathhead	Fife	134	H9
Pathhead	Mdloth	128	B7
Pathlow	Warwks	47	N3
Path of Condie	P & K	134	D5
Patmore Heath	Herts	51	K5
Patna	E Ayrs	114	H5
Patney	Wilts	21	L3
Patrick	IoM	80	b5
Patrick Brompton	N York	97	K2
Patricroft	Salfd	82	G5
Patrington	E R Yk	93	P6
Patrington Haven	E R Yk	93	P6
Patrixbourne	Kent	39	L10
Patterdale	Cumb	101	L7
Pattingham	Staffs	57	Q5
Pattishall	Nhants	49	J4
Pattiswick Green	Essex	52	D7
Patton	Shrops	57	K5
Paul	Cnwll	2	D8
Paulerspury	Nhants	49	K5
Paull	E R Yk	93	L5
Paul's Dene	Wilts	21	M8
Paulton	BaNES	20	C3
Paunton	Herefs	46	C4
Pauperhaugh	Nthumb	119	M11
Pave Lane	Wrekin	70	D11
Pavenham	Bed	61	L9
Pawlett	Somset	19	J6
Pawston	Nthumb	118	G4
Paxford	Gloucs	47	N7
Paxton	Border	129	N10
Payden Street	Kent	38	F11
Payhembury	Devon	10	B4
Paynter's Lane End	Cnwll	2	H5
Paythorne	Lancs	96	B10
Paytoe	Herefs	56	G10
Peacehaven	E Susx	25	K10
Peak Dale	Derbys	83	N9
Peak District National Park	Sheff	83	Q6
Peak Forest	Derbys	83	P9
Peak Hill	Lincs	74	E7
Peakirk	C Pete	74	C9
Pearson's Green	Kent	25	Q2
Peartree Green	Herefs	46	A8
Peasedown St John	BaNES	20	D3
Peaseland Green	Norfk	76	F8
Peasemore	W Berk	34	E9
Peasenhall	Suffk	65	M8
Pease Pottage	W Susx	24	G4
Peaslake	Surrey	36	C2
Peasley Cross	St Hel	81	Q6
Peasmarsh	E Susx	26	E7
Peasmarsh	Somset	10	G2
Peasmarsh	Surrey	23	Q5
Peathill	Abers	159	M4
Peat Inn	Fife	135	M6
Peatling Magna	Leics	60	C2
Peatling Parva	Leics	60	C3
Peaton	Shrops	57	J7
Pebmarsh	Essex	52	E5
Pebworth	Worcs	47	M5
Pecket Well	Calder	90	B5
Peckforton	Ches E	69	P3
Peckham	Gt Lon	36	H5
Peckleton	Leics	72	D10
Pedairffordd	Powys	68	F10
Pedlinge	Kent	27	K4
Pedmore	Dudley	58	D8
Pedwell	Somset	19	M7
Peebles	Border	117	K2
Peel	IoM	80	b5
Peel	Lancs	88	D4
Peel Common	Hants	14	G6
Peene	Kent	27	L4
Peening Quarter	Kent	26	E6
Peggs Green	Leics	72	C7
Pegsdon	C Beds	50	D4
Pegswood	Nthumb	113	K3
Pegwell	Kent	39	Q9
Peinchorran	Highld	153	J11
Peinlich	Highld	152	G6
Pelcomb	Pembks	40	H7
Pelcomb Bridge	Pembks	40	H7
Pelcomb Cross	Pembks	40	H7
Peldon	Essex	52	G8
Pell Green	E Susx	25	P4
Pelsall	Wsall	58	F4
Pelsall Wood	Wsall	58	F4
Pelton	Dur	113	L10
Pelton Fell	Dur	113	L10
Pelutho	Cumb	109	P11
Pelynt	Cnwll	5	L10
Pemberton	Carmth	28	F4
Pemberton	Wigan	82	C4
Pembles Cross	Kent	26	E2
Pembrey	Carmth	28	D4
Pembridge	Herefs	45	M3
Pembroke	Pembks	41	J10
Pembroke Dock	Pembks	41	J10
Pembrokeshire Coast National Park	Pembks	40	F6
Pembury	Kent	25	P2
Pen-allt	Herefs	45	R9
Penallt	Mons	31	P2
Penally	Pembks	41	M11
Penare	Cnwll	3	P5
Penarth	V Glam	30	G10
Penblewin	Pembks	41	M7
Pen-bont Rhydybeddau	Cerdgn	54	F8
Penbryn	Cerdgn	42	F4
Pencader	Carmth	42	H7
Pencaenewydd	Gwynd	66	G6
Pencaitland	E Loth	128	C6
Pencarnisiog	IoA	78	F10
Pencarreg	Carmth	43	K5
Pencarrow	Cnwll	5	J5
Pencelli	Powys	44	F9
Penclawdd	Swans	28	F5
Pencombe	Herefs	46	A4
Pencoyd	Herefs	45	Q9
Pencraig	Herefs	45	R10
Pencraig	Powys	68	D9
Pendeen	Cnwll	2	B7
Penderyn	Rhondd	29	P3
Pendine	Carmth	41	P9
Pendlebury	Salfd	82	G4
Pendleton	Lancs	89	M3
Pendock	Worcs	46	E8
Pendoggett	Cnwll	4	G6
Pendomer	Somset	11	L2
Pendoylan	V Glam	30	E9
Pendre	Brdgnd	29	P8
Penegoes	Powys	54	H4
Penelewey	Cnwll	3	L5
Pen-ffordd	Pembks	41	L6
Pengam	Caerph	30	G5
Pengam	Cardif	30	H9
Penge	Gt Lon	37	J6
Pengelly	Cnwll	4	H5
Pengorffwysfa	IoA	78	H6
Pengover Green	Cnwll	5	M8
Pen-groes-oped	Mons	31	K3
Pengwern	Denbgs	80	E9
Penhale	Cnwll	4	H10
Penhale	Cnwll	4	E10
Penhale	Cnwll	5	L8
Penhale	Cnwll	5	Q11
Penhallow	Cnwll	3	K3
Penhalurick	Cnwll	3	J6
Penhalvean	Cnwll	3	J6
Penhill	Swindn	33	N7
Penhow	Newpt	31	M6
Penhurst	E Susx	25	Q7
Peniarth	Gwynd	54	E3
Penicuik	Mdloth	127	N5
Peniel	Carmth	42	H10
Peniel	Denbgs	68	D2
Penifiler	Highld	152	H9
Peninver	Ag & B	120	E7
Penisarwaun	Gwynd	67	K2
Penistone	Barns	90	G10
Penjerrick	Cnwll	3	K7
Penketh	Warrtn	82	C7
Penkill	S Ayrs	114	D8
Penkridge	Staffs	58	D2
Penlean	Cnwll	5	L2
Penleigh	Wilts	20	G4
Penley	Wrexhm	69	M6
Penllergaer	Swans	28	H5
Pen-llyn	IoA	78	F8
Penllyn	V Glam	30	C9
Pen-lon	IoA	78	G11
Penmachno	Conwy	67	P4
Penmaen	Caerph	30	G5
Penmaen	Swans	28	F7
Penmaenan	Conwy	79	N9
Penmaenmawr	Conwy	79	N9
Penmaenpool	Gwynd	67	M11
Penmark	V Glam	30	E11
Penmon	IoA	79	L8
Penmorfa	Gwynd	67	J6
Penmount Crematorium	Cnwll	3	L5
Penmynydd	IoA	79	J10
Penn	Bucks	35	P6
Penn	Wolves	58	C5
Pennal	Gwynd	54	F4
Pennan	Abers	159	K4
Pennant	Cerdgn	43	K2
Pennant	Denbgs	68	D8
Pennant	Powys	55	K5
Pennant-Melangell	Powys	68	D9
Pennard	Swans	28	G7
Pennerley	Shrops	56	F5
Pennicott	Devon	9	L4
Pennines		90	B3
Pennington	Cumb	94	F5
Pennington	Hants	13	P5
Pennington Green	Wigan	89	J9
Pennorth	Powys	44	G9
Penn Street	Bucks	35	P5
Pennsylvania	S Glos	32	D10
Penny Bridge	Cumb	94	G4
Pennycross	Ag & B	137	N10
Pennygate	Norfk	77	L7
Pennyghael	Ag & B	137	N10
Pennyglen	S Ayrs	114	E5
Penny Green	Derbys	84	H5
Penny Hill	Lincs	74	G5
Pennymoor	Devon	9	L2
Pennywell	Sundld	113	N9
Penparc	Cerdgn	42	D5
Penparcau	Cerdgn	54	D8
Penpedairheol	Caerph	30	G5
Penpedairheol	Mons	31	K4
Penperlleni	Mons	31	K4
Penpethy	Cnwll	4	H4
Penpillick	Cnwll	4	H10
Penpol	Cnwll	3	L6
Penpoll	Cnwll	5	J11
Penponds	Cnwll	2	G6
Penpont	Cnwll	4	H7
Penpont	D & G	108	H2
Penpont	Powys	44	D9
Penquit	Devon	6	H7
Penrest	Cnwll	5	N6
Penrherber	Carmth	41	Q3
Pen-rhiw	Pembks	41	P2
Penrhiwceiber	Rhondd	30	E5
Pen Rhiwfawr	Neath	29	K2
Penrhiw-llan	Cerdgn	42	G5
Penrhiw-pal	Cerdgn	42	F5
Penrhos	Gwynd	66	E8
Penrhos	IoA	78	D8
Penrhos	Mons	31	M2
Penrhos	Powys	29	M3
Penrhos garnedd	Gwynd	79	K10
Penrhyn Bay	Conwy	79	Q8
Penrhyn Castle NT	Gwynd	79	L10
Penrhyncoch	Cerdgn	54	E8
Penrhyndeudraeth	Gwynd	67	L7
Penrhyn-side	Conwy	79	Q8
Penrice	Swans	28	E7
Penrioch	N Ayrs	120	G3
Penrith	Cumb	101	P4
Penrose	Cnwll	4	D7
Penruddock	Cumb	101	M5
Penryn	Cnwll	3	K7
Pensarn	Conwy	80	D9
Pensax	Worcs	57	N11
Pensby	Wirral	81	K8
Penselwood	Somset	20	E8
Pensford	BaNES	20	B2
Pensham	Worcs	46	H6
Penshaw	Sundld	113	M10
Penshurst	Kent	25	M2
Penshurst Station	Kent	37	M11
Pensilva	Cnwll	5	M7
Pensnett	Dudley	58	D7
Penstone	Devon	9	J4
Penstrowed	Powys	55	P6
Pentewan	Cnwll	3	Q4
Pentir	Gwynd	79	K11
Pentire	Cnwll	4	B9
Pentlepoir	Pembks	41	M9
Pentlow	Essex	63	P11
Pentlow Street	Essex	63	P11
Pentney	Norfk	75	P8
Penton Grafton	Hants	22	B5
Penton Mewsey	Hants	22	B5
Pentraeth	IoA	79	J9
Pentre	Flints	68	E2
Pentre	Flints	81	L11
Pentre	Mons	31	K3
Pentre	Mons	31	M4
Pentre	Powys	55	P7
Pentre	Powys	56	B7
Pentre	Powys	56	D6
Pentre	Rhondd	69	C5
Pentre	Shrops	69	L11
Pentre	Wrexhm	69	J6
Pentre bach	Cerdgn	43	L5
Pentre Bach	Flints	81	J9
Pentrebach	Myr Td	30	E4
Pentre-bach	Powys	44	C8
Pentrebeirdd	Powys	56	B2
Pentre Berw	IoA	78	H10
Pentre-bont	Conwy	67	N4
Pentrebychan Crematorium	Wrexhm	69	K5
Pentre-cagel	Carmth	42	F6
Pentre-celyn	Denbgs	68	F4
Pentre-celyn	Powys	55	K3
Pentre-chwyth	Swans	29	J6
Pentre-clawdd	Shrops	69	J8
Pentre-cwrt	Carmth	42	G7
Pentredwr	Denbgs	68	G5
Pentrefelin	Gwynd	67	J7
Pentrefelin	IoA	78	G6
Pentre Ffwrndan	Flints	81	K10
Pentrefoelas	Conwy	67	R4
Pentregalar	Pembks	41	N4
Pentregat	Cerdgn	42	F4
Pentre-Gwenlais	Carmth	43	M11
Pentre Gwynfryn	Gwynd	67	K9
Pentre Halkyn	Flints	81	J10
Pentre Hodrey	Shrops	56	E9
Pentre Isaf	Conwy	80	D10
Pentre Llanrhaeadr	Denbgs	68	E2
Pentre Llifior	Powys	56	B5
Pentre-llwyn-llwyd	Powys	44	D4
Pentre-llyn	Cerdgn	54	E9
Pentre-llyn-cymmer	Conwy	68	C4
Pentre-Maw	Powys	55	K4
Pentre Meyrick	V Glam	30	C9
Pentre-piod	Torfn	31	J4
Pentre-poeth	Newpt	31	J7
Pentre'rbryn	Cerdgn	42	G4
Pentre'r-felin	Cerdgn	43	M5

Place	County	Page	Grid
Pentre'r Felin	Conwy	79	Q11
Pentre'r-felin	Powys	44	C8
Pentre Saron	Denbgs	68	D2
Pentre-tafarn-y-fedw	Conwy	67	Q2
Pentre ty gwyn	Carmth	43	R7
Pentrich	Derbys	84	E10
Pentridge	Dorset	21	K11
Pen-twyn	Caerph	30	H4
Pen-twyn	Mons	31	P3
Pen-twyn	Torfn	31	J4
Pentwynmaur	Caerph	30	G5
Pentyrch	Cardif	30	F8
Penwithick	Cnwll	4	G10
Penwood	Hants	22	D2
Penwyllt	Powys	44	B11
Penybanc	Carmth	43	M10
Penybont	Powys	44	G2
Pen-y-bont	Powys	68	H10
Pen-y-bont-fawr	Powys	68	E10
Pen-y-bryn	Pembks	41	N2
Pen-y-cae	Powys	29	M2
Penycae	Wrexhm	69	J5
Pen-y-cae-mawr	Mons	31	M5
Penycaerau	Gwynd	66	B9
Pen-y-cefn	Flints	80	G9
Pen-y-clawdd	Mons	31	N3
Pen-y-coedcae	Rhondd	30	E7
Pen-y-cwn	Pembks	40	G6
Pen-y-fai	Brdgnd	29	N8
Pen-y-felin	Flints	80	H11
Penyffordd	Flints	69	K2
Penyffridd	Gwynd	67	J3
Pen-y-garn	Cerdgn	54	E7
Pen-y-Garnedd	Powys	68	F10
Pen-y-genffordd	Powys	44	H9
Pen-y-graig	Gwynd	66	C8
Penygraig	Rhondd	30	D6
Penygroes	Carmth	28	G2
Penygroes	Gwynd	66	H4
Pen-y-Gwryd	Gwynd	67	M3
Pen-y-lan	V Glam	30	C9
Pen-y-Mynydd	Carmth	28	E4
Penymynydd	Flints	69	K2
Pen-y-pass	Gwynd	67	L3
Pen-yr-Heol	Mons	31	M2
Pen-yr-Heolgerrig	Myr Td	30	D3
Penysarn	IoA	78	H6
Pen-y-stryt	Denbgs	68	H4
Penywaun	Rhondd	30	C4
Penzance	Cnwll	2	D7
Peopleton	Worcs	46	H4
Peover Heath	Ches E	82	G10
Peper Harow	Surrey	23	P6
Peplow	Shrops	70	A10
Pepper's Green	Essex	51	P8
Pepperstock	C Beds	50	C7
Perceton	N Ayrs	125	K9
Percyhorner	Abers	159	N4
Pereile	Guern	10	b2
Periton	Somset	18	C5
Perivale	Gt Lon	36	E4
Perkins Village	Devon	9	P6
Perkinsville	Dur	113	L10
Perlethorpe	Notts	85	K6
Perranarworthal	Cnwll	3	K6
Perranporth	Cnwll	3	K3
Perranuthnoe	Cnwll	2	E8
Perranwell	Cnwll	3	K3
Perranwell	Cnwll	3	K6
Perran Wharf	Cnwll	3	K6
Perranzabuloe	Cnwll	3	K3
Perrott's Brook	Gloucs	33	K3
Perry	Birm	58	G6
Perry Barr	Birm	58	G6
Perry Barr Crematorium	Birm	58	G6
Perry Green	Essex	52	D7
Perry Green	Herts	51	K7
Perry Green	Wilts	33	J7
Perrystone Hill	Herefs	46	B9
Perry Street	Somset	10	G3
Pershall	Staffs	70	E9
Pershore	Worcs	46	H5
Pertenhall	Bed	61	N7
Perth	P & K	134	E3
Perth Crematorium	P & K	134	D2
Perthy	Shrops	69	L8
Perton	Herefs	46	A6
Perton	Staffs	58	C5
Pertwood	Wilts	20	G7
Peterborough	C Pete	74	C11
Peterborough Crematorium	C Pete	74	C10
Peterborough Services	Cambs	61	P2
Peterchurch	Herefs	45	L7
Peterculter	C Aber	151	L7
Peterhead	Abers	159	R8
Peterlee	Dur	104	D2
Petersfield	Hants	23	K10
Peter's Green	Herts	50	D7
Petersham	Gt Lon	36	E6
Peters Marland	Devon	16	H9
Peterstone Wentlooge	Newpt	31	J9
Peterston-super-Ely	V Glam	30	E9
Peterstow	Herefs	45	R10
Peter Tavy	Devon	8	D9
Petham	Kent	39	K11
Petherwin Gate	Cnwll	5	M4
Petrockstow	Devon	17	J10
Petsoe End	M Keyn	49	N5
Pett	E Susx	26	E9
Pett Bottom	Kent	39	L11
Petterden	Angus	142	G9
Pettinain	S Lans	116	D2
Pettistree	Suffk	65	L10
Petton	Devon	18	D10
Petton	Shrops	69	M9
Petts Wood	Gt Lon	37	L7
Pettycur	Fife	134	H10
Petty France	S Glos	32	E7
Pettymuk	Abers	151	N3
Petworth	W Susx	23	Q10
Pevensey	E Susx	25	P9
Pevensey Bay	E Susx	25	Q10
Pewsey	Wilts	21	N2
Pheasant's Hill	Bucks	35	L7
Phepson	Worcs	46	H3
Philadelphia	Sundld	113	M10
Philham	Devon	16	D7
Philiphaugh	Border	117	N5
Phillack	Cnwll	2	F6
Philleigh	Cnwll	3	M6
Philpot End	Essex	51	P7
Philpstoun	W Loth	127	K2
Phocle Green	Herefs	46	B9
Phoenix Green	Hants	23	L3
Phones	Highld	148	C9
Pibsbury	Somset	19	M9
Pica	Cumb	100	D6
Piccadilly	Warwks	59	K5
Piccotts End	Herts	50	B9
Pickburn	Donc	91	N9
Pickering	N York	98	F4
Picket Piece	Hants	22	C5
Picket Post	Hants	13	L3
Pickford	Covtry	59	L8
Pickford Green	Covtry	59	L8
Pickhill	N York	97	M4
Picklescott	Shrops	56	G5
Pickmere	Ches E	82	E9
Pickney	Somset	18	G9
Pickstock	Wrekin	70	C10
Pickup Bank	Bl w D	89	L6
Pickwell	Devon	16	H3
Pickwell	Leics	73	K8
Pickwick	Wilts	32	G10
Pickworth	Lincs	73	Q4
Pickworth	Rutlnd	73	P8
Picton	Ches W	81	N10
Picton	Flints	80	G8
Picton	N York	104	D9
Piddinghoe	E Susx	25	K10
Piddington	Bucks	35	M4
Piddington	Nhants	49	M4
Piddington	Oxon	48	H11
Piddlehinton	Dorset	11	Q5
Piddletrenthide	Dorset	11	Q5
Pidley	Cambs	62	D5
Piercebridge	Darltn	103	P7
Pierowall	Ork	169	d2
Piff's Elm	Gloucs	46	H9
Pigdon	Nthumb	113	J3
Pigeon Green	Warwks	47	P2
Pig Oak	Dorset	12	H4
Pig Street	Herefs	45	M5
Pikehall	Derbys	71	M3
Pilford	Dorset	12	H4
Pilgrims Hatch	Essex	51	N11
Pilham	Lincs	85	Q2
Pill	N Som	31	P9
Pillaton	Cnwll	5	P9
Pillatonmill	Cnwll	5	P9
Pillerton Hersey	Warwks	47	Q5
Pillerton Priors	Warwks	47	Q5
Pilleth	Powys	56	D11
Pilley	Barns	91	J10
Pilley	Hants	13	P5
Pilley Bailey	Hants	13	P5
Pillgwenlly	Newpt	31	K7
Pillhead	Devon	16	H6
Pilling	Lancs	95	J11
Pilling Lane	Lancs	94	H11
Pilning	S Glos	31	Q7
Pilot Inn	Kent	27	J8
Pilsbury	Derbys	71	L2
Pilsdon	Dorset	11	J5
Pilsgate	C Pete	73	R9
Pilsley	Derbys	84	B6
Pilsley	Derbys	84	F8
Pilson Green	Norfk	77	M9
Piltdown	E Susx	25	K6
Pilton	Devon	17	K5
Pilton	Nhants	61	M4
Pilton	Rutlnd	73	N10
Pilton	Somset	19	Q6
Pilton Green	Swans	28	D7
Pimlico	Lancs	89	L2
Pimlico	Nhants	48	H6
Pimperne	Dorset	12	F3
Pinchbeck	Lincs	74	D5
Pinchbeck Bars	Lincs	74	C5
Pinchbeck West	Lincs	74	D6
Pincheon Green	Donc	91	R7
Pinchinthorpe	R & Cl	104	F8
Pincock	Lancs	88	G7
Pinfold	Lancs	88	D8
Pinford End	Suffk	64	A10
Pinged	Carmth	28	D4
Pingewood	W Berk	35	J11
Pin Green	Herts	50	F5
Pinhoe	Devon	9	N6
Pinkett's Booth	Covtry	59	L8
Pinkney	Wilts	32	G7
Pinley	Covtry	59	N9
Pinley Green	Warwks	59	K11
Pin Mill	Suffk	53	M4
Pinminnoch	S Ayrs	114	C9
Pinmore	S Ayrs	114	D9
Pinn	Devon	10	C7
Pinner	Gt Lon	36	D3
Pinner Green	Gt Lon	36	D3
Pinsley Green	Ches E	69	Q5
Pinvin	Worcs	47	J5
Pinwherry	S Ayrs	114	D10
Pinxton	Derbys	84	G10
Pipe and Lyde	Herefs	45	Q6
Pipe Aston	Herefs	56	H10
Pipe Gate	Shrops	70	C6
Pipehill	Staffs	58	G3
Piperhill	Highld	156	F7
Pipers Pool	Cnwll	5	M5
Pipewell	Nhants	60	H3
Pippacott	Devon	17	J4
Pippin Street	Lancs	88	H4
Pipton	Powys	44	H7
Pirbright	Surrey	23	P3
Pirbright Camp	Surrey	23	P3
Pirnie	Border	118	C5
Pirnmill	N Ayrs	120	H3
Pirton	Herts	50	D4
Pirton	Worcs	46	G5
Pisgah	Cerdgn	54	F9
Pishill	Oxon	35	K7
Pistyll	Gwynd	66	E6
Pitagowan	P & K	141	K4
Pitblae	Abers	159	N5
Pitcairngreen	P & K	134	D2
Pitcalnie	Highld	156	E3
Pitcaple	Abers	151	J2
Pitcarity	Angus	142	E4
Pitchcombe	Gloucs	32	G3
Pitchcott	Bucks	49	L10
Pitcher Row	Lincs	74	E4
Pitchford	Shrops	57	J4
Pitch Green	Bucks	35	L4
Pitch Place	Surrey	23	N7
Pitch Place	Surrey	23	P4
Pitchroy	Moray	157	N10
Pitcombe	Somset	20	C8
Pitcot	V Glam	29	N10
Pitcox	E Loth	128	G3
Pitfichie	Abers	150	H4
Pitglassie	Abers	158	G6
Pitgrudy	Highld	162	H8
Pitlessie	Fife	135	J6
Pitlochry	P & K	141	M6
Pitmachie	Abers	150	H2
Pitmain	Highld	148	C7
Pitmedden	Abers	151	M2
Pitmedden Garden	Abers	151	M2
Pitminster	Somset	18	H11
Pitmuies	Angus	143	K8
Pitmunie	Abers	150	H5
Pitney	Somset	19	N9
Pitroddie	P & K	134	G2
Pitscottie	Fife	135	L5
Pitsea	Essex	38	B4
Pitses	Oldham	83	K4
Pitsford	Nhants	60	G7
Pitstone	Bucks	49	P11
Pitt	Devon	18	D11
Pitt	Hants	22	E9
Pittarrow	Abers	143	N3
Pitt Court	Gloucs	32	D5
Pittenweem	Fife	135	P7
Pitteuchar	Fife	134	H8
Pittington	Dur	104	B2
Pittodrie House Hotel	Abers	150	H3
Pitton	Wilts	21	P8
Pitt's Wood	Kent	37	P11
Pittulie	Abers	159	N4
Pityme	Cnwll	4	F6
Pity Me	Dur	113	L11
Pivington	Kent	26	F2
Pixey Green	Suffk	65	J6
Pixham	Surrey	36	E10
Plains	N Lans	126	D4
Plain Street	Cnwll	4	F6
Plaish	Shrops	57	J5
Plaistow	Gt Lon	37	K4
Plaistow	W Susx	24	B4
Plaitford	Hants	21	Q11
Plank Lane	Wigan	82	D5
Plas Cymyran	IoA	78	D9
Plastow Green	Hants	22	F2
Platt	Kent	37	P9
Platt Bridge	Wigan	82	D4
Platt Lane	Shrops	69	P7
Platts Heath	Kent	38	E11
Plawsworth	Dur	113	L11
Plaxtol	Kent	37	P10
Playden	E Susx	26	F7
Playford	Suffk	53	M2
Play Hatch	Oxon	35	K9
Playing Place	Cnwll	3	L5
Playley Green	Gloucs	46	E8
Plealey	Shrops	56	G3
Plean	Stirlg	133	N10
Pleasance	Fife	134	G5
Pleasington	Bl w D	89	J5
Pleasington Crematorium	Bl w D	89	J5
Pleasley	Derbys	84	H8
Pleasleyhill	Notts	84	H8
Pleck	Dorset	11	Q2
Pledgdon Green	Essex	51	N5
Pledwick	Wakefd	91	J7
Pleinheaume	Guern	10	b1
Plemont	Jersey	11	a1
Plemstall	Ches W	81	P10
Plenmeller	Nthumb	111	P8
Pleshey	Essex	51	Q8
Plockton	Highld	153	Q11
Plowden	Shrops	56	F7
Plox Green	Shrops	56	F4
Pluckley	Kent	26	F2
Pluckley Station	Kent	26	F3
Pluckley Thorne	Kent	26	F3
Plucks Gutter	Kent	39	N9
Plumbland	Cumb	100	G3
Plumgarths	Cumb	95	K2
Plumley	Ches E	82	F10
Plumpton	Cumb	94	G5
Plumpton	Cumb	101	N5
Plumpton	E Susx	25	J8
Plumpton	Nhants	48	G5
Plumpton End	Nhants	49	K6
Plumpton Green	E Susx	25	J7
Plumpton Head	Cumb	101	P3
Plumstead	Gt Lon	37	K5
Plumstead	Norfk	76	G4
Plumstead Green	Norfk	76	G4
Plumtree	Notts	72	G4
Plumtree Green	Kent	26	D2
Plungar	Leics	73	K4
Plurenden	Kent	26	F4
Plush	Dorset	11	Q4
Plushabridge	Cnwll	5	N7
Plwmp	Cerdgn	42	G4
Plymouth	C Plym	6	D8
Plymouth Airport	C Plym	6	E6
Plympton	C Plym	6	E8
Plymstock	C Plym	6	E8
Plymtree	Devon	9	Q4
Pockley	N York	98	E3
Pocklington	E R Yk	98	G11
Pode Hole	Lincs	74	D6
Podimore	Somset	19	P10
Podington	Bed	61	K8
Podmore	Staffs	70	D7
Point Clear	Essex	53	K9
Pointon	Lincs	74	B4
Pokesdown	Bmouth	13	K6
Polbain	Highld	160	H4
Polbathic	Cnwll	5	N10
Polbeth	W Loth	127	J5
Polbrock	Cnwll	4	G8
Poldark Mine	Cnwll	2	H7
Polebrook	Nhants	61	N3
Pole Elm	Worcs	46	F4
Polegate	E Susx	25	N10
Pole Moor	Kirk	90	D7
Polesworth	Warwks	59	L4
Polgiga	Cnwll	2	B9
Polglass	Highld	160	G5
Polgooth	Cnwll	3	N5
Polgown	D & G	115	P7
Poling	W Susx	24	B10
Poling Corner	W Susx	24	B9
Polkerris	Cnwll	4	H11
Pollard Street	Norfk	77	L5
Pollington	E R Yk	91	Q7
Polloch	Highld	138	D4
Pollokshaws	C Glas	125	P5
Pollokshields	C Glas	125	P5
Polmassick	Cnwll	3	P4
Polmear	Cnwll	4	H11
Polmont	Falk	126	G2
Polnish	Highld	145	N11
Polperro	Cnwll	5	M11
Polruan	Cnwll	5	J11
Polsham	Somset	19	P6
Polstead	Suffk	52	G4
Polstead Heath	Suffk	52	G3
Poltalloch	Ag & B	130	C9
Poltescoe	Cnwll	3	J10
Poltimore	Devon	9	N5
Polton	Mdloth	127	P5
Polwarth	Border	129	J9
Polyphant	Cnwll	5	M5
Polzeath	Cnwll	4	F6
Pomathorn	Mdloth	127	N6
Pomeroy	Derbys	83	P11
Ponde	Powys	44	G7
Pondersbridge	Cambs	62	C2
Ponders End	Gt Lon	51	J11
Ponsanooth	Cnwll	3	K6
Ponsonby	Cumb	100	E9
Ponsongath	Cnwll	3	K10
Ponsworthy	Devon	7	J4
Pont Abraham Services	Carmth	28	G3
Pontac	Jersey	11	c2
Pontamman	Carmth	28	H2
Pontantwn	Carmth	28	D2
Pontardawe	Neath	29	K4
Pontarddulais	Swans	28	G4
Pont-ar-gothi	Carmth	43	K10
Pont-ar-Hydfer	Powys	44	B9
Pont-ar-llechau	Carmth	43	P10
Pontarsais	Carmth	42	H9
Pontblyddyn	Flints	69	J2
Pont Cyfyng	Conwy	67	N3
Pont Dolgarrog	Conwy	79	P11
Pontdolgoch	Powys	55	N6
Pont-Ebbw	Newpt	31	J7
Pontefract	Wakefd	91	M6
Pontefract Crematorium	Wakefd	91	L6
Ponteland	Nthumb	113	J6
Ponterwyd	Cerdgn	54	G8
Pontesbury	Shrops	56	F3
Pontesbury Hill	Shrops	56	F3
Pontesford	Shrops	56	G3
Pontfadog	Wrexhm	68	H7
Pontfaen	Pembks	41	K4
Pont-faen	Powys	44	D8
Pontgarreg	Cerdgn	42	F4
Pontgarreg	Pembks	41	M2
Ponthenry	Carmth	28	E3
Ponthir	Torfn	31	K6
Ponthirwaun	Cerdgn	42	E5
Pontllanfraith	Caerph	30	G5
Pontlliw	Swans	28	H5
Pontllyfni	Gwynd	66	G4
Pont Morlais	Carmth	28	F3
Pontneddfechan	Neath	29	P3
Pontnewydd	Torfn	31	J5
Pontnewynydd	Torfn	31	J4
Pont Pen-y-benglog	Gwynd	67	M2
Pontrhydfendigaid	Cerdgn	54	G11
Pont Rhyd-y-cyff	Brdgnd	29	N7
Pont-rhyd-y-fen	Neath	29	L6
Pontrhydygroes	Cerdgn	54	G10
Pontrhydyrun	Torfn	31	J5
Pontrilas	Herefs	45	M9
Pont Robert	Powys	55	Q2
Pont-rug	Gwynd	67	J2
Ponts Green	E Susx	25	Q7
Pontshaen	Cerdgn	42	H5
Pontshill	Herefs	46	B10
Pontsticill	Myr Td	30	D3
Pont Walby	Neath	29	N3
Pontwelly	Carmth	42	H6
Pontyates	Carmth	28	D4
Pontyberem	Carmth	28	F2
Pont-y-blew	Wrexhm	69	K7
Pontybodkin	Flints	69	J3
Pontyclun	Rhondd	30	D8
Pontycymer	Brdgnd	29	P6
Pontyglasier	Pembks	41	M3
Pontygwaith	Rhondd	30	D6
Pontygynon	Pembks	41	M3
Pont-y-pant	Conwy	67	P4
Pontypool	Torfn	31	J4
Pontypool Road	Torfn	31	K5
Pontypridd	Rhondd	30	E7
Pont-yr-hafod	Pembks	40	H5
Pont-yr-Rhyl	Brdgnd	29	P7
Pontywaun	Caerph	30	H6
Pool	Cnwll	2	H6
Pool	IoS	2	b2
Pool	Leeds	97	K11
Poole	Poole	12	H6
Poole Crematorium	Poole	12	H5
Poole Keynes	Gloucs	33	J5
Poolewe	Highld	160	D10
Pooley Bridge	Cumb	101	N6
Pooley Street	Norfk	64	F5
Poolfold	Staffs	70	F2
Pool Head	Herefs	45	R4
Poolhill	Gloucs	46	D9
Pool of Muckhart	Clacks	134	C7
Pool Quay	Powys	56	D2
Pool Street	Essex	52	C4
Pooting's	Kent	37	L11
Popham	Hants	22	G6
Poplar	Gt Lon	37	J4
Poplar Street	Suffk	65	N8
Porchfield	IoW	14	D8
Poringland	Norfk	77	K11
Porkellis	Cnwll	2	H7
Porlock	Somset	18	C4
Porlock Weir	Somset	17	R2
Portachoillan	Ag & B	123	N8
Port-an-Eorna	Highld	153	P11
Port Appin	Ag & B	138	G8
Port Askaig	Ag & B	122	F6
Portavadie	Ag & B	124	A4
Port Bannatyne	Ag & B	124	D4
Portbury	N Som	31	P9
Port Carlisle	Cumb	110	D8
Port Charlotte	Ag & B	122	C8
Portchester	Hants	14	H5
Portchester Crematorium	Hants	14	H5
Port Clarence	S on T	104	E6
Port Driseach	Ag & B	124	B3
Port Ellen	Ag & B	122	E10
Port Elphinstone	Abers	151	K3
Portencalzie	D & G	106	D3
Portencross	N Ayrs	124	F8
Port Erin	IoM	80	a8
Portesham	Dorset	11	N7
Portessie	Moray	158	B4
Port e Vullen	IoM	80	g3
Port Eynon	Swans	28	E7
Portfield Gate	Pembks	40	H7
Portgate	Devon	5	Q4
Port Gaverne	Cnwll	4	G5
Port Glasgow	Inver	125	J3
Portgordon	Moray	158	A5
Portgower	Highld	163	N4
Porth	Cnwll	4	C9
Porth	Rhondd	30	D6
Porthallow	Cnwll	3	K9
Porthallow	Cnwll	5	L11
Porthcawl	Brdgnd	29	M9
Porthcothan	Cnwll	4	D7
Porthcurno	Cnwll	2	B9
Port Dinllaen	Gwynd	66	D6
Porth Henderson	Highld	153	N4
Porthgain	Pembks	40	F4
Porthgwarra	Cnwll	2	B9
Porthill	Staffs	70	E5
Porthkea	Cnwll	3	L5
Porthkerry	V Glam	30	E11
Porthleven	Cnwll	2	G8
Porthmadog	Gwynd	67	K7
Porthmeor	Cnwll	2	C6
Porth Navas	Cnwll	3	K8
Portholland	Cnwll	3	P5
Porthoustock	Cnwll	3	L7
Porthpean	Cnwll	3	Q3
Porthtowan	Cnwll	2	G6
Porthwgan	Wrexhm	69	L5
Porthyrhyd	Carmth	43	K11
Porth-y-Waen	Shrops	69	J10
Portincaple	Ag & B	131	J2
Portinfer	Jersey	11	a1
Portington	E R Yk	92	C4
Portinnisherrich	Ag & B	131	K5
Portinscale	Cumb	101	J6
Port Isaac	Cnwll	4	F5
Portishead	N Som	31	N9
Portknockie	Moray	158	C4
Portland	Dorset	11	P10
Portlethen	Abers	151	N8
Portling	D & G	109	J10
Portloe	Cnwll	3	—
Port Logan	D & G	106	E9
Portlooe	Cnwll	5	L11
Portmahomack	Highld	163	L10
Portmeirion	Gwynd	67	K7
Portmellon	Cnwll	3	Q5
Port Mor	Highld	144	F12
Portmore	Hants	13	P5
Port Mulgrave	N York	105	L7
Portnacroish	Ag & B	138	G8
Portnaguran	W Isls	168	k4
Portnahaven	Ag & B	122	A9
Portnalong	Highld	152	E11
Port nan Giuran	W Isls	168	k4
Port nan Long	W Isls	168	d10
Port Nis	W Isls	168	k1
Portobello	C Edin	127	Q3
Portobello	Gatesd	113	L9
Portobello	Wolves	58	D5
Port of Menteith	Stirlg	132	H7
Port of Ness	W Isls	168	k1
Porton	Wilts	21	N7
Portontown	Devon	5	—
Portpatrick	D & G	106	C7
Port Quin	Cnwll	4	F5
Port Ramsay	Ag & B	138	F8
Portreath	Cnwll	2	H4
Portree	Highld	152	H9
Port St Mary	IoM	80	b8
Portscatho	Cnwll	3	M6
Portsea	C Port	14	H6
Portskerra	Highld	166	F3
Portskewett	Mons	31	N7
Portslade	Br & H	24	G9
Portslade-by-Sea	Br & H	24	G9
Portslogan	D & G	106	C6
Portsmouth	C Port	14	H7
Portsmouth	Calder	89	Q5
Port Soderick	IoM	80	d7
Port Solent	C Port	14	H5
Portsonachan Hotel	Ag & B	131	K3
Portsoy	Abers	158	E4
Port Sunlight	Wirral	81	L8
Portswood	C Sotn	14	D4
Port Talbot	Neath	29	L7
Port Tennant	Swans	29	K6
Portuairk	Highld	137	L2
Portway	Herefs	45	P6
Portway	Herefs	45	P7
Portway	Sandw	58	E7
Portway	Worcs	58	G10
Port Wemyss	Ag & B	122	A9
Port William	D & G	107	K9
Portwrinkle	Cnwll	5	P11
Portyerrock	D & G	107	N10
Posbury	Devon	9	K5
Posenhall	Shrops	57	M4
Poslingford	Suffk	63	N11
Posso	Border	117	J4
Postbridge	Devon	8	G9
Postcombe	Oxon	35	K4
Post Green	Dorset	12	G5
Postling	Kent	27	K4
Postwick	Norfk	77	K10
Potarch	Abers	150	G8
Potsgrove	C Beds	49	Q9
Potten End	Herts	50	B9
Potten Street	Kent	39	N8
Potter Brompton	N York	99	K5
Potterhanworth	Lincs	86	E7
Potterhanworth Booths	Lincs	86	E7
Potter Heigham	Norfk	77	N8
Potterne	Wilts	21	J3
Potterne Wick	Wilts	21	J3
Potters Bar	Herts	50	F10
Potters Brook	Lancs	95	K10
Potter's Cross	Staffs	58	B8
Potter's Crouch	Herts	50	D9
Potter's Forstal	Kent	26	E2
Potters Green	Covtry	59	N8
Potter's Green	E Susx	25	M6
Potter's Green	Herts	51	J6
Pottersheath	Herts	50	F7
Potters Marston	Leics	72	D11
Potterspury	Nhants	49	L6
Potterton	Abers	151	N4
Potterton	Leeds	91	L3
Potthorpe	Norfk	76	E7

Pottle Street - Rhigos 295

Pottle Street Wilts 20 F6
Potto N York 104 E10
Potton C Beds 62 B11
Pott Row Norfk 75 P6
Pott's Green Essex 52 F7
Pott Shrigley Ches E 83 K9
Poughill Cnwll 16 C10
Poughill Devon 9 L3
Poulner Hants 13 L3
Poulshot Wilts 21 J3
Poulton Gloucs 33 L4
Poulton Wirral 81 L6
Poulton-le-Fylde Lancs 88 C3
Poulton Priory Gloucs 33 L5
Pound Bank Worcs 57 N10
Poundbury Dorset 11 P6
Poundffald Swans 28 G6
Poundgate E Susx 25 L5
Pound Green E Susx 25 M6
Pound Green Suffk 63 M10
Pound Green Worcs 57 P9
Pound Hill W Susx 24 G3
Poundon Bucks 48 H9
Poundsbridge Kent 25 M2
Poundsgate Devon 7 J4
Poundstock Cnwll 5 L2
Pound Street Hants 22 E2
Pounsley E Susx 25 M6
Pouton D & G 107 N8
Pouy Street Suffk 65 M7
Povey Cross Surrey 24 G2
Powburn Nthumb 119 L7
Powderham Devon 9 N8
Powerstock Dorset 11 L5
Powfoot D & G 109 P7
Pow Green Herefs 46 D6
Powhill Cumb 110 D9
Powick Worcs 46 F4
Powmill P & K 134 C8
Poxwell Dorset 12 B8
Poyle Slough 36 B5
Poynings W Susx 24 G8
Poyntington Dorset 20 C10
Poynton Ches E 83 K8
Poynton Wrekin 69 Q11
Poynton Green Wrekin 69 Q11
Poyston Cross Pembks 41 J7
Poystreet Green Suffk 64 D10
Praa Sands Cnwll 2 F8
Pratt's Bottom Gt Lon 37 L8
Praze-an-Beeble Cnwll 2 G6
Predannack Wollas
Cnwll 2 H10
Prees Shrops 69 Q8
Preesall Lancs 94 H11
Prees Green Shrops 69 Q8
Preesgweene Shrops 69 J7
Prees Heath Shrops 69 Q7
Prees Higher Heath
Shrops 69 Q7
Prees Lower Heath
Shrops 69 Q8
Prendwick Nthumb 119 K8
Pren-gwyn Cerdgn 42 H6
Prenteg Gwynd 67 K6
Prenton Wirral 81 L7
Prescot Knows 81 P6
Prescott Devon 10 B2
Prescott Shrops 57 M8
Prescott Shrops 69 M10
Presnerb Angus 142 B4
Pressen Nthumb 118 F3
Prestatyn Denbgs 80 F8
Prestbury Ches E 83 J9
Prestbury Gloucs 47 J10
Presteigne Powys 45 L2
Prestleigh Somset 20 B6
Prestolee Bolton 89 M9
Preston Border 129 K8
Preston Br & H 24 H9
Preston Devon 7 M4
Preston Dorset 11 Q8
Preston E R Yk 93 L4
Preston Gloucs 33 K4
Preston Herts 50 E6
Preston Kent 38 H9
Preston Kent 39 M9
Preston Lancs 88 G5
Preston Nthumb 119 N5
Preston Rutlnd 73 M10
Preston Shrops 57 J2
Preston Somset 18 E7
Preston Suffk 64 C11
Preston Torbay 7 M6
Preston Wilts 33 K9
Preston Wilts 33 Q10
Preston Bagot Warwks 59 J11
Preston Bissett Bucks 49 J9
Preston Bowyer Somset 18 F9
Preston Brockhurst
Shrops 69 P10
Preston Brook Halton 82 C8
Preston Candover Hants 22 H6
Preston Capes Nhants 48 G4
Preston Crematorium
Lancs 88 H4
Preston Crowmarsh
Oxon 34 H6
Preston Deanery Nhants 60 G9
Preston Green Warwks 59 J11
Preston Gubbals Shrops 69 N11
Preston Montford
Shrops 56 G2
Preston on Stour
Warwks 47 P5
Preston on Tees S on T 104 D7
Preston on the Hill
Halton 82 C8
Preston on Wye Herefs 45 M6
Prestonpans E Loth 128 B5
Preston Patrick Cumb 95 L4
Preston Plucknett
Somset 19 P11
Preston Street Kent 39 N9
Preston-under-Scar
N York 96 G2
Preston upon the
Weald Moors Wrekin 70 B11
Preston Wynne Herefs 45 R5
Prestwich Bury 82 H4
Prestwick Nthumb 113 J6
Prestwick S Ayrs 114 G2
Prestwick Airport S Ayrs 114 G2
Prestwood Bucks 35 N4
Prestwood Staffs 58 C7
Price Town Brdgnd 29 P6
Prickwillow Cambs 63 J4
Priddy Somset 19 P4
Priestacott Devon 8 B3
Priestcliffe Derbys 83 P10
Priestcliffe Ditch Derbys 83 P10
Priest Hutton Lancs 95 L6
Priestland E Ayrs 125 P10
Priestley Green Calder 90 E5
Priest Weston Shrops 56 D5
Priestwood Green Kent 37 Q8
Primethorpe Leics 60 B2
Primrose Green Norfk 76 F8
Primrosehill Border 129 K8
Primrose Hill Cambs 62 E3
Primrose Hill Derbys 84 F9
Primrose Hill Dudley 58 D7
Primrose Hill Lancs 88 D9
Primsidemill Border 118 F5
Princes Gate Pembks 41 M8
Princes Risborough
Bucks 35 M4
Princethorpe Warwks 59 P10
Princetown Devon 6 F4
Prinsted W Susx 15 L5
Prion Denbgs 68 E2
Prior Rigg Cumb 111 J7
Priors Halton Shrops 56 H9
Priors Hardwick Warwks 48 E3
Priorslee Wrekin 57 N2
Priors Marston Warwks 48 E3
Priors Norton Gloucs 46 G10
Priory Vale Swindn 33 M7
Priory Wood Herefs 45 K5
Prisk V Glam 30 D9
Priston BaNES 20 C2
Pristow Green Norfk 64 G4
Prittlewell Sthend 38 E4
Privett Hants 23 J9
Prixford Devon 17 K4
Probus Cnwll 3 M4
Prora E Loth 128 E4
Prospect Cumb 100 F2
Prospidnick Cnwll 2 G7
Protstonhill Abers 159 K5
Prudhoe Nthumb 112 G8
Prussia Cove Cnwll 2 F8
Publow BaNES 20 B2
Puckeridge Herts 51 J6
Puckington Somset 19 L11
Pucklechurch S Glos 32 C9
Puckrup Gloucs 46 G7
Puddinglake Ches W 82 F11
Puddington Ches W 81 L10
Puddington Devon 9 K2
Puddledock Norfk 64 F3
Puddletown Dorset 12 C6
Pudleston Herefs 45 R3
Pudsey Leeds 90 G4
Pulborough W Susx 24 B7
Puleston Wrekin 70 C10
Pulford Ches W 69 L3
Pulham Dorset 11 Q3
Pulham Market Norfk 64 H4
Pulham St Mary Norfk 65 J4
Pullens Green S Glos 32 B6
Pulloxhill C Beds 50 C4
Pumpherston W Loth 127 K4
Pumsaint Carmth 43 N6
Puncheston Pembks 41 K5
Puncknowle Dorset 11 L7
Punnett's Town E Susx 25 P6
Purbrook Hants 15 J5
Purfleet Thurr 37 N5
Puriton Somset 19 K6
Purleigh Essex 52 D11
Purley Gt Lon 36 H8
Purley W Berk 35 J9
Purlogue Shrops 56 D9
Purlpit Wilts 32 G11
Purls Bridge Cambs 62 G3
Purse Caundle Dorset 20 C11
Purshull Green Worcs 58 C10
Purslow Shrops 56 F8
Purston Jaglin Wakefd 91 L7
Purtington Somset 10 H3
Purton Gloucs 32 C3
Purton Gloucs 32 C4
Purton Wilts 33 L7
Purton Stoke Wilts 33 L6
Pury End Nhants 49 K5
Pusey Oxon 34 C5
Putley Herefs 46 B7
Putley Green Herefs 46 B7
Putloe Gloucs 32 E3
Putney Gt Lon 36 F6
Putney Vale
Crematorium Gt Lon 36 F6
Putsborough Devon 16 G3
Puttenham Herts 35 N2
Puttenham Surrey 23 P5
Puttock End Essex 52 D3
Putton Dorset 11 N8
Puxley Nhants 49 L6
Puxton N Som 19 M2
Pwll Carmth 28 E4
Pwllcrochan Pembks 40 H10
Pwll-du Mons 30 H2
Pwll-glâs Denbgs 68 F4
Pwllgloyw Powys 44 E8
Pwllheli Gwynd 66 F7
Pwllmeyric Mons 31 P6
Pwll Trap Carmth 41 Q7
Pwll-y-glaw Neath 29 L6
Pydew Conwy 79 Q9
Pye Bridge Derbys 84 F10
Pyecombe W Susx 24 G8
Pye Corner Newpt 31 K7
Pye Green Staffs 58 E2
Pyle Brdgnd 29 M8
Pyleigh Somset 18 F8
Pylle Somset 20 B7
Pymoor Cambs 62 G3
Pymore Dorset 11 K6
Pyrford Surrey 36 B9
Pyrton Oxon 35 J5
Pytchley Nhants 61 J6
Pyworthy Devon 16 E11

Q

Quabbs Shrops 56 C8
Quadring Lincs 74 D4
Quadring Eaudike Lincs 74 D4
Quainton Bucks 49 K10
Quaker's Yard Myr Td 30 E5
Quaking Houses Dur 113 J10
Quantock Hills Somset 18 G7
Quarff Shet 169 r10
Quarley Hants 21 Q6
Quarndon Derbys 72 A2
Quarr Hill IoW 14 G8
Quarrier's Village Inver 125 K4
Quarrington Lincs 73 R2
Quarrington Hill Dur 104 B3
Quarrybank Ches W 82 C11
Quarry Bank Dudley 58 D7
Quarrywood Moray 157 M5
Quarter N Ayrs 124 F5
Quarter S Lans 126 C7
Quatford Shrops 57 N6
Quatt Shrops 57 P7
Quebec Dur 103 N2
Quedgeley Gloucs 32 F2
Queen Adelaide Cambs 63 J4
Queenborough Kent 38 F7
Queen Camel Somset 19 Q10
Queen Charlton BaNES 32 B11
Queen Dart Devon 17 Q8
Queen Elizabeth Forest
Park Stirlg 132 G7
Queenhill Worcs 46 G7
Queen Oak Dorset 20 E8
Queen's Bower IoW 14 G10
Queensbury C Brad 90 E4
Queensferry Flints 81 L11
Queen's Head Shrops 69 K9
Queenslie C Glas 126 B4
Queen's Park Bed 61 M11
Queen's Park Nhants 60 G8
Queen Street Kent 37 Q11
Queen Street Wilts 33 K7
Queenzieburn N Lans 126 B2
Quendon Essex 51 M4
Queniborough Leics 72 G8
Quenington Gloucs 33 M4
Quernmore Lancs 95 L8
Queslett Birm 58 G6
Quethiock Cnwll 5 N9
Quick's Green W Berk 34 G9
Quidenham Norfk 64 E4
Quidhampton Hants 22 F4
Quidhampton Wilts 21 M8
Quina Brook Shrops 69 P8
Quinbury End Nhants 48 H4
Quinton Dudley 58 E8
Quinton Nhants 49 L4
Quinton Green Nhants 49 L4
Quintrell Downs Cnwll 4 C9
Quixhall Staffs 71 L6
Quixwood Border 129 K7
Quoditch Devon 5 Q2
Quoig P & K 133 N3
Quorn Leics 72 F7
Quothquan S Lans 116 D3
Quoyburray Ork 169 e6
Quoyloo Ork 169 b4

R

Raasay Highld 153 K9
Rabbit's Cross Kent 26 C2
Rableyheath Herts 50 F7
Raby Cumb 110 C10
Raby Wirral 81 L9
Rachan Mill Border 116 G4
Rachub Gwynd 79 L11
Rackenford Devon 17 R8
Rackham W Susx 24 B8
Rackheath Norfk 77 K9
Racks D & G 109 M6
Rackwick Ork 169 b7
Radbourne Derbys 71 P7
Radcliffe Bury 89 M9
Radcliffe Nthumb 119 Q10
Radcliffe on Trent Notts 72 G3
Radclive Bucks 49 J8
Radcot Oxon 33 Q5
Raddery Highld 156 C6
Raddington Somset 18 D9
Radernie Fife 135 M6
Radford Covtry 59 M8
Radford Semele Warwks 48 B2
Radlet Somset 18 H7
Radlett Herts 50 E10
Radley Devon 17 N7
Radley Oxon 34 F5
Radley Green Essex 51 P9
Radmore Green Ches E 69 Q3
Radnage Bucks 35 L5
Radstock BaNES 20 C4
Radstone Nhants 48 G6
Radway Warwks 48 C5
Radwell Bed 61 M9
Radwell Herts 50 F3
Radwinter Essex 51 P3
Radwinter End Essex 51 P3
Radyr Cardif 30 F8
RAF College (Cranwell)
Lincs 86 D11
Rafford Moray 157 K6
Ragdale Leics 72 H7
Ragdon Shrops 56 H6
Raginnis Cnwll 2 D8
Raglan Mons 31 M3
Ragnall Notts 85 P6
Raigbeg Highld 148 E2
Rainbow Hill Worcs 46 G3
Rainford St Hel 81 P4
Rainham Gt Lon 37 M4
Rainham Medway 38 D8
Rainhill St Hel 81 P6
Rainhill Stoops St Hel 81 Q6
Rainow Ches E 83 K9
Rainsough Bury 82 H4
Rainton N York 97 N5
Rainworth Notts 85 J9
Raisbeck Cumb 102 B9
Raise Cumb 111 P11
Raisthorpe N York 98 H8
Rait P & K 134 G2
Raithby Lincs 87 K4
Raithby Lincs 87 L7
Raithwaite N York 105 N8
Rake Hants 23 M9
Rakewood Rochdl 89 Q8
Ralia Highld 148 C8
Ram Carmth 43 L5
Ramasaig Highld 152 B9
Rame Cnwll 3 J7
Rame Cnwll 6 C9
Ram Hill S Glos 32 C9
Ram Lane Kent 26 G2
Rampisham Dorset 11 M4
Rampside Cumb 94 E7
Rampton Cambs 62 F7
Rampton Notts 85 P5
Ramsbottom Bury 89 M7
Ramsbury Wilts 33 Q10
Ramscraigs Highld 167 K11
Ramsdean Hants 23 K10
Ramsdell Hants 22 G3
Ramsden Oxon 48 C11
Ramsden Worcs 46 H5
Ramsden Bellhouse
Essex 38 B3
Ramsden Heath Essex 38 B2
Ramsey Cambs 62 C3
Ramsey Essex 53 M5
Ramsey IoM 80 g3
Ramsey Forty Foot
Cambs 62 D3
Ramsey Heights Cambs 62 B4
Ramsey Island Essex 52 F10
Ramsey Island Pembks 40 D6
Ramsey Mereside Cambs 62 C3
Ramsey St Mary's Cambs 62 C3
Ramsgate Kent 39 Q8
Ramsgill N York 96 H6
Ramshaw Dur 103 M5
Ramshaw Dur 112 E11
Ramsholt Suffk 53 P3
Ramshope Nthumb 118 D10
Ramshorn Staffs 71 K5
Ramsley Devon 8 G6
Ramsnest Common
Surrey 23 P8
Ranby Lincs 86 H5
Ranby Notts 85 L4
Rand Lincs 86 F5
Randalls Park
Crematorium Surrey 36 E9
Randwick Gloucs 32 F3
Ranfurly Rens 125 K4
Rangemore Staffs 71 M10
Rangeworthy S Glos 32 C7
Rankinston E Ayrs 115 J5
Ranksborough Rutlnd 73 L8
Rank's Green Essex 52 B8
Rannoch Station P & K 140 B6
Ranscombe Somset 18 B6
Ranskill Notts 85 L3
Ranton Staffs 70 F10
Ranton Green Staffs 70 E10
Ranworth Norfk 77 M9
Raploch Stirlg 133 M9
Rapness Ork 169 e2
Rapps Somset 19 K11
Rascarrel D & G 108 G11
Rashfield Ag & B 131 N11
Rashwood Worcs 58 D11
Raskelf N York 97 Q6
Rassau Blae G 30 G2
Rastrick Calder 90 E6
Ratagan Highld 145 R4
Ratby Leics 72 E9
Ratcliffe Culey Leics 72 A11
Ratcliffe on Soar Notts 72 D5
Ratcliffe on the Wreake
Leics 72 G8
Ratfyn Wilts 21 N6
Rathen Abers 159 N5
Rathillet Fife 135 K3
Rathmell N York 96 B9
Ratho C Edin 127 L3
Ratho Station C Edin 127 L3
Rathven Moray 158 B4
Ratlake Hants 22 D10
Ratley Warwks 48 C5
Ratling Kent 39 M11
Ratlinghope Shrops 56 G5
Rattan Row Norfk 75 K8
Rattar Highld 167 N2
Ratten Row Cumb 101 K2
Ratten Row Cumb 110 G11
Ratten Row Lancs 88 E2
Rattery Devon 7 J6
Rattlesden Suffk 64 D10
Ratton Village E Susx 25 N10
Rattray P & K 142 B8
Raughton Cumb 110 G11
Raughton Head Cumb 110 G11
Raunds Nhants 61 L6
Ravenfield Rothm 91 M11
Ravenglass Cumb 100 E11
Ravenhills Green Worcs 46 D4
Raveningham Norfk 65 M2
Ravenscar N York 105 Q10
Ravenscraig N Lans 126 D6
Ravensdale IoM 80 e3
Ravensden Bed 61 N10
Ravenseat N York 102 G10
Ravenshead Notts 85 J10
Ravensmoor Ches E 69 R4
Ravensthorpe Kirk 90 G6
Ravensthorpe Nhants 60 E6
Ravenstone Leics 72 C8
Ravenstone M Keyn 49 M4
Ravenstonedale Cumb 102 D10
Ravenstruther S Lans 126 G8
Ravensworth N York 103 M9
Raw N York 105 P9
Rawcliffe C York 98 B10
Rawcliffe E R Yk 92 A6
Rawcliffe Bridge E R Yk 92 A6
Rawdon Leeds 90 G3
Rawdon Crematorium
Leeds 90 G3
Rawling Street Kent 38 F10
Rawmarsh Rothm 91 L11
Rawnsley Staffs 58 F2
Rawreth Essex 38 C3
Rawridge Devon 10 E3
Rawtenstall Lancs 89 N6
Raydon Suffk 52 H4
Raylees Nthumb 112 D2
Rayleigh Essex 38 D3
Raymond's Hill Devon 10 G5
Rayne Essex 52 B7
Raynes Park Gt Lon 36 F7
Reach Cambs 63 J7
Read Lancs 89 M4
Reading Readg 35 K10
Reading Crematorium
Readg 35 K9
Reading Services W Berk 35 J11
Reading Street Kent 26 F5
Reading Street Kent 39 Q8
Reagill Cumb 102 B7
Realwa Cnwll 2 G6
Rearquhar Highld 162 G8
Rearsby Leics 72 H8
Rease Heath Ches E 70 A4
Reay Highld 166 G4
Reculver Kent 39 M8
Red Ball Devon 18 E11
Redberth Pembks 41 L10
Redbourn Herts 50 D8
Redbourne N Linc 92 G11
Redbrook Gloucs 31 P3
Redbrook Wrexhm 69 P6
Redbrook Street Kent 26 F4
Redburn Highld 156 G8
Redburn Nthumb 111 Q8
Redcar R & Cl 104 H6
Redcastle D & G 108 H7
Redcastle Highld 155 Q8
Red Dial Cumb 110 E11
Redding Falk 126 G2
Reddingmuirhead Falk 126 G2
Reddish Stockp 83 J6
Redditch Worcs 58 F11
Redditch Crematorium
Worcs 58 F11
Rede Suffk 63 P9
Redenhall Norfk 65 K5
Redenham Hants 22 B5
Redesmouth Nthumb 112 C4
Redford Abers 143 P3
Redford Angus 143 K9
Redford W Susx 23 N9
Redfordgreen Border 117 M7
Redgate Rhondd 30 D7
Redgorton P & K 134 D2
Redgrave Suffk 64 E6
Redhill Abers 151 K7
Red Hill Bmouth 13 J5
Redhill Herts 50 H4
Redhill N Som 19 N2
Redhill Surrey 36 G10
Red Hill Warwks 47 M3
Redisham Suffk 65 N5
Redland Bristl 31 Q9
Redland Ork 169 c4
Redlingfield Suffk 64 H7
Redlingfield Green Suffk 64 H7
Red Lodge Suffk 63 L6
Red Lumb Rochdl 89 N7
Redlynch Somset 20 D8
Redlynch Wilts 21 P10
Redmain Cumb 100 F4
Redmarley Worcs 57 P11
Redmarley D'Abitot
Gloucs 46 E8
Redmarshall S on T 104 C6
Redmile Leics 73 K3
Redmire N York 96 F2
Redmyre Abers 143 P2
Rednal Birm 58 F9
Rednal Shrops 69 L9
Redpath Border 118 A3
Redpoint Highld 153 N4
Red Post Cnwll 16 D10
Red Rock Wigan 88 H9
Red Roses Carmth 41 P8
Red Row Nthumb 119 Q11
Redruth Cnwll 2 H5
Redstocks Wilts 20 H2
Redstone P & K 142 B11
Redstone Cross Pembks 41 M7
Red Street Staffs 70 E4
Redvales Bury 89 N9
Red Wharf Bay IoA 79 J8
Redwick Newpt 31 M8
Redwick S Glos 31 P7
Redworth Darltn 103 P6
Reed Herts 51 J3
Reedham Norfk 77 N11
Reedness E R Yk 92 C6
Reeds Beck Lincs 86 H7
Reeds Holme Lancs 89 N6
Reepham Lincs 86 D6
Reepham Norfk 76 G7
Reeth N York 103 K11
Reeves Green Solhll 59 L9
Regaby IoM 80 f2
Regil N Som 19 P2
Reiff Highld 160 F4
Reigate Surrey 36 G10
Reighton N York 99 N5
Reisque Abers 151 M4
Reiss Highld 167 P6
Rejerrah Cnwll 4 B10
Releath Cnwll 2 H7
Relubbus Cnwll 2 F7
Relugas Moray 156 H8
Remenham Wokham 35 L8
Remenham Hill Wokham 35 L8
Rempstone Notts 72 F6
Rendcomb Gloucs 33 K3
Rendham Suffk 65 L9
Rendlesham Suffk 65 L11
Renfrew Rens 125 N4
Renhold Bed 61 N10
Renishaw Derbys 84 G5
Rennington Nthumb 119 P7
Renton W Duns 125 K2
Renwick Cumb 101 Q2
Repps Norfk 77 N8
Repton Derbys 71 Q9
Resaurie Highld 156 C8
Rescassa Cnwll 3 P5
Rescorla Cnwll 3 P4
Resipole Highld 138 C5
Reskadinnick Cnwll 2 G5
Resolis Highld 156 B4
Resolven Neath 29 M4
Rest and be thankful
Ag & B 131 Q6
Reston Border 129 M7
Restronguet Cnwll 3 L6
Reswallie Angus 143 J7
Reterth Cnwll 4 E9
Retford Notts 85 M4
Retire Cnwll 4 G9
Rettendon Essex 38 C2
Retyn Cnwll 4 D10
Revesby Lincs 87 J8
Rew Devon 7 J11
Rew Devon 7 K4
Rewe Devon 9 M5
Rew Street IoW 14 E8
Rexon Devon 5 Q4
Reydon Suffk 65 P6
Reymerston Norfk 76 E10
Reynalton Pembks 41 L9
Reynoldston Swans 28 E7
Rezare Cnwll 5 P6
Rhadyr Mons 31 L4
Rhandirmwyn Carmth 43 Q6
Rhayader Powys 55 M11
Rheindown Highld 155 P8
Rhes-y-cae Flints 80 H10
Rhewl Denbgs 68 F2
Rhewl Denbgs 68 G6
Rhewl-fawr Flints 80 G8
Rhewl Mostyn Flints 80 H8
Rhicarn Highld 164 C11
Rhiconich Highld 164 G6
Rhicullen Highld 156 B3
Rhigos Rhondd 29 P3

Place	County	Page	Grid
Rhireavach	Highld	160	G7
Rhives	Highld	163	J6
Rhiwbina	Cardif	30	G8
Rhiwbryfdir	Gwynd	67	M5
Rhiwderyn	Newpt	31	J7
Rhiwen	Gwynd	67	K2
Rhiwinder	Rhondd	30	D7
Rhiwlas	Gwynd	68	B7
Rhiwlas	Gwynd	79	K11
Rhiwlas	Powys	68	G8
Rhiwsaeson	Rhondd	30	E8
Rhode	Somset	19	J8
Rhoden Green	Kent	37	Q11
Rhodesia	Notts	85	J5
Rhodes Minnis	Kent	27	L3
Rhodiad-y-brenin	Pembks	40	E5
Rhonehouse	D & G	108	F9
Rhoose	V Glam	30	E11
Rhos	Carmth	42	G7
Rhos	Denbgs	68	F2
Rhos	Neath	29	K4
Rhosbeirio	IoA	78	F6
Rhoscefnhir	IoA	79	J9
Rhoscolyn	IoA	78	D9
Rhoscrowther	Pembks	40	H10
Rhosesmor	Flints	81	J11
Rhos-fawr	Gwynd	66	F7
Rhosgadfan	Gwynd	67	J3
Rhosgoch	IoA	78	G7
Rhosgoch	Powys	44	H5
Rhos Haminiog	Cerdgn	43	K2
Rhoshill	Pembks	41	N2
Rhoshirwaun	Gwynd	66	C9
Rhoslan	Gwynd	66	H6
Rhoslefain	Gwynd	54	D3
Rhosllanerchrugog	Wrexhm	69	J5
Rhôs Lligwy	IoA	78	H7
Rhosmaen	Carmth	43	M10
Rhosmeirch	IoA	78	H9
Rhosneigr	IoA	78	E10
Rhosnesni	Wrexhm	69	L4
Rhôs-on-Sea	Conwy	79	Q8
Rhosrobin	Wrexhm	69	K4
Rhossili	Swans	28	D7
Rhostryfan	Gwynd	66	H3
Rhostyllen	Wrexhm	69	K5
Rhosybol	IoA	78	G7
Rhos-y-brithdir	Powys	68	F10
Rhosygadfa	Shrops	69	K8
Rhos-y-garth	Cerdgn	54	E10
Rhos-y-gwaliau	Gwynd	68	B8
Rhos-y-llan	Gwynd	66	C7
Rhosymedre	Wrexhm	69	J6
Rhos-y-meirch	Powys	56	D11
RHS Garden Wisley	Surrey	36	C9
Rhu	Ag & B	132	B11
Rhuallt	Denbgs	80	F9
Rhubodach	Ag & B	124	C3
Rhuddall Heath	Ches W	69	Q2
Rhuddlan	Cerdgn	43	J6
Rhuddlan	Denbgs	80	E9
Rhulen	Powys	44	G5
Rhunahaorine	Ag & B	123	M10
Rhyd	Gwynd	67	L6
Rhydargaeau	Carmth	42	H9
Rhydcymerau	Carmth	43	L7
Rhydd	Worcs	46	F5
Rhyd-Ddu	Gwynd	67	K4
Rhydding	Neath	29	K5
Rhydgaled	Conwy	68	C2
Rhydlanfair	Conwy	67	Q4
Rhydlewis	Cerdgn	42	F5
Rhydlios	Gwynd	66	B9
Rhyd-lydan	Conwy	68	A4
Rhydowen	Cerdgn	42	H5
Rhydrosser	Cerdgn	54	D11
Rhydspence	Herefs	45	J5
Rhydtalog	Flints	68	H4
Rhyd-uchaf	Gwynd	68	B7
Rhyd-y-clafdy	Gwynd	66	E8
Rhydycroesau	Shrops	68	H8
Rhydyfelin	Cerdgn	54	D9
Rhydyfelin	Rhondd	30	E7
Rhyd-y-foel	Conwy	80	C9
Rhydyfro	Neath	29	K3
Rhyd-y-groes	Gwynd	79	K11
Rhydymain	Gwynd	67	Q10
Rhyd-y-meirch	Mons	31	K3
Rhydymwyn	Flints	81	J11
Rhyd-y pennau	Cerdgn	54	E2
Rhyd-yr-onnen	Gwynd	54	E4
Rhyd-y-sarn	Gwynd	67	M6
Rhyl	Denbgs	80	E8
Rhymney	Caerph	30	F3
Rhynd	P & K	134	F3
Rhynie	Abers	150	D2
Rhynie	Highld	163	J11
Ribbesford	Worcs	57	P10
Ribbleton	Lancs	88	H4
Ribby	Lancs	88	E4
Ribchester	Lancs	89	K3
Riber	Derbys	84	D9
Riby	Lincs	93	L9
Riccall	N York	91	Q3
Riccarton	Border	111	K2
Riccarton	E Ayrs	125	L10
Richards Castle	Herefs	56	H11
Richings Park	Bucks	36	B5
Richmond	Gt Lon	36	E6
Richmond	N York	103	N10
Richmond	Sheff	84	F3
Richmond Fort	Guern	10	b2
Rich's Holford	Somset	18	F8
Rickerscote	Staffs	70	G10
Rickford	N Som	19	N3
Rickham	Devon	7	K11
Rickinghall	Suffk	64	E6
Rickling	Essex	51	L4
Rickling Green	Essex	51	M5
Rickmansworth	Herts	36	C2
Riddell	Border	117	Q6
Riddings	Derbys	84	F10
Riddlecombe	Devon	17	L9
Riddlesden	C Brad	90	D2
Ridge	BaNES	19	Q3
Ridge	Dorset	12	F7
Ridge	Herts	50	F10
Ridge	Wilts	21	J8
Ridgebourne	Powys	44	F2
Ridge Green	Surrey	36	H11
Ridge Lane	Warwks	59	L6
Ridge Row	Kent	27	M3
Ridgeway	Derbys	84	F4
Ridgeway	Worcs	47	K2
Ridgeway Cross	Herefs	46	D5
Ridgewell	Essex	52	B3
Ridgewood	E Susx	25	L7
Ridgmont	C Beds	49	Q7
Riding Mill	Nthumb	112	H8
Ridley	Kent	37	P8
Ridley	Nthumb	111	Q8
Ridley Green	Ches E	69	Q4
Ridlington	Norfk	77	L5
Ridlington	Rutlnd	73	L10
Ridlington Street	Norfk	77	L5
Ridsdale	Nthumb	112	D4
Rievaulx	N York	98	B3
Rievaulx Abbey	N York	98	B4
Rigg	D & G	110	E7
Riggend	N Lans	126	D3
Righoul	Highld	156	F7
Rigmadon Park	Cumb	95	N4
Rigsby	Lincs	87	M5
Rigside	S Lans	116	B3
Riley Green	Lancs	89	J5
Rileyhill	Staffs	58	H2
Rilla Mill	Cnwll	5	M7
Rillaton	Cnwll	5	M7
Rillington	N York	98	H6
Rimington	Lancs	96	B11
Rimpton	Somset	20	B10
Rimswell	E R Yk	93	P5
Rinaston	Pembks	41	J5
Rindleford	Shrops	57	N5
Ringford	D & G	108	E9
Ringinglow	Sheff	84	C4
Ringland	Norfk	76	G9
Ringles Cross	E Susx	25	L6
Ringlestone	Kent	38	E10
Ringley	Bolton	89	M9
Ringmer	E Susx	25	K8
Ringmore	Devon	6	H9
Ringmore	Devon	7	N4
Ring o'Bells	Lancs	88	F8
Ringorm	Moray	157	P9
Ring's End	Cambs	74	G10
Ringsfield	Suffk	65	N4
Ringsfield Corner	Suffk	65	N4
Ringshall	Herts	35	Q2
Ringshall	Suffk	64	E11
Ringshall Stocks	Suffk	64	F11
Ringstead	Nhants	61	L5
Ringstead	Norfk	75	P2
Ringwood	Hants	13	L3
Ringwould	Kent	27	Q2
Rinsey	Cnwll	2	F8
Rinsey Croft	Cnwll	2	G8
Ripe	E Susx	25	M8
Ripley	Derbys	84	E10
Ripley	Hants	13	L5
Ripley	N York	97	L8
Ripley	Surrey	36	C9
Riplingham	E R Yk	92	G4
Riplington	Hants	23	J10
Ripon	N York	97	M6
Rippingale	Lincs	74	A5
Ripple	Kent	39	Q11
Ripple	Worcs	46	G7
Ripponden	Calder	90	C7
Risabus	Ag & B	122	D11
Risbury	Herefs	45	Q4
Risby	N Linc	92	F8
Risby	Suffk	63	P7
Risca	Caerph	30	H6
Rise	E R Yk	93	L2
Riseden	E Susx	25	P4
Riseden	Kent	26	B4
Risegate	Lincs	74	D5
Riseholme	Lincs	86	C5
Risehow	Cumb	100	D4
Riseley	Bed	61	M8
Riseley	Wokham	23	K2
Rishangles	Suffk	64	H8
Rishton	Lancs	89	L4
Rishworth	Calder	90	C7
Rising Bridge	Lancs	89	M5
Risley	Derbys	72	D3
Risley	Warrtn	82	E6
Risplith	N York	97	K7
Rivar	Wilts	22	B2
Rivenhall End	Essex	52	D8
River	Kent	27	N3
River	W Susx	23	P10
River Bank	Cambs	62	H7
Riverford	Highld	155	P7
Riverhead	Kent	37	N9
Rivers Corner	Dorset	12	C2
Rivington	Lancs	89	J8
Rivington Services	Lancs	89	J8
Roachill	Devon	17	R7
Roade	Nhants	49	L4
Road Green	Norfk	65	K3
Roadhead	Cumb	111	K6
Roadmeetings	S Lans	126	F8
Roadside	E Ayrs	115	L4
Roadside	Highld	167	L4
Roadwater	Somset	18	D7
Roag	Highld	152	D9
Roa Island	Cumb	94	E7
Roan of Craigoch	S Ayrs	114	E7
Roast Green	Essex	51	L4
Roath	Cardif	30	G9
Roberton	Border	117	N8
Roberton	S Lans	116	C5
Robertsbridge	E Susx	26	B7
Robertstown	Moray	90	F6
Robeston Wathen	Pembks	41	J7
Robgill Tower	D & G	110	D6
Robin Hill	Staffs	70	G3
Robin Hood	Lancs	88	G8
Robin Hood	Leeds	91	J5
Robin Hood Crematorium	Solhll	58	H8
Robin Hood Doncaster Sheffield Airport	Donc	91	R11
Robinhood End	Essex	52	B4
Robin Hood's Bay	N York	105	N9
Roborough	Devon	6	E6
Roborough	Devon	17	K8
Roby	Knows	81	N6
Roby Mill	Lancs	88	G9
Rocester	Staffs	71	L7
Roch	Pembks	40	G6
Rochdale	Rochdl	89	P8
Rochdale Crematorium	Rochdl	89	P8
Roche	Cnwll	4	F9
Rochester	Medway	38	B8
Rochester	Nthumb	118	F11
Rochford	Essex	38	E3
Rochford	Worcs	57	L11
Roch Gate	Pembks	40	G6
Rock	Cnwll	4	E6
Rock	Neath	29	L6
Rock	Nthumb	119	P6
Rock	W Susx	24	D8
Rock	Worcs	57	N10
Rockbeare	Devon	9	P6
Rockbourne	Hants	21	M11
Rockcliffe	Cumb	110	G8
Rockcliffe	D & G	108	H10
Rockcliffe Cross	Cumb	110	F8
Rock End	Staffs	70	F3
Rockend	Torbay	7	N6
Rock Ferry	Wirral	81	L7
Rockfield	Highld	163	L10
Rockfield	Mons	31	N2
Rockford	Devon	17	P2
Rockford	Hants	13	L3
Rockgreen	Shrops	57	J9
Rockhampton	S Glos	32	C6
Rockhead	Cnwll	4	H5
Rockhill	Shrops	56	D9
Rock Hill	Worcs	58	E10
Rockingham	Nhants	61	J2
Rockland All Saints	Norfk	64	D2
Rockland St Mary	Norfk	77	L11
Rockland St Peter	Norfk	64	D2
Rockley	Notts	85	M6
Rockley	Wilts	33	N10
Rockliffe	Lancs	89	P6
Rockville	Ag & B	131	Q9
Rockwell End	Bucks	35	L7
Rockwell Green	Somset	18	F10
Rodborough	Gloucs	32	F4
Rodbourne	Swindn	33	M7
Rodbourne	Wilts	32	H8
Rodd	Herefs	45	L2
Roddam	Nthumb	119	K6
Rodden	Dorset	11	N8
Roddymoor	Dur	103	N3
Rode	Somset	20	F4
Rode Heath	Ches E	70	E3
Rode Heath	Ches E	83	J11
Rodel	W Isls	168	f9
Roden	Wrekin	69	Q11
Rodhuish	Somset	18	D7
Rodington	Wrekin	57	K2
Rodington Heath	Wrekin	57	K2
Rodley	Gloucs	32	D2
Rodley	Leeds	90	G3
Rodmarton	Gloucs	32	H5
Rodmell	E Susx	25	K9
Rodmersham	Kent	38	F9
Rodmersham Green	Kent	38	F9
Rodney Stoke	Somset	19	N5
Rodsley	Derbys	71	N6
Rodway	Somset	19	J6
Roecliffe	N York	97	N7
Roe Cross	Tamesd	83	L5
Roe Green	Herts	50	F9
Roe Green	Herts	51	H4
Roe Green	Salfd	82	G4
Roehampton	Gt Lon	36	F6
Roffey	W Susx	24	E4
Roger Ground	Cumb	101	L11
Rogate	W Susx	23	M10
Rogerstone	Newpt	31	J7
Roghadal	W Isls	168	f9
Rogiet	Mons	31	N7
Roke	Oxon	34	H6
Roker	Sundld	113	P9
Rollesby	Norfk	77	N8
Rolleston	Leics	73	J10
Rolleston	Notts	85	M10
Rolleston on Dove	Staffs	71	N9
Rolston	E R Yk	93	M2
Rolstone	N Som	19	L2
Rolvenden	Kent	26	D5
Rolvenden Layne	Kent	26	E5
Romaldkirk	Dur	103	J6
Romanby	N York	97	N2
Romanno Bridge	Border	127	M8
Romansleigh	Devon	17	N7
Romden Castle	Kent	26	E3
Romesdal	Highld	152	G7
Romford	Dorset	13	J3
Romford	Gt Lon	37	M3
Romiley	Stockp	83	K6
Romney Street	Kent	37	N8
Romsey	Hants	22	C10
Romsley	Shrops	57	P8
Romsley	Worcs	58	E8
Rona	Highld	153	L6
Ronachan	Ag & B	123	M9
Rood Ashton	Wilts	20	G3
Rookhope	Dur	102	H2
Rookley	IoW	14	F10
Rookley Green	IoW	14	F10
Rooks Bridge	Somset	19	L4
Rooks Nest	Somset	18	E8
Rookwith	N York	97	K3
Roos	E R Yk	93	N4
Roose	Cumb	94	E7
Roosebeck	Cumb	94	F7
Roothams Green	Bed	61	N9
Ropley	Hants	22	H8
Ropley Dean	Hants	22	H8
Ropley Soke	Hants	23	J8
Ropsley	Lincs	73	P4
Rora	Abers	159	Q7
Rorrington	Shrops	56	E4
Rosarie	Moray	158	A7
Rose	Cnwll	3	K3
Roseacre	Lancs	88	E3
Rose Ash	Devon	17	P7
Rosebank	S Lans	126	E8
Rosebush	Pembks	41	L5
Rosecare	Cnwll	5	K2
Rosecliston	Cnwll	4	C10
Rosedale Abbey	N York	105	K11
Rose Green	Essex	52	F6
Rose Green	Suffk	52	F4
Rose Green	Suffk	52	G3
Rose Green	W Susx	15	P7
Rosehall	Highld	162	B6
Rosehearty	Abers	159	M4
Rose Hill	E Susx	25	L7
Rose Hill	Lancs	89	N4
Rosehill	Shrops	69	N5
Roseisle	Moray	157	L4
Roselands	E Susx	25	P10
Rosemarket	Pembks	41	J9
Rosemarkie	Highld	156	C6
Rosemary Lane	Devon	10	D2
Rosemount	P & K	142	B9
Rosenannon	Cnwll	4	F8
Rosenithon	Cnwll	3	L9
Roser's Cross	E Susx	25	M6
Rosevean	Cnwll	4	G10
Rosevine	Cnwll	3	M6
Rosewarne	Cnwll	2	G6
Rosewell	Mdloth	127	P5
Roseworth	S on T	104	D6
Roseworthy	Cnwll	2	G6
Rosgill	Cumb	101	P7
Roskestal	Cnwll	2	B9
Roskhill	Highld	152	D9
Roskorwell	Cnwll	3	K9
Rosley	Cumb	110	H10
Roslin	Mdloth	127	P5
Rosliston	Derbys	71	N11
Rosneath	Ag & B	132	B11
Ross	D & G	108	D12
Ross	Nthumb	119	M3
Rossett	Wrexhm	69	L3
Rossett Green	N York	97	L3
Rossington	Donc	91	Q11
Rossland	Rens	125	L3
Ross-on-Wye	Herefs	46	A10
Roster	Highld	167	N9
Rostherne	Ches E	82	F8
Rosthwaite	Cumb	101	J3
Roston	Derbys	71	L6
Rosudgeon	Cnwll	2	F8
Rosyth	Fife	134	E11
Rothbury	Nthumb	119	L10
Rotherby	Leics	72	H7
Rotherfield	E Susx	25	N5
Rotherfield Greys	Oxon	35	K6
Rotherfield Peppard	Oxon	35	K8
Rotherham	Rothm	84	F2
Rotherham Crematorium	Rothm	84	G2
Rothersthorpe	Nhants	60	F9
Rothersthorpe Services	Nhants	60	F9
Rotherwick	Hants	23	K3
Rothes	Moray	157	P8
Rothesay	Ag & B	124	C5
Rothiebrisbane	Abers	158	H10
Rothiemay	Moray	158	E8
Rothiemurchus Lodge	Highld	148	H6
Rothienorman	Abers	158	H10
Rothley	Leics	72	F8
Rothley	Nthumb	112	F3
Rothmaise	Abers	158	G11
Rothwell	Leeds	91	J5
Rothwell	Lincs	93	K11
Rothwell	Nhants	60	H4
Rotsea	E R Yk	99	M10
Rottal Lodge	Angus	142	F4
Rottingdean	Br & H	25	J10
Rottington	Cumb	100	C8
Roucan	D & G	109	M5
Roucan Loch Crematorium	D & G	109	M5
Roud	IoW	14	F10
Rougham	Norfk	76	A7
Rougham Green	Suffk	64	C9
Rough Close	Staffs	70	G7
Rough Common	Kent	39	K10
Roughlee	Lancs	89	N2
Roughpark	Abers	149	Q5
Roughton	Lincs	86	H8
Roughton	Norfk	77	J4
Roughton	Shrops	57	P6
Roughway	Kent	37	P10
Roundbush	Essex	52	E11
Round Bush	Herts	50	D11
Roundbush Green	Essex	51	N8
Round Green	Luton	50	D6
Roundham	Somset	11	J3
Roundhay	Leeds	91	J3
Rounds Green	Sandw	58	E7
Round Street	Kent	37	Q7
Roundstreet Common	W Susx	24	C5
Roundway	Wilts	21	K2
Roundyhill	Angus	142	F7
Rousay	Ork	169	c3
Rousdon	Devon	10	F6
Rousham	Oxon	48	E10
Rous Lench	Worcs	47	K4
Routenburn	N Ayrs	124	F3
Routh	E R Yk	93	J2
Rout's Green	Bucks	35	L5
Row	Cnwll	4	H6
Row	Cumb	95	K3
Row	Cumb	102	B4
Rowanburn	D & G	110	H5
Rowardennan	Stirlg	132	D8
Rowarth	Derbys	83	M7
Row Ash	Hants	14	F4
Rowberrow	Somset	19	N3
Rowborough	IoW	14	E10
Rowde	Wilts	21	J2
Rowden	Devon	8	D6
Rowen	Conwy	79	P10
Rowfield	Derbys	71	M5
Rowfoot	Nthumb	111	N8
Rowford	Somset	18	H9
Row Green	Essex	52	B7
Rowhedge	Essex	52	H7
Rowhook	W Susx	24	D4
Rowington	Warwks	59	K11
Rowland	Derbys	84	B6
Rowland's Castle	Hants	15	K4
Rowland's Gill	Gatesd	113	J9
Rowledge	Surrey	23	M6
Rowley	Dur	112	G11
Rowley	E R Yk	92	G4
Rowley	Shrops	56	E3
Rowley Hill	Kirk	90	F8
Rowley Regis	Sandw	58	E7
Rowley Regis Crematorium	Sandw	58	E7
Rowlstone	Herefs	45	M9
Rowly	Surrey	24	B2
Rowner	Hants	14	G6
Rowney Green	Worcs	58	F10
Rownhams	Hants	22	C11
Rownhams Services	Hants	22	C11
Rowrah	Cumb	100	E7
Rowsham	Bucks	49	M11
Rowsley	Derbys	84	C7
Rows of Trees	Ches E	82	H9
Rowstock	Oxon	34	D7
Rowston	Lincs	86	E9
Rowthorne	Derbys	84	G8
Rowton	Ches W	69	M2
Rowton	Shrops	56	F4
Rowton	Shrops	56	G8
Rowton	Wrekin	69	R11
Row Town	Surrey	36	B8
Roxburgh	Border	118	C4
Roxby	N Linc	92	G7
Roxby	N York	105	L7
Roxton	Bed	61	Q10
Roxwell	Essex	51	P9
Royal Botanic Gardens, Kew	Gt Lon	36	E5
Royal Leamington Spa	Warwks	59	M11
Royal Oak	Darltn	103	P6
Royal Oak	Lancs	81	N4
Royal's Green	Ches E	69	R6
Royal Tunbridge Wells	Kent	25	N3
Royal Wootton Bassett	Wilts	33	L8
Roy Bridge	Highld	146	H11
Roydhouse	Kirk	90	G8
Roydon	Essex	51	K8
Roydon	Norfk	64	G5
Roydon	Norfk	75	P6
Roydon Hamlet	Essex	51	K8
Royston	Barns	91	K8
Royston	Herts	51	J3
Royton	Oldham	89	Q9
Rozel	Jersey	11	c1
Ruabon	Wrexhm	69	K6
Ruaig	Ag & B	136	D6
Ruan High Lanes	Cnwll	3	N6
Ruan Lanihorne	Cnwll	3	M5
Ruan Major	Cnwll	3	J10
Ruan Minor	Cnwll	3	J10
Ruardean	Gloucs	46	B11
Ruardean Hill	Gloucs	46	B11
Ruardean Woodside	Gloucs	46	B11
Rubery	Birm	58	E9
Rubha Ban	W Isls	168	c16
Ruckcroft	Cumb	101	P2
Ruckhall	Herefs	45	P7
Ruckinge	Kent	26	H5
Ruckland	Lincs	87	K5
Ruckley	Shrops	57	J4
Rudby	N York	104	F9
Rudchester	Nthumb	112	H7
Ruddington	Notts	72	F3
Ruddle	Gloucs	32	C2
Ruddlemoor	Cnwll	3	Q3
Rudford	Gloucs	46	E10
Rudge	Somset	20	F4
Rudgeway	S Glos	32	B7
Rudgwick	W Susx	24	C4
Rudhall	Herefs	46	B9
Rudheath	Ches W	82	E10
Rudheath Woods	Ches E	82	F10
Rudley Green	Essex	52	D11
Rudloe	Wilts	32	F10
Rudry	Caerph	30	H7
Rudston	E R Yk	99	M7
Rudyard	Staffs	70	H3
Ruecastle	Border	118	B4
Rufford	Lancs	88	F7
Rufforth	C York	98	A10
Rug	Denbgs	68	E6
Rugby	Warwks	60	B5
Rugeley	Staffs	71	J11
Ruishton	Somset	19	J9
Ruislip	Gt Lon	36	C3
Rùm	Highld	144	E8
Rumbach	Moray	158	A7
Rumbling Bridge	P & K	134	C8
Rumburgh	Suffk	65	L5
Rumby Hill	Dur	103	N4
Rumford	Cnwll	4	D7
Rumford	Falk	126	G2
Rumney	Cardif	30	H9
Rumwell	Somset	18	G10
Runcorn	Halton	81	Q8
Runcton	W Susx	15	N6
Runcton Holme	Norfk	75	M9
Runfold	Surrey	23	N5
Runhall	Norfk	76	F10
Runham	Norfk	77	N9
Runham	Norfk	77	Q10
Runnington	Somset	18	F10
Runsell Green	Essex	52	C10
Runshaw Moor	Lancs	88	G7
Runswick	N York	105	M7
Runtaleave	Angus	142	G4
Runwell	Essex	38	C3
Ruscombe	Wokham	35	L9
Rushall	Herefs	46	B7
Rushall	Norfk	64	H5
Rushall	Wilts	21	M3
Rushall	Wsall	58	F4
Rushbrooke	Suffk	64	B9
Rushbury	Shrops	57	J6
Rushden	Herts	50	H4
Rushden	Nhants	61	L7
Rushenden	Kent	38	F7
Rusher's Cross	E Susx	25	P5
Rushford	Devon	8	C9
Rushford	Norfk	64	C4
Rush Green	Gt Lon	37	M3
Rush Green	Herts	50	F6
Rush Green	Warrtn	82	E4
Rushlake Green	E Susx	25	P7
Rushmere	Suffk	65	N4
Rushmere St Andrew	Suffk	53	L2
Rushmoor	Surrey	23	N6
Rushock	Herefs	45	L3
Rushock	Worcs	58	C10
Rusholme	Manch	83	J6
Rushton	Ches W	69	Q2
Rushton	Nhants	60	H4
Rushton	Shrops	57	L3
Rushton Spencer	Staffs	70	G2
Rushwick	Worcs	46	F4
Rushyford	Dur	103	Q5
Ruskie	Stirlg	133	J7
Ruskington	Lincs	86	E10
Rusland	Cumb	94	G3
Rusper	W Susx	24	F3
Ruspidge	Gloucs	32	C2
Russell Green	Essex	52	B9
Russell's Water	Oxon	35	K7
Russel's Green	Suffk	65	K7
Russ Hill	Surrey	24	F2
Rusthall	Kent	25	N3
Rustington	W Susx	24	B10
Ruston	N York	99	J4
Ruston Parva	E R Yk	99	M8
Ruswarp	N York	105	N9
Ruthall	Shrops	57	K6
Rutherford	Border	118	B4
Rutherglen	S Lans	125	Q5
Ruthernbridge	Cnwll	4	F8
Ruthin	Denbgs	68	F3
Ruthrieston	C Aber	151	N7
Ruthven	Abers	158	D8
Ruthven	Angus	142	D8
Ruthven	Highld	148	D8

Ruthvoes Cnwll 4 E9
Ruthwaite Cumb 100 H3
Ruthwell D & G 109 N7
Ruxley Corner Gt Lon 37 L6
Ruxton Green Herefs 45 Q11
Ruyton-XI-Towns
  Shrops 69 L10
Ryal Nthumb 112 F6
Ryall Dorset 11 J5
Ryall Worcs 46 G6
Ryarsh Kent 37 Q8
Rycote Oxon 35 J3
Rydal Cumb 101 L9
Ryde IoW 14 G8
Rye E Susx 26 F7
Ryebank Shrops 69 P8
Ryeford Herefs 46 B10
Rye Foreign E Susx 26 E7
Rye Harbour E Susx 26 F8
Ryehill E R Yk 93 M5
Ryeish Green Wokham 35 K11
Rye Street Worcs 46 E7
Ryhall Rutlnd 73 Q8
Ryhill Wakefd 91 K8
Ryhope Sundld 113 P10
Rylah Derbys 84 G7
Ryland Lincs 86 D5
Rylands Notts 72 E3
Rylstone N York 96 F9
Ryme Intrinseca Dorset 11 M2
Ryther N York 91 P3
Ryton Gatesd 113 J8
Ryton N York 98 F5
Ryton Shrops 57 P4
Ryton Warwks 59 P7
Ryton-on-Dunsmore
  Warwks 59 N10
Ryton Woodside Gatesd 112 H8

S

Sabden Lancs 89 M3
Sabine's Green Essex 51 M3
Sacombe Herts 50 H7
Sacombe Green Herts 50 H7
Sacriston Dur 113 K11
Sadberge Darltn 104 B7
Saddell Ag & B 120 E5
Saddington Leics 60 E2
Saddle Bow Norfk 75 M7
Saddlescombe W Susx 24 G8
Sadgill Cumb 101 N9
Saffron Walden Essex 51 M3
Sageston Pembks 41 L10
Saham Hills Norfk 76 C11
Saham Toney Norfk 76 B11
Saighton Ches W 69 M2
St Abbs Border 129 N6
St Agnes Border 128 H7
St Agnes Cnwll 3 J4
St Agnes IoS 2 b3
St Albans Herts 50 D9
St Allen Cnwll 3 L3
St Andrew Guern 10 b2
St Andrews Fife 135 N4
St Andrews Botanic
  Garden Fife 135 N4
St Andrew's Major
  V Glam 30 F10
St Andrews Well Dorset 11 K6
St Anne's Lancs 88 C5
St Ann's D & G 109 N2
St Ann's Chapel Cnwll 5 Q9
St Ann's Chapel Devon 6 H9
St Anthony Cnwll 3 K8
St Anthony's Hill E Susx 25 P10
St Arvans Mons 31 P5
St Asaph Denbgs 80 E10
St Athan V Glam 30 D11
St Aubin Jersey 11 b2
St Austell Cnwll 3 Q3
St Bees Cumb 100 C8
St Blazey Cnwll 3 R3
St Blazey Gate Cnwll 3 R3
St Boswells Border 118 A4
St Brelade Jersey 11 a2
St Brelade's Bay Jersey 11 a2
St Breock Cnwll 4 F7
St Breward Cnwll 4 H6
St Briavels Gloucs 31 Q4
St Brides Pembks 40 F8
St Bride's Major V Glam 29 N10
St Brides Netherwent
  Mons 31 M7
St Brides super-Ely
  V Glam 30 E9
St Brides Wentlooge
  Newpt 31 J8
St Budeaux C Plym 6 D7
Saintbury Gloucs 47 M7
St Buryan Cnwll 2 C8
St Catherine BaNES 32 E11
St Catherines Ag & B 131 N6
St Chloe Gloucs 32 F4
St Clears Carmth 41 Q7
St Cleer Cnwll 5 L8
St Clement Cnwll 3 M5
St Clement Jersey 11 c2
St Clether Cnwll 5 L5
St Colmac Ag & B 124 C4
St Columb Minor Cnwll 4 C9
St Columb Minor Cnwll 4 C9
St Columb Road Cnwll 4 E10
St Combs Abers 159 Q5
St Cross South Elmham
  Suffk 65 K5
St Cyrus Abers 143 N5
St David's P & K 133 Q3
St David's Pembks 40 E5
St Day Cnwll 3 J5
St Decumans Somset 18 E6
St Dennis Cnwll 4 F10
St Devereux Herefs 45 N8
St Dogmaels Pembks 42 C5
St Dogwells Pembks 41 J6
St Dominick Cnwll 5 Q8
St Donats V Glam 29 P11
St Edith's Marsh Wilts 21 J2
St Endellion Cnwll 4 F6
St Enoder Cnwll 4 D10
St Erme Cnwll 3 L4
St Erney Cnwll 5 P10
St Erth Cnwll 2 E7
St Erth Praze Cnwll 2 F6
St Ervan Cnwll 4 D7
St Eval Cnwll 4 D8
St Ewe Cnwll 3 P4
St Fagans Cardif 30 F9

St Fagans: National
  History Museum
  Cardif 30 F9
St Fergus Abers 159 Q7
St Fillans P & K 133 K3
St Florence Pembks 41 L10
St Gennys Cnwll 5 J2
St George Conwy 80 D9
St Georges N Som 19 L2
St George's V Glam 30 F9
St George's Hill Surrey 36 C8
St Germans Cnwll 5 P10
St Giles in the Wood
  Devon 17 J8
St Giles-on-the-Heath
  Devon 5 P3
St Gluvia's Cnwll 3 K7
St Harmon Powys 55 M10
St Helen Auckland Dur 103 N5
St Helens Cumb 100 D4
St Helens E Susx 26 D9
St Helens IoW 14 H9
St Helens St Hel 81 Q5
St Helens Crematorium
  St Hel 81 P5
St Helier Gt Lon 36 G7
St Helier Jersey 11 b2
St Hilary Cnwll 2 E7
St Hilary V Glam 30 D10
Saint Hill Devon 10 B3
Saint Hill W Susx 25 J3
St Illtyd Blae G 30 H4
St Ippollitts Herts 50 E5
St Ishmael's Pembks 40 F9
St Issey Cnwll 4 E7
St Ive Cnwll 5 N8
St Ive Cross Cnwll 5 N8
St Ives Cambs 62 D6
St Ives Cnwll 2 E5
St Ives Dorset 13 K4
St James Norfk 77 K7
St James's End Nhants 60 F8
St James South Elmham
  Suffk 65 L5
St Jidgey Cnwll 4 E8
St John Cnwll 5 Q11
St John Jersey 11 b1
St Johns Dur 103 L4
St John's IoM 80 c5
St Johns Kent 37 M9
St Johns Surrey 23 Q3
St Johns Worcs 46 F4
St John's Chapel Devon 17 J6
St John's Chapel Dur 102 G3
St John's Fen End Norfk 75 K8
St John's Highway Norfk 75 K8
St John's Kirk S Lans 116 D3
St John's Town of Dalry
  D & G 108 D4
St John's Wood Gt Lon 36 G4
St Jude's IoM 80 e2
St Just Cnwll 2 B7
St Just-in-Roseland
  Cnwll 3 L6
St Katherines Abers 159 J11
St Keverne Cnwll 3 K9
St Kew Cnwll 4 G6
St Kew Highway Cnwll 4 G6
St Keyne Cnwll 5 L9
St Lawrence Cnwll 4 G8
St Lawrence Essex 52 G11
St Lawrence IoW 14 F11
St Lawrence Jersey 11 b1
St Lawrence Kent 39 Q8
St Leonards Bucks 35 P3
St Leonards Dorset 13 K4
St Leonards E Susx 26 D10
St Leonard's Street Kent 37 Q9
St Levan Cnwll 2 B9
St Lythans V Glam 30 F10
St Mabyn Cnwll 4 G7
St Madoes P & K 134 F3
St Margarets Herefs 45 M8
St Margarets Herts 51 J8
St Margaret's at Cliffe
  Kent 27 Q3
St Margaret's Hope Ork 169 d7
St Margaret South
  Elmham Suffk 65 L5
St Marks IoM 80 c7
St Martin Cnwll 3 J9
St Martin Cnwll 5 M10
St Martin Guern 10 b2
St Martin Jersey 11 c1
St Martin's IoS 2 c1
St Martin's P & K 142 B11
St Martins Shrops 69 K7
St Martin's Moor Shrops 69 K7
St Mary Jersey 11 a1
St Mary Bourne Hants 22 D4
St Marychurch Torbay 7 N5
St Mary Church V Glam 30 D10
St Mary Cray Gt Lon 37 L7
St Mary Hill V Glam 30 C9
St Mary in the Marsh
  Kent 27 J6
St Marylebone
  Crematorium Gt Lon 36 G3
St Mary's IoS 2 c2
St Mary's Ork 169 d6
St Mary's Bay Kent 27 J6
St Mary's Grove N Som 31 N11
St Mary's Hoo Medway 38 D6
St Maughans Mons 45 P11
St Maughans Green
  Mons 45 P11
St Mawes Cnwll 3 L7
St Mawgan Cnwll 4 D8
St Mellion Cnwll 5 P8
St Mellons Cardif 30 H8
St Merryn Cnwll 4 D7
St Mewan Cnwll 3 N3
St Michael Caerhays
  Cnwll 3 P5
St Michael Church
  Somset 19 K8
St Michael Penkevil
  Cnwll 3 M5
St Michaels Kent 26 E4
St Michaels Worcs 57 K11
St Michael's on Wyre
  Lancs 88 F2
St Michael South
  Elmham Suffk 65 L5
St Minver Cnwll 4 F6
St Monans Fife 135 N7
St Neot Cnwll 5 K8
St Neots Cambs 61 Q8
St Nicholas Pembks 40 H3
St Nicholas V Glam 30 E10

St Nicholas at Wade
  Kent 39 N8
St Ninians Stirlg 133 M9
St Olaves Norfk 65 P2
St Osyth Essex 53 K8
St Ouen Jersey 11 a1
St Owens Cross Herefs 45 Q10
St Pauls Cray Gt Lon 37 L7
St Paul's Walden Herts 50 E6
St Peter Jersey 11 a1
St Peter Port Guern 10 c2
St Peter's Guern 10 b2
St Peter's Kent 39 Q8
St Peter's Hill Cambs 62 B6
St Petrox Pembks 41 J11
St Pinnock Cnwll 5 L9
St Quivox S Ayrs 114 G3
St Ruan Cnwll 3 J10
St Sampson Guern 10 c1
St Saviour Guern 10 b2
St Saviour Jersey 11 b2
St Stephen Cnwll 3 N3
St Stephens Cnwll 5 N4
St Stephens Cnwll 5 Q10
St Teath Cnwll 4 H5
St Tudy Cnwll 4 H6
St Twynnells Pembks 41 J11
St Veep Cnwll 5 J10
St Vigeans Angus 143 L9
St Wenn Cnwll 4 F9
St Weonards Herefs 45 P10
St y-Nyll V Glam 30 E9
Salcombe Devon 7 J11
Salcombe Regis Devon 10 D7
Salcott-cum-Virley Essex 52 F9
Sale Traffd 82 G6
Saleby Lincs 87 N5
Sale Green Worcs 46 H3
Salehurst E Susx 26 C7
Salem Carmth 43 M9
Salem Cerdgn 54 F8
Salen Ag & B 137 P7
Salen Highld 138 B5
Salesbury Lancs 89 K4
Salford C Beds 49 P7
Salford Oxon 47 Q9
Salford Salfd 82 H5
Salford Priors Warwks 47 L4
Salfords Surrey 36 G11
Salhouse Norfk 77 L9
Saline Fife 134 C9
Salisbury Wilts 21 M9
Salisbury Cathedral Wilts 21 M9
Salisbury Crematorium
  Wilts 21 N8
Salisbury Plain Wilts 21 L6
Salkeld Dykes Cumb 101 P3
Salle Norfk 76 G7
Salmonby Lincs 87 K6
Salperton Gloucs 47 L10
Salph End Bed 61 N10
Salsburgh N Lans 126 E5
Salt Staffs 70 H9
Salta Cumb 109 N11
Saltaire C Brad 90 E3
Saltash Cnwll 6 C7
Saltburn Highld 156 C3
Saltburn-by-the-Sea
  R & Cl 105 J6
Saltby Leics 73 M5
Salt Coates Cumb 110 C10
Saltcoats Cumb 100 E11
Saltcoats N Ayrs 124 G9
Saltcotes Lancs 88 D5
Saltdean Br & H 25 J10
Salterbeck Cumb 100 C5
Salterforth Lancs 96 C11
Salterswall Ches W 82 D11
Salterton Wilts 21 M7
Saltfleet Lincs 87 N2
Saltfleetby All Saints
  Lincs 87 N2
Saltfleetby St Clement
  Lincs 87 N2
Saltfleetby St Peter
  Lincs 87 M3
Saltford BaNES 32 C11
Salthouse Norfk 76 F3
Saltley Birm 58 H7
Saltmarsh Newpt 31 K8
Saltmarshe E R Yk 92 C6
Saltney Flints 69 L2
Salton N York 98 E5
Saltrens Devon 16 H7
Saltwell Crematorium
  Gatesd 113 L8
Saltwick Nthumb 113 J4
Saltwood Kent 27 L4
Salvington W Susx 24 D9
Salwarpe Worcs 46 G2
Salway Ash Dorset 11 K5
Sambourne Warwks 47 L2
Sambrook Wrekin 70 C10
Samlesbury Lancs 88 H4
Samlesbury Bottoms
  Lancs 89 J5
Sampford Arundel
  Somset 18 F11
Sampford Brett Somset 18 E6
Sampford Courtenay
  Devon 8 F4
Sampford Moor Somset 18 F11
Sampford Peverell
  Devon 9 P2
Sampford Spiney Devon 6 E4
Samsonlane Ork 169 f4
Samson's Corner Essex 53 J8
Samuelston E Loth 128 D5
Sanaigmore Ag & B 122 B5
Sancreed Cnwll 2 C8
Sancton E R Yk 92 H3
Sand Somset 19 M5
Sandaig Highld 145 M7
Sandale Cumb 100 H2
Sandal Magna Wakefd 91 J7
Sandavore Highld 144 G11
Sanday Ork 169 f2
Sanday Airport Ork 169 f2
Sandbach Ches E 70 D2
Sandbach Services
  Ches E 70 D2
Sandbank Ag & B 131 P11
Sandbanks Poole 12 H7
Sandend Abers 158 E4
Sanderstead Gt Lon 36 H8
Sandford Cumb 102 D7
Sandford Devon 9 K4
Sandford Dorset 12 F7
Sandford Hants 13 L4
Sandford IoW 14 F10

Sandford N Som 19 M3
Sandford S Lans 126 C9
Sandford Shrops 69 K10
Sandford Shrops 69 Q8
Sandford-on-Thames
  Oxon 34 F4
Sandford Orcas Dorset 20 B10
Sandford St Martin Oxon 48 D9
Sandgate Kent 27 M4
Sandhaven Abers 159 N4
Sandhead D & G 106 E8
Sandhill Rothm 91 L11
Sandhills Dorset 11 M4
Sandhills Dorset 11 P2
Sandhills Leeds 91 K3
Sandhills Oxon 34 G3
Sandhills Surrey 23 P7
Sandhoe Nthumb 112 E7
Sandhole Ag & B 131 L8
Sand Hole E R Yk 92 D3
Sandholme E R Yk 92 D4
Sandholme Lincs 74 F3
Sandhurst Br For 23 M2
Sandhurst Gloucs 46 F10
Sandhurst Kent 26 D6
Sandhurst Cross Kent 26 C6
Sandhutton N York 97 N4
Sand Hutton N York 98 D9
Sandiacre Derbys 72 D3
Sandilands Lincs 87 P4
Sandiway Ches W 82 D10
Sandleheath Hants 21 M11
Sandleigh Oxon 34 E4
Sandley Dorset 20 E10
Sandling Kent 38 C10
Sandlow Green Ches E 82 G11
Sandness Shet 169 n8
Sandon Essex 52 B11
Sandon Herts 50 H4
Sandon Staffs 70 G9
Sandon Bank Staffs 70 G9
Sandown IoW 14 G10
Sandplace Cnwll 5 M10
Sandridge Herts 50 E8
Sandridge Wilts 32 H11
Sandringham Norfk 75 N5
Sands Bucks 35 M6
Sandsend N York 105 N8
Sand Side Cumb 94 E4
Sandside Cumb 95 K4
Sandtoft N Linc 92 B9
Sandway Kent 38 E11
Sandwich Kent 39 P10
Sandwick Highld 101 M7
Sandwick Shet 169 r11
Sandwick W Isls 168 j4
Sandwith Cumb 100 C8
Sandwith Newtown
  Cumb 100 C8
Sandy C Beds 61 Q11
Sandy Bank Lincs 87 J9
Sandycroft Flints 81 L11
Sandy Cross E Susx 25 N6
Sandy Cross Herefs 46 C3
Sandyford D & G 110 D2
Sandygate Devon 7 M4
Sandygate IoM 80 e2
Sandy Haven Pembks 40 G9
Sandyhills D & G 109 J9
Sandylands Lancs 95 J8
Sandy Lane C Brad 90 E3
Sandy Lane Staffs 70 C7
Sandylane Swans 28 G7
Sandy Lane Wilts 33 J11
Sandy Lane Wrexhm 69 M6
Sandy Park Devon 8 H7
Sandysike Cumb 110 G7
Sandyway Herefs 45 P9
Sangobeg Highld 165 K3
Sangomore Highld 165 K3
Sankey Bridges Warrtn 82 C7
Sankyn's Green Worcs 57 P11
Sanna Bay Highld 137 L2
Sanndabhaig W Isls 168 j4
Sannox N Ayrs 124 C8
Sanquhar D & G 115 Q6
Santon Cumb 100 F10
Santon IoM 80 d7
Santon Bridge Cumb 100 F10
Santon Downham Suffk 63 P3
Sapcote Leics 59 Q6
Sapey Common Herefs 46 D2
Sapiston Suffk 64 C6
Sapley Cambs 62 B6
Sapperton Derbys 71 M8
Sapperton Gloucs 32 H4
Sapperton Lincs 73 Q4
Saracen's Head Lincs 74 F5
Sarclet Highld 167 P8
Sarisbury Hants 14 F5
Sarn Brdgnd 29 P8
Sarn Gwynd 66 C8
Sarn Powys 55 M5
Sarn Powys 55 C6
Sarnau Carmth 42 F11
Sarnau Cerdgn 42 F4
Sarnau Gwynd 68 C7
Sarnau Powys 44 E8
Sarnau Powys 68 H11
Sarn Bach Gwynd 66 E9
Sarnesfield Herefs 45 M4
Sarn Park Services
  Brdgnd 29 P8
Sarn-wen Powys 69 J11
Saron Carmth 28 H2
Saron Carmth 42 G7
Saron Gwynd 66 H3
Saron Gwynd 79 J11
Sarratt Herts 50 B11
Sarre Kent 39 N8
Sarsden Oxon 47 Q10
Sarson Hants 22 B6
Satley Dur 103 M2
Satmar Kent 27 N4
Satron N York 102 H11
Satterleigh Devon 17 M7
Satterthwaite Cumb 94 G2
Satwell Oxon 35 K8
Sauchen Abers 151 J5
Saucher P & K 142 B11
Sauchieburn Abers 143 M4
Saul Gloucs 32 D3
Saundby Notts 85 N3
Saundersfoot Pembks 41 M10
Saunderton Bucks 35 L4
Saunton Devon 16 H4
Sausthorpe Lincs 87 L7
Saveock Cnwll 3 K4
Saverley Green Staffs 70 H7
Savile Town Kirk 90 G6

Sawbridge Warwks 60 B7
Sawbridgeworth Herts 51 L8
Sawdon N York 99 J3
Sawley Derbys 72 D4
Sawley Lancs 96 A11
Sawley N York 97 K7
Sawston Cambs 62 G11
Sawtry Cambs 61 Q4
Saxby Leics 73 L7
Saxby Lincs 86 D3
Saxby All Saints N Linc 92 G7
Saxelbye Leics 72 H6
Saxham Street Suffk 64 E9
Saxilby Lincs 85 Q5
Saxlingham Norfk 76 E4
Saxlingham Green Norfk 65 J2
Saxlingham Nethergate
  Norfk 65 J2
Saxlingham Thorpe
  Norfk 65 J2
Saxmundham Suffk 65 M9
Saxon Street Cambs 63 L9
Saxtead Suffk 65 K8
Saxtead Green Suffk 65 K9
Saxtead Little Green
  Suffk 65 J8
Saxthorpe Norfk 76 G5
Saxton N York 91 M3
Sayers Common W Susx 24 G7
Scackleton N York 98 C6
Scafell Pike Cumb 100 H9
Scaftworth Notts 85 L2
Scagglethorpe N York 98 G6
Scalasaig Ag & B 136 b3
Scalby E R Yk 92 D5
Scalby N York 99 L2
Scald End Bed 61 M9
Scaldwell Nhants 60 G6
Scaleby Cumb 110 H8
Scalebyhill Cumb 110 H8
Scale Houses Cumb 111 L11
Scales Cumb 94 F6
Scales Cumb 101 K5
Scalesceugh Cumb 110 H11
Scalford Leics 73 K6
Scaling N York 105 K8
Scaling Dam R & Cl 105 K8
Scalloway Shet 169 r10
Scalpay Highld 153 L11
Scamblesby Lincs 87 J5
Scammonden Kirk 90 D7
Scamodale Highld 138 E3
Scampston N York 98 H5
Scampton Lincs 86 C5
Scaniport Highld 156 A10
Scapegoat Hill Kirk 90 D7
Scarba Ag & B 130 D7
Scarborough N York 99 L3
Scarcewater Cnwll 3 N3
Scarcliffe Derbys 84 G7
Scarcroft Leeds 91 K2
Scarfskerry Highld 167 N2
Scargill Dur 103 L8
Scarinish Ag & B 136 C7
Scarisbrick Lancs 88 D8
Scarness Cumb 100 H4
Scarning Norfk 76 D9
Scarrington Notts 73 J2
Scarth Hill Lancs 88 E9
Scarthingwell N York 91 M3
Scartho NE Lin 93 N9
Scatsta Airport Shet 169 q6
Scawby N Linc 92 G8
Scawsby Donc 91 N10
Scawthorpe Donc 91 N9
Scawton N York 98 A4
Scayne's Hill W Susx 25 J6
Scethrog Powys 44 G9
Scholar Green Ches E 70 E3
Scholemoor
  Crematorium C Brad 90 E4
Scholes Kirk 90 F5
Scholes Kirk 90 F9
Scholes Leeds 91 K3
Scholes Rothm 91 K11
Scholes Wigan 88 H9
School Aycliffe Dur 103 Q6
School Green C Brad 90 E4
School Green Ches W 70 A2
Schoolgreen Wokham 35 K11
School House Dorset 10 H4
Scissett Kirk 90 G8
Scleddau Pembks 40 H4
Scofton Notts 85 K4
Scole Norfk 64 H6
Scone P & K 134 E2
Sconser Highld 153 J11
Scoonie Fife 135 K7
Scopwick Lincs 86 E9
Scoraig Highld 160 G7
Scorborough E R Yk 99 J11
Scorrier Cnwll 3 J5
Scorriton Devon 7 J5
Scorton Lancs 95 L11
Scorton N York 103 Q10
Sco Ruston Norfk 77 K7
Scotby Cumb 110 H9
Scotch Corner N York 103 P9
Scotforth Lancs 95 K9
Scot Hay Staffs 70 D5
Scothern Lincs 86 D5
Scotland Lincs 73 Q4
Scotland Gate Nthumb 113 L4
Scotlandwell P & K 134 F7
Scot Lane End Bolton 89 J9
Scotscalder Station
  Highld 167 J5
Scotsdike Cumb 110 G6
Scot's Gap Nthumb 112 F3
Scotsmill Abers 150 F4
Scotstoun C Glas 125 N4
Scotswood N u Ty 113 K8
Scotter Lincs 92 E10
Scotterthorpe Lincs 92 E10
Scottlethorpe Lincs 73 R6
Scotton Lincs 92 E11
Scotton N York 97 M9
Scotton N York 103 N11
Scottow Norfk 77 K7
Scott Willoughby Lincs 73 R3
Scoulton Norfk 76 D11
Scounslow Green Staffs 71 K9
Scourie Highld 164 E6
Scourie More Highld 164 D6
Scousburgh Shet 169 q12
Southead Oldham 90 B9
Scrabster Highld 167 K2
Scraesburgh Border 118 C7
Scrafield Lincs 87 K7

Scrainwood Nthumb....119 J9
Scrane End Lincs....74 G2
Scraptoft Leics....72 G9
Scratby Norfk....77 Q8
Scrayingham N York....98 E9
Scrays E Susx....26 C8
Scredington Lincs....74 A2
Scremby Lincs....87 M7
Scremerston Nthumb....129 Q10
Screveton Notts....73 J2
Scrivelsby Lincs....87 J7
Scriven N York....97 M9
Scrooby Notts....85 L2
Scropton Derbys....71 M8
Scrub Hill Lincs....86 H9
Scruton N York....97 L2
Scuggate Cumb....110 H6
Scullomie Highld....165 P4
Sculthorpe Norfk....76 B5
Scunthorpe N Linc....92 E8
Scurlage Swans....28 E7
Sea Somset....10 G2
Seaborough Dorset....11 J3
Seabridge Staffs....70 E6
Seabrook Kent....27 L4
Seaburn Sundld....113 P9
Seacombe Wirral....81 L6
Seacroft Leeds....91 K3
Seacroft Lincs....87 Q8
Seadyke Lincs....74 F3
Seafield Highld....152 H9
Seafield W Loth....127 J4
Seafield Crematorium C Edin....127 P2
Seaford E Susx....25 L11
Seaforth Sefton....81 L5
Seagrave Leics....72 G7
Seagry Heath Wilts....33 J8
Seaham Dur....113 P11
Seahouses Nthumb....119 P4
Seal Kent....37 N9
Seale Surrey....23 N5
Seamer N York....99 L4
Seamer N York....104 E8
Seamill N Ayrs....124 G8
Sea Palling Norfk....77 N6
Searby Lincs....93 J9
Seasalter Kent....39 J9
Seascale Cumb....100 D10
Seathwaite Cumb....100 H11
Seathwaite Cumb....100 H8
Seatle Cumb....94 H4
Seatoller Cumb....100 H8
Seaton Cnwll....5 N11
Seaton Cumb....100 D4
Seaton Devon....10 E6
Seaton Dur....113 N11
Seaton E R Yk....99 P11
Seaton Kent....39 M10
Seaton Nthumb....113 M5
Seaton Rutlnd....73 N11
Seaton Burn N Tyne....113 K6
Seaton Carew Hartpl....104 F5
Seaton Delaval Nthumb....113 M5
Seaton Ross E R Yk....92 C2
Seaton Sluice Nthumb....113 M5
Seatown Dorset....11 J6
Seave Green N York....104 G10
Seaview IoW....14 H8
Seaville Cumb....110 C10
Seavington St Mary Somset....11 J2
Seavington St Michael Somset....19 M11
Sebastopol Torfn....31 J5
Sebergham Cumb....101 L2
Seckington Warwks....59 L3
Sedbergh Cumb....95 P2
Sedbury Gloucs....31 P6
Sedbusk N York....96 C2
Sedgeberrow Worcs....47 K7
Sedgebrook Lincs....73 M3
Sedge Fen Suffk....63 L4
Sedgefield Dur....104 C5
Sedgeford Norfk....75 P3
Sedgehill Wilts....20 G9
Sedgemoor Services Somset....19 L4
Sedgley Dudley....58 D6
Sedgley Park Bury....82 H4
Sedgwick Cumb....95 L3
Sedlescombe E Susx....26 C8
Sedrup Bucks....35 M2
Seed Kent....38 F10
Seend Wilts....20 H2
Seend Cleeve Wilts....20 H2
Seer Green Bucks....35 Q6
Seething Norfk....65 L2
Sefton Sefton....81 M4
Sefton Town Sefton....81 L4
Seghill Nthumb....113 L6
Seighford Staffs....70 F9
Seion Gwynd....79 J11
Seisdon Staffs....58 B5
Selattyn Shrops....69 J8
Selborne Hants....23 K8
Selby N York....91 Q4
Selham W Susx....23 P10
Selhurst Gt Lon....36 H7
Selkirk Border....117 P5
Sellack Herefs....45 R9
Sellafirth Shet....169 s4
Sellan Cnwll....2 C7
Sellick's Green Somset....18 H11
Sellindge Kent....27 J4
Selling Kent....38 H10
Sells Green Wilts....20 H2
Selly Oak Birm....58 F8
Selmeston E Susx....25 M9
Selsdon Gt Lon....37 J8
Selsey Gloucs....32 F4
Selsey W Susx....15 N8
Selsfield Common W Susx....24 H4
Selside Cumb....101 P11
Selside N York....96 A5
Selsted Kent....27 M3
Selston Notts....84 G10
Selworthy Somset....18 B5
Semer Suffk....52 G2
Semington Wilts....20 G2
Semley Wilts....20 G9
Sempringham Lincs....74 B4
Send Surrey....36 B9
Send Marsh Surrey....36 B9
Senghenydd Caerph....30 F6
Sennen Cnwll....2 B8
Sennen Cove Cnwll....2 B8
Sennybridge Powys....44 C9
Serlby Notts....85 K3

Sessay N York....97 Q5
Setchey Norfk....75 M8
Setley Hants....13 P4
Seton Mains E Loth....128 C4
Settle N York....96 B8
Settrington N York....98 G6
Seven Ash Somset....18 G8
Sevenhampton Gloucs....47 K10
Sevenhampton Swindn....33 P6
Seven Hills Crematorium Suffk....53 M3
Seven Kings Gt Lon....37 L3
Sevenoaks Kent....37 M9
Sevenoaks Weald Kent....37 M10
Seven Sisters Neath....29 M3
Seven Springs Gloucs....47 J11
Seven Star Green Essex....52 F6
Severn Beach S Glos....31 P8
Severn Stoke Worcs....46 G6
Severn View Services S Glos....31 Q7
Sevick End Bed....61 N10
Sevington Kent....26 H3
Sewards End Essex....51 N3
Sewardstonebury Essex....51 J11
Sewell C Beds....49 Q10
Sewerby E R Yk....99 P7
Seworgan Cnwll....3 J7
Sewstern Leics....73 M6
Sexhow N York....104 E9
Sezincote Gloucs....47 N8
Sgiogarstaigh W Isls....168 k1
Shabbington Bucks....35 J3
Shackerley Shrops....57 Q3
Shackerstone Leics....72 B9
Shacklecross Derbys....72 C4
Shackleford Surrey....23 P5
Shade Calder....89 Q6
Shader W Isls....168 i2
Shadforth Dur....104 B2
Shadingfield Suffk....65 N5
Shadoxhurst Kent....26 G4
Shadwell Leeds....91 J3
Shadwell Norfk....64 C5
Shaftenhoe End Herts....51 K3
Shaftesbury Dorset....20 G10
Shaftholme Donc....91 P9
Shafton Barns....91 K8
Shafton Two Gates Barns....91 K8
Shakerley Wigan....82 E4
Shalbourne Wilts....22 B2
Shalcombe IoW....14 C9
Shalden Hants....23 J6
Shalden Green Hants....23 K6
Shaldon Devon....7 N4
Shalfleet IoW....14 D9
Shalford Essex....52 B6
Shalford Surrey....36 B11
Shalford Green Essex....52 B6
Shallowford Staffs....70 F9
Shalmsford Street Kent....39 J11
Shalstone Bucks....48 H7
Shamley Green Surrey....24 B2
Shandford Angus....142 H5
Shandon Ag & B....132 B10
Shandwick Highld....156 F2
Shangton Leics....73 J11
Shankhouse Nthumb....113 L5
Shanklin IoW....14 G10
Shap Cumb....101 Q7
Shapinsay Ork....169 e5
Shapwick Dorset....12 F4
Shapwick Somset....19 M7
Shard End Birm....59 J7
Shardlow Derbys....72 C4
Shareshill Staffs....58 D3
Sharlston Wakefd....91 K7
Sharlston Common Wakefd....91 K7
Sharman's Cross Solhll....58 H9
Sharnal Street Medway....38 C7
Sharnbrook Bed....61 L9
Sharneyford Lancs....89 P6
Sharnford Leics....59 Q6
Sharnhill Green Dorset....11 Q3
Sharoe Green Lancs....88 G4
Sharow N York....97 M6
Sharpenhoe C Beds....50 C4
Sharperton Nthumb....119 J10
Sharp Green Norfk....77 M7
Sharpness Gloucs....32 C4
Sharpthorne W Susx....25 J4
Sharptor Cnwll....5 M7
Sharpway Gate Worcs....58 E11
Sharrington Norfk....76 E4
Shatterford Worcs....57 P8
Shatterling Kent....39 N10
Shatton Derbys....84 B4
Shaugh Prior Devon....6 E6
Shave Cross Dorset....11 J5
Shavington Ches E....70 B4
Shaw C Brad....90 C3
Shaw Oldham....89 Q9
Shaw Swindn....33 M7
Shaw W Berk....34 E11
Shaw Wilts....32 G11
Shawbirch Wrekin....57 L2
Shawbost W Isls....168 h3
Shawbury Shrops....69 Q10
Shawclough Rochdl....89 P8
Shaw Common Gloucs....46 C9
Shawdon Hill Nthumb....119 L8
Shawell Leics....60 B4
Shawford Hants....22 E9
Shawforth Lancs....89 P6
Shaw Green Herts....50 H4
Shaw Green Lancs....88 G7
Shaw Green N York....97 L10
Shawhead D & G....109 J5
Shaw Mills N York....97 L8
Shawsburn S Lans....126 D7
Shear Cross Wilts....20 G6
Shearington D & G....109 M7
Shearsby Leics....60 D2
Shearston Somset....19 J8
Shebbear Devon....16 G10
Shebdon Staffs....70 D9
Shebster Highld....166 H4
Sheddens E Rens....125 P6
Shedfield Hants....14 G4
Sheen Staffs....71 L2
Sheepbridge Derbys....84 E6
Sheep Hill Dur....113 J9
Sheepridge Kirk....90 F7
Sheepscar Leeds....91 J4
Sheepscombe Gloucs....32 G2
Sheepstor Devon....6 F5
Sheepwash Devon....8 C3
Sheepwash Nthumb....113 L3

Sheepway N Som....31 N9
Sheepy Magna Leics....72 A10
Sheepy Parva Leics....72 A10
Sheering Essex....51 M8
Sheerness Kent....38 F7
Sheerwater Surrey....36 B8
Sheet Hants....23 L10
Sheffield Cnwll....2 D7
Sheffield Sheff....84 E3
Sheffield Bottom W Berk....34 H11
Sheffield City Road Crematorium Sheff....84 E3
Sheffield Green E Susx....25 K5
Shefford C Beds....50 D3
Sheigra Highld....164 E4
Sheinton Shrops....57 L4
Shelderton Shrops....56 G9
Sheldon Birm....59 J8
Sheldon Derbys....83 Q11
Sheldon Devon....10 C3
Sheldwich Kent....38 H10
Sheldwich Lees Kent....38 H10
Shelf Calder....90 E5
Shelfanger Norfk....64 G5
Shelfield Warwks....47 M2
Shelfield Wsall....58 F4
Shelfield Green Warwks....47 M2
Shelford Notts....72 H2
Shelford Warwks....59 P7
Shellacres Nthumb....118 G2
Shelley Essex....51 N9
Shelley Kirk....90 G8
Shelley Suffk....52 H4
Shelley Far Bank Kirk....90 G8
Shellingford Oxon....34 B6
Shellow Bowells Essex....51 P9
Shelsley Beauchamp Worcs....46 D2
Shelsley Walsh Worcs....46 D2
Shelton Bed....61 M7
Shelton Norfk....65 J3
Shelton Notts....73 K2
Shelton Shrops....56 H2
Shelton Green Norfk....65 J3
Shelton Lock C Derb....72 B4
Shelton Under Harley Staffs....70 E7
Shelve Shrops....56 E5
Shelwick Herefs....45 Q6
Shenfield Essex....51 P11
Shenington Oxon....48 C6
Shenley Herts....50 E10
Shenley Brook End M Keyn....49 M7
Shenleybury Herts....50 E10
Shenley Church End M Keyn....49 M7
Shenmore Herefs....45 M7
Shennanton D & G....107 K5
Shenstone Staffs....58 H4
Shenstone Worcs....58 C10
Shenstone Woodend Staffs....58 H4
Shenton Leics....72 B11
Shenval Moray....149 N2
Shepeau Stow Lincs....74 F8
Shephall Herts....50 G6
Shepherd's Bush Gt Lon....36 F4
Shepherd's Green Oxon....35 K8
Shepherds Patch Gloucs....32 D4
Shepherdswell Kent....27 N2
Shepley Kirk....90 F9
Shepperdine S Glos....32 B5
Shepperton Surrey....36 C7
Shepperton Green Surrey....36 C7
Shepreth Cambs....62 E11
Shepshed Leics....72 D7
Shepton Beauchamp Somset....19 M11
Shepton Mallet Somset....20 B6
Shepton Montague Somset....20 C8
Shepway Kent....38 C11
Sheraton Dur....104 D3
Sherborne Dorset....20 B11
Sherborne Gloucs....33 N2
Sherborne Somset....19 Q3
Sherborne St John Hants....22 H3
Sherbourne Warwks....47 Q2
Sherburn Dur....104 B2
Sherburn N York....99 K5
Sherburn Hill Dur....104 B2
Sherburn in Elmet N York....91 M4
Shere Surrey....36 C11
Shereford Norfk....76 B6
Sherfield English Hants....21 Q10
Sherfield on Loddon Hants....23 J3
Sherfin Lancs....89 M5
Sherford Devon....7 K10
Sherford Dorset....12 F6
Sheriffhales Shrops....57 P2
Sheriff Hutton N York....98 D7
Sheringham Norfk....76 H3
Sherington M Keyn....49 N5
Shermanbury W Susx....24 F7
Shernborne Norfk....75 P4
Sherrington Wilts....21 J7
Sherston Wilts....32 G7
Sherwood C Nott....72 F2
Sherwood Forest Notts....85 K9
Sherwood Forest Crematorium Notts....85 L7
Shetland Islands Shet....169 r8
Shettleston C Glas....125 Q5
Shevington Wigan....88 G9
Shevington Moor Wigan....88 G8
Shevington Vale Wigan....88 G9
Sheviock Cnwll....5 P10
Shibden Head C Brad....90 D5
Shide IoW....14 F9
Shidlaw Nthumb....118 F3
Shiel Bridge Highld....146 A4
Shieldaig Highld....153 Q7
Shieldhill D & G....109 M3
Shieldhill Falk....126 F2
Shieldhill House Hotel S Lans....116 E2
Shields N Lans....126 D6
Shielfoot Highld....138 B3
Shielhill Angus....142 G6
Shielhill Inver....124 G3
Shifford Oxon....34 C4
Shifnal Shrops....57 N3
Shilbottle Nthumb....119 N9
Shildon Dur....103 P5
Shillford E Rens....125 M6
Shillingford Devon....18 C10

Shillingford Oxon....34 G6
Shillingford Abbot Devon....9 M7
Shillingford St George Devon....9 M7
Shillingstone Dorset....12 D2
Shillington C Beds....50 D4
Shillmoor Nthumb....118 G9
Shilton Oxon....33 Q3
Shilton Warwks....59 P8
Shimpling Norfk....64 H5
Shimpling Suffk....64 B11
Shimpling Street Suffk....64 B11
Shincliffe Dur....103 Q2
Shiney Row Sundld....113 M10
Shinfield Wokham....35 K11
Shingay Cambs....62 D11
Shingle Street Suffk....53 Q3
Shinnersbridge Devon....7 K6
Shinness Highld....162 C4
Shipbourne Kent....37 N10
Shipdham Norfk....76 D10
Shipham Somset....19 M4
Shiphay Torbay....7 M5
Shiplake Oxon....35 K9
Shiplake Row Oxon....35 K9
Shiplate N Som....19 L3
Shipley C Brad....90 F3
Shipley Derbys....72 C2
Shipley Shrops....57 Q5
Shipley W Susx....24 D6
Shipley Bridge Surrey....24 H2
Shipley Hatch Kent....26 H4
Shipmeadow Suffk....65 M3
Shippea Hill Station Cambs....63 K4
Shippon Oxon....34 E5
Shipston on Stour Warwks....47 Q6
Shipton Bucks....49 L9
Shipton Gloucs....47 K11
Shipton N York....98 B9
Shipton Shrops....57 K6
Shipton Bellinger Hants....21 P5
Shipton Gorge Dorset....11 K6
Shipton Green W Susx....15 M7
Shipton Moyne Gloucs....32 G7
Shipton-on-Cherwell Oxon....48 E11
Shiptonthorpe E R Yk....92 E2
Shipton-under-Wychwood Oxon....47 Q11
Shirburn Oxon....35 J5
Shirdley Hill Lancs....88 D8
Shire Cumb....102 B3
Shirebrook Derbys....84 H7
Shiregreen Sheff....84 E2
Shirehampton Bristl....31 P9
Shiremoor N Tyne....113 M6
Shirenewton Mons....31 N6
Shire Oak Wsall....58 G4
Shireoaks Notts....85 J4
Shirkoak Kent....26 F4
Shirland Derbys....84 F9
Shirlett Shrops....57 L5
Shirley C Sotn....14 D4
Shirley Derbys....71 N6
Shirley Gt Lon....37 J7
Shirley Solhll....58 H9
Shirl Heath Herefs....45 N3
Shirrell Heath Hants....14 G4
Shirvan Ag & B....123 Q3
Shirwell Devon....17 L4
Shiskine N Ayrs....120 H6
Shittlehope Dur....103 K3
Shobdon Herefs....45 N2
Shobley Hants....13 L3
Shobrooke Devon....9 L4
Shoby Leics....72 H6
Shocklach Ches W....69 M5
Shocklach Green Ches W....69 M5
Shoeburyness Sthend....38 F4
Sholden Kent....39 Q11
Sholing C Sotn....14 E4
Shoot Hill Shrops....56 G2
Shop Cnwll....4 D7
Shop Cnwll....16 C9
Shopwyke W Susx....15 N5
Shore Rochdl....89 Q7
Shoreditch Gt Lon....36 H4
Shoreditch Somset....18 H10
Shoreham Kent....37 M8
Shoreham Airport W Susx....24 F9
Shoreham-by-Sea W Susx....24 F9
Shoreswood Nthumb....129 N10
Shorley Hants....22 G9
Shorncote Gloucs....33 K5
Shorne Kent....37 Q6
Shorta Cross Cnwll....5 M10
Shortbridge E Susx....25 L6
Shortfield Common Surrey....23 M6
Shortgate E Susx....25 L7
Short Heath Birm....58 G6
Shortheath Hants....23 L7
Short Heath Wsall....58 E4
Shortlanesend Cnwll....3 L4
Shortlees E Ayrs....125 L11
Shortstown Bed....61 N11
Shorwell IoW....14 E10
Shoscombe BaNES....20 D3
Shotesham Norfk....65 J2
Shotgate Essex....38 C3
Shotley Suffk....53 M4
Shotley Bridge Dur....112 G10
Shotleyfield Nthumb....112 G10
Shotley Gate Suffk....53 M5
Shotley Street Suffk....53 M4
Shottenden Kent....38 H11
Shottermill Surrey....23 N8
Shottery Warwks....47 N4
Shotteswell Warwks....48 D5
Shottisham Suffk....53 N3
Shottle Derbys....71 Q5
Shottlegate Derbys....71 Q5
Shotton Dur....104 C5
Shotton Dur....104 D3
Shotton Flints....81 L11
Shotton Colliery Dur....104 C2
Shotts N Lans....126 F6
Shotwick Ches W....81 L10
Shouldham Norfk....75 N9
Shouldham Thorpe Norfk....75 N9
Shoulton Worcs....46 F3
Shover's Green E Susx....25 Q4

Shraleybrook Staffs....70 D5
Shrawardine Shrops....69 L11
Shrawley Worcs....57 Q11
Shreding Green Bucks....36 B4
Shrewley Warwks....59 K11
Shrewsbury Shrops....56 H2
Shrewton Wilts....21 L6
Shripney W Susx....15 P6
Shrivenham Oxon....33 Q8
Shropham Norfk....64 D3
Shrub End Essex....52 G7
Shucknall Herefs....46 A6
Shudy Camps Cambs....51 P2
Shuna Ag & B....130 F6
Shurdington Gloucs....46 H11
Shurlock Row W & M....35 M10
Shurnock Worcs....47 K2
Shurrery Highld....166 H5
Shurrery Lodge Highld....166 H5
Shurton Somset....18 H6
Shustoke Warwks....59 K6
Shute Devon....9 L4
Shute Devon....10 F5
Shutford Oxon....48 C6
Shut Heath Staffs....70 F10
Shuthonger Gloucs....46 G7
Shutlanger Nhants....49 K5
Shutterton Devon....9 N7
Shutt Green Staffs....58 C3
Shuttington Warwks....59 L3
Shuttlewood Derbys....84 G6
Shuttleworth Bury....89 N7
Siabost W Isls....168 h3
Siadar W Isls....168 i2
Sibbertoft Nhants....60 E4
Sibdon Carwood Shrops....56 G8
Sibford Ferris Oxon....48 C7
Sibford Gower Oxon....48 C7
Sible Hedingham Essex....52 B4
Sibley's Green Essex....51 P5
Siblyback Cnwll....5 L7
Sibsey Lincs....87 L10
Sibsey Fenside Lincs....87 K10
Sibson Cambs....74 A11
Sibson Leics....72 B10
Sibster Highld....167 P6
Sibthorpe Notts....85 M6
Sibthorpe Notts....85 N11
Sibton Suffk....65 M8
Sicklesmere Suffk....64 C9
Sicklinghall N York....97 N11
Sidbrook Somset....19 J9
Sidbury Devon....10 C6
Sidbury Shrops....57 M7
Sid Cop Barns....91 K9
Sidcot N Som....19 M3
Sidcup Gt Lon....37 L6
Siddick Cumb....100 D4
Siddington Ches E....82 H10
Siddington Gloucs....33 K5
Sidemoor Worcs....58 E10
Sidestrand Norfk....77 K4
Sidford Devon....10 C6
Sidlesham W Susx....15 N7
Sidlesham Common W Susx....15 N7
Sidley E Susx....26 B10
Sidmouth Devon....10 C7
Siefton Shrops....56 H8
Sigford Devon....7 K4
Sigglesthorne E R Yk....99 P11
Sigingstone V Glam....30 C10
Signet Oxon....33 P2
Silchester Hants....22 H2
Sileby Leics....72 G7
Silecroft Cumb....94 C4
Silfield Norfk....64 G2
Silian Cerdgn....43 L4
Silkstead Hants....22 D10
Silkstone Barns....90 H9
Silkstone Common Barns....90 H10
Silk Willoughby Lincs....73 R2
Silloth Cumb....109 P10
Silpho N York....99 K2
Silsden C Brad....96 F11
Silsoe C Beds....50 C3
Silton Dorset....20 E9
Silverburn Mdloth....127 N5
Silverdale Lancs....95 K6
Silverdale Staffs....70 E5
Silver End Essex....52 D7
Silverford Abers....159 J5
Silvergate Norfk....76 H6
Silverlace Green Suffk....65 L9
Silverley's Green Suffk....65 K6
Silverstone Nhants....49 J6
Silver Street Kent....38 E9
Silver Street Somset....19 P8
Silverton Devon....9 N4
Silverwell Cnwll....3 J4
Silvington Shrops....57 L9
Simister Bury....89 N9
Simmondley Derbys....83 M6
Simonburn Nthumb....112 C6
Simonsbath Somset....17 P4
Simonsburrow Devon....18 F11
Simonstone Lancs....89 M4
Simonstone N York....96 C2
Simprim Border....129 J11
Simpson M Keyn....49 N7
Simpson Cross Pembks....40 G7
Sinclair's Hill Border....129 L9
Sinclairston E Ayrs....115 J4
Sinderby N York....97 M4
Sinderhope Nthumb....112 D10
Sinderland Green Traffd....82 F7
Sindlesham Wokham....35 L11
Sinfin C Derb....72 A4
Singleborough Bucks....49 L8
Single Street Gt Lon....37 K8
Singleton Kent....26 H3
Singleton Lancs....88 D3
Singleton W Susx....15 N4
Singlewell Kent....37 Q6
Sinkhurst Green Kent....26 D3
Sinnarhard Abers....150 D5
Sinnington N York....98 E3
Sinton Worcs....46 F2
Sinton Green Worcs....46 F2
Sipson Gt Lon....36 C5
Sirhowy Blae G....30 F2
Sissinghurst Kent....26 C4
Siston S Glos....32 C9
Sitcott Devon....5 P3
Sithney Cnwll....2 G8
Sithney Common Cnwll....2 G8
Sithney Green Cnwll....2 G8
Sittingbourne Kent....38 F9
Six Ashes Shrops....57 P7

Six Bells Blae G...........30 H4
Sixhills Lincs..........86 G3
Six Mile Bottom Cambs...63 J9
Sixmile Cottages Kent....27 K3
Sixpenny Handley
  Dorset.............21 J11
Six Rues Jersey.........11 b1
Sizergh Castle Cumb....95 K5
Sizewell Suffk.........65 P9
Skaill Ork............169 a6
Skares E Ayrs.........115 K4
Skateraw Abers........151 N9
Skateraw E Loth.......129 J5
Skeabost Highld.......152 G8
Skeeby N York.........103 N10
Skeffington Leics......73 J10
Skeffling E R Yk.......93 Q7
Skegby Notts..........84 G8
Skegby Notts..........85 N7
Skegness Lincs........87 Q8
Skelbo Highld.........162 H7
Skelbo Street Highld...162 H8
Skelbrooke Donc.......91 N8
Skeldyke Lincs........74 F3
Skellingthorpe Lincs....86 B6
Skellorn Green Ches E..83 K8
Skellow Donc..........91 N8
Skelmanthorpe Kirk.....90 G8
Skelmersdale Lancs....88 F9
Skelmorlie N Ayrs.....124 F4
Skelpick Highld.......166 B5
Skelston D & G........108 H3
Skelton C York........98 B9
Skelton Cumb.........101 N3
Skelton E R Yk........92 C5
Skelton N York........97 N7
Skelton N York.......103 L10
Skelton R & Cl.......105 J7
Skelwith Bridge Cumb..101 K10
Skendleby Lincs.......87 M7
Skene House Abers.....151 K5
Skenfrith Mons.........45 P10
Skerne E R Yk.........99 L3
Skerray Highld........165 Q4
Skerricha Highld......164 F4
Skerton Lancs.........95 K8
Sketchley Leics........59 P6
Sketty Swans..........28 H6
Skewen Neath..........29 K5
Skewsby N York........98 C6
Skeyton Norfk.........77 J6
Skeyton Corner Norfk...77 K6
Skiall Highld.........166 H3
Skidbrooke Lincs.......87 M2
Skidbrooke North End
  Lincs.............93 R11
Skidby E R Yk.........92 H4
Skigersta W Isls......168 k1
Skilgate Somset........18 C9
Skillington Lincs......73 M5
Skinburness Cumb.....109 P9
Skinflats Falk.......133 Q11
Skinidin Highld.......152 C8
Skinners Green W Berk..34 D11
Skinningrove R & Cl...105 K7
Skipness Ag & B.......123 R8
Skipper's Bridge D & G.110 G4
Skiprigg Cumb........110 G11
Skipsea E R Yk.........99 P10
Skipsea Brough E R Yk..99 P10
Skipton N York........96 E10
Skipton-on-Swale N York..97 N5
Skipwith N York.......91 R3
Skirlaugh E R Yk.......93 K3
Skirling Border.......116 F3
Skirmett Bucks.........35 L6
Skirpenbeck E R Yk.....98 E9
Skirwith Cumb........102 B3
Skirwith N York.......95 Q6
Skirza Highld........167 Q3
Skitby Cumb.........110 H7
Skittle Green Bucks....35 L4
Skokholm Island Pembks.40 D10
Skomer Island Pembks..40 D9
Skulamus Highld......145 K3
Skyborry Green Shrops..56 D10
Skye Green Essex.......52 E7
Skye of Curr Highld...148 H3
Skyreholme N York......96 G8
Slack Calder..........90 B5
Slackcote Oldham.......90 B9
Slack Head Cumb.......95 K5
Slackholme End Lincs...87 P6
Slacks of Cairnbanno
  Abers............159 K8
Slad Gloucs...........32 G3
Slade Devon...........10 C3
Slade Devon...........17 J2
Slade Devon...........17 Q6
Slade End Oxon........34 G6
Slade Green Gt Lon....37 M5
Slade Heath Staffs.....58 D3
Slade Hooton Rothm....84 H4
Sladesbridge Cnwll......4 G7
Slades Green Worcs....46 F8
Slaggyford Nthumb....111 N10
Slaidburn Lancs.......95 Q10
Slaithwaite Kirk.......90 D8
Slaley Derbys.........84 C9
Slaley Nthumb........112 E9
Slamannan Falk.......126 F3
Slapton Bucks.........49 P10
Slapton Devon..........7 L9
Slapton Nhants........48 H5
Slattocks Rochdl.......89 P9
Slaugham W Susx.......24 G5
Slaughterford Wilts....32 F10
Slawston Leics........60 G2
Sleaford Hants.........23 M7
Sleaford Lincs........86 E11
Sleagill Cumb........101 Q7
Sleap Shrops..........69 N9
Sleapford Wrekin.......70 A11
Sleapshyde Herts......50 E9
Sleasdairidh Highld...162 E7
Slebech Pembks........41 K7
Sledge Green Worcs....46 F8
Sledmere E R Yk.......99 J8
Sleetbeck Cumb.......111 K5
Sleight Dorset.........12 G5
Sleightholme Dur.....103 J8
Sleights N York......105 N9
Slepe Dorset..........12 H7
Slickly Highld.......167 N3
Sliddery N Ayrs......120 H7
Sligachan Highld.....144 G2
Sligrachan Ag & B....131 P9
Slimbridge Gloucs.....32 D4
Slindon Staffs.........70 E8
Slindon W Susx........15 Q5

Slinfold W Susx........24 D4
Sling Gwynd...........79 L11
Slingsby N York........98 D6
Slip End C Beds........50 C7
Slip End Herts.........50 G3
Slipton Nhants.........61 L5
Slitting Mill Staffs.....71 J11
Slockavullin Ag & B...130 G8
Sloley Norfk...........77 K7
Sloncombe Devon........8 H7
Sloothby Lincs.........87 N6
Slough Slough..........35 Q9
Slough Crematorium
  Bucks.............35 Q8
Slough Green Somset....19 J11
Slough Green W Susx....24 G5
Slumbay Highld.......154 A10
Slyfield Green Surrey...23 Q4
Slyne Lancs...........95 K7
Smailholm Border......118 B3
Smallbridge Rochdl.....89 Q7
Smallbrook Devon........9 L5
Smallbrook Gloucs......31 Q4
Smallburgh Norfk.......77 L7
Smalldale Derbys.......83 N9
Smalldale Derbys.......83 Q8
Small Dole W Susx......24 F8
Smalley Derbys.........72 C2
Smalley Common Derbys..72 C2
Smalley Green Derbys...72 C2
Smallfield Surrey......24 H2
Small Heath Birm.......58 H7
Small Hythe Kent.......26 E5
Smallridge Devon.......10 G4
Smallthorne C Stke.....70 F4
Smallways N York......103 M8
Smallwood Ches E.......70 E2
Small Wood Hey Lancs...94 H11
Smallworth Norfk.......64 E5
Smannell Hants.........22 C5
Smardale Cumb........102 D9
Smarden Kent..........26 E3
Smarden Bell Kent......26 E3
Smart's Hill Kent......25 M2
Smeafield Nthumb......119 L3
Smearisary Highld.....138 A2
Smeatharpe Devon.......10 D2
Smeeth Kent...........27 J4
Smeeton Westerby Leics..60 E2
Smelthouses N York.....97 J8
Smerral Highld.......167 L10
Smestow Staffs.........58 C6
Smethwick Sandw.......58 F7
Smethwick Green Ches E..70 E2
Smisby Derbys.........72 A7
Smitheclose IoW........14 F8
Smith End Green Worcs..46 E4
Smithfield Cumb......110 H7
Smith Green Lancs......95 K9
Smithies Barns........91 K9
Smithincott Devon.......9 Q2
Smith's Green Essex....51 K3
Smith's Green Essex....51 N6
Smith's Green Essex....51 Q2
Smithstown Highld....160 B11
Smithton Highld......156 C8
Smithy Bridge Rochdl...89 Q7
Smithy Green Ches E....82 F10
Smithy Green Stockp....83 J7
Smithy Houses Derbys...84 E11
Smockington Leics......59 Q7
Smoo Highld..........165 K3
Smythe's Green Essex....52 F8
Snade D & G..........108 H3
Snailbeach Shrops......56 F4
Snailwell Cambs........63 K7
Snainton N York........99 J4
Snaith E R Yk.........91 Q6
Snake Pass Inn Derbys..83 P6
Snape N York..........97 L4
Snape Suffk...........65 M10
Snape Green Lancs......88 D8
Snape Street Suffk.....65 M10
Snaresbrook Gt Lon.....37 K3
Snarestone Leics.......72 A9
Snarford Lincs.........86 D4
Snargate Kent.........26 G6
Snave Kent............26 H6
Sneachill Worcs........46 H4
Snead Powys...........56 E6
Sneath Common Norfk...64 H4
Sneaton N York.......105 N9
Sneatonthorpe N York..105 P9
Snelland Lincs.........86 E4
Snelson Ches E.........82 H10
Snelston Derbys........71 M6
Snetterton Norfk.......64 D3
Snettisham Norfk.......75 N4
Snibston Leics.........72 C8
Snig's End Gloucs......46 E9
Snitter Nthumb.......119 K10
Snitterby Lincs........86 C2
Snitterfield Warwks....47 P3
Snitterton Derbys......84 C8
Snitton Shrops.........57 K9
Snoadhill Kent.........26 F3
Snodhill Herefs........45 L6
Snodland Kent.........38 B9
Snoll Hatch Kent.......37 Q11
Snowden Hill Barns.....90 H10
Snowdon Gwynd........67 L4
Snowdonia
  National Park Gwynd...67 Q9
Snow End Herts........51 K4
Snowshill Gloucs.......47 L8
Snow Street Norfk......64 F5
Soake Hants...........15 J4
Soar Cardif...........30 E8
Soar Devon.............7 J11
Soar Powys...........44 D8
Soay Highld..........144 F5
Soberton Hants.........22 H11
Soberton Heath Hants...14 H4
Sockbridge Cumb......101 N5
Sockburn Darltn......104 B9
Sodom Denbgs..........80 F10
Sodylt Bank Shrops.....69 K7
Soham Cambs...........63 J6
Soham Cotes Cambs......63 J5
Solas W Isls.........168 d10
Solbury Pembks........40 G8
Soldon Devon..........16 E9
Soldon Cross Devon.....16 E9
Soldridge Hants........23 J7
Sole Street Kent.......27 J3
Sole Street Kent.......37 Q7
Solihull Solhll........59 J9
Sollers Dilwyn Herefs..45 N3
Sollers Hope Herefs....46 B8
Sollom Lancs..........88 F7

Solva Pembks..........40 F6
Solwaybank D & G.....110 F5
Somerby Leics.........73 K8
Somerby Lincs.........93 J9
Somercotes Derbys......84 F10
Somerford Dorset.......13 L6
Somerford Keynes
  Gloucs............33 K5
Somerley W Susx.......15 M7
Somerleyton Suffk......65 P2
Somersal Herbert Derbys.71 L7
Somersby Lincs.........87 K6
Somersham Cambs.......62 E5
Somersham Suffk........53 J2
Somerton Oxon.........48 E9
Somerton Somset........19 N9
Somerton Suffk........63 P10
Somerwood Shrops.......57 K2
Sompting W Susx........24 E9
Sonning Wokham........35 L9
Sonning Common Oxon....35 K8
Sonning Eye Oxon.......35 K9
Sontley Wrexhm........69 K5
Sopley Hants..........13 L5
Sopworth Wilts.........32 F7
Sorbie D & G.........107 M8
Sordale Highld.......167 K4
Sorisdale Ag & B......136 H3
Sorn E Ayrs..........115 L2
Sortat Highld........167 N4
Sotby Lincs...........86 H5
Sots Hole Lincs........86 F8
Sotterley Suffk........65 N5
Soughton Flints........81 J11
Soulbury Bucks.........49 N9
Soulby Cumb..........101 N5
Soulby Cumb..........102 D8
Souldern Oxon.........48 F8
Souldrop Bed..........61 L8
Sound Ches E..........70 A5
Sound Muir Moray.....157 R7
Soundwell S Glos.......32 C9
Sourton Devon...........8 D6
Soutergate Cumb........94 E4
South Acre Norfk.......75 R8
South Alkham Kent......27 M3
Southall Gt Lon.......36 D5
South Allington Devon...7 K11
South Alloa Falk.....133 P9
Southam Gloucs.........47 J9
Southam Warwks........48 D2
South Ambersham
  W Susx............23 P10
Southampton C Sotn....14 D4
Southampton Airport
  Hants.............22 E11
Southampton
  Crematorium Hants....22 D11
South Anston Rothm.....84 H4
South Ascot W & M......35 P11
South Ashford Kent.....26 H3
South Baddesley Hants..14 C7
South Ballachulish
  Highld...........139 K6
South Bank C York......98 B10
South Bank R & Cl....104 F6
South Barrow Somset....20 B9
South Beddington
  Gt Lon............36 G8
South Beer Cnwll........5 N3
South Benfleet Essex....38 C4
South Bersted W Susx...15 P6
South Bockhampton
  Dorset............13 L5
Southborough Gt Lon....37 K7
Southborough Kent......25 N2
Southbourne Bmouth.....13 K6
Southbourne W Susx.....15 L5
South Bowood Dorset....11 J5
South Bramwith Donc....91 Q8
South Brent Devon.......6 H6
South Brewham Somset...20 D7
South Bristol
  Crematorium Bristl...31 Q11
South Broomhill
  Nthumb...........119 P11
Southburgh Norfk.......76 E10
South Burlingham Norfk.77 M10
Southburn E R Yk.......99 K10
South Cadbury Somset...20 B9
South Carlton Lincs.....86 B5
South Carlton Notts.....85 J4
South Cave E R Yk.......92 F4
South Cerney Gloucs....33 K5
South Chailey E Susx...25 J7
South Chard Somset.....10 G3
South Charlton Nthumb..119 N6
South Cheriton Somset..20 C10
South Church Dur......103 P5
Southchurch Sthend.....38 F4
South Cleatlam Dur....103 M8
South Cliffe E R Yk.....92 E3
South Clifton Notts.....85 P6
South Cockerington
  Lincs.............87 L3
South Cornelly Brdgnd..29 M8
Southcott Cnwll.........5 K2
Southcott Devon.........5 D5
Southcott Devon.........9 J8
Southcott Devon........16 G8
Southcott Wilts........21 N3
Southcourt Bucks.......35 M2
South Cove Suffk.......65 P5
South Creake Norfk.....76 B4
South Crosland Kirk....90 E8
South Croxton Leics....72 H8
South Dalton E R Yk.....99 K11
South Darenth Kent.....37 N7
South Downs
  National Park Br & H...25 J7
South Duffield N York...92 A4
Southease E Susx.......25 K9
South Elkington Lincs...87 J3
South Elmsall Wakefd...91 M8
Southend Ag & B.......120 C10
South End E R Yk.......93 Q7
South End Hants........21 M11
South End Herefs.......45 P8
South End N Linc.......93 K6
South End Norfk........64 D3
South End Wilts........33 N10
Southend Airport Essex..38 E4
Southend Crematorium
  Sthend............38 E4
Southend-on-Sea
  Sthend............38 E4
Southerndown V Glam...29 N10
Southerndown V Glam...29 N10
Southerness D & G.....109 L10

South Erradale Highld..153 N3
Southerton Devon.......10 B6
Southery Norfk.........63 K2
South Essex
  Crematorium Gt Lon....37 N3
South Fambridge Essex..38 E3
South Fawley W Berk....34 C8
South Ferriby N Linc....92 G6
South Field E R Yk......92 H5
Southfleet Kent........37 P6
Southford IoW..........14 F11
Southgate Gt Lon.......36 G2
Southgate Norfk........76 N4
Southgate Norfk........76 B4
Southgate Norfk........76 G7
Southgate Swans.......28 G7
South Godstone Surrey..37 J11
South Gorley Hants.....13 L2
South Gosforth N u Ty..113 K7
South Green Essex......37 Q2
South Green Essex......52 H8
South Green Kent.......38 E9
South Green Norfk......76 F9
South Green Suffk......64 H6
South Gyle C Edin.....127 M3
South Hanningfield
  Essex.............38 B2
South Harting W Susx...23 L11
South Hayling Hants....15 K7
South Hazelrigg Nthumb.119 L4
South Heath Bucks......35 P4
South Heighton E Susx..25 K10
South Hetton Dur......113 M11
South Hiendley Wakefd..91 K8
South Hill Cnwll........5 N7
South Hill Somset......19 N9
South Hinksey Oxon.....34 F4
South Hole Devon.......16 C7
South Holmwood Surrey..24 E1
South Hornchurch
  Gt Lon............37 M4
South Horrington
  Somset............19 Q5
South Huish Devon.......6 H10
South Hykeham Lincs....86 B8
South Hylton Sundld...113 N9
Southill C Beds........50 E2
Southington Hants......22 F5
South Kelsey Lincs.....92 H11
South Kessock Highld..156 B8
South Killingholme
  N Linc............93 K6
South Kilvington N York.97 P4
South Kilworth Leics...60 D4
South Kirkby Wakefd....91 L8
South Knighton Devon....7 L4
South Kyme Lincs.......86 G11
South Lanarkshire
  Crematorium S Lans...126 B6
Southleigh Devon.......10 E6
South Leigh Oxon.......34 C3
South Leverton Notts...85 N4
South Littleton Worcs..47 L5
South London
  Crematorium Gt Lon....36 G7
South Lopham Norfk.....64 E5
South Luffenham Rutlnd..73 N10
South Malling E Susx...25 K8
South Marston Swindn...33 N7
South Merstham Surrey..36 G10
South Middleton
  Nthumb...........119 J6
South Milford N York...91 M4
South Milton Devon......6 J10
South Mimms Herts......50 F10
South Mimms Services
  Herts.............50 F10
Southminster Essex.....38 G2
South Molton Devon.....17 N6
South Moor Dur.......113 J10
Southmoor Oxon........34 C5
South Moreton Oxon.....34 G7
Southmuir Angus......142 F7
South Mundham W Susx...15 N6
South Muskham Notts....85 N9
South Newbald E R Yk...92 F3
South Newington Oxon...48 D8
South Newton Wilts.....21 L8
South Normanton
  Derbys............84 F9
South Norwood Gt Lon...36 H7
South Nutfield Surrey...36 H11
South Ockendon Thurr...37 N4
Southoe Cambs.........61 Q8
Southolt Suffk.........64 H8
South Ormsby Lincs.....87 L5
Southorpe C Pete.......74 A10
South Ossett Wakefd....90 H7
South Otterington
  N York............97 N3
Southover Dorset.......11 N6
Southover E Susx.......25 Q5
South Owersby Lincs....86 E2
Southowram Calder......90 E6
South Park Surrey......36 F11
South Perrott Dorset...11 K3
South Petherton Somset.19 M11
South Petherwin Cnwll...5 N5
South Pickenham Norfk..76 B11
South Pill Cnwll........5 Q10
South Pool Devon........7 K10
South Poorton Dorset...11 L5
Southport Sefton.......88 C7
Southport Crematorium
  Lancs.............88 D8
South Queensferry
  C Edin...........127 L2
South Radworthy Devon..17 N5
South Rauceby Lincs....86 D11
South Raynham Norfk....76 B7
Southrepps Norfk.......77 K4
South Reston Lincs......87 M4
Southrey Lincs.........86 F7
South Ronaldsay Ork...169 d8
Southrop Gloucs........33 N4
Southrope Hants........23 J6
South Runcton Norfk....75 M9
South Scarle Notts.....85 P8
Southsea C Port........15 J7
Southsea Wrexhm........69 K4
South Shian Ag & B....138 G9
South Shields S Tyne..113 N7
South Shields
  Crematorium S Tyne..113 M8
South Shore Bpool......88 C4
Southside Dur.........103 M5
South Somercotes Lincs.87 M2
South Stainley N York...97 M8

South Stifford Thurr....37 N5
South Stoke BaNES......20 D2
South Stoke Oxon.......34 G8
South Stoke W Susx.....24 B9
South Stour Kent.......26 H4
South Street Kent.......37 P8
South Street Kent.......39 J10
South Street Kent.......39 K8
South Tarbrax S Lans..127 J7
South Tawton Devon......8 G6
South Tehidy Cnwll......2 H5
South Thoresby Lincs...87 M6
South Thorpe Dur......103 M8
South Town Hants.......23 J7
Southtown Norfk........77 Q10
Southtown Somset.......19 K11
South Uist W Isls.....168 d14
Southwaite Cumb......110 H11
Southwaite Services
  Cumb.............110 H11
South Walsham Norfk....77 M9
Southwark Gt Lon.......36 H5
South Warnborough
  Hants.............23 K5
Southwater W Susx......24 E5
Southwater Street
  W Susx............24 D5
Southway Somset.......19 P6
South Weald Essex......37 N2
Southwell Dorset.......11 P10
Southwell Notts........85 L10
South West Middlesex
  Crematorium Gt Lon....36 D6
South Weston Oxon......35 K5
South Wheatley Cnwll....5 L3
Southwick Hants........14 H5
Southwick Nhants.......61 M2
Southwick Somset.......19 L5
Southwick Sundld......113 N9
Southwick W Susx.......24 F9
Southwick Wilts........20 F3
South Widcombe BaNES...19 Q3
South Wigston Leics....72 F11
South Willesborough
  Kent..............26 H3
South Willingham Lincs..86 G4
South Wingate Dur.....104 D3
South Wingfield Derbys..84 E9
South Witham Lincs.....73 N7
Southwold Suffk........65 Q6
South Wonston Hants....22 E7
Southwood Norfk.......77 M10
Southwood Somset.......19 Q8
South Woodham
  Ferrers Essex........38 D2
South Wootton Norfk....75 M6
South Wraxall Wilts....20 F2
South Zeal Devon........8 G6
Sowerby Calder........90 C6
Sowerby N York........97 P4
Sowerby Bridge Calder..90 D6
Sowerby Row Cumb.....101 L2
Sower Carr Lancs.......88 D2
Sowerhill Somset.......18 A10
Sowhill Torfn..........31 J4
Sowley Green Suffk.....63 M10
Sowood Calder.........90 D7
Sowton Devon...........6 E5
Sowton Devon...........9 N6
Soyland Town Calder....90 C6
Spa Common Norfk.......77 K5
Spain's End Essex......51 Q3
Spalding Lincs.........74 D6
Spaldington E R Yk.....92 C4
Spaldwick Cambs........61 P6
Spalford Notts.........85 P7
Spanby Lincs..........74 A3
Spanish Green Hants....23 J3
Sparham Norfk..........76 F8
Sparhamill Norfk.......76 F8
Spark Bridge Cumb......94 G4
Sparket Cumb.........101 M5
Sparkford Somset......20 B9
Sparkhill Birm.........58 H8
Sparkwell Devon.........6 F7
Sparrow Green Norfk....76 C9
Sparrowpit Derbys......83 N8
Sparrows Green E Susx..25 P4
Sparsholt Hants........22 D8
Sparsholt Oxon.........34 B7
Spartylea Nthumb......112 C11
Spath Staffs...........71 K7
Spaunton N York........98 E3
Spaxton Somset........18 H7
Spean Bridge Highld...146 G11
Spear Hill W Susx......24 D7
Spearywell Hants.......22 B9
Speen Bucks...........35 M5
Speen W Berk..........34 E11
Speeton N York.........99 P6
Speke Lpool...........81 N8
Speldhurst Kent........25 N2
Spellbrook Herts.......51 L7
Spelmonden Kent........26 B4
Spelsbury Oxon.........48 B10
Spen Kirk.............90 F5
Spencers Wood Wokham...35 K11
Spen Green Ches E......70 E2
Spennithorne N York....96 H3
Spennymoor Dur.......103 Q4
Spernall Warwks........47 L2
Spetchley Worcs........46 G4
Spetisbury Dorset......12 F4
Spexhall Suffk.........65 M5
Spey Bay Moray.......157 R4
Speybridge Highld.....149 J2
Speyview Moray.......157 P9
Spilsby Lincs..........87 M7
Spindlestone Nthumb...119 N4
Spinkhill Derbys.......84 G5
Spinningdale Highld...162 F9
Spion Kop Notts........85 J7
Spirthill Wilts........33 J9
Spital Wirral..........81 L8
Spital Hill Donc.......85 K2
Spital in the Street Lincs..86 C2
Spithurst E Susx.......25 K7
Spittal E Loth........128 D4
Spittal E R Yk.........92 F10
Spittal Highld........167 L6
Spittal Nthumb........129 Q9
Spittal Pembks.........41 J6
Spittalfield P & K.....141 R9
Spittal of Glenmuick
  Abers............149 Q10
Spittal of Glenshee P & K.141 R4
Spittal-on-Rule Border.118 A7
Spixworth Norfk........77 J8
Splatt Cnwll...........4 E6
Splatt Cnwll...........5 L4

Splatt Devon........8 F3
Splayne's Green E Susx..25 K6
Splottlands Cardif........30 H9
Spofforth N York....97 N10
Spondon C Derb........72 C3
Spon Green Flints....69 J2
Spooner Row Norfk....64 F2
Sporle Norfk........76 A9
Spott E Loth........128 H4
Spottiswoode Border..128 G10
Spratton Nhants........60 F7
Spreakley Surrey....23 M6
Spreyton Devon........8 G5
Spriddlestone Devon..6 E8
Spridlington Lincs....86 D4
Springburn C Glas....125 Q4
Springfield D & G....110 F7
Springfield Essex....52 B10
Springfield Fife........135 J5
Springhill Staffs....58 E4
Springhill Staffs....58 G3
Springholm D & G....108 H6
Springside N Ayrs....125 K10
Spring Vale Barns....90 H10
Springwell Sundld....113 L9
Springwood
   Crematorium Lpool..81 N7
Sproatley E R Yk....93 L4
Sproston Green Ches W..82 F11
Sprotbrough Donc....91 N10
Sproughton Suffk....53 K3
Sprouston Border....118 E3
Sprowston Norfk....77 K9
Sproxton Leics........73 M6
Sproxton N York....98 C4
Spunhill Shrops........69 M8
Spurstow Ches E........69 Q3
Spyway Dorset........11 L6
Square & Compass
   Pembks........40 F4
Stableford Shrops....57 P5
Stableford Staffs....70 E7
Stacey Bank Sheff....84 C2
Stackhouse N York....96 B7
Stackpole Pembks....41 J11
Stacksford Norfk....64 F3
Stacksteads Lancs....89 P6
Staddiscombe C Plym..6 E8
Staddlethorpe E R Yk..92 D5
Staden Derbys........83 N10
Stadhampton Oxon....34 H5
Stadhlaigearraidh W Isls..168 C14
Staffield Cumb........101 P2
Staffin Highld........152 H4
Stafford Staffs........70 G10
Stafford Crematorium
   Staffs........70 H10
Stafford Services
   (northbound) Staffs..70 F8
Stafford Services
   (southbound) Staffs..70 F8
Stagsden Bed........49 Q5
Stainborough Barns..91 J10
Stainburn Cumb........100 D5
Stainburn N York....97 L11
Stainby Lincs........73 N6
Staincross Barns....91 J8
Staindrop Dur........103 M6
Staines-upon-Thames
   Surrey........36 B6
Stainfield Lincs....74 A6
Stainfield Lincs....86 F6
Stainforth Donc....91 Q8
Stainforth N York....96 B7
Staining Lancs........88 C3
Stainland Calder....90 D7
Stainsacre N York....105 P9
Stainsby Derbys........84 G7
Stainton Cumb........95 L3
Stainton Cumb........101 N5
Stainton Cumb........110 G9
Stainton Donc........85 J2
Stainton Dur........103 L7
Stainton Middsb....104 E8
Stainton N York....103 M11
Stainton by Langworth
   Lincs........86 E5
Staintondale N York..105 Q11
Stainton le Vale Lincs..86 G2
Stainton with Adgarley
   Cumb........94 E6
Stair Cumb........100 H6
Stair E Ayrs........114 H3
Stairfoot Barns....91 K9
Stairhaven D & G....106 H7
Staithes N York....105 L7
Stakeford Nthumb....113 L3
Stake Pool Lancs....95 J11
Stakes Hants........15 J5
Stalbridge Dorset....20 D11
Stalbridge Weston
   Dorset........20 D11
Stalham Norfk........77 M6
Stalham Green Norfk..77 M7
Stalisfield Green Kent..38 G11
Stalland Common Norfk..64 E2
Stallen Dorset........20 B11
Stallingborough NE Lin..93 L8
Stalling Busk N York..96 D3
Stallington Staffs....70 G7
Stalmine Lancs........94 H11
Stalmine Moss Side
   Lancs........94 H11
Stalybridge Tamesd..83 L5
Stambourne Essex....52 B4
Stambourne Green
   Essex........51 Q3
Stamford Lincs........73 Q9
Stamford Nthumb....119 P7
Stamford Bridge Ches W..81 P11
Stamford Bridge E R Yk..98 F3
Stamfordham Nthumb..112 G6
Stamford Hill Gt Lon..36 H3
Stanah Lancs........88 D2
Stanborough Herts....50 F8
Stanbridge C Beds....49 Q10
Stanbridge Dorset....12 H4
Stanbury C Brad....90 C3
Stand Bury........89 M9
Stand N Lans........126 G5
Standburn Falk....126 G3
Standeford Staffs....58 D3
Standen Kent........26 E3
Standen Street Kent..26 D5
Standerwick Somset..20 F4
Standford Hants....23 M8
Standingstone Cumb..100 E4
Standish Gloucs....32 E3
Standish Wigan....88 H8

Standish Lower Ground
   Wigan........88 H9
Standlake Oxon........34 C4
Standon Hants........9 D9
Standon Herts........51 J6
Standon Staffs........70 E7
Standon Green End
   Herts........51 J7
Standwell Green Suffk..64 G8
Stane N Lans........126 F6
Stanford C Beds........50 E2
Stanford Kent........27 K4
Stanford Shrops....56 F2
Stanford Bishop Herefs..46 C4
Stanford Bridge Worcs..57 N11
Stanford Bridge Wrekin..70 C10
Stanford Dingley W Berk..34 G10
Stanford in the Vale
   Oxon........34 B6
Stanford le Hope Thurr..37 Q4
Stanford on Avon
   Nhants........60 C5
Stanford on Soar Notts..72 E6
Stanford on Teme Worcs..57 N11
Stanfree Derbys........84 G6
Stanghow R & Cl....105 J7
Stanground C Pete....74 D11
Stanhill Lancs........89 L5
Stanhoe Norfk........75 R3
Stanhope Border....116 G5
Stanhope Dur........103 J3
Stanhope Kent........26 H3
Stanhope Bretby Derbys..71 P10
Stanion Nhants........61 K3
Stanklin Worcs........58 C10
Stanley Derbys........72 C2
Stanley Dur........113 J10
Stanley Notts........84 G8
Stanley P & K........141 R11
Stanley Shrops........57 N8
Stanley Staffs........70 G4
Stanley Wakefd........91 J6
Stanley Common Derbys..72 C2
Stanley Crook Dur....103 N3
Stanley Ferry Wakefd..91 K6
Stanley Gate Lancs....88 E9
Stanley Moor Staffs....70 G4
Stanley Pontlarge
   Gloucs........47 K8
Stanmer Br & H........24 H9
Stanmore Gt Lon........36 E2
Stanmore Hants........22 E9
Stanmore W Berk....34 E9
Stannersburn Nthumb..111 P3
Stanningfield Suffk....63 B10
Stanningley Leeds....90 G4
Stannington Nthumb..113 K5
Stannington Sheff....84 C3
Stannington Station
   Nthumb........113 K4
Stansbatch Herefs....45 L2
Stansfield Suffk........63 N10
Stanshope Staffs....71 L4
Stanstead Suffk....52 D2
Stanstead Abbotts Herts..51 J8
Stansted Kent........37 P8
Stansted Airport Essex..51 M6
Stansted Mountfitchet
   Essex........51 M5
Stanton Derbys........71 P11
Stanton Gloucs........47 L8
Stanton Mons........45 L10
Stanton Nthumb....112 H4
Stanton Staffs........71 L5
Stanton Suffk........64 D7
Stanton by Bridge
   Derbys........72 B5
Stanton by Dale Derbys..72 D3
Stanton Drew BaNES....19 Q2
Stanton Fitzwarren
   Swindn........33 N6
Stanton Harcourt Oxon..34 D3
Stanton Hill Notts....84 G8
Stanton in Peak Derbys..84 B8
Stanton Lacy Shrops....56 H9
Stanton Lees Derbys....84 C8
Stanton Long Shrops....57 K6
Stanton on the Wolds
   Notts........72 G4
Stanton Prior BaNES....20 C2
Stanton St Bernard Wilts..21 L2
Stanton St John Oxon..34 G3
Stanton St Quintin Wilts..32 H9
Stanton Street Suffk..64 D8
Stanton under Bardon
   Leics........72 D8
Stanton upon Hine
   Heath Shrops........69 Q10
Stanton Wick BaNES....20 B2
Stanwardine in the
   Field Shrops........69 M10
Stanwardine in the
   Wood Shrops........69 M9
Stanway Essex........52 F7
Stanway Gloucs........47 L8
Stanway Green Essex..52 G7
Stanway Green Suffk..65 J2
Stanwell Surrey........36 C6
Stanwell Moor Surrey..36 B6
Stanwick Nhants........61 L6
Stanwix Cumb........110 H9
Staoinebrig W Isls....168 C14
Stape N York........98 F2
Stapehill Dorset....13 J4
Stapeley Ches E........70 B5
Stapenhill Staffs....71 P10
Staple Kent........39 N10
Staple Cross Devon....18 D10
Staple Cross E Susx....26 C7
Staplefield W Susx....24 G5
Staple Fitzpaine Somset..19 J11
Stapleford Cambs....62 G10
Stapleford Herts....50 H7
Stapleford Leics....73 L7
Stapleford Lincs....85 Q9
Stapleford Notts....72 D3
Stapleford Wilts....21 L7
Stapleford Abbotts
   Essex........37 M2
Stapleford Tawney
   Essex........51 M11
Staplegrove Somset....18 H9
Staplehay Somset....18 H10
Staple Hill Worcs....58 E10
Staplehurst Kent....26 C3
Staplers IoW........14 F9
Staplestreet Kent....39 J9

Stapleton Cumb........111 K6
Stapleton Herefs....56 E11
Stapleton Leics....72 C11
Stapleton N York....103 Q8
Stapleton Shrops....56 H4
Stapleton Somset....19 N10
Stapley Somset........10 D2
Staploe Bed........61 Q8
Staplow Herefs........46 C6
Star Fife........135 J7
Star Pembks........41 P4
Star Somset........19 M3
Starbeck N York....97 M9
Starbotton N York....96 E6
Starcross Devon....9 N8
Stareton Warwks....59 M10
Starkholmes Derbys....84 D9
Starlings Green Essex..51 L4
Starr's Green E Susx....26 C9
Starston Norfk........65 J5
Start Devon........7 L10
Startforth Dur........103 K7
Startley Wilts........32 H8
Statenborough Kent....39 P10
Statham Warrtn....82 E7
Stathe Somset........19 L9
Stathern Leics........73 L4
Station Town Dur....104 D3
Staughton Green Cambs..61 P7
Staughton Highway
   Cambs........61 P8
Staunton Gloucs........31 Q2
Staunton Gloucs........46 E9
Staunton in the Vale
   Notts........73 L2
Staunton on Arrow
   Herefs........45 M2
Staunton on Wye Herefs..45 M4
Staveley Cumb........94 H3
Staveley Cumb........101 N11
Staveley Derbys....84 F6
Staveley N York....97 N8
Staverton Devon....7 K6
Staverton Gloucs....46 G10
Staverton Nhants....60 B8
Staverton Wilts....20 G2
Staverton Bridge Gloucs..46 G10
Stawell Somset....19 L7
Stawley Somset........18 E10
Staxigoe Highld....167 Q6
Staxton N York........99 L5
Staylittle Cerdgn....54 E7
Staylittle Powys....55 K6
Staynall Lancs....88 D2
Staythorpe Notts....85 N10
Stead C Brad........96 H11
Stean N York........96 G6
Stearsby N York....98 C6
Steart Somset........19 J5
Stebbing Essex........51 Q6
Stebbing Green Essex..51 Q6
Stechford Birm....58 H7
Stede Quarter Kent....26 E4
Stedham W Susx........23 N10
Steel Nthumb........112 D9
Steel Cross E Susx....25 M4
Steelend Fife........134 C9
Steele Road Border....111 K2
Steel Green Cumb....94 D5
Steel Heath Shrops....69 P7
Steen's Bridge Herefs..45 Q3
Steep Hants........23 K9
Steephill IoW........14 F11
Steep Lane Calder....90 C6
Steeple Dorset........12 F8
Steeple Essex........52 F11
Steeple Ashton Wilts..20 H3
Steeple Aston Oxon....48 E9
Steeple Barton Oxon..48 D10
Steeple Bumpstead
   Essex........51 Q2
Steeple Claydon Bucks..49 K9
Steeple Gidding Cambs..61 P4
Steeple Langford Wilts..21 K7
Steeple Morden Cambs..50 G2
Steeton C Brad........90 C2
Stein Highld........152 D6
Stella Gatesd........113 J8
Stelling Minnis Kent....27 K2
Stembridge Somset....19 M10
Stenalees Cnwll....4 G10
Stenhouse D & G....115 R9
Stenhousemuir Falk....133 P11
Stenigot Lincs........86 H4
Stenscholl Highld....152 H4
Stenson Fields Derbys..72 A4
Stenton E Loth........128 G5
Steornabhagh W Isls..168 j4
Stepaside Pembks....41 M9
Stepney Gt Lon........37 J4
Stepping Hill Stockp..83 K7
Steppingley C Beds....50 B3
Stepps N Lans........126 B4
Sternfield Suffk....65 M9
Stert Wilts........21 K3
Stetchworth Cambs....63 K9
Stevenage Herts....50 F5
Steven's Crouch E Susx..26 B8
Stevenston N Ayrs....124 H9
Steventon Hants....22 F5
Steventon Oxon....34 E6
Steventon End Essex..51 N2
Stevington Bed....49 Q4
Stewartby Bed........50 B2
Stewartfield S Lans..125 Q6
Stewarton E Ayrs....125 L9
Stewkley Bucks....49 N9
Stewley Somset....19 L11
Stewton Lincs........87 L3
Steyne Cross IoW....14 H9
Steyning W Susx....24 E8
Steynton Pembks....40 H9
Stibb Cnwll........16 C9
Stibbard Norfk........76 D6
Stibb Cross Devon....16 G9
Stibb Green Wilts....21 P2
Stibbington Cambs....61 A11
Stichill Border........118 D3
Sticker Cnwll........3 P3
Stickford Lincs........87 L8
Sticklepath Devon....8 F6
Sticklepath Somset....18 D7
Stickling Green Essex..51 L4
Stickney Lincs........87 K9
Stiffkey Norfk........76 D3
Stifford's Bridge Herefs..46 D5
Stiff Street Kent....38 E9
Stile Bridge Kent....26 C2
Stileway Somset....19 N6

Stilligarry W Isls....168 C14
Stillingfleet N York....91 P2
Stillington N York....98 B7
Stillington S on T....104 C6
Stilton Cambs........61 Q3
Stinchcombe Gloucs....32 D5
Stinsford Dorset....11 Q6
Stiperstones Shrops....56 F4
Stirchley Birm........58 G8
Stirchley Wrekin....57 N3
Stirling Abers........159 R9
Stirling Stirlg........133 M9
Stirling Services Stirlg..133 N10
Stirtloe Cambs........61 Q7
Stirton N York........96 E10
Stisted Essex........52 D7
Stitchcombe Wilts....33 P11
Stithians Cnwll....3 J6
Stivichall Covtry....59 M9
Stixwould Lincs....86 G7
St Margaret's Bay Kent..27 Q3
Stoak Ches W........81 N10
Stobo Border........116 H3
Stoborough Dorset....12 F7
Stoborough Green
   Dorset........12 F7
Stobs Castle Border....117 Q9
Stobswood Nthumb....119 P11
Stock Essex........51 Q11
Stock N Som........19 N2
Stockbridge Hants....22 C7
Stockbriggs S Lans..126 D10
Stockbury Kent....38 D9
Stockcross W Berk....34 D11
Stockdalewath Cumb..110 G11
Stocker's Hill Kent....38 G11
Stockerston Leics....73 L11
Stock Green Worcs....47 J3
Stocking Herefs....46 B8
Stockingford Warwks..59 M6
Stocking Pelham Herts..51 L5
Stockland Devon....10 E4
Stockland Bristol Somset..18 H6
Stockland Green Kent..25 N2
Stockleigh English
   Devon........9 L3
Stockleigh Pomeroy
   Devon........9 L4
Stockley Wilts........33 J11
Stockley Hill Herefs....45 M7
Stocklinch Somset....19 L11
Stockmoor Herefs....45 M4
Stockport Stockp....83 J6
Stockport Crematorium
   Stockp........83 K7
Stocksbridge Sheff....90 H11
Stocksfield Nthumb....112 G8
Stockton Herefs....45 Q2
Stockton Norfk........65 M3
Stockton Shrops....56 D4
Stockton Shrops....57 N5
Stockton Warwks....48 D2
Stockton Wilts....21 J7
Stockton Wrekin....70 D11
Stockton Brook Staffs..70 G4
Stockton Heath Warrtn..82 D7
Stockton-on-Tees S on T..104 D7
Stockton on Teme Worcs..57 N11
Stockton on the Forest
   C York........98 D9
Stockwell Gloucs....32 H2
Stockwell End Wolves..58 C4
Stockwell Heath Staffs..71 K10
Stockwood Bristl....32 B11
Stockwood Dorset....11 M3
Stock Wood Worcs....47 K3
Stodday Lancs........95 K9
Stodmarsh Kent........39 M9
Stody Norfk........76 F4
Stoer Highld........164 B11
Stoford Somset........11 M2
Stoford Wilts........21 L7
Stogumber Somset....18 E7
Stogursey Somset....18 H6
Stoke Covtry........59 N9
Stoke Devon........16 C7
Stoke Hants........15 K6
Stoke Hants........22 D4
Stoke Medway........38 D7
Stoke Abbott Dorset..11 K4
Stoke Albany Nhants..60 H3
Stoke Bardolph Notts..72 G2
Stoke Bliss Worcs....46 C2
Stoke Bruerne Nhants..49 K5
Stoke by Clare Suffk..52 B3
Stoke-by-Nayland Suffk..52 H4
Stoke Canon Devon....9 M5
Stoke Charity Hants..22 E7
Stoke Climsland Cnwll..5 P7
Stoke Cross Herefs....46 B4
Stoke D'Abernon Surrey..36 D9
Stoke Doyle Nhants....61 M3
Stoke Dry Rutlnd....73 M11
Stoke Edith Herefs....46 B6
Stoke End Warwks....59 J5
Stoke Farthing Wilts..21 L9
Stoke Ferry Norfk....75 P10
Stoke Fleming Devon....7 M9
Stokeford Dorset....12 E7
Stoke Gabriel Devon....7 M7
Stoke Gifford S Glos..32 B9
Stoke Golding Leics....72 B11
Stoke Goldington
   M Keyn........49 M5
Stoke Green Bucks....35 Q8
Stokeham Notts....85 M5
Stoke Hammond Bucks..49 N9
Stoke Heath Shrops....70 B9
Stoke Heath Worcs....58 D11
Stoke Holy Cross Norfk..77 J11
Stokeinteignhead Devon..7 N4
Stoke Lacy Herefs....46 B5
Stoke Lyne Oxon....48 E9
Stoke Mandeville Bucks..35 M2
Stokenchurch Bucks....35 L5
Stoke Newington Gt Lon..36 H3
Stokenham Devon....7 M10
Stoke-on-Trent C Stke..70 F5
Stoke Orchard Gloucs..46 H9
Stoke Poges Bucks....35 Q8
Stoke Pound Worcs....58 D11
Stoke Prior Herefs....45 Q3
Stoke Prior Worcs....58 D11
Stoke Rivers Devon....17 L4
Stoke Rochford Lincs..73 N5
Stoke Row Oxon....35 J8
Stoke St Gregory Somset..19 K9
Stoke St Mary Somset..19 J10
Stoke St Michael Somset..20 C5

Stoke St Milborough
   Shrops........57 K8
Stokesay Shrops....56 G8
Stokesay Castle Shrops..56 G8
Stokesby Norfk........77 N9
Stokesley N York....104 F9
Stoke sub Hamdon
   Somset........19 N11
Stoke Talmage Oxon....35 J5
Stoke Trister Somset..20 D9
Stoke upon Tern Shrops..70 B9
Stoke-upon-Trent C Stke..70 F5
Stoke Wake Dorset....12 C3
Stoke Wharf Worcs....58 E11
Stolford Somset....18 H5
Stondon Massey Essex..51 N10
Stone Bucks........35 L2
Stone Gloucs........32 C5
Stone Kent........37 N6
Stone Rothm........85 J3
Stone Somset........19 Q8
Stone Staffs........70 G8
Stone Worcs........58 C9
Stonea Cambs........62 G3
Stone Allerton Somset..19 L4
Ston Easton Somset....20 B4
Stonebridge N Som....19 L3
Stonebridge Norfk....64 C3
Stonebridge Warwks..59 K8
Stone Bridge Corner
   C Pete........74 E10
Stonebroom Derbys....84 F9
Stone Chair Calder....90 F4
Stone Cross E Susx....25 M5
Stone Cross E Susx....25 P4
Stone Cross Kent....25 M5
Stone Cross Kent....26 H4
Stone Cross Kent....39 P10
Stonecross Green Suffk..64 A10
Stonecrouch Kent....26 B5
Stone-edge-Batch
   N Som........31 N10
Stoneferry C KuH....93 K4
Stonefield Castle Hotel
   Ag & B........123 Q5
Stonegate E Susx....25 Q5
Stonegate N York....105 L9
Stonegrave N York....98 D5
Stonehall Worcs....46 G5
Stonehaugh Nthumb....111 Q5
Stonehaven Abers....151 M10
Stonehenge Wilts....21 M6
Stone Hill Donc....92 A9
Stonehouse C Plym....6 D6
Stone House Cumb....95 R3
Stonehouse Gloucs....32 E4
Stonehouse Nthumb....111 N9
Stonehouse S Lans....126 D8
Stone in Oxney Kent....26 F6
Stoneleigh Warwks....59 M10
Stoneley Green Ches E..69 R4
Stonely Cambs........61 P7
Stoner Hill Hants....23 K9
Stonesby Leics....73 L6
Stonesfield Oxon....48 C11
Stones Green Essex....53 L6
Stone Street Kent....37 N10
Stone Street Suffk....52 G4
Stone Street Suffk....52 H3
Stone Street Suffk....65 M5
Stonestreet Green Kent..27 J4
Stonethwaite Cumb....101 J8
Stonewells Moray....157 P3
Stonewood Kent....37 N6
Stoneybridge W Isls..168 C14
Stoneybridge Worcs....58 C9
Stoneyburn W Loth....126 H5
Stoney Cross Hants....13 N2
Stoneygate C Leic....72 G10
Stoneyhills Essex....38 C2
Stoneykirk D & G....106 E7
Stoney Middleton
   Derbys........84 B5
Stoney Stanton Leics..59 N8
Stoney Stoke Somset..20 D8
Stoney Stratton Somset..20 C7
Stoney Stretton Shrops..56 F3
Stoneywood C Aber....151 M5
Stoneywood Falk....133 M11
Stonham Aspal Suffk..64 G10
Stonnall Staffs....58 G4
Stonor Oxon........35 K7
Stonton Wyville Leics..73 J11
Stony Cross Herefs....46 D5
Stony Cross Herefs....57 J11
Stonyford Hants....22 B11
Stony Houghton Derbys..84 G7
Stony Stratford M Keyn..49 L6
Stonywell Staffs....58 G2
Stoodleigh Devon....17 M5
Stoodleigh Devon....18 B11
Stop 24 Services Kent..27 K4
Stopham W Susx....24 B7
Stopsley Luton....50 C5
Stoptide Cnwll....4 E6
Storeton Wirral....81 L8
Storeyard Green Herefs..46 D6
Stornoway W Isls....168 j4
Stornoway Airport W Isls..168 j4
Storridge Herefs....46 E5
Storrington W Susx....24 C8
Storth Cumb........95 K5
Storwood E R Yk....92 C3
Stotfield Moray....157 N3
Stotfold C Beds....50 F3
Stottesdon Shrops....57 M8
Stoughton Leics....72 G10
Stoughton Surrey....23 Q4
Stoughton W Susx....15 M4
Stoulton Worcs........46 H5
Stourbridge Dudley....58 C8
Stourbridge
   Crematorium Dudley..58 C8
Stourpaine Dorset....12 E3
Stourport-on-Severn
   Worcs........57 Q10
Stour Provost Dorset..20 E10
Stour Row Dorset....20 F10
Stourton Leeds........91 J4
Stourton Staffs....58 C8
Stourton Warwks....47 Q7
Stourton Wilts........20 E8
Stourton Caundle Dorset..20 D11
Stout Somset........19 M8
Stove Shet........169 r11
Stoven Suffk........65 N5
Stow Border........117 P2
Stow Lincs........85 Q4
Stow Bardolph Norfk..75 M9

Stow Bedon Norfk 64 D2
Stowbridge Norfk 75 M9
Stow-cum-Quy Cambs 62 H8
Stowe Gloucs 31 Q3
Stowe Shrops 56 E10
Stowe by Chartley Staffs ...71 J9
Stowehill Nhants 60 D9
Stowell Somset 20 C10
Stowey BaNES 19 Q3
Stowford Devon 8 B5
Stowford Devon 8 B7
Stowford Devon 10 C7
Stowford Devon 17 M3
Stowlangtoft Suffk 64 D8
Stow Longa Cambs 61 P6
Stow Maries Essex 38 D2
Stowmarket Suffk 64 E10
Stow-on-the-Wold
  Gloucs 47 N9
Stowting Kent 27 K3
Stowting Common Kent 27 K3
Stowupland Suffk 64 F9
Straanruie Highld 148 H4
Strachan Abers 150 H9
Strachur Ag & B 131 M7
Stradbroke Suffk 65 J7
Stradbrook Wilts 20 H4
Stradishall Suffk 63 N10
Stradsett Norfk 75 N9
Stragglethorpe Lincs 86 B10
Stragglethorpe Notts 72 H3
Straight Soley Wilts 34 B10
Straiton Mdloth 127 P4
Straiton S Ayrs 114 G7
Straloch Abers 151 M3
Straloch P & K 141 P5
Stramshall Staffs 71 K7
Strang IoM 80 e6
Strangeways Salfd 82 H5
Strangford Herefs 46 A9
Stranraer D & G 106 E5
Strata Florida Cerdgn 54 G11
Stratfield Mortimer
  W Berk 23 J4
Stratfield Saye Hants 23 J2
Stratfield Turgis Hants 23 J3
Stratford C Beds 61 Q11
Stratford Gt Lon 37 J4
Stratford St Andrew
  Suffk 65 M9
Stratford St Mary Suffk 52 H5
Stratford sub Castle
  Wilts 21 M8
Stratford Tony Wilts 21 L9
Stratford-upon-Avon
  Warwks 47 P3
Strath Highld 160 B11
Strathan Highld 160 H2
Strathan Highld 165 N4
Strathaven S Lans 126 C9
Strathblane Stirlg 125 P2
Strathcanaird Highld 161 K6
Strathcarron Highld 154 B9
Strathcoil Ag & B 138 B11
Strathdon Abers 150 B5
Strathkinness Fife 135 M4
Strathloanhead W Loth 126 G3
Strathmashie House
  Highld 147 P9
Strathmiglo Fife 134 G6
Strathpeffer Highld 155 N6
Strathtay P & K 141 M7
Strathwhillan N Ayrs 121 K4
Strathy Highld 166 D4
Strathy Inn Highld 166 D3
Strathyre Stirlg 132 H4
Stratton Cnwll 16 C10
Stratton Dorset 11 P6
Stratton Gloucs 33 K4
Stratton Audley Oxon 48 H9
Stratton-on-the-Fosse
  Somset 20 C4
Stratton St Margaret
  Swindn 33 N7
Stratton St Michael
  Norfk 65 J3
Stratton Strawless Norfk ...77 J7
Stream Somset 18 E7
Streat E Susx 25 J7
Streatham Gt Lon 36 H6
Streatley C Beds 50 C5
Streatley W Berk 34 G8
Street Devon 10 D7
Street Lancs 95 L10
Street N York 105 K10
Street Somset 19 N7
Street Ashton Warwks 59 Q8
Street Dinas Shrops 69 K7
Street End E Susx 25 P6
Street End Kent 39 K11
Street End W Susx 15 N7
Street Gate Gatesd 113 K9
Streethay Staffs 58 H2
Street Houses N York 98 A11
Streetlam N York 104 B11
Street Lane Derbys 84 E11
Streetly Wsall 58 G5
Streetly Crematorium
  Wsall 58 G5
Streetly End Cambs 63 K11
Street on the Fosse
  Somset 20 B7
Strefford Shrops 56 G7
Strelitz P & K 142 B10
Strelley Notts 72 E2
Strensall C York 98 C8
Strensham Worcs 46 H6
Strensham Services
  (northbound) Worcs 46 G6
Strensham Services
  (southbound) Worcs 46 H6
Stretcholt Somset 19 J6
Strete Devon 7 L9
Stretford Herefs 45 N3
Stretford Herefs 45 Q3
Stretford Trafd 82 G6
Strethall Essex 51 L3
Stretham Cambs 62 H6
Strettington W Susx 15 N5
Stretton Ches W 69 M4
Stretton Derbys 84 E8
Stretton Rutlnd 73 N7
Stretton Staffs 58 C2
Stretton Staffs 71 P9
Stretton Warrtn 82 D8
Stretton en le Field Leics ...59 M2
Stretton Grandison
  Herefs 46 B6
Stretton-on-Dunsmore
  Warwks 59 P10

Stretton on Fosse
  Warwks 47 P7
Stretton Sugwas Herefs 45 P6
Stretton under Fosse
  Warwks 59 Q8
Stretton Westwood
  Shrops 57 K5
Strichen Abers 159 M6
Strines Stockp 83 L7
Stringston Somset 18 G6
Strixton Nhants 61 K8
Stroat Gloucs 31 Q5
Stroma Highld 167 Q1
Stromeferry Highld 153 R11
Stromness Ork 169 b6
Stronachlachar Stirlg 132 E5
Stronafian Ag & B 131 L11
Stronchrubie Highld 161 L3
Strone Ag & B 131 P11
Strone Highld 146 E11
Strone Highld 147 N2
Stronenaba Highld 146 G11
Stronmilchan Ag & B 131 P2
Stronsay Ork 169 f4
Stronsay Airport Ork 169 f4
Strontian Highld 138 E5
Strood Kent 26 E5
Strood Medway 38 B8
Strood Green Surrey 36 F11
Strood Green W Susx 24 B6
Stroud Gloucs 32 G3
Stroud Hants 23 K10
Stroude Surrey 36 B7
Stroud Green Essex 38 E3
Stroud Green Gloucs 32 F3
Stroxton Lincs 73 N4
Struan Highld 152 E10
Struan P & K 141 K4
Strubby Lincs 87 N4
Strumpshaw Norfk 77 L10
Strutherhill S Lans 126 D8
Struthers Fife 135 K6
Struy Highld 155 M9
Stryd-y-Facsen IoA 78 E8
Stryt-issa Wrexhm 69 J5
Stuartfield Abers 159 N8
Stubbers Green Wsall 58 F4
Stubbington Hants 14 G6
Stubbins Lancs 89 M7
Stubbs Green Norfk 65 K2
Stubhampton Dorset 12 F2
Stubley Derbys 84 D5
Stubshaw Cross Wigan 82 C5
Stubton Lincs 85 Q11
Stuckton Hants 13 L2
Studfold N York 96 B7
Stud Green W & M 35 N9
Studham C Beds 50 B7
Studholme Cumb 110 E9
Studland Dorset 12 H8
Studley Warwks 47 L2
Studley Wilts 33 J10
Studley Common
  Warwks 47 L2
Studley Roger N York 97 L7
Studley Royal N York 97 L6
Stuntney Cambs 63 J5
Sturbridge Staffs 70 E8
Sturgate Lincs 85 Q3
Sturmer Essex 51 Q2
Sturminster Common
  Dorset 12 C2
Sturminster Marshall
  Dorset 12 G4
Sturminster Newton
  Dorset 12 C2
Sturry Kent 39 L9
Sturton N Linc 92 G10
Sturton by Stow Lincs 85 Q4
Sturton le Steeple Notts 85 N4
Stuston Suffk 64 G6
Stutton N York 91 M2
Stutton Suffk 53 L5
Styal Ches E 82 H8
Stydd Lancs 88 K3
Stynie Moray 157 Q5
Styrrup Notts 85 K2
Succoth Ag & B 132 B6
Suckley Worcs 46 D4
Suckley Green Worcs 46 D4
Sudborough Nhants 61 L4
Sudbourne Suffk 65 N11
Sudbrook Lincs 73 P2
Sudbrook Mons 31 P7
Sudbrooke Lincs 86 D5
Sudbury Derbys 71 M8
Sudbury Gt Lon 36 E3
Sudbury Suffk 52 E3
Sudden Rochdl 89 P8
Sudgrove Gloucs 32 H3
Suffield N York 99 K2
Suffield Norfk 77 J5
Sugdon Wrekin 69 R11
Sugnall Staffs 70 D8
Sugwas Pool Herefs 45 P6
Suisnish Highld 145 J4
Sulby IoM 80 e3
Sulgrave Nhants 48 G6
Sulgrave Manor Nhants 48 G5
Sulham W Berk 34 H10
Sulhamstead W Berk 34 H11
Sulhamstead Abbots
  W Berk 34 H11
Sulhamstead Bannister
  W Berk 34 H11
Sullington W Susx 24 C8
Sullom Shet 169 q6
Sullom Voe Shet 169 r6
Sully V Glam 30 G11
Sumburgh Airport Shet 169 q12
Summerbridge N York 97 K8
Summercourt Cnwll 4 D10
Summerfield Norfk 75 Q3
Summerfield Worcs 58 B10
Summer Heath Bucks 35 K6
Summerhill Pembks 41 N9
Summerhill Staffs 58 G3
Summer Hill Wrexhm 69 K4
Summerhouse Darltn 103 P7
Summerlands Cumb 95 L3
Summerley Derbys 84 E5
Summersdale W Susx 15 N5
Summerseat Bury 89 M8
Summertown Oxon 34 F3
Summit Oldham 89 Q9
Summit Rochdl 89 Q7
Sunbiggin Cumb 102 C9
Sunbury Surrey 36 D7
Sundaywell D & G 108 H4

Sunderland Ag & B 122 B7
Sunderland Cumb 100 G3
Sunderland Lancs 95 J9
Sunderland Sundld 113 N9
Sunderland Bridge Dur 103 Q3
Sunderland
  Crematorium
  Sundld 113 N9
Sundhope Border 117 L5
Sundon Park Luton 50 C5
Sundridge Kent 37 L9
Sunk Island E R Yk 93 N7
Sunningdale W & M 35 Q11
Sunninghill W & M 35 P11
Sunningwell Oxon 34 E4
Sunniside Dur 103 M3
Sunniside Gatesd 113 K9
Sunny Brow Dur 103 N4
Sunnyhill C Derb 72 A4
Sunnyhurst Bl w D 89 K6
Sunnylaw Stirlg 133 M8
Sunnymead Oxon 34 F3
Sunton Wilts 21 P4
Surbiton Gt Lon 36 E7
Surfleet Lincs 74 E5
Surfleet Seas End Lincs 74 E5
Surlingham Norfk 77 L10
Surrex Essex 52 E7
Surrey & Sussex
  Crematorium W Susx 24 G3
Sustead Norfk 76 H4
Susworth Lincs 92 D10
Sutcombe Devon 16 E9
Sutcombemill Devon 16 E9
Suton Norfk 64 F2
Sutterby Lincs 87 L6
Sutterton Lincs 74 E3
Sutton C Beds 62 B11
Sutton C Pete 74 A11
Sutton Cambs 62 F5
Sutton Devon 7 J10
Sutton Devon 7 P5
Sutton Donc 91 P8
Sutton E Susx 25 L11
Sutton Gt Lon 36 G8
Sutton Kent 27 P2
Sutton N York 91 M5
Sutton Norfk 77 M7
Sutton Notts 73 K3
Sutton Oxon 34 D3
Sutton Pembks 16 H7
Sutton Shrops 57 J2
Sutton Shrops 57 N7
Sutton Shrops 69 L9
Sutton Shrops 70 B8
Sutton St Hel 82 B6
Sutton Staffs 70 D10
Sutton Suffk 53 P2
Sutton W Susx 23 Q11
Sutton Abinger Surrey 36 D11
Sutton at Hone Kent 37 N7
Sutton Bassett Nhants 60 G2
Sutton Benger Wilts 32 H9
Sutton Bingham Somset 11 L2
Sutton Bonington
  Notts 72 E6
Sutton Bridge Lincs 75 J6
Sutton Cheney Leics 72 C10
Sutton Coldfield Birm 58 H5
Sutton Coldfield
  Crematorium Birm 58 H5
Sutton Courtenay Oxon 34 F6
Sutton Crosses Lincs 74 H6
Sutton cum Lound
  Notts 85 L4
Sutton Fields Notts 72 D5
Sutton Green Surrey 36 B10
Sutton Green Wrexhm 69 M5
Sutton Howgrave N York 97 M5
Sutton in Ashfield Notts 84 G9
Sutton-in-Craven N York 90 C2
Sutton in the Elms Leics 60 B2
Sutton Lane Ends Ches E 83 K10
Sutton Maddock Shrops 57 N4
Sutton Mallet Somset 19 L7
Sutton Mandeville Wilts 21 J9
Sutton Manor St Hel 81 Q6
Sutton Marsh Herefs 45 R6
Sutton Montis Somset 20 B10
Sutton-on-Hull C KuH 93 K4
Sutton on Sea Lincs 87 P4
Sutton-on-the-Forest
  N York 98 B8
Sutton on the Hill Derbys 71 N8
Sutton on Trent Notts 85 N7
Sutton Poyntz Dorset 11 Q8
Sutton St Edmund Lincs 74 G8
Sutton St James Lincs 74 G7
Sutton St Nicholas
  Herefs 45 Q5
Sutton Scotney Hants 22 E7
Sutton Street Kent 38 D10
Sutton-under-Brailes
  Warwks 48 B7
Sutton-under-
  Whitestonecliffe
  N York 97 Q4
Sutton upon Derwent
  E R Yk 98 E11
Sutton Valence Kent 26 D2
Sutton Veny Wilts 20 H6
Sutton Waldron Dorset 20 G11
Sutton Weaver Ches W 82 B9
Sutton Wick BaNES 19 Q3
Sutton Wick Oxon 34 E6
Swaby Lincs 87 L5
Swadlincote Derbys 71 P11
Swaffham Norfk 75 R9
Swaffham Bulbeck
  Cambs 63 J8
Swaffham Prior Cambs 63 J8
Swafield Norfk 77 K5
Swainby N York 104 E10
Swainshill Herefs 45 P6
Swainsthorpe Norfk 77 J11
Swainswick BaNES 32 E11
Swalcliffe Oxon 48 C7
Swalecliffe Kent 39 K8
Swallow Lincs 93 L10
Swallow Beck Lincs 86 B7
Swallowcliffe Wilts 21 J9
Swallowfield Wokham 35 K2
Swallow Nest Rothm 84 G3
Swallows Cross Essex 51 P11
Swampton Hants 22 D4
Swanage Dorset 12 H9
Swanbourne Bucks 49 M9
Swanbridge V Glam 30 G11
Swancote Shrops 57 N6
Swan Green Ches W 82 F10

Swanland E R Yk 92 G5
Swanley Kent 37 M7
Swanley Village Kent 37 M7
Swanmore Hants 22 G11
Swannington Leics 72 C7
Swannington Norfk 76 G8
Swanpool Garden
  Suburb Lincs 86 C7
Swanscombe Kent 37 P6
Swansea Swans 29 J6
Swansea Swans 28 G6
Swansea Airport Swans 28 G6
Swansea Crematorium
  Swans 29 J5
Swansea West Services
  Swans 28 H5
Swan Street Essex 52 E6
Swanton Abbot Norfk 77 K6
Swanton Morley Norfk 76 E8
Swanton Novers Norfk 76 E5
Swanton Street Kent 38 E10
Swan Village Sandw 58 E6
Swanwick Derbys 84 F10
Swanwick Hants 14 F5
Swarby Lincs 73 Q2
Swardeston Norfk 77 J11
Swarkestone Derbys 72 B5
Swarland Nthumb 119 N10
Swarraton Hants 22 G7
Swartha C Brad 96 C11
Swarthmoor Cumb 94 F5
Swaton Lincs 74 B3
Swavesey Cambs 62 E7
Sway Hants 13 N5
Swayfield Lincs 73 P6
Swaythling C Sotn 22 D11
Sweet Green Worcs 46 B2
Sweetham Devon 9 L5
Sweethaws E Susx 25 M5
Sweetlands Corner
  Kent 26 C2
Sweets Cnwll 5 K2
Sweetshouse Cnwll 4 H5
Swefling Suffk 65 L9
Swepstone Leics 72 B8
Swerford Oxon 48 C8
Swettenham Ches E 82 H11
Swffryd Blae G 30 H5
Swift's Green Kent 26 E3
Swilland Suffk 64 H11
Swillbrook Lancs 88 F4
Swillington Leeds 91 K4
Swimbridge Devon 17 L5
Swimbridge Newland
  Devon 17 L5
Swinbrook Oxon 33 Q2
Swincliffe Kirk 90 G5
Swincliffe N York 97 K9
Swincombe Devon 17 M3
Swinden N York 96 C10
Swinderby Lincs 85 Q8
Swindon Gloucs 46 H9
Swindon Nthumb 119 J11
Swindon Staffs 58 C6
Swindon Swindn 33 M8
Swine E R Yk 93 K3
Swinefleet E R Yk 92 C6
Swineford S Glos 32 C11
Swineshead Bed 61 N7
Swineshead Lincs 74 D2
Swineshead Bridge
  Lincs 74 D2
Swiney Highld 167 M9
Swinford Leics 60 C5
Swinford Oxon 34 D3
Swingfield Minnis
  Kent 27 M3
Swingfield Street
  Kent 27 M3
Swingleton Green
  Suffk 52 G2
Swinhoe Nthumb 119 P5
Swinhope Lincs 93 M11
Swinithwaite N York 96 F3
Swinmore Common
  Herefs 46 C6
Swinscoe Staffs 71 L5
Swinside Cumb 100 H6
Swinstead Lincs 73 Q6
Swinthorpe Lincs 86 E4
Swinton Border 129 L10
Swinton N York 97 K5
Swinton N York 97 F6
Swinton Rothm 91 M11
Swinton Salfd 82 G4
Swithland Leics 72 F8
Swordale Highld 155 Q4
Swordland Highld 145 N9
Swordly Highld 166 B4
Sworton Heath Ches E 82 E8
Swyddffynnon Cerdgn 54 F11
Swyncombe Oxon 35 J6
Swynnerton Staffs 70 F7
Swyre Dorset 11 L7
Sycharth Powys 68 H9
Sychnant Powys 55 M9
Sychtyn Powys 55 M3
Sydallt Wrexhm 69 K3
Syde Gloucs 33 J2
Sydenham Gt Lon 37 J6
Sydenham Oxon 35 J4
Sydenham Damerel
  Devon 5 Q4
Sydenhurst Surrey 23 Q8
Syderstone Norfk 76 A5
Sydling St Nicholas
  Dorset 11 N5
Sydmonton Hants 22 E3
Sydnal Lane Shrops 57 Q3
Syerston Notts 85 M11
Sygun Copper Mine
  Gwynd 67 L5
Syke Rochdl 89 P7
Sykehouse Donc 91 Q7
Syleham Suffk 65 J6
Sylen Carmth 28 H7
Symbister Shet 169 s7
Symington S Ayrs 125 K11
Symington S Lans 116 D3
Symondsbury Dorset 11 J6
Symonds Yat Herefs 45 P11
Sympson Green C Brad 90 F3
Synderford Dorset 10 H4
Synod Inn Cerdgn 42 H4
Syre Highld 165 Q8
Syreford Gloucs 47 K10
Syresham Nhants 48 H6
Syston Leics 72 G8
Syston Lincs 73 N2
Sytchampton Worcs 58 B11
Sywell Nhants 60 H7

T

Tabley Hill Ches E 82 F9
Tackley Oxon 48 E11
Tacolneston Norfk 64 G2
Tadcaster N York 91 M2
Taddington Derbys 83 P10
Taddington Gloucs 47 L8
Taddiport Devon 16 H8
Tadley Hants 22 H4
Tadlow Cambs 62 C11
Tadmarton Oxon 48 C7
Tadwick BaNES 32 D10
Tadworth Surrey 36 F9
Tafarnaubach Blae G 30 F2
Tafarn-y-bwlch Pembks 41 L4
Tafarn-y-Gelyn Denbgs 68 G2
Taff's Well Rhondd 30 F8
Tafolwern Powys 55 K4
Taibach Neath 29 L7
Tain Highld 162 H10
Tain Highld 167 M3
Tai'n Lôn Gwynd 66 G4
Tairbeart W Isls 168 g7
Tai'r Bull Powys 44 D9
Takeley Essex 51 N6
Takeley Street Essex 51 M6
Talachddu Powys 44 F8
Talacre Flints 80 G8
Talaton Devon 9 Q5
Talbenny Pembks 40 F8
Talbot Green Rhondd 30 D8
Talbot Village Bmouth 13 J6
Taleford Devon 10 B5
Talerddig Powys 55 L4
Talgarreg Cerdgn 42 H4
Talgarth Powys 44 H8
Talisker Highld 152 E11
Talke Staffs 70 E4
Talke Pits Staffs 70 E4
Talkin Cumb 111 L9
Talladale Highld 154 B3
Talla Linnfoots Border 116 G6
Tallaminnock S Ayrs 114 H8
Tallarn Green Wrexhm 69 M6
Tallentire Cumb 100 F3
Talley Carmth 43 M8
Tallington Lincs 74 A9
Tallwrn Wrexhm 69 J5
Talmine Highld 165 N4
Talog Carmth 42 F4
Talsarn Cerdgn 43 K3
Talsarnau Gwynd 67 L7
Talskiddy Cnwll 4 E8
Talwrn IoA 78 H9
Talwrn Wrexhm 69 L5
Tal-y-bont Cerdgn 54 F7
Tal-y-bont Conwy 79 P11
Tal-y-bont Gwynd 67 K10
Tal-y-bont Gwynd 79 L10
Talybont-on-Usk Powys 44 G10
Tal-y-Cafn Conwy 79 P10
Tal-y-coed Mons 45 N11
Tal-y-garn Rhondd 30 D9
Tal-y-llyn Gwynd 54 G3
Talysarn Gwynd 66 H4
Tal-y-Waun Torfn 31 J4
Talywern Powys 55 J4
Tamer Lane End Wigan 82 D4
Tamerton Foliot C Plym 6 D6
Tamworth Staffs 59 K4
Tamworth Green Lincs 74 G2
Tamworth Services
  Warwks 59 K4
Tancred N York 97 M3
Tancredston Pembks 40 G5
Tandridge Surrey 37 J10
Tanfield Dur 113 J9
Tanfield Lea Dur 113 J10
Tangiers Pembks 41 J7
Tangley Hants 22 B4
Tangmere W Susx 15 P5
Tangusdale W Isls 168 b17
Tan Hill N York 102 G9
Tankerness Ork 169 e6
Tankersley Barns 91 J11
Tankerton Kent 39 K8
Tannach Highld 167 P7
Tannachie Abers 151 K11
Tannadice Angus 142 H6
Tanner's Green Worcs 58 G10
Tannington Suffk 65 J8
Tannochside N Lans 126 C5
Tansley Derbys 84 D9
Tansor Nhants 61 N2
Tantobie Dur 113 J10
Tanton N York 104 F8
Tanwood Worcs 58 D10
Tanworth in Arden
  Warwks 58 H10
Tan-y-Bwlch Gwynd 67 M6
Tan-y-fron Conwy 68 C2
Tan-y-fron Wrexhm 69 J4
Tan-y-grisiau Gwynd 67 M5
Tan-y-groes Cerdgn 42 E5
Taobh Tuath W Isls 168 e9
Taplow Bucks 35 P8
Tarbert Ag & B 123 L9
Tarbert Ag & B 123 Q6
Tarbert W Isls 168 g7
Tarbet Ag & B 132 C7
Tarbet Highld 145 N9
Tarbet Highld 164 C10
Tarbock Green Knows 81 P7
Tarbolton S Ayrs 114 H2
Tarbrax S Lans 127 J6
Tardebigge Worcs 58 E11
Tarfside Angus 142 H2
Tarland Abers 150 D7
Tarleton Lancs 88 E6
Tarlscough Lancs 88 E8
Tarlton Gloucs 33 J5
Tarnock Somset 19 L4
Tarns Cumb 109 P11
Tarnside Cumb 95 J2
Tarporley Ches W 69 Q2
Tarr Somset 17 R5
Tarrant Crawford Dorset 12 F4
Tarrant Gunville Dorset 12 F2
Tarrant Hinton Dorset 12 F2
Tarrant Keyneston
  Dorset 12 F4
Tarrant Launceston
  Dorset 12 F3
Tarrant Monkton Dorset 12 F3
Tarrant Rawston Dorset 12 F3
Tarrant Rushton Dorset 12 F4
Tarring Neville E Susx 25 K10
Tarrington Herefs 46 B6

Tarskavaig Highld 145 J5
Tarves Abers 159 L11
Tarvin Ches W 81 P11
Tarvin Sands Ches W 81 P11
Tasburgh Norfk 64 H2
Tasley Shrops 57 M6
Taston Oxon 48 C10
Tatenhill Staffs 71 N10
Tathall End M Keyn 49 M5
Tatham Lancs 95 N7
Tathwell Lincs 87 K4
Tatsfield Surrey 37 K9
Tattenhall Ches W 69 N3
Tatterford Norfk 76 B6
Tattersett Norfk 76 A6
Tattershall Lincs 86 H9
Tattershall Bridge Lincs 86 G9
Tattershall Thorpe Lincs 86 H9
Tattingstone Suffk 53 K4
Tattingstone White Horse Suffk 53 K4
Tatworth Somset 10 G3
Tauchers Moray 157 R8
Taunton Somset 18 H10
Taunton Deane Crematorium Somset 18 H10
Taunton Deane Services Somset 18 G10
Taverham Norfk 76 H9
Taverners Green Essex 51 N7
Tavernspite Pembks 41 N8
Tavistock Devon 6 D4
Taw Green Devon 8 G5
Tawstock Devon 17 K6
Taxal Derbys 83 M9
Taychreggan Hotel Ag & B 131 L3
Tay Forest Park P & K 141 J5
Tayinloan Ag & B 123 L10
Taynton Gloucs 46 D10
Taynton Oxon 33 P2
Taynuilt Ag & B 139 J11
Tayport Fife 135 M2
Tayvallich Ag & B 130 E10
Tealby Lincs 86 G2
Tealing Angus 142 G10
Team Valley Gatesd 113 K9
Teangue Highld 145 L6
Teanord Highld 155 Q5
Tebay Cumb 102 B10
Tebay Services Cumb 102 B9
Tebworth C Beds 49 Q9
Tedburn St Mary Devon 9 K6
Teddington Gloucs 47 J8
Teddington Gt Lon 36 E6
Tedstone Delamere Herefs 46 C3
Tedstone Wafer Herefs 46 C3
Teesport R & Cl 104 F6
Teesside Crematorium Middsb 104 E7
Teesside Park S on T 104 E7
Teeton Nhants 60 E6
Teffont Evias Wilts 21 J8
Teffont Magna Wilts 21 J8
Tegryn Pembks 41 P4
Teigh Rutlnd 73 M7
Teigncombe Devon 8 G7
Teigngrace Devon 7 M4
Teignmouth Devon 7 N4
Teindside Border 117 N9
Telford Wrekin 57 M3
Telford Crematorium Wrekin 57 N2
Telford Services Shrops 57 N3
Tellisford Somset 20 F3
Telscombe E Susx 25 K10
Telscombe Cliffs E Susx 25 K10
Tempar P & K 140 G6
Templand D & G 109 N3
Temple Cnwll 5 J7
Temple Mdloth 127 Q6
Temple Balsall Solhll 59 K9
Temple Bar Cerdgn 43 K4
Temple Cloud BaNES 20 B3
Templecombe Somset 20 D10
Temple End Suffk 63 L10
Temple Ewell Kent 27 N3
Temple Grafton Warwks 47 M3
Temple Guiting Gloucs 47 L9
Temple Hirst N York 91 Q6
Temple Normanton Derbys 84 F7
Temple of Fiddes Abers 151 L11
Temple Sowerby Cumb 102 B5
Templeton Devon 9 L2
Templeton Pembks 41 M8
Templetown Dur 112 H10
Tempsford C Beds 61 Q10
Tenbury Wells Worcs 57 K11
Tenby Pembks 41 M10
Tendring Essex 53 K7
Tendring Green Essex 53 K6
Tendring Heath Essex 53 K6
Ten Mile Bank Norfk 75 L11
Tenpenny Heath Essex 53 J7
Tenterden Kent 26 E5
Terling Essex 52 C8
Tern Wrekin 69 R11
Ternhill Shrops 70 A8
Terregles D & G 109 K5
Terrington N York 98 D6
Terrington St Clement Norfk 75 L6
Terrington St John Norfk 75 K8
Terry's Green Warwks 58 H10
Teston Kent 38 B11
Testwood Hants 14 C4
Tetbury Gloucs 32 G6
Tetbury Upton Gloucs 32 G5
Tetchill Shrops 69 L8
Tetcott Devon 5 N2
Tetford Lincs 87 K6
Tetney Lincs 93 P10
Tetney Lock Lincs 93 P10
Tetsworth Oxon 35 J4
Tettenhall Wolves 58 C4
Tettenhall Wood Wolves 58 C5
Teversall Notts 84 G8
Teversham Cambs 62 G9
Teviothead Border 117 N9
Tewin Herts 51 G8
Tewin Wood Herts 50 G7
Tewkesbury Gloucs 46 G8
Teynham Kent 38 G9
Thackley C Brad 90 F3
Thackthwaite Cumb 100 F6
Thackthwaite Cumb 101 M5
Thakeham W Susx 24 D7
Thame Oxon 35 K3

Thames Ditton Surrey 36 E7
Thamesmead Gt Lon 37 L4
Thanet Crematorium Kent 39 Q8
Thanington Kent 39 K10
Thankerton S Lans 116 D3
Tharston Norfk 64 H3
Thatcham W Berk 34 F11
Thatto Heath St Hel 81 Q6
Thaxted Essex 51 P4
Theakston N York 97 M3
Thealby N Linc 92 E7
Theale Somset 19 N5
Theale W Berk 34 H10
Thearne E R Yk 93 J3
The Bank Ches E 70 E3
The Bank Shrops 57 L5
The Beeches Gloucs 33 K4
Theberton Suffk 65 N8
The Beth Chatto Gardens Essex 53 J7
The Blythe Staffs 71 J9
The Bog Shrops 56 F5
The Bourne Worcs 47 J3
The Braes Highld 153 J11
The Bratch Staffs 58 C6
The Broad Herefs 45 P2
The Brunt E Loth 128 H5
The Bungalow IoM 80 e4
The Burf Worcs 57 Q11
The Butts Gloucs 46 G11
The Camp Gloucs 32 H3
The Chequer Wrexhm 69 N6
The City Bed 61 P9
The City Bucks 35 L5
The Common Oxon 47 Q9
The Common Wilts 21 P8
The Common Wilts 33 K7
The Corner Kent 26 B3
The Counties Crematorium Nhants 60 F9
The Cronk IoM 80 d2
Theddingworth Leics 60 E3
Theddlethorpe All Saints Lincs 87 N3
Theddlethorpe St Helen Lincs 87 N3
The Den N Ayrs 125 J7
The Forest of Dean Crematorium Gloucs 32 B2
The Forge Herefs 45 L3
The Forstal Kent 26 H4
The Fouralls Shrops 70 B8
The Garden of England Crematorium Kent 38 E8
The Green Cumb 94 D4
The Green Essex 52 C8
The Green N York 105 L9
The Green Wilts 20 G8
The Grove Worcs 46 G6
The Haven W Susx 24 C4
The Haw Gloucs 46 F9
The Headland Hartpl 104 F4
The Hill Cumb 94 D4
The Holt Wokham 35 M9
The Hundred Herefs 45 Q2
Thelbridge Cross Devon 9 J2
The Leacon Kent 26 G5
The Lee Bucks 35 P4
The Lhen IoM 80 e1
The Linn Crematorium E Rens 125 P6
Thelnetham Suffk 64 E6
The Lochs Moray 157 Q5
Thelveton Norfk 64 H5
Thelwall Warrtn 82 E7
The Manchester Crematorium Manch 82 H6
The Marsh Powys 56 E5
Themelthorpe Norfk 76 F7
The Middles Dur 113 K10
The Moor Kent 26 C6
The Mumbles Swans 28 H7
The Murray S Lans 125 Q7
The Mythe Gloucs 46 G8
The Narth Mons 31 P3
The Neuk Abers 151 J8
Thenford Nhants 48 F6
Theobald's Green Wilts 33 K11
The Park Crematorium Hants 23 N5
The Quarry Gloucs 32 D5
The Quarter Kent 26 E3
The Reddings Gloucs 46 H10
Therfield Herts 50 H3
The Rhôs Powys 44 H8
The Rose Hill Crematorium Donc 91 Q10
The Ross P & K 133 M3
The Sands Surrey 23 N5
The Shoe Wilts 32 F10
The Smithies Shrops 57 M5
The Spike Cambs 62 G11
The Spring Warwks 59 L10
The Square Torfn 31 J5
The Stair Kent 37 P11
The Stocks Kent 26 F6
The Straits Hants 23 L7
The Strand Wilts 20 H3
The Tank Museum (Bovington) Dorset 12 D7
Thetford Norfk 64 B5
Thetford Forest Park 63 P3
Thethwaite Cumb 101 J3
The Towans Cnwll 2 F6
The Vale Crematorium Luton 50 D6
The Vauld Herefs 45 Q5
The Wyke Shrops 57 N3
Theydon Bois Essex 51 K11
Thicket Priory N York 92 A2
Thickwood Wilts 32 F10
Thimbleby Lincs 86 H6
Thimbleby N York 104 D11
Thingwall Wirral 81 K8
Thirkleby N York 97 Q5
Thirlby N York 97 Q4
Thirlestane Border 128 F3
Thirn N York 97 K3
Thirsk N York 97 P4
Thirtleby E R Yk 93 L4
Thistleton Lancs 88 E3
Thistleton Rutlnd 73 N7
Thistley Green Suffk 63 L5
Thixendale N York 98 G8
Thockrington Nthumb 112 E5
Tholomas Drove Cambs 74 H9
Tholthorpe N York 97 Q7
Thomas Chapel Pembks 41 M9
Thomas Close Cumb 101 M2

Thomastown Abers 158 E10
Thomas Town Warwks 47 L2
Thompson Norfk 64 C2
Thong Kent 37 Q6
Thoralby N York 96 F3
Thoresby Notts 85 K6
Thoresthorpe Lincs 87 N5
Thoresway Lincs 93 L11
Thorganby Lincs 93 M11
Thorganby N York 92 A2
Thorgill N York 105 K11
Thorington Suffk 65 N7
Thorington Street Suffk 52 H4
Thorlby N York 96 E10
Thorley Herts 51 L7
Thorley IoW 14 C9
Thorley Houses Herts 51 L6
Thorley Street IoW 14 C9
Thormanby N York 97 Q6
Thornaby-on-Tees S on T 104 E7
Thornage Norfk 76 F4
Thornborough Bucks 49 K8
Thornborough N York 97 L5
Thornbury C Brad 90 F4
Thornbury Devon 16 H9
Thornbury Herefs 46 B3
Thornbury S Glos 32 B6
Thornby Cumb 110 E10
Thornby Nhants 60 E5
Thorncliff Staffs 71 J3
Thorncliffe Crematorium Cumb 94 D6
Thorncombe Dorset 10 H4
Thorncombe Street Surrey 23 Q6
Thorncott Green C Beds 61 Q10
Thorncross IoW 14 D10
Thorndon Suffk 64 G8
Thorndon Cross Devon 8 D6
Thorne Donc 92 A8
Thorne Coffin Somset 19 P11
Thornecroft Devon 7 K5
Thornehillhead Devon 16 G8
Thorner Leeds 91 K2
Thornes Staffs 58 G4
Thornes Wakefd 91 J7
Thorne St Margaret Somset 18 F10
Thorney Bucks 36 B5
Thorney C Pete 74 E10
Thorney Notts 85 Q6
Thorney Somset 19 M10
Thorney Hill Hants 13 M5
Thorney Island W Susx 15 L6
Thorney Toll Cambs 74 F10
Thornfalcon Somset 19 J10
Thornford Dorset 11 N2
Thorngrafton Nthumb 111 Q7
Thorngrove Somset 19 L8
Thorngumbald E R Yk 93 M5
Thornham Norfk 75 P2
Thornham Magna Suffk 64 G7
Thornham Parva Suffk 64 G7
Thornhaugh C Pete 73 R10
Thornhill C Sotn 14 E4
Thornhill Caerph 30 G8
Thornhill Cumb 100 D9
Thornhill D & G 116 B11
Thornhill Derbys 83 Q8
Thornhill Kirk 90 H7
Thornhill Stirlg 133 K7
Thornhill Crematorium Cardif 30 G8
Thornhill Lees Kirk 90 G7
Thornhills Calder 90 F6
Thornholme E R Yk 99 N8
Thornicombe Dorset 12 E4
Thornington Nthumb 118 G4
Thornley Dur 103 M3
Thornley Dur 104 C3
Thornley Gate Nthumb 112 B9
Thornliebank E Rens 125 P6
Thorns Suffk 63 M9
Thornsett Derbys 83 M7
Thorns Green Ches E 82 G8
Thornthwaite Cumb 100 H5
Thornthwaite N York 97 J9
Thornton Angus 142 F8
Thornton Bucks 49 K7
Thornton C Brad 90 D4
Thornton E R Yk 98 F11
Thornton Fife 134 H8
Thornton Lancs 88 C2
Thornton Leics 72 D9
Thornton Lincs 86 H7
Thornton Middsb 104 E8
Thornton Nthumb 129 P10
Thornton Pembks 40 H9
Thornton Sefton 81 L4
Thornton Curtis N Linc 93 J7
Thornton Garden of Rest Crematorium Sefton 81 L4
Thorntonhall S Lans 125 P6
Thornton Heath Gt Lon 36 H7
Thornton Hough Wirral 81 L8
Thornton-in-Craven N York 96 D11
Thornton in Lonsdale N York 95 P6
Thornton-le-Beans N York 97 N2
Thornton-le-Clay N York 98 D7
Thornton le Dale N York 98 G4
Thornton le Moor Lincs 92 H11
Thornton-le-Moor N York 97 N3
Thornton-le-Moors Ches W 81 N10
Thornton-le-Street N York 97 P3
Thorntonloch E Loth 129 K5
Thornton Rust N York 96 E3
Thornton Steward N York 97 J3
Thornton Watlass N York 97 K3
Thornwood Common Essex 51 L10
Thornydykes Border 128 G10
Thornythwaite Cumb 101 L6
Thoroton Notts 73 K2
Thorp Arch Leeds 91 M4
Thorpe Derbys 71 M4
Thorpe E R Yk 99 K4
Thorpe Lincs 87 N4
Thorpe N York 96 F8
Thorpe Norfk 65 N2
Thorpe Notts 85 N11
Thorpe Surrey 36 B7
Thorpe Abbotts Norfk 64 H6

Thorpe Acre Leics 72 E7
Thorpe Arnold Leics 73 K6
Thorpe Audlin Wakefd 91 M7
Thorpe Bassett N York 98 H6
Thorpe Bay Sthend 38 F4
Thorpe by Water Rutlnd 73 M11
Thorpe Common Rothm 91 K11
Thorpe Constantine Staffs 59 L3
Thorpe End Norfk 77 K9
Thorpe Green Essex 53 L7
Thorpe Green Lancs 88 H6
Thorpe Green Suffk 64 C11
Thorpe Hesley Rothm 91 K11
Thorpe in Balne Donc 91 P8
Thorpe Langton Leics 60 F2
Thorpe Larches Dur 104 C5
Thorpe Lea Surrey 36 B6
Thorpe le Fallows Lincs 86 B4
Thorpe-le-Soken Essex 53 L7
Thorpe le Street E R Yk 92 D2
Thorpe Malsor Nhants 60 H5
Thorpe Mandeville Nhants 48 F6
Thorpe Market Norfk 77 J4
Thorpe Marriot Norfk 76 H8
Thorpe Morieux Suffk 64 C11
Thorpeness Suffk 65 P10
Thorpe on the Hill Leeds 91 J5
Thorpe on the Hill Lincs 86 B7
Thorpe Park Surrey 36 B7
Thorpe St Andrew Norfk 77 K10
Thorpe St Peter Lincs 87 N8
Thorpe Salvin Rothm 84 H4
Thorpe Satchville Leics 73 J8
Thorpe Thewles S on T 104 C6
Thorpe Tilney Lincs 86 F9
Thorpe Underwood N York 97 Q9
Thorpe Underwood Nhants 60 G4
Thorpe Waterville Nhants 61 M4
Thorpe Willoughby N York 91 P4
Thorpland Norfk 75 M9
Thorrington Essex 53 J8
Thorverton Devon 9 M4
Thrales End C Beds 50 D7
Thrandeston Suffk 64 G6
Thrapston Nhants 61 L5
Threapland Cumb 100 G3
Threapland N York 96 E8
Threapwood Ches W 69 M6
Threapwood Staffs 71 J6
Threapwood Head Staffs 71 J6
Threave S Ayrs 114 F6
Threave Castle D & G 108 F8
Three Ashes Herefs 45 Q10
Three Bridges W Susx 24 G3
Three Burrows Cnwll 3 J4
Three Chimneys Kent 26 D4
Three Cocks Powys 44 H7
Three Counties Crematorium Essex 52 C6
Three Crosses Swans 28 G6
Three Cups Corner E Susx 25 P6
Three Gates Worcs 46 C2
Threehammer Common Norfk 77 L8
Three Hammers Cnwll 5 L4
Three Holes Norfk 75 K10
Threekingham Lincs 74 A3
Three Leg Cross E Susx 25 Q4
Three Legged Cross Dorset 13 J3
Three Mile Cross Wokham 35 K11
Threemilestone Cnwll 3 K6
Three Miletown W Loth 127 K2
Three Oaks E Susx 26 D9
Threlkeld Cumb 101 K5
Threshers Bush Essex 51 L9
Threshfield N York 96 E8
Thrigby Norfk 77 P9
Thringarth Dur 102 H6
Thringstone Leics 72 C7
Thrintoft N York 97 M2
Thriplow Cambs 62 F11
Throapham Rothm 84 H3
Throckenhalt Lincs 74 G9
Throcking Herts 50 H4
Throckley N u Ty 113 J7
Throckmorton Worcs 47 J4
Throop Bmouth 13 K5
Throop Dorset 12 D6
Throphill Nthumb 112 H3
Thropton Nthumb 119 K10
Throsk Stirlg 133 N7
Througham Gloucs 32 H3
Throughgate D & G 109 J4
Throwleigh Devon 8 G6
Throwley Kent 38 G10
Throwley Forstal Kent 38 G11
Thrumpton Notts 72 E4
Thrumpton Notts 85 M4
Thrumster Highld 167 P7
Thrunscoe NE Lin 93 P9
Thrunton Nthumb 119 J8
Thrup Oxon 33 Q5
Thrupp Gloucs 32 G4
Thrupp Oxon 48 E11
Thrushelton Devon 8 B7
Thrussington Leics 72 H7
Thruxton Hants 21 Q5
Thruxton Herefs 45 N8
Thrybergh Rothm 91 M11
Thulston Derbys 72 C4
Thurcaston Leics 72 F8
Thurcroft Rothm 84 G3
Thurdon Cnwll 16 D9
Thurgarton Norfk 76 H5
Thurgarton Notts 85 L11
Thurgoland Barns 90 H10
Thurlaston Leics 72 E11
Thurlaston Warwks 59 Q10
Thurlbear Somset 19 J10
Thurlby Lincs 74 A7
Thurlby Lincs 86 B8
Thurlby Lincs 87 N5
Thurleigh Bed 61 N9
Thurlestone Devon 6 H10
Thurloxton Somset 19 J8
Thurlstone Barns 90 G10
Thurlton Norfk 65 N2
Thurlwood Ches E 70 E3
Thurmaston Leics 72 G9
Thurnby Leics 72 G10

Thurne Norfk 77 N8
Thurnham Kent 38 D10
Thurning Nhants 61 N4
Thurning Norfk 76 F6
Thurnscoe Barns 91 M9
Thurrock Services Thurr 37 N5
Thursby Cumb 110 F10
Thursden Lancs 89 Q4
Thursford Norfk 76 D5
Thursley Surrey 23 N7
Thurso Highld 167 K3
Thurstaston Wirral 81 J8
Thurston Suffk 64 C8
Thurston Clough Oldham 90 B9
Thurstonfield Cumb 110 F9
Thurstonland Kirk 90 F8
Thurston Planch Suffk 64 C9
Thurton Norfk 77 L11
Thurvaston Derbys 71 N4
Thuxton Norfk 76 E10
Thwaite N York 102 G11
Thwaite Suffk 64 G8
Thwaite Head Cumb 94 G2
Thwaites C Brad 90 D2
Thwaite St Mary Norfk 65 L2
Thwaites Brow C Brad 90 D2
Thwing E R Yk 99 L5
Tibbermore P & K 134 C3
Tibbers D & G 116 B11
Tibberton Gloucs 46 E10
Tibberton Worcs 46 H3
Tibberton Wrekin 70 B10
Tibbie Shiels Inn Border 117 J6
Tibenham Norfk 64 G4
Tibshelf Derbys 84 F8
Tibthorpe E R Yk 99 K9
Ticehurst E Susx 25 Q4
Tichborne Hants 22 G8
Tickencote Rutlnd 73 P9
Tickenham N Som 31 N10
Tickford End M Keyn 49 N6
Tickhill Donc 85 J2
Ticklerton Shrops 56 H6
Ticknall Derbys 72 B6
Tickton E R Yk 93 J2
Tidbury Green Solhll 58 H9
Tidcombe Wilts 21 Q3
Tiddington Oxon 34 H4
Tiddington Warwks 47 P3
Tiddleywink Wilts 32 G9
Tidebrook E Susx 25 P4
Tideford Cnwll 5 P10
Tideford Cross Cnwll 5 N9
Tidenham Gloucs 31 Q5
Tideswell Derbys 83 Q9
Tidmarsh W Berk 34 H10
Tidmington Warwks 47 Q7
Tidpit Hants 21 L11
Tidworth Wilts 21 P5
Tiers Cross Pembks 40 H8
Tiffield Nhants 49 K4
Tigerton Angus 143 J5
Tigh a Ghearraidh W Isls 168 c10
Tigharry W Isls 168 c10
Tighnabruaich Ag & B 124 B3
Tigley Devon 7 K6
Tilbrook Cambs 61 N7
Tilbury Thurr 37 P5
Tilbury Green Essex 52 B3
Tilbury Juxta Clare Essex 52 C3
Tile Cross Birm 59 J7
Tile Hill Covtry 59 L9
Tilehouse Green Solhll 59 J9
Tilehurst Readg 35 J10
Tilford Surrey 23 N6
Tilgate W Susx 24 G3
Tilgate Forest Row W Susx 24 G4
Tilham Street Somset 19 Q7
Tillers Green Gloucs 46 C8
Tillicoultry Clacks 133 Q8
Tillietudlem S Lans 126 E8
Tillingham Essex 52 G11
Tillington Herefs 45 P6
Tillington W Susx 23 Q10
Tillington Common Herefs 45 P5
Tillybirloch Abers 150 H6
Tillyfourie Abers 150 G5
Tillygreig Abers 151 M3
Tillyrie P & K 134 E6
Tilmanstone Kent 39 P11
Tilney All Saints Norfk 75 L7
Tilney High End Norfk 75 L7
Tilney St Lawrence Norfk 75 K8
Tilshead Wilts 21 K5
Tilstock Shrops 69 P7
Tilston Ches W 69 N4
Tilstone Bank Ches W 69 Q3
Tilstone Fearnall Ches W 69 Q2
Tilsworth C Beds 49 Q10
Tilton on the Hill Leics 73 J9
Tiltups End Gloucs 32 F5
Tilty Essex 51 N5
Timberland Lincs 86 F9
Timbersbrook Ches E 70 F2
Timberscombe Somset 18 C6
Timble N York 97 J10
Timewell Devon 18 C9
Timpanheck D & G 110 F2
Timperley Traffd 82 G7
Timsbury BaNES 20 C3
Timsbury Hants 22 B10
Timsgarraigh W Isls 168 f4
Timsgearraidh W Isls 168 f4
Timworth Suffk 64 B8
Timworth Green Suffk 64 B8
Tincleton Dorset 12 C6
Tindale Cumb 111 M9
Tindale Crescent Dur 103 P5
Tingewick Bucks 49 J8
Tingley Leeds 90 H5
Tingrith C Beds 50 B4
Tingwall Airport Shet 169 r9
Tinhay Devon 5 P4
Tinker's Hill Hants 22 D5
Tinkersley Derbys 84 C8
Tinsley Sheff 84 F2
Tinsley Green W Susx 24 G3
Tintagel Cnwll 4 H4
Tintagel Castle Cnwll 4 H4
Tintern Abbey Mons 31 P4
Tintern Parva Mons 31 P4
Tintinhull Somset 19 N11
Tintwistle Derbys 83 M5
Tinwald D & G 109 M4
Tinwell Rutlnd 73 Q9
Tippacott Devon 17 P2
Tipp's End Norfk 75 K11

Tiptoe - Tunstall 303

Tiptoe Hants 13 N5
Tipton Sandw 58 E6
Tipton Green Sandw 58 E6
Tipton St John Devon 10 B6
Tiptree Essex 52 E8
Tiptree Heath Essex 52 E8
Tirabad Powys 44 B6
Tiree Ag & B 136 C7
Tiree Airport Ag & B 136 C7
Tiretigan Ag & B 123 M7
Tirley Gloucs 46 F9
Tirphil Caerph 30 F4
Tirril Cumb 101 P5
Tir-y-fron Flints 69 J3
Tisbury Wilts 20 H9
Tisman's Common W Susx 24 C4
Tissington Derbys 71 M4
Titchberry Devon 16 C6
Titchfield Hants 14 F5
Titchfield Common Hants 14 F5
Titchmarsh Nhants 61 M5
Titchwell Norfk 75 Q2
Tithby Notts 72 H3
Titley Herefs 45 L2
Titmore Green Herts 50 F5
Titsey Surrey 37 K10
Titson Cnwll 16 C11
Tittensor Staffs 70 F7
Tittleshall Norfk 76 B7
Titton Worcs 58 B11
Tiverton Ches W 69 Q2
Tiverton Devon 9 N2
Tivetshall St Margaret Norfk 64 H4
Tivetshall St Mary Norfk 64 H4
Tivington Somset 18 B5
Tivy Dale Barns 90 H9
Tixall Staffs 70 H10
Tixover Rutlnd 73 P10
Toab Shet 169 q12
Toadhole Derbys 84 E9
Toadmoor Derbys 84 D10
Tobermory Ag & B 137 N4
Toberonochy Ag & B 130 E6
Tobha Mor W Isls 168 c14
Tocher Abers 158 G11
Tochieneal Moray 158 D4
Tockenham Wilts 33 K9
Tockenham Wick Wilts 33 K8
Tocketts R & Cl 104 H7
Tockholes Bl w D 89 K6
Tockington S Glos 32 B7
Tockwith N York 97 Q10
Todber Dorset 20 E11
Todburn Nthumb 119 M11
Toddington C Beds 50 B5
Toddington Gloucs 47 K8
Toddington Services C Beds 50 B5
Todds Green Herts 50 F5
Todenham Gloucs 47 P7
Todhills Angus 142 G10
Todhills Cumb 110 G8
Todhills Dur 103 P4
Todhills Services Cumb 110 G8
Todmorden Calder 89 Q6
Todwick Rothm 84 G4
Toft Cambs 62 E9
Toft Ches E 82 G9
Toft Lincs 73 R7
Toft Shet 169 r6
Toft Warwks 59 Q10
Toft Hill Dur 103 N5
Toft Hill Lincs 86 H8
Toft Monks Norfk 65 N3
Toft next Newton Lincs 86 D3
Toftrees Norfk 76 B6
Toftwood Norfk 76 D9
Togston Nthumb 119 P10
Tokavaig Highld 145 K5
Tokers Green Oxon 35 K9
Tolastadh W Isls 168 k3
Toldish Cnwll 4 E10
Tolland Somset 18 F8
Tollard Farnham Dorset 21 J11
Tollard Royal Wilts 20 H11
Toll Bar Donc 91 P9
Tollbar End Covtry 59 N9
Toller Fratrum Dorset 11 M5
Toller Porcorum Dorset 11 M5
Tollerton N York 97 R8
Tollerton Notts 72 G4
Toller Whelme Dorset 11 L4
Tollesbury Essex 52 G9
Tolleshunt D'Arcy Essex 52 F9
Tolleshunt Knights Essex 52 F9
Tolleshunt Major Essex 52 F9
Tolpuddle Dorset 12 C6
Tolsta W Isls 168 k3
Tolworth Gt Lon 36 E7
Tomatin Highld 148 E2
Tomchrasky Highld 146 H5
Tomdoun Highld 146 F7
Tomich Highld 147 J2
Tomich Highld 155 P8
Tomich Highld 156 B3
Tomich Highld 162 E5
Tomintoul Moray 149 M4
Tomlow Warwks 48 E2
Tomnacross Highld 155 P9
Tomnavoulin Moray 149 N2
Tompkin Staffs 70 G4
Ton Mons 31 K4
Ton Mons 31 L5
Tonbridge Kent 37 N11
Tondu Brdgnd 29 N8
Tonedale Somset 18 F10
Ton fanau Gwynd 54 D4
Tong C Brad 90 G4
Tong Kent 38 G10
Tong Shrops 57 P3
Tonge Leics 72 C6
Tong Green Kent 38 G11
Tongham Surrey 23 N5
Tongland D & G 108 E10
Tong Norton Shrops 57 P3
Tongue Highld 165 N5
Tongue End Lincs 74 C7
Tongwynlais Cardif 30 F8
Tonmawr Neath 29 M5
Tonna Neath 29 L5
Ton-teg Rhondd 30 E7
Tonwell Herts 50 H7
Tonypandy Rhondd 30 C6
Tonyrefail Rhondd 30 D7
Toot Baldon Oxon 34 G4
Toot Hill Essex 51 M10
Toothill Hants 22 C11
Toothill Swindn 33 M8
Tooting Gt Lon 36 G6
Tooting Bec Gt Lon 36 G6
Topcliffe N York 97 N5
Topcroft Norfk 65 K3
Topcroft Street Norfk 65 K3
Top End Bed 61 M8
Topham Donc 91 Q7
Top of Hebers Rochdl 89 P9
Toppesfield Essex 52 B4
Toppings Bolton 89 L8
Toprow Norfk 64 H2
Topsham Devon 9 N7
Top-y-rhos Flints 69 J3
Torbeg N Ayrs 120 G6
Torboll Highld 162 H7
Torbreck Highld 156 A9
Torbryan Devon 7 L5
Torcastle Highld 139 L2
Torcross Devon 7 L10
Tore Highld 155 R7
Torfrey Cnwll 5 J11
Torinturk Ag & B 123 P7
Torksey Lincs 85 P5
Tormarton S Glos 32 E9
Tormore N Ayrs 120 G5
Tornagrain Highld 156 D7
Tornaveen Abers 150 G6
Torness Highld 147 P2
Toronto Dur 103 N4
Torpenhow Cumb 100 H3
Torphichen W Loth 126 H3
Torphins Abers 150 G7
Torpoint Cnwll 6 C7
Torquay Torbay 7 N6
Torquay Crematorium Torbay 7 N5
Torquhan Border 128 C10
Torr Devon 6 F8
Torran Highld 153 K8
Torrance E Duns 125 Q3
Torranyard N Ayrs 125 K9
Torre Somset 18 D7
Torridon Highld 154 B6
Torridon House Highld 153 R6
Torrin Highld 145 J3
Torrisdale Ag & B 120 E4
Torrisdale Highld 165 Q4
Torrish Highld 163 M3
Torrisholme Lancs 95 K8
Torrobull Highld 162 D6
Torry C Aber 151 N6
Torryburn Fife 134 C10
Torteval Guern 10 a2
Torthorwald D & G 109 M5
Tortington W Susx 24 B10
Torton Worcs 58 B10
Tortworth S Glos 32 D6
Torvaig Highld 152 H9
Torver Cumb 94 F2
Torwood Falk 133 N10
Torwoodlee Border 117 P3
Torworth Notts 85 L3
Tosberry Devon 16 D7
Toscaig Highld 153 N10
Toseland Cambs 62 B8
Tosside Lancs 95 R9
Tostock Suffk 64 D9
Totaig Highld 152 C7
Tote Highld 152 G8
Tote Highld 153 J5
Tote Hill W Susx 23 N10
Totford Hants 22 G7
Tothill Lincs 87 M4
Totland IoW 13 P7
Totley Sheff 84 D5
Totley Brook Sheff 84 D4
Totnes Devon 7 L6
Toton Notts 72 E4
Totronald Ag & B 136 F4
Totscore Highld 152 F4
Tottenham Gt Lon 36 H2
Tottenhill Norfk 75 M8
Totteridge Gt Lon 36 F2
Totternhoe C Beds 49 Q10
Tottington Bury 89 M8
Tottleworth Lancs 89 L4
Totton Hants 14 C4
Touchen End W & M 35 N9
Toulston N York 91 M2
Toulton Somset 18 G8
Toulvaddie Highld 163 K10
Tovil Kent 38 C11
Towan Cnwll 3 Q4
Towan Cnwll 4 D7
Toward Ag & B 124 E4
Toward Quay Ag & B 124 E4
Towcester Nhants 49 J5
Towednack Cnwll 2 D6
Towersey Oxon 35 K3
Towie Abers 150 C5
Tow Law Dur 103 M3
Town End Cambs 74 H11
Town End Cumb 95 J4
Town End Cumb 101 K9
Town End Cumb 102 B5
Townend W Duns 125 K2
Towngate Cumb 111 K11
Towngate Lincs 74 B8
Town Green Lancs 88 E9
Town Green Norfk 77 M9
Townhead Barns 83 Q4
Townhead Cumb 100 E3
Town Head Cumb 101 M10
Townhead Cumb 102 B4
Townhead D & G 109 M3
Town Head N York 96 B9
Townhead of Greenlaw D & G 108 F8
Townhill Fife 134 E10
Town Kelloe Dur 104 C3
Townlake Devon 5 Q7
Town Lane Wigan 82 E5
Town Littleworth E Susx 25 K7
Town of Lowton Wigan 82 D5
Town Row E Susx 25 N4
Towns End Hants 22 G3
Townsend Somset 10 H2
Townshend Cnwll 2 F7
Town Street Suffk 63 N3
Townwell S Glos 32 D6
Town Yetholm Border 118 F5
Towthorpe C York 98 C9
Towthorpe E R Yk 98 H8
Towton N York 91 M3
Towyn Conwy 80 D9
Toxteth Lpool 81 M7
Toynton All Saints Lincs 87 L8
Toynton Fen Side Lincs 87 L8
Toynton St Peter Lincs 87 M8
Toy's Hill Kent 37 L10
Trabboch E Ayrs 114 H3
Trabbochburn E Ayrs 115 J3
Traboe Cnwll 3 J9
Tracebridge Somset 18 E10
Tradespark Highld 156 F6
Trallong Powys 44 D9
Tramway Museum Derbys 84 D9
Tranent E Loth 128 C5
Tranmere Wirral 81 L7
Trantelbeg Highld 166 E6
Trantlemore Highld 166 E6
Tranwell Nthumb 113 J4
Trapp Carmth 43 N11
Traprain E Loth 128 F4
Trap's Green Warwks 58 H11
Trapshill W Berk 22 C2
Traquair Border 117 L4
Trash Green W Berk 35 J11
Trawden Lancs 89 Q3
Trawscoed Cerdgn 54 F10
Trawsfynydd Gwynd 67 N7
Trealaw Rhondd 30 D6
Treales Lancs 88 E4
Trearddur Bay IoA 78 D9
Treaslane Highld 152 F7
Treator Cnwll 4 E6
Tre Aubrey V Glam 30 D10
Trebanog Rhondd 30 D6
Trebanos Neath 29 K4
Trebartha Cnwll 5 M6
Trebarwith Cnwll 4 H4
Trebeath Cnwll 5 M4
Trebetherick Cnwll 4 E6
Treborough Somset 18 D7
Trebudannon Cnwll 4 D9
Trebullett Cnwll 5 N6
Treburgett Cnwll 4 H6
Treburley Cnwll 5 P6
Treburrick Cnwll 4 D7
Trebyan Cnwll 4 H9
Trecastle Powys 44 B9
Trecogo Cnwll 5 N5
Trecott Devon 8 F4
Trecwn Pembks 41 J4
Trecynon Rhondd 30 C4
Tredaule Cnwll 5 L5
Tredavoe Cnwll 2 D8
Tredegar Blae G 30 F3
Tredethy Cnwll 4 H7
Tredington Gloucs 46 H9
Tredington Warwks 47 Q6
Tredinnick Cnwll 4 E7
Tredinnick Cnwll 4 G10
Tredinnick Cnwll 5 K8
Tredinnick Cnwll 5 L10
Tredinnick Cnwll 5 M10
Tredomen Powys 44 G8
Tredrissi Pembks 41 L2
Tredrizzick Cnwll 4 F6
Tredunnock Mons 31 L6
Tredustan Powys 44 G8
Treen Cnwll 2 B9
Treen Cnwll 2 C6
Treesmill Cnwll 4 H10
Treeton Rothm 84 F3
Trefasser Pembks 40 G3
Trefdraeth IoA 78 G10
Trefecca Powys 44 G8
Trefeglwys Powys 55 M6
Trefenter Cerdgn 54 E11
Treffgarne Pembks 41 J6
Treffgarne Owen Pembks 40 G5
Trefforest Rhondd 30 E7
Treffynnon Pembks 40 G5
Trefil Blae G 30 F2
Trefilan Cerdgn 43 K3
Trefin Pembks 40 F4
Treflach Wood Shrops 69 J9
Trefnannau Powys 68 H11
Trefnant Denbgs 80 F10
Trefonen Shrops 69 J9
Trefor Gwynd 66 F5
Trefor IoA 78 F8
Trefrew Cnwll 5 J5
Trefriw Conwy 67 P2
Tregadillett Cnwll 5 M5
Tre-gagle Mons 31 P3
Tregaian IoA 78 H8
Tregare Mons 31 M2
Tregarne Cnwll 3 K9
Tregaron Cerdgn 43 N3
Tregarth Gwynd 79 L11
Tregaswith Cnwll 4 D9
Tregatta Cnwll 4 H4
Tregawne Cnwll 4 G8
Tregeare Cnwll 5 L4
Tregeiriog Wrexhm 68 G8
Tregele IoA 78 F6
Tregellist Cnwll 4 G6
Tregenna Cnwll 3 M5
Tregeseal Cnwll 2 B7
Tregew Cnwll 3 L7
Tre-Gibbon Rhondd 30 C3
Tregidden Cnwll 3 K9
Tregiskey Cnwll 3 Q4
Treglemais Pembks 40 F5
Tregole Cnwll 5 K2
Tregolls Cnwll 3 J6
Tregonce Cnwll 4 E7
Tregonetha Cnwll 4 F9
Tregony Cnwll 3 N5
Tregoodwell Cnwll 5 J5
Tregorrick Cnwll 3 Q3
Tregoss Cnwll 4 F9
Tregoyd Powys 44 H7
Tregrehan Mills Cnwll 3 Q3
Tre-groes Cerdgn 42 H6
Tregullon Cnwll 4 H9
Tregunna Cnwll 4 F7
Tregunnon Cnwll 5 L5
Tregurrian Cnwll 4 D8
Tregynon Powys 55 P5
Tre-gynwr Carmth 42 H11
Trehafod Rhondd 30 D6
Trehan Cnwll 5 Q10
Treharris Myr Td 30 E5
Treharrock Cnwll 4 G6
Trehemborne Cnwll 4 D7
Treherbert Carmth 43 L5
Treherbert Rhondd 29 P5
Trehunist Cnwll 5 N9
Trekenner Cnwll 5 N6
Treknow Cnwll 4 H4
Trelan Cnwll 3 J10
Trelash Cnwll 5 K3
Trelassick Cnwll 3 M3
Trelawne Cnwll 5 L11
Trelawnyd Flints 80 F9
Treleague Cnwll 3 K9
Treleaver Cnwll 3 K10
Trelech Carmth 41 Q4
Trelech a'r Betws Carmth 42 F9
Treleddyd-fawr Pembks 40 E5
Trelew Cnwll 3 L6
Trelewis Myr Td 30 F5
Treligga Cnwll 4 G5
Trelights Cnwll 4 F6
Trelill Cnwll 4 G6
Trelinnoe Cnwll 5 N5
Trelion Cnwll 3 N3
Trelissick Cnwll 3 L6
Trelissick Garden Cnwll 3 L6
Trellech Mons 31 P3
Trelleck Grange Mons 31 N4
Trelogan Flints 80 G8
Trelow Cnwll 4 E8
Trelowarren Cnwll 3 J9
Trelowia Cnwll 5 M10
Treluggan Cnwll 3 M6
Trelystan Powys 56 D4
Tremadog Gwynd 67 K7
Tremail Cnwll 5 K4
Tremain Cerdgn 42 D5
Tremaine Cnwll 5 L4
Tremar Cnwll 5 M8
Trematon Cnwll 5 P10
Trembraze Cnwll 5 M8
Tremeirchion Denbgs 80 F10
Tremethick Cross Cnwll 2 C7
Tremore Cnwll 4 G9
Tre-Mostyn Flints 80 G9
Trenance Cnwll 3 L9
Trenance Cnwll 4 D8
Trenance Cnwll 4 E7
Trenarren Cnwll 3 Q4
Trench Wrekin 57 M2
Trench Green Oxon 35 J9
Trendeal Cnwll 3 M3
Trendrine Cnwll 2 D6
Treneague Cnwll 4 F7
Trenear Cnwll 2 H7
Treneglos Cnwll 5 L4
Trenerth Cnwll 2 G6
Trenewan Cnwll 5 K11
Trenewth Cnwll 4 H6
Trengune Cnwll 5 K3
Treninnick Cnwll 4 C9
Trenowah Cnwll 4 B10
Trenoweth Cnwll 3 K7
Trent Dorset 19 Q11
Trentham C Stke 70 F6
Trentishoe Devon 17 L2
Trentlock Derbys 72 D4
Trent Port Lincs 85 P4
Trent Vale C Stke 70 F6
Trenwheal Cnwll 2 G7
Treoes V Glam 29 P9
Treorchy Rhondd 30 C5
Trequite Cnwll 4 G6
Tre'r-ddol Cerdgn 54 F6
Trerhyngyll V Glam 30 D9
Trerulefoot Cnwll 5 N10
Tresaith Cerdgn 42 E4
Tresawle Cnwll 3 M4
Tresco IoS 2 b2
Tresco Heliport IoS 2 b2
Trescott Staffs 58 C5
Trescowe Cnwll 2 F7
Tresean Cnwll 4 B10
Tresham Gloucs 32 E6
Treshnish Isles Ag & B 136 G7
Tresillian Cnwll 3 M4
Tresinney Cnwll 5 J5
Treskinnick Cross Cnwll 5 L2
Tresmeer Cnwll 5 L4
Tresparrett Cnwll 5 J3
Tressait P & K 141 K5
Tresta Shet 169 q8
Tresta Shet 169 t4
Treswell Notts 85 N5
Treswithian Cnwll 2 G5
Treswithian Downs Crematorium Cnwll 2 G5
Tre Taliesin Cerdgn 54 F6
Trethevey Cnwll 4 H4
Trethewey Cnwll 2 B9
Trethomas Caerph 30 G7
Trethosa Cnwll 3 N3
Trethurgy Cnwll 4 G10
Tretio Pembks 40 E5
Tretire Herefs 45 Q10
Tretower Powys 44 H10
Treuddyn Flints 69 J3
Trevadlock Cnwll 5 M6
Trevalga Cnwll 4 H3
Trevalyn Wrexhm 69 L3
Trevanger Cnwll 4 F6
Trevanson Cnwll 4 F7
Trevarrack Cnwll 2 D7
Trevarren Cnwll 4 E9
Trevarrian Cnwll 4 D8
Trevarrick Cnwll 3 P5
Trevarth Cnwll 3 J5
Trevaughan Carmth 41 P7
Tre-Vaughan Carmth 42 G10
Treveal Cnwll 2 D5
Treveal Cnwll 4 B10
Treveighan Cnwll 4 H6
Trevellas Downs Cnwll 3 J3
Trevelmond Cnwll 5 L9
Trevemper Cnwll 4 C10
Treveor Cnwll 3 P5
Treverbyn Cnwll 3 M4
Treverbyn Cnwll 4 G10
Treverva Cnwll 3 K7
Trevescan Cnwll 2 B9
Trevethin Torfn 31 J4
Trevia Cnwll 4 H5
Trevigro Cnwll 5 N8
Trevilla Cnwll 3 L6
Trevilson Cnwll 4 C10
Treviscoe Cnwll 4 E10
Treviskey Cnwll 3 N5
Trevithick Cnwll 3 P4
Trevithick Cnwll 4 D9
Trevoll Cnwll 4 C10
Trevone Cnwll 4 D6
Trevor Wrexhm 69 J6
Trevorgans Cnwll 2 C8
Trevorrick Cnwll 4 E7
Trevose Cnwll 4 D6
Trew Cnwll 2 G8
Trewalder Cnwll 4 H5
Trewalkin Powys 44 H8
Trewarmett Cnwll 4 H4
Trewassa Cnwll 5 J4
Trewavas Cnwll 2 F8
Treween Cnwll 5 L5
Trewellard Cnwll 2 B7
Trewen Cnwll 5 M5
Trewennack Cnwll 2 H8
Trewent Pembks 41 K11
Trewern Powys 56 D2
Trewetha Cnwll 4 G5
Trewethern Cnwll 4 G6
Trewidland Cnwll 5 M10
Trewillis Cnwll 3 K10
Trewint Cnwll 5 L5
Trewint Cnwll 5 M9
Trewithian Cnwll 3 M6
Trewoodloe Cnwll 5 N7
Trewoon Cnwll 2 H10
Trewoon Cnwll 3 P3
Treworga Cnwll 3 M5
Treworgan Cnwll 3 L4
Treworlas Cnwll 3 M6
Treworld Cnwll 5 J3
Treworthal Cnwll 3 M6
Tre-wyn Mons 45 L10
Treyarnon Cnwll 4 D7
Treyford W Susx 23 M11
Trickett's Cross Dorset 13 J4
Triermain Cumb 111 L7
Triffleton Pembks 41 J6
Trillacott Cnwll 5 M4
Trimdon Dur 104 C4
Trimdon Colliery Dur 104 C3
Trimdon Grange Dur 104 C3
Trimingham Norfk 77 K4
Trimley Lower Street Suffk 53 N4
Trimley St Martin Suffk 53 N4
Trimley St Mary Suffk 53 N4
Trimpley Worcs 57 P9
Trimsaran Carmth 28 E4
Trims Green Herts 51 L7
Trimstone Devon 17 J3
Trinafour P & K 140 H5
Trinant Caerph 30 H5
Tring Herts 35 P2
Tringford Herts 35 P2
Tring Wharf Herts 35 P2
Trinity Angus 143 L5
Trinity Jersey 11 b1
Trinity Gask P & K 134 B4
Triscombe Somset 18 G7
Trislaig Highld 139 K3
Trispen Cnwll 3 L3
Tritlington Nthumb 113 K2
Troan Cnwll 4 D10
Trochry P & K 141 N9
Troedrhiwfuwch Caerph 30 F4
Troedyraur Cerdgn 42 F5
Troedyrhiw Myr Td 30 E4
Trofarth Conwy 80 B10
Trois Bois Jersey 11 b1
Troon Cnwll 2 H6
Troon S Ayrs 125 J11
Tropical World Roundhay Park Leeds 91 J3
Trossachs Stirlg 132 G6
Trossachs Pier Stirlg 132 F6
Troston Suffk 64 B7
Troswell Cnwll 5 M3
Trotshill Worcs 46 G3
Trottiscliffe Kent 37 P8
Trotton W Susx 23 M10
Troughend Nthumb 112 C2
Trough Gate Lancs 89 P6
Troutbeck Cumb 101 L5
Troutbeck Cumb 101 M10
Troutbeck Bridge Cumb 101 M10
Troway Derbys 84 E5
Trowbridge Wilts 20 G3
Trowell Notts 72 D3
Trowell Services Notts 72 D2
Trowle Common Wilts 20 F3
Trowley Bottom Herts 50 C8
Trowse Newton Norfk 77 J10
Troy Leeds 90 G3
Trudoxhill Somset 20 D6
Trull Somset 18 H10
Trumfleet Donc 91 Q8
Trumpan Highld 152 C5
Trumpet Herefs 46 C7
Trumpington Cambs 62 F10
Trumpsgreen Surrey 35 Q11
Trunch Norfk 77 K5
Trunnah Lancs 88 C2
Truro Cnwll 3 L5
Truro Cathedral Cnwll 3 L5
Truscott Cnwll 5 M4
Trusham Devon 9 L8
Trusley Derbys 71 P7
Trusthorpe Lincs 87 P4
Trysull Staffs 58 C6
Tubney Oxon 34 D5
Tuckenhay Devon 7 L7
Tuckhill Shrops 57 P7
Tuckingmill Cnwll 2 H5
Tuckingmill Wilts 20 H9
Tuckton Bmouth 13 K6
Tucoyse Cnwll 3 P4
Tuddenham Suffk 53 L2
Tuddenham Suffk 63 M6
Tudeley Kent 37 P11
Tudhoe Dur 103 Q3
Tudorville Herefs 46 A10
Tudweiliog Gwynd 66 C7
Tuesley Surrey 23 Q6
Tuffley Gloucs 32 F2
Tufton Hants 22 E5
Tufton Pembks 41 K5
Tugby Leics 73 K10
Tugford Shrops 57 K7
Tughall Nthumb 119 P5
Tullibody Clacks 133 P8
Tullich Highld 147 Q2
Tullich Highld 156 F2
Tulliemet P & K 141 P7
Tulloch Abers 159 K11
Tullochgorm Ag & B 131 K8
Tulloch Station Highld 147 K11
Tullymurdoch P & K 142 B7
Tullynessle Abers 150 F4
Tulse Hill Gt Lon 36 H6
Tumble Carmth 28 F2
Tumbler's Green Essex 52 D6
Tumby Lincs 86 H9
Tumby Woodside Lincs 87 J9
Tummel Bridge P & K 141 J6
Tunbridge Wells Kent 25 N3
Tundergarth D & G 110 C4
Tungate Norfk 77 K6
Tunley BaNES 20 C3
Tunstall C Stke 70 F4

Tunstall E R Yk ... 93 P4
Tunstall Kent ... 38 E9
Tunstall Lancs ... 95 N6
Tunstall N York ... 103 P11
Tunstall Norfk ... 77 N10
Tunstall Staffs ... 70 D9
Tunstall Suffk ... 65 M10
Tunstall Sundld ... 113 N10
Tunstead Derbys ... 83 P10
Tunstead Norfk ... 77 K7
Tunstead Milton Derbys ... 83 M8
Tunworth Hants ... 23 J5
Tupsley Herefs ... 45 Q6
Turgis Green Hants ... 23 J3
Turkdean Gloucs ... 47 M11
Tur Langton Leics ... 60 F2
Turleigh Wilts ... 20 F2
Turleygreen Shrops ... 57 P7
Turn Lancs ... 89 N7
Turnastone Herefs ... 45 M7
Turnberry S Ayrs ... 114 D6
Turnchapel C Plym ... 6 D8
Turnditch Derbys ... 71 P5
Turner Green Lancs ... 89 J4
Turner's Green E Susx ... 25 P7
Turner's Green Warwks ... 59 J11
Turner's Hill W Susx ... 24 H3
Turners Puddle Dorset ... 12 D6
Turnford Herts ... 51 J10
Turnhouse C Edin ... 127 M3
Turnworth Dorset ... 12 D3
Turriff Abers ... 158 H7
Turton Bottoms Bl w D ... 89 L7
Turves Cambs ... 74 F11
Turvey Bed ... 49 P4
Turville Bucks ... 35 L6
Turville Heath Bucks ... 35 K6
Turweston Bucks ... 48 H7
Tushielaw Inn Border ... 117 L7
Tutbury Staffs ... 71 N9
Tutnall Worcs ... 58 E10
Tutshill Gloucs ... 31 P6
Tuttington Norfk ... 77 J6
Tutwell Cnwll ... 5 P6
Tuxford Notts ... 85 M6
Twatt Ork ... 169 b4
Twatt Shet ... 169 q8
Twechar E Duns ... 126 B2
Tweedbank Border ... 117 Q4
Tweedmouth Nthumb ... 129 P9
Tweedsmuir Border ... 116 G6
Twelveheads Cnwll ... 3 K5
Twelve Oaks E Susx ... 25 Q6
Twemlow Green Ches E ... 82 G11
Twenty Lincs ... 74 C6
Twerton BaNES ... 20 D2
Twickenham Gt Lon ... 36 E6
Twigworth Gloucs ... 46 F10
Twineham W Susx ... 24 G7
Twineham Green W Susx ... 24 G6
Twinhoe BaNES ... 20 E3
Twinstead Essex ... 52 E4
Twitchen Devon ... 17 P5
Twitchen Shrops ... 56 F9
Twitham Kent ... 39 N10
Two Bridges Devon ... 6 G4
Two Dales Derbys ... 84 C8
Two Gates Staffs ... 59 K4
Two Mile Oak Cross Devon ... 7 L5
Two Pots Devon ... 17 J3
Two Waters Herts ... 50 C9
Twycross Leics ... 72 A10
Twycross Zoo Leics ... 59 M3
Twyford Bucks ... 49 J9
Twyford Hants ... 22 E10
Twyford Leics ... 73 J8
Twyford Lincs ... 73 N6
Twyford Norfk ... 76 E7
Twyford Wokham ... 35 L9
Twyford Common Herefs ... 45 Q7
Twyn-carno Caerph ... 30 F3
Twynholm D & G ... 108 E10
Twyning Green Gloucs ... 46 H7
Twynllanan Carmth ... 43 Q10
Twyn-yr-Odyn V Glam ... 30 F10
Twyn-y-Sheriff Mons ... 31 M3
Twywell Nhants ... 61 L5
Tyberton Herefs ... 45 M7
Tyburn Birm ... 58 H6
Tycroes Carmth ... 28 H2
Ty Croes IoA ... 78 E10
Tycrwyn Powys ... 68 F11
Tydd Gote Lincs ... 75 J7
Tydd St Giles Cambs ... 74 H7
Tydd St Mary Lincs ... 74 H7
Tye Hants ... 15 K6
Tye Green Essex ... 51 M6
Tye Green Essex ... 51 N3
Tye Green Essex ... 52 C7
Tyersal C Brad ... 90 F4
Tyldesley Wigan ... 82 E4
Tyler Hill Kent ... 39 K9
Tylers Green Bucks ... 35 P6
Tyler's Green Essex ... 51 M9
Tylers Green Surrey ... 37 J10
Tylorstown Rhondd ... 30 D5
Tylwch Powys ... 55 M8
Ty-nant Conwy ... 68 C6
Ty-nant Gwynd ... 68 B9
Tyndrum Stirlg ... 139 Q11
Ty'n-dwr Denbgs ... 68 H6
Tynemouth N Tyne ... 113 N7
Tynemouth Crematorium N Tyne ... 113 M7
Tynewydd Rhondd ... 29 P5
Tyninghame E Loth ... 128 G4
Tynron D & G ... 115 R9
Tyntesfield NT N Som ... 31 P10
Ty'n-y-bryn Rhondd ... 30 D7
Ty'n-y-Groes Conwy ... 79 P10
Tyn-y-nant Rhondd ... 30 E7
Tyringham M Keyn ... 49 N5
Tyseley Birm ... 58 H8
Tythegston Brdgnd ... 29 N9
Tytherington Ches E ... 83 K9
Tytherington S Glos ... 32 C7
Tytherington Somset ... 20 E6
Tytherington Wilts ... 20 H6
Tytherleigh Devon ... 10 G4
Tytherton Lucas Wilts ... 32 H10
Tyttenhanger Herts ... 50 E9
Tywardreath Cnwll ... 4 H11
Tywardreath Highway Cnwll ... 4 H10
Tywyn Conwy ... 79 P9
Tywyn Gwynd ... 54 D4

U

Ubbeston Green Suffk ... 65 L7
Ubley BaNES ... 19 P3
Uckerby N York ... 103 P10
Uckfield E Susx ... 25 L6
Uckinghall Worcs ... 46 G7
Uckington Gloucs ... 46 H10
Uckington Shrops ... 57 K2
Uddingston S Lans ... 126 B5
Uddington S Lans ... 116 B4
Udimore E Susx ... 26 E8
Udny Green Abers ... 151 M2
Udny Station Abers ... 151 N3
Uffcott Wilts ... 33 M9
Uffculme Devon ... 9 Q2
Uffington Lincs ... 73 R9
Uffington Oxon ... 34 B7
Uffington Shrops ... 57 J2
Ufford C Pete ... 74 A10
Ufford Suffk ... 65 K11
Ufton Warwks ... 48 C2
Ufton Nervet W Berk ... 34 H11
Ugadale Ag & B ... 120 L6
Ugborough Devon ... 6 H7
Uggeshall Suffk ... 65 N5
Ugglebarnby N York ... 105 N9
Ughill Sheff ... 84 C2
Ugley Essex ... 51 M5
Ugley Green Essex ... 51 M5
Ugthorpe N York ... 105 L8
Uibhist A Deas W Isls ... 168 d14
Uibhist A Tuath W Isls ... 168 C10
Uig Ag & B ... 136 F5
Uig Highld ... 152 B7
Uig Highld ... 152 F5
Uig W Isls ... 168 f4
Uigshader Highld ... 152 G8
Uisken Ag & B ... 137 K12
Ulbster Highld ... 167 P8
Ulcat Row Cumb ... 101 M6
Ulceby Lincs ... 87 M6
Ulceby N Linc ... 93 K8
Ulceby Skitter N Linc ... 93 K7
Ulcombe Kent ... 26 D2
Uldale Cumb ... 100 H3
Uley Gloucs ... 32 E5
Ulgham Nthumb ... 113 K2
Ullapool Highld ... 161 J8
Ullenhall Warwks ... 58 H11
Ullenwood Gloucs ... 46 H11
Ulleskelf N York ... 91 N3
Ullesthorpe Leics ... 60 B3
Ulley Rothm ... 84 G3
Ullingswick Herefs ... 46 A5
Ullinish Lodge Hotel Highld ... 152 E10
Ullock Cumb ... 100 E6
Ullswater Cumb ... 101 M6
Ulpha Cumb ... 94 D2
Ulpha Cumb ... 95 K4
Ulrome E R Yk ... 99 P9
Ulsta Shet ... 169 r5
Ulva Ag & B ... 137 K7
Ulverley Green Solhll ... 58 H8
Ulverston Cumb ... 94 F5
Ulwell Dorset ... 12 H8
Ulzieside D & G ... 115 Q6
Umberleigh Devon ... 17 L7
Unapool Highld ... 164 F10
Underbarrow Cumb ... 95 K2
Under Burnmouth Border ... 111 J4
Undercliffe C Brad ... 90 F4
Underdale Shrops ... 57 J2
Underling Green Kent ... 26 C2
Under River Kent ... 37 N10
Underwood Notts ... 84 G10
Undley Suffk ... 63 L4
Undy Mons ... 31 M7
Union Mills IoM ... 80 e6
Union Street E Susx ... 26 B5
Unst Shet ... 169 s3
Unstone Derbys ... 84 E5
Unstone Green Derbys ... 84 E5
Unthank Cumb ... 101 N3
Unthank Cumb ... 102 B2
Unthank Cumb ... 110 G11
Unthank Derbys ... 84 D5
Unthank Nthumb ... 129 P10
Upavon Wilts ... 21 M4
Up Cerne Dorset ... 11 P4
Upchurch Kent ... 38 D8
Upcott Devon ... 17 P6
Upcott Herefs ... 45 L4
Upend Cambs ... 63 M9
Up Exe Devon ... 9 M4
Upgate Norfk ... 76 G8
Upgate Street Norfk ... 64 F3
Upgate Street Norfk ... 65 K3
Uphall Dorset ... 11 M4
Uphall W Loth ... 127 K3
Upham Devon ... 9 L3
Upham Hants ... 22 F10
Uphampton Herefs ... 45 M2
Uphampton Worcs ... 46 F2
Uphill N Som ... 19 K3
Up Holland Lancs ... 88 G9
Uplawmoor E Rens ... 125 L6
Upleadon Gloucs ... 46 E9
Upleatham R & Cl ... 104 H7
Uplees Kent ... 38 H9
Uploders Dorset ... 11 L6
Uplowman Devon ... 18 D11
Uplyme Devon ... 10 G6
Up Marden W Susx ... 15 L4
Upminster Gt Lon ... 37 N3
Up Mudford Somset ... 19 Q11
Up Nately Hants ... 23 J4
Uppottery Devon ... 10 E3
Upper Affcot Shrops ... 56 G7
Upper Ardchronie Highld ... 162 E9
Upper Arley Worcs ... 57 P8
Upper Arncott Oxon ... 48 H11
Upper Astrop Nhants ... 48 F7
Upper Basildon W Berk ... 34 G9
Upper Batley Kirk ... 90 G5
Upper Beeding W Susx ... 24 E8
Upper Benefield Nhants ... 61 L3
Upper Bentley Worcs ... 58 E11
Upper Bighouse Highld ... 166 E5
Upper Birchwood Derbys ... 84 F9
Upper Boat Rhondd ... 30 F7
Upper Boddington Nhants ... 48 E4
Upper Borth Cerdgn ... 54 E7
Upper Brailes Warwks ... 48 B7
Upper Breakish Highld ... 145 L3
Upper Breinton Herefs ... 45 P6
Upper Broadheath Worcs ... 46 F3
Upper Broughton Notts ... 72 H5
Upper Bucklebury W Berk ... 34 F11
Upper Burgate Hants ... 21 N11
Upper Bush Medway ... 37 Q7
Upperby Cumb ... 110 H10
Upper Caldecote C Beds ... 61 Q11
Upper Canada N Som ... 19 L3
Upper Canterton Hants ... 13 N2
Upper Catesby Nhants ... 60 B9
Upper Catshill Worcs ... 58 D10
Upper Chapel Powys ... 44 E6
Upper Chicksgrove Wilts ... 21 J9
Upper Chute Wilts ... 21 Q4
Upper Clapton Gt Lon ... 36 H3
Upper Clatford Hants ... 22 C6
Upper Coberley Gloucs ... 47 J11
Upper Cokeham W Susx ... 24 D9
Upper Cotton Staffs ... 71 K5
Upper Cound Shrops ... 57 K3
Upper Cudworth Barns ... 91 K9
Upper Cumberworth Kirk ... 90 G9
Upper Dallachy Moray ... 157 R5
Upper Deal Kent ... 39 Q11
Upper Dean Bed ... 61 M7
Upper Denby Kirk ... 90 G9
Upper Denton Cumb ... 111 M7
Upper Dicker E Susx ... 25 N9
Upper Dinchope Shrops ... 56 H8
Upper Dounreay Highld ... 166 H3
Upper Dovercourt Essex ... 53 M5
Upper Drumbane Stirlg ... 133 M6
Upper Dunsforth N York ... 97 P8
Upper Eashing Surrey ... 23 Q6
Upper Eathie Highld ... 156 D5
Upper Egleton Herefs ... 46 B6
Upper Elkstone Staffs ... 71 K3
Upper Ellastone Staffs ... 71 L6
Upper End Derbys ... 83 N9
Upper Enham Hants ... 22 C4
Upper Farmcote Shrops ... 57 P6
Upper Farringdon Hants ... 23 K7
Upper Framilode Gloucs ... 32 E2
Upper Froyle Hants ... 23 L6
Upperglen Highld ... 152 E7
Upper Godney Somset ... 19 N6
Upper Gravenhurst C Beds ... 50 D3
Upper Green Mons ... 45 M11
Upper Green Suffk ... 63 M8
Upper Green W Berk ... 22 C2
Upper Grove Common Herefs ... 45 R9
Upper Hackney Derbys ... 84 C8
Upper Hale Surrey ... 23 M5
Upper Halliford Surrey ... 36 C7
Upper Halling Medway ... 37 Q8
Upper Hambleton Rutlnd ... 73 N9
Upper Harbledown Kent ... 39 K10
Upper Hardres Court Kent ... 39 L11
Upper Hardwick Herefs ... 45 N3
Upper Hartfield E Susx ... 25 L4
Upper Hartshay Derbys ... 84 E10
Upper Hatherley Gloucs ... 46 H10
Upper Hatton Staffs ... 70 E7
Upper Haugh Rothm ... 91 L11
Upper Hayton Shrops ... 57 J8
Upper Heaton Kirk ... 90 F7
Upper Helmsley N York ... 98 D9
Upper Hergest Herefs ... 45 K4
Upper Heyford Nhants ... 60 E9
Upper Heyford Oxon ... 48 E9
Upper Hill Herefs ... 45 P4
Upper Hockenden Kent ... 37 M7
Upper Hopton Kirk ... 90 F7
Upper Howsell Worcs ... 46 E5
Upper Hulme Staffs ... 71 J2
Upper Ifold Surrey ... 24 B4
Upper Inglesham Swindn ... 33 P5
Upper Kilcott Gloucs ... 32 E7
Upper Killay Swans ... 28 G6
Upper Kinchrackine Ag & B ... 131 P2
Upper Lambourn W Berk ... 34 B8
Upper Landywood Staffs ... 58 E3
Upper Langford N Som ... 19 N3
Upper Langwith Derbys ... 84 H7
Upper Largo Fife ... 135 L7
Upper Leigh Staffs ... 71 J7
Upper Littleton N Som ... 19 Q2
Upper Lochton Abers ... 150 H8
Upper Longdon Staffs ... 58 G2
Upper & Lower Stondon C Beds ... 50 E4
Upper Ludstone Shrops ... 57 Q5
Upper Lybster Highld ... 167 N9
Upper Lydbrook Gloucs ... 46 B11
Upper Lyde Herefs ... 45 P6
Upper Lye Herefs ... 56 F11
Upper Maes-coed Herefs ... 45 L8
Upper Midhope Sheff ... 90 G11
Uppermill Oldham ... 90 B9
Upper Milton Worcs ... 57 Q10
Upper Minety Wilts ... 33 K6
Upper Moor Worcs ... 47 J5
Upper Moor Side Leeds ... 90 G4
Upper Mulben Moray ... 157 R7
Upper Netchwood Shrops ... 57 L6
Upper Nobut Staffs ... 71 J7
Upper Norwood W Susx ... 23 P11
Upper Padley Derbys ... 84 B5
Upper Pennington Hants ... 13 P5
Upper Pollicott Bucks ... 35 K2
Upper Poppleton C York ... 98 B9
Upper Quinton Warwks ... 47 N5
Upper Ratley Hants ... 22 B10
Upper Rissington Gloucs ... 47 P11
Upper Rochford Worcs ... 57 L11
Upper Ruscoe D & G ... 108 C8
Upper Sapey Herefs ... 46 C2
Upper Seagry Wilts ... 32 H8
Upper Shelton C Beds ... 49 Q6
Upper Sheringham Norfk ... 76 G3
Upper Skelmorlie N Ayrs ... 124 L3
Upper Slaughter Gloucs ... 47 N10
Upper Soudley Gloucs ... 32 C2
Upper Spond Herefs ... 45 L4
Upper Standen Kent ... 27 M3
Upper Staploe Bed ... 61 P9
Upper Stoke Norfk ... 77 K11
Upper Stowe Nhants ... 60 D9
Upper Street Hants ... 21 N11
Upper Street Norfk ... 64 H6
Upper Street Norfk ... 77 L8
Upper Street Norfk ... 77 M8
Upper Street Suffk ... 53 K5
Upper Street Suffk ... 65 N10
Upper Street Suffk ... 64 G11
Upper Strensham Worcs ... 46 G6
Upper Sundon C Beds ... 50 B5
Upper Swell Gloucs ... 47 N9
Upper Tankersley Barns ... 91 J11
Upper Tasburgh Norfk ... 65 J2
Upper Tean Staffs ... 71 J7
Upperthong Kirk ... 90 E9
Upperthorpe N Linc ... 92 C10
Upperton W Susx ... 23 Q10
Uppertown Derbys ... 84 D8
Uppertown Dur ... 103 L3
Uppertown Highld ... 167 Q1
Upper Town N Som ... 31 P11
Upper Town Suffk ... 64 C8
Upper Tumble Carmth ... 28 F2
Upper Tysoe Warwks ... 48 B6
Upper Ufford Suffk ... 65 K11
Upperup Gloucs ... 33 K5
Upper Upham Wilts ... 33 P9
Upper Upnor Medway ... 38 C7
Upper Victoria Angus ... 143 J10
Upper Vobster Somset ... 20 D5
Upper Wardington Oxon ... 48 E5
Upper Weald M Keyn ... 49 M7
Upper Weedon Nhants ... 60 D9
Upper Welland Worcs ... 46 E6
Upper Wellingham E Susx ... 25 K8
Upper Weston BaNES ... 32 D11
Upper Weybread Suffk ... 65 J6
Upper Wick Worcs ... 46 F4
Upper Wield Hants ... 22 H7
Upper Winchendon Bucks ... 35 K2
Upperwood Derbys ... 84 C9
Upper Woodford Wilts ... 21 M7
Upper Wootton Hants ... 22 G4
Upper Wraxall Wilts ... 32 F10
Upper Wyche Worcs ... 46 E6
Uppincott Devon ... 9 M3
Uppingham Rutlnd ... 73 M11
Uppington Dorset ... 12 H3
Uppington Shrops ... 57 K3
Upsall N York ... 97 Q4
Upsettlington Border ... 129 M10
Upshire Essex ... 51 K10
Up Somborne Hants ... 22 C8
Upstreet Kent ... 39 M9
Up Sydling Dorset ... 11 N4
Upthorpe Suffk ... 64 D7
Upton Bucks ... 35 L2
Upton C Pete ... 74 B10
Upton Cambs ... 61 Q5
Upton Ches W ... 81 N11
Upton Cnwll ... 5 M7
Upton Cnwll ... 16 C11
Upton Cumb ... 101 K3
Upton Devon ... 7 J10
Upton Devon ... 10 B4
Upton Dorset ... 12 B8
Upton Dorset ... 12 G6
Upton E R Yk ... 99 N10
Upton Halton ... 81 P7
Upton Hants ... 22 C11
Upton Hants ... 22 C3
Upton Leics ... 72 B11
Upton Lincs ... 85 Q3
Upton Nhants ... 60 F9
Upton Norfk ... 77 M9
Upton Notts ... 85 N10
Upton Notts ... 85 M5
Upton Oxon ... 34 F7
Upton Pembks ... 41 K10
Upton R & Cl ... 105 K7
Upton Slough ... 35 Q9
Upton Somset ... 18 C9
Upton Somset ... 19 N9
Upton Wakefd ... 91 M8
Upton Warwks ... 47 M3
Upton Wilts ... 20 G8
Upton Wirral ... 81 K7
Upton Bishop Herefs ... 46 C9
Upton Cheyney S Glos ... 32 C10
Upton Cressett Shrops ... 57 M6
Upton Crews Herefs ... 46 B9
Upton Cross Cnwll ... 5 M7
Upton End C Beds ... 50 D4
Upton Grey Hants ... 23 J5
Upton Heath Ches W ... 81 N11
Upton Hellions Devon ... 9 K4
Upton Lovell Wilts ... 20 H6
Upton Magna Shrops ... 57 K2
Upton Noble Somset ... 20 D7
Upton Pyne Devon ... 9 M5
Upton St Leonards Gloucs ... 46 G11
Upton Scudamore Wilts ... 20 G5
Upton Snodsbury Worcs ... 46 H4
Upton Towans Cnwll ... 2 F5
Upton upon Severn Worcs ... 46 G6
Upton Warren Worcs ... 58 D11
Upwaltham W Susx ... 15 P4
Upware Cambs ... 62 H6
Upwell Norfk ... 75 J10
Upwey Dorset ... 11 P7
Upwick Green Herts ... 51 L6
Upwood Cambs ... 62 C4
Urchfont Wilts ... 21 K3
Urdimarsh Herefs ... 45 Q5
Ure Bank N York ... 97 M7
Urlay Nook S on T ... 104 D8
Urmston Traffd ... 82 G5
Urquhart Moray ... 157 P5
Urra N York ... 104 G10
Urray Highld ... 155 P7
Usan Angus ... 143 N7
Ushaw Moor Dur ... 103 P2
Usk Mons ... 31 L4
Usselby Lincs ... 86 E2
Usworth Sundld ... 113 M9
Utkinton Ches W ... 82 B11
Utley C Brad ... 90 D2
Uton Devon ... 9 K5
Utterby Lincs ... 87 K2
Uttoxeter Staffs ... 71 K8
Uwchmynydd Gwynd ... 66 B9
Uxbridge Gt Lon ... 36 C4
Uyeasound Shet ... 169 s3
Uzmaston Pembks ... 41 J8

V

Vale Guern ... 10 c1
Vale of Glamorgan Crematorium V Glam ... 30 F10
Vale of Rheidol Railway Cerdgn ... 54 G9
Valley IoA ... 78 D9
Valley End Surrey ... 23 Q2
Valley Truckle Cnwll ... 4 H5
Valtos Highld ... 153 J5
Valtos W Isls ... 168 f4
Vange Essex ... 38 B4
Varteg Torfn ... 31 J3
Vatsetter Shet ... 169 s5
Vatten Highld ... 152 D9
Vaynor Myr Td ... 30 D2
Vazon Bay Guern ... 10 b2
Veensgarth Shet ... 169 r9
Velindre Powys ... 44 H7
Vellow Somset ... 18 E7
Velly Devon ... 16 D7
Venngreen Devon ... 16 F9
Vennington Shrops ... 56 F3
Venn Ottery Devon ... 10 B6
Venny Tedburn Devon ... 9 K5
Venterdon Cnwll ... 5 P7
Ventnor IoW ... 14 G11
Venton Devon ... 6 F7
Vernham Dean Hants ... 22 B3
Vernham Street Hants ... 22 B3
Vernolds Common Shrops ... 56 H8
Verwood Dorset ... 13 J3
Veryan Cnwll ... 3 N6
Veryan Green Cnwll ... 3 N5
Vicarage Devon ... 10 E7
Vickerstown Cumb ... 94 D7
Victoria Barns ... 90 F9
Victoria Blae G ... 30 G3
Victoria Cnwll ... 4 F9
Vidlin Shet ... 169 r7
Viewfield Moray ... 157 P5
Viewpark N Lans ... 126 C5
Vigo Kent ... 37 P8
Village de Putron Guern ... 10 c2
Ville la Bas Jersey ... 11 a1
Villiaze Guern ... 10 b2
Vinehall Street E Susx ... 26 C7
Vines Cross E Susx ... 25 N7
Vinters Park Crematorium Kent ... 38 C10
Virginia Water Surrey ... 36 B7
Virginstow Devon ... 5 P3
Vobster Somset ... 20 D5
Voe Shet ... 169 r7
Vowchurch Herefs ... 45 M7
Vulcan Village St Hel ... 82 C6

W

Waberthwaite Cumb ... 94 C2
Wackerfield Dur ... 103 N6
Wacton Norfk ... 64 H3
Wadborough Worcs ... 46 H5
Waddesdon Bucks ... 49 K11
Waddeton Devon ... 7 M7
Waddicar Sefton ... 81 M5
Waddingham Lincs ... 92 G11
Waddington Lancs ... 89 L2
Waddington Lincs ... 86 C8
Waddon Devon ... 9 L9
Waddon Dorset ... 11 N7
Wadebridge Cnwll ... 4 F7
Wadeford Somset ... 10 G2
Wadenhoe Nhants ... 61 M4
Wadesmill Herts ... 51 J7
Wadhurst E Susx ... 25 P4
Wadshelf Derbys ... 84 D6
Wadswick Wilts ... 32 F11
Wadworth Donc ... 91 P11
Waen Denbgs ... 68 C2
Waen Denbgs ... 80 C11
Waen Powys ... 68 H11
Waen Fach Powys ... 68 H11
Waen-pentir Gwynd ... 79 K11
Waen-wen Gwynd ... 79 K11
Wagbeach Shrops ... 56 F4
Wainfelin Torfn ... 31 J4
Wainfleet All Saints Lincs ... 87 N9
Wainfleet Bank Lincs ... 87 N9
Wainfleet St Mary Lincs ... 87 N9
Wainford Norfk ... 65 L3
Wainhouse Corner Cnwll ... 5 K2
Wainscott Medway ... 38 B7
Wain's Hill N Som ... 31 L10
Wainstalls Calder ... 90 C5
Waitby Cumb ... 102 F9
Waithe Lincs ... 93 N10
Wakefield Wakefd ... 91 J6
Wakefield Crematorium Wakefd ... 91 J7
Wake Green Birm ... 58 G8
Wakerley Nhants ... 73 P11
Wakes Colne Essex ... 52 E6
Walberswick Suffk ... 65 P7
Walberton W Susx ... 15 P5
Walbottle N u Ty ... 113 J7
Walbutt D & G ... 108 F7
Walby Cumb ... 110 H8
Walcombe Somset ... 19 Q5
Walcot Lincs ... 73 R3
Walcot N Linc ... 92 E6
Walcot Shrops ... 56 F7
Walcot Shrops ... 57 K2
Walcot Swindn ... 33 N8
Walcot Warwks ... 47 M3
Walcote Leics ... 60 C4
Walcot Green Norfk ... 64 G5
Walcott Lincs ... 86 F9
Walcott Norfk ... 77 M5
Walden N York ... 96 F4
Walden Head N York ... 96 E4
Walden Stubbs N York ... 91 P7
Walderslade Medway ... 38 C9
Walderton W Susx ... 15 L4
Walditch Dorset ... 11 K6
Waldley Derbys ... 71 L7
Waldridge Dur ... 113 L11
Waldringfield Suffk ... 53 N2

Waldron E Susx....25 M7
Wales Rothm....84 G4
Wales Somset....19 Q10
Walesby Lincs....86 F2
Walesby Notts....85 L6
Walford Herefs....46 A10
Walford Herefs....56 F10
Walford Shrops....69 M10
Walford Staffs....70 E8
Walford Heath Shrops....69 M11
Walgherton Ches E....70 B5
Walgrave Nhants....60 H6
Walhampton Hants....13 P5
Walkden Salfd....82 F4
Walker N u Ty....113 L8
Walkerburn Border....117 M3
Walker Fold Lancs....89 K2
Walkeringham Notts....85 N2
Walkerith Lincs....85 N2
Walkern Herts....50 G5
Walker's Green Herefs....45 Q5
Walker's Heath Birm....58 G9
Walkerton Fife....134 G2
Walkford Dorset....13 M6
Walkhampton Devon....6 E5
Walkington E R Yk....92 G3
Walkley Sheff....84 D3
Walk Mill Lancs....89 P5
Walkwood Worcs....47 K2
Wall Nthumb....112 D7
Wall Staffs....58 H3
Wallacetown S Ayrs....114 E7
Wallacetown S Ayrs....114 F3
Wallands Park E Susx....25 K8
Wallasey Wirral....81 K6
Wall End Cumb....94 E4
Wall End Herefs....45 N3
Wallend Medway....38 E6
Waller's Green Herefs....46 C7
Wallhead Cumb....111 J8
Wall Heath Dudley....58 C7
Wall Houses Nthumb....112 F7
Wallingford Oxon....34 H7
Wallington Gt Lon....36 G8
Wallington Hants....14 G5
Wallington Herts....50 G4
Wallington Heath Wsall....58 E4
Wallis Pembks....41 K5
Wallisdown Poole....13 J6
Walliswood Surrey....24 D3
Walls Shet....169 p9
Wallsend N Tyne....113 L7
Wallthwaite Cumb....101 L5
Wall under Haywood Shrops....57 J6
Wallyford E Loth....128 B5
Walmer Kent....39 Q11
Walmer Bridge Lancs....88 F6
Walmersley Bury....89 N8
Walmestone Kent....39 N10
Walmley Birm....58 H6
Walmley Ash Birm....58 H6
Walmsgate Lincs....87 L5
Walpole Somset....19 K6
Walpole Suffk....65 M7
Walpole Cross Keys Norfk....75 K7
Walpole Highway Norfk....75 K8
Walpole St Andrew Norfk....75 K7
Walpole St Peter Norfk....75 K7
Walrow Somset....19 K5
Walsall Wsall....58 F5
Walsall Wood Wsall....58 F4
Walsden Calder....89 Q6
Walsgrave on Sowe Covtry....59 N8
Walsham le Willows Suffk....64 E7
Walshaw Bury....89 M8
Walshford N York....97 P10
Walsoken Norfk....75 J8
Walston S Lans....127 K8
Walsworth Herts....50 E4
Walter's Ash Bucks....35 M5
Walters Green Kent....25 M2
Walterston V Glam....30 E10
Walterstone Herefs....45 L9
Waltham Kent....27 K2
Waltham NE Lin....93 N10
Waltham Abbey Essex....51 J10
Waltham Chase Hants....14 G4
Waltham Cross Herts....51 J10
Waltham on the Wolds Leics....73 L6
Waltham St Lawrence W & M....35 M9
Waltham's Cross Essex....51 Q4
Walthamstow Gt Lon....37 J3
Walton C Pete....74 C10
Walton Cumb....111 K8
Walton Derbys....84 E7
Walton Leeds....97 P11
Walton Leics....60 C3
Walton M Keyn....49 N7
Walton Powys....45 K3
Walton Shrops....56 H9
Walton Somset....19 N7
Walton Staffs....70 F8
Walton Staffs....70 F9
Walton Suffk....53 N4
Walton W Susx....15 M6
Walton Wakefd....91 K7
Walton Warwks....47 Q4
Walton Wrekin....69 Q11
Walton Cardiff Gloucs....46 H8
Walton East Pembks....41 K6
Walton Elm Dorset....20 E11
Walton Grounds Nhants....48 F8
Walton-in-Gordano N Som....31 M10
Walton Lea Crematorium Warrtn....82 D7
Walton-le-Dale Lancs....88 H5
Walton-on-Thames Surrey....36 D7
Walton-on-the-Hill Staffs....70 H10
Walton on the Hill Surrey....36 F9
Walton on the Naze Essex....53 N7
Walton on the Wolds Leics....72 F7
Walton-on-Trent Derbys....71 N11
Walton Park N Som....31 M10
Walton West Pembks....40 G8
Waltonwrays Crematorium N York....96 E10
Walwen Flints....80 G9
Walwen Flints....80 H10
Walwen Flints....81 J9

Walwick Nthumb....112 D6
Walworth Darltn....103 P7
Walworth Gt Lon....36 H5
Walworth Gate Darltn....103 P6
Walwyn's Castle Pembks....40 G8
Wambrook Somset....10 F3
Wampool Cumb....110 D10
Wanborough Surrey....23 P5
Wanborough Swindn....33 P8
Wandon End Herts....50 D6
Wandsworth Gt Lon....36 G6
Wangford Suffk....65 P6
Wanlip Leics....72 F8
Wanlockhead D & G....116 B8
Wannock E Susx....25 N10
Wansford C Pete....73 R11
Wansford E R Yk....99 M9
Wanshurst Green Kent....26 C2
Wanstead Gt Lon....37 K3
Wanstrow Somset....20 D6
Wanswell Gloucs....32 C4
Wantage Oxon....34 C7
Wants Green Worcs....46 E3
Wapley S Glos....32 D9
Wappenbury Warwks....59 N11
Wappenham Nhants....48 H5
Warbleton E Susx....25 P7
Warborough Oxon....34 G6
Warboys Cambs....62 D4
Warbreck Bpool....88 C3
Warbstow Cnwll....5 L3
Warburton Traffd....82 F7
Warcop Cumb....102 D7
Warden Kent....38 H7
Warden Nthumb....112 D7
Ward End Birm....58 H7
Ward Green Suffk....64 E9
Ward Green Cross Lancs....89 J3
Wardhedges C Beds....50 C3
Wardington Oxon....48 E5
Wardle Ches E....69 R3
Wardle Rochdl....89 Q7
Wardley Gatesd....113 M8
Wardley Rutlnd....73 L10
Wardley Salfd....82 G4
Wardlow Derbys....83 Q10
Wardsend Ches E....83 K8
Wardy Hill Cambs....62 G4
Ware Herts....51 J8
Wareham Dorset....12 F7
Warehorne Kent....26 G5
Warenford Nthumb....119 M5
Waren Mill Nthumb....119 M4
Warenton Nthumb....119 M4
Wareside Herts....51 J7
Waresley Cambs....62 C10
Waresley Worcs....58 B10
Ware Street Kent....38 C10
Warfield Br For....35 N10
Warfleet Devon....7 M8
Wargate Lincs....74 D4
Wargrave Wokham....35 L9
Warham Herefs....45 P7
Warham All Saints Norfk....76 D3
Warham St Mary Norfk....76 C3
Wark Nthumb....112 C5
Wark Nthumb....118 F3
Warkleigh Devon....17 L7
Warkton Nhants....61 J5
Warkworth Nhants....48 E6
Warkworth Nthumb....119 P9
Warlaby N York....97 M2
Warland Calder....89 Q6
Warleggan Cnwll....5 K8
Warleigh BaNES....20 E2
Warley Town Calder....90 D6
Warlingham Surrey....37 J9
Warmbrook Derbys....71 P4
Warmfield Wakefd....91 K6
Warmingham Ches E....70 C2
Warmington Nhants....61 N2
Warmington Warwks....48 D5
Warminster Wilts....20 G5
Warmley S Glos....32 C10
Warmsworth Donc....91 N10
Warmwell Dorset....12 C7
Warndon Worcs....46 G3
Warner Bros Studio Tour Herts....50 C10
Warnford Hants....22 H10
Warnham W Susx....24 E4
Warnham Court W Susx....24 E4
Warningcamp W Susx....24 B9
Warninglid W Susx....24 F5
Warren Ches E....83 J10
Warren Pembks....40 H11
Warrenby R & Cl....104 G5
Warrenhill S Lans....116 C3
Warren Row W & M....35 M8
Warren's Green Herts....50 G5
Warren Street Kent....38 F11
Warrington M Keyn....49 N4
Warrington Warrtn....82 D7
Warriston C Edin....127 P2
Warriston Crematorium C Edin....127 P2
Warsash Hants....14 E5
Warslow Staffs....71 K3
Warsop Vale Notts....84 H7
Warter E R Yk....98 H10
Warthermaske N York....97 K5
Warthill N York....98 D9
Wartling E Susx....25 Q9
Wartnaby Leics....73 J6
Warton Lancs....88 E5
Warton Lancs....95 K6
Warton Nthumb....119 K10
Warton Warwks....59 L4
Warwick Warwks....59 L11
Warwick Bridge Cumb....111 J9
Warwick Castle Warwks....47 Q2
Warwick-on-Eden Cumb....111 J9
Warwick Services Warwks....48 B3
Warwicksland Cumb....111 J5
Wasbister Ork....169 c3
Wasdale Head Cumb....100 G9
Wash Derbys....83 N8
Washall Green Herts....51 K4
Washaway Cnwll....4 G8
Washbourne Devon....7 K8
Washbrook Somset....19 M4
Washbrook Suffk....53 K3
Washfield Devon....18 B11
Washfold N York....103 L10
Washford Somset....18 E6
Washford Pyne Devon....9 K2
Washingborough Lincs....86 D6
Washington Sundld....113 M9

Washington W Susx....24 D8
Washington Services Gatesd....113 L9
Washwood Heath Birm....58 H7
Wasing W Berk....22 G2
Waskerley Dur....112 F11
Wasperton Warwks....47 Q3
Wasps Nest Lincs....86 E8
Wass N York....98 B5
Watchet Somset....18 E6
Watchfield Oxon....33 P6
Watchfield Somset....19 K5
Watchgate Cumb....101 P11
Watchill Cumb....100 G2
Watcombe Torbay....7 N5
Watendlath Cumb....101 J7
Water Devon....9 J8
Water Lancs....89 N5
Waterbeach Cambs....62 G7
Waterbeach W Susx....15 N5
Waterbeck D & G....110 D5
Waterden Norfk....76 B4
Water Eaton Oxon....34 F2
Water Eaton Staffs....58 D2
Water End Bed....61 P10
Water End Bed....61 P11
Water End C Beds....50 C3
Waterend Cumb....100 F6
Water End E R Yk....92 C3
Water End Essex....51 N2
Water End Herts....50 B8
Water End Herts....50 F10
Waterfall Staffs....71 K4
Waterfoot E Rens....125 P6
Waterford Herts....50 H8
Water Fryston Wakefd....91 M5
Watergate Cnwll....5 J5
Waterhead Cumb....101 L10
Waterheads Border....127 N7
Waterhouses Dur....103 N2
Waterhouses Staffs....71 K4
Wateringbury Kent....37 Q10
Waterlane Gloucs....32 H4
Waterloo Cnwll....5 J7
Waterloo Derbys....84 F8
Waterloo Herefs....45 L5
Waterloo Highld....145 L3
Waterloo N Lans....126 E7
Waterloo Norfk....77 J8
Waterloo P & K....141 Q10
Waterloo Pembks....41 J10
Waterloo Poole....12 H6
Waterloo Sefton....81 L5
Waterloo Cross Devon....9 Q2
Waterloo Port Gwynd....66 H2
Waterlooville Hants....15 J5
Watermillock Cumb....101 M6
Water Newton Cambs....74 B11
Water Orton Warwks....59 J6
Waterperry Oxon....34 H3
Waterrow Somset....18 E9
Watersfield W Susx....24 B7
Waterside Bl w D....89 L6
Waterside Bucks....35 Q4
Waterside Cumb....110 D11
Waterside Donc....91 R8
Waterside E Ayrs....114 H6
Waterside E Ayrs....125 M9
Waterside E Duns....126 B3
Water's Nook Bolton....89 K9
Waterstein Highld....152 A8
Waterstock Oxon....34 H3
Waterston Pembks....40 H9
Water Stratford Bucks....49 J8
Water Street Neath....29 M8
Waters Upton Wrekin....70 A11
Water Yeat Cumb....94 F3
Watford Herts....50 D11
Watford Nhants....60 D7
Watford Gap Services Nhants....60 D7
Wath N York....96 H7
Wath N York....97 M5
Wath upon Dearne Rothm....91 L10
Watlington Norfk....75 M8
Watlington Oxon....35 J6
Watnall Notts....84 H11
Watten Highld....167 M6
Wattisfield Suffk....64 E7
Wattisham Suffk....64 E11
Watton Dorset....11 K6
Watton E R Yk....99 L11
Watton Norfk....76 C11
Watton-at-Stone Herts....50 H7
Watton Green Norfk....76 C11
Wattons Green Essex....51 M11
Wattston N Lans....126 D3
Wattstown Rhondd....30 D6
Wattsville Caerph....30 H6
Wauldby E R Yk....92 G5
Waulkmill Abers....150 G9
Waunarlwydd Swans....28 H5
Waunfawr Cerdgn....42 E8
Waunfawr Gwynd....67 J3
Waungron Swans....28 G4
Waunlwyd Blae G....30 G3
Wavendon M Keyn....49 P7
Waverbridge Cumb....110 D11
Waverton Ches W....69 N2
Waverton Cumb....110 D11
Wawne E R Yk....93 J3
Waxham Norfk....77 N6
Waxholme E R Yk....93 P5
Way Kent....39 P8
Waye Devon....7 K4
Wayford Somset....11 J3
Waytown Dorset....11 K5
Way Village Devon....9 L2
Way Wick N Som....19 L2
Weacombe Somset....18 F6
Weald Oxon....34 B4
Wealdstone Gt Lon....36 E3
Weardley Leeds....90 H2
Weare Somset....19 M4
Weare Giffard Devon....16 H7
Wearhead Dur....102 G3
Wearne Somset....19 M9
Wear Valley Crematorium Dur....103 Q4
Weasdale Cumb....102 C10
Weasenham All Saints Norfk....76 A7
Weasenham St Peter Norfk....76 B7
Weaste Salfd....82 H5
Weatheroak Hill Worcs....58 G10
Weaverham Ches W....82 D10
Weaverslake Staffs....71 L11
Weaverthorpe N York....99 K6

Webbington Somset....19 L3
Webb's Heath S Glos....32 C10
Webheath Worcs....58 F11
Webton Herefs....45 N7
Wedderlairs Abers....159 L11
Wedding Hall Fold N York....96 D11
Weddington Kent....39 N10
Weddington Warwks....59 N6
Wedhampton Wilts....21 L3
Wedmore Somset....19 M5
Wednesbury Sandw....58 E6
Wednesfield Wolves....58 D4
Weecar Notts....85 P7
Weedon Bucks....49 M10
Weedon Nhants....60 D9
Weedon Lois Nhants....48 H5
Weeford Staffs....58 H4
Week Devon....7 K6
Week Devon....17 K6
Week Devon....17 N8
Weeke Devon....J3
Weeke Hants....22 E8
Weekley Nhants....61 J4
Week St Mary Cnwll....5 L2
Weel E R Yk....93 J3
Weeley Essex....53 K7
Weeley Crematorium Essex....53 K7
Weeley Heath Essex....53 L7
Weem P & K....141 K8
Weeping Cross Staffs....70 G10
Weethley Warwks....47 L3
Weeting Norfk....63 N3
Weeton E R Yk....93 Q6
Weeton Lancs....88 D4
Weeton N York....97 L11
Weetwood Leeds....90 H3
Weir Lancs....89 P5
Weirbrook Shrops....69 K10
Weir Quay Devon....6 C5
Weisdale Shet....169 q8
Welborne Norfk....76 F9
Welbourn Lincs....86 C10
Welburn N York....98 E7
Welbury N York....104 C10
Welby Lincs....73 P3
Welches Dam Cambs....62 G3
Welcombe Devon....16 C8
Weldon Bridge Nthumb....119 M11
Welford Nhants....60 D4
Welford W Berk....34 D10
Welford-on-Avon Warwks....47 M4
Welham Leics....60 G2
Welham Notts....85 M4
Welham Green Herts....50 F9
Well Hants....23 L5
Well Lincs....87 M6
Well N York....97 L4
Welland Worcs....46 E6
Wellbank Angus....142 H10
Well End Bucks....35 N7
Well End Herts....50 F11
Wellesbourne Warwks....47 Q3
Wellesbourne Mountford Warwks....47 Q3
Well Head Herts....50 E5
Well Hill Kent....37 L8
Wellhouse W Berk....34 F10
Welling Gt Lon....37 L5
Wellingborough Nhants....61 J7
Wellingham Norfk....76 B7
Wellingore Lincs....86 C9
Wellington Cumb....100 E10
Wellington Herefs....45 P5
Wellington Somset....18 F10
Wellington Wrekin....57 M2
Wellington Heath Herefs....46 D6
Wellington Marsh Herefs....45 P5
Wellow BaNES....20 D3
Wellow IoW....14 C9
Wellow Notts....85 L7
Wellpond Green Herts....51 K6
Wells Somset....19 P5
Wellsborough Leics....72 B10
Wells Green Ches E....70 B4
Wells Head C Brad....90 D4
Wells-next-the-sea Norfk....76 C3
Wellstye Green Essex....51 P7
Well Town Devon....9 M3
Welltree P & K....134 B3
Wellwood Fife....134 D10
Welney Norfk....75 H2
Welshampton Shrops....69 M7
Welsh Bicknor Herefs....46 A11
Welsh End Shrops....69 P7
Welsh Frankton Shrops....69 L8
Welsh Hook Pembks....40 H5
Welsh Newton Herefs....45 Q11
Welshpool Powys....56 C3
Welsh St Donats V Glam....30 D9
Welton Cumb....101 L2
Welton E R Yk....92 G5
Welton Lincs....86 D5
Welton Nhants....60 C7
Welton le Marsh Lincs....87 M7
Welton le Wold Lincs....87 J3
Welwick E R Yk....93 P6
Welwyn Herts....50 F7
Welwyn Garden City Herts....50 F8
Wem Shrops....69 P9
Wembdon Somset....19 J7
Wembley Gt Lon....36 E3
Wembury Devon....6 D9
Wembworthy Devon....17 M10
Wemyss Bay Inver....124 F4
Wenallt Cerdgn....54 F10
Wendens Ambo Essex....51 M3
Wendlebury Oxon....48 G11
Wendling Norfk....76 C9
Wendover Bucks....35 N3
Wendron Cnwll....2 H7
Wendy Cambs....62 D11
Wenfordbridge Cnwll....4 H6
Wenhaston Suffk....65 N6
Wennington Cambs....62 B5
Wennington Gt Lon....37 M4
Wennington Lancs....95 N7
Wensley Derbys....84 C8
Wensley N York....96 G3
Wentbridge Wakefd....91 M7
Wentnor Shrops....56 F6
Wentworth Cambs....62 G5
Wentworth Rothm....91 K11
Wentworth Castle Barns....91 J10
Wenvoe V Glam....30 F10
Weobley Herefs....45 N4

Weobley Marsh Herefs....45 N4
Wepham W Susx....24 B9
Wereham Norfk....75 N10
Wergs Wolves....58 C4
Wern Gwynd....67 J7
Wern Powys....44 G11
Wern Powys....56 D2
Wern Powys....69 J8
Werneth Low Tamesd....83 L6
Wernffrwd Swans....28 F6
Wern-y-gaer Flints....81 J11
Werrington C Pete....74 C10
Werrington Cnwll....5 M3
Werrington Staffs....70 G5
Wervin Ches W....81 N10
Wesham Lancs....88 E4
Wessex Vale Crematorium Hants....22 E11
Wessington Derbys....84 E9
West Aberthaw V Glam....30 D11
West Acre Norfk....75 Q7
West Allerdean Nthumb....129 N10
West Alvington Devon....7 J10
West Amesbury Wilts....21 M6
West Anstey Devon....17 R6
West Appleton N York....97 K2
West Ashby Lincs....87 J6
West Ashling W Susx....15 M5
West Ashton Wilts....20 G3
West Auckland Dur....103 N5
West Ayton N York....99 K4
West Bagborough Somset....18 G8
West Bank Blae G....30 H3
West Bank Halton....81 Q8
West Barkwith Lincs....86 G4
West Barnby N York....105 M8
West Barns E Loth....128 H4
West Barsham Norfk....76 C5
West Bay Dorset....11 K6
West Beckham Norfk....76 G4
West Bedfont Surrey....36 C6
Westbere Kent....39 L9
West Bergholt Essex....52 G6
West Berkshire Crematorium W Berk....34 F11
West Bexington Dorset....11 L7
West Bilney Norfk....75 P7
West Blatchington Br & H....24 G9
West Boldon S Tyne....113 N8
Westborough Lincs....73 M2
Westbourne Bmouth....13 J6
Westbourne W Susx....15 L5
West Bourton Dorset....20 E9
West Bowling C Brad....90 F4
West Brabourne Kent....27 J3
West Bradenham Norfk....76 C10
West Bradford Lancs....89 L2
West Bradley Somset....19 Q7
West Bretton Wakefd....90 H8
West Bridgford Notts....72 F3
West Briscoe Dur....103 J7
West Bromwich Sandw....58 F6
West Bromwich Crematorium Sandw....58 F6
Westbrook Herefs....39 P7
Westbrook W Berk....34 D10
Westbrook Wilts....33 J11
West Buckland Devon....17 M5
West Buckland Somset....18 G10
West Burton N York....96 F3
West Burton W Susx....15 Q4
Westbury Bucks....48 H7
Westbury Shrops....56 F3
Westbury Wilts....20 G4
Westbury Leigh Wilts....20 G5
Westbury on Severn Gloucs....32 D2
Westbury-on-Trym Bristl....31 Q9
Westbury-sub-Mendip Somset....19 P5
West Butsfield Dur....103 M2
West Butterwick N Linc....92 D9
Westby Lancs....88 D4
West Byfleet Surrey....36 B8
West Cairngaan D & G....106 F11
West Calder W Loth....127 J5
West Camel Somset....19 Q10
West Chaldon Dorset....12 C8
West Challow Oxon....34 C7
West Charleton Devon....7 K10
West Chelborough Dorset....11 L3
West Chevington Nthumb....119 P11
West Chiltington W Susx....24 C7
West Chinnock Somset....11 K2
West Chisenbury Wilts....21 M4
West Clandon Surrey....36 B10
West Cliffe Kent....27 P3
Westcliff-on-Sea Sthend....38 E4
West Coker Somset....11 L2
West Combe Devon....7 K6
Westcombe Somset....20 D6
West Compton Somset....19 Q6
West Compton Abbas Dorset....11 M6
Westcote Gloucs....47 P10
Westcote Barton Oxon....48 D9
Westcott Bucks....49 K11
Westcott Devon....9 P4
Westcott Surrey....36 D11
West Cottingwith N York....92 A2
Westcourt Wilts....21 P2
West Cowick E R Yk....91 R6
West Cross Swans....28 H7
West Curry Cnwll....5 M3
West Curthwaite Cumb....110 F11
Westdean E Susx....25 M11
West Dean W Susx....15 N4
West Dean Wilts....21 Q9
West Deeping Lincs....74 B9
West Derby Lpool....81 M6
West Dereham Norfk....75 N10
West Ditchburn Nthumb....119 M6
West Down Devon....17 K3
Westdowns Cnwll....4 H5
West Drayton Gt Lon....36 C5
West Drayton Notts....85 M6
West Dunnet Highld....167 M2
Wested Kent....37 M7
West Ella E R Yk....92 H5
West End Bed....49 Q4
West End Br For....35 N10
West End Caerph....30 H5
West End Cambs....62 G3
West End Cumb....110 F9

West End E R Yk........92 F4
West End E R Yk........93 L4
West End E R Yk........93 N5
Westend Gloucs........32 E3
West End Hants........14 E4
West End Hants........22 H7
West End Herts........50 G9
West End Herts........50 H9
West End Lancs........89 L5
West End Leeds........90 G3
West End Lincs........93 Q11
West End N Som........31 N11
West End N York........91 N2
West End Norfk........76 C10
West End Norfk........77 Q9
West End Oxon........34 G7
West End S Glos........32 D7
West End Somset........20 C8
West End Surrey........23 P2
West End Surrey........36 D8
West End W & M........35 M9
West End W Susx........24 F7
West End Wilts........20 H10
West End Wilts........21 J10
West End Wilts........33 J9
West End Green Hants........23 J2
Westend Town Nthumb........111 Q7
Westenhanger Kent........27 K4
Westerdale Highld........167 K6
Westerdale N York........105 J9
Westerfield Suffk........53 L2
Westergate W Susx........15 P5
Westerham Kent........37 K10
Westerhope N u Ty........113 J7
Westerland Devon........7 M6
Westerleigh S Glos........32 C9
Westerleigh
   Crematorium S Glos........32 D9
Western Isles W Isls........168 f8
Wester Ochiltree W Loth........127 J3
Wester Pitkierie Fife........135 P6
Wester Ross Highld........160 F11
Westerton N York........15 N5
Westerton of Rossie
   Angus........143 M7
Westerwick Shet........169 p9
West Ewell Surrey........36 F8
West Farleigh Kent........38 B11
West Farndon Nhants........48 F4
West Felton Shrops........69 K9
Westfield BaNES........20 C4
Westfield Cumb........100 C5
Westfield E Susx........26 D8
Westfield Highld........167 J4
Westfield N Lans........126 C3
Westfield Norfk........76 D10
Westfield W Loth........126 G3
Westfields Dorset........12 B3
Westfields Herefs........45 P6
Westfields of Rattray
   P & K........142 B8
Westfield Sole Kent........38 C9
West Flotmanby N York........99 M5
Westford Somset........18 F10
Westgate Dur........102 H3
Westgate N Linc........92 C9
Westgate Norfk........76 D3
Westgate Hill C Brad........90 G5
Westgate on Sea Kent........39 P7
Westgate Street Norfk........76 H7
West Ginge Oxon........34 D7
West Grafton Wilts........21 P2
West Green Hants........23 K3
West Grimstead Wilts........21 P9
West Grinstead W Susx........24 E6
West Haddlesey N York........91 P5
West Haddon Nhants........60 D6
West Hagbourne Oxon........34 F7
West Hagley Worcs........58 D8
Westhall Suffk........65 N5
West Hallam Derbys........72 C2
West Hallam Common
   Derbys........72 C2
West Halton N Linc........92 F6
Westham Dorset........11 P9
Westham E Susx........25 P10
West Ham Gt Lon........37 J4
Westham Somset........19 M5
Westhampnett W Susx........15 N5
West Handley Derbys........84 E5
West Hanney Oxon........34 D6
West Hanningfield Essex........38 B2
West Harnham Wilts........21 M9
West Harptree BaNES........19 Q3
West Harting W Susx........23 L10
West Hatch Somset........19 J10
West Hatch Wilts........20 H9
West Haven Angus........143 K10
Westhay Somset........19 M6
Westhead Lancs........88 E9
West Head Norfk........75 L9
West Heath Birm........58 F9
West Heath Hants........22 G3
West Helmsdale Highld........163 N3
West Hendred Oxon........34 D7
West Hertfordshire
   Crematorium Herts........50 D10
West Heslerton N York........99 J5
West Hewish N Som........19 L2
Westhide Herefs........46 A6
Westhill Abers........151 L6
West Hill Devon........9 Q6
West Hoathly W Susx........25 J4
West Holme Dorset........12 E7
Westholme Somset........19 Q6
Westhope Herefs........45 P4
Westhope Shrops........56 H7
West Horndon Essex........37 P3
Westhorpe Nhants........48 F4
Westhorpe Lincs........74 D4
Westhorpe Suffk........64 E8
West Horrington Somset........19 Q5
West Horsley Surrey........36 C10
West Horton Nthumb........119 K4
West Hougham Kent........27 N3
Westhoughton Bolton........89 K9
Westhouse N York........95 P6
Westhouses Derbys........84 F9
West Howe Bmouth........13 J5
West Howetown Somset........18 B8
Westhumble Surrey........36 E10
West Huntingtower
   P & K........134 D3
West Huntspill Somset........19 K6
West Hyde C Beds........50 D7
West Hyde Herts........36 B2
West Hythe Kent........27 K5
West Ilkerton Devon........17 N2
West Ilsley W Berk........34 E8
West Itchenor W Susx........15 L7

West Keal Lincs........87 L8
West Kennett Wilts........33 M11
West Kilbride N Ayrs........124 G8
West Kingsdown Kent........37 N8
West Kington Wilts........32 F9
West Kirby Wirral........81 J7
West Knapton N York........98 H5
West Knighton Dorset........12 B7
West Knoyle Wilts........20 G8
West Kyloe Nthumb........119 L2
Westlake Devon........6 G8
West Lambrook Somset........19 M11
Westland Green Herts........51 K6
West Langdon Kent........27 P2
West Lavington W Susx........23 N10
West Lavington Wilts........21 K4
West Layton N York........103 M8
West Leake Notts........72 E5
West Learmouth
   Nthumb........118 F3
West Lees N York........104 E10
West Leigh Devon........8 G3
Westleigh Devon........16 H6
Westleigh Devon........18 E11
West Leigh Somset........18 F8
Westleton Suffk........65 N8
West Lexham Norfk........76 A8
Westley Shrops........56 F3
Westley Suffk........63 P8
Westley Waterless
   Cambs........63 K9
West Lilling N York........98 C8
Westlington Bucks........35 L2
West Linton Border........127 M7
Westlinton Cumb........110 G8
West Littleton S Glos........32 E9
West Lockinge Oxon........34 D7
West London
   Crematorium Gt Lon........36 F4
West Lulworth Dorset........12 D8
West Lutton N York........99 J7
West Lydford Somset........19 Q8
West Lyn Devon........17 N2
West Lyng Somset........19 K9
West Lynn Norfk........75 M6
West Malling Kent........37 Q9
West Malvern Worcs........46 E5
West Marden W Susx........15 L4
West Markham Notts........85 M6
Westmarsh Kent........39 N9
West Marsh NE Lin........93 N9
West Marton N York........96 C10
West Melbury Dorset........20 G10
West Melton Rothm........91 L10
West Meon Hants........22 H10
West Meon Hut Hants........23 J9
West Meon Woodlands
   Hants........22 H9
West Mersea Essex........52 H9
Westmeston E Susx........24 H8
West Mickley Nthumb........112 G8
West Midland Safari
   Park Worcs........57 Q9
Westmill Herts........50 H7
Westmill Herts........51 J5
West Milton Dorset........11 L5
Westminster Gt Lon........36 G5
West Minster Kent........38 F7
West Molesey Surrey........36 D7
West Monkton Somset........19 J9
West Moors Dorset........13 J4
West Morden Dorset........12 F5
West Morriston Border........118 B2
West Morton C Brad........90 D2
West Mudford Somset........19 Q10
Westmuir Angus........142 F7
West Ness N York........98 D5
West Newbiggin Darltn........104 C7
Westnewton Cumb........100 F2
West Newton E R Yk........93 M3
West Newton Norfk........75 N5
West Newton Somset........19 J9
West Norwood Gt Lon........36 H6
West Norwood
   Crematorium Gt Lon........36 H6
Westoe S Tyne........113 N7
West Ogwell Devon........7 L4
Weston BaNES........32 D11
Weston Ches E........70 C4
Weston Devon........10 C4
Weston Devon........10 D7
Weston Dorset........11 P10
Weston Halton........81 Q8
Weston Hants........23 K10
Weston Herefs........45 M3
Weston Herts........50 G4
Weston Lincs........74 E6
Weston N York........97 J11
Weston Nhants........48 G5
Weston Notts........85 N7
Weston Shrops........56 E10
Weston Shrops........57 L6
Weston Shrops........69 J9
Weston Staffs........70 H9
Weston W Berk........34 C10
Weston Beggard Herefs........46 A6
Westonbirt Gloucs........32 G7
Weston by Welland
   Nhants........60 G2
Weston Colley Hants........22 F7
Weston Colville Cambs........63 K10
Weston Corbett Hants........23 J5
Weston Coyney C Stke........70 G6
Weston Favell Nhants........60 G8
Weston Green Cambs........63 K10
Weston Heath Shrops........57 P2
Weston Hills Lincs........74 E6
Weston in Arden Warwks........59 N7
Westoning C Beds........50 B4
Weston-in-Gordano
   N Som........31 M10
Westoning Woodend
   C Beds........50 B4
Weston Jones Staffs........70 D10
Weston Longville Norfk........76 G8
Weston Lullingfields
   Shrops........69 M10
Weston Mill
   Crematorium C Plym........6 D7
Weston-on-Avon Warwks........47 N4
Weston-on-the-Green
   Oxon........48 F11
Weston Patrick Hants........23 J5
Weston Rhyn Shrops........69 J7
Weston-sub-Edge Gloucs........47 M6
Weston-super-Mare
   N Som........19 K2
Weston-super-Mare
   Crematorium N Som........19 L2
Weston Turville Bucks........35 N2

Weston-under-Lizard
   Staffs........57 Q2
Weston under Penyard
   Herefs........46 B10
Weston-under-
   Redcastle Shrops........69 Q9
Weston under
   Wetherley Warwks........59 N11
Weston Underwood
   Derbys........71 P6
Weston Underwood
   M Keyn........49 N4
Weston-upon-Trent
   Derbys........72 C5
Westonzoyland Somset........19 L8
West Orchard Dorset........20 F11
West Overton Wilts........33 M11
Westow N York........98 F7
West Panson Devon........5 N3
West Park Abers........151 K8
West Parley Dorset........13 J5
West Peckham Kent........37 P10
West Peeke Devon........5 N3
West Pelton Dur........113 K10
West Pennard Somset........19 P7
West Pentire Cnwll........4 B9
West Perry Cambs........61 P7
West Porlock Somset........17 R2
Westport Somset........19 L10
West Pulham Dorset........11 Q3
West Putford Devon........16 F8
West Quantoxhead
   Somset........18 F6
Westquarter Falk........126 G2
Westra V Glam........30 F10
West Raddon Devon........9 L4
West Rainton Dur........113 M11
West Rasen Lincs........86 E3
West Ravendale NE Lin........93 M11
Westray Ork........169 d2
Westray Airport Ork........169 d1
West Raynham Norfk........76 B6
West Retford Notts........85 L4
Westridge Green W Berk........34 G9
West Rounton N York........104 D10
West Row Suffk........63 L5
West Rudham Norfk........75 R5
West Runton Norfk........76 H3
Westruther Border........128 G10
Westry Cambs........74 H11
West Saltoun E Loth........128 D6
West Sandford Devon........9 K4
West Sandwick Shet........169 r5
West Scrafton N York........96 G4
West Sleekburn Nthumb........113 L4
West Somerton Norfk........77 P7
West Stafford Dorset........11 Q7
West Stockwith Notts........92 C11
West Stoke W Susx........15 M5
West Stonesdale N York........102 G10
West Stoughton Somset........19 M5
West Stour Dorset........20 E10
West Stourmouth Kent........39 N9
West Stow Suffk........63 P6
West Stowell Wilts........21 M2
West Stratton Hants........22 F6
West Street Kent........38 F11
West Street Kent........39 P11
West Street Medway........38 B6
West Street Suffk........64 D7
West Suffolk
   Crematorium Suffk........63 P7
West Tanfield N York........97 L5
West Taphouse Cnwll........5 J9
West Tarbert Ag & B........123 P6
West Tarring W Susx........24 D10
West Thirston Nthumb........119 N11
West Thorney W Susx........15 L6
Westthorpe Derbys........84 G5
West Thorpe Notts........72 G5
West Thurrock Thurr........37 N5
West Tilbury Thurr........37 Q5
West Tisted Hants........23 J9
West Torrington Lincs........86 F4
West Town BaNES........19 P2
West Town Hants........15 K7
West Town Herefs........45 N2
West Town N Som........31 N11
West Town Somset........19 P7
West Town Somset........20 D6
West Tytherley Hants........21 Q9
West Walton Norfk........75 J8
West Walton Highway
   Norfk........75 J8
Westward Cumb........101 J2
Westward Ho! Devon........16 G6
Westwell Kent........26 G2
Westwell Oxon........33 P3
Westwell Leacon Kent........26 G2
West Wellow Hants........21 Q11
West Wembury Devon........6 E9
West Wemyss Fife........135 J9
Westwick Cambs........62 F7
Westwick Dur........103 L2
West Wick N Som........19 L2
Westwick Norfk........77 K6
West Wickham Cambs........63 K11
West Wickham Gt Lon........37 J7
West Williamston
   Pembks........41 K9
West Wiltshire
   Crematorium Wilts........20 H3
West Winch Norfk........75 M7
West Winterslow Wilts........21 P8
West Wittering W Susx........15 L7
West Witton N York........96 G3
Westwood Devon........9 P5
Westwood Kent........27 P6
Westwood Kent........39 Q8
Westwood Notts........84 G10
Westwood Nthumb........111 Q7
Westwood Wilts........20 F3
West Woodburn
   Nthumb........112 C3
West Woodhay W Berk........22 C2
Westwood Heath Covtry........59 L9
West Woodlands Somset........20 E6
Westwoodside N Linc........92 B10
West Worldham Hants........23 K7
West Worthing W Susx........24 D10
West Wratting Cambs........63 K10
West Wycombe Bucks........35 M6
West Wylam Nthumb........112 H8
West Yatton Wilts........32 G9
West Yoke Kent........37 P7
West Youlstone Cnwll........16 D8

Wetham Green Kent........38 D8
Wetheral Cumb........111 J10
Wetherby Leeds........97 P11
Wetherby Services
   N York........97 P10
Wetherden Suffk........64 E8
Wetheringsett Suffk........64 G8
Wethersfield Essex........52 B5
Wetherup Street Suffk........64 G9
Wetley Rocks Staffs........70 H5
Wettenhall Ches E........69 R2
Wetton Staffs........71 L3
Wetwang E R Yk........99 J9
Wetwood Staffs........70 D8
Wexcombe Wilts........21 Q3
Wexham Slough........35 Q8
Wexham Street Bucks........35 Q8
Weybourne Norfk........76 G3
Weybourne Surrey........23 N5
Weybread Suffk........65 J5
Weybread Street Suffk........65 J6
Weybridge Surrey........36 C8
Weycroft Devon........10 G5
Weydale Highld........167 L4
Weyhill Hants........22 B5
Weymouth Dorset........11 P9
Weymouth
   Crematorium Dorset........11 P9
Whaddon Bucks........49 M8
Whaddon Cambs........62 E11
Whaddon Gloucs........32 F2
Whaddon Wilts........20 G2
Whaddon Wilts........21 N9
Whale Cumb........101 P6
Whaley Derbys........84 H6
Whaley Bridge Derbys........83 M8
Whaley Thorns Derbys........84 H6
Whaligoe Highld........167 P8
Whalley Lancs........89 L3
Whalley Banks Lancs........89 L3
Whalsay Shet........169 s7
Whalton Nthumb........112 H4
Whaplode Lincs........74 F6
Whaplode Drove Lincs........74 F8
Wharf Warwks........48 D3
Wharfe N York........96 A7
Wharles Lancs........88 E3
Wharley End C Beds........49 P6
Wharncliffe Side Sheff........84 C2
Wharram-le-Street
   N York........98 H7
Wharton Ches W........82 E11
Wharton Herefs........45 Q3
Whashton N York........103 N9
Whasset Cumb........95 L4
Whatcote Warwks........47 Q6
Whateley Warwks........59 K5
Whatfield Suffk........52 H2
Whatley Somset........10 H3
Whatley Somset........20 D5
Whatley's End S Glos........32 C8
Whatlington E Susx........26 C8
Whatsole Street Kent........27 K3
Whatstandwell Derbys........84 D10
Whatton Notts........73 J3
Whauphill D & G........107 M8
Whaw N York........103 J10
Wheal Rose Cnwll........3 J5
Wheatacre Norfk........65 P3
Wheatfield Oxon........35 J5
Wheathampstead Herts........50 E8
Wheathill Shrops........57 L8
Wheathill Somset........19 Q8
Wheatley Calder........90 D5
Wheatley Hants........23 L6
Wheatley Oxon........34 G3
Wheatley Hill Dur........104 C3
Wheatley Hills Donc........91 P10
Wheatley Lane Lancs........89 N3
Wheaton Aston Staffs........58 C2
Wheatsheaf Wrexhm........69 K4
Wheddon Cross Somset........18 B7
Wheelbarrow Town
   Kent........27 K2
Wheeler End Bucks........35 M6
Wheeler's Green
   Wokham........35 L10
Wheeler's Street Kent........26 D3
Wheelerstreet Surrey........23 P6
Wheelock Ches E........70 D3
Wheelock Heath Ches E........70 D3
Wheelton Lancs........89 J6
Wheldrake C York........92 A2
Whelford Gloucs........33 N5
Whelpley Hill Bucks........35 Q4
Whelpo Cumb........101 K3
Whelston Flints........81 J9
Whempstead Herts........50 H6
Whenby N York........98 C7
Whepstead Suffk........64 A10
Wherstead Suffk........53 L3
Wherwell Hants........22 C6
Wheston Derbys........83 P9
Whetsted Kent........37 Q11
Whetstone Gt Lon........36 G2
Whetstone Leics........72 F11
Wheyrigg Cumb........110 C11
Whicham Cumb........94 C4
Whichford Warwks........48 B8
Whickham Gatesd........113 K8
Whiddon Devon........8 C5
Whiddon Down Devon........8 G6
Whight's Corner Suffk........53 K3
Whigstreet Angus........142 H9
Whilton Nhants........60 D8
Whimble Devon........16 F11
Whimple Devon........9 P5
Whimpwell Green Norfk........77 M6
Whinburgh Norfk........76 E10
Whin Lane End Lancs........88 D2
Whinnie Liggate D & G........108 F10
Whinnow Cumb........110 F10
Whinnyfold Abers........159 Q11
Whinny Hill S on T........104 C7
Whippingham IoW........14 F8
Whipsnade C Beds........35 B7
Whipton Devon........9 M6
Whirlow Sheff........84 D4
Whisby Lincs........86 B7
Whissendine Rutlnd........73 L8
Whissonsett Norfk........76 C7
Whistlefield Ag & B........131 Q3
Whistlefield Inn Ag & B........131 N5
Whistley Green Wokham........35 L10
Whiston Knows........81 P6
Whiston Nhants........60 H8
Whiston Rothm........84 F3
Whiston Staffs........58 C2
Whiston Staffs........71 J5

Whiston Cross Shrops........57 P4
Whiston Eaves Staffs........71 J5
Whitacre Fields Warwks........59 L6
Whitbeck Cumb........94 C4
Whitbourne Herefs........46 D3
Whitburn S Tyne........113 P8
Whitburn W Loth........126 G5
Whitby Ches W........81 M9
Whitby N York........105 N8
Whitbyheath Ches W........81 M10
Whitchester Border........129 J8
Whitchurch BaNES........32 B11
Whitchurch Bucks........49 M10
Whitchurch Cardif........30 G9
Whitchurch Devon........6 D4
Whitchurch Hants........22 E5
Whitchurch Herefs........45 R11
Whitchurch Oxon........34 H9
Whitchurch Pembks........40 F5
Whitchurch Shrops........69 P6
Whitchurch
   Canonicorum Dorset........10 H5
Whitchurch Hill Oxon........34 H9
Whitcombe Dorset........11 Q7
Whitcot Shrops........56 F6
Whitcott Keysett Shrops........56 D8
Whiteacre Kent........27 K2
Whiteacre Heath Warwks........59 K6
Whiteash Green Essex........52 C5
White Ball Somset........18 F11
Whitebridge Highld........147 M4
Whitebrook Mons........31 P3
Whitecairns Abers........151 N4
Whitechapel Gt Lon........36 H4
White Chapel Lancs........88 H2
Whitechurch Pembks........41 N3
Whitecliffe Gloucs........31 Q3
White Colne Essex........52 E6
White Coppice Lancs........89 J7
Whitecraig E Loth........127 G3
Whitecroft Gloucs........32 B3
Whitecross Cnwll........2 E7
White Cross Cnwll........2 H9
Whitecross Cnwll........4 F7
Whitecross Falk........126 H2
White End Worcs........46 E8
Whiteface Highld........162 G9
Whitefarland N Ayrs........120 G3
Whitefaulds S Ayrs........114 E6
Whitefield Bury........89 N9
Whitefield Devon........17 N4
Whitefield Somset........18 E9
Whitefield Lane End
   Knows........81 P7
Whiteford Abers........151 J2
Whitegate Ches W........82 D11
Whitehall Hants........23 K4
Whitehall Ork........169 f4
Whitehall W Susx........24 D6
Whitehaven Cumb........100 C7
Whitehill Kent........38 H10
Whitehill Leics........72 C8
Whitehill and Bordon
   Hants........23 L8
Whitehills Abers........158 G4
Whitehouse Abers........150 G5
Whitehouse Ag & B........123 P7
Whitehouse Common
   Birm........58 H5
Whitekirk E Loth........128 F3
White Kirkley Dur........103 K3
White Lackington Dorset........11 Q5
Whitelackington Somset........19 L11
White Ladies Aston
   Worcs........46 H4
Whiteleaf Bucks........35 M4
White-le-Head Dur........113 J10
Whiteley Hants........14 F5
Whiteley Bank IoW........14 G10
Whiteley Green Ches E........83 K9
Whiteley Village Surrey........36 C8
Whitemans Green
   W Susx........24 H5
White Mill Carmth........43 J10
Whitemire Moray........156 H7
Whitemoor C Nott........72 E2
Whitemoor Cnwll........4 F10
Whitemoor Derbys........84 E11
Whitemoor Staffs........70 F2
Whiteness Shet........169 q6
White Notley Essex........52 C8
Whiteoak Green Oxon........34 B2
White Ox Mead BaNES........20 D3
Whiteparish Wilts........21 P10
White Pit Lincs........87 L5
Whiterashes Abers........151 M3
White Roding Essex........51 N8
Whiterow Highld........167 Q7
Whiterow Moray........157 J6
Whiteshill Gloucs........32 F3
Whitesmith E Susx........25 M8
White Stake Lancs........88 G5
Whitestaunton Somset........10 F2
Whitestone Devon........9 L6
White Stone Herefs........45 R6
Whitestone Cross Devon........9 L6
Whitestreet Green Suffk........52 G4
Whitewall Corner N York........98 F7
White Waltham W & M........35 M9
Whiteway BaNES........20 D2
Whiteway Gloucs........32 H2
Whitewell Lancs........95 P11
Whiteworks Devon........6 G4
Whitfield C Dund........142 G10
Whitfield Kent........27 P2
Whitfield Nhants........48 H7
Whitfield Nthumb........111 Q9
Whitfield S Glos........32 C6
Whitfield Hall Nthumb........111 Q9
Whitford Devon........10 F5
Whitford Flints........80 G9
Whitgift E R Yk........92 D6
Whitgreave Staffs........70 G9
Whithorn D & G........107 M9
Whiting Bay N Ayrs........121 K6
Whitkirk Leeds........91 K4
Whitland Carmth........41 N7
Whitlaw Border........117 Q8
Whitletts S Ayrs........114 G3
Whitley N York........91 P6
Whitley Readg........35 K10
Whitley Sheff........84 D2
Whitley Wilts........32 G11
Whitley Bay N Tyne........113 N6
Whitley Bay
   Crematorium N Tyne........113 M6
Whitley Chapel Nthumb........112 D9
Whitley Heath Staffs........70 E9
Whitley Lower Kirk........90 G7

Whitley Row - Woodhouses 307

Whitley Row Kent 37 L10
Whitlock's End Solhll 58 H9
Whitminster Gloucs 32 E3
Whitmore Dorset 13 J3
Whitmore Staffs 70 E6
Whitnage Devon 18 D11
Whitnash Warwks 48 B2
Whitney-on-Wye Herefs 45 K5
Whitrigg Cumb 100 H3
Whitrigg Cumb 110 D9
Whitrigglees Cumb 110 D9
Whitsbury Hants 21 M11
Whitsome Border 129 M9
Whitson Newpt 31 L8
Whitstable Kent 39 K8
Whitstone Cnwll 5 M2
Whittingham Nthumb 119 L8
Whittingslow Shrops 56 G7
Whittington Derbys 84 E5
Whittington Gloucs 47 K10
Whittington Lancs 95 N5
Whittington Norfk 75 P11
Whittington Shrops 69 K8
Whittington Staffs 58 C8
Whittington Staffs 59 J3
Whittington Warwks 59 L5
Whittington Worcs 46 G4
Whittington Moor Derbys 84 E6
Whittlebury Nhants 49 J6
Whittle-le-Woods Lancs 88 H6
Whittlesey Cambs 74 E11
Whittlesford Cambs 62 G11
Whittlestone Head Bl w D 89 L7
Whitton N Linc 92 F6
Whitton Nthumb 119 L10
Whitton Powys 56 D11
Whitton S on T 104 C6
Whitton Shrops 57 K10
Whitton Suffk 53 K2
Whittonditch Wilts 33 Q10
Whittonstall Nthumb 112 G9
Whitway Hants 22 E3
Whitwell Derbys 84 H5
Whitwell Herts 50 E6
Whitwell IoW 14 F11
Whitwell N York 103 Q11
Whitwell Rutlnd 73 N9
Whitwell-on-the-Hill N York 98 E7
Whitwell Street Norfk 76 G7
Whitwick Leics 72 C7
Whitwood Wakefd 91 L6
Whitworth Lancs 89 P7
Whixall Shrops 69 P8
Whixley N York 97 P9
Whorlton Dur 103 M8
Whorlton N York 104 E10
Whyle Herefs 45 R2
Whyteleafe Surrey 36 H9
Wibdon Gloucs 31 Q5
Wibsey C Brad 90 E4
Wibtoft Warwks 59 Q7
Wichenford Worcs 46 E2
Wichling Kent 38 F10
Wick Bmouth 13 L6
Wick Devon 10 D4
Wick Highld 167 Q6
Wick S Glos 32 D10
Wick Somset 18 H6
Wick Somset 19 M9
Wick V Glam 29 P10
Wick W Susx 24 B10
Wick Wilts 21 N10
Wick Worcs 47 J5
Wicken Cambs 63 J6
Wicken Nhants 49 K7
Wicken Bonhunt Essex 51 L4
Wickenby Lincs 86 E4
Wick End Bed 49 Q4
Wicken Green Village Norfk 76 A5
Wickersley Rothm 84 G2
Wicker Street Green Suffk 52 G3
Wickford Essex 38 B3
Wickham Hants 14 G4
Wickham W Berk 34 C10
Wickham Bishops Essex 52 D9
Wickhambreaux Kent 39 M10
Wickhambrook Suffk 63 N10
Wickhamford Worcs 47 L6
Wickham Green Suffk 64 F8
Wickham Green W Berk 34 D10
Wickham Heath W Berk 34 D11
Wickham Market Suffk 65 L10
Wickhampton Norfk 77 N10
Wickham St Paul Essex 52 D4
Wickham Skeith Suffk 64 F8
Wickham Street Suffk 63 N10
Wickham Street Suffk 64 F8
Wick John o' Groats Airport Highld 167 Q6
Wicklewood Norfk 76 F11
Wickmere Norfk 76 H5
Wick St Lawrence N Som 31 L11
Wickstreet E Susx 25 M9
Wickwar S Glos 32 D7
Widdington Essex 51 M4
Widdop Calder 89 Q4
Widdrington Nthumb 119 Q11
Widdrington Station Nthumb 113 K2
Widecombe in the Moor Devon 8 H9
Widegates Cnwll 5 M10
Widemouth Bay Cnwll 16 C11
Wide Open N Tyne 113 K6
Widford Essex 51 Q10
Widford Herts 51 K7
Widham Wilts 33 L7
Widley Hants 15 J5
Widmer End Bucks 35 N5
Widmerpool Notts 72 G5
Widmore Gt Lon 37 K7
Widnes Halton 81 Q8
Widnes Crematorium Halton 81 Q7
Widworthy Devon 10 E5
Wigan Wigan 88 H9
Wigan Crematorium Wigan 82 C4
Wigborough Somset 19 M11
Wiggaton Devon 10 C6
Wiggenhall St Germans Norfk 75 L8
Wiggenhall St Mary Magdalen Norfk 75 L8
Wiggenhall St Mary the Virgin Norfk 75 L8
Wiggens Green Essex 51 Q2
Wiggenstall Staffs 71 K2
Wiggington Shrops 69 K7
Wigginton C York 98 C9
Wigginton Herts 35 P2
Wigginton Oxon 48 C8
Wigginton Staffs 59 K3
Wigginton Bottom Herts 35 P3
Wigglesworth N York 96 B9
Wiggonby Cumb 110 E10
Wiggonholt W Susx 24 C7
Wighill N York 97 Q11
Wighton Norfk 76 C4
Wightwick Wolves 58 C5
Wigley Derbys 84 D6
Wigley Hants 22 B11
Wigmore Herefs 56 G11
Wigmore Medway 38 C9
Wigsley Notts 85 Q6
Wigsthorpe Nhants 61 M4
Wigston Leics 72 G11
Wigston Fields Leics 72 G10
Wigston Parva Leics 59 Q7
Wigthorpe Notts 85 J4
Wigtoft Lincs 74 E3
Wigton Cumb 110 E11
Wigtown D & G 107 M6
Wigtwizzle Sheff 90 G11
Wike Leeds 91 J2
Wilbarston Nhants 60 H3
Wilberfoss E R Yk 98 E10
Wilburton Cambs 62 G5
Wilby Nhants 61 J7
Wilby Norfk 64 E4
Wilby Suffk 65 J7
Wilcot Wilts 21 M2
Wilcott Shrops 69 L11
Wilcrick Newpt 31 M7
Wilday Green Derbys 84 D6
Wildboarclough Ches E 83 L11
Wilden Bed 61 N9
Wilden Worcs 58 B10
Wilde Street Suffk 63 M5
Wildhern Hants 22 C4
Wildhill Herts 50 G9
Wildmanbridge S Lans 126 E7
Wildmoor Worcs 58 E9
Wildsworth Lincs 92 D11
Wilford C Nott 72 F3
Wilford Hill Crematorium Notts 72 F3
Wilkesley Ches E 70 A6
Wilkhaven Highld 163 L9
Wilkieston W Loth 127 L4
Wilkin's Green Herts 50 E9
Wilksby Lincs 87 J8
Willand Devon 9 P2
Willards Hill E Susx 26 B7
Willaston Ches E 70 B4
Willaston Ches W 81 L9
Willen M Keyn 49 N6
Willenhall Covtry 59 N9
Willenhall Wsall 58 E5
Willerby E R Yk 92 H4
Willerby N York 99 L5
Willersey Gloucs 47 M7
Willersley Herefs 45 L5
Willesborough Kent 26 H3
Willesborough Lees Kent 26 H3
Willesden Gt Lon 36 F4
Willesleigh Devon 17 K5
Willesley Wilts 32 G7
Willett Somset 18 F8
Willey Shrops 57 M5
Willey Warwks 59 Q8
Willey Green Surrey 23 P4
Williamscot Oxon 48 E5
Williamstown Rhondd 30 D6
Willian Herts 50 F4
Willicote Warwks 47 N5
Willingale Essex 51 N9
Willingdon E Susx 25 N10
Willingham Cambs 62 F6
Willingham by Stow Lincs 85 Q4
Willingham Green Cambs 63 K10
Willington Bed 61 P10
Willington Derbys 71 P9
Willington Dur 103 N3
Willington Kent 38 C11
Willington Warwks 47 Q7
Willington Corner Ches W 82 B11
Willington Quay N Tyne 113 M7
Willitoft E R Yk 92 B4
Williton Somset 18 E6
Willoughby Lincs 87 N6
Willoughby Warwks 60 B7
Willoughby Hills Lincs 87 L11
Willoughby-on-the-Wolds Notts 72 G5
Willoughby Waterleys Leics 60 C2
Willoughton Lincs 86 B2
Willow Green Ches W 82 D9
Willows Green Essex 52 B8
Willsbridge S Glos 32 C10
Willsworthy Devon 8 D8
Willtown Somset 19 L10
Wilmcote Warwks 47 N3
Wilmington BaNES 20 C2
Wilmington Devon 10 E5
Wilmington E Susx 25 M10
Wilmington Kent 37 M6
Wilmslow Ches E 82 H8
Wilnecote Staffs 59 K4
Wilpshire Lancs 89 K4
Wilsden C Brad 90 D3
Wilsford Lincs 73 Q2
Wilsford Wilts 21 M3
Wilsford Wilts 21 M7
Wilsham Devon 17 P2
Wilshaw Kirk 90 E9
Wilsill N York 97 J8
Wilsley Green Kent 26 C4
Wilsley Pound Kent 26 C4
Wilson Herefs 45 R10
Wilson Leics 72 C6
Wilsontown S Lans 126 G6
Wilstead Bed 50 C2
Wilsthorpe Lincs 74 A8
Wilstone Herts 35 P2
Wilstone Green Herts 35 P2
Wilton Cumb 100 D8
Wilton Herefs 46 A10
Wilton N York 98 H4
Wilton R & Cl 104 G7
Wilton Wilts 21 L8
Wilton Wilts 21 Q2
Wilton Dean Border 117 P8
Wimbish Essex 51 N3
Wimbish Green Essex 51 P3
Wimbledon Gt Lon 36 F6
Wimblington Cambs 62 F2
Wimboldsley Ches W 70 B2
Wimborne Minster Dorset 12 H5
Wimborne St Giles Dorset 12 H2
Wimbotsham Norfk 75 M9
Wimpole Cambs 62 E11
Wimpstone Warwks 47 P5
Wincanton Somset 20 D9
Winceby Lincs 87 K7
Wincham Ches W 82 E9
Winchburgh W Loth 127 K3
Winchcombe Gloucs 47 K9
Winchelsea E Susx 26 F8
Winchelsea Beach E Susx 26 F8
Winchester Hants 22 E9
Winchester Services Hants 22 F7
Winchet Hill Kent 26 B3
Winchfield Hants 23 L4
Winchmore Hill Bucks 35 P5
Winchmore Hill Gt Lon 36 H2
Wincle Ches E 83 L11
Wincobank Sheff 84 E2
Winder Cumb 100 D7
Windermere Cumb 101 M11
Winderton Warwks 48 B6
Windhill Highld 155 P8
Windlehurst Stockp 83 L7
Windlesham Surrey 23 P2
Windmill Cnwll 4 D7
Windmill Derbys 83 Q9
Windmill Hill E Susx 25 P8
Windmill Hill Somset 19 K11
Windrush Gloucs 33 N2
Windsole Abers 158 E5
Windsor W & M 35 Q9
Windsor Castle W & M 35 Q9
Windsoredge Gloucs 32 F4
Windsor Green Suffk 64 B11
Windy Arbour Warwks 59 L10
Windygates Fife 135 J7
Windyharbour Ches E 82 H10
Windy Hill Wrexhm 69 K4
Wineham W Susx 24 F6
Winestead E R Yk 93 N6
Winewall Lancs 89 Q2
Winfarthing Norfk 64 G4
Winford IoW 14 G10
Winford N Som 19 P2
Winforton Herefs 45 K5
Winfrith Newburgh Dorset 12 D8
Wing Bucks 49 N10
Wing Rutlnd 73 M10
Wingate Dur 104 D3
Wingates Bolton 89 K9
Wingates Nthumb 119 L11
Wingerworth Derbys 84 E7
Wingfield C Beds 50 B5
Wingfield Suffk 65 J6
Wingfield Wilts 20 F3
Wingfield Green Suffk 65 J6
Wingham Kent 39 M10
Wingmore Kent 27 L2
Wingrave Bucks 49 N11
Winkburn Notts 85 M9
Winkfield Br For 35 P10
Winkfield Row Br For 35 N10
Winkhill Staffs 71 K4
Winkhurst Green Kent 37 L11
Winkleigh Devon 17 L10
Winksley N York 97 L6
Winkton Dorset 13 L5
Winlaton Gatesd 113 J8
Winlaton Mill Gatesd 113 J8
Winless Highld 167 P6
Winllan Powys 68 H10
Winmarleigh Lancs 95 K11
Winnall Hants 22 E9
Winnersh Wokham 35 L10
Winnington Ches W 82 D10
Winscales Cumb 100 D5
Winscombe N Som 19 M3
Winsford Ches W 82 E11
Winsford Somset 18 B8
Winsham Devon 17 J4
Winsham Somset 10 H3
Winshill Staffs 71 P10
Winshwen Swans 29 J5
Winskill Cumb 101 Q4
Winslade Hants 23 J5
Winsley Wilts 20 E2
Winslow Bucks 49 L9
Winson Gloucs 33 L3
Winsor Hants 13 P2
Winster Cumb 95 J2
Winster Derbys 84 B8
Winston Dur 103 M7
Winston Suffk 64 H9
Winstone Gloucs 33 J3
Winswell Devon 16 H9
Winterborne Came Dorset 11 Q7
Winterborne Clenston Dorset 12 D4
Winterborne Herringston Dorset 11 P7
Winterborne Houghton Dorset 12 D4
Winterborne Kingston Dorset 12 E5
Winterborne Monkton Dorset 11 P7
Winterborne Stickland Dorset 12 D4
Winterborne Tomson Dorset 12 E5
Winterborne Whitechurch Dorset 12 D4
Winterborne Zelston Dorset 12 E5
Winterbourne S Glos 32 B8
Winterbourne W Berk 34 E10
Winterbourne Abbas Dorset 11 N6
Winterbourne Bassett Wilts 33 L10
Winterbourne Dauntsey Wilts 21 N8
Winterbourne Earls Wilts 21 N8
Winterbourne Gunner Wilts 21 N7
Winterbourne Monkton Wilts 33 L10
Winterbourne Steepleton Dorset 11 N7
Winterbourne Stoke Wilts 21 L6
Winterbrook Oxon 34 H7
Winterburn N York 96 D9
Winteringham N Linc 92 F6
Winterley Ches E 70 C3
Wintersett Wakefd 91 K7
Winterslow Wilts 21 P8
Winterton N Linc 92 F7
Winterton-on-Sea Norfk 77 P8
Winthorpe Lincs 87 Q7
Winthorpe Notts 85 P9
Winton Bmouth 13 J6
Winton Cumb 102 E8
Winton E Susx 25 M10
Winton N York 104 D11
Wintringham N York 98 H6
Winwick Cambs 61 P4
Winwick Nhants 60 D6
Winwick Warrtn 82 D6
Wirksworth Derbys 71 P4
Wirral 81 K7
Wirswall Ches E 69 P6
Wisbech Cambs 75 J9
Wisbech St Mary Cambs 74 H9
Wisborough Green W Susx 24 C5
Wiseman's Bridge Pembks 41 M9
Wiseton Notts 85 M3
Wishanger Gloucs 32 H3
Wishaw N Lans 126 D6
Wishaw Warwks 59 J6
Wisley Surrey 36 C9
Wispington Lincs 86 H6
Wissenden Kent 26 F3
Wissett Suffk 65 M6
Wissington Norfk 75 N11
Wissington Suffk 52 G5
Wistanstow Shrops 56 G7
Wistanswick Shrops 70 B9
Wistaston Ches E 70 B4
Wistaston Green Ches E 70 B4
Wisterfield Ches E 82 H10
Wiston Pembks 41 K7
Wiston S Lans 116 D4
Wiston W Susx 24 D8
Wistow Cambs 62 C4
Wistow Leics 72 G11
Wistow N York 91 P3
Wiswell Lancs 89 L3
Witcham Cambs 62 G4
Witchampton Dorset 12 G3
Witchford Cambs 62 H5
Witcombe Somset 19 N10
Witham Essex 52 D9
Witham Friary Somset 20 D6
Witham on the Hill Lincs 73 R7
Witham St Hughs Lincs 85 Q8
Withcall Lincs 87 J4
Withdean Br & H 24 H9
Witherenden Hill E Susx 25 P5
Witheridge Devon 9 K2
Witherley Leics 72 A11
Withern Lincs 87 M4
Withernsea E R Yk 93 P5
Withernwick E R Yk 93 L2
Withersdale Street Suffk 65 K5
Withersfield Suffk 63 L11
Witherslack Cumb 95 J4
Withiel Cnwll 4 F8
Withiel Florey Somset 18 C8
Withielgoose Cnwll 4 G8
Withington Gloucs 47 K11
Withington Herefs 45 R6
Withington Manch 82 H6
Withington Shrops 57 K2
Withington Staffs 71 J7
Withington Green Ches E 82 H10
Withington Marsh Herefs 45 R6
Withleigh Devon 9 M2
Withnell Lancs 89 J6
Withybed Green Worcs 58 F10
Withybrook Warwks 59 P8
Withycombe Somset 18 D6
Withyham E Susx 25 L3
Withy Mills BaNES 20 C3
Withypool Somset 17 Q4
Withywood Bristl 31 Q11
Witley Surrey 23 P7
Witnesham Suffk 64 H11
Witney Oxon 34 C2
Wittering C Pete 73 R10
Wittersham Kent 26 F6
Witton Birm 58 G6
Witton Norfk 77 L10
Witton Norfk 77 L5
Witton Gilbert Dur 113 K11
Witton Green Norfk 77 N11
Witton le Wear Dur 103 M4
Witton Park Dur 103 N4
Wiveliscombe Somset 18 E9
Wivelrod Hants 23 J7
Wivelsfield E Susx 24 H6
Wivelsfield Green E Susx 25 J7
Wivelsfield Station W Susx 24 H7
Wivenhoe Essex 52 H7
Wivenhoe Cross Essex 52 H7
Wiveton Norfk 76 E3
Wix Essex 53 L6
Wixford Warwks 47 L4
Wix Green Essex 53 L6
Wixhill Shrops 69 Q9
Wixoe Suffk 52 B3
Woburn C Beds 49 P8
Woburn Abbey C Beds 49 Q8
Woburn Sands M Keyn 49 P7
Wokefield Park W Berk 35 J11
Woking Surrey 36 B9
Woking Crematorium Surrey 23 Q3
Wokingham Wokham 35 M11
Wolborough Devon 7 M4
Woldingham Surrey 37 J9
Wold Newton E R Yk 99 L6
Wold Newton NE Lin 93 M11
Wolfclyde S Lans 116 E3
Wolferlow Herefs 46 C2
Wolferton Norfk 75 N5
Wolfhampcote Warwks 60 B7
Wolfhill P & K 142 B11
Wolf Hills Nthumb 111 P9
Wolf's Castle Pembks 41 J5
Wolfsdale Pembks 40 H6
Wollaston Dudley 58 C8
Wollaston Nhants 61 K8
Wollaston Shrops 56 E2
Wollaton C Nott 72 E3
Wolleigh Devon 9 K8
Wollerton Shrops 69 R8
Wollescote Dudley 58 D8
Wolseley Bridge Staffs 71 J10
Wolsingham Dur 103 L3
Wolstanton Staffs 70 F5
Wolstenholme Rochdl 89 N8
Wolston Warwks 59 P9
Wolsty Cumb 109 P10
Wolvercote Oxon 34 E2
Wolverhampton Wolves 58 D5
Wolverhampton Halfpenny Green Airport Staffs 58 B6
Wolverley Shrops 69 N8
Wolverley Worcs 58 B9
Wolverton Hants 22 G3
Wolverton Kent 27 N3
Wolverton M Keyn 49 M6
Wolverton Warwks 47 P2
Wolverton Wilts 20 E8
Wolverton Common Hants 22 G3
Wolvesnewton Mons 31 N5
Wolvey Warwks 59 P7
Wolvey Heath Warwks 59 P7
Wolviston S on T 104 E5
Wombleton N York 98 D4
Wombourne Staffs 58 C6
Wombwell Barns 91 L10
Womenswold Kent 39 M11
Womersley N York 91 N7
Wonastow Mons 31 N2
Wonersh Surrey 36 B11
Wonford Devon 9 M6
Wonson Devon 8 G7
Wonston Dorset 12 B3
Wonston Hants 22 E7
Wooburn Bucks 35 P7
Wooburn Green Bucks 35 P7
Wooburn Moor Bucks 35 P7
Woodacott Devon 16 F10
Woodale N York 96 F5
Woodall Rothm 84 G4
Woodall Services Rothm 84 G4
Woodbastwick Norfk 77 L8
Woodbeck Notts 85 N5
Wood Bevington Warwks 47 L4
Woodborough Notts 85 K11
Woodborough Wilts 21 M3
Woodbridge Devon 10 D5
Woodbridge Dorset 20 G11
Woodbridge Suffk 53 N2
Wood Burcote Nhants 49 J5
Woodbury Devon 9 P7
Woodbury Salterton Devon 9 P7
Woodchester Gloucs 32 F4
Woodchurch Kent 26 F5
Woodchurch Wirral 81 K7
Woodcombe Somset 18 C5
Woodcote Gt Lon 36 G8
Woodcote Oxon 34 H8
Woodcote Wrekin 70 D11
Woodcote Green Worcs 58 D10
Woodcott Hants 22 D4
Woodcroft Gloucs 31 P5
Woodcutts Dorset 21 J11
Wood Dalling Norfk 76 F6
Woodditton Cambs 63 L9
Woodeaton Oxon 34 F2
Wood Eaton Staffs 70 E11
Wooden Pembks 41 M9
Wood End Bed 61 M11
Wood End Bed 61 N7
Wood End Cambs 62 E5
Wood End Gt Lon 36 D4
Wood End Herts 50 H5
Woodend Highld 138 D5
Woodend Nhants 48 H5
Woodend Staffs 71 M9
Woodend W Loth 126 G4
Woodend W Susx 15 M5
Wood End Warwks 58 H10
Wood End Warwks 59 K5
Wood End Warwks 59 L7
Wood End Wolves 58 D4
Wood Enderby Lincs 87 J8
Woodend Green Essex 51 N5
Woodfalls Wilts 21 N10
Woodford Cnwll 16 C9
Woodford Devon 7 K8
Woodford Gloucs 32 C5
Woodford Gt Lon 37 K2
Woodford Nhants 61 L5
Woodford Stockp 83 J8
Woodford Bridge Gt Lon 37 K2
Woodford Halse Nhants 48 F4
Woodford Wells Gt Lon 37 K2
Woodgate Birm 58 E8
Woodgate Devon 18 F11
Woodgate Norfk 76 B8
Woodgate Norfk 76 E8
Woodgate W Susx 15 P6
Woodgate Worcs 58 E11
Wood Green Gt Lon 36 H2
Woodgreen Hants 21 N11
Woodgreen Oxon 34 C2
Woodhall N York 96 E2
Woodhall Hill Leeds 90 G3
Woodhall Spa Lincs 86 G8
Woodham Bucks 49 K11
Woodham Dur 103 Q5
Woodham Surrey 36 B8
Woodham Ferrers Essex 38 C2
Woodham Mortimer Essex 52 D11
Woodham Walter Essex 52 D10
Wood Hayes Wolves 58 D4
Woodhead Abers 159 J10
Woodhill Shrops 57 N8
Woodhill Somset 19 L9
Woodhorn Nthumb 113 L3
Woodhorn Demesne Nthumb 113 M3
Woodhouse Leeds 90 H4
Woodhouse Leics 72 E8
Woodhouse Sheff 84 F4
Woodhouse Wakefd 91 K6
Woodhouse Eaves Leics 72 E8
Woodhouse Green Staffs 70 G2
Woodhouselee Mdloth 127 N5
Woodhouselees D & G 110 G6
Woodhouse Mill Sheff 84 F3
Woodhouses Cumb 110 F10

Woodhouses Oldham..........83 K4
Woodhouses Staffs.............58 G3
Woodhouses Staffs.............71 M11
Woodhuish Devon.................7 N8
Woodhurst Cambs................62 D5
Woodingdean Br & H..........25 J9
Woodkirk Leeds....................90 H5
Woodland Abers................151 M3
Woodland Devon...................6 G7
Woodland Devon...................7 K5
Woodland Dur....................103 L5
Woodland Kent....................27 K3
Woodland S Ayrs...............114 C8
Woodland Head Devon..........9 J5
Woodlands Abers...............151 N8
Woodlands Donc.................91 N9
Woodlands Dorset...............13 J3
Woodlands Hants.................13 P2
Woodlands Kent...................37 N8
Woodlands N York...............97 M10
Woodlands Somset..............18 G6
Woodlands (Coleshill)
   Crematorium Warwks.....59 J7
Woodlands Park W & M.....35 N9
Woodlands St Mary
   W Berk.............................34 B9
Woodlands
   (Scarborough)
   Crematorium N York......99 L3
Woodlands
   (Scunthorpe)
   Crematorium N Linc.......92 E8
Woodland Street Somset....19 P7
Woodland View Sheff..........84 D3
Wood Lane Shrops..............69 M8
Wood Lane Staffs................70 E5
Woodleigh Devon..................7 J9
Woodlesford Leeds..............91 K5
Woodley Stockp...................83 K6
Woodley Wokham................35 L10
Woodmancote Gloucs..........32 E5
Woodmancote Gloucs..........33 K3
Woodmancote Gloucs..........47 J9
Woodmancote W Susx.........15 L5
Woodmancote W Susx.........24 F8
Woodmancote Worcs...........46 H6
Woodmancott Hants.............22 G6
Woodmansey E R Yk...........93 J3
Woodmansgreen W Susx.....23 N9
Woodmansterne Surrey.......36 G9
Woodmanton Devon...............9 P7
Woodmarsh Wilts..................20 G3
Woodmill Staffs....................71 L10
Woodminton Wilts................21 K10
Woodnesborough Kent........39 P10
Woodnewton Nhants............61 M2
Woodnook Notts...................84 G10
Wood Norton Norfk..............76 E6
Woodplumpton Lancs..........88 F4
Woodrising Norfk.................76 D11
Wood Row Leeds.................91 K5
Woodrow Worcs...................58 C9
Wood's Corner E Susx.........25 Q7
Woods Eaves Herefs............45 K5
Woodseaves Shrops.............70 B8
Woodseaves Staffs..............70 D9
Woodsend Wilts....................33 P9
Woodsetts Rothm.................84 H4
Woodsford Dorset................12 C6
Wood's Green E Susx...........25 P4
Woodside Br For..................35 P10
Woodside Cumb..................100 D4
Woodside Essex...................51 L10
Woodside Fife....................135 L6
Woodside Gt Lon.................36 H7
Woodside Hants...................13 P6
Woodside Herts....................50 F9
Woodside P & K..................142 C10
Woodside Green Kent...........38 F11
Woodstock Oxon..................48 D11
Woodstock Pembks...............41 K5
Woodston C Pete.................74 C11
Wood Street Norfk...............77 M7
Wood Street Village
   Surrey..............................23 Q4
Woodthorpe Derbys..............84 G6
Woodthorpe Leics................72 E7
Woodthorpe Lincs................87 M4
Woodton Norfk.....................65 K3
Woodtown Devon..................16 G7
Woodvale Sefton..................88 C8
Woodvale Crematorium
   Br & H..............................24 H9
Woodville Derbys.................71 Q11
Woodwall Green Staffs.........70 D8
Wood Walton Cambs............62 B4
Woodyates Dorset................21 K11
Woody Bay Devon................17 M2
Woofferton Shrops...............57 J11
Wookey Somset....................19 P5
Wookey Hole Somset............19 P5
Wool Dorset.........................12 D7
Woolacombe Devon..............16 H3
Woolage Green Kent............27 M2
Woolage Village Kent..........39 M11
Woolaston Gloucs................31 Q5
Woolaston Common
   Gloucs..............................31 Q4
Woolavington Somset...........19 K6
Woolbeding W Susx..............23 N10
Woolbrook Devon.................10 C7
Woolcotts Somset.................18 C8
Wooldale Kirk.......................90 F9
Wooler Nthumb..................119 J5
Woolfardisworthy
   Devon..................................9 K3
Woolfardisworthy
   Devon................................16 E7
Woolfold Bury......................89 M8
Woolfords S Lans...............127 J6
Woolhampton W Berk...........34 G11
Woolhope Herefs..................46 B7
Woolland Dorset...................12 C3
Woollard BaNES...................20 B2
Woollensbrook Herts.............51 J9
Woolley BaNES....................32 D11
Woolley Cambs.....................61 Q6
Woolley Cnwll......................16 D8
Woolley Derbys....................84 E8
Woolley Wakefd....................91 J8
Woolley Bridge Derbys.........83 M6
Woolley Edge Services
   Wakefd..............................91 J8
Woolley Green W & M.........35 M8
Woolmere Green Worcs........47 J2
Woolmer Green Herts...........50 G7
Woolmerston Somset............19 J8
Woolminstone Somset...........11 J3
Woolpack Kent......................26 E4
Woolpit Suffk........................64 D9

Woolpit Green Suffk.............64 D9
Woolscott Warwks................60 B7
Woolsgrove Devon..................9 J4
Woolsington N u Ty.............113 J6
Woolstaston Shrops..............56 H5
Woolsthorpe Lincs................73 L4
Woolsthorpe-by-
   Colsterworth Lincs.........73 N6
Woolston C Sotn..................14 D4
Woolston Devon.....................6 C9
Woolston Devon.....................7 J8
Woolston Shrops...................56 G7
Woolston Shrops...................69 K10
Woolston Somset.................18 E7
Woolston Somset.................20 C9
Woolston Warrtn...................82 D7
Woolstone Gloucs.................47 J8
Woolstone M Keyn................49 N7
Woolstone Oxon....................33 Q7
Woolston Green Devon..........7 K5
Woolton Lpool......................81 N7
Woolton Hill Hants...............22 D2
Woolverstone Suffk...............53 L4
Woolverton Somset...............20 E4
Woolwich Gt Lon..................37 K5
Woonton Herefs....................45 M4
Woonton Herefs....................45 R2
Wooperton Nthumb............119 K6
Woore Shrops.......................70 C6
Wootten Green Suffk............65 J7
Wootton Bed.........................50 B2
Wootton Hants......................13 M5
Wootton Herefs....................45 L4
Wootton IoW.........................14 F8
Wootton Kent........................27 M2
Wootton N Linc.....................93 J7
Wootton Nhants....................60 G9
Wootton Oxon.......................34 E4
Wootton Oxon.......................48 D11
Wootton Shrops....................69 K9
Wootton Staffs......................70 E9
Wootton Staffs......................71 L6
Wootton Bassett Wilts..........33 L8
Wootton Bridge IoW.............14 F8
Wootton Broadmead
   Bed...................................50 B2
Wootton Common IoW..........14 F8
Wootton Courtenay
   Somset..............................18 B6
Wootton Fitzpaine
   Dorset...............................10 H5
Wootton Rivers Wilts............21 N2
Wootton St Lawrence
   Hants.................................22 G4
Wootton Wawen
   Warwks..............................47 N2
Worcester Worcs..................46 G4
Worcester Park Gt Lon.........36 F7
Wordsley Dudley..................58 C7
Worfield Shrops....................57 P5
Worgret Dorset.....................12 F7
Workhouse End Bed.............61 P10
Workington Cumb...............100 D5
Worksop Notts......................85 J5
Worlaby Lincs.......................87 K5
Worlaby N Linc.....................92 H8
Worlds End Bucks.................35 N3
Worlds End Hants.................14 H4
World's End W Berk..............34 E9
Worlds End W Susx..............24 H6
Worle N Som.........................19 L2
Worleston Ches E.................70 B3
Worlingham Suffk.................65 N4
Worlington Devon...................9 J2
Worlington Suffk...................63 L6
Worlingworth Suffk...............65 J8
Wormald Green N York.........97 M7
Wormbridge Herefs..............45 N8
Wormegay Norfk...................75 N8
Wormelow Tump Herefs........45 P8
Wormhill Derbys...................83 P10
Wormhill Herefs....................45 N7
Wormingford Essex..............52 F5
Worminghall Bucks..............34 H3
Wormington Gloucs..............47 K7
Worminster Somset..............19 Q6
Wormit Fife........................135 L2
Wormleighton Warwks..........48 E4
Wormley Herts......................51 J9
Wormley Surrey....................23 P7
Wormleybury Herts...............51 J9
Wormley Hill Donc...............91 R7
Wormshill Kent.....................38 E10
Wormsley Herefs..................45 N5
Worplesdon Surrey...............23 Q4
Worrall Sheff........................84 D2
Worrall Hill Gloucs...............32 B2
Worsbrough Barns................91 K10
Worsbrough Bridge
   Barns................................91 K10
Worsbrough Dale Barns........91 K10
Worsley Salfd.......................82 G4
Worstead Norfk.....................77 L6
Worsthorne Lancs.................89 P4
Worston Devon.......................6 F8
Worston Lancs......................89 M2
Worth Kent...........................39 P10
Worth Somset.......................19 P6
Worth W Susx......................24 H3
Wortham Suffk......................64 F6
Worthen Shrops....................56 E4
Worthenbury Wrexhm...........69 M5
Worthing Norfk.....................76 D8
Worthing W Susx..................24 D10
Worthing Crematorium
   W Susx..............................24 D9
Worthington Leics................72 C6
Worth Matravers Dorset.......12 G9
Worthybrook Mons...............31 N2
Worting Hants......................22 G4
Wortley Barns......................91 J11
Wortley Leeds......................90 H4
Worton N York......................96 E3
Worton Wilts.........................21 J3
Wortwell Norfk.....................65 K5
Wotherton Shrops................56 D4
Wothorpe C Pete..................73 Q9
Wotter Devon..........................7 F6
Wotton Surrey.......................36 D11
Wotton-under-Edge
   Gloucs..............................32 E6
Wotton Underwood
   Bucks................................49 J11
Woughton on the
   Green M Keyn...................49 N7
Wouldham Kent.....................38 B9
Woundale Shrops.................57 P6
Wrabness Essex....................53 L5
Wrafton Devon......................16 H4
Wragby Lincs........................86 F5

Wragby Wakefd....................91 L7
Wramplingham Norfk............76 G10
Wrangaton Devon...................6 H7
Wrangbrook Wakefd.............91 M8
Wrangle Lincs.......................87 M10
Wrangle Common Lincs........87 M10
Wrangle Lowgate Lincs........87 M10
Wrangway Somset................18 F11
Wrantage Somset.................19 K10
Wrawby N Linc.....................92 H9
Wraxall N Som......................31 N10
Wraxall Somset.....................20 B7
Wray Lancs...........................95 N7
Wray Castle Cumb..............101 L10
Wraysbury W & M.................36 B6
Wrayton Lancs......................95 N6
Wrea Green Lancs.................88 D4
Wreaks End Cumb................94 E3
Wreay Cumb.......................101 M6
Wreay Cumb........................110 H11
Wrecclesham Surrey.............23 M6
Wrekenton Gatesd..............113 L9
Wrelton N York....................98 F3
Wrenbury Ches E..................69 Q5
Wrench Green N York...........99 K3
Wreningham Norfk................64 H2
Wrentham Suffk....................65 P5
Wrenthorpe Wakefd..............91 J6
Wrentnall Shrops..................56 G4
Wressle E R Yk.....................92 B4
Wressle N Linc......................92 G9
Wrestlingworth C Beds.........62 C11
Wretton Norfk.......................75 N10
Wrexham Wrexhm.................69 K4
Wribbenhall Worcs...............57 P9
Wrickton Shrops...................57 L7
Wrightington Bar
   Lancs................................88 G8
Wright's Green Essex...........51 M7
Wrinehill Staffs.....................70 D5
Wrington N Som...................19 N2
Writhlington BaNES..............20 C4
Writtle Essex........................51 Q9
Wrockwardine Wrekin...........57 L2
Wroot N Linc........................92 B10
Wrose C Brad.......................90 F3
Wrotham Kent.......................37 P9
Wrotham Heath Kent............37 P9
Wrottesley Staffs..................58 B4
Wroughton Swindn...............33 M8
Wroxall IoW..........................14 G11
Wroxall Warwks....................59 K10
Wroxeter Shrops..................57 K3
Wroxham Norfk.....................77 L8
Wroxton Oxon.......................48 D6
Wyaston Derbys....................71 M6
Wyatt's Green Essex............51 N11
Wyberton East Lincs............74 F2
Wyberton West Lincs...........74 F2
Wyboston Bed......................61 Q9
Wybunbury Ches E...............70 B5
Wychbold Worcs...................58 D11
Wych Cross E Susx..............25 K4
Wychnor Staffs.....................71 M11
Wyck Hants..........................23 L7
Wyck Rissington Gloucs.......47 N10
Wycliffe Dur........................103 M8
Wycoller Lancs......................89 Q3
Wycomb Leics......................73 K6
Wycombe Marsh Bucks.........35 N6
Wyddial Herts.......................51 J4
Wye Kent..............................27 J2
Wyesham Mons....................31 P2
Wyfordby Leics.....................73 K7
Wyke C Brad.........................90 F5
Wyke Devon...........................9 L5
Wyke Devon..........................10 F5
Wyke Dorset.........................20 E9
Wyke Shrops........................57 L4
Wyke Surrey..........................23 P4
Wyke Champflower
   Somset..............................20 C8
Wykeham N York..................99 K4
Wyken Covtry.......................59 N8
Wyken Shrops.......................57 P5
Wyke Regis Dorset...............11 P9
Wykey Shrops.......................69 L10
Wykin Leics..........................72 C11
Wylam Nthumb...................112 H8
Wylde Green Birm................58 H6
Wylye Wilts...........................21 K7
Wymeswold Leics.................72 G6
Wymington Bed....................61 L8
Wymondham Leics...............73 L7
Wymondham Norfk...............76 G11
Wyndham Brdgnd.................29 P6
Wynford Eagle Dorset..........11 M5
Wynyard Park S on T...........104 D5
Wynyard Village S on T.......104 D5
Wyre Forest
   Crematorium Worcs.......57 Q10
Wyre Piddle Worcs...............47 J5
Wysall Notts.........................72 G5
Wyson Herefs.......................57 J11
Wythall Worcs......................58 G9
Wytham Oxon.......................34 E3
Wythburn Cumb..................101 K8
Wythenshawe Manch...........82 H7
Wythop Mill Cumb..............100 G5
Wyton Cambs.......................62 C6
Wyton E R Yk.......................93 L4
Wyverstone Suffk.................64 E8
Wyverstone Street Suffk.......64 E8
Wyville Lincs........................73 M5

Y

Yaddlethorpe N Linc............92 E9
Yafford IoW..........................14 D10
Yafforth N York....................97 M2
Yalberton Torbay....................7 M7
Yalding Kent.........................37 Q10
Yanwath Cumb...................101 P5
Yanworth Gloucs..................33 L2
Yapham E R Yk.....................98 F10
Yapton W Susx.....................15 Q6
Yarborough N Som...............19 L3
Yarbridge IoW......................14 H9
Yarburgh Lincs......................87 L2
Yarcombe Devon..................10 E3
Yard Devon...........................17 P7
Yardley Birm........................58 H7
Yardley Crematorium
   Birm.................................58 H8
Yardley Gobion Nhants.........49 L6
Yardley Hastings Nhants......61 J9
Yardley Wood Birm..............58 H9
Yardro Powys.......................45 J3

Yarford Somset.....................18 H9
Yarkhill Herefs.....................46 B6
Yarley Somset.......................19 P6
Yarlington Somset.................20 C9
Yarm S on T.......................104 D8
Yarmouth IoW......................14 C9
Yarnacott Devon...................17 L5
Yarnbrook Wilts....................20 G4
Yarner Devon..........................9 J9
Yarnfield Staffs.....................70 F8
Yarnscombe Devon...............17 K7
Yarnton Oxon.......................34 E2
Yarpole Herefs.....................45 P2
Yarrow Border....................117 M5
Yarrow Somset.....................19 L5
Yarrow Feus Border............117 L5
Yarrowford Border..............117 N4
Yarsop Herefs......................45 N5
Yarwell Nhants.....................73 R11
Yate S Glos..........................32 D8
Yateley Hants.......................23 M9
Yatesbury Wilts....................33 L10
Yattendon W Berk................34 G10
Yatton Herefs.......................56 G11
Yatton N Som.......................31 M11
Yatton Keynell Wilts.............32 G9
Yaverland IoW......................14 H9
Yawl Devon..........................10 G6
Yawthorpe Lincs...................85 Q2
Yaxham Norfk.......................76 E9
Yaxley Cambs.......................61 Q2
Yaxley Suffk.........................64 G7
Yazor Herefs........................45 N5
Yeading Gt Lon....................36 D4
Yeadon Leeds......................90 G2
Yealand Conyers Lancs........95 L6
Yealand Redmayne
   Lancs................................95 L5
Yealand Storrs Lancs...........95 K5
Yealmbridge Devon................6 F8
Yealmpton Devon...................6 F8
Yearby R & Cl....................104 G6
Yearngill Cumb...................100 F2
Yearsley N York...................98 B6
Yeaton Shrops......................69 M11
Yeaveley Derbys...................71 M6
Yeavering Nthumb..............118 H4
Yedingham N York................98 H5
Yelford Oxon........................34 C4
Yell Shet.............................169 r5
Yelland Devon......................16 H5
Yelling Cambs......................62 C8
Yelvertoft Nhants.................60 C5
Yelverton Devon.....................6 E5
Yelverton Norfk....................77 K11
Yenston Somset....................20 D10
Yeoford Devon........................9 J5
Yeolmbridge Cnwll.................5 N4
Yeo Mill Devon.....................17 Q6
Yeo Vale Devon....................16 G7
Yeovil Somset.......................19 Q11
Yeovil Crematorium
   Somset..............................19 P11
Yeovil Marsh Somset............19 P11
Yeovilton Somset..................19 P10
Yerbeston Pembks................41 L9
Yesnaby Ork.......................169 b5
Yetlington Nthumb..............119 K9
Yetminster Dorset................11 M2
Yetson Devon.........................7 L7
Yettington Devon....................9 Q7
Yetts o'Muckhart
   Clacks.............................134 C7
Yews Green C Brad...............90 D4
Yew Tree Sandw...................58 F5
Y Felinheli Gwynd.................79 J11
Y Ferwig Cerdgn...................42 C5
Y Ffor Gwynd.......................66 F7
Y Gyffylliog Denbgs..............68 E3
Yielden Bed..........................61 M7
Yieldingtree Worcs...............58 C9
Yieldshields S Lans.............126 F7
Yiewsley Gt Lon...................36 C4
Y Maerdy Conwy..................68 D6
Y Nant Wrexhm.....................69 J4
Ynysboeth Rhondd...............30 E5
Ynysddu Caerph...................30 G6
Ynysforgan Swans................29 J5
Ynyshir Rhondd....................30 D6
Ynyslas Cerdgn....................54 E6
Ynysmaerdy Rhondd.............30 D8
Ynysmeudwy Neath..............29 K3
Ynystawe Swans...................29 J4
Ynyswen Powys....................29 M2
Ynyswen Rhondd..................30 C5
Ynysybwl Rhondd.................30 E6
Ynysymaengwyn
   Gwynd..............................54 D4
Yockenthwaite N York..........96 D5
Yockleton Shrops..................56 F2
Yokefleet E R Yk..................92 D6
Yoker C Glas......................125 N4
York C York..........................98 C10
York Lancs...........................89 L4
York City Crematorium
   C York...............................98 B11
Yorkletts Kent......................39 J9
Yorkley Gloucs.....................32 B3
York Minster C York.............98 C10
Yorkshire Dales
   National Park N York........96 C5
York Town Surrey..................23 N2
Yorton Heath Shrops............69 P10
Youlgreave Derbys...............84 B8
Youlthorpe E R Yk................98 F9
Youlton N York.....................97 Q8
Youngsbury Herts.................51 J7
Young's End Essex................52 B8
Yoxall Staffs.........................71 L11
Yoxford Suffk.......................65 M8
Y Rhiw Gwynd......................66 C9
Ysbyty Cynfyn Cerdgn..........54 H9
Ysbyty Ifan Conwy...............67 Q5
Ysbyty Ystwyth Cerdgn.........54 G10
Ysceifiog Flints....................80 H10
Ysgubor-y-Coed
   Cerdgn..............................54 F5
Ystalyfera Neath...................29 L3
Ystrad Rhondd.....................30 C5
Ystrad Aeron Cerdgn............43 K3
Ystrad Ffin Carmth...............43 Q5
Ystradgynlais Powys.............29 L2
Ystrad Meurig Cerdgn..........54 G11
Ystrad Mynach Caerph.........30 F6
Ystradowen V Glam..............30 D9
Ystumtuen Cerdgn................54 G9
Ythanbank Abers................159 M11
Ythanwells Abers................158 F10
Ythsie Abers......................159 L11

Z

Zeal Monachorum
   Devon..................................8 H4
Zeals Wilts............................20 E8
Zelah Cnwll............................3 L3
Zennor Cnwll..........................2 D6
Zoar Cnwll..............................3 K10
Zouch Notts..........................72 E6
ZSL Whipsnade Zoo
   C Beds..............................50 B7